THE COLUMBIA COMPANION TO AMERICAN HISTORY ON FILM

★ ★ ★ ★ ★ ★ ★

Edited by **PETER C. ROLLINS**

THE COLUMBIA COMPANION TO AMERICAN HISTORY ON FILM

How the Movies Have Portrayed the American Past

COLUMBIA UNIVERSITY PRESS *New York*

Columbia University Press
Publishers Since 1893
New York Chichester, West Sussex

Library of Congress Cataloging-in-Publication Data
The Columbia companion to American history on
film : How the movies have portrayed the American past / edited by Peter C. Rollins
p. cm.
Includes bibliographical references and index.
ISBN 0-231-11222-X (cloth : alk. paper)
1. United States—In motion pictures. 2. United States—History—Miscellanea. I. Rollins, Peter C.
II. Title.
PN1995.9.U64 C65 2004
791.43/658 21
2003053086

♾ Columbia University Press books are printed on
permanent and durable acid-free paper.
Printed in the United States of America
c 10 9 8 7 6 5 4 3 2 1
p 10 9 8 7 6 5 4 3 2 1

To John E. O'Connor and Martin A. Jackson, cofounders of *Film & History: An Interdisciplinary Journal of Film and Television History* (www.filmandhistory.org)

★ CONTENTS

IV. Groups

V. Institutions and Movements

VI. Places

VII. Themes and Topics

VIII. Myths and Heroes

★ ACKNOWLEDGMENTS

Susan Rollins, Leslie Fife, and Deborah Carmichael helped prepare materials for this book, and they have my great thanks. Throughout the project, James Warren of Columbia University Press was a demanding and hard-working colleague. Gregory McNamee was a joy to work with and enhanced both the consistency and insight of the manuscript. William F. Waters of Films for the Humanities provided authors with relevant documentaries from its collection; both he and Films for the Humanities deserve an emphatic note of thanks for making these resources available (www.films.com). I thank, too, Oklahoma State University for honoring my work by appointing me Regents Professor. A long series of department heads have promoted my efforts, among them Jack Crane, Leonard Leff, Jeffrey Walker, Edward Walkiewicz, and Carol Moder. I am most grateful for their support and faith. Finally, the staff of *Film & History* (www.filmandhistory.org) was ever generous with suggestions, help with documentation and filing, and production of the final manuscript.

★ INTRODUCTION

Film and television define our perceptions of our time and of historical experience. In 1973, John Harrington warned about the power of visual media to shape the contemporary sensibility, estimating that "by the time a person is fourteen, he will witness 18,000 murders on the screen. He will also see 350,000 commercials. By the time he is eighteen, he will stockpile nearly 17,000 hours of viewing experience and will watch at least twenty movies for every book he reads. Eventually, the viewing experience will absorb ten years of his life" (v). Nearly thirty years later, psychologists Robert Kubey and Mihaly Csikszentmihalyi described contemporary viewing as a form of addiction: "The amount of time people spend watching television is astonishing. On average, individuals in the industrial world devote three hours a day to the pursuit—fully half of their leisure time, and more than on any single activity save work and sleep. At this rate, someone who lives to seventy-five would spend nine years in front of the tube" (76).

Through video rentals and reruns, film and television recycle themselves to consummate their impact on popular memory. All citizens need to ponder the implications of such statistics, but historians should be particularly concerned about this phenomenon, for what millions see on theater and television screens defines what is called "popular memory," the informal—albeit generally accepted—view of the past. Indeed, visual media define history for many Americans. *The Columbia Companion to American History on Film,* a collection of essays that explore how major eras, institutions, peoples, wars, leaders, social groups, and myths of our national culture have been portrayed on film, offers readers and researchers an unparalleled resource on a vital source of historical interpretation and reflection.

Many scholars welcome the plethora of films and television programs that depict our history. They see film as a way of introducing and dramatizing the events, ideas, and forces that have shaped history and identity. But the use of films as sources of historical interpretation is not without problems or detractors. Take, for example, the case of the HBO feature film *A Bright Shining Lie* (1998), which purported to adapt a Pulitzer Prize–winning book to the screen. In the process so many changes were made that author Neil Sheehan and a major character, Daniel Ellsberg, threatened to sue the filmmakers for misrepresentation because the complex and ambiguous story of America's role in Vietnam had been reduced to a cinematic diatribe against American intervention. (For Ellsberg's trenchant discussion of the subject, consult the *Film & History* web site, www.filmandhistory.org.) Yet very few viewers are worried about "poetic license," inventions, and deletions by filmmakers. Most are more interested in good stories about the past than accuracy of analysis. As filmmakers will tell you, they constitute an audience that simply wants to be "entertained."

Since their inception, motion pictures and television have exerted a profound impact on our understanding of the past. As historical sources they can be very useful and revealing, but they must be "read" with sensitivity, care, and discrimination. During the silent era, directors such as D. W. Griffith helped to define the meaning of westward expansion and the significance of the Civil War. Silent-era director James Cruze contributed his vision of an Anglo-Saxon West in his adaptation of Emerson Hough's *The Covered Wagon* (1923). These ambitious early films spoke volumes about American values in an era anxious about the impact of immigration, and *The Covered Wagon* in particular helped smooth the way for the Immigration Restriction Act of 1928. Throughout the so-called Studio Era (1930–48), leading producers and moguls took pride in underwriting historical films as part of the "quality" work of their corporations; David O. Selznick's *Gone with the Wind* (1939) is perhaps the most famous example of a lavish film made to interpret American history to a large audience, an immensely popular project about which film scholars have been quarreling ever since. Such films were made as a gesture toward defining our national past, and some were made without concern for profit. Whether aimed at making money or not, they taught memorable lessons.

In recent decades, Oliver Stone has pilloried the American system in films such as *Platoon* (1986) and *Wall Street* (1987). Some critics consider him a history teacher, and in 1997, assuming that role, he spoke to the American Historical Association in a packed hall of more than 1,200 academics. He did not win over many of his critics. Historians deplore Stone's mélange of fact and speculation. As George Will, a noted columnist and former professor of politics, has observed rancorously, "Stone falsifies so much that he may be an intellectual sociopath, indifferent to the truth." In the feature film *JFK* (1991), what disturbed historians most can be identified early in the film where Stone edits factual footage—the famous Zapruder film of the assassination—with reenactments so similar in their documentary texture that it is almost impossible to distinguish what is fact and what is fiction. Among filmmakers, this technique has been condemned since the mid-1930s, when the famous *March of Time* newsreel series (1935–53) exploited it to a ridiculous extreme. Historians are especially sensitive about this kind of fraudulence because they are taught to identify sources accurately so that others can verify the accuracy of their findings. Within the films of Oliver Stone, no such option is available, even for the most alert viewers. In addition, most trained historians have warned that conspiracy theories rarely stand up to rigorous analysis; they oversimplify complex historical problems. In

Stone's case, without his all-pervasive conspiracy theory about the assassination of John F. Kennedy, the filmmaker's historical interpretation self-destructs. As *Time* observed in a highly critical review, "So, you want to know, who killed the President and connived in the cover-up? Everybody! High officials in the CIA, the FBI, the Dallas constabulary, all three armed services, Big Business and the White House. Everybody done it—everybody but Lee Harvey Oswald." Stone offers similar errors of interpretation in his *Platoon* and *Wall Street,* yet the popularity of these clever films poses a serious challenge to historians. They are powerfully convincing as screen narratives, often more convincing than attempted classroom rebuttals by history teachers.

Over the history of motion pictures, there have been isolated attempts to critique historical films—usually by those with strong objections to the content. When D. W. Griffith's *The Birth of a Nation* was released in 1915, African American activists organized demonstrations and published condemnations of the epic film's depiction of the Old South, an imaginary place where slaves supposedly enjoyed leisure and plenty. During World War I (1914–18), it became problematic to depict the American Revolution on film because Britain was a vital European ally. Within this context, films critical of England were suppressed by government censors. In one infamous case, a producer was imprisoned because he had been so subversive as to make the British the villains of his film about America's struggle for independence. Not all censorship comes from outside the film project, however. Self-criticism softened the radicalism of *Native Land* (1941), a film designed to expose the injustices of American capitalism. Shortly before the release of the picture, Germany attacked the Soviet Union, leading to a (temporary) support of capitalist nations that would fight against the Axis enemy. Within this context of what was called a "Popular Front," director Leo Hurwitz reedited the film, transforming it into a positive celebration of the Constitution and the Bill of Rights—even the Pilgrims! Hurwitz's revision was a case of obedient rewriting of history to fit a changing party line. The option to make the same film teach such opposite lessons stands as a classic example of how malleable the film medium can be as an interpreter of history.

At least in the United States, little was done to evaluate historical films until 1970, when the Historians Film Committee was created as an affiliated society of the American Historical Association (AHA). Pressured by the obvious interest in film and television by the general population and concerned about the competition of the media of a "media age," the AHA approved the creation of the society and its publication, *Film & History: An Interdisciplinary Journal of Film and Television Studies.* The journal has published articles that explore the relationship between America's favorite art form and America's historical legacy as defined by those academically trained to research and write history.

What is the value of such studies? At the beginning of the twentieth century, philosopher George Santayana made the lasting observation, that "those who do not remember the past are condemned to repeat it." We know the importance of a sense of history for insight into the economic, political, and foreign-policy issues of our time, but there is often the chance that decisions will be made on the basis of popular memory and reel history rather than the authentic insights of real history. Motion pictures are often made with the objective of telling good stories in a way that makes sense to a contemporary audience. In contrast, the best history is written to investigate the truth about the past without the intrusion of melodramatic, entertainment, or ideological concerns. Films, as the essays in this volume demonstrate at many points, reflect their times, along with the prejudices, misconceptions, and fixations of the periods in which they were made. For this reason, they are wonderful exempla for those who would seek to understand the ways Americans in the past have thought about critical events and themes in their history. Yet this virtue as documents of the past limits the value of motion pictures as truly insightful studies of history. To cite another observation by Santayana, historical motion pictures often can be characterized as "a pack of lies about events that never happened told by people who weren't there." Those who rely on historical films for their understanding of the past are often in danger of learning the wrong lessons—and, as a result, using the wrong models for interpreting the present.

The essays in this collection should help teachers, students, and general readers to avoid such pitfalls. Furthermore, reminders about the multiple perspectives of the past are always valuable because they force us to build and shape our own understanding of history. As an Internet announcement for a 2002 London conference on history and media observed, "For those who deplore these developments, the take-over of history by the media has resulted in a facile vision of the past, which is by turns intellectually unexciting and condescending towards its audience." Each essay in this collection should both illuminate and complicate the subject matter examined by motion pictures; the result should be both a better understanding of both history and film—not to mention the process by which history is interpreted.

The Nature of the Essays

Each essay in *The Columbia Companion to American History on Film* reflects the outlook and sensibility of the contributor. Many, though not all essays, compare and contrast the interpretations of filmmakers with those of professional historians. Most contributors are from history or film departments, but some are in American studies and communications; all of the scholars who have contributed follow an interdisciplinary methodology with the goal of linking historical themes with related motion pictures.

The contributors to this volume were asked to keep a number of questions in mind while researching and writing their essays. Some of these questions were more important to certain essays than to others. The first question was this: Broadly speaking, how has the subject been treated by historians and by filmmakers? To which are added two corollary questions: What was the interpretation to be found in the accepted historical sources of the time in which the film was made? Is there a "take" on those sources in the film, or is there direct borrowing? For example, D. W. Griffith was a direct borrower of "tragic era" interpretations of post–Civil War Reconstruction, histories written by such authorities as William Dunning (1857–1922) and Claude Bowers (1878–1958). Their highly tendentious histories painted a portrait of a stable and happy slave society before the Civil War and the agony that resulted when war destroyed the Plantation Ideal. Griffith subscribed to both the vision of the antebellum harmony and the "tragic era" approach to Reconstruction (1865–77)—which, according to Dunning and Bowers, was an era in which an imposed government violated the political and civil rights of southern whites. Thus, it is clear that Griffith was methodologically faithful in his borrowing of historical interpretation, but, in this infamous case, the historians and the filmmaker were equally guilty of historical distortion.

The fourth question is: How do the film interpretations deviate from their sources? Surprisingly, the film adaptation of *The Grapes of Wrath* (1940) wanders widely from John Steinbeck's classic novel (1939) in ways that Steinbeck himself did not notice when he inspected Nunnally Johnson's preproduction script, thanks to his own lack of visual literacy (Owens, 98). Whereas Steinbeck was outraged about the suffering of his "Okies," and pessimistic about government efforts to help the unemployed, the film by director John Ford and producer Darryl F. Zanuck seems almost Pollyannaish in its optimism. The Hollywood version discloses its politics when a director of a government-run migrant camp is an intentional look-alike for Franklin Delano Roosevelt, the president (1933–45) whose "New Deal" promised to save the American system. Steinbeck's book offered far less hope for an America in search of justice during hard times, a pessimism reflected in the very title of the epic—an allusion to the American Civil War and its famous "Battle Hymn of the Republic."

The fifth question is: What was the impact of contemporary issues on the film or films under consideration? Contemporary issues and assumptions shape film projects. Historical films such as *The Birth of a Nation* (1915) and *Roots* (1977) address the same historical topic, yet both interpretations reflect their own times—one the racially segregating Progressive Era (1900–17), the other the era of civil rights and rebellion against existing social customs and mores related to race and ethnicity (1954–68). Both films were made to shape popular memory and influence current politics: in the first case, D. W. Griffith was explicit about his desire to show the evils of "the war of Northern aggression"; in the second, Alex Haley clearly wished to share a sense of racial pride he experienced after tracing his family tree back to its African roots. Both were dependent upon the reigning historical wisdom of their times—as a result, the same story is shaped entirely differently. (See the entries "Slavery" and "African Americans After World War II.")

Contemporary pressures clearly shaped *On the Waterfront* (1954), by writer Budd Schulberg and director Elia Kazan. As an act of conscience, Kazan testified against former friends about his and their involvement in the American Communist movement during the 1930s. Not surprisingly, Kazan and other "friendly witnesses"—including Schulberg and director Edward Dmytryk—before the House Committee on Un-American Activities (HUAC) were lambasted by the artistic community. Arthur Miller even wrote an allegorical play about the "witch hunt," *The Crucible* (1953). In Miller's play, the evils of such testimony were thrust back into the context of the Massachusetts Bay Colony of the Puritans during the infamous Salem witch trials of 1692 (see "The Puritan Era and the Puritan Mind"). To answer this kind of criticism, Kazan and Schulberg shaped the plot of *On the Waterfront* to tell the story of Terry Malloy (Marlon Brando), who, as a matter of conscience, goes before the federal crime commission to expose the unlawful and immoral behavior of the union bosses—many of whom are his relatives, friends, or patrons. To do so, Terry must go through a spiritual conversion from an ally of the longshoremen's union to a citizen of conscience concerned about the rights of fellow dockworkers. As Kenneth Hey observes, Father Barry (Karl Malden) gives a funeral sermon that "challenges silent liberals to speak out against past totalitarian activities" (173). As far as Kazan was concerned, he and Terry had made the right decision—the resulting film effectively captured that connection in a production that was also a powerful narrative. For our purposes, the point is that Kazan made the film to construe contemporary history from his viewpoint—a viewpoint still unpopular in Hollywood and New York.

The sixth question is: How do the important films on the subject convey meaning and theme? Although a film's messages are often conveyed by dialogue and narration, it is also true that some of the most effective communication is accomplished by nonverbal means—imagery and symbolism, editing, mise-en-scène, and sound and music. For example, many have noted the sexual symbolism at the opening of Stanley Kubrick's *Dr. Strangelove* (1964). The B-52 bombers refueling in midair appear to be mating in the sky in some perverse, technological copulation. This moment has special meaning within Kubrick's Freudian vision; it connects with the filmmaker's view of man's place in a high-tech age where machines are becoming more like people while people are becoming more robotic. In *The Grapes of Wrath,* a section on "The Cats" (the Caterpillar tractors that replace individual farmers and their plows) early in the film says volumes about John Ford's interpretation of the Joads and their dilemma: they are American Adams, and their pastoral garden is being disrupted by machines. (See "The American Adam" and "The Machine in the Garden.") Many interpreters have argued that the prominence of this myth of the machine in the garden, a theme key to the entire oeuvre of director John Ford, mutes the radical vision of Steinbeck's American epic. Although Steinbeck was not uninterested in misuses of the land, he focused more on the revolutionary potential of class conflict.

Music and sound are often important vehicles of meaning. The music from director Pare Lorentz's *The Plow That Broke the Plains* (1935) and *The River* (1937) are still broadcast staples for National Public Radio. Composer Virgil Thomson drew his inspiration from the folk music and hymns of Middle America, while Lorentz celebrated the dignity of the ordinary rural people. The result was a powerful marriage of image and sound still worthy of study in both history and film classes; indeed, any textbook on the history of American documentary will have a section about the Lorentz productions, made for the Farm Services Administration to project a positive image for Roosevelt's New Deal. (See "The 1930s.") Filmmakers know that music can penetrate viewer defenses, and they enlist this aesthetic option to stir up the emotions; likewise, as all filmmakers know, documentaries are designed to arouse audiences, not merely to inform them. Feature films have even greater opportunity to employ this aural device, and some—such as Oliver Stone's *Platoon* (1986)—make maximum use of music to promote political messages. In *Platoon,* Stone's recurring employment of the heartrending "Adagio for Strings" by Samuel Barber as a leitmotif is unforgettable, as are the filmmaker's clever uses of popular tunes to evoke the cultural clashes of the 1960s. (See "The 1960s" and "The Vietnam War.")

The seventh question is: What is the role of production history in shaping the films? Knowledge of production history will often resolve apparently contradictory messages in a film—or at least explain their presence. Often in historical films with a political intent, after a message has been conceived, the creative forces behind the film search for a "vehicle" to carry that idea. For example, it seems clear that Warren Beatty's film *Reds* (1981), ostensibly about American John Reed's involvement in the Russian Revolution of 1917 and the subsequent founding of the Bolshevik state, was designed to romanticize twentieth-century radical movements in the United States. To make this connection, documentary-style interviews with radicals young and old (called "the witnesses") are intercut by editor Dede Allen with narrative about Reed's involvement with Soviet Communism. A typical viewer leaves the theater inspired by the idea of the Soviet experiment and angry about the repression of dissidents within the United States. Although *Reds* was far from a blockbuster at the box office, the poor financial showing was not a total disaster—at least for the director. Beatty's film was admired by the cognoscenti of Hollywood, the most important audience for some filmmakers. Although it is an engaging screen history, there are problems with *Reds*; what appears to be a historical study is really a cinematic manifesto designed to arouse complacent audiences during the presidency of Ronald Reagan (1981–89).

For a film like *The Grapes of Wrath,* the production history tells much about the intentions of the filmmakers and the gap between the goals of the social epic and the goals for the film. The social visions of John Ford and Darryl Zanuck are central to these differences from Steinbeck's literary original, leading to significant changes in plot, characterization, and imagery. Many questions are answered when attention is focused on how a film project moves from book to script to screen. As Lewis Owens has observed, "Zanuck and Ford succeeded in more than muting the political message of the novel and producing a film that—brilliant though it may be in many ways—turns Steinbeck's call for a rebirth of national consciousness into a sentimental celebration of the American 'salt of the earth'" (98).

The eighth question is: How was the film received by its contemporaries? And, as corollaries: Were there major disagreements at the time about its historical and entertainment values? What did the disagreement reflect about the gap between academic history and popular memory? As an example, what was there about the political atmosphere of the late 1930s that caused the federal government to withdraw *The Plow That Broke the Plains* from public distribution? (It was not reissued until 1964.) Conceived as a film to address environmental issues, the documentary was interpreted by many in Congress as an unfair attack on the American heartland. How could such a pioneering classic in the art of documentary filmmaking receive such treatment? The answer says much about the interface between art and politics in America. As has been mentioned, the epic film *The Birth of a Nation* (1914) was, in its historical interpretation, consonant with the then "new" history about Reconstruction. Even President Woodrow Wilson, a leading historian himself, greeted the film as an epic "history written with lightning." We now realize that both the history and the film history of the time were clouded by regional, class, and racial prejudices. As a southerner, Woodrow Wilson was blinded by regional mores as much as was filmmaker Griffith.

Goals and Structure of the Book

It is vital at the outset to define what this collection does *not* attempt to do: it does not attempt to be a comprehensive history of American films with historic themes and it does not attempt to be an encyclopedic in its coverage of motion pictures for the topics we have chosen to explore.

The book has been written with a broad audience in mind, to include thoughtful members of the general public who wish to pursue historical issues by way of video rentals and library loans; high school and college students and teachers who may wish to amplify their studies with appropriate—and intelligently critiqued—motion pictures; and graduate students and specialists in American culture studies. For all of these users, the essays in this book strive to be well-crafted interpretive reviews of the topics they cover. They can be used as a starting point for research and reflection. The essays should prove to be excellent maps of the territory, but neither the survey of films on the topic in question nor the discussion of written works of history is comprehensive. Rather, the essays offer particular ways of "reading" the film record, of exploring cinematic approaches to our past. Students reading about particular decades and leaders will profit from studying the ways in which time periods and personalities have been depicted by Hollywood, although such portrayals should always be compared with print historical sources, starting with the discussions in this volume. Graduate students writing theses and dissertations should sample the "popular memory" constructed of their topics by Hollywood, even when their research projects are not devoted to film or television. Teachers can turn to the book to find a few choice films that will add pedagogical tension to their classes. And these classes need not only be in film or history; for example, Charles J. Maland's essay "The American Adam" could be used as a starting point for research into the relationship of American literature to American film. Conversely, teachers of film and history could use that essay to make linkages with cultural patterns established by literature. The primary and secondary works cited, along with the films listed, could be a pool for further pursuit of the topic of one of the great American myths—the myth of individual and national innocence.

The essays are divided into eight parts, covering eras, major historical events, individuals of note, groups, institutions, places, themes, and myths of the American experience. Columbia University Press executive editor James Warren and I selected the topics after an extensive survey of existing textbooks in American history and such classic reference works as *The Harvard Guide to American History, An Encyclopedia of World History, The Reader's Companion to American History, The Columbia Literary History of the United States,* and the journal *Film & History.* We consulted with a number of outside scholars as well. The goal was to cover topics with a substantial film record now being studied in social studies and history classrooms. As the project advanced, we noticed—as we had hoped—that there are many instances where coverage overlapped, and therefore the same films may be examined in several different parts of the book for different reasons. As these overlapping instances multiplied, we decided to rely on a detailed index as the key for researching topics by keyword, film title, or director. We urge readers of the *Companion* to make use of the table of contents, but we believe that even more can be gleaned from a thoughtful use of the index, which will prove to be a valuable navigational instrument. If readers are interested in "the environment," they will discover through the index that films about the West, films from the Depression, films about the self-made man, and films from many other categories are relevant. The military-history enthusiast will find topics and films in the obvious places, but also in regional essays and in the section about myths; here, again, the index will be the best tool for a complete investigation of any topic.

Each essay is followed with a detailed filmography that lists relevant films for the topic; this list will help those wishing to construct a viewing agenda for personal enrichment or further research. The filmographies comprise three categories: feature films, abbreviated as "F"; documentaries, abbreviated as "D"; and television programs, series, or made-for-television movies, abbreviated as "TV." Each entry indicates the year a production was released, except in the rare instances where this datum is unknown. Following the filmography for each essay is a bibliography of sources, along with additional works of interest to anyone wanting to pursue the topic in further depth.

Part I, "Eras," covers obvious chronological periods of the American experience, beginning with the Puritans of the seventeenth century and continuing to the present. Although historians often quibble about what they may be, it is customary for us to associate clusters of attitudes with particular decades and eras of our history; this section looks at Hollywood versions of the special events, people, and values of America's crucial decades.

Part II, "Wars and Other Major Events," contains essays on major crises in our history, including America's major military conflicts. Beginning with the American Revolution, it surveys conflicts that are interminably—and sometimes mindlessly—used as fodder for programs on America's cable channels. The Civil War is one of the most-studied clashes for amateur historians. World War II receives two separate entries—one for the many documentaries made during (and, later, about) the struggle, and another for the large body of feature films about the conflict. The American war film is a highly politicized genre, explicitly addressing—depending upon the stage of the conflicts—the nation's prewar anxieties, wartime aggressions, and postwar reconsiderations.

Events in the American West have fascinated both Americans and Hollywood, and films about westward expansion—both the early stages in the Appalachians as well as the later reaches into the Northwest and California—

are excellent tools for gauging the nation's morale. This section surveys the formula westerns of the silent era, moving forward to "New Westerns" such as George Roy Hill's *Butch Cassidy and the Sundance Kid* (1969) and Clint Eastwood's *Unforgiven* (1992)—which, like many other genre films, reflect their own eras as much as they depict the past. In our time of burgeoning Native American awareness and political autonomy, the depiction of the Indian Wars has a vital place in any motion picture survey. Like other depictions of the West, these films reflect contemporary attitudes—so that whereas *They Died with Their Boots On* (1941) was a celebration of George Armstrong Custer (Errol Flynn), *Little Big Man* (1970) excoriates the famed military leader as a pompous fool in an attempt to comment on the suffering inflicted by western expansion as well as to make an antiwar statement about the ongoing Vietnam conflict. Yet both films claim to be about the very same public figure.

Part III, "Notable People," looks at cinematic depictions of selected prominent Americans, beginning with Indian leaders and Columbus and moving forward in time to John F. Kennedy and Richard Nixon. America adores its notables, and Hollywood has obliged with films sometimes made with little hope of financial return—proving again that Hollywood works for more than money. Such hagiographic studies can emerge with far different interpretations of the great people in our history.

Part IV, "Groups," offers essays on films that depict ethnic peoples within the United States. Over the decades, even though the motion picture studios were owned or managed by scions of ethnic groups, Hollywood had difficulty getting the story right about minorities. Often there was a fear that films that did not play to stereotypes would not be acceptable as "entertainment" by mainstream audiences. In some cases, the writers and filmmakers willingly perpetuated prejudice and bigotry. African Americans, Asian Americans, and Native Americans, among others, have legitimate complaints about derogatory stereotyping. The existing film record gives a fascinating window on how Americans have seen themselves—and others—on motion picture screens across the land. Women and children, too, have had major roles in the movies of America; here again, the depiction of these groups serves as an important social barometer.

Part V, "Institutions and Movements," examines major building blocks of the nation—government at the local and national levels, civil rights and labor groups, the family, and schools. Of perennial interest, of course, is the American presidency, a topic of such blockbuster films as *The American President* (1994) and the award-winning television series *The West Wing* (1999–). What Americans think about their presidents reflects our own self image—so that *Gabriel Over the White House* (1934) speaks volumes about America's jitters during the early days of the Great Depression, while *Primary Colors* (1998) accurately reveals the nation's ambivalent support for William Jefferson Clinton. (The film ends on Inauguration Eve with the voiceover warning, "Don't break our hearts!")

How have films reported on reporters? The entry "Journalism and Media" answers this provocative question. America has been a success as a society because of a plethora of what sociologists now call "mediating structures." As far back as *Democracy in America* (1835), Alexis de Tocqueville noted the proliferation of grass-roots organizations and predicted that they would be the basis for a dynamic nation. A number of these engines of our "civil society" are explored here as well.

Part VI, "Places," travels from region to region within the United States, looking at the manner in which filmmakers have interpreted our varied national landscapes. Because mise-en-scène (that is, the use of physical details of the environment) is a primary aesthetic device for filmmakers, there has been much emphasis on this element—to the point where the land, itself, can become a character in a film. For example, in Michael Cimino's *The Deer Hunter* (1978), the landscape is so important to the Leatherstocking motif of the film that the director created Rocky Mountain–style vistas for hunting scenes set in the less-than-sublime Appalachians. On the other hand, such films as *Giant* (1956) clearly stress the epic growth of a society on a land rich in natural resources (cattle and oil) and steeped in traditions—not all of them acceptable to the modern sensibility. Not to be left out are the heavens, the topic of some memorable motion pictures—some fantastic and others approaching documentary realism. Space films continue the exploration of a physical frontier, thereby appealing to a national obsession that has been operative since at least 1893, when historian Frederick Jackson Turner announced that American character was linked to the nation's ongoing frontier experience.

Part VII, "Themes and Topics," addresses a potpourri of important issues, including obvious topics such as slavery and sexuality, but also less noticed subjects such as drugs and crime. Hollywood has cast key lights on unexpected—and in some cases, forbidden—areas of our national existence for a multitude of reasons, only some of which have to do with prurient interest. Especially in the 1940s, filmmakers made special efforts to reconsider the nature of the American family; later, teenagers became a preoccupation because they were an identifiable ticket-buying audience and because Americans were perplexed about how postwar economic and social changes were affecting an affluent generation. Of course, how feminism has been depicted should be of interest to all thoughtful citizens; clearly, there has been revision of judgment since the early days when suffragettes were objects of ridicule.

Part VIII, "Myths and Heroes," brings this volume to a conclusion with a collection of essays on American myths that have been embedded in the film legacy. A people lives by its myths, and what reaches mythic status says much about its values. Americans fervently believe in democracy, and American culture often links that theme with a place called the frontier. (Indeed, the "frontier thesis" was a dominant paradigm of the historical profession before motion pictures became a mass medium.) American culture celebrates the self-made man and sings the praises of entrepreneurial innovation. On the other hand, Americans worry about the negative impact of technology and deplore unbridled individualism. In one of our most pervasive romantic myths, we believe in the American Adam in his New World garden. Yet hard-boiled detective novels such as *The Maltese Falcon* (book 1930, film 1941) and their cinematic adaptations explore the noir side of the American Dream, where morality is defunct and corruption pervasive. Yet, in times of crisis, we pay homage to ordinary Americans in uniform—as did noir director John Huston in his gripping World War II documentaries.

The Columbia Companion to American History on Film should help readers gain an understanding of the malleability of the "facts" of history in documentaries and feature films. Discerning interpretation and point of view is the beginning of a wise use of visual resources about America's past and its present culture. If we spend as much as nine years of our lives in movie theaters and before our television sets, we need to be media-literate. The essays in this collection will help guide readers toward a responsible use of films as portals to America's past.

PETER C. ROLLINS

References

Filmography

The Birth of a Nation (1915, F)
A Bright Shining Lie (1998, TV)
The Covered Wagon (1923, F)
The Deer Hunter (1978, F)
Dr. Strangelove, or: How I Stopped Worrying and Learned to Love the Bomb (1964, F)
Giant (1956, F)
Gone with the Wind (1939, F)
The Grapes of Wrath (1940, F)
JFK (1991, F)
Native Land (1941, F)
On the Waterfront (1954, F)
Platoon (1986, F)
The Plow That Broke the Plains (1936, D)
Reds (1981, F)
The River (1937, D)
Roots (1977, F)
Wall Street (1987, F)
The West Wing (1999– , TV)

Bibliography

Elliott, Emory, ed. *Columbia Literary History of the United States.* New York: Columbia University Press, 1988.

Film & History: An Interdisciplinary Journal of Film and Television Studies. www.filmandhistory.org.

Foner, Eric, and John Garraty, eds. *The Reader's Companion to American History.* Boston: Houghton Mifflin, 1991.

Freidel, Frank, ed. *The Harvard Guide to American History.* 2 vols. Rev. ed. Cambridge, MA: Belknap Press, 1974.

Harrington, John. *The Rhetoric of Film.* New York: Holt, Rinehart, and Winston, 1973.

Hey, Kenneth. "Ambivalence as a Theme in *On the Waterfront* (1954): An Interdisciplinary Approach to Film Study." In Peter Rollins, ed., *Hollywood as Historian: American Film in a Cultural Context,* 159–189. Lexington: University Press of Kentucky, 1998.

Kubey, Robert, and Mihaly Csikszentmihalyi. "Television Addiction Is No Mere Metaphor." *Scientific American,* February 2002.

Langer, William, ed. *An Encyclopedia of World History.* Boston: Houghton Mifflin, 1952.

O'Connor, John E. *American History/American Film.* New York: Frederick Ungar, 1979.

——. *Image as Artifact: The Historical Analysis of Film and Television.* Malabar, FL: Krieger, 1990.

Owens, Lewis. *The Grapes of Wrath: Trouble in the Promised Land.* Boston: G. K. Hall, 1989.

Rollins, Peter. *Will Rogers: A Bio-Bibliography.* Westport, CT: Greenwood, 1983.

——, ed. *Hollywood as Historian: American Film in a Cultural Context.* 2d ed. Lexington: University Press of Kentucky, 1998.

Rollins, Peter, and John E. O'Connor. *Hollywood's White House: The American Presidency in Film and Television.* Lexington: University Press of Kentucky, 2003.

——, eds. *The West Wing: The American Presidency as Television Drama.* Syracuse, NY: Syracuse University Press, 2003.

Will, George. "'JFK' Makes Hash of History." *Time,* 26 December 1991.

I.
Eras

★ ★ ★ ★ ★ ★ ★

[EDWARD J. INGEBRETSEN]

The Puritan Era and the Puritan Mind

The Puritans who organized the 1630 Great Migration to Boston—and the Pilgrim Separatists who, a few years earlier, had settled in Plymouth, twenty miles south—sought protection from the religious harassment they experienced in England and the Netherlands. Neither group had much use for principles that would later be thought especially "American": religious toleration, individualism, separation of church and state. On the contrary, as their sobriquet implied, they separated themselves to the wilds of Massachusetts in order to purify their religious practice. In exile they sought to make that practice more, rather than less, strict. In conformity with biblical warrant, they simplified liturgical practice and emphasized the preaching of the biblical Word, in general turning away from high-church ritual. The Puritans, as well as the stricter Pilgrims, intended their religious society to constitute more—rather than less—of the civil state.

For much of its postcolonial history, American intellectual culture has been concerned with distancing itself from the perceived narrowness of "Puritanism"—or "The New England Way," as their theocratic order would be remembered. This is particularly visible in the literature of the American Renaissance (1830–1865). Emerson and Hawthorne, for instance, alternately apologize for the Puritan past or envelop it in nostalgia. Hawthorne's treatment is wistfully apologetic, particularly in his numerous short sketches and in *The Scarlet Letter* (1850) and *The House of the Seven Gables* (1851). Emerson, on the other hand, after leaving the Unitarian ministry, transformed the legacy of Puritan spiritual thought into the more expansive moral idealism of romanticism.

Nevertheless, the Puritans play an extraordinary part in the mythology of America. They are idealized in some quarters and demonized in others. Numerous scholars on the Puritans have demonstrated that even as the Puritan theocratic order declined in authority with the passing of years, the rhetoric, energy, and expectant messianism of the Puritan vision both shaped and was appropriated by a civic rhetoric of progress. The "city set on a mountain," for example, is an image used by Jesus (Matthew 5:14–15) in the Sermon on the Mount. The first governor of the Massachusetts Bay Colony, John Winthrop, borrowed the image with polemical intent at the landing of the *Arbella* in Boston (1630). The phrase would later find echoes in theologian Jonathan Edwards's (1703–1758) language of civic destiny, while a rationalist reworking of similar apocalyptic rhetoric shapes Thomas Jefferson's Declaration of Independence. At a further remove, Puritan millennial expectations provided impetus and justification for the Revolutionary War and even ground the terms of Manifest Destiny as well as the American Dream. In his remarks at Gettysburg Cemetery and in his Second Inaugural Address, the avowedly secular Abraham Lincoln would find the Puritans' covenantal language of fidelity and guilt appropriate to his postwar elegiac needs.

Yet, despite Lincoln's example, the recognition of the Puritans as valuably "American" was late in coming. The religious fundamentalism of the Puritans was considered by many to be an embarrassment to America's democratic sensibility. Further, the strict moralism credited to the Puritans and their single-minded religious vision made them a scapegoat for late-nineteenth-century capitalism and intellectual liberalism. Such well-known intellectuals as Oliver Wendell Holmes Sr. and William James excoriated their seventeenth-century forebears. Holmes took particular exception to Jonathan Edwards. His theology, Holmes wrote, "shocks the sensibilities of a later generation" (384). Similarly, in *The Varieties of Religious Experience,* James argued that Edwards's sovereign God was, "if sovereignly anything, sovereignly irrational and mean" (330).

After the traumatic years of World War I and following the short-lived economic boom of the 1920s, the country sank into the Depression. Models of American heroism were in short supply during these years, and the Puritan legacy was revived. Harvard historian Samuel Eliot Morison played an important role in this project. In his worshipful *Builders of the Bay Colony* (1930), Morison rehabilitated the Puritans as examples of struggle, courage, and spiritual integrity. Morison also built on this rehabilitation by editing William Bradford's *Of Plymouth Plantation, 1620–1647.* The rediscovery of the Puritans was broadened in the years following World War II, when the United States found itself again embodying the "city on a hill." The performance was a complicated one, however, inasmuch as the city on the hill was being watched as well as watching—a guardian and exemplar of national moralities as well as world securities.

The discovery of the Puritan past as contemporary American ideal owes its current force to these years. Particularly through the work of Harvard University's Perry Miller (1905–1963), a direct intellectual line was drawn from the early Puritan founders to thinkers of the nineteenth and twentieth centuries. In the two volumes of Miller's *The New England Mind* (1939, 1953), New England's regional history became "national" history. Miller fit the moral enthusiasm of the Puritans to the secular idealism of a newly self-aware, world-policing nation. In colleges and universities across the land, the nascent American studies movement—a celebration of American themes, disciplines, and issues—would capitalize upon this refurbishing. John Winthrop's "Cittee on the Hill" was understood to be American now, and progressive, rather than Puritan and millenarian. In this manner it was used to define, as well as to justify, conceptions of American exceptionalism. Such an image remained strongly influential through the Cold War years and beyond, as typified by President Ronald Reagan's reflexive use of the image in nearly all of his major addresses to the nation.

Thus, a conflicted energy to forget as well as to remember finds the Puritan legacy—indeed, New England itself—at once underrepresented and overdetermined in film. That is, although Puritan rhetoric and example have been useful in presidential speeches from Lincoln through Eisenhower and Reagan, very few attempts were made to translate these historical experiences into popular twentieth-century media, including film and television.

The Frontier and the Vanished Puritan

The Puritans and their descendants do figure slightly off-camera in various "frontier" narratives. However, the particularly religious intensity of their lives remained cinematically untouchable, given an American defensiveness around such notions as religious tolerance and separation of church and state. Nonetheless, construed as an aspect of frontier life, as in *The Last of the Mohicans* (1920, 1936) and *Drums along the Mohawk* (1939), or as an exercise in nostalgia, as in *Last of the Red Men* (1947), a derivative Puritan ethos was used to emphasize stalwart loyalty and courage against natural forces and human enemies. These explicitly nationalistic films silently elide any overt religious reference. Indeed, creedal or spiritual ideas of any sort were erased from these Hollywood productions in order to underscore truly "American values" of courage, endurance, and reliance upon inner strength. These were the emotional tools necessary in Depression-era America, and consequently the Puritan theocentric vision had to be reconceptualized as "democratic individualism," which it surely had not been.

Cinematic representations of Puritan history are scarce, except where a Puritan sensibility is useful as aesthetic backdrop. For example, *The Pursuit of Happiness* (1934) is a historical romance about revolutionary times. The film shows how the shadow of war touched a rural community in Connecticut. This civil order (highly romanticized) is by implication Puritan—narrow and restrictive and so, as the title suggests, against the pursuit of happiness. In this case, happiness is the formulaic love affair developing between a rural Connecticut maid, Prudence, and a Hessian soldier, a mercenary outsider to the community. In this secular vision of the American past, a patina of Puritan feeling is retained, while people who might actually have been Puritans are silently erased.

The expanding cinema industry also sought out "American" adventures that could be translated to the screen. Certain episodes associated with the Puritans were found useful. Although its title refers specifically to the founding of Plymouth Colony, *Plymouth Adventure* (1952), directed by Clarence Brown (from the novel by Ernest Gebler), is more about misadventures at sea than about the landing at Plymouth. The film dramatizes the perilous 1620 journey of the *Mayflower* from Old to New England, with little attention given to the actual fortunes of the colony itself subsequent to landing.

Although Puritan ideology could be trimmed, cut, and celebrated as "proto-American," legendary Puritan intolerance also made the New Englanders easy targets for demonization. To H. L. Mencken, for example, the term "Puritan" was synonymous with provincialism and cultural narrowness. In particular, the Salem witch trials of 1692–93 have been the subject, or perhaps excuse, for many inexpensive horror films, often mixed with political allegory. The Salem events are recast as typically Puritan, but similar ideological use is as old as the sketches in Hawthorne's *Twice-Told Tales* (1842). *Maid of Salem* (1937), directed by Frank Lloyd, is typical of this revisionist history; a prologue states that the story was based on "authentic records of the year 1692." Nonetheless, as in *Plymouth Adventure,* historicity in *Maid of Salem* quickly gives way to a sentimental love formula (starring Claudette Colbert as Barbara Clarke and Fred MacMurray as Roger Coverman).

Hawthorne's revisions of Puritan history are numerous, and so, too, *The Scarlet Letter* (1850) has been treated variously in film. Hawthorne's classic text, like the Puritan history itself, was trimmed to fit a variety of polemical needs. Three in particular deserve note. The 1934 production, directed by Robert G. Vignola, has its own mix of ideology and Hollywood formula, as an opening title indicates: "This is more than the story of a woman—it is a portrait of the Puritan period in American life." The Puritans come in for conventional criticism. Centered on work and courting customs, scenes comically portray Puritans as relentlessly literal-minded. The scenes most directly related to Hawthorne's text, however, are generally faithful to his original narrative. Chillingworth is portrayed as cerebral and malevolent in seeking revenge, Arthur Dimmesdale as inwardly torn and ineffectual. Hester's nobility—her mercy and compassion under great duress—are shown triumphing over the sin-obsessed narrow-mindedness of the Puritan villagers.

The 1979 PBS *Scarlet Letter* (directed and produced by Rick Hauser) remains the most complex and nuanced treatment of all versions. Hauser portrays better than others Hawthorne's layered ambiguity, in whose

FIGURE 1. *The Scarlet Letter* (1995). Condemned by the townspeople of Salem for adultery, Hester Prynne (Demi Moore) remains dignified and defiant as she walks with her baby. Courtesy Allied Stars, Cinergi, Lighthouse, and Moving Pictures.

treatment of an actual political crisis in early Puritan history the rigidity of Puritan idealism comes under scrutiny. Although Hauser remains true to Hawthorne, his baroque presentation has some drawbacks. It is long on meditation—especially the almost nuanced portrayal of Chillingworth (wronged, but compassionate and understanding, as played by Kevin Conroy) and Dimmesdale (timid but literally self-flagellating, as played by John Heard). Hester (Meg Foster) is represented as type rather than individual; she is stoic and proud, silently enduring all abuse from the citizens of the town. The Hawthornean indictment of disassociated idealism comes through most clearly in the repeated confrontations between proud Hester and the town magistrate, Mr. Wilson, who is determined to break her spirit. Similarly, Hauser remains true at least to the spirit of Hawthorne in the attention he pays to Hester's daughter's (Elisa Erali) willful personality. He also shows, as Hawthorne made clear, that the pressure leveraged against Dimmesdale by his religious superiors and secular authorities results from a mix of envy as well as solicitousness.

In 1995, Hollywood Pictures released *The Scarlet Letter,* "freely adapted from the novel," directed by Roland Joffe. The Puritans come in for the usual bashing. Governor Bellingham (Edward Hardwicke) says to the stylishly dressed Hester Prynne (Demi Moore), as she disembarks in Salem, "You would do well here to use less lace in your dressmaking." In this adaptation Hawthorne's tale becomes one narrow part of the history of the Puritan colony at Salem. Narrated from the retrospective viewpoint of Pearl, now a young woman, the colony of Salem is situated between two crises—the growing distrust of the Indians on one hand (in 1666, when the film opens, King Philip's War is a decade in the future) and, on the other hand, the witch hunts of a later generation (1692–93). Hawthorne's narrative remains submerged for the first half of the film. It is midway through the film before Hester is found with child, and only much later does her husband Roger (Robert Duvall)—supposedly long dead in an Indian raid—make his appearance.

The conflation of the Puritans and the Salem witch hunts is standard literary practice from Hawthorne onward, and the newer media are no exception. Witchcraft films are perennial favorites in the Gothic as well as comedy genres (for horror, see *The Craft* [1996] and *The Blair Witch Project* [1999]). Typically, Salem and the Puritans provide the framing narrative in many of them, such as *Maid of Salem* (1937) and *Warlock* (1989). The association of Puritanism and witchery can be found in the earliest cinematic productions, both in the United States and abroad; Arthur Miller returns to the theme of witchcraft and the Puritan past in *The Crucible* (1953). Cold War concerns about infiltrating communists brought Miller to the attention of the House Committee on Un-American Activities (HUAC). Miller's stage version of a tense and divided Salem played first on Broadway in 1953 against this American backdrop; the play was clearly designed to editorialize about contemporary concerns.

Although popular in school dramatic productions, and other than two productions intended for television, there was no major English film version of Miller's *The Crucible* until

FIGURE 2. *The Crucible* (1996). Teenage girls in Salem (1692), led by Abigail Williams (Winona Ryder, center), hurl false accusations of witchcraft. Courtesy Twentieth Century-Fox.

the 1996 Twentieth Century–Fox production, directed by Nicholas Hytner. Daniel Day-Lewis plays John Proctor; Winona Ryder plays his nemesis, the love-struck, self-centered Abigail Williams, while Paul Scofield plays the sternly righteous Judge Danforth. Arthur Miller wrote the screenplay for this production, and, though he keeps Proctor's adultery as motive, it is subsidiary to other emotions—town rivalries, land tensions, and, finally, the spiritual zealotry and inhumanity of the Colony leaders. Nevertheless, Miller's 1996 adaptation, like the original stage play in this respect, presents a nuanced view of the Puritans. Although many officials, civil and religious, are portrayed as flawed, power-hungry, and inflexible, a few are depicted as decent, thoughtful people. Likewise, some townspeople are land-grabbing, greedy, and contentious, but others are fearful and trusting—wanting to do right but often confused as to how.

Puritan Gothic

Many, perhaps most, of the Gothic films that feature New England or the Puritans are versions of literary works. Indeed, after Hawthorne, H. P. Lovecraft is to be credited with popularizing the genre of New England Gothic, and he credits at length its Puritan legacy. In *Supernatural Horror in Literature,* Lovecraft cites "all manner of notions respecting man's relation to the stern and vengeful God of the Calvinists, and to the sulphurous Adversary of that God." Such a climate, the fervent materialist Lovecraft claimed, was one in which "tales of witchcraft and unbelievable secret monstrosities lingered long after the dread days of the Salem nightmare" (60–61). A number of Lovecraft's New England tales (twenty-two, to be precise) have been reimagined as films, including the John Carpenter release *In the Mouth of Madness* (1995). Of particular interest are *The Unnamable* (1988, Jean-Paul Ouellette, dir.) and *The Dunwich Horror* (1969, Daniel Haller, dir.).

The Disney Versions

Two of Disney's recent films have some bearing in this discussion of a usable Puritan past. *Squanto: A Warrior's Tale* (1994) derives its name from an Indian who was taken captive by British colonists and later exhibited in London. In Disney's film, Squanto escapes in England and returns to the New World. There he finds that remnants of the Mayflower colony have taken over his destroyed village—now renamed "Plymouth." Squanto helps the colonists adapt to the New World while convincing local tribes to accept them. More distantly, there are a variety of children's versions of the Pocahontas story. Disney's *Pocohantas* [*sic*] (1995) retells that anxiety-laden originary myth of racial encounter between Captain John Smith and the daughter of Wahunsonacook, dubbed Chief Powhatan (the tribal name)—at the landing at Jamestown. These animated versions of events in early American history demonstrate the pattern noted earlier by which historical memory, already a vexed enterprise, becomes further complicated when its events become pressed into service as allegory and civic self-narrative.

It is probably impossible to draw with any accuracy a portrait of the original English settlers of New England. Ideological imperatives, varying in needs and energy, insure that any portrayal of the Puritans in film and literature will exploit current social concerns. This exploitation, of course, is not limited to cinema or to the present. In the prologue to *The Scarlet Letter,* Hawthorne discusses how the Puritan past serves him. As a grandson of one of the Salem judges, John Hathorne, he recognizes the distance between his grandfather's generation and his own: "No aim, that I have ever cherished, would they recognize as laudable; no success of mine . . . would they deem otherwise than worthless." And yet, Hawthorne writes, "Let them scorn me as they will, strong traits of their nature have intertwined themselves with mine" (10). Hawthorne's mix of misplaced guilt, regret, and envy still has its place in the reconstruction of memory. The Puritans will always be available to play out those emotions, as CBS demonstrated in its 1999 sitcom about the Puritans and Thanksgiving, entitled *Thanks.*

References

Filmography

Arthur Miller and The Crucible (1981, D)
Blair Witch Project (1999, F)
Burn, Witch, Burn (a.k.a. *Night of the Eagle,* 1961, F)
City of the Dead (a.k.a. *Horror Hotel,* 1960, F)
The Craft (1996, F)
The Crucible (1967, TV; 1980, TV; 1996, F)
The Devil's Hand (a.k.a. *Naked Goddess, Live to Love,* 1959, F)
Drums along the Mohawk (1939, F)
The Dunwich Horror (1969, F)
Hocus Pocus (1993, F)
House of the Seven Gables (1940, F)
In the Mouth of Madness (1995, F)
The Last of the Mohicans (1920, F; 1936, F)
Last of the Red Men (1947, F)
The Little Puritan (1915, F)
Maid of Salem (1937, F)
My Mother, the Witch (n.d., F)
Natural Born Puritan (1994, D)
Pilgrim Journey (n.d., D)
Plymouth Adventure (1952, F)
Pocohantas (1995, F)
The Promised Land (1997, D)
The Puritan (1914, F)
Puritan Passions (1923, F)
The Pursuit of Happiness (1934, F)
Rosemary's Baby (1968, F)
Salem Witch Trials (1992, D)
The Scarlet Letter (1909, F; 1917, F; 1926, F; 1934, F; 1950, TV; 1954, TV; 1979, F; 1995, F)
Squanto: A Warrior's Tale (1994, F)
Thanks (1999, TV)
The Unnamable (1988, F)
The Unnamable Returns (1992, F)
Unnamable II: The Statement of Randolph Carter (1993, F)
Warlock (1989, F)
The Witch of Salem (1913, F)
A Witch of Salem Town (1915, F)
The Witch Woman (1918, F)
Witchcraft (a.k.a. *Witch and Warlock,* 1964, F)
Witchcraft (1988, F)
Witchcraft, Part II: The Temptress (1989, F)
Witchcraft III: The Kiss of Death (1991, F)
Witchcraft IV: Virgin Heart (1992, F)
The Witches (a.k.a. *The Devil's Own,* 1966, F)
The Witches (1990, F)
The Witches of Eastwick (1987, F)
Witchfinder General (a.k.a. *The Conqueror Worm,* 1968, F)

Bibliography

Anonymous. Review of *Maid of Salem. Literary Digest,* February 1937.
Bercovitch, Sacvan. *The Puritan Origins of the American Self.* New Haven: Yale University Press, 1975.
Colacurcio, Michael. *Doctrine and Difference: Essays in the Literature of New England.* New York: Routledge, 1997.
Conforti, Joseph A. *Jonathan Edwards: Religious Tradition and American Culture.* Chapel Hill: University of North Carolina Press, 1996.
Demos, John. *Entertaining Satan: Witchcraft and the Culture of Early New England.* Oxford: Oxford University Press, 1982.
Heimert, Alan, ed. *The Puritans in America: A Narrative Anthology.* Cambridge, MA: Harvard University Press, 1985.
Holmes, Oliver Wendell. *Pages from an Old Volume of Life: A Collection of Essays, 1857–1881.* Boston: Houghton Mifflin, 1892.
James, William. *The Varieties of Religious Experience: A Study in Human Nature.* Ed. Martin E. Marty. New York: Penguin, 1983.
Lovecraft, H. P. *Supernatural Horror in Literature.* New York: Dover, 1973.

Maslin, Janet. Review of *The Crucible. New York Times,* 27 November 1996.
Miller, Perry. *Errand into the Wilderness.* Cambridge, MA: Belknap Press, 1956.
——. *The New England Mind: From Colony to Province.* Cambridge, MA: Harvard University Press, 1953.
——. *The New England Mind: The Seventeenth Century.* Boston: Beacon Press, 1961.
Morison, Samuel Eliot. *Builders of the Bay Colony.* Boston: Houghton Mifflin, 1930.
——. *The Intellectual Life of Colonial New England.* New York: New York University Press, 1956.
Pitts, Michael R. *Hollywood and American History: A Filmography of Over 250 Motion Pictures Depicting U.S. History.* Jefferson, NC: McFarland, 1984.
Santayana, George. *The Last Puritan: A Memoir in the Form of a Novel.* New York: Scribner's, 1936.

[JOSEPH MILLICHAP]

The 1890s

The final decade of the nineteenth century would prove conclusive in America's transition from the rural and agrarian simplicity of the early republic to the urban and industrial complexity of the twentieth-century superpower. A period of rapid changes, major dislocations, and extreme tensions, the 1890s were subsumed in the American cultural consciousness as the last flowering of an innocent age. The American sobriquet "the Gay Nineties," though created by the same reaction against Victorian mores that named it *le fin de siècle* abroad, was soon transmuted into a wistful evocation of a lost time of simpler pleasures by the new century's nostalgia.

During the 1890s, largely unacknowledged tensions of gender, race, and class exploded in a number of historically important and socially significant conflicts. Among these were the first emergence of major agitation for and resistance to women's rights, the majority acceptance of a "separate but equal" facade and a "Jim Crow" reality in racial relations, and widespread antagonism between rich and poor, native and immigrant, and big business and labor. In particular, these economic tensions determined the important historical events of the decade: the literal warfare of the Homestead (1892), the Pullman (1894), and several other strikes; the financial Panic of 1893, the nation's worst business collapse before the Great Depression; and the Spanish-American War (1898), our first flirtation with imperialism, colonialism, and world power status. Thus, the shaping realities of the American 1890s were anything but "gay," in the parlance of those times.

Perhaps as important in a cultural sense was the more subtle conflict between traditional human values inherent in the land itself and the emerging power of technology represented in the new machinery of the era. Chicago's Columbian Exposition (1892–93) showcased these innovative technologies and elicited the recognition that our culture had changed fundamentally as the era of expansion closed forever. Frederick Jackson Turner's classic statement of his "Frontier Thesis" appeared in connection with the great exposition and in direct response to the census data of 1890, which declared the western experiment finished in cultural terms. The first year of the decade also saw the Wounded Knee Massacre, the final assault on the independent Native cultures trying to dance back the buffalo against the forces of civilization represented by the transcontinental railroad, barbed wire, and the repeating rifle.

Among these many emerging technologies were the pioneering efforts of Thomas A. Edison and others on the new frontier of film. This prehistory of the movies is somewhat obscure, but, at the decade's beginning, Edison was perfecting his Kinetoscope, a sort of home "peep show" that he saw as a visual complement to his phonograph. In 1893 he built the first film studio, and by 1895 the first theaters for public projection of his Kinematographs, or "flickers." For subjects, Edison and his competitors turned their cameras on the America of the 1890s that surrounded them. A catalogue of early film titles parallels a popular history of the period: *Empire State Express* (1896), the fastest train of the era; *The Kiss* (1896), which records the osculatory antics of the popular Broadway actor Fred Ott; and *Rough Riders at Guantanamo* (1898), directly before the famous charge up San Juan Hill in the Cuban theater of the war against the Spanish.

Unfortunately, later American film would be less inclined to record the realities of the 1890s. As national film production shifted from New York to Los Angeles in the early decades of the twentieth century, it came to reflect and to recreate the national amnesia about the actual history of the nineteenth century, including its last decade. Nor would the Hollywood studio system ever be much interested in the struggles of suffragettes, the bloody reign of Jim Crow and lynch law, or organized labor's or populist farmers' battles with unbridled big business.

Indeed, the popular revolt against the social and sexual restraints of a lingering Puritanism in the "Gay Nineties" would be transformed into a smirking, repressed amusement at the quaint doings in the age of corset and bustle. In fact, the major movie response to the 1890s was a simplistic "good old days" reading of the era. Sentimental recreations of the period dominated the central decades of the twentieth century, perhaps in response to their own harsh realities; however, the 1930s of the Depression, the 1940s of World War II, and the 1950s of the Cold War were also the central decades of the Hollywood studio system. Even in more liberated times since the demise of the studios, this reading of the period has hardly changed on the American screen.

A representative though undistinguished example in point is *The Naughty Nineties* (1945), featuring the comedic pairing of Bud Abbott and Lou Costello in a rambling anthology of variety pieces set aboard a superannuated showboat. The title captures Hollywood's take on this pivotal decade: nostalgic humor, including the filmic version of the stars' trademark "Who's On First" routine, chorines in flora-dora outfits and can-can corsets, and minstrel-show blacks and slow-talking "poor white trash." Of course, the Abbott and Costello features were program fillers, with little more substance than a television variety show; yet the clichés evident in *The Naughty Nineties* pervade Hollywood's versions of the 1890s, whether low-budget programs or big-budget features.

For example, the immensely popular features of Will Rogers very consciously project the same historical take on the 1890s, one which Rogers himself developed during his frontier youth in Oklahoma and iterated in his famous radio talks (Rollins, 211). *David Harum* (1934) provides the best filmic view of the time, with Rogers becoming a "Dutch Uncle" to a younger protagonist who flees the city during an economic downturn and discovers true American values in symbolically Homeville, U.S.A. Although the names and places change, the same images appear in other Rogers features such as *Steamboat 'Round the Bend* (1935), which pairs Rogers with humorist Irvin S. Cobb, and *In Old Kentucky* (1935), Rogers's last feature before his untimely death. His first important movie, *A Connecticut Yankee in King Arthur's Court* (1931), was rereleased in 1936 as a confirmation of his popularity. This literary adaptation proves doubly ironic; Mark Twain's 1889 novel satirizes romantic attitudes about the good old days in Bridgeport and Camelot, while Rogers's take sentimentalizes both places and times—much as the humorist did with 1930s America.

Some other movie examples in confirmation of these general tendencies might start with the Mae West classic *She Done Him Wrong* (1933), the source of her trademark line: "Why don't you come up sometime and see me?" The target of Mae's famous come-on is a very young and virile Cary Grant as an ineffective vice-squad operative in the Bowery during the 1890s. West wrote her own script from her earlier play, *Diamond Lil* (1928), a loosely based re-creation of the career of 1890s glamour girl

Lillian Russell. Her characterization of the turn of the century sexpot was reprised in *Belle of the Nineties* (1934), though the scene shifted to New Orleans, and *Klondike Annie* (1934), where she runs off to the Yukon with the San Francisco constabulary in hot pursuit.

San Francisco, the glamour capitol of the West in the last decade of the nineteenth century, was balanced on the East Coast by New York City, then as now the Big Apple of the entertainment business. Tin Pan Alley, then just coming into its own, provided a venue for nostalgic tunes, as in *Sweet Rosie O'Grady* (1945), featuring Betty Grable and Adolphe Menjou, or *Belle of New York* (1952), with Fred Astaire and Vera Ellen. Hollywood versions of the decade changed little, even if the scene shifted, with the same ubiquitous Ms. Grable showing off her long, silk-stockinged legs at Chicago's Columbian Exhibition in *Wabash Avenue* (1950).

These "show biz" stories were often based on real personalities, ranging from famous stars to obscure songwriters. More earnest film biographies, often categorized as "biopics," reached the height of their popularity in the 1930s and 1940s and presented some of the more interesting Hollywood images of the American 1890s. For example, Diamond Lil was more demurely portrayed by Alice Faye in *Lillian Russell* (1940), which also featured a very young Henry Fonda as romantic rival to Edward Arnold's "Diamond Jim" Brady. In another area of popular entertainment, *Gentleman Jim* (1942) starred Errol Flynn as 1890s heavyweight boxing champion James J. Corbett. Perhaps the best example of this neglected genre remains *The Story of Alexander Graham Bell* (1939), which starred veteran character actor Don Ameche in his most famous role as the inventor of the telephone.

A sophisticated variant of the standard filmed biography is Orson Welles's classic *Citizen Kane* (1941), the fictionalized history of newspaper mogul William Randolph Hearst. Welles's brash rich boy Charles Foster Kane comes of age with the 1890s, taking over a staid New York daily on a lark and making it the most popular tabloid in the era that invented "yellow journalism." Kane reprises Hearst's putative statement to his reporters when they complained that they could discover no revolution in Spanish-held Cuba; they were to stay in place to furnish the stories and pictures, as he would soon furnish the war. The film reflects Hearst's jingoist editorial stance favoring a war with Spain in a brilliant scene of a stag dinner replete with chorus girls wearing both corsets and campaign caps, an image toying with several of the era's conflated and conflicting interests.

Welles's literate interest in the 1890s continued in his next effort, *The Magnificent Ambersons* (1942), an adaptation of Booth Tarkington's novel of the same title. Literary adaptations generally produced some of the more realistic images of the decade in film. For example, one of pioneer *auteur* D. W. Griffith's first important films is *A Corner in Wheat* (1911), which combines plot lines and image patterns from several narratives by the naturalist writer Frank Norris. In some ways, Griffith's briefer and more focused version emphasizes the economic conflicts of the decade more effectively than Norris's diffuse, symbolic fictions. The debut novel of another important writer of naturalism, Theodore Dreiser's *Sister Carrie* (1900), was adapted in 1952 under the shorter title *Carrie,* with Jennifer Jones interpreting the title role under the able direction of William Wyler. Jack London's naturalistic *Call of the Wild* (1903) also elicited multiple adaptations: in 1935 with Clark Gable as the rugged hero, and in 1972 with Charlton Heston in that role.

The subject of both London's novel and its two filmed versions is the Alaska Gold Rush of the later 1890s. Adventures in the frozen North became a variation of the western in both the silent and in the sound eras. On the silent screen, the most notable example is Charles Chaplin's seriocomic epic *The Gold Rush*

(1925), with its wonderfully realistic opening sequences. Aside from the two adaptations of London's classic novel, other notable examples include *The Spoilers* (1942) with John Wayne and Marlene Dietrich. *Belle of the Yukon* (1944), with western stalwart Randolph Scott and burlesque star Gypsy Rose Lee, essentially mined the same territory, as did a plot reprised even less seriously by John Wayne and single-named phenoms Capucine and Fabian in *North to Alaska* (1960).

Another subgenre of the western, one concerned with the ending of the frontier, may be associated quite naturally with the 1890s. The frontier West did close during the last decade of the nineteenth century, both in pragmatic and theoretical terms. The coming of civilization and its discontents is often associated with the same sentimentalizing of realistic history that characterized Hollywood's attitude toward the whole period. In the early westerns this development is found in more comic variations such as *Ruggles of Red Gap* (1935), with Charles Laughton in the title part, which was later remade as *Fancy Pants* (1950), with Bob Hope in the featured role of a British "gentleman's gentleman" transported to the Wild West.

More sardonic versions emerged in later decades, seemingly in response to the decline of the western, of the American ideals encapsulated by the genre, as well as the aging of the Hollywood icons who portrayed archetypal western heroes. Some examples include Robert Altman's *McCabe & Mrs. Miller* (1971), which stars Warren Beatty and Julie Christie; George Roy Hill's self-consciously "kicky" *Butch Cassidy and the Sundance Kid* (1969), with Paul Newman and Robert Redford; and John Huston's offbeat *The Life and Times of Judge Roy Bean* (1972), with Newman as the self-appointed guardian of law west of the Pecos. John Wayne's geriatric efforts struck a sentimental note somewhere in between, as in *True Grit* (1969), with Kim Darby as his youthful companion, or its sequel, *Rooster Cogburn* (1975), with Katherine Hepburn as another virtuous example for the Duke.

All in all, American film for the most part ignored the 1890s, and when it did consider the decade, it refashioned it in Hollywood's sentimentalized version of the past. Such interpretation seems natural enough to the comedy or the musical, but even the film biography, the literary adaptation, and the western all conform to the same pattern. The exceptions that prove the rule are the occasional serious depictions of cultural conflict, such as Joan Micklin Silver's *Hester Street* (1975), an adaptation of a play by Abraham Cahan about the difficulties and disappointments of Jewish immigrant life on New York's Lower East Side. Literary critic Fredric Jameson reminds us that history is available only as narrative or text and that all of these narratives or texts are created by the exigencies of the present as much as the determinations of the past. In Hollywood's depiction of the 1890s, the needs of the present overbalance the responsibilities to the past, as this disturbing decade was stereotyped into the "good old days," helping to determine its enduring image in the American cultural consciousness.

References

Filmography

Belle of New York (1952, F)
Belle of the Nineties (1934, F)
Belle of the Yukon (1944, F)
Butch Cassidy and the Sundance Kid (1969, F)
The Call of the Wild (1935, F; 1972, F)
Carrie (1952, F)
Citizen Kane (1941, F)
Coney Island (1943, F)
A Connecticut Yankee in King Arthur's Court (1931, F)
A Corner in Wheat (1911, F)
David Harum (1934, F)
Destiny of Empires: The Spanish-American War of 1898 (1998, D)

Fancy Pants (1950, F)
Gentleman Jim (1942, F)
The Gold Rush (1925, F)
Hester Street (1975, F)
In Old Kentucky (1935, F)
Klondike Annie (1934, F)
The Life and Times of Judge Roy Bean (1972, F)
Lillian Russell (1940, F)
The Magnificent Ambersons (1942, F)
McCabe & Mrs. Miller (1971, F)
The Naughty Nineties (1945, F)
North to Alaska (1960, F)
Rooster Cogburn (1975, F)
Ruggles of Red Gap (1935, F)
She Done Him Wrong (1933, F)
The Spoilers (1942, F)
Steamboat 'Round the Bend (1935, F)
The Story of Alexander Graham Bell (1939, F)
Sweet Rosie O'Grady (1945, F)
True Grit (1969, F)
Wabash Avenue (1950, F)

Bibliography

Handlin, Oscar. *The Uprooted.* 2d ed. New York: Little, Brown, 1973.

Hofstadter, Richard. *The Age of Reform: From Bryan to FDR.* New York: Random House, 1960.

Rollins, Peter C. *Hollywood as Historian: American Film in a Cultural Context.* 2d ed. Lexington: University Press of Kentucky, 1998.

——. *Will Rogers: A Bio-Bibliography.* Westport, CT: Greenwood, 1984.

Toplin, Robert B. *History by Hollywood: The Use and Abuse of the American Past.* Urbana: University of Illinois Press, 1996.

[JOHN C. TIBBETTS]

The 1920s

The decade of the 1920s was both text and context for American movies. The nation and the film industry had returned home from World War I tested and strengthened. Immediately, however, both faced new tensions, challenges, and opportunities. A new conservatism was replacing progressive politics, a burgeoning industrial growth was signaling an unparalleled prosperity, and new technologies were changing the face of society and communications. Amid this welter of confusion and change, the American cinema, like the nation at large, was ready to take its first great strides from an awkward adolescence toward a global maturity.

There were obstacles along the way, to be sure. Despite the lofty idealism of President Woodrow Wilson's justifications for intervention in what was then called the Great War—an agenda that minimized America's more selfish and self-regarding interests, historian Richard Hofstadter asserts—returning soldiers had found the European struggle to be a filthy, disillusioning business. The nation's enthusiasm for the League of Nations faltered. A new isolationism pervaded the country. The Progressive movement stalled. "The pressure for civic participation was followed by widespread apathy," writes Hofstadter, "the sense of responsibility by neglect, the call for sacrifice by hedonism" (282). With the virtual collapse of the Democratic Party came an old style of conservative leadership that had not been seen since the turn of the century. The new president in 1920 was Warren G. Harding, whose assets included affability, good looks, and a professed agenda of "normalcy." He was succeeded by another Republican, Calvin Coolidge, a prudent man with a genius for inactivity and laissez-faire politics. Together, they benefited the "plutocrats" and large corporations with advantageous tax policies, and, in general, they promoted the continued process of business consolidation.

Progressive idealism faltered. Although it blazed bravely in the Harlem Renaissance—that awakening of black culture when artists such as writers Jean Toomer and Langston Hughes and musicians Duke Ellington and Louis Armstrong looked back to Africa for identity and difference from white America—it also surfaced in several misbegotten forms. The Ku Klux Klan was largely the result of a misplaced rural Anglo-Saxon Protestant protest against the seeming corruption in the fast-growing city centers of the purity of race and ideals by immigrants, blacks, Catholics, and Jews. Another misplaced relic of an earlier moral frenzy was Prohibition. Enacted by the passing of the Volstead Act in January 1920, Prohibition soon was flouted and exploited by bootleggers and gangsters, inaugurating a decade of organized crime.

The inevitable rebellion against encroaching Puritanism and conventional respectability was spearheaded by the satiric *Prejudices* of H. L. Mencken; the "voices" of T. S. Eliot's J. Alfred Prufrock and "The Waste Land" (1922) and Hugh Selwyn Mauberley in Ezra Pound's eponymous poem (1920); the novels of Sinclair Lewis (*Main Street,* 1920; *Babbitt,* 1922); Theodore Dreiser (*An American Trag-*

edy, 1925); the plays of the young Eugene O'Neill (*The Emperor Jones,* 1920; *The Hairy Ape,* 1922); and the jazz-inflected classicism of George Gershwin's symphonic rhapsodies and Tin Pan Alley songs (legacies of the late James Europe) and the machines and gunshots in the music of George Antheil. F. Scott Fitzgerald proclaimed the decade the Jazz Age in *The Great Gatsby* (1926), and Ernest Hemingway, borrowing from Gertrude Stein, pronounced its citizens a Lost Generation in the epigraph to *The Sun Also Rises* (1926). Both were correct. The character of Jay Gatsby, in Fitzgerald's *The Great Gatsby*—at once the brash, opportunistic hero and the failed idealistic victim of his times—most typified what Frederick Jackson Turner had described as the essential American spirit: "That practical, inventive turn of mind, quick to find expedients; that masterful grasp of material things, lacking in the artistic but powerful to effect great ends; that restless, nervous energy; that dominant individualism, working for good and for evil."

The changing roles of women were among the most visible results of this flux and ferment. Advances in women's rights, as Molly Haskell has written in *From Reverence to Rape,* "made the twenties seem closer to our time than any intervening decade. They seem, indeed, the antecedent to the current women's liberation movement and the 'new morality' and, more, to anticipate the split between the two" (44). Newly empowered by the vote, young women abandoned ankle-length dresses, corsets, and long tresses and eagerly took up hip flasks, flesh-colored stockings, smoking, and careers in all professions.

Maintaining one's balance in such a chaotically changing world required the agility and endurance of a marathon runner. Even though Gatsby's ideals had fallen victim to the siren songs of money, social status, and material success, the rest of the nation eagerly embraced the brittle novelties, foibles, and fantasies of the age. Reports of crimes, disasters, and scandals—Al Capone's bootlegging, the Scopes trial, the newest dance crazes, thrill seekers, and the exploits of evangelist Aimee Semple McPherson and the Four Horsemen of Notre Dame—commanded the biggest headlines.

The motion picture industry lost no time in taking up the challenge of Pound's "Hugh Selwyn Mauberley":

> The age demanded an image
> Of an accelerated grimace,
> Something for the modern stage,
> Not, at any rate, an Attic grace. . . .
> The "age demanded" chiefly a mould in plaster,
> Made with no loss of time,
> A prose kinema, not, not assuredly, alabaster
> Of the "sculpture" of rhyme.

In their variety, technical polish, star power, and global proliferation, American films proclaimed America's new place in the international scene. As Peter Rollins declares in his study of Will Rogers, "The message of these films was that older civilizations may have posted their claims to preeminence before the United States, but postwar realities dictated that the United States was the only country whose spirit had not been broken by World War I" (80).

What has come to be labeled by historians David Bordwell, Kristin Thompson, and Janet Staiger as the "classical" period of the Hollywood studio film—an integral system defined by products consistently displaying "respect for tradition, mimesis, self-effacing craftsmanship, and cool control of the perceiver's response" (4)—the modern American movie industry was now entering its mature phase. Maintaining its financial operations on the East Coast, the studios had long since relocated their production facilities to Southern California, scattered from Santa Monica to Edendale to Pasadena; as far north as San Francisco; and as far east as Phoenix, Arizona. By the middle of the decade, most of the Big Five studios were in place; by 1929 the last of the majors, RKO, was established as a result of the talkie boom. Patterning these studios after the

Ford-Taylor assembly line production system, entrepreneurs such as Adolph Zukor, Louis B. Mayer, the Warner brothers, Carl Laemmle, and William Fox were successfully exploiting their backgrounds in sales and retail and their understanding of public tastes to establish, by mid-decade, vertically integrated structures that controlled the production, distribution, and exhibition of films. Pictures were shaped, manufactured, and implemented by most of the supporting technical developments still relevant today (various color processes, camera and sound recording equipment, optical effects); by the self-imposed protocensorship policies established by the Motion Picture Producers and Distributors Association of America (MPPDA) in 1922, 1927, and 1929; by the rise of company unions, particularly the Motion Picture Academy; by the proliferation of publicity departments, trade papers, and fan magazines; and by the consolidation of exhibition chains and the modern movie theaters (including the picture palaces). Reflecting the nation's dominant political and social climate, the resulting products were dedicated, for the most part, to promoting the decade's "mainstream" American image of conservative Anglo-Saxon values. Indeed, that collective entity known as "Hollywood" was flexing its muscles. The opening title of Joseph von Sternberg's *The Last Command* (1928) described Hollywood as "The Magic Empire of the Twentieth Century! The Mecca of the World!"; the motto of *American Cinematographer* magazine boasted, "Give Us a Place to Stand and We Will Film the Universe."

While many pictures supported vestiges of a prewar progressive idealism that was tenuously linked, at the same time, with the politics, literature, and lifestyle of the modern age, an equally significant subset of films reflected resistance to conventional mores. Epitomizing the first category are the most commercially popular filmmakers of the day. Whereas D. W. Griffith, Mary Pickford, Douglas Fairbanks, and Charles Chaplin had initially distinguished themselves by their fierce individualism and satiric social visions from the mid- to late 1910s, they spent the decade of the 1920s in retrenchment, making lavishly produced, studio-bound blockbusters and fairy tales. Distancing himself from the acerbic social commentary that marked many of his Biograph shorts and features such as *The Mother and the Law* (1916), D. W. Griffith turned increasingly to theatrical melodramas (*Way Down East*, 1920; *Sally of the Sawdust*, 1925) and historical reenactments (*America*, 1924). Pickford's *Pollyanna* (1920) and *Little Annie Rooney* (1925) consolidated her "little girl" image, and her *Dorothy Vernon of Haddon Hall* (1925) and *My Best Girl* (1927) retreated into the realms of the costume drama and the shop-girl romance, respectively. Fairbanks's *The Mark of Zorro* (1920) inaugurated his cycle of costume swashbucklers, which included *The Three Musketeers* (1921), *Robin Hood* (1922), *The Black Pirate* (1926), and *The Gaucho* (1928). Chaplin's *The Kid* (1921) was his most insistently Victorian melodrama to date, and the remaining work of the decade, *The Gold Rush* (1925) and *The Circus* (1927), was awash in a cozily Victorian nostalgia.

Other directors and stars, by contrast, invested their films with more contemporary bite and explored new genres. Erich von Stroheim, Cecil B. De Mille, and Mal St. Clair invested their "Old World" films with a suggestively biting social and sexual commentary. *The Merry Widow* (1925), *Male and Female* (1922), and *The Grand Duchess and the Waiter* (1926), respectively, wedded the old-fashioned contexts of European-based manners, settings, and class distinctions with a jazzier sensibility. Will Rogers's silent films took his homespun wisdom and satire to Washington (*Going to Congress*, 1924) and Europe (*They Had to See Paris*, 1929). Émigré directors F. W. Murnau, Victor Seastrom, Ernst Lubitsch, and Paul Leni reversed the process, bringing European "art" prestige to America in *Sunrise* (1927), *The Scarlet Letter* (1926), *Lady Windemere's Fan*

(1925), and *The Cat and the Canary* (1927), respectively. Among the younger American directors, John Ford began his estimable cycle of American "manifest destiny" westerns with *The Iron Horse* (1924) and *Three Bad Men* (1928); Tod Browning teamed up with Lon Chaney for a new kind of psychological horror chiller with *The Unholy Three* (1925) and *The Unknown* (1928); Joseph von Sternberg heralded the modern cycle of gangster pictures with *Underworld* (1927), and Robert Flaherty took his cameras to far-flung places such as Alaska and the South Seas in *Nanook of the North* (1922) and *Moana* (1926).

The "new woman" in society—the emancipated "flapper" figure vaguely derived from the real-life exploits of Zelda Fitzgerald and from the spate of "new woman" plays currently enjoying success on Broadway—found her screen incarnation in films scripted by women who enjoyed enormous clout and prestige in the industry at the time, including Anita Loos, Frances Marion, and Clara Beranger. Their stories were crafted for young actresses such as Clara Bow, Colleen Moore, Marion Davies, and Joan Crawford. Exuberant and sexy as *Our Dancing Daughters* (1928) and Dorothy Arzner's *The Wild Party* (1929) seemed, however, they were, as Molly Haskell reminds us, essentially ambivalent in their sexual liberation, like the age that produced them: "They made stars of heroines who, with their ruthless insistence on having a good time, were the very embodiment of a spirit that was more the way an age liked—or feared—to see itself than the way it actually was" (333). It is worth noting that actress Louise Brooks had to emigrate to Germany to make, under the guidance of G. W. Pabst, *Pandora's Box* (1928), the only film of the time that did not flinch from the essential amorality of this character type.

World War I, still a vivid memory, was not deemed commercial box-office material until King Vidor's landmark *The Big Parade* (1925), with its gritty realism, became a popular sensation. In quick succession followed Raoul Walsh's *What Price Glory?* (1926), William Wellman's aviation epic *Wings* (1927), George Fitzmaurice's *Lilac Time* (1928), and Lewis Milestone's antiwar classic *All Quiet on the Western Front* (1930).

It was no coincidence that many films reflected a society newly galvanized and in constant motion, both in the air, à la Lindbergh, and on the ground, courtesy of Barney Oldfield. It was an age of speed and thrills. New modes of transportation such as the automobile and the airplane resulted in a plethora of airports, automatic traffic lights, concrete roads, one-way streets, officially numbered highways, tourist homes, roadside hotels, roadside diners, hot-dog stands, fruit and vegetable stalls, filling stations, and, of course, traffic congestion and parking problems. Construction boomed, prefabricated homes sprang up, suburbs spread out, and the newfangled skyscrapers towered over the streets. Slapstick comedians Charlie Chase, Harold Lloyd, and Buster Keaton, in films such as *Speedy* (1928), *Safety Last* (1923), and *Seven Chances* (1925), converted this new landscape into a gymnasium. Emulating the exploits of real-life thrill seekers, high-wire performers, wing-walkers, and "human flies," they climbed buildings, raced cars, fell out of airplanes, and tumbled from buses, motorcycles, ocean liners, and locomotives.

Although the preceding discussion reflects a cross-section of mainstream American films from this period, historian Kevin Brownlow, in his books *The War, the West and the Wilderness* and *Behind the Mask of Innocence*, is quick to remind us that fictional and documentary films of social consciousness and ethnographic concerns were indeed made throughout the 1920s, even if they came from the margins of the industry and received limited exposure. "In the twenties, if a film set out to educate rather than to entertain," writes Brownlow, "audiences knew, by some sixth sense, how to avoid it" (xvii). Nonetheless, many brave examples include the "race movies," such as *Scar of Shame* (1927), produced by the Lincoln Motion Picture Company, which was dedicated to making movies with black performers for black audiences. These productions, like the films of black filmmaker Oscar Micheaux, chronicled what Thomas Cripps has termed the "black bourgeois success myth." (Recent studies by historians Mark A. Reid and Pearl Bowser are currently reexamining Micheaux's work, including three titles that survive, *Within Our Gates,* 1920; *Symbol of the Unconquered,* 1920; and *Body and Soul,* 1925). With unflinching directness, they examined issues of bigotry, lynch-mob justice, Uncle Tomism, and the activities of the Klan. Among the few female filmmakers was Alice Weber, who devoted her career to films examining the societal inequities and double standards facing women. *The Angel of Broadway* (1927), for example, blended a jazz-age nightclub setting with a story about slum reform. Among the pioneering ethnographic documentarians were Martin and Osa Johnson, whose "camera safaris" recorded the life, landscapes, and peoples of Africa and Borneo.

The contrasts, turmoil, and sheer exuberance of the 1920s era have long been favorite subjects of filmmakers and television producers. King Vidor's *The Crowd* (1928) was not just a story set in the 1920s; it has become something of a time capsule of the look and texture of the time. The cycle of gangster films of the 1930s, including Mervyn LeRoy's *Little Caesar* (1931), William Wellman's *The Public Enemy* (1931), and Howard Hawks's *Scarface* (1932), dissected the roots of gangland violence in the racketeering that grew up around Prohibition. *The Roaring Twenties* (1939), produced by Warner Bros. barely six years after the repeal of Prohibition, set the seal on the this type of gangster picture as it rehashed the by-now familiar story of the rise and fall of a bootlegger, from the trenches of wartime to the bloody streets of gangland and the crash of the stock market. Brian De Palma's *The Untouchables* (1987) and Roger Corman's *St. Valentine's Day Massacre* (1967) reprised the saga of Chicago's gangland. (On television, *The Untouchables,* 1959–63, and *The Roaring Twenties,* 1960–62, brought Prohibition alive once again for home viewing.) Films chronicling the swashbuckling days of aviation and tabloid journalism include George Roy Hill's *The Great Waldo Pepper* (1975) and numerous adaptations of the hit Ben Hecht–Charles MacArthur 1927 play *The Front Page.* John Sayles's *Matewan* (1987) told the story of a bitter 1920 strike in the coalmines of southern West Virginia. A far rosier romance and nostalgia marked Blake Edwards's *Thoroughly Modern Millie* (1967) and George Roy Hill's *The Sting* (1973), both veritable catalogues of pertinent topics, including white slavery, the liberated flapper, gangland activities, and Prohibition. And, of course, Fitzgerald's *Great Gatsby,* which sums up the bittersweet romance of the whole era, has been adapted three times, in 1926, 1949, and 1974.

The decade ended badly for the country and for the movies. Until the stock market crash of October 1929, American industry and business had marched on, unhampered by a government little concerned with regulatory legislation and a labor movement that had not only stalled but also dwindled. Attempts to halt the panic by leading bankers failed and, five days later, more than sixteen million shares of stock were thrown on the market by frantic sellers. An amount of money larger than the national debt vanished. The Great Depression was on its way. It broke the optimistic mood of the 1920s as surely and abruptly as the postwar years broke the back of progressive fervor.

Meanwhile, the talkie revolution of 1927–28 was wreaking its own havoc on the silent film industry. The talking picture revolution, begun with the DeForest Phonofilms and the Vitaphone shorts of the mid-1920s and culminating in the first synchronized-sound features from Warner Bros. and Fox in 1927–29 (Alan Crosland's *The Jazz Singer* and Raoul Walsh's

In Old Arizona, respectively), was a by-product of the developing communications technologies of the day. As Donald Crafton demonstrates in his authoritative *The Talkies,* the new talking picture technology was marketed and imaged as one more new development in "thermionics," or electrical science—as part of a burgeoning age of communications (telephone, wireless radio, television, amplifiers, microphones, and public-address systems): "By 1928 most of the popular press writers saw the perfected talkies as an inevitable outgrowth of modern science—a predestined consequence of other communication technologies." With incredible rapidity, technically mature talkies such as Rouben Mamoulian's *Applause* (1929) and Sternberg's *Thunderbolt* (1929) not only superseded the form of the silent film, but the immediacy of their sounds and the suggestiveness of their words also provoked renewed calls for censorship that eventually resulted in the writing of the Motion Picture Code of 1930. Suddenly, abruptly, completely, the industry suffered a complete technological overhaul, and a "panic" of sorts threw studios into disarray and put thousands of technicians, actors, and musicians out of work. Unlike the Depression, however, the effect would prove to be short-term. Hollywood bounced back by 1930 and faced with renewed confidence a new decade of expansion and consolidation.

References

Filmography

All Quiet on the Western Front (1930, F)
America (1924, F)
The Angel of Broadway (1927, F)
Applause (1929, F)
The Big Parade (1925, F)
The Black Pirate (1926, F)
Body and Soul (1925, F)
The Circus (1927)
The Crowd (1928)
Dorothy Vernon of Haddon Hall (1925, F)
The Front Page (1929, F)
The Gaucho (1928, F)
Going to Congress (1924, F)
The Gold Rush (1925, F)
The Grand Duchess and the Waiter (1926, F)
The Great Gatsby (1926, F; 1949, F; 1974, F)
The Great Waldo Pepper (1975, F)
In Old Arizona (1929, F)
The Iron Horse (1924, F)
The Jazz Singer (1927, F)
The Kid (1921, F)
Lady Windemere's Fan (1925, F)
The Last Command (1928, F)
Lilac Time (1928, F)
Little Annie Rooney (1925, F)
Little Caesar (1931, F)
Male and Female (1922, F)
The Mark of Zorro (1920, F)
Matewan (1987, F)
The Merry Widow (1925, F)
Moana of the South Seas (1926, F)
The Mother and the Law (1916, F)
My Best Girl (1927, F)
Nanook of the North (1922, F)
One Week (1920, F)
Our Dancing Daughters (1928, F)
Pandora's Box (1928, F)
Pollyanna (1920, F)
The Public Enemy (1931, F)
The Roaring Twenties (1939, F; 1960–62, TV)
Robin Hood (1922, F)
Safety Last (1923, F)
Sally of the Sawdust (1925, F)
Scarface (1932, F)
The Scarlet Letter (1926, F)
Scar of Shame (1927, F)
Seven Chances (1925, F)
Speedy (1928, F)
The Sting (1973, F)
The St. Valentine's Day Massacre (1967, F)
Sunrise (1927, F)
Symbol of the Unconquered (1920, F)
They Had to See Paris (1929, F)
Thoroughly Modern Millie (1967, F)
Three Bad Men (1928, F)
The Three Musketeers (1921, F)
Thunderbolt (1929, F)
Underworld (1927, F)
The Unholy Three (1925, F)
The Unknown (1928, F)
The Untouchables (1987, F; 1959–63, TV)
Way Down East (1920, F)
What Price Glory? (1926, F)
The Wild Party (1929, F)
Wings (1927, F)
Within Our Gates (1920, F)

Bibliography

Allen, Frederick Lewis. *The Big Change: America Transforms Itself, 1900–1950.* New York: Harper & Brothers, 1952.

Bordwell, David, Janet Staiger, and Kristin Thompson. *The Classical Hollywood Cinema: Film Style and Mode of Production to 1960.* New York: Columbia University Press, 1985.

Bowser, Pearl, Jane Gaines, and Charles Musser. *Oscar Micheaux and His Circle: African-American Filmmaking and Race Cinema of the Silent Era.* Princeton: Princeton University Press, 2001.

Brownlow, Kevin. *Behind the Mask of Innocence.* New York: Knopf, 1990.

——. *The War, the West and the Wilderness.* New York: Knopf, 1979.

Crafton, Donald. *The Talkies: American Cinema's Transition to Sound, 1926–1931.* New York: Simon & Schuster, 1997.

Cripps, Thomas. "'Race Movies' as Voices of the Black Bourgeois." In John E. O'Connor and Martin A. Jackson, eds., *American History/ American Film: Interpreting the Hollywood Image,* 39–55. New York: Frederick Ungar, 1979.

Haskell, Molly. *From Reverence to Rape: The Treatment of Women in the Movies.* New York: Penguin, 1975.

Hofstadter, Richard. *The Age of Reform.* New York: Random House, 1955.

Koszarski, Richard. *An Evening's Entertainment: The Age of the Silent Feature Picture, 1915–1928.* Los Angeles: University of California Press, 1990.

Massa, Ann. *American Literature in Context, 1900–1930.* London: Methuen, 1982.

May, Lary. *The Big Tomorrow: Hollywood and the Politics of the American Way.* Chicago: University of Chicago Press, 2000.

Reid, Mark A. *Redefining Black Film.* Berkeley: University of California Press, 1993.

Rollins, Peter. "Will Rogers and the Relevance of Nostalgia." In John E. O'Connor and Martin A. Jackson, eds., *American History/American Film: Interpreting the Hollywood Image,* 77–96. New York: Frederick Ungar, 1979.

Sklar, Robert. *Movie-Made America: A Cultural History of American Movies.* New York: Random House, 1975.

Tibbetts, John C. "The 'New Woman' on Stage." *Helicon 9: The Journal of Women's Arts and Letters* 7 (1982): 6–19.

[CARLTON JACKSON]

The 1930s

The stock market crash of October 29, 1929, "Black Tuesday," heralded the onset of the Great Depression, which lasted for most of a decade and influenced social and governmental policies for the rest of the century. Nationwide, unemployment rose to 25 percent, while in the industrial cities of Cleveland and Toledo it climbed to 50 and 80 percent, respectively. The gross national product fell from $104 billion in 1929 to $76.4 billion in 1932, a 25 percent decline. In human terms, the Depression spelled disaster for millions, with soup kitchens and street-corner apple sellers becoming commonplace. "Families" writes historian Arthur M. Schlesinger, "slept in tarpaper shacks and tin-lined caves and scavenged like dogs for food in the city dump." One-fifth of New York's schoolchildren suffered from malnutrition, while millions of people went undernourished in the American South and elsewhere.

Historian Albert U. Romasco, in *The Poverty of Abundance,* likens the Depression to a rainstorm: "a sensible man acknowledged his inability to stop the rain [and] sought shelter while waiting for the storm to pass" (viii). Romasco further observes that the Depression "made man's dependence [on other people and the government] fully evident; and it thoroughly exposed the impotence of the individual in modern society" (viii). Fellow sufferers came together, hoping to work in concert for the common good. And this "concert" ultimately led much of the American public to expect entitlement programs from Washington. Both movies and academia helped delineate this trend. Even many years after the Depression it appeared that many, if not most, of the New Deal's social programs had become "permanent institutions" (Bernstein, 8). Local governments and charities were no longer sufficient for the problems facing the country.

Frank Capra's *American Madness,* made in 1932, the worst year of the Depression, evoked the plight of the "Little People," but the focus was on a heroic small-business owner. At least at this stage, Capra preferred "Hoover voluntarism" to other solutions to the Depression: "No need for government aid; better individual behavior will solve the massive economic slump." Capra offered in his Depression films a "concerned, small-proprietor individualism" (Stricker, 458). The message was direct and simple: honest bankers would turn the economy around. But, as Robert Sobel writes in *The Great Bull Market,* many Americans began to believe that Wall Street—and, by extension, banks—caused "most of the problems facing the nation" (159). Indeed, in the Depression, banks were among the greatest villains, and they continued to hold this unsavory reputation for years to come.

As the Depression continued, Hollywood directors—including Capra—took the country's economic failures more seriously. They began to depict an intractable Depression that displaced citizens, fostered venal gangsters, and brought into power political grafters and corrupted officials.

The Road People

During the Depression, large numbers of Americans lost their jobs and started drifting, making the 1930s the "golden years" of hoboing in the United States. Men, and sometimes women, wandered here and there, looking for sustenance—both physical and moral. Hollywood took an interest in these uprooted citizens. Among the first of the "traveling" films was *Wild Boys of the Road* (1933), depicting a new phenomenon of American social history: young boys whose parents had been bankrupted by the Depression seeking their own solutions to economic problems. Eddie (Frankie Darro) sells his car, "Leapin' Lena," to help his father. When this sacrifice proves to be only temporarily helpful, he and his best friend Tommie (Edwin Phillips) "hit the road," soon joined by dozens of other youths as they look for work and food. Like most other Depression movies, *Wild Boys of the Road* has a happy ending, for anything else would add to the audience's gloom; a compassionate judge (Robert Barrat)—who sits beneath the Blue Eagle of the National Recovery Administration—gives the boys, who have been charged as runaways, a "second chance."

FIGURE 3. *The Petrified Forest* (1936). Alan Squires (Leslie Howard, left) confronts gangster Duke Mantee (Humphrey Bogart, right), venting his anger at the society that produced criminals like Mantee. Gabby (Bette Davis, seated) the daughter of the inn's owner, looks on. The inn itself, isolated on a high plateau in the Arizona desert, becomes the unlikely setting for philosophical inquiry. Courtesy Warner Bros.

The Petrified Forest (1936), filmed from Robert Sherwood's last play, brings together hoboing and gangsterism. Alan Squier (Leslie Howard), having once married into wealth but now down and out, has been hitching rides after being dumped by a tourist group because he could not pay his way. Hoping, he declares, to find something to believe in, he comes to a gas station/café at the edge of the Petrified Forest in the Arizona desert. There he finds "Gabby" Maple (Bette Davis) and is smitten by her beauty and philosophical bent. After she reads some of her poetry, they talk about the world's chaos. The Depression, Alan says, is "nature hitting back" with instruments called neuroses, afflicting humankind "with the jitters." The republic, he continues, "is in bad need of saving," but our "fine excuse" for a government cannot keep law and order, as is evident by the numerous criminals spawned by Prohibition.

One such thug is Duke Mantee (Humphrey Bogart), who, according to radio reports, is headed toward the Petrified Forest. Mantee arrives and waits at the café for an old flame to arrive and join him in an escape to Mexico. Over the course of the film, Alan, who has secretly signed over a $5,000 life-insurance policy to Gabby, talks Mantee into shooting him. He believes that his death will make a creative life possible for Gabby, thus salvaging at least one positive value from the Depression. Just as Mantee shoots Alan, a posse arrives. Mantee and his gang flee, but the other hostages at the café soon hear over the radio that the gang leader has been killed.

The Petrified Forest reflects forms of humanity within the framework of the Depression. Alan's gesture of bestowing his life-insurance policy on Gabby is a heroic sacrifice for a stranger to make. Although Duke Mantee is a desperate criminal, the movie even depicts a degree of benevolence on his part. *The Petrified Forest* shows humanity in its various moods: love, hate, greed, avarice, and redemption. It is a nearly perfect movie for the Depression years—not least because of Humphrey Bogart's resemblance to the "public enemy number 1" of the time, John Dillinger.

The most "depressing" of all the Depression movies was *I Am a Fugitive from a Chain Gang* (1932). James Allen (Paul Muni) is so destitute that he tries to sell the medals he has earned for his service in World War I. An exasperated pawnbroker shows him a drawerful of medals from other down-and-out veterans; there is no monetary value to his patriotic service. Allen learns to survive any way he can. Eventually he is falsely implicated in a robbery that lands him on a chain gang. He escapes and in time becomes an important engineer in the Chicago area. His landlady, Marie Woods (Glenda Farrell), discovers his background, saying, "I wouldn't tell if I had a reason to protect you. If you were my husband." Not surprisingly, the subsequent shotgun marriage is not a happy one. When Allen falls in love with Helen (Helen Vinson), he asks Marie for a divorce, a request she vehemently rejects. Intensely angry, she reports her husband to the authorities. Believing that he has to serve only a token ninety days before being pardoned, Allen returns to prison. Discovering that he has been tricked by the authorities, he escapes again, going all the way from war hero to criminal outsider and fugitive.

Fugitive, unlike most other Depression films, does not have a happy ending. Allen slips through the shadows but enjoys neither rest nor peace. When he comes to see Helen one dark night after a year on the run, she asks him, "How do you live?" His answer: "I steal." The movie is a provocation rather than a reassurance. The country's mood was not good in 1932, and *Fugitive* reflected that situation. According to film scholar Andrew Bergman, if *Fugitive* had been made just a year later, "the chances are good that James Allen would have encountered a sympathetic federal official at picture's end, with a just solution in sight" (97). By late 1933, Franklin Roosevelt's New Deal was taking hold and, at least in the minds of many people, the economy was improving, so such a salvation might well have been possible.

The Grapes of Wrath (1940), based on John Steinbeck's novel and directed by John Ford, includes almost every Depression motif. It is a "road" movie, a "collectivist" one, with strong themes of "family," and—unlike the book—it has a happy ending. The Joads, "Okies," lose their property in Oklahoma and head for the "Promised Land" of California. Tom Joad (Henry Fonda) gathers the family into a dilapidated truck, and they travel along Route 66 through Texas, New Mexico, and Arizona to California. The family stops at numerous transient stations. At a work site, the Keene Ranch, vigilantes decide to clear out a nearby "Hooverville" made up of migrant workers looking for jobs. In self-defense, Tom kills one of the vigilantes and becomes a fugitive.

After more travel, the Joads come to the Farm Workers Wheat Patch Camp, sponsored by the United States Department of Agriculture (regarded by many locals as "a bunch of Reds"). There the family obtains food, clothing, and shelter, and something it has long been deprived of: a social life and, above all else, dignity. In fact, the Joads gain the treatment in *The Grapes of Wrath* that was denied James Allen in *Fugitive.* A New Deal program, in effect, comes to their rescue. Unfortunately, the police are still hot on Tom's trail for killing the guard at Keene, so he once more has to take flight. He announces to Ma (Jane Darwell) that he would be "everywhere" there is injustice. As the movie ends, Ma tells Pa (Charley Grapewin)—in a speech written by Darryl Zanuck to give the conclusion of the film an upbeat message—that "We'll go on forever, Pa. We're the People." This thought of "We the People" consorting with the government to end the Depression became a powerful one, and movies such as *The Grapes of Wrath* reinforced the vision.

Political Movies

When the Depression began in 1929, Robert and Helen Merrell Lynd maintain in *Middletown in Transition,* individuals may have blamed themselves for their economic predicaments. A latter-day historian, William Leuchtenburg, echoes their thoughts when he observes that "The unemployed worker almost always experienced feelings of guilt and self-deprecation" (118). As time passed, however, it was increasingly clear that the public hoped for a government-led, macroeconomic solution to the Depression.

Probably the most intense "leftist" Depression movie from Hollywood was King Vidor's *Our Daily Bread* (1934), which attacked just about every traditional American value: rugged individualism, monetary gain, and capitalism itself. Called by many critics a "pinko" movie (it won awards from the League of Nations and the Soviet Union), *Our Daily Bread* "stressed the elimination of competition and the fulfillment of the individual in the group, rather than his submergence in the mass" (Bergman, 79). In the movie, a young couple flees the city to occupy a rundown farm they have inherited. Migrants come to the farm, and the owners, Tom and Mary, decide to turn it into a cooperative. Before long, farmers, masons, plumbers, tailors, bricklayers—even a concert violinist—make their home in this new society. Each takes on an "expert" role in a spontaneous division of labor. The movie climaxes with the opening of an irrigation ditch that everyone has worked on together. They cheer as the life-giving water saturates their land. Despite the collectivist thrust of the film, critic Terry Christensen maintains, the residents of the cooperative still wanted a strong leader to guide them in their various pursuits. One of the subtexts of *Our Daily Bread* is that there is a natural need of humans en masse to demand strong, even undemocratic leadership in times of crisis.

The "strong leadership" theme emerged in numerous Depression movies, but never more potently—albeit fantastically—than in *Gabriel Over the White House* (1933), directed by Gregory La Cava. In it, President Judson Hammond (Walter Huston) shows little interest in solving the country's problems until he suffers a near-death experience in an auto accident and comes under the protective wing of the archangel Gabriel. He then becomes "benevolent"—at least by his own definition. Trampling on the Bill of Rights, he ends crime by declaring martial law, puts gangsters up against firing squads, forces the rest of the world to join America in disarmament, and, when disarmament is accomplished everywhere except in the United States, scuttles the U.S. Navy.

Many Americans saw *Gabriel Over the White House* as friendly to fascist ideals, implying that only a single strongman could save the nation, and just as dangerous ideologically as *Our Daily Bread* had been, albeit at the other end of the political spectrum. President Hammond uses the newly developed technology of radio to get his messages across to the American people, in effect, prophetic of Franklin Roosevelt's "fireside chats" (Roosevelt took office a few weeks after *Gabriel* appeared in movie theaters). The loudest applause in the president's first inaugural address came when he asked for "broad executive power," in effect a mandate from the American people to deal with the Depression (Schlesinger, 8).

Documentaries

Not far removed from political films were social documentaries whose creators commented upon the country's economic conditions. One major director was Pare Lorentz, who made two films for the federal government that fit Depression themes: *The Plow That Broke the Plains* (1936) and *The River* (1937). Lorentz "believed that film should be used to clarify public perception of issues" (Rollins, 38); both of these documentaries exemplified his notions of "clarification."

The federal government's Farm Security Administration (previously called the Resettlement Administration), sponsored both *Plow* and *The River,* causing some critics to view them as blatant attempts to convince Americans that salvation lay in big government. Supporters, however, argued that the two films would help to "bridge the communications gap between government and the public" (Rollins, 39), especially in an era when most major dailies were hostile to Roosevelt's experiments.

Plow deals with the Great Plains, stretching from Texas to Canada, covering more than 400 million acres, a land of "high winds and sun, but little rain." By 1933 the "old grassland" that had "bound the soil together" was the "new wheatland." Drought and poor farming practices had created severe erosion, and a constant wind removed the soil in great billowing clouds of silt, turning portions of the Great Plains into a "dust bowl" and forcing thousands of its inhabitants—the real-life counterparts of the Joads—to flee. Many Depression audiences got their first look at the "Dust Bowl" when they viewed *The Plow That Broke the Plains.* Indeed, the final segment of the movie foreshadows *The Grapes of Wrath,* depicting columns of old cars and trucks moving westward, their occupants looking for shelter and work (O'Connor, 286). The movie ends despondently with the image of an abandoned bird's nest in the branches of a dead tree. Apparently, there had been a New Deal "upbeat" ending to *Plow,* for in the Depression even documentaries needed happy resolutions, but, all the same, the movie was withdrawn from circulation in 1939 after South Dakota Senator Karl Mundt claimed it had insulted him. *The Plow That Broke the Plains* was not made public again until 1961 (Rollins, 41).

A year after *Plow,* Lorentz shot *The River* (1937), about the Mississippi and its tributaries. The narrator focused on the damage the Mississippi had wrought over the years through floods and erosion. The film's saving message was that if "we had the power to take the [Mississippi] Valley apart, we have the power to put it back together again." In "putting it back together," a technocratic government built dams in many areas drained by the Mississippi. Citing disastrous floods from 1903 to 1937, the narration justifies the federal government's massive program of dam and levee construction, which changed the face of the American landscape. The movie's final scenes show newly built houses in places where flood control devices had been installed, houses financed by generous loans from a benevolent federal government. As with *Plow,* critics saw *The River* primarily as New Deal propaganda. *The River,* however, was not pulled from circulation as *Plow* would be; in fact, *The River* won numerous prizes, and no less a person than James Joyce said that its narrative contained "the most beautiful prose I have heard in ten years" (Rollins, 40). Resonating with the evangelical culture of Depression audiences, Virgil Thomson's music for *The River* matches the scenes portrayed on the screen. "How Firm A Foundation," a well-known and beloved hymn, was played in variations throughout the film, as well as " 'Tis So Sweet to Trust in Jesus." To symbolize the destruction of forests, Thomson's score also played loud variations of "Hot Time in the Old Town Tonight" (Rollins, 42).

Another documentary is *Native Land* (1942). A mixture of narration and acting, its contemporary appeal lay in the drive during the 1930s to unionize the American worker, a movement portrayed from a far-left perspective by a group of activists who organized a studio called Frontier Films. Its members were proud to be Communists, and their marxism was a point of honor. The film speaks to how the Bill of Rights had been steadily undermined by those who opposed labor and racial harmony in the United States, and it mirrors many previous themes of Depression movies when the announcer proudly proclaims, "You can't blacklist a whole people."

Films as Depression "Historian"

The Great Depression has also been "revisited" by filmmakers of the generations following World War II. Director Arthur Penn made *Bonnie and Clyde* (1967), a glorification of two hardened bank robbers and murderers who, in real life, were not at all "glamorous." Clyde Barrow (Warren Beatty) and Bonnie Parker (Faye Dunaway) "tried" to move their lives off the Depression "standstills" that historian Caroline Bird describes in *The Invisible Scar* (xiv). Regrettably, they endeavored to accomplish their goals by robbing banks and killing anyone who got in their way.

Banks of the 1930s were regular Depression villains; one of the most compelling scenes in *Bonnie and Clyde* depicts its former owner's joining Clyde in shooting out the windows of a foreclosed house. Later, when Clyde robs a bank, he allows a poor farmer to keep his money. After one heist, Clyde counts the haul and laments its smallness. His brother Buck (Gene Hackman) philosophizes, "Well, times is hard."

The 1987 movie *Ironweed,* directed by Hector Babenco and starring Jack Nicholson and Meryl Streep, was almost as depressing as *Fugitive,* made half a century earlier. It offers starkly realistic portrayals of down-and-outers on the cold streets of Albany, New York, in the middle of the Depression. They hurt because of hard economic times and personal shortcomings, and their chief comfort is the bottle. Such depictions were quite relevant to the *real* Depression, where the mood gradually grew that "suffering is suffering no matter the victim, no matter the reason," a thought that would gain as much currency in the 1980s and 1990s as in the 1930s.

Robert Benton's *Places in the Heart* (1984) reflects the determination of some in the Depression not only to live through hard times but also to prosper. Edna Spalding's (Sally Field) life is changed forever when her husband, the sheriff of Waxahachie, Texas, is accidentally shot to death by a drunken African American. Afterward, she and a black man, Moses (Danny Glover), harvest the first bale of cotton of the season and thus gain the best price at the local cotton gin, though their partnership is broken when local members of the Ku Klux Klan intimidate Moses into leaving. The movie touches on another sensitive subject of the 1930s as, indeed, of the 1980s and 1990s, insisting that white and black Americans had to pull together to fight economic deprivation.

A 1998 documentary, *The Great Depression* (Tower Productions), narrated by former New York Governor Mario Cuomo, gives a useful summary of the traumatic events of the 1930s. The experiences of the "road people" are recounted here, as well as the need for collective and mutual cooperation as a way out of the Depression. Hoboes, soup kitchens, dust-bowl victims, labor strife, gangsterism, and corrupt government—all are described, interspersed with learned comments from John Kenneth Galbraith, Upton Sinclair, Howard Zinn, and Kitty Carlisle Hart. The ultimate "message" of this documentary is that Roosevelt's New Deal administration saved the day by, as Leuchtenburg remarks, creating "a new emphasis on social security and collective action" (340).

In the end, filmmakers and historians have not greatly diverged in describing and explaining the Great Depression. Directors, in much the way of a good historical novelist, have created fictional characters and put them into real-life situations. Documentaries have portrayed the devolution of "rugged individualism" into "ragged individualism" (Meltzer, 160) during the Depression and have shown how Franklin Roosevelt resurrected "rugged individualism" in a distinctly changed form to allow increased governmental scrutiny of social and economic life. No longer, for example, could that symbol of capitalist fraud and corruption, the New York Stock Exchange, "operate as a private club free of national supervision" (Leuchtenburg, 336). And by controlling Wall Street, banks, big business, and other special interest groups could perhaps be harnessed as well.

Movies and historians alike have depicted Roosevelt as the architect of a government that serves as "the affirmative instrument of the people" (Schlesinger, 483), representing general rather than specific interests. Whatever ended the Depression—the New Deal or World War II—will forever be debated, and neither the movies nor the historians have ever reached a consensus on this question.

References

Filmography

American Madness (1932, F)
Bonnie and Clyde (1967, F)
Gabriel Over the White House (1933, F)
Gone with the Wind (1939, F)
The Grapes of Wrath (1940, F)
The Great Depression (1998, D)
I Am a Fugitive from a Chain Gang (1932, F)
I'm No Angel (1933, F)
Ironweed (1987, F)
Little Caesar (1931, F)
Native Land (1942, D)
Our Daily Bread (1934, F)
The Petrified Forest (1936, F)
Places in the Heart (1984, F)
The Plow That Broke the Plains (1936, D)
Public Enemy (1931, F)
The River (1937, D)
Scarface (1932, F)
Wild Boys of the Road (1933, F)

Bibliography

Bergman, Andrew. *We're in the Money: Depression America and Its Films.* New York: New York University Press, 1971.

Bernstein, Michael A. *The Great Depression: Delayed Recovery and Economic Change in America, 1929–1939.* New York: Cambridge University Press, 1987.

Bird, Caroline. *The Invisible Scar.* New York: David McKay, 1966.

Christensen, Terry. "Politics and the Movies: The Early Thirties." *San Jose Studies* 31 (1985): 9–24.

Ellis, Edward Robb. *A Nation in Torment: The Great American Depression, 1929–1939.* New York: Coward & McCann, 1978.

Leuchtenburg, William E. *Franklin Roosevelt and the New Deal, 1932–1940.* New York: Harper & Row, 1963.

Lynd, Robert, and Helen Merrill. *Middletown in Transition.* New York: Harcourt, Brace, 1937.

Mast, Gerald, ed. *The Movies in Our Midst: Documents in the Cultural Heritage of Film in America.* Chicago: University of Chicago Press, 1982.

Meltzer, Milton. *Brother, Can You Spare a Dime? The Great Depression, 1929–1933.* New York: Knopf, 1969.

Miller, Don. *"B" Movies: An Informal Survey of the American Low Budget Film, 1933–1945.* New York: Curtis Books, 1973.

O'Connor, John E., ed. *Image as Artifact: The Historical Analysis of Film and Television.* Malabar, FL: Robert E. Krieger, 1990.

Roffman, Peter, and Jim Purdy. *The Hollywood Social Problem Film: Madness, Despair, and Politics from the Depression to the Fifties.* Bloomington: Indiana University Press, 1981.

Rollins, Peter C., ed. *Hollywood as Historian.* Lexington: University Press of Kentucky, 1983.

Romasco, Albert U. *The Poverty of Abundance: Hoover, the Nation, the Depression.* New York: Oxford University Press, 1965.

Schlesinger, Arthur M. *The Crisis of the Old Order.* Boston: Houghton Mifflin, 1957.

Schwarz, Jordon A. *The Interregnum of Despair: Hoover, Congress, and the Depression.* Urbana: University of Illinois Press, 1970.

Sobel, Robert. *The Great Bull Market: Wall Street in the 1920s.* New York: Norton, 1968.

Stott, William. *Documentary Expression and Thirties America.* New York: Oxford University Press, 1973.

Stricker, Frank. "Repressing the Working Class: Individualism and the Masses in Frank Capra's Films." *Labor History* 31 (1990): 454–467.

[CHRISTOPHER C. LOVETT]

The 1960s

The 1960s—an era of social upheaval and youthful rebellion—has become a battleground in America's collective memory, and Hollywood films produced during that dynamic decade or with themes from that era reflect the struggle to interpret what was once optimistically called the Age of Aquarius. Historians and filmmakers are divided; interpretations of events such as Vietnam, civil rights, feminism, and the campus wars often turn on an individual's political orientation at the time. Todd Gitlin, a former Students for a Democratic Society (SDS) activist, and now a sociologist and historian, is correct when he observes, "Fantasy revolutions, withdrawals, media-driven dismissals . . . all the easy reactions obscured the more elusive and ambiguous results, the triumphs and precedents that the New Left left behind as it broke up" (421). Many former radicals challenge Gitlin's interpretation of the decade's spirit. For instance, Peter Collier and David Horowitz dispute any positive spin on the era, including Gitlin's. To them, the student radicals of the New Left "set out to destroy America from within" (243). The debate continues.

The public's interest in the 1960s remains strong and is evident in the popularity of "oldies" music and a wave of nostalgic histories about the decade. In the 1980s, Hollywood attempted to capture this nostalgia craze with Lawrence Kasdan's *The Big Chill* (1983), a film about the "good old days" of commitment and student activism, but *The Big Chill* and other such nostalgic films told only part of the story. During and following the Reagan era (1980–88), Hollywood reexamined the dark side of the 1960s in a series of films depicting the years of hope, days of sorrow, and the pain the American public experienced between 1960 and 1973, a true watershed in American history. James Patterson, a respected historian, agrees, noting that the ever-increasing demands for an expansion of civil rights for women, minorities, and the underprivileged, as well as the riots that plagued the decade, "did more than bewilder people." Those issues not only divided America, but "also aroused a backlash, the most vivid of the many reactions that arose amid the polarization of the era. It long outlasted the 1960s" (668). It was this backlash that brought forth the Reagan revolution and the conservative reaction that followed.

The Silent Generation and the Origins of the Youth Rebellion

With the onset of the Cold War, Americans became perplexed: how could the Arsenal of Democracy win a global conflict with Germany and Japan, yet find itself besieged by the threat of Communism? Before Senator Joseph R. McCarthy announced on February 12, 1950, in Wheeling, West Virginia, that he had a list of 205 Communists in the State Department, Hollywood had been under attack by the House Committee on Un-American Activities (HUAC). Nineteen screenwriters and directors scorned the investigation, and ten who refused to testify were imprisoned. The proscription of the Hollywood Ten and the blacklist in Hollywood—which quickly spread to radio, television, and the theater—cast a cloud over the entertainment industry. In 1951, Irwin Shaw, a veteran of World War II and author of *The Young Lions,* published his second novel, *The Troubled Air,* dealing with the blacklist in the radio industry. John Henry Faulk, a CBS radio writer, chronicled his own experiences in *Fear on Trial* (1975), which was made into a TV docudrama in the 1970s. The lesson of McCarthyism, accurately portrayed in Shaw's book and Faulk's film, was obvious: conform or suffer the consequences. Later, historian Stuart Samuels would summarize the fallout, noting that "three concepts dominated the decade: conformity, paranoia, and alienation" marked the films Hollywood produced (207). Many directors and screenwriters played it safe and avoided controversial films for fear of losing their positions. Now that the Cold War nightmare is over, it remains difficult to comprehend the fear and trepidation that the Red Scare caused among intellectuals and writers in academia and in the entertainment industry.

It has been long suspected, and only recently acknowledged by historians, that the Communist Party USA (CPUSA) was funded by the Soviet Union. As Harvey Klehr, James Earl Haynes, and Fridrikh Igorevich Firsov have noted, Soviet intelligence agencies actively recruited agents from the CPUSA into the Communist underground for Soviet covert operations (195). Much of this has become known with the availability of the Venona decrypts, a top-secret American effort to decode Soviet message traffic from 1943 to 1980.

Venona showed that the Soviets had penetrated the U.S. government from the Justice Department to the War Department during the 1930s and 1940s. To protect the most secret source of intelligence, the chairman of the Joint Chiefs of Staff, Omar Bradley, did not inform Harry Truman of the project, according to former Senator Daniel Patrick Moynihan (71). Moynihan claims, after an examination of the evidence, that "by the onset of the Cold War the Soviet attack in the area of espionage and subversion had been blunted and turned back" (Weinstein, 340). Still, as historian Robert Ferrell emphasizes, "There was fire behind McCarthy's smoke, for the Soviet Union had infiltrated the U.S. government with spies, but McCarthy . . . never managed to find a single one, save possibly an Army dentist" (19). Even Herbert Romerstein, a former staff member to HUAC, asserts that "to a very great degree Senator Joseph R. McCarthy was, in fact, irrelevant to the anti-Communist cause" because of Venona (451). So, although it was true that the Communist threat had existed earlier, prior to 1950, McCarthy's demagoguery succeeded only in damaging the anticommunist cause to such an extent that Christopher Andrew considers McCarthy as the greatest agent of influence the Kremlin had during the Cold War (164).

In the 1950s young people silently rebelled against the conformity of their parents. The coming of rock 'n' roll, particularly the advent of Elvis Presley, helped mobilize this rebellion. In Nicholas Ray's 1955 film *Rebel Without a Cause,* James Dean defined the mood: American youth was frustrated yet could not identify a target for its anger. In the meantime, parents in the 1950s were warned of juvenile delinquency as depicted in Hollywood productions. The related issues of alienation and identity were also raised by sociologists such as David Riesman in *The Lonely Crowd* and William Whyte in *The Organization Man.* Riesman and Whyte pointed to the serious feelings of alienation and a change in American character that were evident among not only middle-class youth but also their parents.

Still, a few films addressed real social concerns, as when Hollywood forced the American public to remember the internment of Japanese Americans during World War II in films such as John Sturges's *Bad Day at Black Rock* (1955). Indirectly, Hollywood required the public to address not only the issue of internment but also its willing compliance in the national hysteria in the early 1950s that resulted in legislation such as the McCarran Act (1950), which permitted the government to arrest and intern enemies of the state without due process of law. Congress passed the McCarran Act over Harry Truman's veto and warning that it "would make a mockery of our Bill of Rights" (Hamby, 549).

Even more remarkable, filmmakers had urged men of principle to stand up against evil—and not as HUAC perceived it. By 1959, "young people with a great deal of sophistication, tolerance, and eagerness were looking *for* something in literature," as Morris Dickstein notes, "not simply looking at it" (13). In high school and college, American youth gravitated to Arthur Miller's *The Crucible,* a depiction of the Salem witchcraft trials as a metaphor for the evils of McCarthyism. A new age of focused rebellion was born.

Dr. Strangelove and How We Learned to Love the Bomb

America's nuclear monopoly ended in 1949, when the Soviet Union tested its first atomic device. As the 1950s ended and politicians debated first a "bomber gap" and then a "missile gap," an increasingly insecure public slowly became aroused by the threat of nuclear war. It is difficult for later generations to imagine the panic that gripped the country, but Americans came to realize that nuclear weapons—ostensibly developed to protect the land—posed a danger to the nation's survival. At the time, the media accurately reported that radioactive isotopes were being found in cows' milk and that a danger existed to the public health owing to atmospheric nuclear testing.

What the public did not know was that its own government systematically tested the sick and the infirm with high levels of nuclear radiation to gauge the long-term effects of exposure during some future nuclear war. The Eisenhower administration established a top-secret, blue-ribbon committee—composed of Bernard Brodie, Arthur Compton, James B. Conant, John Hersey, Clark Kerr, Arthur Krock, Charles Mayo, Karl Menninger, and many others—in order to evaluate human testing. According to Eileen Welsome, the plutonium experiments "were not just immoral science, they were bad science" (9). A PBS documentary, *The Atomic Café* (1982), satirizes how people in the 1950s viewed nuclear weapons—sometimes sophomorically, sometimes with odd optimism that by "ducking and covering" they could survive an atomic a holocaust. Another warning came with the publication of Pat Frank's 1959 novel *Alas, Babylon,* depicting the survival of a small Florida town following a nuclear exchange between the Soviet Union and the United States.

The possibility of nuclear accidents existed before Hollywood dramatized the dangers of unintentional nuclear war. Most Americans were oblivious to the risks. The citizens of Roswell, New Mexico, were no exception; until 1988, they did not realize that thirty-three years earlier a U.S. Navy attack aircraft had jettisoned a fully armed atomic device not far from their city. In order to avoid panic, the Navy issued a press release to local papers that a "practice bomb" had been dropped not far from the now-famous town. Quickly, the FBI rushed to the scene and helped cordon the area from the media and onlookers as bomb-disposal teams retrieved the unexploded weapon. By the 1960s, public attitudes had changed concerning weapons of mass destruction, and Hollywood was willing to exploit the issue.

The fear of nuclear war escalated during the presidency of John F. Kennedy—in Berlin and, much closer to home, during the Cuban missile crisis in 1962. Hollywood addressed the possibility of combat with the Soviet Union in Stanley Kramer's adaptation of Nevil Shute's *On the Beach* (1959), in which an American submarine crew decides to return home to die rather than survive in the desolation of a post-nuclear world; in *The Bedford Incident* (1965), about an aggressive American destroyer commander, portrayed by Richard Widmark, who precipitates an accidental nuclear confrontation between his ship and a Soviet submarine;

and in *Fail-Safe* (1964), in which a faulty computer system sends U.S. bombers to attack the Soviet Union. These films convinced the public that despite American technological superiority over the Soviet Union, neither side would "win" a nuclear exchange. As a corollary, the films indirectly supported the Kennedy administration's view of limited war: If war had to come between East and West, it would be better if it were fought far from home, with conventional weapons and in a Third World setting.

As the public reflected on the dangers of a possible nuclear Armageddon in the 1960s, the film industry next challenged American nuclear strategy. Stanley Kubrick's *Dr. Strangelove* (1964) was a devastating comedy depicting the irrationality of mutually assured destruction (MAD), the operative U.S. nuclear strategy best formulated in Henry Kissinger's *Nuclear Weapons and Foreign Policy* (1957) and Herman Kahn's *On Thermonuclear War* (1960), *Thinking About the Unthinkable* (1962), and *On Escalation* (1965). Although not accurate in a historical sense, *Dr. Strangelove* captures, according to Paul Boyer, "a specific moment and offers a satiric but recognizable portrait of the era's strategic thinking and cultural climate" (266). Likewise, Norman Jewison's *The Russians Are Coming! The Russians Are Coming!* (1966), starring Alan Arkin and Carl Reiner, played on American fears of a Soviet attack, turning such antics into a hilarious spoof. In the end, the Russians and the Americans of the film learn to value cooperation over confrontation—and to make love, not war.

Sex, Drugs, and Rock 'n' Roll

By the mid-1960s Hollywood was in trouble. American youth was listening to a different beat and was tuned in to such best-sellers as Joseph Heller's *Catch-22* and, later, Charles Reich's *The Greening of America.* Reich assumed that the crisis began as the meritocracy twisted American life into a rat race, turning youth and the enlightened into "strangers to themselves" (9). Timothy Leary, the guru of LSD, swayed many students with his seductive appeal "to tune in, turn on, and drop out." Thousands sought refuge in San Francisco's Haight-Ashbury, the East Village in New York, or the communes that dotted the nation's landscape. The sexual revolution even reached the heartland, where birth control reshaped sexual relations on university campuses. The major studios initially failed to exploit those trends. Indeed, the only studio actually making money was United Artists, with spaghetti westerns, the *Pink Panther* series, and James Bond films. United Artists, sensing the shift of the youth culture, secured rights to The Beatles before they became a household word with *A Hard Day's Night* (1964) and *Help!* (1965). Events passed Hollywood by, and it was not until 1967, when headlines increasingly proved that the optimistic world of the Frankie Avalon–Annette Funicello beach movies and even of The Beatles had disappeared, that filmmakers produced movies that reflected stresses in America's cultural and social fabric. (George Lucas would resurrect something of that innocence in his 1973 celebration of the early 1960s, *American Graffiti.*)

Warren Beatty, the handsome star of Elia Kazan's *Splendor in the Grass* (1961), had yet to make his mark in American cinema, despite acclaim for his acting in the William Inge story. For the most part, Beatty was his own worst enemy, believing that he was too good for most of the parts offered to him—until he saw the script for *Bonnie and Clyde* (1967). Beatty sold *Bonnie and Clyde* as an outlaw film; however, it was unlike any of the classic gangster films of the 1930s. Instead of a traditional cops-and-robbers picture, director Arthur Penn produced a film that dramatically reflected the social upheaval in the late 1960s, replacing the traditional criminal with a 1960s-style revolutionary pushing the envelope of rebellion and violence to the limit.

Bonnie and Clyde projected on the screen an allegory of the cultural and social revolution that was taking place on college campuses and cities across the land. At almost the same time, Peter Fonda called his friend Dennis Hopper about a biker film, which would follow two outlaws traveling cross-country after making a big score selling drugs. This film, however, much like *Bonnie and Clyde,* would not only revolutionize Hollywood but would also reflect the emerging counterculture during the Summer of Love, 1967. The film *Easy Rider* (1969) was largely improvised (despite Terry Southern's script) and gave Middle America its first cinematic view of the youth revolution. Much has been made of Captain America's (Peter Fonda) statement to Billy (Dennis Hopper): "We blew it." Did "it" mean that the characters failed to accept the communal lifestyle of the counterculture? If Fonda and Hopper accepted that premise, then there was no need for the bloody ending to the picture, in which Captain America and Billy were murdered by southern rednecks. Still, Fonda and Hopper—unlike the studios, which attempted to exploit the youth culture with *Wild in the Streets* (1968), *Joe* (1970), and *The Strawberry Statement* (1970)—further condemned the conformist social values that, according to the youth culture, dominated the American scene in the late 1960s.

The Graduate (1967), directed by Mike Nichols, was a comedy involving a recent college graduate, Benjamin Braddock (Dustin Hoffman), experiencing an identity crisis. The initial advice given to Benjamin, as a college graduate, was to seek his fortune in "plastics," a famous statement satirizing 1960s materialism in an age of affluence. (Ironically, Benjamin never worried about the draft at a time when hundreds of thousands of his contemporaries had been shipped off to fight in Southeast Asia). Moviegoers, for the most part, focused on either the comedy or the love story between Benjamin and Elaine (Katharine Ross). When they did, they overlooked another subplot of the film, the radicalization of Mrs. Robinson (Ann Bancroft), who was willing to risk her dignity to escape the constraints of the traditional female role. The songs sung by Simon and Garfunkel dramatically added to the popularity of the picture and ensured an Oscar for director Mike Nichols.

Bonnie and Clyde, Easy Rider, and *The Graduate* portrayed the 1960s in fictionalized form. It was not until Warner Bros. released Michael Wadleigh's *Woodstock* (1970) that the public had the opportunity to experience visually the hippie lifestyle during the much-publicized Festival of Life outside Saugerties, New York, in June 1969. Although the free love, drugs, and bare bodies of the youthful participants shocked some parents, the rockumentary was a hit with younger audiences and grossed over $16.4 million. To Charles Reich, the Woodstock Nation became "the revolution of the new generation" (4). For Abbie Hoffman, Woodstock represented anarchy for anarchy's sake (Burner, 131). But in many ways, *Woodstock* marked a high point of the counterculture. The ensuing Tate–LaBianca murders by Charles Manson and his "family" in August 1969 revealed the dark side of the counterculture not only for the public at large, but also for the film community. Still more tragedies were to unfold, particularly the murder of an African American at a Rolling Stones concert at the Altamont Raceway in December 1969, captured on film for Albert Maysles's documentary *Gimme Shelter* (1970)—a film intentionally designed to "answer" the optimism of *Woodstock.*

Hollywood did not create the counterculture, but, as Peter Biskind argues in *Easy Riders, Raging Bulls,* the values and rebellion of the counterculture saved Hollywood and expanded the creative opportunities for the film industry. Not everyone agrees with Biskind's analysis. One strident critic of Hollywood and its impact on American culture since the 1960s, Michael Medved, notes that Hollywood created an unhealthy environment that has contaminated American society. Using a popular 1960s metaphor, Medved claims that "The

FIGURE 4. *Woodstock* (1970). Camera crews prepare for filming under the direction of filmmaker Michael Wadleigh (seated at center right, with headset). Although many fictional films in the 1960s depicted aspects of the "youth rebellion" of the time, the concert movie gave the counterculture its greatest and most widespread visibility on the screen. Courtesy Wadleigh-Maurice and Warner Bros.

popular culture is unhealthy for children—and other living things" (344). The debate goes on.

Judging the 1960s

The films of the 1960s attempted to depict a new age of redefinition, liberation, and social activism in a visualization and celebration of change. Filmmakers were not concerned with nitpicking details of historical truth; instead, they sought to give meaning to the social revolution that they witnessed in the streets, on university campuses, among men and women, and on the distant battlefields where young Americans fought and died in a controversial war. Hollywood provided an instrument for future generations, often too young to understand the dynamics of the 1960s, to conceptualize the divisiveness of the decade. Yet an element of distortion, somehow overlooked, occurs when society relies on film to explain historical reality.

Oliver Stone, the point man for Hollywood's effort to reinterpret the 1960s, believes that historians, like many directors, are overly defensive "and come at filmmakers with an attitude of hostility." Stone argues that historians presume that directors "pervert the paradigm with emotion, sentimentality, and so on." No doubt speaking for other filmmakers, the director of *Platoon, The Doors, Born on the Fourth of July, JFK,* and *Nixon* contends "historians exhibit much pomposity whey they think that they alone are in custody of the 'facts,' and take it upon themselves to guard 'the truth' as zealously as the high priests of ancient Egypt" (Toplin, 51).

Still, the decade divides Americans. David Burner argues that social activism alienated the traditional Democratic coalition and directly aided the forces of reaction, a point Charles Reich supports in *The Greening of America* (312). Maurice Isserman, a respected liberal historian, grudgingly agrees that the student radicals, those who alienated the political mainstream, failed to learn a fundamental lesson from their seniors—"the need for a patient, long-term approach to building movements; an emphasis upon the value of winning small victories . . . [and] the need to work with others with differing viewpoints" (219).

Some scholars of the antiwar movement and responses to it have reached different conclusions, arguing that defiant protests may have prolonged the war by hardening public attitudes of the middle class about Vietnam (Garfinkle, 1). Michael Medved not only agrees but also notes that "Hollywood paints only the most glowing portrait of the contemporaries who stayed home and protested American policy" (230). Tom Wells believes that it was the antiwar movement, and particularly college protesters, that altered, for one, Notre Dame University president Theodore Hesburgh's views about Vietnam. Hesburgh, a Catholic priest and nearly iconic representative of Middle America, recalled, "I think the young people really turned the tide on this one. . . . Most of us underwent a complete transformation from A to Z" (Wells, 303).

The youthful rebels on college campuses and in Hollywood never anticipated the counterrevolution that came with Richard Nixon's election in 1968 (see "Richard Nixon"), when, Lewis Gould writes, "American politics was changed for the worse in ways that the nation has not fully absorbed or resolved nearly a quarter century after Richard Nixon's narrow victory over Hubert Humphrey" (169). The triumphant liberalism that defeated the Depression and won World War II was, ironically, a victim of the 1960s. From the ashes came the neoconservatives, who, according to Paul Lyons, "understood the ways in which the radical challenges concerning race, gender, values, nation, and nature were unsettling to hardworking Middle Americans" (211).

How do we judge the 1960s? Historians remain divided. Maurice Isserman and Michael Kazin compare the decade to the American Civil War, writing that "many of the key conflicts of the 1960s had neither healed nor driven either side from the field of battle" (294). Even Todd Gitlin, writing closer to the decade than many other historians, believes that "the Sixties' returns are not in, the activists now [as of 1987] in their thirties and forties [are] not necessarily finished." Gitlin, unlike many others of his generation, still harbors the dream that "there are still movements waiting to happen" (438). Horowitz and Collier argue, on the other hand, "the radical future is an illusion," and the Left's resilience "is primarily a result of the fact that it has built its political religion on liberal precepts: its luminous promise—equality, fraternity, and social justice" (335). Consequently, the real battle for conservative writers remains, Horowitz and Collier believe, "between those who have had second thoughts about their experiences in the Sixties, and those who have not" (334). Regardless, the "aftershocks are still felt," according to Jules Witcover, "not only in the country at large but particularly in the lives of the millions, and in their memories of a year that rocked a bitterly divided nation to its core—and set it on a course that keeps it divided still" (507).

References

Filmography

The Atomic Café (1982, D)
Bad Day at Black Rock (1955, F)
The Bedford Incident (1965, F)

The Big Chill (1983, F)
Bonnie and Clyde (1967, F)
Catch-22 (1970, F)
Cold War (1998–99, D)
Dr. Strangelove, or: How I Learned to Stop Worrying and Love The Bomb (1964, F)
Easy Rider (1969, F)
Fail-Safe (1964, F)
Fear on Trial (1975, TV)
The Front (1976, F)
Gimme Shelter (1970, D)
The Graduate (1967, F)
Hollywood on Trial (1976, D)
Joe (1970, F)
Legacy of the Hollywood Blacklist (1997, D)
Making Sense of the Sixties (1991, D)
On the Beach (1959, F)
Rebel Without a Cause (1955, F)
The Russians Are Coming! The Russians Are Coming! (1966, F)
Splendor in the Grass (1961, F)
The Strawberry Statement (1970, F)
Wild in the Streets (1968, F)
The Wild One (1954, F)
Woodstock (1970, D)

Bibliography

Andrew, Christopher M., and Vasili Mitrokhin. *The Sword and the Shield: The Mitrokhin Archive and the Secret History of the KGB.* New York: Basic Books, 1999.

Biskind, Peter. *Easy Riders, Raging Bulls: How the Sex-Drugs-and-Rock 'n' Roll Generation Saved Hollywood.* New York: Simon & Schuster, 1999.

Boyer, Paul. "Dr. Strangelove." In Mark C. Carnes, ed., *Past Imperfect: History According to the Movies,* 266–269. New York: Henry Holt, 1995.

Burner, David. *Making Peace with the 60s.* Princeton: Princeton University Press, 1996.

Collier, Peter, and David Horowitz. *Destructive Generation: Second Thoughts About the 60s.* New York: Summit, 1988.

Dickstein, Morris. *Gates of Eden: American Culture in the Sixties.* New York: Basic Books, 1977.

Ferrell, Robert H., ed. *The Eisenhower Diaries.* New York: Norton, 1981.

Garfinkle, Adam. *Telltale Hearts: The Origins and Impact of the Vietnam Antiwar Movement.* New York: St. Martin's, 1995.

Gitlin, Todd. *The Sixties: Years of Hope, Days of Rage.* New York: Bantam, 1987.

Gould, Lewis L. 1968*: The Election That Changed America.* Chicago: Ivan R. Dee, 1993.

Hamby, Alonzo L. *Man of the People: A Life of Harry S. Truman.* New York: Oxford University Press, 1995.

Isserman, Maurice. *If I Had a Hammer: The Death of the Old Left and the Birth of the New Left.* New York: Basic Books, 1987.

Isserman, Maurice, and Michael Kazin. *America Divided: The Civil War of the 1960s.* New York: Oxford University Press, 2000.

Klehr, Harvey, John Earl Haynes, and Fridrikh Igorevich Firsov. *The Secret World of American Communism.* New Haven: Yale University Press, 1995.

Lyons, Paul. *New Left, New Right and the Legacy of the Sixties.* Philadelphia: Temple University Press, 1996.

Medved, Michael. *Hollywood vs. America: Popular Culture and the War on Traditional American Values.* New York: HarperCollins, 1992.

Moynihan, Daniel Patrick. *Secrecy.* New Haven: Yale University Press, 1998.

Patterson, James T. *Grand Expectations: The United States, 1945–1974.* New York: Oxford University Press, 1996.

Reich, Charles A. *The Greening of America: How the Youth Revolution Is Trying to Make America Livable.* New York: Random House, 1970.

Rollins, Peter C., ed. *Hollywood as Historian: American Film in a Cultural Context.* 2d ed. Lexington: University Press of Kentucky, 1998.

Romerstein, Herbert, and Eric Breindel. *The Venona Secrets: Exposing Soviet Espionage and America's Traitors.* Washington, DC: Regnery, 2000.

Roszak, Theodore. *The Making of a Counter Culture: Reflections on the Technocratic Society and Its Youthful Opposition.* Garden City, NY: Doubleday, 1969.

Samuels, Stuart. "The Age of Conspiracy and Conformity: Invasion of the Body Snatchers (1956)." In John E. O'Conner and Martin A. Jackson, eds., *American History/American Film: Interpreting the Hollywood Image,* 200–215. Rev. ed. New York: Continuum, 1989.

Toplin, Robert Brent, ed. *Oliver Stone's USA: Film, History, and Controversy.* Lawrence: University Press of Kansas, 2000.

Weinstein, Allen. *The Haunted Wood: Soviet Espionage in America—The Stalin Era.* New York: Random House, 1999.

Wells, Tom. *The War Within: America's Battle Over Vietnam.* Berkeley: University of California Press, 1994.

Welsome, Eileen. *The Plutonium Files: America's Secret Medical Experiments in the Cold War.* New York: Dial Press, 1999.

Witcover, Jules. *The Year the Dream Died: Revisiting 1968 in America.* New York: Warner Books, 1997.

[ZIA HASAN]

The 1970s

The 1970s was a turbulent time, and it has been rightly labeled the "Media Decade": The Vietnam War, the Watergate scandal, the election of Jimmy Carter, the growing power of the antinuclear movement, and the crisis in Iran were all media events in the sense that the public perception of these events was shaped by the reports of network television news. The quest for higher ratings was often a very strong motivating factor behind television's delineation of events.

The 1970s also saw the emergence of the first generation of children who grew up on television. When television began broadcasting in the 1950s, its credo was a blend of public service and entertainment, and the results were classic programs such as *Victory at Sea, Omnibus,* and *Kraft Television Theatre.* In the 1970s, commercial television became big business; sex and violence began to undergird successful programs, both reflecting and causing a change in social mores, and a "TV" generation emerged—a cohort that was passive, prone to accept violence casually, and insensitive to social issues (Comstock, 249).

The decade also saw the growth of the women's liberation movement. The movement, which started to gather momentum in the 1960s, found pervasive support from diverse sections of society and, as a political force, was instrumental in bringing fundamental changes in social attitudes. More women had jobs previously held only by men, and such visible bastions of male dominance as West Point and Annapolis saw the graduation of the first classes of female officers in the armed forces. The transformation of an essentially passive and dependent image of women also brought about marked changes in male/female relationships. The movement led to what Christopher Lasch called a "flight from feeling" in the female's attitude toward relationships with males. Some observers feared a slide toward promiscuity. Feminists also cited the findings of Masters and Johnson, which destroyed the "myth" of vaginal orgasm and announced that females were multi-orgasmic; many ideologues saw this as liberating women from dependence on men and, indeed, pointing toward women's biological superiority. These findings destroyed the concept of the traditional role of women and shifted the "pressure to perform" from the female to the male. In effect, interpersonal relations were threatened because of the inversion of roles and, in the process of role reversal, men, for many, became the sex object.

Tom Wolfe labeled the 1970s "The Me Decade" for self-evident reasons. According to Wolfe and other critics, the basic precepts of a narcissistic personality implied that an individual was only concerned with the progression and development of one's own career. The "me" personality shirked permanent relationships and simply ignored everybody else in the quest for "self glorification" (Wolfe, 156).

Perhaps the most significant phenomenon of the 1960s, which culminated as the major issue of the early 1970s, was the Vietnam War. A public perception that this was America's first major defeat meant that veterans of the war were denied the heroic welcome and status bestowed upon veterans of other wars, perhaps because "losing" was not acceptable in the American tradition. This rejection greatly amplified the problems of readjustment for the returning soldier, already burdened by the guilt about what he had been told by public spokesmen and his radical peers was an immoral war.

Many of the returning soldiers exhibited symptoms of what was diagnosed as "post-traumatic stress disorder" (PTSD), a state characterized by self-doubt, aggression, and genuine fear of intimate relationships. Thus the process of readjustment into a hostile society involved not only overcoming the physical and emotional difficulties but also finding a constructive new direction in life. Many veterans, such as John Kerry, who later served in the U.S. Senate, sought self-expression by becoming demonstrators against the very war in which they had served. These "prophet-heroes," as Robert Lifton characterizes them, contributed in large measure to the reevaluation of America's role in Vietnam and changed society's attitude toward any such future involvement. Others, such as Navy flyer James Webb, went on to government service and continued to defend America's failed efforts in Indochina.

Motion Pictures About the 1970s Media

It was within this extended backdrop that many significant films of the 1970s were created. Sidney Lumet's *Network* (1976) and Alan J. Pakula's *Parallax View* (1974) and *All the President's Men* (1976) focused on the growing power of the media and the marked impact of television on human behavior and on public perception. *Network* is very explicit in its depiction of the evils of television, the depersonalization of American society, and the fate of resistant individuals enmeshed within the system. The film raised a flag about the impact of television on thinking processes and behavior patterns—and thus the fabric of American society. *All the President's Men,* which traced the investigative reporting of two young *Washington Post* reporters who were instrumental in exposing the Watergate break-in and the subsequent cover-up, underlined the impact of the print news media, as did *The Parallax View,* which focuses on a journalist who attempts to probe the assassination of a presidential candidate. Both films validated the power of the fourth estate and the far-reaching influence of television on America's future.

Feminism

The undercurrent of the feminist movement, which in many ways was a vital part of the 1970s mise-en-scène, was also the thematic focus of a range of important films. Jane Kramer observes that the focus on male-female relationships in these movies reveals "their longing to discover an archetype of the modern woman—one that will hold, one that will move in some pure female space" (30). Such films include Joan Micklin Silver's *Hester Street* (1975), Robert Benton's *Kramer vs. Kramer* (1979), James Bridge's *The China Syndrome* (1979), Paul Mazursky's *An Unmarried Woman* (1978), Richard Brooks's *Looking for Mr. Goodbar* (1977), and the Woody Allen films *Annie Hall* (1977) and *Manhattan* (1979).

In *An Unmarried Woman,* Erica (Jill Clayburgh) is a thirty-seven-year-old woman whose husband has deserted her. She meets Saul Kaplan (Alan Bates), a famous painter who is looking for a permanent relationship. Unfortunately, Erica's "flight from feeling," resulting from the disappointing experience in her marriage, finally causes the relationship to crumble. In *Looking for Mr. Goodbar,* Theresa Dunn (Diane Keaton) is a young schoolteacher who instructs deaf children during the day and at night "cruises" the singles bars for temporary liaisons aimed at satisfying her narcissistic sexuality. In both *Manhattan* and *Annie Hall,* the protagonists embody the sexual anxieties of modern men, which, when transposed on interpersonal relationships, imbue them with the tasks of not only adjusting to the changing image of the liberated woman but also of justifying themselves as men.

Vietnam

That the Vietnam War and our involvement are examined in many of the memorable films of the 1970s is not accidental. As the decade opened, the national mood was wrenchingly altered by the perception that the war was widening into Laos and Cambodia. Films such as Michael Cimino's *The Deer Hunter* (1978), Francis Ford Coppola's *Apocalypse Now* (1979), and Hal Ashby's *Coming Home* (1978) explored the effects of the war both on the front line and at home.

The last film, while taking an antiwar stance, focuses on the problems confronting the returning Vietnam veteran, graphically projecting the conflict between a traditional America accustomed to winning and a new, hip society that had to come to terms with loss. Among the victims of the Vietnam War were the warriors who had to learn to live in a society that rejected them. In *Coming Home,* Luke Martin (Jon Voight) is wounded, but his healing brings new insights about life; on the other hand, Captain Bob Hyde (Bruce Dern) is destroyed because he cannot reconcile old values with the world of Woodstock.

The Vietnam War also yielded more than four hundred documentaries that examined the war from various perspectives. Among the important ones produced in the 1970s were *Saigon* (1970), *Vietnam: Voices in Opposition* (1970), *Where We Stand in Cambodia* (1971), *Lyndon Johnson Talks Politics* (1972), *Indochina 1975: The End of the Road?* (1975), *POWs: The Pawns of War* (1971), *The World of Charlie Company* (1970), *The Boat People* (1979), and *The Selling of the Pentagon* (1971). *Vietnam: Voices in Opposition* was filmed in compliance with an FCC ruling that CBS must provide an opportunity for administration critics to reply to President Nixon's televised statements on Vietnam, with CBS correspondents offering their analysis. *Where We Stand in Cambodia* examines the expansion of the war in Vietnam, and *Indochina 1975: The End of the Road?* assesses the gains made by Communist forces in South Vietnam and Cambodia and looks at the plight of refugees in both countries. Finally, *The Boat People* reports on the plight of thousands of homeless Vietnamese refugees stranded along the coast of Malaysia and Southeast Asia and examines U.S. policies concerning these people.

Documentaries made in the 1980s focus more on the aftermath of Vietnam. Memorable among these include *Frontline: Bloods of 'Nam* (1986), *Frank: A Vietnam Veteran* (1981), *The Problems of Peace* (1981), *Are You Listening: Indochina Refugees* (1981) and *Becoming American* (1982). *Frontline: Bloods of 'Nam* examines the fact that although blacks made up only 10 percent of the soldiers in combat, they accounted for 23 percent of the casualties. *Frank* is a returning soldier's monologue describing the horrors of his experience, while *The Problems of Peace* analyzes the problems of Vietnam from a postwar perspective. Finally, *Are You Listening* and *Becoming American* highlight the heartaches and joys of the American experience. The diversity of perspectives in the films underscores the impact of the Vietnam experience on the American psyche.

Compensatory Vision

In a decade where many of the societal problems continued to fester, the most successful films were often wish-fulfillment fantasies, which offered solutions to pervasive pressures. Perhaps the most significant among these are John Avildsen's *Rocky* (1976) and George Lucas's *Star Wars* (1977). The original *Rocky* was the first in a series of films that featured Rocky Balboa (Sylvester Stallone) as an underdog boxer from Philadelphia. In this recurring role, "Cinderella" Balboa becomes an American cultural icon by overcoming insurmountable odds through the strength of the human spirit—a veritable success story, triumphing over incredible odds.

Star Wars–type films such as *Close Encounters of the Third Kind* (1977), *Battlestar: Galactica* (1978), and *Star Trek: The Motion Picture* (1979) heralded a new, futuristic direction for the genre, which Robert Aldiss has defined as a "space opera": "Ideally, the earth must be in peril, there must be quest and a man to meet the mighty hour. . . . There must be a woman fairer than the skies and a villain darker than the Black Hole. And all must come right in the end" (10). *Star Wars* fits this description neatly yet manages to convey a deeper meaning, as the narrator of the documentary *The Making of Star Wars* notes: "Its power is to rise from something simpler to something rarer, the romantic spirit. Before it we are young again and everything seems possible."

Star Wars recreated a myth out of our own past and carried it into the future, making "the old fable of fateful youth rising to combat universal tyranny with a paean of communal hope" (Collins, 6), a theme reiterated in *The Empire Strikes Back* (1980). Coming in the 1970s, when Americans were buffeted by the repercussions of the Vietnam War, the disintegrating family, and the polarization of interpersonal relationships and feared being replaced and dehumanized by technological extensions of the self, *Star Wars* offered appealing, mystical solutions to problems of great magnitude. In the process, it restored the American dream and reaffirmed the American way of life.

Behind this sociocultural backdrop, the 1970s was also a watershed era in many critical aspects. The decade saw the renewal and rebirth of the film industry and was, in contrast to the 1950s and the 1960s, a box office–oriented period, with megablockbusters like *Jaws* (1975) and *Star Wars* standing among the highest grossing films in history. It was also in this decade that subsidiary markets—cable television and video sales and rentals—for Hollywood films emerged as result of new technology such as Sony's Betamax and Japanese Victor's VHS videocassette players.

The decade also witnessed the emergence of a new breed of directors, "Movie Brats" who had formal film school training and were able to create films that were both critically and commercially successful. They brought in an audiovisual rather than narrative approach to filmmaking, which often favored style, loud soundtracks, and action, stressing form and style as much as content. Among them were Martin Scorsese, George Lucas, Bob Rafelson, Alan Pakula, Brian De Palma, Peter Bogdanovich, and Robert Altman. These new talents were responsible for the most creative and artistically significant films of the period: *Mean Streets* (1973), *Star Wars* (1977), *Five Easy Pieces* (1970), *Klute* (1971), *Carrie* (1976), *The Last Picture Show* (1971), and *MASH* (1970).

The films of the 1970s range from the political to the apathetic, from the mundane to the speculative, from the philosophical to the mindless. Altogether, as Peter Lev has argued, the films of the decade represent a form of discussion about the nature and the direction of American society in the era: "open, diverse, and egalitarian, or stubbornly resistant to change" (36). It is an apt assessment that reinforces the relationship between film and history.

References

Filmography

All the President's Men (1976, F)
Annie Hall (1977, F)
Apocalypse Now (1979, F)
Are You Listening: Indochina Refugees (1981, D)
Battlestar: Galactica (1978, F)
Becoming American (1982, D)
The Boat People (1979, D)
Carrie (1976, F)

The China Syndrome (1979, F)
Close Encounters of the Third Kind (1977, F)
Coming Home (1978, F)
The Deer Hunter (1978, F)
The Empire Strikes Back (1980, F)
Five Easy Pieces (1970, F)
Frank: A Vietnam Veteran (1981, D)
Frontline: Bloods of 'Nam (1986, D)
Hester Street (1975, F)
Indochina 1975: The End of the Road? (1975, D)
Jaws (1975, F)
Klute (1971, F)
Kramer vs. Kramer (1979, F)
The Last Picture Show (1971, F)
Looking for Mr. Goodbar (1977, F)
Lyndon Johnson Talks Politics (1972, D)
Manhattan (1979, F)
MASH (1970, F)
Mean Streets (1973, F)
Network (1976, F)
The Parallax View (1974, F)
POWs: The Pawns of War (1971, D)
The Problems of Peace (1981, D)
Rocky (1976, F)
Saigon (1970, D)
The Selling of the Pentagon (1971, D)
Star Trek: The Motion Picture (1979, F)
Star Wars (1977, F)
An Unmarried Woman (1978, F)
Vietnam: Voices in Opposition (1970, D)
Where We Stand in Cambodia (1971, D)
The World of Charlie Company (1970, D)

Bibliography

Aldiss, Robert. *Space Opera.* London: Futura, 1974.

Biskind, Peter. *Easy Riders, Raging Bulls: How the Sex-Drugs-and Rock 'n' Roll Generation Saved Hollywood.* New York: Simon & Schuster, 1999.

Collins, Robert G. "*Star Wars:* The Pastiche of Myth and Yearning for a Past Future." *Journal of Popular Culture* 12 (1977): 3.

Comstock, George, et al. *Television and Human Behavior.* New York: Columbia University Press, 1978.

Freeman, Jo, ed. *Social Movements of the Sixties and Seventies.* New York: Longman, 1983.

Kramer, Jane. "The So-Called New Woman in Film." *Horizon,* May 1978.

Lasch, Christopher. *The Culture of Narcissism.* New York: Norton, 1978.

Lev, Peter. *American Films of the 70s: Conflicting Visions.* Austin: University of Texas Press, 2000.

Lifton, Robert J. *Home from the War.* New York: Simon & Schuster, 1973.

Monaco, James. *American Film Now.* New York: New American Library, 1979.

Olson, James S., ed. *Historical Dictionary of the 1970s.* Westport, CT: Greenwood, 1999.

Sklar, Robert. *Movie-Made America: A Cultural History of American Movies.* Rev. ed. New York: Vintage, 1994.

Wolfe, Tom. *Mauve Gloves & Madmen, Clutter & Vine.* New York: Farrar, Straus & Giroux, 1976.

Zinman, David. *Fifty Grand Movies of the 1960s and 1970s.* New York: Crown, 1986.

[WILLIAM J. PALMER]

The 1980s

It is fitting that the central figure of 1980s social history and the trendsetter for 1980s film representations of that history is Ronald Reagan, a former film actor who repeatedly employed film images and references to advance his historical goals. The major social, political, and historical issues of the 1980s—winning the Vietnam War ten years after the fact, the New Patriotism, saber-rattling détente with Russia's "evil empire," renewed fears of nuclear holocaust, the federal deficit, the self-indulgent Yuppie lifestyle, a "neo-racism" against Asians much different from that of the World War II era—were in many respects both inspired and exploited by Reagan and his cohort. Other film reflections on social history, such as a strikingly focused cluster of farm-crisis films, a redefinition of feminist roles, and a proliferation of films about gangs and drugs, were all reactions to specific cultural events and trends. However, the greatest historical undermining of any 1980s illusion of 1950s, Eisenhower-era stability was the growing threat of an international terrorist community, organized on the two models of the "big event" and the "death squad." The emergence of this invisible international villain, increasingly sponsored by national entities, either terrorist states or fascist governments, served as a violent dialogic denial of the grandfatherly illusion of prosperity and rededication to old-fashioned American values of the Reagan years.

Coincident with the spun imagery of the Reagan era, at the very beginning of the 1980s, a new approach to historical discourse—named the "New Historicism" by Stephen Greenblatt in a 1980 essay—came into vogue. It emphasized that the texts of history needed to be more diverse and more attuned to the "marginalized" voices of the poor and working classes of society as well as the politically, racially, and sexually disenfranchised members of society than the master-text, power-centered traditional histories of the past had been (1). Despite long-standing and consistent charges of the film industry's traditional exploitation of historical fact and romanticizing of historical realism, Hollywood in the 1980s proved quite reactive and timely in its representation of social history. When the New Historicists presented their arguments that historical "fact" is always much more complex than conventional histories have portrayed it and that historical "reality" is extremely difficult to recreate, past charges of Hollywood's historical inaccuracy and exploitation of history were rendered increasingly moot. If, as Graeme Turner writes, film "is a social practice for its makers and its audience, in its narratives and meanings we can locate evidence of the ways in which our culture makes sense of itself" (xiv–xv), then the films of the 1980s proved a highly reactive, analytic, and accessible body of representations of the historical climate, the social trends, and the political violence of the 1980s. In other words, in this decade the mirroring of society was one of the things that films did best.

A literariness marked by films such as *The French Lieutenant's Woman* (1981) and *Ragtime* (1981) proved a false start to the decade's film consciousness, but by 1982 the first real gatherings of sociohistorical film texts around contemporary life texts began. Films such as *Testament* (1983) and *Silkwood* (1983), perhaps inspired by Israel's preemptive strike against an Iraqi nuclear reactor in 1981, actually predicted (as *The China Syndrome* had in 1979) real-life toxic disasters such as the gas leak in Bhopal, India, that killed 3,400 people in 1984 and the Chernobyl nuclear plant explosion in 1986. The years 1983 and 1984 saw a newfound emphasis on the family farm with the release of *Places in the Heart, Country,* and *The River,* while 1987 was the year of Vietnam with Oliver Stone's Academy Award–winning *Platoon* serving as an antidote to the politically fantasized winning of the lost Vietnam War in earlier films such as *Rambo II* (1985) and *Uncommon Valor* (1983). Comedy reasserted itself as a vibrant social commentator upon the triumphs and tragedies of Reagonomics in 1988, the year of the Yuppie hit *Baby Boom.* But if Vietnam was put to rest in the deficit-flaunting excess of the Yuppie lifestyle, other wars of a very different sort were asserting their sociocultural presence in the films of the 1980s. The resurgence of Cold War antagonism toward Russia and the emergence of organized international terrorism became prominent film texts.

For the New Historicists, movies are what Dominick LaCapra calls "mechanisms of diffusion" (80). They are one of the means whereby complex historical texts are circulated, interpreted, and used in society. For example, film diffuses the social history of the 1980s by defining those trends or texts—such as Vietnam guilt or Yuppie cynicism—that people of the time were trying to understand.

Two of the major film texts of the 1980s—the large group of Vietnam War films and the smaller cluster of nuclear-holocaust films—were holdovers from earlier decades. The Vietnam War films took two different shapes in the 1980s. Early in the decade, led by the hit *Rambo* series, a body of films espoused the militarist fantasy that the Vietnam War was not really lost in the 1960s and 1970s but merely placed on hold until 1980s heroes portrayed by Sylvester Stallone, Chuck Norris, Gene Hackman, and the like could go back and redeem the national pride, exorcise the national shame. Later in the decade, however, Oliver Stone's *Platoon* (1986) became the most famous of a group of films—*Full Metal Jacket* (1987), *Hamburger Hill* (1987), *Gardens of Stone* (1987), *Good Morning, Vietnam* (1988), *Off Limits* (1988), *Some Kind of Hero* (1981), *Birdy* (1985), *Cutter's Way* (1981), *Cease Fire* (1986), and *The Killing Fields* (1984)—that attempted to interpret the American experience in Vietnam and the "coming home" experience of the veterans of that war.

Another violent echo out of America's past, the doomsday fear of nuclear Armageddon, also reasserted itself in the films of the 1980s and helped to generate another group of films that explored America's slippery and fragile détente with Russia leading up to the fall of that "evil empire" in 1989. Early in the decade, one of the most important (and most watched) films of the 1980s appeared on television. *The Day After* (1983) may not have been as complex or well made as *Testament* (1983), *Silkwood* (1983), or *War Games* (1983), but it was seen by more people than any other movie of the decade. Its warning was unmistakably clear and was taken to heart immediately as the Reagan administration (which had threatened to place medium-range missiles in Europe) intensified nuclear disarmament negotiations with Russia, culminating in Reagan's going to the Moscow Summit in 1988. Throughout the decade, these ongoing U.S. relations with Russia were explored in another group of films—*Gorky Park* (1983), *Moscow on the Hudson* (1984), *Rocky IV* (1985), *White Nights* (1985), *Russkies* (1987), and *Little Nikita* (1988)—that commented on the neo–Cold War brittleness of 1980s détente with a Soviet Union that was growing desperate in its economic failure.

But if the old devils of Vietnam and Russia were being exorcised in 1980s films, a new villain was casting its huge shadow (in the form of a threatening and frightening film text) over the whole decade. It was the shadow of international terrorism. Terrorism in its varied forms (from organized, state-supported, international terrorism to government, "death squad," control terrorism to commercial, drug-trade terrorism) escalated throughout the decade and became commonplace. Hostages were taken, planes and cruise ships were hijacked and bombed, American soldiers abroad were attacked in discos and their own barracks, political figures and judges were assassinated, and finally a terrorist Jihad or "holy war" was declared against the United States. Films such as *The Formula* (1980), *Rollover* (1981), *Nighthawks* (1981), *The Little Drummer Girl* (1984), *Half Moon Street* (1987), and *Die Hard* (1988) examined the dynamics, the personalities and the motives of international terrorists. Another set of films—*Missing* (1982), *The Year of Living Dangerously* (1983), *Under Fire* (1983), *Beyond the Limit* (1983), *The Killing Fields* (1984), *Under the Volcano* (1984), *Kiss of the Spider Woman* (1985), *The Official Story* (1985), and *Salvador* (1986)—represented the terrorist control tactics of "death squad" fascist governments. Of this set of government terrorist texts, *Under Fire* and *The Official Story* are the two most perceptive. *Under Fire* is mainstream Hollywood filmmaking at its most commercial, but it tellingly engages one of the historical, moral struggles of our time, the control-terrorism text. *The Official Story* is the ultimate "New Historicist" film of the 1980s, for not only does it explore the plight of the "*desaparecidos*" of Argentina, but it also unfolds a striking subtext concerning the very nature of history itself, of how "the official story" intentionally obscures the real story of history.

But films of the 1980s focused on things other than international historical issues. Domestic issues such as the ascent of a neofeminism and a newly defined (in economic terms) form of racism against Asians found cinematic expression. Appropriate to the Reagan years, the films of the 1980s—beginning with the farm films of 1983 and 1984, all three of which focus on a working farm wife struggling to keep her family's world together in the face of economic and natural disasters—championed a neoconservative redefinition of feminism as opposed to the radical and economic feminisms of the 1960s and 1970s. Other films, such as *Atlantic City* (1980), *Personal Best* (1983), and *Educating Rita* (1983), keyed on the attempts of working-class feminist heroines to find success in the competitive world of the 1980s. Still other films, such as *Private Benjamin* (1980), *Urban Cowboy* (1980), *Swing Shift* (1984), *Betrayed* (1988), and *Working Girl* (1989), signaled the success of neoconservative women in what were formerly male domains. Finally, some excellent female biopics were made in the decade—*Coal Miner's Daughter* (1980), *Heart Like a Wheel* (1983), *Eleni* (1984), *Marie* (1985), *Out of Africa* (1986), and *Gorillas in the Mist* (1988)—that offered feminist profiles in courage for a new generation.

Less palatable, yet sociologically acute, was a group of films that represented American society's growing resentment toward Asian immigrants and Asian Americans in the midst of Asian success in the economic exploitation of American markets. Films such as *Alamo Bay* (1985), *Gung Ho* (1986), and, especially, *Year of the Dragon* (1985) examine different versions of generalized anti-Asian racist tensions that were a clear residue from the Vietnam War.

But by far the major domestic film text of the 1980s was the Yuppie lifestyle text, a large grouping of films exploring the cynical angst and the economic excess of the Yuppie world. *Bright Lights, Big City* (1988) and *Wall Street* (1987) are the two marquee films exploring the Reagonomics phenomenon whereby all the money is grabbed and spent before it ever has a chance to trickle down. Perhaps *The Big Chill* (1983), however, is the ultimate checklist film for the Yuppie generation. Its conversational vignettes between its eight Yuppie stereotypes define the angst, anger, exhilaration, and confusion of the time.

Although the films of the 1980s were heavily influenced by eight years of Ronald Reagan's neoconservative reimaging of America, they also engaged history, politics, and economics in some highly perceptive ways. They may have represented that burgeoning neoconservatism, but they also powerfully critiqued it. Perhaps Oliver Stone's work in the decade—*Salvador* (1986), *Platoon* (1986), *Wall Street* (1987), *Talk Radio* (1989), and *Born on the Fourth of July* (1989)—is the best testament to the analytic critique of social history that film carried on in that turbulent time.

References

Filmography

Alamo Bay (1985, F)
Atlantic City (1980, F)
Baby Boom (1988, F)
Betrayed (1988, F)
Beyond the Limit (1983, F)
The Big Chill (1983, F)
Birdy (1985, F)
Born on the Fourth of July (1989, F)
Bright Lights, Big City (1988, F)
Cease Fire (1986, F)
The China Syndrome (1979, F)
Coal Miner's Daughter (1980, F)
Country (1984, F)
Cutter's Way (1981, F)
The Day After (1983, TV)
Die Hard (1988, F)
Educating Rita (1983, F)
Eleni (1984, F)
The Formula (1980, F)
The French Lieutenant's Woman (1981, F)
Full Metal Jacket (1987, F)
Gardens of Stone (1987, F)
Good Morning, Vietnam (1988, F)
Gorillas in the Mist (1988, F)
Gorky Park (1983, F)
Gung Ho (1986, F)
Half Moon Street (1987, F)
Hamburger Hill (1987, F)
Heart Like a Wheel (1983, F)
The Killing Fields (1984, F)
Kiss of the Spider Woman (1985, F)
The Little Drummer Girl (1984, F)
Little Nikita (1988, F)
Marie (1985, F)
Missing (1982, F)
Moscow on the Hudson (1984, F)
Nighthawks (1981, F)
The Official Story (1985, F)
Off Limits (1988, F)
Out of Africa (1986, F)
Personal Best (1983, F)
Places in the Heart (1984, F)
Platoon (1986, F)
Private Benjamin (1980, F)
Ragtime (1981, F)
Rambo II (1985, F)
The River (1984, F)
Rocky IV (1985, F)
Rollover (1981, F)
Russkies (1987, F)
Salvador (1986, F)
Silkwood (1983, F)
Some Kind of Hero (1981, F)
The Stunt Man (1980, F)
Swing Shift (1984, F)
Talk Radio (1989, F)
Testament (1983, TV)
Uncommon Valor (1983, F)
Under Fire (1983, F)
Under the Volcano (1984, F)
Urban Cowboy (1980, F)
Wall Street (1987, F)
War Games (1983, F)
White Nights (1985, F)
Working Girl (1989, F)
Year of the Dragon (1985, F)
The Year of Living Dangerously (1983, F)

Bibliography

Greenblatt, Stephen. "Towards a Poetics of Culture." In H. Aram Veeser, ed., *The New Historicism,* 1–14. New York: Routledge, 1989.
LaCapra, Dominick. *History and Criticism.* Ithaca, NY: Cornell University Press, 1985.
Palmer, William J. *The Films of the Eighties: A Social History.* Carbondale: Southern Illinois University Press, 1992.
Quart, Leonard, and Albert Auster. *American Film and Society Since 1945.* New York: Praeger, 1991.
Turner, Graeme. *Film as Social Practice.* London, New York: Routledge, 1988.
White, Hayden. *Metahistory.* Baltimore: Johns Hopkins University Press, 1973.

II.
Wars and Other Major Events

★ ★ ★ ★ ★ ★ ★

[COTTEN SEILER]

The American Revolution

Gordon Wood opens *The Radicalism of the American Revolution* by noting, "We Americans like to think of our revolution as not being radical; indeed, most of the time we consider it downright conservative." The names of prominent early American personae and the events in which they participated fail to conjure up images we typically associate with the term *revolution*: "We cannot quite conceive of revolutionaries in powdered hair and knee breeches. The American revolutionaries seem to belong in drawing rooms or legislative halls, not in cellars or in the streets. They made speeches, not bombs, they wrote learned pamphlets, not manifestos. . . . The American Revolution does not seem to have the same kinds of causes—the social wrongs, the class conflict, the grossly inequitable distributions of wealth—that presumably lie behind other revolutions. There were no peasant uprisings, no jacqueries, no burning of chateaux, no storming of prisons" (3).

Given this conception of the American Revolution, the scarcity of films treating it should come as little surprise. The revolution featured few dramatic events of the type Wood mentions—riots, conflagrations, executions—little of the chaotic, compelling imagery, in other words, in which the French and Russian revolutions abounded. It may be objected here that the American Revolution was, nonetheless, a war, and that military events have been vividly represented onscreen. There are differences, however, between narratives of war and those of revolution, and the military aspects of the American Revolution, despite their importance, did not define the event in any essential way. Instead, what distinguishes the era was the production and recognition of a new political ideology. According to Bernard Bailyn, the revolutionaries' aims and grievances stemmed from the perceived suspension of rights guaranteed them by the British constitution. They sought "not the overthrow or even the alteration of the existing social order but the preservation of political liberty threatened by the apparent corruption of the constitution, and the establishment in principle of the existing conditions of liberty. . . . What was essentially involved in the American Revolution was not the disruption of society, with all the fear, despair, and hatred that that entails" (19).

Bailyn asserts the primary causes of the revolution to be ideals, not social discontent or tyranny. To make the point that the American Revolution was fundamentally a revolution of ideology and of *language*—communicating new understandings of social class, political power, and identity—in no way diminishes its significance. The preeminence of language, however, seems to have presented obstacles to constructing strong films.

Wood describes the popular notion of the American Revolution as a musty museum exhibit, a place one visits to gaze at the documents under glass and pay homage to the "Founding Fathers" whose faces grace our money. This presentation of history is more conducive to genuflection than fascination. One reason for this conception may be that the revolution has too often been interpreted in mythic and moralistic terms, as a narrative of men and women of unassailable character and vision inhabiting a utopia of American righteousness in conflict with British tyranny. This view tends to turn the era into a ready-made symbol of all that was right with America, a symbol generally used by those who assert that a great deal is currently wrong.

Of course, this narrow interpretation frustrates historians of the American Revolution, such as Wood and Gary Nash, who view the period as one of the most intellectually, socially, economically, and politically protean, fractious, and fertile in American history. Others, such as Howard Zinn, can be grouped under the headings of "People's History" or "Social History." These scholars regard the writing of history as a potentially radical political act, and they tend to focus on the suppressed stories of minorities, women, and the poor, challenging dominant interpretations to create "a history disrespectful of governments and respectful of people's movements of resistance" (Zinn, 570). Whatever their focus, these historians have generally engaged with, and often been radicalized by, theoretical approaches generated outside the discipline of history since the 1960s, in departments of philosophy, women's studies, sociology, ethnic studies, literature, and film. These new approaches have challenged historians to think thematically about the experiences of marginalized groups in American history, and practically about the textual nature of the past, the power embedded in historical knowledge, and the construction of historical truth. The new historiography, in problematizing and radicalizing the American Revolution, has attempted to rescue the era from both sacralization and irrelevance.

Struggles between historians over the meaning and political import of the revolution eventually find their way onto the screen; indeed, film serves as a more transparent medium in terms of illustrating the political uses of the past. Films, unlike most written history, tend to wear their ideology openly, often dispensing with objectivity in exchange for a more dramatic and accessible narrative. In defense of this tendency to interpret, it is important to note, as Robert Rosenstone has, that the best historical films are not necessarily those that "get it right," but those that "offer a new relationship to the world of the past" (12). The most compelling historical films do more than render in visual terms the familiar names and events of history; they also hazard a vision of an alternate past and, with it, an alternate future.

One reason for the scarcity of films on the American Revolution lies in the conception of it that Wood ridiculed—as staid, cerebral, and, unlike the Civil War, very much *over.* The recent popularity of the Civil War and the accompanying plethora of films with Civil War themes have much to do with racial politics in the United States over the past decade. In many ways, the issues surrounding the Civil War remain unresolved, the reconciliation of regions and races unfinished. The Revolution, however, is perceived as a finished product: independence declared, British expelled, freedom enshrined—end of story. At their worst, both academic and cinematic historians merely restate these myths; at their best, they challenge such an erroneous and complacent relationship to the past.

Monuments to Americanism

The list of fictional and documentary films and television programs about the American Revolution is relatively short and, with a few exceptions, not terribly distinguished. Two major Revolutionary War films, *America* and *Janice Meredith,* were released in the spring and fall, respectively, of 1924. These films were extravagant monuments to Americanism, and demonstrated the newly arrived legitimacy of film as a middle-class entertainment. What is most remarkable about *Janice Meredith* and *America* is their spectacle—the sumptuous set and costume designs, the grand ballroom and battle scenes—and not their fealty to historical accuracy. The mission of D. W. Griffith's

America (alternate title, *Love and Sacrifice*) was "to stir the patriotic hearts of the nation as . . . no other picture has ever done" (Henderson, 249). *Janice Meredith*, produced by William Randolph Hearst, set about a similar task, though his film (also known as *The Beautiful Rebel*), starring his paramour Marion Davies in the title role, was not above taking a few titillating liberties with American history, including a portrayal of George Washington as a seeker of Miss Meredith's affections.

John Ford's *Drums Along the Mohawk* (1939) enjoyed a rare success in drawing audiences for a story set during the Revolutionary War. Adapted from Walter Edmonds's popular 1936 novel, the film tells the story of a young couple (played by Claudette Colbert and Henry Fonda) on the upstate New York frontier. Though set in the Mohawk Valley in the early years of the war, the film employs genre conventions of the western. As John O'Connor has argued, this film enabled a vital reconnection to the American past and patriotic symbolism during the hard times of the Great Depression (100).

Johnny Tremain, John Paul Jones, and *The Devil's Disciple* were produced in the late 1950s, and they remain among the most engaging films on the subject. *Johnny Tremain* (1957), a Disney film directed by Robert Stevenson, tells a fictional story of a young Massachusetts silversmith's apprentice who becomes involved in the struggle for independence. *John Paul Jones* (1959), directed by John Farrow (and featuring his young daughter, Mia), stars an appropriately gruff Robert Stack as the father of the U.S. Navy. *The Devil's Disciple* (1959), the most interesting of the three, will be examined in greater detail later in this essay. Also during this time, the French produced *Lafayette* (1961), which recounts the story of Washington's young aide-de-camp, the marquis de Lafayette, and features Orson Welles as Benjamin Franklin.

1776 (1972) was adapted from the eponymous Broadway musical. Produced at a time when patriotic feeling ebbed for some Americans because of the Vietnam War, *1776* is ironically one of the more nuanced and insightful films depicting the Revolutionary era. Hugh Hudson's *Revolution* (1985) emerged during a very different decade politically, at a time when Ronald Reagan's presidency emphasized American myths once again. Yet this film, judged by most to be a flop of epic proportions, is nonetheless praiseworthy for its reluctance to recycle clichés. Instead, *Revolution* assumes the point of view of its least-heralded participants, the urban poor.

Television has perennially visited the subject of the American Revolution. Notable among these small-screen treatments are *The Adams Chronicles* (1976), *George Washington* and *George Washington II: Forging a New Nation* (1984–85), *Liberty! The American Revolution* (1997), and *History Alive: The American Revolution* (1998). The critically acclaimed PBS series *The Adams Chronicles* portrays the famous family from Quincy, Massachusetts. By stipulation of the executors of the Adams estate, the dialogue was restricted to the actual words written by the Adams themselves, giving the production a stiff, literary feel. The ABC-produced *George Washington* miniseries, in contrast, turns the revolution into substandard TV melodrama. The History Channel's *History Alive: The American Revolution* combines Ken Burns–style talking-head narration and celebrity voiceover with re-creations of significant events. Another PBS series, *Liberty! The American Revolution,* is perhaps most successful in its merging of dramatic readings by actors, interviews with historians, re-creations of historical events, and still cinematography of period paintings and artifacts. It is important to emphasize that the majority of these works, unlike most cinema productions, sought out the counsel of academic historians. For example, among those enlisted by PBS for the *Liberty!* project were Bailyn, Wood, Pauline Maier, Margaret Washington, Dave Edmunds, and Michael Zuckert, scholars whose views diverge widely but whose expertise enhanced the production enormously.

Several films produced for school or institutional viewing manage to both edify and amuse. The Eastern National Park and Monument association, for example, managed to secure cinematic luminary John Huston to direct *Independence* (1972), a short film shown at Independence National Historical Park in Philadelphia. Various revolutionary leaders return to twentieth-century Philadelphia to remember the tumultuous events of the late eighteenth century. The film is well acted and informative, yet it glosses over the more contentious issues of the era, depicting an illusory consensus among the Continental Congress and colonists alike. Few educational films deviate from the standard historical model of the American Revolution as an ideological and intellectual feat performed by a handful of colonial elites, despite new historical evidence conflicting with this view.

A Racialized Revolution: *America*

The 1920s saw a historiographic trend in "debunking" the mythological interpretation of early American history, a trend that suffered a backlash in the history and historical films of the 1930s (see O'Connor). Historians such as Carl Becker (1915) and Charles Beard (1925) stressed class conflict and domestic political inequality as defining characteristics of a previously hallowed era and pointed out the economic self-interest that guided the Founding Fathers—those "pillars of the temple of liberty" whom Abraham Lincoln had praised in the previous century. This historiography paralleled the critique of economic inequality, class strife, and untrammeled corporate power associated with the Progressive Era.

D. W. Griffith's epic *America,* however, displays little influence of the Progressive historians. The project began with a request from Will H. Hays, of the Motion Picture Producers and Distributors of America, that Griffith make a patriotic film about the American Revolution. The movie industry had recently been sullied by scandal, and this type of film could help restore Hollywood's reputation. Loosely based on Griffith's unproduced play *War* and Robert Chambers's novel *The Reckoning,* the film was developed in consultation of nationalistic organizations such as the Daughters of the American Revolution; the United States War Department contributed troops and materiel for the battle scenes. In addition to Chambers, who is credited for the story, the director enlisted John L. E. Pell, a specialist on Ethan Allen, for "historical arrangement." Griffith was known to seek out such historical verification, but only from those sources and materials "that bore out his own preconceived ideas" (Henderson, 150). In fact, *America* largely recycled the moralism and didacticism in Griffith's controversial *Birth of a Nation* (1914).

The narrative proceeds from the first stirrings of resistance in the early 1770s in Boston and Virginia to the defeat of Cornwallis at Yorktown in 1781. In typical Griffith style, these historic events serve as the backdrop for a romance between a common farmer, Nathan Holden (Neil Hamilton), and a Tory debutante, Nancy Montague (Carol Dempster). Besides the obvious obstacles of class, the romance is further hamstrung by the onset of the War of Independence: Nancy's father, Justice Montague (Erville Alderson), remains faithful to the Crown, despite the family's friendship with fellow Virginian George Washington. Escaping north to Canada, the family finds itself at ground zero—Lexington, Massachusetts, where the shooting war begins. Family loyalties are divided further when Nancy's brother Charles (Charles Mack) joins the rebel cause at Lexington and is killed in Boston at the Battle of Bunker Hill. When Justice Montague is wounded in a mob incident outside a Lexington Inn, the blame falls on Nathan, whom Nancy scorns—until he is vindicated.

Holden and the Montagues embody American virtues: Nathan's strength, bravery, love of liberty, and humility mark him as a hero, and Nancy epitomizes the ideal of pure American womanhood; yet Griffith also admires Justice Montague, with his steadfast devotion to monarchy, his respect for the rule of law and political order. For all its patriotic fervor, *America* is curiously unconcerned with the British, deciding instead to rewrite the revolution as a battle between virtuous and decadent Americans. Thematically, in other words, *America* revisits the conflicts of *The Birth of a Nation.* The villains are all either "savage" Native Americans or traitorous American loyalists who fought alongside British forces. Yet, as we see in the sympathetic portrayal of Justice Montague, not all Tories are depicted as villains.

Griffith's moral world view, abundantly demonstrated in *The Birth of a Nation,* divided cleanly down racial lines: the darker races threatened the moral rectitude of the lighter; they represented vice, mongrelization, chaos. Yet more damnable were those whites who allied themselves with other races in a gambit for power. Treason against one's nation was, in Griffith's view, far less heinous than treason against one's race. Nowhere is this type of villainy more clearly depicted than in the character Captain Walter Butler (Lionel Barrymore), a "Tory ranger" responsible for the infamous Cherry Valley Massacre of 1778. The first scenes featuring Butler show him first making a war pact with the Iroquois, then carousing in his hunting lodge with his men, Indians, and a group of slatternly, fawning women. Butler "dreams of an opportunity through which he may become leader, betray his King, and over the ruins of his country establish a new empire with himself as Viceroy." A young Mohawk woman, barely clad, dances erotically before him as he whips the crowd into a fury. The scene tells all: Butler, who dreams of "autocratic" power, would turn America into his own decadent, violent, and miscegenated kingdom.

Consonant with Griffith's anglophilia, the film ends with Montague and Washington, "again friends, to help solidify the power of the English speaking peoples in the work of the world." While the film does not identify this "work," it likely alludes to the alliance of the United States and Britain in the then-recent world war of 1914–18. Finally, Holden enters the ranks of the elite when he marries Nancy, reinforcing the belief in American class mobility. *America* ultimately does little to illuminate the American Revolution, yet it speaks volumes about the racial and political sensibilities of the most prominent American filmmaker of the 1920s and his audience.

A Fable of Individualism: *The Devil's Disciple*

The 1950s saw a resurgence in the nationalistic historiography of the 1930s, a movement fueled by the Pax Americana and rising prosperity. This new affluence, along with a dominant sociological "consensus" model of American society fueled, it could be argued, a desire to see a similar consensus in America's past. Pulitzer Prize–winning historian Henry Steele Commager, for example, attempted to overturn Charles Beard's economic interpretation of the Constitution, arguing that its intended purpose was one of equitably distributing power, whatever the pecuniary interests of its framers. Yet consensus, as social critics of the 1950s warned, can verge on conformity, an especially loaded term during the Cold War. The most compelling popular culture products and developments of the 1950s (the James Dean of *Rebel without a Cause,* the rock 'n' roll of Chuck Berry) can be partially understood as reactions to the conformity and standardization of a highly developed, consumer society.

Guy Hamilton's *The Devil's Disciple* (1959) features the unlikely trio of Kirk Douglas, Burt Lancaster, and Laurence Olivier. A British production based on George Bernard Shaw's play, the film examines moral obligation, conformity, individualism, and masculine identity in small-town Massachusetts during the war. Lancaster plays the Presbyterian minister Anthony Anderson, though not very convincingly. The story begins with the hanging of one of the parson's flock, a patriarch of the town who was falsely accused of treason. The hanged man's itinerant, ne'er-do-well son, Richard Dudgeon (Douglas), steals the body from the gallows. Dudgeon is everything the parson is not: reckless, bold, physically and mentally agile. Dudgeon boasts to Anderson of having sworn his soul to "his captain and friend," the Devil, "and that oath and promise made a man of me!" Dudgeon's raffish appeal is not lost on Anderson's young wife, Judith (Janette Scott), a character who serves only to recommend his more preferable dynamic virility over Reverend Anderson's pacifism and piety.

FIGURE 5. *The Devil's Disciple* (1959). Richard Dudgeon (Kirk Douglas), about to be executed on the orders of General John Burgoyne, the British commander, who seeks to quell rebellious rumblings in a small New York town in 1777. Based on George Bernard Shaw's satirical play of the same name, *The Devil's Disciple* depicts a series of mishaps set off by the British occupation. Courtesy Brynapod and Hecht, Hill, & Lancaster Production.

If Anderson and Dudgeon represent two types of masculinity, a third is presented in the character of General "Gentleman Johnny" John Burgoyne (Olivier). Foppish and sarcastic, Burgoyne was nonetheless one of Britain's most effective commanders until his defeat at Saratoga in 1777. Olivier portrays Burgoyne, ostensibly the villain, as a voice of reason and civility in a pointless war. The general's climactic confrontation with Dudgeon, mistakenly arrested as Anderson, is a volley of witticisms ranking among Shaw's best. Meanwhile, after stumbling through a firefight, Parson Anderson suddenly takes to combat with unwonted skill and vigor for a (former) pacifist. When he rides into Burgoyne's headquarters demanding Dudgeon's release, Burgoyne is puzzled (as is the viewer) at the sight of the buckskin-clad clergyman, who declares, "In the hours of trial, sir, a man finds his true profession."

The film ends with Lancaster exuding the same hammy nobility, but Olivier and Douglas are the true heroes here, as they make plans to dine together later. Burgoyne and Dudgeon are individualists, beholden to none, impatient with the stupidity and mediocrity of wars, nations, causes, and humanity at large. They care little for society's approval but are so masterful in deed and bearing that they receive it anyway. The combination of Burgoyne's military efficacy and gentlemanly mien, Dudgeon's chaotic spontaneity, and Anderson's rectitude and faith provided a template for contemporary masculinity in the 1950s.

The Devil's Disciple plays fast and loose with the facts of Burgoyne's campaign, which menaced Continental forces up until the British surrender at Saratoga. Also, the film ends with Burgoyne remarking that Britain will certainly give up its American colonies, a rather nonsensical pronouncement for a British general in 1777. Shaw's irreverent play and Hamilton's film are more interested in human folly than historical truth. "But what will history say?" a lieutenant asks Burgoyne at the film's conclusion. He responds, "History, as usual, will tell lies."

The Reagan Era Looks Back: *Revolution*

The resurgence of the American economy in the 1980s and the policies of the Ronald Reagan and George Bush administrations spurred a revival of conservative ideology and a new willingness to "feel good about America again." It was a decade in which "The Age of Reagan and the Age of Hollywood merged not only in policies and rhetoric but also in popular images" (Sklar, 345). However, the 1980s were also a decade of resistance, a time during which gender and racial minorities found new strategies to combat what many regarded as a regression in civil rights and social justice. Not surprisingly, historiography reflected the era's ideological battles. The prevailing conservatism resuscitated the myths of the American Revolution for the justification of some controversial policies (for example, President Reagan's description of the Nicaraguan Contras as "the moral equivalent of our founding fathers"). Within academia, however, the scope of historical analysis of the American Revolution expanded, with scholars increasingly interested in "history from the bottom up"—the stories of the poor, women, and minorities.

Hugh Hudson's *Revolution* appears, in many ways, to be a product of the new social and people's history of recent decades. Hudson and screenwriter Robert Dillon seem to have drawn on new scholarship emphasizing the radical strains in the colonial era, the complexity of race, gender, and class relations in the eighteenth century, and the historical agency of marginalized groups. Mary Beth Norton, Gary Nash, Gordon Wood, Eric Foner, Ira Berlin, and Joan Hoff Wilson are among the group of historians who stress the radical democratic ferment of the late eighteenth century. Though not necessarily directly informed by such works, the film shares their sensibilities.

Revolution attempts to represent the world of the eighteenth century in a new way, both thematically and visually, and was beautifully designed and photographed. Bernard Lutic's cinematography works with available light, mimicking the shadowy, torch-lit interiors of the era. The battle scenes are appropriately grim and horrifying, and the landscapes—especially what serve here as the Hudson Valley and Yorktown—are breathtaking. The socially "low" perspective of the film and its stark depiction of the eighteenth century may have accounted for its lack of box-office success. A less theoretical reason lies in its being a bad movie, with woeful miscasting, poor dialogue, inexplicable relationships, and underdeveloped characters.

The year is 1776, and New York is "goin' crazy," in the words of fisherman Tom Dobb (Al Pacino), with General Washington's evacuation notice and the expected arrival of British troops. A mob topples a statue of George III and throws Tories into the harbor. Shot from a vantage amid the crowd, this opening scene comes as close as any film has in asserting that the revolution *was* a radical movement of the common people. As Gary Nash has noted, the urban crowds of the era, much feared by elites on both sides of the conflict, "included a broad range of city dwellers, from slaves and servants through laborers and seamen to artisans and shopkeepers" (*Race,* 216). Similar scenes in *Revolution* bear out Nash's contention that the "developing consciousness and political sophistication of ordinary city dwellers came rapidly to fruition in the early 1760s and thereafter played a major role in the advent of the Revolution" (216).

After the crowd confiscates Tom's boat for the cause, his young son, Ned (Sid Owen, later Dexter Fletcher), is tricked into enlisting in the Continental Army. Tom follows, and the two depart with the army for Brooklyn. Daisy McConnahay (Nastassja Kinski) is an idealistic young patrician caught up in the radical chic of independence, much to the chagrin of her family. For reasons untold, she is drawn to the monosyllabic Dobb, and brings him food after the Continentals are routed at Brooklyn Heights.

Back in New York, the British humiliate Dobb by forcing him to play the fox in a mock hunt. Ned is arrested as a guerrilla and tortured by a British noncommissioned officer (Donald Sutherland). Sutherland takes to his role with real aplomb, and his Sergeant Major

Peasy, although a tough, battle-scarred veteran, reveals a dimension of class consciousness and compassion. Tom rescues Ned from the British camp, and, pursued by Iroquois trackers, escapes with him into the Hudson Valley. Dobb ambushes and kills the Iroquois, earning the trust of nearby Oneida, who take the escapees in and care for Ned. Some months later, Daisy is reunited briefly with Tom and Ned at Valley Forge when she arrives bearing supplies for the troops; she and Tom enjoy a brief (and unconvincing) romantic moment—a critical fault of the film is its inability to generate any motivation for the attraction between Tom and Daisy.

The choice of an Italian American actor for the part of the Scottish-born Tom Dobb is an interesting one, fitting the multicultural sensibility of *Revolution,* but Pacino never gets the feel of the eighteenth century—its social politics of deference, its manners and sensibilities. Ned's marriage to a young Jewish woman he meets at Valley Forge is a similarly admirable attempt to show the ethnic diversity of the Continentals. The handling of ethnic integration, however, subscribes to an earlier, "melting pot" model of American heterogeneity. Despite more recent sociological models of the continuing cultural integrity of minority groups in American history, *Revolution* defines American identity as a racial and ethnic cipher. While minorities and women are represented, none—except, perhaps, Daisy—is given any abiding perspective as either an agent or an observer of historical change. Ultimately, the filmmakers failed to create a compelling film from the ingredients of social and people's history, however commendable the intentions of screenwriter Dillon and director Hudson.

The Revolutionary Museum

As any museum visitor knows, touching the artifacts on display is against the rules. Given the power of the American Revolution to symbolize American ideals, perhaps it has been similarly marked as off-limits for revision and reconstruction in film. Yet historians, and especially historical filmmakers, must "touch" the past in order to bring it to life, and sometimes this means putting one's fingerprints on it. *America, The Devil's Disciple,* and *Revolution* are not exactly films about the American Revolution; rather, they involve attempts by their respective writers and directors to interpret the era in the light of contemporary social and political conditions. Griffith used the American Revolution to justify an ethnocentric worldview; Shaw and Hamilton used it to illustrate human folly and encourage individualism; Hudson and Dillon tethered its struggles and diversity to those of the present.

References

Filmography

The Adams Chronicles (1976, TV)
America (1924, F)
The Devil's Disciple (1959, F)
Drums Along the Mohawk (1939, F)
George Washington (1984, TV)
George Washington II: Forging a New Nation (1985, TV)
History Alive: The American Revolution (1998, TV)
The Howards of Virginia (1940, F)
Independence (1972, D)
Janice Meredith (1924, F)
Johnny Tremain (1957, F)
John Paul Jones (1959, F)
Lafayette (1961, F)
Liberty! The American Revolution (1997, TV)
The Patriot (2000, F)
Revolution (1985, F)
1776 (1972, F)

Bibliography

Bailyn, Bernard. *The Ideological Origins of the American Revolution.* Rev. ed. Cambridge, MA: Harvard University Press, 1992.

Beard, Charles. *An Economic Interpretation of the Constitution.* New York: Macmillan, 1925.

Becker, Carl L. *Beginnings of the American People.* Boston: Houghton Mifflin, 1915.

Berlin, Ira. "The Revolution in Black Life." In Alfred F. Young, ed., *The American Revolution: Explorations in the History of American Radicalism,* 349–382. DeKalb: Northern Illinois University Press, 1976.

Commager, Henry Steele. "The Constitution: Was It an Economic Document?" *American Heritage* 10 (December 1958): 58–61, 100–103.

Henderson, Robert M. *D. W. Griffith: His Life and Work.* New York: Oxford University Press, 1972.

Nash, Gary B. *Race, Class, and Politics: Essays on Colonial and Revolutionary Society.* Urbana: University of Illinois Press, 1986.

——. "Social Change and the Growth of Prerevolutionary Urban Radicalism." In Alfred F. Young, ed., *The American Revolution: Explorations in the History of American Radicalism,* 3–36. DeKalb: Northern Illinois University Press, 1976.

Norton, Mary Beth. *Founding Fathers & Mothers: Gendered Power and the Forming of American Society.* New York: Knopf, 1996.

O'Connor, John E. "A Reaffirmation of American Ideals: *Drums Along the Mohawk.*" In John E. O'Connor, ed., *American History/American Film: Interpreting the Hollywood Image,* 92–112. New York: Frederick Ungar, 1979.

Rosenstone, Robert A. *Visions of the Past: The Challenge of Film to Our Idea of History.* Cambridge, MA: Harvard University Press, 1995.

Sklar, Robert. *Movie-Made America: A Cultural History of American Movies.* Rev. ed. New York: Vintage, 1994.

Wilson, Joan Hoff. "The Illusion of Change: Women and the American Revolution." In Alfred F. Young, ed., *The American Revolution: Explorations in the History of American Radicalism,* 383–446. DeKalb: Northern Illinois University Press, 1976.

Wood, Gordon S. *The Radicalism of the American Revolution.* New York: Vintage, 1993.

Zinn, Howard. *A People's History of the United States.* New York: Harper & Row, 1980.

[ALICIA R. BROWNE AND LAWRENCE A. KREISER JR.]

The Civil War and Reconstruction

The people and events of the Civil War and Reconstruction eras long have captured the American imagination, but nowhere more so than in the movies. As Bruce Chadwick points out in *The Reel Civil War,* more than seven hundred Hollywood productions have portrayed Americans' attempts to define the future of the nation between 1861 and 1877, more than any other period in the nation's history. Civil War and Reconstruction films have had mixed success in making money at the box office. But whatever their financial fate, movies that depict the Civil War and the Reconstruction era have played major roles in shaping and reflecting popular and scholarly attitudes toward these watershed events in American history.

The Silent Era and Nationalist Historians

Americans sought to heal the lingering wounds of the Civil War during the early twentieth century. Appomattox still lay fresh within the living memory of many in the country, but Union and Confederate veterans had begun to meet in joint reunions that stressed their shared experiences and common bravery. During the same years, the Spanish-American War (1898) had brought the nation together in a common cause and demonstrated the tremendous power of a united country. In academia, historians such as James Ford Rhodes and John Burgess pioneered a nationalist school that sought to establish a usable past on which both North and South could agree. By the turn of the century, scholars from both regions of the country had reached a consensus that, although secession was constitutionally unjustifiable, the South had been more than punished by the excesses of the Reconstruction.

The theme of reconciliation dominated the flood of silent films about the war, and stories that both Northerners and Southerners identified with became common. Courage in the face of battle was one sectionally unifying theme. In Thomas Ince's *The Coward* (1915), a Southern deserter redeems himself when he smuggles valuable Union plans to the Confederates. In D. W. Griffith's *The Battle* (1911), a frightened young soldier proves his bravery to his sweetheart by bringing needed supplies to his regiment through enemy lines. Families and sweethearts separated by the war also were popular unifying themes. Rarely had immediate family members fought on opposite sides, but the image of brother fighting brother served as a symbolic representation of the divided Union. In *The Sting of Victory* (1916), a Southerner is rejected by his family and sweetheart after he fights for the Union, while *In the Days of War* (1913) follows brothers-in-law who fight on opposite sides but make their peace after they wound one another in battle. Lovers are divided in Herbert Blache's *Barbara Frietchie* (1915), the most gripping version of the oft-retold romance, loosely based on the famous poem by John Greenleaf Whittier.

D. W. Griffith's *The Birth of a Nation* (1915) is the most important, as well as controversial, silent film on the Civil War era. The Kentucky-born son of a Confederate veteran, Griffith was raised on stories of the South's wartime bravery and home front sacrifices. Griffith featured these images in many of his early Civil War films, but Reconstruction dominates *The Birth of a Nation.* Based on Thomas Dixon's virulently racist novel and play *The Clansman* (1905), the movie tells the story of the Camerons of South Carolina and the Stonemans, their Northern friends. The Stonemans move to the South after the war, led by their patriarch, Austin (who was based on Thaddeus Stevens, the Radical Republican congressman). They find the Camerons' entire way of life destroyed by arrogant carpetbaggers and ignorant freedmen, all of whom have gained political power during Reconstruction. Among their tormentors is Austin Stoneman's protégé, Silas Lynch, a mulatto who becomes lieutenant governor. Stoneman eventually gets his comeuppance when Lynch proposes to his daughter, Elsie, while blacks rampage through the streets, drunk on their newfound power. The Camerons' young daughter also falls victim to a black man's sexual aggression, when, after a protracted pursuit, she leaps from a cliff to avoid being raped. Order is reestablished only by the Ku Klux Klan, whose members save Elsie Stoneman from Lynch's clutches, avenge Flora Cameron's death, and restore white control. At the end of the movie, North and South are reunited symbolically by marriages between the Cameron and Stoneman children.

Griffith used several innovative production techniques to heighten the drama of his story. He made viewers part of chase and battle scenes by filming with cameras placed on moving trucks, while irising reduced rectangular images to circles of various sizes to highlight characters and action. Rapid cross-cutting between two locales built excitement by allowing audiences to view events happening simultaneously, a particularly effective technique in the sequences where Lynch forces himself on Elsie and the Klan gathers for her rescue. Successive generations of filmmakers have followed the path forged by Griffith, and today many of his production techniques have become commonplace.

The Birth of a Nation drew mainly favorable reviews and large crowds, both because of Griffith's cinematic innovations and because he effectively dramatized the prevailing views about the Civil War era. The early intertitle that reads, "The bringing of the African to America planted the first seed of disunion," was in accord with nationalist historians who argued that the war was an unavoidable conflict and that slavery was one of its primary causes. But the film is most notable because of Griffith's now-discredited version of Reconstruction. His portrayal reveals the influence of the Dunning school, the dominant scholarly interpretation of the period until World War II. Historian William Dunning and his students described Reconstruction as a "tragic era" characterized by black excesses and white suffering. Carpetbaggers were villains, scalawags were traitors, and freedmen were woefully unprepared to exercise the political rights thrust upon them. Most of Griffith's black characters (played primarily by white actors in blackface) are stereotyped as sexual aggressors or as fools and dupes of the carpetbaggers. In one provocative scene, Griffith showed the South Carolina legislature dominated by blacks (which is accurate) who legalize interracial marriage while they prop bare feet on their desks, drink whiskey, and eat chicken. The images roused only limited audience protest because, by the 1910s, oppressive "Jim Crow" laws severely limited the rights of blacks in the South and discrimination prevailed throughout much of the nation. White viewers found common ground in the depiction of blacks as the cause of the war and the villains of the peace.

Scholarly reassessments of Reconstruction and changes in popular thinking about race have made *The Birth of a Nation* outdated and controversial. A small number of scholars first challenged the Dunning school as early as the 1930s and 1940s, but the most influential shifts in thinking occurred in conjunction with the civil rights movement of the 1960s. Revisionist scholars argued that black politicians pursued ambitious reform agendas, including civil rights and the establishment of public schools. Postrevisionist historians later minimized the lasting reforms of the era by arguing that the Southern power structure remained essentially unchanged by the war. Most recently, a new generation of scholars, led by Eric Foner, has tried to strike a balance that acknowledges both the genuine accomplishments of the era, particularly by African Americans, and the failure to affect sweeping changes. Although shifts in thinking about race make *The Birth of a Nation* unfashionable to modern audiences, the movie is a significant part of film history. In 1998, the American Film Institute placed Griffith's masterpiece forty-fourth on its list of the one hundred best films in American history.

Moonlight and Magnolias

In contrast to the wealth of silent films about the Civil War, the 1920s and 1930s proved a barren period for the blue and gray. During the interwar period, the nationalist school broke down, and historians increasingly argued about the origins of the conflict. Some historians of the time, among them Charles and Mary Beard, explained the war as an economic struggle between the Southern planter aristocracy and capitalists of the North and West. Others historians, dismayed by what seemed to be the senseless tragedy of World War I, looked back and saw America's sectional warfare as a "repressible conflict" that resulted from inept political leadership and fanaticism on both sides. For the public, however, the emergence of the nation from the carnage of the fighting in Europe brought primarily a desire for lighthearted and fast-paced entertainment. Hollywood avoided the events of the mid- and late nineteenth century, especially the serious social and political themes found in *The Birth of a Nation.* The war functioned occasionally as a backdrop in films, exemplified by two outstanding comedies. In 1926, Paramount released *Hands Up!,* a well-made satire of Civil War spy dramas. The next year, United Artists released Buster Keaton's classic *The General,* loosely based on an 1862 raid by Union spy James Andrews. Keaton portrays a bumbling Southern engineer who wins glory and his sweetheart's hand when he foils the raiders' plans. With these notable exceptions, the Civil War and Reconstruction made little headway on the silver screen until 1939, when they returned in the blockbuster *Gone with the Wind.*

Producer David O. Selznick made a leap of faith when he paid a record $50,000 for the rights to Margaret Mitchell's novel in 1936. Movies about the Civil War had gained a reputation as box-office poison, and when Louis B. Mayer reportedly expressed interest in acquiring the book, MGM's Irving Thalberg convinced him otherwise. "Don't do it, Louis," Thalberg declared in one of the great miscalculations of film history. "No Civil War picture ever made a nickel!" (Hay, 183). Thalberg was correct about most Civil War movies, but the epic based on the triumphs and tragedies of Scarlett O'Hara was not most movies. Scarlett's travails captivated audiences, and whether she wins back Rhett Butler has become one of the enduring questions in American popular culture. (Alexandra Ripley made an ill-conceived attempt to answer the question in her novel *Scarlett,* which was published in 1991 and aired on television three years later and which demonstrated that the characters' fate is best left to the individual imagination.)

Selznick faced a daunting task in bringing the lengthy novel to the screen, and stories about the process have passed into legend. Vivien Leigh was chosen to play Scarlett only after a well-publicized national search; the original director was replaced during filming; and at least ten writers, including F. Scott Fitzgerald, tried their hand at the script. The film lost some of the subtlety and nuance of the book in the process. According to Mitchell's biographer, the novelist considered herself a revisionist who saw Southern white society as more complex and multilayered than the one-dimensional planter elite commonly featured in popular entertainment. Selznick, however, perpetuated the "moonlight and magnolias" view that 1930s audiences expected. He transformed Tara, the O'Hara home, from the ordinary house of an Irish immigrant into the white-columned mansion of an established and prosperous planter. The elegance of Tara and the splendor of Twelve Oaks, the Wilkes's plantation, disturbed Mitchell, who in a tour of Clayton County, Georgia, the setting for the two plantations, found only one antebellum home with columns. "When I think of the healthy, hearty country and somewhat crude civilization I depicted," Mitchell wrote, "and then of the elegance that is to be presented, I cannot help yelping with laughter" (Pyron, 370–71).

In addition to romanticizing the image of Tara to fit audience expectations, Selznick altered the story to make the film more palatable to a national audience. Mitchell perceived herself to be a revisionist, but she held many of the racial and regional prejudices of her time. To avoid controversy, Selznick removed the author's direct references to the Ku Klux Klan, as well as certain negative depictions of black characters. Additionally, in the scene where Scarlett shoots a Federal soldier who has entered Tara, the latter character is a deserter and looter, a character unsympathetic to both North and South. Nevertheless, Selznick retained much of the novel's flavor, and the movie remains an accurate Southern view of the war and its aftermath.

Gone with the Wind opened in December 1939 to glowing reviews and strong box office returns. The sweeping love story appealed to audiences, and the theme of triumph over adversity resonated with viewers still reeling from the effects of the Depression. Although it is difficult to compare its profits to those of more recent films, by all estimations the movie has earned hundreds of millions of dollars. The film is set apart from pedestrian Civil War romances like *So Red the Rose,* a 1935 flop, by riveting characters; its attention to detail (California's black soil was colored red, for example, to mimic Georgia's); and Academy Award–winning performances by Vivien Leigh (Scarlett) and Hattie McDaniel (Mammy).

McDaniel made history as the first black performer to win an Academy Award, but her character finds less approval with modern audiences. As in *The Birth of a Nation* and other early films, black characters in *Gone with the Wind* are portrayed mainly as "happy darkies," and their stereotypical performances now cause viewers to blanch. Prissy (Butterfly McQueen), the silly and indolent slave who "don't know nuthin' 'bout birthin' babies," is one of the more egregious examples. Although Selznick removed some of Mitchell's objectionable depictions of blacks, he, like the author, reflected his times. Only in the 1960s and 1970s did historians such as Stanley Elkins, Eugene Genovese, and Herbert Gutman seriously explore the experience of slavery. Despite these limitations, the American Film Institute recognized the film's enduring audience appeal and ranked *Gone with the Wind* fourth among its one hundred best films.

War had erupted in Europe and American involvement was on the horizon when *Gone with the Wind* appeared in theaters. Hollywood turned away from the mid-nineteenth century and created propaganda films to support the conflict at hand. The lack of attention to the Civil War continued after 1945, and few notable films about the era appeared for the remainder of the decade. Of note are *Virginia City* (1940), which stars Errol Flynn as a Union officer who escapes from a Confederate prison; *Tap Roots* (1948), a romance that repeats tired images of the Old South; and *A Southern Yankee* (1948), a comedic farce that employed the down-on-his-luck Buster Keaton as a gag writer.

The Rise of Consensus History

After the Allied victory in World War II and the rise of the United States as a world power,

FIGURE 6. *Gone with the Wind* (1939). At the close of the Civil War, Scarlett O'Hara (Vivien Leigh, right) and her housekeeper, Mammy (Hattie McDaniel, left), enter the Atlanta jail in the hope of convincing Rhett Butler (Clark Gable) to loan them money to pay the mortgage on the O'Hara plantation, Tara. Scarlett wears a dress made of old velvet drapes to disguise her poverty. Courtesy Selznick International Pictures.

a new school of historical thought emerged that discouraged the lively debate over the causes of the Civil War that had dominated the interwar years. Consensus historians viewed America's past as a steady march of progress, emphasizing factors that had united, rather than divided, the country. According to historian David Donald, consensus scholars eschewed analysis of the Civil War because "so appalling an aberration is inexplicable, easiest to pass over in silence" (354). Instead, many historians began new topics of exploration. Of particular note was Bell Wiley's pioneering work on the experiences of the common soldier. John Huston brought the enlisted man's story to the screen in 1951 in his faithful adaptation of Stephen Crane's novel *The Red Badge of Courage* (1895). Audie Murphy portrays Henry Fleming, a Union soldier who flees from his first battle but performs heroically the following day. Huston accurately captured Civil War soldiers' everyday experiences, including their boredom in camp and their desire to go into combat. "All we ever do is drill," Fleming lamented before his first battle. "I'm getting mighty sick of it. Thunder! I joined up to fight. Smell gunsmoke for once. What are these here guns for anyway, to shoot or to drill with? Might as well be broomsticks." Although studio editing dramatically changed Huston's original version and the movie failed at the box office, *Red Badge of Courage* remains a superb portrayal of the common soldier at war.

William Wyler's *Friendly Persuasion* (1956) also explores the common person's reaction to the war. Gary Cooper and Dorothy McGuire star as Indiana Quakers who struggle to remain true to their faith as John Hunt Morgan's Confederate cavalry raiders surge closer to their community in 1863. Whether their son (Anthony Perkins) will fight in the Home Guard is one in a series of moral dilemmas that confronts the family. The plot will disappoint viewers looking for a significant exploration of pacifism during wartime, although the film itself is charming and well acted.

In addition to portraying the experiences of the common soldier, Hollywood used the Civil War to exploit the popularity of westerns during the 1950s and 1960s. In many of these films the war provides the excuse for soldiers to be out west, where they fight Indians, Mexicans, and outlaws. A standard plot features Union and Confederate soldiers joining forces to face a common enemy, as portrayed in *Major Dundee* (1965), starring Charlton Heston, and *The Undefeated* (1969), with Rock Hudson and John Wayne. The rough-and-tumble Wayne also stars in John Ford's *The Horse Soldiers* (1959), which invokes many of the elements of the typical western. Loosely based on an 1863 Union cavalry raid through Mississippi and Louisiana commanded by Benjamin Grierson, the film finds Wayne leading his troopers against a more numerous foe.

Jimmy Stewart starred in many westerns throughout the 1960s, but *Shenandoah* (1965) found him in the more thoughtful role of a Virginia father who attempts to keep his family neutral amid the turmoil of the war. *Shenandoah* lays the blame for the war firmly on slavery, and the charge of "rich man's war, poor man's fight," recurs throughout the film, as it did during the conflict. The movie accurately captures the internal dissent that some historians blame for the Confederacy's defeat, in stark contrast to many earlier films that portrayed the South united behind the war. Like most highland Southerners, Stewart's Charlie Anderson owns no slaves, and he believes that the war is not his concern. When a Confederate soldier attempts to enlist the six Anderson boys, their father rebuffs him with, "This war is not mine, and I take no notice of it." Anderson must take notice when Federal soldiers mistake his youngest son for a Rebel and take him prisoner. Anderson's isolation from the war is screen fiction, for few Virginia farms remained untouched while the opposing armies swirled around them. Additionally, few young males avoided conscription in the post-Gettysburg South, with the exception of large slaveholders.

Shenandoah harkens back to scholars Avery Craven and James G. Randall, who argued that a "blundering generation" dragged the country into an avoidable conflict full of needless death and destruction. This school of thought had encountered challenges by the 1960s, but the interpretation found an articulate spokesman in Charlie Anderson. The plain-speaking farmer sums up the folly of the war in a monologue to his wife's grave: "I don't even know what to say to you anymore, Martha. There is nothin' much I can tell you about this war. It's like all wars, I suppose. The undertakers are winning it. The politicians will talk a lot about the glory of it. And the old men will talk about the need of it. The soldiers, they just want to go home."

An Occurrence at Owl Creek Bridge (1961), an Academy Award–winning short subject film, also depicts a grim reality of war. Based on the story by Ambrose Bierce, a Union veteran, Robert Enrico's film features an anonymous Civil War soldier at the moment of his execution by hanging. Miraculously, the noose appears to break and, as the soldier escapes from his executioners, thoughts of home and family swirl through his mind. Scenes in which dialogue is conspicuously absent contrast the condemned man's past happiness with his present danger, and the unexpected ending effectively conveys Bierce's bitter view of war. The movie later appeared as an episode on the CBS television series *The Twilight Zone.*

Although the war sparked introspective films and action-packed westerns, for many Hollywood producers the conflict remained the ultimate vehicle for the great romantic epic. MGM released Edward Dmytryk's *Raintree County* in 1957, in an overt attempt to recreate the success of *Gone with the Wind.* Set in rural Indiana before and during the war, the movie traces the romance of a would-be writer (Montgomery Clift) and a beautiful Southern belle (Elizabeth Taylor). The couple briefly travels through the South after they marry, and the romantic images of the region reprise many earlier films. Unlike most of these movies, however, made when abolitionists were villains to both North and South, *Raintree County* portrays them in a sympathetic light. Clift plays a vocal critic of slavery, and he has the audience on his side as he forces his bride to free her slaves. The movie also openly addresses miscegenation, and Taylor portrays a woman who is driven slowly mad by her fear that her mother was black. A budget of more than $5 million and spectacular costumes and sets failed to compensate for a tedious script, and the movie fared poorly with audiences. Nevertheless, the Civil War remained an obvious setting for romantic epics, and long costume dramas would later thrive on television.

Television and New Social History

Television revolutionized popular media during the 1960s, and the Civil War found a home away from the silver screen. TV provided an accommodating venue for lengthy examinations and, beginning in the 1970s, miniseries about the era flourished. In 1977, the television version of Alex Haley's *Roots* (1976), a fictionalized account of the author's slave ancestors, brought new insights about slavery to the screen. The series aired for eight consecutive nights and stimulated unprecedented popular consideration of slavery. As scholars Eugene Genovese and Herbert Gutman had long been documenting, *Roots* vividly showed that slaves developed a community and a culture that existed outside of their relationship with whites. The series also portrayed Reconstruction from the perspective of emancipated slaves. Their determination to achieve an economic livelihood and to implement their political rights in the face of tremendous resistance provided a necessary correction to the portrait of childlike and unruly freedmen in *The Birth of a Nation* and the unflinchingly loyal slaves in *Gone with the Wind.*

While *Roots* challenged viewers to reconsider their perceptions of slavery, miniseries such as *The Blue and the Gray* (1982), *North and South* (1986), and its sequel, *North and South Book II* (1986) entertained viewers with familiar clichés. In these series, the conflict separates families and friends and forces them to make painful choices between region and loved ones. The success of these films demonstrates that the image of American fighting American was as poignant in the 1980s as it was seventy years before.

The most significant television film about the era is Ken Burns's *The Civil War* (1990). Burns vividly brings to life the war's civilian and military participants through photographs, music, letters, and diaries. Burns focuses on stories of individual failure and accomplishment because, as one prominent film historian describes, they create the "emotional connections [that] become a kind of glue which makes the most complex of past events stick in our minds and our hearts" (Toplin, 160). The film starts with the causes of the conflict, and, although Burns blames neither side, he attributes the war to slavery. The film then proceeds chronologically from battle to battle, and while Burns emphasizes the brutality and horror of these engagements, he also highlights many of the individual acts of honor and courage displayed by the participants. In the last episode, Burns examines veterans' reunions and other acts of national unity that occurred in the late nineteenth and early twentieth centuries. His focus glosses over much of the ill will that followed the fighting, but historian Robert Brent Toplin suggests that the focus on reconciliation is in keeping with late-twentieth-century Americans' desire to emphasize their common heritage rather than their past differences.

Fourteen million people watched the initial run of *The Civil War* on PBS, and even more read the companion book or saw subsequent airings. Historians recognized that Burns had reached an audience underexposed to academic histories, and many were vocal with criticisms large and small. In an indication of the current dominance of social history, whose proponents study history "from the bottom up" by examining the everyday experiences of ordinary men and women, Burns was taken to task for emphasizing battles and generals. Many scholars believed that Burns and writer Geoffrey Ward gave short shrift to their particular areas of interest, including Reconstruction and the wartime roles of women. Some of Burns's critics noted valid shortcomings and errors while others only nitpicked, but their attention to the series and its record-setting audience for public television suggest how relevant the war remains to Americans.

Among the many prominent individuals featured in Burns's series, none is more important than Abraham Lincoln. (See "Abraham Lincoln.") The sixteenth president was an immensely popular figure during the early years of the movie industry, and films such as *The Land of Opportunity* (1920) and *Abraham Lincoln* (1924) dramatized periods of his life and political career. In *The Birth of a Nation,* D. W. Griffith calls Lincoln the "Great Heart" and portrays him as a fatherly figure who pardons Confederate prisoners, a popular image in silent films. Griffith's sympathetic image of Lincoln reflected a general sentiment that, had the President lived, he would have enacted more benign Reconstruction policies than did the Radical Congress. Griffith made *Abraham Lincoln* in 1930, a full-length talking film whose chief failing is an episodic approach to the president's life. *Young Mr. Lincoln* (1939) and *Abe Lincoln in Illinois* (1940) focus on the president's early career, and both perpetuate images of his frontier resourcefulness. The last few decades have generally found Lincoln on the periphery of Civil War films. Scholars are now less likely to portray Lincoln as a flawless leader, and some have sought to debunk his image as the "Great Emancipator." The only recent full-length screen biography is *Gore Vidal's Lincoln* (1987), based on Vidal's fictionalized version of the Lincoln presidency. Vidal offers a very human portrait of a folksy yet shrewd president who is ultimately a heroic figure.

Few films that examine Lincoln as wartime president mention his decisive role in the recruitment of black soldiers. By 1865, 74 percent of free northern blacks of military age had volunteered, and these 179,000 men constituted nearly 10 percent of the Union military (Duncan, 20). The 54th Massachusetts was the first Northern black regiment, and its history came to the public's attention in *Glory* (1989). The movie follows the unit's organization under Colonel Robert Gould Shaw (Matthew Broderick) during the winter of 1862–63 through the ill-fated attack the following summer on Fort Wagner, which guarded the harbor at Charleston, South Carolina. The regiment suffered nearly 50 percent casualties, but the courage of its members helped to convince the Northern public that blacks would fight bravely and skillfully for the Union. To make an already poignant story even more so, the film's regiment is filled with ex-slaves who initially labor in ill-fitting shoes and without uniforms. In reality, freeborn blacks dominated the 54th Massachusetts, and, as Governor John Andrew's model black regiment, they received adequate supplies and equipment. *Glory*'s stirring score, performed by the Boys Choir of Harlem, and its gripping battle scenes dramatically bring forth the magnitude of the regiment's accomplishments.

Like black soldiers, prisoners of war are underrepresented in the movies. One of the only films to explore this subject is the television film *Andersonville* (1996), the story of the infamous Southern prison in Georgia. Established in the late winter of 1864, the prison quickly exceeded its capacity, and malnutrition and disease ran rampant. The film accurately portrays the hellish conditions that led to the deaths of nearly one-third of the 45,000 inmates. Criminal gangs of prisoners, called Raiders, exacerbated the already deplorable conditions, and the film dramatizes a true incident in which the Confederate guards gave permission to the prisoners to try their tormentors and to execute the ringleaders. *Andersonville* depicts Captain Heinrich Wirz, the controversial commandant whom the War Department executed after the war, as vindictive and slightly crazy. Although he may have been both, historians now generally agree that Wirz was hampered by a lack of supplies and a deteriorating Confederate infrastructure.

The lingering pain of slavery became a silver screen topic in 1998, when Oprah Winfrey put her tremendous popularity behind a film adaptation of Toni Morrison's Pulitzer Prize–winning novel *Beloved* (1987). In addition to producing the film, Winfrey portrayed Sethe, a former runaway slave who is haunted by memories of the daughter she killed rather than allow her to be captured by slave catchers. The film failed dismally at the box office, despite Winfrey's moving performance. The poor showing was due more to Thandie Newton's off-putting portrayal of Beloved, the murdered child, and to an overly long and confusing script than to audience resistance to the issue of slavery. Appearing concurrently and

FIGURE 7. *Gettysburg* (1993). Involving hundreds of reenactors, *Gettysburg* chronicles the massive, detailed, and violent three-day battle of July 1863, which ended a Confederate invasion of the North. Courtesy Esparza/Katz Productions and Turner Pictures.

demonstrating the continued viability of the topic were *Slavery in America* (1998) a PBS documentary, and *Remembering Slavery* (1998), a book and companion audio tapes featuring slave reminiscences gathered in the 1930s by the Federal Writers' Project.

Despite Hollywood's recent forays into new topics, many audiences still want to hear the crash of gunfire and the roar of artillery, and the ultimate Civil War movie occurs on the battlefield. *Gettysburg* (1993), based on Michael Shaara's Pulitzer Prize–winning novel *The Killer Angels* (1974), is one of the most vivid depictions of Civil War combat, as is its prequel *Gods and Generals* (2003). *Gettysburg* portrays the decisive three-day battle during the summer of 1863 that ended the South's last invasion of the North and marked the high-water mark of Robert E. Lee's Confederate army. Filmed on the battlefield, the movie features thousands of reenactors and gives tremendous attention to accuracy of details. Effective camera techniques vividly convey the size and scope of the battle, most poignantly as line after line of Confederate soldiers sweep forward during Pickett's Charge. But despite the presence of so many enlisted soldiers, the film is most concerned with explaining the actions and motivations of their officers. One of the more controversial portrayals is that of Lee, played by Martin Sheen in *Gettysburg* (but by Robert Duvall in *Gods and Generals*). Both sides revered the Confederate commander after his death in 1870, and his battlefield skill and sense of duty made him an American hero. In the past twenty years, however, Lee has come under increased fire from scholars such as Thomas Connelly and Alan Nolan, who criticize the general's excessive confidence in the abilities of his men and his obsession with winning the war through a single, climactic battle. The movie suggests these deficiencies and portrays Lee as less capable than General James Longstreet (Tom Berenger), his chief subordinate—and a controversial figure in his own right.

Gettysburg is again examined in a series of documentaries by Greystone Communications. The topics are diverse and include episodes on the Irish soldiers who fought on both sides; Jennie Wade, the only civilian killed during the fighting; and the leading officers. *Chamberlain at Gettysburg* (1998), which focuses on the hero of Little Round Top, demonstrates the strength of the series, with sequences filmed on the battlefield, well-executed computer graphics, and a balanced combination of historians and United States Park Service experts.

Hollywood has explored the events of the era in hundreds of films since the advent of the film industry. The drama inherent in a war in which Americans fought their fellow countrymen has captured the public's imagination. Just as audiences lined up to see *Gone with the Wind,* their grandchildren remained glued to their televisions throughout the Ken Burns series. In contrast to the attention given to the war, Reconstruction is rarely depicted in film. Many Americans know little about the war's aftermath, except to perceive it dimly as a time of corruption, dishonor, and failure. Public understanding probably will lag behind scholarly reinterpretation until Hollywood challenges the outdated images of Griffith and Selznick with honest portrayals of the successes and failures of the era. Continued attention to the varied events of the entire period remains important, for, as Shelby Foote elegantly declares in *The Civil War,* "Any understanding of this nation has to be based, and I mean really based, on an understanding of the Civil War. . . . It defined us."

References

Filmography

Abe Lincoln in Illinois (1940, F)
Abraham Lincoln (1924, F; 1930, F)
Africans in America (1998, D)
Andersonville (1996, TV)
Barbara Frietchie (1915, F)
The Battle (1911, F)
Beloved (1998, F)
The Birth of a Nation (1915, F)
The Blue and the Gray (1982, TV)
The Bridge (1931, F)
Chamberlain at Gettysburg (1998, D)
The Civil War (1990, D)
The Coward (1915, F)
The Filmmakers' Gettysburg (1998, D)
Friendly Persuasion (1956, F)
The General (1927, F)
Gettysburg (1993, F)
Glory (1989, F)
Gods and Generals (2003, F)
Gone with the Wind (1939, F)
Gore Vidal's Lincoln (1987, TV)
Hands Up! (1926, F)
The Horse Soldiers (1959, F)
In the Days of War (1913, F)
The Land of Opportunity (1920, F)
Major Dundee (1965, F)
North and South (1986, TV)
North and South Book II (1986, TV)
An Occurrence at Owl Creek Bridge (F, 1961)
Raintree County (1957, F)
The Red Badge of Courage (1951, F; 1974, TV)
Roots (1977, TV)
Santa Fe Trail (1940, F)
Scarlett (1994, TV)
Seven Angry Men (1955, F)
Shenandoah (1965, F)
So Red the Rose (1935, F)
A Southern Yankee (1948, F)
The Sting of Victory (1916, F)
Tap Roots (1948, F)
The Undefeated (1969, F)
The Unknown Civil War (1998, D)
Virginia City (1940, F)
Young Mr. Lincoln (1939, F)

Bibliography

Berlin, Ira, Marc Fureau, and Steven F. Miller. *Remembering Slavery: African Americans Talk about Their Personal Experiences of Slavery and Freedom.* New York: Norton, 1998.

Carnes, Mark C., ed. *Past Imperfect: History According to the Movies.* New York: Henry Holt, 1995.

Chadwick, Bruce. *The Reel Civil War: Mythmaking in American Film.* New York: Knopf, 2001.

Cullen, Jim. *The Civil War in Popular Culture: A Reusable Past.* Washington, DC: Smithsonian Institution Press, 1995.

Donald, David. "American Historians and the Causes of the Civil War." *South Atlantic Quarterly* 59 (1960): 351–355.

Duncan, Russell, ed. *Blue-Eyed Child of Fortune: The Civil War Letters of Colonel Robert Gould Shaw.* Athens: University of Georgia Press, 1992.

Foner, Eric. *Reconstruction: America's Unfinished Revolution: 1863–1877.* New York: Harper & Row, 1988.

Hay, Peter. *MGM: When the Lion Roars.* Atlanta: Turner, 1991.

Kinnard, Roy. *The Blue and the Gray on the Silver Screen: More Than Eighty Years of Civil War Movies.* Secaucus, NJ: Carol, 1996.

Lang, Robert, ed. *The Birth of a Nation: D. W. Griffith, Director.* New Brunswick, NJ: Rutgers University Press, 1994.

Marvel, William. *Andersonville: The Last Depot.* Chapel Hill: University of North Carolina Press, 1994.

McPherson, James M. *Battle Cry of Freedom: The Civil War Era.* New York: Oxford University Press, 1988.

Pyron, Darden Asbury. *Southern Daughter: The Life of Margaret Mitchell.* New York: Oxford University Press, 1991.

Rachels, David, and Robert Baird. "Andersonville Goes to Hollywood—Courtesy of Ted Turner." *Film & History* 25.1 (1995): 54–57.

Spears, Jack. *The Civil War on the Screen and Other Essays.* New York: A. S. Barnes, 1977.

Spehr, Paul C. *The Civil War in Motion Pictures: A Bibliography of Films Produced in the United States since 1897.* Washington, DC: U.S. Government Printing Office, 1961.

Toplin, Robert Brent, ed. *Ken Burns's* The Civil War: *Historians Respond.* New York: Oxford University Press, 1996.

[PHILIP J. LANDON]

The Cold War

The Cold War was the name given to the decades-long political and economic conflict between the United States and the Soviet Union. It began in the wake of World War II as the two superpowers sought to determine the political and economic futures of the European nations devastated by the war, and it continued until the political disintegration of the Soviet Union in 1991. Walter Lippman's *The Cold War* (1947), an analysis of American foreign policy, gave a name to the escalating hostilities between the Soviet Union, together with its Eastern European satellite states, and the United States, in alliance with the nations of Western Europe. George F. Kennan's famous "long telegram," published as "Sources of Soviet Conduct" in *Foreign Affairs* (1947), argued that the Cold War could be attributed to Soviet expansionism in Europe, and he advised a strategy of "containment" to thwart the spread of Soviet communism. The subsequent decisions by the administration of President Harry S. Truman to intervene on the side of the anticommunists in the Greek civil war (the Truman Doctrine) and to rebuild the war-devastated economies of western Europe along the lines of democratic capitalism (the Marshall Plan) exemplified Kennan's strategy, and for the next four decades the doctrine of "containment" shaped both American foreign policy and American interpretations of the origins of Cold War.

Events of the late 1940s and early 1950s (the Soviet blockade of Berlin in 1948; the communist victory in China in 1949; the testing of nuclear weapons in Russia in 1949; the invasion of South Korea by the communist-led North in 1950 [see "The Korean War"]; and revelations of Soviet espionage activities in the United States) seemed to confirm the widespread assumption in America that the Cold War was precipitated by the Soviet Union's plans for global domination. A massive rearmament program and the creation of a network of military and political alliances—including the North Atlantic Treaty Organization (NATO), the Southeast Asia Treaty Organization (SEATO), and the Organization of American States (OAS)—aimed at stemming aggression abroad, while a concern for internal security lead to zealous (and often excessive) attempts to root out subversives at home.

The House Committee on Un-American Activities (HUAC) hunted for communists and communist sympathizers in government, in universities, and in the mass media. The committee's investigations of the film industry led to the conviction of the "Hollywood Ten" and the blackballing of others for their leftist political affiliations in the 1930s and 1940s. Many of these investigations proceeded with little regard for rules of evidence or the constitutional rights of the accused, but it was Senator Joseph McCarthy, chairman of the Senate Permanent Investigations Subcommittee, who lent his name to the practices that soon came to be regarded as "witch hunts."

By the late 1950s, as Stephen Whitfield points out in *The Culture of the Cold War*, attitudes toward the Cold War were undergoing significant changes. The excesses of "McCarthyism" had discredited the anticommunist crusades of the previous decade, making it difficult to stifle criticism of the country's Cold War policies by labeling them un-American. Witnesses such as Dagmar Wilson, the leader of Women's Strike for Peace, openly defied HUAC, and the comedian Mort Sahl ridiculed the hunt for subversives (Whitfield, 125). More important, perhaps, the idea of winning a war between the United States and the Soviet Union became suspect. No ideological differences seemed to justify a nuclear holocaust, and the arms race had created a world in danger of being plunged into war accidentally.

These new attitudes are evident in the responses to increased East-West tensions during the early 1960s. After a thaw in American-Soviet relations in the last years of the Eisenhower administration, the downing of an American spy plane over Russia in 1960 and the building of the Berlin Wall in 1961 intensified the Cold War, and, a year later, the Cuban Missile Crisis brought the countries to the brink of war. Instead of uniting the country in opposition to communist aggression, critics became even more vocal in their criticism of the doctrine of mutually assured destruction (MAD). The disastrous outcome of the war in Vietnam (see "The Vietnam War") left even more Americans disillusioned with pursuing the Cold War, and the Nixon administration's desire to seek détente with the Soviet Union and its plan to implement a nuclear nonproliferation agreement seemed to herald an end to the Cold War.

Unfortunately, as the 1970s drew to a close, new weapons, principally the deployment of missiles with multiple warheads (MIRVs), threatened any nonproliferation agreement. President Jimmy Carter's administration, fearing a Soviet military buildup, laid the groundwork by expanding American forces. At the same time, attitudes toward the Cold War were undergoing another change. These new attitudes and the desire to have America reclaim its place as the preeminent world power would define the administration of President Ronald Reagan and mark the final phase of the Cold War.

The Reagan administration increased military spending and championed the development of new weapons systems (including the highly publicized "Star Wars" antimissile project) to defend against an increasingly militant Soviet Union, which was described by the President as the "Evil Empire." While the threat of another nuclear standoff alarmed America's ideological allies as well as her enemies, the response at home never duplicated the grim determination to stem the tide of international communism at all costs that characterized the early years of the Cold War.

A primary goal of renewing the Cold War often seems to have been a desire to rekindle a sense of national pride, patriotism, and purpose that had been weakened by the war in Vietnam and the cultural upheavals of the 1960s. When the president entered New York harbor aboard a recommissioned World War II battleship to celebrate the renovation of the Stature of Liberty in 1986, *Time* magazine invoked a 1984 Republican campaign slogan to sum up the public mood: "America Is Back." By the mid-1980s, however, the "Evil Empire" had begun to collapse. Soviet satellite states—including Poland and Czechoslovakia—unseated communist regimes; in 1989 the Berlin Wall dividing East and West Germany fell; and in 1991 the Soviet Union itself ceased to exist, bringing an end to the Cold War.

Perspectives on the Cold War

American attempts to account for the origins and the progress of the Cold War vary widely in their ideological, political, and economic perspectives, as John Lewis Gaddis has demonstrated in *The Long Peace* (1987) and in *The United States at the End of the Cold War* (1992). During the first decade and a half of the Cold War, the division between East and West was blamed on the Soviet Union's desire to control the countries of Eastern Europe and to foster the growth of socialism throughout the world, a view forcefully articulated by the architects of American Cold War policy, including George Kennan and Paul Nitze. In the late 1950s and 1960s, increasing skepticism toward Cold War policies was reflected in the work of left-leaning revisionist historians who saw the Soviet Union's behavior in the years following World War II as a response to plans by America and its Western allies aimed at creating political systems favorable to free-market capitalism. In 1959, William Appleton Williams offered a version of this revisionist argument in *The Tragedy of American Diplomacy,* and Noam Chomsky's writings exemplify the view that the United States is primarily responsible for the Cold War (see, for example, *Towards a New Cold War,* 1982). During the 1980s, as the Cold War drew to a close, historians like Gaddis sought to arrive at a balance between the early hard-line and the revisionist interpretations. A genuine historical consensus regarding the causes of the Cold War, however, has yet to be established. A decade after its conclusion, historians and cultural critics were still fighting the ideological battles it inspired.

Cold War Films: Documentaries

American documentaries dealing with the Cold War not only reflect the widely differing interpretations of the underlying causes of the hostilities, but they also parallel the importance of those interpretations in the political discourse of the Cold War era. Several episodes of *The March of Time* series (1948–51) covered various aspects of the Cold War, exemplifying the doctrine of "containment" espoused by George Kennan. A three-part series ("The Cold War: Act I—France," "The Cold War: Act II—Crisis in Italy," and "Cold War: Act III—Battle for Greece") released in 1948 focuses on the expansionist policies of the Soviet Union, the need for an American military buildup, and the possibility of thermonuclear war as a final defense against that expansion. "Crisis in Iran" (1951), one of the last *March of Time* productions, suggests that the Cold War had become a global struggle.

During the 1950s, the Cold War served as the subtext for a number of documentaries devoted to the accomplishments of the military services. The most memorable of these films was NBC's twenty-six-episode *Victory at Sea* (1953–54). Based on Samuel Eliot Morrison's history of naval operations during World War II, the series combined archival footage of the war at sea with a superior musical score by Richard Rodgers both to celebrate the heroic accomplishments of the U.S. Navy and to dramatize the importance of military vigilance as essential to the preservation of democracy. The political implications of *Victory at Sea* were well suited to the tastes of "a cold-war television audience" (Rollins, 135). Four years later, NBC once again portrayed America as the enemy of tyranny in *Air Force,* a compilation film tracing the history of the U.S. Air Force.

Nightmare in Red (1955), another example of an early Cold War documentary, depicts the rise of Soviet Communism from a militantly anticommunist perspective. The Bolshevik Revolution in Russia, viewers are urged to believe, merely exchanged the tyranny of the tsarist regime for the tyranny of Stalinism, which is equated with Nazism in Germany under Adolf Hitler. As Peter Rollins points out in his analysis of *Nightmare in Red,* the ideological presuppositions of the film's producers and their desire to create a dramatic narrative in which good is pitted against evil led them to take considerable liberties with historical fact. For example, in order to suggest that the Russian people saw their Soviet leaders as oppressors, *Nightmare in Red* includes footage from World War II Nazi propaganda films which show Soviet citizens welcoming German invaders as liberators. These distortions, however misleading they may be, do suggest the intensity of the anticommunist passions during the early years of the Cold War. In addition, these documentaries also point to the manner in which militant anticommunism became a way of attacking domestic political enemies. New Deal social reforms, cultural cosmopolitanism, and the renascent civil rights movement were all attacked as "un-American" and, often, communist-inspired. *Anarchy USA* (1966), for example, attributes racial unrest to the work of communist agitators.

By 1966, however, old-fashioned anticommunism had become suspect, and the prospects of an all-out war with the Soviet Union were viewed with increasing skepticism. Emile De Antonio's *Point of Order* (a.k.a. *McCarthy: Death of a Witchhunter*) (1964) is a compilation film covering the McCarthy-Army hearings of 1954. In it, Senator McCarthy appears as a boorish opportunist, a comic figure who exemplifies the folly of anticommunist witch hunts. Irony, satire, and black comedy became familiar techniques in documentaries that shared the revisionist views of Cold War policies and politics. In *The Atomic Café* (1982), for example, filmmakers Kevin Rafferty and Jayne Loader have edited familiar documentary footage from the 1940s through the 1960s in a way that makes the nuclear arms race and Cold War that underlay the arms race appear foolish, naive, brutal, delusional, and—above all—unnecessary. Not all revisionist documentaries were exercises in satire. Julia Reichart's and Jim Klein's *Seeing Red* (1983) is a sympathetic, even sentimental, examination of the lives of Americans who were attracted to the Communist Party during the 1930s and early 1940s. They are treated as idealists seeking answers to the economic devastation of the Depression and a way to oppose fascism, who turned to the Soviet Union only to be disillusioned by the excesses of the Stalinist era. Interpretations of the Cold War appear in a variety of documentaries devoted to the people and events which shaped American history in the years following World War II. *David Halberstam's The Fifties* (1997), a miniseries based on Halberstam's best-selling account of the decade, devotes a segment to the Cold War that is critical of American policies at home and abroad.

Post–Cold War Perspectives

The end of the Cold War in 1991 encouraged a more balanced view of the East-West conflict that had defined American political life for nearly five decades. New interpretations rejected both the hard-line anticommunism that laid the blame for the hostilities on the expansionist policies of the Soviet Union and the revisionist perspective that saw the Cold War originating in the political and economic policies of the capitalist nations in the West. *The Birth of the Cold War* (1997), one of the documentaries in NBC's *White Papers* series, is sympathetic to the idea of containing the spread of Soviet communism while at the same time critical of the excesses that often ignored civil liberties and brought the world to the brink of nuclear war.

The most ambitious documentary treatment of the era has been CNN's *Cold War* (1998–99). In twenty-four hour-long episodes, it chronicles events from the Russian Revolution, which brought the Communist Party to power, to the final collapse of the Soviet Union. A joint production by television companies in the United States, Great Britain, Germany, and Russia, the series scrupulously avoids siding with any of the nations involved. Many of the episodes (the one covering the Berlin Airlift, for example) are very effective. Others seem to be rather misleading in their ideological evenhandedness. The sixth episode, which covers the domestic effects of the Cold War, tends to equate the Red Scare in the United States with the Stalinist repression in the Soviet Union, and the narrator, Kenneth Branagh, who serves as a mediating and interpreting voice for the series, encourages viewers to see a sort of moral equivalence. The images, however, tell another story. The disregard for constitutional rights demonstrated by HUAC and the shameful (and racist) treatment of Paul Robeson remain a national disgrace, but they are hardly a match for persecution of religious leaders such as Hungary's Roman Catholic prelate Cardinal Josef Mindszenty after the country was taken over by communists in 1948 or for the creation of the Soviet Gulag. Despite these shortcomings, however, *Cold War* is a valuable series for the breadth of its coverage and the interviews with the men and women who both shaped and endured the Cold War.

Feature Films

The influence on the American film industry was deep and long lasting. Hollywood became a highly visible target of HUAC during the late 1940s and 1950s. Uncooperative witnesses were blacklisted by the studios, and some, like the Hollywood Ten, served time in jail. To prove their "Americanism," studio bosses not only fired and blacklisted employees, but they also turned out a string of films warning against the dangers of communism at home and abroad, films that reflect the same political attitudes evident in the documentaries of the early Cold War years. Less than a year after Walter Lippman coined the term "Cold War," Twentieth Century–Fox released William Wellman's *Iron Curtain* (a.k.a. *Behind the Iron Curtain*) (1947), adapted from the life story of Russian code clerk Igor Gouzenko (Dana Andrews), who had defected to the West with evidence of Soviet espionage operations in North America. Felix Feist's *Guilty of Treason* (1949) recounts the fate of Cardinal Mindszenty (Charles Bickford), who endures arrest, torture, and prison rather than capitulate to his godless enemies.

Contemporary Cold War events continued to provide material for filmmakers throughout the 1950s. George Seaton's *The Big Lift* (1950) dramatizes the lives of fliers serving with the Berlin Airlift. Shot on location in Berlin using documentary techniques, the film focuses on the ability of American technology to carry the day, love affairs between the central characters (Paul Douglas and Montgomery Clift) and two German women, and stresses the importance of seeing Germany not as a totalitarian enemy but as a fledgling democracy and an ally in the struggle against communism.

At the same time that Hollywood films were busy exposing life behind the Iron Curtain and defending the nation's interests abroad, they were also ferreting out spies and subversives at home. Alfred Werker's *Walk East on Beacon* (1952) recounts the efforts of Soviet spies to penetrate a top-secret scientific project. The Reds prove no match, however, for a team of FBI agents led by Inspector Belden (George Murphy). The film owes much of its sense of realism to the clever blending of a fictional narrative with the style of a documentary, a technique that had been used with great success in Louis de Rochemont's *March of Time* series. Although the project the communists seek to penetrate is never explicitly identified, it has something to do with atomic secrets, a subject very much in the news at a time when Julius and Ethel Rosenberg had been charged with passing atomic secrets to the Russians.

While *Walk East on Beacon* enthusiastically endorsed the FBI's relentless pursuit of suspected communists, Gordon Douglas's *I Was a Communist for the FBI* (1951) cast Frank Lovejoy as undercover agent Matt Cvetic, who suffers estrangement from family and friends in order to infiltrate the Communist Party as part of the bureau's plan to expose disloyal Americans. John Wayne joined the hunt for communists in Hawaii as the title character in Edward Ludwig's *Big Jim McLain* (1952). Wayne and his assistant (James Arness) interview repentant ex-communists as they seek out Soviet agents for interrogation by HUAC. The film celebrates the committee's activities, but it plays fast and loose with historical facts. Unlike the fate of uncooperative witnesses called before HUAC, who were jailed for contempt or blacklisted for invoking the Fifth Amendment, the agents rounded up by Big Jim escape punishment by what he describes as "abusing" their constitutional rights and refusing to testify. Similar narratives became the subject of television series, and one of the most popular was *I Led Three Lives* (1953–56), which was based on Herbert A. Phil-

FIGURE 8. *Walk East on Beacon* (1952). The FBI's relentless efforts to ferret out Soviet spies even in the cellars of suburban homes were presented in a documentary-like style. Courtesy Columbia Pictures Corporation and RD-DR Productions.

brick's best-selling account of his years as an FBI undercover agent posing as a member of the Communist Party.

The importance of denouncing friends and relatives with communist associations became a theme central to several films of the period, including Victor Saville's Anglo-American production *Conspirator* (1949) and Robert Stevenson's *I Married a Communist* (a.k.a. *The Woman on Pier 13*) (1950). Perhaps the most revealing of these films is Leo McCarey's *My Son John* (1952). It verges on self-parody in its anticommunist zeal, but it still "feverishly [reflected] the political traumas of the Cold War" (Whitfield, 136). John Jefferson (Robert Walker), the son of hard-working, patriotic, and religious parents, is a member of what seems to be the State Department where, presumably, his communist sympathies, his intellectual arrogance, and his nasty temperament go unnoticed. Rejected by members of his family after they discover he is a Soviet spy, he plans to flee the country with government secrets. A sudden change of heart prompts him to reveal his treachery, and, in retribution, he is murdered by communist agents.

A large number of B films featuring American citizens serving as communist agents helped create the impression that the country was overrun by Soviet spies. They infiltrate the government in Harold Schuster's *Security Risk* (1954), penetrate a secluded California research site in Edward Dein's *Shack out on 101*, and gain control of a Washington, D.C., advertising agency in Jacques Tourneur's *The Fearmakers* (1958). Most of these films failed as both anticommunist propaganda and as thrillers. Two, however, became film noir classics. In Sam Fuller's *Pickup on South Street* (1953), a petty criminal, Skip McCoy (Richard Widmark), steals a wallet containing scientific secrets. His theft touches off a series of events in which he and his acquaintances are hunted by both federal agents and Soviet spies. The action unfolds in a dark, urban environment where characters find themselves caught up in events they neither control nor fully understand. McCoy, who claims no political allegiances, finally decides to cooperate with the federal agents after Soviet agents have murdered a friend (Thelma Ritter) and savagely beaten his lover (Jean Peters).

The second film, Robert Aldrich's adaptation of Mickey Spillane's best-selling novel *Kiss Me Deadly* (1952), is set in Los Angeles rather than New York City, but it remains a part of the same noir world. Like McCoy, Mike Hammer stumbles upon a case of nuclear espionage and cooperates with a team of federal agents whose leader, Pat Chambers (Wesley Addy), appears to be as mysterious and sinister as the Soviet agents pursuing a box of radioactive material. Hammer's motives for cooperating with Chambers have little to do with patriotism and very much to do with his desire to turn a profit, wreak personal vengeance, and rescue his assistant, Velda (Maxine Cooper), who has been kidnapped by the spies. His search leads him deeper into a dark underworld of multiple deceptions and sadistic cruelty from which there appears to be no escape.

Although Cold War espionage triggers the events that set these last two narratives in motion, neither of the central characters is motivated by patriotism or by anticommunism.

McCoy, like Hammer, finally cooperates with the federal agents for personal motives. Moreover, Aldrich's Hammer is a familiar noir hero, alienated and contemptuous of all forms of idealism—in sharp contrast with the hero of Spillane's novel, who was a zealous anticommunist. Both films reveal how easily Cold War tensions could be invoked for narrative rather than ideological purposes.

Cold War Allegories

If *Pickup on South Street* and *Kiss Me Deadly* reduce Cold War ideology to narrative convention, Fred Zinneman's *High Noon* (1952) and Elia Kazan's *On the Waterfront* (1954) were profoundly influenced by those ideological conflicts, though manifested only indirectly. On the surface, *High Noon* is a classic western that pits Will Kane (Gary Cooper), the Hadleyville town marshal, against a murderous band of gunmen bent on revenge. The film focuses on Kane's futile effort to enlist the aid of the townspeople who, out of a combination of cowardice and self-interest, leave him to face Frank Miller (Ian McDonald) and his three henchmen alone. The film was written by Carl Foreman, his last before being blacklisted for refusing to testify before HUAC. He intended the film as a political allegory in which Hadleyville represented Hollywood and its citizens the cowardly studio executives who refused to resist what he considered the unlawful behavior of the committee, which had cited him for contempt.

Unlike Foreman, Elia Kazan had been a cooperative committee witness, giving it the names of eight friends and colleagues who had been associated with communist organizations in the past, and, in *On the Waterfront,* he treats informing as an act of heroism. Terry Malloy (Marlon Brando) is a washed-up boxer working as a longshoreman on the Hoboken docks. Jobs on the docks are controlled by a corrupt labor union that uses violence and murder to keep workers in line. Under the moral influence of his priest (Karl Malden) and the sister (Eva Marie Saint) of a murdered worker, Malloy risks his life to testify against the union leaders who were previously his friends and benefactors. Like *High Noon,* the film has been read as a metaphor for Cold War politics and—in this case—a justification for Kazan's naming names.

By the mid-1950s, the threat from the enemy within tended to give way to the threat from the enemy without. Senator McCarthy's increasingly reckless and often baseless attacks led to his Senate censure and subsequent fall from power, and the anticommunist crusade began to lose momentum. Reflecting this shift in political attitudes, Hollywood turned its attention from the communist subversion to communist expansion around the world. Resisting the latter demanded, in the minds of policymakers, a strong military and a willingness to go to war if necessary. The anxieties aroused by the prospect of a permanent struggle between East and West that might erupt into a third world war fought with nuclear weapons were evident in all the major Hollywood film genres, including the musical (*Silk Stockings,* 1957), but these fears were most fully expressed in science fiction films such as Christian Nyby's *The Thing from Another World* (1951) and Don Siegel's *The Invasion of the Body Snatchers* (1956). Anxieties aroused by the ubiquitous presence of the Bomb were largely displaced onto the horror film. The effects of radiation spawned a variety of gigantic sea creatures (*The Beast from 20,000 Fathoms,* 1953), ants (*Them,* 1954), and even grasshoppers (*The Beginning of the End,* 1957). But films that depicted life after a nuclear holocaust either ignored the political implications (*The Day the World Ended,* 1956) or attributed the devastation to an accident (*The World, the Flesh, and the Devil,* 1959).

If Cold War tensions found indirect and symbolic expression in the science fiction/horror film, they are made manifest in the war film. The genre, which had virtually disappeared from the screen at the end of World

War II, was revived as the Cold War intensified in the late 1940s. With a few exceptions, the settings of these films were World War II, the Korean War, or the Cold War itself. Those set in World War II show how the virtues of patriotism, professionalism, and teamwork have saved America from totalitarian predators; the Korean War films raised questions about the willingness and the ability of Americans to live up to those ideals; and the Cold War films showed how those ideals can be called on to prevent war while at the same time containing the Soviet Union. They also favored subjects that featured those weapons most closely associated with the nuclear war they were designed to prevent: the long-range bomber and the nuclear submarine.

The first and most successful of the Air Force films, *Strategic Air Command* (1955), was directed by Anthony Mann at the urging of the film's star, ex–bomber pilot Jimmy Stewart, who remained an officer in the Air Force Reserve and wanted to make a film honoring the Air Force's cold warriors. Stewart plays "Dutch" Holland, a professional baseball player who is recalled to active duty and comes to realize that serving with the Strategic Air Command is more important than returning to the baseball diamond. The narrative is divided between Holland's duties as an aircraft commander and the effect his decision to stay in the service has on his marriage. His wife (June Allyson) wants him to return to civilian life, but she understands the importance of defending America and remains steadfastly loyal. The same choice between the successful civilian career desired by his family and the more Spartan demands of the Strategic Air Command faces the central characters of Gordon Douglas's *Bombers B-52* (1957) and Delbert Mann's *A Gathering of Eagles* (1963). All of these films depict a tight-knit, patriarchal family as an ideal to be emulated. Such families, Elaine Tyler May has explained in *Homeward Bound* (1988), were considered essential to a strong America.

Reevaluating Cold War Policies

By the late 1950s the developing revisionist interpretations of the Cold War were encouraged by a thaw in East-West hostilities and the increasing tendency to regard the nuclear standoff less as a frightening possibility than as an unnecessary threat to human survival. This shift in the Cold War culture found its way into Hollywood features of the late 1950s. Stanley Kramer's *On the Beach* (1959) recounts the final months of the human race after an exchange of hydrogen bombs between the United States and the Soviet Union. The crew of an American submarine has taken refuge in Australia to await the arrival of a deadly atomic cloud moving south from the northern hemisphere. Despite its sensational subject and its all-star cast (Gregory Peck, Ava Gardner, Anthony Perkins, Fred Astaire), *On the Beach* reduces the narrative to a rather flat moral fable. It is perhaps more significant as a film that marks the ideological shift in Hollywood's depiction of Cold War politics evident in the films of the 1960s.

A destroyer captain (Richard Widmark) in James Harris's *The Bedford Incident* (1964) engages in the furious pursuit of a Soviet submarine and threatens to plunge the world into nuclear war. John Sturges's *Ice Station Zebra* (1968) depicts a race between an American and a Soviet submarine to retrieve the data aboard a Soviet spy satellite downed in the Arctic. Once again the drama stops just short of armed conflict when another submarine commander (Rock Hudson) destroys the data and persuades the Soviets to publicize the incident as a joint search for the lost satellite. Both films imply that neither the Americans nor the Soviets can claim the moral high ground and that the threat of nuclear war outweighs the claims of any ideology.

Although the Cold War intensified again in the early 1960s with the erection of the wall dividing East and West Berlin (1961) and the Cuban Missile Crisis (1962), the renewed threat of war only sharpened the criticism of

Cold War policies, criticisms embodied in two of the most memorable of Cold War films: Sidney Lumet's *Fail-Safe* (1964) and Stanley Kubrick's *Dr. Strangelove* (1964). In both films American bombers attack the Soviet Union, and the American president and his military advisors try to prevent the attack from escalating into a thermonuclear war. Events in Lumet's film unfold with a grim solemnity and end with the president's (Henry Fonda) ordering a nuclear attack on New York City to compensate the earlier (and unintended) attack on Moscow. Kubrick had also planned a serious adaptation of Peter George's novel *Red Alert,* but as he developed his screenplay he decided that the very idea of nuclear warfare was suicidal and absurd, a subject best suited to a satiric black comedy. Consequently, from the moment a demented right-wing SAC general (Sterling Hayden) orders an attack on the Soviet Union, the film mounts a comic attack on Cold War ideologues, ineffectual politicians, doomsday planners, and military brass. Dr. Strangelove (Peter Sellers), the wheelchair-bound scientific advisor, combines the intellectual arrogance and the urge to destroy that Kubrick suggests is at the heart of nuclear policymaking. The desperate attempts to recall or destroy the attacking B-52s fail when a single aircraft gets to its target, triggering a Soviet "doomsday machine" capable of destroying all human life.

Thrillers in which the Cold War adversaries met in the labyrinthine world of espionage rather than on the battlefield saw a similar ideological transformation. One of the earliest, Carol Reed's *The Third Man* (1949), based on Graham Greene's novel and set in postwar Vienna, blends Cold War spy drama with a complex tale of black marketeering and betrayal; by film's end, the viewer cannot easily distinguish good guys from bad. In 1954, Nunnally Johnson's *Night People* used postwar Berlin as the setting for a battle of wits between a colonel in the U.S. Army's Counter Intelligence Corps (Gregory Peck) and his Russian counterparts, who behave as badly as the Nazis they defeated (and with whom they are linked in the film). Peck prevails because he can be as ruthless as the Soviets, but, as the film makes clear, he does it in the service of democratic ideals. By 1961 Billy Wilder could use Berlin to satirize the Cold War culture in both East and West. In *One, Two, Three,* America is represented not by a tough professional military officer but by the head of Coca Cola's Berlin office (James Cagney), who employs the skills of a spy to distribute Coke in East Germany and to transform a Communist student (Horst Buchholz) into a suitable husband for the boss's daughter by converting him to capitalism. Wilder's witty dialogue is so dependent on highly topical allusions to the Cold War rhetoric of the period that his film may seem dated, but, along with Carol Reed's *Our Man in Havana* (1960), it remains far superior to the numerous parodies of the genre that proliferated during the 1960s and 1970s.

Martin Ritt's *The Spy Who Came in from the Cold* (1965), adapted from the John Le Carré novel, paints a far darker picture of intelligence operations in the city that had become the epicenter of Cold War. A disillusioned British agent, Alec Lemeas (Richard Burton), is sent on a final mission into East Berlin, where he discovers that he has been set up by his superiors to preserve the cover of a "mole" (Peter Van Eyck) they have planted in East German intelligence. When the one person he still has faith in (Claire Bloom) is treacherously gunned down at the Berlin Wall, Lemeas refuses to escape alone and is shot dead. The same themes of betrayal, double-dealing, and entrapment are played out in another film adaptation of a Le Carré novel, Sidney Lumet's *A Deadly Affair* (1966), an underrated example of the genre. The Cold War's influence can be seen in Alfred Hitchcock's *The Man Who Knew Too Much* (1956) and *North by Northwest* (1959), and he addresses East-West espionage activities in two of his less successful films: *Torn Curtain* (1966) and *Topaz* (1969).

During the later 1960s, as the war in Vietnam escalated, the Cold War political consensus gave way to bitter political and ideological divisions. Consequently, Hollywood avoided making films about the Cold War and the hot war in Vietnam. Neither promised to be good box office.

Cold War Nostalgia

The Cold War intensified at the end of the decade as the United States and the Soviet Union embarked on a new arms race and financed local wars in the Third World. In 1980, long-time cold warrior Ronald Reagan was elected president, and he lost no time in denouncing the Soviet Union and her allies as an "evil empire" and urging America to reclaim its place as the defender of democratic values. Despite the accelerating arms race, the renewed East-West tensions never revived the fears of communist expansion and imminent nuclear war that had defined America's Cold War culture during the 1950s and 1960s. Invoking the specter of the "evil empire" did more to recall an era when America was more prosperous, more unified, and more capable of heroic action than the nation that had endured defeat in Vietnam and a general disillusionment with national institutions.

The sense of the Cold War as theater or as an exercise in nostalgia informs many films dealing with Cold war subjects, such as the recent comedy *Blast from the Past* (1999). Sam Peckinpah's *The Osterman Weekend* (1983) and Richard Benjamin's *Little Nikita* (1988) are tales of espionage that echo films of an earlier generation without either the ideological agendas or the narrative skill of their predecessors. Peckinpah's last feature focuses on the adventures of a talk-show host (Rutger Hauer) whom the CIA recruits to spy on friends suspected of being Soviet undercover agents, while Benjamin's thriller dramatizes a young man's (River Phoenix) discovery that his parents are Soviet agents in deep cover. He is persuaded by a fatherly FBI agent (Sidney Poitier) to aid in foiling a communist plot.

FIGURE 9. *The Spy Who Came in from the Cold* (1965). In West Berlin, disillusioned British secret agent Alex Leamus (Richard Burton, right) watches and waits apprehensively as a colleague attempts to flee from East Berlin. Courtesy Salem Productions.

The best examples of Cold War nostalgia may be found in the films of Clint Eastwood, who directed and/or starred in several films that express a longing for the period when, as the hero (Eastwood) of *In the Line of Fire* (1993) announces, "The country was different [and better] then." In *Heartbreak Ridge* (1986), which is based on a film from the early years of the Cold War (Allan Dwan's *Sands of Iwo Jima,* 1949), Sgt. Tom Highway, an anachronistic survivor of the old Marine Corps, manages to instill in an insolent, undisciplined, and very 1980s group of young Marines the virtues exemplified by John Wayne and his men in the earlier film. Their training serves them well during the invasion of Grenada, where victory, Highway makes clear, has redeemed the defeat in Vietnam.

While a number of the Cold War films of the 1980s may share a longing for the good old days, they remain ideologically diverse, ranging from the right-wing jingoism of John Milius's *Red Dawn* (1984) to the revisionism of John Schlesinger's *The Falcon and the Snowman* (1985), in which the CIA proves more villainous than the young Californians who betray their country to the Soviet Union. Brian De Palma explores the same theme in *Mission Impossible* (1996), a film based on the popular

Cold War TV series (1966–73). In the original series, a team of Impossible Mission Force operatives led by Jim Phelps (Peter Graves) carry out extralegal missions to defend freedom-loving peoples from the machinations of totalitarian aggressors who are clearly identified with the Soviet Union and their client nations. In the De Palma film, however, the archvillain proves to be Phelps (Jon Voight) himself, a narrative shift that exemplifies a significant change in post–Cold War American culture: the widely held belief that the enemy of traditional democratic values is the very government once seen as essential to protecting them.

In other, perhaps more prophetic films, Russians and American become partners in hunting down criminals or preserving world peace (Michael Apted's *Gorky Park,* 1983; Walter Hill's *Red Heat,* 1988; and John McTiernan's *The Hunt for Red October,* 1990). McTiernan's adaptation of the Tom Clancy novel about a Soviet naval officer's decision to defect with his country's newest and most powerful nuclear submarine was the last of Hollywood's Cold War films. When it went into production, the Russia's underwater fleet posed a major threat to the United States. The year of its release saw the collapse of the Soviet Union and the end of the Cold War.

Neither the documentaries nor the feature films have been particularly accurate in their accounts of the Cold War years. Both have been compromised by tailoring historical evidence to fit dominant political and cultural assumptions, by preferring dramatic simplicity to political complexity, and by avoiding controversies that might reduce box office receipts or advertising revenues. As historical documents, however, they are quite successful in reflecting the same ideological perspectives held by the historians of the Cold War. From the late 1940s through the early 1960s, films accepted, if they did not always enthusiastically endorse, the need to contain communism through patriotic vigilance. From the later 1960s through the 1970s, films embodied the revisionist interpretations of the Cold War that dominated public discourse. When, in the 1980s, a revived Cold War promised to return America to an era when the country was stronger and united against a common enemy, Hollywood produced films that reflected that sense of nostalgia. Since the end of the Cold War in 1991, no Hollywood epic, no documentary (not even the twenty-four hours of CNN's *Cold War*) has managed to capture the complexity of an era that continues to be the subject of historical debate.

References

Filmography

Anarchy USA (1966, D)
The Atomic Café (1982, D)
Big Jim McLain (1952, F)
The Big Lift (1950, F)
The Birth of the Cold War (1997, D)
Blast from the Past (1999, F)
Cold War (1998–99, D)
David Halberstam's The Fifties (1997, D)
Dr. Strangelove, or: How I Learned to Stop Worrying and Love the Bomb (1964, F)
Fail-Safe (1964, F)
The Falcon and the Snowman (1985, F)
Guilty of Treason (1949, F)
Heartbreak Ridge (1986, F)
High Noon (1952, F)
The Hunt for Red October (1990, F)
Invasion of the Body Snatchers (1956, F; 1978, F)
Iron Curtain (a.k.a. *Behind the Iron Curtain*) (1947, F)
I Was a Communist for the FBI (1951, F)
Kiss Me Deadly (1955, F)
The March of Time (1948–51, D)
Mission Impossible (1996, F)
My Son John (1952, F)
Nightmare in Red (1955, D)
Night People (1954, F)
On the Beach (1959, F)
On the Waterfront (1954, F)
Our Man in Havana (1960, F)
Pickup on South Street (1953, F)
Point of Order (1964, D)
Red Dawn (1984, F)

Seeing Red (1983, D)
The Spy Who Came in from the Cold (1965, F)
Strategic Air Command (1955, F)
Stripes (1981, F)
The Thing from Another World (1951, F)
The Third Man (1949, F)
Torn Curtain (1966, F)
Victory at Sea (1953–54, D)
Walk East on Beacon (1952, F)

Bibliography

Chomsky, Noam. *Towards a New Cold War: Essays on the Current Crisis and How We Got There.* New York: Pantheon, 1982.

Gaddis, John Lewis. *The Long Peace: Inquiries into the History of the Cold War.* New York: Oxford University Press, 1987.

——. *The United States and the End of the Cold War: Implications, Reconsiderations, Provocations.* New York: Oxford University Press, 1992.

Kennan, George F. "The Sources of Soviet Conduct." *Foreign Affairs* 25 (July 1947): 566–582.

Lippmann, Walter. *The Cold War: A Study in U.S. Foreign Policy.* New York: Harper, 1947.

May, Elaine Tyler. *Homeward Bound: American Families in the Cold War Era.* New York: Basic Books, 1988.

May, Lary, ed. *Recasting America: Culture and Politics in the Age of the Cold War.* Chicago: University of Chicago Press, 1989.

Nitze, Paul H. *From Hiroshima: At the Center of Decision.* New York: Grove Weidenfeld, 1989.

Patterson, James T. *Grand Expectations: The United States, 1945–1974.* New York: Oxford University Press, 1996.

Quart, Leonard, and Albert Auster. *American Film and Society Since 1945.* New York: Praeger, 1991.

Rogin, Michael. *Ronald Reagan, the Movie: And Other Episodes in Political Demonology.* Berkeley: University of California Press, 1987.

Rollins, Peter. "*Nightmare in Red*: A Cold War View of the Communist Revolution." In John E. O'Connor and Martin A. Jackson, eds., *American History/American Film: Interpreting the Hollywood Image,* 134–158. New York: Frederick Ungar, 1979.

Sayre, Nora. *Running Time: Films of the Cold War.* New York: Dial Press, 1982.

Whitfield, Stephen J. *The Culture of the Cold War.* 2d ed. Baltimore: Johns Hopkins University Press, 1996.

Williams, William Appleman. *The Tragedy of American Diplomacy.* New York: Norton, 1959.

[PHILIP J. LANDON]

The Korean War

As Clay Blair explains in his appropriately entitled *The Forgotten War* (1987), the American public never regarded the Korean War (1950–53) as a heroic crusade. An advisor to President Harry S. Truman familiar with events in Korea referred to it as a "nasty little war" (Halberstam, 62). From the moment that the North Korean forces crossed the thirty-eighth parallel into the Republic of South Korea on June 25, 1950, the progress of the fighting gave rise to misgivings about the necessity of the war (see Cumings, *The Origins of the Korean War*), the strategic goals to be achieved (see Foot, *The Wrong War*), and the battlefield performance of American fighting men (see Leckie, *Conflict*). The war began with a series of defeats for the South Koreans and the American troops sent from Japan to aid them. Although the communist-dominated North and their supporters, the Soviet Union and Communist China, claimed to be defending itself against the aggressive policies of South Korea's President Syngman Rhee, President Truman interpreted the attack as another example of the dangerously expansionist policies of the Soviet Union. The desire to contain the spread of communism throughout the world, a policy articulated in what became known as the Truman Doctrine, prompted a massive buildup of American forces in the southern tip of the Korean Peninsula.

Within a week, the United Nations authorized an international force to halt the North's aggression, and the war became officially known as a "police action." Led by General Douglas MacArthur, the overwhelmingly American UN forces staged a series of successful counterattacks, and by the end of September the North Koreans had been badly defeated and pushed back across the thirty-eighth parallel. MacArthur continued driving north and by November had nearly reached the Manchurian border at the Yalu River when the Chinese joined in the fighting. By the spring of 1951, the Americans and their allies had retreated to the thirty-eighth parallel; Truman had dismissed MacArthur from his command; and the war had reached a stalemate that continued until the truce arrived at in July 1953.

Feature Films

Americans, who had little enthusiasm for the Korean War when it began, were increasingly disillusioned with its progress. A country that had emerged triumphant from World War II had little taste for a limited war that would not end in victory. It became even more unpopular as disagreements over its conduct led to the sacking of a popular general, as information about American POWs' collaborating with the Communists surfaced, and as Americans continued dying on the battlefield because truce talks stalled. The mood of disillusioned resignation is captured in Sam Fuller's *The Steel Helmet* (1951), released just six months after the war began. The central character, Sgt. Zack (Gene Evans), is a tough, cynical veteran of World War II who trusts no one and regards war not as a noble enterprise but as condition of existence. He sees little difference between his Korean enemies and his Korean allies. Events appear to confirm his suspicion when a group of enemy soldiers arrives disguised as Buddhist monks fleeing the communists. Unlike in the films of World War II, the furious combat achieves no noticeable goal, and the film ends with the ominous epitaph: "There is no end to this story." Fuller's next film, *Fixed Bayonets* (1951), uses the Korean conflict to explore the responsibilities of leadership in a brutal war without clearly defined goals. Cpl. Denno (Richard Basehart), embittered by what he sees as the futile sacrifice of fellow soldiers, refuses to lead them until the death of his platoon sergeant (the same Sgt. Zack from *The Steel Helmet*) makes him realize that "no one looks for responsibility" and leads the survivors of his platoon back to their regiment.

Fuller not only made two of the best-crafted Korean War films, but he also revealed the ways in which the generic conventions established during World War II could be adapted to the circumstances of the fighting in Korea. The war films of the 1940s focused on small groups of military men representing a cross-section of American society. Their ability to transcend internal conflicts and fight as a team proved the key to success in a climactic battle, and winning that battle was portrayed as crucial to America's ultimate victory (see "World War II: Feature Films" and "The American Fighting Man"). But in Fuller's films there are no climactic battles, and there is no assurance of a final victory, only the hope for survival. Those best suited to fight such a war are cold-blooded professionals like Zack or the hero (Robert Mitchum) of Dick Powell's *The Hunters* (1958). Nicknamed "the Iceman," he declares, "I'm regular Air Force. I don't have to be told [why we are fighting]."

More frequently, however, the protagonist's doubts about his mission become central to Korean War films and are exemplified in Mark Robson's *The Bridges at Toko-Ri* (1954) and Lewis Milestone's *Pork Chop Hill* (1959). Based on James Michener's well-received novella published a year earlier, *The Bridges at Toko-Ri* focuses on Lieutenant Harry Brubaker (William Holden), a naval aviator stationed on an aircraft carrier off the coast of Korea. The World War II veteran is understandably bitter at having been recalled to duty at the expense of his successful law practice. Nevertheless, he refuses to use his father-in-law's political influence to secure a noncombat assignment and takes part in the attack on the bridges at Toko-Ri. The operation is a success, but Brubaker's plane is forced down behind enemy lines. He dies wondering how he wound up "in a smelly ditch in Korea" fighting "the wrong war in the wrong place." American Admiral Tarrant (Frederick March) praises the dead lieutenant (who reminds him of a son killed in World War II) for selflessly helping to stop the spread of Communism. But the desolate image of Brubaker's body lying in the Korean streambed encourages an ironic reading of this concluding eulogy.

The same ambivalence concerning the lives sacrificed in Korea appears in *Pork Chop Hill*. The film recounts a fierce struggle to recapture a hill of no strategic value, a struggle that had come to symbolize the American dilemma in Korea, as military historian S. L. A. Marshall points out in his 1956 book of the same title. The peace negotiators at Panmunjon hope the effort will symbolize American resolve, convincing the Communists that the UN forces will not accede to improper Communist demands in order gain an early cease-fire. Despite his own doubts and his awareness that his men see their mission as futile, Lieutenant Joe Clemons (Gregory Peck) orders his company to attack and defend Pork Chop Hill. The assault succeeds, but his company is decimated by the Chinese defenders and then—in a command that bewilders and angers the combatants—ordered to abandon their prize.

Rapid advances followed by equally rapid retreats marked the sudden reversal of fortunes in the Korean fighting, and one of the consequences of these swift movements was that both sides took many prisoners. Widespread public discussions of Americans being brainwashed and of collaborating with their captors became the dominant themes of a subgenre of the war film: narratives of life as a POW. Although early evidence suggests that, despite the harsh life they were forced to endure, the vast majority (perhaps 95 percent) of American prisoners resisted their captors (Harrison), the few who did collaborate were used as examples of a decline in military discipline and the general decline of American cultural values (Kinkead). The first of the Korean prison camp films, Andrew Morton's *Prisoner of War* (1954), focuses on both collaboration with the enemy and Communist brainwashing techniques. An American intelligence agent (Ronald Reagan) allows himself to be captured in order to see firsthand conditions in the North Korean prison camps. He sees the brutalities suffered by American prisoners, but it turns out that an apparent collaborator is also an American agent on the same mission, and the Americans establish their immunity to Communist manipulation. Not much better than this facile and improbable piece of propaganda is Lewis Seiler's *Bamboo Prison* (1955), a Korean War version of Billy Wilder's World War II POW drama *Stalag 17* (1953), in which a falsely accused collaborator proves to be a loyal American.

Films that dealt more thoughtfully with the issues of brainwashing and collaboration were equally anxious to vindicate the accused. In Arnold Lavin's *The Rack* (1956), an ex-prisoner (Paul Newman) is guilty of collaboration, but the blame is attributed to his traumatic childhood. Similarly, an American officer (Richard Basehart) accused of signing a false confession in Karl Malden's *Time Limit* (1957), is defended at his trial by an attorney who reveals that the ex-POW has acted to save the lives of sixteen prisoners.

The most famous film to dramatize the themes of collaboration and brainwashing (and arguably one of the two best American films dealing with the Korean War) is John Frankenheimer's *The Manchurian Candidate*

FIGURE 10. *Pork Chop Hill* (1959). Lt. Joe Clemons (Gregory Peck, left foreground) stands in stoic ambivalence at the thought of leading his men on a pointless strategic mission in Korea that will surely kill many in the company. Courtesy Melville Production.

(1962). Part psychological thriller and part political satire, it is the story of Raymond Shaw (Lawrence Harvey), a decorated Korean War veteran who, after being kidnapped and subjected to brainwashing by his Chinese Communist captors, returns to the United States with no memory of the experience. He has been programmed to obey commands given to him by his American handler, and his mission is to assassinate an American presidential candidate. His handler turns out to be his own dominating mother (Angela Lansbury), a deep cover agent married to a right-wing, communist-hunting senator (James Gregory) selected to run on the ticket with the targeted candidate. With the help of a counterintelligence officer (Frank Sinatra), the plot is foiled, and Raymond manages to shoot his nefarious mother and McCarthy-like stepfather instead of the presidential candidate. The cartoonish characters and the improbable sequence of events diminish the film as a thriller, but it offers an insight into the political paranoia of Cold War America while foreshadowing the acts of Lee Harvey Oswald a year later.

The other film classic set in Korea, Robert Altman's *MASH* (1970), is probably more concerned with the political issues of the 1960s than with the Korean War itself. The film's many anachronisms (smoking marijuana, for example) suggest that the war in Vietnam rather than in Korea inspired the filmmakers. The focus of the film is a mobile surgical hospital, an innovation in treating battle casualties that saved many lives during the war and was the subject of an earlier film, Richard Brooks's *Battle Circus* (1953), a serious if pedestrian treatment. *MASH,* on the other hand, is a black comedy that satirizes the hollow ideals and windy pieties that justify both the war and the military system conducting it. A pair of surgeons, Hawkeye Pierce (Donald Sutherland) and Trapper John McIntyre (Elliott Gould), battles the bureaucratic hypocrisies and medical incompetence embodied in a superior officer (Robert Duvall). The film established Altman as a major director and served as the model for one of television's most popular and longest-running series (*M*A*S*H,* 1972–83). By the early 1970s, the cycle of Korean War films had run its course. Except for Terence Young's *Inchon* (1981), a U.S.-Korean production that has found its way onto all-time-worst-movies lists, Korea was no longer the subject of American feature films. Hollywood had lost interest in a war that the American public had largely forgotten.

Documentaries

As the fortieth anniversary of the Korean War approached, historians began to reappraise the conflict, and television networks, sensing a renewed interest in Korea, turned out a number of documentaries that reflected the widespread influence of historical revisionism. The earliest of the Korean War documentaries, which began to appear shortly after the hostilities began, were staunchly pro-American. John Ford's *This Is Korea* (1951) explains why it is necessary to resist Communist aggression in Korea, as does Joseph Browne's *Korea and Communism in the Pacific* (1953). The latter, which was produced by the Army Signal Corps and broadcast on NBC's *Youth Wants to Know* television series, features James Michener, the author of *The Bridges at Toko-Ri,* answering young people's questions about the necessity of an unpopular war.

Irving Lerner's *Suicide Attack* (1951) deplores the Chinese Communists' disregard for the value of human life, while Owen Crump's *Cease Fire* (1954), reenacts a battle fought just hours before the 1953 armistice is to begin. Like the fictional *Pork Chop Hill,* which dramatizes a similar battle, *Cease Fire* praises the resolution of UN forces and blames the Chinese and North Korean aggressiveness and treachery for the continuing bloodshed. The same Cold War ideology informed the documentary treatments of the Korean War, whether found in portraits of policy makers (Robert Foster's survey of Harry Truman's presidency, *H.S.T., Days of Decision* [1963]; and Louis Tetunic's eulogy to General Douglas MacArthur, *Old Soldier* [1964]) or reports on the continuing tensions in the divided Korea (for example, the CBS account of the tenth anniversary of the armistice, *Korea: The War That Didn't End,* 1963).

By the 1990s, however, the end of the Cold War and the increasing popularity of historical revisionism brought a very different political mood to documentary treatments of the Korean War. The CBS production *Korea—Forgotten War* (1987) and the History Channel's five-episode miniseries *The Korean War: Fire and Ice* (1999) focus more on the sacrifices made by the participants than on ideological issues in much the same way that films dealing with Vietnam managed to honor the frontline soldiers without staking out an ideological position on the war itself. *Korea: The Unknown War* (1990), a six-part effort produced by Thames Television in association with WGBH, Boston, lays much of the blame for the Korean War (and the Cold War in general) on the aggressively anticommunist policies of a United States determined to preserve its post–World War II hegemony in world affairs. *An Arrogant Display of Strength,* the title of the episode describing the United Nations counterattacks that drove the North Korean forces back to the Yalu River, exemplifies *The Unknown War's* ideological perspective. CNN's massive twenty-four-hour documentary, *Cold War* (1998–99), tries to achieve greater objectivity (or at least avoid contentious issues) by granting equal weight to the opposing interpretations.

These Korean War documentaries tend to use the same familiar film footage to exemplify radically different interpretations of the conflict. For example, the images of exhausted, nearly frozen American infantrymen retreating from North Korea has been used to illustrate the sacrifices necessary to contain communism *(This Is Korea),* the stoic resolve of the common soldier *(The Korean War: Fire and Ice),* and the bitter consequences of Douglas MacArthur's hubris *(The Unknown War).* As a result, although none of the films can match the scope and ideological balance of Clay Blair's book *The Forgotten War,* they provide examples of the ideological battles waged by journalists and historians over the past half century. In addition, the best of the feature films (*The Steel Helmet, The Bridges at Toko-Ri, Time Limit,* and *Pork Chop Hill*) offer rich and complex insights into the ambivalent and conflicted responses of the Americans who reluctantly supported a war in which the objectives were not clear and in which victory was impossible.

References

Filmography

All the Young Men (1960, F)
Bamboo Prison (1955, F)
Battle Circus (1953, F)
The Bridges at Toko-Ri (1954, F)
Cease Fire (1954, D)
Cold War (1998–99, TV)
Fixed Bayonets (1951, F)
H.S.T., Days of Decision (1963, TV)
The Hunters (1958, F)
Inchon (1981, F)
Korea—Forgotten War (1987, TV)
Korea: The War That Didn't End (1963, TV)
The Korean War: Fire and Ice (1999, TV)
The Manchurian Candidate (1962, F)
MASH (1970, F; 1972–83, TV)
The Men of the Fighting Lady (1952, F)
Mission over Korea (1953, F)
Old Soldier (1964, F)
Pork Chop Hill (1959, F)
Prisoner of War (1954, F)
The Rack (1956, F)
The Reluctant Heroes (1971, F)
Sabre Jet (1953, F)
The Steel Helmet (1951, F)
Suicide Attack (1951, F)
This Is Korea (1951, D)
Time Limit (1957, F)
Torpedo Alley (1953, F)
War Is Hell (1963, F)

Bibliography

Blair, Clay. *The Forgotten War: America in Korea, 1950–1953.* New York: Times Books, 1987.
Cumings, Bruce. *The Origins of the Korean War.* 2 vols. Princeton, NJ: Princeton University Press, 1981.
——. *War and Television.* London: Verso, 1992.
Edwards, Paul M. *A Guide to Films on the Korean War.* Westport, CT: Greenwood, 1997.
Foot, Dorothy. *The Wrong War: American Policy and the Dimensions of the Korean Conflict, 1950–1953.* Ithaca, NY: Cornell University Press, 1985.
Halberstam, David. *The Fifties.* New York: Villard, 1993.
Harrison, Thomas D., with Bill Stapleton. "Why Did Some GI's Turn Communist?" *Colliers,* April 1953.
Kaufman, Burton I. *The Korean War: Challenges in Crisis, Credibility, and Command.* 2d ed. New York: McGraw-Hill, 1997.
Kinkead, Eugene. *In Every War but One.* New York: Norton, 1959.
Leckie, Robert. *Conflict: The History of the Korean War, 1950–1953.* New York: Putnam, 1962.
Marshall, S. L. A. *Pork Chop Hill.* New York: Morrow, 1956.
Michener, James A. *The Bridges at Toko-Ri.* New York: Random House, 1953.

[JAMES YATES]

The Mexican-American War and the Spanish-American War

Two of the most prominent and controversial of America's smaller military conflicts remain the war with Mexico (1846–48) and the war with Spain (1898). Their ramifications still reverberate more than a century later as immigration to the United States and trade alliances transform the complexion of U.S.–Latin American relations.

The War with Mexico

Effective in its execution, yet intensely ambiguous for national consciousness, the American conflict with Mexico remains a controversial episode in our military and political history. Though now considered a "forgotten war," it was a defining moment which forged new identities for both the United States and Mexico. For America, which at midcentury was a nation still in search of a national identity, the war became an important step in self-definition. As America's first foreign war, the conflict with Mexico, which engendered both public enthusiasm and remarkable military successes pushed national pride to the point of chauvinism. Ultimately, the war reinforced popular convictions concerning the superiority of an exuberant nation, its republican government, and its Manifest Destiny.

The origins of the American conflict with Mexico are rooted in the expansionist ideology of Manifest Destiny and dramatic socioeconomic change—the older values of patriotism and heroism were seemingly threatened by commercial, industrial, and material advancement. The outcome of the war with Mexico added more than a million square miles of territory to the United States—including the present states of Texas, New Mexico, Arizona, and California. As the first war "fought in the media," the conflict fueled popular passions through heroic songs, plays, paintings, and lithographs, bringing the first reassurance since the War of 1812 that Americans could still act heroically in the service of their republic. However, a darker consequence—internal division—threatened the Union. The conflict—denounced as a cruel act of aggression (by New Englanders as diverse as Henry David Thoreau and Daniel Webster) and celebrated as a necessary step in expansion and development (by presidents James K. Polk and John C. Calhoun)—fueled the slavery debate that eventually led to the Civil War.

From the Mexican perspective, insatiable American ambition, aided and abetted by the Mexican government's own internal weaknesses, brought about the war and "the massive theft" of half of its territory through the 1848 Treaty of Hidalgo (Lopez, 22). In response to President Polk's annexation of Texas, coupled with his gradual push of U.S. troops into disputed territory, the Mexican government retaliated for what it saw as acts of aggression. For Mexico, the end of the war ushered in demoralization and turmoil, social restructuring, and economic collapse for Mexico and the creation of what we now call Chicano culture. In this vibrant border culture, the war is not forgotten. According to Mexican historian Jesus Velasco-Marquez, Mexicans still "feel aggrieved that the United States invaded their country and occupied their capital" (Christensen and Christensen, 4).

The Mexican War escalated gradually: first came the Texas Revolt of 1836, with the massacre at the Alamo followed quickly by a stunning victory for Sam Houston's forces at the Battle of San Jacinto; later came a more sustained conflict, involving the American armed forces in such well-remembered actions as the U.S. Marines' assault on "the Halls of Montezuma"—that is, Mexico City.

The Mexican-American War on Film

Hollywood's treatment of the Mexican War largely concentrates on the 1836 revolt of Texas settlers against "Mexican tyranny," usually centering on the siege and massacre at the Alamo. Filmmakers forfeit historical accuracy for patriotic posturing in films ranging from Frank Lloyd's *The Last Command* (1956) and Byron Haskin's *The First Texan* (1956) to Burt Kennedy's woeful 1987 TV miniseries based on Lon Tinker's classic *Thirteen Days to Glory* and the banal 1993 miniseries based upon James Michener's *Texas.* Although not without its critics, John Wayne's 1960 three-hour account serves as the most durable and successful mythic portrayal. Using hundreds of extras and sparing no expense (he financed the production) in recreating the historical details of the siege, Wayne's *Alamo* is stirring in its sense of patriotic vision and heroic sacrifice, as is the IMAX version, *Alamo: The Price of Freedom,* which is shown on a six-story screen with six-track stereo sound every two hours at the Rivercenter in San Antonio—only some five hundred yards from the Alamo's historic remains.

During 1998, three Mexican War films were released: a two-hour cable television film, entitled *Two for Texas,* focusing on the Battle of San Jacinto; a four-hour PBS documentary on the 1846–48 conflict; and a History Channel documentary examining the history of Mexico. Based on James Lee Burke's novel, Turner Network Television's *Two for Texas* (directed by Rod Hardy and written by Larry Brothers) concentrates on the events immediately following the siege, emphasizing that Sam Houston's Texas Volunteer Army avenged the Alamo defeat less than thirty days after the tragedy. Though closely attentive to historic detail, *Two for Texas* fails as an epic because of its excessive attention to the melodramatic plight of its protagonists, two Louisiana prison escapees (played by Kris Kristofferson and Scott Barstow) accidentally swept up by the winds of war.

More ambitious in both scope and substance, the PBS documentary *The U.S. War with Mexico, 1846–48* is a meticulously researched and engrossing examination of the origins, events, figures, impact, and remembrance of the conflict. Produced by KERA Dallas/Ft. Worth, the four-hour film (which debuted nationally on September 13–14, 1998) blends interviews, period photographs and drawings, personal letters, and diary entries into the most significant cinematic treatment available. Sylvia Komatsu, executive producer of the series, resolved to present multiple perspectives in order to produce an accurate, balanced, and compelling story of a disputed history. According to Rob Tranchin, the program's coproducer and writer, "The binational nature of the project was our biggest challenge—it always, in a way, had two heads. We were trying to account for both the U.S. and Mexican perspectives without having each cancel out the other point of view" (Stabile, 12).

The extensive collaboration of experts from the United States and Mexico did indeed produce a wide range of interpretations. KERA also provided a number of teaching materials, including a companion book, a curriculum kit designed for middle and secondary schools, and a fascinating Web site (http://www.pbs.org/kera/usmexicanwar/) amplifying the issues broached by the documentary. The conflicting legacies resulted in complicated storytelling that KERA strived to overcome by including historians and resources from both countries. Thus, a significant element of the KERA documentary is its emphasis on the Mexican perspective; some Mexican scholars view the conflict as not merely a war fought over territory but a metaphysical violation on the part of expansionist America—a violation of language, labor, and culture. Other Mexican sources view the war as a matter of security that Mexican authorities were unable to meet—in addition to fighting the Americans, many Mexican factions were fighting each other. Others come very close to echoing nineteenth-century Mexican nationalist José Maria Lafragua's demand that the United States return the unjustly acquired territory to Mexico. "Did Polk have a vision of how the war was going to take place when he sent Taylor to the Rio Grande?" Tranchin asks rhetorically. "In the main, our American scholars felt that he didn't know—that he was reacting as much as acting. Our Mexican scholars felt Polk had a plan and was carrying out that plan. These are tricky shoals to navigate. When the narrator is involved, we make sure that the narrator doesn't plant a seed where we can't be sure" (Stabile, 13).

The History Channel aired in 1998 a four-part documentary, *Mexico,* a comprehensive historical overview. The film's second episode, "From Independence to the Alamo," thoroughly examines the initial conflict between Mexico and the United States and its origins in slavery, taxation, and Yankee settler rebelliousness toward Mexico City control. This conflict flares into open hostility leading to the Mexican siege of the Alamo and the later surprise attack at San Jacinto. Along the way, the filmmakers provide commentary from Mexican scholars, who maintain that the Alamo has been overemphasized and should be seen as merely one chapter in a long history of American incursions into Mexico. For Americans, the battle was a defining moment that provided a rallying cry for vengeance; especially for filmmakers, the Alamo provides an opportunity to condense sixteen years of Texas history into a compact narrative. The third episode, "Battle for North America," treats the Mexican War as a product of Polk's obsession with Manifest Destiny and Mexico's refusal to accept the annexation of Texas by another country. "War," the film holds, "is what Polk wanted. Mexico was an obstacle of the dream of an America 'from sea to shining sea.'" Polk found a convenient excuse for war in an old border dispute between Texas and Mexico. The film also discusses internal opposition to the war on both sides of the border.

In 1999, MGM released *One Man's Hero,* starring Tom Berenger, which chronicles the life of Major John Riley and the Saint Patrick's Battalion, a unit consisting of Irish Catholic immigrants who deserted from the U.S. Army during the Mexican-American War to take up arms against their former countrymen. According to the fact-based storyline, President Polk, with the backing of Southern slave states, raised an army using the sons of Irish immigrants, who joined with the promise of full citizenship for their families and forty acres of western land. After encountering pervasive nativism and anti-Catholic prejudice, the Irish troops deserted and fought for the Mexicans. Since the monumental *volte face,* generations of Mexicans have regarded Riley as a folk hero, though director Lance Hool, who labored for three decades to bring the story to the screen, doubts whether American audiences would have the same sympathetic reaction: "After all, the Saint Patrick's were deserters. But they were also fighting for a cause they believed in [i.e., freedom from intolerance], a quality Americans still appreciate today" (Wherry, 89). The film follows on the heels of the 1996 documentary by Mark Day called *The San Patricios,* which was shot on location in Texas, Mexico, and Ireland. The documentary includes interviews with American and Mexican historians, writers, and journalists and has been broadcast by RTE in Ireland, Televisa in Mexico, and more than a dozen PBS stations in the United States. In September 1997, the St. Patrick's Battalion was honored in a commemoration ceremony in Mexico City with

Mexican President Ernesto Zedillo, Ireland's ambassador to Mexico, and other government dignitaries.

The Spanish-American War

Originating in the Cuban struggle for independence from Spain, the Spanish-American War, inflamed by yellow-press sensationalism, became America's first military conflict with a foreign power since the War with Mexico. It "wasn't much of a war, but it was the best one we had" reported one American official (Williams, 317). Military hostilities commenced in April 1898 and ended only five months later. The Spanish conflict was, in Secretary of State John Hay's famous words, "a splendid little war," with low casualties (385 U.S. soldiers killed in battle) and a quick and decisive victory. The most important battles for ground forces lasted only one month, with the press reporting each action extravagantly. More than five thousand servicemen died of malaria and yellow fever because—against recommendations from the army—the war was fought during the months of summer contagion. In spite of the brevity of the conflict, the Spanish-American War is a turning point in the national experience because it thrust America into world politics and spurred the opening of Latin America to Yankee influence. The subsequent expansion of trade and security proved problematic in the Pacific and Caribbean regions, so much so that the nation eventually turned away from the adventurism and empire building of 1898. More important, the war hastened the nation's acceptance of international responsibilities commensurate with its might while effectively ending Spain's long history as a colonial power.

Beginning in 1895, with rebellion breaking out in the jewel in the crown of Spain's shrinking empire, Cuba, Americans supported the rebels attempting to overthrow Spanish rule. A relatively recent U.S. tariff on sugar plunged the island into depression, jeopardizing U.S. investments. A cry of "Cuba Libre" resounded throughout the island as poet José Martí parlayed the growing peasant dissatisfaction into a revolutionary movement and began guerilla attacks on cane fields and mills. Spanish officials retaliated by herding 300,000 suspects into squalid concentration camps. America's "yellow press," seeing an opportunity to increase circulation, fanned public opinion and built sympathy for the Cubans by highlighting Spain's brutal excesses. In early 1898, pro-Spanish loyalists rioted in Havana, prompting the arrival of the battleship *Maine* to protect American citizens. Late in the evening of February 15, the ship mysteriously exploded and sank, killing 266 Americans. The sinking outraged the American public and, with reconciliation between Spain and Cuba remote, President William McKinley asked Congress to authorize the use of force.

Although more than 288,000 Americans served, one infantry action in the four-month conflict has been enshrined in the American consciousness. "The Rough Riders," the 1st U.S. Volunteer Calvary Regiment and their leader, Lieutenant Colonel Theodore Roosevelt, underwent a transformation into mythic warriors when their most decisive engagement, the Battle of San Juan Hill (actually Kettle Hill) on July 1, was celebrated by the press as a heroic microcosm of the entire war. Earlier, on May 1, in aiding the Filipino insurrection against Spain, Commodore George Dewey steamed into Manila Bay in the Philippines and briskly annihilated the Spanish fleet. Previously, American plantation owners in Hawaii had aided in the overthrow of Queen Liliuokalani's government and appealed to Congress to annex the islands. In July, McKinley successfully pushed an annexation bill through Congress, capturing the islands as an important strategic and commercial gateway. With American forces in both Cuba and the Philippines, Spanish resistance quickly collapsed; after the invasion of Puerto Rico, Spain, realizing the war was a lost cause, sued for peace. With the Treaty of Paris on December 10, America and Spain agreed on terms: independence for Cuba and cession of the Philippines, Puerto Rico, and Guam to the United States in return for a $20 million payment to Madrid. The formal annexation of Hawaii, Wake Island, and, in 1899, Samoa completed the agreement. With control of the Philippines, the United States believed it possessed a good check against Japanese and German expansion in the region; on the Caribbean side, it gained port facilities at Guantanamo Bay, a base considered indispensable for the defense of the soon-to-be-built Panama Canal.

The Spanish-American War on Film

Writer-director John Milius, an aficionado whose *The Wind and the Lion* (1976) had offered a respectful portrait of Teddy Roosevelt, brought the Rough Riders to television in a four-hour film for Turner Network Television, *Rough Riders* (1997), Hollywood's most comprehensive cinematic treatment of the war. The film, which stars Tom Berenger as Roosevelt, along with Sam Elliot, Chris Noth, and Buck Taylor, accurately traces the formation of the volunteer unit, its training, and its battles in Cuba, climaxing with the famous charge up San Juan Hill. The opening montage blends newspaper headlines, political cartoons, and footage of the *Maine* to evoke the origins of the conflict. Reflecting the multicultural sensibility of the 1990s, the film stresses the ethnic diversity of the unit, a rainbow mixture of cowboys, outlaws, Mexican Americans, and Ivy Leaguers. It also features fairly accurate discussions among characters regarding the reasons for the war, and the texture of the conflict, including details about the infamous promotional efforts of yellow journalist William Randolph Hearst (George Hamilton).

In 1998, the History Channel presented the two-hour *The Spanish-American War: Birth of a Super Power* to commemorate the hundredth anniversary of the conflict. The Lou Reda production depicts the war as changing the United States from "a political pygmy to a dominating world power." Beginning with the sinking of the *Maine,* the "most controversial beginning of an American war," and the ruthless counterinsurgency policy of Spain against Cuban insurrectionists, the documentary traces the conflict in the Pacific and in Cuba against the backdrop of a "new American restlessness," using archival footage, reenactments, and comments from historians. The film explores the underlying conflict in American motivations between idealism (to help abused people) and realpolitik (to gain territory). The two-part series *Destiny of Empires: The Spanish-American War of 1898* solidly explores the causes, characters, and political consequences of the war; *"Remember the Maine": The Roots of the Spanish-American War* uses archival footage, newspaper excerpts, and historical documents to trace the roots of the conflict, while *The Spanish-American War: A Conflict in Progress* competently examines the conduct of the war from Roosevelt's Rough Riders to the Treaty of Paris.

On August 23, 1999, PBS aired *Crucible of Empire: The Spanish-American War,* which combined historical footage, crisp narration by actor Edward James Olmos, and interviews, including one with historian Stephen Ambrose, who exonerates American actions: "We had to find some new outlet for our energy, for our dynamic nature, for this coiled spring that was the United States. With the frontier gone, there was something akin to a panic among people." The documentary, though not a diatribe against American imperialism, traces how the nation grappled with its new role as a colonial power. In Spain, defeat meant not only the loss of territory but also a deep examination of its political and military institutions by what would be called "the generation of '98"; indeed, the war still rankles Spaniards a century later.

From Romance to History

Through cinematic treatments of the conflicts with Mexico and Spain, filmmakers have moved from the more romantic approaches to historical accuracy. Whereas John Wayne's sprawling 1960 account of *The Alamo* resounds with heroic and patriotic fervor in its treatment of U.S.-Mexican relations a decade before open hostilities erupted, the 1998 PBS/KERA documentary *The U.S. War with Mexico: 1846–48* presents an engrossing, thoroughly researched account of the origins and continual impact of the conflict. Likewise, the History Channel's comprehensive history, *Mexico,* illuminates not only the development of the nation but also the crunching economic and cultural effects of its conflict with the United States. Lance Hool's recent theatrical interpretation *One Man's Hero,* though controversial, uncovers an often overlooked aspect of the war—that of the Irish immigrant—and its relation to both sides of the conflict. With the centenary of the Spanish-American War, filmmakers presented both dramatic and documentary treatments of the conflict that established the United States as a major global player in the twentieth century. John Milius's dramatic and accurate depiction of *Rough Riders,* the History Channel's examination of *The Spanish-American War: Birth of a Super Power,* and PBS's *Crucible of Empire* examine not only the central causes and events of the brief conflict but also America's subsequent superpower status and its effect on the national consciousness. Throughout each treatment, basic themes emerge: expansion and assimilation, loss and transformation, and shifting individual and national perception. As the cinematic history of these two conflicts reveals, the ramifications continue to resound not only in U.S. relations with Mexico and Spain but also with its own citizens and its own national memory.

References

Filmography

The Alamo (1960, F)
The Alamo: Thirteen Days to Glory (1987, TV)
Captains and the Kings (1974, TV)
Crucible of Empire: The Spanish-American War (1999, D)
Destiny of Empires: The Spanish-American War of 1898 (1998, D)
The First Texan (1956, F)
The Last Command (1956, F)
Mexico (1998, D)
One Man's Hero (1999, F)
Rough Riders (1997, TV)
The San Patricios (1996, D)
The Spanish-American War (1998, D)
Texas (1993, TV)
Two for Texas (1998, TV)
The U.S. War with Mexico: 1846–48 (1998, D)
The West of the Imagination: The Golden Land (1997, D)
The Wind and the Lion (1976, F)

Bibliography

Berner, Brad K. *The Spanish-American War.* Englewood Cliffs, NJ: Scarecrow, 1998.
Christensen, Carol, and Thomas Christensen. *The U.S.-Mexican War.* San Francisco: Bay Books, 1998.
Collier, Christopher, and James L. Collier. *Hispanic America, Texas, and the Mexican War, 1835–1850.* London: Marshall Cavendish, 1998.
Cosmas, Graham A. *An Army for Empire.* College Station: Texas A&M University Press, 1998.
Davis, William C. *Three Roads to the Alamo: The Lives and Fortunes of David Crockett, James Bowie, and William Barrett Travis.* New York: HarperCollins, 1998.
Johannsen, Robert W. *To the Halls of the Montezumas: The Mexican War in the American Imagination.* New York: Oxford University Press, 1985.
Lopez, Lalo. "Legacy of a Land Grab." *Hispanic,* September 1997.
McCullough, David. *Mornings on Horseback.* New York: Simon & Schuster, 1981.
Miller, Nathan. *Theodore Roosevelt: A Life.* New York: William Morrow, 1992.
Millis, Walter. *Arms and Men: America's Military History and Military Policy from the Revolution to the Present.* New York: Capricorn, 1956.
Musicant, Ivan. *Empire by Default: The Spanish-American War and the Dawn of the American Century.* New York: Henry Holt, 1998.
Santoni, Pedro. *Mexicans at Arms.* Dallas: Texas Christian University Press, 1996.
Stabile, Tom. "Crossroad of Conflict: Exploring the Legacy of the U.S.-Mexican War." *Humanities* (September–October 1998): 12–16.

Stevens, Peter. *The Rogue's March: John Riley and the St. Patrick's Battalion.* Dallas: Brassey, 1998.

Trask, David F. *The War with Spain in 1898.* Lincoln: University of Nebraska Press, 1996.

Wherry, Rob. "Tale of the Turncoats." *George,* September 1998.

Williams, T. Harry. *The History of American Wars from 1745 to 1918.* New York: Knopf, 1981.

[PETER C. ROLLINS]

The Vietnam War

The Vietnam war pitted the United States and the Republic of Vietnam (South Vietnam) against the National Liberation Front (also known as the Vietcong) and the Democratic Republic of Vietnam (North Vietnam) in a struggle for control of South Vietnam, which in 1954 had been partitioned as a separate political entity by the Geneva Accords. The conflict was viewed by U.S. policymakers as a "test case" of American institutions and a demonstration of American resolve in the global fight against international communist expansion. SEATO allies agreed: Australia, New Zealand, Thailand, and South Korea sent troops, while the Philippines provided civilian personnel. In the early days of the conflict (1954–64), the United States provided advisors and economic support; in 1965, as the communist insurgency grew in strength (accompanied by political instability within the south), U.S. infantry units were committed. The number of U.S. forces peaked in 1969 with the deployment of 543,400 troops. Unlike most of their cinematic counterparts, U.S. troops aggressively pursued their missions. As historian George Herring has concluded: "American troops fought well, despite the miserable conditions under which the war was waged—dense jungles and deep swamps, fire ants and leeches, booby traps and ambushes, an elusive, but deadly enemy. In those instances where main units were actually engaged, the Americans usually prevailed, and there was no place in Vietnam where the enemy enjoyed security from American firepower" (153). Yet, by 1975, the war was lost, owing to a number of factors—many of them diplomatic and political—that are still the subject of heated discussion and debate. Ironically, Hollywood would virtually ignore the conflict while it was a contemporary controversy, but, after the debacle in 1975, it would exploit the military clash in a series of major feature films and documentaries.

Background

Vietnam, a French colony since the 1880s, was one of the first targets for the Japanese in the opening days of World War II. After the war, the French regained control of their former Indochina colony. In part because of fears that Communists would take over in France itself, the United States shunned the forces for independence in Vietnam (Herz, 15). The French-Vietnamese war (1946–54) ended in France's defeat at the hands of Ho Chi Minh's Communist Viet Minh. The Geneva Accords of 1954 divided the country into two parts—with the North occupied by the Communists and the South under the authoritarian regime of Ngo Dinh Diem, one of the last living noncommunist nationalists—who governed with benefit of extensive support from the United States.

In the meantime, Premier Nikita Khrushchev announced that the Soviet Union would spread Communism through "wars of national liberation." In 1959, the North Vietnamese initiated such an offensive, and, after a series of reversals for the South, American troops were brought into the conflict in force in 1965. Although there are different interpretations of its meaning, the Tet offensive of 1968 marked a turning point: despite a disaster for the Vietcong on the battlefields of South Vietnam, the media reports of Tet eroded public support for the conflict in the United States and seemed to confirm the worst predictions of the antiwar movement. American troops fought on, but morale in the field eroded steadily after February 1968. When Richard Nixon assumed the presidency in 1969, he vowed to "Vietnamize" the fighting and to withdraw U.S. forces gradually. By March 1973, all U.S. combat units had departed Vietnam. With the passage of the Case-Church Amendment in 1973, all U.S. support of the South ceased, despite previous pledges during the Paris Peace negotiations by President Nixon and Secretary of State Kissinger. After some false starts, the North invaded the South in a traditional, cross-border assault in the spring of 1975 and took possession of Saigon (now Ho Chi Minh City) at the end of April, bringing the military phase of the struggle to an end. In response to the subsequent repression by the North, hundreds of thousands of South Vietnamese took to the sea, becoming "boat people." Many would die in this desperate flight to avoid Communist tyranny and "reeducation," but many others would become American citizens—immigrants who are now among our most hard-working and successful neighbors.

America's involvement in Vietnam was an outgrowth of what was called "the doctrine of containment," elaborated by diplomat George Kennan. It called for the United States to resist Soviet expansionism where it affected vital interests. In 1947, President Harry S. Truman announced what was called "The Truman Doctrine," an unambiguous statement that the United States would oppose Communist aggression. Much of the disagreement about the meaning of the Vietnam conflict stems from the varying interpretations of the putative threat—or nonthreat—of the Soviet Union and Communist China. McGeorge Bundy and Walt W. Rostow, national-security advisors to Presidents Kennedy and Johnson, saw their Vietnam strategy as a logical extension of the stance defined for America by Kennan and Truman.

For many reasons, the U.S. government decided against "selling" the commitment to Vietnam as it had the struggle of World War II. Most historians believe that Lyndon B. Johnson, who inherited Vietnam when he became president in 1963, feared that too much beating on the war drums would distract attention away from his Great Society programs; both Johnson and his secretary of state, Dean Rusk, also feared that the delicate efforts to win the struggle through gradual escalation would be disrupted if the American people became too aroused. (Many would later regret this decision to soft-pedal public information.)

Meanwhile, commercial television reported the war. Believing that the press would serve them in a patriotic fashion, the armed forces provided reporters with helicopter rides and full access to military operations. That assumption proved to be misguided. Night after night, American viewers saw their boys hurt or dying on the nation's television screens in a conflict insufficiently justified by their government. Especially during the Tet offensive of 1968, the stories from Vietnam stressed ineptitude and defeat, disaffecting the public permanently. Vietnam has been called America's first television war, and the ramifications of that novelty are still being explored by scholars and filmmakers. Referring to Walter Cronkite's famous special reports during the offensive, one insightful commentator with a gift for exaggeration described the Vietnam War as the first American military conflict to be called off by a television anchor.

Vietnam was a watershed event in modern American history; the war had a profound impact on American national identity. Indeed, the "Vietnam Syndrome" still casts a shadow over the country's foreign policy. The much-vaunted "Powell Doctrine" concerning the commitment of U.S. forces is a direct outgrowth of Secretary of State Colin Powell's experience as an infantry company commander in Vietnam and was formulated to avoid the "quagmire" that sullied the international reputation of a superpower with the best of intentions.

Historical Scholarship

The rationale for U.S. involvement in Vietnam is most succinctly described in Martin F. Herz's *The Vietnam War in Retrospect.* Ambassador Herz explores the historical roots of the conflict, the Geneva Accords, the concerns about "Wars of National Liberation," the Tet offensive, and television, together with the post–Tet offensive trends. He clearly links the defeat of the South to America's failure to live up to its commitments. Henry Kissinger's monumental volume *Diplomacy* (1994) devotes considerable attention to the Truman Doctrine and the doctrine of containment—to include their successful application in Korea from 1950 on as opposed to their inept application in Vietnam. It was Kissinger, of course, who extricated America from Vietnam and who led the negotiations with Hanoi during the Paris Peace talks of 1973. Long before Kissinger's overview, Guenter Lewy in *America in Vietnam* (1978) studied the moral issues in relation to the war and concluded that the repression imposed by the Communists after 1975 "lends strength to the view that the American attempt to prevent a communist domination of the area was not without moral justification" (441).

The interpretations of the war are varied, but—in relation to U.S. policy—they tend to stress that either the United States miscalculated how difficult it would be to win its war (while simultaneously reforming an authoritarian regime in the South) or that our involvement was both politically and morally wrong—that we were meddling in a civil war in which the Vietnamese people were struggling to determine their political destiny. Still others have argued that the destiny of Vietnam was not of vital interest to the United States—and, therefore, the U.S. commitment was a mistake from the beginning.

The most strident attack on U.S. motives and policies is Gabriel Kolko's *Anatomy of a War: Vietnam, The United States, and the Modern Historical Experience* (1986). For Kolko, every Vietcong is a self-effacing nationalist yearning for freedom and every South Vietnamese official a corrupt and dictatorial puppet of the American exploiters. Also stridently critical, albeit less ideological, is Neil Sheehan's Pulitzer Prize–winning volume *A Bright Shining Lie: John Paul Vann and America in Vietnam* (1988), a monumental work adapted for television by HBO in 1998. So much of the writing from this perspective takes America to task for its (supposed) arrogance after the great victory in World War II. The Kolko approach stresses our unconscious transformation into a society that promotes the interests of exploitative corporations over people—a trend Kolko traces back to domestic developments during the Progressive Era at the end of the nineteenth century. The Sheehan approach condemns America for losing its democratic roots and sense of humanity in our blustering efforts, after World War II, to transform other cultures into mirror images of our own.

In recent days, there has developed among military historians what might be labeled a "Krepinevich School" of criticism—named for Andrew F. Krepinevich, whose *The Army and Vietnam* (1988) attracted much attention because the critical study was written by an Army officer on active duty. According to the Krepinevich critique, General William Westmoreland, the commander in Vietnam from 1964 to 1968, made a fundamental strategic error by focusing on destruction (attrition) of main force units rather than concentrating on pacifying—and occupying—individual villages. Neil Sheehan supports this analysis, attributing this alternative approach to General Victor Krulak, a close advisor to President Kennedy, whose innovative ideas about counterinsurgency were rebuffed by the Army. Rebuttals of these criticisms can be found in books by General Phillip Davidson, Westmoreland's intelligence chief. Colonel Harry Summers (d. 1999) took the position that the United States should have blocked infiltration into the South, leaving to the army of the Republic of South Vietnam (ARVN) the task of village pacification. The military strategists continue their debate with Westmoreland as the villain. Not even mea culpa books by major players such as Robert S. McNamara have relieved the shadow over a caring leader's legacy.

Documentary Films

The documentary record of the Vietnam war is rich and reflects the kinds of debates found in scholarship about the conflict. Although the U.S. government made a deliberate decision not to propagandize the American public, one film, *Why Vietnam?* (1965), closely follows the Frank Capra World War II model. The film opens with President Lyndon B. Johnson reading a letter from the mother of a young soldier in Vietnam. She wants an explanation of why her son is hazarding his life in a faraway land; the film uses Lyndon Johnson, Secretary of State Dean Rusk, and an omniscient narrator to explain the doctrine of containment and the threat of wars of national liberation. It argues that America has learned from the Munich Crisis before World War II—and in Berlin and Korea after the war—that "aggression unopposed is aggression unleashed." *Why Vietnam?* promises that all will end well if America learns from the past and takes a firm stand.

Peter Davis's *Hearts and Minds* (1974) is a powerful documentary that takes the Kolko/Sheehan approach to the war, with special emphasis on the notion that Americans have lost their sensitivity to other cultures. According to Davis, our obsession with communism has blinded us to the real nature of the struggles in the Third World; indeed, our wealth, our competitiveness, and our racism make us a menace to aspiring peoples around the globe. Through intercutting techniques and by pulling clips from hokey anticommunist feature films of the Cold War era, Davis creates a devastating portrait of a misguided superpower. When the producer, Bert Schneider, read a thank-you note from Hanoi at the 1974 Academy Awards presentations, his action spoke volumes about the Hollywood creative community's "spin" on the war. Michael DeAntonio's *In the Year of the Pig* (1968) is a more honest film by a declared radical who clearly and unequivocally opposed what he saw as American colonialism. Unlike Davis, DeAntonio does not sneer at his country and its warriors in the style of *Hearts and Minds* but opposes its policies with clear and powerful arguments. (De Antonio was a severe critic of *Hearts and Minds,* albeit from a leftist perspective.)

In 1983, the Public Broadcasting Service (PBS) aired a thirteen-part series about the war entitled *Vietnam: A Television History.* (The series was recycled at least three times during the next five years and purchased by countless schools and universities across the land.) The series was supposedly based on Stanley Karnow's *Vietnam: A History,* but many who have seen the series and read the book hold that the latter is a far more balanced presentation of the war and its complexities. The television series was so unbalanced that it sparked public protests by Vietnamese refugee groups in Washington, Houston, and Los Angeles. An outgrowth of these protests was a book entitled *Losers Are Pirates* (1985), a critique—episode by episode—of the errors and distortions of the series. In 1985, a Washington-based media watchdog group, Accuracy in Media, came forward with two programs that attempted to counter the PBS version: *Television's Vietnam: The Real Story* uses interviews with diplomats and historians—some of whom had been consulted by PBS and then ignored—to refute the PBS series. *Television's Vietnam: The Impact of Media* looks at the Tet offensive of 1968 in an attempt to examine, through specific stories, the impact of reporting on the American viewing audience, to include people working within the Johnson White House. Both films draw heavily from the work of Peter Braestrup, whose two-volume *Big Story* (1977) provided a scholarly foundation of media criticism by a working member of the media itself. (Braestrup, who died in 1997, had been a Marine infantry officer in Korea; in Vietnam, he served as *Washington Post* bureau chief. His previous combat exposure gave him a less alarmist perspective on battlefront pyrotechnics.)

With the explosion of the video market, the major networks have produced multiepisode boxed sets from their archives; unfortunately, they have not, for the most part, revised the errors and distortions of their reporting during the war years but recapitulate the same egregious misrepresentations—this time in the service of "history." A significant exception to this stale video record is a PBS series entitled *Battlefield: Vietnam*—a cluster of three programs that maintained an admirable objectivity toward both sides of the conflict as it presents detailed studies of specific engagements. (The series Web site included equally praiseworthy resources for study at www.pbs.org/battlefieldvietnam.)

Feature Films

Other than John Wayne's much-maligned *Green Berets*, which reached theaters in 1968, Hollywood was so afraid to cover the war *during* the conflict that Julian Smith wrote an entire book about the avoidance, *Looking Away: Hollywood and Vietnam* (1975). Smith concluded that if Vietnam themes emerged in motion pictures during and immediately after the war, they did so indirectly in such "historical" productions as *Little Big Man* (1970) and *Soldier Blue* (1970), where contemporary clashes between first- and third-world cultures were projected into the American past.

Boot Camp: Indoctrination of Killers?

During the 1960s, opposition to the "Establishment" was one of the most important themes in the counterculture. For that reason, it is not surprising to find that boot camp and infantry training are assailed in films about the era. These forms of indoctrination seemed to embody the regimentation and conformity demanded by those on the other side of America's "generation gap."

In the motion picture version of the musical *Hair* (1979), the Oklahoma protagonist, Clod (John Savage), participates in the love and freedom of the Age of Aquarius but is then drafted and sent to Vietnam. The Establishment's attack on Clod's individuality is symbolized by his hair*cut*. Naturally, not long after he is shipped out to Vietnam, he dies—an innocent victim of a senseless war machine. The screen adaptation of Philip Caputo's autobiographical novel *A Rumor of War* (1977; film 1980) carefully establishes that Marine Corps hazing misled young Philip, turning him into a callous, small-unit leader who forgot the morality of his Catholic upbringing. These portrayals in *Hair* and *A Rumor of War* are both a comment on the ostensible subject—the impact of the military regimen on impressionable, young men—and a statement about the nature of American institutions in the era of Woodstock.

The most devastating motion picture portrayal of military training is Stanley Kubrick's *Full Metal Jacket* (1987). The title refers to the cover of the 7.62-mm bullet fired by the M-14 rifle used by the Marines in the film, but it relates as well to the hard carapace with which the armed forces (supposedly) coat the sensibilities of raw recruits. Some of the young are destroyed by the unrelenting harassment of their stentorian drill sergeant; others succumb to the training and become distorted, amoral monsters when they reach the battlefield—confusing sex and violence, love and death in ways that could only be unraveled by a disciple of Freud. As an outsider to the Corps, Kubrick missed the positive effects of boot camp on most young Marines. They typically gain a sense of pride and self-confidence in having

FIGURE 11. *Full Metal Jacket* (1987). Stanley Kubrick depicts the vicious and unrelenting training of the marines. Gunnery Sergeant Hartman's (R. Lee Ermey, center front) constant abuse of recruit Leonard Lawrence (Vincent D'Onofrio, left) will finally incite the private to kill the sergeant and himself. The recruit known as "Joker" (Matthew Modine, center rear), the narrator and moral center of Kubrick's film, looks on. Courtesy Warner Bros.

completed a physically and mentally challenging thirteen weeks of training. As a film experience, Kubrick's version of Vietnam, based on the novel *The Short-Timers* by Marine combat veteran Gustav Hasford, is a powerful (and unfair) indictment of the Marine Corps and its sacrifices on the battlefield. For an entirely different view of Marine boot camp, see Jack Webb's 1957 film *The DI,* a post–Korean War paean to the tough training and discipline of a proud Corps. Webb's film was updated, though with an antiwar twist, in the 1970 made-for-TV movie *Tribes,* in which a tough-as-nails drill instructor (Darren McGavin) and a rebellious hippie draftee (Jan-Michael Vincent) face off with tragic consequences.

Small Units in Combat

Elsewhere in this volume, Robert C. Doyle speaks of the small unit as the core for war stories (see "The American Fighting Man"). Early in the war, two documentaries attempted to convey the textures of experience for soldiers in small units. In *A Face of War* (1968), Eugene Jones distills a three-month experience with a Marine unit into an hour-length cinema verité film. Half of the unit was injured during that period, as was the filmmaker, who was wounded twice. There is fighting, the pain and excitement of combat, but there is also the birth of a child—an event the tough, young Marines witness in awe. The company's gunnery sergeant has a prominent role in the film and exemplifies the kind of professionalism (and caring) that veterans associate with people in that venerable role—tough, but fatherly. An Army counterpart to this film is Pierre Schoendorffer's *The Anderson Platoon* (1967). The unit is named for its African American platoon leader, and this slice-of-life production—like *A Face of War*—shows how cooperatively combat soldiers lived and worked. There are firefights and wounds, but there is also time for play and for humor. No fraggings, no rapes, no shooting of prisoners or civilians enter this record of a typical U.S. Army unit in Vietnam. Indeed, both of these black-and-white documentaries convey an accurate portrait of American combat troops in Vietnam, 90 percent of whom told Harris pollsters in 1980 that they were happy to have served, and nearly 80 percent of whom denied that the United States had taken advantage of them (Rollins, "Popular Culture," 334).

Two feature films explore the war in close-up, taking two diametrically opposed perspectives: John Irvin's *Hamburger Hill* (1987) and Oliver Stone's *Platoon* (1986). *Hamburger Hill* focuses on an infantry squad (twelve men), part of a platoon (thirty-eight men) from the 101st Airborne Division involved in a ten-day assault on a North Vietnamese position near the Laotian border during May 1969. This battle was debated in the U.S. Senate as it was being fought and was condemned by Senator Edward Kennedy for its waste of American lives during a period in which the American military was supposed to be disengaging. The Army's response to the senator's criticism was that Hill 937 (Ap Bia Mountain) was fortified and occupied by an enemy regiment and that

FIGURE 12. *Hamburger Hill* (1987). An infantry squad and a platoon are ordered to take Hill 937 even as the U.S. military was under a call for disengagement. Courtesy RKO Pictures.

the U.S. Army's role in Vietnam was to seek out the enemy regular forces—with luck, away from built-up areas where civilians might be hurt—and to destroy them, especially during a time of disengagement. When the Americans finally reached the summit of the fortified mountain, they had lost fifty-six soldiers while killing more than six hundred of the enemy. Sam Zaffiri's eponymous book explores both the home- and warfront dimensions of the battle, while Irvin's feature film—not based on the book—examines the weapons, tactics, frustrations, hopes, and comradeship of Americans in battle. Black and white, schooled and unschooled, the soldiers of the 101st do their best to survive the maelstrom of war while completing their perilous mission. Michael L. Lanning, a Vietnam veteran who is also a military historian, has said that "this picture is extremely accurate in weaponry, equipment, [and] the use of artillery and air support" (240). Lanning also praises the film for showing the dedication and discipline of our troops in battle—factors foreign to most Hollywood histories.

Labeled by Lanning "the unkindest movie yet made about the Vietnam war," Oliver Stone's *Platoon* (1986) is a powerful study of a small unit in combat—but it is much more, in that the director depicts the unit as a microcosm for the cultural changes affecting American society in the 1960s. Viewers are led to believe that American troops regularly shot civilians, that our field commanders used troops as "bait," and that our servicemen were so undisciplined that they spent more time "fragging" each other than fighting an elusive enemy. ("Fragging" was a slang term during the era for attacks on officers and noncommissioned officers by disgruntled subordinates—who used fragmentation grenades to kill or injure their victims.) Stone, himself a combat veteran, comments broadly about American history when the most sympathetic father figure in the film, Sergeant Elias, explains, "We've been kicking ass for so long, it's about time we had ours kicked." The central character, Chris Taylor (Charles Sheen), is torn between the polarized values in the unit—he admires the grit and tenacity of Staff Sergeant Barnes (Tom Berenger), but he also aspires to the New Age masculinity represented by Elias (Willem Dafoe). Naturally, the two father figures are icons of the cultural forces of the day; significantly, Chris Taylor has to murder Barnes (the old values) to begin his new life. Unfortunately, along the way, the American platoon rapes Vietnamese villagers and shoots civilians indiscriminately—all at odds with the actual behavior of most American troops in Vietnam. Exasperated by Stone's distortions, Lanning concludes: "What is a shame for the viewer and an insult to every Vietnam veteran is that the vast majority of those who see it believe it is the ultimate true story of what really happened in the war" (293). To unmask Stone's claims about the autobiographical basis for *Platoon,* Robert Hemphill—Oliver Stone's company commander in Vietnam—produced a narrative entitled *Platoon: Bravo Company* (1998). Hemphill wrote the book, in part, because Stone's film had been successful in depicting "the average American soldier in Vietnam as a cruel, racist, pot-headed malcontent" (9), a view which the author tries to refute by narrating the events of a busy, painful, but professional year in combat with Bravo Company, 3d Battalion, 25th Division of the U.S. Army in Vietnam, 1967–68.

The Vietnam Veteran

There are almost 3.5 million veterans of the Southeast Asian conflict. Their attitudes toward country and service were plumbed by Harris pollsters in 1980—with results that inevitably surprise students because of the misrepresentation of veterans in popular Hollywood productions. Vietnam stories are stories of losers who return to our country as pathetic remnants, "walking wounded." Vietnam veterans (VVs) are rapists in *Platoon* and *Casualties of War* (1989)—indeed, the latter film is an extended rape over two hours in length; VVs are a "haunted generation" in the *Rambo* series starring Sylvester Stallone and in the Chuck Norris *Missing in Action* films; the VVs are psychologically haunted in *The House, Jacob's Ladder, Jackknife,* and *Taxi Driver* (in the last, Robert De Niro plays a troubled young man obsessed by violence); VVs are emotional loose cannons in *Welcome Home, Soldier Boys* (1972), where veterans go berserk and destroy a town; future VVs become enamored with "the Horror" in *Apocalypse Now* (1979)and the omnipresence of death in *The Deer Hunter* (1978); VVs (at least the unrepentant ones) suffer from masculinity problems—witness the Bruce Dern character in *Coming Home* (1978), the Henry Winkler character in *Heroes* (1977), and the John Terry character in *In Country* (1989); VVs are "guns for hire" in a Mafia underworld in *The Stone Killer* (1973). Little wonder that the public perceives VVs as victims at best and walking time bombs at worst. In marked contrast to these macabre portraits of veterans is an HBO documentary entitled *Dear America: Letters Home from Vietnam* (1987), produced by the New York City Vietnam Veterans Memorial. This television program shows sensitivity to the variety of

FIGURE 13. *Coming Home* (1978). An angry Captain Bob Hyde (Bruce Dern, left) confronts Luke Martin (Jon Voight, right), a paraplegic former infantryman in Vietnam who has been having an affair with Hyde's wife. Courtesy Jayne Productions and Jerome Hellman Productions.

Vietnam experiences while paying homage to all who served in a controversial overseas conflict.

In *Coming Home,* Jon Voight plays a paraplegic infantryman who is brought back to health and sexual fulfillment by the wife (Jane Fonda) of a Marine officer serving in Vietnam. Much of the dialogue for the film was extemporized; once into the production, Bruce Dern (who plays the Marine officer and husband) realized that his character was being trashed by Fonda and Voight. In response, Dern stopped telling his fellow actors what the Marine officer would say, hoping to rescue a modicum of dignity for his character. Like *Platoon,* director Hal Ashby's *Coming Home* propagandizes for countercultural values: the old kind of masculinity (Dern) is on the way out, to be replaced with a softer manhood represented by the paraplegic veteran (Voight), who has come to peace with himself by joining the antiwar movement. As Michael Lanning has observed, "Regardless of the merits of the film, anyone seeing it will understand why many Vietnam veterans are not 'fonda' Jane" (196).

Ron Kovic assisted Hal Ashby with details about paralyzed Vietnam veterans. His own story would reach the screen under the guidance of Oliver Stone in *Born on the Fourth of July* (1989). This biography of a young patriot turned antiwar protestor taps a powerful national myth, the myth of the American Adam. Ron Kovic was a gung-ho Marine who was a squad leader and a two-tour veteran. He protested against the Vietnam war only after he was wounded and lost his faith in God and country, in part because—the story explains—he was mistreated by an uncaring Veterans Administration. Rather than turning inward for strength, Kovic turned outward and became a spokesman for Vietnam Veterans Against the War—a role that culminates in his protest at the 1968 Republican convention in Florida and his opportunity to speak at the 1972 Democratic national convention. Oliver Stone created a powerful story of an American innocent who was first hoodwinked by patriotic slogans and then crushed by an impersonal government; in the end, however, the victim triumphs by talking back to power. In shaping this personal story, Kovic and Stone vindicated the rebellion of all who embraced the counterculture in the 1960s—especially Abbie Hoffman, an activist who appears in the film and to whom the film is dedicated. Hoffman, whose antiwar activities receive near-mythic treatment in the 2000 biopic *Steal This Movie,* died of an overdose of drugs shortly before *Born on the Fourth of July* was released—a sad ending, to be sure, but one more appropriate to the counterculture than to the experience of most Vietnam combat veterans.

Reconciling Visions

In spring 1999, the *Chronicle of Higher Education* reported that two professors at Barat College, in Lake Forest, Illinois, were team-teaching a course entitled "The Politics and History of the Vietnam War." James Brask was a reluctant draftee during the war, Robert Arnoldt a volunteer. The two veterans said that their chronological distance from the war has allowed them to disagree without being disagreeable. Ideally, such binocular vision will lead to dispassionate and detached studies that explain America's tragic loss in Vietnam—with luck, without explaining it away. Brask and Arnoldt's willingness to entertain complex analysis is exemplary, although this ecumenical attitude will take some time to reach America's newspapers, cable networks, and movie theaters.

References

Filmography

The Anderson Platoon (1967, D)
Apocalypse Now (1979, F)
Battlefield: Vietnam (1999, TV)
*Bat*21* (1988, F)
Born on the Fourth of July (1989, F)
Casualties of War (1989, F)
Coming Home (1978, F)
Dear America: Letters Home from Vietnam (1987, D)
The Deer Hunter (1978, F)
The DI (1957, F)
A Face of War (1968, D)
First Blood (1982, F)
Full Metal Jacket (1987, F)
Gardens of Stone (1987, F)
Good Morning, Vietnam (1987, F)
The Green Berets (1968, F)
Hair (1979, F)
Hamburger Hill (1987, F)
The Hanoi Hilton (1987, F)
Hearts and Minds (1974, D)
Heroes (1977, F)
In Country (1989, F)
In the Year of the Pig (1968, D)
Jackknife (1989, F)
Jacob's Ladder (1990, F)
The Killing Fields (1984, F)
Little Big Man (1970, F)
Magnum, P.I. (1980, TV)
Missing in Action (1984, F)
Missing in Action 2—The Beginning (1985, F)
1969 (1988, F)
Operation Tailwind (1998, TV)
Platoon (1986, F)
The Quiet American (1958, F; 2002, F)
Rambo II: First Blood (1985, F)
Rambo III (1988, F)
Return of the Secaucus 7 (1981, F)
Rolling Thunder (1977, F)

A Rumor of War (1980, F)
Running on Empty (1988, F)
Soldier Blue (1970, F)
The Stone Killer (1973, F)
The Strawberry Statement (1970, F)
Taxi Driver (1976, F)
Television's Vietnam: The Impact of Media (1986, D)
Television's Vietnam: The Real Story (1985, D)
Trial of the Catonsville Nine (1972, F)
Tribes (1970, TV)
Uncommon Valor (1983, F)
Vietnam: A Television History (1983, D)
The War at Home (1978, D)
Welcome Home, Soldier Boys (1972, F)
When Hell Was in Season (1979. F)
Why Vietnam? (1965, D)

Bibliography

Anderegg, Michael. *Inventing Vietnam: The War in Film and Television.* Philadelphia: Temple University Press, 1991.

Banarian, James. *Losers Are Pirates: A Close Look at the PBS Series* Vietnam: A Television History. Phoenix: Sphinx, 1985.

Braestrup, Peter. *Big Story: How the American Press and Television Reported and Interpreted the Crisis of Tet 1968 in Vietnam and Washington.* 2 vols. Boulder, CO: Westview, 1976.

Buhl, Paul M., and Edward Rice-Maximin. *William Appleton Williams: The Tragedy of Empire.* New York: Routledge, 1995.

Cleland, Max. *Strong at the Broken Places: A Personal Story.* Atlanta: Cherokee, 1989.

Davidson, Phillip B. *Secrets of the Vietnam War.* Novato, CA: Presidio, 1990.

——. *Vietnam at War: The History, 1946–1975.* Novato, CA: Presidio, 1988.

Eilert, Rick. *For Self and Country.* New York: Simon & Schuster, 1983.

Harris, Louis, and Associates, Inc. *Myths and Realities: A Study of Attitudes Toward Vietnam Era Veterans.* Washington, DC: Veterans Administration, 1980.

Hemphill, Robert. *Platoon: Bravo Company.* Fredericksburg, VA: Sergeant Kirkland's, 1998.

Herring, George. *America's Longest War: The United States and Vietnam, 1950–1975.* 2d ed. New York: Knopf, 1986.

Herz, Martin F. *The Vietnam War in Retrospect: Four Lectures.* Washington, DC: School of Foreign Service, 1984.

Jason, Philip. *The Vietnam War in Literature: An Annotated Bibliography of Criticism.* Pasadena, CA: Salem Press, 1992.

Karnow, Stanley. *Vietnam: A History.* New York: Viking, 1983.

Kennan, George. *American Diplomacy: 1900–1950.* Chicago: University of Chicago Press, 1951.

Kissinger, Henry. *Diplomacy.* New York: Simon & Schuster, 1994.

Kolko, Gabriel. *Anatomy of a War: Vietnam, the United States, and the Modern Historical Experience.* New York: Pantheon, 1985.

Krepinevich, Andrew F. *The Army and Vietnam.* Baltimore: Johns Hopkins University Press, 1988.

Lanning, Michael Lee. *Vietnam at the Movies.* New York: Ballantine, 1994.

Lewy, Guenter. *America in Vietnam.* New York: Oxford University Press, 1978.

Malo, Jean-Jacques, and Tony Williams, eds. *Vietnam War Films: Over 600 Feature, Made-For-TV, Pilot, and Short Movies, 1939–1992.* Jefferson, NC: McFarland, 1994.

McNamara, Robert S. *Vietnam in Retrospect: The Tragedies and Lessons of Vietnam.* New York: Times Books, 1995.

Podhoretz, Norman. *Why We Were in Vietnam.* New York: Simon & Schuster, 1982.

Powers, Richard Gid. *Not Without Honor: The History of American Anticommunism.* New York: Free Press, 1996.

Reich, Charles. *The Greening of America.* New York: Random House, 1970.

Rollins, Peter. "Using Popular Culture to Study the Vietnam War: Perils and Possibilities." In Peter Freese and Michael Porsche, eds., *Popular Culture in the United States,* 315–337. Essen: Die Blau Eule, 1994.

——. *The Vietnam War: Experiences and Interpretations in American Popular Culture.* Binghamton, NY: Haworth Press, 2003.

Schmidt, Peter. "Two Veterans Animate a Class on Vietnam." *Chronicle of Higher Education,* 5 March 1999.

Sheehan, Neil. *A Bright and Shining Lie: John Paul Vann and America in Vietnam.* New York: Random House, 1988.

Smith, Julian. *Looking Away: Hollywood and Vietnam.* New York: Scribner's, 1975.

Westmoreland, William C. *A Soldier Reports.* Garden City, NY: Doubleday, 1976.

Williams, William Appleton. *The Tragedy of American Diplomacy.* Rev. ed. New York: Norton, 1972.

Zaffiri, Samuel. *Hamburger Hill: May 11–20, 1969.* New York: Pocket Books, 1988.

[JAMES A. SANDOS]

Westward Expansion and the Indian Wars

White America's conquest of Native Americans on the plains and in the Southwest is an integral and tragic part of the settlement of the American West. Until the 1980s it had been, in many respects, an overlooked chapter in American history, often inaccurately told when recounted at all. Hollywood's treatment of the North American Indian Wars after the Civil War, however, reveals the complex interplay between academic and popular history, the emergence in the popular mind of the director as authoritative storyteller of the past, and the steadily expanding role of television—first in helping to instill stereotypes, and then in trying to revise them.

After the end of the Civil War, American movement west grew from a steady migration into a stampede. In an area where fewer than two million whites had lived before the war, an undaunted drive to seize prosperity from new land brought newcomers westward in unprecedented numbers. In twenty-five years, the white population increased to nearly 8.5 million. In the process, whites and their allies displaced or destroyed many of the Native American peoples, grouped in distinct cultures, who stood in the way. Violent struggle swept over the West for nearly three decades, with the occasional battle among military equals far outnumbered by one-sided massacres on the part of white civilians and soldiers alike. The final major episode in the Indian Wars came as a dreadful massacre by the U.S. Army of a group of desperately hungry Sioux surrendering at Wounded Knee, South Dakota, in late December 1890. That year the frontier closed, according to its chief historian, Frederick Jackson Turner, because the era of "free land" for Americans had come to a close. They had taken it all. But, in the process of white westward expansion and contact with "the simplicity of primitive society," Turner argued, "the forces dominating American [national] character" had emerged (28). Hollywood took that concept as inspiration for hundreds of films while downplaying the cost paid by Indians.

The military history of the Indian Wars following the Civil War in film focuses on two areas, the plains and the Southwest, and on two principal groups and their allies, the Sioux (now called the Lakota) and the Apache. (It should be noted in passing that two important campaigns are generally omitted: one against the Modocs in 1872–73 and another against the Nez Perce in 1877.) Occupying the northern plains were the Sioux (a congeries of Souian-speaking peoples including the Hunkpapa, Oglala, and Brulé), the Cheyenne, the Arapaho, and the Kiowa. The Comanche people held the southern plains. From 1866 to 1875, the U.S. Army fought more than two hundred battles, mainly against the Sioux; the second phase, from 1880 to 1887, centered on the Apache and its best-known tribe, the Chiricahua. The names of many Indian leaders remain in American memory: Red Cloud, Sitting Bull, and Crazy Horse from the Sioux; Cochise, Victorio, and Geronimo from the Apache.

The Indian Wars to the 1980s

Hollywood portrayal of Indians in these wars is often more complex than conventional wisdom about stereotypes suggests. Three sources, two literary and one experiential, mainly informed the Indian image on film. James Fennimore Cooper in *The Last of the Mohicans* (1826) gave Hollywood two Indian types: the noble forest dweller and the brutal savage. Many film students, however, overlook the other two sources. Helen Hunt Jackson wrote *Ramona* (1884) as a novel of social protest against what American "civilization" had done to California Indians. Hers was an anti-Turnerian view of the West written a decade before Turner. Three silent versions of *Ramona* were made, and the novel later became the subject of the first Cinemascope film; it was an important influence on other filmmakers who were to tackle the subject.

D. W. Griffith made the first version in 1910, with seventeen-year-old Mary Pickford as Ramona and Henry Walthall as the Indian, Alessandro. Griffith, who had played Alessandro on stage, drew from Walthall a mannered portrayal of stoic resignation in the face of injustice. Walthall's gestures (arms folded across his chest; arm around Ramona, face buried in her hair, free arm at his side; back to camera, head bent, arms slowly raised high above his head with fists clenched) formed an ongoing counterpoint to the Cooper-influenced dualism of Indian nobility and savagery.

The simulated "experience" of the frontier through the vehicle of "Buffalo Bill's Wild West Show," however, gave to millions of Americans and to the screen many of its lasting Indian images. For thirty years, twice a day and three times on weekends, William F. "Buffalo Bill" Cody's drama depicted four stock themes. First, the Deadwood Stage was attacked by mounted, gun-firing Indians and its passengers saved by Buffalo Bill; then a settler family's house was attacked by Indians, and again Buffalo Bill saved them; third, a wagon train was attacked by Indians, and again Buffalo Bill came to the rescue—but, following George Armstrong Custer's "Last Stand," Buffalo Bill rode into the arena with a sign behind him reading, "Too Late." As historian Richard White notes in an episode of the series *The West* (1996), there is something "deeply weird" about this view of American conquest of the West; instead of portraying the victors as conquering heroes, they are depicted as victims of Indian savagery. Such depictions became standard in filmmaking from the beginning while also sharing time with both the Cooper and Jackson visions. Thus Griffith could make *Ramona* (1910) for Biograph, telling his audience, "This is the story of the white man's injustice to the Indian" and three years later for the same company make *The Battle at Elderbush Gulch* around the "Indians-attack-the-settlers'-cabin" theme of Buffalo Bill's show, a contradiction that apparently did not trouble studio executives or directors.

John Ford's Western Campaigns

While "budget films" (B movies) recapitulated Buffalo Bill's stories endlessly, the upper tier of Hollywood productions showed a somewhat different West. The army—rather than the cowboy or settler—engaged the Indian in battle, and some serious films addressed that fact. John Ford devoted a trilogy to the army in *Fort Apache* (1948), *She Wore a Yellow Ribbon* (1949), and *Rio Grande* (1950), depicting a struggling military training raw recruits and trying to protect settlers from Indian depredations. Ford drew these plots from short stories by James Warner Bellah that first appeared in the *Saturday Evening Post.* Ford changed them to suit his own ideas, but they were infused with the Turnerian notion of the frontier and the inevitability of the triumph of civilization, interlaced with the Wild West shows' depictions of Indian savagery. In these films Ford raises the specter of a pan-Indian threat to destroy whites. Such a menace casts the army as victim and elicits audience sympathy for the expansionist cause. Ford filmed in Monument Valley of Utah and Arizona, and used Navajos (cousins to the Apache) for the non-speaking Indian roles. These Indians, like nature, are in the background, obstacles to be overcome; Army life on a frontier post is in the foreground. John Wayne appeared in all three Ford productions, a cavalry "everyman" imparting the wisdom of the Indian fighter. In these films women are dutiful and subordinate; men are generally correct. Sergeant Brittles (John Wayne), for example, repeatedly tells the young men in *She Wore a Yellow Ribbon,* "Never apologize—it's a sign of weakness," inculcating a male value by which error—especially error in conquering native peoples of the West—cannot be acknowledged.

Yet Ford made two films that go against such stereotypes, examining squarely the legacy of white racism in conquering the West: *The Searchers* (1956) and *Sergeant Rutledge* (1960). John Wayne portrays ex-Confederate Ethan Edwards in *The Searchers,* a man who recalls Herman Melville's description, in *The Confidence Man,* of the Indian hater par excellence as one "the hate of which is a vortex from whose suction scarce the remotest chip of the guilty race [Indian] may feel reasonably secure." Edwards knows the Comanche, whose name he pronounces repeatedly without the final "e," like an insider, one who has lived among them long enough to know their customs. But familiarity has produced hatred, not love. When Comanches kill his brother and family and kidnap two nieces, Edwards pursues them relentlessly. Early in the chase he finds his elder niece stripped, raped, and murdered. For six years he continues the search for the younger girl, obsessed with the thought that by then she will have mated with an Indian and therefore must be killed.

Two examples underscore the viciousness of Edwards's racism. Coming upon a dead brave, Edwards shoots the eyes out of the corpse; he knows that, according to their religion, the warrior will never find the next world without them. Edwards uses the term "religion" rather than "superstition" or "belief," further testifying to his intimate knowledge of his foe. At another point he comes upon a buffalo herd and shoots the animals, not from need, but to deny the Comanche food. At the fade he rescues, rather than kills, his remaining niece. He then disappears into the vastness of the land to continue his vendetta against any Indian he might encounter. Ford and Wayne drew a portrait of a truly repellent antihero whose existence runs counter to the "hero as victim" scenario.

FIGURE 14. *The Searchers* (1956). John Wayne, as ex-Confederate Ethan Edwards, personifies the evils of the white racist as he pursues Comanche Indians who have abducted his niece. Edwards's rage against any Indian in his path intensifies as he draws closer to the Comanche encampment. Courtesy C.V. Whitney Pictures and Warner Bros.

Woody Strode portrays *Sergeant Rutledge,* a distinguished "buffalo soldier" accused of the rape and murder of a teenage girl and the murder of her father, his post commander. Whites are willing to believe this heinous charge, despite Rutledge's impeccable record for bravery and fidelity as a soldier, because he is black and a white woman is the victim. Rutledge is not guilty of the rape-murder, but his trial and the widespread appeals to racism to convict him present a far different, and undoubtedly more accurate, view of post life than Ford depicted in his earlier cavalry trilogy. Both *The Searchers* and *Sergeant Rutledge* are good departure points for demythologizing the traditional cinematic renderings of the West.

Delmer Daves attempted a sympathetic portrayal of the Apache and one of their leaders,

Cochise, in the highly influential *Broken Arrow* (1950). Generally seen as a "breakthrough" film for its time, partly because of its depiction of white racism, Daves sought to present the Apache viewpoint, reflecting the *Ramona* film tradition. The film takes liberties with history, implying that the peace was long-lasting and that Geronimo broke it; in fact, Cochise died two years following the conclusion of this story, and Geronimo observed the peace of Cochise and fled the reservation only after his death. Subsequent raids against whites by Geronimo reflected his standing as a war leader informed by the visions of his power and of his standing among some segments of his people. Moviemakers, like Americans generally, have managed to confuse the title of "chief" with an absolute ruler over all Indians bearing the tribal name. Thus, in calling Geronimo "chief" they impute more authority and control to him than he actually had.

The Northern Plains

Regarding Northern Plains Indians, filmmakers took a different course. A coalition of Sioux and Cheyenne dealt the American people a stunning blow to their national confidence on the centennial observation of their independence; the Indians defeated and killed George Armstrong Custer and nearly 250 members of his Seventh Cavalry on June 25, 1876. Known to whites as the Battle of the Little Big Horn and to Indians as the Battle of Greasy Grass, warriors under the command of Gall, Two Moons, and Crazy Horse annihilated Custer and his men with superior numbers, tactics, and firepower. Chief Sitting Bull, never on the battlefield, served as their mentor, medicine man, and prophet. The greatest Indian victory, however, was followed by their relentless destruction by a revenge-driven army.

Custer's encounters on the plains provided the fodder for many silent and B western films. A major film of Custer's life by Raoul Walsh, *They Died with Their Boots On,* was released in late 1941. While historically inaccurate in many parts, it features a performance by Errol Flynn that captured the magnetism, along with the bravado and vanity, of the historic Custer. The "Last Stand" is portrayed as a noble act, not a reckless blunder. Appearing as it did on the eve of America's entry into World War II, the film portrays Custer's death as a necessary national sacrifice so that Americans can finish settling the West in peace, a message of comfort in the days following the Japanese attack on Pearl Harbor.

After the war, Ford presented his thoughts on Custer in *Fort Apache* (1948). Although Ford shifted the scene to the Southwest and substituted Apache for Sioux, Colonel Owen Thursday (Henry Fonda) fits the description of Custer in every detail, except that he lacks Custer's magnetism. Thursday is a strict disciplinarian, hard on his men, a martinet in search of a general's star, and no man of his word where Indians are concerned. Nevertheless, he is brave and intent upon protecting settlers. Thursday and his command are wiped out by the Apache after he recklessly refuses to take the advice of fellow officer Captain York (John Wayne). Nevertheless, York still stands by the posthumous depiction of Thursday as gallant and correct—deliberately overlooking his faults—because Thursday's goal of subduing the Apache was noble.

Portraying Custer changed again with American involvement in Vietnam. Arthur Penn depicted Custer as insane in *Little Big Man* (1970) and presented cavalry raids on Cheyenne villages as an antiwar critique of contemporary "search and destroy" assaults on Vietnamese villages. The joking quality of the film, however, based upon a novel written as parody, flirts with nihilism. It inaccurately depicts the army as having superior firepower over the Indians in all its campaigns. Penn's view is also misogynistic. Indian women are depicted as promiscuous, as when the hero's wife has him sleep with her three sisters, or when Chief Lodge Poles remarks that his Snake Indian wife is strange to him because she copulates with horses. While the last line is played for a laugh, it nonetheless recalls the belief prevalent among many whites in the eighteenth and nineteenth centuries that African women copulated with apes. Both beliefs depict women of color as possessed by unwholesome sexual appetites.

The negative portrayal of Custer and the U.S. Army in *Little Big Man* anticipated the subsequent anti-Turnerian view of those writing the "New Western" history in the late 1980s. So did Robert Altman in another important film of the 1970s, *Buffalo Bill and the Indians* (1976). Based loosely on Arthur Kopit's play *Indians* (1969), Altman presents Buffalo Bill (Paul Newman) as the "father of the new show business" and focuses on a five-month period when Chief Sitting Bull appeared with the show. It is a meditation on cultural conflict as well as on personal and national aggrandizement at the expense of Indians; it can be used in the classroom with the proper readings and videos for context.

From the 1950s, television provided a progressively greater volume of contradictory western images through screening B westerns and then by developing television series. Television reached a larger audience more frequently than movie houses and played a powerful role in inscribing visions of Indians on at least two American generations. In the 1970s television turned away from westerns, just as Hollywood did, in response to growing viewer apathy. The western seemed dead. Its return in the 1990s in a very different form derived from rediscovered American interest in Indian lifestyles and values.

Dances with Wolves and Its Impact

Kevin Costner's *Dances with Wolves* (1990) resonated with audiences influenced by the New Age movement's interest in all things Indian. By reversing typical storylines, Costner made his Civil War veteran, Union officer John Dunbar, a man who goes native. He joins the Sioux and comes to see the world through their eyes. As a result of this transvaluation, whites are recast as the villains, and the audience roots for the Indians when they attack the soldiers. While the Sioux are sensitively portrayed, their Indian enemies, the Pawnee, are molded into the old "bloodthirsty savage" stereotype. Indian women and their tribal roles are slighted. Indians are major actors in this film, however, building upon the breakthroughs won by Salish Chief Dan George in *Little Big Man* and Creek Will Sampson in *Buffalo Bill and the Indians.* It seems unthinkable now that Hollywood or television will ever again cast non-Indians in Indian parts. The enormous popularity of *Dances with Wolves* and the availability of a "director's cut" provide multiple options for teaching.

The impact of *Dances with Wolves* coincided with an innovation in filmic "truth telling" through the revitalization of the documentary. Films entertain by telling stories through character development and conflict. Plot lines must be clear and simple. Lived human experience over many years, however, such as the Plains Indian wars, has far more complexity than one film can depict. The documentary, with its narrative structure and opportunity for commentary can present a more nuanced portrait of the past. In the PBS series *The Civil War* (1990), Ken Burns took old photographs, newspaper headlines, documents, songs from the era, interviews with historians, and contemporary photographs of battle sites along with limited re-creations to bring alive the most important historical event in America's past. The successful enterprise proved overwhelming; Americans wanted more of this new documentary, and Indians and western history quickly became its subjects.

The Indian Wars in the 1990s

Commercial channels "discovered" the West first. In 1993, the Arts and Entertainment (A&E) network produced *The Real West,* covering soldiers, Indians, settlers, lawmen, and desperadoes, while the Discovery Channel made *How the West Was Lost,* focusing on the Indian Wars. Stephen Ives, with Ken Burns producing, presented *The West* (1996) on PBS, an ostensibly omnibus history of the subject that, surprisingly, omitted the Southwest and the Apache campaigns. New Western historians made significant contributions to these projects. This spate of solid, important historical documentaries removed in a stroke the conventional historian's complaint that the West was inadequately covered by film.

Biopics (biographical pictures) also appeared, frequently sponsored by Ted Turner and his Turner Network Television (TNT) channel, offering further consideration of major Indian figures in films such as *Geronimo* (1993) and *Crazy Horse* (1993). Turner also encouraged Danny Glover to make *The Buffalo Soldiers* (1997), about African American cavalrymen fighting in the campaign against the Apache Victorio. On the big screen, Cherokee Wes Studi, who had previously played the Pawnee in *Dances with Wolves* and Red Cloud in *Crazy Horse,* portrayed the title role in Walter Hill's *Geronimo* (1993). This is the best of the new biopics, but it needs material from the documentaries to put the film in historical perspective.

The Indian Wars after the Civil War have now become an important part of our visual memory; Frederick Jackson Turner's previously familiar tale cannot be told now without serious qualification. The challenge before us is to use the new tools from the visual media and fresh insights from the New Western history to teach a more inclusive and accurate national history.

References

Filmography

Battle at Elderbush Gulch (1913, F)
Broken Arrow (1950, F)
Buffalo Bill and the Indians (1976, F)
The Buffalo Soldiers (1997, TV)
Crazy Horse (1993, TV)
Dances with Wolves (1990, F)
Fort Apache (1948, F)
Geronimo (1993, F)
How the West Was Lost (1993, D)
Little Big Man (1970, F)
Lonesome Dove (1990, TV)
Ramona (1910, F)
The Real West (1993, D)
Rio Grande (1950, F)
The Searchers (1956, F)
Sergeant Rutledge (1960, F)
She Wore a Yellow Ribbon (1949, F)
Son of the Morning Star (1991, TV)
They Died with Their Boots On (1941, F)
The West (1996, D)

Bibliography

Faulk, Odie B. *The Geronimo Campaign.* New York: Oxford University Press, 1969.

Hutton, Paul A., ed. *The Custer Reader.* Lincoln: University of Nebraska Press, 1992.

Lamar, Howard R., ed. *The New Encyclopedia of the American West.* New Haven: Yale University Press, 1998.

Pearson, Roberta E. *Eloquent Gestures.* Berkeley: University of California Press, 1992.

Rollins, Peter C., and John E. O'Connor, eds. *Hollywood's Indian.*Lexington: University Press of Kentucky, 1998.

Rosa, Joseph G., and Robin May. *Buffalo Bill and His Wild West.* Lawrence: University Press of Kansas, 1989.

Sturtevant, William C., ed. *Handbook of North American Indians,* vol. 4. Washington, DC: U.S. Government Printing Office, 1988.

Turner, Frederick Jackson. *The Significance of the Frontier in American History.* Harold P. Simonson, ed. New York: Frederick Ungar, 1991.

Tuska, Jon. *The American West in Film.* Lincoln: University of Nebraska Press, 1988.

Utley, Robert, and Wilcomb Washburn. *The American Heritage History of the Indian Wars.* New York: Simon & Schuster, 1977.

White, Richard. *"It's Your Misfortune and None of My Own": A New History of the American West.* Norman: University of Oklahoma Press, 1991.

[PETER C. ROLLINS]

World War I

World War I—in its own time called "The Great War"—may have been the most important event of the early twentieth century; it decimated a lost generation and silenced the optimistic voices of the Victorian era. The sheer numbers are staggering. The Allies (Great Britain, France, Russia, and, in the last two years of the war, the United States) suffered 2.3 million battle deaths. On the side of the Central Powers (Germany and Austria-Hungary in alliance with the Ottoman Empire and Bulgaria), often-victorious armies suffered 2.7 million battle deaths between 1914 and November 1918, when hostilities terminated. Along the way an influenza pandemic struck and, among the Americans alone, there were nearly thirty thousand deaths from the highly contagious disease in home-front training camps, aboard troop transports, and in rear-echelon training facilities in France and in the United States.

Renewed interest in World War I stems from the 1975 publication of a truly exciting study of the war's cultural legacy, Paul Fussell's *The Great War in Modern Memory.* Fussell took a fresh approach to the war's fiction, poetry, and aesthetics as well as to the literary fallout from the war—which Fussell claims extends into our own time, most notably in the literature of the Vietnam War. Another brilliant study of cultural patterns based on fresh research is *A War Imagined* (1991) by Samuel Hynes. These reconsiderations prompted a 1993 conference on the films of World War I in Amsterdam, from which two books emerged: *Film and the First World War* (1995) takes an internationalist look at developments, with special attention to the work of Russian, German, Britain, and French filmmakers; *Hollywood's World War I* (1997) concentrates on the relationship of American morale to the developing conflict, while considering how the war was interpreted after 1919 by nearly twenty key productions. All of this creative activity gives clear evidence that the study of World War I is, to use a military metaphor, on the advance rather than in retreat.

Motion pictures depicting the war reflect America's changing attitudes toward involvement. When the European war began in the summer of 1914, the United States took the stance of a neutral nation concerned primarily with freedom of the seas. Once President Woodrow Wilson committed the nation to military preparedness—the Selective Service Act of 1917 initiated the first military draft since the Civil War—the motion picture industry began to project heroic images of battle: stars such as Charlie Chaplin, Douglas Fairbanks Sr., Lillian Gish, and Marie Dressler toured the nation promoting the sale of war bonds; meanwhile, the screens of America's theaters welcomed government and Hollywood productions designed to incite a fighting spirit. After the war, the cinematic memory would be divided between those who remembered a heroic struggle and those who bemoaned a noble crusade that became a catastrophe.

"Too Proud to Fight," 1914–1916

Woodrow Wilson was elected in 1916 (as was Lyndon Johnson some fifty years later) under the slogan that "he kept us out of war." A high-minded idealist, Wilson was famous for proclaiming that America was "too proud to fight." Before 1917, Hollywood productions reflected the antiwar sentiments of both the nation and its chief executive. In a major example of the antiwar films, a work entitled *Civilization* (1916), Director Thomas Ince pleaded for sympathy "to the vast pitiful army whose tears have girdled the universe—The Mothers of the Dead." In a particularly dramatic moment of the film, a U-boat captain sinks his craft rather than carry out a torpedo attack on a civilian liner. (Most readers have not seen *Civilization,* but the footage of the liner being sunk has been borrowed by countless subsequent filmmakers to represent the fate of the *Lusitania,* most notably in *The Great War* [1965].) The antiwar message remained dominant until Germany announced a policy of unrestricted submarine warfare in February 1917.

Owing to a complex combination of diplomatic and military factors, the president and the movie industry moved toward involvement. Films such as *Civilization* and D. W. Griffith's *Intolerance* (1916)—an extended plea for peace that joined the Ince production in invoking Christ as a spokesman—were withdrawn from circulation. More militaristic fare emerged from a Hollywood bent on supporting the president's mobilization program. Yet the most lasting—and contradictory—cinematic renderings of the war would be produced after the conflict.

The Heroic Vision

During the 1920s, Hollywood contributed to the heroic image of the recent struggle. King Vidor's *The Big Parade* (1925) was the first financially successful postwar film about the military conflict. The famous battle scenes of the film (reenacting American Expeditionary Force actions in the Argonne forest during the Meuse-Argonne campaign of September–November 1918, the subject as well of the Arts & Entertainment network's excellent and historically accurate production *The Lost Battalion* [2001]) employed inventive visual and editing techniques. The director asked his actors to walk, shoot, and fall to the cadence of an on-set drum, thereby creating a metronomic rhythm that, to the surprise of everyone except Vidor, gave the battle scenes a strange, balletic quality. (Those who have not seen *The Big Parade* need to be told that the title of the film does not refer to a military ceremony, but to the ineluctable march to victory on the western front of American troops, trucks, tanks, and planes.) When the "doughboys" fight and die in this film, they do so as democratic heroes for their nation's cause. Vidor had worked closely with World War I veterans in planning the film, and many former doughboys reenacted their wartime exploits for Vidor's cameras. Not surprisingly, veterans were delighted with Vidor's efforts to tell their patriotic story with both artistry and verisimilitude.

The Marine Corps' contribution was celebrated in *What Price Glory?* (1926), director Raoul Walsh's adaptation of Laurence Stallings's stage play of the same title. This paean to Marine Corps manliness—both on and off the battlefield—(accurately) celebrated the battle record of the 4th Marine Brigade at Belleau Wood (also called the Aisne-Marne Defensive, June 4–July 10, 1918) while (distractingly) pursuing the amatory exploits of the two main characters from China to the Philippines to their arrival on the western front. (A later version by John Ford in 1952, starring James Cagney and Dan Dailey, further obfuscated history by stressing macho rivalry rather than war issues; it was roundly criticized when it was released.)

In *Wings* (1927), William Wellman followed the evolution of two aviators from their first days of flight training. Wellman had been a pilot in the war and sought to make the Army Air Corps look every bit as romantic as the infantry had in *The Big Parade* and the Marine Corps did in *What Price Glory?* The War Department provided a cast of thousands for a film that, even with government help, cost over $2 million. No expense was spared; for example, reenactment of the St. Mihiel campaign (September 12–16, 1918) cost Paramount over $250,000. All aerial duels were filmed aloft with cameras mounted on the planes. As with *The Big Parade,* the film combined drama with a stringent adherence to details of aviation technology. Distributed soon after Charles Lindbergh crossed the Atlantic, *Wings* exploited and encouraged America's fascination with the military potential of aviation. Indeed, Lindbergh is quoted in a heroic lead. Through written titles, he dedicates the film "to those young warriors of the sky, whose wings are folded about them forever." America's young pilots could have had no memorial more heroic than this monument in celluloid. *Wings* is an action film that still rents well in video stores across the nation. It is a testimony to the power of film art in the 1920s; even the visually "hip" students of Generation X are impressed by the epic grandeur of *Wings.* (John Guillermin's *The Blue Max* [1966], starring George Peppard and James Mason, borrowed some of the imagery of *Wings* to recount the air war from the German point of view; in *The Great Waldo Pepper* [1975], director George Roy Hill and actor Robert Redford would pay homage simultaneously to both World War I pilots and William Wellman's epic.)

The Nightmare Vision

During World War I, the machine gun, the tank, poison gas, the airplane, barbed wire, and the submarine suddenly brought mechanization into world of horse-drawn artillery, men on foot, and the chivalric officers celebrated in French director Jean Renoir's *Grand Illusion* (1937); the horrors of this new, deadly efficient machine age form a subtext to many movies of World War I, including such recent pieces as *Legends of the Fall* (1994) and *Gods and Monsters* (1998) as well as classics such as *Lawrence of Arabia* (1962). The dimensions of the nightmare were registered as early as the Battle of the Somme in 1916, a six-month struggle that military historian S. L. A. Marshall has described as "the most soulless battle in British annals. . . . It was a battle not so much of attrition as of mutual destruction" (260). A feature-length documentary called *The Battle of the Somme* was released in late summer of 1917. According to Paul Fussell, by this time the war had become "a hideous embarrassment to the prevailing Meliorist myth which had dominated the public consciousness for a century. It reversed the Idea of Progress" (8). The cloud of melancholia would drift toward America after the war as public spokesmen reflected on the significance of what was proclaimed, retrospectively, to be a misguided attempt to fight "a war to end all wars."

After the Versailles Treaty, a host of exposés convinced many Americans that their country had been pulled into a European conflict that had not been their business. George Creel described his role in *How We Advertised America* (1922). Creel had been America's chief propagandist, and he gleefully explains how carefully orchestrated media blitzes had mobilized public support. Walter Lippmann's *Public Opinion* (1922) voiced a more sardonic evaluation of what he called "the myth of the omnicompetent citizen." Lippmann's reading of the war record led him to advise the nation to give up its traditional notion of democracy. America would be better served by a government of experts—professionals who were not susceptible to the wiles of propaganda. Within this context, Erich Maria Remarque's *All Quiet on the Western Front* (1928) crystallized an existing disillusionment. The protagonist, German infantryman Paul Baumer, enters the struggle as an idealist, but months of shelling and death convince him that "when it comes to dying for your country, it is better not to die at all." Some critics scrutinized Remarque's war record in an attempt to challenge the book's authenticity, but no one could deny that the German author had captured the mood of a worldwide "lost generation."

In just two years, director Lewis Milestone would transform the disconsolate German book into a devastating American film. His screen adaptation of *All Quiet on the Western Front* (1930) shared the nightmare vision with mass audiences across the globe. During a famous battle segment, Paul Baumer finds himself trapped for the night in a muddy shell crater with a dead French soldier. As a result of this horrific experience, Baumer—and presumably the audience—comes to realize that the world's little people are victims of bureaucracy, the nation state, industrialism, and "progress." The fact that the film won awards for best picture and best director was a sign that the nightmare vision was (temporarily) au courant in Hollywood. In Germany, Nazis under Joseph Goebbels first disrupted screenings of the "American propaganda," and then found legislative methods to prevent distribution. By 1933, the Third Reich was burning Remarque's antiheroic books.

FIGURE 15. *Paths of Glory* (1957). Three military men remain immovable in their positions and perspectives on war. Colonel Dax (Kirk Douglas, left) seeks to protect his regiment from the corrupt, ambitious General Mireau (George Macready, center), as Major Saint-Auban (Richard Anderson, right) stands aloof, resigned to go ahead with General Mireau's pointless advance of Colonel Dax's men. The dress and posture of each man reveal their social class. Courtesy Bryna Productions.

The Cold War era produced a very powerful indictment of putative injustices during the earlier conflict, a film by Stanley Kubrick entitled *Paths of Glory* (1957). Starring Kirk Douglas as Colonel Dax, a regimental commander who seems unique in caring about the welfare of his men, the film seeks to expose the callousness fostered by class divisions within the allied armies. On one of the less-than-glorious "paths of glory" presented, the French high command executes three soldiers drawn by lot from a unit that displayed cowardice (according to its corrupt leader, General Mureau, the division commander). An outraged Colonel Dax pleads for his troops against this barbarity, but to no avail. The Establishment is entrenched and cannot be challenged. Many have praised Kubrick's social analysis (drawn, in part, from a 1935 novel of the same title by Humphrey Cobb, but also inspired by the work of C. Wright Mills, a popular sociologist), but others have found the film to be a satire that neglects the complexity of unit, battlefield, and political realities. Still, most viewers have praised the gritty realism—as well as the cinematic dexterity—of the film's battle scenes. (Even Winston Churchill voiced approval.) The black-and-white film stock selection enhanced the apparent documentary quality of this forceful film. Historically, there were executions during World War I, but these draconian measures usually followed outright mutiny in the trenches rather than mere cowardice. To use the execution of troops by an unfeeling officialdom as a microcosm of World War I for any of the contending armies—to include the German army—is to misrepresent the social dynamics of the conflict. World War I, alas, was a people's conflict; shifting blame to an elite simply cannot be sustained by evidence. Still, *Paths of Glory* is a powerful drama whose commentary on the past would later be embellished by the antiwar movement during America's military involvement in Vietnam (1965–73).

During the Vietnam era, two historian-filmmakers, R. C. Raack and Patrick Griffin, released a challenging film entitled *Goodbye Billy: America Goes to War, 1916–17* (1972).

This nonnarrative compilation film would trace the American ethos from optimism to confusion to disillusionment in a film that reflected both a lost generation's approach to the Great War and America's mood swings before, during, and after the Tet offensive of 1968. The interanimation of past and present in the award-winning documentary confirms many of the assertions made by Paul Fussell about the long-term cultural reverberations of the Great War.

The Heroic Version Returns

The cynical version of World War I was wheeled off the set as World War II approached. Back in New York, Louis de Rochemont's newsreel staff at *The March of Time* produced a feature-length docudrama entitled *The Ramparts We Watch* (1940). A plea for military preparedness, the film tried to establish parallels between World War I and the coming conflict. Fast-moving events in Poland and France reinforced lessons about unpreparedness. Hoping to win battles before they were fought, the Nazis distributed impressive documentaries about the success of their blitzkrieg. As experts in the editing of newsreels, de Rochement's crew made full use of World War I and Nazi footage to put the fear of God in the American audience. De Rochement's message was that Americans needed to stop watching from their protected ramparts and start building their own war machine so that they would not be caught off guard again.

In 1941, Warner Bros. came forward with *Sergeant York,* the landmark picture for the new American mood. Alvin York was a Tennessee boy who killed twenty Germans at the Argonne forest and captured another 132—a spectacular feat on any battlefield. For these exploits, York was awarded a host of medals, including the Medal of Honor. Director Howard Hawks took this story about a man of natural virtue and exploited it to highlight the flaws of isolationism. York's "conversion scene," powerfully acted by Gary Cooper, was aimed directly at those who said we should remain out of the fray. (As late as July 1941, polls showed that this meant 70 percent of Americans.) Here was a spin on the war that flashed back to 1917, when a newly mobilized President Woodrow Wilson spoke idealistically about "a war to make the world safe for democracy."

Near the time of the film's premier, the real Sergeant York—who joined Franklin Roosevelt and Warner Bros. in endorsing its message about preparedness—called for aid to Britain. As concerned Citizen York, the nation's poster hero explained that Americans must stand up for democracy; if they did not, "then we owe the memory of George Washington an apology, for if we have stopped, then he wasted his time at Valley Forge." In a speech to the Veterans of Foreign Wars, York noted that the last war had been fought to make the world safe for democracy, "and it did—for a while" (Rollins and O'Connor, 137, 138). At such a moment, we can safely say that the memory of World War I had come full circle.

In an effort to dramatize the need for a United Nations after World War II, Darryl Zanuck produced his *Wilson* (1944), an unabashed glorification of Woodrow Wilson's crusade to sell the League of Nations to American voters. Teachers and students will profit greatly from this biographical film, especially because so many documents from the 1920s and 1930s exaggerate Wilson's failings as both a human being and national leader. *Wilson* provides fascinating (and highly accurate) details about the various phases of America's experience with war: neutrality (1914–17), preparedness and involvement (1917–18), and Wilson's failed peacemaking efforts (1918–21). Although viewers must keep in mind the internationalist intent of the film as propaganda for a nascent United Nations, all can profit from the historical scrupulousness of the film for each historical phase. Although *Wilson* may be excessive in its celebration of the president's virtues, it is far more reliable than better-known debunking treatments by Wilson's bitter contemporaries. (Zanuck went to great lengths to verify both the production's details and historiography.)

Perhaps in homage to the excellence of the African American contributions to combat units in the Vietnam war, *Men of Bronze* (1977) looked back at the contribution of the 369th Regiment (of the 93d Division), a New York City unit that sailed to France in December 1917. The unit served in combat with French units for 191 days—which set a record for any American unit under fire during the war. In the process, the 369th suffered 1,500 casualties. Indeed, the 93d Division had a casualty rate of 32 percent. Using historical footage and interviews with historians—as well as some articulate, surviving veterans—*Men of Bronze* celebrates the heroism of men who displayed the ultimate "grace under pressure." African Americans performed marvels on the battlefields of France, winning numerous personal and unit citations. The 369th Regiment received an exultant welcome as its members marched down New York's Fifth Avenue; later that day, a testimonial dinner was held in their honor, but their legacy remains unremembered—or at least underremembered. This documentary goes far toward reviving a proud record, albeit at a very late date.

Was World War I a heroic crusade, or was it a traumatic nightmare? We are beginning to discern that it was both—and more. We have yet to fully track the impact of the Great War on basic beliefs and myths of our postmodernist world. As recently as 1997, PBS came forward with a multiepisode series entitled *The Great War and the Shaping of the 20th Century*, an Emmy Award–winning attempt to link the military struggle and suffering to the cultural history of the time—and our time.

References

Filmography

Aces: The Story of the First Air War (1996, D)
All Quiet on the Western Front (1930, F; 1979, TV)
The American Siberian Expeditionary Force (1989, D)
Battle of the Somme (1916, D)
The Big Parade (1925, F)
The Blue Max (1966, F)
Civilization (1916, F)
A Farewell to Arms (1932, 1957, F)
The Frozen War—America Intervenes in Russia, 1918–20 (1973, D)
Gods and Monsters (1998, F)
Goodbye Billy: America Goes to War, 1917–1918 (1972, D)
Grand Illusion (1937, F)
The Great War (1965, F)
The Great War and the Shaping of the 20th Century (1996, TV)
Homefront, 1917–1918—War Transforms American Life (1967, D)
Intolerance (1916, F)
Lawrence of Arabia (1962, F)
The League of Nations: The Hope of Mankind (1976, D)
Legends of the Fall (1994, F)
The Lost Battalion (2001, TV)
Men in Crisis: Wilson Versus the Senate (1964, D)
Men of Bronze (1977, D)
Paths of Glory (1957, F)
The Pershing Story (1975, D)
The Ramparts We Watch (1940, D)
Sergeant York (1941, F)
Shipwreck: The Lusitania (1997, D)
Soldier's Home (1977, F)
Versailles—The Lost Peace (1978, D)
What Price Glory? (1926, 1952, F)
Wilson (1944, F)
Wings (1927, F)
World War I (1965, TV)

Bibliography

Campbell, Craig. *Reel America and World War I: A Comprehensive Filmography and History of Motion Pictures in the United States, 1914–1920.* Jefferson, NC: McFarland, 1985.
DeBauche, Leslie Midkiff. *Reel Patriotism: The Movies and World War I.* Madison: University of Wisconsin Press, 1997.
Dibbets, Karel, and Bert Hogenkamp, eds. *Film and the First World War.* Amsterdam: Amsterdam University Press, 1995.
Ferrell, Robert H. *Woodrow Wilson and World War I, 1917–1921.* New York: HarperCollins, 1986.
Fussell, Paul. *The Great War and Modern Memory.* New York: Oxford University Press, 1975.
Hynes, Samuel. *A War Imagined: The First World*

War and English Culture. New York: Atheneum, 1991.

Kennedy, David M. *Over Here: The First World War and American Society.* New York: Oxford University Press, 1986.

Marshall, S. L. A. *World War I.* New York: American Heritage, 1964.

Rollins, Peter, and John O'Connor, eds. *Hollywood's World War I: The Motion Picture Images.* Bowling Green: Bowling Green University Press, 1997.

Venzon, Anne Cipriano, ed. *The United States in the First World War: An Encyclopedia.* New York: Garland, 1995.

Ward, Larry Wayne. *The Motion Picture Goes to War: The United States Government Film Effort During World War I.* Ann Arbor: UMI Research Press, 1985.

Winter, Jay, and Blaine Baggett. *The Great War and the Shaping of the 20th Century.* New York: Penguin, 1996.

[PETER C. ROLLINS]

World War II: Documentaries

World War II, far more than its predecessor (see "World War I"), was a worldwide conflagration that changed the lives of all Americans: millions of youths were drafted into the armed forces; family men who remained at home were asked to perform homeland service and to observe rationing restrictions on consumer items such as meat, gasoline, and rubber; children zealously collected scrap metal and rubber for the war effort; and women—both married and single—joined a work force that had previously shunned their talents. (Many a Rosie left her ironing board and became a riveter!) Minorities were affected in dramatically different ways: more than 100,000 Japanese Americans were forcibly removed to internment camps in Utah, Arizona, Wyoming, Arkansas, and the California desert, away from their West Coast homes and businesses, some of which were looted in their absence. More fortunate were the thousands of rural African American families that gravitated to production centers near Los Angeles and Detroit, where they found lucrative jobs in aircraft and armaments plants. The result was an ineradicable redefinition of race and gender roles in American society.

At the end of the war, America had lost approximately 405,000 service men and women, a tragic toll for a nation that otherwise had been largely untouched by battle—allowing it to develop an unprecedented industrial capacity—since the Civil War. Wealthier, and stirred by victory, the nation's minorities resisted a return to the prewar status quo; great changes lay ahead for a nation still seeking to fulfill President Franklin Delano Roosevelt's wartime promise of four great freedoms: freedom of speech and expression; freedom of worship; freedom from want; freedom from fear. Artist Norman Rockwell commemorated these aspirations in his famous series of paintings entitled "Four Freedoms," but the nation as a whole knew the significance of its corporate efforts to defeat fascism. According to historian William O'Neill (and many observers at the time), the war was a great challenge to the nation's sincerity: "By passing this greatest of tests, America also won the right to become a better nation. Though social reform was not why servicemen took the risks that they did, it would be one of the outcomes" (433). As America has gained perspective on the conflict, it has created a monument on the National Mall in Washington, D.C. (completed in 2003), and conferred a proud label, "the Greatest Generation," upon the cohorts who successfully navigated both the Great Depression (1929–41) and World War II (1941–45). Oral histories edited by NBC broadcaster Tom Brokaw and popular narratives by historian Stephen Ambrose have codified this memory of the Americans who struggled through unprecedented home and warfront challenges.

World War II was a people's war, and leaders of the major antagonists—Japan, Germany, Russia, England, the United States—enlisted their best filmmakers to produce documentary and propaganda productions that would both inform and move what, in those pioneer days of social science, was described as a "mass audience." Many of these films would become classics, films worthy of study in university classes decades later; the quality of the American work should come as no surprise, for some of Hollywood's best directors—John Ford, William Wyler, John Huston, Frank Capra, Garson Kanin, Darryl Zanuck, and George Stevens among them—brought their skills to these projects.

Documentaries of the war era had many objectives. Some were designed to convince Americans that isolationism was irresponsible in a world at war; others were more specifically focused on indoctrinating service personnel preparing for overseas duty; special campaign and battle films sought to justify the costs of the conflict. At the same time, home-front films explained the principles that Americans should treasure during the war. After the conflict, readjustment films tried to sensitize audiences to the problems of returning veterans. Later generations would reflect on the war through documentary as an exercise of public memory. The retrospection began soon after the war with the NBC television series *Victory at Sea* and the contemporary CBS offering *Air Power,* narrated by Walter Cronkite.

Many American boys remember watching such multiepisode television epics with their fathers (recent veterans in many cases). Unfortunately, most viewers would miss the ways in which these hagiographic compilation films from the archives were reflections of the times in which they were made rather than valid interpretations of the past. The advent of cable alternatives such as C-SPAN and The History Channel at the end of the twentieth century would tap both the best and worst of the documentary legacy of World War II.

Dispelling Isolationism, 1940–41

On the evening of December 6, 1941, the Gallup Poll found that almost 70 percent of Americans were in favor of remaining detached from the military conflicts in Europe and Asia. Much of this noninterventionist attitude stemmed from disillusionment with the Versailles Treaty and failure of the League of Nations to restrain the expansionism of Japan, Italy, and Germany. Earlier bestsellers such as Walter Millis's *Road to War: America, 1914–1917* (1935) had convinced many that isolationism had failed only because it had not been followed faithfully. That same year, the Neutrality Act placed an embargo on the sale of arms and munitions to all combatants. In answer to such arguments and policies, Louis de Rochement and the staff of the newsreel magazine *March of Time* produced a feature-length docudrama entitled *The Ramparts We Watch* (1940) to reconsider America's preparations for World War I and the failure of President Woodrow Wilson's initial policy of being "too proud to fight." Americans in 1917 were portrayed as having many similar challenges as the Americans in the audience in 1940, with a chief lesson that delay—rather than promoting peace—led to more suffering than rapid military preparations to confront aggression. During production of the film, German blitzkrieg victories motivated the filmmakers to turn *Ramparts* into an even harder-hitting argument for U.S. intervention. The resulting work, which included daunting Wehrmacht combat footage, has been described by film historian R. M. Barsam as "superceded only by the *Why We Fight* series in its attempt to inform Americans about the war" (180).

The surprise Japanese air raid on Pearl Harbor had an instant impact on the American public. To explain and dramatize the significance of the attack, leading filmmaker John Ford, with the help of cinematographer Greg Toland, produced *December 7th* (1942). We now know that much of the footage was fabricated in Hollywood: there are colorful reenactments of gunners firing back at the Japanese attackers, of strafings and bombings, of American bravery and suffering. Although the fabrication of evidence is understandable within the context of the time and the rush to production, Ford's footage was later recycled in countless subsequent documentary and feature productions—including the oft-used scene of sailors tossing a baseball and then looking up to observe the enemy planes. Thus, the famous John Ford quote about what should happen if the facts conflict with a nice story ("When the legend becomes fact, print the legend") seems applicable to this "documentary" about what President Roosevelt called America's "Day of Infamy." Though heavy with narration and full of preachments about Japanese perfidy, little is said about why the attack caught Americans so unprepared on that Sunday morning. Ford was quite successful, however, in portraying the attack in personal terms, turning the struggle into something human and understandable—which audiences could take away with them from the theatres. Emphasis on American heroism provided an important microcosm for all U.S. citizens during the initial year of mobilization for war. President Roosevelt, who had commissioned the work, was particularly happy to have such a timely government production in America's theatres.

Indoctrination and Propaganda, 1942–1945

Because many Americans were isolationists before the attack on Pearl Harbor, it was essential that troops going into battle be reoriented to the international struggle. General George C. Marshall, knowing the Sicilian immigrant Frank Capra to be the all-American director of such films as *Mr. Deeds Goes to Town* (1936) and *Mr. Smith Goes to Washington* (1939), called Capra to Washington and commissioned him to produce a series of indoctrination films designed for both service personnel and civilians. Film scholar David H. Culbert has said that the resulting series, *Why We Fight* (seven episodes), was "the most comprehensive set of war aims released by the U.S. government in *any medium* during World War II" (188). The effectiveness of these outstanding compilation films was further enhanced by the innovative use of graphics produced by the Disney Studios.

In *Prelude to War* (1942), isolationism is rejected as a policy that permitted the Axis antagonists to gain momentum after the Munich Crisis of 1938. Americans are now in a struggle for national existence, narrator Walter Huston intones: "The chips are down; it's us or them." In *The Nazis Strike* (1943), the Germans show their "passion for conquest." Despite the setbacks in Czechoslovakia and Poland, Winston Churchill promised that "out of the depths of sorrow and of sacrifice will be born again the glory of mankind." *Divide and Conquer* (1943) traces the debacles in France, Denmark, Norway, Belgium, and Holland. *The Battle of Britain* (1943) focuses on the air war, showing that, despite enormous losses, the Germans were unsuccessful in terrorizing the British people. This important film helped to dispel the myth of German invincibility. *The Battle of Russia* (1944) sidesteps the "C" word (Communism) to lavish praise on the culture and bravery of the Soviet peoples. In the face of the German war machine, the Russian folk arose to defend the motherland, proving that "generals win battles, but peoples win wars." (A similar film, *The Battle of China* [1944] promoted empathy for America's Asian ally.) In the final episode of the series, *War Comes to America* (1945), America's multicultural experience is celebrated, as are the ideas of freedom and equality: "Without the idea, the country would have remained a wilderness; without the country, the idea may have remained only a dream." The *Why We Fight* series was shown to every fighting man and woman going abroad and to millions of civilians across the land. The films offer later viewers great insight into the thoughts and objectives of the times.

Capra would oversee the production of many other nonfiction films, but *The Negro Soldier* (1944) deserves special attention because of its subject and impact. Nearly 540,000 African Americans were inducted into the U.S. Army during the war, and this film was designed for two purposes: first, to show the soldiers of color what their stake was in terms of U.S. history and in relation to the racist policies of the Axis powers; second, to convince white soldiers and civilians of the human dignity of the African Americans in uniform. Thomas Cripps and David Culbert conclude that the film was successful in both efforts; furthermore, the film laid the groundwork for such "problem films" (films considering social problems in the United States) after the war as *Home of the Brave* (1949), *The Defiant Ones* (1958), and *Guess Who's Coming to Dinner* (1967). Cripps and Culbert realize the ironies of this development: "Who would have thought that the Army, officially committed to segregation, would end up with a film which symbolically promoted the logic of integration?" (133)

Battle and Campaign Films

Americans were told about the heroism and dedication of their troops in a great number of impressive films whose titles often identified the service and the battle zone. As part of the war effort, these films convinced home-front audiences to commit themselves to active participation. Furthermore, in a civilian world untouched by war, they brought home the harsh realities of combat—reaffirming the nobility of the young Americans fighting for freedom.

John Ford's *Battle of Midway* (1942) was shot in color on the strategic island rather than at the ocean site of the battle, yet the film—much of it shot by Ford, himself, with a handheld 16mm camera—has a gritty realism. Upfront and personal are the heroic, defensive efforts of American troops responding to a Japanese air attack. In the process of filming the events at Midway, Ford became one of the many seriously wounded marines and sailors.

John Huston was responsible for a number of battle films, including *Report from the Aleutians* (1943), the story of a fairly uneventful series of encounters between the Americans and the Japanese in a hostile natural environment. More important as documentary was Huston's *The Battle of San Pietro* (1945), a film so "realistic" that the U.S. Army withdrew it from circulation to modify the editing. We now know that many scenes in the film were staged for the camera—indeed, it would have been impossible to film many of them. On the other hand, through artful editing, these very scenes, combined with combat footage, convey a powerful message about war and its toll on both civilians and combatants in the Liri Valley of Italy. R. M. Barsam calls the film "an indictment of modern warfare in general" (194), but he misses the point: *The Battle of San Pietro* is a somber paean to the painful sacrifices of American troops in World War II—epitomized by the stark scenes of battlefield reclamation of dead American soldiers.

William Wyler's documentary about the twenty-fifth (and, by regulation, last) mission of a B-17 bomber crew stationed in Britain has received retrospective attention after the success of a feature film also entitled *Memphis Belle* (1990), starring Matthew Modine, John Lithgow, and Harry Connick Jr. With the completion of their last combat mission, the crew qualified for rotation stateside. Again, employing a number of staged sequences to allow the camera intimacy with the crew and its functions aboard a B-17, Wyler created an intensely realistic, color portrait of men and machine at work in *Memphis Belle* (1944), giving a sense of what it meant to fly through flak over Hitler's "Fortress Europe." Not long after the war, director Henry King's *Twelve O'Clock High* (1949), starring Gregory Peck, gave a poignant report of the psychological stress of those who flew such raids. (Although not a documentary, the film has been used at the Air Force Academy to teach leadership skills and to comprehend the pressures on those in command.) Most of these films, according to O'Neill, promote an American fixation with hygienic "war from the air," a "democratic delusion" that continues into our own time (306). (Walt Disney's feature-length *Victory Through Air Power* [1943], based on a book by Major Alexander P.

de Seversky, would best exemplify America's sanguine attitude toward strategic bombing during the war and after.)

In the Pacific, documentaries, using footage shot by military cameramen and edited by anonymous groups of dedicated filmmakers reached millions of Americans in local theatres, showing the kind of sacrifice endured by their neighbors in uniform. *With the Marines at Tarawa* (1944) recounts a victory that cost many lives; like many other islands, Tarawa had been heavily fortified by the Japanese. The marines in the first waves of the invasion suffered horrendous casualties. Indeed, this was the first wartime documentary to include graphic scenes of battlefield carnage, including American war dead littering the beach. Subsequent amphibious landings are recounted in *The Battle for the Marianas* (1944); *The Battle of New Britain* (1944); and the all-color *To the Shores of Iwo Jima* (1944). Some of the filmmakers still take pride in their accomplishments, viewing their work as a pure "slice of life" from battles that might otherwise have been ignored by the public. The great loss of life (6,821 killed and close to 20,000 wounded at Iwo Jima alone) required justification, and, it should be noted, the debate over some of these campaigns still goes on; O'Neill, for example, asserts that "Iwo was a costly blunder at the least, a waste of precious riflemen" (407). For most Americans, however, the famous Joe Rosenthal photograph of five marines and one navy corpsman raising an American flag on Mount Suribachi symbolized the entire war effort by a united people. Later use of the photograph in bond drives and as a U.S. postage stamp would further implant this image of World War II in the American consciousness. The Marine Memorial adjacent to Arlington National Cemetery in Washington, D.C., has codified that indelible icon of patriotic service. Indeed, the image has become an icon of the U.S. Marines because it seems to embody the traits that make up America's view of the smallest and boldest of America's military services—determination, courage, teamwork, esprit, aggressiveness, and the steadfast commitment to accomplishing an assigned mission.

Naval contributions to victory in the Pacific were recorded in such films as *The Fighting Lady* (1944), a quiet hymn to life aboard an (unnamed) Essex-class aircraft carrier (to represent all carriers) during the naval battles late in the war. The Technicolor film was directed by Louis de Rochemont, the *March of Time* producer who had so valiantly criticized isolationism prior to the war in his *Ramparts We Watch.* Admiral Chester W. Nimitz was so impressed by *The Fighting Lady* that he advocated dropping copies of it on the Japanese mainland in an effort to awaken our adversary to the potent naval force being assembled for the final invasion of the war.

Home-Front Films

Civilians needed to know what their duty was in the war effort, and the Office of War Information told them in hundreds of productions. The more obvious kind showed civilians contributing to the war effort through indirect efforts such as conserving rubber, tin, and aluminum or in more direct efforts at munitions and aircraft plants across the country. *Salvage* showed exactly what happened to the materials conserved by citizens by following iron, tin, and rubber from collection points to the finished tanks, airplanes, or tires at the end of the production cycle. Other films explored the details of home-front contributions, carrying such titles as *Fuel Conservation, Food for Fighters, Farm Manpower, Send Your Tin Cans to War,* and *Get a War Job.* In *Every Two and a Half Minutes* (1944), an American soldier dies, while home-front workers are urged to make the factories more productive to "get the job done."

Less obvious were films focusing on American values—centered on studies of small towns. During the Great Depression, the feature films of Will Rogers had promoted a fond, sentimental view of America before big cities, flappers, and industrialism. Films such as *Da-*

vid Harum (1934), *In Old Kentucky* (1935), and *Steamboat Round the Bend* (1935) exploited the nostalgia of audiences for earlier—and apparently simpler—times when people were remembered for their intrinsic virtues rather than for their wealth or possessions. New Deal documentaries such as *Power and the Land* (1940), by Joris Ivens, pitched rural electricity as a means to enhance—rather than transform—the traditional values of a representative rural farm family, the Parkinsons.

A number of nostalgic celebrations of small town life were produced during the war. In *The Town* (1944), Joseph von Sternberg told the story of a small community as yet untouched by industrialism and urbanization. Even *Steel Town* (1945) seemed to ignore the industrial aspects of the story of Youngstown, Ohio, in favor of celebrating the cultural diversity and economic prosperity of representative American workers. *The Cummington Story* (1945) was Helen Grayson's attempt to show that recent immigrants, fleeing the collapsing democracies of Europe, fit comfortably into the town meetings of rural America and were no threat to our democratic institutions. As film scholar Hans Borchers has observed, "Demographic reality had once and for all relegated the American small town to the storehouse of all those venerable legends surrounding the founding of American democracy" (174). *War Town* (1943) depicts the problems a typical Alabama town faced with overcrowding created by defense industries. In these films, American beliefs in the small town myth triumphed over sociological nostrums and impersonal statistics.

Readjustment Films: Trauma and Recovery

Elsewhere in this volume (see "World War II: Feature Films"), film scholar Robert Fyne discusses an uplifting readjustment film entitled *The Best Years of Our Lives* (1945). William Wyler followed three fictional servicemen back into civilian life, exploring the challenges and pitfalls of readjustment in a film which received Oscars for best picture, best director, and best actor (Fredric March). Eschewing flag waving and propaganda, the film accurately reassessed the pain and anguish of war—not to mention the readjustment problems of citizen-soldiers who had been plucked out of the workforce and given momentous challenges to overcome, only to return to a nation too busy to pay homage to their sacrifices.

More strictly documentary in approach was John Huston's unforgettable *Let There Be Light* (1946), a film about the phenomenon now known as post–traumatic stress disorder but described at the time as "battle fatigue." In black-and-white footage and with loving concern, Huston and his camera crews visited army hospitals where severe cases of PTSD were being treated. (The resulting film so shocked army supervisors that it was not released for general viewing until 1980, although it was available in government archives and had been written about as early as 1946.) Today, it seems clear that filmmakers placed too much faith in the powers of psychoanalysis to cure those affected, but the painful film's message is that previously healthy-minded young Americans who saw too much combat could be returned to civilian life after caring, psychoanalytic treatment. As film scholar Greg Garrett has said, "*Let There Be Light,* even with its affirmation of the power of the wounded psyche to heal, was simply too raw and too powerful for its time. Fifty years after its making, it remains one of the most moving and thought-provoking films about the effects of war on the people who fight it" (31).

A Screen Epic on TV: New Life for Old Footage

Without question, *Victory at Sea* (1952) was the most creative use of World War II footage in the immediate postwar period. Produced as a public service by NBC, the series used archival footage to tell the story of U.S. naval operations worldwide during the recent war. As the first of a now long-standing television tradition, the series used fiction footage (including scenes from John Ford's *December 7th*), training film footage, and actual footage from other battles to tell its story with maximum drama and impact. Later, a theatrical version of some ninety minutes was released for large-screen audiences (and is available in many video stores).

Victory at Sea was a magnificent success when it came out in 1952, and it is still aired on television. (The complete set of twenty-six episodes is commercially available.) Richard Rodgers provided orchestrator Robert Russell Bennett with twelve tunes, which Bennett, a gifted composer in his own right, embellished to interpret the footage in rough cut. Editor Isaac Kleinerman then refined the editing to better support the music. The result was an aural and visual experience that teaches many uplifting lessons about America's role as the world's policeman, although some observers—including this author—have taken the series to task as overbearing in its celebration of war to advance American ideals and interests. The series succeeds as drama because it addresses concerns of the American audience at the beginning of the Cold War, when many felt the need to be reminded of the virtue of its cause and the worthwhile sacrifices we had made during World War II. Though it was purported to be based on Admiral Samuel Eliot Morison's famous multivolume history of U.S. naval operations, the series is actually a celebration of simple American righteousness in conflict with the pernicious Axis powers. The simplification from book to film was so great that it would be unfair to seriously claim a close connection—even though the producer, Henry Salomon, had worked with Morison on the official history. Like its wartime predecessors, *Victory at Sea* featured a polished script (by Richard Hanser) delivered by an offscreen narrator (Leonard Graves); it is unlike the typical documentary format of later decades—which includes interviews with participants when possible and/or clips of experts or scholars, so-called talking heads.

During the World War II celebrations of 1995, *Victory at Sea* returned to the screen and became a major draw for veterans and their families. Its stirring message of courage and sacrifice transcends time and represents the kind of message World War II veterans would like to have in the mainstream media.

Later Retrospections and Acts of Public Memory

With the classroom in mind, Films for the Humanities distributes *World War II,* a thirty-three-minute overview from the invasion of Poland to the Nuremberg trials. *Hidden Army—Women in World War II* (1995) stresses the contribution of women during the struggle, a record that has finally come to the surface and is proudly embodied in the Women in Military Service for America Memorial, completed in 2000, which stands on the grounds of Arlington National Cemetery.

The fiftieth anniversary of the Normandy landing, "Operation Overlord," brought many visitors to European battle sites to participate in solemn commemorations. President Bill Clinton spoke at the cemetery above Omaha Beach on June 6, 1994, and C-SPAN captured the moving ceremony on video. Other events included honoring the U.S. Rangers who scaled Pointe du Hoc, a feat that seems superhuman to any visitor to that vertical cliff on the Normandy coast. These commemorations say as much about the times in which they were made, the 1990s, as they do about the events themselves. (*The Longest Day* [1962] was a major effort to produce a faithful narrative of the greatest invasion in human history. Steven Spielberg's later production, *Saving Private Ryan* [1998], starring Tom Hanks, took many liberties with the events, but has been praised for its "realistic" rendering of the Omaha Beach landing, actually shot in Scotland.) During 2000, historian Stephen Ambrose and others opened a D-Day museum in New Orleans. Linked with the opening of the museum was an episode in the History Channel series *Save Our History.* The one-hour program investigated the artifacts and rationale for this act of memory by veterans, academics, and celebrities such as Tom Brokaw, whose books of oral history had been so favorably embraced by the veteran community. Related History Channel productions examined the role of LSTs (ships that carried landing craft and vehicles), the construction of Hitler's "Atlantic Wall," D-Day deceptions and code breaking, and the nature of Operation Overlord's commander, Dwight D. Eisenhower. C-SPAN was also present to record seminars with Ambrose, Brokaw, Tom Hanks, and other speakers honoring the sacrifices of the WWII generation.

The World War II Memorial on the National Mall was completed in 2003. The purposes and intentions of the memorial are studied in *Save Our History: The World War II Memorial.* Bob Dole, chairman of the Memorial Committee, shares the screen with former presidents Gerald Ford and George Bush and historian Stephen Ambrose. Bob Dole was severely wounded during the Italian campaign, and his story of recovery is detailed in the film, as are the varied stories of America's "greatest generation." Programs of this nature can serve as history lessons and as texts for students to analyze: How do Americans remember their history? Which elements are stressed and which elements are left in the background? How do these films—made long after the conflict—compare and contrast with some of the classic documentaries? Teachers have a wonderful opportunity with these readily available cinematic texts.

Documentaries and Democracy

America's documentary and propaganda film record of World War II reveals a democracy concerned with purpose and cohesion. Films about the home front stressed the rootedness of democratic institutions; if the town meeting was idealized in productions such as *The Cummington Story,* it was also true that the exaggeration was a product of hope more than of deception. Filmmakers wanted self-government and intellectual freedom to prevail in a world where such principles were under attack. On the other hand, documentaries about the front lines—for example, *With the Marines at Tarawa*—provided citizens with a fundamental service urged upon all documentarians by a pioneer of the documentary medium, John Grierson: these films brought citizens into contact with each other and provided a stirring picture of the common struggle. Without such portraits, the sacrifice would have gone unvalued; with such stirring depictions, ordinary citizens could understand their place in the big picture. And, for all its rhetoric and simplification, Frank Capra's series for the U.S. Army really did explain America's war aims in pictures and language that even uneducated farm boys (or city boys, for that matter) could understand. No lecture, few books, and not even the best radio chats of an eloquent president could have matched the stirring messages and historical insights of *Why We Fight.*

As later generations came back to inspect the meaning of the conflict, many found values that needed to be highlighted for the children and grandchildren of veterans. Spokesmen such as Bob Dole and Stephen Ambrose worked mightily to highlight the principles of self-sacrifice and patriotism. The contrast between the hard-edged messages of the 1940s documentaries and the hagiography of the later films is striking and deserves further study.

References

Filmography

The Battle for the Marianas (1944, D)
The Battle of Midway (1942, D)
The Battle of New Britain (1944, D)
The Battle of San Pietro (1945, D)

The Best Years of Our Lives (1945, F)
The Cummington Story (1945, D)
December 7th (1942, D)
The Fighting Lady (1944, D)
Hidden Army—Women in World War II (1995, TV)
Home of the Brave (1949, F)
Let There Be Light (1946, D)
Memphis Belle (1944, D; 1990, F)
The Negro Soldier (1944, D)
Prelude to War (1942, D)
The Ramparts We Watch (1940, F)
Report from the Aleutians (1943, D)
Save Our History: The Making of the National D-Day Museum (2000, TV) and *The World War II Memorial* (2000, TV)
Saving Private Ryan (1998, F)
Steel Town (1945, D)
To the Shores of Iwo Jima (1944, D)
The Town (1944, D)
Twelve O'Clock High (1949, F)
Victory at Sea (1952, D)
Victory Through Air Power (1943, D)
With the Marines at Tarawa (1944, D)
World War II (n.d., D)
Why We Fight (1942–45, D)

Bibliography

Adams, Michael C. C. *The Best War Ever: America and World War II.* Baltimore: Johns Hopkins University Press, 1994.

Ambrose, Stephen. *Band of Brothers: E Company, 506th Regiment, 101st Airborne, from Normandy to Hitler's Eagle's Nest.* New York: Simon & Schuster, 2001.

——. *D-Day, June 6, 1944: The Climactic Battle of World War II.* New York: Simon & Schuster, 1995.

Barsam, Richard Meran. *Nonfiction Film: A Critical History.* New York: E. P. Dutton, 1973.

Basinger, Jeanine. *The World War II Combat Film: Anatomy of a Genre.* New York: Columbia University Press, 1986.

Borchers, Hans. "Myths Used for Propaganda: The Small Town in Office of War Information Films, 1944–1945." In Lewis Carlson and Kevin Vichcales, eds., *American Popular Culture at Home and Abroad,* 161–175. Kalamazoo: Western Michigan University Press, 1996.

Brokaw, Tom, *The Greatest Generation.* New York: Random House, 1998.

Cripps, Thomas and David H. Culbert. "*The Negro Soldier* (1944): Film Propaganda in Black and White." In Peter C. Rollins, ed., *Hollywood as Historian: American Film in a Cultural Context,* 109–133. 2d ed. Lexington: University Press of Kentucky, 1998.

Culbert, David H. "'Why We Fight': Social Engineering for a Democratic Society at War." In K. R. M. Short, ed., *Film & Radio Propaganda in World War II,* 173–191. Knoxville: University of Tennessee Press, 1983.

Dick, Bernard. *The Star-Spangled Screen: The American World War II Film.* Lexington: University Press of Kentucky, 1985.

Fussell, Paul. *Wartime: Understanding and Behavior in the Second World War.* New York: Oxford University Press, 1989.

Garrett, Greg. "*Let There Be Light* and Huston's *film noir.*" *Proteus* 7.2 (1990): 30–33.

——. "Muffling the Bell of Liberty: Censorship and the World War Two Documentary." *Journal of the American Studies Association of Texas* 22 (1991): 63–73.

Keegan, John. *The Second World War.* New York: Viking, 1990.

Koppes, Clayton R., and Gregory D. Black. *Hollywood Goes to War: How Politics, Profits, and Propaganda Shaped World War II Movies.* New York: Free Press, 1987.

Maslowski, Peter. *Armed with Cameras: American Military Photographers of World War II.* New York: Free Press, 1993.

O'Neill, William L. *A Democracy at War: America's Fight at Home and Abroad in World War II.* New York: Free Press, 1993.

Roeder, George H. *The Censored War: American Visual Experience During World War Two.* New Haven: Yale University Press, 1993.

Rollins, Peter C. "Frank Capra's *Why We Fight* Series and Our American Dream." *Journal of American Culture* 19.4 (1996): 81–86.

——. "*Victory at Sea:* Cold War Epic." *Journal of Popular Culture* 6.4 (1972): 463–482.

Wheal, Elizabeth-Anne, and James Taylor, eds. *A Dictionary of the Second World War.* New York: Peter Bedrick, 1990.

[ROBERT FYNE]

World War II: Feature Films

Without question, World War II—the greatest social, political, and economic upheaval of the twentieth century—completely altered the life of every American. From 1941 to 1945, workers suddenly found high-paying jobs at plants making airplanes in California, tanks in Wisconsin, or rifles in Massachusetts, creating unprecedented demographic shifts as thousands of once-impoverished rural workers moved to cities such as Los Angeles and Chicago, where defense jobs beckoned. African Americans, victims of Jim Crow prejudices in the southern states, joined that exodus. Women of all ages were quickly recruited to work in those assembly plants, too, and a new sobriquet, "Rosie the Riveter," entered the wartime jargon. At the same time, millions of young men—the nation's volunteers and conscripts—were uprooted from life and drawn into the military world, where they met compatriots from around the nation, from all ethnicities, religions, and walks of life.

World War II historians have put forward varying interpretations of the conflict and its significance for Americans. Right after the war, tomes such as Samuel Eliot Morison's fifteen-volume *History of the United States Naval Operations in World War II* took a heroic view of the fight, proclaiming that America had rescued the world from the threat of barbarism. In 1999 this hagiographic interpretation resurfaced in Tom Brokaw's best-seller *The Greatest Generation.* Other explanations offered more modulated insights. William O'Neill's *A Democracy at War* (1993) reiterated that we fought a just war, but he tempered his enthusiasm by delineating the inequitable treatment of women and African Americans during the struggle for democracy.

Chicago journalist Studs Terkel elaborates on individual achievements in the ironically titled *"The Good War"* (1984). Terkel reaffirms that World War II completely changed the psyche, as well as the face, of the United States and the world, while Marine Corps veteran William Manchester's first-person narrative *Goodbye, Darkness* (1979), argues that the leathernecks who fought with him on Okinawa, young men who had been tempered and strengthened in the 1930s Depression by a struggle for survival, still maintained a strong sense of patriotism. Another veteran's memoir, E. B. Sledge's *With the Old Breed at Peleliu and Okinawa* (1981), claims that despite the realization that combat itself was pure insanity, he was still proud to be a marine who had served his country.

Philip D. Beidler's *The Good War's Greatest Hits* (1998) describes how the media have fostered a mythology blurring the fine line between fact and fiction, allowing Hollywood's version of the war to become enshrined as historical fact in the nation's collective memory. John W. Dower's *War Without Mercy* (1986) argues that existing racial prejudices encouraged American military strategists to advocate a policy of eradication in the Pacific. Michael C. C. Adams's *The Best War Ever* (1994) lauds the nation's patriotic fervor, but notes that there was also selfishness by corporations, organized labor, and individuals. Finally, Paul Fussell's debunking *Wartime: Understanding and Behavior in the Second World War* (1989) sees the military operations as a series of blunders, wishful thinking, and petty humiliations clouded by bureaucratic euphemisms. These negative qualities were sanitized by Hollywood's treatment of the war—for, as Fussell observes—motion pictures provided a silver lining where unalloyed good always triumphed over unprincipled evil (ix).

Hollywood Goes to War, 1941–45

The Pearl Harbor attack transformed Hollywood. Early in the war, President Roosevelt averred that motion pictures were the most effective medium to keep the nation informed about the worldwide hostilities. Promising no censorship, Roosevelt called for a continuous output of screenplays and appointed Elmer Davis to run the Office of War Information (the OWI), an agency that established film industry guidelines. These regulations were designed to insure screenplay conformity and—for the most part—did not disavow Roosevelt's pledge. True, all scripts required OWI approval, and occasionally changes were mandated, but in the end Hollywood and government bureaucracy formed a cooperative relationship. These photoplays, as Jordan Braverman acknowledges, would "make the public understand what was at stake in the conflict" (161).

For the next four years, the cameras kept rolling as one movie after another documented a world at war. Some screenplays were major productions with big-name stars and directors. Other photodramas came from small B-movie studios, companies working on a shoestring budget, which hacked out their sixty-minute products in less than a week. And although many titles became classics, others were relegated—like points, war stamps, and victory gardens—to oblivion. In all, more than four hundred propaganda films that reaffirmed America's righteousness were made by V-J Day. These motion pictures, as Swedish historians Leif Furhammer and Folke Isaksson observe, were aimed "at audiences which already shared their values" (231). Without question, Hollywood's contribution played an important role in sustaining morale and optimism.

How did the motion picture industry accomplish all this? How did its popular films reiterate America's determination to win the war? First of all, Hollywood was not caught flat-footed on December 7, 1941. For more than two years, most studios had produced dozens of antifascist titles—such as *Confession of a Nazi Spy* (1939), *Foreign Correspondent* (1940), and *Man Hunt* (1940)—warning of Axis aggression in Europe. After Pearl Harbor, Hollywood simply ordered full speed ahead.

Released just six weeks after Pearl Harbor, *A Yank on the Burma Road* sets the stage for the dozens of anti-Japanese movies that followed. Here Barry Nelson, a former New York City cabby, risks everything to deliver medical supplies to his Chinese allies, outwitting the Nipponese attackers on every serpentine turn of the famous mountain highway. Similar photoplays depict U.S. forces routing their Asian enemy. In *Flying Tigers* (1942), John Wayne and his airmen destroy much of the Japanese air force, while Anthony Quinn, now a Chinese chieftain, decimates his invaders in *China Sky* (1945). Other contemporary screenplays depicting American prowess against the Japanese include *Gung Ho, Wing and a Prayer, Guadalcanal Diary, Back to Bataan, Thirty Seconds Over Tokyo,* and *Wake Island.*

In their fight against Japan, Hollywood reduced America's Pacific adversary to a two-dimensional caricature, the butt of numerous racial epithets. The American people, outraged by a "sneak attack," clamored for revenge. On the screen, the Japanese soldier often wears thick eyeglasses and shouts "banzai!" while his officers—frail, diminutive men waving samurai swords—volunteer their lives to Emperor Hirohito by leading a suicide attack or committing hara-kiri. The Japanese are depicted as a simian enemy who tortures and mutilates American GIs without remorse in *The Purple Heart, Objective Burma,* and *Marine Raiders* or violates Red Cross nurses in *So Proudly We Hail* and *Cry Havoc.* Frequently, these characterizations seemed ludicrous because so many Western actors, wearing exaggerated makeup, portrayed these Asians not as assailants but as comic-strip fanatics.

On the European front, members of the Third Reich were often derided as strutting clowns in a manner that seemed callous and macabre. The Nazi soldier appears as a buffoon, a gangster, or a heel-clicking martinet—and sometimes all three, as in *Casablanca* (1942)—while in Italy, Il Duce's soldiers sing nineteenth-century arias and refrain from armed combat completely. Motion pictures such as *To Be or Not to Be, Invisible Agent, Once upon a Honeymoon,* and *Desperate Journey* reduce the German officer to an incompetent who fidgets with his suede gloves or polishes his monocle while mispronouncing his v's and w's. When confronted by an American GI (Humphrey Bogart in *Sahara*) or a British Tommy (Franchot Tone in *Five Graves to Cairo*), the Nazi war machine simply falls apart. Only late in the war, with such realistic dramas as Lewis Milestone's *A Walk in the Sun* (1945), were German soldiers reckoned as determined and difficult foes who were not likely to give up easily.

For the Soviet Union, the Allies' new partner, Hollywood employed its best talents to finesse a touchy situation. As far back as 1919, American filmgoers were regularly warned about the expansionist policies of communist Russia and its goal of world domination in such titles as *Red Salute* (1935), *Tovarich* (1937), and *He Stayed for Breakfast* (1940). Now, as brothers in arms, a softer image was quickly formed to cement this alliance. The Russian soldier emerges as brave, intrepid, and venturesome, relying on his mettle to rout Hitler's armies. Always outnumbered and lacking proper equipment, the Red Army defeats the Axis at every turn in *The North Star, Song of Russia, Days of Glory,* and *The Boy from Stalingrad.* In *Mission to Moscow*—a film that would later receive congressional scrutiny—every misdeed committed under Bolshevism is swept under the rug, including Stalin's purge trials, the invasion of Finland, and the Hitler-Stalin Pact, as the former American ambassador, Joseph E. Davies, in an introductory trailer, lauds Soviet gallantry. The picture, as historians Clayton Koppes and Gregory Black recall, "fed a genuine hunger on the part of millions of Americans to know more about their heroic but little understood and still mistrusted allies" (185).

The Chinese—now an integral part of the Allied forces—were battling a superior enemy, but Hollywood quickly came to their rescue by sending American pilots into the combat zone. Dennis Morgan (*God Is My Co-Pilot*) John Carroll (*Flying Tigers*) and George Montgomery (*China Girl*)destroy countless Japanese Zeroes, while on the ground two rice farmers, Katherine Hepburn and Walter Huston, poison the food of an entire Japanese regiment in *Dragon Seed.* Other titles—*Night Plane from Chungking, Escape from Hong Kong,* and *China's Little Devils*—depict American fighters, with Chinese assistance, halting the invaders.

The Home Front

Back on the home front, while the civilian population slowly adjusted to the new war regulations that included rationing, blackout shades, and air-raid drills, Hollywood produced numerous titles reminding audiences that the battles fought on some remote Pacific island were first won at home. American workers, especially the distaff factory assemblers, are praised for their wartime contributions in *Sweethearts of the U.S.A.* and *Rosie the Riveter,* while other titles—*Joe Smith, American, Watch on the Rhine,* and *Saboteur*—warn of fifth columnists. Some levity emerged in two Preston Sturges pictures, *The Miracle of Morgan's Creek* and *Hail the Conquering Hero,* while Hollywood mogul David O. Selznick's *Since You Went Away* focuses on the problems germane to upper-class America when the breadwinner, now in the officer corps, departs for overseas duty.

Occasionally, some pictures touch upon the self-sacrifice and hardship found on the home front. *Pride of the Marines, I'll Be Seeing You,* and *The Enchanted Cottage* take a hard look at the problems associated with the returning veteran, while *The Fighting Sullivans* (also called *The Sullivans*) poignantly traces the lives of five brothers, born and bred in the Norman Rockwell world of Waterloo, Iowa, who enlisted together in the navy and were assigned to the same ship; during an early naval battle off Guadalcanal, all five were killed. In reenacting this disaster, Hollywood created one of the most memorable images of the war. Character actor Ward Bond, playing a naval commander, informs the Sullivan family of its loss in a scene that offers dignity to a terrible event. The screenplay's propaganda message—that freedom is not cheap—offers quiet solace to a nation experiencing combat casualties.

There were lighthearted moments on the home front as the Hollywood musical provided additional escapism from the uncertainty associated with the war. Pictures such as *Up in Arms, The Fleet's In, Stage Door Canteen,* and *Yankee Doodle Dandy* entertained theatergoers everywhere with their fancy tap dancing, standup comedy, pratfalls, and popular melodies. But one scene certainly brought down the house: Kate Smith, the doyenne of popular vocalists, singing the inspirational "God Bless America" in *This Is the Army.* By V-J Day, more than seventy-five Hollywood war musicals had been released, providing enough flag-waving lyrics for everyone. As William Tuttle observes, theater attendance "soared during the war. Most people wanted escape and with fat pay checks they could go to the movies several times a week" (154).

The B Films of World War II

Developed as a gimmick to boost sales during the Depression years, the B (for budget) movie—using unknown actors, limited capital, and standard backdrops—required about seven working days to complete. Now on a wartime footing, the B movie took aim at America's enemies.

Out on the frontier, B cowboys nab Axis saboteurs, protect their cattle ranches, and deliver horses to military installations in *Cowboy Commandoes, Black Market Rustlers,* and *Texas to Bataan.* On another open prairie, Roy Rogers and Gene Autry—two popular singing cowboys—foil Nazi espionage while crooning patriotic melodies in *King of the Cowboys* and *Bells of Capistrano.*

Other titles that reminded audiences of Axis treachery are *Secret Enemies, Spy Train, Secret Command,* and *Nazi Spy Ring.* Additional movies—with similar-sounding names—include *Madame Spy, Unseen Enemy, Underground Agent,* and *Foreign Agent.* Each picture follows a similar format: enemy spies threaten America but are caught and punished by quick-thinking patriots. Even well-known detectives—Charlie Chan, Ellery Queen, Dick Tracy, and Sherlock Holmes—entered the fray, with their numerous contributions proving once again, as film historians Michael Shull and David Wilt have noted, that America was safe from all spies and saboteurs (253).

As a major component to the war effort, these low-budget potboilers played an important role in the overall propaganda effort by releasing titles that framed basic American homilies: watch out for foreign spies, find a job in a defense plant, obey rationing edicts, and always defend your home, flag, and country.

After four difficult years, the fighting was over. Back in Hollywood, the moguls could shift their production plans. War film production came to a screeching halt as new screenplays highlighted frivolity and extravagance. American audiences, now savoring the material goods that came with peace, wanted old-fashioned fun, entertainment, and escapism.

Postwar Productions

Only a handful of war pictures appeared in 1946, mostly titles that were carryovers from 1945. Three photodramas—*O.S.S., Thirteen*

Rue Madeline, and *Cloak and Dagger*—emphasize Allied espionage activities in the European Theater, while *Till the End of Time* focuses on a new problem created by combat: the readjustment of handicapped veterans coming home. But one additional title seemed to say it all: the Academy Award–winning *Best Years of Our Lives.* William Wyler's film traces the joys, sorrows, and self-realizations of three combat veterans as they return to their thriving mid-American city months after the war. Dana Andrews is outstanding as a decorated B-17 bombardier; Fred Derry discovers that the postwar boom has no place for the men who dropped their explosives on German targets; while Frederic March plays Al Stephenson, a former sergeant back from the Pacific who grudgingly returns to his executive banking position, a job he now finds incongruous. "Last year," he reminds his wife (Myrna Loy), "it was kill Japs; and this year it's make money."

But Harold Russell's portrayal of Homer Parrish, a young sailor who lost both hands when his ship was attacked, steals the show as a shy, sensitive, gee-whiz, hometown boy hoping for a modicum of normalcy. (Russell, who really did lose his hands in a munitions explosion, would go on to appear in other films over the years, including a final appearance in the anti-Vietnam drama *Cutter's Way* [1981].) Replete with numerous social criticisms that blast draft-dodgers, war profiteering, unfaithful wives, America First committees, and short memories, *Best Years* calls to task the various modes of opportunism on the home front. Without question, this highly acclaimed motion picture makes one thing abundantly clear: the days of the propaganda film, touting unequivocal American virtues, were over.

For the next few years, World War II titles trickled out of Hollywood as new screenplays took a hard and sometimes critical look at the terrible cost of the Allied victory. Both *Command Decision* (1948) and *Twelve O'Clock High* (1949) scrutinize the high casualty rate of Air Corps bombing raids over Europe as officers and politicians—frequently at odds with each other—argue over strategy. Back in the foxholes, *Battleground* (1949), *An American Guerrilla in the Philippines* (1950), and *Halls of Montezuma* (1950) describe, in graphic terms, the uncertainty every foot soldier felt as bombs and shells fell nearby.

But the quintessential combat film of the postwar period that—in a quiet, dignified manner—honored the Marine Corps for its many island victories was *Sands of Iwo Jima* (1949). Only John Wayne could portray a tough squad leader who teaches his young charges the meaning of loyalty, teamwork, and *semper fidelis.* Soon the marines assault Iwo Jima and, along with John Agar and Forrest Tucker, push inland to witness the historic flag raising on Mount Suribachi. Here a Japanese sniper fells John Wayne. After a short eulogy, the marines—mindful of their sergeant's sacrifice—continue their attack. Using three actual members from the iconic Joe Rosenthal photograph in the cast, the movie reaffirms the high human cost of the South Pacific fighting and the value of the U.S. Marines, then under fire as an expensive anachronism by President Harry S. Truman.

The 1950s and 1960s

When the Korean War broke out in June 1950, Hollywood again pushed the go button and for the next three years produced a new generation of World War II films, titles that once more reminded American audiences of past sacrifices and victories. Patriotic screenplays—such as *Flying Leathernecks, The Frogmen, Go for Broke,* and *Destination Gobi*—highlight Yankee intransigence. Now that the Cold War had turned hot, screenwriters sent a strong nuclear warning in *Above and Beyond* (1952) to their new enemy, communist Russia. Here Robert Taylor, a fly-by-the-book, Army Air Corps pilot, trains a specialized crew to drop the first atomic bomb. The movie's message needed no decoding for the Soviets: we did it before and we can do it again.

After the 1953 Panmunjon peace accord, World War II films began to scrutinize old battles and past glories. Many films of the 1950s and 1960s, such as John Huston's *Heaven Knows, Mr. Allison* (1957) and Raoul Walsh's *Battle Cry* (1955), celebrate the heroism of ordinary soldiers, while the officer class—once portrayed as sacrosanct—receives some nasty swipes in dramas such as *The Caine Mutiny* (1954), *Mister Roberts* (1955), and *The Dirty Dozen* (1967).

Many other films are heavily critical of the military caste system. *From Here to Eternity* (1953), based on James Jones's acclaimed novel, is a strong indictment of the spit-and-polish mentality at a U.S. Army base a few miles from Pearl Harbor, where favoritism, bullying, and torture are the order of the day. Another screenplay, *The Naked and the Dead* (1958)—an elaborate adaptation of Norman Mailer's controversial book—also points the finger at some troubled personalities among officers as an army unit advances inland on a Japanese-held island during a 1943 offensive. *The Bridge on the River Kwai* (1957), a blockbuster directed by David Lean and the winner of seven Academy Awards, describes the ordeal of Allied POWs building a Japanese railway bridge in the Malaysian jungle, an all but impossible project dictated by the brutal Japanese officer played by Sessue Hayakawa but made all the more difficult by the prisoner's own remote, unbending commander, portrayed by Alec Guinness. And Edward Dmytryk's *The Young Lions* (1958) suggests that all generals, whether Allied or Axis, are incompetent, whereas all soldiers, whether Allied or Axis, are inherently noble, if sometimes misunderstood.

But not every picture disparaged America's leadership. Titles such as *To Hell and Back* (1955), *Battle Cry* (1955), *The Guns of Navarone* (1961), and *The Great Escape* (1963) reinforce traditional U.S. values, as military forces, using skill and initiative, pulverize their enemies. Other photoplays emphasizing superior leadership are *The Gallant Hours* (1960), *Merrill's Marauders* (1962), *PT 109* (1962), and *The Longest Day* (1962).

As an elaborate, black-and-white blockbuster, Darryl F. Zanuck's *The Longest Day*—based on the best-selling book by Cornelius Ryan—documents the June 6, 1944, invasion of Normandy as witnessed by both Allied and Axis forces at numerous battle sites and command headquarters. Using a large contingency of famous stars, the storyline details the successes, good fortune, tragedy, and dumb luck that both sides experienced during the invasion. The screenplay is noteworthy for its attempt to render participants and battle sites with detailed accuracy. This D-Day portrait, as motion picture historian Steven Jay Rubin observes, represents the perfect image of what D. W. Griffith originally viewed as a history lesson on film (45).

The Vietnam Era

By 1968 the Vietnam War had polarized the nation, and flag-waving war films lost much of their appeal. Screenplays such as *Beach Red* (1967), *Hell in the Pacific* (1968), *Castle Keep* (1969), and *Catch-22* (1970)—while ostensibly World War II titles—are obvious anti-Nixon, anti-Vietnam parables. Together, all three pictures elaborate one common theme: war's absurdity.

As a strong antiwar statement, *Beach Red*—based on the novel by Peter Bowman—downplays stereotypical heroics and, instead, focuses on folly and egomania. Here, a stalwart marine officer, Captain MacDonald (Cornel Wilde, who directed) cautiously guides his men through the uncharted jungles on some unnamed South Pacific island only to witness violent death at every turn. As a complex parable, John Boorman's *Hell in the Pacific* offers similar editorial statements about survival, friendship, and tolerance. Portraying a Japanese officer marooned on a remote South Pacific atoll during the closing months of the war, Toshiro Mifune maintains a solitary existence in a harsh environment. Eventually, a naval pilot, Lee Marvin, washes ashore, and the two men—initially hostile to each other and unable to communicate verbally—reach a truce, if one with an ironic denouement.

Another screenplay offering a combined ontological and mystical look at war's futility, Sidney Pollack's *Castle Keep* (based on the novel by William Eastlake), employs various forms of mysticism, spiritualism, and rationalism during the precarious 1944 Battle of the Bulge offensive. Likewise, Mike Nichols's *Catch-22,* a black comedy based on Joseph Heller's best-selling novel, fires off both barrels at the lunacy of military life, blasting away at the nepotism, opportunism, goldbricking, and bureaucracy. Praising its satirical tone, psychiatrist Robert Lifton and historian Gregory Mitchell note that even though *Catch-22* is a World War II topic, in reality it is about Vietnam (379).

Realizing that flag-waving patriotism still appealed to pro-Vietnam supporters, two titles emerged that waved the red, white, and blue with multimillion dollar extravagance: *Patton* (1970) and *Tora! Tora! Tora!* (1970). Both titles were box-office smashes and reminded audiences of the heroic past, even though the latter highlighted the Pearl Harbor defeat. Franklin J. Schaffner's *Patton* is a controversial, 171-minute hagiography to the flamboyant and controversial four-star general known to his men as "Old Blood-and-Guts" (or, as one of the soldiers in the film ironically comments, "our blood, his guts"), the larger-than-life, egomaniacal officer responsible for many important battlefield victories in Europe after D-Day. In an Academy Award–winning performance, George C. Scott captures the mannerisms of the unconventional George S. Patton—from his Bible-quoting oratory down to his pearl-handled revolver—beginning with his 1942 North African campaign. In a similar vein *Tora! Tora! Tora!* is a quasi-documentary, both-sides-of-the-story examination of the events leading up to the Japanese attack on Pearl Harbor.

After Vietnam

After the Vietnam hostilities came to end, with most Americans still divided over the outcome, Hollywood—with its eye on the bottom line—relegated World War II to the archives. Although *Midway* (1976), *A Bridge Too Far* (1977), and *Force 10 from Navarone* (1978) retell certain aspects of the American combat adventure, other screenplays turn the tables. Both *Cross of Iron* (1977) and *The Eagle Has Landed* (1977) glamorize the exploits of the German soldier, portraying these men as heroes, lending support to Peter C. Rollins's observation that Hollywood often attempts to influence history by producing films consciously designed to change public attitudes (1). In *Cross of Iron,* directed by Sam Peckinpah, Wehrmacht sergeant James Coburn is something of a German John Wayne, a deft soldier leading his men to victory on the eastern front. Michael Caine's cockney accent is incongruous for a Nazi commando ordered to kill Winston Churchill in *The Eagle Has Landed*; even more distorted is the way in which the film sugarcoats every facet of Hitlerism.

In the 1980s, only a handful of motion pictures recalled the global conflict. While some movies, such as Sam Fuller's *The Big Red One* (1980), examined the war, others fooled around with history. In *The Final Countdown* (1980)—a high-flying, science-fiction yarn that shows off the U.S. Navy's modern carrier power in a manner usually found in the eerie scripts that made the television series *The Twilight Zone* so popular—Kirk Douglas stars as the captain of the U.S.S. *Nimitz,* a flattop cruising west of the Hawaiian Islands in late 1979, while Martin Sheen, a civilian observer, studies military protocol. Soon a phantasmagoric sea storm transposes the ship back into the time zone of late 1941. The carrier's reconnaissance planes spot the Japanese armada, but, unable to upset the course of history, the *Nimitz* must reluctantly return to the present, allowing the sneak attack to culminate. Replete with pithy hindsight observations, this offbeat tale glamorizes every facet of life aboard an electronically operated fighting ship.

Another subject—the controversial issue of using nuclear weapons on two Japanese cities—is examined in *Fat Man and Little Boy* (1989). Written from a military point of view, the film examines the design, building, and delivery of the atomic bomb. Paul Newman portrays project commander General Leslie Groves, while Dwight Schultz sparkles as noted physicist Dr. J. Robert Oppenheimer. Brimming with philosophical arguments, this motion picture offers strong rationalizations regarding the thorny issue of the necessity for obliterating Hiroshima and Nagasaki. This was not the first screenplay, however, to deal with the *Enola Gay's* early morning mission over Japan. In *The Beginning or the End* (1947) Hume Cronyn, in the Oppenheimer role, proffers a conservative approach. One scene—depicting the Los Alamos implosion—seems macabre as Oppenheimer and his staff, unaware of nuclear energy's potential, rub suntan lotion on their skin as protection against the blast from the first atomic test. Another title, *Day One* (1989), a made-for-TV docudrama, offers a centrist interpretation of the events that unfolded at the top-secret New Mexico site.

The Last Decade

By 1990, World War II had become a distant memory for most Americans. But films continued to probe the conflict. In *The Plot to Kill Hitler* (a made-for-TV drama), numerous Nazi officers, led by Brad Davis, mastermind the elaborate assassination attempt of the Führer. They fail. *For the Boys* (1991) tells the story of two entertainers, played by James Caan and Bette Midler, and their adventures as U.S.O. performers in the combat zone, while another made-for-TV indictment, *Mission of the Shark,* recounts the harrowing events after the U.S.S. *Indianapolis* was torpedoed—on July 30, 1945, just before V-J Day—forcing most of its crew to bobble helplessly in the shark-infested Pacific for four days before rescuers arrived.

Memphis Belle (1990) is an elaborate testimony to the first crew in the Eighth Air Force to fly the coveted twenty-fifth mission, a feat that qualified the men for stateside duty. As the youthful leader of a B-17, Captain Dennis Dearborn (Matthew Modine) guides his aircraft from the quiet plains of southern England to the German port of Bremen to bomb the city's industrial area on May 17, 1943. Constantly under attack by Luftwaffe fighters or antiaircraft fire, the bomber—damaged in its critical landing section—limps back home to the acclaim of the senior officers and public relations staff. While elements of the storyline are pure Hollywood fiction, it is nevertheless a paean to William Wyler's 1944 aerial documentary *The Memphis Belle,* a film that glorifies this famous twenty-fifth crossing. In 1995, an HBO production, *The Tuskegee Airmen,* honored the African American pilots who provided fighter support for the *Memphis Belle* and its sister aircraft.

Not every screenplay has kind words about American behavior in World War II. Recalling some of the themes of John Sturges's 1955 drama *Bad Day at Black Rock,* Alan Parker's *Come See the Paradise* (1990) is a strongly worded indictment of Executive Law 9066—quickly passed after the Pearl Harbor attack—that sent thousands of West Coast Japanese American citizens to internment centers for the war's duration—the worst violation of civil liberties in wartime America, as historian Allan M. Winkler documents (73). Here, an outspoken labor organizer, Jack McGurn (Dennis Quaid), married to a nisei, watches helplessly as federal agents, brandishing newly printed warrants, round up his wife and in-laws, claiming they represent a threat to the nation's security.

Another picture that takes a caustic, surrealistic, and ontological look at war, death, and friendship—*A Midnight Clear* (1992)—demeans the caste system separating enlisted men from their officers. Ethan Hawke sparkles as a young, pensive soldier, Sergeant Will

Knott, who, along with five other GIs from an intelligence and reconnaissance squad, squirrels himself away in the Ardennes Forest during the Christmas 1944 German offensive, while *Schindler's List* (1993) retells the Holocaust tragedy in a dignified, poignant, and harrowing manner. A financial success and Academy Award winner, *Schindler's List* became the twentieth century's exclamation point, restating the horror of the Final Solution with great poignancy.

Most viewers ignored *Mother Night* (1996), the film version of Kurt Vonnegut's black comedy about an American spy working as a German radio announcer, proving again that World War II themes were hit or miss affairs in the eyes of fickle, youthful audiences. In 1998, though, Spielberg returned to the war much more successfully with *Saving Private Ryan,* a mega-blockbuster depicting the Normandy invasion. The same year saw the return of the acclaimed director Terrence Malick, whose *The Thin Red Line,* set on the Japanese-held island of Guadalcanal, is a pensive meditation on the folly of war—and a decidedly more downbeat film than Spielberg's celebration of men at arms.

FIGURE 16. *Memphis Belle* (1990). *Memphis Belle* celebrates the feats and personalities of a B-17 bomber crew under the command of Capt. Dennis Dearborn (Matthew Modine) as it fulfills its twenty-fifth and final mission. Courtesy Warner Bros.

Hollywood as Historian

Probably no other Hollywood genre has experienced such diverse interpretations as the World War II film. Appearing weeks after Pearl Harbor, the early titles—such as *Joan of Paris, Captains of the Clouds, To the Shores of Tripoli,* and *Across the Pacific*—render the Axis foes in strict two-dimensional terms. Visual clichés, stock characters, and stereotypes abound, using the same message of morale: we may have lost the first battle, but we will win the last. Most of these motion pictures, John W. Jeffries observes, portray the armed forces stressing both teamwork and diversity (181), while Jeanine Basinger—noting the influence of genre on filmmaking—concludes that the World War II screenplays create images of power that would and could not be forgotten. These are the photodramas, she asserts, that speak to the American soul (81).

When the war ended, Hollywood, now free of all propaganda restraints, offered different interpretations. Titles such as *All My Sons* (1948) expose opportunism, while *Home of the Brave* (1949) details military racism. *The Men* (1950) and *Bright Victory* (1951) probe the ordeal of the wounded veteran. Standard combat melodramas—*Flying Leathernecks* (1951), *The Tanks are Coming* (1951), and *Eight Iron Men* (1952)—retell stories of battle heroism. The list seems endless as Hollywood continued to churn out one picture after another.

Are they historically accurate? Some, such as *D-Day: The Sixth of June* (1956), are half fact, half soap opera, as Robert Taylor, about to embark on his great crusade, behaves like a lovesick cow because his married British girlfriend will not give him a straight answer to his proposal of marriage. Others are farfetched, such as *The Sea Wolves* (1980), in which a motley group of over-the-hill British civilians, living in Calcutta, forms a commando team that destroys three Nazi warships moored in nearby Goa, a neutral Portuguese port.

After television emerged as the dominant tool of communication, World War II films went off in all directions—a symphony orchestra captured by the Nazis in *Counter-*

point (1968); a visit to a faraway planet in *Slaughterhouse-Five* (1972); a glorification of American generals in *MacArthur* (1977) and *Ike* (1979); an updated Gothic thriller in *A Time of Destiny* (1988); and private-school remembrances in *December* (1991). Even the likes of Cary Grant and Frank Sinatra rout the Axis in, respectively, *Father Goose* (1964) and *Never So Few* (1959), *None but the Brave* (1965), and *Von Ryan's Express* (1965). Some titles reexamine old enemies, almost washing the slate clean for their Axis misdeeds: *The Desert Fox* (1951), *The Enemy Below* (1957), *The Best of Enemies* (1962), *Is Paris Burning?* (1965), and *Eye of the Needle* (1981). Other topics include the home front in *Summer of '41* (1971), *The Way We Were* (1973), *Swing Shift* (1984), and *Racing with the Moon* (1984); even spoofs appeared with *1941* (1979), *Dead Men Don't Wear Plaid* (1982), *To Be or Not to Be* (1983), and *Top Secret!* (1984).

Beginning with a shaky start, right after Pearl Harbor, the filmmakers—inspired by President Roosevelt's declaration that motion pictures were the most effective medium to inform all citizens—pooled their talents to produce hundreds of titles that explained the international conflict to America. After the final surrender of the Axis, Hollywood took an in-depth look at the war itself and offered a multifaceted appraisal, mixing praise and condemnation. With each decade, the tone of these screenplays—like the society they mirrored—changed. As historians John Chambers and David Culbert note, audiences for moving images are so great that more people have experienced the war through feature films and television docudramas than actually participated in it (viii). Some screenplays are right on target; others are pure fiction, even hokum. It may be true, as Paul Fussell laments, that "America has not yet understood what the Second World War was like" (268), but one thing is certain: for better or worse, Hollywood has become our primary teacher about World War II.

References

Filmography

Above and Beyond (1952, F)
Across the Pacific (1942, F)
All My Sons (1948, F)
An American Guerrilla in the Philippines (1950, F)
The Americanization of Emily (1964, F)
Attack (1956, F)
Back to Bataan (1945, F)
Bad Day at Black Rock (1955, F)
Bataan (1943, F)
Battle Cry (1955, F)
Battleground (1949, F)
Beach Red (1967, F)
The Beginning or the End (1947, F)
A Bell for Adano (1945, F)
Bells of Capistrano (1942, F)
The Best of Enemies (1962, F)
The Best Years of Our Lives (1946, F)
The Big Red One (1980, F)
Biloxi Blues (1988, F)
Black Market Rustlers (1943, F)
The Boy from Stalingrad (1943, F)
The Bridge on the River Kwai (1957, F)
A Bridge Too Far (1977, F)
Bright Victory (1951, F)
The Caine Mutiny (1954, F)
Captains of the Clouds (1942, F)
Casablanca (1942, F)
Castle Keep (1969, F)
Catch-22 (1970, F)
China Girl (1942, F)
China Sky (1945, F)
China's Little Devils (1945, F)
Cloak and Dagger (1946, F)
Come See the Paradise (1990, F)
Command Decision (1948, F)
Confessions of a Nazi Spy (1939, F)
Counterpoint (1968, F)
Cowboy Commandoes (1943, F)
Cross of Iron (1977, F)
Cry Havoc (1943, F)
Day One (1989, F)
Days of Glory (1944, F)
D-Day: The Sixth of June (1956, F)
Dead Men Don't Wear Plaid (1982, F)
December (1991, F)
The Desert Fox (1951, F)
Desperate Journey (1942, F)
Destination Gobi (1953, F)

The Dirty Dozen (1967, F)
The Eagle Has Landed (1977, F)
Eight Iron Men (1952, F)
The Enchanted Cottage (1945, F)
The Enemy Below (1957, F)
Escape from Hong Kong (1942, F)
Eye of the Needle (1981, F)
Father Goose (1964, F)
Fat Man and Little Boy (1989, F)
The Fighting Seabees (1944, F)
The Fighting Sullivans (1944, F)
The Final Countdown (1980, F)
Five Graves to Cairo (1943, F)
The Fleet's In (1942, F)
Flying Leathernecks (1951, F)
Flying Tigers (1942, F)
Force 10 from Navarone (1978, F)
Foreign Agent (1942, F)
Foreign Correspondent (1940, F)
For the Boys (1991, F)
The Frogmen (1951, F)
From Here to Eternity (1953, F)
The Gallant Hours (1960, F)
God Is My Co-Pilot (1945, F)
Go for Broke (1951, F)
The Great Escape (1963, F)
Guadalcanal Diary (1943, F)
Gung Ho (1943, F)
The Guns of Navarone (1961, F)
The Gypsy Warriors (1978, F)
Hail the Conquering Hero (1944, F)
Halls of Montezuma (1950, F)
Heaven Knows, Mr. Allison (1957, F)
Hell in the Pacific (1968, F)
He Stayed for Breakfast (1940, F)
Home of the Brave (1949, F)
Ike (1979, F)
I'll Be Seeing You (1944, F)
Invisible Agent (1942, F)
Is Paris Burning? (1965, F)
Joan of Paris (1942, F)
Joe Smith, American (1942, F)
King of the Cowboys (1943, F)
The Longest Day (1962, F)
MacArthur (1977, F)
Madame Spy (1942, F)
Man Hunt (1940, F)
Marine Raiders (1944, F)
Memphis Belle (1944, D; 1990, F)
The Men (1950, F)
Merrill's Marauders (1962, F)
A Midnight Clear (1992, F)
Midway (1976, F)
The Miracle of Morgan's Creek (1944, F)
Mission of the Shark (1991, F)
Mission to Moscow (1943, F)
Mister Roberts (1955, F)
Mother Night (1996, F)
The Naked and the Dead (1958, F)
Nazi Spy Ring (1943, F)
Never So Few (1959, F)
Night Plane from Chungking (1943, F)
1941 (1979, F)
None but the Brave (1965, F)
The North Star (1943, F)
Objective, Burma! (1945, F)
Once upon a Honeymoon (1942, F)
O.S.S. (1946, F)
Patton (1970, F)
Pearl Harbor (2001, F)
The Plot to Kill Hitler (1990, F)
Pride of the Marines (1945, F)
PT 109 (1962, F)
The Purple Heart (1944, F)
Racing with the Moon (1984, F)
Red Salute (1935, F)
Rosie the Riveter (1944, F)
Saboteur (1942, F)
Sands of Iwo Jima (1949, F)
Saving Private Ryan (1998, F)
Schindler's List (1993, F)
The Sea Wolves (1980, F)
Secret Command (1944, F)
Secret Enemies (1942, F)
Since You Went Away (1944, F)
Slaughterhouse-Five (1972, F)
Song of Russia (1943, F)
So Proudly We Hail (1943, F)
Spy Train (1943, F)
Stage Door Canteen (1943, F)
Stalag 17 (1953, F)
Summer of '41 (1971, F)
Sweethearts of the U.S.A. (1944, F)
Swing Shift (1984, F)
The Tanks Are Coming (1951, F)
Texas to Bataan (1942, F)
The Thin Red Line (1998, F)
Thirteen Rue Madeline (1946, F)
Thirty Seconds Over Tokyo (1944, F)
This Is the Army (1943, F)
Till the End of Time (1946, F)
A Time of Destiny (1988, F)
To Be or Not to Be (1983, F)
Top Secret (1984, F)
Tora! Tora! Tora! (1970, F)
To the Shores of Tripoli (1942, F)
Tovarich (1937, F)
The Tuskegee Airmen (1995, F)
Twelve O'Clock High (1949, F)
Underground Agent (1942, F)
Unseen Enemy (1942, F)
Up in Arms (1944, F)
The Victors (1963, F)
Von Ryan's Express (1965, F)
Wake Island (1942, F)
A Walk in the Sun (1945, F)

Watch on the Rhine (1943, F)
The Way We Were (1973, F)
Wing and a Prayer (1944, F)
Yankee Doodle Dandy (1942, F)
A Yank on the Burma Road (1942, F)
The Young Lions (1958, F)

Bibliography

Adams, Michael C. C. *The Best War Ever: American and World War II.* Baltimore: Johns Hopkins University Press, 1994.

Basinger, Jeanine. *The World War II Combat Film: Anatomy of a Genre.* New York: Columbia University Press, 1986.

Beidler, Philip D. *The Good War's Greatest Hits: World War II and American Remembering.* Athens: University of Georgia Press, 1998.

Braverman, Jordan. *To Hasten the Homecoming: How Americans Fought World War II Through the Media.* Lanham, MD: Madison, 1996.

Brokaw, Tom. *The Greatest Generation.* New York: Random House, 1999.

Butler, Ivan. *The War Film.* New York: A. C. Barnes, 1974.

Chambers, John Whiteclay, and David Culbert. *World War II: Film and History.* New York: Oxford University Press, 1996.

Dick, Bernard F. *The Star-Spangled Screen: The American World War II Film.* Lexington: University Press of Kentucky, 1985.

Dower, John W. *War Without Mercy: Race and Power in the Pacific War.* New York: Pantheon, 1986.

Furhammar, Leif, and Folke Isaksson. *Politics and Film.* New York: Praeger, 1971.

Fussell, Paul. *Wartime: Understanding and Behavior in the Second World War.* New York: Oxford University Press, 1989.

Fyne, Robert. *The Hollywood Propaganda of World War II.* Metuchen, NJ: Scarecrow, 1994.

Jeffries, John W. *Wartime America: The World War II Home Front.* Chicago: Ivan R. Dee, 1996.

Jones, Ken D., and A. F. McClure. *Hollywood at War: The American Motion Picture and World War II.* New York: Castle, 1973.

Kagan, Norman. *The War Film.* New York: Pyramid, 1974.

Kane, Kathryn. *Visions of War: Hollywood Combat Films of World War II.* Ann Arbor: UMI Research Press, 1982.

Koppes, Clayton R., and Gregory D. Black. *Hollywood Goes to War: How Politics, Profits, and Propaganda Shaped World War II Movies.* New York: Free Press, 1987.

Langman, Larry, and Ed Borg. *Encyclopedia of America War Films.* New York: Garland, 1974.

Lifton, Robert Jay, and Gregory Mitchell. *Hiroshima in America: Fifty Years of Denial.* New York: Putnam, 1995.

Manchester, William. *Goodbye Darkness: A Memoir of the Pacific War.* Boston: Little Brown, 1979.

Manvell, Roger. *Films and the Second World War.* New York: Dell, 1974.

Morison, Samuel Eliot. *History of United States Naval Operations in World War II.* 15 vols. Boston: Little Brown, 1951.

O'Neill, William. *A Democracy at War: America's Fight at Home and Abroad in World War II.* New York: Free Press, 1993.

Parish, James Robert. *The Great Combat Pictures: Twentieth-Century Warfare on the Screen.* Metuchen, NJ: Scarecrow, 1990.

Rollins, Peter, ed. *Hollywood as Historian: American Film in a Cultural Context.* 2d ed. Lexington: University Press of Kentucky, 1998.

Rubin, Steven Jay. *Combat Films: American Realism, 1945–1970.* Jefferson, NC: McFarland, 1981.

Shull, Michael S. and Wilt, David E. *Hollywood War Films, 1937–1945.* Jefferson, NC: McFarland, 1996.

Sledge, E. B. *With the Old Guard at Peleliu and Okinawa.* Novato, CA: Presidio, 1981.

Strada, Michael J., and Harold R. Troper. *Friend or Foe? Russians in American Film and Foreign Policy, 1933–1991.* Lanham, MD: Scarecrow, 1997.

Terkel, Studs. *"The Good War": An Oral History of World War II.* New York: Pantheon, 1984.

Tuttle, William. *Daddy's Gone to War: The Second World War in the Lives of America's Children.* New York: Oxford University Press, 1993.

Winkler, Allan M. *Home Front U.S.A.: America During World War II.* Arlington Heights, IL: Harlan Davidson, 1986.

Woll, Allen L. *The Hollywood Musical Goes to War.* Chicago: Nelson, 1983.

III. Notable People

★ ★ ★ ★ ★ ★ ★

WELCOME
SAM and Mrs SAM

[**MICHAEL BIRDWELL**]

The Antebellum Frontier Hero

Hollywood's antebellum hero owes an incalculable debt to James Fenimore Cooper (1789–1851), creator of the archetypal American frontier hero of the trans-Appalachian West. Inspired by Daniel Boone, Cooper created a solitary, taciturn hero, more comfortable in the wilderness than in an advancing, civilized society. This peculiarly American Adam was "an individual emancipated from history, happily bereft of ancestry, untouched and undefiled by the usual inheritances of family and race; an individual standing alone, self-reliant, self-propelling, ready to confront whatever awaited him with the aid of his own unique and inherent resources" (Lewis, 5). Slow to anger, he overcame insurmountable odds with artful ease; yet he acted selflessly, seeking no personal rewards for his endeavors. Daniel Boone became the "emblematic hero of Manifest Destiny," the equivalent of an American Moses, "leading his people to the Promised Land" (Hughes, 191–192). Cooper's fictionalized Boone (variously known as Natty Bumppo, Hawkeye, Leatherstocking, and Deerslayer) idealized an American piety and unfettered freedom on a contested frontier; this archetypal hero continues to exist in movies ranging from frontier epics to science fiction films. The heroes evoke values Americans hold dear—freedom, love of country, and a sense of humor.

Sometimes self-effacing, sometimes a device to catch his prey off guard, and other times a potent weapon, the American hero employed humor to his advantage. A product of the frontier itself, this humor can be traced to a number of sources. From the Whig almanacs attributed to Davy Crockett to tall-tale characters such as Mike Fink, Captain Simon Suggs, Sut Lovingood, or Ransey Sniffle, humor softened and humanized—and sometimes satirized—the brutality of the frontier experience. Davy Crockett's boast that he was "half-horse, half-alligator" reflected the braggadocio and bluster of the pioneer spirit. The frontier provided a wild, sprawling expanse that needed larger-than-life characters to subdue it. As Constance Roarke notes in *American Humor*, real humans such as Davy Crockett or Mike Fink "grew supersized" (54). Numerous retellings of their exploits, real and imagined, encouraged embellishment. Thus, the frontier hero was bigger, meaner, sneakier, smarter, braver, sillier, and possessed a larger ego than any opponent. Often inventing and spreading his own notoriety, as David Crockett did in his various autobiographies (which remain classic examples of self-promotion and mythmaking), the hero played a key role in the public's perception of him.

Daniel Boone (1734–1820)

As biographer John Mack Faragher observes, Daniel Boone's image was often reinvented, beginning with Boone's own conversations as an elderly man with John Filson. Boone has represented everything from a symbol of American progress to a benighted primitivist, racist, and litigious land speculator (320–362). Though a staple of the silent screen, Boone appeared with far less frequency in sound pictures before World War II. He makes a cameo appearance in *The Great Meadow* (1931), an unusual film that examines the role of women on the frontier and argues (quite correctly, we now know) that the frontier could not have flourished without brave pioneer women who often assumed traditional male roles. A civilizing force, women deserve credit for their assistance in "taming" the trans-Appalachian West. Based on Elizabeth Madox Roberts's novel of the same name, the film centers on the intrepid Virginians who followed Daniel Boone along the Wilderness Road through the Cumberland Gap into Kentucky.

Daniel Boone (1936) continues to be one of the best film portrayals of the legendary hero. Originally made as one of the RKO studio's low-budget westerns, the film rose above its limitations. The story focuses on Boone (George O'Brien) in 1775 as he leads a group of pioneers (including an African American) from Yadkin County, North Carolina, into Kentucky. After Boone establishes a modest community along the Kentucky River at Fort Boonesboro, Wyandot Indians attack. The community struggles to eke out an existence in the hostile wilderness. Later captured by British troops through the duplicity of a greedy frontiersman, Simon Girty (John Carradine), Boone is dragged off to Detroit, where he uses his formidable survival skills to escape. Upon his return to Kentucky, he finds Boonesboro again besieged by hostile Indians; providentially, inclement weather works to the settlers' advantage, and the attack fails. The film reflects the can-do spirit of New Deal America, stressing the need for the people of America to pull together in times of difficulty and work together for the common good. (John Ford's *Drums Along the Mohawk* would reiterate this historical message three years later.)

No significant film made during the war years used Boone as a primary character, though his spirit is invoked in Howard Hawks's *Sergeant York* (1941). York, who was born in the Tennessee backwoods in 1887, grew up in a quasi-frontier society that depended upon hunting skills to supplement diet and income. Visual and aural references to Boone pepper the film, implying that Alvin York is a twentieth-century equivalent of Daniel Boone and the embodiment of the frontier virtues that made this country moral and strong.

FIGURE 17. *Daniel Boone* (1936). George O'Brien (center) plays the heroic Daniel Boone, who has just founded Fort Boonesboro in Kentucky. He is captured and taken away to Detroit by the British but soon escapes, returning to Boonesboro to protect the settlement against attacking Indians. Courtesy George A. Hirliman Productions and RKO Radio Productions.

A fictionalized account of Boone's legendary rise as a pioneer and Indian fighter, Monogram studio produced *Young Daniel Boone* (1950), starring David Bruce. Though the real Boone was in his mid-thirties before he crossed the Appalachians, the film ignores that fact to depict the frontiersman as a budding youth. Aimed at a teenaged audience, the film underscores the difficulties of growing up in hard times; Boone, the intrepid youth, overcomes adversity while embodying the essence of true Americanism. This message came at a time when films such as *Rebel without a Cause* focused on teenagers struggling for identity and acceptance.

Bruce Bennett plays the pioneer in *Daniel Boone, Trailblazer* (1957), a color feature filmed in Mexico. Retelling Boone's story, it follows pioneers from North Carolina into Kentucky for the creation of Fort Boonesboro.

Unwelcomed by local inhabitants, the settlers fall under attack from vicious Shawnee under the command of villainous Chief Blackfish (Lon Chaney Jr.). This unpretentious, formulaic film reflects the unease that gripped a Cold War America yearning for dependable heroes and clearly identifiable villains.

The Daniel Boone most familiar to the baby boomers and subsequent generations came from television. In 1964 Fess Parker (who had played Davy Crockett in three popular films for Walt Disney) tackled the role of Boone for NBC. Using his abilities for humor and drama, Parker's television series proved popular and successful for six years. Essentially a family drama that used the frontier as a backdrop, *The Daniel Boone Show* mixed history with the television conventions of the day to create a backwoods version of *Father Knows Best.* The catchy theme song declared Daniel Boone "the rippin'est, roarin'est, fightin'est man / the frontier ever knew." Initially, the series was a carbon copy of the Disneyfied frontier. Fortunately, Parker's Boone evolved and grew distinctly different from his depiction of Crockett. The show was timely in a number of ways, for it matured as the country underwent the devastating upheavals of the civil rights movement, debates over the war in Vietnam, the women's movement, and other confrontations in the American culture of the 1960s.

Reflective of the era in which it was made, *The Daniel Boone Show* often dealt with contemporary themes. In many episodes, the self-sufficient Rebecca Boone (Patricia Blair) plays a key role in Boonesboro's defense during her husband's frequent absences. In many other episodes, Boone's best friend Mingo (Ed Ames), an Oxford-educated Native American, helps the frontier hero to recognize the importance of cultural and ethnic diversity. As the series developed, the characters grew more rounded and the storylines more complex. Unfortunately, as the series progressed, again perhaps reflecting the times, some episodes became more serious, the liveliness and humor modulated into stiff though well-meaning didacticism.

Andrew Jackson (1767–1845)

Andrew Jackson was a curious variation on the frontier hero motif. The historical Jackson possessed a number of character flaws that usually render a person unfit for leadership—he was poorly educated, hot-tempered, a gambler, duelist, racist, and bigamist. Yet he, like Crockett, had charisma. As historian John William Ward notes, "Andrew Jackson captured the American imagination at the Battle of New Orleans, which rightfully stands for the point in history when America's consciousness turned westward, away from Europe toward the interior" (77). Jackson, in Ward's estimation, became a force of nature to be reckoned with, an America in miniature with all its myriad contradictions and possibilities. Jackson represented Manifest Destiny in the flesh; in 1814 he defeated the Creeks at Horseshoe Bend (with the help of Cherokees whom he would later force west), and in 1818 he deliberately misinterpreted orders from the federal government and set in motion the American annexation of Florida. Such actions further advanced Old Hickory's popularity.

Andrew Jackson—in all his larger-than-life ardor—has yet to be accurately portrayed on film. Perhaps the first representation of Jackson was in the silent feature *The Frontiersman* (1927). One of the few films to examine the Jackson's destruction of the Creek Confederation during the War of 1812, it was primarily an action vehicle for Tim McCoy (portraying a Tennessee militiaman, John Dale). Jackson (Russell Simpson) serves as a catalyst for the romance between Dale and his ward, Lucy (Claire Windsor), later kidnapped by Creeks. The film culminated in her rescue and the exciting destruction of the Creek Confederation at the Battle of Horseshoe Bend on March 27, 1814—which is represented as a glorious American victory.

The formidable actor Lionel Barrymore played Jackson twice, first in *The Gorgeous Hussy* (1936), a dramatization of the Peggy Eaton affair, and later in *Lone Star* (1952). Based on Samuel Hopkins Adams's novel of the same name, *The Gorgeous Hussy* romanticizes the first serious sex scandal in U.S. presidential politics. Set in 1831, the film uses the Eaton affair as the event that destroyed the relationship between Andrew Jackson and his erstwhile vice president, John C. Calhoun. Joan Crawford portrays the clever and beautiful Margaret Eaton in a film that takes liberties with the facts. Rachel Donelson Robards Jackson (Beulah Bondi) follows her husband to Washington, only to be snubbed by polite society. In truth, Rachel never made it to Washington; she died during Jackson's campaign for the presidency in 1828. Furthermore, Jackson and Calhoun parted company over the so-called Nullification Crisis of 1833, not the Eaton affair (although it is true that on the social level the Calhouns would have nothing to do with Margaret Eaton).

In *The Buccaneer* (1938) Jackson (Hugh Sothern) takes a back seat to the heroics of pirates Jean Lafitte (Frederic March) and his brother Dominic (Akim Tamiroff). The film depicts events leading up to the battle of New Orleans, where General Jackson's "hunters of Kentucky" humiliated the elite British troops that had defeated Napoleon three years earlier. On January 8, 1815, Jackson's outnumbered militia killed or wounded more than two thousand British soldiers while suffering one-tenth as many casualties (Remini, 136–168). Jackson, however, plays only a minor role in *The Buccaneer.* Directed by Cecil B. De Mille, the film focuses on both the real events that caused Jackson to rely on pirates to help him defeat the British and a contrived love story between Lafitte and a belle of New Orleans.

In *The President's Lady* (1953) and the remake of *The Buccaneer* (1958) Charlton Heston portrays Jackson as both a charismatic president and a levelheaded, even regal, military commander. In both films Heston proved more polished and reserved than the historic Jackson. Just as Heston's Jackson is more refined than the historical Old Hickory, Susan Hayward in *The President's Lady* presents a more glamorous Rachel Jackson than her historical original. On the other hand, the film accurately captures the intensity of Jackson's devotion to his wife and is one of the few screen attempts to examine his private life; many believe that *The President's Lady* is one of Hollywood's best screen biographies.

The remake of *The Buccaneer* in 1958 differs in some respects from the 1938 De Mille production and marks Anthony Quinn's first directorial effort. Andrew Jackson plays a more central role in the story, and Yul Brynner's subtle depiction of Jean Lafitte reflects more natural acting styles emerging from post-studio Hollywood. The sprawling film is notable for capturing the spirit of the climactic battle of the War of 1812. Quinn's film features an ethnically textured cast, more representative of the Creole culture of Louisiana, including Governor Claiborne's house slave Cato, who fought in the battle against the British. Though the remake retains the various love interests of the original feature, it also raises concerns about class and race in the America pondering a growing civil rights movement.

Davy Crockett (1786–1836)

Of all the trans-Appalachian frontier heroes, Davy Crockett best fits the mold of the hero as humorist. Enlarging upon a persona that David Crockett created in print and on stage, the backwoods politician became a folk icon in his own lifetime. Though the historical Crockett was constantly moving west to avoid creditors, the folk Crockett sought to tame the wilderness on his own terms: he could grin down a bear or an entire tribe of hostile Indians; he could joke with Andrew Jackson or disarm Congress (in which he served two terms) with his humor. Davy could slay the ladies with his smile or take on the likes of Mike Fink in a rough-and-tumble wrestling match. Half-alligator, half-horse, and possessing an indefatigable confidence, Davy entertained adults and children alike with his antics.

A recurring motif in Crockett films was his martyrdom at the Alamo in 1836. Two silent film treatments stand out. In *Martyrs of the Alamo* (1915), Davy represents the apotheosis of American patriotism, needlessly slain by Mexican general Santa Anna. Depicted as a reprobate addicted to drugs, Santa Anna's licentious tastes eventually lead to his own demise at the Battle of San Jacinto—just forty-six days after the siege at the Alamo. *Davy Crockett at the Fall of the Alamo* (1926) proved significant because it argued (accurately) that the annexation of Texas was as much for the expansion of slavery as it was the extension through Manifest Destiny of the territorial holdings of the United States.

Just as Daniel Boone made few film appearances during the 1930s, Crockett, too, was conspicuous in his absence. Davy (Lane Chandler) said his first words on screen in *Heroes of the Alamo* (1938), the only film to feature the Tennessean in a prominent role, which was produced "to take advantage of the national attention afforded the centennial of the siege" (Roberts and Olson, 457). In what is primarily an action picture, Crockett is depicted as a rough-hewn product of the frontier, intent upon expanding American interests and wresting Texas from inept Mexican control. The film is of interest because it violated the Roosevelt administration's "Good Neighbor" policy, which tried to enlist the film community's aid in improving U.S. relations with Latin America.

Crockett, like Boone, made an important reentry into American popular culture during the 1950s. *The Last Command* (1955), another Alamo picture, features a solid script and credible acting. Significantly, this is the only film to examine the difficult choices of the Texas pioneers who had family or business dealings with Mexicans. Sterling Hayden, who prolonged his career by naming names before the House Committee on Un-American Activities (HUAC), gives a believable performance as Jim Bowie. Veteran character actor Arthur Hunnicut's rendition of Davy Crockett stands head and shoulders above all the other Crocketts of the 1950s—except Fess Parker's—balancing both the humor and the grit associated with the frontier legend. Hunnicut's Crockett, no callow youth but a seasoned, grisly veteran of the frontier, is aware of his own mortality but is still in search of the American Dream.

The most prevalent incarnation of Davy Crockett from the late 1950s was created by Fess Parker. Originally airing on ABC television as a part of the *Wonderful World of Disney*, the Disney Crockett did double duty on the big screen. The Disneyfication of Crockett capitalized on the traditions of the buddy picture, coupling him with a worthy sidekick, Georgie Russell (Buddy Ebsen). This Crockett embodies the humor and pathos associated with a doomed hero. The Disney version caught the imagination of a nation contemplating the possibility of nuclear holocaust, looking backward to a putatively safer era of muskets and tomahawks.

One of the appealing virtues of Parker's Crockett is his willingness to defy authority. In a period of conformity (and at a studio noted for its corporate discipline), Crockett communicated a message of individualism. As J. W. Williamson notes, "the Davy played by Fess Parker was downright subversive, jokey, askew; he was more a trickster than an overwhelmingly testosteronized fighter; Fess Parker's bravery seemed offhand and nothing special . . . like a classic fool, this Davy assumed a democratic equality and acted on it" (83). In *Davy Crockett, King of the Wild Frontier,* the hero disregards a direct order from General Andrew Jackson and threatens mutiny. The contrast between Crockett and Jackson struck a resonant chord with young television viewers. Crockett, dressed casually, exuded youthful self-confidence. Andrew Jackson (Basil

Ruysdael), by contrast, was old, ponderous, dripping gold braid from his uncomfortable wool uniform. The episode is based on an incident in 1814 when Tennessee volunteers mutinied because their enlistments had expired after the battle of Horseshoe Bend. In reality, Jackson quelled the rebellion by turning cannons on his own troops, but in the Disney version, Crockett charms the general with his frontier wit and common sense.

Though the first installment in the series ends with Crockett's heroic death at the Alamo, Disney quickly resurrected its buckskin Lazarus. The short-lived series launched a veritable Crockett mania, as young and old alike sang its infectious theme song, "The Ballad of Davy Crockett."

In *Davy Crockett Goes to Congress* (1955), Fess Parker took his frontier charms to the nation's capital, providing a backwoods antidote to an entrenched bureaucracy. Disney's Crockett proved a far more capable statesman than his historic counterpart, for the real Crockett lost his bid for reelection in 1835. Disney's Crockett is a man of the people who can articulate their needs: dressed in buckskin, Crockett sits among professional politicians in their fine clothes, and the contrast is arresting. Crockett, comfortable with himself and his station, feels no need to put on airs. He is a fitting symbol of the common man, rising to the occasion by virtue of his innate abilities. In an era when people feared Communist subversion and nuclear annihilation, *Davy Crockett Goes to Congress* presented something of a latter-day *Mr. Smith Goes to Washington.* The film called for Americans to restore their faith in the republic and taught that though bad men sometimes populate the national assembly, it can still work for the public good.

Reflecting popular attitudes, politicians paid lip service to the homespun wisdom of Disney's Crockett, chief among them Tennessee senator and vice presidential hopeful Estes Kefauver, who sported a coonskin cap during his 1956 bid for the presidency. What was both peculiar and significant about the Crockett craze was that it struck a resonant chord with both conservatives and liberals. The Disney version appealed because it represented so many things that both sides could rally around—nostalgia for a better time, national pride, heroic struggle in the face of dangers real and imagined, and values that Americans want to believe in—making it possible for either side to define those values and claim to be their true protector.

The only rendition of Davy Crockett to give Fess Parker serious competition was produced, and written in part, by John Wayne. *The Alamo* (1960), a picture that Wayne had wanted to make for nearly twenty years, followed closely upon the heels of the Disney version. Wayne spent more than $15 million of his own money to bring the story to the screen, building a full-scale replica of the Alamo (one that has become a tourist attraction in its own right) and employing an army of actors and extras. Wayne's testament to Americanism, it is often preachy and unevenly paced, though helped along by an admirable supporting cast (including Richard Boone, Richard Widmark, and Laurence Harvey) and an Academy Award–winning soundtrack. Where Fess Parker's Crockett is playful, John Wayne's portrayal is deadly serious. Wayne's buckskinned hero fights for abstract ideas such as the virtues of a republic—difficult things to represent visually—rather than the independence of Texas. Wayne wanted to "sell America to countries threatened with Communist domination" as well as the domestic audience "who should appreciate the struggle our ancestors made for the precious freedom we enjoy" (Roberts and Olson, 470–471).

Sam Houston (1793–1863)

Richard Dix portrays Sam Houston in the compelling and forthright remake of the *Conqueror* (1917), *Man of Conquest* (1939). The film opens at the climactic battle of Horseshoe Bend, where Houston was wounded in the process of defeating the Creek Nation. Befriended by General Andrew Jackson (Edward Ellis), the relationship changes over the course of both men's tempestuous lives. The film covers Houston's rise to the governorship of Tennessee; his disastrous (and still controversial) marriage to Eliza Allen, which led to his resignation as governor; and his subsequent life among the Cherokees. Urged by Jackson to leave his adopted Cherokee family, Houston agrees to head to Texas to fight with other Tennesseans against the Mexican army. It features Houston's move west to Indian Territory (now Oklahoma) and his impressive victory over General Santa Anna's forces at the Battle of San Jacinto in 1836. Concluding with Houston's helping shepherd Texas into the union, *Man of Conquest* celebrates American initiative and resolve in the face of a continuing depression and troubled times overseas. It includes sympathetic portrayals of Native Americans and recognizes that the Texas Houston fought to liberate represented a culturally diverse American microcosm.

FIGURE 18. *Man of Conquest* (1939). Sam Houston (Richard Dix), campaigning for the governorship of Tennessee, is greeted by voters. Houston's marriage to Eliza Allen (Joan Fontaine) will soon generate rumors and controversy, contributing to Houston's resignation as governor. Courtesy Republic Pictures Corporation.

The 1950s presented a variety of Houston films, with most centering on Davy Crockett's death and Houston's vow to avenge him. These films, including *The Man from the Alamo* (Universal, 1953), *The Last Command* (Republic, 1955), *The First Texan* (Allied Artists, 1956), and the aforementioned Disney Crockett films, reflect consensus attitudes developing in America during the Cold War. The 1950s proved to be an incredibly rich period for defining the American mission in a world divided by what Winston Churchill called an "Iron Curtain." The late 1940s and early 1950s were indeed frightful times owing to the Greek crisis, the Berlin Blockade, the detonation of the Soviet atomic bomb, Mao Zedong's triumph in China, and the Korean War. Fear of Communist subversion manifested itself in the hearings of HUAC and Senator Joseph McCarthy; the execution of the Rosenbergs for espionage; and the requirement of loyalty oaths. Fears that gripped the American people often found their way into films of the period, and the federal government sought the assistance of the film capital to sell Americanism abroad (Saunders, 284–301).

The Man from the Alamo focuses on the fictional story of Johnny Stroud (Glenn Ford), who had escaped the Alamo in order to save his family, featuring Sam Houston (Howard Negley) in a supporting role. Accused of cowardice for having fled, Stroud spends the rest of the film proving his worth as he and other Texans fight for independence. After saving the same community that had ostracized him, Stroud is allowed to rejoin Houston's army in its decisive victory at San Jacinto. Houston personally welcomes the prodigal back into the fold, insuring audiences that true Americans know how to forgive and forget. The film communicates a number of Cold War themes: patriotism, duty to one's family and community, the importance of one's reputation, and forgiveness.

The First Texan features Joel McCrae as Sam Houston in an earnest, understated performance. This wide-screen production includes some excellent action sequences that heighten the drama of Texas independence. It depicts an embattled nation (Texas as America) under siege and draws direct parallels between the threats of the Texas frontier and the dangers of Cold War America.

The Frontiersman's Filmic Descendants

Antebellum frontier heroes—Boone, Jackson, Crockett, and Houston—acted as the spiritual forebears of a number of character types that continue to surface in American films. Dennis Hopper has evoked characteristics of the frontier hero in a number of films. In *Easy Rider* (1969), which he also directed, Hopper, with his sidekick Captain America (Peter Fonda), sets out in search of a modern frontier, clad in a buckskin jacket astride his chopped Harley, even tramping over some of Andrew Jackson's own territory in New Orleans. Hopper took the frontier sensibility abroad in Wim Wenders's existential film *The American Friend* (1977) nearly a decade later. In *Apocalypse Now* (1979) Hopper emerges from Colonel Kurtz's (Marlon Brando) compound as a hippie on a more sinister frontier, the jungles of Vietnam and Cambodia. His character, the dazed photographer in awe of Kurtz who has gone native, is based in part on Sean Flynn, the photojournalist son of Errol Flynn, who rode a motorcycle off into the jungles of Cambodia, never to be seen again. In *Hoosiers* (1986), Hopper plays a besotted former high school basketball star who wears eighteenth-century garb and yearns for a lost frontier lifestyle and values. The recurring Hopper version is more antihero than hero in search of a vitality and frontier individualism that modern-day America often seems to suppress.

The wise-cracking, live-by-the-wits attributes of the frontier hero continue to flourish and manifest themselves in a number of ways, from Groucho Marx in *Duck Soup* or Elvis Presley's dual role in *Kissing Cousins* to George Clooney in *O Brother, Where Art Thou?* Elements of the trans-Appalachian frontier hero have emerged in two characters associated with Harrison Ford—Han Solo and Indiana Jones. Though neither wears coonskin caps nor wields a muzzleloader, both characters look back to Daniel Boone and Davy Crockett. Han Solo, the self-serving Crockett of the future, ends up doing the right thing by coming to the aid of the community. Indiana Jones brandishes his bullwhip with ease while evincing an aw-shucks attitude in spite of his credentials as an archaeologist. Likewise, Mel Gibson has also created characters from Mad Max (*Mad Max, Road Warrior,* and *Thunderdome*) to Officer Riggs (the *Lethal Weapon* series) who use weapons and "gonzo" humor to defeat their opponents. Max operates in a postapocalyptic dystopia that has reverted to a frontier state, while Riggs uses his wits in an urban frontier. As such, the trans-Appalachian frontier hero will continue to fascinate and no doubt undergo new permutations. As the post–Cold War world seeks to redefine itself, new versions of Boone, Crockett, Jackson, and Houston will no doubt emerge. They embody basic values Americans hold dear—freedom, self-determination, loyalty, love of country, and a sense of humor.

References

Filmography

The Alamo (1960, F)
The American Friend (1977, F)
Apocalypse Now (1979, F)
Attack on Fort Boonesborough (1906, F)
The Buccaneer (1938, F; 1958, F)
The Conqueror (1917, F)
Daniel Boone (1906, F; 1907, F; 1936, F)
The Daniel Boone Show (1964–70, TV)
Daniel Boone Through the Wilderness (1926, F)
Daniel Boone, Trailblazer (1957, F)
Davy Crockett (1910, F; 1916, F; 1955, F)
Davy Crockett and the Last of the River Pirates (1957, F)
Davy Crockett at the Alamo (1955, TV)
Davy Crockett at the Fall of the Alamo (1926, F)
Davy Crockett Goes to Congress (1955, TV)
Davy Crockett, Indian Fighter (1954, TV)
Davy Crockett, Indian Scout (1950, F)

Davy Crockett in Hearts United (1909, F)
Davy Crockett, King of the Wild Frontier (1956, F)
Easy Rider (1969, F)
The First Texan (1956, F)
The Frontiersman (1927, F)
The Gorgeous Hussy (1936, F)
The Great Meadow (1931, F)
Heroes of the Alamo (1938, F)
Hoosiers (1986, F)
Immortal Alamo (1912, F)
In the Days of Daniel Boone (1923, F)
The Last Command (1955, F)
The Man from the Alamo (1953, F)
Man of Conquest (1939, F)
Martyrs of the Alamo (1915, F)
Old Hickory (1939, F)
The President's Lady (1953, F)
Sergeant York (1941, F)
Young Daniel Boone (1950, F)

Bibliography

Aron, Stephen. *How the West Was Lost: The Transformation of Kentucky from Daniel Boone to Henry Clay.* Baltimore: Johns Hopkins University Press, 1996.

Carnes, Mark C., ed. *Past Imperfect: History According to the Movies.* New York: Henry Holt, 1995.

Davis, William C. *Three Roads to the Alamo: The Lives and Fortunes of David Crockett, James Bowie, and William Travis.* New York: HarperCollins, 1999.

Dooley, Roger. *From Scarlett to Scarface: American Films in the 1930s.* New York: Harcourt Brace, 1981.

Faragher, John Mack. *Daniel Boone: The Life and Legend of an American Pioneer.* New York: Henry Holt, 1992.

Hughes, Robert. *American Visions: The Epic History of Art in America.* New York: Knopf, 1997.

Leab, Daniel. "I Was a Communist for the FBI." In David W. Ellwood, ed., *The Movies as History: Visions of the Twentieth Century,* 89. London: Sutton, 2000.

Lewis, R. W. B. *The American Adam: Innocence, Tragedy, and Tradition in the Nineteenth Century.* Chicago: University of Chicago Press, 1955.

Lofaro, Michael, ed. *Davy Crockett: The Man, The Legend, The Legacy, 1786–1986.* Knoxville: University of Tennessee Press, 1985.

Marszalek, John F. *Petticoat Affair: Manners, Mutiny, and Sex in Andrew Jackson's White House.* New York: Free Press, 1997.

Remini, Robert. *The Battle of New Orleans: Andrew Jackson and America's First Military Victory.* New York: Viking, 1999.

Roarke, Constance. *American Humor: A Study of the National Character.* New York: Harcourt, Brace, 1931.

Roberts, Randy, and James Olson. *John Wayne: American.* New York: Free Press, 1995.

Saunders, Frances Stonor. *The Cultural Cold War: The CIA and the World of Arts and Letters.* New York: New Press, 2000.

Shockley, Megan Taylor. "King of the Wild Frontier vs. King Andrew I: Davy Crockett and the Election of 1831." *Tennessee Historical Quarterly* 62.3 (1997): 158–169.

Ward, John William. *Andrew Jackson: Symbol for an Age.* New York: Oxford University Press, 1953.

Williamson, J. W. *Hillbillyland: What the Movies Did to the Mountains and What the Mountains Did to the Movies.* Chapel Hill: University of North Carolina Press, 1995.

Wills, Garry. *John Wayne's America.* New York: Simon & Schuster, 1997.

[ANTHONY CHASE]

Christopher Columbus

In 1492, according to a line in Winifred Stoner's memorable poem "The History of the United States" (1919), Columbus sailed the ocean blue and discovered a new world. Or, at least, so children learned, generation in and out, from their elementary primers and public school teachers. Whatever the relation between this particular story of adventure and real history, pupils were engaged in something weightier than mere social studies. They were mastering a myth and, at the same time, learning to be Americans. They were engaged in one of the fundamental and characteristic rituals of sharing a common culture.

Much of that has now changed, at least within the educational system. A popular high school textbook—Thomas Bailey, David M. Kennedy, and Lizabeth Cohen's *The American Pageant*—for example, still refers to Columbus as a "skilled Italian seafarer," but one immediately recognizes a tentativeness in the observation that "Columbus's discovery would eventually convulse four continents" (14). The note of ambiguity is extended when we read that for "Europeans as well as for Africans and Native Americans, the world after 1492 would never be the same, for better or worse" (14). Hard facts are then permitted to make their grim appearance: "In the century after Columbus's landfall, nearly 90 per cent of the Native Americans perished" (15). Schools adopting revised and updated history readers may nevertheless be in recess on Columbus Day.

Conflicting interpretations of the Columbian legacy reached a boiling point in 1992, in conjunction with widespread quincentennial celebrations. Whereas many Italian American organizations proudly recalled Columbus's extraordinary seamanship and prominently proclaimed his contribution to American history, the National Council of Churches issued a formal statement indicating that for the descendants and survivors of the invasion and "genocide" that followed on the heels of 1492, celebration was an inappropriate form of observation. The council, representing a broad constituency of American Anglican, Orthodox, and Protestant church communities, called on Christians to mark the occasion with reflection and repentance. The city of Berkeley, California, officially replaced Columbus Day with Indigenous People's Day. Still others bemoaned the fact that Columbus Day had effectively been banned by the mandarins of "political correctness." A decade later, arguments over what to do with Columbus Day remained sufficiently acrimonious to send fists flying in an episode of HBO television's popular series *The Sopranos.*

Motion-picture treatments of the age of exploration generally, and of Columbus in particular, reflect the same tensions that mark public debates over acts of official commemoration and the content of school textbooks. In *The Conquest of Paradise: Christopher Columbus and the Columbian Legacy* (1990), Kirkpatrick Sale devotes several hundred pages to chronicling the development of mythology surrounding the "Columbia experience"—before 1625! Film scholar and screenwriter Peter Wollen outlines three further periods of development of the Columbus myth beyond

1625. The first "significant stirrings of the cult were felt with the advent of American Independence, as the new nation began to construct its new identity and history" (22). From King's College being renamed Columbia University through the publication of Washington Irving's quasi-official three-volume biography in 1828, Columbus was reconstructed as "a romantic genius and an embattled underdog" (22). Although riddled with pure mythology, Irving's history of the life and voyages of Columbus was frequently reprinted throughout the following century and achieved a grand readership.

The second stage, which accompanied westward expansion and waves of Italian immigration to the United States, brought in its wake Columbus Day, Columbus Circle in New York, and the Columbian Exposition (or world's fair) of 1893 in Chicago, which, according to Wollen, featured "Arawaks from British Guiana in a thatched hut. Presumably these were the best available stand-ins for the Taino," who Wollen acknowledges were wiped out, soon after the arrival of Columbus, by "forced labour, famine, slavery, slaughter and disease" (22). Wollen's third stage, which arrives with the quincentenary, witnesses the emergence of historical circumspection. "The reticence of 1992 reflects," he believes, "not a diminution of Columbus' mythic role but a reevaluation" (22).

Movies about the (presumably) Genoa-born, Cristoforo Colombo, also known as Cristobal Colón, have almost uniformly retained the essentials of the mythic role, the romantic underdog, "harried by flat-earthers and envious hidalgos, betrayed by perfidious royalty" (Wollen, 22). Fredric March, who starred in the award-winning *The Best Years of Our Lives* in 1946, played the master mariner in *Christopher Columbus* (1949). Although produced by Gainsborough Pictures, which was founded in 1924 by Michael Balcon and brought Alfred Hitchcock's *The Lady Vanishes* to the screen in 1938, *Christopher Columbus* was not a success. "Gainsborough's flailing attempts to add 'class' and international prestige to their more interesting low-key 'domestic' output," says Paul Taylor in his capsule review of *Christopher Columbus,* "resulted in this expensively mounted dodo," which, Taylor urges, should have been consigned to "the scrap heap of film history" (148). Kirkpatrick Sale refers to the image of Columbus and his mates as they set out on their uncertain voyage, crossing themselves and kneeling "as they passed by La Rabida, listening to the last chorus of the friars' morning hymn," as part of the "fantasy put forward as fact in Samuel Eliot Morison's 1942 Pulitzer Prize–winning biography" (20).

Carla Rahn Phillips and William D. Phillips Jr., however, argue that more recent films on Columbus fail to capture the bold seafarer's "character or his probable physical appearance as well as the eponymous 1949 film biography" (65). "The physical description of Columbus," argues Samuel Eliot Morison, "shows that he was of a North Italian type frequently seen today in Genoa; tall and well-built, red-haired with a ruddy and freckled complexion, hawk-nosed and long of visage, blue-eyed and with high cheekbones" (47). To be sure, this rather concrete image is derived from memories of Columbus recorded after his death, and the Phillipses acknowledge that with respect to Columbus no authenticated portrait, painted during his lifetime, exists.

So historians know more about the social consequences of the Columbian expedition than they do about what Columbus looked like. This does not mean, of course, that either Columbus historians or biographers necessarily find themselves in agreement. One highly contentious debate revolves around the role of disease in the destruction of Native American civilizations. Some historians assert that microbes were far more deadly enemies of Indian societies than were the Europeans who followed in Columbus's wake. "Disease and genocide," responds historian David E. Stannard, "were interdependent forces acting dynamically—whipsawing their victims between plague and violence, each one feeding upon the other" (xii). Scholars still dispute (possibly irresolvable) issues, such as those of Columbus's true nationality and his ultimate place of burial. Another question about whose answer historians disagree is whether Columbus faced a mutiny on ship just before arriving in the West Indies.

Although this problem may seem a small matter, it turns out not to be—at least not with respect to a cinematic retelling of the Columbus legend. Here is the dilemma filmmakers confront: dramatizing Columbus's civilizing mission in the New World is plagued by a certain uneasiness with the Columbus/Indian relationship. The temptation to fall back on tried-and-true generic solutions is considerable. Peter Wollen points to westerns as a classic narrative model for the retelling of American myths of all kinds—including the one about initial contact between Europeans and Native Americans. Here, the formula is applied so that a good soldier or scout (Columbus) has to deal with damage wrought by unscrupulous reservation store traders or gunrunners (the Europeans Columbus leaves behind to manage Hispaniola) who sell firewater to the local natives, turning them savage and bloodthirsty.

With this kind of canned narrative constituting the second half of Columbus films, the climax tends to come in the middle or earlier, at the moment when the cry of "Land ho!" is first raised. In other words, filmmakers are able to subordinate the less appealing—or, perhaps, least inspiring—aspects of the Columbus saga simply by making the discovery of land itself, and the conflicts at sea that precede that crucial turning point in the story, the essence of their tale. It is the sighting of land in these pictures that would be shown in previews on television, designed to attract excited viewers to the theater.

Three things make the actual sighting of land thrilling. First, Columbus encounters considerable opposition when trying to organize his expedition (the "flat-earthers") that he must overcome. Second, there is the empty expanse of water itself, which symbolizes everything that is unknown to science and cartography, an ocean that literally must be crossed. Finally, closely allied with the uncertainty of the voyage and constituting its visceral expression is the fear that grips these sailors: a fear of falling off the edge of the earth, of monsters lurking beneath the waves, or of the fate of castaways—starvation and a harsh death at sea. Land, any land, in this context represents salvation. Among feature-length films on Columbus, *1492: The Conquest of Paradise* (1992) stands out for its visual splendor. Directed by Ridley Scott, *1492* is studded with sequences as breathtaking as sparkling stones, especially the film's depiction of the ultimate moment of discovery. Clouds of mist part magically, suddenly revealing a tropical island landscape. This undulating image, filled with intense greens and blues, is "certainly true to Columbus' own experience," as Peter Wollen points out, inasmuch as "his diary is full of expressions of wonder at the proliferation and verdancy of trees on the Caribbean islands" (21).

Dramatic tension mounts in *Christopher Columbus: The Discovery* (1992), as well as in *Christopher Columbus* (1985), a made-for-television feature with Gabriel Byrne in the title role, as risky transatlantic voyages appear to be going nowhere. In the latter film, Oliver Reed, as Martin Pinzon, inspires a mutiny of almost laughably confused and frightened sailors who seem to have been recruited for this arduous assignment from a Popeye cartoon. The mutineers, their weapons drawn, are reminded that they will be hanged when they get back to Spain (something that appears not to have occurred to them)—and immediately Columbus's life is in jeopardy: apparently, no admiral, then no evidence of mutiny. But Columbus draws a line on the deck of the ship, and enough loyalists (including, inexplicably, the most outspoken rebel) join their leader to

FIGURE 19. *1492: Conquest of Paradise* (1992). Before departing for the New World, Spanish nobleman Sanchez (Armand Assante, right) introduces Christopher Columbus (Gerard Depardieu, center) to Don Francisco de Bobadilla (Mark Margolis, left), who is seeking a governorship in the West Indies. Columbus has encountered much opposition to his expedition. Courtesy Paramount Pictures and Touchstone Pictures.

justify postponing the threatened mutiny for three days, just long enough to enable the three little ships to make landfall.

There are even more swashbuckling antics in *Christopher Columbus: The Discovery,* including a man overboard eaten by a shark and the actual placing of Columbus's neck on the chopping block by extremely disgruntled seamen. The sighting of land, not surprisingly, provides an outrageously melodramatic, last-minute reprieve. Carla and William Phillips regard the two near-mutinies shown in *Christopher Columbus: The Discovery* as based on "real" historical events, but the near-execution of Columbus they characterize as "fictitious" (63). Zvi Dor-Ner, executive producer of the PBS series *Columbus and the Age of Discovery,* quotes the entry Columbus made in his log on October 10, 1492: "They grumbled and complained of the long voyage, and I reproached them for their lack of spirit, telling them that for better or worse, they had to complete the enterprise on which the Catholic sovereigns had sent them" (145). But grumbling and complaining are not the same as mutiny at sea. "All of this mutiny story," observes Kirkpatrick Sale, "has once more the smell of deception, perhaps even self-deception—of [Columbus] trying, through self-serving stories to his son and gullible chroniclers, to create the image of the valiant lone visionary against the disbelieving multitude" (61). Without the mutinies, however, it is hard to imagine that these Columbus films could retain the interest of their audience, admittedly unlikely to be mesmerized simply by the sound of rope stretching and the color blue.

The valiant, lone visionary, however, survives in the documentary film *The Italians in America* (1998), made for the Arts & Entertainment television network. Although the film leaps from the discovery of America to Ellis Island in a single bound, it leaves no doubt as to the heroic role played by Columbus in American history. This conventional, if venerable, portrait is preserved, as well, by Ingri Mortenson d'Aulaire and Edgar Parin d'Aulaire in their picture book *Columbus,* published by Doubleday in 1955. Thirty years later, Spoken Arts made a delightful film from this book, *Christopher Columbus* (1987), adding the video to their "historical adventures" series—which includes biographies of Washington, Franklin, and Lincoln, all based on d'Aulaire titles. The Spoken Arts rendition of the Columbus tale is visually enchanting and provides a modern equivalent of the classic N. C. Wyeth illustrations accompanying favorite stories and poems in long-forgotten but cherished elementary school readers.

Perhaps not surprisingly, in the d'Aulaires' children's version Columbus returns on his second voyage to the new world only to find that the "fortress on Haiti was in ruins and all the men gone." In fact, as *1492* reveals in appalling detail, the men Columbus had left behind were slaughtered. The fate of those Native Americans, for whom the "New World" was, in reality, an old world is only hinted at in one line from the Spoken Arts film: "Columbus and his men ate so much the Indians said, 'No more food.'" That is as close as youthful viewers of the d'Aulaires' *Christopher Columbus* will get to an initial confrontation with what historian David E. Stannard calls the "American Holocaust." Reconciliation of the picture-book version with the one they study later, in "historically corrected" high school texts, is a task the youngsters themselves will have to shoulder.

Is there any solid ground, however, on which viewers of Columbus films can stand? Are there any aspects of this drama about which historians, and history teachers, can say something with confidence, with certainty? The Society of American Historians–sponsored *Reader's Companion to American History* (1991) states that Columbus referred to the native peoples waiting for him in the new world as "Indians" because "he assumed he had been sailing in the Indian Ocean" (374). Daniel K. Richter goes farther, and, citing Moffitt and Sebastian's *O Brave New People* (1996), suggests that what Columbus meant by describing his discovery as "Paradise-on-Earth" was that he had found "a specific place described in the Book of Genesis as having been initially inhabited by Adam and Eve" (1581). From such extraordinary expectations came the first actual European confrontation with the Americas.

References

Filmography

Blade Runner (1982, F)
Christopher Columbus (1949, F; 1985, TV; 1987, TV)
Christopher Columbus: The Discovery (1992, F)
1492: The Conquest of Paradise (1992, F)
Italians in America (1998, D)

Bibliography

Bailey, Thomas A., David M. Kennedy, and Lizabeth Cohen. *The American Pageant: A History of the Republic.* 11th ed. Boston: Houghton Mifflin, 1998.

Bodnar, John. *Remaking America: Public Memory, Commemoration, and Patriotism in the Twentieth Century.* Princeton: Princeton University Press, 1992.

d'Aulaire, Ingri M., and Edgar P. d'Aulaire. *Columbus.* New York: Doubleday, 1995.

Dor-Ner, Zvi. *Columbus and the Age of Discovery.* New York: William Morrow, 1991.

Lucas, Paul R. "Exploration of North America." In Eric Foner and John A. Garraty, eds., *The Reader's Companion to American History,* 372–377. Boston: Houghton Mifflin, 1991.

Mancall, Peter C. "The Age of Discovery." *Reviews in American History* 26.1 (1998): 6–53.

Moffitt, John F., and Sebastian Santiago. *O Brave New People: The European Invention of the American Indian.* Albuquerque: University of New Mexico Press, 1996.

Morison, Samuel Eliot. *Admiral of the Ocean Sea: A Life of Christopher Columbus.* Boston: Little, Brown, 1942.

Phillips, Carla Rahn, and William D. Phillips Jr. "Christopher Columbus: Two Films." In Mark C. Carnes, ed., *Past Imperfect: History According to the Movies,* 60–65. New York: Henry Holt, 1995.

Richter, Daniel K. "Book Review." *American Historical Review* 103.5 (1998): 1580–1581.

Sale, Kirkpatrick. *The Conquest of Paradise: Christopher Columbus and the Columbian Legacy.* New York: Knopf, 1990.

Stannard, David E. *American Holocaust: Columbus and the Conquest of the New World.* New York: Oxford University Press, 1992.

Taviani, Paolo Emilio. *Christopher Columbus: The Grand Design.* London: Orbis, 1985.

Taylor, Paul. "Christopher Columbus." In John Pym, ed., *Out Film Guide,* 148. 6th ed. London: Penguin, 1998.

Wollen, Peter. "Cinema's Conquistadors." *Sight and Sound* 2.7 (1992): 21–23.

[COTTEN SEILER]

The Founding Fathers

Although Thomas Jefferson's claim that "all men are created equal" certainly seems "self-evident" today, it was at the time a novel—even radical—assertion. Jefferson's statement is an expression of the political and philosophical world that we have come to call "modern," emerging between the seventeenth and nineteenth centuries and propelled by an intellectual movement known as the Enlightenment. Thinkers such as Jefferson, Thomas Hobbes, John Locke, and Jean-Jacques Rousseau questioned a social order dominated by religious orthodoxy and arbitrary political authority and theorized about the origin of society and the "natural rights" of all individuals. The collective project of Enlightenment thinkers was universal human emancipation from the "benighted" ideas and practices of the past. They asserted that human behavior was subject to the same natural and rational laws that governed celestial motion and the circulation of the blood and that these laws—rather than scripture and theology—would provide the blueprints for a just society.

Though sharing these general themes, the sensibilities and modes of Enlightenment thought were many and diverse and tied to specific places and local traditions. Rousseau's work, for example, was overwhelmingly influenced by and directed at the distinctive hierarchy and rarefied social protocols of French society. A similar claim can be made about the strain of Enlightenment thought originating in British North America, that it was "defined by the selective attention to some particular themes chosen from the range of questions and concerns taken up by the larger Enlightened world" (Shuffleton, ix–x).

America's initial participation in the Enlightenment was largely symbolic. The European philosophes (radical philosophers) saw the vast "New World" as a sort of abstract "laboratory" for their theories. This territory, they speculated, existed in a pure state, untouched by "civilization" and therefore could be the site of society's remaking. These hopes paralleled those of the New England Puritans, who believed their divine mission to be one of taming a physical and spiritual wilderness. However unfounded or exclusionary these beliefs, which ignored the complex and ancient civilizations of indigenous people, they gave America its central place in the Enlightenment.

Yet America's role did not remain merely symbolic; rather, the founding of the United States was a momentous political achievement of the Enlightenment. Colonial American enlighteneners were "unabashedly prudential" (Lerner, 20), primarily concerned with commerce and with the preservation of political rights to which they, as English subjects, felt themselves entitled. By the mid-eighteenth century, American thinkers began to connect their own struggle for colonial autonomy to abstract Enlightenment ideals of human liberty. Enlightenment theory aided them in thinking about and articulating their grievances and desires and in determining how to reconfigure their society to better ensure the rights of all. We continue to use the language of the Enlightenment to describe the uniqueness and promise of American society—"life, liberty, and the pursuit of happiness"—and to combat persisting ills, as in Martin Luther King Jr.'s assertion that "the goal of America is freedom" (97).

Historical Film: Confounding the Founding Fathers?

Popular history tends to privilege individual historical actors, the "great figures" of history. Thus the mainstream historiography of the American Enlightenment features that assortment of social elites, philosophers, politicians and political theorists, intellectuals, landowners, slaveholders, soldiers, merchants, diplomats, and scientists known as the "Founding Fathers." The membership list of this cadre is occasionally redrawn, but it usually includes John Adams, George Washington, Thomas Jefferson, Benjamin Franklin, Alexander Hamilton, Samuel Adams, John Hancock, and James Madison.

The peripheral status of women in the canon of Enlightenment thinkers (with the possible exception of Abigail Adams) testifies to the decidedly *un*enlightened gender relations of the era. Also left out are the lower and artisan classes (with the possible exceptions of Thomas Paine and Paul Revere) and minorities. These exclusions are ironic and rankling in a nation steeped in an ideology of class mobility and unfettered meritocracy, and the attempts by historians to reconstruct the lives of marginalized groups in early America have only recently begun.

Although the Founding Fathers are held to be exemplars of American ideals, genius, and virtue, representing them through a medium such as film involves some ideological risk. The figure of George Washington, for example, has been used as a paragon of American virtue. Could an inaccurate and/or unflattering portrayal in film, one that reduced Washington to human scale, damage the myth? What would be the consequences? Historical film has played a role in contesting and destabilizing the myths surrounding the Founding Fathers, and in so doing it has humanized the august pantheon of American history and challenged audiences to draw connections between past and present. Depictions of the American Enlightenment such as *1776, Thomas Jefferson, Jefferson in Paris,* and *The Adams Chronicles* combine patriotic representations of the Founding Fathers with the more recent—often critical—historical accounts of their lives and times.

1776

The 1970s, with its shocks of Watergate, Vietnam, and recession, witnessed a decline in patriotic feeling, despite the attempts at Bicentennial ballyhoo in 1976. The antiestablishment politics of the 1960s fostered new ideas about the founders of the republic. On one hand, these advocates of inalienable human rights and equality were held up as symbols by the civil rights movement and the New Left. The attempt here was not to dethrone the Founding Fathers but rather to identify and cultivate a radical tradition in American history, one that legitimated the current dissent and activism. On the other hand, they were also vilified for their racism, sexism, and elitism—problems with which America continued to grapple.

Historians and mythmakers had made grand claims about the Founding Fathers—Parson Weems's fable of Washington and the cherry tree springs to mind—but few had yet lauded the Founding Fathers for their ability to sing. Peter Stone's musical *1776* had been a Broadway hit before making its way to the screen in 1972. Notwithstanding the abysmal songs, the film portrays the debate in the Continental Congress over independence with sophistication and aplomb.

Inaccuracies pervade *1776*, though few are very troubling. The film exaggerates the Congress's lack of confidence in Washington's forces: in the summer of 1776, the conventional wisdom held that the war would be won by year's end. As Thomas Fleming has written, *1776* is also somewhat capricious in its characterization of the congressmen. Personages are altered, usually for dramatic or comic effect; some are omitted altogether. The hero here is John Adams (William Daniels), the chief proponent of independence, repeatedly (and accurately) described as "obnoxious and disliked." Despite the fact that Benjamin Franklin could barely stand Adams, Franklin is depicted here as his sage sidekick. Richard Henry Lee, the Virginia delegate known for his austerity and commitment to the cause of independence, is portrayed as a good-natured bumpkin wholly in the sway of Adams and Franklin. In the film's worst moments, the writers of the film, Sherman Edwards and Peter Stone, "seem to view the Continental Congress as an early version of *Animal House*" (Fleming, 92).

1776 is most interesting in its treatment of Jefferson (Ken Howard). In order to inspire the young Virginian in writing the Declaration of Independence, Adams sends for Martha Jefferson (Blythe Danner) to come to Philadelphia. The visit, of course, never occurred: Martha was too ill at the time to make such a journey. Nonetheless, Adams and Benjamin Franklin (Howard Da Silva) wait outside Jefferson's quarters during the conjugal tryst. Martha emerges, and intimates to them that Jefferson "plays the violin," a reference to his sexual prowess. Both song and scenario are contrived and rather silly, but they are part of the film's overarching attempt to humanize the founding fathers, to redraw them to human scale.

One figure spared the revisionism of the musical comedy is George Washington. Historiography critical of Washington is rare; rarer still are the films which would subject the "Father of Our Country" to speculation or even critique. Most films, documentary or narrative, echo Benson Bobrick's claim that "the myth is that there is a myth about [Washington]. And those looking to tear down an idol in order to find the 'real' man will, as they find him, have to build him back up" (132). The solution to Washington's "untouchability" as a national symbol has generally been to move him to the periphery or not to represent him at all. Washington never appears onscreen in the whimsical *1776;* he is represented only through his dispatches to Congress—the thought of the severe, taciturn American Cincinnatus breaking into song was apparently too much for the filmmakers.

The Adams Chronicles

The Adams family of Massachusetts certainly merits inclusion in the story of the American Enlightenment and its legacy. A prodigious political dynasty, the Adams family was instrumental in securing independence for the United States and guiding the young republic through its early crises. In addition, the family—notable among them John, Samuel, Abigail, John Quincy, Charles Francis, and Henry—produced voluminous and insightful written commentary on a century and a half of American political life. This enormous body of documents has been available to scholars since 1954 and is expected to generate more than 150 published volumes of Adams family letters, diaries, political papers, poetry, and assorted scribblings (see Bailyn, 3–4). It was from this trove of material that the producers of the PBS series *The Adams Chronicles* (1976) drew.

Produced by WNEW for the Public Broadcasting Service and funded by the National Endowment for the Humanities, the Mellon Foundation, and the Atlantic Richfield Corporation, the thirteen-part series, broadcast over the course of the bicentennial year 1976, traced the lives of the Adams family over 150 years. Like the more recent PBS series *Liberty!* (1997), the release of *The Adams Chronicles* was accompanied by the publication of companion works designed to complement and enlarge the historical vision of the series (see Janes; Rothman; and Shepherd). Indeed, more than any other filmic work on the American Enlightenment, *The Adams Chronicles* is painstakingly documented and scrupulously authentic in both its words and images.

The series hews closely to the (plentiful) textual evidence and the established academic historical canon. A press release emphasizes the extraordinary care and attention to factuality that went into all aspects of the production, including locations (the mansions of Newport, Rhode Island, the Capitol in Washington, and Congress Hall in Philadelphia), costumes (based on Adams portraits), makeup, and casting (according to the release, the series employed "800 period faces"). In the ultimate genuflection to authenticity, *The Adams Chronicles* screenplays were assembled from the 300,000-page compendium of the Adams family's written work. Yet historical dramas that overemphasize verisimilitude, as Robert Rosenstone has noted in reference to the series, "have tended to be visually and dramatically inert, better as aids to sleep than to the acquisition of historical consciousness" (7). In the case of this production, the commendable quest for realism became a monomania, and ended up stifling the narrative, however accurate the sets, costumes, and dialogue.

Yet there are strengths to the production—which enjoyed large audiences during its run—as well. One critic notes that the series' creators "deserve congratulations for their daring in presenting a family almost totally deficient in charm or grace" (Grier et al., 78). John Adams (George Grizzard) is depicted more or less as he constructed himself in his writings, as a man of contradictory character—by turns self-righteous and self-effacing, inhibited and sensuous, ornery and generous of spirit. The series also flirts with depicting the Founding Fathers (especially John Hancock) as self-interested plutocrats rather than enlightened pragmatists. *The Adams Chronicles,* in other words, grants the Adams family their complexities in their time and indulges in only a little dramatic fancy, as in Kathryn Walker's portrayal of Abigail Adams, one of the most articulate and intelligent protofeminist voices in the early republic. The production, however, tends to depict her as little more than the sensual counterpart to her husband's intellect.

The final effect of *The Adams Chronicles* on the viewer may be one of puzzlement: why was this series produced? As one writer observed in 1978, the series came about as a "chance to exploit bicentennial-generated enthusiasm for safe revolutionary themes" and as part of the larger project of using film and television to demonstrate the relevance of the past to a broad public audience (Grier et al., 81). Yet the viewer is left with little notion about what forces propelled the Adams family and the era and how the ideas and the individuals continue to drive American culture; moreover, in encouraging little interpretive or imaginative work on the part of the viewer, the series is often boring. Ultimately, *The Adams Chronicles* explores few of the potential innovations for presenting history on film, settling instead for a guided tour of a musty archive.

Thomas Jefferson

"Unfortunately and tragically," says the African American historian John Hope Franklin in Ken Burns's 1996 documentary *Thomas Jefferson,* "I would say that in a sense Thomas Jefferson personifies the United States and its history." Despite innumerable investigations of his character, his philosophical and political beliefs, and, recently, his sexual conduct, Jefferson remains a protean and contradictory figure. As Andrew Burstein writes, "whether he was the mellow and erudite *philosophe* he posed as or an earthy and unblushing slave owner like many other Virginians of his class, or something in between—is simply not known" (Burstein, Isenberg, and Gordon-Reed, 24). The struggle among historians for the true character of Jefferson is in many ways a struggle over the moral and ethical foundations of American culture (see Ellis; Gordon-Reed; and O'Brien).

Jefferson continues to interest Americans for his rhetorical brilliance, militantly democratic vision, and stewardship of the early republic; but the most compelling Jeffersonian legacy is, to use W. E. B. DuBois's famous phrase, "the problem of the color line." Jefferson's ambiguous impact on American race relations makes his legacy, at the beginning of the twenty-first century, particularly fascinating and vexing. The same hand that penned the famous opening lines of the Declaration of Independence also wrote virulently racist descriptions of slaves in his *Notes on the State of Virginia.* The former, echoed in the words of Dr. Martin Luther King Jr., would become a touchstone for those who demand that America live up to its egalitarian promise; the latter would help legitimate the most vicious racist polemic of the next two centuries. Even by the standards of his own time, Jefferson's views on race were reactionary (certainly less progressive than those of his fellow Virginian George Washington, who fulfilled his promise to free his slaves). If the injustice and hypocrisy of Jefferson's owning slaves haunts his legacy, it is because race remains an issue of tremendous import to the inheritors of that legacy.

Certainly such a life provides material for a compelling film; yet Jefferson remains underrepresented and poorly represented in the medium, most likely due to the contradictions and ambiguity that make him interesting in the first place. Burns's three-part series *Thomas Jefferson* stands as a fine example of artistic documentary filmmaking, and it is currently the "last word" on Jefferson committed to film. As in previous Burns productions, *Thomas Jefferson* combines cinematography, period music, interviews, and actor voiceovers to re-create the world of the eighteenth century. It is not easy to portray cinematically a world vacant of photographic images, and Burns's integration of portraiture, genre painting, and location cinematography is generally skillful. The production features interviews with prominent American historians and scholars of Jeffersoniana, including Franklin, Garry Wills, Jan Lewis, Joseph Ellis, and Gore Vidal. The shots of Monticello and of the Philadelphia room in which Jefferson drafted the Declaration of Independence are haunting and beautiful, and actor Sam Waterston proves a suitably low-key conduit for Jefferson's words.

The depth and thoughtfulness with which the producers crafted *Thomas Jefferson* is evident. What is less evident is whether the filmmakers accomplished their goal of illuminating the personality behind the national icon, or whether they merely updated the icon for the late twentieth century. Ken Burns's productions have been notable for their commitment to a full engagement with the contradictory record of history, and *Thomas Jefferson* does not obscure its subject's most egregious words and acts. Rather, the most confounding and regrettable aspects of Jefferson's life are foregrounded, especially his racism and slaveholding. As Sean Wilentz notes, when confronting the gray areas of Jefferson's life and career, such as his alleged affair with his slave Sally Hemings, "the film presents all possibilities and wisely suspends final judgment" (39). However, in this and his earlier works on baseball and the Civil War, Burns has demonstrated his facility for reconstructing, upgrading, and reinvigorating the animating myths of the nation. His purchase on the viewer is ultimately an emotional one, and his films in their worst moments willingly trade critique for sentimentality.

At one point in the film, John Hope Franklin urges the audience to find in their hearts the same forgiveness he has given Jefferson. The comment is a powerful one, and it seems to point to a way out of the historiographic trench warfare in which historians have engaged over the past few decades. Burns's film presents itself as an olive branch extended to the bashers of Jefferson and his apologists, and it tries to incorporate the arguments of both. But at the end of *Thomas Jefferson,* one is left with the sense that the icon has emerged more or less unscathed; that Jefferson, for all his faults, remains a figure worthy of the investment the culture has made in him.

Jefferson in Paris

As in *The Adams Chronicles,* the lavish sets and costumes of *Jefferson in Paris* (1995) reproduce the eighteenth-century aristocratic world with grand verisimilitude. Yet for all the authenticity of the set design, costumes, and music, the Enlightenment as a period of social and political upheaval is barely evident in the film. As Darren Stoloff notes, "Hardly an oppressive, corrupt, or decadent social order, Merchant and Ivory's French high society resembles a slightly saucy Euro-Disney period recreation" (750). The filmmaking trio of Ismail Merchant, James Ivory, and Ruth Prawer-Jhabvala, despite some admirable gestures toward rethinking Jefferson, ended up sacrificing edification for titillation.

Thomas Jefferson *wrote* his way into history—more than the other major figures of the American Enlightenment, he is best remembered for his acts of writing. Jefferson was known to spend up to ten hours a day at the writing desk—an estimable habit, but not the most riveting spectacle, to say the least. Rather than sidestep this cinematic obstacle, the makers of *Jefferson in Paris* (1995) confront it directly with an opening shot of Jefferson's duplication machine at work, the writer's hand in motion. The implications of this image (the pen nib dipping the ink, the words produced by the automatic pen) are provocative, as it suggests Jefferson's production—and reproduction—of himself through writing.

Having foregrounded Jefferson's defining practice, the film returns to the writing desk only infrequently and only to give Jefferson's mostly superfluous commentary on the conditions in France and the state of Franco-American relations. Instead, *Jefferson in Paris* focuses largely on the romantic diversions of the American diplomat. Despite the multitude of concerns on Jefferson's mind during his years in Paris, from refinancing of the American war debt to the cataloguing of European plants to the promotion of the cause of liberty among the French, the filmmakers would have the viewer believe that the American polymath's mind was overwhelmingly occupied by *l'amour.* Inspired by Fawn Brodie's 1974 *Thomas Jefferson: An Intimate Biography,* screenwriter Prawer-Jhabvala and director Ivory portray Jefferson as a sensualist surrounded by a trio of women competing for his exclusive affections.

Maria Cosway (Greta Scacchi), the cultured and beautiful wife of an English painter, is the first woman of whom Jefferson becomes enamored; their affair (allegedly never consummated) produced one of Jefferson's most famous letters, addressed to Cosway and known as the "Dialogue between My Head and My Heart." The film suggests that Cosway was ousted from Jefferson's heart by an unlikely rival, Jefferson's fifteen-year-old slave Sally Hemings (Thandie Newton). Completing the triangle is his teenage daughter Martha (Gwyneth Paltrow), a symbolic as well as vocal reminder of his late wife and his promise never to remarry.

Far from offering a window into Jefferson's character, *Jefferson in Paris* manages to mystify him further—or worse, render him insipid—through his romantic entanglements. For all the intimation of sex and passion, an overwhelming sterility prevails. The film wants to interrogate Jefferson's "dual nature"—his warring intellect and passions—and it does so by making Cosway and Hemings predictable symbols of, respectively, mind and body. It should come as no surprise to any student of American culture that this dichotomy is figured here in terms of race. The affair with Hemings is "the equivalent of a tin can tied to Jefferson's reputation that has continued to rattle through the ages and the pages of the history books" (Ellis, 217). Newton's "Dusky Sally," as she was called by Jefferson's political enemies, tempts him with an earthy sexuality for which Cosway's cultivation and wit are no match. The film implies that Sally's seduction of the man who owned her was a matter of charming him with song and dance, not to mention the ample bosom threatening to burst through the top of her calico dress. In the end, Jefferson "chooses" Hemings, and with this choice the film clunks to a halt (after he has agreed to free Hemings and her brother).

"Whatever the truth," writes Annette Gordon-Reed, "the story of the liaison between Thomas Jefferson and Sally Hemings persists because it humanizes the eloquent Jefferson, when the alternative is to imagine him sexless and therefore less human" (Burstein, Isenberg, and Gordon-Reed, 24). The film arrives at the verdict that the twentieth century, after Freud and the sexual revolution, the civil rights movement and the O. J. Simpson trial, seems to want: the truth about Jefferson can be found at the complex intersection of sex and race in America.

The Enlightenment: More Than Wigs and Knee Breeches?

There is a legendary anecdote about Harry Cohn, the former head of Columbia Pictures, and his dismay at the earnings of a particular eighteenth-century epic produced by his studio. Cohn allegedly issued a moratorium on further studio forays into the stuffy and unsalable era, with its "men in wigs and knee breeches writing with quill pens" (Schickel). Filmmakers since Harry Cohn have unfortunately done little to prove him wrong: since his edict in the 1930s, the American Enlightenment has remained a place rarely visited by the mainstream film industry.

Harry Cohn understood movies, but the importance of representing the past eluded him. Despite its foreign character, its alien practices, fashions, and customs, the eighteenth century remains a time with which each generation of Americans strives to find its affinity. The United States is ideologically funded by the achievements of the Enlightenment—the Declaration of Independence, the Constitution—and, unlike other nations, ideas are all we have for solidarity. The films discussed here succeed or fail not necessarily by how accurate they are but to the degree that they tie the founding ideas of the American past to the environment of the present.

References

Filmography

The Adams Chronicles (1976, TV)
Against the Odds: Samuel Adams, American Revolutionary (1988, D)
Alexander Hamilton (1961, F)
America (1924, F)
Benjamin Franklin: Citizen of the World (1994, D)
George Washington (1984, TV)
George Washington: The Man Who Wouldn't Be King (1992, TV)
George Washington II: The Forging of a Nation (1986, TV)
History Alive: The American Revolution (1998, TV)
The Howards of Virginia (1940, F)
Independence (1976, F)
Janice Meredith (1924, F)
Jefferson in Paris (1995, F)
Johnny Tremaine (1957, F)
Lafayette (1961, F)
The Legacy of Thomas Jefferson (1995, D)
Liberty! The American Revolution (1997, TV)
Magnificent Doll (1946, F)
Meet George Washington (1990, TV)
Old Louisiana (1937, F)
1776 (1972, F)
Thomas Jefferson (1996, D)
Thomas Jefferson: The Pursuit of Liberty (1991, D)

Bibliography

Bailyn, Bernard. *Faces of Revolution: Personalities and Themes in the Struggle for American Independence.* New York: Vintage, 1992.

Bobrick, Benson. *Angel in the Whirlwind: The Triumph of the American Revolution.* New York: Simon & Schuster, 1997.

Burstein, Andrew, Nancy Isenberg, and Annette Gordon-Reed. "Three Perspectives on America's Jefferson Fixation." *The Nation,* 30 November 1998.

Ellis, Joseph J. *American Sphinx: The Character of Thomas Jefferson.* New York: Knopf, 1998.

Fleming, Thomas. "1776." In Mark C. Carnes, ed., *Past Imperfect: History According to the Movies*, 85–93. New York: Henry Holt, 1996.

Gordon-Reed, Annette. *Thomas Jefferson and Sally Hemings: An American Controversy.* Charlottesville: University Press of Virginia, 1997.

Grier, Edward F., et al. "TV Viewing Guide: The Adams Chronicles." *American Studies* 19.2 (1978): 75–84.

Janes, Regina. *Adams Chronicles: A Student Guide.* New York: Educational Associates, 1976.

King, Martin Luther, Jr. *Why We Can't Wait.* New York: Harper & Row, 1963.

Lerner, Ralph. *Revolutions Revisited: Two Faces of the Politics of the Enlightenment.* Chapel Hill: University of North Carolina Press, 1994.

O'Brien, Conor Cruise. *The Long Affair: Thomas Jefferson and the French Revolution, 1785–1800.* Chicago: University of Chicago Press, 1997.

Rosenstone, Robert. *Visions of the Past: The Challenge of Film to Our Idea of History.* Cambridge, MA: Harvard University Press, 1995.

Rothman, David J., ed. *The World of the Adams Chronicles: Forging Our Nation.* New York: Educational Associates, 1976.

Schickel, Richard. "The Pursuit of Stuffiness." *Time,* 10 April 1995.

Shepherd, Jack. *The Adams Chronicles: Four Generations of Greatness.* New York: Little, Brown, 1976.

Shuffleton, Frank, ed. *The American Enlightenment.* Rochester: University of Rochester Press, 1993.

Stoloff, Darren. "Film Review: *Jefferson in Paris.*" *William and Mary Quarterly* 52.4 (1995): 750–753.

Wilentz, Sean. "Life, Liberty, and the Pursuit of Thomas Jefferson." *The New Republic,* 10 March 1997.

[ROBERT BAIRD]

Indian Leaders

The popular conception of the "Indian chief" remains a simplified caricature. Derived from dime novels, sensational journalism, and B movies, popularized Indian chiefs are, following the familiar Western model of political and military hierarchy, the sole and ultimate rulers of their various tribes, their status signaled by wearing the headdress with the most feathers. The caricature of the chief is perpetuated at colleges around the country; for example, at the University of Illinois, home of the "Fighting Illini," an undergraduate poses each year as "The Chief," dressed in fringed buckskin and flowing headdress, responsible for performing an inspiring dance at major sporting events. Illinois's Chief, and many of the Indian-theme school mascots around the country, came into being in the first half of this century, when popular interest in and concern over the "vanishing American" was at its peak.

In contrast, academic and tribal historians have shed light on the quite varied forms of leadership found in historical and contemporary Native American tribes, making it clear that in most historical tribes, power was informally distributed among a diverse group of peace chiefs, war chiefs, religious leaders, medicine men, and prophets. The informality of Indian political power was frequently accompanied in many tribes with a respect for individual discretion so great as to be alien to Euro-Americans. David Roberts clarifies this point in *Once They Moved Like the Wind*: "The autonomy that lay at the heart of Apache life, dictating that each band had the right to seek its own battles, eluded the grasp of Americans who had just fought a great war to preserve their own nationhood. Among the Apache, even so great a chief as Cochise had no authority to order the humblest warrior into battle: the choice must be made of each man's free will each time" (92).

Such individual autonomy played a key role in the tactical success of Apache warriors (considered by some military historians to be the greatest guerrilla fighters ever). This same autonomy, however, ultimately undermined the Apache's strategic hopes of mounting a lasting, pantribal defense against the United States, whose race-based allegiances powerfully unified individual civilians and military agents on the frontier.

When historical chiefs are depicted in film, they are most frequently chosen from the patriot war chiefs of the Plains tribes, whose heroic resistance during the end of the nineteenth century was dramatic, well publicized at the time, and recent enough to allow for historical recovery. Eastern chiefs of great historical stature such as Tecumseh (Shawnee, 1768–1813) and Pontiac (Ottawa, 1720?–1769) are rarely depicted. The great peace chiefs and culture brokers, such as Quanah Parker (Comanche, 1853–1911) and Sequoyah (Cherokee, 1770–1843), have also been neglected. Influential contemporary Indian leaders do not seem to exist at all within the Hollywood mindset.

Hollywood's Indian chiefs grow out of a very long, popular infatuation with the Plains tribes, especially the Sioux, who gave us Red Cloud (Oglala, 1821/22–1909); Crazy Horse

(Oglala, 1840–1877); and Sitting Bull (Hunkpapa, 1831?–1890). With Geronimo (Bedonkohe Apache, 1829–1909) and Cochise (Chiricahua Apache, 1810–1874) deriving from the Apache people, America's mainstream perception of "the Indian chief" emerges from a handful of leaders representing only a small part of North America's native legacy. Although Apache leaders and the conflict of the Southwest are popularly known, it is the Plains tribal iconography of horses, buffalo, war bonnet, and teepees that dominates popular culture representations, serving as a generic model in motion pictures for all Native Americans.

The historical chiefs famous enough to inspire Hollywood's attention have frequently been played by nonnative actors. The great Cochise, for instance, was played three times by Jeff Chandler (born Ira Grossel), and a survey of other Hollywood depictions of Cochise reveals not a single Native American performance. Alongside Hollywood's century-long tradition of casting non-Indians in native roles ran a tradition of casting real Indian chiefs (but usually only for cameos and background). Chief John Big Tree (Onondaga, 1865–1967), who was the model for James Earle Fraser's relief work used for the Indian Head nickel, appeared as a warrior or chief in more than a hundred films, from *The Primitive Lover* (1922) to *Devil's Doorway* (1950). The most successful and skilled native chief actor was likely Chief Dan George (Salish, 1899–1982), whose roles in *Little Big Man* (1970), *Harry and Tonto* (1974), and *The Outlaw Josey Wales* (1976) were widely celebrated. George's characters and performances cut against the grain of the stereotypically stoic, suffering, silent Indian and indulged humor, self-deprecation, and playfulness—even as his outward appearance confirmed the popular model of the noble, sagacious chief.

Hollywood biographies of Indian chiefs typically warp, omit, and invent history for the sake of drama. Film documentaries, less concerned with "character development" and dramatic logic than Hollywood features, are much more respectful of the facts of historical chiefs' lives. Although documentaries usually avoid fabrication, they nonetheless often fixate on one dominating interpretation of their biographical figure at the expense of other valid perspectives. These simplifications of character are a product of both historical attitudes toward Indians as well as film and narrative form, which tends to collapse and condense the complexity of actual lives and historical records. As war chiefs engaged in armed conflict with the United States up until the final years of the Indian wars, Cochise, Sitting Bull, and Geronimo have always inspired conflicting and ambivalent responses from contemporaries and later historians and filmmakers. The known facts about Geronimo have in particular challenged the art of biography and clear-cut moral judgment. At once a victim and perpetrator of the most horrific atrocities, a medicine man with power but not an actual war or peace chief, now idolized as *the* figure of Native American military resistance, but a man who spent more time on reservations, peaceably, than most other warrior leaders, Geronimo resists unified categorization and understanding. Historian Angie Debo captures the surreal irony of Geronimo's life when she describes the old warrior's role in Theodore Roosevelt's inaugural parade:

> Geronimo was on his favorite pony, carefully shipped there for the occasion. He held himself erect, completely calm and self-possessed, while men threw their hats into the air and shouted, "Hooray for Geronimo!" "Public Hero No. 2," said the disgusted Woodworth Clum. This son of the Apache agent, hating Geronimo with all the intensity of his father, had been a member of the inaugural committee, and Roosevelt's request for Geronimo's presence had been made to him. Now he was privileged to stand near the president as he reviewed the parade in front of the White House, and he took the opportunity to ask, "Why did you select Geronimo to march in the parade, Mr. President? He is the greatest single-handed murderer in American history." "I wanted to

> give the people a good show," answered the irrepressible Teddy. (419)

Geronimo's valued place in American show business and popular culture was largely attributable to his status as one of the last (safely vanquished) Indian military threats to the United States. Geronimo himself, however, did not hide from "show business" and the public stage and spent his years of captivity signing autographs, visiting various fairs and public gatherings, and speaking out about his people's continued imprisonment and loss of ancestral land.

The most historically accurate depictions of Geronimo's life followed a *Dances with Wolves*–inspired return of the western. Ted Turner's made-for-television production (1993) makes Geronimo (Joseph Runningfox) the central character and presence of the film. Providing his own voiceover narration (typically assigned to a white character in such films), Geronimo recounts his life (in flashback) to a young Apache. Like nearly all films dealing with the Indian Wars, this one chooses sides, with Mexican and American perfidy toward the Apache shown (accurately) to motivate Geronimo's revenge and militancy. Following the emphasis and rhetorical strategy of Geronimo's autobiography, the film centers on Mexican-Apache relations, diplomatically downplaying American-Apache troubles.

In creating a heroic Geronimo, the film suppresses the brutality of Apache raiding and warfare tradition. Raiding is treated in the film only when Geronimo steals horses (without harming anyone) for his bride price—raiding, then, is treated in the context of courting. Apache offensive warfare is never shown on camera, although Geronimo's rhetorical skills (and deep hatred) are displayed when he rallies his fellows for vengeance on the garrison town harboring the Mexican troops (and families) that massacred his family. In the end, though, Ted Turner's Geronimo (or any other Apache) never raises his hand against noncombatants, a significant historical omission, but a fundamental requirement of a western cinema hero. Like *Dances with Wolves,* Ted Turner's *Geronimo* "revises" the western by inverting the traditional, simplistic us/them binary, making Indians the us and Mexican and European Americans the them.

Ted Turner's interest in Native American history led to the development of a series of films, including the aforementioned *Geronimo,* as well as *Tecumseh: The Last Warrior* (1995). Like *Geronimo, Tecumseh* is a heroic, post–*Dances with Wolves* treatment, well funded, nicely acted, and more accurate than Hollywood fare of an earlier generation. Nonetheless, *Tecumseh* frequently simplifies the complex, ambiguous record of its subject. For instance, the film leaves the impression that Tecumseh was greeted enthusiastically by every tribe he visited during his famous pantribal tours, which is not surprising as this conforms with contemporary appreciation for Tecumseh's political savvy and feelings regarding what *should have been done* by tribes fighting western expansion. In reality, during one tour of the Five Southern Tribes in 1811, only the Creeks were receptive to Tecumseh's pro-British pleas. Then, too, *Tecumseh* ends in political correctness or, perhaps, simple wish fulfillment, with the slain warrior receiving a traditional and beautifully staged Shawnee burial. Most historians, though, knowing that Tecumseh was killed in battle on October 5, 1813, believe that Kentucky militiamen mutilated his body and buried it in a mass grave.

The most significant Hollywood biography of a patriot chief is Walter Hill's *Geronimo: An American Legend* (1993), which presents a much more angry and violent Geronimo than does Ted Turner's film, a difference achieved, in part, through casting actor Wes Studi, a Cherokee, as Geronimo. Director Walter Hill, known for tough-minded buddy films, centers his film on American-Apache relations and creates an undeniably revisionist western, although he still employs the traditional narrative strategy of framing the Indian story through white characters, all based (somewhat) on actual participants in the Geronimo campaigns: Briton Davis (Matt Damon), Lieutenant Charles Gatewood (Jason Patrick), General George Crook (Gene Hackman), and tracker Al Sieber (Robert Duvall). With a script by John Milius (*Jeremiah Johnson, Apocalypse Now, Red Dawn, Patton,* and other political and historical pieces), *Geronimo: An American Legend* unflinchingly depicts massacres, executions, revenge, and debilitating hatreds that many works gloss over or suppress. Although the dramatic license of this film is more carefully constrained than westerns of earlier decades, there are some instances of narrative invention and audience pandering. In one scene, Gatewood and Geronimo work as a semicomic Lone Ranger–Tonto team to hold off a posse of Tombstone Rangers. In another, a standard barroom shootout, Davis, Gatewood, Sieber, and Apache scout Chato (Steve Reevis) are confronted by a gang of scalphunters, only to gun them down. As Gerald Thompson makes clear in his historical analysis of the film, "Nothing like this episode ever occurred" (211). Both incidents, however, allow viewers to enjoy this Geronimo within familiar and comfortable western scene types, where the good and bad are clearly marked and dealt with accordingly. In one way, though, *Geronimo: An American Legend* remains more challenging to the historical record than the most typical B western. By presenting actual historical figures and incidents and being promoted as a historical, revisionist motion picture, *Geronimo* creates an expectation of historical fidelity that Saturday matinee features and singing cowboys likely never assumed.

Although *Geronimo: An American Legend* is one of the best Hollywood treatments of an Indian leader to date, there are real problems in viewing the film, or any narrative feature, as a work of historical verisimilitude. Hollywood treatments of historical figures never abandon their emphasis on storytelling and mythmaking. They remain devoted to a dramatic coherence and contemporary cultural relevance that frequently betrays actual lives and the best textual biographies.

Robert Altman's *Buffalo Bill and the Indians, or Sitting Bull's History Lesson* (1976) attempts to recast the heroic myths of the west by contrasting a blustering, drunken William F. Cody (Paul Newman) with a quiet, modest, and prophetic Sitting Bull (Frank Kaquitts). Like other revisionist "Vietnam westerns" of the late 1960s and 1970s, which metaphorically associate nineteenth-century mistreatment of Native Americans with America's mistreatment of the Vietnamese, *Buffalo Bill* devotes itself to ironic harpooning of American institutions, myths, and ideals. Historian Wayne Sarf offers a blistering critique of the film in *God Bless You, Buffalo Bill,* finding that the film's debunking "degenerates into overkill, although Altman does manage to avoid having Cody rape a child or steal from a blind beggar" (251). Part of Altman's strategy seems to be the casting of Sitting Bull with Frank Kaquitts, a slight, unknown actor lacking the presence or photogenic qualities of the actual Sitting Bull. Indeed, Altman slyly introduces Sitting Bull into the film so that both the audience and Buffalo Bill confuse a much taller, more conventionally imposing warrior (Will Sampson) for him. Throughout the film, Sampson plays interpreter to Kaquitts's Sitting Bull, affecting a contrast between Sampson's Hollywood-style Indian and Kaquitts's banal figure.

The best film biographies of Indian chiefs can be found in educational television documentaries. *Geronimo and the Apache Resistance* (1988) balances historical appraisals with contemporary Native American perspectives, including an emphasis on Geronimo's shamanism. Interviews with tribal members help convey Geronimo's legacy to contemporary Indians. Critical of American treatment of the Apaches, the film nonetheless balances and

FIGURE 20. *Geronimo: An American Legend* (1993). This revisionist, violent portrait of the legendary Apache leader Geronimo (Wes Studi) focuses on the final months of the U.S. Army's campaign of 1885–1886 and the tragic events leading to his surrender. Courtesy Columbia Pictures Corporation.

complicates its history, acknowledging the decency of General Crook's relations with the Apaches and the unpopularity of Geronimo among his own tribe, some of whom were embittered over the great cost of his militarism. Most surprisingly, the years of confinement at Fort Sill, Oklahoma, are presented positively as a safe period during which the tribe was able to stabilize and begin rebuilding its strength.

Respected documentarian Ken Burns has treated the great Indian chiefs of the Plains tribes in his series *The West* (1996), especially in the episodes "Fight No More Forever" and "The Geography of Hope." Burns's documentary style incorporates a cinematic (moving-camera) treatment of historical photographs, beautifully arranged music of the particular era under study, and a balance of great-man historiography with a populist's celebration of little known but eloquent individuals, their words drawn from diaries and memoirs, read by the very best actors. Burns has occasionally been criticized for relying too strongly on a single historical text or author, but his treatment of Native Americans typically balances a cache of the best academic scholars and tribal historians.

In "Fight No More Forever," Burns and director Stephen Ives offer a Sitting Bull who is foremost a medicine man and spiritual leader, who scorns "agency Indians" as "slaves to bacon," and who contributes decisively to the Little Big Horn victory through his Sun Dance vision of soldiers falling upside down into a great Indian camp. Burns's film celebrates Sitting Bull, but the most heroic Indian chief of the episode is Chief Joseph of the Nez Perce, whose eloquent surrender speech provides the episode's title. It is not difficult to see why Burns would celebrate Chief Joseph above all others: Joseph's intelligence, eloquence, diplomacy, and concern for his people were the equal of his outstanding military skills. Essentially a peace chief, Joseph fought only as a last resort. The little-known, made-for-TV *I Will Fight No More Forever* (1975) provides a poignant, surprisingly accurate treatment of Joseph's long, fighting retreat, enlisting heartfelt performances from James Whitmore as General Howard and Ned Romero as Chief Joseph, the two intractable but respectful adversaries of that campaign.

In "The Geography of Hope," Burns returns to Sitting Bull, beginning with the chief's wish that he would "rather die an Indian than live a white man." Sitting Bull's final, defiant retreat into Canada is traced, and then his return to the reservation. Burns presents a proud, defiant, even petulant Sitting Bull. When U.S. senators visit the Standing Rock reservation in 1883, it is Sitting Bull who says, "Do you know who I am? I want to tell you that if the Great Spirit has chosen anyone to be the chief of their country, it is myself." Burns has a fondness for the complexities and ironies of history. He points out that for all his defiance, Sitting Bull made sure that his son attended the Carlyle Indian Training and Industrial School in Pennsylvania, having seen, while traveling with William Cody in his Wild West Show, the breadth of the wider world. The episode ends hauntingly with another of Sitting Bull's visions: a meadowlark tells him, "Your own people will kill you."

The Way West: The War for the Black Hills, 1870–1876 (1995), written, produced, and directed by Ric Burns—Ken's brother—focuses on the frontier context of the battle of the Little Big Horn in June 1876. The lives of Red Cloud, Crazy Horse, and Sitting Bull are carefully sketched with the help of the respected, mainstream historians and advocates of the topic—Dee Brown, Robert Utley, Stephen E. Ambrose—and their words embodied through the narration of professional actors such as Rodney Grant, Graham Greene, Wes Studi, and others. With original and evocative music by Brian Keane, *The War for the Black Hills* is as emotionally compelling as any Hollywood feature. Crazy Horse—who was never photographed and certainly did not sell his portrait, as did Geronimo and Sitting Bull—is presented as a mysterious, almost magical spirit of Native American vengeance. Sitting Bull is presented as "the chief holy man of the Hunkpapa Sioux," and his Sun Dance–inspired dream dominates this narrative.

Historically, women chiefs were rare among Indian tribes. Spanish contact with Mississippian tribes suggested some women held power through a type of monarchy. Among eastern tribes, Iroquois women were well known for wielding matrilineal powers, which included selecting and counseling male chiefs, or sachems. The two most famous American Indian women—Pocahontas (Algonquin, 1596–1617) and Sacagawea (Shoshone, 1786?–1812/84)—were not chiefs per se but were leaders of a sort.

Pocahontas was the daughter of the chief whom local whites called Powhatan (Algonquin, ?–1618), who was paramount leader of a tribal confederation in eastern Virginia. Historians concur that Pocahontas, famous worldwide for the legendary rescue of Captain John Smith from death at the hands of her fellow tribesmen, *did* serve as a peacemaker, eventually marrying John Rolfe in a diplomatic union that helped end conflicts between natives and newcomers. *Pocahontas: Her True Story* (1995), an Arts & Entertainment biography, is recommended in lieu of Disney's fairytale rendering.

Sacagawea, likewise, is known more in legend than in fact. Frequently claimed as the principal guide of the Lewis and Clark expedition, Sacagawea was more accurately an occasional guide and interpreter. Ken Burns's *Lewis & Clark: The Journey of the Corps of Discovery* (1997) undercuts the legendary Sacagawea without failing to credit the young woman's bravery and her threefold significance to the expedition. First, Sacagawea was able to locate and gather native plants, roots, and berries, which provided valuable nutritional and medical supplements to the expedition. Second, her presence, including that of her infant child, signaled wary tribes along the route that the expedition was not a war party. Third, Sacagawea's value as a Shoshone interpreter became even more significant when it was discovered that, in her long absence, her brother had become chief of a tribe strategically located and equipped for helping travelers cross the Bitterroot Mountains.

Hollywood has yet to offer a significant depiction of a contemporary Indian chief. A few documentaries are available. *Wilma P. Mankiller: Woman of Power,* a twenty-nine-minute film, uses interviews with contemporary Cherokee leader Mankiller to foreground her trailblazing role as a woman chief. *Oren Lyons, the Faithkeeper,* Bill Moyers's interview with Onondaga Chief Oren Lyons, an important advocate in the international environmental movement, provides a glimpse of the role of a contemporary chief. Lyons details his tribal history, especially the Great Law of the Six Nations, a legacy of carefully shared power and consensus building, which, Lyons believes, helped ground a new nation many years ago—one that came to call itself the United States.

References

Filmography

Annie Get Your Gun (1950, F)
The Battle at Apache Pass (1952, F)
Broken Arrow (1950, F)
Buffalo Bill and the Indians, or Sitting Bull's History Lesson (1976, F)
Conquest of Cochise (1953, F)
Dances with Wolves (1990, F)
Fight No More Forever: Ken Burns Presents the West (1996, D)
Fort Apache (1948, F)
40 Guns to Apache Pass (1966, F)
The Geography of Hope: Ken Burns Presents the West (1996, D)
Geronimo (1939, F; 1962, F; 1993, TV)
Geronimo: An American Legend (1993, F)
Geronimo and the Apache Resistance (1988, D)
Geronimo's Revenge (1960, F)
Ghost Dance: Ken Burns Presents the West (1996, D)
The Great Sioux Massacre (1965, F)
Harry and Tonto (1974, F)
I Killed Geronimo (1950, F)
I Will Fight No More Forever (1975, TV)
Kenny Rogers as The Gambler, Part III, The Legend Continues (1987, TV)
The Last Outpost (1951, F)
Lewis & Clark: The Journey of the Corps of Discovery (1997, D)
Little Big Man (1970, F)
One Flew Over the Cuckoo's Nest (1975, F)
Oren Lyons, the Faithkeeper (1997, D)
The Outlaw Josey Wales (1976, F)
Pocahontas: Her True Story (1995, D)
Sitting Bull (1954, F)
Sitting Bull and the Great Sioux Nation (1993, D)
Son of Geronimo (1952, F)
Stagecoach (1939, F)
Taza, Son of Cochise (1954, F)
Tecumseh: The Last Warrior (1995, F)
Tonka (1958, F)
Valley of the Sun (1942, F)
Walk the Proud Land (1956, F)
The Way West: The War for the Black Hills, 1870–1876 (1995, D)
Wilma P. Mankiller: Woman of Power (1992, D)

Bibliography

Barrett, S. M. *Geronimo: His Own Story.* New York: Dutton, 1970.
Clark, Ella A., and Margot Edmonds. *Sacagawea of the Lewis and Clark Expedition.* Berkeley: University of California Press, 1979.
Debo, Angie. *Geronimo: The Man, His Time, His Place.* Norman: University of Oklahoma Press, 1976.
Deloria, Philip J. Review of *Geronimo: An American Legend. American Historical Review* 100.4 (1995): 1194–1198.
Friar, Ralph E., and Natasha A. Friar. *The Only Good Indian: The Hollywood Gospel.* New York: Drama Book Specialists, 1972.
Hilger, Michael. *The American Indian in Film.* Metuchen, NJ: Scarecrow, 1986.
Jojola, Theodore S. "Movies." In Frederick E. Hoxie, ed., *Encyclopedia of North American Indians,* 402–405. Boston: Houghton Mifflin, 1996.
Mankiller, Wilma, and Michael Wallis. *Mankiller: A Chief and Her People.* New York: St. Martin's, 1993.
Roberts, David. *Once They Moved Like the Wind: Cochise, Geronimo, and the Apache Wars.* New York: Simon & Schuster, 1993.
Rollins, Peter C., and John E. O'Connor, eds. *Hollywood's Indian: The Portrayal of the Native Ameri-*

can in Film. Lexington: University Press of Kentucky, 1998.

Sarf, Wayne Michael. *God Bless You Buffalo Bill: A Layman's Guide to History and the Western Film.* East Brunswick, NJ: Associated University Presses, 1983.

Sweeney, Edwin R. *Cochise: Chiricahua Apache Chief.* Norman: University of Oklahoma Press, 1991.

Thompson, Gerald. "Hollywood as History: *Geronimo—An American Legend,* A Review Essay." *Journal of Arizona History* 35.2 (1994): 205–212.

Utley, Robert M. *The Lance and the Shield: The Life and Times of Sitting Bull.* New York: Henry Holt, 1993.

Vestal, Stanley. *Sitting Bull: Champion of the Sioux.* Norman: University of Oklahoma Press, 1957.

[HARRIS J. ELDER]

The Kennedys

Few families loom larger in the American popular imagination than the Kennedys, about whom historians have written prolifically. In *The Fitzgeralds and the Kennedys,* Doris Kearns Goodwin offers a Kennedy family history from its arrival in the United States as Irish immigrants in the mid-nineteenth century to the assassination of John Fitzgerald Kennedy (JFK) on November 22, 1963. Like many others of the "Second American Revolution," she writes, the Kennedys "had fashioned an image of themselves as an invigorating new breed of men, risen out of the blend of a half-dozen lesser breeds" (810–811). The Kennedy story is the American story in Peter Collier and David Horowitz, *The Kennedys: An American Drama.* Putting JFK and his brother Robert Francis Kennedy (RFK) in the context of the civil rights movement, Vietnam, and events in 1968 Chicago is Harris Wofford's *Of Kennedys and Kings: Making Sense of the Sixties.* An assessment of the adverse effects of the family's success is Garry Wills, *The Kennedy Imprisonment: A Meditation on Power,* in which the Kennedys become prisoners of family, image, and charisma.

The family's success matched its aspirations. Joseph Patrick Kennedy (1888–1969) graduated from Boston Latin School and Harvard College—no mean feat at the time for an Irish Catholic. He insinuated himself, and later his family, into Boston society, going into banking and moving to the "Yankee" suburb of Brookline. The Kennedy family entered national consciousness while Joseph was ambassador to England (1938–40). Kennedy and his family of nine appealing children fascinated Americans and even the British. Kennedy viewed public service as both duty and a means to prestige—a family belief that persists. More than money, power, or prestige, Joseph Kennedy was motivated by a strong commitment to family prowess, pushing his children to compete and achieve. The Kennedy legacy of success has become legendary. Richard J. Whalen, who admires his subject, quotes a Kennedy friend who said, "his ideal in life was the success of his children" (486).

John Fitzgerald Kennedy's (1917–1963) senior thesis at Harvard was published as *Why England Slept* (1940), a best-seller; his *Profiles in Courage* (1956) won a Pulitzer Prize. Carrying the Kennedy torch of public service, JFK served in the U.S. House of Representatives and Senate. He failed in an attempt for the 1956 vice-presidential nomination, but in 1960 was elected as the youngest—and first Catholic—president. Energy, optimism, and zeal for public service marked Kennedy's presidency. The Kennedy White House emphasized culture and grace and had a cabinet and advisors of great intellect; a charismatic leader; a beautiful and charming first lady; and a wealthy and glamorous (extended) family. They seemed to satisfy yearning for an American royal family.

Some historians are satisfied, others not. Kennedy family friend William Manchester shares personal stories, traits, and habits in *Portrait of a President: John F. Kennedy in Profile.* In *Kennedy,* celebrity historian Theodore C. Sorensen ("special counsel to the late President") concludes that "what mattered most" to Kennedy was "the strength of his ideas and ideals, his courage and judgment" (7); JFK "stood for excellence in an era of indifference" (757). Arthur M. Schlesinger Jr. offers a personal memoir of his observations while on the White House staff in *A Thousand Days: John F. Kennedy in the White House.* All three books are tributes. Nigel Hamilton is critical, yet sympathetic, in *JFK: Reckless Youth.* In *A Question of Character,* Thomas C. Reeves writes that the president "arrogantly and irresponsibly violated his covenant [of high moral values] with the people" (421). In *The Dark Side of Camelot,* exposé journalist Seymour Hersh concludes that JFK's "personal weaknesses limited his ability to carry out his duties as president" (ix).

Kennedy surprised many when he appointed his brother Robert (1925–1968) attorney general. Continuing the family tradition of public service, RFK had served in government and managed his brother's presidential campaign. While a U.S. senator (1965–68), he reversed his position on Vietnam, entered the 1968 presidential election, and won the California primary. The popular belief is that his brother's death, as James W. Hilty puts it, "had deepened Robert Kennedy's concerns for social inequalities, until he finally became champion of the outcasts, the Jeremiah of the sixties" (498). Ronald Steel is skeptical about the depth of RFK's transformation in *In Love with Night: The American Romance with Robert Kennedy.* In *Robert Kennedy and His Times,* though, Schlesinger concludes that by November 1967, RFK "was the most original, enigmatic, and provocative figure in mid-century American politics" (804). He was assassinated on June 6, 1968. Now the Kennedy saga was being seen as a Greek tragedy.

Edward Moore "Ted" Kennedy (b. 1932) was elected to JFK's Senate seat in 1962. As a staunch liberal, he has sponsored bills on reform in housing, education, and healthcare. Most Democrats regarded him a potential presidential candidate after his brothers' assassinations; his conduct following a highly publicized 1969 automobile accident in Chappaquiddick, Massachusetts, in which a young woman drowned, destroyed his chances. Just as RFK's transformations from Cold Warrior to dove and from Establishment Democrat to champion of civil rights made him an emblem of the 1960s, so the youngest brother's behavior mirrored the self-indulgence of the "me decade" of the 1970s.

The descendants of Joseph and Rose Kennedy are now numerous and scattered, not all enjoying the family's earlier concentration of wealth but some benefiting from the family name. Some continue the Kennedy tradition of public service and, occasionally, recklessness and self-indulgence. The family name remains very much in the public consciousness, as evidenced by the public's response to John F. Kennedy Jr.'s fatal airplane crash in July 1999. The John F. Kennedy Library and Museum in Boston features many Kennedy exhibits that help explain the charisma.

Films about the Kennedys

American-studies scholar John Hellmann traces the history of JFK mythmaking in fiction and film, which "has endured as the fevered dreams of a nation reading the history of his life and death" (147). The war-hero movie *PT 109* (1963) is an early example of the mythmaking surrounding John F. Kennedy, here as a young navy lieutenant whose plywood vessel sinks after colliding at night with a Japanese destroyer. In the film, Kennedy (portrayed by Cliff Robertson, whom JFK reputedly requested be given the role) displays character in keeping up the spirits of his men and courage in leading a brave rescue of stranded marines, adventures that *New York Times* film reviewer Bosley Crowther thought portrayed "in a noticeably overblown order." Robertson's JFK is "a pious and pompous bloke who stands up straight, looks at you squarely, and spouts patriotic platitudes" (23).

In *Executive Action* (1973), wealthy right-wing conspirators plan to kill Kennedy because

FIGURE 21. *P. T. 109* (1963). John F. Kennedy (Cliff Robertson) receives exuberant praise after leading a successful rescue of marines. *P.T. 109* was the first feature in cinema's mythological construction of JFK. Courtesy Warner Bros.

he will withdraw United States personnel from Vietnam—a theme that resurfaces in Oliver Stone's *JFK* (1991). The former film uses TV footage of Kennedy's speeches and home life. *Winter Kills* (1979) is a black comedy that takes place fifteen years after the assassination of a young American president whose half-brother suspects and investigates conspiracy. These Kennedy-related films were part of a zeitgeist: the 1970s was a decade of conspiracy films in general, with *The Conversation* (1974) a prominent—and chilling—example. *The House of Yes* (1997) depicts twins who believe they are JFK and Jacqueline. The film intercuts footage of Jacqueline Kennedy on her televised tour of the White House. The film's "Jackie O" shoots her brother at the end of the film.

Kennedys Don't Cry (1975) is a typical Kennedy documentary in that it embellishes the JFK myth and portrays other members of the family as courageous leaders. The Kennedys "made it seem, in a world struggling for survival, that anything was possible." Home-movie footage shows the children "in constant competition." JFK is presented as a hero in the Bay of Pigs fiasco, a conclusion at odds with most historical interpretations but typical of film portrayals of the Kennedy family for nearly thirty years after JFK's assassination. The second half of the documentary stresses RFK's desire to "discard what has proven a fallacy" in Vietnam. After his brothers' deaths Edward Kennedy "began to emerge in some ways as a better politician than either of the others." Chappaquiddick "rivaled the tragedies of the Greeks," a take at odds with what historians see as, at very least, an act of serious negligence by Ted Kennedy.

Other Kennedy family films touch sympathetically on these themes and events. A Kennedy documentary longer and more complete than most is the three-hour PBS series *The American Experience: The Kennedys* (1991). This three-hour history of the family departs from earlier mainstream portrayals in that it looks askance at Kennedy misbehavior and political acumen; the family's image is not an ideal one for lesser beings to emulate. Writing in this vein, Ralph G. Martin finds the family guilty of "an arrogance of invulnerability" (xxi).

Films about the marriage of JFK and Jacqueline Bouvier typically offer a positive spin. *Person to Person* provides a brief look at the newlyweds. *Jackie: Behind the Myth* promises to "go behind the headlines and the hype for a rare glimpse at the extraordinary life of this woman." In *John F. Kennedy and the Media: The First Television President,* Joseph P. Berry Jr. treats JFK's use of the media to achieve political goals. For a look at JFK thinking on his feet, *Thank You, Mr. President* (1983) offers an excellent melding of the president's press conferences. *Life in Camelot: The Kennedy Years* (1988) features Kennedy home movies, the 1960 campaign, news footage—some on JFK's Catholicism—and radio spots. The new president's low point was the Bay of Pigs; his moment of triumph the Cuban missile crisis. JFK is presented as a self-effacing man, kind to his children, even in the Oval Office. His funeral evokes the fallen president's idealism, remembered in voiceovers.

Initial reaction to the Warren Commission report on John F. Kennedy's assassination was generally positive. To make *Four Days in No-*

vember (1964) David Wolper selected 123 minutes of footage from more than eight million feet of film, stills, and snapshots in a narrative less suspicious than mournful. An early challenge to the lone assassin conclusion appears in *Rush to Judgment: The Plot to Kill JFK* (1966). In this version, Mark Lane, author of the eponymous book, charges the government with covering up and tampering with evidence and pursuing too narrow an inquiry. Interviews with "experts" and witnesses juxtaposed with Warren Commission findings argue that the official version of the assassination should not be trusted. Another Mark Lane product, *Two Men in Dallas* (1987), features a Dallas police officer who questions the lax security surrounding JFK. The film alleges that the FBI and CIA destroyed evidence. In *Best Evidence* (1990), eyewitnesses to the JFK autopsy reveal "new" information about tampering. *Reasonable Doubt* (1990) uses historical and interview footage to prove that the single bullet theory "contradicts the laws of physics, ballistics, and common sense."

The History Channel regularly broadcasts *Missing Files: The JFK Assassination,* in which one investigator claims that out there are "shoeboxes full of photos" to be found; he suspects a conspiracy to hide revealing evidence from public view. The cable channels continue to produce new Kennedy "documentaries" of varying quality, which usually recycle footage and keep the controversy going. Thomas Brown analyzes a chronology of JFK images since the president's death, concluding that "revisionists depicted him as a cleverly stylized and somewhat updated adherent of conventional assumptions and attitudes" (105).

Oliver Stone's compelling feature film *JFK,* released in 1991, casts doubt on the Warren Commission's findings. It presents four stories in parallel action: Jim Garrison's investigation, Lee Harvey Oswald's murky identity, the assassination itself, and the conspiracy formed by a "military-industrial complex." Assassination images, taken from both actual documentary and reenacted footage, appear in the four story lines. The deftly edited mix forces audiences to see the assassination in an entirely different way. *JFK* creates the illusion of actual footage to provide plausible "documentation" for its conspiratorial interpretation. The narration usually identifies historical re-creations, but the distinction is blurred because the footage is recapitulated in different orders and contexts. Mixing archival materials with *JFK*'s historical revision of the present gives the film an authentic feel. Many see Stone's interpretation as provocative and forceful, if others have taken issue with its liberties with hard fact.

Indeed, *JFK* elicited a torrent of reactions to its main theme: that the assassination was a conspiracy involving right-wingers in and out of government. Responses to those reactions quickly followed, many by Stone himself. Public forums debated issues generated by the film. Television news stories and documentaries appeared. Print and broadcast media condemned the film as manipulative and irresponsible. Others agreed wholly or in part with the film's conclusions. In an important legislative response to the controversy, the 102d Congress passed a joint resolution that authorized the release of additional records pertaining to the assassination. As yet, nothing of great significance has come out of newly exposed materials from federal archives. To help viewers understand the film, Stone and screenwriter Zachary Sklar prepared *JFK: The Book of the Film* (1992), which includes a fully documented screenplay with photographs and historical annotations. One of the ablest critics of *JFK*'s conspiracy theme is Arthur Schlesinger, who concedes that although the premise of *JFK* is defensible, its conclusion is not. Complaining of the film's "explosive style," Schlesinger concludes that *JFK*'s case for a second gunman "both makes that case and impairs it, since the viewer can never tell at any point . . . where fact ends and fiction begins" (Stone, 394–395).

The "documentaries" that appear on television with regularity boost ratings and satisfy a voracious public appetite for the Kennedys, but their quality is irregular at best. The paucity of feature films about the Kennedys suggests that as a subject for big-screen audiences, they have been difficult to approach. Now that the family's wealth and power have begun to diffuse and assassinations and Chappaquiddick become more distant, feature films about the Kennedys may occur with more frequency. At the Williamstown (Massachusetts) Film Festival on June 26, 1999, for example, director John Frankenheimer, whose presidential films include *The Manchurian Candidate* (1962) and *Seven Days in May* (1964), announced his interest in making a feature on RFK for HBO or Showtime. (In its place, perhaps, he made *Path to War* [2002], which takes a hard view at the Johnson administration's Vietnam policies.) In October 2000, CBS Television broadcast a "miniseries event" entitled *Jacqueline Bouvier Kennedy Onassis,* which presents its subject as a survivor. And in late November 2000, the History Channel presented *The Men Who Killed Kennedy,* its five-hour content indicated by subtitles ("The Coup d'État," "The Forces of Darkness," "The Cover-Up," "The Patsy," and "The Witnesses"). We do not know how the family's myth will be reshaped and formed, but we can predict that America's appetite for all things Kennedy will persist for some time.

References

Filmography

The American Experience: The Kennedys (1991, TV)
America Remembers JFK (1983, D)
Being with Kennedy (1983, D)
Best Evidence (1990, D)
The Best of "Person to Person" (1993, TV)
Blood Feud (1983, D)
Bobby Kennedy: In His Own Words (1990, D)
The Conversation (1974, F)
Dangerous World: The Kennedy Years (1998, D)
Edward M. Kennedy: Tragedy, Scandal, and Redemption (1998, TV)
Four Days in November 1964, D)
The House of Yes (1997, F)
Jackie: Behind the Myth (1999, TV)
Jacqueline Bouvier Kennedy Onassis (2000, TV)
JFK (1991, F)
Johnny, We Hardly Knew Ye (1977, TV)
The Journey of RFK (1970, D)
Kennedy (1988, D)
The Kennedys: The Next Generation (1991, TV)
Kennedys Don't Cry: The Real-Life Saga of America's Most Powerful Dynasty (1995, D)
Life in Camelot: The Kennedy Years (1988, D)
The Making of the President (1960, D)
The Men Who Killed Kennedy (2000, TV)
The Missiles of October (1974, D)
Missing Files: The JFK Assassination (1998, TV)
The Parallax View (1974, F)
PT 109 (1963, F)
Reasonable Doubt (1990, F)
RFK Remembered (1968, D)
Robert Kennedy and His Times (1984, D)
Rose F. Kennedy: A Life to Remember (1990, D)
Rush to Judgment: The Plot to Kill JFK (1966, D)
The Speeches Collection: John F. Kennedy (1983, D)
Thank You, Mr. President (1983, D)
Thirteen Days (2000, F)
A Thousand Days (1964, D)
Two Men in Dallas (1987, D)
Winter Kills (1979, F)
The World of Jacqueline Kennedy (1962, TV)

Bibliography

Berry, Joseph P., Jr. *John F. Kennedy and the Media: The First Television President.* Lanham, MD: University Press of America, 1987.
Briley, Ron. "Teaching *JFK* (1991): Potential Dynamite in the Hands of Our Youth?" *Film and History* 28.1–2 (1998): 8–15.
Brown, Thomas. *JFK: History of an Image.* Bloomington: Indiana University Press, 1988.
Collier, Peter, and David Horowitz. *The Kennedys: An American Drama.* New York: Summit, 1984.
Crowther, Bosley. Review of *PT 109. New York Times,* 27 June 1963.
Goodwin, Doris Kearns. *The Fitzgeralds and the Kennedys: An American Saga.* New York: Simon & Schuster, 1987.
Hamilton, Nigel. *JFK: Reckless Youth.* New York: Random House, 1992.
Hellman, John. *The Kennedy Obsession: The American Myth of JFK.* New York: Columbia University Press, 1997.

Hersh, Seymour. *The Dark Side of Camelot.* Boston: Little, Brown, 1997.

Hilty, James W. *Robert Kennedy, Brother Protector.* Philadelphia: Temple University Press, 1997.

Manchester, William. *Portrait of a President: John F. Kennedy in Profile.* Boston: Little, Brown, 1962.

Martin, Ralph G. *Seeds of Destruction: Joe Kennedy and His Sons.* New York: Putnam's, 1995.

Reeves, Thomas C. *A Question of Character: A Life of John F. Kennedy.* New York: Free Press, 1991.

Schlesinger, Arthur M. *Robert Kennedy and His Times.* New York: Houghton Mifflin, 1978.

——. *A Thousand Days: John F. Kennedy in the White House.* Boston: Houghton Mifflin, 1965.

Sorensen, Theodore C. *Kennedy.* New York: Harper & Row, 1965.

Steel, Ronald. *In Love with Night: The American Romance with Robert Kennedy.* New York: Simon & Schuster, 2000.

Stone, Oliver, and Zachary Sklar. *JFK: The Book of the Film.* New York: Applause, 1992.

Whalen, Richard J. *The Founding Father: The Story of Joseph P. Kennedy.* New York: New American Library, 1964.

Wills, Garry. *The Kennedy Imprisonment: A Meditation on Power.* Boston: Houghton Mifflin, 1994.

Wofford, Harris. *Of Kennedys and Kings: Making Sense of the Sixties.* New York: Farrar, Straus & Giroux, 1980.

[MARTIN A. JACKSON]

Abraham Lincoln

Since his assassination, as in his lifetime, Abraham Lincoln has fascinated Americans. For the generation of scholars and writers after the Civil War, Lincoln was an unavoidable subject. Many writers and historians since then have explored well the enduring nature of Lincoln's legacy and his impact on the succeeding generations of thinkers and politicians, as well as of average Americans. It was Lincoln who gave shape and energy to America's vision of itself as the hope of humankind for representative government and as proof of the resilience of a democratic society. For more than a century, when we think of American values, we (consciously or not) are drawn to Lincoln's legacy.

The centrality of Lincoln to America's history started early and gathered momentum in the twentieth century, enriching popular culture and calling forth exemplary scholarship. As early as the 1870s, his law partner, James Herndon, drew a portrait of Lincoln as a skilled politician, a man driven by ambition and talent who worked hard for the presidency. Other early biographers embellished a log-cabin legend that remained standard for many years. In the 1920s, Carl Sandburg enshrined the Lincoln myth of the prairie savior who embodied the central values of American life: hard work, honesty, innate intelligence, and faith in the common people. During the tumultuous years of the Depression, Lincoln (like so many other national icons) was reevaluated by historians such as Charles Beard and Vernon Parrington, who probed into the free-soil, free-market side of Lincoln's record and placed him in the context of rising capitalism. Political parties on both the right and left tried to enlist Lincoln in their causes: the American Communist Party, for example, celebrated Lincoln-Lenin Day each February, while Herbert Hoover appealed to the Lincoln legend when denouncing the New Deal.

During the 1950s, Harvard's David Donald updated the Lincoln hagiography, trimming it to suit the times. Donald wrote of Lincoln as a complex man and leader, distinguished by his refusal to be classified ideologically: Lincoln, in other words, as an Eisenhower Republican, a perfect model for the feel-good era of the 1950s. "In our age of anxiety, it is pertinent to remember," says Donald, "that our most enduring political symbolism derives from Lincoln, whose one dogma was an absence of dogma" (16). Equally influential among the post–World War II writers was Richard Hofstadter, who argued that Lincoln himself had created his own mythology: "The first author of the Lincoln legend and the greatest of the Lincoln dramatists was Lincoln himself," writes Hofstadter in *The American Political Tradition* (117).

A contrary vision of Lincoln emerged during the 1960s, when his views on race were challenged and often found wanting. The radical historian Howard Zinn, for example, declared, "It was Abraham Lincoln who combined perfectly the needs of business, the political ambition of the new Republican party, and the rhetoric of humanitarianism" (182). African American historians and scholars in the 1960s and 1970s took exception to Lincoln's racial utterances and wondered aloud about the completeness of his opposition to slavery. In this revisionist light, Lincoln emerged as a conservative in racial matters.

In recent years there have been Freudian studies of Lincoln; discussions of his medical condition (he probably had Marfan's disease); and unsettling questions asked about his record on civil liberties. But the Lincoln legacy lives on into the twenty-first century, still capable of inspiring notable scholarship. In 1992 Garry Wills wrote a subtle and laudatory exegesis of the Gettysburg Address, *Lincoln at Gettysburg,* casting Lincoln as a philosopher of democracy and a political theorist. According to Wills, Lincoln's words have shaped our self-definition: "The Gettysburg Address has become an authoritative expression of the American spirit. . . . For most people now, the Declaration [of Independence] means what Lincoln told us it means. . . . By accepting the Gettysburg Address . . . we have been changed. Because of it, we live in a different America" (147). In 1999, Frank Thompson produced what is probably the most comprehensive study of the Lincoln iconography in relation to film and other contemporary visual media such as television and video recording. Thompson demonstrates convincingly that the visual power of Lincoln has continued unabated into the age of electronic media, with roots extending back to the earliest days of film.

The Movies and Mr. Lincoln

In the early 1900s, moviemakers were powerfully attracted to Lincoln. It is well to remember that many of the pioneer filmmakers grew up in an America where Lincoln was still a part of oral history, not a dim historical figure. D. W. Griffith was no exception. Although his view of Lincoln was shaped by his southern heritage and was, in general, an ambivalent acceptance, it did not deter Griffith from making Lincoln a sympathetic character in *Birth of a Nation* (1915), where Lincoln is referred to as "the great Heart," and portrayed as a leader with compassion for ordinary mortals.

The silent film industry made Lincoln a frequent "star" in the early years. Vitagraph Studios in particular seemed to have a penchant for Lincoln stories, releasing one such film each year from 1911 to 1914, including such titles as *Battle Hymn of the Republic* (1911), *Lincoln's Gettysburg Address* (1912), and even *Lincoln the Lover* (1913), the last about Lincoln and Anne Rutledge, of course. In 1915 the Edison Company produced *The Life of Abraham Lincoln, The Greatest of Americans.* An awkward and stagy film, *Life* starred Frank McGlynn, with a script by James Oppenheim. It is, to a DVD-era viewer, painfully static, but its adoring portrait of Lincoln seems to have won a contemporary audience.

In the 1920s, Lincoln adulation accelerated. There were scores of companies, products, towns, and books that used the Lincoln name and image, sometimes with embarrassing results. The Lincoln Life Insurance company was formed in the 1920s, only one of many efforts to tap the Lincoln legend of unshakable virtue. When Edsel Ford promoted a luxury automobile in the 1920s, in vivid contrast to his father's humble Model T, he chose the president's honored name because, while the car was expensive, it was still quintessentially American and trustworthy. There were Lincoln Logs (still a familiar toy), Lincoln Day sales, Lincoln theaters, Lincoln bacon, and Lincoln pajamas. Abraham Lincoln had become the nation's common cultural touchstone—even in the marketplace.

The booming film industry did not—could not—ignore Abraham Lincoln. In 1924, for instance, the Rockett Brothers produced *Abraham Lincoln,* a silent biography in twelve reels subtitled "a dramatic life of Abraham Lincoln." Directed by Phil Rosen, *Abraham Lincoln* was a birth-to-death film biography of the sixteenth president with the standard stops along the way, from the Kentucky log cabin to Ford's Theater. Lincoln was a featured presence in John Ford's *Iron Horse* in 1924. Indeed, the movie is dedicated to Lincoln, who, ennobled as "The Builder," is apparently responsible for the creation of the transcontinental railroad; even as far back as his Springfield days, Ford asserts that the young Lincoln saw the need for linking East and West by rail in an effort to unify a progressive, industrial nation.

In 1930, the aging and ill D. W. Griffith chose Lincoln as the focus of his last movie, *Abraham Lincoln,* a screen biography that Merrill Peterson called "the first major historical film of the sound era" (344). Walter Huston got the part of the president despite having not very much resemblance to Lincoln, but he was a strong actor with a sonorous voice. The screenplay was by Stephen Vincent Benét, a celebrated midwestern poet of the early 1930s. In fact, Griffith had hoped to get Carl Sandburg to write the film script, but Sandburg had doubts (probably justified by the controversies over Griffith's earlier historical films) and turned down a $30,000 fee for the project.

Lincoln continued to appear in American movies during the middle and late 1930s. *A Perfect Tribute,* for example, was a well-produced short released by MGM in 1935; it related the famous (albeit untrue) story of Lincoln reciting his Gettysburg Address to a wounded Confederate soldier. Two very successful films of the time gave Lincoln, or at least his words, a central part: *Ruggles of Red Gap* (1935) and *Mr. Smith Goes to Washington* (1939). In *Ruggles,* an imported British butler (Charles Laughton) brings the rough American crowd to awed silence by reciting, from memory, the Gettysburg Address. His embrace of American democratic values after a life of stuffy subservience is beautifully captured by his recitation, and it remains a fine performance of those memorable words of the American creed. In Frank Capra's *Mr. Smith Goes to Washington* (1939), one of the classic social-problem films of the 1930s, Lincoln has a crucial role. When the novice Senator Jefferson Smith (James Stewart) is confused and overwhelmed by the corruption of modern Washington, he finds his way to the Lincoln Memorial, where the towering seated figure sculpted by Daniel Chester French brings him back to his true faith. With Lincoln watching over him, Smith reminds himself (and the audience) that Lincoln's words—of the Gettysburg Address and the Second Inaugural—still apply. Few in the late 1930s could watch those scenes and remain uninspired.

Capra's iconic Lincoln reappeared again in the director's *Why We Fight* series during World War II. Capra invoked Lincoln the war president, again, to unite the nation in a time of crisis, and reminded his viewers of the Lincoln legacy. It should not be surprising that Frank Capra, the immigrant from Sicily, should find the Lincoln legend so appealing. Capra arrived in a nation where Lincoln mythology was in full flower, and he cherished that inspiring myth throughout his life and career as a leading Hollywood celebrant of the American Dream.

By the end of the Depression, the world was spiraling into war, and America nervously faced a dangerous world. Not by accident did Abraham Lincoln reappear on the movie screens, in two of the best film treatments of the subject. In 1939, John Ford directed *Young Mr. Lincoln,* with Henry Fonda as the young president-to-be; in 1940, John Cromwell directed *Abe Lincoln in Illinois,* taken from the Pulitzer Prize–winning play by Robert Sherwood.

It is instructive to note that these film biographies, both powerful shapers of the Lincoln mythology, appeared within months of each other. By the time *Abe Lincoln in Illinois* reached American screens, the war in Europe had begun and Paris had fallen; Britain stood alone while Hitler seemed destined for victory. America seemed in grave danger and, in this time of crisis, the uplifting Lincoln myth was needed. Ford's *Young Mr. Lincoln* was a lyrical story of frontier Illinois and the formation of

Lincoln's noble character. Henry Fonda is superb as the young Lincoln, a shy but clever backwoods philosopher who loves Ann Rutledge and defends an innocent boy in a murder trial. Ford is in his element with this tale of the new nation, and the movie retains its humanity and power after six decades; the final scene, when Abe strides off into the horizon with the words "I think I'll go on a little ways," has become part of American folklore: Lincoln, the exemplar of the American soul, is not seeking glory but is destined for it.

In *Abe Lincoln in Illinois,* Raymond Massey plays the future president with striking verisimilitude. (Of all the actors who have taken the role, Massey best matches Lincoln's physical appearance.) The story itself was adapted from Robert Sherwood's hit play of the 1939 season and covered much the same period as the earlier *Young Abe Lincoln,* namely the New Salem years with Ann Rutledge and his fledgling political efforts. Lincoln beats the town bully in a wrestling match, spins tales, tells jokes, and generally lives up to the highest expectations of the 1940 viewer, badly in need of a larger-than-life national hero. Massey's Lincoln is the reluctant hero, the wholesome boy of the Midwest, whom Fate has chosen for leadership.

Not surprisingly, Lincoln's screen image underwent changes in the postwar world. In 1951, a film with the blunt title *The Tall Target* was released, dealing with an early assassination attempt on Lincoln as he rides to Washington in 1861. In 1952, television took on the subject of Lincoln, too, with a controversial five-part series written by critic and journalist James Agee. Funded by the Ford Foundation for the distinguished *Omnibus* series, this effort ran into trouble for its progressive views on race; in fact, the series was never broadcast past its first episode.

In 1977, *The Lincoln Conspiracy* was made for television and was far better received. It probed the plot against Lincoln and raised some doubts about many of the leading characters. Gore Vidal's popular book *Lincoln* became a television film in 1988 and presented again a more complex and modern portrait of the president. In 1992 yet another television series, *Lincoln,* told the story of the eponymous hero's humble birth to his tragic end, but with a distinct late-twentieth-century sensibility. Ken Burns's *Civil War* series for PBS naturally dealt with Lincoln and showed him as a tragic yet noble figure who labored mightily to preserve the Union. The remarkable public acclaim for Burns's effort rekindled an interest in Civil War matters, and still further interest in Lincoln; after its initial broadcast, the fifteen-part series was eagerly adopted by schools and universities.

Among the many classroom films dealing with Lincoln, two from Films for the Humanities may serve as examples of the genre: *Lincoln of Illinois* (1965), and *Abraham Lincoln: Against the Odds* (1973). The latter is a ten-minute survey of Lincoln's life and career, emphasizing his victory over initial hardships, while the former is a more comprehensive, thirty-minute exploration of Lincoln's role in the history of the nation. These teaching films are a rich store of Lincoln material available for the student. Most are now available on video tape or CD-ROM. The Lincoln Library in Springfield (www.lincolnlibrary.org) offers a list of teaching aids, both visual and aural, and scarcely a library in America is without some tape, film, or computer material concerning Lincoln's life and work.

The Myth Lives On

Lincoln will not fade soon from America's movie or television screens. He continues to evoke deep feelings and to stimulate debate on a wide range of issues from race to political conspiracy, and he has yet to be replaced as a national symbol. That famous stovepipe hat and somber beard will surely be seen again as new generations of filmmakers and writers explore his meaning and fate (and perhaps even have a little fun with the president, as did director Stephen Herek in *Bill and Ted's Excellent*

Adventure). The symbolism is still potent in contemporary America, as we have seen in more recent times. The choice of the Lincoln Memorial as the venue for Martin Luther King's epic "I Have a Dream" speech in 1963 was hardly accidental, and the lasting image of King, watched over by a seated Lincoln, is indelible in American consciousness—and neatly echoes the inspiration provided to Capra's Jefferson Smith. In 1970, as antiwar protesters gathered in Washington, President Richard Nixon made a strained effort to engage them and chose as his meeting place the Lincoln Memorial. The site seemed appropriate as a gathering place for those who cared about America and its future.

Historians, scholars, and filmmakers will no doubt continue their normal efforts to revise, reconsider, and rediscover the meaning and nature of Abraham Lincoln because he continues to matter. The timeless summation of the democratic faith in Lincoln's invocation of a government "of the people, by the people, and for the people" resonates into the twenty-first century and has influenced the lives of people all over the world. He has become a historical figure for all time, and the inescapable symbol of the American nation.

References

Filmography

Abe Lincoln in Illinois (1940, F)
Abraham Lincoln (1924, F; 1930, F; 1988, D)
Abraham Lincoln: Against the Odds (1973, D)
Battle Hymn of the Republic (1911, F)
Bill and Ted's Excellent Adventure (1989, F)
The Civil War (1997, D)
The Day Lincoln Was Shot (1998, TV)
Gore Vidal's Lincoln (1988, TV)
The Iron Horse (1924, F)
The Life of Abraham Lincoln, the Greatest of Americans (1915, F)
Lincoln (1992, TV)
The Lincoln Conspiracy (1977, TV)
Lincoln of Illinois (1965, D)
Lincoln's Gettysburg Address (1912, F)
Lincoln the Lover (1913, F)
Mr. Lincoln of Illinois (1993, TV)
Mr. Smith Goes to Washington (1939, F)
Of Human Hearts (1938, F)
A Perfect Tribute (1935, D)
Ruggles of Red Gap (1935, F)
The Tall Target (1951, F)
Young Mr. Lincoln (1939, F)

Bibliography

Donald, David. *Lincoln Reconsidered.* New York: Anchor, 1965.
Hofstadter, Richard. *The American Political Tradition.* New York: Vintage, 1974.
Peterson, Merrill. *Lincoln in American History.* New York: Oxford University Press, 1994.
Thompson, Frank. *Abraham Lincoln: Twentieth-Century Popular Portrayals.* Dallas: Taylor, 1999.
Wills, Garry. *Lincoln at Gettysburg: The Words That Remade America.* New York: Simon & Schuster, 1992.
Zinn, Howard. *A People's History of the United States.* New York: HarperCollins, 1995.

[DONALD M. WHALEY]

Richard Nixon

When Richard Milhous Nixon (1913–1994), thirty-seventh president of the United States, prepared to resign in disgrace as a result of the Watergate affair, a scandal involving abuses of power by the president and his aides, his secretary of state, Henry Kissinger, told Nixon that history would treat him kindly. Nixon responded that would depend on who wrote the history. He might have added that it would also depend on who made the films.

Nixon's career was filled with spectacular victories and defeats. From modest beginnings—he was the son of a failed California grocer—Nixon enjoyed a rapid political ascent. He was first elected, as a Republican, to the United States House of Representatives in 1946, to the Senate in 1950, and to the vice presidency in 1952. Defeated by John Kennedy in the presidential election of 1960, Nixon also lost the California governor's race in 1962. After spending time as a lawyer for a Wall Street firm, he returned to politics. He was elected president in 1968 and overwhelmingly reelected in 1972.

From the first, Nixon was controversial. In his early campaigns he distorted his opponents' records to make them seem procommunist, while he presented himself as a family man who believed in hard work, religious values, and respect for authority. He made his national reputation with his dogged pursuit—as a member of the House Committee on Un-American Activities (HUAC)—of Alger Hiss, a former State Department official accused of spying for the Soviet Union. Hiss's supporters saw Nixon as advancing his career by persecuting an innocent man (in fact, documents declassified after the Cold War suggest Hiss's guilt). Nixon also drew criticism for the "Checkers" speech in which, during his 1952 vice presidential campaign, Nixon defended himself against charges that he benefited from a secret fund collected by California businessmen. While the American public was won over, critics viewed the speech as self-righteous, shameless, and manipulative. As Garry Wills describes in *Nixon Agonistes* (1970), by the 1950s Democrats and many journalists began to regard Nixon as "Tricky Dick"—a sanctimonious, unprincipled, ruthless con artist.

Watergate reinforced this perception of Nixon. The scandal began when a group of operatives working for Nixon's 1972 campaign were arrested while breaking into the headquarters of the Democratic National Committee. Subsequent investigations revealed other "White House horrors." Some of the Watergate burglars had been involved in a break-in at a psychiatrist's office in an effort to find damaging information about Daniel Ellsberg, a former government official and a critic of Nixon's handling of the Vietnam War, who had leaked what became known as the "Pentagon Papers," a secret Defense Department study of the war, to the *New York Times*. The White House kept an enemies list; some on the list had been targeted for tax audits. Nixon secretly taped conversations in the Oval Office. Tapes revealed Nixon's use of profanity, which undermined the upright image Nixon had always tried to project. One tape provided evidence that Nixon obstructed justice by participating in a cover-up of his aides' involvement in the Watergate burglary. Faced with impeachment, Nixon resigned in 1974.

Bob Woodward and Carl Bernstein, who covered Watergate for the *Washington Post,* published *All the President's Men* (1974), an account of their investigation. Guided by "Deep Throat," an official in the Nixon administration whose identity they have continued to keep secret, the reporters came to understand Watergate as part of a larger campaign of political sabotage. Stanley Kutler based *The Abuse of Power* (1998) on tapes released in 1996, which revealed Nixon making anti-Semitic remarks and participating in raising money to buy the Watergate burglars' silence. James David Barber, writing in *Political Science Quarterly,* argues that, in the Watergate crisis, the American people had had a close call with tyranny.

Historians in a 1996 survey rated Nixon in the lowest category of presidents, the "failures." But some historians put forward a more sympathetic interpretation of Nixon. In *Nixon: The Triumph of a Politician, 1962–1982* (1989), Stephen Ambrose praises Nixon's foreign policy achievements, especially the president's trip to China, which began the process of restoring diplomatic relations between China and the United States, and "détente," Nixon's policy of easing Cold War tensions by negotiating nuclear arms control agreements with the Soviet Union. Ambrose concludes that Nixon "had shown potential to be a great world statesman" (408). Joan Hoff, in *Nixon Reconsidered* (1994), emphasizes Nixon's domestic achievements, especially progress in desegregating the South, an increase in social-welfare spending, revenue sharing in which federal funds were sent to state and local governments, and establishment of the Environmental Protection Agency. By 2000, the arguments of these historians apparently had had an effect. A survey of historians taken by C-SPAN in that year ranked Nixon twenty-fifth among forty-one presidents, and eighth among presidents in leadership in international relations.

This changing assessment of Nixon by historians finds a parallel in the changing treatment of Nixon by filmmakers. As early as the 1960s, filmmakers had taken as their subject matter Nixon's political excesses. Watergate inspired a number of films from the 1970s through the 1990s. By the late 1980s, however, some filmmakers had begun to examine Nixon's accomplishments as president.

Feature films have presented three versions of Nixon: evil, comic, and tragic. The evil Nixon first appears in *The Best Man* (1964), written by Gore Vidal. Vidal had been a Democratic candidate for Congress and, like most Democrats, viewed Nixon as "Tricky Dick." Vidal based one of his characters, presidential candidate Joe Cantwell (Cliff Robertson), on this stereotype of Nixon. Cantwell wraps himself in middle-class pieties (his name symbolizes his character), promotes his career by "exposing" a Mafia-Communist alliance he has made up, and distorts his opponent's psychiatric history.

An evil Nixon is also on display in *All the President's Men* (1976), based on the book by Woodward and Bernstein. Nixon appears in the film only on television or in newspaper headlines. The movie follows the reporters' investigation into the burglary at Democratic headquarters. As they pursue their inquiry, Woodward (Robert Redford) and Bernstein (Dustin Hoffman) come to realize that the burglary and other acts of espionage and sabotage against the Democrats have been financed by a secret fund controlled by John Mitchell, Nixon's former attorney general, who heads Nixon's reelection campaign, and H. R. Haldeman, Nixon's chief of staff. The film implies that the actions of Nixon and his aides threatened to undermine constitutional government. The film also implies that the reporters' lives were in danger (in an interview, Woodward conceded that he did not know if their lives were actually in danger, but he argued that the film did re-create accurately the fear the reporters felt at the time).

Nixon's physical awkwardness made him a target for comic mimicry, just as his political excesses made him a target for satire. Director Robert Altman's *Secret Honor* (1984) presents a clumsy, profane Nixon (Philip Baker Hall) tape recording a Checkers-style speech to defend himself during Watergate. In *Elvis Meets Nixon* (1997), Nixon (Bob Gunton) is inspired by *The Godfather* to go after his political enemies, spends the Christmas season making an enemies list instead of a Christmas list, and joins Elvis Presley (Rick Peters) in a duet of "My Way." *Dick* (1999) not only shows Nixon and his aides as comic bumblers but also satirizes *All the President's Men.* In the film, two teenage girls (Kirsten Dunst, Michelle Williams) stumble upon the Watergate burglary. To keep them quiet, Nixon (Dan Hedaya) arranges for them to work in the White House. One of the girls develops a crush on Nixon, but both girls are disillusioned when they accidentally hear Nixon's tapes. The girls become Deep Throat, whose identity the satirized Woodward and Bernstein keep secret out of embarrassment.

Writing in *Presidential Studies Quarterly,* Joan Hoff argues that director Oliver Stone's *Nixon* (1995) was "an attempt to implant an even worse image of Nixon in the public mind than existed when he was forced to resign" (8). To be sure, Nixon's dark side is on display in the film: the ruthless ambition, the insecurity about his social background that led him to rage at anything he perceived as a slight, the petty vindictiveness, the willingness to abuse power. But, drawing upon the revisionist view of Nixon (including the work of Joan Hoff), the film also cites Nixon's accomplishments.

In fact, Stone's Nixon is more tragic than evil. Stone's film implicitly compares Nixon to Abraham Lincoln. Nixon (Anthony Hopkins) first appears in the film in the Lincoln Sitting Room of the White House, where a portrait of Lincoln hangs over the fireplace. Later, Nixon visits the Lincoln Memorial, where he talks with war protesters. Nixon looks up at the statue of Lincoln and says, "That man up there lived in similar times. He had chaos and civil war and hatred between the races." Toward the end of the film, Nixon's daughter Julie (Annabeth Gish) tells him, "You've done what Lincoln did. You've brought this country back from civil war!" In comparing Nixon to Lincoln, the film suggests that Nixon had the potential to be a great president but that his inner flaws doomed his presidency. Henry Kissinger (Paul Sorvino) states the film's point when, near the end of the movie, he says about Nixon, "It's a tragedy, because he had greatness in his grasp, but he had the defects of his qualities."

Nixon has been the subject of a number of documentary films. *Speeches of Richard Nixon* (1990) includes the Checkers speech; excerpts from interviews with Nixon about Watergate; and the press conference Nixon, angry at his treatment by reporters, gave after his 1962 gubernatorial loss. The Kennedy-Nixon presidential debates (1960) are part of the video record (radio listeners thought Nixon won; television viewers gave the edge to Kennedy). *Millhouse: A White Comedy* (1971) uses video clips of Nixon to create a bitter satire. Also critical of Nixon is *Watergate: The Corruption of American Politics and the Fall of Richard Nixon* (1994), produced by the BBC for The Discovery Channel, which shows Nixon deeply involved in dirty campaign tricks against the Democrats and participating in the cover-up almost immediately after the Watergate burglary. *Nixon: The Arrogance of Power* (2000), made for the History Channel, provides evidence that Nixon, to gain political advantage in the presidential election of 1968, covertly sabotaged the Johnson administration's Vietnam peace negotiations and speculates that the purpose of the Watergate burglary was to discover how much Democratic officials knew about what Nixon had done.

Nixon (1989), part of the PBS *American Experience* series, portrays Nixon's legacy as an ambiguous mixture of Watergate scandal and foreign policy triumph. *Nixon's China Game* (2000), part of the same series, credits Nixon's diplomatic opening to China with bringing an isolated China back into the world community and with putting pressure on the Soviets to negotiate arms control agreements with the United States. *Detente, 1969–1975* (1998), an episode in CNN's *Cold War* series, credits Nixon with making an all-out war between the United States and the Soviet Union less likely. The documentary most sympathetic to Nixon is C-SPAN's *Life Portrait of Richard Nixon* (1999), which features interviews with Joan Hoff and with John Taylor, executive director of the Nixon Presidential Library, who vigorously defends Nixon.

In the years after he resigned from the presidency, Richard Nixon wrote eight books, in which he put forward his vision of international relations. As Joan Hoff has written in *Presidential Studies Quarterly:* "His early post-presidential books, *The Real War, The Real Peace,* and *No More Vietnams,* all implied that détente and other geopolitical maneuvers of his administration . . . laid out the best hope that the United States could wage the Cold War differently than it had since 1945" (123). After the fall of the Soviet Union, both President Bush and President Clinton sought Nixon's advice on dealing with Russia. Nixon had succeeded in rehabilitating himself as a foreign policy expert. Four former presidents attended his funeral (actual footage of the funeral appears at the end of Oliver Stone's *Nixon*). President Bill Clinton delivered a eulogy in which he argued that Nixon should be judged on his entire life and career.

At the end of the twentieth century, historians and filmmakers had begun to do that. Both groups had come to see the Nixon administration as more than just the Watergate scandal. Historians and filmmakers alike had begun to examine—even to praise—Nixon's achievements, especially in foreign policy.

References

Filmography

All the President's Men (1976, F)
The Best Man (1964, F)
Detente, 1969–1975 (1998, TV)
Dick (1999, F)
Elvis Meets Nixon (1997, TV)
The Final Days (1989, TV)
Forrest Gump (1994, F)
Life Portrait of Richard Nixon (1999, TV)
Millhouse: A White Comedy (1971, D)
Nixon (1989, TV; 1995, F)
Nixon: The Arrogance of Power (2000, TV)
Nixon's China Game (2000, TV)
Secret Honor (1984, F)
Sleeper (1973, F)
Speeches of Richard Nixon (1990, D)
Watergate: The Corruption of American Politics and the Fall of Richard Nixon (1994, TV)

Bibliography

Ambrose, Stephen E. *Nixon: The Education of a Politician, 1913–1962.* New York: Simon & Schuster, 1987.

——. *Nixon: Ruin and Recovery, 1973–1990.* New York: Simon & Schuster, 1991.

——. *Nixon: The Triumph of a Politician, 1962–1972.* New York: Simon & Schuster, 1989.

Barber, James David. "The Nixon Brush with Tyranny." *Political Science Quarterly* 92.4 (winter 1977–78): 510.

Hamburg, Eric, ed. *Nixon: An Oliver Stone Film.* New York: Hyperion, 1995.

Hoff, Joan, "About This Issue" and "A Revisionist View of Nixon's Foreign Policy." *Presidential Studies Quarterly* 26.1 (1996): 8–10, 107–29.

——. *Nixon Reconsidered.* New York: Basic Books, 1994.

Kutler, Stanley. *The Abuse of Power.* New York: Simon & Schuster, 1998.

Monsell, Thomas. *Nixon on Stage and Screen: The Thirty-Seventh President as Depicted in Films, Television, Plays and Opera.* Jefferson, NC: McFarland, 1998.

Wills, Garry. *Nixon Agonistes.* Boston: Houghton Mifflin, 1970.

Woodward, Bob, and Carl Bernstein. *All the President's Men.* New York: Simon & Schuster, 1974.

[MICHAEL S. SHULL]

Franklin and Eleanor Roosevelt

Probably no other modern president of the United States has been as represented in fictional film and documentaries as the thirty-second, Franklin Delano Roosevelt (1882–1945). FDR's iconographic image, distinctive voice or references to him as the president, the New Deal's NRA (National Recovery Administration) and WPA (Works Progress Administration), the wartime Allied leadership, and so on appear in an extraordinary number of films made during or representing the period from 1933 to 1945—encompassing both the horrific Depression and the monumental struggle to defend democracy during World War II. Though recent presidents have dominated the mass media while in office, few have had more than a couple of fictional cinematic or made-for-TV treatments, and none has been warmly identified with a particular era, other than the so-called Camelot associated with John Fitzgerald Kennedy's ephemeral administration.

The image of FDR that evolved was one of a smiling, reassuringly avuncular man, witty and energetic, wearing pince-nez glasses and often smoking a cigarette in a holder jauntily clenched between his teeth. During his twelve-year presidency, Roosevelt was portrayed, impersonated, or caricatured by Hollywood in scores of fictional feature-length motion pictures, a few animated cartoons, fictional shorts, documentaries, numerous nonfiction shorts, and countless newsreels—including filmed reproductions of his famous "Fireside Chats."

Roosevelt was the first truly radio-savvy president. He developed a broadcast persona that highlighted his seductively soothing voice, tremendously enhanced by the verisimilitude of intimacy imparted by the comparatively new radio and sound-newsreel media. FDR's vocal delivery seemed to reach out over the airwaves or onscreen soundtracks and touch his audience as though he were addressing them personally—"my friends" sounded sincere, inclusive, and not patronizing, despite his patrician upbringing.

What is also intriguing is the visual representation of FDR—one that does not acknowledge his partial paralysis after a 1921 bout with polio. Only a single nonfiction short, *Roosevelt, the Man of the Hour* (MGM, 1933), is known to have made a direct reference to this condition during his presidency. In fact, it would not be until 1960, with the Warner Bros. production *Sunrise at Campobello,* that Roosevelt's physical challenge would be frankly addressed. But that biopic, featuring Ralph Bellamy in the lead role, ends with his decision to deliver the 1924 Democratic presidential nomination speech for Al Smith. It would be another forty-one years until a theatrically released film portraying FDR in office, *Pearl Harbor* (2001), would clearly show that the nation's leader was dependent for his mobility upon a wheelchair or thirty-pound metal braces and the muscular assistance of aides.

What amounted to a constructed identity of Roosevelt was valorized through the new twentieth-century media. With the active collusion of the political establishment, the press, and Hollywood during the 1930s, 1940s, and beyond, Americans were presented with a less

FIGURE 22. *Sunrise at Campobello* (1960). Director Vincent J. Donehue was the first filmmaker to picture Franklin Delano Roosevelt in a wheelchair. Many other films have depicted FDR, who was paralyzed by a bout of polio that struck in 1921; most have sidestepped controversial issues of a nation in war under the leadership of a physically challenged president and the complicity of the press in hiding his condition. Courtesy Schary Productions and Warner Bros.

than true image of FDR—as either standing in a stationary position, perhaps the two most mythic moments being his March 1933 inaugural address ("We have nothing to fear but fear itself") and his December 8, 1941, "Date which will live in infamy" war message, or as seated behind a desk in his "Fireside Chat" mode, adopted several times in fictional films (but altered with behind-the-head shots). However, the most familiar visual image of the president was in formal portraits or newsreel footage. Yet the majority of the American people, irrespective of their political orientation, were probably not receptive to an alternate Roosevelt identity—preferring a wishful vision of a restored, economically fit, national self as embodied by a seemingly robust president.

The creation of this image, or myth, of FDR was fully established within a few months into his administration's first term. Roosevelt and the New Deal became inextricably linked with confidence in a democratic nation whose citizens would now work together to ameliorate the worst aspects of the Great Depression (1929–40). Certain songs and symbols likewise became emblematic of this optimistic spirit and were directly linked to FDR and the Democratic Party: "Happy Days Are Here Again" and "We're in the Money," the NRA Blue Eagle ("We Do Our Part"), and so on. The freedom from fear became, among other things, a freedom to sing again—to embrace democracy as the all-American antidote to authoritarian solutions for alleviating the Depression's woes. The cumulative effect of this on the public significantly contributed to its perceptions of the "reality" that had become FDR. In effect, the iconography of the New Deal subsumed the physical person.

After his 1932 landslide victory, Roosevelt became "Dr. New Deal," the man with the cure for the Depression's ills. This theme is treated literally in *Confidence,* an animated short released in July 1933 by Universal, featuring Oswald the Rabbit. The cartoon opens with the dark cloud of the Depression rising out of the city dump, creating a bank scare, and then settling down upon Oswald's farm. Oswald goes for a cure to "Dr. Pill," who promptly points to FDR's photo. When the rabbit flies to Washington and asks Roosevelt for the cure, a singing and dancing president leads Oswald in performing the title song.

An overt reference to reading FDR's first inaugural address is made by the unemployed war veteran protagonist of *Heroes for Sale* (1933), implying that the president's speech should inspire hope in all the "forgotten men" wandering across the countryside. In director Frank Capra's *Lady for a Day* (1933), the Damon Runyonesque Apple Annie tells a fellow panhandler to stop "yapping" about the parsimonious passersby: "Didn't you hear the president over the radio?" The message was obvious, as well as tendentious: Americans should stop complaining, because there was less to fear now that Roosevelt was in office.

One of the best-remembered phrases from a 1932 Roosevelt campaign speech, intoning that America cannot fail in its attempt to restore "the forgotten man at the bottom of the economic pyramid," receives a stylized interpretation, "Remember My Forgotten Man," in *Gold Diggers of 1933.* This film is invariably cited as the quintessential Depression-era musical owing to its opening number, with a chorus line, dressed in cutout silver dollars, singing the upbeat "We're in the Money." But the most blatant early cinematic homage to FDR occurs during the finale of a 1933 Warner release *Footlight Parade,* starring James Cagney as a movie-palace stage director and self-proclaimed "New Dealer." In an overhead shot, the chorus uses flash cards to display, in succession, a screen-filling American flag, FDR's beaming face, and the NRA eagle.

The legislative onslaught of the Roosevelt administration's first hundred days resulted in the proliferation of New Deal agencies, identified by their acronyms. With many in Hollywood enthusiastically embracing the NRA concept of reducing individual job hours to expand the workforce, several studios even began including the NRA logo in the opening or end credits of their films. Throughout the latter half of 1933, MGM's popular *Our Gang* series displayed the NRA seal.

Many Hollywood productions would incorporate into their scripts more discreet references to New Deal agencies—unambiguously reinforcing an iconographic linkage to FDR. In *Mr. Skitch* (1933), with Will Rogers in the title role, the impecunious Skitch wryly states when offered the "CM" (car manager) job at an auto park: "There are a lot of initials in the country now." *Wild Boys of the Road,* an oft-cited 1933 Warner Bros. release, chronicles the lives of homeless teenagers. Following their infamous "sewer pipe city" battle with police, the downtrodden youth appear before a kindly judge (an FDR surrogate). After admonishing them, he points to the NRA eagle on the wall, suggesting it should become their inspiration. Even the classic melodrama, *Imitation of Life* (1934), featuring a rags-to-riches businesswoman, includes this frustrated suitor's comment: "In the name of the National Recovery Act, will you give her a day free?" Ironically, in just over a year the Supreme Court would declare the NRA unconstitutional.

Soon afterward, the Works Progress Administration (WPA) would supersede the NRA as the paramount New Deal agency. Likewise, it became the most commonly evoked symbol of FDR's governance. Numerous films would reflect this, usually incorporating casual references to a character on relief work at a WPA project. A typical example is from *Next Time I Marry* (1938), a screwball comedy featuring an heiress, played by Lucille Ball, who meets a college man digging a ditch on a WPA road gang.

Because of an ill-advised attempt by Roosevelt to "pack" the Supreme Court, another economic downturn, and labor unrest throughout 1936–1937, the president's popularity declined. Despite his reelection to a second term, the virulence of FDR's critics increased, particularly amongst the business elite. Although this was mainly reflected by a reduction in those fictional releases that referred to his leadership, at least one film contained negative allusions to Roosevelt, albeit in a comedy format. In *Soak the Rich* (1936) a frustrated tycoon concedes that FDR has "charm," but adds, "Our president is blind to the woes of millionaires." This stereotyped capitalist antithesis to the New Deal spirit, who is also plagued by an unruly daughter in college, later moans, "Rockefeller, Ford . . . even Roosevelt has good children."

One of the more intriguing feature films from the later 1930s that unabashedly refers to the Roosevelt administration is *Ali Baba Goes to Town* (1937). Singer-comedian Eddie Cantor plays an extra named Aloysius Babson on a desert picture set who, after overdosing on painkillers, hallucinates being in Arabia in 937. He encounters the troubled sultan, who fears that his starving people will revolt. Appointed his advisor, "Ali Baba" suggests that the sultan run for president, promising New Deal–style reforms. Ali Baba then mimics FDR's phrases and gestures of public address, with such campaign slogans as "Put the people to work on government projects. . . . Start federal theaters. . . . Tax your wives to pay."

Throughout FDR's second term, his most common appearance in fictional films was that of the presidential portrait, usually placed in some governmental setting. A typical example is *Gambling on the High Seas* (1940), a gangster tale that contains scenes at a district attorney's office, featuring side-by-side portraits of Roosevelt and George Washington. During the wartime years, this type of onscreen appearance multiplied. In *Margin for Error* (1943), a comedy with an espionage motif, the smiling photo of FDR at a police station serves as a stark counterimage to the pretentious portrait of a uniformed Hitler in the Nazi spies' quarters.

By early 1940 the "comforting" image of FDR had more fully evolved. In John Ford's film adaptation of the John Steinbeck novel *The Grapes of Wrath* (1940), a well-known scene unequivocally portrays a compassionate government, thus making an associative linkage with the New Deal and FDR. The migrant Joad family, after suffering many indignities, discovers the refuge provided at a sanitary, democratically administered Department of Agriculture motor camp. The dispirited family's hope for their own future and faith in the country is restored through the kindness with which they are treated by the camp's "caretaker," an ambulatory Roosevelt look-alike wearing pince-nez glasses.

As active participation of the United States in World War II neared, this increasing identification with or reverence for FDR, with unmistakable patriotic overtones, was manifested in many films. A fall 1939 MGM musical, featuring Mickey Rooney and Judy Garland, *Babes in Arms,* concludes with the number "In God's Country." As the chorus sings in a stage setting, the juvenile stars, posing as Franklin and Eleanor Roosevelt, are driven up to the Capitol in an open car—a grinning Mickey with FDR's trademark cigarette holder clamped in his mouth.

Through her numerous public appearances and her weekly "My Day" newspaper column, Eleanor Roosevelt (1884–1962) became recognized as a spokesperson for FDR—much to the chagrin of conservative critics, who repeatedly attacked her outspoken liberal views. One of the earliest fictional film references to Mrs. Roosevelt occurs in *Woman of the Year* (1942), when an award-winning female journalist comments on interviewing the First Lady. During the war years Eleanor became the president's legs, tirelessly traveling around the world visiting America's troops. Bob Hope even delivers a one-liner about these trips in *They Got Me Covered* (1943). But Eleanor Roosevelt would not be cinematically portrayed by an actress until her appearance as Franklin's dutiful "missus" in *Sunrise at Campobello,* played by Greer Garson. The personal as well as political life of the Roosevelts, from Mrs. Roosevelt's perspective, is chronicled in the two-part made-for-TV film *Eleanor and Franklin* (1976–77). Both the first episode of the TV film and *Sunrise at Campobello* dramatize Eleanor's defying her domineering mother-in-law's attempt to persuade her paraplegic son to abandon politics—the implication being that Eleanor's actions may have changed the course of history—a point that was further elaborated on in the second part ("Fear Itself") of PBS's 1994 documentary, *The American Experience: The Presidents—FDR.* Today Mrs. Roosevelt is most often remembered as a civil rights champion. In a poignant scene from *The Tuskegee Airmen* (1995), set in the middle of World War II, Eleanor visits the black flying cadets' base and insists on taking a flight with one.

FDR's "Day of Infamy" war declaration was both broadcast and recorded live and captured on newsreel film. This seminal moment in millions of Americans' lives is recreated in several prominent films. In both *The Sullivans* (1944) and *Pride of the Marines* (1945), families solemnly listen to the actual speech in the intimacy of their own homes. On occasion, expressions of near veneration for FDR would also occur in Hollywood's wartime productions, epitomized by the comment of a tough merchant marine sailor in *Action in the North Atlantic* (1943): "I got faith in God, FDR, and the Brooklyn Dodgers."

Yet the myth of Roosevelt as the approachable leader remained the most cinematically appealing. In *Yankee Doodle Dandy* (1942), starring James Cagney as actor, composer, and director George M. Cohan (1878–1942), there is a stage sequence of Cohan impersonating FDR, musically exchanging quips with the press while doing a lively dancing routine. The presidential repartee is punctuated by the reprise that his comments are strictly "off the record"—a parody of the actual restrictions placed on the White House press corps regarding directly quoting Roosevelt at news conferences. This patriotic spectacular, which metaphorically wraps FDR in the "Grand Old Flag," is framed by scenes of a personal visit to the Oval Office by Cohan to receive a medal. The almost casual nature of the meeting shows Cohan as deferential but in no way obsequious. Likewise, FDR engages the entertainer in an informal yet respectful manner—further emphasized by a very lifelike impersonation of Roosevelt's voice.

The symbolism of FDR's image, even following his death in April 1945, could imply powerful social connotations. The film noir classic *Crossfire,* RKO's top grosser of 1947, centers on a psychopathic soldier who savagely kills a "Jew boy" veteran. A fellow member of his platoon exposes the murderer after being lectured on prejudice by a detective. During most of this darkly lit scene, a highlighted portrait of Roosevelt looms in the background—suggesting that FDR's spirit continues to demand the elimination of all forms of bigotry.

The omnipresence of references to FDR and his administration in movie theatres during his presidency was followed by his virtual absence from the screen until 1960—aside from relevant actuality footage incorporated into documentaries. Fictional exceptions would be confined to the odd formal portrait and a few topical remarks referring to him in historical dramas. A good example of the latter would be *A Man Called Peter* (1955), a biography of Peter Marshall, the beloved pastor of "the church of the presidents" in Washington. FDR is referred to on several occasions, including one instance regarding a presidential visit, and his death is mourned, but Roosevelt is never actually portrayed.

In fact, casual iconic referents became the most typical postwar portrayal of Roosevelt in period films—vestigial visual or audio reminders of his greatness—most particularly his portrait or passing comments referring to the president or the New Deal. In *The Group* (1966), which centers on a group of 1933 Vassar graduates, one particularly vocal FDR supporter works for the NRA (posters of the Blue Eagle and FDR side by side); in the small town where the eponymous heroes of *Bonnie and Clyde* (1967) share some intimate moments before their final bloody rendezvous with the law, a large portrait of Roosevelt seems to watch over them; and in *The Green Mile* (1999) Tom Hanks's humane death-row officer sits in his office beneath the benevolent gaze from a wall-mounted photograph of FDR.

Interestingly, among Depression-era films released since 1945, the more downbeat the portrayal of 1930s America, the more likely the film will not include specific references to the New Deal or FDR. *Ironweed* (1987), featuring an alcoholic drifter, is an obvious example. Two more compelling films are *Night of the Hunter* (1955) and *Bound for Glory* (1976). Although both eschew overt references to FDR's administration, one could argue that their protagonists capture the New Deal spirit. For instance, in the former film, Lillian Gish's simple farmwoman defends homeless children imperiled by an evil, predatory preacher. The latter film focuses on the wanderings of singer-composer Woody Guthrie (1912–1967), whose music came to symbolize the American people's struggle to surmount the Depression's hardships.

One might suppose that the first major postwar Hollywood production to depict the Pearl Harbor attack fictionally, *Tora! Tora! Tora!* (1970), would include scenes with Roosevelt. But FDR is absent from this film, despite its docudrama recounting of the activities of virtually all other key participants. However, there are numerous verbal references to "the president," including those by aides who are frantically attempting to keep him informed of Japan's intentions. Perhaps, because these scenes tend to imply vacillation on the part of the administration, the filmmakers chose to downplay Roosevelt's direct involvement in the decision-making process.

When *Pearl Harbor* was released in 2001, much was made of its candid portrayal of FDR, as well as its special-effects re-creation of Japan's assault on the U.S. Pacific Fleet on December 7, 1941. Although one might dispute the film's historical accuracy, *Pearl Harbor* pointedly acknowledges Roosevelt's physical condition. In every scene in which he appears, the camera focuses on his wheelchair. This is epitomized by the dramatic (and totally fictional) scene in which a grimacing president, played by Jon Voight, having listened to excuses from his advisors pertaining to the difficulty of militarily responding to the attack, struggles out of his wheelchair, his braces clearly visible, to a standing position, histrionically proclaiming, "Do not tell me it can't be done!"

Fortunately, the previously mentioned documentary, *The American Experience: The Presidents—FDR,* provides a more historically reliable full biography of Franklin D. Roosevelt. Narrated by David McCullough, and with useful insights by such individuals as one of the president's grandsons and the historian Doris Kearns Goodwin, it provides a balanced portrait of both the private and public lives of FDR and Eleanor. The first part, "The Center of the World," examines the Roosevelts' early years, including a frank discussion of FDR's affair with Lucy Mercer Rutherford and its profound impact on his relationship with Eleanor. The next episode, "Fear Itself," centers on FDR's struggle with polio, incorporating some of the very rare footage and extant photo stills that clearly show him coping with his disability. The last two parts, "The Grandest Job Ever" and "The Juggler," deal with FDR's presidency. Though FDR is described as "deeply shaken" by the attack on Pearl Harbor, the audience is shown, in its entirety, the newsreel footage of a determined FDR at the podium before the Congress delivering his stirring "Day of Infamy" war speech on December 8, 1941.

References

Filmography

Action in the North Atlantic (1943, F)
Ali Baba Goes to Town (1937, F)
The American Experience: The Presidents—FDR (1994, TV)
Babes in Arms (1939, F)
Bonnie and Clyde (1967, F)
Bound for Glory (1976, F)
Confidence (1933, F)
Crossfire (1947, F)
Eleanor and Franklin (1976, TV)
Eleanor and Franklin: The White House Years (1977, TV)
Footlight Parade (1933, F)
Gambling on the High Seas (1940, F)
Gold Diggers of 1933 (1933, F)
The Grapes of Wrath (1940, F)
The Green Mile (1999, F)
The Group (1966, F)
Heroes for Sale (1933, F)
Imitation of Life (1934, F)
Ironweed (1987, F)
Lady for a Day (1933, F)
A Man Called Peter (1955, F)
Margin for Error (1943, F)
Mr. Skitch (1933, F)
Next Time I Marry (1938, F)

Night of the Hunter (1955, F)
Pearl Harbor (2001, F)
Pride of the Marines (1945, F)
Roosevelt, the Man of the Hour (1933, F)
Soak the Rich (1936, F)
The Sullivans (1944, F)
Sunrise at Campobello (1960, F)
They Got Me Covered (1943, F)
Tora! Tora! Tora! (1970, F)
The Tuskegee Airmen (1995, TV)
Wild Boys of the Road (1933, F)
Woman of the Year (1942, F)
Yankee Doodle Dandy (1942, F)

Bibliography

Bergman, Andrew. *We're in the Money: Depression America and Its Films.* New York: New York University Press, 1971.

Blum, John Morton. *V Was for Victory: Politics and American Culture During World War II.* New York: Harcourt Brace Jovanovich, 1976.

Boime, Albert. *The Unveiling of National Icons: A Plea for Patriotic Iconoclasm.* Cambridge: Cambridge University Press, 1998.

Burns, James MacGregor. *Roosevelt: The Lion and the Fox.* New York: Harcourt, Brace & World, 1956.

——. *Roosevelt: The Soldier of Freedom, 1940–1945.* New York: Harcourt Brace Jovanovich, 1970.

Cook, Blanche Wiesen. *Eleanor Roosevelt, 1884–1933.* New York: Viking, 1991.

——. *Eleanor Roosevelt, 1933–1938.* New York: Viking, 1999.

Craig, Douglas B. *Fireside Politics: Radio and Political Culture in the United States, 1920–1940.* Baltimore: Johns Hopkins University Press, 2000.

Dick, Bernard F. *The Star Spangled Screen: The American World War II Film.* Lexington: University Press of Kentucky, 1985.

Erenberg, Lewis A., and Susan E. Hirsch, eds. *The War in American Culture: Society and Consciousness During World War II.* Chicago: University of Chicago Press, 1996.

Fleming, Thomas. *The New Dealer's War: Franklin D. Roosevelt and the War Within World War II.* New York: Basic Books, 2001.

Goodwin, Doris Kearns. *No Ordinary Time: Franklin and Eleanor Roosevelt—The Home Front in World War II.* New York: Simon & Schuster, 1994.

Kennedy, David M. *Freedom from Fear: The American People in Depression and War, 1929–1945.* New York: Oxford University Press, 1999.

Ketchum, Richard M. *The Borrowed Years, 1938–1941: America on the Way to War.* New York: Random House, 1989.

Leuchtenburg, William E. *Franklin Roosevelt and the New Deal.* New York: Harper & Row, 1963.

McElvaine, Robert S. *The Great Depression: America, 1929–1941.* New York: Random House, 1984.

Muscio, Giuliana. *Hollywood's New Deal.* Philadelphia: Temple University Press, 1997.

Olson, James S., ed. *Historical Dictionary of the New Deal: From Inauguration to Preparation for War.* Westport, CT: Greenwood, 1985.

Roffman, Peter, and Jim Purdy. *The Hollywood Social Problem Film: Madness, Despair, and Politics from the Depression to the Fifties.* Bloomington: Indiana University Press, 1981.

Shindler, Colin. *Hollywood in Crisis: Cinema and American Society, 1929–1939.* London: Routledge, 1996.

Shull, Michael S., and David Edward Wilt. *Hollywood War Films, 1937–1945.* Jefferson, NC: McFarland, 1996.

Winfield, Betty Houchin. *FDR and the News Media.* Urbana: University of Illinois Press, 1990.

Wolfskill, G., and John A. Hudson. *All but the People: Franklin D. Roosevelt and His Critics.* London: Macmillan, 1969.

[DOUGLAS A. NOVERR]

Babe Ruth and Lou Gehrig

Sportswriters have never been accused of trying to write history. Their time-bound daily columns, reports, and features have been largely snapshots or the game-by-game record of a season. But contained within this journalistic process and emanating from it are the mythmaking and legend formulation central to American sports, especially professional baseball. The accumulation of personal records of performance and the detailing of special exploits or events allow for the emergence of myth and legend. In baseball, well into the modern era, sportswriters served as reporters, official scorers, and record keepers. The term "scribe" fit them perfectly.

With the advent of newsreels covering the World Series and early silent feature films about baseball stars and with the beginning of national and local broadcasts of games, the mythmaking machinery found new, powerful means of transmission and dissemination. Novels and stories spun out by the magazine syndicates fed the imaginations of young boys.

George Herman "Babe" Ruth and Lou Gehrig, two of the greatest legends of professional baseball, were created by their own athletic exploits and records, by their visibility as the star players of what became a two-part New York Yankees dynasty in the 1920s and 1930s, and by their personal publicity agents, sportswriters, and first biographers.

Their personal backgrounds and stories were dramatic opposites. Ruth came out of the background of a family saloon in Baltimore and the St. Mary's Industrial Home, where he grew up and became a pro ballplayer by age seventeen, with Baltimore Orioles owner Jack Dunn as his legal guardian. Gehrig, the son of German immigrants, grew up in New York City and attended Columbia University, where he was a star athlete in baseball. Ruth spent almost no time in the minor leagues before being sold to the Boston Red Sox and helping them, as their ace pitcher, win World Championships in 1915 and 1916, Ruth's first full seasons with the club. Ruth came to the Yankees with great fanfare in 1920 as part of a $425,000 financial deal and a newly acquired reputation as a slugging home-run hitter, having powered a then amazing twenty-nine round-trippers in his last season with the Red Sox. Ruth then cranked up the home-run output to fifty-four and then fifty-nine in his first two seasons with the Yankees. Gehrig came to the Yankees after two seasons in the minors with brief but impressive visits with the parent club at the ends of the 1923 and 1924 seasons. He became a regular two years after signing a contract and showed promise of extra-bases power and runs-batted-in capacity in the 1925 and 1926 seasons.

In the 1927 season, on a team most baseball historians consider the greatest of all time, Ruth and Gehrig combined forces to take the Yankees to 110 regular-seasons wins and a World Series sweep over the Pittsburgh Pirates. Ruth slammed sixty home runs and scored 159 runs, while Gehrig drove in a league-leading 175 runs with a .373 batting average (up sixty points from his 1926 average). The two stars came into conjunction and would play ten full seasons together (1925 through 1934), with the Yankees winning four league pennants and three World Series (each time in a sweep) during that span. After Ruth was released from New York in 1934, Gehrig would play four more full seasons and in three consecutive World Series (1936–38) that the Yankees won and dominated.

Gehrig as Common-Man Hero

The first feature-film biographies of Ruth and Gehrig were prompted by the debilitating illnesses and by the actual or impending deaths of these two greats. The films commemorated their rise to stardom and their amazing individual success stories.

Pride of the Yankees was released in July 1942, a year after Lou Gehrig died at age thirty-seven of a rare muscular disease. The screenplay, by veteran writers Jo Swerling and Herman J. Mankiewicz, was based on Paul Gallico's moving biographical tribute published the same year. Gehrig's quiet heroism and modesty, his consistency and reliability (with 2,130 consecutive games played between 1925 and 1939), his team leadership as captain, and his overcoming social and physical awkwardness to find a loving and beloved wife are all celebrated in the film. Eleanor Twitchell Gehrig provided special assistance to the film, and Teresa Wright (as Eleanor) and Gary Cooper (as Lou) gave dignity and sensitivity to the story. Christy Walsh, Gehrig's public relations agent and good friend, also helped on the film.

Samuel Goldwyn was persuaded to make the film after first saying a baseball story was "box-office poison" and then that "if people want baseball they go to the ballpark" (Berg, 370). But when Niven Bush, a story editor, showed Goldwyn newsreels of the Lou Gehrig Appreciation Day held at Yankee Stadium on July 4, 1939, Goldwyn was moved to tears and ordered the project into production. In the film's text prologue, Gehrig's life and courageous facing of death with "valor and fortitude" are connected to the American soldiers then dying on the far-flung battlefields of World War II. Gary Cooper, who was too old to enlist, went on a five-week tour of American bases in New Guinea in 1943, and in his appearances before the troops he recited Gehrig's famous and eloquent Yankee Stadium speech, bringing the men to tears and then to a standing ovation (Berg, 373). The film was widely distributed overseas and seen by servicemen. *Pride of the Yankees* proved to be a box-office success and a popularly embraced film because it celebrated common American values of consistency, dedication, and satisfaction gained from family and marriage. Gehrig's romance with Eleanor Twitchell and their mutual love and devotion are treated in the film as just as significant an accomplishment as Gehrig's "Iron Horse" consecutive-game record, his 1934 Triple Crown achievement, and his success as a member of two great generations of Yankee ball clubs—the Murderer's Row and Bronx Bombers teams. What gives Gehrig the composure and dignity in his farewell speech, in which he considers himself "the luckiest man on the face of the earth," is his knowledge of a job well done, of the respect of fellow players and fans, and of the love and support of a remarkable partner.

Babe Ruth, Bill Dickey (who was Gehrig's roommate), Bob Meusel, and Mark Koenig all played themselves in *Pride,* with Ruth doubling for Cooper in the long shots. The film was superbly edited by Daniel Mandell, with documentary footage seamlessly woven in and the staging of Gehrig's day of honor and speech done with careful and exact re-creation.

Film Hagiography for the Babe

The Babe Ruth Story was released in late July 1948. Babe Ruth, dying of cancer in a New York City hospital, saw the premier of the film but, because of pain, was unable to sit through it (Creamer, 424). The film was based on a book by veteran sportswriter Bob Considine, who cowrote the script with George Callahan. Ruth traveled to California to assist in the filming. His death on August 16, 1948, completed the story of the film, which in the final scene saw him courageously accept the use of a "serum never before used in medicine" in the hope of stemming the ravages of his cancer. As the doctors wheel a hopeful Babe down the hospital corridor, the voiceover narration describes "the Babe who had performed miraculous feats" making now the "greatest play of his life" by offering "his life to help them [the fans] and theirs."

The film is filled with misrepresentations and fictions about Babe's life and career. Babe did not submit to an untested experimental cancer treatment serum, nor did he show up in the hospital room of the just-deceased Yankee manager Miller Huggins to say he was sorry for giving Huggins grief, worry, and strain and to ask for his manager's forgiveness. The film's story of the "called shot" home run in the 1932 World Series has Ruth hitting it for a seriously ill boy named Johnny in Gary, Indiana, with Claire Ruth shouting to him from the stands, "Don't forget Johnny." William Bendix, playing the Babe, emphasizes the called shot by gesturing three times to the centerfield bleachers where he would hit the next pitch. The biopic also downplays Ruth's private dissipation and excesses and his challenges to authority and instead focuses on the celebration of his rise to fame as the "Superman of baseball" and as a personification of all that is essentially American. His redeeming qualities are his love of baseball, his fondness for children and generosity toward them, and his incredible ability to inspire hope and even effect miracles. At one point, Claire Hodgson, who is not yet Mrs. Ruth, tells a drunken Babe, dressed as Santa Claus to give gifts to waiting hospitalized children, "Whether you asked for it or not, you represent the dreams and ambitions of millions of kids. How you act, they act. Never forget that." Chastened, Babe sends his agent in to distribute the presents.

The film evokes sympathy for the Babe when his abilities begin to decline and he can no longer deliver on the field. He has to deal with the deep disappointment of never becoming a big-league manager and with his rapidly declining health. The game rejects him, but fans gather outside the hospital to sing a slow, dirgelike "Take Me out to the Ballgame," while thousands of letters fill his room and give him hope even in the darkest hours. In the end, this story of a commoner's rising to the status of national hero and icon is based on the theme of never quitting and never forgetting that baseball is about the faith and support of the fans. Ruth's actual life is elevated to a national tale about success and about aging, illness, and dying.

The Babe Ruth Story was not as successful or popular as the Gehrig biopic because it lacked the high production qualities, was not as skillfully edited, and did not have the immediate connection to current history that *Pride of the Yankees* had in its connection to the war and battlefield heroism in 1942. The Ruth film story seemed more contrived and staged, and the Babe's death overshadowed a film about his life. Grief and a national sense of loss made the film seem ill timed and even inappropriate.

Modern Updates of the Two Legends

The original Gehrig story was updated in 1978 with an NBC feature called *A Love Affair: The Eleanor and Lou Gehrig Story*, with Blythe Danner and Edward Herrmann. Based on the 1976 book *My Luke and I,* by Eleanor Gehrig and Joseph Durso, the film offers Mrs. Gehrig's perspective and focuses on their six years of marriage and two years of courtship. It is a sensitive and compelling love story that deepens an appreciation for Gehrig's character, his quiet heroism, and his deep attachment to his home life.

In 1992 John Goodman starred in *The Babe,* with Kelly McGillis as Claire and Trini Alvarado as Helen Woodford, Ruth's first wife. This film shows in full measure all of Ruth's faults and excesses: his boorishness and crudity, unrestrained indulgence in food and sex, arrogance and self-centeredness, and almost infantile and juvenile personality, which constantly sought novelty and sensual gratification. Ruth is even shown coming apart emotionally, attacking umpires and fans. Unsettled and restless, Ruth refuses to accept rules and boundaries. He prevails only as long as his power and hitting eye can be drawn upon. The story ends with his final game in 1935 for the lowly Boston Braves, when he belts three consecutive home runs against the Pittsburgh Pirates, takes the salute from the fans, and then deliberately drops his cap at the feet of the Braves' owner. As he leaves the field, he meets an adult Johnny Sylvester, a boy he had earlier saved from death with a promised home run, and Babe says, "I'm gone, Johnny, I'm gone," while Johnny says "You're the best. You're the best there's ever been." In the 1948 film, Babe hits the three round-trippers and then singles. He calls a young rookie into running for him and says "Run for me kid. Play for me too. . . . Be good to the game, kid. Give it everything you've got. Baseball will be good for you."

Directed by Arthur Hiller, the 1992 film truncates Ruth's life, noting only in an afterword that he "never managed" and "died of throat cancer." Goodman's Babe is a flawed and pathetic individual looking for the love, acceptance, and family he was denied as a boy orphan. While he does gain a family life with Claire and two adopted daughters, Ruth is shown as cheated and misused by the owners and, in the end, completely disillusioned by the game he loved. Critics and reviewers blasted the film for its inaccuracies and fabrications, with Stephen Jay Gould saying the film "chose to follow the most vulgar, cardboard, clichéd version of the [Ruth] myth" (34).

The story of Lou Gehrig has been treated sensitively and movingly in two notable films, whereas Babe Ruth biopics have been less well received. Ruth's life and career are more entangled in myth and legend and in a larger-than-life picture filled with irresolvable contradictions and complexities. The best dramatization of Ruth's life turned out to be not a feature-length film but a 1984 play, *The Babe,* written by Bob and Ann Acosta, with Max Gail as Babe Ruth. Broadcast on ESPN, this one-character show, set in the Yankees locker room, has three scenes and allows the Babe to speak for himself in his own voice with a poignancy and humanity neither Ruth biopic achieved. These films show that Gehrig is eminently more understandable and easier to identify with, while the Babe eludes our grasp and we stand in awe and wonder at his feats and the extremes in his life. In our imaginations and fantasies we dream of being capable of Ruthian exploits and having an insatiable zest for life, but in our waking hours we know that Gehrig-like consistency, responsibility, and reliability will earn us true esteem and personal rewards.

References

Filmography

The Babe (1984, TV; 1992, F)
Babe Ruth (1991, TV)
The Babe Ruth Story (1948, F)
Headin' Home (1920, F)
Lou Gehrig's Greatest Day (1955, TV)
The Lou Gehrig Story (1956, TV)
A Love Affair: The Eleanor and Lou Gehrig Story (1978, TV)
Pride of the Yankees (1942, F)
Slide, Babe, Slide (1932, D)

Bibliography

Berg, A. Scott. *Goldwyn: A Biography.* New York: Ballantine, 1989.
Bergan, Ronald. *Sports in the Movies.* New York: Proteus, 1982.
Creamer, Robert W. *Babe: The Legend Comes to Life.* New York: Simon & Schuster, 1974.
Gallico, Paul. *Lou Gehrig: Pride of the Yankees.* New York: Grosset & Dunlap, 1942.
Good, Howard. *Diamonds in the Dark: America, Baseball and the Movies.* Lanham, MD: Scarecrow, 1997.

Gould, Stephen Jay. "Say It Ain't So, 'Babe': Myth Confronts Reality." *New York Times,* 26 April 1992.

Manchel, Frank. *Great Sports Movies.* New York: Franklin Watts, 1980.

Mote, James. *Everything Baseball.* Englewood Cliffs, NJ: Prentice-Hall, 1989.

Smelser, Marshall. *The Life That Ruth Built: A Biography.* New York: Quadrangle, 1975.

Trachtenberg, Leo. *The Wonder Team: The True Story of the Incomparable 1927 New York Yankees.* Bowling Green, OH: Bowling Green State University Popular Press, 1995.

Williams, Peter. *The Sports Immortals: Deifying the American Athlete.* Bowling Green, OH: Bowling Green State University Popular Press, 1994.

[MARTIN A. JACKSON]

Harry S. Truman

Harry S. Truman's historical stock stands high in the new millennium. He is routinely listed among the "great" or "near great" presidents in America's past, and, even thirty years after his death and a half century after his presidency (1945–52), he exerts a powerful attraction on historians, political experts, and ordinary Americans alike. David McCullough's Pulitzer Prize–winning biography *Truman* (1989) was a surprise best-seller, and Truman's autobiography *Memoirs* (1955–56) won a large popular readership, as have other books about Truman such as Merle Miller's *Plain Speaking* (1974). Scholarly work about Truman is considerable and ranges from the laudatory to the critical, with debate continuing on such matters as the use of the atomic bomb and Truman's civil rights record. Despite such controversy, in the years since his presidency Truman has achieved that rarest of distinctions: standing as a politician who was genuinely popular with the American people. The unassuming young man from Missouri, a haberdasher and local judge, came late to national attention, but once in the Oval Office he displayed unimagined powers and depth. Simply and vigorously, Harry Truman reached out to the average American, taking the reins of government in the midst of war and in the footsteps of the awesome Franklin Roosevelt. His strength was in speaking his mind, in making hard choices (the famous "The Buck Stops Here" sign on his desk speaks volumes about his own image), and in appearing to be an ordinary man in extraordinary circumstances.

As a twentieth-century president, Harry S. Truman was often captured by the motion picture camera. The newsreels of the mid-1940s, when Truman was a Missouri senator and later vice president, give him ample footage, and there is much to see of the prepresidential Truman in these reels. Fox Movietone, Hearst, and Pathé all have extensive listings for Truman before April 1945, when he succeeded Franklin Roosevelt in the Oval Office. Once he was president, of course, the image of a feisty Truman became familiar around the world, and especially in American theaters. Films for the Humanities, for example, offers a useful compilation in *1945: Year of Victory* (1992), an overview that covers the crowded events of that watershed year, including Truman at Potsdam, Truman and the atomic-bomb decision, and the announcement of victory over Japan. On the controversial matter of the atomic bomb, Truman himself defends his decision in *Hiroshima: The Legacy* (1986) from Films for the Humanities. As he did throughout his life, Truman argued that the bomb saved lives, both American and Japanese, by avoiding the perils of an invasion of the Japanese homeland in 1945.

The Cold War and the collisions of the late 1940s may be seen in *Superpowers Collide,* also from Films for the Humanities. This episode from *Inside the Cold War* (1990), hosted by David Frost, explores the Berlin Airlift and other early Cold War issues in which Truman was prominently involved. The *New York Times* series *Origins of the Cold War* (1990) features several programs about Truman's presidency, covering such issues as the Truman Doctrine and the outbreak of the Korean War. Most pertinent is *The Cold War: Containing the Soviet Threat,* in which Truman plays a central role during the crisis in Korea and the early Soviet-American confrontations in Europe. Truman figures prominently in another series, *The Cold War,* produced in twenty-four episodes by CNN and aired on that network in 1998 and 1999.

Hollywood has not yet portrayed Truman in any feature films, but he is the subject of two excellent made-for-TV films: *Give 'Em Hell, Harry!,* starring James Whitmore (1975), and *Truman,* starring Gary Sinise (1995). The first is taken from a successful one-man Broadway play based on the book by Merle Miller. Whitmore speaks the words of Harry Truman as he reminisces to the audience about a remarkable life, from his frontier childhood in the Midwest to the meetings with world leaders during his term. The exuberance and solid values that made Truman a popular figure are underlined in the show, and although some of the controversies are sidestepped, a rounded portrait of the man does emerge.

The HBO feature-film production, with Sinise as a striking Truman portrayer, weaves together the career, both public and private, of the "Man from Missouri." Truman's happy marriage, his relations with Kansas City's "Boss" Pendergast, and his recognition of Israel are among the subjects dealt with in this powerful biographical drama. Sinise achieves a form of theatrical magic by taking on the appearance and voice of Truman, and it is not hard to imagine that the man himself is speaking to the camera.

FIGURE 23. *Truman* (1995). The HBO docudrama realistically reenacts the famous moment when newly elected President Harry S. Truman (Gary Sinise), who many people thought would be soundly defeated by Thomas Dewey, holds up the premature newspaper headline announcing his defeat. Courtesy HBO and Spring Creek Productions.

The Harry S. Truman Presidential Library in Independence, Missouri, commissioned a film in 1997 to orient visitors, and it offers a vigorous (if hagiographic) account of his career. Directed by Charles Guggenheim, *Harry Truman, 1884–1972* is a forty-five-minute exploration of Truman's progress from Missouri to the White House and afterward.

References

Filmography

The Cold War (1998–99, TV)
Give 'Em Hell, Harry! (1975, TV)
Harry Truman, 1884–1972 (1997, D)
Hiroshima: The Legacy (1986, D)
H.S.T., Days of Decision (1963, TV)
Inside The Cold War (1990, D)
1945: Year of Victory (1992, D)
Truman (1995, TV)

Bibliography

Hamby, Alonzo L. *Man of the People: A Life of Harry S. Truman.* New York: Oxford University Press, 1995.

McCullough, David. *Truman.* New York: Simon & Schuster, 1989.

Miller, Merle. *Plain Speaking.* New York: Putnam, 1974.

Zinn, Howard. *A People's History of the United States.* 2d ed. New York: HarperCollins, 1999.

[JOHN D. THOMAS]

George Washington

"Be courteous to all, intimate with few." George Washington gave those words of advice to his nephew, but they can also easily be applied to the relationship our first president has had with the American people. Almost every citizen knows Washington as the mythic father of our nation, but very few have a notion of what the man was really like. Americans commonly know Washington as the tenacious military leader whose defensive strategies helped the fledgling nation win independence. During his presidency (1789–97), Washington kept the nation out of war, created our cabinet and currency, and, perhaps more than any other Founding Father, helped keep the country unified. The United States named its capital for him, built the towering Washington Monument in his honor, and put his solemn face on the ubiquitous dollar bill.

But that is all most Americans know. A great number would certainly be shocked to learn that Washington was also sensitive, unschooled, emotional, pessimistic, and not an overwhelming intellect. The reason so many people have such a sketchy impression of Washington is that he was a victim of his own good (and frequently apocryphal) press. Many of the common myths about Washington—that he could not tell a lie, that he threw a coin across the Rappahannock, that he kneeled in prayer at Valley Forge looking for divine guidance—were perpetrated by nineteenth-century biographer Parson Weems. As a result, Washington is now seen by many as remote, aloof, and not particularly interesting.

After examining how historians currently view Washington, a considerably different, more complicated and contradictory picture emerges. Because so many portraits of Washington depict him as regal and reserved—which he quite often was—few people have any inkling of how volatile the man could be. In fact, Washington had quite a temper and was prone to fits of cursing. He was also a very proud man who was deeply concerned with how history would remember him. In contrast to this pride and self-assurance, Washington was quite insecure, not only because of the death of his father when he was eleven, but also because of his almost complete lack of formal education and his rural upbringing. He took great umbrage when anyone questioned his authority. In spite of his lack of schooling and lack of exposure to culture as a youth, he grew to love theater and music, became an accomplished amateur architect, and earned a reputation as an experimental farmer, one of whose projects was to introduce the mule to this country. Washington was also quite stoic personally, but he spent lavishly on entertaining. A slaveholder, he was strict and demanding with his slaves, but he grew to find slavery repugnant. (He took the radical step of freeing his slaves in his will.) Another surprising fact is that Washington was anything but a commanding speaker.

The popular impression of Washington as a flawless military commander is something of a myth. Although his army eventually wore down the superb British forces in what amounted to a war of attrition, during the

Revolutionary War the general fought in merely nine major battles and won only a third of them. Washington was not beyond criticism even in his own time. For example, in 1778, Pennsylvania attorney general Jonathan Dickinson Sergeant corresponded with Congressman James Lovell, telling him that "thousands of lives and millions of property are yearly sacrificed to the inefficiency of the commander-in-chief. Two battles he has lost for us by two such blunders as might have disgraced a soldier of three months' standing" (Randall, 354).

But if Washington was such a flawed individual, how did he manage to have such a profound impact on the founding of our nation? Part of the answer rests in his disciplined character. As Robert F. Jones notes, "His talents in most fields were relatively commonplace; what he did was to raise those talents to the level of superlative accomplishment by self-discipline, a character trait in which he was certainly extraordinary. This enabled him, in turn, to pay unremitting attention to details, essential to coordinating all the disparate parts of an organization so they worked toward the accomplishment of a goal, whether it be the lands and slaves of Mount Vernon toward the attaining of personal wealth or the resources of the States and the soldiers of the Continental Army toward a victory over the English" (157).

With such a fascinating and complicated subject with which to work, one might assume that the Hollywood film industry would produce compelling cinema about the father of our new nation. Regrettably, this has not been the case.

The Dramatic Washington

Though no Hollywood feature film has ever been made primarily about the life and times of Washington, America's first chief executive has appeared in supporting roles in about a dozen movies. Of those films, three are available on video featuring Washington as more than merely a spectral presence—*America* (1924), *Unconquered* (1947), and *John Paul Jones* (1959). Close examination reveals that films about Washington's life and character unconsciously reflect the eras in which they were made and that his image was manipulated to meet the rhetorical needs of the project. All of these films present Washington very much in the tradition of Parson Weems. And, keeping in mind the impact that Weems had on Washington's legacy, it is important to note how these sorts of portrayals have kept those myths alive. As film scholar George F. Custen writes, "While most biopics do not claim to be the definitive history of an individual or era, they are often the only source of information many people will ever have on a given historical subject" (7).

The *New York Times* described D. W. Griffith's *America* (1924) as a movie "that will stir the patriotic hearts of the nation as probably no other picture ever has done." Apparently American patriotism was not stirring enough for Griffith, because he contrived a love story to carry the plot. Two scenes are crucial to understanding how Washington was shaped as a symbolic figure and contrived to fit the purposes of this film.

In addition to chopping down the cherry tree and crossing the Delaware, one of the most persistent images of Washington is of his time spent at Valley Forge during the winter of 1777–78. On one hand, Washington expert Willard Sterne Randall writes, "The pain and suffering that Washington's troops suffered that winter . . . have become a cliché in American history. . . . It was not an unusually cold winter: in fact, it was one of the warmest in memory" (351). But warm memories are exactly what many people have of Valley Forge, thanks to the apocryphal image of Washington kneeling in the snow, praying for guidance. The myth lives on into our time in a manner clearly designed to inspire national admiration: that image of Washington on bended knee with hands clenched in prayer has graced two postage stamps (1928 and 1977) as well as J. C. Leyendecker's famous cover of the *Sat-*

urday Evening Post in 1935. Like the U.S. Postal Service, Griffith was not timorous about using fiction to reinforce the American belief that Washington was a divinely inspired hero. Through an intertitle, *America* informs the audience that at Valley Forge "Washington's army suffered through the winter of 1777–78, the worst in fifteen years." Then the film cuts to the classic shot of Washington (Arthur Dewey) kneeling in the snow, hands folded in prayer, eyes to the sky, seeking guidance from the Lord.

The final scene in *America* depicts the inauguration of Washington in New York City. The image itself is not incorrect—Washington standing on a balcony with ecstatically cheering crowds below him. The intent of the final tableau is to show America's first president as an icon of strength and power, showered with adulation. But at the time, Washington was feeling anything but strong and powerful. Describing the new president's mood as "pessimistic and gloomy," Harrison Clark writes that, "for Washington, the thought that his countrymen expected him to be a living god served only to deepen his human worries" (132). That apprehension, however, was certainly not a color on the palette from which Griffith painted his epic portrait. Still, at the time *America* was released, the country was dealing with corruption in Warren G. Harding's administration, including the infamous Teapot Dome scandal, and the resplendent, unimpeachable image of Washington on movie screens would certainly have been received as assuring and restorative. In addition, *America* was released the same year the xenophobic Immigration Act of 1924 was passed. The law was designed to maintain America's putatively Nordic bloodlines through immigration restrictions, and the image of the heroic, ever-so-white Washington in *America* could easily have been seen as underscoring the sentiment behind the law. It should also not be forgotten that *America* was made by the same filmmaker who created *The Birth of a Nation* (1915), a racist picture that proudly displayed its nativist sentiments.

A similarly iconic Washington appears in Cecil B. De Mille's *Unconquered* (1947). The movie focuses on Captain Christopher Holden (Gary Cooper), a frontiersman who saves both a fort and his love from the evil clutches of a rogue (Howard Da Silva) attempting to undermine America's march toward independence.

One scene is key in showing how De Mille worked to manipulate Washington's life in order for it to match the hagiographic myth. Washington (Richard Gaines) finds Holden staring uneasily at an auction of white indentured servants brought over from Britain (Holden's love object, played by Paulette Goddard, is one of them), and Washington ventures this bit of personal information: "One of my teachers was an indentured convict, Chris, a fine man, but he never could teach me to spell."

Although it is true that Washington did receive much of his education from an indentured servant, the film does not explain that the man was owned by Washington's father, that Washington's father also owned dozens of slaves, and that Washington himself would own some 350 after his marriage. *Unconquered* premiered in 1947, when an offhand remark about Washington's being schooled by a white indentured servant was one thing, but opening the Pandora's box of slavery at a time before the nation had begun to deal adequately with its racial divisions was quite another. De Mille, for his part, kept the box hermetically sealed. It is also important to note that the Cold War–inspired anticommunist investigations began in Hollywood around the time of this film's release and that the film's moral, dignified portrait of Washington could easily be seen as an artistic salvo from the film industry to underscore its faith in classic American (that is, anticommunist) values.

In 1959, Washington once again appeared on the screen, this time playing muse to heroic sea captain John Paul Jones (Robert Stack) in a portrait not very different from that of *Unconquered.* As a clue to understanding how America felt about Washington during the 1950s, historian Karal Ann Marling writes that "in his appearance as a kind of historical mirage praying in the cold of Valley Forge on Norman Rockwell's 1950 Boy Scout calendar, George Washington was a holy picture" (378).

In director John Farrow's *John Paul Jones,* Washington (John Crawford) is held in divine reverence. The movie also underscores how filmmakers never allow facts to get in the way of national myths. The key scene in *John Paul Jones* occurs as the captain, fed up with the bureaucratic balderdash that is keeping him from fighting the good fight on the high seas, travels to Valley Forge during that historic winter of 1777–78 to deliver his letter of resignation personally. The future first president lectures Jones like a naughty schoolboy, asking him, "What are you fighting for, the principle of liberty or promotion?"

In fact, that dramatic encounter never happened, because that winter Jones had already sailed to France to see Benjamin Franklin. Bosley Crowther of the *New York Times,* for one, felt that Farrow's historic tinkering was over the top: "The old Hollywood disposition to reconstruct American history in the spirit and style of steel engravings or large patriotic lithographs is exercised again in [producer] Samuel Bronston's pseudo-biographical 'John Paul Jones.'" However, that type of portrait may have been psychologically reassuring for many Americans at the time. President Eisenhower, a Washingtonesque war hero whose administrations were characterized by peace and prosperity, was about to finish his second and final term, potentially leaving the nation without a strong, experienced leader to deal with critical issues including an international Cold War and increasing domestic racial tensions.

The Comic Washington

Washington has also appeared as a flat character in a number of comic farces. A good example is *Monsieur Beaucaire,* a 1946 Paramount release starring Bob Hope as the eponymous barber who flees France to set up shop in the colonies. At the end of the picture, Washington (Douglass Dumbrille) trots into Beaucaire's barber shop for a shave and a haircut, and, when Beaucaire asks him what his plans for the day are, Washington replies, "Oh, Jefferson and the boys are cooking up some sort of a declaration or something. I thought I might go over and watch them sign it." Comic irony has never been so rich.

Washington once again plays the fool in the 1942 Jack Benny film *George Washington Slept Here.* The story hinges on the fact that Bill Fuller's (Benny) wife (Ann Sheridan) buys a dilapidated house in the countryside, mostly because she is in awe of the fact that Washington once spent the night there. When they begin renovating, the couple goes wildly into debt, and things never stop going awry. At one point, once again perpetuating the Weemsian myth of Washington and his ax, the frustrated family maid declares, "George Washington should have chopped this house down instead of the cherry tree."

Watching and reading the critical responses to these films featuring Washington as a character, one is left with the feeling that a great injustice has been done to our first president. Washington has been portrayed as a ridiculously virtuous one-trick political pony. In the same way that Jefferson Smith stands in naive awe before the Washington Monument in Frank Capra's *Mr. Smith Goes to Washington,* filmmakers have also treated Washington with a reverence that has done little more than perpetuate the Washington of Weems's didactic tales.

The Washington Myth

Whatever Happened to George Washington? (1996) has attempted to right some of these cinematic and historical wrongs. In it, Ben Wattenberg moderates a roundtable discussion with a quartet of Washington experts

(Daniel Boorstin, Stanley Elkins, Edwin Yoder, and James Rees) to "look beyond the mythology of the father of our country."

The participants discuss matters including Washington's lackluster military record and his intellectual limitations; however, the issue they continually return to is Washington's character, which was most crucial to his success in helping to establish this nation. For example, as Yoder explains, "People forget that at this time the infant United States was surrounded by hostile and alien powers—the British in Canada, the French in the Mississippi Valley, the Spanish in Florida . . . and Washington had the vision and character to keep this struggling young nation out of this vortex of European rivalries and ambitions."

Although these experts do a good job of humanizing Washington, their reliance on such an amorphous term as "character" makes their arguments somewhat imprecise. Even Washington demythologizer Marcus Cunliffe is wary of attaching the term to our first president, writing pejoratively that, in the work of Weems, "character is the key word" (8).

A more solid, substantive and precise examination of Washington was presented by the C-SPAN series *American Presidents: George Washington.* It ran for more than six hours, and segment topics included Washington's boyhood home, Washington and slavery, Washington's relationship with the first Congress, Washington's relationship with women, and Washington's connection to modern-day America. Perhaps the most compelling portion of the programming was a two-hour segment during which historian Richard Norton Smith answered questions of callers from all over America. Smith fielded questions that touched on everything from Washington's sense of humor (he had a quite developed one) to whether or not he had sexual relations with his slaves (he did not). A twelve-year-old boy even called to ask if the first president had indeed chopped down the fabled cherry tree. Many of the callers expressed a desire to know more about the real Washington, as opposed to the saccharine myths that have been disseminated so widely.

Judging from the hunger for knowledge about Washington expressed by those callers, it seems as if America is now ready and eager to get to know and truly understand its first president. Hollywood films have shortchanged Washington over the years, inflating his image beyond recognition. Certainly, such studies as Willard Sterne Randall's *George Washington: A Life* and William M. S. Rasmussen and Robert S. Tilton's *George Washington: The Man Behind the Myths* provide a basis of fact for future films about our first president. When such films are produced, Americans will rediscover Washington as a man much less precious than they were led to believe, but just as important in the founding of our country as they knew.

References

Filmography

Alexander Hamilton (1931, F)
America (1924, F)
American Presidents: George Washington (1999, D)
Are We Civilized? (1934, F)
The Battle Cry of Peace (1915, F)
Betsy Ross (1917, F)
The Dawn of Freedom (1916, F)
George Washington Slept Here (1942, F)
Give Me Liberty (1936, F)
John Paul Jones (1959, F)
Monsieur Beaucaire (1946, F)
The Phantom President (1932, F)
The Remarkable Andrew (1942, F)
Sons of Liberty (1939, F)
The Spy (1914, F)
Unconquered (1947, F)
Whatever Happened to George Washington? (1996, D)
Where Do We Go from Here? (1945, F)

Bibliography

Brookhiser, Richard. *Founding Father: Rediscovering George Washington.* New York: Free Press, 1996.
Clark, Harrison. *All Cloudless Glory: The Life of*

George Washington from Youth to Yorktown. Washington, DC: Regnery, 1995.
Crowther, Bosley. Review of *John Paul Jones. New York Times,* 17 June 1959.
Cunliffe, Marcus. *George Washington: Man and Monument.* Boston: Little, Brown, 1958.
Custen, George F. *Bio/Pics: How Hollywood Constructed Public History.* New Brunswick, NJ: Rutgers University Press, 1992.
Fraser, George MacDonald. *The Hollywood History of the World.* New York: Ballantine, 1988.
Jones, Robert F. *George Washington.* New York: Fordham University Press, 1986.
Marling, Karal Ann. *George Washington Slept Here: Colonial Revivals and American Culture, 1876–1986.* Cambridge, MA: Harvard University Press, 1988.
Potter, David M. *People of Plenty: Economic Abundance and the American Character.* Chicago: University of Chicago Press, 1954.
Randall, Willard Sterne. *George Washington: A Life.* New York: Henry Holt, 1997.
Rasmussen, William M. S., and Robert S. Tilton. *George Washington: The Man Behind the Myths.* Charlottesville: University of Virginia Press, 1999.
Smith, Richard Norton. *Patriarch: George Washington and the New American Nation.* Boston: Houghton Mifflin, 1993.

IV.
Groups

★ ★ ★ ★ ★ ★ ★

[DAVID E. WILT AND MICHAEL SHULL]

African Americans After World War II

Although slavery ended with the Civil War, progress toward racial equality was slow, especially because of the so-called Jim Crow laws enacted to maintain white supremacy (see "The South"). African Americans made some progress over the eighty years following the Civil War, but it took the total-war environment of World War II—"requiring black assistance, against an enemy that led U.S. elites to stress their more egalitarian principles, reinforced by internal pressures to live up to those principles" (Klinkner, 73)—to set in motion major changes in society.

However, the process was still a slow and difficult one. The milestones are well known today: President Truman's executive orders prohibiting discrimination in employment and integrating the armed forces (1948); *Brown vs. Board of Education* (1954); the Montgomery bus boycott sparked by Rosa Parks's action (1955); federal troops helping integrate a school in Little Rock, Arkansas (1957); the March on Washington (1963); the Civil Rights Act of 1964 and the Voting Rights Act of 1965; race riots (1964–68); and the assassination of Dr. Martin Luther King Jr. (1968). The process may not yet be complete, but few would deny that enormous strides were made in a relatively short period, as if to make up for nearly two centuries of neglect (see "Civil Rights").

Post–World War II Hollywood was not unaware of the gradual move toward social justice and racial equality, but neither could it ignore the resistance to this movement in some segments of the population. Consequently, the African American image in films underwent a variety of changes that were not necessarily synchronized with the slow but fairly steady progress being made in society.

Although the most offensive black stereotypes generally vanished from Hollywood movies after World War II, filmmakers were slow to replace them with positive images. Major African American roles in the 1950s and 1960s were largely but not exclusively restricted to "message films" in which race played an important part in the film's plot. The 1970s saw the reemergence of films with predominantly African American casts, but—whether "serious" movies or the so-called blaxploitation genre productions—these movies were, like the black-cast movies of the 1930s and 1940s, primarily intended for African American audiences. Mainstream Hollywood began to introduce African American performers and themes into its productions. These included "color-blind" parts for black professionals, black policemen, and so forth, in which a character's race was not relevant to the plot; the presence of these minority roles signified a desire for a more realistic portrayal of a multiethnic America. Major films with African American stars or costars were also produced, and these were expected to appeal to audiences white and black. This three-way split continues to the present: mainstream movies with African American performers, serious films about the African American experience (some of which have a chance of becoming "crossover" hits), and popular films aimed at a predominantly African American audience (which only rarely find a broader audience).

Social Problem Films

In the early 1940s, as the world crisis drew closer to the shores of the United States, it became obvious that all Americans would have to cooperate if the forces of democracy were going to prevail against the totalitarian aggressors. Still, it took the threat of a massive protest march on Washington to prompt President Franklin D. Roosevelt to sign, in June 1941, an executive order prohibiting racial or religious discrimination in defense industries. When war came, African Americans served in the armed forces and worked on the home front, although often in segregated positions and frequently in the face of prejudice.

The need for a united front during wartime translated to the Hollywood screen. Immediately before and during World War II, a handful of films made a particular point of including atypically strong and admirable African American characters. For instance, *In This Our Life* (1942) features an African American law clerk (Ernest Anderson) who is framed by the unsympathetic protagonist (Bette Davis) for a hit-and-run accident. In *Syncopation* (1942), a young white musician learns jazz from an African American trumpeter (Todd Duncan). Other movies, notably *Bataan, Sahara,* and *Crash Dive,* were clearly an attempt to illustrate and foster national solidarity during wartime.

Ironically, one of the first postwar films with a major African American role almost completely reversed this trend and prompted numerous protests as a result: one historian indicates the film was "picketed more heavily than any film since *The Birth of a Nation*" (Leab, 37). This movie was *Song of the South* (1946), a part-animated, part-live action film from the Disney Company, starring James Baskett as Uncle Remus, who tells stories to entertain and educate a young white boy. The paternalistic "Uncle Tom" stereotype, while not without its positive aspects, offended many African Americans. Although it was not the last such holdover from prewar Hollywood images, *Song of the South* was one of the most egregious examples, and has been called "a great leap backwards" (Nesteby, 228).

More in line with trends in society as a whole were the "social problem" films produced later in the decade. In addition to pictures dealing with anti-Semitism (*Gentleman's Agreement* and *Crossfire,* 1947), mental illness (*The Snake Pit,* 1948), and juvenile delinquency (*Knock on Any Door,* 1949), the issue of racial equality was also addressed. These films were undoubtedly produced for a variety of reasons, not all of them altruistic, and they are more well intentioned than realistic or groundbreaking, but the very fact that they were made suggests a growing awareness of the societal problems that needed to be addressed.

The reason for the "social problem" films of the immediate postwar years is varied. The race hatred of the Nazis and its horrendous results were widely known, as were the contributions of African Americans to the war effort. Furthermore, almost as soon as the war ceased, the NAACP began a series of lawsuits challenging legalized discrimination and segregation. In December 1945, President Truman formed the Committee on Civil Rights; its report, issued the following October, condemned racial injustice in the United States. World War II had made racism undesirable, at least in principle.

The most noteworthy of the postwar era films with racial themes are *Home of the Brave* (1949), *Lost Boundaries* (1949), *Pinky* (1949), *Intruder in the Dust* (1949), and *No Way Out* (1950). *Home of the Brave,* directed by Stanley Kramer, deals with Peter Moss (James Edwards), an African American soldier who was stricken with hysterical paralysis after a wartime mission in the Pacific. A sympathetic psychiatrist discovers that Moss feels guilty for abandoning a fellow GI who had called him "nigger" to the advancing Japanese. The doctor shocks Moss into walking by repeating the slur and says that a history of social injustice predisposed the soldier to react as he did. The film was released two years after President

Truman's order mandating equality of treatment in the armed forces, a belated tribute to African American fighting men during war. It was not until October 1954, however, that the last all-black unit was disbanded.

Intruder in the Dust, based on a novel by William Faulkner, was shot on location in Mississippi and contains a fairly realistic portrayal of conditions in the South at the time. Lucas Beauchamp (Juano Hernandez) is accused of shooting a white man. Lucas is proud and stubborn, and he knows what to expect from the white man's justice. However, a coalition consisting of a white teenager, his African American friend, the white boy's lawyer uncle, and an elderly white spinster manages to prevent Lucas from being lynched and proves his innocence.

Lost Boundaries and *Pinky* both deal with light-skinned African Americans who "pass" as white. The first film, based on an actual case, tells the story of a doctor and his family who live and work in a white community in the North, where they are assumed to be white (the doctor's children are not even aware that they are African American). There is some controversy when the truth comes out, but the film's conclusion—which leaves a number of issues unresolved—suggests that in this particular case, the family's race is irrelevant to their friends and associates. However, earlier scenes did clearly show that discrimination and prejudice were still present in the United States. *Pinky,* directed by Elia Kazan, was a major studio (Twentieth Century–Fox) production with a "name" star (Jeanne Crain) in the title role. Pinky is a light-skinned African American who attended nursing school in the North. After a white doctor proposes marriage, Pinky goes home to the South to think things over. Her grandmother (Ethel Waters) criticizes Pinky for "passing," feeling it is wrong to deny one's identity and live a lie. Pinky inherits a mansion from the white Miss Em, whom she nursed in the older woman's final days; she decides to stay in the South and open a clinic and nursing school in the house. As with *Lost Boundaries,* there are scenes that overtly depict discrimination and prejudice; however, the issue was once more personalized, suggesting that racism could be overcome with good intentions and that institutional racism was vanishing (Pinky wins a court case against Miss Em's white relatives).

No Way Out was the last major entry in the first wave of racially oriented social problem films. Sidney Poitier, in his screen debut, plays Luther Brooks, a newly certified doctor who loses an emergency patient in a hospital prison ward and is accused of murder by the dead man's virulently racist brother, Ray Biddle (Richard Widmark). Biddle foments a race riot (interestingly enough, the African American targets of the planned attack stage a preemptive strike rather than wait passively to be assaulted). In the end, Brooks proves his moral superiority by refusing to kill the racist when he has the chance, even after he is shot and wounded himself. While Ray Biddle's racism is explained away as a result of his "sick mind" (he is also referred to as a "mental case"), the bitter and hostile actions of other white and black residents of the city (one woman spits in Luther's face and says "keep your black hands off my boy") are not as easy to overlook. Nonetheless, the film does portray some open-minded and reasonable characters of both races, and the scenes of Luther and his family were a rare Hollywood glimpse into middle-class African American life.

Hollywood's brief flirtation with liberal causes faltered in the face of economics (the challenge of television to some extent influenced the types of films being made, and socially aware movies became somewhat more rare), and the emergence of more pressing issues (the Korean War, McCarthyism). While images of African Americans did not revert to prewar stereotypes, major movies about race relations in the United States, or even those with significant African American characters, became scarce, if not nonexistent. A handful of sports films exalted the prowess of boxer Joe Louis (*The Joe Louis Story,* 1953), baseball player Jackie Robinson (*The Jackie Robinson Story,* 1950), and the Harlem Globetrotters basketball team (*The Harlem Globetrotters,* 1950; *Go, Man, Go!* 1953). Although they contained positive images of African Americans, these films were not aimed at a mass audience: only a limited number of whites with special interests would be expected to view these pictures, in addition to African American filmgoers.

This relative eclipse came at a time when legal barriers to equality were beginning to fall, although not without considerable resistance. *Brown vs. Board of Education,* the landmark Supreme Court decision declaring school segregation unconstitutional, was heard in May 1954. Within a few months, school systems around the country were forced to desegregate, a process that led to the use of federal troops in September 1957 in Little Rock, Arkansas, where local officials refused to comply. The same year saw the passage of the Voting Rights Act. In 1955 and 1956 the first wave of sit-ins and boycotts protesting discriminatory policies and laws took place. These steps irrevocably altered the United States, but the change did not come overnight. Understandably, the controversy was frightening to Hollywood: although they were in favor of "equality" and "brotherhood," the studios saw nothing to gain from making films about the civil rights struggle. Motion pictures produced in this era dealt with race obliquely, if at all.

A number of movies did prominently feature African Americans, but these films generally fell into two categories: mainstream movies with Sidney Poitier (or perhaps Harry Belafonte), and specialty pictures such as *Bright Road* (1953), *Porgy and Bess* (1959), and *Carmen Jones* (1954). The latter two pictures were major studio productions (MGM made *Bright Road,* but on a low budget) with serious, respectful depictions of African Americans, but in terms of their place in the overall scheme of Hollywood productions they were little more than updated versions of prewar black-cast movies such as *Green Pastures* or *Cabin in the Sky.*

Sidney Poitier, on the other hand, played roles in films that could not have been released before World War II. Many of his films dealt overtly with racial issues, including *The Defiant Ones* (1958), *A Raisin in the Sun* (1961), *In the Heat of the Night* (1967; five Academy Awards, including best picture), and *Guess Who's Coming to Dinner* (1967). Nonetheless, he was generally cast as such exceptional individuals that his race was, if not irrelevant and never ignored, then certainly subordinate to his characters' other traits. Poitier earned a place in mainstream Hollywood never before achieved by an African American actor, but also a certain amount of hostility from members of his own race: "At the height of his star power . . . Poitier's 'ebony saint' image was increasingly wearing thin for African Americans; it did not speak to the aspirations or anger of the new black social consciousness that was emerging" (Guerrero, 72).

One of Poitier's most famous roles—Dr. John Prentice in *Guess Who's Coming to Dinner*—illustrates both aspects of the controversy. Prentice is black, and the film's raison d'être hinges on his race, but he is also a world-famous surgeon who lives in Switzerland. His engagement to the white Joey Drayton (Katharine Houghton) shocks both her parents and his parents, but the only argument against the marriage is patently specious—namely, that they are of different races. John and Joey are culturally compatible, and because they plan to live in Switzerland after they are married, even the argument that their lives would be difficult in racially intolerant America is irrelevant. The film thus boils down the racial issue to its lowest, most superficial level (skin color), while at the same time ignoring many real questions about race relations in the United States.

Perhaps in response to comments from the African American community, Poitier tried a

FIGURE 24. *Guess Who's Coming to Dinner* (1967). Actor Sidney Poitier was at the height of his appeal and craft in this landmark 1960s film about racial tolerance. Joey (Katharine Houghton) shows Dr. John Prentice (Poitier) photographs depicting her idyllic family, an example of how the film skillfully deflects attention from important racial issues. Courtesy Columbia Pictures.

few change-of-pace roles such as the romantic *For the Love of Ivy* (1968) and *The Lost Man* (1969), a remake of *Odd Man Out,* substituting Poitier for James Mason and black militants for the Irish Republican Army. By shedding his "ebony saint" image, Poitier also gave up mainstream stardom, and since the 1970s he has appeared in relatively few movies (he also started directing films, which has occupied much of his time).

Aside from Poitier, Harry Belafonte was the only other African American performer who even came close to sustained leading-man status before the 1970s. After roles in *Bright Road* and *Carmen Jones,* Belafonte appeared in three major movies (the latter two produced by his own independent company) that, while using his race as a plot point, were not overt "social problem" movies. *Island in the Sun* (1957), set on a Caribbean island, stars Belafonte as a politically ambitious young man in love with a rich society woman, played by Joan Fontaine. Although this film broke the interracial-romance barrier (another "mixed" couple is also featured in the movie), setting it in an exotic locale diffused the impact considerably. In *The World, the Flesh, and the Devil* (1959), Belafonte, Inger Stevens, and Mel Ferrer are the only three people left alive on the earth after an atomic disaster. The racial symbolism was obvious but muted, subordinate to the romantic triangle (Stevens meets Belafonte first and falls in love with him, which causes trouble when Ferrer shows up, but in the end they manage to work out their differences). Belafonte's third starring film in a row—and his last for over a decade—was *Odds Against Tomorrow* (1959). Slater (Robert Ryan), a racist southerner, and Ingram (Belafonte), a middle-class African American with gambling debts, are hired by a third man (Ed Begley) to carry out a robbery scheme. The heist fails due to Slater's racist attitudes, and he and Ingram are incinerated in a climactic explosion.

As the civil rights struggle continued in the latter part of the 1950s and throughout the 1960s, a handful of films emerged that began to look at the issue of race or featured predominantly black casts, including *Take a Giant Step* (1958), *Nothing but a Man* (1964), and *Hurry Sundown* (1967). One interesting independent production was *Black Like Me* (1964), an adaptation of a nonfiction book by John Howard Griffin. John Horton (James Whitmore) is a white Texas journalist who undergoes medical treatments to change his skin color because "I want to find out what it's like to be a Negro in the South" (his publisher's response is "You're kidding!"). Although Whitmore never really looks like an African American (especially when he shares the screen with actual African American actors), the film is undeniably powerful in its depiction of racism. After weeks of discrimination and abuse, Horton is touched by the slightest example of fair-mindedness he encounters from a Southern white man, but this is an extremely rare event: the film's white characters are overwhelmingly overtly hostile, condescending, or fearfully apologetic but unwilling to break the color barrier. *Black Like Me* makes it clear that "it doesn't matter who you are or what you are, the color of your skin is all that matters."

Black Exploitation and Black Filmmaking

After the landmark legal rulings, laws, and civil unrest of the 1950s and 1960s, the civil rights movement seemed to fade into the background in the 1970s. Progress was still being made but much more slowly and without the fanfare that had accompanied earlier efforts, and there were some who believed momentum had been lost: "In spite of all the court decisions, the sit-ins, marches and boycotts, the average black American was disillusioned with his status in American society, for he still found himself . . . segregated and discriminated against . . . in all walks of American life" (Hornsby, xxxiv). The racial unrest of the late 1960s and the burgeoning "black militant" movement came about after the major laws and court decisions of the 1950s and 1960s, suggesting the process of achieving equality was far from complete.

FIGURE 25. *Black Like Me* (1964). Too risky and daring for Hollywood, this story, adapted from John Howard Griffin's nonfiction book, could be made only as an independent production. Investigative journalist John Horton (James Whitmore) changes skin color to be confronted with despicable and vicious racism, a concept many Americans, especially Southerners, had yet to confront. Courtesy The Hilltop Company.

Similarly, the African American image in Hollywood films continued to evolve. The blaxploitation films of the early 1970s may be viewed as an outgrowth of the civil rights movement: Hollywood was aware of the potential African American audience, and this audience was waiting for films specifically tailored for it. Ironically, these movies were often made by white film-industry veterans, and the profits went back to the Hollywood establishment. One exception was *Sweet Sweetback's Baadasssss Song* (1971), directed by Melvin Van Peebles, an independent production usually cited as the film that signified the existence and box-office potential of an urban, minority audience. *Shaft* (1971) and *Superfly* (1972) were also made by African American directors (Gordon Parks and Gordon Parks Jr., respectively), but for major studios. Dozens of other, lesser films followed, mostly adhering to "the central narrative ingredients of the blaxploitation formula: violent expressions of black manhood or womanhood, and a black-white confrontation that ends with the oppressed black coming out spectacularly victorious" (Guerrero, 110). These films created their own set of stereotypes, particularly the African American superman (or, more rarely, superwoman), capable of defeating (mostly white) oppressors and performing prodigious feats of lovemaking. However, less admirable stereotypes also abounded in these films, including gangsters, pimps, and women utilized as sex objects. A few of these films managed to cross over to whites, but the blaxploitation genre was largely aimed at a minority audience.

At the same time, mainstream Hollywood continued the gradual integration of its casts, and even a few "serious"—or at least non-blaxploitation—films about black topics were produced, often by African American filmmakers. These include *The Learning Tree* (1969), directed by Gordon Parks; Sidney Poitier's directorial debut, *Buck and the Preacher* (1972); *Sounder* (1972), directed by Martin Ritt; *Aaron Loves Angela* (1975), directed by Gordon Parks Jr.; *Cornbread, Earl and Me* (1975), directed by Joe Manduke; and *Cooley High* (1975), directed by Michael Schultz. Though well received critically, these films failed to attract a significant crossover audience, suggesting that whites were willing to accept African Americans in significant roles in mainstream movies but were not particularly interested in viewing films with predominantly black casts. Ironically, later in the decade, *Roots* (1977) would earn record-breaking ratings during its eight-night run on ABC television, with nearly half the country (100 million people) watching the final episode.

During the presidencies of Richard Nixon and Gerald Ford, there were few major breakthroughs in race relations, and the topic ceased to be of major interest to Hollywood. During the Carter administration, "President Carter's gestures . . . were not only hampered by a slow economy, but also by a growing white backlash against affirmative action" (Hornsby, xxxix). During the two terms of President Ronald Reagan, the administration's conservative judiciary helped codify this opposition to programs and policies like affirmative action. Ironically, it was during this period that African American performers achieved an unprecedented prominence in mainstream Hollywood productions.

The Rise of the African American Crossover Star

Sidney Poitier—and, to a much lesser extent, Harry Belafonte and even Sammy Davis Jr.—had crossed over to stardom in mainstream Hollywood, but their successors were not immediately forthcoming. Bill Cosby achieved considerable success on television, but his film career was insignificant. Jim Brown became a leading player in action films of the late 1960s but was rarely asked to carry a film as the star until the blaxploitation era. The first African American performer to sustain crossover success in the 1970s was Richard Pryor. After an apprenticeship in supporting roles, Pryor first achieved mainstream attention as Gene Wilder's costar in *Silver Streak* (1976). Over the next few years he alternated appearances in predominantly black-cast pictures such as *The Bingo Long Traveling All-Stars and Motor Kings* (1976), *Car Wash* (1976), *Which Way Is Up?* (1977), *Greased Lightning* (1977), *The Wiz* (1978), *Some Kind of Hero* (1981), and *Bustin' Loose* (1981), with roles—generally paired with white actors—in mainstream films such as *Blue Collar* (1978), *Stir Crazy* (1980), *Superman III* (1983), *Brewster's Millions* (1985), and *See No Evil, Hear No Evil* (1989). Pryor's most successful films at the box office were his crossover pictures, where he was either supported by or in support of white performers. Pryor did not have a single, signature screen persona, which allowed him to avoid stereotyping, although his quick wit was often used to portray him as street-smart, particularly in contrast to naive white characters.

Eddie Murphy, like Pryor a comedian before he became an actor, followed Pryor into films. His first movie was *48 Hours* (1982), a mainstream "buddy" film teaming convict Reggie (Murphy) with police detective Jack Cates (Nick Nolte). *Trading Places* (1983) featured another white-black combination, Murphy and Dan Aykroyd. In *Beverly Hills Cop* (1984), Murphy was elevated to stardom, with white actor Judge Reinhold playing a supporting role. Even more than Pryor, Murphy capitalized on a brash, smart-aleck persona, in some ways a version of the folktale "trickster" who mocks, fools, and manipulates his victims. Murphy's film career faltered for a time, and his mere presence could not guarantee a film's success. *The Nutty Professor* (1996), *Dr. Dolittle* (1998), and *The Nutty Professor 2: The Klumps* (2000) were crossover hits, but *Metro* (1997), *Holy Man* (1998), and *Life* (1999) were relative failures.

A third African American performer who achieved mass-market popularity in the 1980s was Whoopi Goldberg. Although best known for comedy, Goldberg had major dramatic roles in a variety of films, most notably *The Color Purple* (1985), *Ghost* (1990)—for which she won an Academy Award—*The Long Walk Home* (1990), *Sister Act* (1992), and *Sarafina!* (1992). Several of these films dealt with racial issues or the African American experience, but Goldberg usually works in mainstream films where her race is not an issue. She often plays outspoken, brash characters. Goldberg has also appeared in a number of mainstream films as housekeepers (*Clara's Heart,* 1988; *Corinna Corinna,* 1994) or nurses (*Girl, Interrupted,* 1999) who are employed by, or care for, whites. Regardless of the thrust of these films and the strength of Goldberg's characters, some might consider such roles as throwbacks to older Hollywood images of African Americans. Conversely, Goldberg's role as a maid in *The Long Walk Home* is justified by the historical context and the film's plot, set during the 1955 bus boycott in Montgomery, Alabama.

In the 1990s and beyond, a number of African American actors have risen to positions of prominence. Rapper and TV sitcom star Will Smith transferred his hip, urban image to a number of popular films, including *Independence Day* (1996), *Men in Black* (1997), *Wild Wild West* (2000), *Men in Black II* (2002), and *Ali* (2001). Smith seemed to have become a bankable star, but even his presence in *The Legend of Bagger Vance* (2000) could not help that film—about an African American who helps a World War I veteran regain his lost golfing prowess—find an audience or turn a profit. Danny Glover achieved stardom with *Lethal Weapon* (1987) and its sequels. Denzel Washington has forged a career in mainstream films as a handsome leading man, but it is interesting to note that pictures such as *The Pelican Brief* (1993), *Crimson Tide* (1995), *Fallen* (1998), *The Bone Collector* (1999), *Remember the Titans* (2000), and *Training Day* (2001) do not present him in "romantic" leading man roles, and thus the issue of an interracial romance is never raised. Samuel L. Jackson, Morgan Freeman, and Wesley Snipes have also starred in films intended for a mass audience. All of these actors have also worked in serious "black" movies.

Mainstream Films and the African American Experience

Since the 1980s, a three-way division in films about or starring African Americans has been evident. There are mainstream Hollywood films starring African Americans but aimed at the mass audience, films about the African American experience or other racial topics that are expected to cross over to the mass audience, and movies produced specifically for the African American audience. Each of these types of films contains a variety of images of African Americans.

Mainstream films such as *Men in Black, Lethal Weapon* and its three sequels, *Kiss the Girls,* and *Enemy of the State* feature African American stars or costars, but for the most part these films are color-blind—the plot and characterizations may take notice of the race of the performers, but this is not a significant aspect of the film. A movie such as *The Bodyguard* (1992) may star a white actor (Kevin Costner) and an African American actress (Whitney Houston), but the interracial component of their romance is most definitely not the focus of the film; either of the two major stars could have been replaced with a performer of another race and the film would have been essentially the same. The actress Halle Berry has similarly crossed over into color-blind romantic roles such as in *Swordfish* (2001) and *Die Another Day* (2002), though her Academy Award–winning role in Marc Forster's film *Monster's Ball* (2001) certainly made ethnicity an issue.

In the past several decades Hollywood has produced a fair number of films dealing with racial themes and intended for a mass (white as well as black) audience. It may be significant, however, that a number of these movies are period pictures—thus avoiding a direct discussion of the state of current race relations in the United States. Examples include *The Color Purple* (1985), *Driving Miss Daisy* (1989), *Glory* (1989), *Ghosts of Mississippi* (1996), *Rosewood* (1997), *Amistad* (1997), and *Beloved* (1998). Most of these films were directed by whites: whether the race of the director influenced the portrayal of African Americans in these films is open to debate, but the fact remains that most African American directors work in the third category, films aimed at African American audiences.

Whether serious dramas—*Daughters of the Dust* (1991), *Malcolm X* (1992), and *Eve's Bayou* (1997), for example—or commercial action films and comedies, one writer argues, "Hollywood makes these modestly budgeted black features with the expectation of recovering the capital invested and turning a profit from the black audience alone" (Guerrero, 166). Only rarely does one of these films cross over to the white audience. The most prolific African American filmmaker today, Spike Lee, has had very little success with white audiences, *Do the Right Thing* (1989) excepted. Films such as *She's Gotta Have It* (1986) and *School Daze* (1988) explore the African American experience in terms that may be too nuanced for whites: *School Daze,* for example, is set at an all-black university and highlights the competition between "jigaboos" and "wannabes," cliques of students defined by their skin color and hairstyles, which signify their degree of cultural "blackness."

Features made by African American filmmakers display their own sets of stereotypes, including rappers, "gangstas," sexually objectified women, and "buppies" (black urban professionals) in popular films such as *I'm Gonna Git You Sucka* (1988), *House Party* (1990), *Boyz N the Hood* (1991), *Menace II Society* (1993), *Booty Call* (1997), *Next Friday* (2000), *Scary Movie* (2000), *The Original Kings of Comedy* (2000), and *Barbershop* (2002). Images that might be perceived as racist if produced by white filmmakers are more acceptable if created by African Americans for an internal audience because the motivations and portrayals originate in, and are intended for, a different cultural context. Spike Lee's *Bamboozled* (2000) nonetheless drew considerable criticism for its resurrection of black stereotypes from the minstrel show and early Hollywood eras, even though the director used these offensive images to make a satirical and political point.

Reluctant Progress

Since World War II, the visibility of African Americans in motion pictures has increased significantly. Although Hollywood is still reluctant—with very few exceptions—to produce big-budget films with predominantly black casts, this appears to be a function of the (perceived or real) limited audience for such movies, rather than a decision based on racist motives. African American performers are regularly cast in major roles, and race stereotyping is extremely rare. The debate may now be between proponents of "color blindness" in films and those who want greater attention paid to African American subjects. Although the struggle for absolute racial justice has not concluded, in Hollywood movies as in real life, significant progress has certainly been made.

References

Filmography

Aaron Loves Angela (1975, F)
Ali (2001, F)
Amistad (1997, F)
Bamboozled (2000, F)
Barbershop (2002, F)
Bataan (1943, F)
Beloved (1998, F)
Beverly Hills Cop (1984, F)
The Bingo Long Traveling All-Stars and Motor Kings (1976, F)
Black Like Me (1964, F)
Blue Collar (1978, F)
The Bodyguard (1992, F)
The Bone Collector (1999, F)
Booty Call (1997, F)
Boyz N the Hood (1991, F)
Brewster's Millions (1985, F)
Bright Road (1953, F)
The Brother from Another Planet (1984, F)
Buck and the Preacher (1972, F)
Bustin' Loose (1981, F)
Carmen Jones (1954, F)

Car Wash (1976, F)
Clara's Heart (1988, F)
The Color Purple (1995, F)
Cooley High (1975, F)
Corinna, Corinna (1994, F)
Cornbread, Earl and Me (1975, F)
Cotton Comes to Harlem (1970, F)
Crash Dive (1943, F)
Crimson Tide (1995, F)
Daughters of the Dust (1991, F)
The Defiant Ones (1958, F)
Do the Right Thing (1989, F)
Dr. Dolittle (1998, F)
Driving Miss Daisy (1989, F)
Enemy of the State (1999, F)
Eve's Bayou (1997, F)
Eyes on the Prize (1986, TV)
Fallen (1998, F)
For the Love of Ivy (1968, F)
48 Hours (1982, F)
Ghost (1990, F)
Ghosts of Mississippi (1996, F)
Girl, Interrupted (1999, F)
Glory (1989, F)
Go, Man, Go! (1953, F)
Greased Lightning (1977)
Guess Who's Coming to Dinner (1967, F)
The Harlem Globetrotters (1950, F)
Holy Man (1998, F)
Home of the Brave (1949, F)
House Party (1990, F)
Hurry Sundown (1967, F)
I'm Gonna Git You Sucka (1988, F)
Independence Day (1996, F)
In the Heat of the Night (1967, F)
In This Our Life (1942, F)
Intruder in the Dust (1949, F)
Island in the Sun (1957, F)
The Jackie Robinson Story (1950, F)
The Joe Louis Story (1953, F)
Kiss the Girls (1997, F)
The Learning Tree (1969, F)
The Legend of Bagger Vance (2000, F)
Lethal Weapon (1987, F)
Life (1999, F)
The Long Walk Home (1990, F)
Lost Boundaries (1949, F)
The Lost Man (1969, F)
Malcolm X (1992, F)
Menace II Society (1993, F)
Men in Black (1997, F)
Men in Black II (2002, F)
Metro (1997, F)
Monster's Ball (2001, F)
New Jack City (1991, F)
Next Friday (2000, F)
Night of the Living Dead (1968, F)
Nothing but a Man (1964, F)
No Way Out (1950, F)
The Nutty Professor (1996, F)
The Nutty Professor 2: The Klumps (2000, F)
Odds Against Tomorrow (1959, F)
The Original Kings of Comedy (2000, F)
Panther (1995, F)
The Pelican Brief (1993, F)
Pinky (1949, F)
Porgy and Bess (1959, F)
The Quiet One (1948, F)
A Raisin in the Sun (1961, F)
Remember the Titans (2000, F)
Roots (1977, TV)
Rosewood (1997, F)
Sahara (1943, F)
Sarafina! (1992, F)
Scary Movie (2000, F)
School Daze (1988, F)
See No Evil, Hear No Evil (1989, F)
Sergeant Rutledge (1960, F)
Sergeants Three (1962, F)
Shaft (1971, F)
She's Gotta Have It (1986, F)
Silver Streak (1976, F)
Sister Act (1992, F)
A Soldier's Story (1984, F)
Some Kind of Hero (1981, F)
Song of the South (1946, F)
Sounder (1972, F)
Stir Crazy (1980, F)
Superfly (1972, F)
Superman III (1983, F)
Sweet Sweetback's Baadasssss Song (1971, F)
Syncopation (1942, F)
Take a Giant Step (1958, F)
To Kill a Mockingbird (1962, F)
Trading Places (1983, F)
Training Day (2001, F)
Which Way Is Up? (1977, F)
White Man's Burden (1995, F)
Wild, Wild West (2000, F)
The Wiz (1978, F)
The World, the Flesh, and the Devil (1959, F)

Bibliography

Anderson, Lisa M. *Mammies No More: The Changing Image of Black Women on Stage and Screen.* Lanham, MD: Rowman & Littlefield, 1997.

Bogle, Donald. *Blacks in American Films and Television: An Encyclopedia.* New York: Garland, 1988.

——. *Toms, Coons, Mulattoes, Mammies, and Bucks: An Interpretive History of Blacks in American Films.* 3d ed. New York: Continuum, 1994.

Cripps, Thomas. *Slow Fade to Black: The Negro in American Film, 1900–1942.* New York: Oxford University Press, 1977.

Diawara, Manthia. *Black American Cinema.* New York: Routledge, 1993.

Ellison, Mary. *The Black Experience: American Blacks Since 1865.* London: Batsford, 1974.

Franklin, John Hope, and Alfred A. Moss, Jr. *From Slavery to Freedom.* 8th ed. New York: Knopf, 2000.

George, Nelson. *Blackface: Reflections on African-Americans and the Movies.* New York: HarperCollins, 1994.

Guerrero, Ed. *Framing Blackness: The African American Image in Film.* Philadelphia: Temple University Press, 1993.

Hornsby, Alton, Jr. *Chronology of African-American History.* Detroit: Gale Research, 1991.

Klinkner, Philip A., and Rogers M. Smith. *The Unsteady March: The Rise and Decline of Racial Equality in America.* Chicago: University of Chicago Press, 1999.

Klotman, Phyllis R., and Janet K. Cutler, eds. *Struggles for Representation: African American Documentary Film and Video.* Bloomington: Indiana University Press, 1999.

Leab, Daniel J. *From Sambo to Superspade: The Black Experience in Motion Pictures.* Boston: Houghton Mifflin, 1975.

Levine, Michael L. *African Americans and Civil Rights.* Phoenix: Oryx Press, 1996.

Mungazi, Dickson A. *The Journey to the Promised Land: The African American Struggle for Development since the Civil War.* Westport, CT: Praeger, 2001.

Nesteby, James R. *Black Images in American Films, 1896–1954.* Lanham, MD: University Press of America, 1982.

Null, Gary. *Black Hollywood: From 1970 to Today.* Secaucus, NJ: Carol, 1993.

Reid, Mark A. *Redefining Black Film.* Berkeley: University of California Press, 1993.

Richards, Larry. *African American Films Through 1959.* Jefferson, NC: McFarland, 1998.

Rocchio, Vincent F. *Reel Racism.* Boulder, CO: Westview, 2000.

Sampson, Henry T. *Blacks in Black and White: A Source Book on Black Films.* 2d ed. Metuchen, NJ: Scarecrow, 1995.

Smith, Valerie, ed. *Representing Blackness: Issues in Film and Video.* New Brunswick, NJ: Rutgers University Press, 1997.

Snead, James A. *White Screens/Black Images.* New York: Routledge, 1994.

Thernstrom, Stephan, and Abigail Thernstrom. *America in Black and White: One Nation, Indivisible.* New York: Simon & Schuster, 1997.

Willis, Sharon. *High Contrast: Race and Gender in Contemporary Hollywood Film.* Durham, NC: Duke University Press, 1997.

[JACK G. SHAHEEN]

Arab Americans

As of 2002, there were 3.5 million Arab Americans in the United States. Four in five were born in the country, and the vast majority—75 percent—were Christians. Arabs have been in America since at least 1854, when Antonius Bishallany, a Syrian, went to study in New York. From the turn of the nineteenth century through the early 1920s, there followed successive waves of immigrants—between five thousand and eight thousand annually. Most of them came from Mount Lebanon and Greater Syria. Contributing to a growing America were Eastern Orthodox, Maronite, and Melkite Christians, as well as some Muslims and Druze. The newcomers were so fond of America that they would frequently repeat the phrase, "May God continue to bless this country."

Like other immigrants passing through Ellis Island, most Arab immigrants were desperately poor and discriminated against early on for the mere fact that they were foreigners. Malicious name-calling was commonplace. In 1903, *The Pittsburgh Leader* described them as "undesirable Syrians, many degrading inhabitants of dives of disgusting depravity" (Pannbacker, 48). In St. Louis, the press tagged them "Street Arabs" and "wandering Bedouins . . . worthless of character in parents, immoral and drunken fathers and mothers. What can they become? Only vagrants, tramps and prostitutes" (Dacus, 407–408). Fearful that their swarthy color and Arabic names might deny them admittance to and acceptance in the country, some immigrants Americanized their names: my cousin, Albert Shaheen, became Mr. Green. Butros became Peter; Haddad became Smith, and Peter Smith was born.

From the beginning, many engaged in peddling. Fellow Arabs showed the new immigrants the routes and the ropes. They extended credit and gave the beginners needed supplies, enabling them to fill their suitcases with a wide range of items, from notions to linens, that an isolated farmer's wife or city dweller might want to buy. It was common to see family members working side by side, sixteen hours a day, seven days a week. Peddling required little capital, but it necessitated learning English, which helped the immigrants to become more quickly Americanized. This peddler image was used for comedic purposes in the stage and screen version of Rodgers and Hammerstein's musical *Oklahoma.*

The immigrants soon established trading networks throughout the country. After World War I, they came to own and operate grocery, fruit, and dry goods stores, offering much of the same merchandise they sold as peddlers. These entrepreneurs established a model for the residence and assimilation of later Arab immigrants, notably those escaping Ottoman conscription after 1909. Gradually, as family members brought over friends and relatives, whole village networks were created in the New World's urban centers. In Pittsburgh and Birmingham they worked the railroad freight yards and steel mills; in Detroit, the automobile assembly lines; in Kansas City, the meat packing plants; and in New England, the textile mills.

Arab Americans have since excelled as teachers, physicians, members of the armed services, congressional representatives, journalists, athletes, homemakers, lawyers, and clergy. Among thousands of notables are the poet and philosopher Kahlil Gibran; Dr. Michael DeBakey, heart specialist; Helen Thomas, dean of the White House Press Corps; Colonel James Jabara, our nation's first jet ace; Donna Shalala, educator and secretary of health and human services in the Clinton administration; actor Danny Thomas, founder of St. Jude's Research Center; clothing designer Joseph Abboud; radio personality Casey Kasem; and Ralph Nader, presidential candidate and consumer advocate.

Motion Pictures

Despite the rich history and numerous contributions of Americans of Arab descent, motion pictures have singled them out for discrimination, portraying them as the Other. Hollywood has failed to reveal their individual accomplishments; nor have movies humanized them. I am still in search of a film that has projected an Arab American family, with grandparents and children, as an integral part of America's cultural mosaic. And, though most of America's Arabs are Christians, no movie has ever shown them worshiping in a church. In fact, films display most Americans of Arab heritage as Muslims and link the Islamic faith—a religion of peace—with violence. Nor do films project Arab Americans distinguishing themselves in the military.

In contrast to these omissions and stereotypes, consider, for example, two typical families—the Jacobs and the Rafeedies. My grandfather, Jacob Mike Jacob, was a chanter at our church; he also worked in the mills outside of Pittsburgh for nearly two decades. Albert Rafeedie, my father-in-law, served in the U.S. Army during World War I. Following the war he ran dry goods stores in Minneapolis and Los Angeles. Both Albert and Jacob emigrated to America in the early 1900s. Their families served their country during World War II and the Korean War.

Inexplicably, the presence of Americans of Arab heritage and their innumerable contributions to our nation have been invisible. Fourteen of the twenty films surveyed in this essay display them not as they are—typical hardworking Americans—but as carbon copies of Hollywood stereotypes. These fourteen films project Americans of Arab descent as crude, disorderly, and burnoosed foreigners, covetous male rogues; bumbling buffoons; shady shysters; terrorists killing fellow Americans, even children; and mute submissive maidens.

The Arab American in Film

Ironically, the first and only silent film to feature an Arab American character, Paramount's *Anna Ascends* (1922), stands in stark contrast to the injurious stereotypes. This rags-to-riches immigrant story is, in fact, the only movie ever to feature as the principal character an Arab American woman. The setting for this lost film, which is based on Harry Ford's successful Broadway play, is New York City's "Little Syria," where the newly arrived Anna Ayoub works as a waitress in Said Coury's coffeehouse. After Anna bravely fends off the advances of a hustling pimp, she runs off to attend night school, where she excels. Eventually, Anna goes on to write a best-selling novel. In the end she weds her long-lost suitor, a wealthy New Yorker; they go on to live happily ever after. "The idea of writing *Anna Ascends*," Ford told a *Variety* reporter, "came first into my mind during the winter of 1912, when I met and finally knew very intimately a Syrian family living in Washington, D.C. Their family life . . . impressed me. . . . Hence I figured why not write a Syrian [American] drama?"

Not until 1976, fifty-four years after the debut of *Anna Ascends*, did Arab American characters appear again on silver screens. This time the portraits were unsightly and heinous. *The Next Man* (1976), *Cheech and Chong's Next Movie* (1980), and *Wrong Is Right* (1982) lambaste Arab Americans. Set in New York City, *The Next Man* and *Wrong Is Right* present Arab

American students not as regular college kids, but rather as shrill, militant radicals. They flaunt signs reading "Arabia for the Arabians," "No More Lies, the Jews Own Television," "Death to the Jews," and "Kill the Jews." Eventually New York City police officers subdue the protestors. Arab American agitators and students in *Wrong Is Right* are seen protesting America's Mideast policies. How? Not peacefully, like other Americans, but by blowing themselves up on Manhattan streets and launching terrorist attacks in Washington, Chicago, and Detroit.

Instead of projecting an archetypal American, *Cheech and Chong's Next Movie* demeans a mustached Arab American gas station owner. Quips Cheech: He's "a [mute] dude too busy watching his money." As the credits roll, he and Chong pilfer gas from the Arab American's Texaco station. To ally the proprietor with stereotypical oil-rich Arabs, the camera cuts to the Arab American's tow truck. Emblazoned on the door is the logo "Saydis and Saydat." Chuckling, Cheech walks off with a garbage can filled with stolen gas, singing: "Ahab the Ayrab, sheikh of the burning sands." Taken together, the gas theft, truck logo, and "Ahab" tune unfairly equate an American proprietor with rich, desert Arabs.

Wild Geese II (1985), a drama set in Berlin, depicts John Haddad (Scott Glenn), a grim and unappealing Arab American mercenary from Pittsburgh. The dreadful film focuses on Haddad and his cohorts as they attempt to kidnap Rudolf Hess from the infamous Spandau prison. The drama has absolutely nothing to do with the Arab-Israeli conflict. Yet, the producers inject unmerited dialogue. For example, instead of having Haddad express concerns for Palestinians under occupation, cliché-ridden lines contend that Haddad hates them, for Palestinians, goes the stale scenario, killed his family.

Not until *Baby Boom* (1987) did Hollywood release another film featuring an Arab American woman—no heroic Anna Ayoub–type character, but a submissive caricature. The opening frames show a liberal Manhattan executive (Diane Keaton) interviewing prospective nannies to care for her infant daughter. Instead of introducing an Arab American woman applicant patterned after women's-rights advocate Marlo Thomas, the producers present a nameless and rigid woman; she wears a black *abaya* that covers her from head to toe. Hoping to be employed as the little girl's nanny, the cloaked Arab American boasts not about the importance of equal rights for women, but rather about female subservience: "I do not need a bed. I prefer to sleep on the floor." And, "I speak only when spoken to. . . . I will teach your daughter to properly respect a man." The executive grimaces; out the door goes this backward applicant.

Another film of 1987, *Wanted Dead or Alive*, deals with Arab Americans residing in Los Angeles. In the film they function not as dignified neighbors but as deceitful villains. The grubby Arab Americans who own Amir's restaurant are terrorists; they willingly assist a Palestinian militant, Malak (Gene Simmons). Scenes reveal Malak and Americans of Arab descent blowing up hundreds of civilians. At Amir's restaurant several sadists beat, torture, and murder a CIA agent. The same kuffiyeh-clad Arab Americans operate a Los Angeles bomb factory. They conspire with Malak to ignite fifty-plus bombs, the devastation in Los Angeles intended to make "Bhopal, India, look like a minor traffic accident." In time, the CIA and the Los Angeles Police Department collar them. Earlier, UCLA's Arab American students are tagged "desert dwellers and animals"; the slurs are not contested. Would *Wanted Dead or Alive*'s producers even think about—let alone release—a similar film showing America's Asians, blacks, Jews, or Latinos being so unfairly vilified?

Though most critics failed to address *Wanted Dead or Alive*'s stereotypes, one vocal Hollywood reviewer strongly objected to the film's hateful depictions. On January 30, 1987, columnist Michael Medved wrote to me, saying that Arab Americans "are shown to be active supporters of a bloody vicious terrorist kingpin. This disturbed me precisely because it bears no connection with reality." Medved's criticisms notwithstanding, one year later *Terror in Beverly Hills* (1988) advanced *Wanted Dead or Alive*'s hateful theme: Arab Americans are terrorists. Instead of presenting generic terrorists, *Terror,* too, shows Arab American fanatics bringing panic to California's streets. In Beverly Hills they and their Palestinian cohorts shoot and torture innocents. In addition, they kidnap and hold hostage the American president's daughter, as well as a Los Angeles policeman's wife. Ultimately, the LAPD frees the hostages and wipes out the swarthy villains. Instead of showing America's Arabs bonding with America's blacks to eradicate the kidnapers, *Terror*'s closing scenes show present a hateful confrontation. An African American policeman corners an Arab American thug. Smiling, the officer empties his shotgun, boasting, "You've made my day!"

Nearly all Arab American cab drivers in New York City function as other cabbies do—they are honest, helpful, and multilingual. Not so in *Quick Change* (1990). This film projects a dim-witted New York cabby (Tony Shalhoub) who listens to Arab music and mumbles only in Arabic. An angry passenger tries but fails to direct the sheepishly smiling cabby to the airport. "What da ya got, sand in your ears?" he screams. Frustrated, the passenger exits the moving cab. The anxious cabby speeds through a red light, nearly injuring pedestrians. The police arrive. Feeling degraded, the cabby falls to his knees, cries, and begs the officers to arrest him.

Navy SEALs (1990) displays heroic U.S. forces wiping out hundreds of Palestinian insurgents. The film also reveals brief images of an Arab American reporter, Claire (Joanne Whalley-Kilmer). When Claire meets with the SEAL leader, Hawkins (Charlie Sheen), he barks, "Beirut [is a] shithole filled with ragheads." Claire allows the slur to stand. Claire sympathizes with the enemy. She knows where the lead terrorist, Shaheed, and his Palestinians are hiding out, but she refuses to help the SEALs track the terrorists. To justify her behavior, Claire declares, "I'm a journalist." Only after she watches a report on gun-toting "Algerians" shooting up a civilian jet does Claire grudgingly agree to assist the SEALs. Instead of having an Arab American journalist refuse to help her country track down terrorists, the producers should have featured a patriotic reporter, someone like *Newsweek* columnist Lorraine Ali, eagerly assisting the SEALs.

Ever since the Spencer Tracy/Elizabeth Taylor *Father of the Bride* debuted in 1950, each and every *Bride* movie has successfully projected a wholesome and universal theme—loving fathers being overly concerned about losing their "little girls." These same fathers also fret that outrageous price tags for simple weddings will bankrupt them. Never had a *Father of the Bride* movie strayed off course and injected shady manipulators until Disney's *Father of the Bride Part II* (1995). Set in Los Angeles, this family film depicts, among its minor characters, the rich and miserly Mr. Habib (Eugene Levy), who speaks broken English with a thick Arab accent. When Habib's wife tries to speak—she appears for only seconds—her husband becomes furious. Mr. Habib shouts gibberish at her, a mix of Farsi and Arabic. Instantly, Mrs. Habib heels, reinforcing the stereotype of the Arab woman as a subservient nonentity. Throughout *Bride II* Mr. Habib functions as an unkempt swindler. He purchases a neat house from the protagonists, the Banks family. The sentimental Mr. Banks, however, decides he wants his house back. The next day he offers Habib a $50,000 bonus—not bad for a day's profit. Yet, Habib demands even more cash. Only after Banks offers Habib a $100,000 bonus does the covetous crook sell the home back to its "rightful owner."

Another Disney family film, *Kazaam* (1996), projects Arab Americans as gluttonous, greedy gangsters; they speak with guttural accents, have a penchant for blondes, and are intent on acquiring "all the money in the world." The antagonist is Malik (Marshal Manesh), a black marketeer engaged in "pirating tapes and CD's." The camera shows Malik voraciously devouring "goat's eyes" as a pig swallows dung. Malik and his two scruffy henchmen, Hassem and El-Baz, are 100 percent evil; these Arab Americans not only exploit the good genie (Shaquille O' Neal), but they also trounce a teenager's father then toss the boy down an elevator shaft. Fortunately, the genie restores the fatally injured teen to life. In Disney's close, the genie transforms the Arab American into a bouncing ball, tossing him into a trash bin. Audiences frequently howl at this scene.

The movies *Mother* (1996) and *Kingpin* (1996) advance myths that Americans of Arab descent speak with funny accents. *Kingpin* presents, briefly, Sayed, a gas station mechanic called "Fatima." *Mother* displays two unpleasant TV installers, one of whom (Richard Assad) is a dimwit who does not understand English and speaks with a thick Arab accent. When the homeowner asks whether he is married, he chuckles, "Hee, hee, hee." When she asks whether the TV picture is too green, he grins, and says, "Yes, thank you." His colleague, who is all business, screams at his coworker in Arabic, slaps him hard on the shoulder, calls him a *majnoon* (idiot), and then shows him the door. Asks the homeowner, "What's wrong with him?" Quips the installer, "He's mentally ill, ma'am." These bits of "humor" give rise to several questions: why insert and paint Arab Americans as dumb and disagreeable? Why mock their ethnicity? Why not display them like the film's other "regular" characters?

Notably absent are Arab American women. Films such as *Baby Boom* (1987), *Navy SEALs* (1990), and *Father of the Bride Part II* (1995) offer fleeting and derogative portraits. *Escape from L.A.* (1996) features, albeit briefly, a bright, attractive Arab American Muslim woman, Tasmila (Valerie Golina), as a casualty. After the U.S. government has initiated an undemocratic profiling policy, officials decide that Tasmila and other law-biding Americans are "undesirable and unfit to live in moral America." They are removed from their homes and shipped off to "Los Angeles Island." On the island, Tasmila befriends and then guides the movie's protagonist (Kurt Russell) to a safe place. The protagonist fails to understand how the government could classify a decent and intelligent woman like Tasmila as an "undesirable." He asks, "Why are you here?" Sighs Tasmila, "I was a Muslim in South Dakota. All of a sudden they made it a crime." Suddenly, she is shot dead. Credit goes to producer-director John Carpenter for revealing how unjust profiling damages innocents.

Movies of the 1980s, such as *Wanted Dead or Alive* and *Terror in Beverly Hills,* featured Arab Americans murdering residents of Los Angeles. Fast forward to 1998. This time around, auto mechanics, university students, and a Brooklyn College professor of "Arab Studies" link up with Arab Muslim fanatics in *The Siege* (1998) and kill more than seven hundred New Yorkers. The extremists blow up FBI agents, blast theatergoers, bomb a crowded bus, and try to murder schoolchildren. Writes film critic Roger Ebert, "The prejudicial attitudes embodied in the film are insidious, like the anti-Semitism that infected fiction and journalism in the 1930s—not just in Germany but in Britain and America. . . . There's a tendency to lump together 'towelheads' (a term used in the movie)," he notes. "Given how vulnerable Arab Americans are to defamation, was this movie really necessary?" (Shaheen, 430)

Denzel Washington portrays the FBI agent responsible for eradicating terrorists in *The Siege.* His sidekick is an Arab American agent, played by Tony Shalhoub. Shalhoub does a fine job portraying a "good" Arab American. But one minor supporting actor does not compensate for the movie's numerous Arab stereotypes. The Arab American's character brings to mind producers trying to justify their pervasive, hostile depictions of Native Americans. Hollywood protestations notwithstanding and "Indian sympathy films" taken into account, it is still true that the savage image of Native Americans has not been counterbalanced. What if *The Siege* had projected Irish or Jewish Americans as undesirables? What if, writes *Washington Post* reporter Sharon Waxman, "A nefarious rabbi exhorts his extremist ultra-Orthodox followers to plant bombs against Arab sympathizers in America. Innocents are killed and maimed." Would not "such a provocative narrow-minded scenario suggesting every Jew was a terrorist . . . spark protests from Jews? Would Hollywood choose to portray them in the first place?"

Given the false lesson fiction films teach us about Americans of Arab heritage, it is not surprising that many Americans believe that real Arab Americans are the same as those reel bad Arabs. Note this November 6, 1998, conversation between *Today* host Matt Lauer and actor Denzel Washington about *The Siege.* Lauer told Washington, "You're getting some heat from Arab groups"—not "Arab Americans." Instead of correcting Lauer's mistake, Washington concurred, quipping, "[In] certain countries they wouldn't even be allowed to do that!" By declaring "they" and "certain countries," Washington linked real Arab Americans with *The Siege*'s villainous movie Arabs. If media-savvy Lauer and Washington cannot differentiate between our nation's Americans of Arab heritage and Hollywood's reel Arabs, how many moviegoers are making the same mistake?

Three turn-of-the-century movies not demeaning Arab Americans are *A Perfect Murder* (1998), *The Kitchen* (2001), and *Enough* (2002). They present Americans of Arab descent as everyday, neighborly Americans. The set-in-Manhattan *Murder,* a remake of the 1954 thriller *Dial M for Murder,* features in a supporting role a bright and soft-spoken bilingual detective, Mohamed "Mo" Karaman (David Suchet). Mo befriends and speaks Arabic with the heroine, Emily (Gwyneth Paltrow). When Emily's husband tries to murder her, Emily protects herself, killing him. Instead of arresting Emily, Mo comes to her defense, saying, "*Allah ma cum*" (God be with you). Emily replies, "And with you as well." Emily's response solidifies her trust and faith in the Arab American.

Andre Degas's *The Kitchen* (2001), an independent film telecast only a few times in New York and San Francisco, is the only American motion picture to display an Arab American male lead character. The movie focuses on the relationship of two regular New Yorkers—a shopkeeper named Farid (Mark Margolis) and his son Jamal (Jason Raize). The Arab Americans function as an integral part of America's rainbow. Their roots become apparent only when words like *babaganoush* (eggplant) are spoken, or when the camera cuts to "Ali Baba's," the store's neon sign, or when Farid tells Jamal, "I will get you an Egyptian girl" to marry. Though most films allow slurs against Arabs to remain, when the antagonist in *The Kitchen* spews out slurs such as "camel jockeys," they are contested.

The Jennifer Lopez film *Enough* (2002) is the first feature following the September 11 tragedy to display an Arab American character. In lieu of advancing stereotypes, screenwriter Nicholas Kazan and director Michael Apted present fresh images. Credit them for portraying Phil (Christopher Maher), an Arab American restaurateur, as a heroic father figure. When Phil finds out that his former waitress Slim (Lopez) is trapped inside her own house and being viciously beaten by Mitch, her husband, he moves to save her. Acting as Slim's "surrogate father . . . who really loves her," Phil and his friends crash into the house. Wielding a baseball bat, Phil charges Mitch, then runs away with the injured Slim and her baby girl. Next, Phil pays for their plane fare, dispatching them to Michigan. On arrival, Phil's Arab American friends warmly greet Slim and her daughter, then guide them to a safe place—proving the humanity of the real American Arab community.

The Cultural Other

Fourteen of the twenty movies discussed here do not present Americans of Arab descent as they should—as neighbors, friends, classmates, and coworkers. Instead, the industry has misrepresented and maligned them. Yet openness to change is an American tradition. Not so many years ago filmmakers projected other ethnic Americans—Asians, Blacks, Italians, Jews, and Latinos—as the cultural Other. No longer. Aware that these heinous stereotypes injure innocents, these Americans and others formed pressure groups and acted aggressively against discriminatory portraits. Minorities also became a key part of the industry's creative work force, functioning as executives, producers, writers, and directors.

Not many Arab Americans are involved in the film industry; not one is a famous Hollywood mogul. And Arab Americans have been slow to mobilize, although the depiction of Arab Americans as born terrorists in the Arnold Schwarzenegger vehicle *True Lies* (1994) did stir widespread, vocal criticism that shows the possibilities of organized resistance to ethnic profiling. Mainstream movies such as *A Perfect Murder* and *Enough* show that inclusion of Arab American characters is profitable and possible. These films suggest that Hollywood is beginning to address hurtful stereotypes, and that some producers are projecting Americans of Arab descent as regular folk. As for the future, when Americans of Arab heritage become an integral part of the industry, when they begin forming lobbying groups in Los Angeles, and when producers display them in family films on a par with *I Remember Mama* (1948) and *My Big Fat Greek Wedding* (2002), perhaps moviegoers will finally begin to view them honestly—as true Americans.

References

Filmography

Anna Ascends (1922, F)
Baby Boom (1987, F)
Cheech and Chong's Next Movie (1980, F)
Enough (2002, F)
Escape from L.A. (1996, F)
Father of the Bride Part II (1995, F)
Kazaam (1996, F)
Kingpin (1996, F)
The Kitchen (2001, F)
Mother (1996, F)
Navy SEALs (1990, F)
The Next Man (1976, F)
A Perfect Murder (1998, F)
Quick Change (1990, F)
The Siege (1998, F)
Terror in Beverly Hills (1988, F)
True Lies (1994, F)
Wanted Dead or Alive (1987, F)
Wild Geese II (1985, F)
Wrong Is Right (1982, F)

Bibliography

Abraham, Nabeel, and Sameer Abraham, eds. *Arabs in the New World.* Detroit: Wayne State University Press, 1983.

Dacus, J. A. *A Tour of St. Louis.* St. Louis: Western, 1878.

Kasem, Casey, "I Want My Son to Be Proud." *Parade,* 16 January 1994.

Naff, Alexia. *The Arab Americans.* New York: Chelsea House, 1988.

Pannbacker, Alfred Ray. *The Levantine Arabs of Pittsburgh, Pennsylvania.* Ann Arbor: University Microfilms International, 1981.

Rollins, Peter C., ed. *Hollywood as Historian: American Film in a Cultural Context.* 2d ed. Lexington: University Press of Kentucky, 1998.

Saeed, Ahmed. "Overcoming the Stereotypes." *Atlanta Journal-Constitution,* 4 October 2001.

Shaheen, Jack. *Reel Bad Arabs: How Hollywood Vilifies a People.* Northampton, MA: Interlink, 2001.

[TERRY HONG]

Asian Americans

In 1587 the Spanish galleon *Nuestra Senora de Esperanza* (Our Lady of Hope) landed in California, bringing Filipino crewmembers who acted as scouts for the landing party. Almost two centuries later, in the mid-1700s—well before the signing of the U.S. Declaration of Independence—other Filipino sailors, escaping the brutal conditions of conscripted labor on Spanish ships, arrived on the shores of Louisiana, where they founded coastal fishing villages. They were the first Asians known to have come to North America and stayed.

In the next century, Chinese laborers arrived in California, marking the first large-scale wave of Asian immigration. Although the common belief is that these immigrants came to "Gold Mountain" (in Mandarin Chinese, *gum san*) to escape the hardships in their home country and take advantage of the potential wealth found in a land where the streets were rumored to be paved with gold, the more accurate explanation of the origins of Chinese immigration is mutual economic need between two countries.

With the end of legal slavery throughout the United States, the growing labor needs of a burgeoning nation—especially the West Coast, where there was no legacy of African American enslavement—turned to other "colored" workers for manpower. Chinese laborers, along with smaller populations of South Asian, Japanese, and later Korean laborers, provided muscle to build the transcontinental railroad, develop the agricultural industry (including revolutionary irrigation systems), and work in newly established factories and canneries. They were paid a fraction of what their white counterparts received then heavily taxed on what little they earned. Excluded from other forms of employment, they opened businesses such as "Chinese laundries," often providing services that their white neighbors disdained to do.

The influx of these Asian laborers led to racial tension, for many white Americans saw these immigrants as a threat to their jobs and their security. The "yellow peril" had to be contained, lest American—read white—rule be challenged. Such racially motivated prejudice and fears against Asians led to the 1882 Chinese Exclusion Act, which banned the immigration of Chinese laborers to the United States. It was the first—although unfortunately not the last—institutionalized racist law to single out Asians in America.

Even birth on American soil did not guarantee U.S. citizenship, even though the Fourteenth Amendment asserted that right. Not until 1898, when California-born Wong Kim Ark challenged the Supreme Court, did American-born Asians irrefutably earn the right to citizenship.

In 1904, Congress amended the 1882 law to exclude immigrants from the Philippines, Guam, Samoa, and even Hawaii. In 1907, the so-called Gentlemen's Agreement put an end to Japanese labor immigration. The Immigration Act of 1917, also known as the Barred Zone Act, established a zone of countries that excluded most of Asia, as well as parts of Russia, the Middle East, and Afghanistan. In 1922, the Cable Act stripped American women of their citizenship if they married "aliens ineligible for naturalization," meaning Asians. In 1922 as well, the

Japanese-born Takao Ozawa was denied naturalization, in accordance with the 1790 Naturalization Act, which allowed only "free White persons" to become U.S. citizens. In 1923, citing that he was biologically Caucasian and therefore white, Bhagat Singh Thind applied for naturalization, but the *U.S. vs. Bhagat Singh Thind* decision officially barred Asian Indians as well from citizenship.

By 1924, the National Origins Act effectively ended all Asian immigration, except from the Philippines, which was by then a U.S. territory. But that, too, came to a virtual end with the 1934 Tydings-McDuffie Act, which promised independence in ten years but limited Filipino immigration to a mere fifty individuals a year.

Less than ten years later, on February 19, 1942, Franklin D. Roosevelt signed Executive Order 9066, sending 120,000 Americans of Japanese descent into concentration camps for the duration of World War II. Ironically, the 442d Regimental Combat Team, predominantly made up of second-generation Japanese Americans and led by a Korean American, Colonel Young Oak Kim, became the most decorated military unit in U.S. history.

For Asian-born American residents, moreover, the 1790 Naturalization Act remained in effect until 1952, in essence relegating Asian Americans to foreigner status for almost two centuries following the American Revolution, a war fought for and by immigrants to the then-new world.

Not until 1965, with the Immigration and Nationality Act, were anti-Asian immigration laws finally lifted. The result was drastic: from less than 1 percent of the U.S. population in 1970, Asian Americans made up 4 percent of the population in 2000. Today, Asian Americans are the nation's fastest-growing minority population after Hispanics. But even with a history older than the nation, Asian Americans are, for the most part, still perceived as foreign, as "other," and continue to face racism that runs the spectrum from blatant exotification to complete ostracism.

Asian Americans in Film

Just as Asian Americans are a part of American history from the beginning, so, too, are Asian Americans participants in American film history literally since its inception. In 1899, when Thomas Alva Edison began making the very first films with his newly invented Kinetograph, among his simple attempts were at least four films dramatizing the Philippines campaign of 1899, when the United States acquired the Philippine Islands at the end of the Spanish-American War. (The films can be viewed at http://memory.loc.gov/ammem/edhtml/edre.html.) Shot in New Jersey, the reenactments show the American army subduing the cowardly, weak Filipinos. That depiction of the great white man conquering the yellow enemy in effect laid the foundation for the representation of Asians and Asian Americans for over a century of American celluloid history. As the U.S. government sought to control Asian Americans through exclusionary and racist laws, Hollywood, too, attempted to control the Asian American image on film.

Despite anti-Asian sentiment, three Asian American actors managed to establish longstanding careers during the twentieth century: Sessue Hayakawa (1890–1973), a Japanese-born American who became a silent film actor and was later nominated for an Academy Award in 1957 for *The Bridge on the River Kwai*; Philip Ahn (1905–1978), the son of Korean patriot Ahn Chang Ho, who was the first U.S.-born Korean American; and the legendary Anna May Wong (1905–1961), who was Asian America's first internationally recognized actor.

In spite of their unmistakable talents, all three could not escape the trap of Hollywood's stereotypes. Hayakawa's first great success was in Cecil B. De Mille's *The Cheat* (1915), in which he played a villain who victimized a wealthy white woman. Variations of the dark, evil, plotting villain would be Hayakawa's signature role throughout his career. Ahn was originally rejected for his first major role in

Anything Goes (1934) because, as a native-born American, his English was too good for the part. Only when he mimicked an artificial Asian accent did he get the role. Wong's frustration over being cast in limiting roles such as a sacrificial Lotus Blossom in *Toll of the Sea* (1922), a slave girl in *The Thief of Baghdad* (1924), the ultimate dragon lady in *Daughter of the Dragon* (1931), and a prostitute in *Shanghai Express* (1932), in addition to her defeat over not getting the lead in the film version of Pearl S. Buck's *The Good Earth* (1937), led her to leave Hollywood for international travel and performance. She returned in the 1950s to a television series, *The Gallery of Madame Liu-Tsong,* but it lasted only a few weeks.

Overall, anti-Asian sentiment persisted in the United States in various forms throughout most of the twentieth century and was well reflected on the silver screen. As white America had first perceived the immigrant laborers—the fear of yellow peril—Hollywood's Asian characters, too, were cunning, evil, and untrustworthy. These Asian roles were not even played by actors of Asian descent but by white actors in hideous yellowface, complete with plastic prosthetics and overdone makeup. The Swedish-born Walter Oland spent the majority of his career as the evil-incarnate Fu Manchu in such films as *The Mysterious Fu Manchu* (1929) and as the faux-Chinese detective Charlie Chan in such films as *Charlie Chan Carries On* (1931). Similarly, Myrna Loy was often cast as an exotic Asian woman (e.g., *Mask of Fu Manchu,* 1933), whose dark sensuality threatened white America. Of course, in the end, the honesty and purity of the white American hero could not be overcome, and all yellow evil was vanquished.

In addition to anti-immigration laws, antimiscegenation laws emerged to fuel yellowface on film, and with them, new stereotypes emerged in the 1930s and beyond. With interracial marriage now illegal, Hollywood's Motion Picture Industry Code prohibited any scenes suggesting miscegenation as desirable. Leading white actresses with faces altered by cosmetic tape, rather than Asian American actresses, were chosen for major Asian roles. By casting such actresses as Luise Rainer in *The Good Earth* (1937), Katharine Hepburn in *Dragon Seed* (1944), and Shirley MacLaine in *My Geisha* (1962), Hollywood redefined the notion of Asian beauty. To be a beautiful Asian meant having more Caucasian features. On the other hand, famous Hollywood men continued to don yellowface as well, although their portrayals of Asian men were hardly complimentary: see, for example, John Wayne as the war-crazed Genghis Khan in *The Conqueror* (1956); Marlon Brando as the sneaky, backstabbing Japanese interpreter in *Teahouse of the August Moon* (1956); Ricardo Montalban as the sexless dancing eunuch in *Sayonara* (1957); and Mickey Rooney as the squinty-eyed, buck-toothed Japanese landlord in *Breakfast at Tiffany's* (1961)—whose hideous caricature has recently resurfaced as Icebox.com's objectionable Mr. Wong.

As late as 1995, *The Complete Make-Up Artist,* by Penny Delamar, explained how to do "Caucasian to oriental" and "Caucasian to Indian," complete with illustrations of a young blonde woman transformed to resemble Fu Manchu, still one of Hollywood's favorite fake Asians. Yellowface also received international attention in the 1990s when non-Asian actor Jonathan Pryce was cast as a Eurasian engineer in *Miss Saigon,* a theatrical spectacle whose producers insisted that no Asian American actors talented enough could be found to play the London-originated role on Broadway. Even more recently, the character of Miss Swan on Fox's *Mad TV* has come under attack for non-Asian actor Alex Borstein's recurring portrayal of an English-challenged nail-salon owner in heavy Asian-like makeup. Despite adamant claims that the character is not of Asian origin, that she originally appeared in the first sketch as the unmistakably Asian-sounding Miss Kwan makes denials suspect.

Indeed, yellowface is, most unfortunately, alive and well.

Beyond Yellowface and the Birth of New Stereotypes

In addition to the use of yellowface, Hollywood continued to control the celluloid image of Asian America through new, insidious stereotypes. Beyond the yellow peril of the first Asian American immigrants, world events began to further shape depictions of Asians and Asian Americans in film.

With Japan's expansion into Korea at the turn of the century and into China in the 1930s came new fears of Asian domination. Now under siege, the Chinese were more favorably depicted in Hollywood. Suddenly they were the "good Asian," being threatened by the "bad Asian"—the Japanese. The Chinese suffered most nobly as worthy peasants in *The Good Earth* (1937). Anna May Wong was twice the loyal Chinese ally plotting against the Japanese enemy in *Bombs over Burma* (1942) and *Lady from Chungking* (1943). Anthony Quinn played a Chinese guerilla fighting the Japanese in *China Sky* (1945), while Chinese children helped save American pilots in *China's Little Devils* (1945). With Japan's bombing of Pearl Harbor in 1941, the vilification of the Japanese intensified. The Asian face in American film was associated with the cruel, non–English speaking caricature of the demonized Japanese soldier, as in films like *The Purple Heart* (1944), *Back to Bataan* (1945), and *First Yank in Tokyo* (1945).

When World War II ended, leaving Japan in utter devastation, Hollywood abandoned its version of the evil Japanese and reinstated the Chinese into the "bad Asian" slot just in time for the Red Scare of early 1950s McCarthyism. *Flash Gordon,* which debuted as a film in 1936 with evil Ming the Merciless, emperor of futuristic Mongo—Mongolia? as in China?—returned in 1952 as a full-blown television series. *Shanghai Story* (1954) had evil Red Chinese trapping innocent Americans. Furthermore, in a complete turnaround from less than ten years earlier, *The House of Bamboo* (1955) found the Japanese working together with the Americans, even falling in love with them in *Three Stripes in the Sun* (1955). In 1955 as well, John Sturges's *Bad Day at Black Rock,* starring Spencer Tracy, addressed anti-Japanese racism and internment of the war years. What a difference a decade made.

With the 1947 amendment to the 1945 War Brides Act, which granted U.S. entry for the Asian wives and children of U.S. military, Hollywood discovered the box-office potential of the love affair between the white male and the Asian female, as witnessed by the success of *Love Is a Many-Splendored Thing* (1955), in which William Holden made his Asiaphile debut, falling for a Eurasian doctor played by Jennifer Jones. That Eurasian angle was key, as it was deemed permissible for non-Asian actresses in yellowface to be swept away by the conquering white hero—but not permissible for the truly Asian women to be so desired, much less conquered.

Hollywood exploited the demand for the interracial relationship, marked by the larger-than-life debut of the geisha in such films as *Teahouse of the August Moon* (1956) and *Sayonara* (1957)—she was beautiful and subservient, a lotus blossom ready to please. Then came *The World of Suzie Wong* (1960), in which William Holden returned to fall in love with Nancy Kwan, herself a Eurasian actress—in this case, Kwan was just Asian enough and yet not Asian enough to pose any sort of threat. Suzie Wong became the ultimate Hollywood-created Asian woman, a prostitute with a heart of gold, ever ready to offer pleasure to the white man who could pay the highest price. She was a sexual dynamo, more mysterious, sultrier, more desirable than her earlier incarnations. She remains, unfortunately, one of the most pernicious stereotypes today.

Fast forward to the mid-1960s, when exclusionary immigration laws were finally lifted to allow for large numbers of Asians to enter the

United States and anti-miscegenation laws were abolished nationwide with *Loving vs. Virginia* in 1967. The decade ended with the civil rights movement, when Orientals became Asian Americans. Finally, despite various backgrounds, cultures, and experiences, Asian Americans began to find a united, organizing voice. With greater numbers came better representation. In a few surprising instances, the Asian man got the Asian girl, as in *Walk Like a Dragon* (1960), when James Shigeta won Nobu McCarthy from Jack Lord, or in *Bridge to the Sun* (1961) when James Shigeta even got the white girl Carroll Baker. Also in 1961, *Flower Drum Song,* based on the 1958 Rodgers and Hammerstein Broadway musical about life in San Francisco's Chinatown, became the first Hollywood film with an almost-all Asian cast. *Song* was not without controversy: detractors hated it for creating a whitewashed version of Chinatown filled with misconceptions and stereotypes, while supporters adored it because it was the first time stage and screen featured Asian-looking faces.

The 1970s saw the meteoric rise of Bruce Lee, who ironically had to abandon the United States (he was born in San Francisco) to create the ultimate Hollywood fighting machine. After enduring growing racism in Hollywood, Lee finally left for Hong Kong in disgust after David Carradine was cast in *Kung Fu*—yellowface never dies—as the wandering monk character that Lee originally created for himself. Lee's legacy—stereotypes and all—remains timeless with Dragon-wannabes.

Throughout the 1980s and 1990s, Hollywood continued to churn out new variations of old stereotypes. One of the worst offenders was *Year of the Dragon* (1985), complete with a Connie Chung–like reporter who must be tamed, then dominated by the white man who is busy fighting the evil Chinese mafia who have overrun New York City. The film's rampant, insulting stereotypical depictions of Asian Americans earned it nationwide objections and protests, and even an admission of racism two years later by its screenwriter, Oliver Stone, in *American Film* magazine: "I got the rap of racism . . . the complaints were certainly legitimate about *Dragon.*" Additionally, even well-intentioned films ostensibly about Asian or the Asian American experience did not have Asian American lead roles. While one might argue that yellowfacing is no longer rampant, the audience must still question why Asian Americans are still subordinated even in their own stories: *The Killing Fields* (1984), about the horrors in Cambodia during the Khmer Revolution in which Haing S. Ngor played a supporting role to Sam Waterston and John Malkovich, or *Seven Years in Tibet* (1997) in which Brad Pitt was surrounded by extras in their own country, or *The Lost Empire* (2001), in which a white businessman was the vehicle to tell the tale of the legendary (and Chinese) Monkey King. Perhaps the worst offender of all was Hollywood's version of the Japanese internment, *Come See the Paradise* (1990), starring Dennis Quaid as the white husband of the imprisoned Tamlyn Tomita.

Good intentions aside, other films continued to find commercial success by furthering new stereotypes. *The Karate Kid* series, which began in 1983, was one of many titles featuring the wise Asian sage with mystical powers rooted in martial arts. *Sixteen Candles* (1984) introduced audiences to the sexless Asian geek. The Asian/Japanese work ethic was lampooned in *Gung Ho* (1986). The Japanese became the ultimate mobsters in *Black Rain* (1989). The Japanese businessman was vilified in *Rising Sun* (1993). The stingy Korean shopkeeper got his due in *Falling Down* (1993). Unfortunately, the list goes on.

Asian American Filmmaking

In reaction to Hollywood's many irresponsible depictions, Asian American filmmakers continue to reclaim the Asian American image. Three organizations have been essential in that effort, beginning with Visual Communications (VC), founded in 1970 in Los Angeles as a community organization promoting media arts by and about Asian Americans. Asian CineVue (ACV) followed six years later in New York, supporting the production and exhibition of Asian American media, including the founding of the Asian American International Film Festival which today is the longest-running Asian American film festival in the country. In San Francisco, the National Asian American Telecommunications Association (NAATA) was established in 1980 to fund, produce, and distribute films that encompass the diversity of Asian America. NAATA also sponsors the annual San Francisco International Asian American Film Festival. Film festivals, especially Asian American–specific film festivals, proved to be a remarkable venue for reaching inquisitive, growing audiences. In recent years, Asian- and Asian American–centered festivals have sprouted in cities throughout the country, including Honolulu, Seattle, Los Angeles, San Diego, Washington, Chicago, and Dallas. Furthermore, the watchdog group Media Action Network for Asian Americans (MANAA) was founded in 1992 to monitor portrayals of Asian Americans in the media so that damaging stereotypes do not go unnoticed and unprotested by the public.

The advent of these media-specific organizations marked a major milestone in Asian Americans in film. In addition to media organizations, Asian American actors proved to be some of the most effective advocates for more accurate Asian American representation. Walking a fine line between not perpetuating stereotypes and the artistic and economic need to work, the post–World War II generation of Asian American actors, among them Mako, Soon-Tek Oh, Sab Shimono, James Shigeta, James Hong, Wood Moy, Nobu McCarthy, and Beulah Quo, gave voice to the fight against demeaning roles. In more recent years, distinctive actors such as Kelvin Han Yee, Lane Nishikawa, John Lone, Amy Hill, Jodi Long, Joan Chen, Dennis Dun, and Rosalind Chao remained committed to the fight. Together, they helped reclaim the Asian American image.

One of those initial reclamations was Duane Kubo and Robert A. Nakamura's first all–Asian American full-length film, *Hito Hata: Raise the Banner* (1980), which captured the contributions and hardships of Japanese Americans since the early 1900s through the life of an immigrant Japanese laborer, Oda, played by the veteran actor/director Mako. The film opens with a wizened Oda and his elderly friends—all men without families kept single by the long-lasting exclusionary immigration laws—who are out in Little Tokyo celebrating Nisei Week. Through flashbacks, the film traces Oda's experiences from a Southern Pacific railroad worker to his experiences as a community organizer struggling to keep developers from destroying the affordable residential hotels that are home to a generation of elderly single Japanese American men. From a young disadvantaged immigrant to an old man fighting for his rights, the character Oda bore absolutely no resemblance to the fake, Hollywood-created Asians and Asian Americans.

One year later came Wayne Wang's debut, *Chan Is Missing,* about a Chinese American cabbie and his nephew's search for a friend who has gone missing with $4,000 of their savings. On the surface, *Chan* is a clever detective story without an easy ending. But starting with the film's title—an obvious reference to the fake Charlie Chans populating the screens, including Peter Ustinov in the title role of *Charlie Chan and Curse of the Dragon Queen* just one year earlier—Wang's film is also a definitive statement about Asian Americans in film. In Wang's world, Chan is truly of Chinese descent. But just as the true Chan was never found—much less seen—in Hollywood's versions, so, too, must he remain missing in Wang's version. Because Chan is missing, his Asian American friends and relatives must continue to search for him, just as Asian Americans must continue to search for fair and accurate representation in film and elsewhere.

Social politics aside, Wang made an inventive, enjoyable film—which also marked the birth of the independent Asian American film movement. *Chan Is Missing* remains one of the most widely distributed Asian American titles in film history. Wang went on to direct *Dim Sum: A Little Bit of Heart* (1984), now a classic about the relationship between an Asian American mother and daughter, and *Eat a Bowl of Tea* (1989), based on the novel by Louis Chu about a young couple in Chinatown starting their lives together. Then came *Joy Luck Club* (1993), based on Amy Tan's best-selling novel and still the only major Hollywood studio–made film specifically about a slice of the Asian American experience, featuring a stellar Asian American cast. The mother-daughter relationship, which was at the heart of the film, proved a resonating theme with all audiences, regardless of ethnic makeup. Indeed mothers and daughters have intricate, complicated relationships in any culture, and in *Joy Luck Club,* those mothers and daughters happened to be Asian American. Given its universal theme, the film was a bona fide hit—and remains the only Asian American–themed film, made by and with Asian Americans, from a major Hollywood studio.

In addition, documentary filmmaking by Asian Americans grew especially quickly with great strength, led by such seminal works as *Unfinished Business* (1985) by Steven Okazaki and *Who Killed Vincent Chin?* (1988) by Christine Choy and Renee Tajima-Peña. Stories of immigration, internment, isolation and separation, family history, and first-person narratives emerged and multiplied. Gone were the stereotypes: Asian Americans told their Asian American stories in earnest, with Asian American themes and subjects played out by Asian American actors. Asian American filmmakers continued to fracture and break out of Hollywood's suffocating molds while winning Hollywood's accolades including several Academy Awards: Steven Okazaki for *Days of Waiting* in 1990, Frieda Lee Mock for *Maya Lin: A Strong Clear Vision* in 1994, Jessica Yu for *Breathing Lessons* in 1996, Chris Tashima for *Visas and Virtue* in 1997, and Keiko Ibi for *The Personals: Improvisations on Romance in the Golden Years* in 1998.

Asian American filmmakers also found success with a hybrid form that was part history and part feature film. One of the most successful titles is Kayo Hatta's *Picture Bride* (1995), which introduced the picture-bride phenomenon to mainstream audiences. Between 1908 and 1924, more than twenty thousand Asian women arrived in Hawaii to marry immigrant plantation workers, sight unseen, with the exception of a single, often aged photograph sent by the bridegroom back to the home country in hopes of a making a long-distance match. The film focuses on the relationship between young, expectant Riyo, who arrives in Hawaii in 1918 to marry weathered, hard-working Matsuji, who is twenty years older than his photograph. A beautifully rendered, tender film, *Picture Bride* follows the relationship that blossoms between the mismatched pair while offering a glimpse of immigration life in the early twentieth century.

Today, the latest feature films are just on the cusp of breakout superstardom, led by Justin Lin's *Better Luck Tomorrow,* which won international acclaim for its depiction a group of overprivileged Asian American honor students who steal, cheat, lie, and more in their free time. A major success at Sundance 2002, the film was acquired by MTV for national distribution, making Asian American film history along the way: it was not only the first Asian American film ever to be picked up at Sundance, but it also became the first film ever—regardless of ethnic background—purchased for distribution by MTV Films.

At a question-and-answer session following a Sundance screening, Lin was criticized by a film critic for making "such a bleak, negative, amoral film," referring to the film's main characters, the Ivy-bound boys gone amok. "Don't you have a responsibility to paint a more positive and helpful portrait of your community?" the critic demanded. Lin replied that he made the film he wanted to make, that what he depicted was a reality among teenagers of any ethnicity. Then came *Chicago Sun-Times* film critic Roger Ebert (he of international thumbs-up fame), to Lin's defense, later devoting a column to the Sundance incident. "You would never make a comment like that to a white filmmaker," Ebert chastised the detractor. "If Justin Lin had a responsibility to 'his community,' it was to make the best film he possibly could," Ebert wrote—which certainly earned him countless thumbs-up from many communities.

Better Luck Tomorrow owes its success, in part, to previous, smaller, no less notable films that capture Asian American life, with an emphasis on the "American." Whether coming-of-age in Los Angeles on the eve of graduation for eight teenagers in Chris Chan Lee's *Yellow* (1996); or finding unexpected connections between a lonely gay man, a quirky waitress and a distraught housewife in Quentin Lee and Justin Lin's *Shopping for Fangs* (1997); or a final-year medical student coping with the demands of his domineering mother in Francisco Aliwalas's *Disoriented* (1997); or two young men spending a last summer together before they go their separate ways in Michael Idemoto and Eric Nakamura's *Sunsets* (1997); or a straight-faced, Tony Award–winning playwright David Henry Hwang irreverently hawking porn featuring "positive images of confident Asian-American men and women" in Greg Pak's parody *Asian Porn Pride* (1999), today's Asian American films are best described as just films—that happen to be populated with Asian American characters, crafted by makers whose ethnic background is Asian American.

Moreover, with growing interest in the foreign-film market, especially films from Asia, the definition of Asian American film has blurred and grown. The commercial success of Asian directors such as Zhang Yimou (*Red Sorghum,* 1991; *Raise the Red Lantern,* 1997) and Chen Kaige (*Farewell My Concubine,* 1993), along with the luminous actress Gong Li, has created a new and viable celluloid niche. Additionally, the 1997 Hong Kong handover sent reverberations through Hollywood, as seen in the box-office success of Hong Kong director John Woo and his blockbusters *Broken Arrow* (1995), *Face/Off* (1997), *Mission: Impossible 2* (2000), and, most recently, *Windtalkers* (2002). Jackie Chan is the comic answer to the Dragon—although one still has to ask, how come he never gets the girl? The phenomenal success of in-between Asian/Asian Americans such as Asian-born, U.S.-educated, U.S.-domiciled directors Ang Lee and Mira Nair further blurs the lines of Asian American film. Regardless of definitions, the phenomenal success of Lee's *Crouching Tiger, Hidden Dragon* (2000) and Nair's *Monsoon Wedding* (2002)—that the former film won an Academy Award for best foreign film speaks volumes—can only further the efforts of Asian Americans working in film.

The latest crop of Asian American actors, too, have benefited from the Asian crossovers: the most visible, such as Tamlyn Tomita, Margaret Cho, Ming-Na Wen, Rick Yune, Russell Wong, Jason Scott Lee, John Cho, Eddie Shin, Garrett Wang, Keiko Agena, B. D. Wong, Alec Mapa, and Sandra Oh, have been joined by the likes of Chow Yun Fat, Michelle Yeoh, Bai Ling, Zhang Ziyi, and Tsui Hark, to name but a few.

Ironically, with growing exposure, the most successful Asian American directors have taken on projects that are out of the Asian American realm and are of the so-called Hollywood mainstream: Wayne Wang with *Smoke* (1995) and *Maid in Manhattan* (2003), Joan Chen with *Autumn in New York* (2002), Ang Lee with *Sense and Sensibility* (1995), *The Ice Storm* (1997), and *The Hulk* (2003). The criticism has been unnecessarily harsh. Asian American filmmakers, like any others, deserve to choose their projects. Would Steven Spielberg be attacked for not making only Jewish-centered films?

Clearly and steadily, the new generation of Asian American filmmakers, directors, producers, and actors and a growing Asian American audience are helping to dismantle Hollywood-created, Hollywood-insisted images of what it means to be Asian and Asian American. Certainly more progress needs to be made. In a Hollywood-dominated celluloid industry, Asian Americans are still facing the same challenges they did a hundred years ago—the lack of opportunity coupled with the denial of accurate representation. But lest that glass be considered half-empty, be assured: we've come a long way, baby.

References

Filmography

Ancestors in the Americas (2001, D)
Arirang: The Korean American Century (2003, D)
Asian Porn Pride (1999, F)
Better Luck Tomorrow (2002, D)
Breathing Lessons (1996, D)
Bridge to the Sun (1961, F)
Chan Is Missing (1981, F)
The Cheat (1915, F)
Days of Waiting (1990, D)
Dim Sum: A Little Bit of Heart (1984, F)
Disoriented (1997, F)
Eat a Bowl of Tea (1989, F)
First Person Plural (2000, D)
Flower Drum Song (1961, F)
The Good Earth (1937, F)
History and Memory (1991, D)
Hito Hata: Raise the Banner (1980, F)
Joy Luck Club (1993, F)
Love Is a Many-Splendored Thing (1955, F)
Maya Lin: A Strong Clear Vision (1994, D)
Mississippi Masala (1992, F)
Monsoon Wedding (2002, F)
My America (. . . or honk if you love Buddha) (1997, D)
The Personals: Improvisations on Romance in the Golden Years (1998, D)
Picture Bride (1995, F)
Sa-I-Gu: From Korean Women's Perspectives (1993, D)
Salaam Bombay! (1988, F)
Shopping for Fangs (1997, F)
Slaying the Dragon (1988, D)
Sunsets (1997, F)
Unfinished Business (1985, D)
Visas and Virtue (1997, D)
Walk Like a Dragon (1960, F)
Who Killed Vincent Chin? (1988, D)
Yellow (1996, F)

Bibliography

Eng, David. *Racial Castration: Managing Masculinity in Asian America.* Durham, NC: Duke University Press, 2001.
Feng, Peter X. *Identities in Motion: Asian American Film and Video.* Durham, NC: Duke University Press, 2002.
——. "In Search of Asian American Cinema." *Cineaste* 21.1–2 (1995): 32.
——, ed. *Screening Asian Americans.* New Brunswick, NJ: Rutgers University Press, 2002.
Garcia, Roger. *Out of the Shadows: Asians in American Cinema.* Milan: Olivares, 2001.
Hamamoto, Darrell Y., and Sandra Liu, eds. *Countervisions: Asian American Film and Criticism.* Philadelphia: Temple University Press, 2000.
Ito, Robert. "'A Certain Slant': A Brief History of Hollywood Yellowface." http://www.brightlightsfilm.com/18/18_yellow.html.
Leong, Russell, ed. *Moving the Image: Independent Asian Pacific American Media Arts.* Los Angeles: UCLA Asian American Studies Center and Visual Communications, 1991.
Marchetti, Gina. *Romance and the "Yellow Peril": Race, Sex and Discursive Strategies in Hollywood Fiction.* Berkeley: University of California Press, 1994.
Odo, Franklin. *The Columbia Documentary History of the Asian American Experience.* New York: Columbia University Press, 2002.
Takaki, Ronald. *Strangers from a Different Shore: A History of Asian Americans.* Boston: Little, Brown, 1989.
Thi Thanh Nga. "The Long March from Wong to Woo: Asians in Hollywood." *Cineaste* 21.4 (1995): 38.
Xing, Jun. *Asian American Through the Lens: History, Representations and Identity.* Walnut Creek, CA: Altamira Press, 1998.

[PETER C. HOLLORAN]

Catholic Americans

As their depiction in movies demonstrates, no other religious minority in America has been as reviled and misunderstood, and then as accepted and admired, as Catholics. The first Europeans to settle in America were Roman Catholics, but North American anti-Catholicism is so deeply rooted that very few Americans realize that Catholics predate Protestants in the New World. In part, the bitter conflict between the British in the Americas and the rival Spanish and French colonial empires may account for this lingering antipathy. The reformation of the Catholic Church in England (1530) under Henry VIII, however, led to an abiding mistrust of Roman Catholics among the English, and this attitude arrived in America with the Pilgrims and the Puritans, who were by definition anti-Anglican and anti-Catholic. The Huron tribes, allies of the French in Canada and converted by Jesuit missionaries, were another reason to fear Catholics, for they raided English and Dutch colonists in New York and New England. As a result, no group was as hated in the British colonies as the Catholics, who were often prohibited from militia service, disarmed, and forced to pay double taxes by colonial legislatures. Despite the alliance with Catholic France and the Continental Army service of the marquis de Lafayette, patriotic "No Popery" parades on Guy Fawkes Day were common in Boston, New York, and Philadelphia before and after the American Revolution. Even prudent John Adams described a Catholic service he attended in Philadelphia in 1774 as "most awful and affecting." This was America's oldest and most abiding prejudice.

Despite the anti-Catholic attitudes of the Protestant majority, Catholics made significant contributions to the colonies and the new states. They numbered only forty thousand in the new nation of four million people in 1780, most in Maryland and scattered German and Irish Catholic communities in Pennsylvania. However, Catholics became the largest denomination in the United States by 1850 as waves of French Canadian, German, and Irish immigrants added to the expanding American Catholic Church. They still encountered deeply rooted prejudice because they resisted assimilation and were suspected of loyalty to the pope, supposedly a foreign potentate. It was not until World War II that American Catholics began to be considered truly acculturated Americans. Catholics appeared on the silver screen only as immigrants or as colorful ethnic background—most often as Mexican peons, sexy señoritas, Irish policemen, Italian gangsters, or Slavic industrial workers. In the silent movie era (1893–1929), the influential director D. W. Griffith included some Catholic images and characters, and Mack Sennett, the pioneer Irish Catholic director and producer, based his Keystone Kops comedies on the ubiquitous Irish American policeman. Leading man Rudolph Valentino, an Italian Catholic, blazed across the silent silver screen, yet the first American Catholic movie actors to achieve megastar status were urban Irish tough guys like James Cagney and Spencer Tracy in the 1930s. It is significant that the popularity of movies coincided with America's rejection of Victorianism during the Jazz Age. Yet, even in Hollywood's Golden Age (1930–40), Catholics were more often than not merely exotic and appealing offbeat screen characters, strangers in the new land.

The Catholic presence in the colonial era, the Revolutionary War, and the early national period has not been explored well by Hollywood. *1492: Conquest of Paradise* (1992), a movie unsuccessful both at the box office and with movie critics, does provide a rich portrait of the First Encounter and the Columbian Exchange from a Spanish viewpoint. *The Mission* (1986), a more popular and dramatic film, offers rich images of the conflict between the Jesuit priests and the avaricious conquistadors in late-eighteenth-century Brazil. On a similar theme in North America, *Black Robe* (1991) traces Jesuit missionaries among Native American tribes in seventeenth-century Quebec.

Some Civil War movies, such as *Gone with the Wind* (1939) and *Gettysburg* (1993), acknowledge the role of Irish Catholic soldiers in the Confederate and Union armies. *The Molly Maguires* (1970) is a memorable portrait of Irish miners who unionized Pennsylvania coalminers in 1876, a year of unprecedented labor violence. Irish and German immigrants dominated the American Catholic Church until the 1880s, when immigration by French Canadians, Italians, Poles, Hungarians, and others from eastern and southern Europe expanded its ranks. The five million Italian Catholics who entered the United States between 1880 and 1925 provided filmmakers with new ethnic stereotypes, first the Sicilian street musician and fruit peddler and then, more ominously, the Mafia gangster. This wave of immigration also brought families of such future filmmakers as John Ford, Frank Capra, and Martin Scorsese.

In the 1940s Hollywood seized upon Latin Americans to add ethnic spice to hundreds of movies. Latin American actors, music, stories, and locations were convenient Catholic flavor, especially in westerns. One reason was that Latin America was the only foreign market that remained available during World War II. Pan-Americanism was popular, and the U.S. government was eager to maintain good relations during the war. Although some South American nations banned or censored Hollywood films deemed offensive—for example, RKO's *Girl of the Rio* (1932)—the Good Neighbor policy had the effect of adding Latin American Catholics to the silver screen in new and popular ways.

In the silent movie era, Ramon Novarro, a Mexican actor, had played a Latin lover (like the Rudolph Valentino icon) but Dolores del Rio and Lupe Velez both made a successful transition from silents to talkies in the 1930s. Carmen Miranda became the best-known Latin America Hollywood actress in the 1940s. All shared an aggressive sexuality American audiences found exotic and appealing. Nonetheless, Hollywood ignored Hispanic Catholics as a central topic until *West Side Story* (1961) translated William Shakespeare's *Romeo and Juliet* into a modern street ballet featuring rival New York City gangs, Puerto Rican and Anglo, in the late 1950s. *West Side Story,* though better choreography than history, reveals some disturbing trends in New York City social history, including ethnic prejudice, poverty, street crime, adolescent turmoil, and the challenge of multiculturalism in modern society. Catholic immigrants from Cuba more recently contributed to the American ethnic salad bowl, providing new exotic topics Hollywood exploited in films such as Brian De Palma's Miami gangster movie *Scarface* (1983) and Mira Nair's romantic comedy about refugees in Miami, *The Perez Family* (1995). The dramatic film *Romero* (1988) depicted the life of Bishop Oscar Romero, a Salvadoran cleric and human rights leader whose assassination fueled dissent among Americans unhappy with the Reagan administration's dictatorship-friendly policies in Central America.

By 2001, Catholics numbered more than one-fourth of the U.S. population and had become integrated into the American mainstream. The Irish and Italian gangsters were, of course, Catholics, giving movies an opportunity to depict exotic Roman rites in baptism, marriage, confession, wake, and funeral scenes, not to mention the caste of celibate priests and nuns. In the post–World War II age of affluence, conformity, and consensus, Catholicism was no longer a hostile worldview; indeed, secularism and pluralism replaced interfaith rivalry for people of all faiths. The election of John F. Kennedy in 1960 encouraged Catholics to abandon their defensive stance and quieted the echoes of anti-Catholic bigotry.

In the 1930s, the first prominent Catholic filmmaker, John Ford, produced films that were documents of Catholic culture. The tough Ford, son of Irish immigrants, was born in Portland, Maine, and was a pious Catholic all his life. From *The Informer* (1935) to *Mary of Scotland* (1936) or *The Fugitive* (1947), John Ford argued that Catholic spiritual values—loyalty to one's faith, obedience to lawful authority, charity, and humility—were superior to material goals. In *The Quiet Man* (1952), Sean Thornton (John Wayne) returns from a career in America as a soldier and boxer, eager to reenter the simple Irish village of his father—a yearning shown not only in his participation in Catholic parish church services, but also in the rituals and mores of a traditional culture (Gallagher, 1986).

In his westerns, Ford evokes a sense of time, place, and Catholic people in the multicultural American frontier. His silent movie *The Iron Horse* (1924) documented the important role the Irish played in taming the Western frontier. In *Rio Grande* (1950), the goodhearted Irish Sergeant Quincannon (Victor McLaglen) comically genuflects when the Indians attack a Mexican Catholic Church. Two other films in John Ford's trilogy honoring the U.S. Cavalry, *Fort Apache* (1948) and *She Wore a Yellow Ribbon* (1949), accurately feature Irish Catholic soldiers taming the Western frontier in the name of a WASP empire. Irish or Irish Americans composed as much as one-third of the post–Civil War army. In each of these films Ford links the outsider status of Catholics to the doomed Native Americans.

American Catholics played a crucial role in World War I, as depicted heroically in *The Fighting 69th* (1940), *Fighting Father Dunne* (1948), and *The Iron Major* (1943). But with the Roaring Twenties and the Prohibition Era (1920–33), Hollywood found more opportunities to depict Irish and Italian immigrants as gangsters and streetwise slum dwellers. Movies such as *Little Caesar* (1930), *Scarface* (1932), and *The Roaring Twenties* (1939) exploited the underworld's mostly Catholic gangsters, unfairly slighting the criminal careers of Jewish, German, and other ethnic bootleggers. The Great Depression (1929–41) saw unemployment rates reach 25 percent in many communities, and the Catholic Church's response to this social upheaval is sensitively depicted in *Entertaining Angels* (1996), the story of Dorothy Day, Peter Maurin, and the radical Catholic Workers movement. *Boys Town* (1938) earned Spencer Tracy an Academy Award for his role as Father Edward Flanagan, but—more important—it demonstrated the Church's concern with social justice and child welfare during the Depression years. Another unforgettable view of the Depression is Ford's *The Grapes of Wrath* (1940), based, according to the director, on parallels between the uprooted Okies and the Irish famine exiles. Both groups were poor, religious, landless tenant farmers forced from their homes and enduring enormous hardships. Social justice is also an important part of Catholic doctrine, and controversial leadership roles by Catholics in the American labor movement are depicted in *On the Waterfront* (1954), *The Molly Maguires* (1970), and *Hoffa* (1992).

World War II saw Catholics in the United States and abroad confronting Nazis, and it gave Hollywood another chance to portray Catholics as loyal and disproportionately brave Americans. *The Sullivans* (1944) is based on the actual story of five Irish Catholic brothers lost when their ship, the USS *Juneau,* went down off Guadalcanal. John Huston's *Heaven Knows, Mr. Allison* (1957) portrays a Catholic nun stranded on a Japanese-occupied Pacific island; she brings a very secular marine closer to spirituality. The future president John F. Kennedy had his own wartime biopic, *PT 109* (1963), an action film based on his heroism in the South Pacific and timed to help Kennedy in his second presidential campaign (Fuchs, 1967).

Hollywood studio bosses, who were often Jewish businessmen, were scrupulous about portraying the clergy in a sympathetic light. This favorable treatment is personified in Bing Crosby, who created the ultimate image of the engaging Catholic parish priest in *Going My Way* (1944) and reprised his role, with Ingrid Bergman as a parochial-school sister, in *The Bells of St. Mary's* (1945). Crosby also played a priest in *Say One for Me* (1959), as did Frank Sinatra in *The Miracle of the Bells* (1948). Pat O'Brien (in *The Fighting 69th, Fighting Father Dunne, The Fireball,* and *Angels with Dirty Faces*) and Spencer Tracy (in *San Francisco, Boys Town, The Men of Boys Town,* and *The Devil at 4 O'Clock*) were Irish American actors who wore the clerical collar in major roles. The list of other Hollywood priests includes Ward Bond, Montgomery Clift, Robert De Niro, Henry Fonda, John Huston, Van Johnson, Jack Lemmon, Karl Malden, Thomas Mitchell, Gregory Peck, Vincent Price, and Tom Tryon. In post-Vietnam Hollywood, many antireligious films attempted to depict a darker side of the Catholic Church—rigid sexual morality in *The Cardinal* (1963), satanic cultism in *The Exorcist* (1973), corruption in *True Confessions* (1981), and homophobia in *Mass Appeal* (1986)—supposedly in the name of realism.

Catholic contributions to American government are seen in Edwin O'Connor's witty political novel *The Last Hurrah* (1956), which was the basis for a highly rated film of the same name by John Ford (1958). It is a thinly veiled account of Massachusetts Governor James Michael Curley's (1874–1958) last campaign to recover the mayor's seat in Boston, capping a colorful career also depicted in the PBS documentary *Scandalous Mayor* (1998), which may be contrasted with the Chicago Irish political machine in *Daley, The Last Boss* (1995). Preston Sturges also found comedy in the urban political machine in *The Great McGinty* (1940). The contributions of Catholics to American urban law enforcement are also numerous, perhaps best depicted in *The Naked City* (1948) and more darkly in Sidney Lumet's *Serpico* (1973) and *Q & A* (1990). Elia Kazan's *On the Waterfront* (1954) features Karl Malden as a Social Gospel priest fighting to raise the moral conscience of longshoremen exploited by a corrupt labor union. These films reveal the central dilemma of American Catholics: they belong to an immigrant, minority community separated from the Protestant mainstream; they must define their own place so that they may make their own contributions to the United States in consonance with Catholic values.

Similarly, Robert Altman, a Catholic born in Kansas City and educated at Jesuit schools, uses a Catholic lens to examine tensions in American culture. In *MASH* (1970), army chaplain Father John Patrick "Dago Red" Mulcahy is ineffectual when the surgeons stage a parody of the Last Supper. Amid the death and turmoil of a "forgotten war" (1950–53), religion and the bumbling padre are powerless to redeem a fallen world. Altman seems to say that in an absurd world, only black humor can help American men and women cope. In *Quintet* (1978), Altman uses science fiction to satirize the Catholic principle of authority, and in *Nashville* (1975) contemporary southern myths and rites are negatively equated with the rituals of Catholicism. *A Wedding* (1978) appropriates Catholic dualism in a mixed marriage of the Protestant Brenner and the Catholic Corelli families. Like John Ford, Robert Altman's vision of America is pervaded by ritual, a rejection of the good vs. evil dialectic, and a preference for universalism, which is profoundly Roman Catholic. They argue that this distinctive spiritual outlook coexists uncertainly with American visions and values.

With *The Godfather* trilogy (1972, 1974, 1990) Francis Ford Coppola created one of the best recent popular epics of any film genre, based on Mario Puzo's popular novels about an Italian American organized-crime dynasty. Like Italian opera, these films are profoundly Catholic, steeped in tensions between innocence and guilt, piety and profanity. Weddings, funerals, and baptisms are opportunities to see evolving Italian Catholic life in the first half of the twentieth century. Similarly, Martin Scorsese's *Mean Streets* (1973) uses its stylized focus on crime, religion, and free enterprise to define the Italian American underworld in New York City's Little Italy. John Huston's *Prizzi's Honor* (1985) also weaves Catholic practices into his romantic Mafia spoof. More contemporary evidence of the non-Catholic fascination with the celibate Catholic clergy is *Mass Appeal* (1986), a film based on a Broadway play by Bill C. Davis. It explores the relationship of a complacent parish pastor, Father Farley (Jack Lemmon), and a zealous seminarian (Zeljke Ivanek) assigned to his affluent suburban church. Like *Lilies of the Field* (1963), *Mass Appeal* voyeuristically pries into the dim corners of a still foreign church. A more controversial view into the Catholic rectory was *The Priest* (1995), treating homosexuality, alcoholism, and adultery by priests, a far cry from Bing Crosby's *Going My Way* (1944) and as provocative as Martin Scorsese's *The Last Temptation of Christ* (1988). Clearly, Hollywood makes these films because American audiences are still curious about the arcane Roman Catholic Church.

Since the era of antebellum nativism, the Catholic nun (in convents) and sisters (in hospitals and schools), like the celibate priest, have a titillating fascination for American filmmakers and audiences. In *Lilies of the Field* (1963), an African American carpenter (Sidney Poitier) builds a chapel for German missionary sisters in Arizona. *Two Mules for Sister Sarah* (1970), a Clint Eastwood western comedy, offers few insights but exploits the whore/virgin dichotomies of a "sister" who was once a prostitute. *Agnes of God* (1985) shows a modern sister superior faced with a skeptical doctor and a secret childbirth in a Canadian convent; in the process, the film poses the issue of faith versus reason. The Whoopi Goldberg comedy *Sister Act* (1992) replays the stern sister superior cliché. Only Fred Zinnemann's *The Nun's Story* (1959) offers an empathetic view of convent and missionary life. The true experiences of a modern sister counseling Louisiana death row inmates traced in *Dead Man Walking* (1995) is a powerful docudrama. Catholic parochial education may be responsible for the irreverent comedy *Dogma* (1999), which assumes religious faith but mocks doctrinal religion. *Heaven Help Us* (1985) is another satire of Catholic education, and, like the more sober Sidney Lumet film *The Verdict* (1982), it questions how relevant Catholic morality may be in modern America.

Our comfort with such sidelong looks at the institutional church, which some believe verge on blasphemy or cross the line entirely, may be evidence that American Catholics have entered mainstream society. Once despised and shunned, American Catholics have achieved remarkable success, perhaps more success than any other immigrant group in the United States. Comparing the film record with the historical record demonstrates the long road Catholics have traveled and reveals the suspicion and scrutiny the Catholic Church has endured.

References

Filmography

Agnes of God (1985, F)
Angels with Dirty Faces (1938, F)
The Bells of St. Mary's (1945, F)
Black Robe (1991, F)
Boys Town (1938, F)
Brother Orchid (1940, F)
The Cardinal (1963, F)
Daley, the Last Boss (1995, D)
Dead Man Walking (1995, F)
The Devil at 4 O'Clock (1961, F)
Dogma (1999, F)
Entertaining Angels (1996, F)
The Exorcist (1973, F)
The Falcon and the Snowman (1985, F)
Fighting Father Dunne (1948, F)
The Fighting 69th (1940, F)
The Fireball (1950, F)
Fort Apache (1948, F)
1492: Conquest of Paradise (1992, F)
The Fugitive (1947, F)
Gettysburg (1993, F)
Girl of the Rio (1932, F)
The Godfather (1972, F)
The Godfather II (1974, F)
The Godfather Part III (1990, F)
Going My Way (1944, F)
Gone with the Wind (1939, F)
The Grapes of Wrath (1940, F)
The Great McGinty (1940, F)
Heaven Help Us (1985, F)
Heaven Knows, Mr. Allison (1957, F)
Hoffa (1992, F)
The Informer (1935, F)
The Iron Horse (1924, F)
The Iron Major (1943, F)
Jesus Christ Superstar (1973, F)
Jesus of Montreal (1989, F)
Jesus of Nazareth (1978, F)
The Last Hurrah (1958, F)
The Last Temptation of Christ (1988, F)
Lilies of the Field (1963, F)
Little Caesar (1930, F)
Mary of Scotland (1936, F)
MASH (1970, F)
Mass Appeal (1986, F)
Mean Streets (1973, F)
The Men of Boys Town (1941, F)
The Miracle of the Bells (1948, F)
The Mission (1986, F)
The Molly Maguires (1970, F)
Monsignor (1982, F)
The Naked City (1948, F)
Nashville (1975, F)
The Nun's Story (1959, F)
On the Waterfront (1954, F)
The Perez Family (1995, F)
The Priest (1995, F)
Prizzi's Honor (1985, F)
PT 109 (1963, F)
Q & A (1990, F)
The Quiet Man (1952, F)
Quintet (1978, F)
Rio Grande (1950, F)
The Roaring Twenties (1939, F)
Romero (1988, F)
San Francisco (1936, F)
Say One for Me (1959, F)
Scandalous Mayor (1998, D)
Scarface (1932, F; 1983, F)
Serpico (1973, F)
She Wore a Yellow Ribbon (1949, F)
The Sign of the Cross (1932, F)
Sister Act (1992, F)
The Sullivans (1944, F)
Three Godfathers (1948, F)
True Confessions (1981, F)
Two Mules for Sister Sarah (1970, F)
The Verdict (1982, F)
A Wedding (1978, F)
We're No Angels (1989, F)
West Side Story (1961, F)

Bibliography

Ahlstrom, Sydney E. *A Religious History of the American People.* 2 vols. Garden City, NY: Doubleday, 1975.

Black, Gregory D. *Hollywood Censored: Morality Codes, Catholics, and the Movies.* New York: Cambridge University Press, 1995.

Cogley, John. *Catholic America.* New York: Dial Press, 1973.

Doherty, Thomas. *Pre-Code Hollywood: Sex, Immorality, and Insurrection in American Cinema, 1930–1934.* New York: Columbia University Press, 1999.

Dolan, Jay P. *The American Catholic Experience: A History from Colonial Times to the Present.* Garden City, NY: Doubleday, 1985.

Friedman, Lester D. *Unspeakable Images: Ethnicity and the American Cinema.* Urbana: University of Illinois Press, 1991.

Fuchs, Lawrence H. *John F. Kennedy and American Catholicism.* New York: Meredith, 1967.

Gallagher, Tag. *John Ford: The Man and His Films.* Berkeley: University of California Press, 1986.

Gillis, Chester. *Roman Catholicism in America.* New York: Columbia University Press, 1999.

Hennesey, James J. *American Catholics: A History of the Roman Catholic Community in the United States.* New York: Oxford University Press, 1981.

Kass, Judith M. *Robert Altman: American Innovator.* New York: Popular Library, 1978.

Keyser, Les, and Barbara Keyser. *Hollywood and the Catholic Church: the Image of Roman Catholicism in American Movies.* Chicago: Loyola University Press, 1984.

Meagher, Timothy J. *Urban American Catholicism: The Culture and Identity of the American Catholic People.* New York: Garland, 1988.

Medved, Michael. *Hollywood vs. America: Popular Culture and the War on Traditional Values.* New York: HarperCollins, 1992.

O'Connor, Edwin. *The Last Hurrah.* Boston: Little, Brown, 1956.

Vizzard, Jack. *See No Evil: Life Inside a Hollywood Censor.* New York: Simon & Schuster, 1970.

Walsh, Frank. *Sin and Censorship: The Catholic Church and the Motion Picture Industry.* New Haven: Yale University Press, 1996.

[RON GREEN]

Children and Teenagers in the Twentieth Century

The twentieth century was fascinated with young people. Seen variously as victims, villains, and the hope of the future, children and teenagers in the United States have been objects of care and concern in both the popular consciousness and academic studies. No longer viewed as miniature grownups or apprentice adults, they have come to be seen—and to see themselves—as distinctive groups with their own subculture and customs. Their portrayal in films throughout the century has reflected changing perceptions and concerns in the society as a whole.

After 1900, children and teenagers increasingly became subjects of academic study. Beginning with G. Stanley Hall's 1904 pioneering work *Adolescence,* sociologists and psychologists have examined the world of the young. The widely read books of Robert Coles have intensified and popularized a long fascination with the psychology of the early stages of life and the meaning of growing up in the changing cultural climate of the developed world. Historians, too, have found much social significance in the institution of childhood. Beginning with Philippe Ariès's *Centuries of Childhood* (1960), which first postulated the "invention" of the notion of childhood as a separate and distinct life stage, the field today includes growing numbers of books, journal articles, college and university courses, and online discussion groups.

The concern for the social construction of childhood and adolescence has also inspired several scholars to examine the cinematic portrayal of the young, notably Kathy Merlock Jackson on children in films, plus David Considine and Thomas Doherty on screen adolescents. They have insightfully analyzed their subjects both as reflections of the time in which the movies were made and as influences on the behavior of youthful members of movie audiences. More recently, a 1998 journal article by Shirley R. Steinberg and Joe L. Kinchloe reviewed some of the scholarship concerning celluloid teenagers, and added provocative cultural analysis of their own.

Children and adolescents have appeared in commercial film productions from the beginning. Their changing roles throughout the twentieth century reflected a society in transition, as traditional adult authority over young people waned and youth culture grew increasingly autonomous. In their earliest appearances, young actors portrayed characters who exemplified both innocence and dependence, love objects needing adult protection and guidance. Although occasionally showing resourcefulness and an ability to help adults—what Kathy Merlock Jackson has called "fix-it" children—their screen presence represented a sentimental, adult view of childhood. Occasionally amused by youthful quirks and often nostalgic, this perspective dominated films for the first half of the century. A shift in the demographics of movie audiences and a rise in power among both children and teenagers, beginning in the 1940s and exploding in the 1950s and 1960s, created a new, more independent—and often more defiant—image.

The Silent Era: Guardians of Innocence

As early as 1903 in *The Great Train Robbery,* a child actor played a significant role. In that film, the plucky little daughter of the overpowered stationmaster revives and frees him, enabling him to raise the alarm after robbers leave him bound and unconscious. In 1908, a child played the title character of D. W. Griffith's *The Adventures of Dolly,* an innocent victim of kidnapping who survives a harrowing trip through river rapids and over a waterfall. Viewers identified with her distraught parents and her brave young rescuers more than with the happy, adorable child herself. Such a point of view typified films throughout this era. Children served alternately as resourceful helpmates or imperiled victims needing protection and rescue. This period in film history coincided with the intense child protection campaigns of the Progressive era (1889–1920).

The Kid (1921), with seven-year-old Jackie Coogan in the title role, was Charlie Chaplin's first feature-length film and the first to star a child actor. Its characteristically Chaplinesque mixture of humor and sentiment appealed to audiences and set a pattern for future films to follow. As in King Vidor's early sound-era production *The Champ* (1931), a child devoted to his loving (but socially unacceptable) father defied the busybodies of social convention who sought to separate them. Though these and similar subsequent films featured strong performances by their child protagonists, the point of view consistently was that of a protective adult. Children in danger gave the adult the opportunity to play the part of rescuer.

The Early Sound Era: A Sense of Loss

When children died, as in *Penny Serenade* (1941) or *Little Women* (1933, 1949, 1994), films focused directly on the sorrow of those left behind more than on the feelings of the languishing child. All of the protagonist's siblings in *The Yearling* (1946) die young, leaving him as his parents' only surviving offspring. The film emphasizes his relationship with his beloved pet fawn, which ultimately he has to put down. After the passing of grief for the loss, his bonds with his parents provide the basis for his own passage to adulthood. As in many films about childhood, its setting in the past emphasizes a strong sense of nostalgia. Two classic films from 1941 invoke this quality as well: John Ford's *How Green Was My Valley* is an achingly poignant memory film, told by the adult Huw Morgan (Roddy McDowall), about his childhood in the Welsh mining community where his family had lived for generations; and Orson Welles's *Citizen Kane,* though not ostensibly a film about children, based its narrative on its title character's dying words "Rosebud," harking back to Charles Foster Kane's childhood innocence in a pristine Colorado from which he was so abruptly torn.

Combining innocence and self-reliance, a "fix-it" child who still needed adult love and care, the biggest box-office attraction for four years in the mid-1930s was a curly-haired moppet named Shirley Temple, who starred in more than twenty-five feature-length films as a child, among them *Stand up and Cheer* (1934), *Curly Top* (1935), *The Little Colonel* (1935), *Captain January* (1936), and *Wee Willie Winkie* (1937). Her characters' inevitable overcoming of obstacles made her especially appealing to Depression-era audiences. Kathy Merlock Jackson attributes the success of Temple's screen persona to an American sense of guilt combined with hope, regretting the misfortunes so many children had to endure and simultaneously seeing these children as promises of a brighter future.

1940–1980: Increasing Complexity

The social upheaval that marked American life from World War II through the 1970s affected children. From *National Velvet* (1944) and *The Yearling* (1946) through *The Member of the Wedding* (1952) and *Shane* (1953), films reflected the effects of this upheaval. The motion picture lives of children became increasingly complex: the demands of the adult world impinged on them ever more severely, and the potential for psychic and physical perils loomed large. The children themselves could become the villains, as they increasingly resisted adult control, in film as well as in life. In *The Bad Seed* (1956), a demonic little girl (Patty McCormack) commits mayhem and murder until finally and fatally stopped by her mother. In *Children of the Damned* (1960), an entire village of monster children conceived by a mysterious extraterrestrial force seeks to dominate and destroy the adult world. In *The Innocents* (1961), based on Henry James's *Turn of the Screw,* Deborah Kerr's governess character uncovers grotesque lasciviousness and corruption in the two children under her care. While the children of *To Kill a Mockingbird* (1962) display traditional resourcefulness and wide-eyed wonder and must be rescued from deadly peril, the playful laughing children in the opening scene of *The Wild Bunch* (1969) find sadistic pleasure in torturing scorpions to death, feeding them to swarming hordes of ants and then setting all the creatures on fire. Suddenly children were suspect: the spawn of Satan in *Rosemary's Baby* (1968) and *The Omen* (1976); possessed by a demon in *The Exorcist* (1973); prostitutes in *Taxi Driver* (1976) and *Pretty Baby* (1978).

1980–2000: Children of Change

Yet, as the 1980s began, some children's roles returned to innocence and vulnerability. *Kramer vs. Kramer* (1979) derives much of its emotional power from the love between the Dustin Hoffman character and his little son (Justin Henry) and the boy's difficulty in understanding the departure of his mother (Meryl Streep). That same year, director Carroll Ballard's *The Black Stallion* reprised many of the themes of the best of the child–animal films such as *National Velvet* in a beautifully realized movie that also emphasizes the pain of the loss of a parent. In *E.T.* (1982), Steven Spielberg depicts a ten-year-old whose father has abandoned the family; the boy (Henry Thomas) finds love with an adorable alien creature. Resembling in many ways the child–animal films, *E.T.* is a remarkable celebration of the world of an innocent childhood, besieged by adult intrusions. As these examples indicate, the fragmented family became increasingly the norm on the screen as it also did in society, and the costs to children were evident even before the publication of Judith Wallerstein's studies of the impact of divorce. In *Irreconcilable Differences* (1984), ten-year-old Casey Brodsky (Drew Barrymore) seeks to divorce herself from her self-absorbed single parents (Ryan O'Neal and Shelley Long). By the mid-1990s, child performers returned to the "cute kid" style on display in *Jerry Maguire* (1996), as a young boy (Jonathan Lipnicki) charms everyone into wanting Tom Cruise for his stepdad. Today's movie children of divorce are neither monsters nor simple innocents, as they embody and reflect the social changes, the single-parent families and the loss of community that have transformed the reality of American childhood.

The First of the Screen Teens

Hollywood's attention to the American teenager has been less enduring than that given to the younger child. Though the American interest in the teen years as a distinct phase of life began with the 1904 publication of G. Stanley Hall's *Adolescence,* motion pictures were slow to include recognizably teenage characters. Comic-strip hero Harold Teen made the transition from the newspaper pages to the movie screen in a 1928 silent feature directed by Mervyn Leroy and in a Warner Bros. musical in 1934. In both these films, and in the subsequent Andy Hardy (e.g., *A Family Affair,* 1937; *You're Only Young Once,* 1938; *Love Finds Andy Hardy,* 1938) and Henry Aldrich (e.g., *Life with Henry,* 1941; *Henry Aldrich for President,* 1941; *Henry and Dizzy,* 1942) series, teenage life seemed to consist largely of comic adventure. The occasional moral or emotional conundrums faced by Andy Hardy (Mickey Rooney) could be resolved with some sage advice from wise old Judge Hardy (Lewis Stone). The beginnings of a distinct adolescent subculture received treatment that was essentially humorous, often affectionately nostalgic and sometimes condescending, with almost none of the poignancy or intense emotion associated with movies about younger children. Teenagers had a more problematic relationship with adults and thus received a less sentimental treatment. Representative of the era's attitude toward youth, Robert and Helen Lynd's widely read *Middletown* (1929) and *Middletown in Transition* (1937) portrayed the growth of a distinctive adolescent subculture in a typical Midwestern American small city—Muncie, Indiana.

The 1940s: Teenagers as Beings Apart

Historian Grace Palladino notes that by 1936 nearly two-thirds of teenagers were in school, creating a social center for the teenage culture that emerged more fully during the early 1940s. As the wartime economy boomed and social upheaval diminished adult supervision of youth, Hollywood took note of increasingly autonomous adolescents. *Youth Runs Wild* (1944), a rare example of the movies sharing the popular press's fears about rampant juvenile delinquency, came out the same year as *Janie*. The latter film, though very much in the comical teenage-hijinks mode typical of the era, also depicts its title character (Joyce Reynolds) as beyond her parents' control. Her father, David Considine writes, "can only denounce 'the way the children of today dance and the records they play.' . . . He looks upon his daughter as an alien; she speaks differently, acts differently, and seems to live in a world with customs and codes totally unknown to him" (37). The comic plot hinges on the father's attempts to keep a precocious Janie and her friends away from romantic associations with soldiers stationed at a nearby base, a situation often played out in wartime America with considerably less amusement. Considine explains Hollywood's "obsession with adolescence . . . and [its] tribal customs" as a product of a cultural crisis: "With the war on, adolescence remained one of the few areas of society left intact" (42). Sociologist A. B. Hollingshead showed adolescent society as a mirror of the class divisions of the adult communities in which its members grew up. His *Elmtown's Youth* (1949) presents a darker view of youth behavior, stressing the secrets teenagers kept from their parents about the breaking of social taboos.

The 1950s: Troubled Teens and Teenpics

Within the next several years, films such as the Henry Aldrich and Andy Hardy series, *Janie, Margie, Junior Miss,* and *A Date with Judy,* were joined by productions featuring a much more troubled take on teenagers. This noir approach began in 1955 with *The Blackboard Jungle, Rebel Without a Cause, Running Wild,* and *Teenage Crime Wave.* These films started what film historian Thomas Doherty calls a glut of "teenpics," often featuring young actors playing juvenile delinquents engaged in exciting adventures designed to thrill the audience. The enduring classic of this genre is Nicholas Ray's *Rebel Without a Cause,* with its remarkably effective ensemble of young actors including Wendell Corey, Dennis Hopper, Sal Mineo, Natalie Wood, and, most especially, James Dean. Though the script seems to emphasize patriarchal values, subversive moments undercut conventionality throughout the film, giving it an edge and an attitude that continue to attract viewers. Its viewpoint resembled that of Paul Goodman's influential book *Growing up Absurd*: teenagers were right to rebel against a deeply flawed social system. In Goodman's words, "the young *really* need a more worthwhile world in order to grow up at all" (xvi).

FIGURE 26. *Janie* (1944). Hollywood capitalized on attracting a wartime demographic, the adolescent, in popular films such as *Janie.* In the simple comedy, Janie's (Joyce Reynolds) father tries constantly to prevent her romantic rendezvous with soldiers from a nearby base. During wartime, this real social problem received no serious attention on film. Courtesy Warner Bros.

The 1960s and 1970s: A Revival of the Teenpic

The movies' teenage werewolves and Frankensteins of the next few years represented a heightened sense of the distinctive youth culture that had emerged and its potential as a market, with a subtext of adult fear of teenagers as alien beings—and counterculture ones at that, as *Village of the Giants* (1965), starring young Ron Howard and Beau Bridges, makes clear. After the late 1950s flood of "teenpics," though, the genre foundered. The youth of the Beach Party movies of the early 1960s and the counterculture rebels of the latter part of the decade seemed well past their teenage years. Then, in 1973, George Lucas recalled his own teenage years in the late 1950s and early 1960s in the groundbreaking *American Graffiti.* As nostalgic and affectionately humorous about its era as *Margie* (1946) had been about teens of the 1920s, *American Graffiti* features a soundtrack of Golden Oldies, great pop songs of the early years of rock and roll. It may have inspired *Cooley High* (1975), with the greatest hits of soul music scoring a film about African American teenagers of the previous decade. Brian De Palma's *Carrie* (1976) displayed the director's penchant for Hitchcockian visions in a film filled with *Psycho* references both in the title character's home and at Bates (as in Norman) High School. In the course of the action, the meanness and the petty exclusiveness of teenage cliques were thoroughly roasted (as were most of the teenagers, literally).

The Late 1970s and 1980s: A New Wave of Teen Movies

A new wave of teenager movies emerged in the late 1970s. Although often cited as a teenage film, *Grease* (1978) is self-consciously ironic and condescending toward 1950s popular culture, mocking its style and its characters. The humor encouraged its audience to feel superior to the young people on display, making the film the antithesis of the warmth and sentiment that characterized *American Graffiti.* Amy Heckerling's humorous, heartfelt *Fast Times at Ridgemont High* (1982) uses a contemporary setting rather than nostalgically sending up the recent past. Sean Penn's performance as the classroom surfer-dude Spicoli set the tone for later awesome, gnarly characters such as Bill and Ted (*Bill & Ted's Excellent Adventure,* 1989) and Wayne and Garth (*Wayne's World,* 1992). Martha Coolidge's *Valley Girl* (1983) came close to matching the effective mixture of humor, sentiment, and insightful commentary on teenage society displayed by Heckerling. That same year, Tom Cruise starred in Paul Brickman's satirical dark comedy *Risky Business,* turning one upscale family's teenage son into entrepreneurial pimp. In another category altogether was the bleak vision of *River's Edge* (1984), portraying the anomie of a teenage wasteland where even murder within the group failed to register on the malfunctioning moral radar of clique members.

For four years in the mid-1980s, the king of the teenager film seemed to be director John Hughes, with his hit movies *Sixteen Candles*

(1984), *The Breakfast Club* (1985), *Weird Science* (1985), *Ferris Bueller's Day Off* (1986), and *Some Kind of Wonderful* (1987). Writer Jonathan Bernstein saw the Hughes films as so emblematic of their era that he named his 1997 book on "The Golden Age of Teenage Movies" after one of them: *Pretty in Pink.* As teenage culture became increasingly autonomous, a trend that had begun in life and film some forty years earlier, adults seemed increasingly irrelevant. The few adult characters appeared as occasional annoyances, largely stereotyped. Mixing teen soul-searching, sentiment, and a somewhat sophomoric sense of humor, Hughes set the tone for many imitators.

Four end-of-decade films probed the outer edges of the genre and showed teenage society in a bitingly satiric light. Two starred the youth culture's version of Jack Nicholson, Christian Slater: *Heathers* (1989) and *Pump up the Volume* (1990). Two others displayed the outrageous, campy vision of John Waters: *Hairspray* (1988) and *Cry-Baby* (1990). All of these movies exhibited considerable filmmaking talent as they examined teenage social conventions from the point of view of adolescent outsiders.

The 1990s: New Directions

Variations in the genre included racial minorities (a theme of *Hairspray*) and an amalgam of teenage movie conventions with those of other film types. Despite the whiteness of most screen teenagers, portrayals of black teenage culture also appeared occasionally, such as the rollicking *House Party* (1990), the bleak *Boyz N the Hood* (1991), and the powerful *Menace II Society* (1993). Another subgenre that should be mentioned is the teenager-in-peril "slasher" film. John Carpenter's classic *Halloween* (1978) spawned a host of less artful imitators such as *Friday the 13th* (1980) and its seemingly endless train of sequels. The underlying premise of the slasher film held that premature sex kills, as sexually active teenagers became the victims of crazed, unstoppable murderers wielding butcher knives and axes. The subgenre's apotheosis came in 1996 with the entertainingly self-referential *Scream,* a virtual *Cliff's Notes* guide to teen slasher film conventions.

The mid-1990s also saw the release of one of the best teenage comedies of many years, written and directed by Amy Heckerling, and loosely based on Jane Austen's *Emma. Clueless* (1995) was even better than Heckerling's *Fast Times at Ridgemont High.* Sensitive, insightful, and witty, *Clueless* simultaneously celebrated and spoofed upscale Southern California teen culture. Though it recognized the cliques and the sometimes mean-spirited exclusiveness of its social milieu, the film's own point of view is generous and kind-hearted. Although its adult figures are typically out of touch and largely irrelevant, they are treated with some amused affection.

From the *Andy Hardy* series to *Janie* to *Bye Bye Birdie* to *Clueless,* viewers can see portraits of a society in transition. Teenagers had created a world of their own, and adult influence on that world decreased dramatically. As films depicted this change, the point of view shifted. Filmmakers had shown teenagers from an adult perspective, as parents and teachers were alternately charmed, amused, alarmed, or even frightened by them. As teenagers became the dominant audience and as a new generation of young filmmakers created the motion pictures, they transformed Hollywood's vision of children and teenagers. Recent cultural studies of youth such as Sydney Lewis's *A Totally Alien Life-Form* (1996), Patricia Hersch's *A Tribe Apart* (1998), and Barbara Schneider and David Stevenson's *The Ambitious Generation* (1999), as well as studies of film such as Jon Lewis's *The Road to Romance and Ruin* (1992), have described a further growth in peer group autonomy and alienation from adults as defining characteristics of teen culture. Young screen characters have become more complex and their situations more challenging, reflecting the changed social reality of coming of age in America.

References

Filmography

The Adventures of Dolly (1908, F)
American Graffiti (1973, F)
The Bad Seed (1956, F)
Bill & Ted's Excellent Adventure (1989, F)
The Blackboard Jungle (1955, F)
The Black Stallion (1979, F)
Boyz N the Hood (1991, F)
The Breakfast Club (1985, F)
Bye Bye Birdie (1963, F)
Carrie (1976, F)
The Champ (1931, F)
Children of the Damned (1960, F)
Citizen Kane (1941, F)
Clueless (1995, F)
Cooley High (1975, F)
Cry-Baby (1990, F)
Curly Top (1935, F)
A Date with Judy (1948, F)
E.T.: The Extraterrestrial (1982, F)
The Exorcist (1973, F)
A Family Affair (1937, F)
Fast Times at Ridgemont High (1982, F)
Ferris Bueller's Day Off (1986, F)
Friday the 13th (1980, F)
Grease (1978, F)
The Great Train Robbery (1903, F)
Hairspray (1988, F)
Halloween (1978, F)
Harold Teen (1928, F; 1934, F)
Heathers (1989, F)
Henry Aldrich for President (1941, F)
Henry and Dizzy (1942, F)
House Party (1990, F)
How Green Was My Valley (1941, F)
The Innocents (1961, F)
Irreconcilable Differences (1984, F)
I Was a Teenage Frankenstein (1957, F)
I Was a Teenage Werewolf (1957, F)
Janie (1944, F)
Jerry Maguire (1996, F)
Junior Miss (1945, F)
The Kid (1921, F)
Kids (1995, F)
Kramer vs. Kramer (1979, F)
Life with Henry (1941, F)
Little Women (1933, F; 1949, F; 1994, F)
Love Finds Andy Hardy (1938, F)
Margie (1946, F)
The Member of the Wedding (1952, F)
Menace II Society (1993, F)
National Velvet (1944, F)
The Omen (1976, F)
Penny Serenade (1941, F)
Pretty Baby (1978, F)
Pretty in Pink (1986, F)
Pump up the Volume (1990, F)
Rebecca of Sunnybrook Farm (1938, F)
Rebel Without a Cause (1955, F)
Risky Business (1983, F)
River's Edge (1984, F)
Rosemary's Baby (1968, F)
Running Wild (1955, F)
Scream (1996, F)
Shane (1953, F)
Sixteen Candles (1984, F)
Some Kind of Wonderful (1987, F)
Stand up and Cheer (1934, F)
Taxi Driver (1976, F)
Teenage Crime Wave (1955, F)
To Kill a Mockingbird (1962, F)
Valley Girl (1983, F)
Village of the Giants (1965, F)
Wayne's World (1992, F)
Weird Science (1985, F)
The Wild Bunch (1969, F)
The Yearling (1946, F)
You're Only Young Once (1938, F)
Youth Runs Wild (1944, F)

Bibliography

Ariès, Philippe. *Centuries of Childhood: A Social History of Family Life.* New York: Vintage, 1965.

Austin, Joe, and Michael Nevin Willard. *Generations of Youth: Youth Cultures and History in Twentieth-Century America.* New York: New York University Press, 1998.

Bernstein, Jonathan. *Pretty in Pink: The Golden Age of Teenage Movies.* New York: St. Martin's, 1997.

Cary, Diana Serra. *Hollywood's Children: An Inside Account of the Child Star Era.* Boston: Houghton Mifflin, 1979.

Coles, Robert. *The Moral Intelligence of Children.* New York: Random House, 1997.

——. *The Moral Life of Children.* Boston: Atlantic Monthly Press, 1986.

——. *The Spiritual Life of Children.* Boston: Houghton Mifflin, 1990.

Considine, David M. *The Cinema of Adolescence.* Jefferson, NC: McFarland, 1985.

Doherty, Thomas. *Teenagers and Teenpics: The Juvenilization of American Movies in the 1950s.* Boston: Unwin Hyman, 1988.

Gaines, Donna. *Teenage Wasteland: Suburbia's Dead-end Kids.* New York: Pantheon, 1990.

Goodman, Paul. *Growing up Absurd.* New York: Vintage, 1960.

Graff, Harvey J. *Conflicting Paths: Growing up in America.* Cambridge, MA: Harvard University Press, 1995.

——, ed. *Growing up in America: Historical Experiences.* Detroit: Wayne State University Press, 1987.

Hall, G. Stanley. *Adolescence: Its Psychology and Its Relation to Physiology, Anthropology, Sociology, Sex, Crime, Religion, and Education.* New York: D. Appleton, 1904.

Hersch, Patricia. *A Tribe Apart: A Journey into the Heart of American Adolescence.* New York: Fawcett, 1998.

Hollingshead, August B. *Elmtown's Youth: The Impact of Social Classes on Adolescents.* New York: John Wiley & Sons, 1949.

Jackson, Kathy Merlock. *Images of Children in American Film: A Sociocultural Analysis.* Metuchen, NJ: Scarecrow, 1986.

Kett, Joseph F. *Rites of Passage: Adolescence in America, 1790 to the Present.* New York: Basic Books, 1977.

Lewis, Jon. *The Road to Romance and Ruin: Teen Films and Youth Culture.* New York: Routledge, 1992.

Lewis, Sydney. *A Totally Alien Life-Form—Teenagers.* New York: New Press, 1996.

Lynd, Robert S., and Helen Merrell Lynd. *Middletown.* New York: Harcourt Brace and World, 1929.

——. *Middletown in Transition.* New York: Harcourt Brace and World, 1937.

Modell, John. *Into One's Own: From Youth to Adulthood in the United States, 1920–1945.* Berkeley and Los Angeles: University of California Press, 1989.

Palladino, Grace. *Teenagers: An American History.* New York: Basic Books, 1996.

Postman, Neil. *The Disappearance of Childhood.* New York: Delacorte, 1982.

Schneider, Barbara, and David Stevenson. *The Ambitious Generation: America's Teenagers, Motivated but Directionless.* New Haven: Yale University Press, 1999.

Shary, Timothy. *Generation Multiplex: The Image of Youth in Contemporary American Cinema.* Austin: University of Texas Press, 2002.

Wallerstein, Judith S., and Sandra Blakeslee. *Second Chances: Men, Women, and Children a Decade After Divorce.* New York: Ticknor and Fields, 1989.

West, Elliott, and Paula Petrick, eds. *Small Worlds: Children and Adolescents in America, 1850–1950.* Lawrence: University Press of Kansas, 1992.

[PETER C. HOLLORAN]

Irish Americans

The Irish may not have discovered America, despite legends of St. Brendan's voyage to the New World or the Galway sailor said to be among Christopher Columbus's crew, but they have made significant contributions to American culture. The Irish first came to colonial America as indentured servants, soldiers, and sailors; thousands of these were Irish Presbyterian immigrants whose labor and skills were needed from New England to Carolina. During America's antebellum era, 200,000 Irish Catholics entered the country, filling many roles both humble and honored in the national pageant. The Irish were the first impoverished group to leave Europe in great numbers in the nineteenth century. Discriminatory British laws, the enclosure movement on the land, and devastating famines sent them on crowded and disease-ridden "coffin" ships to America. Despite virulent ethnic and religious prejudice, four million Irish immigrants arrived by the end of the nineteenth century. Nonetheless, American historians have often ignored the Irish in the master narrative of the nation. Recently, Timothy Meager and Thomas Fleming have attempted to redress the neglect of the Irish, and for good reason. One in five Americans today traces ancestry to "that most distressful nation" celebrated in story, song, and film as the Emerald Isle.

Until recently, the image of Irish Americans derived from nineteenth-century theatrical stereotypes, especially the stage Irishman with a musical lilt in his voice, a witty remark on his lips, and whiskey on his breath. These Paddy and Bridget cartoon figures, like the African American Sambo image, were derogatory ethnic stereotypes passing as humor—and, sometimes, as scholarship. If Pat was the genial stage actor who befriended leprechauns, the pugnacious Mike was his negative counterpart. Following the lead of historians and American popular culture, Hollywood produced many now-forgotten silent movies incorporating these shanty-Irish characters. Fights, broad slapstick, and beer kegs accompanied the stage Irishman as he staggered from vaudeville to movies in the nickelodeon era (1900–15); some popular examples are *The Washerwoman's Daughter* (1903) and *Casey's Christening* (1906).

By the 1920s millions of Irish immigrants and their children had entered mainstream, middle-class society and would no longer tolerate the drunken Paddy buffoon on either the stage or the screen. These assimilated Americans found one film of the 1920s to be most offensive: MGM's *The Callahans and the Murphys* (1927) was condemned by the Ancient Order of Hibernians, the Knights of Columbus, and other Celtic and Catholic organizations. Several cities canceled the movie or forced the studio to make cuts. The prominent creative and gatekeeper roles many Irish Americans filled in the early movie industry—including directors Francis and John Ford, Sidney Olcott, Mack Sennett, Hal Roach, and Rex Ingram or studio executives Jeremiah J. Kennedy, Winfield R. Sheeman, and Joseph P. Kennedy——helped eliminate some discrimination against the Irish.

In Old Chicago (1938) offers a genial view of Irish immigrants in the 1850–70 era, rehashing the legend that Mrs. O'Leary's cow started the devastating Chicago fire of 1871. Tyrone Power and Don Ameche play their roles with a stage Irish brogue, while Alice Brady won an Academy Award for her portrayal of Mrs. O'Leary. Perhaps the best example of the stage Irishman was Chauncey Olcott (1858–1932), an Irish American from Buffalo who achieved fame as an Irish tenor and composer in blackface minstrel shows in the 1880s. His light-opera career in London and America included his own hit songs "My Wild Irish Rose," "Too-Ra-Loo-Ra-Loo-Ral," and "When Irish Eyes Are Smiling." His songs became sentimental classics, and his career was the basis for *My Wild Irish Rose* (1947), a charming biopic with Olcott as a lovable rogue (played by Dennis Morgan) singing his heart out as the stereotypical Irishmen—witty, handsome, and debonair. Although not politically correct today, this sentimental aspect of Irish American culture and Irish contributions to American musical theater deserves recognition, and Olcott's career is worth reconsideration. Perhaps more significant than Olcott was the Irish American song-and-dance-man, actor, director, producer, and composer George M. Cohan (1878–1942). His patriotic songs, such as "Over There" and "You're a Grand Old Flag," marched Americans to war in 1917. Considered the father of the American musical comedy, Cohan produced more than eighty Broadway shows in his fifty-year theatrical career, had a brief Hollywood film career, and as a civilian earned a medal from Congress in 1940. His distinguished career was the subject of the Hollywood biopic *Yankee Doodle Dandy* (1942) and starred another New York City Celt, James Cagney, who won an Academy Award for his role as the "Prince of Broadway." Cohan selected Cagney to star in the movie, and Cagney dubbed Cohan "the real leader of our clan" and a "tough act to follow." Although more hagiography than history, this film is a wartime celebration of an American success story, and even FDR (played by Jack Young) blessed Cohan's musical contributions to the nation. *Yankee Doodle Dandy* and *The Seven Little Foys* (1955), another view of the Irish on Broadway, reminded Americans of the role many Irish vaudeville, Broadway, and Hollywood performers have played in defining popular culture. Cohan, one of the brightest vaudeville stars, the "man who owned Broadway," was also the subject of a hit Broadway musical *George M* (1968).

With James Cagney in the 1930s, however, a new version of the Irishman came to the movies—the tough, streetwise Mick. No one played these parts better than Cagney. The dapper, cocky New York dancer and actor was not overshadowed by the gangster persona; his Irish American character prevailed, especially as Tough Tommy Powers in *Public Enemy* (1931) or as a prohibition racketeer in *The Roaring Twenties* (1939). Cagney defined the role of America's favorite tough guy. Playing a gangster, boxer, truck driver, cabby, pilot, reporter, soldier, sailor, dancer, or G-man, the lithe, handsome, redheaded Cagney invented the antihero and personified a new culturally diverse urban America. Cagney's dynamic swagger took him from New York's Lower East Side to Broadway and Hollywood stardom, reflecting modern America's acceptance of the Irish American contributions in all walks of life. Despite his average stature, the fast-talking Cagney was dynamic on stage or screen with a pugnacious physical style and raspy voice, the most impersonated man in show business. He was the vintage urban man and created a new image of the cocksure Irish American hero in *Angels with Dirty Faces* (1938), *The Fighting 69th* (1940), and *Captains of the Clouds* (1942). Some Irish Americans, however, feared that this stereotype of the "fighting Irish" might retard assimilation into mainstream society.

Many Irish American actors, from Spencer Tracy in *20,000 Years in Sing Sing* (1933) to Robert Mitchum in *The Friends of Eddie Coyle* (1973) and Sean Penn in *We're No Angels* (1989) and *State of Grace* (1990), played Irish criminals on the screen long before Italian Americans became typecast as the CEOs of organized crime. Prohibition era (1920–33) crime was an equal opportunity industry in which Irish Americans, like Germans and Jews, played important roles, as seen in Gabriel Bryne's performance as the Ohio gangster Tom Reagan in Joel and Ethan Coen's drama *Miller's Crossing* (1990). But one rare and realistic view of law-abiding working-class Irish American family life is found in *A Tree Grows in Brooklyn* (1945). The Nolan family enjoys life in Brooklyn at the turn of the century despite the uncertain income from Papa's job as a singing waiter. Labor movement leadership by the Irish Americans is depicted in more serious films with vivid performances by Sean Connery and Richard Harris in *The Molly Maguires* (1970) and John C. Reilly in *Hoffa* (1992). Similarly, the crucial role the Irish played in building the transcontinental railroads is seen in John Ford's silent movie *The Iron Horse* (1924) and Cecil B. De Mille's *Union Pacific* (1939). Recent scholarship on the men who built the Union Pacific Railroad (1863–69) and settled the frontier has recognized the unique role of Irish immigrants and Civil War veterans. Irish American achievements on the football field are depicted in such films as *Knute Rockne, All American* (1940) and *The Iron Major* (1945) and in boxing by *Gentleman Jim* (1942).

Irish contributions to the American labor movement were profound. Consider Terence Powderly (1849–1924), the son of immigrants to Pennsylvania, who worked on railroads at age thirteen, joined the Machinists' and Blacksmiths' National Union in 1871, and became its president at age twenty-three. Moving in 1874 to the Knights of Labor, a secret organization the Catholic Church shunned, Powderly led it skillfully from 1878 to 1893. His ideal was to organize all workers, eliminate strikes or coercion, and establish labor-management relations on a just basis without divisive trade unionism. The Knights was the largest, most diverse, and most powerful union ever created, with more than a million members by 1886. Powderly was later an effective U.S. Commissioner of Immigration and wrote *Thirty Years of Labor* (1889) and *The Path I Trod* (1940). Like Mother Jones, Elizabeth Gurley Flynn, John Boyle O'Reilly, and the McNamara brothers, Terence Powderly brought organizational skills and overlooked Celtic social skills to the American labor movement.

Coming from a revolutionary political tradition, the Irish brought to America a talent for organization and a liberalism far beyond most ethnic groups. Like Powderly, the United Mine Workers' John Mitchell was a union leader in the liberal tradition, but Irish men and women also played key roles in Pennsylvania strikes as early as the 1850s as well as in the Haymarket Riot (1886) and the Pullman Strike (1894), and in the formative years of the United Automobile Workers and United Steel Workers (1930s). Boston's Mary Kenney O'Sullivan (1864–1943) founded the National Women's Trade Union League (1903) and was an effective feminist union organizer for fifty years. Hollywood has yet to tell the story of the Irish contributions to the labor union tradition. Irish political leadership has been explored by filmmakers, though, and contrasting views are seen in the comedy *The Great McGinty* (1940), John Ford's sentimental *The Last Hurrah* (1958), and the documentaries *Daley, the Last Boss* (1995) and *Scandalous Mayor* (1998).

Among the contributions of Irish immigrants to America is their example of religious faith and devotion to the Roman Catholic Church. Movies such as *The Fighting 69th* (1940), with Cagney as a wiseguy New Yorker turned coward and then hero in trenches of World War I and Pat O'Brien as the saintly Irish Catholic chaplain, did much to shape public acceptance of the Irish. There is a long roll call of Hollywood stars who portrayed priests and nuns in movies. From Bing Crosby in *Going My Way* (1944) to Ingrid Bergman in

FIGURE 27. *A Tree Grows in Brooklyn* (1945). Ethnic depictions of the struggles in pre- and postwar America rarely examined family dynamics, opting for stereotypes and violent situations. Director Elia Kazan focused on love as the unifying factor in an Irish American family. Courtesy Twentieth Century-Fox.

The Bells of St. Mary's (1945), Catholic clergy provided examples of the selfless modern heroes; Spencer Tracy defined the role of the civic-minded priest in *Boys Town* (1938) and won an Academy Award as Father Edward Flanagan rescuing Depression-era children from poverty and delinquency; *The Cardinal* (1963), starring Tom Tryon in the title role, is a rather dated but useful film on the rise of an Irish Catholic from working-class Boston to the Vatican. It includes some often-overlooked episodes on the twentieth-century Klan's anti-Catholicism as well as the Church's ambiguous role during the rise of European Fascism. The postwar Catholic Church in affluent Los Angeles is subject to scrutiny in *True Confessions* (1981), focused on the parallel lives of an ambitious Irish priest (Robert De Niro) and his brother, a cynical police detective (Robert Duvall).

John Ford, the son of Irish immigrants, brought an Irish sensibility—unabashed sentimentality, humor, nostalgia, courage, and patriotism—to his films. Ford met John Wayne on the movie set for *Mother Macree* (1928), and their lifelong association produced some of Hollywood's greatest westerns—*Stagecoach* (1939), *Fort Apache* (1948), *She Wore a Yellow Ribbon* (1949), *Rio Grande* (1950), and *The Searchers* (1956). In each film Ford used Maureen O'Hara and Thomas Mitchell, or characters such as Victor McLaglen's Sgt. Mulcahy, to illustrate the Irish side of American history. Ford cast Wayne as a brave PT-boat commander in *They Were Expendable* (1945) and in the story of an American's return to his Irish roots, *The Quiet Man* (1952). In *The Long Gray Line* (1955), Ford celebrated once again Irish immigrants' courage, humor, and patriotic service with Tyrone Power and Maureen O'Hara as affectionate parental figures to the cadets of the U.S. Military Academy. *Far and Away* (1992) is a more recent treatment of the Irish immigrant journey from the old country to the Boston waterfront ending in the multicultural Oklahoma frontier. *The Irish in America: The Long Journey Home* (1998), a popular PBS documentary based on fact rather than cinematic myths, demonstrates the public's interest in the history of Irish Catholics in America.

Bing Crosby—an Irish Catholic baritone from Tacoma, Washington, educated at a Jesuit college—may have been the most popular entertainer in Hollywood history. Although Crosby played an easygoing parish priest in only three movies—*Going My Way* (1944), *The Bells of St. Mary's* (1945), and *Say One for Me* (1959)—the public loved him in a clerical collar. The crooning priest made Catholicism part of the movie and cultural mainstream in the wartime 1940s. Like Spencer Tracy in *San Francisco* (1936), Crosby's priest was as American as he was Irish Catholic. Crosby and Tracy did much to make the Irish Hollywood's favorite ethnic group, a tradition evident in movies and television today.

The long tradition of Irish and Irish American leading men in Hollywood—Errol Flynn, James Cagney, Gregory Peck, Peter O'Toole, Richard Harris, and Sean Penn among them—revived in the 1980s with new talent from Ireland: Patrick Bergin, Pierce Brosnan, Gabriel Byrne, Liam Neeson, Aidan Quinn, and Stephen Rea. They play men's men, but their tough exteriors are tempered by sensitivity and vulnerability.

Although the soldier and the gangster are movie roles often assigned to the Irish, it is certainly the cop who is most often portrayed as an Irishman. From *"G" Men* (1935) to *The Great O'Malley* (1937), *The Naked City* (1948), *The Godfather* (1972), *State of Grace* (1990), and *Q & A* (1990), Irish American contributions to law enforcement have been a Hollywood staple. It was Mack Sennett (1880–1960), an Irish Canadian silent film pioneer, who created the mustachioed Irish American Keystone Kop. Although one might assume most police officers are still Irish, in fact the Irish have advanced to a wide variety of professions since 1940. Nevertheless, Hollywood is fond of using Irish names for ethnically "neutral" characters, but most recent films with Irish leading actors or Irish themes have avoided stereotypes. A touching contemporary view of Irish family life and the ambiguous father-son relationship was *Da* (1988), with Martin Sheen playing an Irish American who returns to Ireland for his father's funeral.

Finally, Irish Catholics have played a major role in movie censorship. Conservative Irish Catholics controlled the Catholic Church in the United States for most of the film industry's first decades (1900–1960), and Celtic organizations were quick to protest anti-Irish stereotypes and immorality in silent movies. To counter these threats to society, the Catholic Legion of Decency was created in 1934 by prominent Irish Catholic leaders Father Daniel Lord, Martin Quigley, and Joseph Breen. Hollywood censorship czar Will Hays was quick to appoint Breen as head of the new Production Code Administration in 1934. By controlling the PCA's seal of approval, Breen had a profound influence in eliminating sex and violence from the screen. His conservative values shaped the American film industry until 1966, when the code was replaced by an age-based rating system.

America's most famous Irish Catholics are certainly the Kennedy family, and with the election of John F. Kennedy as president in 1960 America's deeply rooted anti-Catholic and anti-Irish prejudices were overcome. The biopic *PT 109* (1963) celebrated President Kennedy as a World War II naval hero almost as unrealistically as Oliver Stone exploited his assassination in *JFK* (1991). But the Kennedy clan had arrived, bringing all the other Celtic clans with them to the White House and to respectability. A long social and cultural journey was over.

References

Filmography

Angels with Dirty Faces (1938, F)
The Bells of St. Mary's (1945, F)
Boys Town (1938, F)
The Brothers McMullen (1995, F)
The Callahans and the Murphys (1927, F)
Captains of the Clouds (1942, F)
The Cardinal (1963, F)
Casey's Christening (1906, F)
Da (1988, F)
Daley, the Last Boss (1995, D)
Darby O'Gill and the Little People (1959, F)
Duffy's Tavern (1945, F)
Far and Away (1992, F)
Fighting Father Dunne (1948, F)
The Fighting 69th (1940, F)
The Fighting Sullivans (1944, F)
Fort Apache (1948, F)
The Friends of Eddie Coyle (1973, F)
The Frisco Kid (1935, F)
Gentleman Jim (1942, F)
"G" Men (1935, F)
The Godfather (1972, F)
Going My Way (1944, F)
Gone with the Wind (1939)
The Great McGinty (1940, F)
The Great O'Malley (1937)
Hoffa (1992, F)
In Old Chicago (1938, F)
The Irish in America: The Long Journey Home (1998, D)
The Iron Horse (1924, F)
The Iron Major (1945, F)
The Iron Road (1990, D)
JFK (1991, F)
Knute Rockne, All-American (1940, F)
The Last Hurrah (1958, F)
The Long Gray Line (1955, F)
Miller's Crossing (1990, F)
The Molly Maguires (1970, F)
Mother Macree (1928, F)
My Favorite Year (1982, F)
My Wild Irish Rose (1947, F)
The Naked City (1948, F)
Patriot Games (1992, F)
PT 109 (1963, F)
Public Enemy (1931, F)
Q & A (1990, F)
The Quiet Man (1952, F)
Ragtime (1981, F)
The Roaring Twenties (1939, F)
Rio Grande (1950, F)
San Francisco (1936, F)
Say One for Me (1959, F)
Scandalous Mayor (1998, D)
The Searchers (1956, F)
The Seven Little Foys (1955, F)
She Wore a Yellow Ribbon (1949, F)
Stagecoach (1939, F)
State of Grace (1990, F)
They Were Expendable (1945)
Three Cheers for the Irish (1940, F)
A Tree Grows in Brooklyn (1945, F)
True Confessions (1981, F)
20,000 Years in Sing Sing (1933, F)
Union Pacific (1939, F)
The Washerwoman's Daughter (1903, F)
We're No Angels (1989, F)
Yankee Doodle Dandy (1942, F)

Bibliography

Ambrose, Stephen E. *Nothing Like It in the World: The Men Who Built the Transcontinental Railroad, 1863–1869.* New York: Simon & Schuster, 2000.

Bayor, Ronald H., and Timothy J. Meagher. *The New York Irish.* Baltimore: Johns Hopkins University Press, 1996.

Bergman, Andrew. *We're in the Money: Depression America and Its Films.* New York: New York University Press, 1971.

Brown, Thomas N. *Irish-American Nationalism.* Philadelphia: Lippincott, 1966.

Clark, Dennis. *Hibernian America: The Irish and Regional Cultures.* New York: Greenwood, 1986.

——. *The Irish in Philadelphia: Ten Generations of Urban Experience.* Philadelphia: Temple University Press, 1973.

Curran, Joseph M. *Hibernian Green on the Silver Screen: The Irish and American Movies.* Westport, CT: Greenwood, 1989.

Diner, Hasia R. *Erin's Daughters in America: Irish Immigrant Women in the Nineteenth Century.* Baltimore: Johns Hopkins University Press, 1983.

Doherty, Thomas. *Pre-Code Hollywood: Sex, Immorality, and Insurrection in American Cinema, 1930-1934.* New York: Columbia University Press, 1999.

Friedman, Lester D., ed. *Unspeakable Images: Ethnic-*

ity and the American Cinema. Urbana: University of Illinois Press, 1991.

Greeley, Andrew M. *The Irish Americans: The Rise to Money and Power.* New York: Harper & Row, 1981.

——. *That Most Distressful Nation: The Taming of the American Irish.* Chicago: Quadrangle Books, 1972.

Griffith, William D. *The Book of Irish Americans.* New York: Times Books, 1990.

Higgins, George V. *The Friends of Eddie Coyle.* New York: Knopf, 1972.

Kenny, Kevin. *The American Irish: A History.* New York: Longman, 2000.

Lahue, Kalton C. *Mack Sennett's Keystone: The Man, the Myth, and the Comedies.* South Brunswick, NJ: A. S. Barnes, 1971.

McCabe, John. *George M. Cohan: The Man Who Owned Broadway.* Garden City, NY: Doubleday, 1973.

McCaffrey, Lawrence J. *The Irish Diaspora in America.* Bloomington: Indiana University Press, 1976.

——. *Irish Nationalism and the American Contribution.* New York: Arno, 1976.

Meagher, Timothy J. *From Paddy to Studs: Irish-American Communities in the Turn of the Century Era, 1880 to 1920.* New York: Greenwood, 1986.

O'Connor, Aine. *Hollywood Irish: In Their Own Words.* Boulder, CO: Roberts Rinehart, 1997.

Shannon, William V. *The American Irish.* New York: Macmillan, 1963.

Vizzard, Jack. *See No Evil: Life Inside a Hollywood Censor.* New York: Simon & Schuster, 1970.

Walsh, Frank. *Sin and Censorship: The Catholic Church and the Motion Picture Industry.* New Haven: Yale University Press, 1996.

Williams, William H. A. *'Twas Only an Irishman's Dream: The Image of Ireland and the Irish in American Popular Song Lyrics, 1800–1920.* Urbana: University of Illinois Press, 1996.

[STACEY DONOHUE]

Italian Americans

Most of the Italians who arrived in the United States during the Great Immigration (1880–1920) were peasants who left southern Italy only to exchange rural for urban poverty. Given the corruption of the *padrone* system both in Italy and in urban America with its ethnic labor contractors, the family was considered the only functioning institution; as a result, most Italian immigrants were alienated from both the Italian language and Italy and then from English and America—a double exile. Even the Catholic Church, a potential facilitator of the assimilation process, was closed to Italians, for the American Catholic Church was Irish-dominated. Arriving at a time of economic upheaval in the United States, Italian immigrants were often forced to take the most menial of jobs. Roger Daniels notes that "the pushcart became one of the stereotypes of Italian American life, as did what must have been a relatively rare occupation, that of the organ grinder with monkey" (195).

In the decades following World War I, Italian Americans began to assimilate both socially and economically, though still at slower rates than other ethnics. Many second-generation Italian Americans grew up in communities where gangsters were respected for their power. This misguided admiration, along with the persistent Italian-immigrant distrust of education and politics, kept many second- and even third-generation Italian Americans in the working class. By the 1960s, however, most Italian Americans had become solidly middle class, although the self-destructive devaluation of higher education continued. Although most Italian Americans have achieved success in politics, education, law, and even film, Hollywood persists in depicting only working-class urban Italians, tapping a stereotype that has lingered since the origin of motion pictures.

Hollywood's Italian Immigrants

The Hollywood film industry originated during the largest wave of immigration to the United States: not only were many of the film producers immigrants, but so were their audiences. Many early films, including the first "talkie," *The Jazz Singer,* dramatized the immigrant experience. It is not surprising, then, that immigration has been a popular theme in Hollywood ever since—although Hollywood's perception of the immigrant varied with the varying attitudes toward newcomers in the United States: ambivalence, fear, sympathy, nostalgia. Films not only reflected public opinion about immigrants, but also helped shape it: they "provided audiences with information (including misinformation), interpretations, and frames of reference" for Americans who had no contact with denizens of the ghetto (Cortes, 53). For the most part, Hollywood relied on ethnic stereotypes to define the immigrant experience, and, according to Carlos Cortes, has dealt with the following—not necessarily progressive—themes: the processes of assimilation; the quest for the American Dream as well as the immigrant as valuable to America; and the immigrant as societal victim (54). Although other groups were also stereotyped, perhaps because the Irish and the Jews gained influence in Hollywood before Italians, derogatory myths associated with Italian Americans became entrenched.

Hollywood films reflect several stereotypes about Italians, almost all stemming from the idea of Italian "passion"; thus we see Italian Americans in family melodramas and big weddings, as in *Love with the Proper Stranger* (1963) and *True Love* (1989); the Italian immigrant as passionate Latin lover, from Rudolph Valentino in the 1920s to John Travolta in the 1970s; and the distortion of passion by the violent Italian gangster/working class in movies from the 1930s through today, such as *Little Caesar* (1930) and *The Godfather* (1972). America "forced" the many separate peoples of what is now southern Italy to take on one identity. Hollywood followed suit and created for American viewers the screen "Italian"—not Sicilian, not Calabrian.

Silent Era: Puppets of Fate

The silent films provide clues about the popular attitudes toward immigrants and their families, cultures, and neighborhoods during the period of mass immigration. Silent films portrayed these newcomers as either a potential threat or, more often, as a "cultural oddity" (Cortes, 55). D. W. Griffith's 1909 film *At the Altar* depicted a clichéd—but "good"—Italian family eating spaghetti on a checkered tablecloth while a violin is playing. The film's plot suggests ambivalence toward Italian immigrants, specifically, fear of their fertility and passion, yet also admiration for their strong family values. This fear is more evident in Griffith's *The Avenging Conscience* (1914), based on Edgar Allen Poe's "The Tell Tale Heart," which depicts the Italian as a sneaky blackmailer. However, the 1915 film *The Italian* sympathetically portrayed a quest for the American dream thwarted by prejudice.

The "good" but weak Italian, victimized by society, becomes more prevalent in the 1920s. In *Society Snobs* (1921), socialite Vivian Forrester falls in a trap set by a rejected suitor, with an unemployed Italian as bait. In *Puppets of Fate* (1921), another "good" Italian is cheated by an Anglo-American, yet here his passionate nature is used against him. The owner of a puppet show in Italy is forced to immigrate without his Italian wife. The brunt of the punishment goes to Gabriel, whose bigamy with an Anglo woman is the result of his unrestrained lust.

Three stereotypes of the Italian immigrant male were entrenched during this time: the violent criminal, the victimized working-class family man, and the Latin lover. Rudolph Valentino was one of the few Italian leading men in early Hollywood films, yet in only one film did he play an Italian, an immigrant nobleman in *Cobra* (1925). Count Rodrigo summarizes his fate: "Women fascinate me, as the Cobra does his victim." Again, the fatalistic message is that Italian men are destined to be destroyed by their lust.

By 1920, the United States had absorbed eighteen million immigrants over the previous fifty years, more than four million of them from Italy. Catholicism and ethnicity were seen as threatening by the Anglo majority. But by the mid-1920s, restrictive immigration laws and recognition of the Catholic Church as an Americanizing influence tempered anti-immigrant sentiment in film—but not interest in these "foreign" cultures. (Of course immigrants themselves were a large part of the audience, and that fact enhanced these films' proliferation.) In the decade following the Depression, however, Hollywood returned to depicting the Italian American as uncontrollably violent, reflecting a regressive fear of foreigners during hard times.

The Italian Gangsters

The 1930s urban gangster film focused on the young, usually ethnic, man who uses crime to overcome deprivation and poverty and to achieve wealth and status—and thus, assimilation. These characters confirmed the earlier Hollywood stereotype of the Italian immigrant as criminal and ethnic neighborhoods as dan-

FIGURE 28. *Cobra* (1925). The popular and attractive Rudolph Valentino brought some dignity to the role of an immigrant Italian nobleman. Playing on a stereotype, the film sees lust as a fatal flaw in Italian men. Count Rodrigo Torriani (Valentino) makes his desire perfectly clear with a piercing stare at the secretary. Courtesy Ritz-Carlton Pictures.

gerous (See "Crime and the Mafia" for a more thorough analysis of this popular film genre.)

In films such as *Little Caesar* (1930) and *Scarface* (1932), the gangster is lost in the gap between traditional Italian culture and the American dream of economic and social success. Echoing the silent films, gangster movies of the 1930s suggested that Italian immigrants were too completely "puppets of fate" to successfully join American society. This fatalism was depicted both as a product of their ethnic neighborhood and a result of displaced and dysfunctional Italian survival mechanisms. The traditional Italian cultural baggage either led to a life of crime or a life as an unassimilated outsider.

By the late 1930s, more sympathetic portraits competed with gangster images. An appreciation for the hard-working Italians is seen in Shirley Temple's 1936 film *Poor Little Rich Girl*. A wealthy Anglo-American daughter gets lost in the city and is saved by Tony the organ grinder, who takes her home for spaghetti and meatballs served by his big wife to a large, loving family. His home is not as clean or mannerly as her rich mansion, but "richer" in family love. The film explicitly criticizes those Anglo-Americans, as the gangster films warned Italian Americans, who sacrifice family for wealth, and privilege the family values of poor ethnics.

Becoming American

Although fascist Italy was an enemy power during World War II, Italian Americans were not vilified by Hollywood. Relatively few Italian Americans were incarcerated for treason, and Italian American leaders at the time publicly declared their loyalty to the United States soon after war was declared against Mussolini's regime in 1941; indeed, more than half a million Italian American men served in the armed forces (Mangione and Moreale, 241, 340). Most postwar films were sympathetic portraits of first- and second-generation Italian Americans.

Italian directors and writers, including the Sicilian immigrant Frank Capra, who began making films in 1922, suppressed their ethnicity to conform to the Hollywood studio system. Frank Capra's only explicit depiction of Italian Americans is in *It's a Wonderful Life* (1946), where Italian family values win out. Although Italian immigrants live in Potterville shanties, their family ties and work ethic are strongly emphasized—and rewarded, in that they achieve the American dream of home ownership. James Stewart's character, although clearly Anglo-American, adopts Italian family values, refusing to sell out to Mr. Potter and ultimately saving both the honor of his family and the homes of the newcomers.

Another film of the 1940s that connected Italian family values and the American work ethic was *Give Us This Day* (1949), based on the 1930s novel *Christ in Concrete* by Pietro Di Donato. Di Donato portrayed the Italian-immigrant working man as sympathetically and powerfully as did John Steinbeck the "Okies" in *The Grapes of Wrath*. Immigrant Geremio and his wife Anunciata dream of buying a house in Brooklyn, but they are thwarted by the Depression and then later by Geremio's death in an accident at his construction site.

The money the family receives due to contractor negligence allows them to buy the house: "At the end the grief-stricken widow voices the irony of their immigrant quest, 'At last Geremio has bought us a house'" (Cortes, 64). In a very literal way, Di Donato's immigrants fight to give their children access to an American Dream they cannot share.

Hollywood dramatized the gains and losses associated with assimilation in conflicts between the immigrant generation and their children. In 1955, two popular films dealing with such conflicts were released: *Marty* (based on a Paddy Chayefsky play) and *The Rose Tattoo* (based on the Tennessee Williams play). Marty is a bachelor loner living with his widowed mother, and in *The Rose Tattoo,* Rose is the Americanized daughter of a Sicilian immigrant widow, Serafina. Both films are negative portraits of the asphyxiating Italian American family and its overprotective Italian mama; both depict Americanization as requiring a painful rejection of a traditional culture.

Return of the Gangster

By the 1970s Italian American women no longer worked in the textile industry: instead, 40 percent were now employed in clerical and "women's" professional fields such as nursing, social work, and teaching (Mangione and Morreale, 338–339). Italian American men were also moving from working-class to managerial positions. Yet Hollywood ignored these economic and social advances.

The 1970s saw the advent of film school–trained Italian American directors such as Martin Scorsese and Francis Ford Coppola. Both chose to represent Italian Americans, and both also returned to the fatalism of their forefathers. Paul Giles argues that Scorsese's *Mean Streets* (1973) is about the American Dream, Catholic style: "The representation here of the San Gennaro feast . . . features a shot of a large wheel of fortune, as if to demonstrate how these immigrant communities . . . perceive their life in the New World to be largely a matter of chance" (339). The opening image of the strings of a puppet at the start of *The Godfather* is echoed later in the film when Don Corleone says to his son, Michael, "I refused to dance on a string. . . . I thought it was you who would be controlling all the strings."

The Godfather II (1974) focuses on the immigrant who became Don Corleone (Marlon Brando), comparing his life and values to his son Michael's. The film begins with the death of his mother and young Corleone's (Robert De Niro) emigration to the United States, where his first words are from an aria about maternal love. The film's target is the Italian American son who tragically chooses the corrupting American dream over Italian values. Post-Vietnam America was open to films critical of American institutions, and the first two *Godfather* films appealed to many Americans' sense of anger and mistrust, as well as a hope for a leader who respected *la famiglia* over money.

"Guidos"

Crime and athletics were the means to upward mobility for many immigrants, and thus it is no surprise that these subjects are quite common in films about Italian Americans. Pellegrino D'Acierno also sees a subgenre of blue-collar cinema as "cinema of the Guido"—"a pejorative term applied to lower class, macho, gold-amulet-wearing, self-displaying neighborhood boys"—or the "guidette," "their gum-chewing, big-haired, air-headed female counterpart" (628), in films such as *Saturday Night Fever* (1977), *True Love* (1989), and *My Cousin Vinny* (1992). Although most Italian Americans were solidly middle class, the still-extant urban ghetto setting offered too much dramatic possibility for Hollywood to ignore.

Saturday Night Fever depicts conflict between working-class parents and their secular, upwardly mobile American son (played by John Travolta). The neighborhood and family depicted in the film are particularly ghastly: a community of abusive fathers, mothers who have forgotten how to cook, soulless sex, mindless entertainment, and dead-end jobs. Although there is only a river separating the Italian world of Staten Island and the non-Italian world of Manhattan, most cannot successfully cross it. The American Dream is not dead, but the film does not have the optimism of *Rocky* (1976) and its sequels. In the latter film series, Sylvester Stallone's eponymous character chooses athletics over crime as a ticket out of a stultifying life, yet unlike Travolta's character, Rocky does not have to reject culture and family to succeed. He even gets to marry a nice Italian girl (Talia Shire, née Coppola) whose shared cultural background helps him maintain the positive values of fairness and hard work. However, another boxing film, Martin Scorsese's *Raging Bull* (1980), returns to the theme of what can happen to second-generation Italian Americans obsessed with success. Based on the life and career of boxer Jake LaMotta, *Raging Bull* focuses on Jake's rage and violence that make him virtually unstoppable in the ring. The same anger also drives Jake to beat his wife and his brother Joey and sends Jake down a self-destructive spiral of self-hatred, paranoia, and rage.

With some exceptions, the films of the 1970s and 1980s, including those directed by Italian Americans, returned to the Italian-as-criminal trope for one of two reasons: to challenge the possibility of maintaining cultural and religious ties while pursuing the American dream, or, for parodic purposes, as in *Prizzi's Honor* (1985) and *The Freshman* (1990).

The 1990s

By the end of the 1980s, Hollywood films continued to focus on those urban Italian Americans "still locked in a self-imposed ghetto," continuing to resist education and its resulting social and economic mobility (Mangione and Moreale, 455). In 1986, the neighborhood of Howard Beach, the home of the late mobster John Gotti, was also the scene of an infamous race riot that began when three black men showed up at a pizzeria. African American director Spike Lee depicted the race and class issues facing those working-class Italians and their black neighbors in *Do the Right Thing* (1989) and *Jungle Fever* (1991). Intergenerational conflicts were still the norm.

Robert De Niro's directorial debut, *A Bronx Tale* (1993), depicts the hard-working immigrant father who watches his son won over by a local crime boss. John Turturro's semi-autobiographical *Mac* (1993) is also a portrayal of the working-class father-and-son relationship, yet, for what seems like the first time, a life of crime does not come up as an alternative. The film uses unsubtitled Italian and is set in Brooklyn rather than the grittier streets of Little Italy. It is an update of the Michael Corleone story: Mac, like Michael—albeit in an honest business—chooses power and economic success over family and thus ends up alone.

The 1990s also revealed the talents of Italian American woman director Nancy Savoca, who was born in the Bronx to immigrants from Sicily and Argentina. Her 1993 film *Household Saints* is the story of three generations in two working-class Italian American families in Little Italy. Joseph Santangelo's superstitious, immigrant mother disapproves of his wife Catherine's inability to cook and be a good housewife. After the grandmother dies, Catherine exorcises her presence by modernizing the decor of the home and getting rid of her Catholic icons. Oddly, her daughter Teresa aspires to be a saint, to the horror of her Americanized and secularized parents, and she unpacks and returns her grandmother's religious icons to their original places. The film reflects the sociological phenomenon of the second and third generations of immigrants: the second generation seeks to reject its ethnic heritage, whereas the third and most Americanized generation often returns to it.

It is difficult to ignore the popularity and the controversy of the HBO dramatic series *The Sopranos*. As with Scorsese's *GoodFellas* (1990), the award-winning series both criticizes and idealizes a Mafia boss as the last of a dying breed. Tony Soprano (James Gandolfini), as any second-generation Italian American, wants upward mobility; at the same time, he is well aware that the mob is an anachronistic institution. He moves to the suburbs, his daughter goes to Columbia, and his son plans to apply to West Point. Yet the show disproves the myth that being in the mob is one of the only ways for Italian immigrants to get ahead. Tony's wealthy neighbors are Italian, as is his doctor, and, though he disapproves of their assimilated ways, he also aspires to be like them.

The mobsters on *The Sopranos* love films like *GoodFellas* and *The Godfather,* and it shows in their mimicry of the lines and clothing from these movies. Celia Wren notes that the reason why the mobsters sense that their roles are soon to be out of date is that "the artificiality of their mobster identities—inherited in large part from Francis Ford Coppola—makes their whole existence feel artificial" (20). They are dinosaurs trying to live out a dysfunctional myth.

The Sopranos has led to a resurgence of criticism not seen since the *Godfather* movies. The National Italian American Foundation argues that the show perpetuates unflattering stereotypes. James Bowman, however, recognizes the attraction of *The Sopranos,* noting that Tony's appeal is his devotion to traditional Italian patriarchy and Sicilian values and that "we are drawn in by the assumption that even the scary and solidly established world of organized crime . . . cannot stand up against the overwhelming banality of the consumer culture in turn-of-the-century suburban New Jersey with which it is juxtaposed in a mock-heroic way" (86). Although media outlets gave currency to the criticism of *The Sopranos,* the series continued to be a major success.

Into the Twenty-First Century

Faced with a film history filled with stereotypes and common themes, Italian American writers and directors need to forge new territory. Some will have no need to recover the Italian immigrant experience in their art. Fourth-generation Italian American Sofia Coppola's directorial debut, *The Virgin Suicides* (1999), for example, does not depict the Italian American experience. But others, perhaps, may take on Pellegrino D'Acierno's challenge. He notes that no extant film deals with Italian American political and social history or radical politics: none yet tell the story of immigrant anarchists Sacco and Vanzetti, whose execution shocked the nation in 1927. Nor has there been a generational saga that excludes gangsters, no Italian American equivalent of *Avalon* (Jewish Americans) or *Roots* (African Americans). Perhaps the twenty-first-century image of Italian Americans in film will move from stereotypes to historical realism and the depiction of contemporary Italians who contribute to a diverse and prosperous America.

References

Filmography

Across 110th Street (1972, F)
Angie (1994, F)
At the Altar (1909, F)
The Avenging Conscience (1914, F)
Baby It's You (1983, F)
The Beautiful City (1925, F)
Big Night (1996, F)
The Black Hand (1950, F)
The Bridges of Madison County (1995, F)
A Bronx Tale (1993, F)
The Brotherhood (1969, F)
Cobra (1925, F)
Diane of Star Hollow (1921, F)
Do the Right Thing (1989, F)
The Fortunate Pilgrim (1988, TV)
Full of Life (1957, F)
The Funeral (1996, F)
Give Us This Day (1949, F)
The Godfather (1972, F)
The Godfather II (1974, F)

The Godfather Part III (1990, F)
GoodFellas (1990, F)
The Greatest Love of All (1925, F)
Household Saints (1993, F)
The Italian (1915, F)
Italianamerican (1974, D)
Italian in America (1998, D)
It's a Wonderful Life (1946)
Jungle Fever (1991, F)
Little Caesar (1930, F)
Little Italy (1921, F)
The Lords of Flatbush (1974, F)
Lovers and Other Strangers (1970, F)
Love with a Proper Stranger (1963, F)
Mac (1993, F)
The Man in Blue (1925, F)
Marty (1955, F)
Mean Streets (1973, F)
Moonstruck (1987, F)
My Cousin Vinny (1992, F)
Prizzi's Honor (1985, F)
Puppets (1926, F)
Puppets of Fate (1921, F)
Raging Bull (1980, F)
Rocky (1976, F)
Rose of the Tenements (1926, F)
The Rose Tattoo (1955, F)
Saturday Night Fever (1977, F)
Scarface (1932, F)
Society Snobs (1921, F)
The Sopranos (1999–, TV)
True Love (1989, F)
A View from the Bridge (1962, F)
When the Clock Strikes Nine (1921, F)
Who's That Knocking at My Door? (1969, F)
Wise Guys (1985, F)

Bibliography

Bowman, James. "Mob Hit." *American Spectator,* April 2001.

Caso, A. *Mass Media vs. the Italian Americans.* Boston: Brenden, 1980.

Ciongoli, A. Kenneth, and Jay Parini, eds. *Beyond the Godfather: Italian American Writers on the Real Italian American Experience.* Hanover, NH: University Press of New England, 1997.

Cortes, Carlos E. "Them and Us: Immigration as Societal Barometer and Social Educator in American Film." In Robert Brent Toplin, ed., *Hollywood as Mirror,* 57–73. Westport, CT: Greenwood, 1993.

D'Acierno, Pellegrino, ed. *The Italian American Heritage: A Companion to Literature and Arts.* New York: Garland, 1999.

Daniels, Roger. *Coming to America: A History of Immigration and Ethnicity in American Life.* New York: HarperCollins, 1990.

Gambino, Richard. *Blood of My Blood.* New York: Anchor, 1975.

Giles, Paul. *American Catholic Arts and Fictions: Culture, Ideology, Aesthetics.* New York: Cambridge University Press, 1992.

La Sorte, Michael. *La Merica: Images of Italian Greenhorn Experience.* Philadelphia: Temple University Press, 1985.

Lourdeaux, Lee. *Italian and Irish Filmmakers in America: Ford, Capra, Coppola, and Scorsese.* Philadelphia: Temple University Press, 1990.

Mangione, Jerre, and Ben Moreale. *La Storia: Five Centuries of the Italian American Experience.* New York: HarperPerennial, 1993.

Miller, Randall M., ed. *The Kaleidoscopic Lens: How Hollywood Views Ethnic Groups.* New York: Jerome S. Ozer, 1980.

Novak, Michael. *The Rise of the Unmeltable Ethnics: Politics and Culture in the Seventies.* New York: Macmillan, 1972.

Parillo, V. N. *Strangers to These Shores: Race and Ethnic Relations in the United States.* Boston: Houghton Mifflin, 1980.

Rollins, Peter C., ed. *Hollywood as Historian: American Film in a Cultural Context.* 2d ed. Lexington: University Press of Kentucky, 1998.

Winokur, Mark. *American Laughter: Immigrants, Ethnicity, and 1930s Hollywood Film Comedy.* New York: St. Martin's, 1996.

Wren, Celia. "Melancholy Mobsters." *Commonweal,* 28 January 2000.

[**SOLOMON DAVIDOFF**]

Jewish Americans

There were Jews in America long before the creation of the United States. As Howard Sachar points out in *A History of the Jews in America,* not only were there Jewish settlers arriving in New Amsterdam as early as 1654, but the crew of Christopher Columbus also almost assuredly included *marranos* (Jews who hid their religion to escape the Spanish Inquisition) and *conversos* (Jews who converted during the Inquisition). Jewish people have made a wide variety of contributions to American life and culture, including the blue jeans devised by Levi Strauss (1829–1902), the polio vaccine formulated by Dr. Jonas Salk (1914–1995), and the modern Hollywood film studios, created by men such as Sam Goldwyn (born Samuel Goldfish, 1882–1974), Louis B. Mayer (1891–1957), Jack Warner (1892–1981), and Adolph Zukor (1873–1976). In fact, there have been contributions by Jewish people to every field of endeavor throughout American history. Asser Levy's (1628–1682) early efforts to convince Peter Stuyvesant that Jewish people should have the right to settle in the Dutch colony of New Amsterdam led to a constitutional precedent of immigration law, that people of all religious extractions should have the opportunity to settle in the New World (Koppman, 35). From the scientific explorations of Julius Oppenheimer (1904–1967) to Emma Lazarus's (1849–1887) poem "The New Colossus" at the base of the Statue of Liberty, from the philanthropy and legacy of Meyer Guggenheim (1828–1905) to the sporting achievements of Sandy Koufax (b. 1935), to name but a few, there is no area of life or achievement in the United States that has not benefited from Jewish involvement.

The first major wave of Jewish immigration to the United States took place during the period of western expansion (1880–1924), when approximately ninety thousand Ashkenazi (Jews of Eastern European descent) came to the United States from Germany and Poland. They were followed by settlers from Russia and Poland in a wave of immigrants known as the "Yiddish Migration" (Gonzalez, 352).

There were marked differences between the earlier Jewish settlers (who were not identified as arriving in an identifiable "wave"), the Sephards (Jews of Spanish descent) and the Western European Jews, and the Jews of the Yiddish Migration. Whereas Western European Jews assimilated and blended into American society, the latter group was far more noticeably "Jewish" in appearance and tradition—in large part owing to its unfamiliarity with Western culture as well as its insular experience within ghettoized communities. Once on American shores, this community continued to be close-knit; initially, the vast majority settled in the Lower East Side of New York City. Just before the advent of World War I, nearly half of the 3.5 million Jews in America lived in New York City—the sheer number of Jewish New Yorkers (1.6 million) surpassing the population size of every major American city save for New York, Chicago, and Philadelphia (Sachar, 174).

The era of the Depression was also the start of the era of modern European immigration to the United States. This phase of immigration, from 1925 to 1945, is notable mostly for the exodus of Jews fleeing Nazi persecution. It is during this period that an association between the Jewish people and show business was most clearly formed in the American mind. This connection was fueled by vaudeville performers such as Jack Benny (1894–1974) and Groucho Marx (1890–1977), famed radio performer Gertrude Berg (1899–1966), and Hollywood personalities such as Eddie Cantor (1892–1964) and George Jessel (1898–1981).

The next major phase of Jewish immigration to the United States was the postwar period, which lasted from 1946 to 1980. The most publicized of these Jewish immigrants were refugees from the Soviet bloc nations, although Eastern European and Israeli immigration continued. The final phase, still in process, began in 1980 and continues today. The majority of Jewish immigrants to the United States in this period have come from Israel, itself a nation of immigrants.

The Cinematic History of Jewish Americans

Jewish American history, when explored in American film, focuses primarily on the question of assimilation versus acculturation. Films such as *American Matchmaker* (1940), *Hester Street* (1975), and *Avalon* (1990) portray Jewish lives within the melting pot of the United States and focus on how difficult it can be for Jewish people to meld into American culture. Michael Kassel finds that *Avalon,* "viewed in historical perspective . . . demonstrates that progress and assimilation had a detrimental effect on the Jewish immigrant family" (52). It is notable that assimilation is now one of the greatest worries to the Jewish community in America. Although assimilating into the anglocentric culture of the United States allowed the Jewish people to advance and progress, this advancement has eroded a unique culture, making it more liberal and secular. Furthermore, the Jews of America are different from those in other countries in that in the United States there has never been a national "Chief Rabbi" or dominant voice who speaks for the entire Jewish community. As a result, behavior and attitudes are based more on personal choice that may change with the mores of the time. The current trend is more toward acculturation—that is, concurrent acceptance of the dominant culture of the United States while maintaining and cultivating qualities and traditions that are unique to the Jewish people. Examples of this evolution of attitude can best be seen in the various interpretations of *The Jazz Singer* (1927, 1943, 1980), wherein the main character chooses American popular music over his religion in the original film but in later versions accepts the importance of his heritage more and more; *The Chosen* (1981), which shows the differing worlds of Orthodox and Conservative Judaism at the dawn of World War II; and *A Woman Called Golda* (1982), portraying the influence that American Judaism had on the history of Israel.

Arrival to American's Shores

The earliest portrayal of American Jews in American cinema can be seen within the comedies, ghetto films, and Yiddish films of the early 1900s. The films of this period portrayed both the very isolated community of the Jewish ghettos of the new world, and the anti-Semitic views of the WASP culture in a period of great social change and "status anxiety." These comedies included films such as *Cohen's Advertising Scheme* (1904) and *The Fights of Nations* (1907), which used a negative stereotype of the money-grubbing Jew to evoke laughter. These were not religious characters, but people with large noses and "Jewish" names who were possessed by greed. A wide variety of films during the silent era dealt with this population; a popular formula juxtaposed the immigrant Jewish and Irish populations, as in Edward Sloman's *His People* (1925), Victor Fleming's *Abie's Irish Rose* (1928), and Harry Pollard's *The Cohens and the Kellys* (1926).

The ghetto films, such as D. W. Griffith's *Old Isaacs, the Pawnbroker* (1908) and *A Child of the Ghetto* (1910), focused on the pervasive poverty of the New York immigrants, showing that not all Jews were rich and powerful. These films also differed greatly from the early comedies in presenting a far less stereotypical image of Jews while illustrating the ways in which the people were, in fact, different from WASP America. Joseph Cohen suggests that the Yiddish films served the Jewish community as an aid to transition: "*American Matchmaker* . . . deals with the serious issue of transition in personally reconciling tradition and the modern, finding the "golden mean" between Jewish and secular identity" (41). Outside of these early efforts, this period in Jewish history has been filmed rarely; a fortunate exception is *Hester Street* (1975), an independent production directed by Joan Micklin Silver. An excellent examination of immigration and assimilation, *Hester Street* shows the toll of change not only on individuals but also on the family and tradition. It is the abandonment of his religion and tradition that dooms Yankel's (Steven Keats) marriage to Gitl (Carol Kane), not through small adaptations (such as changing his name to Jake) but major ones (such as an extramarital affair).

Assimilation into American Society

The next phase of Jewish life in the United States, between 1925 and 1945, was marked by attempts at assimilation. Immigration to the United States was a time of new beginnings, and it makes perfect sense that some of these immigrants took advantage of the opportunity to discard some of the more visible aspects of their traditions. To this end, Jewish people embraced new fields and professions, particularly in the sciences and education. But the Jews of the time also tried to maintain a low profile—as in 1939, when several influential Jewish advisors asked President Roosevelt to reconsider the appointment of Felix Frankfurter to the Supreme Court. They were concerned that such an appointment would incite a wave of anti-Semitism (Whitfield, 101). This timidity is also fascinating, in light of how many Jewish people were in the public eye at the time, both as performers and workers behind the scenes in show business.

Jewish people also shared a rich heritage of humor. In fact, the most noticeable contribution to American society by Jews at this point was actually in the arena of light entertainment. The early "talkies" were notable for the number of dialect-oriented ethnic comedies. Parodying and emphasizing the Yiddish accent or the Germanic sentence structure became quite popular in films such as Roy Del Ruth's *Taxi!* (1932) and George Stevens's *The Cohens and Kellys in Trouble* (1933). This form of humor can also be seen in the works of up-and-coming Jewish comedians such as the Marx Brothers. It was during this period that many actors changed their names from "ethnic" to "American" forms: Muni Weisenfreund to Paul Muni, Julius Garfinkle to John Garfield, David Kominski to Danny Kaye, Betty Perske to Lauren Bacall, Bernard Schwartz to Tony Curtis. The studios insisted on these name changes, fearing that audiences would notice a growing Jewish presence in American entertainment.

Modern popular films seldom portray the Jews of the 1920s and 1930s, with a major exception: gangster movies. Jewish presence in the gangster mobs of the Roaring Twenties was quite pronounced, considering the involvement of Benny "Bugsy" Siegel, the Purple Gang, and others. Films such as William Nigh's *Four Walls* (1928), Burt Balaban's *Lepke* (a.k.a. *Murder, Inc.*) (1960), Sergio Leone's *Once Upon a Time in America* (1984), and Barry Levinson's *Bugsy* (1991) highlight some of the Jewish players in organized crime. As in the case of other ethnic groups, there was no objection to this sort of presentation of the real lives of Jewish people, as opposed to the representation of more noteworthy Jewish personages—for example, in the areas of science and politics.

Although the influx of Jewish immigration did not yet affect the content of the movie industry to a remarkable degree, World War II certainly led to changes in the theme and scope of films. One of the first productions to confront the horrors taking place in Europe was Charles Chaplin's *The Great Dictator* (1940), which included Chaplin's only onscreen performance in a clearly identifiable Jewish role. In time, depictions of World War II would lead to productions concerning the Jewish Holocaust; films dramatizing this aspect of the war have grown more numerous. Notable contributions to the genre are Alan J. Pakula's *Sophie's Choice* (1982) and Stephen Spielberg's *Schindler's List* (1993).

If there is a more modern presentation of Judaism in American film, it consists of assimilated Jews, such as the Jewish characters in *Quicksilver* (1986) and *Rebel Without a Cause* (1955). Jewish faith and culture is not a real part of the lives of these characters, and religious identity seems to be inconsequential to them. This is different from the presentation of secular Jewish characters in films such as Otto Preminger's *Exodus* (1960), which depicts the origin of Israel and focuses on secular Jewish characters rather than religious ones. *Exodus* features characters who feel passionately about their Jewish identity, though it lies in culture more than religious beliefs. More modern efforts, such as *Quicksilver,* feature characters who may be portrayed as celebrating Chanukah rather than Christmas, but their religious and cultural differences from mainstream society are normally mentioned only to serve as the springboard for a brief statement, highlighting the similarities between their religion and those of other characters. This trend may be changing, however, as seen by Jewish characters in films such as *Independence Day* (1996) and *Keeping the Faith* (2000) who practice their faith and celebrate their culture while living lives otherwise identical to those of their fellow Americans.

Acculturation

In part influenced by the horrors of World War II, Jewish people in the United States turned toward acculturating themselves—more than assimilating—into mainstream culture. The cries of "Remember," and "Never Forget" in reference to those who died in European concentration camps forced Jewish people to focus on and embrace their differences. Although this change in behavior has increased the cultural visibility of worldwide Jewry, a further result has been more frequent acts of anti-Semitism. Jewish involvement in the creation and success of labor unions and political action organizations, such as the NAACP and the ACLU, have often equated the terms "Jew" and "liberal," which often has led to inflammatory rhetoric and violence. But anti-Semitism was being dealt with for the first time as a matter of civil rights, and civil rights were a new focus for the general population as well.

Films such as Elia Kazan's *Gentleman's Agreement* (1947) and Edward Dmytryk's *Crossfire* (1947) deal with anti-Semitism, just as later films would deal with prejudice against people of color and other minority groups. The importance of these films is the way in which they lay the blame for intolerance at the feet of those responsible, rather than on the persecuted themselves. (This notion, that members of a group should not bear responsibility for unreasonable hatred toward them, is perhaps the first educational step toward understanding of, rather than mere tolerance for, difference.)

Although many humorous films of this period had notable Jewish characters, such as Walter Hart's *The Goldbergs* (1950) and William Wyler's *Funny Girl* (1968), the majority of Jewish characters in comedic films were only incidentally Jewish. Judaism is present primarily in themes and styles of humor, in such films as Larry Peerce's *Goodbye, Columbus* (1969) and Woody Allen's *Annie Hall* (1977). In fact, all the work of Woody Allen, Mel Brooks, and Carl Reiner can be seen as defining the filmed genre of Jewish humor. The early portrayals of stereotypical Jews that focused on businessmen with thick accents changed over to the mother's boy who walks through life hampered by guilt and attached to maternal apron strings—a character best seen in Neil Simon's two autobiographical films *Brighton Beach Memoirs* (1986) and *Biloxi Blues* (1988).

Perhaps it was the influence of Alex Haley's *Roots* (1977) more than any other novel or film that focused the interest of all Americans upon the details of their heritage—and this focus is plainly visible in films dealing specifically with Judaism. Joan Micklin Silver's *Crossing Delancey* (1988) and Barry Levinson's *Avalon* (1990), as noted earlier, deal with the old world intruding on the new, considering which was "better," and how the similarities of these worlds bridge the generations.

From Stereotype to Character

The film industry has progressed from showing Jewish characters as mere stereotypes to fully formed characters who are just as capable as anyone else of committing heresies and heroism. But it must also be noted that, even today, films are aimed at a general audience. For example, in Brenda Chapman and Steve Hickover's animated film *The Prince of Egypt* (1999), Moses leads the Hebrews out of Egypt and beyond; although the story's conclusion may allude to the religion to come, Judaism per se is never explicitly explored or mentioned. The question must be raised: Why create a film about one of the most defining moments of a people without exploring its spiritual significance? In a country that gives "to bigotry no sanction, to persecution no assistance," as George Washington wrote in his famous letter to the Touro Synagogue of Rhode Island in 1790, perhaps it is time for a change.

References

Filmography

Abie's Irish Rose (1928, F)
Almonds and Raisins: A History of the Yiddish Cinema (1983, D)
American Matchmaker (Amerikaner Shadchen) (1940, F)
Annie Hall (1977, F)
Avalon (1990, F)
Biloxi Blues (1988, F)
Brighton Beach Memoirs (1986, F)
Bugsy (1991, F)
The Chosen (1981, F)
Cohen's Advertising Scheme (1904, F)
The Cohens and the Kellys (1926, F)
Crossfire (1947, F)
Crossing Delancey (1988, F)
Exodus (1960, F)
Fiddler on the Roof (1971, F)
The Fights of Nations (1907, F)
Funny Girl (1968, F)
Gentleman's Agreement (1947, F)
The Goldbergs (1950, F)
Goodbye, Columbus (1969, F)
The Great Dictator (1940, F)
Hester Street (1975, F)
His People (1925, F)
Hollywood: An Empire of Their Own (1997, D)
Independence Day (1996, F)
The Jazz Singer (1927, F; 1943, F; 1980, F)
Keeping the Faith (2000, F)
Lepke (a.k.a. *Murder, Inc.*) (1960, F)
Old Isaacs, the Pawnbroker (1908, F)
Once Upon a Time in America (1984, F)
The Prince of Egypt (1999, F)
Quicksilver (1986, F)
Rebel Without a Cause (1955, F)
Roots (1977, F)
Schindler's List (1993, F)
Sophie's Choice (1982, F)
Taxi! (1932, F)
A Woman Called Golda (1982, TV)

Bibliography

Anklewicz, Larry. *Guide to Jewish Films on Video.* Hoboken, NJ: Ktav Publishing, 2000.

Bernheimer, Kathryn. *The 50 Greatest Jewish Movies: A Critic's Ranking of the Very Best.* Secaucus, NJ: Birch Lane, 1998.

Cohen, Joseph. "Yiddish Film and the American Immigrant Experience." *Film & History* 28.1–2 (1998): 30–44.

Cohen, Sarah Blacher, ed. *From Hester Street to Hollywood: The Jewish-American Stage and Screen.* Bloomington: Indiana University Press, 1983.

Cohen, Steven M. *American Assimilation or Jewish Revival?* Bloomington: Indiana University Press, 1988.

Dimont, Max I. *Jews, G——D and History.* New York: Signet, 1962.

Erens, Patricia. *The Jew in American Cinema.* Bloomington: Indiana University Press, 1984.

Fast, Howard. *The Jews: Story of a People.* New York: Dell, 1968.

Friedman, Lester D. *The Jewish Image in American Film.* Secaucus, NJ: Citadel, 1987.

Gabler, Neal. *An Empire of Their Own: How the Jews Invented Hollywood.* New York: Crown, 1988.

Gonzales, Juan L. *Racial and Ethnic Groups in America.* Dubuque, IA: Kendall/Hunt, 1996.

Gordis, David M., and Dorit P. Gary. *American Jewry: Portrait and Prognosis.* West Orange, NJ: Behrman House, 1997.

Gurock, Jeffrey S. *American Jewish History.* 13 vols. New York: Routledge, 1998.

Guttman, Allen. *The Jewish Writer in America: Assimilation and the Crisis of Identity.* New York: Oxford University Press, 1971.

Howe, Irving. *World of Our Fathers.* New York: Schocken, 1976.

Insdorf, Annette. *Indelible Shadows: Film and the Holocaust.* 2d ed. Cambridge: Cambridge University Press, 1989.

Kassel, Michael B. "The American Jewish Immigrant Family in Film and History: The Historical Accuracy of Barry Levinson's *Avalon.*" *Film & History* 26.1–4 (1996): 52–60.

Kemelman, Harry. *Conversations with Rabbi Small.* New York: Fawcett, 1993.

Koppman, Lionel, and Bernard Postal. *Guess Who's Jewish in American History.* New York: Signet, 1978.

Levitan, Tina. *First Facts in American Jewish History: From 1492 to the Present.* Northvale, NJ: Joseph Aronson, 1996.

Lipset, Seymour Martin. *American Pluralism and the Jewish Community.* New Brunswick, NJ: Transaction, 1990.

Mack, Stanley. *The Story of the Jews: A 4,000 Year Adventure.* New York: Villard, 1998.

Marcus, Jacob Rader. *United States Jewry, 1776–1985.* Detroit: Wayne State University Press, 1989.

Sachar, Howard M. *A History of the Jews in America.* New York: Knopf, 1992.

Sklare, Marshall. *American Jews: A Reader.* West Orange, NJ: Behrman House, 1983.

Whitfield, Stephen J. *American Space, Jewish Time.* Hamden, CT: Archon, 1998.

[SCOTT L. BAUGH]

Mexican Americans

Before the Spanish conquest of Mexico in 1521, an assemblage of diverse indigenous societies developed alongside one another in what is now considered North America. Spain saw America as a land to be colonized, and, after conquering the Aztecs, Spanish forces allied with some Native American societies and began establishing New Spain. Spanish-sponsored explorations sought out fabled riches and new settlement locations in what is now the southwestern United States, but in the process they encountered and battled more Native American tribes, including the Apache and Pueblo peoples. Over the next three centuries, although the Spanish throne ruled the land and its imperial power grew, intermarriages between Spanish colonialists and Native Americans spawned significant political, social, and racial mixtures, the phenomenon called *mestizaje.*

By the time Mexico had gained its independence from Spain in the early 1820s, other European immigrants had begun trekking across the ever-growing United States in fulfillment of Manifest Destiny, some homesteading in the Texas portion of the Spanish empire. In 1836, perhaps carried by the spirit of the Alamo, Texas won independence from Mexico and, along with much of the adjacent territory, including portions of New Mexico, Arizona, California, Utah, Nevada, and Colorado, became part of the United States in 1848 with the signing of the Treaty of Guadalupe Hidalgo. In one stroke of the pen, natives of the region became U.S. citizens. Politically, a new identity was formed: what came to be known as the Mexican American or, later, Chicana and Chicano. More importantly, this political event made possible a new cultural enterprise, progressively evolving as *chicanismo.* Echoing Octavio Paz and José Vasconcelos, Arnoldo Carlos Vento and other Chicano historians argue that the definitive characteristic of Chicano culture is its existence in between dominant cultures, assembling the very best of the divergent American cultures into *movidas* or modes of survival (281). In its mixture historically are various Native American, Iberian Spanish, Moorish, Celtic-Gaelic, Jewish, and colonial Mexican influences, all of which play a part in Chicano identity in the face of the larger American society.

Feature films made in the United States have chronicled Mexican American history and Chicano culture in many ways. The earliest period is marked by some social problem melodramas and many westerns that often misrepresented U.S.-Mexican themes and characters, stressing an assimilationist view. After World War II and reaching a fevered pitch in the late 1960s and 1970s, militarist and nationalist separatism marked a new generation of Chicanos and Chicanas who fought for their social rights and expressed the significance of their cultural background; some films treating this period revise cultural statements made by earlier films and social histories and highlight issues of concern often overlooked by studio fare. Finally, from 1980 to the present, films depicting Mexican Americans have crossed over into the mainstream while at the same time allowing mainstream culture to cross over to Mexican

American cultural expressions. This period celebrates American multiculturalism and hints at the benefits of pluralistic social politics through cultural syncretism or *mestizaje* in U.S. films.

Losing Ground: 1848–1940

Traditionally, United States social histories rely upon an immigration narrative, characterizing American society according to what Caroline Ware calls a "common rootlessness" shared by immigrants to the "New World" (62–64). Overlooking indigenous populations and their varied cultures, social histories favor a Eurocentric vision of the United States. Studio films generally have upheld the perdurable Anglo-Saxon vision of America, and this is most easily recognized in the majority of films treating the historical period before World War II.

The very few studio films that treat pre-Columbian America tend to show natives as "savages." *The Fall of Montezuma* (1912), *The Captive God* (1916), and *Kings of the Sun* (1963) generalize Europeans as civilized and the natives as warring, if "noble," brutes. More often than not, however, studios overlook this period in favor of an America with European settlers.

The vast majority of feature films that treat U.S.-Mexican themes and characters from the nineteenth century to World War II are westerns, resulting in easily prescribed and negative stereotypes—for male characters, the greaser-bandit, the lecherous "Latin lover," and the doltish sidekick; for females, the self-sacrificing maiden and the cantina whore. Many of the most popular westerns subsume these stereotypes, as in Howard Hawks's classic *Red River* (1948), when two Tejanos are shot for defending their homeland, or John Ford's classic *The Searchers* (1956), which portrays natives of the region as frighteningly inhuman. By definition, these stereotypes give oversimplified and one-dimensional characterizations, but worse yet they unfairly define natives as being ruled by their passions—both violent and romantic—and reveal contempt on the part of mainstream society for Mexican and Mexican American culture.

These character types appear in the earliest silent westerns, such as Griffith's *The Greaser's Gauntlet* (1908), William S. Hart vehicles like *The Grudge* (1915), and a string of other "greaser" films, and continue in the sound era as the bandit/*bandito* stereotype in *Western Code* (1933), *The Treasure of the Sierra Madre* (1947), and, to violent extremes, in *Ride Vaquero* (1953) and *Bandolero!* (1968). One strand of the western reveals the greaser-bandit in the form of the "good badman," modeling a Hispanic Robin Hood. Perhaps the two most popular of this type are the Cisco Kid series and the Zorro franchise, both inspired by *The White Vaquero* (1913) and *The Caballero's Way* (1914). The Zorro films center on an American of Spanish ancestry in Old California who tirelessly fights tyrannical power in the name of American-style justice with bandit-style methods. The series begins with Douglas Fairbanks starring in the title role in *The Mark of Zorro* (1920) and *Don Q, Son of Zorro* (1925) and subsequently stars Robert Livingston in *The Bold Caballero* (1936), Duncan Renaldo in *Zorro Rides Again* (1937), Reed Hadley in *Zorro's Fighting Legion* (1939), and Tyrone Power in *The Mark of Zorro* (1940). The Cisco Kid series, the more prolific of the two, also features a Robin Hood–type bandit slightly more in touch with his "Latin lover" side. The series stars Warner Baxter, Cesar Romero, Duncan Renaldo, and Gilbert Roland in the title role with such titles as *In Old Arizona* (1929), *The Arizona Kid* (1930), and *The Cisco Kid* (1931). The Cisco Kid and Zorro series both eventually made their way to television and had a lasting influence on the bandit character, for example in Anthony Quinn's martyr character in *The Ox-Bow Incident* (1943) or his dignified marquis character in *California* (1946) and the parodic *Three Mesquiteers* series beginning in 1935.

Over time, as the stereotypes developed, their social functions gradually grew. Two other strands of westerns that treat specifically the Battle of the Alamo and the Mexican Revolution reflect this development in Hispanic characters and their relationship to U.S. citizens of Mexican descent. In treating the Alamo and the events in the mid-1830s surrounding the Texas War for Independence, studio films often portray Mexicans and Tejanos as villains or hapless victims of their nation's social condition; in either form, the characters' downfalls simply allowed studios to appease contemporary mainstream tastes. *Martyrs of the Alamo* (1915), directed by W. Christy Cabanne and produced by D. W. Griffith, remains one of the most controversial inasmuch as it borrows some racist politics from the contemporary Griffith hit film *Birth of a Nation;* as a matter of fact, the production company advertised the film as *The Birth of Texas* to resonate with Griffith's classic Civil War film. In *Martyrs, The Man from the Alamo* (1953), *The Last Command* (1955), and *The Alamo* (1960), historical veracity appears less important than dramatization of a staunch patriotism that has become practically synonymous with the battle's legend. John Wayne's *The Alamo,* for example, provides only glimpses of General Santa Anna and his Mexican troops and instead attacks the disloyalty of a fellow Anglo as a covert statement against the communist threat of the previous decade.

Similarly, *Viva Zapata!* (1952) treats the Mexican Revolution of 1910 but stands instead as an expression of explicitly anticommunist values during the Cold War. Many silent films reveal a racist contempt for Mexican history and, by extension, U.S. citizens of Mexican heritage. Gary D. Keller, Alfred Charles Richard Jr., and other film historians note that because the Mexican Revolution occurred just as the U.S. film industry began gaining power and prestige, the revolution and its characters provided filmmakers with a convenient villain, and consequently these films entrenched negative Hispanic stereotypes in the American collective imagination (Keller, 71; Richard, xxv). *The Mexican Joan of Arc* (1911) and *The Mexican Revolutionists* (1912), although portraying a slightly more sympathetic portrait of the Mexican Indian rebels, still offer stereotypical characters, mostly bandits; others are less politically sensitive through their use of bandit-revolutionary characters, the most sensationalistic of which include *Villa Rides* (1968), *The Professionals* (1966), and *The Wild Bunch* (1969). *The Treasure of Pancho Villa* (1955), *They Came to Cordura* (1959), and *The Old Gringo* (1989) and deal only indirectly with the revolution or its history, using it as a backdrop for romantic adventures with varying degrees of success and, as a result, ignore the significance of the Mexican Revolution to American history.

The most provocative films treating Chicano themes and characters combine the western with the social problem genre, drawing attention to issues of concern to Americans. In *The Man from Del Rio* (1956), Anthony Quinn plays a Texas sheriff of Mexican descent, who never wins over the bigoted townspeople whom he protects, and in *The Outrage* (1964), an adaptation of Akira Kurosawa's classic *Rashomon* set in the Wild West, a Mexican bandit serves as the villain and raises awareness to the stereotypes surrounding the character; both films highlight the discrimination and racial inequity in American culture. *Giant* (1956) symbolizes through the marriage of a white cattle baron's son to a Tejana and the birth of their son the "browning" of the Texas family as well as the fading Eurocentricism of its patriarch. And in the Cold War classic *High Noon* (1952), Katy Jurado's character is introduced as the stereotypical cantina whore with a heart of gold, yet by the end of the story she centralizes the ethic of social responsibility and convinces other wavering characters to deny their own selfishness and to act in the name of justice.

Other social problem films treat contemporary periods and raise consciousness to issues of concern. In *Bordertown* (1935), Paul Muni portrays an intelligent and motivated Mexican American law student, who, in spite of graduating at the top of his class, is thrown out of a courtroom and disbarred for his temper. Although the messages in the film are inconsistent—when the Mexican American tells a white woman of his love for her, her reply is, "We aren't from the same tribe, savage!"—the film draws critical attention to the prevailing attitudes toward the Mexican American generation before World War II and sets the stage for later social problem films. Chicano historians point to the discrimination surrounding the mass deportations of Mexican Americans during the Depression, which is treated in several films. *Break of Dawn* (1988), based on the documentary *Ballad of an Unsung Hero* (1983), tells the story of Pedro J. Gonzalez, a telegraph operator for Villa in the Revolution who comes to the United States after the war and earns a reputation as a popular radio personality. Gonzalez uses his on-air influence to draw attention to the discriminatory practices of the Department of Labor's "Operation Deportation" during the Depression and is subsequently deported himself. Like *Break of Dawn, The Ballad of Gregorio Cortez* (1983) and a short, *Seguin* (1981), employ independent production methods to create more explicitly subversive social statements. *Seguin* revises the history of the landed Tejanos who fought in the Battle of the Alamo. A revisionist western, *Gregorio Cortez* reveals one plot in English that follows a typical western plot of a posse hunting a fugitive Mexican bandit interwoven with a subversive plot in the form of a Spanish-language *corrido,* a border ballad, that provides his perspective and defends his actions. Code-switching English and Spanish, not only in the dialogue but imbedded in the continuity, hints at the multicultural strength inherent in filmed histories. These three films recount historical material treated unfavorably in some studio films and critically revise the stereotypes and themes, while initiating new film forms and aesthetics. These filmmaking strategies appear even more prominently in Chicano films that treat American society during and after World War II.

Moving Forward: 1945–1990

Historians point to World War II as a significant turning point for U.S. citizens of Mexican heritage (Gutiérrez, 312–18). War films that reveal their service and sacrifice in wartime include *A Medal for Benny* (1945) and *Hell to Eternity* (1960), highlighting the irony of ethnic discrimination in American culture. A number of melodramas and social problem films carry forth this point and advocate equality in a statement of American democracy in the post–World War II years.

The noted actor Ricardo Montalbán, founder of NOSOTROS, an organization dedicated to improving the representation of U.S. citizens of Mexican heritage in popular culture, plays in several social problem films. Montalbán brings to the big screen sympathy for characters who struggle against ethnic and class discrimination—in *Right Cross* (1950) as a young Chicano boxer, in *Mystery Street* (1950) as a police officer fighting for justice, and in *My Man and I* (1952) as a fruit picker who is cheated out of his wages. Orson Welles's *Touch of Evil* (1958) dramatizes the injustice that is part of bordertown life for Chicanos and Chicanas in the 1950s, although it indulges in sensationalism and ignores the irony of Mexican immigrants to the United States being political aliens in a land once considered their homeland. From midcentury up through the 1970s, Chicano social history and the films that chronicle it put to test the debate over assimilation and nationalism; this can be seen most clearly in film treatments of immigration.

Only a few films present sympathetic and, at times, accurate depictions of life on the border and the act of crossing the border. Films such as *El Norte* (1983), told from the perspective of a Guatemalan brother and sister, and *The Border* (1982) dramatize injustices in U.S. immigration policy and the horrific extent to which immigrants will go to get to the North. *Esperanza* (1985), directed by Sylvia Morales, and *Despues del Terremoto/After the Earthquake* (1979), directed by Lourdes Portillo and Nina Serrano, are two shorts that offer a uniquely Latina perspective on immigration issues. *Alambrista!* (1977) and *Raices de Sangre* (1976) use border crossing as a trope for a nationalistic argument against economic exploitation of immigrants. Similarly, *Salt of the Earth* (1954), *The Lawless* (1950), and *El Corrido* (1976) treat the conditions of working-class Chicanos after World War II and point to the function of labor-reform activism and unionization as socially acceptable modes of political resistance, a matter revisited in Jeremy Paul Kagan's crime thriller *The Big Fix* (1978).

In opposition to the tradition of immigration suggested by most U.S. histories, historian Rudolfo Acuña argues that, because the American Southwest is a native territory for Chicanos and Chicanas, crossing the border can be a figurative reclamation of Aztlán, their ancient homeland. During the turbulent civil rights movement of the 1960s and 1970s, Acuña's thesis gives rise to Chicano nationalism, a separatist social policy in counterattack against an equally exclusionary U.S. domestic social policy. Much of the literature written at the time by Chicanos and Chicanas professes nationalism, and several films, such as *I Am Joaquin* (1969), which adapted Corky Gonzalez's legendary epic poem and became the first Chicano film, and the documentary-styled *Yo Soy Chicano* (1972), carry forward this social philosophy. Several film scholars, including Chon Noriega, locate oppositional and resistant politics at the core of Chicano film, primarily as these films respond to misrepresentation in mainstream films.

Studio-produced films misrepresent to a large degree the anger and frustration of the Chicano generation, especially in treating gangs—in *Warriors* (1978), *Walk Proud* (1979), *Boulevard Nights* (1979), and *Blood In, Blood Out: Bound by Honor* (1993). Edward James Olmos's *American Me* (1992) subverts the violence of the gang exploitation films by naturalistically depicting the life story of the father of one of the largest gang and prison "families," looking back to the 1940s through the 1970s. The first studio-produced feature film directed by a Chicano, Luis Valdez's *Zoot Suit* (1981) presents a revisionist history of a significant moment in the formation of Chicano culture; *American Me* and many of the most effective Chicano films produced since 1980 enact this strategy. In *Zoot Suit,* as in *Distant Water* (1990), the Southern California zoot-suit riots of the 1940s are dramatized. *Pachucos* and *pachucas* wore "drape shapes" as a self-expressive act of independence and rebellion against a biased society; mainstream society saw their nonconformity, especially during the tense period of World War II, as un-American. *Zoot Suit* further reveals the discrimination that the legal system brought against one zoot-suit gang in the Sleepy Lagoon murder trial. Valdez highlights the biases and subjectivity of mainstream society in the 1940s maltreatment of Chicano youth by counteracting the law and state authority with multiple perspectives and even multiple endings to this film story. After Valdez failed to reach as wide an audience as he had wished with *Zoot Suit,* he was determined to make a film with social relevance that a mainstream audience would appreciate. *La Bamba* (1987) depicts working-class conditions to emphasize the success-story of Ritchie Valens, a Chicano rock and roll singer, and his climb to fame.

Of course, *La Bamba* does more than simply tell this biographical story. Released within months of *Born in East L.A.* (1987), *The Milagro Beanfield War* (1988), and *Stand and Deliver* (1988), *La Bamba* heads what has been called "Hispanic Hollywood," mainly due to

FIGURE 29. *Zoot Suit* (1981). Playwright and director Luis Valdez uses theatrical techniques in the film when he has El Pachuco (Edward James Olmos) directly address the audience, informing them that *Zoot Suit* combines fact and fiction to explore a chapter of Mexican American history. Courtesy Universal Pictures.

its box-office and critical success. Coming on the heels of *Zoot Suit* and *Gregorio Cortez,* these four films and the debates surrounding their production and marketing centralize the most controversial and critical issue involved in Chicano studies. In film as well as social history, the main issue is acculturation: to what extent should a native minority assimilate into or separate from a dominant mainstream? Where most studio films from the first half of the century favor assimilationism and some post–World War II independent films allow Mexican Americans self-expression of nationalism, by the late 1980s, studios and the mass market to which they make appeals showed interest in depictions of Chicano culture, just as many filmmakers—including Luis Valdez, Moctesuma Esparza, Jesús Salvador Treviño, Ramon Menendez, Alfonso Arau, and Robert Rodriguez—have benefited by crossing over to the mainstream. Depictions of Mexican American characters and themes suggest movement away from the traditional stereotypes and toward multiculturalism.

In "crossing over" markets and traditions in the 1980s, Chicano films took advantage of big budget production and distribution methods; more audiences seeing such films made them that much more effective as vehicles for change in a democratic, multicultural society. Moreover, that mainstream audiences had been "crossing over" to traditionally marginalized cultural ideas and values hinted at a shift away from nationalistic debates to pluralistic syncretism in late-twentieth-century American society. The diversity of production methods and stories reflect how many recent Chicano films disrupt previously drawn film types and contribute to American multiculturalism. Films such as *Born in East L.A.* and *A Million to Juan* (1993) use comedy to undercut the greaser-bandit-*vato* stereotype. These two films, along with *Stand and Deliver* and *The Milagro Beanfield War,* effectively appeal to a mass market and present a socially conscious statement about Chicano rights without enacting a defensive, exclusionary nationalism. Moreover, as films reveal specific aspects of Chicano culture for a mainstream audience, such as Valdez's rendition of the Christmas *Pastorela* (1991) or the handful of films on the Day of the Dead holiday like *Anima* (1989), a fuller appreciation of American multiculturalism results. Like *Zoot Suit* and *American Me,* the short *Espejo* (1991) and *Mi Vida Loca* (1994) portray an insider's view of the inner-city social condition and from a Latina perspective. As these topics are treated for a mainstream audience, traditionally ignored viewpoints are shared with more of American society. Films such as *Fools Rush In* (1994), the love story of a Chicana artist and an Anglo architect; *Selena* (1997), a biopic reminiscent of *La Bamba* though offering a Latina hero; and *Spy Kids* (2001), a family-oriented spy spoof, treat the theme of multiculturalism explicitly.

Like *American Me, Zoot Suit, Gregorio Cortez, Seguin,* and several others, *My Family/Mi*

Familia (1995) offers a revisionist history of Chicanos through its story. The film set a weekend per-screen average record when it opened as part of Cinco de Mayo celebrations in 1995, helping to prove its acceptance in American culture. *My Family* comes as close to epic as any Chicano film, covering three generations of Chicanos in California starting before the territory was part of the United States. The father's migration north from "*un otro pais,*" another country and another world, the mother's deportation during the Depression, one son's involvement in World War II, another son's assimilation and upward mobility through becoming a lawyer, one daughter's involvement in the Catholic Church—each family member disrupts a stereotype and becomes part of a larger Mexican American family and an American cultural constellation. Perhaps the most significant part of the family history covers the two youngest sons, the older involved in zoot-suit-type gangs and eventually executed by a policeman, the younger, scarred by witnessing the elder's death, becomes a prison inmate and must overcome a tradition of victimization. In retelling the histories, *My Family* provides mainstream audiences traditionally ignored aspects and viewpoints that are part of American multiculturalism.

Into the Future

The twenty-first century promises a hopeful future for multiculturalism. The 2000 Census reports that Latinos and Latinas, two-thirds of them of Mexican heritage, constitute 12 percent of the U.S population, and it projects that the Hispanic population will increase by more than 2 percent over the next three decades. Across a variety of areas, including politics, education, commerce, and arts, Mexican Americans continue to contribute in increasing numbers to America's multicultural, democratic society. U.S. feature films have become significantly more diverse, especially in terms of themes, characters, production methods, and an ever-growing appreciation by mainstream audiences since World War II. The diversity of film types and characters benefits modern American society as an expression of democracy and multiculturalism. Many of the earliest character types and themes in U.S. film reflect the legacy of colonization. Where the Chicano civil rights movement provided independent cultural expressions, it injected an exclusionary social politics to counteract an equally exclusionary Eurocentric American tradition. The last years of the twentieth century offered hope through cultural syncretism and pluralistic integration of U.S. society, highlighted by film treatments of Mexican American history.

References

Filmography

The Alamo (1960, F)
American Me (1992, F)
The Ballad of Gregorio Cortez (1983, F)
Bandolero! (1968, F)
Blood In, Blood Out: Bound by Honor (1993, F)
The Border (1982, F)
Bordertown (1935, F)
Born in East L.A. (1987, F)
Boulevard Nights (1979, F)
Break of Dawn (1988, F)
The Caballero's Way (1914, F)
California (1946, F)
The Captive God (1916, F)
The Cisco Kid (1931, F)
Despues del Terremoto/After the Earthquake (1979, F)
El Norte (1983, F)
Espejo (1991, F)
Esperanza (1985, F)
The Fall of Montezuma (1912, F)
Fools Rush In (1994, F)
Giant (1956, F)
The Greaser's Gauntlet (1908, F)
The Grudge (1915, F)
Hell to Eternity (1960, F)
High Noon (1952, F)
I Am Joaquin (1969, F)
In Old Arizona (1929, F)
Kings of the Sun (1963, F)
La Bamba (1987, F)
The Last Command (1955, F)

The Man from Del Rio (1956, F)
The Man from the Alamo (1953, F)
The Mark of Zorro (1920, F; 1940, F)
Martyrs of the Alamo (1915, F)
A Medal for Benny (1945, F)
The Mexican Joan of Arc (1911, F)
The Mexican Revolutionists (1912, F)
The Milagro Beanfield War (1988, F)
A Million to Juan (1993, F)
Mi Vida Loca (1994, F)
My Family/Mi Familia (1995, F)
My Man and I (1952, F)
Mystery Street (1950, F)
The Old Gringo (1989, F)
The Outrage (1964, F)
The Ox-Bow Incident (1943, F)
Pastorela (1991, F)
The Professionals (1966, F)
Red River (1948, F)
Ride Vaquero (1953, F)
Right Cross (1950, F)
Salt of the Earth (1954, F)
The Searchers (1956, F)
Spy Kids (2001, F)
Stand and Deliver (1988, F)
Touch of Evil (1958, F)
The Treasure of the Sierra Madre (1947, F)
Villa Rides (1968, F)
Viva Zapata! (1952, F)
Walk Proud (1979, F)
Warriors (1978, F)
Western Code (1933, F)
The White Vaquero (1913, F)
The Wild Bunch (1969, F)
Yo Soy Chicano (1972, F)
Zoot Suit (1981, F)

Bibliography

Acuña, Rodolfo. *Occupied America: The Chicano's Struggle toward Liberation.* New York: Harper & Row, 1972.

Gutiérrez, David. "Ethnic Mexicans and the Transformation of 'American' Social Space: Reflections on Recent History." In Marcelo M. Suárez-Orozco, ed., *Crossings: Mexican Immigration in Interdisciplinary Perspectives,* 309–335. Cambridge, MA: Harvard University Press, 1995.

Keller, Gary D. *Hispanics and United States Film: An Overview and Handbook.* Tempe, AZ: Bilingual Press, 1994.

Noriega, Chon A. *Chicanos and Film: Essays on Chicano Representation and Resistance.* New York: Garland, 1992.

——, ed. *Shot in America: Television, the State, and the Rise of Chicano Cinema.* Minneapolis: University of Minnesota Press, 2000.

Richard, Alfred Charles, Jr. *The Hispanic Image on the Silver Screen: An Interpretive Filmography from Silents to Sound, 1898–1935.* Westport, CT: Greenwood, 1992.

Vento, Arnoldo Carlos. *Mestizo: The History, Culture, and Politics of the Mexican and the Chicano.* Lanham, MD: University Press of America, 1998.

Ware, Caroline. *The Cultural Approach to History.* New York: Columbia University Press, 1940.

[JACQUELYN KILPATRICK]

Native Americans

In 1893 Frederick Jackson Turner presented a paper titled "The Significance of the Frontier in American History," which has provided grist for study and argument ever since. In it he states, "Up to our own day American history has been in a large degree the history of the colonization of the Great West. . . . In the case of most nations . . . development has occurred in a limited area; and if the nation has expanded, it has met other growing people whom it has conquered. But in the case of the United States we have a different phenomenon. . . . The frontier is the outer edge of the wave—the meeting point between savagery and civilization." Historians such as Ray Allan Billington, D. W. Meinig, and Patricia Nelson Limerick have taken various positions on Turner's vision of the frontier, but one thing seems to remain constant—"frontier" and "Indian" (the presumed "savages") have been inextricably connected. If indeed America's idea of itself is the product of the movement of that frontier across the continent, then the way America sees itself is deeply connected to attitudes and ideas about Native Americans. Those ideas fall roughly into three categories: noble savage, bloodthirsty savage, and a nostalgically envisioned part of a vanishing and vanquished nature.

When James Fenimore Cooper wrote *The Leather-Stocking Tales* in the first decades of the nineteenth century, he had a wealth of literature, mostly "nonfiction," filled with good and bad Indians to draw upon. But it was Cooper himself who most thoroughly established the stereotypical extremes of the Indian—the noble savage and the bloodthirsty savage—in the realm of popular fiction. The lasting quality of the expectations for the behavior of Native Americans he introduced are made obvious by the fact that his most famous novel, *The Last of the Mohicans,* was made into a Hollywood film five times, the latest in 1992, a time of supposedly new sensitivity and sensibilities.

In effect, Cooper was building an American nationalist mythology through identification with the natural landscape and its original inhabitants. His work, even when using historical events or characters such as the siege at Fort Henry or the Delaware Chief Tamenund, is an elaborate fabrication of myth. The "history" he presents renders the complex societies of the Native Americans of the northeastern United States into a simple background for a colonial story, and Cooper's creation of the Indianized white intermediary and hero of the new American mythology would later become a buttress of the film industry, with stars such as Gary Cooper, John Wayne, and even Paul Newman playing savvy woodsmen or plainsmen who were raised by Indians. They were, in fact, generally better at being Indian than the Indians, just as Cooper's Natty Bumppo always managed to be a better Indian than either Chingachgook or Uncus.

Robert Montgomery Bird's *Nick of the Woods* (1837) was second in popularity only to Cooper's *Leather-Stocking Tales.* Bird's hero's name was Nathan Slaughter, a one-man genocide squad who made his way through twenty-four American editions, echoing the creed that the Indian race was made up of bru-

FIGURE 30. *The Last of the Mohicans* (1936). Hawkeye (Randolph Scott) must decide whether to side with the British protecting the colonists or honor his long-standing allegiance to the Mohican people. Courtesy Reliance Productions of California.

tal beasts beyond redemption and beneath contempt. Aside from the bloodthirstiness of his savages, Bird's Indians were only slightly more intelligent than the rocks they hid behind. His very effective method for transmitting their lack of intelligence to the reader was the creation of Indianese, which most of us recognize as Tonto-talk. Bird's Indians were the first to discover they were pronoun-challenged. In *Nick of the Woods,* Nathan Slaughter meets Wenonga, a villainous Shawnee. "'Me Injun-man!' . . . 'Me kill all white-man! Me Wnonga: me drink white-man's blood: me no heart!'" (Stedman, 68). Unfortunately, the pronoun fault and the addition of "um" to every other word became the all-purpose Indian speech for authors who came after Bird and for the only recently diminishing dialect of the all-purpose Hollywood Indian.

As the "frontier" moved west, the opening of the Oregon Trail and the gold strikes in California produced a swarm of white men, women, and children moving across Native American lands. Clashes were frequent, and the government assigned thousands of military men to stand between Euroamerican citizens and noncitizen American Indians. It was the stuff of which legends are made, and the excitement of real and imagined dangers assured a reading public that was well prepared for the heroic Indian-fighter of the dime novels, first published by Irwin P. Beadle & Company in 1860. The authors of these short, fast stories took the ingredients in Cooper's works about Woodland and Plains Indians, Bird's negative attitudes about all American Indians, and the romance and danger of the frontier and made them into a mix-and-match recipe for western fiction that has survived well over a hundred years of use in novels and provided the basis for the model Indian in Hollywood's moviemaking.

The time zone for the dime novel and most western films is necessarily at the point of contact between the civilizing white presence and the "savages" of the West, which provides the conflict central to the genre. These stories bear little resemblance to the actual, historical facts of the points of contact, which were well documented by the Board of Indian Commissioners appointed by President Grant. In its report of November 23, 1869, the board stated, "The history of the border white man's connection with the Indians is a sickening record of murder, outrage, robbery, and wrongs committed by the former as the rule, and occasional savage outbreaks and unspeakably barbarous deeds of retaliation by the latter as the exception. . . . The testimony of some of the highest military officers of the United States is on record to the effect that, in our Indian wars, almost without exception, the first aggressions have been made by the white man, and the assertion is supported by every civilian of reputation who has studied the subject" (Prucha, 63).

This was definitely not the picture a nineteenth-century Euroamerican reader received of the interaction between the Native tribes and the white people of the "frontier" borderlands.

The "Indian" as Spectacle

By the late nineteenth century, the bloodthirsty savage was firmly entrenched in the new American mythology, and one of the

American heroes in perpetual confrontation with him was Buffalo Bill Cody. A prolific self-promoter, Buffalo Bill was one of the most popular of the dime novel heroes and an important figure in the rise of the modern cinematic western. A natural showman, he used his popularity to launch his Wild West Show and, later, his film company. The Wild West Show provided the simplified, standardized, and largely erroneous conceptions of what a Native American "is" for American and European audiences of his time and for film audiences around the world since that time. His imaginative, staged encounters have provided grist for the Hollywood mill for over a century.

The Wild West Show lost its glamour and sparkle before it faded away in the early 1900s. It had been replaced with the new invention, the moving picture. But in many ways, the dime novel and the Wild West Show lived on in those movies, a large percentage of which were westerns, and most westerns included at least an Indian or two. Unfortunately, the actual people remained unseen, replaced by the "Hollywood Indian."

By the year 1894, when Thomas Edison presented to the world the first Kinetoscope, Native Americans were no longer perceived as a threat of any kind, and the Euro-American consciousness was ready to look back on the noble savage, the "first" Americans, nostalgically. It was therefore understandable that Edison's first film vignettes would include titles such as *Sioux Ghost Dance* (1894), *Parade of Buffalo Bill's Wild West* (1898), *Procession of Mounted Indians and Cowboys* (1898), *Buck Dance* (1898), *Eagle Dance* (1898), and *Serving Rations to the Indians* (1898). Two years later, in 1896, the peep shows were projected onto a screen at Koster and Bial's Music Hall in New York City, and the strange representation of the American Indian began in earnest, with flickering ghosts of invented as well as real Native people.

Because they lacked the experience to view the images critically, the early audiences largely accepted as true what they saw in the darkened nickelodeons. Moving pictures were persuasive, and they were seen on the same screen as the newsreels that told them of real-world events. Although they understood the stories to be fiction, they trusted in the images. The particular Indian, whether noble or savage, might have been a screenwriter's invention, but they believed completely in the *idea* of Indianness he or she represented.

Filmmakers knew the impact their films had on their audiences. In an article D. W. Griffith wrote for *The Independent* in 1916, he referred to his films as "influential" and noted that "last year in twelve months one of many copies of a single film in Illinois and the South played to more people and to more money than all the traveling companies that put out from New York play to in fourteen months." The sheer volume of viewers, as well as the persuasive nature of film, made the nascent film industry immensely important in perpetuating the Noble Savage and Bloodthirsty Savage stereotypes to new generations of Euro-Americans.

By the second decade of filmmaking, America was involved in or preparing for World War I. Americans wanted to see the all-American hero, the hero best described by the frontier tamer. The war had started in Europe, and although President Woodrow Wilson issued a proclamation of neutrality, the War Department was concerned about the image of the American military as well as with attracting as many volunteers as possible. Three years later the Wilson administration would form the Committee on Public Information, which mobilized 75,000 speakers to deliver patriotic talks across the country. It also distributed 75 million pamphlets, sponsored war expositions in dozens of cities, and produced propaganda films with titles such as *The Kaiser: The Beast of Berlin.*

Actually, the first of those propaganda films was produced in 1914, when the United States was still politically neutral. It was *The Indian Wars,* a highly exaggerated film by Buffalo Bill Cody about the battles he fought against the

Indians, bloodthirsty foes that Americans of the time generally viewed as vanquished and vanishing. The U.S. Army sent troops and equipment for the filming, General Nelson Miles himself agreed to appear in the film, and the War Department put the Pine Ridge Sioux at Cody's disposal. Such astonishing support was possible because the film was to be used for War Department records and to enlist recruits. As the United States prepared, overtly or not, to enter World War I, it was important to bolster morale and present the military as a force with a noble history, invincible, and quintessentially American.

The film, directed by Theodore Wharton, was first shown to cabinet members, congressmen, and other dignitaries in Washington, and it became an "official" government record—a frightening thought, considering the absolute dedication of its primary producers to presenting the battles as unquestionably justifiable and heroic. In particular, the 1890 massacre at Wounded Knee, South Dakota, of more than three hundred Sioux, the majority of whom were women and children, was presented as a valiant victory. As a propaganda piece, the film was a great success. It tied up "the Indian problem" in a neat package to be purchased for the price of a ticket. It validated and valorized the cavalry troops who fought the American Indians, and it showed the generosity and humanity of the U.S. government toward a defeated enemy. This is a blatant rewriting of the history of Indian-white relations, with the cinematic version becoming a hyperreality.

Silent Stereotypes

The one-dimensional stereotyping of Native Americans in silent films was largely due to the melodramatic nature of the early cinema. The dependable happy ending, where the villains get what is coming to them, was also a typical popularization of the ideals and attitudes of the Progressive era.

Louis Reeves Harrison, a very influential reviewer for *Moving Picture World,* was a major proponent of the Progressive attitude in filmmaking. In an article, "The 'Bison 101' Headliners," in the April 27, 1912, issue of *The Moving Picture World,* he described American Indians as "cruel, crafty, and predatory with no universal language, no marks of gradual enlightenment and incapable of contributing anything of value to human evolution.... Race hatred was unavoidable and it is only modified today. The average descendant of colonial families has little use for the red man, regards him with distrust and, with poetic exceptions, considers him hopelessly beyond the pale of social contact" (Friar and Friar, 56). Harrison may have had little use for the "red man," but he did agree with the many directors and producers of silent films that the Indian made an interesting museum piece, if nothing else. He continued, "The Indian, however, remains one of the most interesting and picturesque elements of our national history. . . . He was essentially a man of physical action, using only that part of his brain which enabled him to be crafty in the hunt for food, though he had vague poetic ideals and nebulous dreams of barbaric splendor" (Friar and Friar, 56).

Being a "man of physical action" made the Indian a perfect foil for the heroic white man in the silent films, and it was perhaps those "vague poetic ideals and nebulous dreams of barbaric splendor" that he was suspected of harboring that could occasionally make him Noble, especially in the past tense.

"Friends of the Indians"

However, by the early 1920s many Americans had become frustrated with the government's inability to solve the "Indian problem," and there was widespread misperception of, disagreement about, and dissatisfaction with the treatment of Native Americans. One of the most outspoken critics of the government's treatment of the American Indian was Zane Grey. Grey's novels often depicted the Native Americans as victims of Euroamerican greed, betrayal, and neglect, but the first of his novels to specifically focus on the American Indian was *The Vanishing American.* It must have seemed the perfect time for Grey, who had firsthand knowledge of the American Indians of the Southwest and thought of them as something more than artifacts, to tell an American Indian story through the newest and most persuasive of media, the motion picture. However, the new film industry was concerned with giving audiences what they wanted and expected, not in educating them in the realities of Native American life.

In a letter to William H. Briggs on May 23, 1924, Grey wrote, "I have studied the Navajo Indians for twelve years. I know their wrongs. The missionaries sent out there are almost everyone mean, vicious, immoral useless men [*sic*] . . . and some of them are crooks. They cheat and rob the Indian and more heinously they seduce every Indian girl they can get hold of" (Aleiss, 470). He was not disposed to change his story of reservation reality in favor of purifying the missionaries' image, but the studio that made his story into a film most definitely was.

The final cinematic version of *The Vanishing American* illustrates the noble but doomed savage stereotype, the brave warrior who loses the Darwinian battle for survival, the villainous agent, and missionaries that are plain good folk. Paramount also added an interesting prologue which depicts human evolutionary history, starting with the cavemen, which effectively places the American Indian firmly in the line of development—further along than the cavemen but not as evolved as the white men. The film is decidedly sympathetic to the Natives, but the changes made between Grey's script and Paramount's film very clearly define what was acceptable to the American public at the time of the film's release.

The "Talkies"

In the early sound films, stereotypes of Native Americans were conveyed to a large degree by language or, perhaps more importantly, the lack of language. The signs that accompanied the Indian of the silent film (the scowling face, rigid body, and anything-goes wardrobe) were carried over to the sound western as the "natural" pose of a Native American. Rarely was an articulate Indian heard, and Indians were depressingly devoid of humor. Most Native Americans in western films had very little to say beyond the ubiquitous grunt or war whoop inherited from the dime novel, and it did not get much better when those early directors and scriptwriters did give their Indians voices. Use of an alien-sounding language, rarely genuine native languages, also contributed to the "othering" of the Native American for mainstream audiences. Hollywood had its own ideas of what an Indian sounded like and went to extreme lengths to get the "authentic" sound. In *Scouts to the Rescue* (1939), for instance, the Indians were given a Hollywood Indian dialect by running their normal English dialogue backward. By printing the picture in reverse, a perfect lip-sync was maintained, and a new "Indian" language born.

Historian Patricia Nelson Limerick writes, "If Hollywood wanted to capture the emotional center of Western history, its movies would be about real estate. John Wayne would have been neither a gunfighter nor a sheriff, but a surveyor, speculator, or claims lawyer." She makes the point that the intersection of races and the allocation of property unified Western history, since that history has been an "ongoing competition for legitimacy—for the right to claim for oneself and sometimes for one's group the status of legitimate beneficiary of Western resources" (Wexman, 71–76). Land is at the center of virtually every western ever made in which Indians appear. Even when it is not overtly at issue, its place is irrefutable, and scenes of natural beauty or harsh surroundings abound. Often, the land is impressive but arid or wild and therefore of no value as "raw" land. The value, then, lies in the sacrifice and hard work poured into the land by the settlers. In films such as William Seiter's *Allegheny Uprising* (1939), the appropriation of the land is justified by the labor invested by the settler who has made the uncharted wilderness his home and assumed his position as the "natural" proprietor. The land becomes the fruit of his labor, and his physical and emotional investments give him a moral right to it.

Most early Euroamericans believed that land not used was wasted. The idea was that to use it properly, one should invest oneself in that land, make something of it, as did the settlers in *Allegheny Uprising* (1939). The Euro-American ideal of the family farm is presented as obviously superior to the Native American attitude toward land, where all was held communally. The general assumption was that the Native Americans were not using the land properly and that dispossession was not only inevitable but also righteous. The concept of land as property is one of the fundamental ideas upon which the American ideal of freedom is based. If one *owns* the land one lives upon, security is nearly absolute. American Indians had not generally adhered to the principles of individual ownership, so their claims were easily ignored and the settling of the West became a heroic enterprise, an idea that carried over to the western movie.

Most films made in America that portray Indians take place in the nineteenth century, and virtually all westerns are placed between 1825 and 1880, the time of westward expansion—the ultimate land grab, from the Native American point of view. The result is a perception by the American public that would be, even if the depictions were historically accurate, confined to a period of fifty-five or so years, which is a very short piece of a Native American history that goes back thousands of years. There is no pre-white world in these films, and rarely was a "modern" American Indian seen.

John Price describes the development of the pseudohistory of white/Native interaction as a "movie story told by white American producers and directors to a white North American audience, assuming and building the plot from anti-Indian attitudes and prejudices" (76). Native Americans became part of the landscape as the history of the West became an allegorical history, and the western became a system of symbols supporting a self-justifying history.

Americans of the 1940s and 1950s rarely questioned the images Hollywood provided of the American Indian, and movies with slaughters of and by Native Americans were so accepted that they were used to teach children in public schools. For instance, the 1940 film *Northwest Passage* was chosen by the Department of Secondary Teachers of the National Education Association for study because Rogers, of Rogers' Rangers fame, "comes to personify man's refusal to bow to physical forces, and the success of this hardy band of early pioneers symbolizes our own struggle against bitter enemies in the modern world" (Sterner, 2). The symbol in question, the Indians, are presented as a bloodthirsty bunch of heathen devils who get what they deserve for attacking innocent settlers. The Native American made a perfect stand-in for the enemies of World War II America, especially because it was firmly believed that all "real Indians" had vanished.

The Cold War

In post–World War II America, life was good once more. However, by the early 1950s, concern about the possibility of the communists provoking a nuclear war was sending children scooting under desks in bomb drills, and the Cold War was on. One result of the fear of Communism in America was the development of McCarthyism. Congressional committees were set up to investigate anti-American activities and blacklists were developed. One result of the blacklists was a climate of fear and, in Hollywood, the shock of suddenly finding oneself one of the oppressed. Films of the 1950s, therefore, ran the gamut from racist, political propaganda to a type of enlightenment not seen in Hollywood since the days of the silent film.

Broken Arrow (1950) has been consistently cited as an example of the burgeoning cultural awareness in Hollywood, prompted at least in part by resistance to McCarthyism. Stereotypes were reinvestigated and cultural norms, such as the righteousness of Manifest Destiny, were questioned. There was an attempt in this film to create multidimensional human beings who were Apache—an unusual idea in Hollywood—but five centuries of stereotypes still cast their shadows over *Broken Arrow*. For instance, the idea of miscegenation got the same old treatment. Tom Jeffords (James Stewart) falls immediately in love with Sonseeahray, played by a darkened and contact lens–wearing Debra Paget. They are married and deliriously happy until they are ambushed by villainous whites, and Sonseeahray is killed. Jeffords rides off alone into the sunset, alone once more. It is a touching love story, but it could not continue. The same would hold true in films made through the 1990s.

FIGURE 31. *Tell Them Willie Boy Is Here* (1969). In 1909, a reluctant sheriff, Christopher Cooper (Robert Redford), hunts a California Indian (played by Robert Blake) who has killed his father-in-law in self-defense. Redford has just discovered the body of Willie Boy's Native American girlfriend Lola (Katharine Ross). The film, based on an actual event, is a study in the racist attitudes prevalent at the beginning of the twentieth century. Courtesy Universal Pictures.

Most Americans defined the civil rights movement as the struggle of black people to gain equal status with the white majority, but many Americans in the late 1960s and early 1970s were not yet willing to pay to see a film about an oppressed African American. One "safe" way to tell the story of society oppressing a minority was to make a movie about a Native American. The images and stereotypes of Native Americans during this period made them rather perfect as complex, sympathetic subjects because they were seen as not only poor and oppressed but also mystical and natural, to say nothing of vanished. The Native American was reinstated as Hollywood's favorite metaphor.

For instance, when Abraham Polonsky returned to Hollywood after two decades on the blacklist, the film he chose to make was *Tell Them Willie Boy Is Here* (1969). It shows society's faults, but in a very one-dimensional way—the Paiutes are mere symbols for the oppressed in America, and Willie Boy acts as a stand-in for the youth culture of the late 1960s. (If Willie is the rebel youth, his people emerge as the mindless, oppressed masses who have bought the system, or who have at least given up on fighting it.) Pauline Kael, in a *New Yorker* review, insists that Willie is definitely a metaphor for the militant African American men of the era, and "since a Black man (the Indian pretense isn't kept up for long) can't trust any white man—not even Coop—there can be no reconciliation of the races, so he should try to bring everything down." Although better than most, this film makes the Indians, en masse and in particular, stand-ins for other people and other ideas, as did many other films of the era.

By 1970, the Vietnam War was winding down, and atrocities such as My Lai were becoming public knowledge. Director Ralph Nelson wanted to make a statement about the war and its excesses, and he chose as his vehicle the all-purpose metaphor for the oppressed, the American Indian. *Soldier Blue* has received criticism from various sources for being much too violent and much too graphic in its representation of the 1864 massacre at Sand Creek, where volunteer soldiers from Denver slaughtered a band of Cheyenne, though a filmmaker would be very hard pressed to match the actual violence and cruelty of the actual massacre. Nelson's intention was to sensitize the American public to the "plight" of the Vietnamese by relating the similar atrocities committed by the U.S. government ninety years before. He was evidently at least somewhat successful in that attempt, but it is an unfortunate thing for Native Americans because they are once again presented as victims who lost and then disappeared. If the scene at *Soldier Blue*'s end were not so bloody and horrible, this film would not have found its way onto anyone's list of "meaningful" films about Native Americans.

On the other hand, *Little Big Man* (1970) has been called the "best yet" film about Native Americans. It also used a white hero to depict the Indian experience, but of all the films made in the 1960s, 1970s, and 1980s that were sympathetic portrayals of the American Indian, it has received the most positive response. It is a well-made film—well acted, directed, and edited, and very entertaining.

The 1868 massacre of the Cheyenne at the Washita River in Oklahoma is much less graphic and bloody than the scene of the massacre at Sand Creek in *Soldier Blue,* but it is much more effective. One reason for this is that in *Little Big Man* the Cheyenne are people—not as fully realized as in Thomas Berger's novel but much more so than in previous films. Cheyenne voices, laughter, and cries become real, and it is possible to care about them personally, so their slaughter is more heartrending than the butchery of unknowns in *Soldier Blue.* Perhaps that simple fact makes a better point than any other in the film.

The 1980s and 1990s

In 1986, the Academy Award for best documentary feature was given to Maria Florio and Victoria Mudd for *Broken Rainbow* (1985), a documentary about the forced relocation of the Navajo so that their land in the Four Corners region of the Southwest could be strip-mined. Shots of Black Mesa being ripped apart, old men and women forced into government housing and then evicted for not paying taxes, livestock slaughtered by the government, and federal tractors plowing under the scrub grass necessary for sustaining stock fill the film. It is impossible to view *Broken Rainbow* without emotion, and it is particularly important because it brought into focus for the American people that all those atrocities they came to know about in *Little Big Man, Soldier Blue,* and other films from the 1960s and 1970s were not isolated horrors from the past but part of an ongoing oppression.

Still, as the yuppies replaced the hippies, the very cyclical American fascination for the American Indian definitely waned, but a few decent films from the 1980s had Native Americans as their subject. One of those is *Powwow Highway* (1989), an odd little film that almost everyone likes for one reason or the other. It has been called a comedy, a thriller, a road film, a western, an action film, a buddy film, even a mystical movie, and each of these fits to at least a small degree. This shape-shifting is intentional and very effective in taking apart the old stereotypes of the American Indian.

The "sets" in this film are real locations and include poverty-stricken reservations, a ratty pool room, a powwow in a high school gym, and a middle-class Denver suburb as well as road shots and location shots in Santa Fe, New Mexico. One reason this film was so well received by American Indians is that they *rec-*

ognized the story, the people, and the places—a rare thing in depictions of Native Americans.

The two buddies in the film are Buddy Red Bow (A Martinez) and Philbert Bono (Gary Farmer). Buddy is a Vietnam veteran, an AIM member who was part of the Wounded Knee standoff, a volatile young man who is not shy about expressing his point of view, verbally or physically, and a respected member of his tribe. He is in many ways like his cinematic predecessor Willie Boy. The other buddy, Philbert, initially seems to be Buddy Red Bow's absolute opposite. Phil is a big man with a sweet smile, a soft look, and an open sincerity that seems, at first, very simple. That simplicity is easily misunderstood as simplemindedness, but he is actually quite bright. He has chosen the "old way" and moves to a different rhythm. Usually, the Hollywood Indian who makes that choice, rare though that is, behaves as though he has had a lobotomy and forgotten that he actually lives in the twentieth or twenty-first century. Philbert has no such problem.

Other characters and places are recognizable—for instance, the Pine Ridge "goons" the pair encounters and the family moving away from the reservation for better opportunities and more safety. It is a good film about real people who are Native American—a rarity.

In 1990, the more mainstream *Dances with Wolves* was hailed as a landmark film because it treated the American Indians as fully realized human beings, and it does make a serious attempt to do so. Kevin Costner, the director, producer, and star of the film, chose to use talented Native American actors from the United States and Canada for the Native American parts, with the result that they are believable, likable, and interesting.

However, every positive trait of the Lakota has a correlative and opposite trait in the white world of the film, a white world represented by the U.S. Army. Whereas Ten Bears (Floyd Red Crow Westerman), Kicking Bird (Graham Greene), and Wind in His Hair (Rodney A. Grant) are very individualized, respectable, and intelligent men, the cavalry officers are misfits at best and psychotics at worst. Even Costner's character, Lieutenant John Dunbar, begins the film as one of those whose screws are a bit loose. Given his choice of assignments in payment for his bravery, Dunbar chooses to go west. He wants to see the frontier "before it is gone." He is another white hero going in search of the Vanishing American.

Given that the film attempts to turn around the stereotypes developed over hundreds of years in a little over three hours, it is understandable that the characterizations of the white people in the film would be one-dimensional, but that, too, buys into other stereotypes that are equally unfair. Not all white men of the 1800s were stupid or cruel, and not many were crazy. The mentally unbalanced officer (such as Dunbar's commanding officer at Fort Hays) is quickly becoming stereotypical in films that are supposed to be sympathetic to the American Indians or Vietnamese or other oppressed groups, and this is a problem. It releases the general public from responsibility and relates violence and cruelty to the madness of a few.

The main flaw of *Dances with Wolves*, however, remains the problem of appropriation of identity. John Dunbar is the white narrator of an Native American existence who, when the white men become so loathsome to him he can no longer stand being identified as one of them, shouts, "I am Dances with Wolves!" Like so many "heroes" before him, he becomes a better Indian than the Indians. He also marries a woman from the Sioux camp; however, she does not die at the film's end. This would be a breakthrough for miscegenation in Hollywood films, except that Stands with a Fist (Mary McDonnell) is a white woman saved by the Lakota as a young child, so the taboos apparently still exist in Costner's film. In fact, when Kicking Bird asks his wife, Black Shawl (Tantoo Cardinal), what the people think of the match, she responds, "They like the idea. It makes sense. They're both white."

The film is also set within the "comfort zone"—that fifty-year period of cinematic Indian existence in the "Wild West." As Jan Elliott, editor of *Indigenous Thought,* states, "Indians are the only minority group that the Indian lovers won't let out of the nineteenth century. They love Indians as long as they can picture them riding around on ponies wearing beads and feathers, living in picturesque tepee villages and making long profound speeches. Whites still expect, even now, to see Indians as they once were, living in the forest or performing in the Wild West shows rather than working on the farm or living in urban areas" (Weaver 27). Elliott's description fits Costner's invention very nicely. They are indeed picturesque, like a favorite snapshot in a very old album.

The most positive point about the current Native American image in film is the fact that many Native Americans are now telling their own stories. Writers such as Tom King, Gerald Vizenor, and Sherman Alexie are writing films that tell the story from a contemporary native point of view and that privilege a native audience. Directors such as Lena Carr, George Burdeau, Victor Masayesva, Geraldine Keams, and many more are directing films with native actors and writers. There are also syncretic partnerships between nonnative and Native American artists that produce films with the better parts from each, with fewer stereotypes of either kind. All in all, things are looking up.

References

Filmography

Allegheny Uprising (1939, F)
Bad Bascomb (1946, F)
The Battle at Elderbush Gulch (1914, F)
Broken Arrow (1950, F)
Broken Rainbow (1985, F)
Buffalo Bill (1944, F)
Buffalo Bill and the Indians (1976, F)
Cheyenne Autumn (1964, F)
Cheyenne Warrior (1994, F)
Clearcut (1993, F)
Dances with Wolves (1990, F)
Dead Man (1996, F)
The Emerald Forest (1985, F)
1492: Conquest of Paradise (1992, F)
Geronimo (1993, F)
Harold of Orange (1984, F)
House Made of Dawn (1972, F)
Imagining Indians (1992, F)
Incident at Oglala (1992, F)
The Indian Wars (1914, F)
Itam Hakim Hopitt (1980, F)
Laguna Woman (1992, F)
The Last of the Dogmen (1995, F)
The Last of the Mohicans (1936, F; 1992, F)
Little Big Man (1970, F)
Lonesome Dove (1990, TV)
A Man Called Horse (1970, F)
Massacre (1912, F)
Medicine River (1994, F)
Nanook of the North (1922, F)
Northwest Passage (1940, F)
One Flew Over the Cuckoo's Nest (1975, F)
Pocahontas (1995, F)
Powwow Highway (1989, F)
A Pueblo Legend (1912, F)
Pueblo Peoples: First Contact (1992, F)
The Real People (1976, F)
The Redman and the Child (1908, F)
Renegades (1989, F)
Ritual Clowns (1988, F)
Scalphunters (1968, F)
Scouts to the Rescue (1939, F)
The Searchers (1956, F)
Smoke Signals (1998, F)
Soldier Blue (1970, F)
Stagecoach (1939, F; 1966, F; 1986, F)
The Sunchaser (1996, F)
Tell Them Willie Boy Is Here (1969, F)
They Died with Their Boots On (1942, F)
Thunderheart (1992, F)
Two Rode Together (1961, F)
Ulzana's Raid (1972, F)
The Vanishing American (1925, F)
War Code: Navajo Code Talkers (1996, F)
War Party (1988, F)
White Fawn's Devotion (1910, F)
Witness (1996, F)

Bibliography

Aleiss, Angela. "The Vanishing American." *Journal of American Studies* 25.3 (December 1991): 470.

Bellin, Joshua David. *Demon of the Continent: Indians and the Shaping of American Literature.* Philadelphia: University of Pennsylvania Press, 2001.

Bird, Robert Montgomery. *Nick of the Woods.* 1837. Ed. Curtis Dahl. New Haven: College and University Press, 1967.

Friar, Ralph E., and Natasha A. Friar. *The Only Good Indian: The Hollywood Gospel.* New York: Drama Book Specialists, 1972.

Griffith, David Warik. "Pictures vs. One Night Stands." *The Independent,* 11 December 1916.

Hilger, Michael. *From Savage to Nobleman: Images of Native Americans in Film.* Metuchen, NJ: Scarecrow, 1995.

Huhndorf, Shari M. *Going Native: Indians and the American Cultural Imagination.* Ithaca, NY: Cornell University Press, 2001.

Kilpatrick, Jacquelyn. *Celluloid Indians: Native Americans and Film.* Lincoln: University of Nebraska Press, 1999.

Price, John A. "The Stereotyping of North American Indians in Motion Pictures." In Gretchen Bataille and Charles L. P. Silet, eds., *The Pretend Indians: Images of Native Americans in the Movies,* 75–91. Ames: Iowa State University Press, 1993.

Prucha, Francis Paul, ed. *Documents of United States Indian Policy.* 2d ed. Lincoln: University of Nebraska Press, 1990.

Rollins, Peter. *Hollywood as Historian: American Film in a Cultural Context.* Lexington: University Press of Kentucky, 1983.

Rollins, Peter, and John E. O'Connor. *Hollywood's Indian: The Portrayal of the Native American in Film.* Lexington: University Press of Kentucky, 1998.

Stedman, Raymond William. *Shadows of the Indian: Stereotypes in American Culture.* Norman: University of Oklahoma Press, 1982.

Sterner, Alice P. "A Guide to the Discussion of the Technicolor Screen Version of *Northwest Passage.*" *Photoplay Studies,* vol. 6. New York: Educational and Recreational Guides, 1940.

Weaver, Jace. "Ethnic Cleansing, Homestyle." *Wicazo Sa Review* 10.1 (1994): 25–31.

Wexman, Virginia Wright. *Creating the Couple: Love, Marriage, and the Hollywood Performance.* Princeton: Princeton University Press, 1993.

[MICHAEL SHULL AND DAVID E. WILT]

Radicals and Radicalism

Fears and concerns about radicalism have been a familiar theme in U.S. history. Indeed, David Caute writes, "The great fear, like the threat of upheaval and expropriation that inspires it, has been a recurrent phenomenon in the history of the bourgeoisie since the French Revolution" (17). The United States is not the only nation to have suffered from (and reacted to) anxiety about radicals in its population: England, France, Italy, Germany, and Spain are a few of the other countries that have experienced similar "fears."

In the United States, fear of leftist radicalism, most particularly militant labor, anarchism, and communism, bordered on mass hysteria during brief periods of the twentieth century. This kind of fear flared up after the Russian Revolution in the form of the "Red Scare" of 1918–1920, "a nationwide antiradical hysteria provoked by a mounting fear and anxiety that a Bolshevik revolution in America was imminent" (Levin, 29), and after World War II, when the Soviet Union took control of much of Eastern Europe and the Chinese mainland fell to the Communists, with the resultant anticommunist excesses of the late 1940s and early 1950s, stigmatized by the name "McCarthyism."

Fear of the extreme right—native fascists, ultraright nationalists, even the "military-industrial complex"—has not been so concentrated. The right radicalism of the 1930s—exemplified by the brief popularity of such homegrown radicals as William Dudley Pelley's "Silver Shirts" and the Christian Front of radio priest Father Coughlin, not to mention the notorious German-American Bund—sparked contemporary concern. In the 1960s and 1970s, when such groups as the John Birch Society and the Minutemen sprang up, another wave of anxiety swept the land. And in the 1990s, with the legacy of the Oklahoma City bombing and other acts and plots attributed to the "militia" movement, the radical right has once again become a popular bogeyman.

Despite the ebb and flow of left-radical and right-radical bogeymen, Hollywood has been remarkably consistent in its outlook: radicalism is bad, particularly in the United States. It is the rare film indeed that presents a positive portrait of radicals in a contemporary, domestic setting.

The Early Years

Reflecting the turmoil and diversity of America during the decade preceding World War I, early silent films gave voice to a surprisingly wide spectrum of political viewpoints. In this period the film industry repeatedly questioned the abuses of individual capitalists and their underlings, while simultaneously cautioning the working class to shun militant labor radicalism and to seek peaceful accommodation with the system.

The influence of the Progressive movement, which began in the late nineteenth century, may be seen here. "Progressivism . . . was a 'reform' movement. It aimed not at the radical replacement of existing institutions, but at their peaceable modification" (Kennedy, xiv). Hollywood's distrust of radical solutions to social, economic, and political problems seems consonant with the meliorist approach: while injustices should be addressed, extreme measures should be distrusted. On the Progressive agenda were issues such as prohibition, women's suffrage, an income tax, regulatory commissions, restrictions on child labor, government aid to farmers, and the right of labor to organize (MacKay, 11). Although some at the time felt that the Progressives were radical, and even antibusiness, their ideas struck a responsive chord in many: in the 1912 presidential election, Teddy Roosevelt (the "Bull Moose" party candidate but a long-time spokesman for Progressivism) received 27 percent of the popular vote and eighty-eight electoral votes. Twelve years later, Robert LaFollette polled 4.8 million votes for president on the Progressive ticket. Both Roosevelt and LaFollette were third-party candidates in these elections.

Although Progressivism, socialism, and communism were rarely broached in American films prior to 1918, the capital-labor issue and its linkage to the radical left was addressed in several hundred films; labor strife, most particularly violent strike actions instigated by labor agitators, was a significant factor in more than a hundred of these motion pictures. Unfortunately, few of these films remain extant, and, even among those surviving, many are damaged or incomplete, and some of them may be viewed only in archives or private collections such as the George Eastman House, the Library of Congress, and the Museum of Modern Art.

With that in mind, there remain a few important examples of early silent films that treat the topic of left-wing radicalism. In *The Voice of the Violin* (1909), directed by D. W. Griffith, a German-born violin instructor with socialist tendencies falls in love with his student, a capitalist's daughter. Fired by the young woman's father, the violinist puts down his instrument and picks up a bomb to assist swarthy anarchists in obliterating an evil capitalist. The target, the young man learns just in time, is to be the father of his sweetheart.

Satirical films often ridiculed radicals, sometimes suggesting that only minds made unstable by alcohol or otherwise undeveloped could possibly take seriously the concepts of socialism or labor militancy. An amusing example of this approach is *Bill Joins the WWWs* (1914). An office boy named Bill stops to listen to a "W.W.W." street rally (the initials stand for "We Won't Work," satirizing the anarcho-syndicalist Industrial Workers of the World, or IWW). The message of resistance to the iron heel of capital so impresses Bill that he cannot wait to tell his boss, who turns out to be a very unreceptive audience.

The Red Scare and the 1920s

Films with sociopolitical themes—in which radical messages, although somewhat muted, were given a voice—all but disappeared by the end of 1918. This retrenchment was a direct result of America's participation in the wartime effort to defeat Germany, the fall of tsarist Russia, and the subsequent rise of Red Russia. With the conclusion of the war in November 1918, there arose a coalition determined to subdue labor militancy and destroy left-wing challenges to American institutions. Two right-wing groups during this period were the American Protective League (APL) and the American Legion. From the spring of 1918 through the fall of 1920, the American motion picture industry helped shape, channel, and sustain the nation's collective loathing of foreign enemies and domestic radicals. Screen villains included the radical "new woman," spineless intellectuals, malevolent Jews, and "free lovers." Even the American West was endangered: in *Mr. Logan, U.S.A.* (1918), featuring cowboy star Tom Mix, German agents and World War I agitators collaborate in an attempt to disrupt production at a strategically important tungsten mine.

By the summer of 1919 the Red Scare was in full stride. In *The Undercurrent* (1919), a veteran named Jack (real-life war hero Guy Empey) returns to his old job in the steel mills only to be laid off through Bolshevik machinations. Unemployed and emotionally vulnerable, Jack comes under the influence of a radical intellectual and a lascivious communist vamp. But Jack comes to his senses and embarks on an antiradical rampage, assisted by soldiers from a nearby Army barracks.

The confrontational nature of earlier capital-labor films and the viciousness of World War I propaganda carried over into movies of the Red Scare era. Militant laborers are often punished or killed without remorse. In *Riders of the Dawn* (1920), based on a popular Zane Grey novel, a veteran leads a group of paramilitaries against a group of labor militants threatening the wheat harvest in America's heartland. *Bolshevism on Trial* (1919) features wealthy radical idealists and assorted opportunists who are led astray by a Red ideologue. They finance an experimental socialist community on "Paradise Island," where social harmony quickly degenerates after work assignments are made: a cinematic mockery of Marx's "workers' and peasants' paradise."

After 1920, there was a dramatic decline in political anxiety. As historian M. J. Heale puts it, "the Big Red Scare had largely succeeded in cutting down radicalism" (75), and the prosperity of 1920s America alleviated the public's fear of internal revolution. This lack of interest was directly reflected in motion pictures. Even in those comparatively few films that still touched on radicalism of either the left or the right, the propensity for rhetorical shrillness and graphic violence was substantially toned down. For instance, most relevant films set in America portrayed gangster-like agents of the Soviet state, not domestic radicals. Beyond the occasional reference to "the Revolution," politics and the contemporary leadership of the Soviet regime were seldom mentioned. By the middle of the decade, the Bolshevik revolution was actually the subject of a romantic melodrama, *The Volga Boatman* (1926), featuring a Red hero played by matinee idol William Boyd (who later became the beloved Hopalong Cassidy).

The 1930s: The "Red Decade"

During the early years of the Depression, the economic distress in the United States was so acute—and the government response so slow and restricted—that the virtues and efficacy of capitalism were seriously questioned: "American capitalism was facing the greatest crisis in its history, and there was sporadic talk of revolution both from resuscitated radicals and from conservatives" (Heale, 103). Given the misery and social disruption that accompanied the Depression, it is not surprising that some cast an approving eye on the "order" established in fascist countries like Germany and Italy. *Gabriel Over the White House* (1933) stars Walter Huston as a president who, after undergoing a near-death experience, suspends Congress and temporarily rules the United States as a dictator (with noble motives, of course). His actions include the arrest and summary execution of gangsters, and the military blackmail of foreign nations into signing a disarmament treaty. But such extremist solutions, rare in Hollywood films (aside from individual vigilantes who began to crop up as protagonists in the 1970s and beyond), were ultimately rejected in real life by most Americans, particularly after the initiation of President Franklin Delano Roosevelt's New Deal.

In the early part of the decade there were at least some positive images of the left, along with attacks on right-wing radicalism. In *Our Daily Bread* (1934), a young urban couple is given a small farm; they establish a cooperative, recruiting from people displaced from their homes and jobs by the Depression. Although quite mild overall, the film was severely attacked at the time for its "socialist" ideas. *The Front Page* (1931) mocks the anticommunist political slogan of the city's corrupt sheriff and mayor: "Reform the Reds with a Rope." A notorious police "Red Squad" appears in *Heroes for Sale* (1933), intimidating a World War I veteran who has been falsely convicted of labor agitation. *Modern Times* (1936) burlesques the irrational fear of communists: Charles Chaplin's Tramp character is mistakenly arrested after waving a red flag (actually a construction warning pennant) during a strike march. Such overreaction to innocuous acts mocked the paranoia of the Red-baiters. Another film that condemned right-wing extremism even more strongly is *Black Legion* (1937), which features a xenophobic secret society opposed to foreigners, "anarchists, and the Roman hierarchy." The Black Legion—whose robes and hoods resemble those of the Ku Klux Klan—was excoriated as un-American and harmful, despite its alleged "patriotic" goals.

However, extremists on the left were not spared. A number of films mocked crazy leftists in urban working-class or lower-middle-class settings. *The Merry Frinks* (1934) features Allen Jenkins in a comic supporting role as a self-appointed "peoples' lawyer" who owns a prized portrait of Josef Stalin. Campus radicals and the 1930s student peace movement were attacked in *Fighting Youth* (1935), in which a radical coed (played by Ann Sheridan) is assigned to vamp the quarterback and thereby subvert the football team. *Red Salute* (1935) stars Barbara Stanwyck as a general's daughter enamored of left-wing causes who eventually winds up romantically linked with an Army corporal (Robert Young). Her previous paramour, a foreign-born student radical leader, is taken out of the picture when he is arrested by immigration authorities. The notorious San Francisco general strike of 1934 is featured in *Together We Live* (1935): a group of elderly Civil War veterans help round up alien Red agitators who have duped honest, native-born workers and are planning a terrorist bombing.

Political Filmmaking of the 1930s and 1940s

Out of the commercial mainstream but still worthy of examination were the politically oriented films produced by leftist groups such as the Workers' Film and Photo League, NY Kino, and Frontier Films. From the early 1930s through the end of the decade, filmmakers including Leo Hurwitz and Paul Strand, mostly based in New York City, made movies such as *Bonus March* (1932), *Native Land* (1942), and *Return to Life* (1938). These were mostly documentaries using footage shot at rallies and demonstrations, and they only occasionally received general release. They also differed from standard Hollywood product in that they espouse a particular point of view and do not automatically reject radical action as a solution to society's problems (although they generally stopped short of fomenting armed revolution against the government).

As the decade ended, warfare in Europe and Asia highlighted the international struggle among fascism, democracy, and communism, but Hollywood's depiction of the growing global conflagration stressed melodrama over politics. The leftist documentary *The Spanish Earth* (1937) describes the political nature of the Spanish Civil War, unlike fictional films on the topic such as *Last Train to Madrid* (1937) and *Blockade* (1938)—and it was still controversial during the McCarthy period. On the home front, *The Grapes of Wrath* (1940), while sympathetic to the working class, warns against involvement with organized radicalism and extremism. Tom Joad (Henry Fonda) says, "if only all the folks got together and yelled," but backs away from even this mild stance when his mother objects. In *Meet John Doe* (1941), villain D. B. Norton (Edward Arnold) reveals his true, far-right colors by his admiration of Napoleon, his formation of a motorcycle corps with fascist trappings, and his ruthless destruction of the John Doe movement when it develops a true democratic base.

The Postwar Era and McCarthyism

During World War II, Hollywood concentrated on outside foes and put domestic radicals—both left and right—on the back burner. There were a few portrayals of homegrown

Nazis, but these villains were generally portrayed as mere pawns of their German masters, as in *Confessions of a Nazi Spy* (1939). The fact that the Soviet Union was a cobelligerent sharply reduced anti-left messages in films. Indeed, such films as *Mission to Moscow* (1943) and *Song of Russia* (1943) whitewashed Soviet excesses at the time because at the time it was believed that Americans needed to feel positive about an ally. However, once the war ended, fears resurfaced of internal groups that might threaten the democratic system.

Although the Red Menace was one of the major issues in postwar cinema, there were other films about domestic radicalism: several of these featured right-wing, populist demagogues inspired by Louisiana's Huey Long. *All the King's Men* (1949), based on Robert Penn Warren's Pulitzer Prize–winning novel, is the story of Willie Stark (Broderick Crawford), a country lawyer who claws his way to the governorship of an unnamed southern state by ruthlessly manipulating his friends and associates and by his cynical exploitation of the masses. Like Huey Long, Willie Stark is assassinated in the state capitol building at the height of his power. *A Face in the Crowd* (1957) addresses many of the same issues in its tale of Lonesome Rhodes (Andy Griffith), a hillbilly singer who parlays his television popularity into a political movement promoting the presidential campaign of the right-wing Senator Fuller, "last of the isolationists." Rhodes is betrayed by an open microphone that allows the audience for his nationwide broadcast to hear his contemptuous statements about the "sheep" who believe his speeches.

An anti-McCarthy backlash produced films such as *Storm Center* (1956), in which a small-town librarian (Bette Davis) is attacked by anticommunist zealots for refusing to remove a book entitled *The Communist Dream* from her library. She defends the freedom of expression guaranteed under the Constitution, even though she does not personally subscribe to the book's credo. In *Three Brave Men* (1957), a civilian employee of the Navy is suspended as a security risk on the word of his right-wing neighbor, who has an ax to grind, and discovers that "innocent until proven guilty" does not apply in his case. These films were each directed by a screenwriter turned director, Daniel Taradash and Philip Dunne, respectively. Both men were liberals, although none of their previous work was as politically oriented as these pictures. However, both films take pains to make it clear they are not sympathetic to communism, but point out that irrational persecution is also "un-American." *Salt of the Earth* (1954), on the other hand, was the product of an openly leftist director (Herbert Biberman) and screenwriter (Michael Wilson), both of whom had already been blacklisted by the film industry. Yet its tale of labor strife at a New Mexico copper mine is surprisingly restrained. The miners go on strike, but when they are legally prevented from picketing, they do not resort to violence or other extreme measures. Instead, the miners' wives take their places on the picket line. Thus, even a film with impeccable leftist credentials, made outside the mainstream, eschewed advocating radical action.

The 1960s and Beyond

The Cold War spawned a number of right-wing extremist groups, such as the John Birch Society, named after an Army captain killed by Chinese Communists shortly after the end of World War II, and the undercover Minutemen, who trained themselves to serve as guerrilla fighters in the event of a communist takeover of America. With the abuses of the HUAC witch hunts fresh in their minds, many Americans of more moderate views saw these organizations as threats to democracy: one writer claimed that "Far Right activity has been intense and widespread since 1958," although exact membership numbers for any of the organizations were difficult to obtain (at the far end of the spectrum, the American Nazi Party, though notorious, may have had only a few

FIGURE 32. *All the King's Men* (1955). In a thinly veiled biographical sketch of the demagogue Huey Long, the suspicious Willie Stark (Broderick Crawford) keeps close watch over his campaign workers to win at any cost. Courtesy Metro-Goldwyn-Mayer.

score members). Hollywood was a little behind the curve, but, beginning in the 1960s, a number of pictures with political themes featured extremist characters of the right wing. In *The Manchurian Candidate* (1962), a brainwashed Korean War veteran (Laurence Harvey) is the pawn in a plot—masterminded by his own mother—to assassinate a presidential candidate. Ironically, given that communists are behind the scheme, the film portrays Senator Iselin (James Gregory) as a buffoonish pseudo-McCarthy, ineptly ranting about his list of communists in the State Department.

Seven Days in May (1964) depicts a planned coup d'état, spearheaded by Air Force General Scott (Burt Lancaster) and a right-wing senator, in response to the signing of a nuclear disarmament treaty with the Soviet Union. Scott, an extreme "hawk," feels that the president's desire for peace "has stripped the muscle off this nation." In the end, a loyal Marine colonel (Kirk Douglas) exposes the plan and democracy is preserved. Other examples include *Advise and Consent* (1962), *Billion Dollar Brain* (1967), and *Executive Action* (1972). The last picture portrays a right-wing cabal plotting the assassination of President John F. Kennedy, a response to his alleged liberal policies such as the nuclear test ban treaty and his plans to pull the United States out of Vietnam, thus "turning over Asia to the Communists." The conspirators include an ex-CIA agent, a politician, a business tycoon, and a right-wing college professor. (Oliver Stone's *JFK* would revive this plot.)

On the other side of the political spectrum, leftist—especially student—radicalism also appeared in films of the 1960s and 1970s. An early example is *Take Her, She's Mine* (1963), in which a complacent suburban lawyer (James Stewart) must cope with his daughter's involvement in various "causes" and "movements" when she goes off to college. A "Ban the Bomb" protest, a sit-in, and "beatniks" are featured, but in an essentially harmless, unthreatening context. The antiwar movement and student unrest inspired some films in the late 1960s and early 1970s, such as *The Revolutionary* (1970), *RPM* (1970), and the semidocumentary *Medium Cool* (1969). *The Revolutionary* shows college student "A" (Jon Voight) going from peaceful protest and leaflet-passing to affiliation with a militant group of radicals and, finally, partnership with an anarchist bent on killing a judge. The edge was taken off this film by setting it in an unnamed European country rather than the United States, but its criticism of radicalism was still pointed. Student protests in films of the era were generally shown to be foolish and self-indulgent at best, subversive and dangerously violent at worst. As recently as *Forrest Gump* (1994), there was an unsympathetic portrait of the 1960s radical group Students for a Democratic Society. *Patty Hearst* (1988) is sympathetic to its title character (played by Natasha Richardson), but her kidnapers, the Symbionese Liberation Army, are depicted as unrealistic, self-absorbed, and feckless "revolutionaries."

A few films did feature committed, rational, "radicals." One of the rare films in which radicals—of any stripe—are favorably portrayed in a contemporary U.S. setting is *Shadow on the Land* (1968), a made-for-TV movie that depicts the United States under a military dictatorship in the very near future. Although written by McCarthy-era blacklist figure Nedrick Young, the picture does not present its rebels as identifiably right or left-wing: they just "love freedom." *Shadow on the Land* more closely resembles a film about the European resistance of World War II, but nonetheless it is quite exceptional in making heroes out of Americans trying to overthrow the government. The right-wing equivalent is *Red Dawn* (1984), but in this instance the ideology is clearer: red-blooded American teenagers refuse to submit to Communist rule after Soviet and Cuban troops invade the United States.

Several films dealing with actual historical figures also treat radicals positively. *Reds* (1981) stars Warren Beatty as famed leftist journalist John Reed. A big-budget, romanticized portrayal of radicals in the 1910s and 1920s, *Reds* spends a lot of time on the rocky love relationship between Reed and Louise Bryant (Diane Keaton), although other real-life characters such as Emma Goldman (Maureen Stapleton) and Big Bill Haywood (Dolph Sweet) also appear. Contemporary interviews with "witnesses" (such as Will Durant, Henry Miller, Hamilton Fish, and even George Jessel) add a semidocumentary veneer to the drama. Reed eventually travels to Russia and witnesses the Bolshevik Revolution firsthand. Sixty-odd years after the fact, the "radicalism" presented in *Reds* was not ideologically threatening, softened by time and by the audience's knowledge that the Communist system proposed by the protagonists had failed anyway. *Panther* (1995) is an admittedly fictionalized history of the Black Panthers, glorifying their free lunch programs and their efforts to promote racial awareness among African Americans in the 1960s, and portraying the establishment—especially J. Edgar Hoover and the FBI—as corrupt and racist. The FBI and the Mafia cooperate to end the threat of black revolution by flooding the ghetto with cheap narcotics. The controversy around this film's content was also muted by the passage of time, by downplaying the leftist ideology of the Panther leadership and—once again—by the fact that the group in question is no longer in existence and therefore poses no current threat to American society.

With very few exceptions, however, the film producers—whether established companies or upstart independents—stopped short of endorsing extreme positions on either end of the spectrum. Instead, the dire consequences of radicalism were highlighted. In *WUSA* (1970), the ultraright programming of the eponymous radio station results in protests, a near riot, attempted murder, and a suicide. The abuses of the McCarthy anticommunist witch hunts are depicted in *The Way We Were* (1973), *The Front* (1976), and *Guilty by Suspicion* (1991). Not surprisingly, the impact on the entertainment industry was highlighted over the negative impact in other professions (such as academia).

Hollywood depictions of contemporary domestic radicalism moved firmly to the right in the late 1980s and 1990s, reflecting the public's opinion that "as of the moment, the most terrifying threat to the well-being of the center appears to come from the extremists of the right" (Gardner, 31). *Betrayed* (1988) and *American History X* (1998) deal with the impact of the white supremacy movement. The first film contains a fictionalized representation of the murder of radio talk-show host Alan Berg by militants; an undercover FBI agent (Debra Winger) falls in love with the protagonist (Tom Berenger), a decorated Vietnam veteran who now owns a farm in America's heartland, only to discover that he is a member of a sinister anti-Semitic, racist organization. *American History X* depicts the world of neo-Nazi skinheads, one of whom (Edward Norton) sees the error of his ways and tries to save his younger brother (Edward Furlong) from involvement in the hate group. *Arlington Road* (1999), in which an antiterrorism expert (Jeff Bridges) discovers that his ordinary-Joe next-door neighbor is a radical bomber, makes veiled references to the Ruby Ridge incident (often cited as the catalyst for the upsurge in the militia movement in the United States) and the 1995 Oklahoma City bombing (here transposed to St. Louis).

The Hollywood Extremist

In Hollywood cinema, extremists—including political, religious, and social radicals—are virtually always treated with suspicion. *Citizen Ruth* (1996) is a good example, criticizing both pro-life and pro-choice activists who try to exploit the title character (Laura Dern), a drug-abusing, pregnant woman. Radical attitudes and actions—particularly in a contemporary American setting—are simply not acceptable. As Murray Levin puts it, "a country that loves change but hates revolution is not going to warmly receive radicals and radical ideas" (241).

Despite its liberal reputation, Hollywood generally treats left-wing radicalism as negatively as it does right-wing extremism. After all, films must appeal to a broad audience, and extremist viewpoints are likely to offend at least some portion of the paying audience. Even films that do take an ideological stand draw the line at sympathetically portraying extreme behavior, particularly in contemporary, domestic settings. Regardless of the validity of one's beliefs, violent, illegal, disruptive acts are negatively portrayed. In Hollywood, activism and radicalism are seen as one small step away from fanaticism—and even terrorism.

FIGURE 33. *Reds* (1981). Radical American journalists John Reed (Warren Beatty) and Louise Bryant (Diane Keaton) travel to the epicenter of the Russian Revolution of 1917. The setting and extras generate a semidocumentary, historical look. Courtesy Paramount Pictures.

References

Filmography

Advise and Consent (1962, F)
All the King's Men (1949, F)
American History X (1998, F)
Arlington Road (1999, F)
Betrayed (1988, F)
Billion Dollar Brain (1967, F)
Bill Joins the WWWs (1914, F)
Black Legion (1937, F)
Bolshevism on Trial (1919, F)
Citizen Ruth (1996, F)
Executive Action (1972, F)
A Face in the Crowd (1957, F)
Fighting Youth (1935, F)
Forrest Gump (1994, F)
The Front (1976, F)
The Front Page (1931, F)
The Godless Girl (1927, F)
The Grapes of Wrath (1940, F)
Guilty by Suspicion (1991, F)
Heroes for Sale (1933, F)
Matewan (1987, F)
Medium Cool (1969, F)
Meet John Doe (1941, F)
The Merry Frinks (1934, F)
Modern Times (1936, F)
Mr. Logan, U.S.A. (1918, F)
Our Daily Bread (1934, F)
Panther (1995, F)
Patty Hearst (1988, F)
Red Dawn (1984, F)
Reds (1981, F)
Red Salute (1935, F)
The Revolutionary (1970, F)
Riders of the Dawn (1920, F)
RPM (1970, F)
Seven Days in May (1964, F)
Shadow on the Land (1968, F)
The Spanish Earth (1937, D)
Storm Center (1956, F)
Take Her, She's Mine (1963, F)

Three Brave Men (1957, F)
Together We Live (1935, F)
The Undercurrent (1919, F)
The Voice of the Violin (1909)
The Volga Boatman (1926, F)
The Way We Were (1973, F)
WUSA (1970, F)

Bibliography

Brownlow, Kevin. *Behind the Mask of Innocence: Sex, Violence, Prejudice, Crime—Films of Social Conscience in the Silent Era.* Berkeley: University of California Press, 1990.

Campbell, Russell. *Cinema Strikes Back: Radical Filmmaking in the United States, 1930–1942.* Ann Arbor: UMI Research Press, 1982.

Caute, David. *The Great Fear.* New York: Simon & Schuster, 1978.

Ceplair, Larry, and Steven Englund. *The Inquisition in Hollywood: Politics in the Film Community, 1930–1960.* Berkeley: University of California Press, 1979.

Dees, Morris. *Gathering Storm: America's Militia Threat.* New York: HarperCollins, 1996.

Gardner, James. *The Age of Extremism.* Secaucus, NJ: Carol, 1997.

Goldstein, Robert J. *Political Repression in Modern America: From 1870 to the Present.* Boston: G. K. Hall, 1978.

Hartz, Louis. *The Liberal Tradition in America.* New York: Harcourt, Brace & World, 1955.

Heale, M. J. *American Anticommunism: Combating the Enemy Within, 1930–1970.* Baltimore: Johns Hopkins University Press, 1990.

Hofstader, Richard. *The Age of Reform.* New York: Knopf, 1968.

Horowitz, David. *The Politics of Bad Faith.* New York: Free Press, 1998.

Janson, Donald, and Bernard Eismann. *The Far Right.* New York: McGraw-Hill, 1963.

Kennedy, David M. *Progressivism: The Critical Issues.* Boston: Little, Brown, 1971.

Levin, Murray B. *Political Hysteria in America: The Democratic Capacity for Repression.* New York: Basic Books, 1971.

MacKay, Kenneth Campbell. *The Progressive Movement of 1924.* New York: Octagon, 1966.

Renshaw, Patrick. *The Wobblies.* Garden City, NY: Doubleday, 1967.

Ribuffo, Leo P. *The Old Christian Right: The Protestant Far Right from the Great Depression to the Cold War.* Philadelphia: Temple University Press, 1983.

Roffman, Peter, and Jim Purdy. *The Hollywood Social Problem Film: Madness, Despair, and Politics from the Depression to the Fifties.* Bloomington: Indiana University Press, 1981.

Rosenstone, Robert A. *Visions of the Past: The Challenge of Film to Our Idea of History.* Cambridge, MA: Harvard University Press, 1995.

Sherwin, Mark. *The Extremists.* New York: St. Martin's, 1963.

Shull, Michael Slade. *Radicalism in American Silent Films, 1909–1929.* Jefferson, NC: McFarland, 2000.

Snow, Captain Robert L. *The Militia Threat.* New York: Plenum, 1999.

[DAVID E. WILT AND MICHAEL SHULL]

Robber Barons, Media Moguls, and Power Elites

In post–Civil War America, a new class of mythic character arose in American culture. Described as "fat cats," "robber barons," "titans," "tycoons," or "plutocrats," these business magnates and Wall Street manipulators, Earl Latham writes, were "attacked and defended with violent passion by the struggling partisans of industrialism and of social reform" (v). The "robber barons" of the Gilded Age included J. P. Morgan, Cornelius Vanderbilt, Andrew Carnegie, John D. Rockefeller, and Jay Gould. The foundations of their fortunes were railroads, steel, oil, and banking. These powerful men sometimes became household names: Rockefeller, for instance, "was the most famous American of his day" (Chernow, xiii).

These "Captains of Industry" were both envied and feared: some were real-life Horatio Alger characters who rose from humble origins to positions of fantastic wealth. These tycoons were not necessarily disliked for their immense fortunes and the conspicuous consumption of their lifestyles—the rich may have been envied, but they were not always hated. Rather, it was turn-of-the-century muckrakers who excoriated the robber barons for the way they "exploited national resources . . . made private capital out of the public domain, and used any and every method to achieve their aims" (Mills, 95). But these capitalists were also, paradoxically, admired by those who saw them as "pace-setters of the capitalist motion itself" (Mills, 96), demonstrating the awesome economic power and innovative spirit of the United States. "The whole subject of the grasping, unscrupulous, domineering businessman and his corrupt political ally got into fiction and on the stage" (Flynn, 3) and into a new mass communications medium—the motion picture. By 1910, the primary molder of such images in the popular culture was the movie industry.

However, there was another side of the robber barons that did not as readily become part of the image in popular culture. The father of Standard Oil, John D. Rockefeller, "a semilegendary character . . . appeared to the general public either as a demon of avarice and extortion, crushing without scruple those who stood in his way, or as a high-minded philanthropist, bestowing his bounty with charitable devotion to good works" (Latham, v). The Rockefeller Foundation, created for the "well-being of mankind," has distributed millions of dollars since its inception in 1913, but this largess was discounted by anti-Rockefeller forces, which "succeeded in fixing an ugly stereotype of Rockefeller and the Trust upon the public mind" (Nevins, 334). Andrew Carnegie, a Scots immigrant who amassed an unbelievable fortune in the steel industry, gave 90 percent of his money away during his lifetime (Wall, 882–883). In keeping with the philosophy expressed by Carnegie in his famous 1889 essay (later popularly called "The Gospel of Wealth"), this money was used for the "public benefit," endowing universities, free libraries, parks, halls, and the like so that individuals with superior talents—whatever their socioeconomic status—could rise to positions of leadership.

Given these undeniably altruistic acts, why did the negative stereotype of the robber baron persist? The well-publicized beliefs of the Progressive movement, which spanned the late nineteenth and early twentieth centuries, deserve some credit. The Progressives "saw the central issue of their age as the relation of public to private power, or, more precisely, of the government to the economy. . . . As they depicted it, [Progressivism] was a moral drama, pitting the people, who embodied all that was good about democracy, against big business, which represented the evils of corruption, privilege and exploitation" (Kennedy, vii–viii). And big business, at least in the early part of the century, was identified with the mogul, the tycoon, the robber baron.

Another factor, and one that cannot be discarded out of hand, is the greater dramatic potential in the depiction of a callous, even sinister capitalist as opposed to a saintly philanthropist. Films were quick to seize upon the cigar-puffing, well-dressed, money-obsessed capitalist caricature. These outward attributes were intended to illustrate the robber baron's wealth, power, social status, and separation from the "common man." Early film examples include D. W. Griffith's *A Corner in Wheat* (1909), which portrays a Wall Street financier whose manipulations of the wheat market lead to massive hardships for the working class. Oblivious to the repercussions of his actions, he throws a lavish party to celebrate his success. While the rich revel in decadent excess, Griffith cuts to a suffering working-class mother: after waiting patiently in line to buy a loaf of bread for her starving child, she can no longer afford it, the price having risen during her time in the queue. Justice prevails, ultimately, when the boastful capitalist is accidentally suffocated in one of his silos filled with hoarded grain. The negative portrayal of the wealthy elite is particularly vigorous in the "modern" story section of Griffith's *Intolerance* (1916). When mill owner Jenkins is approached to financially support the "Uplifters Society," the capitalist agrees, coldly noting that he will raise the funds by cutting his workers' wages by 10 percent.

The free enterprise system itself is seldom attacked directly in movie portrayals of robber barons. But a comeuppance for greedy capitalists does occur in a number of films, such as *Money* (1915). After scenes of a lavish "million dollar dinner" for the rich—contrasted with scenes of starving workers on strike—this film concludes with the death of a Rockefeller surrogate named "John D. Maximilian" and the destruction of his palatial home by a climactic storm.

Capitalists were not always beyond redemption. *The Blacklist* (1916) is a thinly veiled dramatization of the 1914 Ludlow massacre, in which the Colorado militia killed nineteen miners and family members. The film depicts the harsh life imposed on workers in the owner's absence. In response to various injustices, the miners protest; when management compiles a "blacklist" of troublemakers, the workers go on strike. In a melodramatic face-off in the company's offices, miner's daughter Vera (Blanche Sweet), shoots and wounds the owner. But, in the end, the injured villain repents and asks Vera to teach him to love her people.

Fat Cats and Radicals: 1910–1940

The struggles between capital and labor abated during the years of America's active participation in World War I as the nation focused on the conflict. During the "Red Scare" at the end of the decade, militant labor was tarred with the "Communist" brush and accordingly crushed by Attorney General A. Mitchell Palmer and federal and state authorities in the so-called Palmer Raids. Film images of "fat cats" also changed: while capitalists were occasionally figures of fun, portrayal of abuses by sinister "robber barons" largely disappeared during an era of widespread prosperity.

Instead, there were some depictions of the rich who "redeem" themselves by joining the working class. In *Triumph* (1924), a young man violates the stipulations of a will and instead of inheriting a cannery, he loses the business to his womanizing half-brother. The new boss, a former socialist sympathizer, adopts ruthless policies that nearly ruin the business, while the disinherited young man achieves redemption by working his way up from the ranks of labor.

Ironically, the Depression, which evolved from the stock market crash in October 1929, did not wipe out the vast fortunes of most of the tycoons, which now included Henry Ford, the richest man in American as of 1925. Instead it was small investors who lost their savings and workingmen who lost their jobs as the economy staggered. Film images of capitalists underwent some changes, although the well-fed tycoon stereotype persisted, often in the persons of actors Edward Arnold, Walter Connolly, Eugene Pallette, and George Barbier. In the early years of the decade, there were some fictionalized "biographies" of tycoons, including *The Conquerors* (1932), starring Richard Dix as a banking magnate in the American West, and *Come and Get It* (1936), with Edward Arnold in Edna Ferber's story of the lumber industry. These films, which frequently show the protagonist making his "long crawl" up the social ladder (Mills, 113), often depict the protagonists as neither wholly villainous nor heroic. One of the most interesting films of this type is *The Power and the Glory* (1933). Tom Garner (Spencer Tracy) starts out as an illiterate railroad trackwalker but eventually rises to fame and fortune as a railroad magnate. Garner is a heroic but flawed character who becomes ruthless and cold as he moves up in the world, abandoning his faithful wife (who had taught him to read). When he finally dies, Garner is mourned by few—a fitting reward for his selfish quest.

As the decade went on, "fat cat" capitalists were frequently figures of fun, whether sympathetic or villainous. In *Paddy O'Day* (1936) the wealthy, inhibited, reclusive Roy Ford (comedian Pinky Tomlin)—spoofing automotive magnate Henry Ford—takes up with a pair of Russian immigrants and finances a chain of numbered restaurants (a reference to the numbered Ford truck factories set up in the Soviet Union a few years earlier). Henry Ford is justly remembered for pioneering mass production of automobiles, but he was not immune to public criticism in this era, especially for his outspoken anti-union views.

Conservative millionaire Humphrey Craig (Walter Connolly), tormented by fears of the New Deal in *Soak the Rich* (1936), becomes so irrationally afraid of the "radical" threat that he drowns a package he believes to be a bomb but that actually contains cigars. Neither these screwball comedies nor the earlier pseudobiographies openly criticize the American free enterprise system, instead choosing to suggest that as people become more rich and powerful, they become removed from the emotions, desires, and pleasures of everyday people—in essence, less human. Hollywood's prescription is that this problem can sometimes be remedied by contact (especially a romance) with the working classes.

World War II, the 1950s, and Beyond

In a spirit of national cooperation—similar to that seen during World War I—labor and management put aside their differences to work on the war effort (at least, this is the image portrayed in films, although in reality there were a number of incidents of labor unrest on the home front). Consequently, the robber baron image was downplayed, except where such characters could be utilized as negative example of "war profiteers." These were balanced by films like *An American Romance* (1944), the rags-to-riches story of an immigrant ironworker turned automobile manufacturer. After Stefan Dangos (Brian Donlevy) builds an industrial empire, he is eased out of power in his own company but returns to lend his managerial expertise to the government's war production effort.

The traditional robber baron image persisted only in isolated films, often period pieces. Henry F. Potter (Lionel Barrymore) in *It's a Wonderful Life* (1946) dominates the town of Bedford Falls and everyone who lives in it, although he is not identified with a particular industry like mining or manufacturing ("I run practically everything in this town," he says). Like earlier versions of the stereotype, Potter cares only for money, and the suffering of others means nothing to him. *Bright Leaf* (1950) features two tycoons: Major James Singleton (Donald Crisp) is the old-fashioned tobacco magnate who loses out to the younger Brant Royle (Gary Cooper) when the latter gains control of a cigarette-rolling machine (new technology wins out over traditional methods). However, Royle is finally defeated when his own wife denounces his harsh, monopolistic practices to the government. As Brant Royle, Gary Cooper is by no means a heroic figure: rather, he is a ruthless business predator.

Post–World War II America underwent enormous changes, and films reflect the social, political, and economic metamorphoses of the era. Along with the postwar baby boom, the growth of suburbs, and the rise of television came the Cold War, McCarthyism, the Korean War, the beginning of the civil rights movement, and a general feeling that the pace of life had accelerated.

The concept of business and industry also evolved away from companies identified with their founder—although "faceless" corporations had existed prior to the 1950s—toward a corporate culture. "The type of the captain of industry no longer runs business. . . . One can see that there are few survivals of the kinds of dealings—with other business, with labor, with the government—that were standard operating practice for the pre–World War I tycoons" (Riesman, 238, 249). A new breed of tycoon emerged, the corporate executive. No longer were companies dominated by, and identified with, a single man. Corporations were depicted as huge and powerful, but the executives at the top were vulnerable to challenges from within and without. Best-selling novels, adapted into such films as *Executive Suite* (1954) and *The Man in the Gray Flannel Suit* (1956), introduced the concept of corporate culture: the president of a company could be deposed and replaced via political infighting with little effect on the company itself, a far cry from the personalized leadership prevalent in earlier screen images. This tended to displace responsibility from a single "robber baron" and focus on the perverse and impersonal nature of the system itself. A more recent and extreme example is *Robocop* (1987): in the near future, the city of Detroit is controlled by a large corporation with an eye toward profits. The powerful CEO (Dan O'Herlihy) is the primary villainous figure, but there is no real suggestion that his death or removal from office would make a significant difference in the situation. Indeed, *The Hudsucker Proxy* (1994) is based on the premise that the head of a corporation can be replaced by a naive newcomer (Tim Robbins) as part of a plot by the sinister chairman of the board (Paul Newman). When the new "boss" outlives his usefulness, his removal by murder is ordered.

The change in focus from individuals to corporations should not suggest tycoons disappeared from films entirely. *The Carpetbaggers* (1964) is based on Harold Robbins's roman à clef about Howard Hughes, here called "Jonas Cord" (George Peppard). Later screen images of the enigmatic Hughes include *Hughes and Harlow: Angels in Hell* (1977) and *Melvin and Howard* (1980). *Billion Dollar Brain* (1967) relates the tale of Texas billionaire General Midwinter's plan to overthrow the communist bloc with a private army. Another evil magnate can be found in *Chinatown* (1974): Noah Cross (John Huston) plots to monopolize the water supply of Southern California—he wants to control "the future"—and is also revealed to be morally corrupt in his personal life, yet no one can stop him. The tycoons of

Trading Places (1983)—the Duke brothers (Ralph Bellamy and Don Ameche)—demonstrate their almost godlike power by switching the lives of a black street hustler (Eddie Murphy) and a yuppie junior executive (Dan Aykroyd). They also scheme to steal government information to corner the orange juice market.

Some films of the past several decades have concentrated on individuals who manipulate the capitalist system to enrich themselves, often disregarding the rights of others, but the traditional, direct linkage between robber baron and worker has been broken. Films like *Wall Street* (1987) and *Head Office* (1986) feature characters who crunch numbers to make (and lose) "paper fortunes" in a sterile office environment, far removed from the companies and employees whose fates they are manipulating. The former picture contains the famous "greed is good" quote, uttered by the unpleasant Gordon Gekko (Michael Douglas), a fitting successor to Henry Potter from *It's a Wonderful Life,* except that Gekko never comes into contact with his victims. An exception to this broken linkage occurs in *Roger & Me* (1989), a semidocumentary directed by and starring Michael Moore, which chronicles Moore's protracted efforts to confront General Motors president Roger Smith with evidence of the poverty and despair afflicting Flint, Michigan, after the closing of many GM plants.

Not all tycoons have vanished or been subordinated to the corporate culture. One of the protagonists of *Meet Joe Black* (1998) is Bill Parrish (Anthony Hopkins), a media mogul who—against type—is depicted as a kind, happy, family-oriented man, respected by even his business rivals. Even before he gets advance notice of his impending death, Parrish is depicted as a caring father and ethical businessman. *The World Is Not Enough* (1999) begins with the murder of an oil tycoon, leaving his daughter Elektra (Sophie Marceau) in charge of his financial empire. Elektra is depicted as competent and ambitious, although she does require the assistance of James Bond (Pierce Brosnan) to preserve her life and wealth, an ironic twist in which the hero works with—rather than against—a corporate magnate. A more traditional tycoon figure appears in *The Big Lebowski* (1998). A case of mistaken identity throws "Dude" Lebowski (Jeff Bridges) into contact with his millionaire namesake (David Huddleston). The rich Lebowski is a crusty, wheelchair-bound, Republican industrialist with an unfaithful young "trophy wife" and an eccentric artist daughter. He sponsors a foundation that helps inner-city youth but is less than charitable toward the Dude.

New technology and business methods breed new moguls, and the computer revolution has its share of techno-tycoons. *Triumph of the Nerds: The Rise of Accidental Empires* (1996) and *Nerds 2.0.1: A Brief History of the Internet* (1998) are TV documentaries directed by Robert X. Cringely. Bill Gates and Steve Jobs, who appear in these films discussing their rise to prominence, were also the subjects of a television docudrama, *Pirates of Silicon Valley* (1999). As the titles of the two documentaries suggest, these new tycoons are seen as "nerds" rather than dangerous "robber barons," although the aggressive business methods of Gates are depicted in some detail.

The Forgotten Robber Baron

Since the 1950s, the concept of personal leadership—good or bad—in business has been supplanted by the idea of wide-reaching, multinational corporations; thus, the "robber baron" character as the individual, antagonistic focus of films has become much less prevalent. In real life, the situation is much the same. Aside from a few notable exceptions such as Bill Gates, Ted Turner, or Rupert Murdoch, the era of the tycoon as public figure has passed. Few can name the presidents of major corporations, and in any case, as noted earlier, corporate leadership is not the same as personal ownership of a company. However, the image of the robber baron has not completely disappeared. Dramatic works prefer to focus upon an individual villain, even if he is merely the representative of a larger organization, so the maleficent magnate who believes his wealth and power place him above the law may still be seen in films. Nonetheless, absent the sociopolitical conditions that led to the creation of the robber baron stereotype, the character lacks much of its previous ideological resonance.

References

Filmography

The Big Lebowski (1998, F)
Billion Dollar Brain (1967, F)
Boy Meets Girl (1938, F)
Bright Leaf (1950, F)
The Carpetbaggers (1964, F)
Chinatown (1974, F)
Citizen Kane (1941, F)
Come and Get It (1936, F)
A Corner in Wheat (1909, F)
Executive Suite (1954, F)
The Great Man (1957, F)
The Hudsucker Proxy (1994, F)
It's a Wonderful Life (1946, F)
The Man in the Grey Flannel Suit (1956, F)
Meet Joe Black (1998, F)
Melvin and Howard (1980, F)
Nerds 2.0.1.: A Brief History of the Internet (1998, D)
Paddy O'Day (1936, F)
Pirates of Silicon Valley (1999, F)
Robocop (1987, F)
Roger & Me (1989, D)
Soak the Rich (1936, F)
Triumph of the Nerds: The Rise of Accidental Empires (1996, D)
Wall Street (1987, F)
The World Is Not Enough (1999, F)

Bibliography

Biskind, Peter. *Seeing Is Believing: How Hollywood Taught Us to Stop Worrying and Love the Fifties.* New York: Pantheon, 1983.

Cagin, Seth, and Philip Dray. *Hollywood Films of the Seventies: Sex, Drugs, Violence, Rock 'n' Roll & Politics.* New York: Harper & Row, 1984.

Cashman, Sean Dennis. *America in the Age of the Titans: The Progressive Era and World War.* New York: New York University Press, 1988.

Chernow, Ron. *Titan: The Life of John D. Rockefeller* New York: Random House, 1998.

Flynn, John T. "The Muckrakers." In Earl Latham, ed., *John D. Rockefeller: Robber Baron or Industrial Statesman,* 1–6. Boston: D. C. Heath, 1949.

Gordon, John Steele. *The Scarlet Woman of Wall Street.* New York: Weidenfeld & Nicolson, 1988.

Hacker, Louis M. *The World of Andrew Carnegie.* Philadelphia: Lippincott, 1968.

Kennedy, David M. *Progressivism: The Critical Issues.* Boston: Little, Brown, 1971.

Latham, Earl, ed. *John D. Rockefeller: Robber Baron or Industrial Statesman?* Boston: D. C. Heath, 1949.

Mills, C. Wright. *The Power Elite.* New York: Oxford University Press, 1956.

Nasaw, David. *The Chief: The Life of William Randolph Hearst.* Boston: Houghton Mifflin, 2000.

Nevins, Alan. *Study in Power: John D. Rockefeller, Industrialist and Philanthropist.* New York: Scribners, 1953.

Palmer, William J. *The Films of the Eighties: A Social History.* Carbondale: Southern Illinois University Press, 1993.

Riesman, David. *The Lonely Crowd: A Study of the Changing American Character.* Rev. ed. New Haven: Yale University Press, 1961.

Schatz, Thomas. *The Genius of the System: Hollywood Filmmaking in the Studio Era.* New York: Pantheon, 1988.

Sklar, Robert. *Movie-Made America: A Cultural History of American Movies.* New York: Random House, 1975.

Toplin, Robert Brent. *History by Hollywood: The Use and Abuse of the American Past.* Urbana: University of Illinois Press, 1996.

Wall, Joseph Frazier. *Andrew Carnegie.* Pittsburgh: University of Pittsburgh Press, 1989.

[SARAH PEARSALL]

Women from the Colonial Era to 1900

Early in John Ford's classic 1939 film *Drums Along the Mohawk,* Gilbert Martin (Henry Fonda) tries to prevent his recently transplanted wife Magdalena (Claudette Colbert) from helping on their frontier farm. When Gilbert asserts that haying is "no job for a woman," she retorts, "Now there you go. Just because a woman is raised in a town she has to be frail. I'm not. I'm strong. You said yourself you couldn't have done without me." As proof, Magdalena goes on to hay, help settlers flee from enemy Indians, locate her husband after battles, nurse him, give birth during a war, and shoot an attacking Indian.

Magdalena Martin embodies a central film image of women in America before 1900: the strong frontierswoman. Historical films generally do not endear themselves to historians, for they rely on such stereotypes and often manipulate history for dramatic effect. Nevertheless, films command vast audiences and often teach people the history they *do* know. Thus, despite films' reliance on stock visions—of strong settlers, bad girls, and women ahead of their times—they are worth studying. The scholarship on American women's lives has blossomed rapidly in the past thirty years. In 1986 Linda Kerber declared that women's history "is now the fastest-growing field within the profession" (vi), and ten years later Carol Berkin added that the field "has flourished during my decade of work" (vii). The thriving condition of American women's history has not been matched by Hollywood, probably because of the traditionally poor box-office performances of films about the distant past. In addition, films reveal more about the sensibility of the times in which they were made than the times they depict. Despite these caveats, filmmakers offer intriguing glimpses of American women's lives.

The Colonial Era

Pocahontas (1995) features a famous early American woman. As reviewers complained, this film misrepresents the sequence of events and cultural mores of both Indians and English. For instance, Pocahontas had no love affair with John Smith. Pocahontas's relationship with nature reflects a strange combination of scholarship by William Cronon and others and the modern idealization of Native life. Pocahontas is also a symbol of the multicultural 1990s. The movie does echo recent scholarship by Helen C. Rountree on the Powhatans, the Indian nation to which Pocahontas belonged. The film places the Native American woman's story at the center, a rarity in films. The film also presents a more compelling narrative than that of the documentary *Pocahontas: Her True Story* (1995), which is guilty of an overdependence on interviews with Pocahontas' descendants, who have their own idealized vision of her life. Nevertheless, this documentary captures her existence with greater accuracy.

Settler women have fared little better. Laurel Thatcher Ulrich, Mary Beth Norton, Carol F. Karlsen, and John Demos have painted vivid portraits of Puritan women in New England. Ulrich declares, "A married woman in early New England was simultaneously a housewife, a deputy husband, a consort, a mother, a mistress, a neighbor, and a Christian" (9). Demi Moore's portrayal of Hester Prynne in *The Scarlet Letter* (1995), "freely adapted" from Nathaniel Hawthorne's novel (a very free adaptation indeed) fails to convey these complex roles. In fact, the film so wildly conflates historical subjects—witchcraft, adultery, slavery, Anne Hutchinson, Quakerism, and the Indian wars—that it creates instead a muddled pastiche. The fit, emancipated Prynne must have been seen by the filmmakers to represent a 1990s ideal. A 1996 film, *The Crucible,* is also based on history and literature. Arthur Miller's original play was less a study of Puritan New England than a condemnation of 1950s McCarthyism. Like *The Scarlet Letter,* this film reflects a 1990s sensibility in which forces of authority repress a woman ahead of her times, along with her sensitive male partner. The film somewhat caricatures the complex interconnections between Puritan theology and women's status explored by historians such as Karlsen, who posits that "Puritans' witchcraft beliefs are finally inseparable from their ideas about women" (181). The film, with its ignorant and slovenly midwives, also bypasses recent scholarship on the skill and respectability of such women. However, the film does convey the status hierarchy of early New England.

Revolutionary Times

Historians such as Linda K. Kerber and Mary Beth Norton have explored women's roles in the revolutionary era. Norton suggests that "as the nature of American government and society had changed during the half-century that witnessed the Revolution, so too had American notions of womanhood" (296–297). Filmmakers have been less ambitious in their coverage. However, the Seven Years' War receives attention in two films: *Allegheny Uprising* (1939) concerns the revolt by American colonists against their British officers, a foreshadowing of the Revolution. It can also be read as American isolationism just before World War II. Jane MacDougall's (Claire Trevor) resourcefulness reflects the "New Woman" persona of the 1930s. A "dead shot," Jane leads the protest against the British. Jane's plucky self-reliance stands in contrast to the limp passivity exhibited by Cora Monroe (Madeline Stowe), in a more recent film about this era, *The Last of the Mohicans* (1992). Based on James Fenimore Cooper's novel, this film's depiction of women leaves much to be desired. Cora does shoot an Indian in self-defense, but her demeanor can best be described as sappy. She relies constantly on men's protection. Indian women fare no better; indeed, they are conspicuous by their near-total absence.

The revolutionary era remains largely neglected by filmmakers. Based on a play by Peter Stone, *1776* (1972) features only two women: Abigail Adams (Virginia Vestoff) and Martha Jefferson (Blythe Danner). The film does attempt to portray the correspondence between Abigail and John Adams. Still, Abigail's complaints about running a farm and Martha Jefferson's dance sequence do not advance an understanding of women's role in the Revolution. Abigail Adams and her experiences receive far better treatment in a popular PBS documentary, *The Adams Chronicles* (1975). A significant innovation in the 1970s, this series gives a much more rounded depiction of this famous first lady.

Two films purport to tell stories about women's lives during the Revolution. One, *The Howards of Virginia* (1940), does so with little success. It tells the story of the freedom-loving Matt Howard (Cary Grant) and his snobby wife, Jane Peyton Howard (Martha Scott). Jane is prone to sob and eager to transplant a hierarchy-based plantation life to the West. Her slave companion, Dicey (Libby Taylor), is in the tradition of eye-rolling, mistress-loving slaves of old Hollywood. This film stands in contrast to *Drums Along the Mohawk.* Although the configuration (privileged wife taken to western farm by independence-minded husband) is similar, the results are different. While both Jane Howard and Magdalena Martin enjoy twentieth century–style weddings (complete with white dresses, bouquets, and bridesmaids), the representation of the wife is more multidimensional in *Drums Along the Mohawk.* Another 1930s "New Woman," Magdalena joins her husband in fighting during the Revolutionary War. The film does an especially fine job of capturing the daily lives of ordinary white people on the frontier, although Indian women make no appearance. In the European Magdalena, director John Ford also tried to recreate, however minimally, multiethnic frontier society. The film's military sequences are undeniably flawed, but the attention to daily life makes this film a strong partner to much recent social history on women.

So, too, do two documentaries. The first, *Mary Silliman's War* (1993) tells the true story of Mary Silliman (Nancy Palk), whose husband was taken captive during the Revolutionary War. Based on a history by Joy Day Buel and Richard Buel Jr., this film employed numerous historians as consultants. The film accurately depicts the suffering of one family during the war, but it also demonstrates that women were not passive victims of either the British or their husbands. It restores the agency of an early American woman, as does *A Midwife's Tale* (1996), which tells the story of Martha Moore Ballard (Kaiulani Lee). Based on a book by Laurel Thatcher Ulrich, the film is most innovative in its techniques. Rather than simply showing Ballard's experiences as a midwife in early republican Maine, the film alternates between Ballard's life and the ways in which Ulrich pieced together Ballard's life from her diary. Ulrich reminds us of the difficulty of this sort of task: "Without documents, there's no history. And women left very few documents." However, Ulrich, along with director Richard P. Rogers and producer Laurie Kahn-Leavitt, capture the life of this midwife with grace and aplomb.

Antebellum Life, the Civil War, and Reconstruction

Few films focus on the American experience in the first half of the nineteenth century. The War of 1812 receives treatment in the two versions of *The Buccaneer* (1938 and 1958). In both films, women are cast as two archetypes: the nice woman and the naughty-but-nice woman. Neither film conveys the complexities of women's lives. The most famous film about the Civil War is of course *Gone with the Wind* (1939), based on Margaret Mitchell's novel. Its portrayal of black women is based on a view of slavery popular at the 1930s: that of Ulrich B. Phillips and the "plantation school" who argued that blacks were happy with their kindly masters. Mammy (Hattie McDaniel), the faithful family retainer, epitomizes this school. The horrors of slavery for black women, and their resistance to it, so eloquently described by later historians such as Deborah Gray White and Ella Forbes, are elided. The film is somewhat more realistic in its depiction of the lives of elite white Southern women. Scholars such as Elizabeth Fox-Genovese and Drew Gilpin Faust have suggested the vital role played by white mistresses in managing households. Faust has postulated that "the harsh realities of military conflict and social upheaval pushed women toward new understandings of themselves and toward reconstructions of the meanings of southern womanhood that would last well beyond the Confederacy's demise" (7–8). Scarlett O'Hara's (Vivien Leigh) strength and her determination to remake herself after the war thus parallel the experience of such women. Bette Davis in *Jezebel* (1938) equally merits applause for her vibrant spirit. Again, these films reflect a 1930s project of featuring strong women in films.

The film version of Toni Morrison's acclaimed novel *Beloved* (1998) also focuses on strong women, in this case African American ones. Sethe (Oprah Winfrey) and Beloved (Thandie Newton) epitomize the agonizing choices inflicted by the brutal slave system.

The film also conveys the challenges African American women continued to face during Reconstruction. Finally, Beloved's daughter Denver (Kimberly Elise) suggests the ways in which African American women overcame these obstacles. These themes echo recent scholarship on women during Reconstruction and capture both the restrictions and the drive for autonomy by black women.

Beloved is very different from the most infamous representation of Reconstruction: D. W. Griffith's *The Birth of a Nation* (1915), based on Thomas Dixon's novel and a deeply flawed view of Reconstruction. Black characters, mostly white actors in blackface, seeking to deprive white women of their virtue prowl throughout the film; black women receive little attention. Indeed, even when Silas Lynch (George Siegman) founds "a Black Empire," he chooses a white woman for his "queen." White women (especially as portrayed by Lillian Gish) are weeping victims of the black man. This pernicious distortion of Reconstruction arose in part from a contemporaneous school of history that argued that Reconstruction represented the "tragic era" of American history in which blacks terrorized whites. Needless to say, historians have thoroughly rejected this interpretation.

Northern women have received less attention than their southern counterparts, although scholars such as Jeanie Attie and Elizabeth D. Leonard have partially rectified this situation. Three versions of Louisa May Alcott's novel *Little Women* (1933, 1949, and 1994) reveal more about their own times than those of Alcott. In the 1933 version, Marmee (Spring Byington) is shown as an active caregiver. Director George Cukor, targeting Depression-era audiences, highlights the Marches' charity toward the hungry Hummels. Katherine Hepburn sparkles as Jo March, another "New Woman" of the 1930s. In contrast, Mervyn LeRoy's 1949 version paints these "little women" as wives of veterans and loving consumers of shop products (the camera pans carefully over each Christmas gift), much as postwar housewives were expected to contribute by purchasing goods. That each of these "poor" girls has a bedroom of her own reflects the dreams of postwar homemakers (and builders), not the reality of nineteenth-century life. The 1995 version, directed by Gillian Armstrong, borrowed aspects of Alcott's life to present a feminist tribute to Alcott as a writer who refused to give up her ambitions for marriage, as embodied by Jo March (Winona Ryder). A preachy Marmee (Susan Sarandon), sounding very modern indeed, instructs her girls to exercise and to avoid staying in "the house bent over their needlework in restrictive corsets." These three versions demonstrate the challenges of using films as sources for the period they purport to depict. Finally, Joan Micklin Silver beautifully captures the nineteenth-century immigrant experience (and a 1970s-style heroine) in *Hester Street* (1975), in which Gitl (Carol Kane) adapts to a new life in New York.

The West

A popular genre, the western has at least included women at a time when few historians considered them. The danger is that historians working on women in the West have had to fight the stock characters perpetuated by filmmakers. Women in westerns tend to fill key stereotypes: the proper, Eastern ingénue; the saucy, singing Mexican woman of easy virtue; the prostitutes and dancehall girls; the disapproving town matrons. Historians such as John Mack Faragher, Glenda Riley, Paula Petrik, and Judy Yung have complicated these stereotypes considerably by exploring the range of women on the frontier. Yung, for example, returns Chinese American women to this narrative. Pascoe conveys the search for female moral authority in the Old West. Petrik has declared that women's move to the West resulted in a "metamorphosis of women's perceptions of their public and private roles and a new definition of womanhood" (xiii). As in other genres, filmmakers have yet to capture these subtle visions.

Native women often inhabit the shadowy backgrounds of films, but a few films do highlight their experiences. *Broken Arrow* (1950) focuses on a Native woman's story at a time when few films did so. The film's concern with ethnic harmony reflects a fascinating post-Holocaust, pre–civil rights movement sensibility. It also mirrors its times in its portrayal of women. Morning Star (Debra Paget), not played by a Native woman, is a good 1950s housewife, despite her fringed leather garments. She prepares food, washes, and finds happiness in marrying Tom Jeffords (James Stewart). A more recent treatment of Native American women is Kevin Costner's *Dances with Wolves* (1990). This film does aim to gain audience sympathy for the plight of Native Americans dispossessed from their lands. The lead female character is in fact a white woman who has been adopted by a tribe of Sioux, but the film does attempt to show the strength of Native American women.

Conversely, white women remain almost exclusively within the domestic sphere. Although they may dress like men at times, they stay at home while their husbands depart to fight the Indians. In *Shane* (1953), for example, Jean Arthur plays Mrs. Joe Starr, who is introduced as the "little woman." She is a good "Baby Boomer" mother, eager to nurture (and cook for) her men. Likewise, in *The Searchers* (1956), women are portrayed as keepers of home and hearth, in contrast to the roving Ethan Edwards (John Wayne). It is up to him to rescue his niece from the Comanches. These films present a 1950s vision in which post–World War II women were expected to stay home while men engaged in more public successes.

There are two types of western women: the "good girl" and the "bad girl." Often the "bad girl" is deliberately rendered as ethnic, usually Mexican. In *High Noon* (1952), for example, Amy Fowler (Grace Kelly) is the demure blonde who arrives from the East to marry Will Kane (Gary Cooper). Already in the town is Helen Ramirez (Katy Jurado), who is dark and sexy, in contrast to the ladylike Fowler. Much the same configuration occurs in the famous John Ford western *My Darling Clementine* (1946). Again, a contrast is drawn between the pale, modest Clementine Carter (Cathy Downs) and the sensual Mexican, Chihuahua (Linda Darnell). These films suggest the 1950s idealization of and ambivalence about the staid "good girl." A similar contrast, without the ethnic dimension, occurs in the early John Ford classic *Stagecoach* (1939). Dallas (Claire Trevor), the prostitute with a heart of gold, learns to be maternal, like the respectable women around her, and so wins the affections of Ringo (John Wayne).

Some white women are vital to the films and are not expected to remain domestic. At the beginning of *Red River* (1948), Tom Dunson (John Wayne) refuses to let his fiancée accompany him to the Red River. She asserts, "I'm strong. I can stand anything you can," but Tom remains unconvinced. However, ultimately, Tom and Matt (Montgomery Clift) realize that women like Tess Millay (Joanne Dru) are strong enough to join them in the conquest of the American West. Although a satire of westerns, *My Little Chickadee* (1940) includes a Flower Belle Lee (Mae West) who is more than a match for men. As the sassy Flower Belle drawls, "Funny. Every man I meet wants to protect me. I can't figure out what from." Westerns from the 1960s and 1970s, such as *Butch Cassidy and the Sundance Kid* (1968) and *McCabe & Mrs. Miller* (1971) echo this earlier portrayal of women who are both sensual and strong. Indeed, Mrs. Miller (Julie Christie), a typical madame, is also a savvy businesswoman. These films offered heroines for this liberated generation.

So does Clint Eastwood's *Unforgiven* (1992), which offers a meditation on the very genre of the western. In the friendship between Will (Clint Eastwood) and Ned (Morgan Freeman), the film also echoes a 1990s multicultural sensibility. These older, reformed killers can be seen as escapees from a past haunted by the Vietnam War. At first glance its portrayal of women appears quite traditional; women are wives or whores. But the film subverts its stereotypes. The prostitutes refuse to accept categorization as property, as when Strawberry Alice (Frances Fisher) cries, "by God, we ain't horses." Equally, the never-seen Mrs. Horn was the redemption of her troubled husband, Will. Salvation lies in men embracing roles as fathers, not killers; it is thus an uneasy acknowledgment of the shifting terrain of masculinity and gender roles in the 1990s.

The most powerful visions of western womanhood occur when the feminist-minded have reinterpreted westerns. A sharp-tongued Ellen (Sharon Stone) overcomes childhood fears to fight equally with men in *The Quick and the Dead* (1995). In *The Ballad of Little Jo* (1993) the heroine (Suzy Amis) dresses as a man and hoodwinks a town into believing that she can run his (her) own affairs. In *Bad Girls* (1994), brutal customers and censorious townspeople attack prostitutes who then turn to violence themselves. In these remakings, the women are victims of male abuse who then resort to similar tactics. Filmmakers, reversing the old formula of westerns, must have thought that women in the 1990s would respond positively to these portraits of women. These films are still not especially inclusive of women of color. However, they have introduced interesting innovations to a traditional genre.

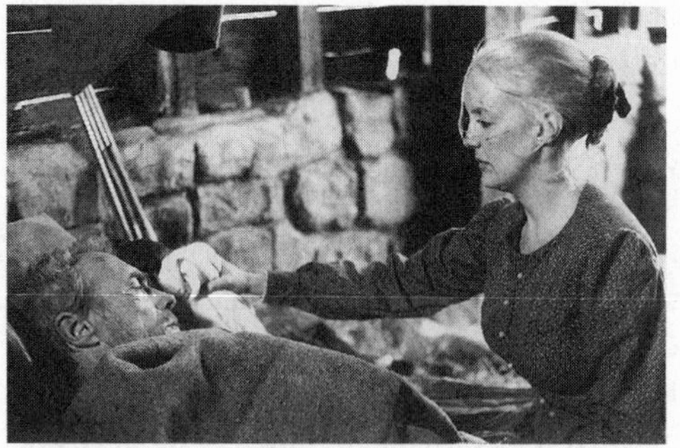

FIGURE 34. *Unforgiven* (1992). Anna Thomson (Anna Levine) comforts the wounded William Munny (Clint Eastwood). Anna's fellow prostitutes have hired Munny to revenge the mutilation of Anna's face by a gang of vigilantes. Munny defends the prostitutes in this revisionist tale of women in the West, insisting that they be treated with respect. Courtesy Malpaso Productions and Warner Bros.

Films as Avenues to the Past

Films simplify a complex and thriving historical literature. Often relying on stereotypes to advance a two-hour narrative, movies nonetheless offer compelling visual and audible representations of the past. Moreover, there is often some slight echo of current scholarly debates (about female agency, for example) in film portraits. In addition, films provide an excellent avenue for understanding representations of women in the eras in which the films were made. Although caution is required, these movies are an entertaining route to learn more about the myriad ways in which women have been represented and understood. Or, as Flower Belle Lee remarks of Cleopatra in *My Little Chickadee,* "She lived way back in the early times. And what a time she had!"

References

Filmography

The Adams Chronicles (1975, D)
Allegheny Uprising (1939, F)
America (1924, F)
Annie Oakley (1935, F)
Bad Girls (1994, F)
The Ballad of Little Jo (1993, F)
Belle Starr (1941, F)
Beloved (1998, F)
The Birth of a Nation (1915, F)
Broken Arrow (1950, F)
The Buccaneer (1938, F; 1958, F)
Butch Cassidy and the Sundance Kid (1968, F)
Calamity Jane (1952, F)
The Crucible (1996, F)
Dances with Wolves (1990, F)
Drums Along the Mohawk (1939, F)
Gettysburg (1993, F)
Gone with the Wind (1939, F)

Hester Street (1975, F)
High Noon (1952, F)
The Howards of Virginia (1940, F)
Jezebel (1938, F)
Johnny Guitar (1954, F)
The Last of the Mohicans (1992, F)
Little Big Man (1970, F)
Little Women (1933, F; 1949, F; 1994, F)
Mary Silliman's War (1993, D)
The Maverick Queen (1956, F)
McCabe & Mrs. Miller (1971, F)
A Midwife's Tale (1996, D)
Montana Belle (1952, F)
My Darling Clementine (1946, F)
My Little Chickadee (1940, F)
The Outlaw (1943, F)
Pocahontas (1995, F)
Pocahontas: Her True Story (1995, D)
The President's Lady (1953, F)
The Quick and the Dead (1995, F)
Red River (1948, F)
The Scarlet Letter (1995, F)
The Searchers (1956, F)
1776 (1972, F)
Shane (1953, F)
Stagecoach (1939, F)
Unconquered (1948, F)
Unforgiven (1992, F)

Bibliography

Attie, Jeanie. *Patriotic Toil: Northern Women and the American Civil War.* Ithaca, NY: Cornell University Press, 1998.

Berkin, Carol. *First Generations: Women in Colonial America.* New York: Hill & Wang, 1996.

Buel, Joy Day, and Richard Buel Jr. *The Way of Duty: A Woman and Her Family in Revolutionary America.* New York: Norton, 1984.

Clinton, Catherine. *The Plantation Mistress: Woman's World in the Old South.* New York: Pantheon, 1982.

Cott, Nancy F. *The Bonds of Womanhood: 'Woman's Sphere' in New England, 1780–1835.* New Haven: Yale University Press, 1977.

Cronon, William. *Changes in the Land: Indians, Colonists, and the Ecology of New England.* New York: Hill & Wang, 1983.

Demos, John Putnam. *Entertaining Satan: Witchcraft and the Culture of Early New England.* Oxford: Oxford University Press, 1982.

Edwards, Laura F. *Gendered Strife & Confusion: The Political Culture of Reconstruction.* Urbana: University of Illinois Press, 1997.

Faragher, John Mack. *Women and Men on the Overland Trail.* New Haven: Yale University Press, 1979.

Faust, Drew Gilpin. *Mothers of Invention: Women of the Slaveholding South in the American Civil War.* New York: Vintage, 1996.

Forbes, Ella. *African American Women during the Civil War.* New York: Garland, 1998.

Fox-Genovese, Elizabeth. *Within the Plantation Household: Black and White Women of the Old South.* Chapel Hill: University of North Carolina Press, 1988.

Jeffrey, Julie Roy. *Frontier Women: The Trans-Mississippi West, 1840–1880.* New York: Hill & Wang, 1979.

Karlsen, Carol F. *The Devil in the Shape of a Woman: Witchcraft in Colonial New England.* New York: Random House, 1987.

Kerber, Linda K. *Women of the Republic: Intellect & Ideology in Revolutionary America.* New York: Norton, 1986.

Lackmann, Ron. *Women of the Western Frontier in Fact, Fiction and Film.* Jefferson, NC: McFarland, 1997.

Leonard, Elizabeth D. *Yankee Women: Gender Battles in the Civil War.* New York: Norton, 1994.

Norton, Mary Beth. *Founding Mothers and Fathers: Gendered Power and the Forming of American Society.* New York: Knopf, 1996.

———. *Liberty's Daughters: The Revolutionary Experience of American Women, 1750–1800.* Boston: Little, Brown, 1980.

Pascoe, Peggy. *Relations of Rescue: The Search for Female Moral Authority in the American West, 1874–1939.* New York: Oxford University Press, 1990.

Petrik, Paula. *No Step Backward: Women and Family on the Rocky Mountain Mining Frontier, Helena, Montana, 1865–1900.* Helena: Montana Historical Society Press, 1987.

Riley, Glenda. *Women and Indians on the Frontier, 1825–1915.* Albuquerque: University of New Mexico Press, 1984.

Rountree, Helen C. *The Powhatan Indians of Virginia: Their Traditional Culture.* Norman: University of Oklahoma Press, 1989.

Scott, Anne Firor. *The Southern Lady: From Pedestal to Politics, 1830–1930.* Chicago: University of Chicago Press, 1970.

Smith-Rosenberg, Carroll. *Disorderly Conduct: Visions of Gender in Victorian American.* New York: Oxford University Press, 1985.

Ulrich, Laurel Thatcher. *Good Wives: Image and Reality in the Lives of Women in Northern New England, 1650–1750.* New York: Vintage, 1980.

White, Deborah Gray. *Ain't I a Woman? Female Slaves in the Plantation South.* Rev. ed. New York: Norton, 1999.

Yung, Judy. *Unbound Feet: A Social History of Chinese Women in San Francisco.* Berkeley: University of California Press, 1995.

[JUNE SOCHEN]

Women in the Twentieth Century

The history of twentieth-century American women is inextricably tied to the history of men and children. As family members, women have lived their lives as part of a larger unit—first as daughters and then as wives and mothers. Only in the last third of this century have large numbers of American women lived alone or in relationships without marriage and worked outside of the home in various occupations and professions. Hollywood movies have always included women in both starring and supporting roles, but always within clearly defined images: as the virginal Mary, such as Mary Pickford in the silent *Pollyanna* (1920); as sexual temptresses or Eves, such as Theda Bara in *A Fool There Was* (1915), in which she defined the vamp; or as an independent woman or Lilith. (All of Katharine Hepburn's movies fit into this last category.)

The most interesting portrayals of women combine two of these images, with the Eve-Lilith synthesis being the most powerful. Greta Garbo in *Flesh and the Devil* (1920), for example, is a temptress who exudes individuality and audacity. Bette Davis in *A Marked Woman* (1937) is a prostitute with integrity and courage willing to stand up to ruthless gangsters. Mary Pickford in *Way Down East* (1920) is a woman seduced by an unscrupulous man who survives, thanks to her tenacity and good spirit.

Women's filmic roles reflect the larger culture's view of women and are shown within familiar film genres. In adventure movies of all sorts, for example, women are the damsels in distress (the Marys) or attractive sexual decorations (the Eves). Less frequently, women are the heroes, the active centers of a thriller, a Lilith among the many Eves and Marys. Occasionally, at certain times in Hollywood history, women have been portrayed as careerists, independent people with identities of their own. Sweet young things and sultry Eves, however, dominated silent film; Bara, Jean Harlow (*China Seas*, 1935), and Garbo starred in film after film where their astonishing beauty baited weak but willing men. Sound movies, beginning in the 1930s, built on the formulaic images of the past but added more renditions of all three types.

Paradoxically, though the material conditions of women's lives have changed enormously during the century, neither dominant cultural values nor cinematic treatments have kept pace. Molly Haskell's classic study of women's roles in the movies, *From Reverence to Rape* (1974), effectively captures this view. Society and Hollywood hold on to traditional values about women simultaneous with observing their new behaviors. Even the fiercely independent Katharine Hepburn falls into Spencer Tracy's arms at the end of *Woman of the Year* (1942), the quintessential Lilith role. More women work outside of the home for more years of their lives than ever before, but recent films rarely show working women in their workplace. *Working Girl* (1988), with Harrison Ford and Melanie Griffith, is a notable exception to this rule. Effective birth control has given women choices as to when, or if, they are to become mothers, yet this very basic subject rarely surfaces in Hollywood films.

Although the relationship between filmic reality and historic reality is not simple, linear, or predictable, there are some correlatives. Strong, independent women were needed during the dark days of the Depression in the 1930s as well as in World War II, for example, so Hollywood delivered with an unprecedented number of films featuring stars such as Katharine Hepburn (*Spitfire,* 1934), Barbara Stanwyck (*Golden Boy,* 1939), Joan Crawford (*Sadie McKee,* 1934), Bette Davis (*Ex-Lady,* 1933), and Rosalind Russell (*His Girl Friday,* 1940) playing professional women as well as working-class women. But there is no simple equation.

During the post-1945 years, America's older stars found few roles open to them. Joan Crawford in *Queen Bee* (1955) plays a manipulative woman, while she is duped by a younger man in *Autumn Leaves* (1956). The problems of mature women were not treated sympathetically on the screen or in the culture. The new generation of stars played classic Eves, no one more effectively than Elizabeth Taylor. Her portrayal of the frustrated wife, Maggie, in Richard Brooks's version of Tennessee Williams's *Cat on a Hot Tin Roof* (1958) displayed her beauty and her unfulfilled yearnings.

In the segregated days of the 1930s and 1940s, Hollywood would not star the beautiful and talented African American actor Lena Horne in a romantic lead role for fear of offending many American moviegoers; indeed, her scenes in *Stormy Weather* (1943) were cut out when the movie played in the South. *Carmen Jones* (1954) starred Dorothy Dandridge opposite Harry Belafonte in a rare offering of a classic story performed with an African American cast. Ignoring race and denying African American actresses job opportunities in film, except for the most predictable and stereotypical roles, became the practice. Hattie McDaniel and Butterfly McQueen could appear on the screen as maids and nursemaids in *Gone with the Wind* (1939), but neither could portray the heroine in a melodrama or drama.

It was not until the early 1970s, and then for a rare and brief moment, that a black actress, Pam Grier, was allowed to play the star in an atypical female role, the adventure heroine, in movies such as *Foxy Brown* (1973) and *Coffy* (1974). The so-called blaxploitation films usually starred Richard Roundtree, but Grier offered a variation on the theme and attracted large audiences; unfortunately, she had few imitators or followers. Latin American actresses fared even worse. A recent documentary on the life and career of Carmen Miranda during the 1940s and 1950s effectively captures both her dilemma and the dilemma of all Latina stars.

Early Film

Silent movies established the pattern for all time with the Mary image dominating. Director D. W. Griffith became a father figure to actresses Dorothy and Lillian Gish, sisters who played sweet young things. Lillian starred in Griffith's The *Birth of a Nation* (1915), *Intolerance* (1916), and *Broken Blossoms* (1919). Mary Pickford, the most popular ingénue, also showed pluck and risk taking in her movies. *Way Down East* (1920) was a good example of a Mary-Lilith role. Mabel Normand departed from the Mary by being a daredevil comic in many silent movies with Charlie Chaplin; she jumped out of airplanes, drove a car, and threw coconut pies in men's faces. She ran with the Keystone Kops and was viewed by her contemporaries as every bit as talented as Keaton and Chaplin. Unfortunately, her fame did not survive the period nor did prints of her movies. Normand was a classic slapstick, a form unbecoming to a lady; it was not until Lucille Ball brought the format to television, a more intimate environment, that slapstick again became acceptable as a woman's genre.

In the adventure serials that were very popular from the early years of the century through the 1930s, *The Perils of Pauline* captured thousands of devoted child viewers. Pearl White, as Pauline, had daring experiences overcoming kidnappings, dangerous physical encounters, and many villains. There was also a series of Nancy Drew serials, based upon the popular novels for adolescent girls and boys; kids thrilled to the multiple escapades engaged in by Nancy and her friends. Both Pauline and Nancy, as young women, could have adventures, but grown-up women had romance. The cultural message clearly stated that young girls grow up to become wives and mothers who then appear in melodramas and domestic comedies.

The Golden Era, 1933–1950

When sound movies took over in the 1930s, movies were still being made for all ages and both sexes; actresses, though caught in predictable images, had many movie roles. Hollywood studios churned out "A" and "B" quality movies. MGM, one of the largest studios, bragged that it had more stars under contract than in the sky. The "weepies," the melodramas of the period (one of the most popular genres, now seen on daytime soap operas), always featured long-suffering women. Barbara Stanwyck in *Stella Dallas* (1937) had to endure many obstacles, but she, like many others, persisted and often prevailed. Joan Crawford became a well-known star playing working-class women whose good looks snared her a wealthy husband, as in *Mannequin* (1937). Clearly the search for romance on a rocky road has lived on as the dominant subject of women in film.

Katharine Hepburn was often a career woman—a pilot in *Christopher Strong* (1933) or a journalist in *A Woman Rebels* (1936) and *Woman of the Year* (1942). Rosalind Russell and Bette Davis also played professional women, both journalists, Russell in *His Girl Friday* (1940) and Davis in *Front Page Woman* (1935). When Hepburn was not pursuing a career, she was an aristocratic woman whose wealth insured her independence. *The Philadelphia Story* (1940) and *Bringing Up Baby* (1936) are good examples of this formula. Greta Garbo played a real-life queen in *Queen Christina* (1933) and a doomed woman in *Anna Karenina* (1935). Her fabulous beauty, however, always determined her outcome. Men flocked to her like bees to clover, but they usually punished her for her seductive power over them. Eves had to be contained.

The stars also played ordinary women who suffered during hard, economic times. They were Liliths out of necessity. Crawford in *Sadie McKee* (1934), Hepburn in *Alice Adams* (1935), and Davis in *A Marked Woman* (1937) represented different social classes and different circumstances, but they were all needy women surviving during the Depression. When Barbara Stanwyck played a world-weary mistress in *Golden Boy* (1939), she did it with both strength and vulnerability, thereby making her enormously popular to her woman fans. Joan Crawford had the largest network of fan clubs around the country.

Mildred Pierce (1945), Crawford's award-winning role, described, rather prophetically, the dilemma many women faced as World War II ended. A weak husband and the need to earn a living and support her two young daughters became the new reality for Mildred Pierce. Her baking skills ultimately led her to open a restaurant, and then a series of successful restaurants. The plot, however, preserved the traditional value system and expected Mildred to remain an at-home mom even after she became an entrepreneur. Her romantic interlude with a playboy, (while her ex-husband was caring for her daughters) led to a family tragedy and what was viewed at the time as apt punishment for an (allegedly) negligent mother.

Mildred Pierce captured many of the new conflicts facing women while preserving the old-time values regarding women's roles. The imaginative universe of a good film enabled audiences to consider competing values, though, in 1945, the consensus upheld the old and rejected the new. Mildred was expected to sacrifice her personal happiness for the sake of her daughters. Working mothers may have

FIGURE 35. *Mildred Pierce* (1945). Mildred Pierce (Joan Crawford, left) confronts her spoiled daughter Veda (Ann Blythe, right), who is ashamed to learn that her mother was once a waitress. The acting captured the differences between the generation of Mildred Pierce and the materialistic generation of her daughter. Courtesy Warner Bros.

been a new reality, but old views die hard and 1945 audiences shared those attitudes. Marjorie Rosen in *Popcorn Venus* (1975) offered analyses of women's films in the 1940s and the new challenges facing women.

The New Generation

As the 1930s generation of actresses matured, a new crop of young stars emerged. Older stars found themselves with few good roles—*All About Eve* (1950) effectively explores the subject—as the general social attitude was that romance and physical beauty was the monopoly of the young. In this sense, films ignored an important stage in women's lives—their mature years. Elizabeth Taylor and Marilyn Monroe dominated the 1950s as superstars, with movie magazines splashing their faces on frequent covers. Romance became the major genre, with women adventurers and careerists finding few role opportunities. Both Taylor (*Butterfield 8,* 1960) and Monroe (*Some Like It Hot,* 1959) learned very quickly that their screen roles were shaped by their physical appearance; they would always be the femmes fatales, the gorgeous women whose attractiveness trumped all other features.

But even beauties projected other characteristics, a sure sign of the multiple meanings produced by movie stars' portrayals. Taylor, as the wife of a cattle baron in *Giant* (1956), director George Stevens's film adaptation of the Edna Ferber novel, defied the stereotype in that she displayed tenacity, tolerance, and independence as well as obvious beauty. The film also discussed anti-Mexican prejudice, a subject rarely shown in American movies. Monroe, on the other hand, played a shrewd blonde playing a dumb blonde in *How to Marry a Millionaire* (1953).

The unfair view that beautiful women have empty heads had existed throughout Hollywood's history, from the silent era onward, and Hollywood's unwillingness to give Monroe roles other than those that emphasized her physical assets perpetuated the image. *Gentlemen Prefer Blondes* (1953) and *The Prince and the Showgirl* (1957) typecast her. Further, this image operated most successfully in comedy and thus remained the genre within which Monroe got most of her parts. While Monroe yearned for serious dramatic roles, projects such as Billy Wilder's *The Seven Year Itch* (1955) were offered to her.

Darker Days Ahead

The 1940s and 1950s also introduced a genre called film noir, a style in which directors emphasized the sinister, the tawdry, and the mean qualities of people. Cinematically, the noir movie often took place at night on dark streets and with dark deeds lurking around every corner. The women in these movies were either the victims of crimes or the perpetrators of them. Barbara Stanwyck wanted to murder her husband for his insurance money in Billy Wilder's adaptation of Raymond Chandler's *Double Indemnity* (1944), but the roles were reversed for her in Anatole Litvak's *Sorry, Wrong Number* (1948) when her husband tried to have her murdered. Even Grace Kelly, the aristocratic beauty of the 1950s, became a victim in Alfred Hitchcock's *Dial M for Murder*

(1954) when she discovered that her husband wanted to kill her.

The easy targets, whatever the reason, were women. As a result, a strange phenomenon occurred: after film noir lost its appeal, sometime in the 1960s, and continuing on to today, the number and type of roles available for women declined precipitously. Film critic Pauline Kael discussed how the male buddy film took over and jokingly called Paul Newman and Robert Redford the romantic duo of the decade. Of the new generation of actresses in the 1960s, only a few got many parts. The best roles went to Jane Fonda, who began as a sweet, young thing in *Barefoot in the Park* (1967), moved into sexual temptress roles (*Barbarella,* 1968), and then to independent women parts (*The China Syndrome,* 1979); Liza Minnelli (*Cabaret,* 1972); and Barbra Streisand, who played in musicals (*Funny Girl,* 1968), comedies (*What's Up Doc?* 1972), and dramas (*The Way We Were,* 1973).

Musicals seemed safe for wary Hollywood producers, and *My Fair Lady* (1964) and *The Sound of Music* (1965) were very popular. In *Cabaret,* Minnelli offered a sexy, decadent young singer in 1920s Berlin. Diana Ross, as legendary blues singer Billie Holiday in *Lady Sings the Blues* (1972), gave audiences a melodrama with music while displaying her acting and singing talent; she was the second African American actress to be nominated for a best actress award (the first was Dorothy Dandridge for *Carmen Jones*). Ross lost to Minnelli. Minority women, Latinas and Asians particularly, continued to be ignored by Hollywood.

Toward the Future

By the end of the 1970s, Hollywood ventured to treat some of the dramatic changes in women's lives. Jill Clayburgh in *An Unmarried Woman* (1977), Jane Fonda in *Coming Home* (1977) and *China Syndrome* (1978), and Sally Field in *Norma Rae* (1979) are among the select few roles that looked at a wife facing life after divorce, a wife of a Vietnam soldier, a reporter, and a working woman fighting for a union.

Sally Field, in the role of Norma Rae, offered a rare portrait of an indomitable working woman in small-town America, a woman raising two children while living uncomfortably with her family. Her awakening as a voice for workers, thanks to the aid of a New York City Jewish union organizer (played by Ron Liebman), was unique because no romance intrudes upon their relationship; they work together, trying to convince apolitical reluctant workers to stand up to the textile company managers. Field's marriage to a fellow worker (played by Beau Bridges) is treated neither extensively nor sentimentally. In fact, because of her increased work for the union, she neglects both her husband and children. (Field won the Academy Award for her performance.) This Martin Ritt film is important for its intrinsic interest, but more so because it was a rare foray into the world of working mothers.

By the 1970s, Hollywood no longer made two hundred movies a year, and the studio system had given way to independent productions. The cost of movies grew each year, and filmmakers seemed content to make Mafia movies (*The Godfather,* 1972), war stories where women were absent (*Patton,* 1970), and thrillers where women were largely extraneous (*Jaws,* 1975). This disturbing trend was fueled by the growth in the youth market, particularly young boys, who had become the major patrons of movies; male adolescents' love for action, destruction, and violence in film as well as their willingness to see the same movie many times encouraged filmmakers to produce the same mindless action movies again and again. In the meantime, adult Americans watched broadcast or cable television or rented classic videos.

By appealing to the market's wishes, film producers can easily justify their continued reliance on tried-and-true formula films starring action heroes. No one can accuse them of willfully ignoring women; rather, they can easily argue that they just make the movies audiences want to see. At the beginning of the twenty-first century, there are still few women producers, directors, or writers, and even fewer male feminists in charge. By the 1980s, the roles for women were so few and far between that the same fine actresses received the slim pickings. Meryl Streep, undeniably one of the great actors of any period, had eight Academy Award nominations between 1981 and 1995, including *Sophie's Choice* (1982) and *Out of Africa* (1985). Jessica Lange had five nominations with stellar performances in films such as *The Postman Always Rings Twice* (1981) and *Blue Sky* (1994).

With fewer movies being made, and fewer starring roles for women, no actress today can compete with the large output of films made by Golden Age stars such as Joan Crawford, Bette Davis, and Barbara Stanwyck. Today's actresses rely on cable movies and theater to occupy themselves between the film offers. Although women are very much alive in real time, they are largely absent in reel time today.

FIGURE 36. *Norma Rae* (1979). Reuben Warshawky (Ron Liebman), a New York union organizer, convinces a factory worker, Norma Rae (Sally Field), to help him unionize her fellow laborers in order to secure better wages and working conditions. Courtesy Twentieth Century-Fox.

References

Filmography

Alice Adams (1935, F)
Barbarella (1968, F)
Barefoot in the Park (1967, F)
Blue Sky (1994, F)
Butterfield 8 (1960, F)
Cabaret (1972, F)
Carmen Miranda: Bananas Is My Business (1995, D)
A Century of Women (1994, D)
China Syndrome (1978, F)
Coming Home (1977, F)
Dial M for Murder (1954, F)
Double Indemnity (1944, F)
Funny Girl (1968, F)
Giant (1956, F)
Golden Boy (1939, F)
The Good, the Bad and the Beautiful (1997, D)
How to Marry a Millionaire (1953, F)
Lady Sings the Blues (1972, F)
Mildred Pierce (1945, F)
Norma Rae (1979, F)
Not a Bedroom War: New Visions of Feminism (1993, D)
Out of Africa (1985, F)
The Postman Always Rings Twice (1981, F)
The Seven Year Itch (1955, F)
Sophie's Choice (1982, F)
Sorry, Wrong Number (1948, F)
Stella Dallas (1937, F)
An Unmarried Woman (1977, F)
The Way We Were (1973, F)
What's Up Doc? (1972, F)

Bibliography

Basinger, Jeanine. *A Woman's View: How Hollywood Spoke to Women, 1930–1960.* Hanover, NH: University Press of New England, 1993.
Haskell, Molly. *From Reverence to Rape.* New York: Holt, Rinehart & Winston, 1974.
Robinson, David. *Hollywood in the Twenties.* New York: A. S. Barnes, 1968.
Rosen, Marjorie. *Popcorn Venus: Women, Movies, and the American Dream.* New York: William Morrow, 1985.
Woloch, Nancy. *Women and the American Experience.* New York: McGraw Hill, 1994.

V.
Institutions and Movements

★ ★ ★ ★ ★ ★ ★

NY
NY

[GREGORY MCNAMEE]

Baseball

Popular legend, repeated in textbooks until very recently, has it that the game of baseball sprang, Athena-like, from Abner Doubleday's thoughtful brow somewhere in the vicinity of Cooperstown, New York, in the spring of 1839. Doubleday (1819–1893) was a man of many accomplishments, to be sure: a capable Union officer, he fought in several major Civil War battles, including Second Manassas and Gettysburg; a capable capitalist, he founded the first cable-car company in San Francisco. But even Doubleday claimed credit, and then quietly, only for codifying and regularizing the rules of a game that had been developing over the course of several centuries, born of a colonial New England game called "town ball" that in turn descended from the English field game called "rounders," an ancestor of not only baseball but also cricket, a game played enthusiastically in every former English colony save the United States. Albert Spalding (1850–1915), a pitcher, manager, and entrepreneur who founded the sporting-equipment company that still bears his name, acknowledged that English descent in his book *America's National Game* (1911), though grudgingly, for it was he who gave Doubleday so much credit to begin with. Having allowed its similarities to cricket, however, Spalding was quick to point out that baseball distinguished our national qualities from those of our former rulers: the English "play Cricket because it accords with the traditions of their country to do so; because it is easy and does not overtax their energy or their thought," whereas, Spalding continued, "Base Ball owes its prestige as our National Game to the fact that as no other form of sport it is the exponent of American Courage, Confidence, and Combativeness; American Dash, Discipline, Determination; American Energy, Eagerness, Enthusiasm; American Pluck, Persistence, Performance; American Spirit, Sagacity, Success; American Vim, Vigor, Virility."

Whatever its ultimate origins, and whatever the claims that can be made for it as an expression of homegrown values as against those of other lands, baseball has been a vitally important American pastime since at least the time of the Civil War, when Union and Confederate soldiers played it among themselves, and sometimes even crossed the lines to play against each other. After Appomattox, those soldiers then spread the game to every corner of the land almost overnight, a development that led Mark Twain to remark that baseball was "the outward and visible expression of the drive and push and rush and struggle of the raging, tearing, booming nineteenth century." External contacts—sometimes war, sometimes peaceful economic exchange—spread the game beyond America's shores as well, and today baseball is flourishing in such places as Japan, Nicaragua, Afghanistan, and even England. The game flows like a mighty river through the nation's, and the world's, history, and millions on millions have bathed in its waters: Geronimo, the famed Apache war leader, who played baseball avidly throughout his years of captivity in Florida and Oklahoma; Fidel Castro, the Cuban revolutionary, who as a young man wanted nothing more than to pitch for a major-league American team; William Howard Taft, the portly president who, it seems, inadvertently invented the seventh-inning stretch and who found sublime pleasure in throwing out the game ball on opening day; Moe Berg, the Sanskrit-speaking scholar who combined an indifferent record as a major-league catcher with a somewhat more illustrious career as a spy on three continents; Johnny Ventura, the Dominican politician and bandleader, who abandoned a promising career in baseball to bring the folk music called merengue to a waiting world; Sadaharu Oh, arguably the greatest player in Japanese baseball history, who brought Zen understanding to the game when he observed, "As the ball makes its high, long arc beyond the playing field, the diamond and the stands suddenly belong to one man. In that brief, brief time, you are free of all demands and complications"; Tallulah Bankhead, the imposing Alabama-born actor, who famously remarked, "There are only two geniuses in the world: Willie Mays and Willie Shakespeare."

Baseball insinuated itself into American folklife early on. Ernest Lawrence Thayer's spirit-crushing poem "Casey at the Bat" (1888) was a part of the national vernacular well before it was translated into the 1896 feature film of that name, and words and phrases from the game (*fan, to root, to strike out*) joined the American lexicon throughout the nineteenth century. Folklife became commodity, too, early on, and baseball grew into a big business almost as soon as the first teams were formed, with squads such as the Brooklyn Atlantics and Cleveland Red Stockings barnstorming their way across the country on newly constructed rail lines and, in the process, building a national following for the professional sport and for individual players such as Amos Rusie, Cap Anson, and Cy Young, the forerunners of today's superstar athletes. Exempted from antitrust laws in the early twentieth century, and sometimes subsidized by municipal levies (which would become standard after the 1960s), major-league baseball proved to be highly profitable for owners and investors, but less so for players, who would struggle for decades to organize themselves in the manner of other skilled trade workers. (See "The Labor Movement and the Working Class.") Fans today grumble about players' inflated salaries and perks—matters of economics that David Ward's altogether pleasing film *Major League* (1989) and Michael Ritchie's worthy comedy-drama *The Scout* (1994) address, if only as subtext—but most are still inclined to agree, along with filmmakers and sports commentators, that the players have at least some inkling of the game's soulful dimensions, whereas, in the words of sportscaster Bob Costas, "baseball owners, by and large, are soulless and incompetent." Those fans have tended to rally to the side of players through thick and thin, and, in the main, to overlook failure and scandal, whether the drug-related arrests of major-league players throughout the 1980s and 1990s or the organized corruption that has flared up from time to time throughout the history of the game, corruption for which the 1919 Chicago "Black Sox" scandal, memorialized in John Sayles's superb film *Eight Men Out* (1988), remains a byword.

Baseball has both reflected the dominant mores of the larger society and served to change them, especially in the troublesome, often shameful matter of ethnic relations. In the early days of the game, a handful of African Americans played in the majors, notably the brothers Welday and Moses Walker, who graced the roster of the Toledo Mud Hens in 1884; games between all-white and all-black clubs were not uncommon, even in the South. Even so, black players were generally not welcomed on white teams or in white leagues, and by the early twentieth century African Americans had been effectively barred from professional baseball, owing to Jim Crow laws, the antipathy of management and some players (Ty Cobb and Cap Anson particularly vocal among them), and, later, the active resistance of baseball commissioner Kenesaw Mountain Landis to integrated play. African American entrepreneurs formed the separate but decidedly unequal Negro League in 1920, an association made up of teams that played a long season in the United States and then barnstormed for the rest of the year in Latin America; among its ranks figured such legendary players as James "Cool Papa" Bell, Josh Gibson, and, most famous of them all, Satchel Paige, the subject of the docudrama *Don't Look Back* (1981). Craig Davidson's documentary *There Was Always Sun Shining Someplace* (1984) traces the history of the Negro League and features interviews with some of its best-known players, including Paige, many of whom figure in fictionalized form in John Badham's excellent film *The Bingo Long Traveling All-Stars & Motor Kings* (1976).

Despite growing resistance to segregation during World War II, the time of the "double-V" campaign—victory, that is, against fascism abroad and inequality at home—the owners of major-league clubs still refused to admit African American players onto their rosters, relaxing their guard enough to consent to a handful of exhibition games with Negro League teams. Worried about declining stadium attendance during the war years, Chicago Cubs owner Philip Wrigley was sympathetic to the desire of African American players to join the show, but, rather than integrate his squad, he put his energies instead into organizing the All-American Girls Professional Ball League, which eventually numbered ten female teams throughout the Midwest. Disbanded almost as soon as male players returned from the war, the All-American Girls are the subject of Penny Marshall's comedy *A League of Their Own* (1992), which drew on interviews with league veterans as background for its historically faithful, good-natured script.

In 1945, Brooklyn Dodgers general manager Branch Rickey recruited former army lieutenant Jackie Robinson, an African American from California, to play for the Montreal Royals, a Dodgers subsidiary. Robinson would not stay with Montreal long, for Rickey had been planning to cross the color line for quite some time, and after gaining a little big-league seasoning Robinson moved south to New York. Rickey "knew that with the war over, things were going to change, that they were going to have to change," recalled Dodgers assistant manager Clyde Sukeforth. "When you look back on it, it's almost unbelievable, isn't it? I mean, here you've had fellows going overseas to fight for their country, putting their lives on the line, and when they come back home again, there are places they're not allowed to go, things they're not allowed to do. . . . Do you know for how long the idea was in Mr. Rickey's head? More than forty years. For more than forty years he was waiting for the right moment, the right man. And that's what he told Robinson."

Rickey's gamble paid off, for in his first season of play for the Dodgers, Robinson racked up an enviable .311 batting average against some of the best pitchers to have ever played the game, an accomplishment he replayed before the cameras in the 1950 biopic *The Jackie Robinson Story*. Other African Americans soon followed Robinson into the major leagues, welcomed onto the field by veterans who themselves had battled discrimination, such as Detroit Tigers first baseman Hank Greenberg, the subject of the documentary *The Life and Times of Hank Greenberg* (2000), who once remarked, "I was representing a couple of million Jews among a hundred million gentiles. . . . As time went by I came to feel that if I, as a Jew, hit a home run I was hitting one against Hitler."

Baseball is by no means free of ethnic tension today, as witness the well-publicized racist outbursts of former Cincinnati Reds owner Marge Schott and the controversy over the cartoonish logos and cheers of the Atlanta Braves and Cleveland Indians. Neither is it untouched by scandal; far from it. All the same, Americans continue to locate many of their popular heroes on the diamond, just as they have over two centuries, which is perhaps why American politicians have for so long thought it advantageous to be seen at the ballpark from time to time. (Indeed, some have made more than passing visits to the stadium: Dwight Eisenhower played minor-league ball; George W. Bush earned a fortune as a club owner; and Ronald Reagan handled the ball admirably before the camera in Lewis Seiler's *The Winning Team* [1952], which treats the troubled life of the legendary pitcher Grover Cleveland Alexander.) Those party operatives and flesh-pressers may make their share of devil's bargains—a matter treated by the immensely popular Broadway play *Damn Yankees* (film, 1958), which finds much pleasure in poking fun at the practical implications of a Washington Senators fan's selling his soul to Lucifer, and which finds a lighthearted opposite in *Angels in the Outfield* (1951 and 1994)—but all the same they have been welcomed alongside the diamond, a secular cathedral where Americans have witnessed countless acts of resurrection, passion, and sacrifice, countless morality plays.

Such life-transforming moments have been grist for the Hollywood mill, which has long taken emblematic baseball figures and remade them into national heroes beyond the field, pressing them into service as living legends that "exemplify the cardinal myths of our culture," in the words of the exemplary fan Stephen Jay Gould. Lou Gehrig was well known even to those who did not follow the fortunes of New York's leading ball club when, in 1939, the debilitating illness that bears his name forced him into retirement and soon thereafter killed him. Gehrig was honored soon after death by the fine film *Pride of the Yankees* (1942), which took some liberties with his famed farewell address to his fans—"People all say I've had a bad break. But today I consider myself the luckiest man on the face of the Earth"—but, thanks to Gary Cooper's memorable portrayal, permanently enshrined Gehrig in the national pantheon of sports heroes. *The Babe Ruth Story* (1948) attempted to do the same for George Herman "Babe" Ruth in its time, though the script erred badly in trying to sugarcoat a life filled with violence, alcoholism, and excess, a reality that fans knew all too well. For its part, *The Pride of St. Louis* (1952) offered a sentimental portrait of the far more sympathetic Jay "Dizzy" Dean, who at the height of segregation reckoned Satchel Paige the greatest pitcher to have ever drawn breath, while *The Stratton Story* (1949) brought to the screen the life of Chicago White Sox pitcher Monty Stratton (played by James Stewart), who lost a leg in a 1938 hunting accident but continued to pitch in the minor leagues into the 1950s.

Hollywood stepped away from the business of hero making in the iconoclastic 1970s, and the subsequent decades have seen few portraits of baseball players as worldly saints, with the notable exception of the tearjerker *Bang the Drum Slowly* (1973), starring a young Robert De Niro as a slow-witted catcher stricken with cancer. The 1992 biopic *The Babe*, starring John Goodman in a startling likeness of the lumpy, hard-living Babe Ruth, comes far closer to telling the truth of the matter than does the 1948 William Bendix vehicle, though, for all its debunking, it does not deny Ruth's inarguable greatness as a baseball virtuoso. Neither does the far harsher *Cobb* (1994) detract from the equally estimable achievements of Tyrus "Ty" Cobb (Tommy Lee Jones), who brought Social Darwinism to the field, proclaiming, "Baseball is something like a war . . . a struggle for supremacy, a survival of the fittest," and who vigorously opposed the integration of the game until his death in 1961. (A teammate of Cobb's from 1905 to 1917, the magnificent power hitter Sam Crawford, sagely recalled, "He came from the South, you know, and he was still fighting the Civil War. As far as he was concerned, we were all damn Yankees before he even met us. Well, who knows, maybe if he hadn't had that persecution com-

FIGURE 37. *Pride of the Yankees* (1942). Lou Gehrig (Gary Cooper, right) brought to baseball dignity and restraint, as well as a sincere appreciation at the public's outpouring of support on learning of the illness that would soon kill him. Cooper exhibits those qualities in the gesture of love and support during the presentation of a plaque by the real-life baseball hero Babe Ruth. Courtesy RKO Radio Pictures and Samuel Goldwyn Company.

plex he never would have been the great ballplayer he was.") Even Billy Crystal's worshipful *61** (2001), which celebrates the race between Roger Maris (Barry Pepper) and Mickey Mantle (Thomas Jane) to beat Babe Ruth's home-run record, takes pains to paint its protagonists as flesh-and-blood figures with the full complement of human frailties, anticipating Mantle's later admission of longtime alcoholism.

But baseball is not only about finding diamond heroes on whom to shower praise or through whom to live vicariously. It is about the simple pleasure of taking the air on a warm day, of trading quips, statistics, and favorite moments with neighbors in the stands. For sandlot players, it is about finding a bit of hope and glory on the field, a dream celebrated by Lloyd Bacon's delightful film *It Happens Every Spring* (1949), which hints that even in the most otherworldly college professor (Ray Milland) the heart of a Babe Ruth lies beating; John Lee Hancock's *The Rookie* (2002), which relates the true, if somewhat romanticized, story of a Texas high school coach, Jimmy Morris (Dennis Quaid), whose students spur him to realize his long-deferred dream of pitching a major-league game; and Brian Robbins's well-played *Hardball* (2001), in which a gambling addict (Keanu Reeves) finds redemption for his manifold sins by coaching a Little League team made up of African American boys from Chicago's battle-scarred Cabrini Green housing project. And baseball is about communing with the past, about dipping a hand into that great river of history. Tom Stanton puts it well, in his memoir *Final Season* (2001), when he writes, "If you listen beyond the silence, if you listen with your heart, you can hear all sorts of things. You can hear your childhood, you can hear your dad and your uncles, you can hear [Tigers batting great Al] Kaline connecting, you can hear the muted cheers of distant, ghost crowds, and you can hear your grandpa calling out from the bleachers."

That joining of personal and cosmic history forms the heart of Phil Alden Robinson's *Field of Dreams* (1989), the most nuanced exploration of the role of baseball in American life and thought. In it, a back-to-the-land, idealistic farmer, Ray Kinsella (Kevin Costner), a veteran of the Berkeley antiwar movement, finds his finances and sanity imperiled when he responds to a mysterious voice that whispers, barely audible among the rustling corn stalks, "If you build it, he will come." "He" is none other than Shoeless Joe Jackson (Ray Liotta), the disgraced victim of the Black Sox scandal, who finds in "it," the diamond that Kinsella carves from his heavily mortgaged field, an earthly paradise. Other ghosts come to join Shoeless Joe, all manner of men whose lives baseball has touched, from the kindly small-town doctor Archibald "Moonlight" Graham (Burt Lancaster) to Kinsella's long-estranged father (Dwier Brown), who once hoped to bridge the gulf between him and his son by playing a simple game of catch, as well as the living and thoroughly disillusioned radical writer Terence Mann (James Earl Jones), who at first rebuffs Kinsella's plea for help with the memorable lines, "Back to the sixties! No place for you in the future! . . . Peace, love, dope—now get the hell out!" (See "The 1960s.") Mann comes around, though, after sharing a telepathic moment with Kinsella at Boston's Fenway Park. When he does, his bitterness over the broken promise of his own era disappears, and Mann is left free to celebrate "the one constant in all the years": baseball, a game that "reminds us of all that was once good and that could be again" in an America "that has been erased like a blackboard"—including, we might imagine, a return to a time of solvent farmers and unbroken families, the vision with which the film's closing shot leaves its viewers.

Also inclining toward an aoristic mysticism in which time has no meaning, though clearly set in the Depression era, is *The Natural* (1984), director Barry Levinson's adaptation of Bernard Malamud's acclaimed 1952 novel. The film loses much of Malamud's carefully constructed Arthurian-cycle symbolism, by which Roy Hobbs's (Robert Redford) lightning-born bat "Wonderboy" is a mythical reflex of the legendary Celtic king's sword Excalibur, his pursuit of the World Series pennant a latter-day quest for the Holy Grail. Even so, and even though it inclines to an awkward sentimentality, and even though Redford is much too old for the part, *The Natural* captures the tremendous affection, inexplicable to many an outside observer, that Americans feel for the game.

But the favorite film of fans today, and arguably the greatest baseball film yet made, is *Bull Durham* (1988), Ron Shelton's lighthearted but on-the-money look at the big business of a game that finds little room for aging men—or, for that matter, simple loyalty. Kevin Costner plays a fading player, Crash Davis, who, having been demoted from the majors, finds a new home on a North Carolina minor-league club whose manager, Skip Riggins (Trey Wilson), is driven to remind his young, untested players of the fundamental simplicity of the game: "You throw the ball, you catch the ball, you hit the ball." It is Crash's task to tame one of those players, a hotheaded pitcher named "Nuke" LaLoosh (Tim Robbins) whose thoughts are less on baseball than on a more vivacious tutor, Annie Savoy (Susan Sarandon), a self-assured, independent woman of a kind too rarely seen onscreen. (See "Feminism and Feminist Films.") But tame him Crash does, expanding on Riggins's simple schematic with sentiments that could have come from a funnier version of *The Grapes of Wrath*: "Quit trying to strike everyone out," he instructs LaLoosh. "Strikeouts are boring. And besides, they're fascist. Throw some ground balls. They're more democratic."

A players' strike and ever-increasing ticket prices diminished public interest in major-league baseball in the 1990s, and Americans' minds were on more pressing matters at the dawn of the twenty-first century. Even so, and even despite the rapid ascent of basketball (another quintessentially American game, invented by a Canadian) as a money-drawing spectator sport, baseball in its many forms—professional, semiprofessional, collegiate, intramural, junior, peewee, and sandlot—remains the most popular of American athletic pastimes. It is comforting to think, with Crash Davis, that this is at least in part because baseball speaks to our better angels: to a vision of life that honors both individual achievement and team play, and always with an insistence on fairness; to our long-held belief that although there are surely winners and losers in life, a reversal of fortunes can make one of the other in an instant; to the American promise of equal opportunity for all, a leveling ethic by which players of all ethnicities and classes can play as one and fans do not hesitate to roar equally for men—and one day, perhaps, women—with names like Alou, Clemente, DiMaggio, Hallahan, Koufax, Lajoie, Nomo, Stahl, and Yastrzemski. Those are all ideals, of course. It remains to be seen whether baseball, Hollywood, and America will rise to the difficult task of making them real.

References

Filmography

Angels in the Outfield (1951, F; 1994, F)
The Babe (1992, F)
The Babe Ruth Story (1948, F)
Bang the Drum Slowly (1973, F)
Baseball (1994, TV)
The Bingo Long Traveling All-Stars and Motor Kings (1976, F)
Bull Durham (1988, F)
Casey at the Bat (1896, F)
Cobb (1994, F)
Damn Yankees (1958, F)
Don't Look Back: The Story of Leroy "Satchel" Paige (1981, TV)
Eight Men Out (1988, F)
Field of Dreams (1989, F)
Hank Aaron: Chasing the Dream (1996, D)
Hardball (2001, F)
It Happens Every Spring (1949, F)
The Jackie Robinson Story (1950, F)
A League of Their Own (1992, F)
The Life and Times of Hank Greenberg (2000, D)
Major League (1989, F)
The Natural (1984, F)
The Pride of St. Louis (1952, F)
Pride of the Yankees (1942, F)
The Rookie (2002, F)
The Scout (1994, F)
*61** (2001, TV)
The Stratton Story (1949, F)
There Was Always Sun Shining Someplace (1984, D)
The Winning Team (1952, F)

Bibliography

Bouton, Jim. *Ball Four.* New York: World, 1970.

Dawidoff, Nicholas. *The Catcher Was a Spy: The Mysterious Life of Moe Berg.* New York: Pantheon, 1994.

Dulles, Foster Rhea. *America Learns to Play: A History of Popular Recreation, 1607–1940.* New York: Appleton-Century, 1940.

Gould, Stephen Jay. *Triumph and Tragedy in Mudville: A Lifelong Passion for Baseball.* New York: Norton, 2003.

Honig, Donald. *Shadows of Summer: Classic Baseball Photographs, 1869–1947.* New York: Viking, 1994.

Isserman, Maurice, and Michael Kazin. *America Divided: The Civil War of the 1960s.* New York: Oxford University Press, 1999.

Mandell, Richard D. *Sport: A Cultural History.* New York: Columbia University Press, 1984.

Peterson, Robert W. *Only the Ball Was White: A History of Legendary Black Players and All-Black Teams.* Englewood Cliffs, NJ: Prentice-Hall, 1970.

Plimpton, George, ed. *Home Run.* San Diego: Harcourt, 2001.

Ritter, Lawrence S. *The Glory of Their Times: The Story of the Early Days of Baseball by the Men Who Played It.* New York: Macmillan, 1966.

Ruth, George Herman. *Babe Ruth's Own Book of Baseball.* 1928. Lincoln: University of Nebraska Press, 1992.

Sklar, Robert. *Movie-Made America: A Cultural History of American Movies.* Rev. ed. New York: Vintage, 1994.

Spalding, Albert G. *America's National Game.* 1911. Lincoln: University of Nebraska Press, 1992.

Stanton, Tom. *Final Season: Fathers, Sons, and One Last Season in a Classic American Ballpark.* New York: St. Martin's, 2001.

Stump, Al. *Cobb: A Biography.* Chapel Hill, NC: Algonquin Books, 1994.

Sullivan, Dean A. *Late Innings: A Documentary History of Baseball, 1945–1972.* Lincoln: University of Nebraska Press, 2002.

Tygiel, Jules. *Past Time: Baseball as History.* New York: Oxford University Press, 2000.

Ward, Geoffrey C., and Ken Burns. *Baseball: An Illustrated History.* New York: Knopf, 1994.

[DOUGLAS MUZZIO, THOMAS HALPER, AND JESSICA MUZZIO]

City and State Government

Hollywood's portrayal of city and state government and politics has tended to reflect its portrayal of American government and politics generally as corrupt, self-interested, and indifferent to the common good, though the subnational levels lack the sinister, omniscient, conspiratorial quality that is often ascribed to the much larger and more powerful national government in films such as *Mr. Smith Goes to Washington* (1939), *The Manchurian Candidate* (1962), *The Parallax View* (1974), and *JFK* (1991).

State and local governments have not widely figured as a central subject of urban films (see, for example, *8 Mile*, 2002), though the city police (*Dead End*, 1937) or the state prison (*Angels with Dirty Faces*, 1938) may represent official authority. Government here is less an actor than a reactor, usually cleaning up a mess created by larger social forces or strong individuals. However, even the police are often presented as unequal to the task, as in the vigilante shoot-'em-up in the early Depression (e.g. *The Secret Six*, 1932) and the early to mid-1970s (e.g., *Death Wish*, 1974), both periods when established authority at all levels seemed overwhelmed by the problems confronting it. Sometimes, cops constrained by weak—usually liberal—administrations must themselves go beyond the law (e.g., *Dirty Harry*, 1971).

Machine-Driven Politics

Political machines govern the reel city, the boss, and his minions following turn-of-the-century New York City ward heeler George Washington Plunkitt's famous adage, "I seen my opportunities and I took 'em" (Riordon, 62). The pols, typically allied with if not subordinate to gangsters, build their machines on graft and deceit, as in such Progressive-era silents as *A Dainty Politician* (1910), *The Grafters* (1913), and *The Politicians* (1915).

With the talkies, Hollywood's stance toward the machine grew ambivalent. On the one hand, numerous movies depicted urban politics as a kind of simple-minded metaphor for evil. This was particularly true of the so-called B movies that were produced in assembly-line fashion to fill out the double features that audiences demanded in the era before television (e.g., *Star Reporter*, 1939; *Boss of Boys Town*, 1943). Typical was a remark in *You and Me* (1938): "The big shots ain't crooks like you and me. They're politicians."

On the other hand, a number of city movies depicted pols as lovable rogues, softening their dishonest image with comedy or tear-jerking sentimentality. What these films communicated was that, though flawed, the machine was human in its creation and operation—and that it performed valuable functions that high-minded reformers were incapable even of recognizing.

The chief example is *The Last Hurrah* (1958), directed by John Ford and based on Edwin O'Connor's (1956) best-selling roman à clef about Boston's notorious James Michael Curley, and starring Spencer Tracy as the eye-twinkling boss with a heart of gold. Lamenting the last days of a colorful and caring Irish machine, the movie looks disdainfully at a future dominated by bland mediocrities whose only

FIGURE 38. *The Last Hurrah* (1958). With the introduction of television into politics, media attention and political corruption follow the political career of Mayor Frank Skeffington (Spencer Tracy) as he fights for election one last time. Courtesy Columbia Pictures.

apparent skill is a bloodless ability to play the ancient game of politics with the modern tool of television. Accompanying the faltering of the machine is a decline in the sense of community on which it rested. Bonds of obligation, tradition, and emotion are replaced by the manipulative tactics of public relations. The most vulnerable, whom the machine looked after for its own interests, are now without protectors. Another example in the pol-as-lovable-rogue genre is *Beau James* (1957), a leaden confection starring Bob Hope as Jimmy Walker, a famous (and crooked) mayor of New York during the Roaring Twenties.

The Rebirth of Cynicism

Since the 1960s, a watershed for cynicism toward authority generally, Hollywood's ambivalence toward city politics and government has all but vanished in a pervasive sense of betrayal, distrust, and greed. This view dominates in period movies such as *Chinatown* (1974), *Kansas City* (1996), *L.A. Confidential* (1997), and *Gangs of New York* (2002) as well as in contemporary movies such as *The Godfather* (1972, 1974), *Serpico* (1973), *Miller's Crossing* (1990), *Q & A* (1990), and *Narc* (2002), and even in fantasies such as *Batman* (1989) and *Dick Tracy* (1990). The economically and politically powerful scam the system for their own aggrandizement. The citizenry, whom the politicians are sworn to serve, is bilked and usually does not even know it.

Of these films, Roman Polanski's *Chinatown* (1974), a noir tale of disgrace, intrigue, and greed, is the most widely praised. Set in the sun-drenched Los Angeles of 1937, it exposes the foundations of rapaciousness upon which the glittering metropolis was built. Los Angeles is a moral and physical wasteland, intensely arid, a virtual desert. In this context, water—the seemingly most innocuous natural substance—becomes a highly prized political commodity, inspiring the most abominable acts. Water, tied to money via economic development, elicits the evil in the film, connecting public scandal with private perversion. Noah Cross (John Huston), city father, water magnate, and land speculator, rapes the land and rapes his daughter (Faye Dunaway). He manipulates the city's water supply to worsen a drought and lower adjacent farmland prices so that he can buy them for a song; he also uses the drought to justify a dam to be built by a public bond issue. The result, he thinks, will be thousands of acres of housing developments that would make a very wealthy man even wealthier.

Cities as Growth Machines

Chinatown was one of the first prominent movies to present the city as a growth machine dominated by "a small, parochial elite whose members have business or professional interests that are linked to local development and growth" (Molotch, 392). These elites use public authority and private power to stimulate economic development in order to enhance their own business interests, although they may also genuinely believe that development serves the public interest. As growth machines seek to provide an environment for private capital accumulation, cities redirect resources away from social programs toward uses benefiting the ambitious wealthy. The city may feel that it has no other choice: it needs private investment to generate jobs and taxes (and to buy off pols). But in any case the elites do very well while telling everyone that they are doing good.

The most realistic and sophisticated growth machine movie is John Sayles's *City of Hope* (1991), perhaps the only important urban film that is not hopelessly personalized. A product of the Reagan-Bush years, when cities seemed to have dropped off the national agenda, the movie neither sought nor won mass audience appeal. However, urbanists continue to work the movie into their conversations the way basketball fans end up discussing Michael Jordan. *City of Hope* revolves around the effort to build a mammoth office and housing complex financed, in part, by foreign (Japanese) capital in a broken-down industrial city in New Jersey. The problem is that the preferred site is occupied by low-income housing. Every effort has been made to remove the tenants—cutting off heat, water, and maintenance—but to no avail. With investors threatening to pull out of the deal, a corrupt district attorney (Bob North) seeking substantial contributions from the investors blackmails a corrupt mayor (Louis Zorich) to clear the site once and for all. The mayor's assistant pressures his brother (Tony Lo Bianco), the developer of the apartments, to "take care of things." The buildings are torched, killing an infant and his mother. The obstacle has been removed.

The governing regime in *City of Hope* is a complex and interdependent growth coalition of property entrepreneurs, financial interests, and politicians. There is a loosely organized and fading white ethnic (Irish and Italian) political machine and a less visible but far more powerful constellation of local, national, and international real estate and financial interests—plus Mafia-controlled construction unions and disaffected racial minorities. In this web of interdependence, no single interest, despite disparities in power, possesses sufficient clout to make growth happen. Government is dependent on the developers (and the financial interests that support them) to resurrect the city—and to provide graft for a multitude of public officials at all levels. Mayor Baci ("the second most indictable mayor in the state") awards contracts, enforces regulations, and distributes city financial assistance in exchange for concessions, legal and otherwise, to those on whom he depends: large-parcel landowners, local developers, and the police. He withholds public services from uncooperative slum-housing residents, physically threatening those who refuse to be displaced or have no other place to go. City politics, in this view, is above all the politics of land use, for land is the factor of production over which city governments exercise the greatest control.

Ethnic and racial inequalities are embedded in the structure of relations in the growth machine. Baci and the Italian American–majority council exploit the racist fears of their constituents. The growth coalition's strategy toward minority groups—as expressed by the principal minority character in the film—is "burn us out, plow us under and drive a wedge through the community." It succeeds because "we are blacks and Hispanics who can't get it together, can't work together, don't even vote."

The political machine is morally repellent, but also a product of history—a vehicle for each new ethnic and racial group to take over the levers of power, build self-esteem, and serve its own. What is striking is the stability of the power relations—the continuity of the regime. Only the faces change, not the arrangements of cooperation and compromise. New York's notorious Boss Tweed builds his Tammany Hall political machine on the murderous muscle of the Irish immigrant gangs of Manhattan's Five Points slum in *Gangs of New York* (2002).

City Hall

City Hall (1995), based on a story by former New York City deputy mayor Kenneth Lipper and cowritten by, among others, prominent investigative urban journalist Nicholas Pileggi, promises a realistic view of big city politics. Mayor John Pappas (Al Pacino) is charming, warm, smart, savvy, literate, and decent. He often dismisses his staff's warnings by declaring that his choice is "the right thing to do." Frank Anselmo (Danny Aiello), the boss of Brooklyn, is a backroom wheeler-dealer and a tool of the Mob, whose hard edges are rounded by his obvious love for his wife and by his obsession with Rodgers and Hammerstein musicals. Anselmo works through his friend, the mayor, to get a judge to grant probation to a violent nephew of a Mafia leader; the nephew kills a policeman and a young black bystander; the media focus on the killings; and the careers of the mayor, the boss, and the judge unravel.

Until the shootings come to dominate the plot, economic development is the main concern. The mayor wants to relocate a corporate megadevelopment to create jobs for the poor; Anselmo, fronting for greedy real estate developers, wants the mayor to commit to an expensive highway off-ramp and subway stop as a price for his support. The mayor finally commits to the infrastructure for the following year, a compromise that satisfies all parties. Such deals, the movies implies, are not wicked, but merely the way the world works. Corruption pervades Borough Hall in Queens, N.Y., in *The Yards* (2000) where bribes, kickbacks, payoffs and contracts are the quid pro quos among the borough president and other pols, cops, labor leaders, and businessmen.

State House

Perhaps because state governments tend to be perceived as less salient and more remote than city governments, movies have only rarely depicted them. An early example was the silent, *Her Honor, the Governor* (1926), a weeper starring Pauline Frederick. A high-minded woman is elected governor of Oklahoma, only to be told by a senior pol that he will wield the real power. She thwarts one of his pet projects; he responds by revealing that her late husband never divorced his first wife, making the governor an unwed mother. After an ensuing fight involving her son, he is charged with murder and she is impeached; but, just in time, the real murderer is caught and a record of her husband's divorce is found. The story, of course, is all stock characters and hokey melodrama. Still, in portraying a woman politician as a strong, independent force and not a "Ma" Ferguson stand-in for her husband—and this only six years after the Nineteenth Amendment gave women the vote—the movie must be considered pathbreaking.

The best-known film on state government is *All the King's Men* (1949), based on Robert Penn Warren's Pulitzer Prize–winning novelization of the life of Louisiana governor Huey P. Long. Scoundrel, charmer, defender of the downtrodden, crook, fighter for progress, foe of democratic accountability, Warren's Huey Long was far more complex than O'Connor's Michael J. Curley—and Long had a capacity for violence and met his death through it. So dominant is the Long character, Willy Stark (Broderick Crawford), that the state government is seen as simply a tool in his hands, as it had been a tool in the hands of the economic oligarchy that preceded him. With this dark portrait, the tendency of movies to personalize politics at the expense of institutions, structures, and processes is carried to its logical conclusion.

Nine years earlier, Preston Sturges's classic comedy *The Great McGinty* (1940) traced the rise of a hobo (Brian Donlevy) from professional voter (casting thirty-seven ballots at two dollars apiece under assumed names in various precincts) to alderman, mayor, and governor. When, pressured by his wife, he decides to reform, confessing to a graft-ridden bridge contract, his honesty is rewarded by a term in jail. For all its charm, however, the movie does not focus long on state politics. Instead, there is a parade of local hacks, one of whom famously remarks, "If it wasn't for graft, you'd see a very low type of people in politics—men without ambition—jellyfish." At the end, the pol-turned-waiter moans, "Here we go again!"

The Documentary Vision

Few movie documentaries focus on American city and state governments; indeed, the best-known of them touch on the subject only tangentially. *Roger & Me* (1989), Michael Moore's polemic against General Motors' lay-offs at its Flint, Michigan plant, attracted an unusually large audience. The film details what Moore sees as the city's victimization at the hands of rapacious capitalism and the banality of the policy responses of the city government. More complex and ambitious is *Public Housing* (1997), by cinema verité director Frederick Wiseman. A many-layered investigation of the residents of a large Chicago housing project, the movie reflects the hopes, fears, and moral ambiguities of real life in the big city. Although neither *Roger and Me* nor *Public Housing* focuses principally on government, both address major public issues affecting modern urban America.

City of Promise (1995), part of a Ford Foundation–funded PBS television series on the rediscovery of poverty in America in the 1960s, looks at Newark, New Jersey. It opens in the summer of 1965, after Lyndon Johnson had declared war on poverty and directed that the war was to be fought primarily in the nation's cities by empowering the poor to design and run antipoverty programs through their "maximum feasible participation." *City of Promise* contrasts the rise of urban black political power with the complacent inertia of the white power structure, recounting the bitter political battles and the racial rioting that erupted over the next several years. In the end, in real life as in the movies, the promise of the city did not materialize.

References

Filmography

All the King's Men (1949, F)
Angels with Dirty Faces (1938, F)
Batman (1989, F)
Beau James (1957, F)
Boss of Boys Town (1943, F)
Chinatown (1974, F)
City Hall (1995, F)
City of Hope (1991, F)
City of Promise (1995, TV)
A Dainty Politician (1910, F)
Dead End (1937, F)
Death Wish (1974, F)
Dick Tracy (1990, F)
Dirty Harry (1971, F)
8 Mile (2002, F)
Exclusive Rights (1926, F)
Far and Away (1992, F)
Gangs of New York (2002, F)
The Glass Key (1935, F)
The Godfather (1972, F)
The Godfather II (1974, F)
The Grafters (1913, F)
The Great McGinty (1940, F)
Her Honor, the Governor (1926, F)
His Girl Friday (1940, F)
JFK (1991, F)
Kansas City (1996, F)
L.A. Confidential (1997)
The Last Hurrah (1958, F)
The Manchurian Candidate (1962, F)
Miller's Crossing (1990, F)
Mr. Smith Goes to Washington (1939, F)
The Parallax View (1974, F)
The Politicians (1915, F)
The Power of the Press (1928, F)
Public Housing (1997, D)
Q & A (1990, F)
Roger & Me (1989, D)
Scandalous Mayor (1991, F)
The Secret Six (1932, F)
Serpico (1973, F)
Star Reporter (1939, F)
This Day and Age (1933, F)
Traffic in Hearts (1924, F)
The Yards (2000, F)
You and Me (1938, F)

Bibliography

Molotch, Harvey. "The City as a Growth Machine: Toward a Political Economy of Place." *American Journal of Sociology* 82.2 (1976): 309–330.
O'Connor, Edwin. *The Last Hurrah.* Boston: Little, Brown, 1956.
Riordon, William L. *Plunkitt of Tammany Hall.* New York: St. Martin's, 1994.

[RAYMOND ARSENAULT]

Civil Rights

The modern American civil rights movement is arguably one of the most important developments of the twentieth century. Rooted in the abolitionist movement and the postemancipation efforts of the Reconstruction era (1865–77), and nurtured by the National Association for the Advancement of Colored People's (NAACP) legal campaign against racial segregation and discrimination, the movement evolved into a sweeping struggle for social justice and human dignity. By prodding the nation to live up to the promises of the Declaration of Independence, the Bill of Rights and the Thirteenth, Fourteenth, and Fifteenth Amendments to the Constitution, civil rights activists redefined the nature of American citizenship, bringing a measure of redemption to a society plagued by racial inequality and injustice. Partially inspired by the ongoing decolonolization of the Third World, including the triumph of Gandhian nonviolence in India and the creation of independent nations in Africa, the battle for civil rights in the United States in turn provided inspiration for liberation movement across the globe. During the 1960s, figures such as Thurgood Marshall (the leader of the NAACP's effort to strike down legalized segregation and the first black to serve on the Supreme Court) and Martin Luther King Jr. (the founder of the Southern Christian Leadership Conference [SCLC] and winner of the Nobel Peace Prize) became international symbols of that came to be known as the "freedom struggle." With the murder of King in 1968, the classic phase of the struggle ended, but the ennobling ideals and innovative tactics of the civil rights movement left an enduring legacy that continues to influence everything from public policy to individual views about race, culture, and citizenship.

The periodization and parameters of the civil rights movement are subjects of continuing debate among scholars, but it is no longer fashionable to limit the movement to the activities following the Brown school desegregation decisions of the mid-1950s. Although the national civil rights movement did not reach maturity until the 1960s, the contributions of early activists such as W. E. B. Du Bois, Paul Robeson, William Hastie, Bayard Rustin, Ella Baker, Pauli Murray, and Mary McLeod Bethune—all of whom were actively working for civil rights in the 1930s and 1940s—are now considered to be an essential part of the civil rights story. However, beyond this recognition of the movement's pioneers there is little consensus about the evolution of the struggle. Among civil rights scholars, there are sharp differences of opinion about King's leadership, the significance of Malcom X and other black nationalists, and the relative importance of various aspects of the movement: local versus national civil rights organizations; federal initiatives versus movement activities; legal versus direct action; and the contributions of the NAACP versus those of SCLC, the Congress of Racial Equality (CORE), and the Student Nonviolent Coordinating Committee (SNCC). Several important recent studies—most notably those of Taylor Branch, John Dittmer, and Adam Fairclough—have acknowledged tensions within the movement and have attempted to demythologize national leaders such as King, Malcolm X, and Marshall. Other works, such as Joanne Grant's biography of Ella Baker, have stressed the critical role of women in the movement.

Civil rights scholarship has become one of the most vital areas of American historiography, but the motion picture industry has not kept pace with growing interest in the civil rights saga. Although a number of interesting films shed light on race relations in modern America, very few focus on civil rights activists or organizations. With few exceptions, the best civil rights films are adaptations of historical fiction, television docudramas, or documentaries. Feature films based on historical accounts of actual incidents or real adventures are rare, and the few high-profile civil rights features that do exist, such as *Mississippi Burning* and *Malcolm X*, have tended to create more confusion and misinformation than enlightenment. Nevertheless, these and other civil rights movies have had a significant impact on American popular culture and thus deserve attention, if not always respect.

Seedtime for Civil Rights: 1930–1945

In recent years, historians have developed a greater appreciation for the scope and vitality of the nascent civil rights movement of the 1930s and 1940s. Unfortunately, only a handful of filmmakers have taken advantage of the growing body of research detailing the early years of the struggle. *Judge Horton and the Scottsboro Boys*, a 1976 NBC docudrama based on historian Dan Carter's groundbreaking study *Scottsboro: A Tragedy of the American South*, provides an accurate and gripping reconstruction of the arrest and trial of nine black men falsely accused of raping two white women on an Alabama train in 1931. The film features Arthur Hill's convincing and sympathetic portrayal of James Horton, the Alabama judge who sacrificed his career in an attempt to save the Scottsboro defendants, and an equally strong performance by Ken Kercheval as prosecuting attorney Thomas Knight. A second docudrama, the 1993 production *Simple Justice*, focuses on the NAACP's early efforts to dismantle the Jim Crow system of legal segregation and discrimination. Based on Richard Kluger's magisterial 1976 book of the same name, the film traces the early life and career of Thurgood Marshall, paying particular attention to the mentoring role of Charles Hamilton Houston, who taught Marshall at Howard University Law School in the 1930s and who later collaborated with him in the development and implementation of the NAACP Legal Defense Fund's complex legal strategies. Another notable and compelling television docudrama, *Miss Evers' Boys* (1997), tells the grim story of the infamous Tuskegee syphilis study initiated by the U.S. Public Health Service in 1932. Alfre Woodard's performance as Miss Evers, the conscience-stricken nurse who helped expose the government's callous disregard for the lives of the black syphilis patients, is riveting, and the entire production—an adaptation of a play by David Feldshuh—is reasonably faithful to the historical record.

The only notable feature film to focus on civil rights during the 1930s is *To Kill a Mockingbird*, the 1962 movie version of Harper Lee's celebrated novel. Though fictional, Horoton Foote's Oscar-winning screenplay presents Atticus Finch, a white lawyer representing a black man charged with rape, as a historically credible (though clearly unusual) character. Gregory Peck's portrayal of Finch is unforgettable, and the entire production, despite obvious touches of sentimentality, successfully captures the mood of the small-town South during the Great Depression.

World War II was an important watershed for black Americans, who witnessed the creation of the Fair Employment Practices Commission in 1941, the Supreme Court's decision outlawing white primaries (*Smith v. Allwright*, 1944), and the proliferation of the Double V campaign—the determination to win twin victories over foreign enemies on the battle field and racial discrimination at home. Clearly, this era of racial transition warrants the attention of filmmakers, but to date such attention has been severely limited. Both during and after the war, Hollywood produced a flood of World War II films, but very few touched upon the experiences of black servicemen or the black home front. The most obvious exception is the classic 1944 documentary *The Negro Soldier*, produced as part of director Frank Capra's memorable *Why We Fight* series. Among World War II feature films, the earliest attempt to deal with the black experience was *Home of the Brave* (1949), a powerful drama based on a play by Arthur Laurents. Produced by Stanley Kramer and directed by Mark Robson, the landmark film depicts the wartime saga of a black soldier named Mossy, played by war veteran James Edwards. Tormented by his fellow GIs' racial prejudices, Mossy survives brutal combat in the Pacific but ends up in an army hospital, where he develops a redemptive friendship with a white amputee,

FIGURE 39. *Judge Horton and the Scottsboro Boys* (1976). Judge Horton (Arthur Hill) listens intensely to a defendant. The NBC docudrama using trial transcripts focused on the human interactions during the trial of the major courtroom figures and the toll it took on their lives. Courtesy Tomorrow Entertainment.

In *A Soldier's Story*, released in 1984, director Norman Jewison offers a less hopeful view of black army life in the 1940s. Based on Charles Fuller's Pulitzer Prize–winning play, the film tells the story of a black officer's murder at a Southern army camp. Strong performances by Howard E. Rollins Jr. and Adolph Caesar dramatize the connection between racial discrimination and pathological interaction among black soldiers during the Jim Crow era. An equally absorbing treatment of black military life can be found in the 1990 television movie *The Court Martial of Jackie Robinson*, based on a 1944 incident in which a black army lieutenant and future Hall of Fame baseball star faced an army court-martial after refusing to comply with a Texas segregated-bus-seating ordinance, this carefully constructed film reveals the indignities of Jim Crow transit, reminding us that the determination of Robinson and others to buck the system antedated the later heroism of Rosa Parks. The persistence of military segregation during the war is also the theme of the 1995 HBO docudrama *The Tuskegee Airmen*. Featuring an all-star cast led by Lawrence Fishburne, Cuba Gooding Jr., Andre Braugher, and John Lithgow, the film makes an honest attempt to depict the exploits of black flyers, the impositions of racial prejudice and condescension, and the common resolve among black servicemen to be treated with respect. Unfortunately, the script is too formulaic to do justice to the complexities of the Tuskegee airmen's bittersweet experiences. A more recent film with similar strengths and weaknesses is *Mutiny*, a 1999 docudrama that profiles the fate of fearful black munitions loaders following a deadly explosion at Port Chicago, California, in 1944, in which more than three hundred black servicemen died.

The Postwar Decade: 1946–1955

The "crucial decade," as historian Eric Goldman dubbed the immediate postwar era, witnessed important developments in civil rights,

FIGURE 40. *A Soldier's Story* (1984). Director Norman Jewison's film explores tensions in the closed community of African American soldiers during World War II. Courtesy Caldix and Columbia Pictures.

including the gradual desegregation of the military and a series of liberal Federal court decisions culminating in the *Brown v. Board of Education* rulings of 1954 and 1955. The first films to explore the changing character of postwar race relations appeared as early as 1946. *It Happened in Springfield* (1946) tells the story of a Massachusetts city rocked by interracial tensions. Based on an actual incident and filmed on location by Warner Bros., the early docudrama traces a grassroots effort to extend the "melting pot" ideal to black Americans. Unfortunately, in the final cut all references to homegrown racism are excised, leaving Nazi propaganda, not traditional American bigotry, as the designated culprit. A more courageous film, one that deals more directly with the social pathology and enforced limitation of Northern black life, is *The Quiet One* (1947), a semidocumentary on the all-black Wiltwyck School in Harlem. Utilizing nonprofessional actors, the film offers an unromanticized look at the life or a ten-year-old boy trapped in a life of crime and neglect.

As the 1940s drew to a close, Hollywood released a spate of "social problem" films focusing on contemporary race relations. *Pinky* (1949), a collaborative effort of producer Darryl F. Zanuck and director Elia Kazan, and *Lost Boundaries* (1949), a Louis DeRochement production starring Mel Ferrer in his first role, both focus on the theme of racial "passing." Jeanne Crain's melodramatic portrayal of a light-skinned "Negro" nurse and Ethel Waters's strong performance as her dark-skinned mother make *Pinky* an interesting if not altogether convincing film. Similarly, *Lost Boundaries*, which received widespread critical acclaim upon its release, is a well-intentioned but flawed production that skirts many of the important issues related to class and the color line.

A less pretentious and ultimately more interesting effort to dramatize the declining years of Jim Crow is the 1949 film adaptation of William Faulkner's novel *Intruder in the Dust.* Filmed in Oxford, Mississippi, and directed by Tennessean Clarence Brown, *Intruder in the Dust* focuses on a small band of fair-minded white Mississippians who prevent the lynching of Lucas Beauchamp, a fiercely proud black farmer falsely accused of murder. Parts of the film have an adolescent Disneyesque quality, but it remains an intriguing piece. Two other notable efforts to capture the racial aura of the 1940s on film are *The Jackie Robinson Story* (1950), a charming and disarmingly straightforward film starring Robinson himself, and *No Way Out* (1950), a Joseph L. Mankiewicz–directed crime drama that marked the film debuts of Sidney Poitier, Ruby Dee, and Ossie Davis. In *No Way Out,* Richard Widmark plays a cold-hearted, racist gangster who avenges his brother's death by inciting a race riot.

The films described above are useful sources for the study of postwar relations, but none of them deals directly with the emerging civil rights movement of this era. Fortunately, three creditable television movies fill part of the gap. *Separate but Equal,* a 1991 production written and directed by George Stevens Jr., is an outstanding dramatization of the final stages (1950–55) of the NAACP Legal Defense Fund's campaign to strike down the separate but equal doctrine of *Plessy v. Ferguson* (1896). With a few minor exceptions, the three-hour film is historically sound, and Sidney Poitier delivers a memorable performance as Thurgood Marshall, the attorney who spearheads the NAACP's efforts in the landmark *Brown* desegregation cases. A second docudrama that offers a somewhat longer view of the NAACP's campaign is *Simple Justice.* The 1993 PBS film's hour-long section on the post–World War II era offers a compressed but generally accurate description of the final twists and turns in the long road to the *Brown* decisions. A third televised docudrama, *The Vernon Johns Story: The Road to Freedom* (1994), profiles the career of one of the postwar South's most courageous black ministers. Brought back to life in a brilliant performance by James Earl Jones, Johns—who preceded Martin Luther King Jr. as pastor of Dexter Avenue Baptist Church in Montgomery, Alabama—is an unforgettable and inspiring character.

The Rise of Massive Resistance: 1955–1960

The tense period following the Brown school-desegregation decisions of the mid-1950s witnessed the emergence of nonviolent direct action during the Montgomery Bus Boycott of 1955–56, the creation of the Southern Christian Leadership Conference in 1957, the crisis at Little Rock's Central High School in 1957, the growth of White Citizens' Councils and the rise of massive resistance among ultrasegragationists in the Deep South, and the birth of the student-led sit-in movement in Greensboro, North Carolina, in 1960. Contemporary filmmakers studiously avoided the subject of the Southern civil rights movement, but they did produce several "race" films that implicitly endorsed racial tolerance and civil rights. Sidney Poitier starred in *Edge of the City* (1957), a provocative tale of working-class life in New York directed by Martin Ritt; *The Defiant Ones* (1958), director Stanley Kramer's masterwork about two shackled convicts, one black and one white, fleeing the police; and *A Raisin in the Sun* (1961), a powerful adaptation of Lorraine Hansberry's celebrated play about survival in black Chicago. Two films featuring Harry Belafonte, *Island in the Sun* (1957) and *Odds Against Tomorrow* (1959), offered, respectively, a comparative look at contemporary racial struggles in the Caribbean and the unhappy story of an interracial band of bank-robbers stymied by racial dissension.

The first feature film to focus squarely on the racial dilemmas of the post-*Brown* South was *Black Like Me,* a 1964 release starring

James Whitmore as investigative journalist John Howard Griffin. From October to December 1959, after temporarily darkening his skin to achieve the appearance of a "Negro," Griffin wandered through Mississippi, Alabama, Georgia, and Louisiana in an attempt to experience the difficult realities of black life. Based on a best-selling 1961 book, Whitmore's Jim Crow odyssey provided moviegoers with a believable and searing portrait of Deep South racism. An even better film, a major production that represents one of the first efforts to deal with the civil rights movement itself, is *The Long Walk Home* (1990). Set in Montgomery, Alabama, in 1956, this carefully scripted drama explores the evolving relationship between a privileged white woman (Sissy Spacek) and her dignified black housekeeper (Whoopi Goldberg) during the bus boycott. John Cook's script is fictional, but the film's depictions of resolute white supremacists, vulnerable Southern moderates, and black Montgomerians discovering the power of a faith-based "movement culture" have the ring of truth. Perhaps most important, the strong and subtle performances by Spacek and Goldberg underscore the key role that women, both black and white, played in sustaining the boycott and other mass protests.

The Montgomery bus boycott also inspired the production of two well-made television docudramas: *Boycott* (2001), and *The Rosa Parks Story* (2002). Shown on the Home Box Office cable channel, *Boycott* successfully combined documentary footage and carefully rendered historical drama. Ably directed by Clark Johnson and filmed on location in Montgomery, it set a new standard for cinematic dramatization of King's emergence as a national civil rights leader and the internal dynamics of the bus boycott. Fine performances by Jeffrey Wright as King, Iris Little-Thomas as Rosa Parks, and Terrence Howard as Ralph Abernathy give the film an emotional power that few civil rights docudramas have been able to muster. The most recent effort to dramatize the boycott, *The Rosa Parks Story*, is somewhat less successful as a re-creation of the complex origins and evolution of the Montgomery Improvement Association. Although the film's depiction of Rosa Parks, the forty-three-year old seamstress and local NAACP leader who became a folk hero after refusing to give up her seat on a crowded Montgomery bus, is generally accurate, the consistently celebratory tone of the script is somewhat problematical.

The only other civil rights film to focus on the mid- or late 1950s is *The Ernest Green Story*, a television docudrama produced for the Disney Channel in 1993. One of the nine black students who desegregated Little Rock's Central High School in 1957, Green survived the taunts and assaults of angry white supremacists and went on to become an important official in the Carter administration and a successful business executive. The film takes a few liberties with chronology and melodramatic dialogue, but overall it offers a balanced and credible picture of the "Little Rock Nine."

The 1960s and Beyond

The sit-in movement that spread across the South in 1960, and the Freedom Rides initiated by CORE in May 1961 kicked off the most intense phase of the civil rights struggle. Throughout the turbulent decade of the 1960s, mass protests and militant activism complemented the NACCP's ongoing legal and legislative challenges to segregation and discrimination. Clashes with demagogic politicians and violent white supremacists attracted the attention of the national media and the Kennedy and Johnson administrations, as thousands of civil rights activists took to the streets demanding an end to Jim Crow. Martin Luther King and the other movement leaders provoked major confrontations in Alabama, where Governor George Wallace "stood in the schoolhouse door" to prevent integration and Birmingham public safety commissioner Bull Connor used fire hoses and attack dogs to control demonstrators, and in Mississippi, where the 1964 Freedom Summer voting rights campaign challenged the traditions of the South's most conservative state.

The passage of the 1964 Civil Rights Act and the 1965 Voting Rights Act represented major movement victories, but disillusionment born of rising expectations, economic hardship, and persistent prejudice helped fuel the Black Power movement and urban riots of the late 1960s. The assassination of Martin Luther King in 1968, the diversions of the Vietnam War, the belated implementation of school desegregation and fair housing and employment laws, and white backlash against groups such as the Black Panthers brought the mass-protest phase of the movement to a close by the end of the decade.

Despite the obvious drama and historical importance of the civil rights struggles of the 1960s, the motion picture industry has made only a half-hearted attempt to put this tumultuous era on film. A notable early effort is *Nothing but a Man* (1964), a powerful dramatization of a romance between a black railroad worker and a black middle-class schoolteacher. This low-budget film makes only passing mention of the civil rights movement but offers a sensitive and moving treatment of the complications of class and race in the early 1960s.

In the Heat of the Night and *Guess Who's Coming to Dinner*—the first major feature films to focus on race relations in the waning years of Jim Crow—broke new ground when they were released in 1967. In both cases, Sidney Poitier's suave upper-middle-class persona limited his character's relevance to the experiences of most black Americans, but the positive response to these films among whites suggested that sensitive topics such as interracial marriage and black empowerment were no longer taboo. In 1968, the release of *Up Tight!*, a remake of the 1935 classic *The Informer* reset in a Cleveland ghetto following the assassination of Martin Luther King, demonstrated that one producer was even willing to make a film on contemporary black revolutionaries. Director Jules Dassin's collaboration with black screenwriters Ruby Dee and Julian Mayfield produced a hard-hitting, if somewhat unrealistic portrait of black militants shredding the remains of a nonviolent movement. A companion film, *Putney Swope*, a farcical comedy about black militants taking over a major New York advertising agency, appeared in 1969. After changing the agency's name to Truth and Soul, Inc., the militants wreak havoc with a clever parody of the Black Power movement. Less satisfying is *The Liberation of L. B. Jones* (1970), the last film of legendary director William Wyler. Based on a popular Jesse Hill Ford novel, the movie profiles the saga of a black, middle-class couple terrorized by white racists in a Tennessee town. Although the film's overall depiction of the black bourgeoisie is somewhat hackneyed, Roscoe Lee Browne's portrayal of the long-suffering undertaker L. B. Jones is convincing, as is Yaphet Kotto's role as a black radical who dispatches a white racist in a hay cropper.

Predictably, Hollywood's brief flirtation with civil rights themes all but disappeared in the early 1970s as the white backlash, propelled by Richard Nixon's "Southern strategy" of soliciting the votes of disaffected segregationists, gained momentum. With the exceptions of *The Man* (1972), a mediocre adaptation of Irving Wallace's bestseller about America's first black president, and *The Klansman* (1974), a sensationalist potboiler based on William Bradford Huie's novel about racial turmoil and white resistance in the contemporary South, feature films studiously avoided the modern civil rights scene until the mid-1980s. Fortunately, in the interim, television took up some of the slack by offering several notable civil rights docudramas. In 1974, the ABC network broadcast a powerful adaptation of Ernest Gaines's novel *The Autobiography of Miss Jane Pittman*. Featuring an unforgettable performance by Cicely Tyson, this Emmy Award–winning film uses the reminiscences of a fictional 110-year-old woman to trace the evolution of civil rights from the Civil War to the 1960s. The script's focus on ordinary individuals involved in local civil rights struggles makes the film especially valuable. Though well intentioned, a second ABC docudrama, *Attack on Terror: The FBI vs. The Ku Klux Klan* (1975), offers a more problematic view of the movement and its alleged allies. The first of several films to explore the murders of three civil rights activists—Andrew Goodman, Michael Schwerner, and James Chaney—during Mississippi's Freedom Summer of 1964, *Attack on Terror* details and glorifies the efforts of white FBI agents but pays only fleeting attention to movement participants, black or white.

Television's most ambitious effort to interpret the civil rights movement—director-writer Abby Mann's lavish four-hour production, *King*—appeared in 1978, on the heels of Arthur Haley's spectacularly successful miniseries *Roots* (1977). Though marred by hagiographic reverence, Mann's script presents a vivid dramatization of Martin Luther King's life. Paul Winfield's portrayal of the martyred civil rights leader is mesmerizing, especially during the film's depictions of King's struggles in Montgomery, Birmingham, and Selma. Unfortunately, the film's tight focus on King and the SCLC leaves little room for a serious treatment of other civil rights leaders and organizations and at times gives the misleading impression that he alone created and led the modern civil rights movement. Despite this limitation, or perhaps because of it, Mann's effort attracted enough viewers to sustain the television industry's interest in civil rights dramas. In 1979 the four-part miniseries *Roots: The Next Generation,* extended Alex Haley's family saga from 1882 to the 1970s, including an episode on Haley's relationship with Malcolm X; in 1986 director John Korty (also the director of *The Autobiography of Miss Jane Pittman*) and screenwriter Morgan Halsey Davis joined forces with actors John Lithgow and Morgan Freeman to produce *Resting Place,* the moving story of a white army officer battling racism during an attempt to bury a black Vietnam War hero in an all-white cemetery in Georgia in the 1970s; a year later Louis Gossett Jr. led an all-star cast in a memorable televised version of *A Gathering of Old Men,* Ernest Gaines's story of a group of aging Louisiana blacks who belatedly take collective responsibility for the murder of a local white supremacist.

Television's reliance on historical fiction to dramatize the civil rights struggle continued in the early 1990s with the airing of a short-lived but remarkable weekly NBC series *I'll Fly Away* (1991–93). Reminiscent of *To Kill a Mockingbird* but more subtle in its depiction of southern race relations, *I'll Fly Away* presents the interrelated stories of two Deep South families in the 1960s. The lead characters—Forrest Bedford, a politically ambitious district attorney played by Sam Waterston, and Lilly Harper, a black housekeeper and single mother played by Regina Taylor—grapple with life's challenges amid the complexities of a changing racial order. Several episodes focus on Lilly's growing awareness of and involvement in civil rights activities, including a voter registration drive and a sit-in on the courthouse steps. Lilly's rising expectations and sense of self-respect clash with her employer's mixed feelings about the civil rights movement, but in the end the series offers a hopeful projection of racial adjustment and redemption. In October 1993, PBS broadcast a two-hour movie sequel featuring Lilly as a successful sixty-year-old novelist recounting the tumultuous civil rights era to her son. Although less satisfying than the original episodes, the sequel represents an interesting attempt to put the series in historical context, using Lilly's encounters with an aging Bedford and other figures from her past as an allegory of the New South.

Hollywood has never produced a civil rights film approaching the quality of *I'll Fly Away,* but after fifteen years of silence it finally re-

FIGURE 41. *I'll Fly Away* (1991–1993). District Attorney Forrest Bedford (Sam Waterson) and his black housekeeper Lilly Harper (Regina Taylor) personify the changing dynamics of southern race relations in the 1960s. Courtesy NBC Television.

turned to civil right themes with the 1988 release of *Mississippi Burning.* Directed by noted British filmmaker Alan Parker, this second attempt to dramatize the Freedom Summer murders of 1964 features a scathing indictment of Mississippi segregationists, Academy Award–winning cinematography, and strong performances by Willem Dafoe and Gene Hackman as the two FBI agents who cracked the case. Regrettably, what it does not feature is historical accuracy. Although marketed as a faithful reconstruction of the FBI's attempt to solve the murders, the film is riddled with factual errors and questionable interpretations. Downplaying the racial and political conservatism that pervaded the J. Edgar Hoover–led FBI in the 1960s, Chris Gerolmo's script offers a seriously distorted view of the bureau's posture toward the Freedom Summer and the civil rights movement in general. The film also grossly understates the role of the media in forcing federal officials to investigate the murders and all but ignores the real sacrifices of the Freedom Summer activists and "local people," who risked their lives to bring a measure of justice to Mississippi. Not surprisingly, *Mississippi Burning*'s highly publicized release triggered a firestorm of criticism among movement veterans and historians, prompting a third attempt to put the Freedom Summer case on film—the 1990 television docudrama *Murder in Mississippi,* a straightforward account that offers the most accurate and balanced treatment to date.

Mississippi is also the setting for four recent efforts to dramatize the interracial violence that punctuated the civil rights struggles of the 1960s. In *A Time to Kill* (1996), a faithful adaptation of John Grisham's first novel, Matthew McConaughey plays a white lawyer representing a black man (Samuel L. Jackson) who murdered two poor whites who had raped his ten-year old daughter. Although pure fiction, the film offers a nuanced and believable picture of Mississippi race relations and invites comparison with the 1949 film *Intruder in the Dust.* The same could be said for *Freedom Song* (2000), a sophisticated and moving exploration of SNCC involvement and local activism in a small Mississippi town during the 1960s. Directed by Phil Alden Robinson and starring Danny Glover, *Freedom Song* is the first film to provide a credible, fiction-based dramatization of SNCC's extraordinary impact on the freedom struggle in Mississippi.

Less concerned with the movement but perhaps more valuable as a cinematic depiction of black life in Mississippi during the post–World War II era is *Once Upon a Time . . . When We Were Colored* (1996). Based upon an autobiographical novel by Clifton L. Taulbert and directed by Tim Reid, this feature film chronicles a decade and a half (1946–62) of cultural and political change among the black residents of Glen Allan, Mississippi. A carefully crafted script and powerful performances by Al Freeman Jr., Richard Roundtree, and Phylicia Rashad make this one of the most emotionally engaging "civil rights films" yet produced by Hollywood. An equally ambitious but ultimately less satisfying film, *Ghosts of Mississippi* (1997), tells the story of Assistant District Attorney Bobby DeLaughter's belated but ultimately successful prosecution of Byron De La Beckwith, the white supremacist who assassinated Mississippi NAACP leader Medgar Evers in 1963. James Woods's portrayal of De La Beckwith is chilling, and Whoopi Goldberg's understated performance as Myrlie Evers, the long-suffering widow who questioned the resolve and integrity of DeLaughter and other white law enforcement officials, is convincing. Even so, for historians of the civil rights movement the film represents a missed opportunity. The filmmaker's decision to focus almost exclusively on DeLaughter and the 1990s retrial of De La Beckwith left no room for even a cursory treatment of Medgar Evers and the civil rights struggle in Mississippi. The film fails to communicate why Evers was willing to risk his life for the civil rights movement or why De La Beckwith was so determined to eliminate Evers. The script's inattention to historical context is consistent with the film industry's longstanding reluctance to explore the passions that animated and divided the contending forces of the civil rights struggle.

This tradition of avoidance has been especially true with respect to the white supremacist side of the struggle. Indeed, the only serious effort to dramatize the segregationist movement of the 1960s are the 1997 miniseries *George Wallace,* a melodramatic screen biography directed by John Frankenheimer, and *The Sins of the Father* (2002), a semifictional account of a man's attempt to come to terms with his father's involvement in the infamous September 1963 church bombing and murder of four young black girls in Birmingham, Alabama. In *George Wallace,* Gary Sinise's riveting portrayal of the race-baiting Alabama governor has an air of authenticity, but invented characters, factual errors, and garbled chronology detract from the film's historical value. These problems are even more apparent in *The Sins of the Father,* though the film does have the virtue of making an honest effort to represent the psychological complexity and cultural context of the white segregationist mindset.

George Wallace's racial demagoguery is an important part of the civil rights story, primarily because his attempt to mobilize disaffected white supremacists in the presidential campaigns of 1964 and 1968 helped to precipitate the fragmentation of the civil rights movement. During the mid- and late 1960s, as Martin Luther King and SCLC conducted campaigns against de facto segregation and discrimination in Chicago and other northern cities, both the politics of white backlash and the civil rights struggle itself became national in scope. At the same time, major "race riots" erupted in Watts and other urban ghettoes, fueling the fires of reaction and bringing black-nationalist groups such as the Nation of Islam and the Black Panthers to the fore. By the end of the decade, the movement had devolved into a welter of competing ideologies and social confusion, which may help to explain why reliable scholarly accounts of this phase of the movement are rare and cinematic treatments are even rarer. Other than the 1968 film *Up Tight!* mentioned earlier, the only feature film to grapple with this subject is Spike Lee's *Malcolm X.* Released with great fanfare in 1992, Lee's three-and-a-half-hour epic recounts the remarkable life and death of the charismatic Black Muslim leader, assassinated in 1965. Anchored by Denzel Washington's riveting performance, Lee's mythic reconstruction of Malcolm X's odyssey from street hustler to prison inmate to national icon offers good drama—but bad history. Invented characters and a heavily politicized and fanciful reinterpretation of Malcolm X's later years compromise the film's value as a work of history. Moviegoers in search of a more faithful account of the political and philosophical adjustments that followed Malcolm X's break with Nation of Islam leader Elijah Muhammad should consult the excellent 1994 Blackside documentary *Malcolm X: Make It Plain.*

Documentaries

The struggle for civil rights has inspired a large number of documentary films. With a few notable exceptions, civil rights documentaries tend to be brief, low-budget productions that focus on a particular incident or individual. Most rely heavily on television news footage and videotaped interviews of activists, and more than a few are makeshift, semiprofessional productions initiated by movement participants. The filmography includes a listing of significant civil rights documentaries, ranging from Frank Capra's seminal 1944 film *The Negro Soldier* to Spike Lee's 1997 Academy Award–nominated documentary *Four Little Girls,* a heartrending account of the September 1963 bombing of Birmingham's Sixteenth Street Baptist Church, as seen through the eyes of friends and relatives of the four young girls killed by the blast. Nearly all of these films include stirring reminders of the sights and sounds of the movement, but only a few provide a contextual framework or serious historical analysis. Among the best are *No Vietnamese Ever Called Me Nigger* (1968), a wrenching look at black soldiers fighting in Vietnam; *King: A Filmed Record . . . From Montgomery to Memphis* (1968), a well-edited biographical portrait produced just after King's death; *Fundi: The Story of Ella Baker* (1981), an inspiring profile of an important but often overlooked movement organizer; *Never Turn Back: The Life of Fannie Lou Hamer* (1983), a biography of the Mississippi Freedom Democratic Party activist who caused a sensation at the 1964 Democratic National Convention; *Malcolm X: Make It Plain* (1994), the best available documentary on the most influential black nationalist of the 1960s; *W.E.B. Du Bois: A Biography in Four Voices* (1996), a carefully rendered study of the legendary black intellectual who helped found the NAACP; *First Person Singular: John Hope Franklin* (1997), an enlightening biographical portrait of a courageous African American historian and activist; *The Promised Land* (1997), an engrossing study of post–World War II black migration to northern cities; *Scottsboro: An American Tragedy* (2001), a beautifully edited collage of photographs and interviews that easily supercedes the 1976 docudrama *Judge Horton and the Scottsboro Boys;* and *Freedom Never Dies: The Legacy of Harry T. Moore* (2000), a sophisticated and eye-opening look at life and death of the controversial Florida NAACP and voting rights leader who, along with his wife Harriet, was murdered by Klansmen in December 1951.

The most ambitious and unquestionably most successful attempt to provide a documentary record of the civil rights movement is African American producer Henry Hampton's monumental PBS series *Eyes on the Prize.* Narrated by movement veteran Julian Bond, the fourteen-part series uses a skillful blend of news footage and retrospective interviews featuring movement participants, government officials, white segregationists, and other observers. In preparing the series, Hampton enlisted several leading civil rights historians as research consultants and assembled hundreds of rare and evocative photographic and video images of the civil rights struggle. The first six episodes, released as *Eyes on the Prize I* in 1986, trace the evolution of the movement from the *Brown* decision of 1954 to the Selma-to-Montgomery march of 1965. All of the episodes offer accurate and balanced accounts of the movement's triumphs, failures, and limitations, but episodes 2 and 3, *Fighting Back (1957–1962)* and *Ain't Scared of Your Jails (1960–1961),* are especially good. *Eyes on the Prize II,* released in 1989, extends the story from the 1965 Voting Rights Act to the early years of the Reagan administration. With the exception of the episodes on the riots and black power movements of the mid- and late 1960s, *Eyes on the Prize II* is less compelling than *Eyes on the Prize I,* but the intellectual quality of the series is uniformly high. For a reliable and comprehensive survey of the modern civil rights movement, there is no better source, in print or on film, than *Eyes on the Prize.*

By proving that it is impossible to put an engaging and sophisticated version of the civil rights story on the screen, Henry Hampton presented a series of challenges to other filmmakers: to overcome the film industry's traditional reluctance to deal with the history of social and political movements; to take full advantage of the recent proliferation of civil rights scholarship; to recapture the history, not the mythology, of the civil rights struggle; and, in general, to fulfill the educational promise of film in an area of American life that affects us all. More than a mere genre, civil rights films carry the potential to illuminate, and perhaps even to enhance, the ongoing effort to resolve the racial dilemmas of America's pas and present.

References

Filmography

Attack on Terror: The FBI vs. the Ku Klux Klan (1975, TV)
The Autobiography of Miss Jane Pittman (1974, TV)
Black Like Me (1964, F)
Boycott (2001, TV)
The Court-Martial of Jackie Robinson (1990, TV)
The Defiant Ones (1958, F)
Driving Miss Daisy (1989, F)
Edge of the City (1957, F)
The Ernest Green Story (1993, TV)
Eyes on the Prize (1986, D)
Eyes on the Prize II (1989, D)
First Person Singular: John Hope Franklin (1997, D)
Four Little Girls (1997, D)
Freedom Never Dies: The Legacy of Harry T. Moore (2000, D)
Freedom Song (2000, TV)
Fundi: The Story of Ella Baker (1981, D)
A Gathering of Old Men (1987, D)
George Wallace (1997, TV)
Ghosts of Mississippi (1997, F)
Guess Who's Coming to Dinner (1967, F)
Having Our Say: The Delaney Sisters' First Hundred Years (1999, TV)
The Home of the Brave (1949, F)
The House I Live In (1946, F)
I'll Fly Away (1991–93, TV)
In the Heat of the Night (1967, F)
Intruder in the Dust (1949, F)
Island in the Sun (1957, F)
It Happened in Springfield (1946, F)
The Jackie Robinson Story (1950, F)
Judge Horton and the Scottsboro Boys (1976, TV)
King (1978, TV)
King: A Filmed Record . . . From Montgomery to Memphis (1968, D)
The Klansman (1974, F)
The Liberation of L. B. Jones (1970, F)
Lilies of the Field (1963, F)
The Long Walk Home (1990, F)
Lost Boundaries (1949, F)
Malcolm X (1992, F)
Malcolm X: Make It Plain (1994, D)
The Man (1972, F)
Miss Evers' Boys (1997, TV)
Mississippi Burning (1988, F)
Murder in Mississipi (1990, TV)
Mutiny (1999, TV)
The Negro Soldier (1944, D)
Never Turn Back: The Life of Fannie Lou Hamer (1983, D)
Nothing but a Man (1964, F)
No Vietnamese Ever Called Me Nigger (1968, D)
No Way Out (1950, F)
Odds Against Tomorrow (1957, F)
Once Upon a Time . . . When We Were Colored (1996, F)
Pinky (1949, F)
The Promised Land (1997, D)
Putney Swope (1969, F)
The Quiet One (1947, F)
A Raisin in the Sun (1961, F)
Resting Place (1986, TV)
Roots: The Next Generation (1979, TV)
The Rosa Parks Story (2002, TV)
Scottsboro: An American Tragedy (2001, D)
Selma, Lord, Selma (1999, TV)
Separate but Equal (1991, TV)
Simple Justice (1993, TV)
The Sins of the Father (2002, TV)
A Soldier's Story (1984, F)
The Strange Demise of Jim Crow (1997, D)
A Time to Kill (1996, F)
To Kill a Mockingbird (1962, F)

The Tuskegee Airmen (1995, TV)
Up Tight! (1968, F)
The Vernon Johns Story (1994, TV)
W.E.B. Du Bois: A Biography in Four Voices (1996, D)

Bibliography

Albert, Peter J., and Ronald Hoffman, eds. *We Shall Overcome: Martin Luther King, Jr. and the Black Freedom Struggle.* New York: Pantheon, 1990.

Bogle, Donald. *Toms, Coons, Mulattoes, Mammies, and Bucks: An Interpretive History of Blacks in American Films.* New York: Viking, 1973.

Branch, Taylor. *Parting the Waters: America in the King Years, 1954–63.* New York: Simon & Schuster, 1988.

——. *Pillar of Fire: America in the King Years, 1963–65.* New York: Simon & Schuster, 1998.

Campbell, Edward D.C., Jr. *The Celluloid South: Hollywood and the Southern Myth.* Knoxville: University of Tennessee Press, 1981.

Carnes, Mark C., ed. *Past Imperfect: History According to the Movies.* New York: Henry Holt, 1995.

Carson, Clayborne. *In Struggle: SNCC and the Black Awakening of the 1960s.* Cambridge, MA: Harvard University Press, 1981.

Cham, Mbye B., and Calire Andrade-Watkins, eds. *Critical Perspectives on Black Independent Cinema.* Cambridge, MA: MIT Press, 1988.

Cripps, Thomas. *Making Movies Black: The Hollywood Message Movie from World War II to the Civil Rights Era.* New York: Oxford University Press, 1993.

Dittmer, John. *Local People: The Struggle for Civil Rights in Mississippi.* Urbana: University of Illinois Press, 1994.

Egerton, John. *Speak Now against the Day: The Generation before the Civil Rights Movement in the South.* New York: Knopf, 1994.

Fairclough, Adam. *Race and Democracy: The Civil Rights Struggle in Louisiana, 1915–1972.* Athens: University of Georgia Press, 1995.

——. *To Redeem the Soul of America: The Southern Christian Leadership Conferences and Martin Luther King, Jr.* Athens: University of Georgia Press, 1995.

Graham, Allison. *Framing the South: Hollywood, Television, and Race During the Civil Rights Struggle.* Baltimore: Johns Hopkins University Press, 2001.

Grant, Joanne. *Ella Baker: Freedom Bound.* New York: Wiley, 1998.

Halberstam, David. *The Children.* New York: Random House, 1998.

King, Richard H. *Civil Rights and the Idea of Freedom.* New York: Oxford University Press, 1992.

Kirby, Jack Temple. *Media-Made Dixie: The South in the American Imagination.* Baton Rouge: Louisiana State University Press, 1978.

Kluger, Richard. *Simple Justice: The History of* Brown v. Board of Education *and Black America's Struggle for Equality.* New York: Knopf, 1976.

Levin, G. Roy. *Documentary Explorations: 15 Interviews with Filmmakers.* Garden City, NY: Doubleday, 1981.

Lewis, John, and Michael D'Orso. *Walking with the Wind: A Memoir of the Movement.* New York: Simon & Schuster, 1998.

Morris, Aldon D. *The Origins of the Civil Rights Movement: Black Communities Organizing for Change.* New York: Free Press, 1984.

Morris, Willie. *The Ghosts of Medgar Evers: A Tale of Race, Murder, Mississippi, and Hollywood.* New York: Random House, 1998.

Olson, Lynne. *Freedom's Daughters: The Unsung Heroines of the Civil Rights Movement from 1830 to 1970.* New York: Scribner, 2001.

Payne, Charles. *I've Got the Light of Freedom.* Berkeley: University of California Press, 1995.

Raines, Howell, ed. *My Soul Is Rested: Movement Days in the Deep South Remembered.* New York: Putnam's, 1977.

Rollins, Peter C., ed. *Hollywood as Historian: American Film in a Cultural Context.* 2d ed. Lexington: University of Kentucky Press, 1998.

Sitkoff, Harvard. *The Struggle for Black Equality, 1954–1980.* New York: Hill & Wang, 1981

Toplin, Robert Brent. *History by Hollywood: The Use and Abuse of the American Past.* Urbana: University of Illinois Press, 1996.

Tyson, Timothy B. *Radio Free Dixie: Robert F. Williams and the Roots of Black Power.* Chapel Hill: University of North Carolina Press, 1999.

Ward, Brian, ed. *Media, Culture, and the Modern African American Freedom Struggle.* Gainesville: University Press of Florida, 2002.

[ANTHONY CHASE]

Congress

"That's right, I don't want to talk about it," says the Thunder Bay Inn bartender (Murray Hamilton), drying glasses and smoking nervously, in Otto Preminger's *Anatomy of a Murder* (1959). The last person he wants to talk to about the night Barney Quill was shot is wily defense attorney Paul Biegler (James Stewart), cornering him behind the bar. But two years earlier Hamilton was more than happy to talk to Stewart, this time playing Charles Lindbergh, when the two paired off as ragamuffin stunt pilots in Billy Wilder's *The Spirit of St. Louis* (1957). Hamilton, as Bud Gurney, confides in Lindbergh that Gurney's dad thinks that a gypsy pilot is basically a bum. "My old man's in the construction business [and] wants me to come home and go to work for him. Says I come from respectable people. . . . Do you come from respectable people?" he asks Lindy. "My father was a lawyer in Minnesota," Lindbergh replies proudly, relaxed beneath a tree on a lazy summer afternoon, "and was in Congress for ten years." "Congress?" exclaims Gurney, much impressed. "Yeah, but that's not for me," Lindy adds quickly. "You can't do it from a plane."

The timing here is significant. The late 1950s—when Wilder and Preminger made these two classics—and the early 1960s represented the golden age for motion picture lawyers and silver screen senators. During the Depression era, lawyers were almost uniformly portrayed as shysters, and politicians were often seen as corrupt windbags. Both real legislators and their motion picture counterparts have been judged harshly in the glare of "post-Watergate morality," and the organized bar understandably worries over the contemporary public image of attorneys. But law and government, perceived as admirable public professions, probably reached their zenith between the Depression and the present during the Kennedy years. There are important elements of continuity and change in Hollywood's history of Congress, and to understand the political landscape fully, both deserve careful attention.

Profiles in Courage and Corruption

Another Preminger film made during this period, *Advise and Consent* (1962), is perhaps the most intelligent American film ever made about the inner workings of the legislative branch of national government. It can be usefully compared with Frank Capra's *Mr. Smith Goes to Washington* (1939). Although separated by only two decades, the films are in some respects like night and day. Capra's Boy Scouts seem more like refugees from a *Little Rascals* episode than the street urchins of William Wyler's *Wild Boys of the Road* (1934), but his *Mr. Smith* is nevertheless, like Wyler's grim picture, painted against a Depression-era canvas. The political dynamics of *Advise and Consent*, on the other hand, are played out against a McCarthy-era backdrop, the film representing a kind of blacklist period piece with issues of frame-up and political blackmail never far from center stage.

Tom Milne describes *Advise and Consent* as a companion piece to Preminger's *Anatomy of a Murder*, "tackling Washington politics with

FIGURE 42. *Advise and Consent* (1962). Director Otto Preminger's film depicts the dynamics of power politics, blackmail, scandal, and personal hatreds in the hallways and rooms of the government's legislative branch. Courtesy Columbia Pictures.

the best-selling mixture of sophistication and evasion characteristic of Preminger in his 'problem picture' mood" (10). The "evasion" Milne alleges no doubt refers to Preminger's failure to specify any more concretely the real-world political analogues of *Advise and Consent*'s shady dealers and intimidation artists. There are better films to watch if the main goal is to learn about the McCarthy period, but there are no better pictures for the purpose of understanding the deeply personal, as well as political, high stakes wagered in the lawmaking process at its summit, the apex of legislative power.

Advise and Consent is loaded with sterling illustrations of what congressmen and congresswomen should be like—profiles in courage, if you will. Mr. Smith of Oregon votes "yes" on confirmation of the president's choice for secretary of state, and then the name of Mr. Smith of Rhode Island is called out. There is a long pause and a rapid zoom-in on the pensive face of Peter Lawford, playing a senator loyal to his party and president and yet, at this key moment, silent. "Mr. Smith of Rhode Island" is called again, and Lawford firmly says "No," sending a ripple of surprise through the chamber. Senator Smith has apparently voted his conscience, placing principle above party, remaining true to a colleague who has committed suicide rather than submit to a nefarious blackmail scheme.

The blackmailer himself, ironically portrayed as a McCarthy-like extreme liberal, will do anything to get the secretary of state nominee through the Congress. Realizing that his plot has failed, he confronts the majority leader, Senator Bob Munson (Walter Pidgeon). "We tolerate about anything here. . . . That's what the Senate's for," Munson instructs his junior. "But you've dishonored us." The youthful true believer snaps back, "What I did was for the good of the country." Munson evenly replies, "Fortunately, our country always manages to survive patriots like you."

In *Mr. Smith Goes to Washington,* Jimmy Stewart's Senator Jefferson Smith and his heroics are at the heart of the film's ultimately optimistic view of congressional politics: one man can make a difference. "The reactionary side of Capra," biographer Joseph McBride observes, "was overshadowed by an urgent burst of idealism in the late 1930s that enabled him to bring forth, at the end of the decade, a ringing patriotic work that celebrated the American political system without flinching from a realistic depiction of its flaws and corruption" (411). McBride also points out, as have others, the "uncomfortable irony" that the chief screenwriter on *Mr. Smith* was, in fact, Sidney Buchman, a member of the Communist Party. Little credit for their patriotic film work was later provided party members when, after World War II had been won by the Allies, they were hauled before the House Un-American Activities Committee (HUAC) or placed on Hollywood's blacklist. So *Mr. Smith* and *Advise and Consent* are made and set in different historical periods, with different contextual issues driving their separate narratives. Nevertheless, the films are similar in their depiction of the underside of legislative process as well as an exemplary tradition of political courage, two different chapters in the story of the U.S. Congress. Historian William Appleman Williams suggests that "some movies of the 1930s, despite the censorship of the Hays office, did offer a deeper reality" (276). And Williams specifically cites a Capra film by way of illustration—but it is *It Happened One Night,* for its sexual candor, and not *Mr. Smith.* Certainly, the New Deal was not short on idealism. But Capra's lone heroes, like Mr. Smith, never had a chance.

"Whatever the rhetoric of liberalism," argues Williams (or, we might say, whatever the rhetoric of Hollywood populism), the substance of New Deal "political economy was a corporate state capitalism increasingly financed by the taxpayer and controlled by a bureaucratic and political elite drawn from the upper class" (249). Frank Capra may have sought, as he put it, simply to "elevate the individual" and, without doubt, as Giuliana Muscio suggests in *Hollywood's New Deal,* the "ritual of the Hollywood happy ending had a reassuring function" (73). But the 1930s did not end with control over American government and society effectively falling into the hands of Senator Jefferson Smith and his anti-establishment constituents. According to Williams, they just paid for it.

The ending of *Advise and Consent,* a more jaded and harder-edged film than *Mr. Smith,* is ambiguous and perhaps more reflective of the political climate and culture from which it emerged. Historian Frank Freidel observes that President John Kennedy "conferred tactfully and tirelessly with key Congressmen, and maintained skilled liaison men at the Capitol. He respected the pride and dignity of Congress, avoided angry words, and demonstrated a willingness to compromise" (584). Although novelist Allen Drury and director Otto Preminger breathe life into Freidel's dry historical description with scenes depicting love and death, sex and suicide, and personal blackmail and political bluff, they nevertheless place in sharp profile the logrolling and craft of accommodation that, in Preminger's Washington, replace the romantic gesture of Jefferson Smith's frenzied, nonstop filibuster.

FIGURE 43. *Mr. Smith Goes to Washington* (1939). After a senator dies, Jefferson Smith (James Stewart), the innocent and idealistic director of a Boy Scouts–like organization, is appointed to take his place by corrupt politicians and a controlling media magnate who wish to use him for their illegal schemes. On the Senate floor, Smith bucks their control in a famous filibustering session. Courtesy Columbia Pictures Corporation.

Congressional Continuity

Beneath and beyond the subtle relationship between these two films and their subject, there remains, of course, a sustained pattern of cynicism and hostility toward legislators and politicians expressed throughout the history of American popular culture. Mark Twain's joke that congressmen are the only inherently criminal class in America is famous. Less well known, but just as representative of at least one strain of thought, are these lines from the sermon preached in a Nantucket chapel at the beginning of Herman Melville's *Moby-Dick:* "Delight is to him, who gives no quarter in the truth, and kills, burns, and destroys all sin though he pluck it out from under the robes of Senators and Judges."

In the early Will Rogers silent film *Our Congressman* (1924), Rogers (as Congressman Alfalfa Doolittle) is tracked down in Washington by some of his hometown constituents. They manage to catch up with him on the golf course. "So this is what politics has done for you?" they inquire contemptuously. "Why," Doolittle responds defensively, "some of our greatest questions are settled on the links."

Pointing to the congressman's baggy plaid golf slacks, one unhappy voter observes, "Laws framed in pants like them would be unconstitutional." Seventy-two years later, in Tim Burton's *Mars Attacks!* (1996) there is a long shot of the U.S. Capitol building in flames after an unprovoked assault by aliens from space. An elderly woman watching on television claps her knees and gleefully bursts out, "They blew up Congress!"

Legislators themselves remain common in American movies, right up to the present, as individuals and committee members, frequently popping up in films drawn from a wide range of movie genres. In Irwin Winkler's *Guilty by Suspicion* (1991), Hollywood attempts to come to terms with its own particular slice of political history, and a congressional committee investigating Communists in the movie industry during the early years of the Cold War is portrayed as itself fundamentally at odds with American democracy. Peter Yates's suspense film *The House on Carroll Street* (1988) begins with a title reading, "U.S. Senate Hearing, New York, 1951," beneath a picture of Emily Crane (Kelly McGillis) being sworn to give testimony before a congressional committee about to grill the *Life* editor for her membership in alleged subversive organizations.

In a crime drama directed by Yates the previous year, *Suspect* (1987), Cher plays public defender Kathleen Riley, secretly working with a criminal trial juror to solve the mystery behind a judicial suicide. Her part-time juror accomplice, played by Dennis Quaid, happens also to be full-time congressional lobbyist Eddie Sanger, who sleeps with Congresswoman Grace Comisky (E. Katherine Kerr) in the hope that she will provide a key vote in behalf of legislation for which he is a paid advocate. The deal remains unstated, however, since both lobbyist and congresswoman are above an overt sexual bribe. Eddie is biting his nails as committee members empty from their private meeting into the corridor when one committee insider walks up to him, shakes his hand, and congratulates him: "Eddie, you lucked out. Her committee chairman must have persuaded Comisky to vote yes." Congresswoman Comisky's eyes barely meet Sanger's as she strides by. Eddie has a pained expression on his face—perhaps because he is not happy with what his job is turning into or perhaps because he is already romantically interested in his public defender coconspirator. But despite the way it sounds, *Suspect* does not present this particular politician–lobbyist relationship as a sordid one: it's just another day at the office, one more angle on the business of government.

Similarly, in Phillip Noyce's *Clear and Present Danger* (1994), there is a somewhat ambiguous Senate committee hearing sequence. CIA agent Jack Ryan (Harrison Ford) is scurrying around his suburban living room trying on different ties, hoping to find one that will make him "look trustworthy." As he walks out the door, he shoves an extra tie into his coat pocket, just to play it safe. The next shot is of the U.S. Capitol, with a voiceover of Senator Mayo (Hope Lange), already beginning her questioning of the CIA official regarding his request for supplemental Congressional funding for the U.S. war-on-drugs program in Colombia. What Senator Mayo wants to know is whether "this increase in funds, this 'escalation' to use your word, will not be used for any covert military action." Ryan acts insulted, as if his credibility has been questioned, and it does seem he is being unfairly accused. As the film unfolds, however, it becomes clear that the senator's concerns are more prophetic than paranoid.

Ray Wise, a veteran of Tim Robbins's *Bob Roberts* (1992), plays Senator John Morton in *Rising Sun* (1993). Morton initially appears on a segment of CNN's *Crossfire,* where, under sharp questioning from real life CNN journalists, he vigorously opposes governmental approval of a contract that would purportedly give Japanese corporations some control over

U.S. military research and development. Later in the film, however, the slick-talking senator claims to have "refined," rather than reversed, his earlier opposition to the sale of Microcon. Wearing a designer tennis outfit reminiscent of Will Rogers's uncharacteristic golf attire in *Our Congressman,* Senator Morton clicks off his TV and explains, "So far, the response has been ten to one in favor of the way I have . . . modified my position." Now the senator is a proponent of foreign trade and free markets, which means the sale should go through. No sucker for this kind of double talk, special police investigator John Connor (Sean Connery) says that it sounds to him like a complete reversal of the senator's original view: "But you were against the sale because it put our advanced weaponry entirely in the control of the Japanese." It comes as no surprise by the end of the film that the senator has been blackmailed into changing his vote on the Microcon deal.

Congressman Sheldon Runyon (Gary Oldman), chairman of a powerful appointments confirmation committee, is a lot smarter than *Rising Sun*'s Senator Morton, but in *The Contender* (2000), he is the one doing the blackmailing. Although motivated by ideology rather than greed, Runyon's confusion of ends and means makes him extremely dangerous and utterly deserving of the dirty trick actually played upon him—a relentless true believer brought down by the very tactics he seemed to have perfected. In spades, his fate proves the familiar saying, "What goes around, comes around." A similar lesson awaits Senator Robert Kelly (Bruce Davison), one of the many bad guys in Bryan Singer's *X-Men* (2000). Kelly uses every means available to him, legal or not, to conduct his McCarthy-like investigations into the lives of the superhuman mutants among us, with the goal of exterminating them in a replay of the Holocaust; high-minded but essentially evil, the senator meets an exceptionally gruesome though well-deserved end for his troubles. By contrast, the congressional representatives pontificating about the war on drugs at a Georgetown cocktail party in *Traffic* (2000) are presented as more naive than evil. Unlike Runyon, they seem not to know where the bodies are buried. In spite of their antidrug rhetoric, their ignorance of the true scope of narcotics trafficking is portrayed as part of the problem, not the solution.

If Cold War congressional investigators (at least nowadays, in contrast to those of the 1950s) and the Shelly Runyons of the (legislative) world tend to be darkly portrayed, and other representatives, such as like *Suspect*'s Congresswoman Comisky or *Clear and Present Danger*'s Senator Mayo, are colored shades of gray, there are lighter versions as well. White-knight congressional committee investigator Dick Goodwin (Rob Morrow), in Robert Redford's *Quiz Show* (1994), provides a perfect example. From the scene where TV producers have initially discussed rigging quiz show questions, Redford cuts to a shot of the Capitol with a telephone voiceover saying "Richard Goodwin. I'm an investigator . . . with the subcommittee on legislative oversight." The tenacious, idealistic, recent Harvard Law graduate is looking into missing rate-schedule documents for the Baltimore & Ohio Railroad, but soon he has bigger fish on the line: high-stakes, big-money, network quiz shows where the fix is in. Goodwin, who would indeed become a Kennedy administration young Turk, is portrayed as embodying all the hope and ambition of Camelot, of the liberal reformers that JFK brought to Washington with him, especially from Cambridge, Massachusetts. And an earlier generation of heroes, those who stood up to McCarthyism, is perhaps symbolized by the role of Senator Ray Clark (Edmond O'Brien) in John Frankenheimer's *Seven Days in May* (1964). Tossing his trusty bottle of bourbon into the wastebasket, Clark survives incarceration on a secret military base, remains the president's steadfast ally when it is hard to know for sure who is and is not a conspirator, and even helps thwart a right-wing military coup.

The Invisible Body

But this spectrum of characters features legislators as individuals or committee members rather than as part of a political body, a branch of government, a separated power under the Constitution. This is the crucial change in the cinematic portrait of federal legislators during the decades subsequent to *Mr. Smith Goes to Washington* and *Advise and Consent.* And the distinction has a specifically visual consequence: audiences are no longer shown the House or Senate in session, no longer shown the U.S. Congress as a governing institution. It was initially thought, in the nineteenth century, that photography would put realist painters out of business. More recently, it could be argued that C-SPAN's "gavel to gavel" coverage of the House of Representatives, not to mention blanket network reporting of the Clinton presidential crisis, provides a televised picture of the legislative process so realistic that movies have, in the face of such a challenge, understandably retreated. But there is a more compelling historical explanation for the decline in motion picture attention to Congress in action, one that is directly related to the declining role of the legislative branch itself within the structure of American governance.

In this regard, Henry King's *Wilson* (1944), produced by Darryl F. Zanuck, becomes a key film. Zanuck's biopic, according to Terry Christensen in *Reel Politics* (1987), suggests that "the League of Nations and collective security might have prevented World War II." And although *Wilson* "deserves credit for taking politics seriously," Christensen asserts that "Wilson himself got the Lincoln treatment: he was wise and good while the Europeans were greedy and vindictive and the American isolationists who opposed the League were fools" (70). Many historians would question how the League of Nations, with or without U.S. membership, could have altered the course of German imperialism and prevented war in Europe. Even if the United States had been an active participant in the League, that would not have prevented Japan from withdrawing from the organization to avoid international legal sanction. But the perception that isolationists in Congress destroyed the League and thus made war more likely left its mark.

The erasure of the House and Senate as governing institutions in American film after *Advise and Consent* simply reflects the actual, long-term decline of the political role of the legislative branch in American public life. That decline begins with the myth that legislative incompetence crippled President Wilson and the League and thereby helped precipitate another world war. The lasting effect of the confrontation between legislative and executive branches depicted in *Wilson,* according to historian James Oliver Robertson, "was to strengthen the Presidency at the expense of the Congress. It created a set of mythic images—of presidential idealism and leadership and responsibility in contrast to congressional shortsightedness, irresponsibility, and venality—which still exist for Americans" (315).

By the time of the Vietnam War, the American executive was able to conduct a "police action" that cost hundreds of thousands of American and Vietnamese lives without consulting either the legislative branch of the U.S. government or the United Nations, the League's successor. James Oliver Robertson argues that the Gulf of Tonkin resolution, which President Johnson used to justify prosecuting a wider war, was passed because "Congress did not consider itself adequately representative, efficient, knowledgeable, expert, or capable of judging American national interests in a crisis—and it is believed, as do most Americans still, that a President is" (317). Little wonder, then, that the "imperial presidency" has elbowed the legislative branch off the historical stage—and, after the humbling of Congress during the Vietnam era, the cinematic stage as well.

Nor is this an exclusively American phenomenon. In his excellent *Legislatures* (1963), British writer K. C. Wheare describes the general subordination of parliaments and legislatures to the omnivorous growth of executive power. Perhaps the best account of the declining role played historically by the legislative branch in the making of U.S. foreign policy is provided by Bill Moyers's PBS documentary *The Secret Government: The Constitution in Crisis* (1987), which was accompanied by publication of the film's transcript, with an introduction by historian Henry Steele Commager. Three years later, in the PBS *Frontline* documentary *High Crimes and Misdemeanors* (1990), Moyers interviewed Michael K. Deaver, one of President Ronald Reagan's key advisors during the Iran-Contra affair. In November 1986, after the presidential election, it was revealed that the United States had been secretly selling arms to Iran in exchange for the release of hostages, as well as to help finance covert operations in Central America. The Nicaraguan Contras were being funded by the Reagan administration in an attempt to overthrow the government of Nicaragua. Moyers asked Deaver if the administration had not sought to avoid public debate about U.S. support for the Nicaraguan Contras during Reagan's reelection campaign. "Never," replied Deaver. "Because if we'd have fought the campaign on Central America, we might have lost." The "governmental problems presented by Iran/contra are not those of rogue operations," concluded independent counsel Lawrence E. Walsh in his final report on the Iran-Contra investigation, "but rather those of Executive Branch efforts to evade congressional oversight" (xxi).

One expects, to be sure, a sober accounting of national affairs from the Public Broadcasting System, but Hollywood, too, has gotten this particular story right, at least in outline. Somewhat ironically, we have a very good example of American movies providing a reliable visual template for understanding a key feature of twentieth century political history: Hollywood's covert realism.

References

Filmography

Advise and Consent (1962, F)
Anatomy of a Murder (1959, F)
Bob Roberts (1992, F)
Clear and Present Danger (1994, F)
Congress: We the People (1984, D)
The Contender (2000, F)
Gabriel Over the White House (1933, F)
Guilty by Suspicion (1991, F)
High Crimes and Misdemeanors (1990, D)
The House on Carroll Street (1988, F)
The Manchurian Candidate (1962, F)
Mars Attacks! (1996, F)
Mr. Smith Goes to Washington (1939, F)
Our Congressman (1924, F)
Point of Order (1963, D)
Quiz Show (1994, F)
Rising Sun (1993, F)
The Secret Government: The Constitution in Crisis (1987, D)
Seven Days in May (1964, F)
The Spirit of St. Louis (1957, F)
Suspect (1987, F)
Traffic (2000, F)
Watergate: The Fall of a President (1994, D)
Wild Boys of the Road (1934, F)
Wild in the Streets (1968, F)
Wilson (1944, F)
X-Men (2000, F)

Bibliography

Chase, Anthony. *Movies on Trial: The Legal System on the Silver Screen.* New York: New Press, 2002.
Christensen, Terry. *Reel Politics.* New York: Basil Blackwell, 1987.
Elving, Ronald D. *Conflict and Compromise: How Congress Makes the Law.* New York: Simon & Schuster, 1996.
Freidel, Frank. *America in the Twentieth Century.* 2d ed. New York: Knopf, 1965.
Harrington, Mona. *The Dream of Deliverance in American Politics.* New York: Knopf, 1986.
Harris, Fred R. *Deadlock or Decision: The U.S. Senate and the Rise of National Politics.* New York: Oxford University Press, 1993.
Kellner, Douglas, and Michael Ryan. *Camera Politica: The Politics and Ideology of Contemporary Hollywood Film.* Bloomington: Indiana University Press, 1988.
McBride, Joseph. *Frank Capra: The Catastrophe of Success.* New York: Simon & Schuster, 1992.
Milne, Tom. "Advise and Consent." In John Pym,

ed., *Time Out Film Guide,* 10. 6th ed. London: Penguin, 1998.

Moyers, Bill. *The Secret Government: The Constitution in Crisis.* Washington, DC: Seven Locks Press, 1989.

Muscio, Giuliana. *Hollywood's New Deal.* Philadelphia: Temple University Press, 1997.

Robertson, James Oliver. *American Myth, American Reality.* New York: Hill & Wang, 1980.

Rosenbaum, Jonathan. *Movies as Politics.* Berkeley: University of California Press, 1997.

Sobchack, Vivian, ed. *The Persistence of History: Cinema, Television, and the Modern Event.* New York: Routledge, 1996.

Walsh, Lawrence E. *Final Report of the Independent Counsel for Iran/Contra Matters.* Washington, DC: U.S. Court of Appeals for the District of Columbia Circuit, 1993.

Wheare, K. C. *Legislatures.* London: Oxford University Press, 1963.

Williams, William Appleman. *Americans in a Changing World: A History of the United States in the Twentieth Century.* New York: Harper & Row, 1978.

[STEVEN MINTZ]

The Family

Many of our most vivid images of families in the past come from the movies. *Drums Along the Mohawk* (1939), which depicts the rugged life of farm families in New York's Mohawk Valley during the era of the American Revolution, helps us visualize family life on the colonial frontier. Similarly, *Little Women* (1933, 1994), the story of a family's struggles during the Civil War, brings to life the trials and the emotional sensibilities of the mid-nineteenth-century middle-class family. In much the same way, *Life with Father* (1947), which shows a benevolent despot trying to maintain order in his 1880s New York household, helps us imagine what family life was like toward the end of the Victorian era.

But if the movies can help us envision families in earlier times, they can also reinforce misleading stereotypes. Cinematic images of strong, supportive, and stable families in the past have the effect of making contemporary family life seem uniquely disordered. In fact, the notion that earlier families were more stable and homogeneous than ours is a myth, based more on nostalgia than on accurate historical knowledge. For example, in colonial America, it was common for parents to send boys and girls as young as seven or eight to work as servants or apprentices in other people's households. A high death rate meant that even as recently as 1900 most families could expect to lose at least one child to premature death, while most children lost at least one parent before they reached their twenty-first birthday.

Recent scholarship on the family has underscored three essential points. The first is that the so-called traditional family, consisting of a breadwinner father and a full-time mother, is a relatively recent invention, dating back less than two hundred years. In fact, it was not until the 1920s that a majority of American families consisted of a breadwinner husband, a homemaker wife, and two or more children attending school.

A second key theme is that American family life has always been diverse and vulnerable to disruption. At the beginning of the twentieth century, the United States had the highest divorce rate in the Western world; one child in ten lived in a single-parent home; and approximately 100,000 children lived in orphanages, in many cases because their mothers and fathers could not support them.

A third major conclusion is that familial change is nothing new. Over the past three hundred years America's families have repeatedly experienced far-reaching shifts in their size and composition, roles and functions, and emotional and power dynamics. Each era in American history has had its own distinctive family patterns. The colonial family was primarily a unit of production in which every member was expected to contribute to the family's support. A hierarchical institution, the colonial family was presided over by the father, who had to consent to his children's marriages and who kept children dependent for years through his control over inheritance.

During the early nineteenth century, the urban middle class created new patterns of family life, in which the father went to work some distance from home, while his wife devoted herself full time to raising her children and keeping house and his children remained home until their late teens or even twenties. Economic conditions made it impossible for working-class and farm families to conform to this middle-class ideal of a sole male breadwinner, a rigid division of gender roles, and a protected childhood. These groups stressed a cooperative family economy in which wives and children contributed to the family's support. During the nineteenth century, children under the age of fifteen provided as much as 20 percent of working-class family income.

In the 1920s marriage counselors popularized a new ideal, known as the "companionate" family, according to which husbands and wives were to be "friends and lovers" and parents and children were to be "pals." This new ideal stressed the couple relationship and family togetherness as the primary sources of emotional satisfaction and personal happiness. The Great Depression and World War II prevented most families from realizing this new ideal.

During the Depression, unemployment and lower wages forced many Americans to share living quarters with relatives, delay marriage, and postpone having children. Many families coped with hard times by returning to a cooperative family economy. Many children took part-time jobs, and many wives supplemented the family income by taking in sewing or laundry, setting up parlor groceries, or housing lodgers. World War II also subjected families to great stresses, among them the severe shortage of housing, schools, and childcare facilities and prolonged separation from loved ones. Five million "war widows" ran their homes and cared for children alone, while millions of older married women went to work in war industries. Wartime stresses contributed to an upsurge in the divorce rate, juvenile delinquency, unwed pregnancy, and truancy.

The postwar era witnessed a sharp reaction to Depression and wartime stress. The average age of marriage for women dropped to twenty, divorce rates stabilized, and the birthrate doubled. Contributing to the emphasis on family togetherness were rapidly rising real incomes; the GI Bill, which allowed many young men to purchase single-family track homes in newly built suburbs; and the relatively modest expectations for personal fulfillment bred by the Depression.

For many Americans, the 1950s family has come to represent a cultural ideal. Yet it is important to recognize that the popular image of 1950s family life is highly unrepresentative. Only 60 percent of children born during that decade spent their childhood in a male-breadwinner, female-homemaker household. In fact, the 1950s family contained the seeds of its own transformation. Youthful marriages, especially by women who cut short their education, contributed to a surge in divorces during the 1960s. The compression of childbearing into the first years of marriage meant that many wives were free of the most intense childrearing responsibilities by their early or mid-thirties. Combined with the rising costs of maintaining a middle-class standard of living, this encouraged many married women to enter the workplace. As early as 1960, a third of married, middle-class women were working part- or full-time. Meanwhile, the expansion of schooling, combined with growing affluence, contributed to the emergence of a youth culture separate and apart from the family.

Between 1960 and 1980, the birth rate fell by half; the divorce rate and the proportion of working mothers doubled, as did the number of single-parent homes; and the number of couples cohabitating outside of wedlock quadrupled. Over a quarter of all children now lived with only one parent, and fewer than half lived with both their biological mother and father. This "domestic revolution" produced alarm, anxiety, and apprehension. It inspired family-values crusaders to condemn careerist mothers, absent fathers, single parents, and unwed parents as the root cause of such social ills as persistent poverty, drug abuse, academic failure, and juvenile crime. The family became a political and cultural battleground, and many of American society's bitterest debates revolved around such family-related issues as the impact of daycare on children and access to same-sex marriage.

Rather than offering realistic portrayals of family life, popular films are better understood as cultural seismographs or barometers that reflect shifts in film audiences and in public values, aspirations, and anxieties. Movies are also educators that have helped give us our images of what ideal families are like.

Families in Film

From the silent era onward, American film has focused its attention on family life, exploring spousal tensions, intergenerational conflict, and dysfunctional family relationships. Filmmakers looked to the family not only to examine the tangled texture of domestic life but also to dramatize larger social, political, and cultural issues, such as the impact of immigration, war, and feminism on American lives. It is revealing that such landmarks of American film history as *The Birth of a Nation* (1915), *The Jazz Singer* (1927), and *Gone with the Wind* (1939) each translate broad cultural themes into family issues. *The Birth of a Nation* uses the threat of miscegenation to symbolize threats to national unity and the marriage of a white Northerner and a white Southerner to represent sectional reconciliation following the Civil War. *The Jazz Singer* personalizes issues involving ethnic identity and the impulse for assimilation by refracting these issues into the story of a jazz lover's effort to break free from his family's restrictive religious traditions while retaining his mother's love. In *Gone with the Wind,* the social upheavals of the Civil War are dramatized through the lives of members of an elite southern family.

In recent years, as anxieties about the breakdown of the so-called traditional family have escalated, many films seemingly about other topics in fact address familial issues. Two of the most popular films of the 1980s, *E.T.: The Extraterrestrial* (1982) and *An Officer and a Gentleman* (1982), illustrate the way that anxieties over the family extended outward from family melodramas into other genres. The backdrop of *E.T.* is the sense of loss and need that grow out of a father's leaving his family for a secretary, and the background of *An Officer and a Gentleman* is a young man's difficulty in developing a capacity for emotional commitment after having been abandoned by his mother and left in his father's care. From science fiction and action films to horror films, anxiety about the family has pervaded recent films.

With their reliance on visual shorthand and caricature, cinematic portrayals of family life have rarely been especially realistic or inclusive. Whole genres, such as the western, are largely devoid of fully developed families, and even today most of Hollywood's protagonists are portrayed as single and childless.

To be sure, contemporary films are far more likely than their predecessors to show single-parent, divorced, or dual-earner families. But in other respects, the images of family life that appear on the screen remain noticeably inaccurate. Mothers, for example, are absent in a disproportionate number of cinematic families, especially those released by the Walt Disney Company; African American, Asian American, and Hispanic families are conspicuous largely in their absence from the screen. Even as family life has grown more fluid in recent years, films dealing with families tend to cling to certain older conventions, especially the notion that female characters are largely defined by their place in the family—as wives or daughters.

For more than a century, American society has been profoundly concerned about the state and fate of the family, especially the threats to familial stability posed by shifts in women's roles and status, the emergence of a distinctive youth culture, an increase in the divorce rate, and the disengagement of many fathers from domestic responsibilities. Films have not only addressed those anxieties, but they have also suggested solutions to them.

The Family in Early Cinema

The birth of film coincided with a nationwide cultural panic over the future of the family. During the last years of the nineteenth century, newly formed temperance organizations and societies for the prevention of cruelty to children awoke many Americans to the prevalence of various forms of domestic violence and child neglect. At the same time, Americans learned that the United States had the highest rate of divorce in the Western world and that one family in ten was headed by a single parent. Child labor, juvenile delinquency, infant and child mortality, and sexual immorality all evoked public concern and prompted enactment of laws criminalizing abortion, restricting the distribution of birth control information, closing down red-light districts, setting up juvenile courts, and reducing the grounds for divorce.

Many early films dealt with issues raised by Progressive reformers. During the 1910s, many films focused on the threats to family stability posed by alcohol, divorce, the double standard of sexual morality, narcotics, the "black plague" of venereal disease, and the "white slave trade." Many of these films were crude polemics whose moralistic themes were clearly revealed in their titles. Thus, a 1916 film on divorce bore the title *The Children Pay*, while the horrors of venereal disease were exposed in *The Sins of the Father* (1913).

It was the director D. W. Griffith who demonstrated that motion pictures that dealt with the family could be more than moralistic tracts or crude attempts at titillation. In *Broken Blossoms* (1919) and *Way Down East* (1920) he showed that family melodramas could be works of art with complex images and compelling narratives. Reflecting the Victorian sensibility of the "genteel tradition," with its stress on rigid gender roles, childhood innocence, and moral propriety, these pictures transform archaic stage melodramas about abusive fathers and the seduction of virginal heroines into timeless stories of love and redemption. They also offer haunting images of child abuse, domestic cruelty, and sexual betrayal that remain powerful decades later.

Griffith's outlook was decidedly Victorian, and his plots often turn on threats to the sanctity of the patriarchal family. A nefarious male villain threatens to harm a child or abuse a young woman and violate her chastity, and a chivalrous male hero must rescue each of these victims. At a time when gender roles were particularly unsettled and discussion of women's suffrage and birth control animated public debate, Griffith offered unambiguous portraits of woman and child victims rescued by virtuous protagonists.

By the 1920s, the intense moralism, reformism, and Victorianism of early film had begun to fade, and many of the most popular films of the 1920s helped to promote the new "companionate" conception of marriage that emphasized partnership, communication, romance, and sexual fulfillment as the hallmarks of a new marital ideal. In a period of sharply rising divorce rates, many experts on the family were convinced that the companionate ideal offered the glue that could hold the family together.

During the 1920s, Hollywood played a significant role in shaping popular notions of romance, love, intimacy, and sexual fulfillment, while Hollywood stars served as models for new forms of behavior. "Flapper" films dealing with the experiences of "flaming youth," such as *The Perfect Flapper* (1924) and *The Plastic Age* (1925), helped disseminate new styles of dress, dancing, and dating. The plots of many of these films revolve around a young woman's efforts to circumvent parental controls and achieve independence. But if these films show young women breaking free from Victorian restrictions, they also tend to conclude on a traditional note, with women finding happiness in romance and marriage.

The Woman's Film and the Family

Popular treatments of cinematic history sometimes suggest that the history of film is the story of simplistic iconic images being replaced by more complex and nuanced imagery. Thus, it has been suggested that images of motherhood have evolved over time from crude, certain caricatures to a more textured acceptance of complexity. Early cinema, which produced films such as *The Eternal Mother* (1912), was filled with paragons of motherhood who provided their families with unconditional love and wise counsel. During the Depression, cinematic mothers, such as O-Lan in *The Good Earth* (1937) and Ma Joad in *The Grapes of Wrath* (1940), were often depicted as sources of stability who kept the family together through hard times, or as paragons of selflessness, as in *Stella Dallas* (1937), who would sacrifice their happiness for their children's sake. During and after World War II, mothers in such films as *Now, Voyager* (1942) and *Psycho* (1960) were portrayed as the sources of their children's psychological problems, resulting from coldness, excessive closeness, or abuse. More multifaceted conceptions motherhood began to appear on the screen with *Terms of Endearment* (1983). Obviously, a view that sees a progression from caricature to complexity contains a kernel of truth, but it also obscures the complex pattern of evolution in cinematic images.

The history of the treatment of the family in film is far too complicated to reduce to a Whiggish story of progress. In certain respects, the most psychologically nuanced and insightful explorations of the tangled texture of family life can be found in the so-called woman's films of the 1930s and 1940s. Directed toward a female audience, these films focus on women's emotions and on such subjects as maternal self-sacrifice, relationships among women, and the tension between motherhood and a career. Maternal self-sacrifice was a central theme in many important woman's films such as *Blonde Venus* (1932) and *Imitation of Life* (1934). Difficult to categorize, the woman's pictures sent mixed messages to female moviegoers, offering images of women acting freely outside the home, partaking in romance, luxury, and careers, even as they ultimately reaffirmed women's roles as wives and mothers.

The woman's picture never disappeared, but, especially during the 1940s, it acquired bleaker and more pathological overtones. Films such as *When Tomorrow Comes* (1939), with its portrait of a married man violating his wedding vows, and *Mildred Pierce* (1945), where maternal self-sacrifice is punished, called into question older notions of family values. In *Now, Voyager,* in which the mousy, repressed, frustrated protagonist suffers under her mother's domination, the family is depicted as a source of psychological pathology.

The Screwball Comedy

Even in a single decade, such as the 1930s, it is extremely difficult to generalize about cinematic representations of the family. Alongside the woman's films, there were a variety of conflicting portrayals of family life, from W. C. Fields's lampooning the family in *The Fatal Glass of Beer* (1933) to John Ford's celebrating family strength in the face of the challenges of frontier life in *Drums Along the Mohawk* (1939). Especially popular were screwball comedies. Taking their name from their subject matter—the madcap adventures of screwball characters—the screwball comedies of the mid- and late 1930s—with their emphasis on confused relationships between men and women, frustrated sexual passions, and comic misunderstandings—offered a superficially lighthearted look at courtship, marriage, and family life. Many screwball comedies, such as *My Man Godfrey* (1936), offered a comic take on the foibles of wealthy but dysfunctional families. Staple characters include a "henpecked" father, a "harebrained" mother, and a jealous sister, and many of these films feature a heroine who is rebelling against her fathers or her snobbish family background (for example, Frank Capra's *It Happened One Night,* 1934).

Other screwball comedies, such as the *Thin Man* series, depicted marriage in a new light, as an adventure in which both husband and wife are true partners. One variation of the screwball comedy emphasized reuniting couples after divorce or separation. With their strong, independent, sophisticated heroines, comedies of remarriage, such as *The Awful Truth* (1937), *His Girl Friday* (1940), and *The Philadelphia Story* (1940), portrayed the battle of the sexes as a battle of equals and raised the question of whether female independence was compatible with marriage.

For Depression-era Americans, screwball comedies offered a number of reassuring messages: that love could triumph over class distinctions, that money is not a prerequisite for marital or familial happiness, and that family conflicts could be resolved. Above all, many of these films conveyed the decidedly unfeminist message that strong-willed, independent, and rebellious women ultimately wanted to marry.

Hollywood and the Emergence of the Teenager

Among the most popular and romanticized portrayals of family life during the late 1930s and early 1940s were the films in Mickey Rooney's Andy Hardy series. Yet for all their crudeness, it is important to recognize that even these films represented an effort to come to terms with a new social phenomenon: the emergence of the teenager.

The Great Depression witnessed intensive efforts to remove teenagers from the workforce in order to provide more jobs for adult breadwinners. Instead of contributing economically to their family's financial well-being, adolescents were increasingly expected to attend high school. By confining adolescents in a single institution, society provided a fertile setting for the development of a distinctive youth culture cutting across class and geographical boundaries.

Beginning with *A Family Affair* (1937), MGM released sixteen films in the low-budget Andy Hardy series, which transformed Mickey Rooney into the country's most popular star in 1939, 1940, and 1941. With its lighthearted focus on family problems and teenage romance, the series provided a prototype for television family situation comedies. These films also played a critical role in shaping and reinforcing cultural stereotypes about teenagers and teenage culture.

Film Noir and the Family

Before World War II, families were usually presented as symbols of normality. Images of family life as joyous and supportive would persist after the war in such films as *It's a Wonderful Life* (1946), *Father of the Bride* (1950), and *Cheaper by the Dozen* (1950). But during World War II, far more critical representations of the family began to appear.

One of the first genres to enter into the tangled recesses of family pathology was film noir. World War II produced far-reaching changes in American life: it accelerated the mobility of the population, raised living standards, and profoundly altered race relations and the roles of women. Film noir metaphorically addressed many anxieties and apprehensions generated by the war, especially a sense of sexual insecurity that was bred by sharply rising divorce rates and fears of sexual infidelity produced by prolonged wartime separations.

The marriages depicted in noir films such as *Double Indemnity* (1944) or *The Postman Always Rings Twice* (1946) are often characterized by mutual hatred, alienation, or simple boredom. The films' protagonists challenge the sanctity of marriage, but the result is often self-destruction.

Family Melodramas of the 1950s

At a time when television presented lighthearted views of working-class families, in which Lucy and Desi or the Kramdens bicker over money and whether the wife should get a job, and suburban middle-class families, such as the Andersons or the Nelsons, in which problems are resolved by a caring father and a supportive mother, film presented a starkly different portrait of family life. In the years before the release of *Gidget* (1959), Hollywood responded to a sharp decline in its audience by producing a significant number of family melodramas that offered powerful portrayals of dysfunctional families.

Reflecting the paranoid style that marked the early Cold War years, these films revealed many previously unexplored problems in family life: infidelity, unwanted pregnancy, drug addiction, emotional cruelty, intergenerational conflict, and mental illness. Unlike the woman's films of the 1930s and 1940s, the family melodramas of the late 1940s and 1950s took a special interest in male psychology.

The popular family melodramas of the period, such as *Rebel Without a Cause* (1955) and *East of Eden* (1955), reveal a pattern of deeply troubled family relationships. These films depict sexual frustration, anxious parents, bitter clashes between generations, alienated children, insensitive or fretful fathers, defiant adolescents, and loveless marriages. In part, this obsession with the theme of marriage and family life as a kind of hell reflected a popularized form of Freudian psychoanalysis, in which Oedipal tensions and sexual repressions are presented as explanations for human behavior. The family melodramas of the 1950s laboriously repeated the theme that sexual frustration inevitably led to neurosis and that harsh, neglectful, or uncomprehending parents produced alienated children. This was very different from the soothing and funny fare available on TV.

According to many of the family melodramas of the 1950s, the source of family woes lay in a lack of familial love. Love is extolled as the solution to problems ranging from juvenile delinquency to schizophrenia. Adolescents in films such as *Splendor in the Grass* (1961) or *Tea and Sympathy* (1956) are rebellious because their parents "won't listen." They crave more love and attention from their mothers and fathers. Husbands and wives drink or take drugs or stray sexually in such films as *The Man with the Golden Arm* (1955), *The Catered Affair* (1956), and *The Dark at the Top of the Stairs* (1960) because they cannot communicate adequately with their spouses. While the films of the 1950s appear to offer a critical and ambivalent view of marriage, their underlying message was hopeful. Even the most severe family problems could be resolved by understanding, perseverance, and love.

FIGURE 44. *Rebel Without a Cause* (1955). Director Nicholas Ray explores the conflicting looks on the faces of Jim Stark (James Dean), his parents, and the police chief. The image personifies teenage alienation and the hopelessness of any future change in family relations. Courtesy Warner Bros.

Nostalgia for the Rural Family

The western, Hollywood's most persistently popular genre from the 1910s through the 1960s, is rarely identified with the family. The classic western hero is a loner who is typically represented as uneasy around women, and many westerns are distinctive in the absence of romance. During the late 1940s and 1950s, the heyday of the western talkie, the family often occupied an important place in such films. But the family patterns displayed differed fundamentally from those portrayed in romantic melodramas. Instead of focusing on spousal relations, many expressed a deep nostalgia for strong rural families. In some of these films, the family is presided over by a patriarchal figure who protects and takes care of the family; others contain a revered mother.

The plots of many postwar westerns revolve around the family. In some cases, the plot centers on relations between a father and a son (*Red River,* 1948) or among brothers (*Broken Lance,* 1954); others feature a wife (like the character played by Jean Arthur in *Shane,* 1953) who is torn between her family obligations and the attraction of a charismatic stranger. Metaphorically, these films reinforced the primacy of the family in postwar culture.

Family Values and Hollywood

As the 1960s began, few would have guessed that this decade and the early years of the next would witness some of Hollywood's most searching explorations of family life. Among the most popular films at the decade's start were Doris Day romantic comedies like *That Touch of Mink* (1962) and such sequels as *Gidget Goes Hawaiian* (1961) and *Gidget Goes to Rome* (1963). Yet even then, there were already glimpses of a more critical perspective on the family in such films as *Splendor in the Grass* (1961), with its critique of sexual repressiveness, *David and Lisa* (1962), which explored the roots of schizophrenia, and *Lolita* (1962), with its examination of a middle-aged man's obsession with a precocious girl. Within a decade, films like *Who's Afraid of Virginia Woolf?* (1966), which depicted the family as a sea of unspoken hatreds and resentments, and *The Graduate* (1967), which laid bare middle-class hypocrisies, viewed family life in highly critical terms. Meanwhile, other films, including *Bob & Carol & Ted & Alice* (1969) and *Carnal Knowledge* (1971), raised searching questions about the consequences of the sexual revolution. Where films such as *Straw Dogs* (1971) appeared to call on men to reassert their authority within the family, other pictures such as *An Unmarried Woman* (1978) exposed the consequences of divorce for women's lives and encouraged women to adopt a heightened feminist consciousness.

By the mid-1970s, the specter of family breakdown haunted many Hollywood genres. Highly negative images of family disintegration, assertive and independent women, and teenage violence proliferated in genres that previously had not been closely associated with family issues. Contributing to these anxieties over the family was a demographic revolution without parallel in American history: in the span of a decade, the divorce rate doubled and the number of single-parent homes tripled.

Following the enormous popular success of *The Godfather* (1972), many films dealing with organized crime began to emphasize the breakdown of family ties. Regardless of the ethnicity of the mob members, family loyalties occupy a central place in these films. The crime organization is typically a "family" enterprise in which members' allegiances are reaffirmed at baptisms, weddings, and funerals. Indeed, in mob films and TV shows such as *The Sopranos,* family loyalty provides the justification for crime and murder. But mob films typically conclude with the destruction of the family as a result of jealousy, treachery, and greed. The implicit message in such films was that the roots of family breakdown were planted in the restless pursuit of money, material possessions, and power.

Horror films, often dismissed as no more than a source of cheap thrills, have often offered thinly veiled critiques of the middle-class family. Even before the 1960s, a growing number of horror films traced the roots of evil to the family: to demonic children (*The Bad Seed,* 1956); monstrous mothers (*Psycho,* 1960); or in the impact of repressive, patriarchal ideologies (*Cat People,* 1942). *I Was a Teenage Werewolf* (1957) illustrates a number of popular themes in 1950s horror films: humans' "animal-like" nature and the fear that teenagers were closer to uncontrollable beasts than civilized adults. Alongside films that located the source of evil within families were others that focused on external threats to family harmony, of which one of the most notable was *Cape Fear* (1962).

Beginning in the late 1960s with the release of *Rosemary's Baby* (1968) and *Night of the Living Dead* (1968), horror films reached new heights of popularity. A theme that pervaded many of these films was the evils that lay hidden within families. Drawing on earlier themes, these films depicted families attacked with brutal violence (*The Texas Chain Saw Massacre,* 1974); raging, sexually repressed, violent children (*Carrie,* 1976; *The Exorcist,* 1973; *The Omen,* 1976); and violent individuals who have deep psychological scars arising from dysfunctional family experiences (*Friday the 13th,* 1980; *Halloween,* 1978; *Poltergeist,* 1982; *Nightmare on Elm Street,* 1984). At least part of the public fascination with recent horror films has to do with the way that they allow viewers to experience family pathologies in a safe context.

During the 1970s and 1980s, family breakdown, the decline of heavy industry, and the expansion of two-earner families posed a special threat to many men's self-conception as the sole family breadwinner. Hollywood responded to a "crisis of masculinity" through a variety of genres, ranging from lighthearted male fantasies of beautiful, utterly compliant women like *10* (1979); frat-house comedies like *Animal House* (1978) that treated women as sex objects; and slasher films in which independent and sexually active women were brutally attacked. Alongside these films were others, such as *Kramer vs. Kramer* (1979) and *Three Men and a Baby* (1987), that suggested that men had the capacity to be as successful as women in mothering children. The box-office success of *Fatal Attraction* (1987), in which a husband's one-night stand is followed by harassment and threats from the woman with whom he had the affair, resulted in a number of pictures, such as *The Hand That Rocks the Cradle* (1992), that portrayed unattached women as a threat to the family.

In his 1992 best-seller *Hollywood vs. America,* the film critic Michael Medved described Hollywood as a "poison factory," befouling America's moral atmosphere and assaulting the country's "most cherished values." Today's films, he argued, use their enormous capacity to influence opinion by maligning marriage, promoting sexual promiscuity, and bombarding viewers with an endless stream of profanity, gratuitous sex, and loutish forms of behavior. Where once the movies offered sentiment, elegance, and romance, now, Medved contends, ideologically motivated producers and directors promote their own divisive antifamily agenda.

In fact, the representations of family in contemporary film are far more diverse, and often more positive, than Medved's generalizations would indicate, even in such silly vehicles as the *National Lampoon's Vacation* series. This is particularly the case in films dealing with the families of African Americans and Hispanics, such as *Sounder* (1972), *Nightjohn* (1996), *La Bamba* (1987), *Selena* (1997), and *Mi Familia* (1995). But even in instances when more negative images of the family appear, as in *American Beauty* (1999), the pictures are best understood not as expressions of an antifamily agenda, but rather as cultural critiques which explore the latent tensions in contemporary American family life. But perhaps the most striking development in recent representations of the family on the screen is that mischievous sons, as in *Home Alone* (1990), have largely displaced parents as the dominant household figures.

During American film's first century, the family repeatedly served as a screen on which Hollywood projected larger social and cultural issues. Families illustrated in microcosm issues ranging from acculturation (*The Jazz Singer,* 1927) and the hardships of the Great Depression (*The Grapes of Wrath,* 1940), to the impact of war (*The Best Years of Our Lives,* 1946), the rise of a semi-autonomous youth culture (*Rebel Without a Cause,* 1955), and racism (*Guess Who's Coming to Dinner,* 1967). Through a process of refraction, Hollywood was able to convey the human meaning of abstract social processes and dilemmas. But since the 1960s, as anxieties over the family have deepened, genres that tended to avoid family issues, notably the gangster film, the horror film, and science fiction, increasingly incorporated fears about the family as a subtext. In recent years, old-fashioned family melodramas, like old-fashioned westerns, have sharply diminished in number. But the concerns that defined the genre—such as maternal sacrifice, sexual confusion, and intergenerational conflict—have frequently been displaced into new settings (*Alien 3,* 1992; *Terminator II,* 1993; *Jurassic Park,* 1993).

References

Filmography

Alien 3 (1992, F)
American Beauty (1999, F)
An American Family (1973, TV)
Animal House (1978, F)
The Awful Truth (1937, F)
The Bad Seed (1956, F)
The Best Years of Our Lives (1946, F)
The Birth of a Nation (1915, F)
Blonde Venus (1932, F)
Bob & Carol & Ted & Alice (1969, F)
Broken Blossoms (1919, F)
Broken Lance (1954, F)
Cape Fear (1962, F; 1991, F)
Carnal Knowledge (1971, F)
Carrie (1976, F)
The Catered Affair (1956, F)
Cat People (1942, F)
Cheaper by the Dozen (1950, F)
The Children Pay (1916, F)
The Dark at the Top of the Stairs (1960, F)
David and Lisa (1962, F)
Double Indemnity (1944, F)
Drums Along the Mohawk (1939, F)
East of Eden (1955, F)
The Eternal Mother (1912, F)
E.T.: The Extraterrestrial (1982, F)
The Exorcist (1973, F)
A Family Affair (1937, F)
Fatal Attraction (1987, F)
The Fatal Glass of Beer (1933, F)
Father of the Bride (1950, F)
Friday the 13th (1980, F)
Gidget (1959, F)
Gidget Goes Hawaiian (1961, F)
Gidget Goes to Rome (1963, F)
The Godfather (1972, F)
Gone with the Wind (1939, F)
The Good Earth (1937, F)
The Good Mother (1988, F)
The Graduate (1967, F)
The Grapes of Wrath (1940, F)
Guess Who's Coming to Dinner (1967, F)
Halloween (1978, F)
The Hand That Rocks the Cradle (1992, F)
His Girl Friday (1940, F)
Home Alone (1990, F)
Imitation of Life (1934, F)
It (1927, F)
It's a Wonderful Life (1946, F)
I Was a Teenage Werewolf (1957, F)
The Jazz Singer (1927, F)
Jurassic Park (1993, F)
Kramer vs. Kramer (1979, F)
La Bamba (1987, F)
Life with Father (1947, F)
Little Women (1933, F; 1994, F)
Lolita (1962, F; 1997, F)
The Man with the Golden Arm (1955, F)
Mi Familia (1995, F)
Mildred Pierce (1945, F)
My Man Godfrey (1936, F)
National Lampoon's Vacation (1983, F)
Nightjohn (1996, TV)
Nightmare on Elm Street (1984, F)
Night of the Living Dead (1968, F; 1990, F)
Now, Voyager (1942, F)
An Officer and a Gentleman (1982, F)
The Omen (1976, F)
The Perfect Flapper (1924, F)
The Philadelphia Story (1940, F)
The Plastic Age (1925, F)
Poltergeist (1982, F)
The Postman Always Rings Twice (1946, F)
Psycho (1960, F)
Rebel Without a Cause (1955, F)
Red River (1948, F)
Rosemary's Baby (1968, F)
Selena (1997, F)
Shane (1953, F)
The Sins of the Father (1913, F)
Sounder (1972, F)
The Sopranos (1999–, TV)
Splendor in the Grass (1961, F)
Stella (1990, F)

Stella Dallas (1937, F)
Stepmom (1998, F)
Straw Dogs (1971, F)
Tea and Sympathy (1956, F)
10 (1979, F)
Terminator II (1993, F)
Terms of Endearment (1983, F)
The Texas Chain Saw Massacre (1974, F)
That Touch of Mink (1962, F)
Three Men and a Baby (1987, F)
An Unmarried Woman (1978, F)
Way Down East (1920, F)
When Tomorrow Comes (1939, F)
Who's Afraid of Virginia Woolf? (1966, F)

Bibliography

Brandon, French. *On the Verge of Revolt: Women in American Films of the Fifties.* New York: Frederick Ungar, 1978.

Brownlow, Kevin. *Behind the Mask of Innocence.* New York: Knopf, 1990.

Byars, Jackie. *All That Hollywood Allows: Re-Reading Gender in 1950s Melodrama.* Chapel Hill: University of North Carolina Press, 1990.

Cavell, Stanley. *Pursuits of Happiness: The Hollywood Comedy of Remarriage.* Cambridge, MA: Harvard University Press, 1984.

Doherty, Thomas. *Teenagers and Teenpics: The Juvenilization of American Movies in the 1950s.* Cambridge, MA: Unwin Hyman, 1988.

Gledhill, Christine, ed. *Home Is Where the Heart Is: Studies in Melodrama and the Woman's Film.* London: British Film Institute, 1987.

Leibman, Nina C. *Living Room Lectures: The Fifties Family in Film and Television.* Austin: University of Texas Press, 1995.

Lewis, Jon. *The Road to Romance and Ruin: Teen Films and Youth Culture.* New York: Routledge: Chapman and Hall, 1992.

Medved, Michael. *Hollywood vs. America: Popular Culture and the War on Traditional Values.* New York: HarperCollins, 1992.

Mintz, Steven, and Susan Kellogg. *Domestic Revolutions: A Social History of American Family Life.* New York: Free Press, 1988.

Williams, Tony. *Hearths of Darkness: The Family in the American Horror Film.* Madison, NJ: Fairleigh Dickinson University Press, 1996.

[DALE HERBECK]

Football

Americans share a collective national obsession with sports. Schoolchildren are encouraged to play sports at an early age, millions of Americans attend sporting events or watch them on television, and the language of sports has permeated daily discourse. Although many different sports claim large and enthusiastic followings, Bob Oates has suggested that "football has evolved into America's most widely accepted major league pastime: first in the polls, first in the ratings" (11). By deftly balancing physical competition, teamwork, and sophisticated strategy, football has become more than a sport; it has become an integral part of our culture.

Despite football's obvious popularity, Deborah Tudor has lamented the "lack of analysis of the representation of sports in North American film and television" (xi). Compounding the problem, when sports films are reviewed in the popular press, they are frequently derided as being trite or inconsequential. This view is mistaken, however, inasmuch as a careful examination of football films reveals attitudes toward winning and losing, offers insights into the character of legends and heroes, and develops perspectives on broader social issues. In the final analysis, sports historian Ronald Bergan suggests, "sports are often only one element in a movie, or as we shall see, a symbol for the human condition" (6).

With several notable exceptions, football films generally reflect broader themes. The early football films of the 1920s and 1930s, made during the heyday of the college football era, focused on the collegiate game and the great teams. These movies gave way to a series of inspirational films in the 1940s and 1950s. Although many of these dramas were also set on college campuses, the films of this era focused less on the nature of the game and more on the character and virtue displayed by legendary coaches and gridiron heroes. Not surprisingly, the football films of the 1960s and 1970s decried the excesses of football and the abuses found in professional sports. In recent years, however, this criticism has given way to a more realistic set of football movies. Although many of these films return to old themes—the college game, the legendary players or coaches, and the violence inherent in the sport—they generally offer a more nuanced portrayal of football, the famous men who played the game, and the place of sport in American culture. By chronicling films and documentaries produced by the National Football League, it is possible to gain insight into football. At the same time, it is possible to understand football as a cultural text worthy of serious scholarly attention.

The College Game: The 1920s and 1930s

The early football movies focused on college teams. In many respects, the titles of these movies tell the story: *The All American* (1932), *Brown of Harvard* (1926), *The College Boob* (1926), *College Coach* (1933), *College Days* (1926), *The College Hero* (1927), *College Humor* (1933), *College Lovers* (1930), *The Forward Pass* (1929), *Hold That Co-Ed* (1938), *Hold 'Em Navy* (1937), *Hold 'Em Yale* (1928 and 1935), *Huddle* (1932), *Makers of Men* (1931), *Making the Varsity* (1928), *Navy Blue and Gold* (1937), *Pigskin Parade* (1936), *Saturday's Millions* (1933), and *The Spirit of Notre Dame* (1931).

Most of these films, Harvey Zucker and Lawrence Babich note, "were as indistinguishable as the titles" (145). Almost without exception, the storyline featured a football hero, a beautiful girl, and a big game against an archrival. Though there are multiple variations, the hero is invariably suspended, kidnapped, or otherwise estranged from his teammates or his romantic interest. Absent the star player, or sometimes because of his temporary ineptitude, the team falls behind in the big game and a bitter defeat to a hated rival appears inevitable. At the last instant, the hero returns and miraculously leads his team to victory. Sometimes this requires the hero to escape from captors, other times it requires the hero to overcome injury or hardship, and occasionally it even requires the hero to engage in some form of trickery or deception. Whatever the variation, however, the story always ends with the hero triumphant, the team victorious, and the romance restored. When depicted in this way, Bergan writes, "Football provided a means of exorcising character deficiencies and pointing the way for young people" (45).

Although the college movies tended to glorify the game, two of the most famous movies of this era are satirical comedies that mock both the sport and higher education. In *The Freshman* (1925), "Speedy" Lamb (Harold Lloyd) arrives at Tate College with the goal of becoming a big man on campus by emulating the star of the later *College Hero* (1927). When these ill-conceived efforts make him into the campus clown, "Speedy" tries to redeem himself by earning a place on the football team. Ordered to substitute himself for a broken tackling dummy, the coach nonetheless makes a place for the inept "Speedy" as the team's waterboy. From the sidelines, the helpless Speedy watches as teammate after teammate is injured in the big game against Union State. Finally, the coach succumbs to the inevitable and sends Speedy into the fray. After the expected comic mayhem, Speedy ends up with the ball on the decisive play of the game and he makes a mad dash to the endzone and victory. In the end, Speedy wins the game, becomes a campus hero, and wins the heart of Peggy (Jobyna Ralston). Commenting on "the comic styles of bourgeois figures like . . . Lloyd," Robert Sklar has observed that they "were nurtured in a particular social setting, where the loosening of the bonds of the old cultural system made space for comic exaggeration and alternative modes of order" (120).

Whereas *The Freshman* was about the exploits of a single player, *Horse Feathers* (1932) features the four Marx Brothers as teammates. Groucho, playing the part of Darwin College's newly installed president, John Quincy Wagstaff, quickly realizes that he must choose between having a good college and having a good football team. He chooses the latter, and, acting on the advice of his son, Zeppo, Groucho hires two star athletes—Chico and Harpo—to play for Darwin in its big game against archrival Huxley College. Learning of Groucho's plan, gamblers backing Huxley arrange to have Chico and Harpo detained. As might be expected, the brothers escape, steal a horse-drawn trash cart, and ride to the game in their new chariot. Showing a total disrespect for the rules, the brothers lead Darwin back from a 12–0 deficit to win a decisive victory. President Wagstaff leaves the sideline and joins his students on the field; Harpo attaches a rubber band to the ball, throws it toward Chico, and scores when the Huxley players mistakenly follow the ball; Harpo scores another touchdown by leaving a trail of slippery banana peels behind him. *Horse Feathers* is properly regarded as a great comedy, and insightful commentators have noted that the movie also develops a sophisticated critique of college football and higher education.

There are, of course, several notable movies that addressed the issues raised in a 1929 report by the Carnegie Foundation, *American*

College Athletics, that contained "a blanket indictment of big-time college athletics and especially the crafty and deceitful practices of college football programs" (Watterson, 165). In *Saturday's Heroes* (1937), for example, the star of Calton University's football team, Val Webster (Van Heflin) is caught selling complimentary tickets. Driven from the team in disgrace, Webster reappears as the assistant coach at tiny Weston College. Appalled by the flagrant professionalism in the college game, Webster persuades Weston's president to subsidize its players openly and to refuse to play schools that decline to abide by this honor code. Webster is vindicated when Weston upsets Calton in the big game. In an ironic twist, however, this victory is obtained in an unscrupulous manner: an angry Weston player stalks toward the sideline, the ball is passed to him, and he races to a touchdown before Calton realizes what has happened. The contrived ending notwithstanding, *Saturday's Heroes* reflects the growing criticism of the college game.

A Time of Legends: The 1940s and 1950s

The best-known movies of the 1940s and 1950s involve legendary figures such as Knute Rockne, Jim Thorpe, and Elroy Hirsch. The most famous of these films, *Knute Rockne, All-American* (1940), begins with the Rockne family's moving from Norway to America in 1892. Young Knute is drawn to football as an undersized child; as a teenager, he earns enough money to enroll at the University of Notre Dame; as a student, he distinguishes himself both as a scholar and as an athlete when he leads the team to a stunning victory over Army by catching a forward pass. After he graduates with honors, Rockne (Pat O'Brien) is forced to choose between a promising career as a research chemist and becoming a football coach at Notre Dame. Rockne opts for football; he distinguishes himself as both a successful coach and strategist by inventing the backfield shift; and, if this were not enough, he defends the integrity of the game before the Carnegie Commission. Vacationing with his family in Florida, Rockne is called to California on business. Despite his wife's fears about his safety, Rockne flies west to save precious vacation days and is tragically martyred when his plane crashes.

Not only did the movie help make Rockne a legend, but it also immortalized his relationship with a young player named George Gipp (Ronald Reagan). Although he initially appears indifferent to Rockne and football, Gipp quickly becomes a triple-threat player—runner, passer, and kicker—and one of the coach's personal favorites. When Gipp is stricken with a mysterious illness (probably strep throat ending in pneumonia), a distraught Rockne visits him in the hospital. In one of the most famous scenes in any sports movie, the dying Gipp opines, "Sometime, Rock, when the team's up against it, when things are wrong and the breaks are beating the boys, tell them to go in there with all they've got and win just one for the Gipper." To consummate the myth, Rockne later includes a reference to the Gipper in a half-time speech that inspires an overmatched Notre Dame team to a surprise victory over favored Army in one of Rockne's worst seasons as a coach.

Jim Thorpe, All American (1951) recounts the life of one of America's greatest athletes. Raised on an Indian reservation, Thorpe (Burt Lancaster) starts playing football at the Carlisle Indian School where he is coached by the famous Pop Warner (Charles Bickford). The movie recounts the famous Carlisle–Pennsylvania game, Thorpe's participation in the 1912 Olympic Games, and his professional career. Thorpe's life takes a turn for the worse when his young son dies and he slips into alcoholism. All is not lost, however, as Pop Warner reappears to absolve Thorpe of his transgressions by telling him that the state of Oklahoma will honor him for his athletic excellence.

The film versions of the lives of Knute Rockne and Jim Thorpe take liberties with the facts, yet they cannot be discounted as simple

FIGURE 45. *Knute Rockne, All American* (1940). Knute Rockne (Pat O'Brien) coaches Notre Dame after a stellar football career. A creative strategist as a coach, Rockne develops the backfield shift, changing football tactics and adding another level of excitement to the game. Courtesy First National Pictures and Warner Bros.

hagiography. After identifying the many errors in the film's rendition of Rockne's life, Michael Steele suggested "the distortions are best understood by keeping in mind that the film reflects the culture better than it portrays Rockne" (196). Both of these films speak to the character of heroes and the formative role that sport plays in the educational process. "Rockne and Thorpe both undergo the process of Americanization," Douglas Noverr writes, "becoming better individuals through sports and becoming national figures symbolic of the best coach and athlete of the early twentieth century. Rockne and Warner represent the national faith Americans had in coaches as institutions and in football as sport" (126).

Although the stories of Rockne and Thorpe may be the most famous, the same conclusion might be drawn from the other films of this area. *Crazylegs* (1954) tells the story of Elroy "Crazylegs" Hirsch. An All-American football player, Hirsch is injured while serving in the Marines. Although it appears that his career is over, Hirsch returns to star with the Los Angeles Rams. Amazingly enough, the aging Hirsch portrays himself in the film, as do several of his teammates on the Rams. In *Harmon of Michigan* (1941), Tom Harmon plays himself, a 1940 All-American at the University of Michigan. All-American quarterback Frankie Albert also played himself in *Spirit of Stanford* (1942). Although he had already agreed to turn pro before the big game, Albert returns to lead Stanford to an important victory. *Spirit of West Point* (1947) recounts the story of Felix "Doc" Blanchard and Glenn Davis, two star players at West Point who resisted the temptation to turn professional. Finally, *The Iron Major* (1943) is a tribute to coach Frank Cavanaugh, a wounded war hero who coached at Boston College and Fordham.

One movie that attempts to challenge these heroic narratives is *Saturday's Hero* (1951). A high school star, Steve Novak (John Derek), hopes to escape a New Jersey mill town by accepting a scholarship from a school known for its high academic standards. With Novak's help, his college becomes a powerhouse, and coaches from opposing schools attempt to buy away the school's best players. Learning that a player from another team was paid to hurt him, Novak begins to question the excesses of the college game. When injuries force him to retire, Novak returns home, finishes his education at night, and wins the girl (Donna Reed). The movie is interesting for another reason, however, as it contains a bitter indictment of college recruiting and the commercialism of the intercollegiate game that neatly foreshadows the football films of the Vietnam era.

Exposing the Game: The 1960s and 1970s

The movies of the 1960s and 1970s were highly critical of football. *The Paper Lion* (1968) is the screen version of a book by journalist George Plimpton describing his preseason experience with the Detroit Lions. By playing the preseason with the team, Plimpton attempted to get beyond the conventional media account of the game on the field. The movie is interesting on several counts: Plimpton (Alan Alda) experiences the game, viewers are invited into the locker room, and the game itself is the center of the movie.

Whereas *The Paper Lion* tries to depict the football experience, *Number One* (1969) focuses on the plight of the aging athlete. Ron Catlan (Charlton Heston) is a forty-year-old quarterback with a bad knee playing for the New Orleans Saints. In an effort to extend his career, Catlan dons a steel brace, wraps himself with yards of tape, and takes serious painkillers. Despite his best efforts, Catlan is mercilessly booed by the fans. Catlan quickly wins over the crowd by marching the Saints down the field. Discovering that all of his receivers are covered, Catlan scrambles for an improbable touchdown. The triumph is fleeting, however, as Catlan's career is ended on the next series of plays when he is viciously tackled by three defenders.

Not regarded as a football film, Robert Altman's *MASH* (1970) is a comedy about an Army hospital during the Korean War. The movie ends, however, with a football game between two rival units. The game itself is hopelessly corrupt, and this fact is sometimes read as an indictment of football. As if to punctuate this fact, the reserve players watch the game from the sideline while smoking marijuana. On closer inspection, however, Robert Sklar has labeled *MASH* a "tragicomedy that satirized the clichés and formulas of war films" (325). Although the movie is ostensibly set in Korea, the look and feel suggest that the film is really a parable about the Vietnam War.

Often dismissed as a comedy, *The Longest Yard* (1974) also raises difficult questions about the nature of authority. The big game in this film takes place in the Citrus State Prison and features a contest between a semipro team that has been handpicked by Warden Rudolph Hazen (Eddie Albert) and a motley collection of inmates organized by Paul "Wrecking" Crewe (Burt Reynolds), a former pro quarterback conveniently serving time for auto theft. "Before this game is over," the Warden taunts, "I want every prisoner in this institution to know what I mean by power . . . and who controls it." In exchange for the secret promise of parole, Crewe agrees to throw the game. Once the game starts, the guards, led by the legendary Bogdanski (played by Ray Nitschke of the Green Bay Packers), brutalize the hapless inmates. Late in the game, Crewe has a sudden change of heart and rallies his demoralized teammates to an improbable victory. Owing to this heroic choice, the audience finds itself rooting for the honorable criminals in a pitched battle against corrupt authority. "Almost everyone in the picture is violent and vicious," Bergan writes, "and the anti-authoritarian stance only leads to the nihilistic view that the violence of authority is indistinguishable from the violence that opposes it" (50).

North Dallas Forty (1979), film critic Leonard Maltin has written, "is one of the best gridirons film ever made and one of the best on any sport." The movie tells the story of Phil Elliott (Nick Nolte), a wide receiver for the North Dallas Bulls. Midway through a difficult season, Elliott arrives at a life crisis. He discovers that he loves the thrill of competition, but he knows his body is breaking down and he needs painkillers to play. This reality comes into sharp focus when he meets Charlotte Caulder (Dayle Haddon), a woman who helps him to see the world beyond football. The stark account offered in *North Dallas Forty* stands in sharp contrast to the football movies of previous generations. Not only is the action violent, but the game is also controlled by wealthy owners primarily concerned with winning championships and making money. "In the world of *North Dallas Forty*," Deborah Tudor writes, "there are no sympathetic management figures; the struggle between the players and management is conceptualized as a strict dichotomy between those who act and those who benefit from their labor" (71). The result is a film that exposes the economics of football as part of a broader critique of capitalism.

Even the lighter fare of the era, the comedies, disparaged the game. In *Semi Tough* (1977),

Bill Clyde Puckett (Burt Reynolds) and Marvin "Shake" Tiller (Kris Kristofferson) share an apartment and a platonic relationship with Barbara Jane Bookman (Jill Clayburgh). Although Clyde leads his team, the Miami Bucks, to victory in the big game, the title correctly implies that this movie is best regarded as a parody. The film features a dim-witted owner named Big Ed Brookman (Robert Preston), a biting critique of a variety of consciousness movements, and a star who would like to marry Barbara Jane and write a book exposing the seamier side of the game.

Another popular comedy of this era, *Heaven Can Wait* (1978), is a remake of *Here Comes Mr. Jordan,* a 1941 movie about boxing. In the football version, a promising young quarterback for the Los Angeles Rams named Joe Pendleton (Warren Beatty) finds himself in heaven when he is prematurely declared dead after an unfortunate accident. Pendleton is reincarnated as an arrogant millionaire named Leo Farnsworth. Unwilling to live out this life story, Farnsworth tries to reclaim Pendleton's place with the Rams. When the team spurns his request for a tryout, Farnsworth solves the problem by buying the team and installing himself as quarterback. Just when it appears that their fifty-year-old player-owner will lead the Rams, heavenly forces intervene again. Although a comedy, the movie also offers some deeper insights into the ethics of business and football. In one of the more telling scenes, Farnsworth tries to convince a skeptical board of directors that it should run the corporation like a football team.

Not all of the films of this era, however, were critical of the sport. *Brian's Song* (1971), for example, recounts the unlikely friendship of two players for the Chicago Bears, the reclusive Gale Sayers (Billy Dee Williams) and the gregarious Brian Piccolo (James Caan). Although they begin their careers as rookies competing for the same position, Sayers and Piccolo become close friends when Piccolo helps Sayers recover from a knee injury that threatens his promising career. The movie has a tragic ending, however, as Sayers is unable to help Piccolo win his battle against cancer. Although football is at the heart of *Brian's Song,* the film also speaks to the nature of friendship between men, race relations (Piccolo and Sayers were the NFL's first interracial roommates), and personal courage in the face of adversity. The movie was particularly powerful because it aired on network television a mere eighteen months after Piccolo died at age twenty-six. In an effort to raise more money for cancer research, *Brian's Song* was remade for television in 2001. Although the new version offers the same football story, the second telling focuses less on football and more on Piccolo (Sean Mahler) and his illness. Gale Sayers (Mekhi Phifer) has a prominent role, but the second film dramatically expands the roles of the player's wives, Joy Piccolo (Paula Cale) and Linda Sayers (Elise Neal).

The New Realism: The 1980s and 1990s

The football movies of the 1980s and 1990s revisited old themes. A number of movies offered moving accounts worthy of earlier generations. Two such movies, *A Triumph of the Heart: The Rickey Bell Story* (1991) and *Rise and Walk: The Dennis Byrd Story* (1994), offer accounts of athletes who overcame great personal hardship to succeed. Most of the movies of this era, however, offered more substantive critiques of athletic heroes, intercollegiate and professional football, and American society.

Everybody's All American (1988) tells the story of Gavin Grey, a legendary player at Louisiana State University. In the first third of the movie, Grey leads the Tigers to victory in the 1957 Sugar Bowl, marries Babs Rogers (Jessica Lange)—the virginal Magnolia Queen—and leads a generally charmed existence. Unlike the heroic movies from an earlier era, the film does not end with the big game, but rather follows the "Grey Ghost" through the next twenty-five years of his life. Unable to replicate his collegiate success with either the Washington Redskins or the Denver Broncos, Grey (Dennis Quaid) eventually becomes a sad parody of himself. Whereas he once resisted trading on his personal fame, he fails at business and is reduced to playing customer golf and selling Astroturf. As Grey tumbles from his lofty pedestal, his cheerleader wife transforms herself from a southern belle majoring in "Gavin and me," to devoted spouse and mother of four children, and finally to a successful businesswoman. While advertised as a "great American love story," *Everybody's All American* exposes both the fragility of our heroes and of the American dream.

Rudy (1993) tells the story of Rudy Ruettiger (Sean Astin), a working-class kid from Joliet, Illinois, who dreams of playing for the University of Notre Dame. Although he is the most improbable of heroes—he suffers from dyslexia, has poor high school grades, less than average athletic skills, and no family support—Rudy is undaunted. Unable to meet the strict admission standards at Notre Dame, he attends Holy Cross Junior College until he can gain admission to the Golden Dome. Realizing that he will never make the traveling team, Rudy distinguishes himself as a player on the scout team with his positive mental attitude. Just when it appears he will never achieve his dream, his teammates convince Coach Dan Devine to include Rudy on the roster for the last game against Georgia Tech. With the game safely in hand and at the enthusiastic urging of the crowd, Rudy is sent in for the final plays of the game. Though he does not lead the Fighting Irish to victory, Rudy does make a tackle and is carried from the field on the shoulders of his triumphant teammates. Although he is not a star player in the traditional sense, Rudy is a hero nonetheless because of his personal character and his selfless dedication to the team.

Remember the Titans (2000) is based on events at a newly integrated high school in Alexandria, Virginia, in 1971. As part of the integration, a new black coach, Herman Boone (Denzel Washington) is hired to replace a successful white coach, Bill Yoast (Will Patton), who becomes his assistant. Knowing that a team divided along racial lines cannot succeed, Coach Boone bullies and cajoles his players into the realization that they can only succeed if they play as a team. In one particularly poignant scene, Boone leads his players through workouts at the Civil War cemetery outside Gettysburg, Pennsylvania. Shrouded in fog, Boone uses the setting to speak out against racial hatred and animosity. Although the integration of the black and white players happens a little too quickly, and although the integrated team breaks out into an anachronistic hip-hop dance during warm-ups, *Remember the Titans* does an admirable job of chronicling the racial issues and the Titans' perfect seasons. He was not commenting on this particular film, but Michael Oriard could have been when he observes, "Racial narratives have moved from the periphery to the center of football's representations, as the racial integration of the game at all levels since the 1960s has made football one of the major American cultural texts of race and racism in the United States" (280–281).

Not all football movies of this era focus on the glory of the game or on heroes. *All the Right Moves* (1983) tells the story of Stef Djordjevic (Tom Cruise), a high school player who hopes an engineering scholarship will allow him to escape life in Ampipe, a dismal Pennsylvania steel town. Just when it appears the dream is within his grasp, the team loses the big game and Stef makes the tragic mistake of criticizing Coach Nickerson (Craig T. Nelson) for calling the wrong play. The outraged coach promptly suspends Stef, and if that is not enough, he tells recruiters that Stef is a problem, thereby ruining his chances of getting a college scholarship. The movie has a happy ending, however, when Stef's girlfriend, Lisa Leitke (Lea Thompson) manages to initiate a reconciliation between player and coach. With their relationship restored, Nickerson conveniently arranges for Stef to get a college scholarship at a school known for the quality of its engineering program. Though this fantasy ending trivializes the film, *All the Right Moves* raises difficult questions about high school football, football coaches and college recruiters, and the excesses of zealous fans.

Varsity Blues (1999) uses an old story to make a new point about high school football. When the star quarterback of the West Canaan Coyotes is hurt, his reluctant backup, Jonathan "Mox" Moxon (James Van Der Beek), is forced into a starring role. While the sudden success of the backup is a familiar theme, the movie also features a loathsome coach named Bud Kilmer (Jon Voight) who is completely obsessed with winning his twenty-third district championship. Although he is a legend within the local community, the movie reveals that the coach encourages players to use steroids, injects injured players with painkillers so that they can return to the game, and uses psychological intimidation to further his own winning record. During halftime of the big game, Mox and his teammates join together to overthrow the coach and put football back in perspective. Winning is important, but *Varsity Blues* argues that it is not so important as to sacrifice the health or the future of high school athletes.

The Program (1993) is a bitter indictment of college football that touches on winning at all costs, alcoholism and steroid abuse, as well as the rivalry between teammates at Eastern State University. In one particularly graphic sequence, players engage in a different sort of game with disastrous consequences. To demonstrate their fearlessness, players lie down on a two-lane highway, risking certain death should an unsuspecting car travel down the road. This unfortunate scene was edited out of the movie after reports that several teenagers may have been killed emulating this "game." Like its predecessors, the film ends with a rousing victory that seems to trivialize much of the bitter criticism leveled against college football.

Jerry McGuire (1996) introduces a new theme, the relationship between a player (Cuba Gooding Jr.) and his agent (Tom Cruise). Although the movie will be forever remembered for its signature line—"Show Me the Money!"—it raises larger issues about what really motivates players. Even though the title character ultimately proves that he cares about more than money, the story suggests that the same cannot be said about many professional athletes. Despite public statements to the contrary, *Jerry Maguire* implies that many professional athletes place their personal fortune ahead of both the game and their teammates.

In *Any Given Sunday* (1999), Oliver Stone uses the Miami Sharks, a professional team in serious decline, to comment on American individualism. The team owner, a young woman named Christina Pagniacci (Cameron Diaz), is determined to prove that she is as ruthless as any man. In an effort to revive her team and prove her own toughness, Pagniacci installs Tony D'Amato (Al Pacino) as head coach. While D'Amato still believes in teamwork, his star player, Willie Beaman (Jamie Foxx), is more concerned with earning individual laurels. The movie also features an injured captain (Dennis Quaid); a doctor (James Woods) more concerned with winning than the health of his players; and a cynical sports reporter (James C. McGinley). The cast also includes an impressive array of football stars, including Dick Butkus, Jim Brown, Lawrence Taylor, and Johnny Unitas. Action scenes from football games permeate *Any Given Sunday,* but Stone uses the game to reach a larger set of issues. "Every human predicament is here," Philip French writes, "and every convention or cliché of the sports movie" (9).

The Replacements (2000) addresses the labor difficulties in professional sports. When the Washington Sentinels go on strike for more money, team owner Edward O'Neil (Jack Warden) hires Jimmy McGinty (Gene Hackman) to field a team of replacement players. The team McGinty assembles includes a quarterback name Shane Falco (Keanu Reeves) who led his college team to ignoble defeat in the Sugar Bowl, a disturbed member of the Los Angeles Police Department, two brothers working as bouncers, a fleet-footed street punk who cannot catch the ball, and a chain-smoking Welsh soccer player with gambling debts. In stark contrast, the striking pros are depicted as spoiled princes obsessed with large contracts, private castles, and exotic cars. John Madden and Pat Summerall appear as themselves, reprising a role created by Bob Uecker in the baseball film *Major League* (1989). They may lack the talent of the striking professionals, but McGinty's misfits have heart and that is enough for them to prevail in the big game. In the final analysis, *The Replacements* is not really about professional football. Rather, the movie is better understood as a sad commentary on the labor troubles in the United States and a biting critique of millionaire athletes seeking ever more money.

Football Documentaries: NFL Films

In addition to movies about football, it is also important to consider football documentaries. Whereas the aforementioned movies use football as a vehicle to comment on society, documentaries produced by the National Football League serve an entirely different purpose; these films are designed to mythologize the sport. "What we see is not the event," Alan and John Clarke write, "but the event transformed into something else—a media event" (70–71).

The idea for NFL Films came from the most humble of origins. Impressed by footage collected by Ed and Steve Sabol—a father and son—using an 8mm Bell & Howell camera, NFL Commissioner Pete Rozelle bought the Sabol's small film company and renamed it NFL Films in the early 1960s. A visionary leader with experience in public relations, Rozelle managed to convince the twelve team owners that NFL Films could preserve the history of the game, promote professional football, and, most significantly, help shape the image of the sport.

To place this decision in historical context, it should be remembered that NFL Films was born at a time when there were no football highlights on television, no instant replays, and no slow-motion effects. All of this quickly changed as NFL Films produced professional highlight reels, introduced three-quarter-speed replays, and introduced viewers to the sounds of the game. At the same time, NFL Films also introduced innovative camera techniques such as ground level angles, tracking a spiraling pass in the air, and close-ups of sweat dripping from a player's helmet. In a particularly fortuitous move, NFL Films hired John Facenda to add dramatic narrative to its documentaries. Sometimes referred to as the "voice of God," Facenda's distinctive baritone became one of the most recognizable voices in sports and many of his signature lines—"the frozen tundra" of Lambeau Field—remained in use long after his death. Finally, NFL Films added stirring music to unify the different elements and reinforce the dramatic effect of the visual images.

One of NFL Films' early efforts, *They Call It Pro Football* (1965), begins with a gripping opening line: "It starts with a whistle and ends with a gun." This vivid language, combined with deftly edited footage, help transform football from a game into a mythic struggle between good and evil. As a testament to its enduring influence, *They Call It Pro Football* has been called the *Citizen Kane* of sports movies. In 1967, Vince Lombardi, legendary coach of the Green Bay Packers, agreed to wear a microphone on a sideline during a game. The result was *Lombardi* (1967), a prime-time special that helped explain how this charismatic leader was able to win five NFL championships and the first two Super Bowls. By melding cinematography, Facenda's narrative, game sounds, and music, these early films transformed football games into sports spectaculars. In the process, they served as propaganda for the NFL and functioned to popularize the professional game.

The new documentaries produced by NFL Films use the latest digital technology, but the formula remains largely the same. All NFL Films feature distinctive cinematography, sounds from the game, symphonic music, and dramatic voiceovers. Recent works include documentaries celebrating the history of the professional game (*75 Seasons: The Story of the National Football League*, 1994), the beauty and violence of the sport (*Best Shots: A Century of Sound and Fury*, 1999), and simple mistakes and tragic blunders (*21st Century NFL Follies*, 2000). NFL Films may be best known, however, for its obsessive coverage of the league's championship game, the Super Bowl (see, for example, *Super Bowl XXXVI*, 2002). These Super Bowl films have become so popular that the National Geographic Society actually did a documentary about the way that NFL Films packages the championship game, and the result was aptly titled *The Idol Makers: Inside NFL Films* (1997).

NFL Films has contributed to the popularity of football, but the significance of these documentaries extends beyond the sport. "NFL highlight reels had a real impact on how movies get made, particularly montages," observes director Ron Howard. "Lots of different images. Images on images. Using the slow-motion, combined with the live action. The hard-hitting sound effects, juxtaposed against incredible music, powerful music, creating a really emotional experience for the viewer" (Strauss, 4).

Football Movies and American Culture

Viewed as a series of related stories, football movies open a window into American culture. The early films speak to the importance of the college game, but they also offer insight into winning and losing. Although the movies of the 1940s and 1950s glorified gridiron heroes, they also testify to our national character and shared values. The movies of the Vietnam era decried the violence and brutality of football, just as many Americans turned against the televised images of the war. Finally, the football movies of the 1980s and 1990s search for new meaning in old stories. Indeed, many of the movies of this era use football as a convenient vehicle for speaking to themes that transcend the game. Through it all, Michael Oriard suggests, football remains a "cultural text in which we read stories about some of the most basic issues that touch our lives" (282).

References

Filmography

The All American (1932, F)
All the Right Moves (1983, F)
Any Given Sunday (1999, F)
Best Shots: A Century of Sound and Fury (1999, D)
Brian's Song (1971, F; 2001, TV)
Brown of Harvard (1926, F)
The College Boob (1926, F)
College Coach (1933, F)
College Days (1926, F)
The College Hero (1927, F)
College Humor (1933, F)
College Lovers (1930, F)
Crazylegs (1954, F)
Everybody's All American (1988, F)
The Forward Pass (1929, F)
The Freshman (1925, F)
Harmon of Michigan (1941, F)
Heaven Can Wait (1978, F)
Here Comes Mr. Jordan (1978, F)
Hold 'Em Navy (1937, F)
Hold 'Em Yale (1928, F; 1935, F)
Hold That Co-Ed (1938, F)
Horse Feathers (1932, F)
Huddle (1932, F)
The Idol Makers: Inside NFL Films (1997, D)
The Iron Major (1943, F)
Jerry Maguire (1996, F)
Jim Thorpe, All American (1951, F)
Knute Rockne, All-American (1940, F)
Lombardi (1967, D)
The Longest Yard (1974, F)
Major League (1989, F)

Makers of Men (1931, F)
Making the Varsity (1928, F)
MASH (1970, F)
Navy Blue and Gold (1937, F)
North Dallas Forty (1979, F)
Number One (1969, F)
The Paper Lion (1968, F)
Pigskin Parade (1936, F)
The Program (1993, F)
Remember the Titans (2000, F)
The Replacements (2000, F)
Rise and Walk: The Dennis Byrd Story (1994, F)
Rudy (1993, F)
Saturday's Hero (1951, F)
Saturday's Heroes (1937, F)
Saturday's Millions (1933, F)
Semi Tough (1977, F)
75 Seasons: The Story of the National Football League (1994, D)
The Spirit of Notre Dame (1931, F)
Spirit of Stanford (1942, F)
Spirit of West Point (1947, F)
Super Bowl XXXVI (2002, D)
They Call It Pro Football (1965, D)
A Triumph of the Heart: The Rickey Bell Story (1991, F)
21st Century NFL Follies (2000, D)
Varsity Blues (1999, F)

Bibliography

Bergan, Ronald. *Sports in the Movies.* New York: Proteus, 1982.

Bernstein, Mark F. *Football: The Ivy League Origins of an American Obsession.* Philadelphia: University of Pennsylvania Press, 2001.

Clarke, Alan, and John Clarke. "'Highlights and Action Replays'—Ideology, Sport and the Media." In Jennifer Hargreaves, ed., *Sport, Culture and Ideology,* 65–77. London: Routledge & Kegan Paul, 1982.

D'Agostino, Annette M. *Harold Lloyd: A Bio-Bibliography.* Westport, CT: Greenwood, 1994.

Davidson, Judith A., and Daryl Adler. *Sport on Film and Video: The North American Society for Sport History Guide.* Metuchen, NJ: Scarecrow, 1993.

French, Philip. "Field of Conflict: All of Life is Here, in Oliver Stone's Take on American Football." *London Observer,* 2 April 2000.

Noverr, Douglas A. "The Coach and the Athlete in Football Sports Films." In Paul Loukides and Linda K. Fuller, eds., *Beyond the Stars: Stock Characters in American Popular Film,* 118–132. Bowling Green, OH: Bowling Green State University Popular Press, 1990.

Oates, Bob. *Football in America: Game of the Century.* Coal Valley, IL: Quality Sports, 1999.

Oriard, Michael. *Reading Football: How the Popular Press Created an American Spectacle.* Chapel Hill: University of North Carolina Press, 1993.

Savage, Howard J. *American College Athletics.* New York: Carnegie Foundation for the Advancement of Teaching, 1929.

Sklar, Robert. *Movie-Made America: A Cultural History of American Movies.* Rev. ed. New York: Vintage, 1994.

Smith, Ronald A. *Sports and Freedom: The Rise of Big Time College Athletics.* New York: Oxford University Press, 1988.

Sperber, Murray. *Onward to Victory: The Crises That Shaped College Sports.* New York: Holt, 1993.

——. *Shake Down the Thunder: The Creation of Notre Dame Football.* New York: Holt, 1993.

Steele, Michael R. *Knute Rockne: A Bio-Bibliography.* Westport, CT: Greenwood, 1983.

Strauss, Robert. "Catching Football on Film." *New York Times,* 29 October 2000.

Thelin, John R. *Games Colleges Play: Scandal and Reform in Intercollegiate Athletics.* Baltimore: Johns Hopkins University Press, 1993.

Tudor, Deborah V. *Hollywood's Vision of Team Sports: Heroes, Race, and Gender.* New York: Garland, 1997.

Watterson, John Sayle. *College Football: History, Spectacle, Controversy.* Baltimore: Johns Hopkins University Press, 2000.

Zucker, Harvey Marc, and Lawrence J. Babich. *Sports Films: A Complete Reference.* Jefferson, NC: McFarland, 1987.

[ROBERT BAIRD]

Journalism and the Media

Early in this nation's history, print materials—broadsides, newspapers, and magazines—were the major medium of communication and entertainment. By the 1930s, motion pictures had become a principal mass medium. During the 1940s radio dominated American media culture, providing continuous news reports and live broadcasts from the various war fronts. At the beginning of the 1960s, television had become the most pervasive mass medium the world had ever seen. Many believe that the Internet will one day replace television. Although particular media have waxed and waned in importance in the last century, the social and economic importance of mass communication continues to increase. Although farms still feed us and foundries and railroads still run, the future pivots on dizzying accelerations in the flow of information.

Hollywood's relation to various types of media follows a revealing pattern: nostalgia for old media; concern and negotiation with contemporary media; and denial, fear, and confusion regarding new media. For instance, when television was a new, rapidly growing medium in the early 1950s, Hollywood refused even to acknowledge it, showing "an almost self-destructive indifference" (Baughman, xvii). But as television rapidly and indisputably asserted itself, Hollywood and the other established media adopted strategies of competition and coexistence. To compete with television, older media "began cultivating the subgroup, segments of the audience denoted by such factors as class, education, or age" (Baughman, xvii). Hollywood also created and marketed films that exploited technological flourishes the small screen could not offer: color, widescreen, epic spectacles. Competition and coexistence led Hollywood to sell feature films for television broadcast and to provide production resources for television shows. The films Hollywood makes about other media are the most visible, public reminders that mass entertainment is at heart a high-stakes, competitive, and often cooperative business.

Newspapers

In *A History of News,* Michael Stephens claims, "Two truths have governed the economics of the newspaper business: one is that well-to-do readers are more attractive to advertisers; the second is that poorer readers build higher circulations" (202). Perhaps because they catered to the same economic class, Hollywood and the popular, tabloid newspapers of America have had something of a century-long love affair. In *Citizen Kane* (1941), the finest newspaper film ever made, the young Charles Foster Kane (Orson Welles) is never again as heroic as when he transforms the respectable, stuffy *Chronicle* into a muckraking, sensational, working-class paper. Hollywood's love for the bustle of the print newsroom, the tenacity of the beat reporter, and the stubborn courage of the newspaper editor are evident in dozens of films: Will Rogers as a folksy small-town editor fighting for the falsely accused in *Life Begins at Forty* (1935); Barbara Stanwyck as a cynical big-city reporter who eventually finds her soul in Frank Capra's *Meet John Doe*

(1941). From the 1930s until today, few character types have been as lauded and loved by Hollywood as the newspaper editor and the investigative reporter. The highlights of this love affair, such as *His Girl Friday, Meet John Doe, Citizen Kane,* and *All the President's Men,* represent some of the finest films ever made.

His Girl Friday (1940) is perhaps the deftest remake in history, updating *The Front Page* (1931), itself based on the very successful 1928 play written by Ben Hecht and Charles MacArthur. For his remake, director Howard Hawks had the brilliant idea of switching the gender of outstanding reporter Hildy Johnson from a man to a woman and making editor Walter Burns (who wants to keep Hildy on staff at all costs) Hildy's ex-husband. The changes allowed Hawks to place the screwball comedy formula within the setting and conventions of a big-city newspaper. In 1974, Billy Wilder remade the tale once again, this time with Jack Lemmon and Walter Matthau. In 1988, *Switching Channels* moved the story into the image-conscious world of television journalism, especially Ted Turner–style, satellite/cable news.

Meet John Doe (1941) shares *His Girl Friday*'s fascination with big-city, tough, cynical news work. Barbara Stanwyck plays a newspaper reporter named Ann Mitchell who invents "John Doe," a workingman populist philosopher in the vein of Will Rogers who speaks up for the little guy against the interests of big money. When the fictive John Doe actually becomes popular, Stanwyck has to find a "real" John Doe, which she does in Long John Willoughby (Gary Cooper), a washed-up minor league pitcher. Capra had earlier developed a wisecracking reporter in *Platinum Blonde* (1931), but the contrast between the homespun Willoughby (and Gary Cooper's All-American image) with Stanwyck's hard-on-the-outside reporter (and the actress's famed toughness) allowed the director to highlight and partially reconcile American cultural tensions of great historical legacy and immediacy.

Hero (1992) is a haphazard borrowing of *Meet John Doe,* with a petty thief (Dustin Hoffman) rescuing passengers, including a TV news reporter (Geena Davis), from a downed airliner. When the "Angel of Flight 49" disappears, Davis's station offers a reward for the hero to come forward, but another man, a drifter (Andy Garcia), claims to be the rescuer. Like *Meet John Doe, Hero* is a cautionary tale, warning how easily public gullibility and sentimentality can be manipulated by the cynical mass media eager to provide larger-than-life, feel-good stories instead of messy, mundane realities or complex social challenges.

By the 1970s, Hollywood was beginning to neglect print journalism for the dramatic possibilities of television news just as two real-life ink-and-paper journalists at *The Washington Post,* Bob Woodward and Carl Bernstein, were beginning investigative work that would eventually unseat a president and capture a Pulitzer Prize. Hip and handsome young reporters toppling an aging, right-wing political dynasty made print journalism very "cool" for students in the nation's colleges and universities. Director Alan J. Pakula wasted no time and brought forward a film called *The Parallax View* (1974), which starred Warren Beatty as just such an investigative reporter (named Joseph Frady) trying to get to the bottom of a senator's assassination. The success of that film led to Pakula's adaptation of Woodward and Bernstein's book *All the President's Men* (1976), where Pakula creatively used film techniques to dramatize the verbal, intellectual, and bookish world of a political news reporter. In the film's famous ending, Nixon's resignation is presented quite effectively via a montage of extreme close ups as the story is spit out on a clattering teletype machine, emphasizing the still substantial power of the written word in the age of video.

It is very easy to forget just how much *Citizen Kane* (1941) is an elaboration of the newspaper genre film. Interestingly, director Orson Welles maintains Hollywood's traditional trust

FIGURE 46. *The Parallax View* (1974). Investigative reporter Joseph Frady (Warren Beatty) steps into a dangerous and clandestine plot to assassinate a senator. Director Alan Pakula's success with *The Parallax View* became the impetus to adapt and direct *All the President's Men.* Courtesy Harbor Productions, Doubleday Productions, and Paramount Pictures.

in newspaper reporters and editors even as he paints a very dark portrait of newspaper publishers. The tragedy of the story, in fact, hinges on Charles Foster Kane's transition from an enthusiastic and idealistic editor and writer to a dogmatic and vindictive media mogul. It should be noted that Kane's great betrayal of his one close friend, Jedediah Leland (Joseph Cotten), occurs over a point of journalistic ethics: Kane's shock over Leland's negative review of Susan Kane's terrible opera debut.

Citizen Kane built on a rich decade of newspaper films: the 1930s, which saw top directors and actors in films like *Five Star Final* (1931), a crime drama involving a sensationalist tabloid (remade in 1936 as *Two Against the World* with radio as its setting); *Blessed Event* (1932), a Walter Winchell–style gossip columnist gets himself into a bit of comic trouble; *The Murder Man* (1935), with Spencer Tracy as a tough crime reporter; *Exclusive* (1937), another comedy romance set amidst competing newspapers; and *Libeled Lady* (1936), starring William Powell, Myrna Loy, Spencer Tracy, and Jean Harlow in a comic treatment of the newsroom.

After the late 1930s, the newspaper genre was so familiar and comfortable that stars not immediately associated with the newsroom began to take their turn at the business. *Nancy Drew—Reporter* (1939) followed the archetypal newspaper formula by having the popular Nancy Drew (Bonita Granville) working a school newspaper beat, trying to clear the name of a girl falsely accused of murder. Comic tandem Bud Abbott and Lew Costello became newspaper photographers in *Hit the Ice* (1943). In *Francis Covers the Big Town* (1953), the talking mule and sidekick Donald O'Connor found themselves on a newspaper reporting a murder trial. Much later in the game, the glossy *Teacher's Pet* (1958) combined the star power of Clark Gable and Doris Day—he is a down-to-earth, big-city editor, she a cerebral journalism teacher, differences that lead to comic and romantic payoffs.

Hollywood has occasionally depicted the underground press, as it did in *Between the Lines* (1977), which dealt with the story of an underground paper in Boston about to be co-opted by a media mogul. The Jerry Bruck Jr. documentary *I. F. Stone's Weekly* (1973) covers one-man, left-wing newspaper publisher I. F. Stone, who raked muck and scooped America's mainstream press countless times. In 1980, *Where the Buffalo Roam* brought the "gonzo" journalism practices of Hunter S. Thompson to the big screen, behind the capable talents of Bill Murray, supplanted in 1998 by Johnny Depp, who played Thompson in the film adaptation of Thompson's famous *Fear and Loathing in Las Vegas.* On a side note, the "new journalism" of Tom Wolfe made its way to the big screen via adaptations of three of his works: *The Last American Hero* (1973), *The Right Stuff* (1983), and *Bonfire of the Vanities* (1990).

The most common beat for the print journalist in Hollywood films has always been the courtroom drama, where reporters typically fight for justice, strive to clear the falsely accused, and help convict the high and mighty. *Absence of Malice* (1981) is interesting for its willingness to present journalists and journalism as less than perfect. Written by Kurt Luedtke, a former reporter, *Absence of Malice* presents an aggressive reporter (Sally Field) who prints a leaked story about Mafia connections that turns out to be false, damaging the reputation of a decent businessman (Paul Newman). Throughout the film, Field's character exceeds the bounds of journalistic ethics in order to make up for her initial mistake.

The May 5, 1969, issue of *New York* magazine contains a dynamic journalistic piece entitled "The Lifestyle of a Pimp." The author, David Freeman, made it all up. Freeman was not fired or forced to return prizes, as were other highly publicized fabricators. In fact, he wrote a screenplay building on the incident that was eventually produced as *Street Smart* (1987). Following the *Meet John Doe* model, Freeman's reporter (Christopher Reeve) is forced to find a flesh-and-blood version of the pimp he invented for his story and settles on "Fast Black" (Morgan Freeman). The film pokes fun at print and television journalism and, like *Absence of Malice,* highlights Hollywood's more complex, post-Watergate stance toward contemporary journalism and media.

FIGURE 47. *The Paper* (1994). Henry Hackett (Michael Keaton), metro editor of the *New York Sun,* and reporter Michael McDougal (Randy Quaid) try to salvage the paper struck by another setback as they try to meet a deadline and possibly save the lives of two African American boys wrongly accused of murder. Courtesy Imagine Entertainment and Universal Pictures.

Although Hollywood has lately begun to critique journalistic practices and transgressions—especially those of television—the old affection for paper-and-ink journalism is still alive, as evident in Ron Howard's *The Paper* (1994). Here, an outstanding cast—Michael Keaton, Robert Duvall, Glenn Close, Randy Quaid, and Jason Robards—gets lives and newspaper back together in an excellent treatment of deadline pressure, journalistic ethics, professional rivalries, work/family conflicts, and old-fashioned investigative do-gooding.

Radio

At the end of the World War II, more American families owned radios than either telephones or indoor plumbing. Radio and film—even when half of radio programming consisted of dramatic shows—were never perceived as being direct and total competitors. Radio relied on advertising sponsors and film relied on ticket sales. In the 1930s and 1940s, there were enough leisure hours in the course of a week for the typical person to patronize both radio and film. Radio advertised and gossiped about movies, incorporated the recognizable voices of Hollywood stars, played movie scores and tunes, and developed radio plays from recently successful Hollywood films. For its part, Hollywood celebrated radio and the big city radio stations in film portrayals that underscored both media's shared allegiance to the same populist, mass audience.

By the early 1960s, radio had abandoned dramatic programming to television, devoting itself almost entirely to music and local news, becoming, in effect, more of an ally than a competitor with Hollywood. Today radio is most significant as a Hollywood advertising mechanism for promoting not only new theatrical and video releases but also hit soundtrack albums, currently one of the most successful and profitable genres of music. Consequently, film treatments of radio are largely loving, comical, and nostalgic, most famously in Woody Allen's *Radio Days* (1987), which effectively evokes the radio drama's powerful engagement of the listener's imagination.

Earlier, in the 1930s and 1940s, the setting of the big-city radio station, with its live, studio performances, provided the perfect backdrop for Hollywood films indulging the romance, the backstage musical, and the vaudeville tradition. The most successful series of this sort was the Paramount Studios, George Burns–led "Big Broadcast" films of 1932, 1936, 1937, and 1938. The last film of the series replaced Burns with Bob Hope, who, in his first feature, won an Academy Award after singing what would become his signature tune: "Thanks for the Memories." The old-style radio studio has been occasionally revisited, as in *Radioland Murders* (1994), with fictional 1940s Chicago radio studio WBN serving as a backdrop for this blend of mystery, comedy, and slapstick. Another period piece is *Tune in Tomorrow* (1990), set in the world of 1950s radio soap operas. *FM* (1978), the best of a number of comic treatments of 1970s radio, nicely captured the mood of the album-oriented Los Angeles rock scene and starred a funny Martin Mull in his first film, a likely inspiration for television's *WKRP in Cincinnati.*

Radio, of course, frequently plays in the background of film scenes, with news, music, and disk jockey commentary serving for historical flavor and thematic enrichment. In the very successful *American Graffiti* (1973), director George Lucas explored the profound significance of local radio to teen culture, mostly by the constancy of radio's presence in their lives and on his soundtrack, but also by having his teens make a late-night pilgrimage to an on-air Wolfman Jack, who, playing himself, offered aid and advice. For later generations, *Pump up the Volume* (1990) presented Christian Slater as a nondescript high school student who, by night, hosts a pirate radio station that offers cool music, coming-of-age advice, and occasional provocations for youthful rebellion. In Jim Jarmusch's *Mystery Train* (1989), the spirit of Elvis and the music of a local radio station dominate the Memphis visit of two rock 'n' roll–crazy Japanese tourists.

Not until the rise of talk radio in the 1980s would Hollywood begin to look less trustingly at radio, most dramatically in Oliver Stone and Eric Bogosian's *Talk Radio* (1988). Derived from Bogosian's one-man stage show, *Talk Radio* is inspired—loosely—by the real-life Alan Berg, a confrontational Denver talk-radio figure assassinated by neo-Nazis in 1984. An earlier film, somewhat ahead of its time in its appreciation of radio's potential for inflammatory rhetoric was Stuart Rosenberg's *WUSA* (1970), starring Paul Newman. A study of a right-wing New Orleans radio station involved in clandestine activities beyond ideological broadcasting, the film was dubbed by Pauline Kael a "garish example of liberal exhibitionism" (851). Alan Rudolph's *Choose Me* (1984) treated talk radio more comically and charitably than *Talk Radio,* with Rudolph orchestrating his typically wacky, Robert Altman–sized troupe of characters around the radio sex therapist "Dr. Love" (Geneviève Bujold) and her relationship with a mysterious drifter played by Keith Carradine. A similar, even sillier treatment of talk radio can be seen in *The Truth About Cats and Dogs* (1996), where Janeane Garofalo plays a lovelorn veterinarian who dishes out pet tips on the local radio. 1997's *Private Parts* treats the rise to fame of "shock-jock" personality Howard Stern. True to form, the older medium of radio, no matter how outrageous the content, is no threat to Hollywood, and the film is a well-made celebration of Stern as a regular guy.

Television

In the early days, television looked to journalism and Broadway for inspiration and talent.

Dependent on bulky, studio-bound cameras, the typical live television drama was like "theater with closeups" (Toll, 63). By the late 1950s, however, television had forced radio to cater to local and regional audiences and was challenging film's hold on the mass audience. In contrast to print and radio, films set in the world of television have frequently displayed a mixture of fear and condescension. Paddy Chayefsky's *Network* (1976) accurately foreshadows many of the sensationalistic and morbid developments of American television. Pointedly hyperbolic, the film is a satiric masterpiece. Its most famous scene—Peter Finch's "I'm as mad as hell and I'm not going to take it anymore!" on-air outburst—is one of the more memorable in all of cinema, a moment that might help future generations realize the sense of power and community that could come when millions upon millions of viewers watched live, spontaneous television on a limited number of broadcast networks—before, that is, the influx of cable in the 1980s. Nominated for ten Academy Awards and given four, *Network* made the cinematic treatment of television acceptable, even imitable. *The Image* (1990) was in the vein of *Network,* with Albert Finney as a news anchorman very cynical about his trade. The influence spread even into the horror genre, where Joe Dante's *The Howling* (1981) smartly mixed werewolves with television news.

The feminist gains of the 1960s and subsequent decades helped extend the role and power of women journalists, even as on-air women journalists continued to be rewarded or fired based on dated notions of youth and beauty. Hollywood found the female journalist a dramatically compelling character. In 1979, Jane Fonda played a journalist in two separate films. *The Electric Horseman* saw Fonda track, find, and befriend a retired rodeo champion (Robert Redford) who rides off with a million-dollar racehorse when he finds it has been drugged and misused by its owners. Redford's character is a pitchman for a breakfast cereal—forced to wear an outrageous cowboy outfit bedecked in electric lights. The film becomes a heroes-on-the-run road picture, with obvious potshots at the dehumanizing influence of corporations, their publicity machines, and pack journalism.

Much more threatening was *The China Syndrome.* In this story, Jane Fonda and Michael Douglas are the Woodward and Bernstein of a California television news team that uncovers some very serious problems at a nuclear power plant. A political thriller without a happy ending, the film pits the investigative reporter against not only the nuclear energy interests but also the higher echelons at her own station. Like *Network, The China Syndrome* finds no comfort in those who control television.

Treatment of women journalists continued in *Broadcast News* (1987), which switched the traditional pattern by having Holly Hunter play the intelligent, highly professional news producer who falls in love with a pretty boy, on-air personality played by William Hurt. *Almost Golden: The Jessica Savitch Story* (1995, TV), offered a biopic of the real-life rise and fall—through drugs and alcohol—of an admired television news anchor. The original script for *Up Close and Personal* (1996), written by Joan Didion and John Gregory Dunne, was, in its earliest drafts, based on the brief, meteoric rise of Savitch, who drowned in her automobile no more than twenty yards from a restaurant where she had just eaten dinner. The final film, following the wishes of Disney executives, dropped the Savitch biography for a fictionalized, rags-to-riches, Pygmalion romance, with an ambitious poor girl (Michelle Pfeiffer) working her way up the television news ladder with the help of a savvy news director (Robert Redford).

The concern with "pack journalism"—an ugly proliferation of "sound bite" journalists and news sources viciously fighting over the same tabloid news stories—is evident in *The Chase* (1994). The falsely accused Charlie Sheen goes behind the wheel of a stolen BMW containing a kidnapped heiress and leads police and television media on a high-speed chase through California. Sound familiar? Not a great drama, the film's treatment of pack journalism in the age of video, satellites, cell phones, and helicopters is simultaneously humorous and frightening.

The six-part documentary *The Dawn of the Eye: The History of Film and TV News* (1997) offers a far-ranging survey of film and television's not-always-respectable role in recording history and reporting news from 1894 to 1997. Commenting on American, British, and Canadian film and television journalism, *Dawn of the Eye* exposes the fakery of newsreels and the suppression of legitimate news in the first half of the century, notes the growing influence and watchdog role of television news from the 1950s through the 1980s, and concludes by exploring the impact of global news events such as the Berlin Wall, Tiananmen Square, and the Gulf War.

1998 saw two of Hollywood's most brilliant treatments of television, both surprisingly rooted in retrospective looks at 1950s-style sitcoms—perhaps impossible to conceive of before cable television's Nickelodeon-led recycling of vintage television. *The Truman Show* was built on the premise of a man who had spent his entire life unaware that he was living inside the world's most popular television show, enclosed in a giant set. When Truman begins to suspect the existence of another world beyond his own, he sets out on a quest that provides viewers with an intelligent exploration of mediated living, linking the film to long traditions of such thought in art, philosophy, cosmology, and theology.

Not as brilliant, but equally earnest, *Pleasantville* built on the premise that two contemporary teens could enter a perfect, 1950s sitcom in the style of *Leave It to Beaver*. Things are too perfect, however, and the new cast members eventually transform the black and white, conforming world of Pleasantville into a multicolored, open society where each person can express him or herself freely. *The Truman Show* and *Pleasantville* make it clear that TV has grown up in the eyes of Hollywood. Now that television is longer a threat but more of an entertainment partner with the studios, we can expect more artful and thoughtful treatments of the small screen on the big screen.

New Media: Computers, Internet, Virtual Reality

In *Hamlet on the Holodeck*, media scholar Janet Murray helps explain Hollywood's bifurcated response toward computer-age new media: "The birth of a new medium of communication is both exhilarating and frightening. Any industrial technology that dramatically extends our capabilities also makes us uneasy by challenging our concept of humanity itself. . . . Half the people I know seem to look upon the computer as an omnipotent, playful genie while the other half see it as Frankenstein's monster" (2).

Although there are outstanding, if hysterical, films that treat computers—*Colossus: The Forbin Project* (1970), *2001: A Space Odyssey* (1968), and *War Games* (1983) among them—Hollywood has yet to present a first-rate film dealing with the Internet or virtual reality, two new technologies that seem to frighten and confuse Hollywood scriptwriters. In movies such as *Hackers* (1995), *Virtuosity* (1995) and *The Lawnmower Man* (1992), filmmakers display computer screens as if they were laser light shows. On film, computer experts program, hack, and debug quicker than most people can type.

Relying on Cassandra-like narratives of impending disaster, the bulk of films treating new media are low-budget genre features, some aimed at the straight-to-video market. *Triumph of the Nerds* (1996), however, is a well-done, three-part documentary on the development of the personal computer, adapted from Silicon Valley insider Robert X. Cringely's 1992 book *Accidental Empires*. *Nerds* gets the technical details of computers correct and balances its appreciation for the wonder kids of personal computers like Bill Gates and Steve Jobs with a not always rosy view of their methods. *Nerds 2.0.1* (1998) returns the whimsically critical Cringely to a history of the Internet. Of the lot of new media films, *Strange Days* (1995) comes closest to offering a believable, if still hysterical, exploration of virtual reality as a dramatically addictive new medium. *The Matrix* (1999), an Orwellian techno-nightmare sporting black-leather-chic action scenes, makes good use of digital special effects work in expressing the possibility that the world as we know it is actually a rather large computer program, with, of course, a few bugs. A more mainstream treatment of computing can be found in *You've Got Mail* (1998), which brings together Tom Hanks and Meg Ryan in a Hollywood romantic comedy of boy meets girls over the Internet—the oldest of Hollywood stories in the context of the newest mass medium.

The most recent medium to affect cinema has already proven to be the most significant. The computer, in the guise of digital editing of digitized 35mm footage; high-end special effects and animation (*Titanic* and *Toy Story II*); the Internet as a medium for cinema and cinemalike marketing, distribution, and presentation; and the "desktop studio" of PC, low-budget editing and effects software, and video/digital camera (*The Blair Witch Project*, 1999) has already so upset the boundaries and traditions of Hollywood production that the October 1999 cover of *Wired* magazine (bible of the information revolution) dubbed its special edition on the future of cinema *Life After Hollywood*. In such a context, the more considerable question might soon focus on how the computer/Internet medium depicts old media such as cinema, television, radio, and print—or, more drastically, whether we should or can distinguish between media at all.

References

Filmography

Absence of Malice (1981, F)
All the President's Men (1976, F)
Almost Golden: The Jessica Savitch Story (1995, TV)
American Graffiti (1973, F)
Between the Lines (1977, F)
The Big Broadcast (1932, F)
The Big Broadcast of 1936 (1935, F)
The Big Broadcast of 1937 (1936, F)
The Big Broadcast of 1938 (1938, F)
Blessed Event (1932, F)
Bonfire of the Vanities (1990, F)
Broadcast News (1987, F)
The Chase (1994, F)
The China Syndrome (1979, F)
Choose Me (1984, F)
Citizen Kane (1941, F)
Colossus: The Forbin Project (1970, F)
The Electric Horseman (1979, F)
Escape from Crime (1942, F)
Exclusive (1937, F)
Fear and Loathing in Las Vegas (1998, F)
Five Star Final (1931, F)
FM (1978, F)
Francis Covers the Big Town (1953, F)
The Front Page (1931, F; 1974, F)
Hackers (1995, F)
Hero (1992, F)
His Girl Friday (1940, F)
Hit the Ice (1943, F)
The Howling (1981, F)
I. F. Stone's Weekly (1973, D)
The Image (1990, F)
It Happens Every Thursday (1953, F)
The Last American Hero (1973, F)
The Lawnmower Man (1992, F)
Libeled Lady (1936, F)
Life Begins at Forty (1935, F)
The Matrix (1999, F)
Meet John Doe (1941, F)
The Murder Man (1935, F)
Mystery Train (1989, F)
Nancy Drew—Reporter (1939, F)
Nerds 2.0.1 (1998, D)
Network (1976, F)
The Paper (1994, F)
The Parallax View (1974, F)
Platinum Blonde (1931, F)
Pleasantville (1998, F)
Pump up the Volume (1990, F)
Radio Days (1987, F)
Radioland Murders (1994, F)
The Right Stuff (1983, F)
Strange Days (1995, F)

Street Smart (1987, F)
Switching Channels (1988, F)
Talk Radio (1988, F)
Teacher's Pet (1958, F)
The Truman Show (1998, F)
The Truth About Cats and Dogs (1996, F)
Tune in Tomorrow (1990, F)
Two Against the World (1936, F)
2001: A Space Odyssey (1968, F)
Up Close and Personal (1996, F)
Virtuosity (1995, F)
Wag the Dog (1997, F)
War Games (1983, F)
The War Room (1993, D)
Where the Buffalo Roam (1980, F)
WUSA (1970, F)
You've Got Mail (1998, F)

Bibliography

Baughman, James L. *The Republic of Mass Culture: Journalism, Filmmaking, and Broadcasting in America since 1941.* 2d ed. Baltimore: Johns Hopkins University Press, 1997.

Cringely, Robert X. *Accidental Empires: How the Boys of Silicon Valley Make Their Millions, Battle Foreign Competition, and Still Can't Get a Date.* New York: Addison-Wesley, 1992.

Good, Howard. *Girl Reporter: Gender, Journalism, and the Movies.* Lanham, MD: Scarecrow, 1998.

——. *Outcasts: The Image of Journalists in Contemporary Film.* Metuchen, NJ: Scarecrow, 1989.

Kael, Pauline. *5001 Nights at the Movies.* New York: Henry Holt, 1982.

Langman, Larry. *The Media in the Movies: A Catalog of American Journalism Films, 1900–1996.* Jefferson, NC: McFarland, 1997.

Murray, Janet H. *Hamlet on the Holodeck: The Future of Narrative in Cyberspace.* Cambridge, MA: MIT Press, 1997.

Stephens, Mitchell. *A History of News: From the Drum to the Satellite.* New York: Viking, 1988.

Toll, Robert C. *The Entertainment Machine: American Show Business in the Twentieth Century.* New York: Oxford University Press, 1982.

[MICHAEL SHULL AND DAVID WILT]

The Labor Movement and the Working Class

The history of organized labor in the United States dates back to the 1790s, when groups of Philadelphia carpenters—and a few years later, shoemakers—banded together and went on strike for better wages. The early nineteenth century saw a significant growth in unions, including some organizations that cut across craft lines and others that attempted to bring together groups from different towns and cities. Business leaders and elected officials frowned upon the idea of organized labor, and numerous trials for conspiracy resulted, seriously undermining the attempts of the unions to consolidate their gains. After the Civil War, labor tried again, business responded, and an era of militant—even violent—labor-management clashes ensued. During this period, strikes occurred in the railroad, mining, textile, and manufacturing industries, to name a few. In 1886, the Haymarket Riot—which broke out following the deaths of six striking workers—left eleven dead, including seven policemen, in Chicago. Four union leaders were convicted of murder and hanged. Other notorious clashes included the 1892 Homestead steel strike, and the 1894 Pullman railroad strike. In many cases the unions—faced with opposition from both their employers and the government—failed to gain their objectives; yet the movement continued to grow. By 1914, total trade union membership in the United States stood at 2.67 million, and it had increased by more than a million by 1920 (Bimba, 226, 308).

After World War I, business made a concerted effort to break the union movement, alarmed by the specter of a "workers' revolt," allegedly under the auspices of the Industrial Workers of the World. Big business promoted the "American plan," nullifying the "closed shop" union concept. Another wave of labor strife ensued, including the violent West Virginia coalfield struggles later memorialized in *Matewan* (1987), and the 1926 Passaic (New Jersey) Textile Strike, which lasted nearly a year. The "virulent anti-union campaign . . . had left the labor movement reeling by the end of the twenties" (Watkins, 211).

The National Industrial Recovery Act (1933), the centerpiece of the Roosevelt administration's early efforts to battle the Depression, stated that employees had the "right to organize and bargain collectively through representation of their own choosing" (Watkins, 189). This sparked a major organizing drive among unions, which not only set out to regain ground they had lost during the 1920s but also moved into areas where they had never been successful before. Another key piece of legislation was the National Labor Relations Act (also known as the "Wagner Act," after its Senate sponsor) of 1935, which labor historian Philip Taft considers "the greatest legislative victory gained by organized labor in American history" (Taft, 451). This major work of New Deal legislation guaranteed the right of workers to organize or join a union without fear of reprisals and codified the right of employees to negotiate with employers. Growth of unions in this period did not come without strife: beginning in 1934, conflicts began to occur frequently, reaching a peak of 4,700 strikes in 1937 (Taft, 853).

World War II and the immediate postwar years marked a watershed for American unions; membership remained steady at around fifteen million in the 1946–50 period (Taft, 631). The percentage of nonagricultural workers who belonged to unions peaked at around 39 percent of the U.S. workforce in the early 1950s. However, since that time, the number of union members has increased only slightly (to just over sixteen million), and the percentage of American workers who belong to unions has decreased to 13.9 percent in 1998 (Bureau of Labor Statistics). The role organized labor plays in American life has also dwindled. In the past, unions and their activities—organizing, negotiating, striking—were national news: "The labor movement is recognized as a factor in national affairs when it breaks out in disturbances or demonstrations of its power; such as strikes, boycotts or riots which make trouble for consumers, employers, the government, and the humanitarians" (Beard, 131). Today, only rare, high-profile organized labor issues are deemed worthy of attention outside of a limited, local sphere. The image of organized labor in Hollywood movies has followed the same curve.

The Hollywood film industry is one of the most heavily unionized work forces in the nation: virtually everyone in the cast and crew of any major Hollywood film belongs to a union. Yet the production companies themselves were resolutely antiunion for many years. A fair amount of strife resulted, and this ongoing conflict contributed to the ambivalent image of labor in movies: unions are sometimes positive forces protecting workers against exploitative bosses but are more often corrupt, misguided, or detrimental to the economy owing to their outrageous demands. William Puette, who has analyzed media images of organized labor, writes that "media sympathy for the working class in the United States is reserved almost exclusively for the utterly powerless and egregiously victimized. To the extent that organized labor is successful at developing bargaining power in any sector of the work force, it is vilified and attacked" (157).

Similarly, blue-collar work is shown to be honest but difficult. It is also not very interesting, which is why very few films—even those ostensibly about blue-collar workers—spend much time showing their protagonists at work. Most "labor" movies concentrate on strikes and corruption or on the personal lives of the protagonists, in keeping with the tendency of Hollywood to prefer personal stories, melodrama, and action to the thorough examination of social problems.

The Early Years of Labor on Film: 1910–1940

In the early years of the century, "Hollywood" had not yet become a monolithic industry, with production, distribution, and exhibition controlled by a handful of major studios. Instead, more than a hundred relatively small companies addressed a wide range of social issues—including the legitimate grievances of labor—often with considerable candor. More than a hundred pre–World War I films depicted strikes (Shull, 145): some are shown to be justifiable responses to exploitation; others are fomented by agitators for their own ends. The dominant message in early capital-versus-labor films is that the working class is inherently good but can be easily led astray by "outside agitators"; it is in the best interests of the nation for labor to abstain from violence and to seek a harmonious relationship with capital. Capitalists must not mistreat faithful workers, and they often share the guilt for labor conflicts.

Some early labor films, including *The Jungle* (1914) and *The Eternal Grind* (1916), contain extended scenes of workers performing their tasks, depicted in ways that create sympathy for their skill and toil. *The Eternal Grind* features Mary Pickford struggling behind a sewing machine in an unsafe sweatshop. *The Jungle* was based on Upton Sinclair's novel about the Chicago meatpacking industry, in which a ruinous strike destroys a family. Unlike most labor films of the era, *The Jungle* openly advocates socialism as an alternative to the exploitative conditions of the present. *The Valley of the Moon* (1914), taken from a Jack London story, includes scenes of a street battle between striking teamsters and replacements; police wagons are later shown trampling over the rebellious workers.

This somewhat balanced—even prolabor at times—treatment dissolved after World War I, the Red Scare that followed, and the consolidation of the movie industry. Numerous strikes occurred after the end of the war: one of the most famous was the Seattle General Strike of 1919. In *The World Aflame* (1919), a fictionalized dramatization of the events, millionaire Carson Burr runs for mayor, upset by the influence of radical propaganda on the city's labor force. The highlight of the film occurs when Burr—aboard an American-flag-draped streetcar—confronts a mob of workers. He breaks the strike, telling the men they have been "misled by alien propagandists."

The protagonist of *Dangerous Hours* (1920) falls under the spell of a foreign vamp, who works for a fanatic Bolshevik named Boris Blotchi. The subversives incite local lowlifes to ransack a small town whose shipyard workers have joined a nationwide strike. The repentant hero joins forces with loyal American working men to combat this bloodthirsty mob. During the denouement, the corrupt labor agitators—who had collaborated with the Bolsheviks—are tarred and feathered and run out of town on rails.

Other films also backed away from the earlier prolabor stance. In *Triumph* (1924), a young wastrel is disinherited and winds up as a worker in his late father's factory; his half-brother, a former agitator, is named head of the factory and overnight becomes an exploiter, suggesting that soi-disant advocates of the workers are really acting out of personal ambition. In *The Whistle* (1921), a factory worker's son is fatally mangled in a mill's improperly protected machinery: yet private enterprise is never challenged, the factory owner is sympathetically portrayed, and the good worker suffers nobly and in silence.

There were some openly prolabor productions such as *The Contrast* (1921), a feature film financed with contributions from nearly a hundred labor and radical organizations. In this picture—based on an actual strike in West Virginia—the conspicuous consumption of absentee mine owners is contrasted with the harsh lives of miners who strike to protest improper safety precautions. At the end, the owners, fearing national disaster, recognize the union. Another union-sponsored picture was *The Passaic Textile Strike* (1926), incorporating actual footage from a real strike in New Jersey. This film is highly sympathetic to labor, showing the strikers' struggle and their resistance to police harassment.

The film industry completed its transformation into big business in the 1930s. The moguls who ran the major companies strenuously resisted attempts by their workers to form new unions. Not surprisingly, this anti-union bias was reflected in some films, an attitude further influenced by the industry's own Breen Office, which asked screenwriters to avoid "radical" themes or attacks on big business. But, given the Depression, the New Deal, and other circumstances that severely affected working Americans, it was impossible for Hollywood to ignore the labor issue entirely or to portray the entire working class as radicals. A significant number of 1930s films feature blue-collar protagonists—miners, steelworkers, truck drivers, longshoremen, and the like. The trick was to make "interesting" films without resorting to the typical capital-versus-labor plot. Sometimes pictures were structured around the dangerous nature of the work, as in *Slim* (1937), in which Henry Fonda plays an electrical lineman. The workplace could serve as a catalyst for various conflicts—in *Black Legion* (1936), an automobile worker (Humphrey Bogart) joins a xenophobic hate group after losing a promotion to an immigrant.

Depression-era films usually portrayed unions as genuinely concerned with the welfare of their members, although at times unsavory or misguided elements took control. "Agitators" generally did not come from within the regular union rank and file, and most workers were portrayed as willing to give an honest day's work for an honest day's pay. Strikes arose out of misunderstandings (or were fomented by third parties), rather than in response to poor pay or dangerous working conditions.

Films actually showing labor strife were rare. In *Black Fury* (1935), Paul Muni plays a simple coal miner who is duped by a dissenter in his union (the agitator is trying to cause trouble because he secretly works for a company supplying guards to mine owners). A strike breaks out, a good union leader is beaten to death by the hired goons, and Muni's character stages a one-man occupation of the mine, threatening to blow it up unless the company and the union negotiate. The original script of this film—based on an actual incident—was toned down at the request of the Breen Office, which had been contacted by an association of mine owners. Breen urged Warner Bros. to downplay scenes of "serious conflict between employer and employee" (American Film Institute 175–176).

Together We Live (1935) was inspired by the 1934 San Francisco General Strike, which began with a bloody confrontation between striking longshoremen and police. In the film, a communist-led strike culminates with a plot to bomb a factory; fortunately, the patriotic residents of a local veterans' home foil the scheme. The Production Code Authority agreed to certify the film only if it contained no "direct attacks on organized labor, capitalism, or constituted forces of law and order" (American Film Institute, 2,224).

FIGURE 48. *Black Fury* (1935). Joe Radek (Paul Muni) and fellow miners stand silently behind steel gates, blocking them from work in a strike where the company and union refuse to negotiate. In anger, Muni finds his way into the mine and threatens its destruction if negotiations do not proceed. Courtesy First National Pictures and Warner Bros.

World War II and Beyond: 1941–1969

Cinematic preparations for the U.S. entry into World War II began even before the actual declaration of hostilities. *Three Girls About Town* (1941) is one such example. It concerns a strike in the aircraft industry and includes a rare depiction of collective bargaining. The need for "national defense" is a deciding issue in settling the strike. Although *Native Land* was released in 1942, this independent production (from Frontier Films) had been on the drawing board for several years. Activist singer and actor Paul Robeson narrates the film, which mixes documentary footage and dramatic re-creations of actual events, such as the brutal repression of black and white sharecroppers who are trying to organize into a union. *Native Land* is overtly patriotic but implies at least a philosophical connection between totalitarians and "fascist-minded corporations," suggesting that the "enemies from within" are as dangerous as the threat from abroad.

Once the United States officially joined the Allies, organized labor made a so-called no-strike pledge. Indeed, there was a reluctance to be perceived as either "war profiteers" (on management's side) or "unpatriotic" (on the part of labor). As the war went on, however, the number of work stoppages increased. Most labor-oriented war films were positive in their outlook, lauding the contributions of manufacturers and workers to the Allied cause. Although these films paid lip service to the contribution of the working man (and woman) to the war effort, the plots of some pictures explicitly depicted factory workers urgently trying to leave their jobs and join the armed forces to "really" serve their country (Shull and Wilt, 258–259).

Man from Frisco (1944) fictionalizes the Liberty Ship program developed by Henry Kaiser, but the only problems encountered are logistical (housing for workers) and technical (assembling prefabricated ships in record time). The entry of women into the industrial labor force was featured in movies such as *Rosie the Riveter* (1944). While women were generally portrayed as effective workers, these films concentrated on romance and only occasionally ventured into the workplace.

Because strikes or salary disputes were rarely touched upon, unions were practically invisible in wartime films. One exception was *Action in the North Atlantic* (1943), about merchant marine ships delivering supplies to Russia. The survivors of a ship sunk by a Nazi submarine return to the United States; some are reluctant to sign up for another dangerous trip, until—in a scene set in the union hiring hall—one of their number makes a speech encouraging them to do their part, both as patriotic Americans and as dedicated workers. During the McCarthy period, this film was involved in a controversy over its alleged radical content: one of the screenwriters was John Howard Lawson, whose Communist affiliations made him one of the "Hollywood Ten."

Although the labor scene had been relatively calm during the war years, the cessation of hostilities was the signal for a new round of conflict between labor and management. The year 1946 was perhaps the most contentious in the history of labor-management relations: there were nearly five thousand work stoppages involving millions of workers. In the wake of this wave of conflict, Congress passed the Taft-Hartley Act: one provision allowed the invocation of a cooling-off period, postponing a strike to give labor and management more time to negotiate.

The anticommunist fervor of the postwar era also had an impact on the public's perception of organized labor. One provision of the Taft-Hartley Act was the requirement that union officers sign a statement denying membership in (or sympathy with) the Communist Party. In 1949 and 1950, the CIO (Congress of Industrial Organizations) expelled eleven unions that were allegedly led or controlled by leftists; nearly one million workers were "unceremoniously dumped" from the CIO (Lorence, 20). The idea that unions could be controlled by communists was featured in pictures like *The Woman on Pier 13* (1950), which dealt with West Coast dock unions, and *I Was A Communist for the FBI* (1951), which depicted communist infiltration of steelworkers' unions in Pittsburgh. In the latter film, the subversives—under the guise of helping the workers—want to incite class and racial violence to destroy America. *Big Jim McLain* (1952) also refers to communist infiltration of unions. All three of these films cite the Korean War as an example of international communist aggression, point out the need for production to help the war effort, and suggest that communists in unions may serve as saboteurs in time of war.

Another trend was the portrayal of unions as pawns of organized crime: honest workers are manipulated and exploited by their mobster union officers. *On the Waterfront* (1954) depicts the brutal treatment of workers by racketeers who demand salary kickbacks from laborers in exchange for the opportunity to work, capped by beatings and even murder of those who dissent. The capital-labor conflict is forgotten: now workers are oppressed by the very organization formed to protect them. This theme also appeared in films like *Edge of the City* (1957) and *Never Steal Anything Small*

(1959). The latter picture stars James Cagney as a waterfront hood who wants to win back control of the stevedores' union from the mafia types currently in office. The picture is a mix of anti- and pro-union messages, alternating references to strikes and union corruption with laudatory invocations of such union heroes as Samuel Gompers, George Meaney, and Walter Reuther.

One pro-union film of the era was *Salt of the Earth* (1954), financed by mineworkers and directed by a blacklisted Hollywood director, Herbert J. Biberman. Based on a real incident and filmed on location, the picture portrays the struggle of zinc miners in New Mexico who want improvements in living and working conditions. They go on strike; in a gesture of solidarity, their wives on the picket line replace them when the company gets a court injunction against the miners themselves. Ironically, the union in question (the International Union of Mine, Mill and Smelter Employees) had been expelled from the CIO. Because of the "tainted" nature of its production, *Salt of the Earth* received very little theatrical distribution in the United States, although its reputation has grown over the years and the film is now a classroom staple.

The 1970s

From the end of the 1950s through the early 1970s, relatively few films dealt with organized labor. The collapse of the studio system—which gave rise to many independent productions—ushered in an era marked by a number of significant movies about labor.

Director Martin Ritt's *The Molly Maguires* (1970), set in 1876 Pennsylvania, portrays a band of Irish miners who sabotage coal company operations when their union fails to win concessions from the owners. An undercover detective (Richard Harris) exposes their plot, and twenty men are executed. Historians question whether the Molly Maguires were actually guilty of a terrorist conspiracy, or if they were railroaded because of their union organizing activities, but Walter Bernstein's script—although it is somewhat ambivalent about the morality of the Pinkerton spy—does not question the guilt of the "Mollies."

In Martin Scorsese's *Boxcar Bertha* (1972), set in the 1930s, Bertha (Barbara Hershey) and "Big Bill" Shelley turn to banditry in the name of poor and oppressed railroad workers. Eventually, Bill is caught and nailed to the side of a boxcar by company goons. David Carradine, who played Big Bill, would also portray folksinger Woody Guthrie in *Bound for Glory* (1976), which details Guthrie's populist, pro-union activities of the 1930s.

Which Way Is Up? (1977), stars Richard Pryor as a fruit picker who falls out of a tree onto a picket line and is photographed with Hispanic labor leader Juarez (that is, Cesar Chavez). His alleged personal relationship with Juarez makes Pryor's character a marked man, threatened and courted by labor and management alike. This film's comedic treatment of farmworkers contrasts strongly with the television documentary *Harvest of Shame* (1960). Made by "CBS Reports," this controversial film examined the plight of migrant workers, living and working in abysmal conditions. *The Fight in the Fields* (1997) was a documentary about the life and struggle of Cesar Chavez and his United Farmworkers Union.

Richard Pryor also appeared in *Blue Collar* (1978), in which three workers at an automobile factory become disillusioned with their ineffectual union and their oppressive jobs. Robbing the union, they find only a small amount of cash and proof the union is engaged in loan sharking. The three hatch a blackmail plot which ends tragically: one man is murdered, another is named union representative in exchange for his silence, and a third is rejected by his fellow workers when he goes to the FBI.

Martin Ritt's *Norma Rae* (1979), based on a real-life incident, takes place in a Southern cotton-mill town dominated by the company.

Norma Rae (Sally Field) works in the mill but gradually becomes radicalized: her mother is losing her hearing from excessive noise levels in the plant, and her father literally drops dead at work, his earlier complaints ignored by the foreman. With the aid of a Jewish labor organizer (Ron Liebman) from New York, Norma fights for unionization despite threats and harassment from the company. At the film's conclusion, the union wins the election among the plant workers. *Norma Rae* is, like *Salt of the Earth,* one of the few completely pro-union sound features: the workers just want fair treatment, while the company is portrayed as both callous and exploitative.

The 1980s and 1990s

Over the past two decades, only a few films have significantly addressed labor issues. One theme, seen in movies such as *Breaking Away* (1979) and *October Sky* (1999), is that "manual labor" is the work of the previous generation, and that youth should aspire to something better. These "escape" films do not criticize those who continue to work in blue-collar professions, but the jobs themselves are shown to be dirty, dangerous, and no longer secure or well paid.

The River (1984) combines the farm crisis and labor: a midwestern farmer, victimized by the economy, by floods, and by a greedy businessman, joins a group of "scabs" in a strike-plagued factory in order to make ends meet. The replacements work in a state of siege and, when the strike is settled, are cast off by the company on a hour's notice and are forced to exit through a hostile gauntlet of the workers whose jobs they had been filling.

U.S. automobile workers had won major concessions in a hundred-day strike against General Motors in 1945–46, but by the 1970s the industry was reeling as a result of foreign competition (the steel industry was similarly threatened by overseas producers). Carmakers tried to fight back, but some of their methods led to new conflicts with labor. The documentary *Roger & Me* (1989) chronicles filmmaker Michael Moore's futile attempt to interview Roger Smith, president of General Motors, after a round of plant closings. In *Gung Ho* (1986), a union shop steward convinces a Japanese automaker to buy a now-shuttered factory. The workers are at first overjoyed to get their jobs back, but then are shocked at the loss of their union-brokered high salaries. Eventually, the Japanese management concept, combined with the promise of a lot of overtime pay, wins over the Americans. *Rising Son* (1990) has a similar basic premise: a family-owned factory in Pennsylvania has been sold to a giant corporation. Among those affected is World War II veteran Gus (Brian Dennehy), who worked his way up through the ranks to a supervisory position but eventually loses his job through layoffs and downsizing. The film points out how Japanese competition and "Reaganomics" (the film is set in the early 1980s) brought about hard times for American manufacturers and, in a domino effect, on labor. In one scene Gus berates his workforce for losing their work ethic; in another, he visits a semi-automated factory where the union representative at his old plant now works (ironically, since the robots will obviously not join unions). The role of organized labor was further marginalized in *Tommy Boy* (1995), where the task of saving an auto-parts factory that has been targeted for takeover and closure by a large corporation is spearheaded not by the union, but by the previously ineffectual son (Chris Farley) of the late owner (also played by Brian Dennehy). The factory workers are reduced to cheerleaders for the earnest but buffoonish junior capitalist.

Mineworkers have been featured in numerous films since the silent era. Director Barbara Kopple won an Academy Award for her documentary *Harlan County U.S.A.* (1977), about a contemporary strike by miners in Kentucky. A decade later, director John Sayles's *Matewan* (1987) returned to the topic. Set in West Virginia in the 1920s, it portrays attempts to organize the workers—whites, African Americans, and immigrant Italians—and the violent reaction of a private security company hired by the mine owners.

Hoffa (1992), a biography of the famed Teamsters leader, contains scenes of labor violence as hired goons and the police assault picketers; later, Hoffa is accused of links to organized crime and jailed. He returns to his post upon his release, but mysteriously disappears in 1975. *Hoffa* is certainly a prolabor film, although it is not a whitewash.

Marginalized Labor

One film historian suggests that "we have failed to appreciate Hollywood's part in shaping the public's image of organized labor" (Walsh, 564). The vague overall message seems to be that companies should not abuse their workers, force them to work in unsafe conditions for low pay, or hire thugs to violently repress union efforts; on the other hand, unions should not demand excessive wages and benefits, should not swindle their members or blackmail employers, and should not strike (except when necessary, for strikes inconvenience the rest of us) or use violence. Labor scholar William Puette argues that "the portrayal of unions in the media, particularly in movies, plays a major role in shaping the attitudes of Americans toward labor unions. With few exceptions, that portrayal has been both unrepresentative and virulently negative" (31).

In recent years, however, the image of organized labor has not been so much negative as absent: unions are increasingly seen as irrelevant. Screen images of working men and women are growing less and less frequent. As organized labor becomes increasingly marginalized, its role in films is also dwindling. Films reflect the status of unions in contemporary America: only one in seven American workers now belongs to a union (one of ten in the private sector) (Bureau of Labor Statistics). Consequently, instead of a policy of active hostility, Hollywood now files "organized labor" in the category of "uninteresting topics" and largely ignores it.

References

Filmography

Action in the North Atlantic (1943, F)
Big Jim McLain (1952, F)
Black Fury (1935, F)
Black Legion (1936, F)
Blue Collar (1978, F)
Bound for Glory (1976, F)
Boxcar Bertha (1972, F)
Breaking Away (1979, F)
The Contrast (1921, F)
Dangerous Hours (1920, F)
Edge of the City (1957, F)
The Eternal Grind (1916, F)
The Fight in the Fields (1997, D)
Gung Ho (1986, F)
Harlan County U.S.A. (1977, D)
Harvest of Shame (1960, TV)
Hoffa (1992, F)
I Was a Communist for the FBI (1951, F)
The Jungle (1914, F)
The Life and Times of Rosie the Riveter (1988, D)
Man from Frisco (1944, F)
Matewan (1987, F)
The Molly Maguires (1970, F)
Native Land (1942, F)
Never Steal Anything Small (1959, F)
Norma Rae (1979, F)
October Sky (1999, F)
On the Waterfront (1954, F)
The Passaic Textile Strike (1926, F)
Rising Son (1990, F)
The River (1984, F)
Roger and Me (1989, F)
Rosie the Riveter (1944, F)
Salt of the Earth (1954, F)
Slim (1937, F)
Three Girls About Town (1941, F)
Together We Live (1935, F)
Tommy Boy (1995, F)
Triumph (1924, F)
The Valley of the Moon (1914, F)
Which Way Is Up? (1977, F)
The Whistle (1921, F)
The Woman on Pier 13 (1950, F)
The World Aflame (1919, F)

Bibliography

American Film Institute. *The American Film Institute Catalog of Motion Pictures Produced in the United States: Feature Films, 1931–1940.* Berkeley: University of California Press, 1993.

Beard, Mary Ritter. *The American Labor Movement: A Short History.* New York: Macmillan, 1931.

Bergman, Andrew. *We're in the Money: Depression America and Its Films.* New York: New York University Press, 1971.

Bimba, Anthony. *The History of the American Working Class.* New York: International Publishers, 1927.

Brownlow, Kevin. *Behind the Mask of Innocence: Sex, Violence, Prejudice, Crime—Films of Social Conscience in the Silent Era.* Berkeley: University of California Press, 1990.

Bureau of Labor Statistics, U.S. Department of Labor. *Monthly Labor Review,* 28 January 1997 and 28 January 1999.

Lorence, James J. *The Suppression of* Salt of the Earth*: How Hollywood, Big Labor, and Politicians Blacklisted a Movie in Cold War America.* Albuquerque: University of New Mexico Press, 1999.

Puette, William J. *Through Jaundiced Eyes: How the Media View Organized Labor.* Ithaca, NY: ILR Press, 1992.

Roffman, Peter, and Jim Purdy. *The Hollywood Social Problem Film: Madness, Despair, and Politics from the Depression to the Fifties.* Bloomington: Indiana University Press, 1981.

Ross, Steven J. *Working-Class Hollywood: Silent Film and the Shaping of Class in America.* Princeton: Princeton University Press, 1998.

Shull, Michael S. *Radicalism in American Silent Films, 1909-1929.* Jefferson, NC: McFarland, 2000.

Shull, Michael S., and David Wilt. *Hollywood War Films, 1937–1945.* Jefferson, NC: McFarland, 1996.

Taft, Philip. *Organized Labor in American History.* New York: Harper & Row, 1964.

Walsh, Francis R. "The Films We Never Saw: American Movies View Organized Labor, 1934–1954." *Labor History* 27.4 (1986): 564–580.

Watkins, T. H. *The Hungry Years: A Narrative History of the Great Depression in America.* New York: Henry Holt, 1999.

Zaniello, Tom. *Working Stiffs, Union Maids, Reds, and Riffraff: An Organized Guide to Films about Labor.* Ithaca, NY: Cornell University Press, 1996.

[MICHAEL J. RILEY]

Militias and Extremist Political Movements

The Constitution of the United States allows for the maintenance of armed militias and—arguably—invests the citizenry with an individual right to keep and bear arms. Furthermore, the Declaration of Independence asserts that citizens have the right to rebel against oppressive tyranny. Indeed, the United States has a long tradition of people banding into armed groups to promote political and ideological aims, beginning with the American Revolution, and continuing through movements as diverse as the Ku Klux Klan after the Civil War, the Black Panthers in the 1960s, and the Symbionese Liberation Army in the 1970s. Indeed, the 1990s witnessed an outpouring of public attention to the rise of a neoconservative "militia movement." For example, Morris Dees's Southern Poverty Law Center in Atlanta tracked more than eight hundred self-proclaimed "militia" or "patriot" groups operating during that decade. These groups tend to believe that power should be dispersed in the hands of the populace via a paramilitary, that the profusion of records documenting the individual threatens liberty, that communism continues to threaten world domination, and that the righteousness of the American character must be protected at all costs. The extreme end of the militia movement steps far beyond beliefs widespread in contemporary American culture to embrace racial separatism, violent insurrection, and belief in the rise of a conspiratorial one-world government often referred to as "ZOG" (Zionist Occupation Government).

Characteristically local, loosely structured, and heavily armed, members of the militia groups believe theirs is a righteous cause: the last stand of traditional "American" ideals in the face of a burgeoning monster—the federal government. Although not all militias are racist, they do include white supremacist organizations such as the Aryan Nations, White Aryan Resistance, and The Order—groups who see their causes as justified by God's higher law and the Constitution. Indeed, the roots of such ideas go deep. According to some scholars, including Bernard Bailyn, the American Revolution was also predicated on the belief that a conspiracy within the colonial government was set to undermine guaranteed personal liberties. Richard Hofstadter has also identified the "paranoid style" as a distinct populist tradition within American politics: "The central image is that of a vast and sinister conspiracy, a gigantic and yet subtle machinery of influence set in motion to undermine and destroy a way of life" ("Paranoid Politics," 161). Yet today, because of fervent racial ideologies and advocacy of violence, the term "militia movement" has acquired ominous connotations in the popular culture, carrying with it dark overtones of racism, paranoia, and political upheaval. To their detractors, militias potentially endanger the stability of the nation and the safety of the people.

The struggle pitting individual against collective rights has long been an important theme in American politics. For example, Hofstadter has stated, "Lynching and vigilantism have so few parallels or equivalents elsewhere that they can be regarded as distinctly American institutions" ("Reflections," 20). Hofstadter's position may be somewhat overstated; certainly, recent times have seen notable mob attacks in many nations, often along ethnic, religious, or nationalistic lines. Nonetheless, such forms of violence have fascinated the public and been reflected in American film, where treatments of militias emerge early and forcefully. One of the most notable examples is D. W. Griffith's silent classic *The Birth of a Nation* (1915). Made only five decades after the Civil War and widely heralded as a cinematic masterwork for its innovative film language, Griffith's epic stirred debate for its sympathetic celebration of the Ku Klux Klan. Although the film opened to a strong response at the box office and largely glowing reviews, John Higham points out in his seminal work *Strangers in the Land,* it became controversial for its portrayal of white victimization during carpetbag regimes—a point of view widespread within the popular consciousness of the day. Wyn Wade further contends that although fiercely opposed by the NAACP and racial activists, only minor changes were made to the film to appease criticism.

Violence in the Wild West

As America stepped up its military and civilian expansion into the West after the Civil War, violent conflict figured recurrently. Indeed, the history of the region is one of warring and domination, and, throughout the twentieth century, Hollywood has demonstrated a particular fondness for portraying the violent side of westward migration. Indeed, the first television generation was steeped in images of conflict in the Wild West. In this regard, author James Gibson suggests that a Wild West mindset became paradigmatic in American culture with the rise of mass media—particularly the moving image. Furthermore, Gibson held that the contemporary militia movement is tied to a cowboy mentality fostered by the media, but in this case the popular mythos of the western mixes with a shoot-'em-up mythology as a means of overcoming unresolved anxieties, such as those stemming from America's loss in the Vietnam War.

At any rate, the cinema is fraught with images of warring in the West, and several westerns depict groups that might be construed as militias. A particularly notable example is *The Big Country* (1958), a powerful tale of two private armies involved in a range war over water. The film ends when retired sea captain James McKay (Gregory Peck), who steadfastly refuses to ally with either side, finally puts his life on the line by stepping between the factions. This is a film about how, in the absence of law and without tolerance, justice becomes subverted by special interests. In contrast, *The Alamo* (1960)—an epic financed and directed by John Wayne—celebrated the violence of history by depicting the last stand of an armed group "selfless patriots," heroes in the fight to divorce Texas from Mexico in 1836. Yet by 1973 a far less optimistic rendering of militias is found in Clint Eastwood's *High Plains Drifter,* where a small town hires a mysterious stranger (played by Eastwood) to train the locals so they can resist outlaws who have been terrorizing the town. Reflecting the moral ambiguity following the 1960s, the formation of a local militia is portrayed as just, yet ultimately ineffectual: the townspeople back down, leaving the gunfighter to stand alone.

A modern-day militia film that continues the tradition of the western is Arthur Penn's *The Chase* (1966), which pits Sheriff Calder (Marlon Brando) against a group of gung-ho vigilantes determined to capture or kill escaped convict Bubber Reeves (Robert Redford). Despite the fact that he must go it alone with little support, the sheriff is eventually able to bring in his prisoner. But the film ends as a vigilante murders the convict in a moment eerily reminiscent of Jack Ruby's execution of accused presidential assassin Lee Harvey Oswald in November 1963. Perhaps the most poignant line of the film is spoken as the lawman seeks to draw a line between justice and vigilantism:

"The State of Texas says everybody can own a gun, and most of you got two, but deputies you ain't. So you just stay drunk and forget about it." Those words crystallize a sense of divisiveness between public officials and self-proclaimed militia groups when authority is in dispute.

Cold War Patriotism

Born of the collective fears surrounding the rise of the "military-industrial complex" during the Cold War, another genre of film has focused on fervent patriotic nationalism but also poses difficult questions about authority. A brilliantly dark picture emerges in John Frankenheimer's *Seven Days in May* (1964), which focuses on a cabal formed within the military by General James Scott (Burt Lancaster), chairman of the Joint Chiefs of Staff, to stage a coup against president Jordan Lyman (Fredric March) after he signs a nuclear disarmament treaty. This film pits two oppositional forms of patriotism: one (governmental) adhering to the established law and authority, and another (military) proclaiming itself representative of the true intentions of the founding fathers and the security interests of the nation. As such, *Seven Days* is excellent for framing questions of patriotism through disputed claims of legitimacy held by political factions.

Another film about defiance of government on moral grounds is *Taps* (1981), in which students at a military academy faced with closure seize the campus and engage in armed confrontation with the National Guard. In one poignant moment, the colonel in charge of the guardsmen (Ronny Cox) tries to explain public sentiment to the cadet major (Timothy Hutton): "They don't see you guys as rebels with a good cause; they think you're home-grown terrorists. And quite frankly, it's got 'em scared shitless. Nice American boys don't act like this." With both sides unwilling to second-guess their self-righteous "might makes right" attitudes, this thought-provoking albeit overstated film ends in tragedy and death wrought by armed confrontation. The kindred—and equally violent—*Red Dawn* (1984), on the other hand, sings the virtues of armed resistance to an imagined invasion of the western United States by Soviet and Cuban paratroopers, an event plausible only in the filmmaker's imagination.

Racial Violence and Civil Rights

The threat of violence is de rigueur in films treating the rise of militias and extremist political movements. Indeed, the ties between political extremism and racism crop up more overtly and more frequently in films produced after the civil rights movement. For example, in *The Chase* the vigilantes attempt to shoot a black man they suspect of sexual involvement with a white woman (Jane Fonda). The systemic racial vigilantism ingrained in communities is the subject of *Mississippi Burning* (1988). A sophisticated period film set in the mid-1960s and based on fact, it pits two FBI agents (Gene Hackman and Willem Dafoe) against the Ku Klux Klan after the disappearance of three youths who had been working to register black voters. However, the film was criticized for its willingness to rewrite historical details for dramatic effect, and for its focus on FBI agents rather than black activists (Toplin, 25–44, 226). The film is brutally violent and ripe with a sense of the fear, vulnerability, and poverty experienced by rural blacks, who often saw federal agents as ineffectual allies only a little less troublesome than the Klansmen. While pursuing themes of domination and the collision of cultures, it builds on divisions within the FBI over the abuse of power, contrasting a local culture seemingly incapable of change against the vague promises of outsiders. In the end the film raises more questions than it answers, when a small, expensive "victory" by government agents leaves the community swathed in destruction and turmoil. The same ambivalence characterizes Michael Apted's *Thunderheart* (1992), in which a

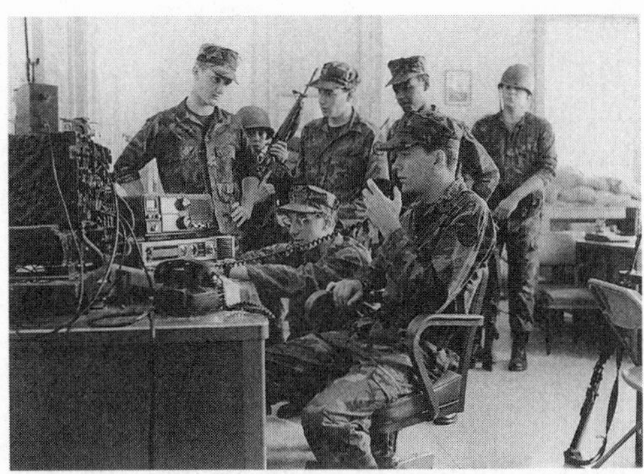

FIGURE 49. *Taps* (1981). Brian Moreland (Timothy Hutton, seated) leads a group of rebellious cadets who refuse to accept the decision to close their military academy for the development of condominiums on the land. Courtesy Twentieth Century-Fox.

part-Indian FBI agent (Val Kilmer) must decide where he stands on the matter of American Indian resistance to both white encroachment and intratribal political corruption.

A less successful portrayal of racial intolerance is *Betrayed* (1988), which also focuses on an FBI investigation. In this case a female agent (Debra Winger) infiltrates a hate group after a Jewish disk jockey is gunned down, recalling the assassination of Denver radio announcer Alan Berg by an Aryan supremacist group, The Order. The film is hampered by its failure to explain a belief system that believes that its actions to bring down a corrupt government are biblically commanded. Instead, it mires in a contrived love affair between the agent and the militia leader (Tom Berenger). Oliver Stone's *Talk Radio* (1988) is also loosely based on the murder of Berg, yet it fails to examine closely the motivations of the killers. Both of these stylized Hollywood undertakings make an interesting contrast to the Bill Moyers documentary *Hate on Trial: Challenging the First Amendment* (1992), which covers a 1990 civil trial of Tom and John Metzger for inciting skinheads in Portland, Oregon, to kill an Ethiopian immigrant. This film, which includes long sessions of testimony interspersed with commentary by legal and civil liberties scholars, is a valuable but often plodding record. Still, it holds considerable potential to spur debate about the relationship between freedom of speech and violence.

Confrontational Politics

Justifiably or not, in some cases violence has also been used by the government to quell personal liberties. *Ambush in Waco* (1995) provides a good example. A dramatization based on an infamous 1993 federal siege of the Branch Davidian compound outside Waco, Texas, which resulted in ninety deaths, it reinforces a popular perspective that the beliefs of extremists can be explained only through madness—hence vindicating the federal attack. Although it represents a position widely believed by the mainstream and espoused in the news media, the film lacks the balanced treatment one might expect from a quality documentary. On the other hand, the highly controversial Academy Award–nominated documentary *Waco: The Rules of Engagement* (1997) presents a provocatively oppositional picture: it suggests that the assault on the compound was in retaliation for the shooting of four federal agents at the beginning of the standoff and that government actions were designed to obscure the truth.

One of the more successful examinations of confrontational politics is *Skokie* (1981), which uses a Hollywood cast led by Danny Kaye to create the feel of a documentary. Factually based on events that occurred in a largely Jewish Chicago suburb, it dramatizes the activities of neo-Nazis planning a march. Legal maneuvers pit the city, which opposed the march, against the ACLU, working on behalf of First Amendment rights. Rather than reveling in bloodshed, however, its violence remains psychological—located in threats and potential skirmishes that never materialize yet create turmoil in a community where many older citizens are Holocaust survivors. One effect is to raise the question of who is the "militia" when neither side represents the government and both seek to wield words and weapons against the other? Narratives of the Holocaust are powerful and poignant elements of this film, but its real strength is its exploration of philosophical underpinnings of law, contrasted with the emotional underpinnings of hate. After viewing *Skokie*, one might hate neo-Nazism all the more while understanding it better.

Racial extremism is allowed to run rampant in the remarkable documentary *Blood in the Face* (1991), which films the militia movement at the ground level. Shot largely at local gatherings of violent, racist groups, this gripping and frank portrayal of hate mongering focuses on the beliefs of the Aryan Movement. Allowing its proponents to speak for themselves, the film is assembled into a collage of bizarre ranting and raving—vague theories that 35,000 Viet Cong are operating in the wilds of British Columbia and pithy quotes like "All I'm gonna say is sieg heil, and let's go eat!" Part of the appeal of the militia movement is that it caters to people who feel they are being victimized; who espouse a xenophobic sentiment that, despite their racial superiority, they are victims of a dark conspiracy to destroy (white) American cultural traditions. As Christian Identity minister Alan Poe states in the film, "They have so misled our people, that truth has become a lie, and the lie is the truth." Drawing on the sentiment of white victimization that infused *The Birth of a Nation*, these militial ideologies are also explored in Tony Kaye's *American History X* (1998), for which Edward Norton, playing a repentant neo-Nazi, earned an Academy Award nomination for best actor.

Radical Politics and the Zeitgeist

Like the multiheaded hydra of Greek mythology, the portrayal of militias within American film takes many forms. Although most cinematic treatments of militias have been based in part on actual events, they tend to blur the lines separating documentary, history, and drama. Often seeking interpretive rather than factual portrayals, they tend to present ideologically driven histories that may be most useful as a litmus test of the salient issues and zeitgeist of their times. Radical political movements bring with them loaded issues as surely as loaded guns. If nothing else, it becomes clear that the film industry has difficulty penetrating fringe and extremist cultures to render them in all their complexities. Given their currency in the United States and their enduring history, militia movements warrant better treatment by visual media than they have received to date.

References

Filmography

The Alamo (1960, F)
Ambush in Waco (1995, F)
American History X (1998, F)
Betrayed (1988, F)
The Big Country (1958, F)
The Birth of a Nation (1915, F)
Blood in the Face (1991, D)
The Chase (1966, F)
Hate on Trial: Challenging the First Amendment (1992, D)
High Plains Drifter (1973, F)
Incident at Oglala (1992, D)
Mississippi Burning (1988, F)
Nightmare in Big Sky Country (1998, F)
Red Dawn (1984, F)
Seven Days in May (1964, F)
Skokie (1981, F)
Talk Radio (1988, F)
Taps (1981, F)
Thunderheart (1992, F)
Waco: The Rules of Engagement (1997, D)

Bibliography

Bailyn, Bernard. *The Origins of American Politics.* New York: Knopf, 1970.
Collier, John, and Malcolm Collier. *Visual Anthropology: Photography as a Research Method.* Albuquerque: University of New Mexico Press, 1986.
Coppola, Vincent. *Dragons of God: A Journey Through Far-Right America.* Atlanta: Longstreet, 1996.
Dees, Morris, and James Corcoran. *Gathering Storm:*

America's Militia Threat. New York: HarperCollins, 1996.

Devereaux, Leslie, and Roger Hillman, eds. *Fields of Vision: Essays in Film Studies, Visual Anthropology, and Photography.* Berkeley: University of California Press, 1995.

Gibson, James. *Warrior Dreams: Paramilitary Culture in Post-Vietnam America.* New York: Hill & Wang, 1994.

Higham, John. *Strangers in the Land: Patterns of American Nativism, 1860–1925.* New York: Atheneum, 1955.

Hofstadter, Richard. "Paranoid Politics." In Gilbert Abcarian, ed., *American Political Radicalism,* 155–171. Waltham, MA: Xerox College Publishing, 1971.

——. "Reflections on Violence in the United States." In Richard Hofstadter and Michael Wallace, eds., *American Violence: A Documentary History,* 3–43. New York: Knopf, 1970.

MacDougall, David. "Films of Memory." *Visual Anthropology Review* 8.1 (1992): 29–37.

Stern, Kenneth S. *A Force Upon the Plain: The American Militia Movement and the Politics of Hate.* New York: Simon & Schuster, 1996.

Toplin, Robert Brent. *History by Hollywood: The Use and Abuse of the American Past.* Urbana: University of Illinois Press, 1996.

Wade, Wyn Craig. *The Fiery Cross: The Ku Klux Klan in America.* New York: Simon & Schuster, 1987.

[JAMES P. HANLAN]

The Political Machine

At least since Lincoln Steffens's muckraking exposé *The Shame of the Cities* (1904), the urban political machine has been viewed with suspicion and derision. Their critics labeled the men who led such machines in cities across the nation "bosses." Progressive reformers regarded these men not as sophisticated leaders but as personally, politically, and financially corrupt defilers of an American tradition of popular government and public service. Richard Hofstadter's Pulitzer Prize–winning *The Age of Reform* (1955) suggested that this moralistic approach stemmed in part from the inability of many Americans to cope with the teeming, impersonal, and ethnic vibrancy of urban life. In particular, Hofstadter pointed to the anxieties of native-born Americans who felt thrust aside by new groups and new forces. Political machines served the interests of these new groups while being instrumental in displacing from power those who assumed that political leadership was their due inheritance.

Professional historians, following in Hofstadter's wake, have borrowed from analytical frameworks provided by the social sciences such as that set forth by Robert K. Merton in *Social Theory and Social Structure* (1957); in this vein, scholars have worked to revise and rehabilitate the reputation of urban political bosses. Urban America was a fragmented society marked by rapid industrialization, explosive physical and demographic growth, the rise of a pluralistic ethnic and racial population, and conflicting demands for attention from neighborhood, city, and business interests. In this setting, the "political boss" has been viewed by these scholars as an important "broker." In this interpretive framework, the "boss" attempts to satisfy competing—and usually directly conflicting—demands. From this perspective, the urban political machine functioned to hold together a pluralistic society always flirting with the potential of disintegration. Stressing functionality rather than exposé, these historians have regarded political machines and bosses as diplomats rather than defilers. The boss unified urban communities, using considerable powers of persuasion and judgment. As a communicator, the machine's leader used humor and an intuitive and often experiential understanding of neighborhood, business, and ethnic life to bypass legalistic frameworks and accomplish pragmatic results.

It was in this framework that Zane L. Miller's *Boss Cox's Cincinnati* (1968) presents its subject. George Barnsdale Cox served as broker and resource allocator, allowing his city to enter the modern world while keeping potentially divisive forces at bay. Similarly Melvin G. Holli, in *Reform in Detroit* (1969), sees Hazen S. Pingree as a "reformer" who stressed lower utility rates for consumers and shifted the tax burden to large corporations. Reform, Holli points out, often served to impose the interests of the business system of the corporation on municipal government while eliminating petty crime and vice. Consistent with Hofstadter's framework, probusiness reformers questioned whether popular rule was a suitable instrument in a pluralistic society.

The approach of scholars diverges sharply from that of novelists and popular filmmakers. Possibly because they were written for middle-class audiences, novels of urban political corruption usually adhere to the muckraking tradition. Such novels portray the stereotypical "boss," glorying in the excesses of personal, political, and financial corruption of both the boss and his coterie of cronies. The classic portrayals of Robert Penn Warren's *All The King's Men* (1946), based on the life and career of Louisiana's Huey Long, and of Edwin O'Connor's *The Last Hurrah* (1956), based on Boston's James Michael Curley, fall into this category. In both instances the authors created literary classics, focusing on the scandals and peccadilloes of their protagonists while neglecting substantive issues of urban politics. For the sake of a good story, the authors overlook the subtle and sophisticated functions of the political system and the "bosses" whom they portray. For Hollywood, as for the novelist, the melodramatic story of "good" versus "evil" proves equally attractive.

Hollywood's focus on the sensationalistic story can be seen in Preston Sturges's *The Great McGinty* (1940). McGinty (Brian Donlevy) was portrayed as a man, utterly corrupted by the system, who sold his vote some thirty-seven times and thus managed to attract the attention of "the boss" (Akim Tamiroff). It was the boss's influence that enabled McGinty to "advance" to the collection of protection money and graft, the position of alderman, and, ultimately, the job of mayor. McGinty was portrayed as utterly without morality—either political or personal, a man whose marriage of convenience was intended only to attract female voters during his candidacy for mayor. Interestingly, McGinty himself could nevertheless be seen as a rather likable figure, corrupted by an urban political system that left the individual with few good choices.

In 1942, Paramount Pictures filmed Dashiell Hammett's tale of political corruption, blackmail, and murder, *The Glass Key* (1931). Director Stuart Heisler used the urban political boss and his world as a backdrop for a film noir tale of amoral complicity. The focus, though, was on the story, the adventure, and human corruption rather than on the functions and methods of the urban political machine itself.

Likewise, respected director John Ford took on the subject of the political boss in 1958 with his screen adaptation of Edwin O'Connor's *The Last Hurrah*. O'Connor's novel portrays the last campaign of an old-time political boss, slightly past his prime. The stars in Ford's cast (Spencer Tracy, Pat O'Brien, and Basil Rathbone) were all at or near the end of their own legendary film careers; thus, the cast matched the elegiac mood of the novel. The utter corruption of the machine is mitigated by the genuine benevolence of Boss Skeffington (Spencer Tracy) toward "his" people and by his sharp perception of their plight. The ethnic and working-class sources of popular support for the boss are far more clearly delineated than are the "contributors" to Skeffington's media-wise rival. As a result, the old-style boss is seen as more human than his telegenic opponent. The film focused nevertheless on stereotypes of rough-and-tumble ward and city politics rather than on the role of the boss as a communicator and broker between various rival groups, each competing for a "fair" share of governmental pork. In fact, the urban boss of the late nineteenth and early twentieth centuries had not one constituency but multiple and complex constituencies. His skill was in his ability to satisfy each group in a complex and often contradictory urban environment while simultaneously perpetuating his own power. Film viewers identify with Skeffington's genuine humanity, realizing the ability of media-based campaigns to manufacture an artificially genuine persona.

As late as 1995, the urban political boss remained a theme for Hollywood filmmakers. Harold Becker's *City Hall* saw Al Pacino portraying a New York mayor as a humane and competent civil servant—a far cry from the villain of Lincoln Steffens's "shame of the cities"—operating amid a society of pervasive corruption. Thus the muckraker theme remained while the flaw was seen as more societal than individual.

The ability of Hollywood to convey a sophisticated sense of what scholars have learned about urban politics is limited by its need to entertain and tell a story that holds and attracts a mass audience. Stolen votes, a threatened or "bought" electorate, and ignorant or amoral politicos make for engaging drama. Documentary filmmakers, in contrast, have managed to take on the topic of the urban political boss in a way that more carefully mirrors the degree of sophistication achieved by historical scholarship.

The treatment of Chicago's late "boss" Richard J. Daley by documentary filmmakers reflects the best of historical scholarship while rejecting the popular, journalistic, and sensational. Mike Royko was one of Daley's local journalistic gadflies. *Boss* (1971) is Royko's "biography" of Daley. Although the author seldom resists the cheap shot, it is cleverly written: in discussing Daley's character, for example, Royko notes that no matter whom Daley stabbed in the back in the afternoon, he always prayed in the morning. Daley is presented as first the creature and then the master of the much-maligned Chicago machine. Royko glosses over Daley's own incisive defense of the primacy of party loyalty: without the party, Daley noted, only the rich could run for office. The party's beneficial function was to assure access of the average person to the mechanism of government. Daley's roots were firmly planted in his Irish neighborhood of Bridgeport. This reminded the "boss" of the reality the progressives would have preferred to downplay. Daley, the intuitive politician, thus echoed the concerns of scholar Richard Hofstadter that, the failures of the old-style political machine notwithstanding, the alternative could be worse.

A far more sophisticated approach was taken by Roger Biles, whose scholarly *Richard J. Daley* (1995) portrays Chicago's mayor as a skilled communications broker who presided over the building of a city well suited for the latter twentieth century—but whose efforts would ultimately founder on the rock of race. The interpretive framework set forth by Biles is reflected in the PBS documentary *Daley: The Last Boss* (1995), which presents the mayor as the last of a dying breed, a man in close touch with both his immigrant neighborhood base and its middle-class aspirations. Like Biles's monograph, the PBS documentary shows how a "local" leader could use party politics to acquire national influence. While other cities fell victim to recurrent crises, Daley's Chicago long remained "the city that works" until it eventually was torn asunder by racial division, a matter that proved beyond Daley's experience and understanding and that, combined with antiwar tensions, exposed his city to national derision in 1968 during the infamous Democratic national convention.

A less successful PBS effort was *Scandalous Mayor* (1991), a portrait of Boston's James Michael Curley. Like the Daley film, this documentary is an episode in the generally excellent series *The American Experience.* Unfortunately, it is unlike the PBS treatment of Daley because it stresses the excesses of a "scandalous mayor." Although it is a more accurate historical portrait than *The Last Hurrah,* the film looks back to the moralistic approach.

PBS has taken on the issue of a new genre of political "boss" in its treatment of Robert Moses. Moses was the ultimate insider, protected by civil service and bureaucracy and immune from the vicissitudes of elections and public opinion. As much as any elected political "boss," Moses the bureaucrat designed and shaped much of New York's metropolitan physical space. Indeed, Moses's bridges, playgrounds, beaches, tunnels, and low-income housing projects would be the envy of any classical "boss." Unfettered by the need to win popular approval by running for office, Moses and his projects used the law of eminent domain to devastate entire neighborhoods. Drawing heavily on Robert Caro's *Power Broker* (1974), the PBS documentary *The World That Moses Built* (1988) raises disturbing questions about the struggle between individual liberty and public order. The elitism of the older order, though without the gentility imagined by many progressives, was reborn in a different guise under Moses. Many New Yorkers would surely have wondered what could "shame" their city more: a benevolent turn-of-the-century boss or a relentless and unfettered twentieth-century builder.

Despite official and media antagonism, the popularity of "scurrilous" urban politicians continued into the 1990s. Washington's infamous Mayor Marion Barry, beset by scandals, was caught on videotape in 1990, in an FBI sting operation, smoking crack cocaine. After release from a brief prison sentence, Barry proved his popularity by again winning elective office. Barry's civil rights activism, together with his tireless battling for rights for the District of Columbia, assured that his luster with poor African American neighborhoods would not be dulled by his scandals. Maligned by the press, Barry remained beloved by his constituents. As with Boston's James Michael Curley, the boss's popularity survived a prison sentence. *The Last Hurrah* had clearly not sounded last at midcentury in Massachusetts, but was loud and strong, albeit less widespread, at century's end.

References

Filmography

All the King's Men (1949, F)
All the President's Men (1976, F)
The Candidate (1972, F)
Citizen Kane (1941, F)
City Hall (1995, F)
Daley: The Last Boss (1995, D, TV)
The Front Page (1931, F)
The Glass Key (1942, F)
The Great McGinty (1940, F)
The Last Hurrah (1958, F)
Scandalous Mayor (1991, D, TV)
The World That Moses Built (1988, D, TV)

Bibliography

Biles, Roger. *Richard J. Daley: Politics, Race and the Governing of Chicago.* DeKalb: Northern Illinois University Press, 1995.

Carnes, Mark C., ed. *Past Imperfect: History according to the Movies.* New York: Henry Holt, 1995.

Caro, Robert A. *Power Broker: Robert Moses and the Fall of New York.* New York: Knopf, 1974.

Christensen, Terry. *Reel Politics: American Political Movies from Birth of a Nation to Platoon.* New York: Basil Blackwell, 1987.

Green, Paul M., and Melvin G. Holli, eds. *The Mayors: The Chicago Political Tradition.* Carbondale: Southern Illinois University Press, 1987.

Hofstadter, Richard. *The Age of Reform.* New York: Knopf, 1955.

Holli, Melvin G. *The American Mayor: The Best and the Worst Big-City Leaders.* University Park: Pennsylvania State University Press, 1999.

——. *Reform in Detroit: Hazen S. Pingree and Urban Politics.* New York: Oxford University Press, 1969.

Merton, Robert K. *Social Theory and Social Structure.* Glencoe, IL: Free Press, 1957.

Miller, Zane L. *Boss Cox's Cincinnati: Urban Politics in the Progressive Era.* New York: Oxford University Press, 1968.

Rosenstone, Robert J. *Visions of the Past: The Challenge of Film to Our Idea of History.* Cambridge, MA: Harvard University Press, 1995.

Royko, Mike. *Boss: Richard J. Daley of Chicago.* New York: Penguin, 1971.

Sarris, Andrew. *Politics and Cinema.* New York: Columbia University Press, 1978.

Sklar, Robert. *Movie-Made America: A Cultural History of American Movies.* New York: Random House, 1975.

[PETER C. ROLLINS]

The Presidency After World War II

The American presidency, like the United States itself, emerged from World War II with enormous powers accumulated during the struggle to defeat fascism. Confronted by the Iron Curtain and Cold War, the chief executive office maintained its wartime activism. From 1945 until the twenty-first century, challenges abroad justified retention of executive prerogatives: the collision with Soviet expansion into Eastern Europe, Chinese adventurism in Korea, Vietnamese militarism in Southeast Asia, and the war on international terrorism that followed the September 11, 2001, disaster at the World Trade Center.

Arthur Schlesinger Jr., the Pulitzer Prize–winning historian, deplored these developments in a book whose title became a watchword for political observers, *The Imperial Presidency* (1994):

> By the early 1970s the American President had become on issues of war and peace the most absolute monarch (with the possible exception of Mao Tse-tung of China) among the great powers of the world. The Indo-China War placed this problem high on the national consciousness. But the end of American military involvement in Southeast Asia would not extinguish the problem. The assertions of sweeping and unilateral presidential authority remained official doctrine in foreign affairs. And, if the President were conceded these life-and-death decisions abroad, how could he be restrained from gathering unto himself the less fateful powers of the national polity? For the claims of unilateral authority in foreign policy soon began to pervade and embolden the domestic presidency. (ix)

Schlesinger, of course, was most disturbed by Lyndon B. Johnson's use of the Gulf of Tonkin Resolution of 1964 to justify a military expedition that cost fifty thousand lives—yet he neglected to note that LBJ repeatedly invited Congress to reconsider and to debate the resolution.

Between 1973 and 1974, most Americans—including a young Oliver Stone—became sensitized to the misuse of executive power by the infamous Watergate scandal. President Richard Nixon's use of federal agencies to harass and punish political opponents disturbed Republicans and Democrats alike—and fostered a suspicion of power that continues into the twenty-first century. In sum, the international challenges of the post–World War II era required executive freedom of action while paradoxically posing a threat to those traditional freedoms the powers were created to preserve and defend.

The Presidency During the Cold War

As the commanders in chief of the armed forces, the presidents of the Cold War era continued to be responsible for the nation's defense. Soviet acquisition of nuclear capability in 1948 and Chinese demonstration of nuclear power in 1964 heightened the need for quick retaliatory power—first through bomber fleets and later in a "triad" of missiles, bombers, and submarines. During this period, consultation with Congress became less frequent and input from the president's cabinet was almost nonexistent; instead, the National Security Council, the secretary of defense, the director of the

CIA, and the chairman of the Joint Chiefs of Staff met frequently to determine the nation's defense policies (Levine, 485).

On the domestic front, the New Deal of Franklin Delano Roosevelt (1932–45) and the Fair Deal of Harry Truman (1945–52) brought about unprecedented increases in executive power. During the Great Depression, the Supreme Court struck down a number of Roosevelt's programs, but war demands vastly expanded the scope of the government. Harry Truman ordered desegregation of the military (a major decision) and was not reticent about forcing big unions and big business to conform to his notion of the national good. Later, Ronald Reagan's tough foreign policy toward the Soviet Union was criticized roundly because he seemed to be practicing "brinkmanship," especially in his fielding of cruise missiles in Europe. When the nation's air traffic controllers union went on strike in 1981, Reagan fired them all in a truly devastating application of executive power. Still later, Bill Clinton's commitment of American troops to operations in the Balkans provoked considerable debate—but only after their deployment. During the midnight hours of his presidency in 2001, Clinton's pardons for prominent businessmen and convicted drug dealers perplexed and angered many who sensed misuse of a presidential prerogative. Many wondered aloud if the office was too powerful and if it posed its own form of threat to true national security.

The Presidency as a Symbolic Office

Beyond its political and economic powers and responsibilities, the presidency has a symbolic role in American life—a role intensified by mass communications and television. The president is a symbol of the nation—its temper, its spirit, its morality. During the formative years of the nation, the authors of the Constitution (such as John Adams) were firm believers in the notion of *civitas*—that the civic character of both leaders and citizens was vital to the health of the republic. Along with the constitutional structure, they saw this civic virtue as the glue that held the nation together.

The president and his wife and children are the "first family" in a nation that values families. People want to empathize with the national leader, to sense that a competent, experienced, and bold chief executive leads them. If nothing else, having an individual at the top of government's chain of command lends a personal touch to what might otherwise be a sterile and depersonalized establishment. Americans want to love (or decry) the man in office, and the singularity of the head of state invites such responses. As President William Howard Taft observed in this context, "the whole government is so identified in the minds of the people with the president's personality, that they make him responsible for all the sins of omission and of commission of society at large" (Schlesinger, *Cycles*, 287). All presidents have felt the gravity—and creative potential—of this symbolic role.

Little wonder that motion pictures have been fascinated with the office. Any presidential story will have available to it the following dramatic tensions: domestic prosperity or depression; foreign war or peace; selfish politics or high statesmanship; personal venality or morality. Within the governmental structures, potential for conflict abounds: there is the presidency versus the Congress; the presidency versus the military; the presidency versus the courts. In the postwar era, various issues have arisen regarding the presidency and the press. Because motion pictures and television thrive on the personifications of abstractions, the White House film genre invites filmmakers to address almost any contemporary issue. As *Air Force One* (1997) proves, even something as apparently dull as a flight on a president's plane can be transformed into an action adventure combining politics, terrorism, and personal heroism. In other words, the checks-and-balances system created by the Founding Fathers provided future dramatists with an elaborate framework for conflict.

Nuclear Confrontation

The United States enjoyed a monopoly in nuclear weaponry until 1949, when the Soviet Union exploded its first nuclear device. Since that time, the threat of nuclear confrontation has been continuous. Americans who lived through the 1950s remember so-called duck and cover drills in the public schools, where children were told to hide under their desks to avoid flying glass. National debates considered the moral questions raised by family fallout shelters. Many children of the era vividly remember nightmares about nuclear annihilation.

The Cuban Missile Crisis of 1962 brought the United States and the Soviet Union closest to nuclear exchange. In 1997, Ernest May of Harvard University edited a book of transcriptions from tapes made by the JFK White House entitled *The Kennedy Tapes: Inside the White House During the Cuban Missile Crisis.* (As perhaps America's senior scholar of the presidency, May was extremely sensitive to the nuances of interpersonal dynamics within the Kennedy administration.) Home Box Office (HBO) brought out a cinematic treatment of those frightening weeks of American history in its docudrama *Thirteen Days* (2000), starring the popular actor Kevin Costner as a special assistant to President Kennedy (Bruce Greenwood). Of necessity, writer David Self and director Roger Donaldson invented transitions and some dialogue; often, the filmmakers cut to black and white footage to signal the use of actual, historical material. The result is a powerful evocation of a climactic moment for the presidency and the nation that is *also* an authentic rendering of history. May reviewed the film and found it unfair to the military of the time in making its leaders appear more devious in their negotiations with JFK than they really were. On the other hand, he was impressed by the film's ability to bring history alive: "It accurately reproduces some of the restrained but anguished debate from the secret tapes, and it intersperses extraordinarily realistic footage of Soviet missile sites being hurriedly readied in jungle clearings, of American U-2s swooping over them, and of bombers, carrier aircraft, and U.S. missiles preparing for action. Viewers who know this movie is about a real event will leave the theater shivering with the understanding of what the Cold War could have brought" (8). May's review was a strong endorsement of the docudrama. (For a documentary treatment of the crisis, see the History Channel's *DEFCON 2*; this version includes interviews with many of the historical personalities involved in the crisis and is a good complement to *Thirteen Days.*)

The dangers of an accidental nuclear missile exchange have plagued the nation and the presidency. In *Fail-Safe* (1964), the American president (Henry Fonda) learns that a flight of bombers has passed its "fail safe" point and, owing to a breakdown in communications, cannot be recalled. In desperation, the president gives the Soviets the destination of the bombers and most of them are intercepted; however, some get through to their primary target, Moscow. In a tragic gesture to validate U.S. intentions during this crisis, the president orders a trusted pilot to release an atomic weapon over New York City, a particularly chilling moment for the film because the first lady is in New York for a day of shopping. By personalizing the decision, *Fail-Safe* effectively dramatizes the gravity of options confronting American presidents in the nuclear age. Alas, as Robert Hunter observes of the portrayal, "If this is the best America can hope for from a model president, what are we likely to get with the real occupants of the White House?" (204).

Stanley Kubrick took a satiric approach to the accidental war story in his *Dr. Strangelove, or: How I Stopped Worrying and Learned to Love the Bomb* (1964), a film that has improved with age. The plot of this film was so close to that of *Fail-Safe* that Kubrick threatened Columbia Pictures with a plagiarism suit. The resemblance between the two films stops at the level of plot: *Dr. Strangelove* is a hilarious black comedy in which some of the most grievous threats to civilization are handled with satiric exaggeration. Most relevant to this discussion is the inability of President Merkin Muffley (Peter Sellers) to control his military establishment, to communicate effectively with his Soviet counterpart over the red telephone, or to have any influence on what becomes an apocalyptic cataclysm. Along the way, Kubrick stresses that the destructive impulses of mankind are retained even in the most "civilized" of settings. (For example, Dr. Strangelove—also played by Sellers—is the leading nuclear scientist, yet he is driven by an atavistic death wish.) The serious message of this hilarious film is that machines and large institutions are out of control and that even the presidency is irrelevant in a high-tech world.

Unconventional Warfare and the White House

One of JFK's campaign promises in 1961 was that the U.S. would back off from its previous brinkmanship and learn to cope with unconventional warfare challenges around the globe. To this end, Kennedy supported the creation of the U.S. Army Special Forces, or Green Berets, an elite unit of multilingual soldiers trained to infiltrate and to live with indigenous peoples. When the counterinsurgency gambit failed in Vietnam, escalation led to a broader struggle—but one that still carefully avoided the nuclear threshold.

In *JFK* (1991) director Oliver Stone connects the Vietnam War to the assassination of a much-beloved president. According to Stone, as articulated by Mr. X (Donald Sutherland), Kennedy was murdered because he planned to withdraw from Vietnam. Apprehensive about the president's second thoughts, a military elite conspired with greedy arms merchants to kill the president; according to Stone, this conspiracy explains the mysteries and contradictions that have continued to surround the assassination. Clearly, in relation to the presidency, the film joins Stone's other presidential production, *Nixon* (1995), in decrying "the beast," by which Stone seems to mean the encroaching powers of corporations on the presidency, which keep the highest office from exercising its proper leadership role. In this pessimistic conclusion, *Dr. Strangelove, JFK,* and *Nixon* seem to be unanimous.

Clear and Present Danger (1994) takes another approach to unconventional warfare and presidential power. Based on a Tom Clancy bestseller of the same title, this exciting thriller looks at how an unscrupulous West Wing might misuse the smart bombs and special forces in its quiver. While not going as far as Chuck Norris's television series *Presidential Man* (2002), in which no restraints are defined for the president's special agent, this feature production examines the misuse of power along precedents set by Lieutenant Colonel Oliver North in Nicaragua in the 1980s. Caught in the middle is the Clancy hero of many novels, Jack Ryan (Harrison Ford), who, as a CIA analyst, discovers and exposes the excesses of his White House colleagues. Like John Dean during the Watergate hearings, Ryan goes before Congress to restore the constitutional balance. The guerilla actions of the American soldiers are accurate in the sense that they show the skill of American fighting men when called upon to perform in nontraditional settings; the unstated implication is disturbing: that our executive branch must circumvent the constitution to defeat drug lords and terrorists.

Director John Frankenheimer's made-for-HBO *Path to War* (2002) traces Lyndon B. Johnson's struggle at first to avoid—and then to lead—the Vietnam conflict. Like *Thirteen Days,* this docudrama is based on a contemporaneous book of transcripts, in this case edited by Michael Beschloss, a volume entitled *Reaching for Glory: Lyndon Johnson's Secret White House Tapes, 1964–1965* (2001). Bent on being remembered as the "Great Society" president, Lyndon Johnson (Michael Gambon) quickly learns that history has forced him to commit American troops to a limited war in a distant land. By 1968, the president is nearly destroyed by the stress of his disappointments and frustrations as a national leader; indeed, rather than being remembered for his aspirations, LBJ leaves office as a dishonored victim. Like *Thirteen Days, Path to War* attempts to be historically accurate; as a drama, it successfully exploits the convincing portrayals of LBJ, Clark Clifford (Donald Sutherland), Robert McNamara (Alec Baldwin), General William Westmoreland (Tom Skerritt), and Lady Bird Johnson (Felicity Huffman). *Path to War* concludes that history controls the presidency rather than the reverse. Whatever the interpretations (see "The Vietnam War"), America failed in its first major experiment with unconventional warfare.

The Bully Pulpit of the Presidency

American presidents are constantly in the public eye, and therefore have hourly opportunities to provide leadership from the "bully pulpit" (a phrase coined by President Theodore Roosevelt) of the White House. Rose Garden speeches announce new policies and plans; talks from shop floors dramatize trade and business initiatives; impromptu comments in hallways or on the White House lawn often suggest the directions of new policies.

Daryl Zanuck's *Wilson* (1944) is about a leader who used the forum of the presidency effectively in a film which, itself, was produced to plead a special cause. At the close of World War II, Darryl Zanuck was passionately in favor of the United Nations, the twentieth century's second attempt to create a supranational peacekeeping organization. To do so, he produced a film about Woodrow Wilson, a Princeton professor and progressive president known for, among other visionary plans, his post–World War I dream of an effective League of Nations. To develop Wilson as a visionary fully, Zanuck felt that he had to show how this activist leader spoke and wrote in favor of other monumental reforms such as the progressive income tax, the Federal Reserve Act (which created the current Federal Reserve system), and vigorous antitrust and civil service reforms. These accomplishments mount up in fast-cut, impact montage sequences. Woodrow Wilson emerges as a dynamic politician whose broad view of the national good is reflected in the panoply of reforms which received his signature in the Oval Office. Don Staples remembers viewing of the film when it came to his local theater: "It was a very patriotic film. We all stood and clapped our hands at the end which was a very unusual reaction for my family. Kids often cheered and yelled at westerns; however, this was a serious movie" (Rollins and O'Connor, *Hollywood's White House*, 124).

Truman (1995) is an HBO docudrama that balances its screen time between the president's war leadership and his domestic agenda. The two-hour study follows the career of Harry S. Truman and adheres closely to the eponymous, Pulitzer Prize–winning biography by David McCullough. The program reminds those who may have forgotten that this earthy man from Independence, Missouri, was a crusader against waste and corruption by war contractors and that he was the president who had the courage to order desegregation of the military (carried out on the Korean battlefield in 1950). Gary Sinise plays a Truman who is strong when he is in the right—for example, in his opposition to Joseph McCarthy—but not flawless as a human being. Like the book on which it is based, *Truman* identifies the presidency as an appropriate office for any patriotic American who wants to lead the nation and not a sinecure reserved for the wealthy scions of the Ivy League—the Wilsons, the Roosevelts, the Kennedys of this world.

Beginning in 1999, an NBC series entitled *The West Wing* began to air and win almost every Emmy Award available. Conceived as a sequel to Rob Reiner's successful feature film *The American President* (1995), the series, created and written by *American President* screenwriter Aaron Sorkin, took America by storm—unaccountably, in the view of some critics. Launched during the Clinton impeachment controversy, *The West Wing* provided an alternative image for the White House. In the very place where Monica Lewinsky became famous for snapping her thong, female workers in Sorkin's West Wing were working long hours; while Bill Clinton was denying that he had had sex with a young intern, the president of *The West Wing* (Martin Sheen) was quoting the Bible, caring for the sick, and treating enlisted personnel of the military with great respect—in other words, supplying a presidential image on television that buoyed faith in the office during an administration that, many felt, failed to live up to John Adams's notion of *civitas.* As *The West Wing* coproducer John Wells has observed, "We'd reached a point in the culture where we assumed that people who want to choose public service have the basest of motives of self-aggrandizement and financial gain. . . . The public wants to believe in the political process, wants to believe in politicians. Wants to believe that the people who are leading us are doing so—even if there are ideological differences—to make the country better" (Lehmann, 354).

The second episode of the second season, entitled "Two Cathedrals," is indicative of the domestic concerns broached by the series. Much of the episode focuses on the agonizing decision of President Bartlet (Martin Sheen) to run for another term, despite health and temporary credibility problems. As part of the character development, the program explores how this "boy king" has his social consciousness raised by Mrs. Delores Landingham (Kathryn Joosten). When Bartlet ascends to high public office, she moves with him as his private secretary and conscience. After she is killed in an automobile accident, the shock and horror force president Bartlet to plumb the depths of his commitment to the nation, drawing up an explicit discussion of domestic priorities. Among them are a jobs program for nearly four million poor people, acquisition of massive tracts of land for conservation, and appointment of liberal and minority judges to the Supreme Court (Sorkin, 343–402). Other episodes examine such issues as gays in the military, election reform, and the economy. In all of these instances, *The West Wing* gives abstract issues a human face. Week after week, the series stresses that the reform instincts of the Bartlet White House go all the way down to the roots of a young Jed Bartlet's schooling, when he learned a code of noblesse oblige. It goes without saying that he has communicated this ethic to those "best and brightest" in the West Wing. Many critics have complained about the liberal political agenda that guides writer Aaron Sorkin's scripts, but even those who might disagree with policy messages of the NBC series can enjoy its refreshing portrait of integrity and idealism.

The Presidency and the Nation

United Airlines 93 was one of the four commercial aircraft commandeered by Islamic terrorists on September 11, 2001. Because of the alertness and courage of passengers aboard, this aircraft was prevented from destroying the White House. The suicidal planners of the attack knew the importance of the building to a democratic republic and hoped that destruction of this symbol of national identity would be a wound to morale—forgetting, of course, the failure of a similar attack during the War of 1812, when British troops set the building on fire. If the twin towers in New York City represented American free enterprise, and if the Pentagon building represented U.S. military might, this small edifice represented America's admiration of virtue and its continued hopes for the "pursuit of happiness" in a free society. Clearly the presidential films produced after World War II exploit a similar concern, with the soul of a proud nation ready to follow the virtuous leaders who live in "the people's house."

References

Filmography

Air Force One (1997, F)
The American President (1995, F; 2000, D)
Clear and Present Danger (1994, F)
DEFCON 2 (2002, D)
Dr. Strangelove, or: How I Stopped Worrying and Learned to Love the Bomb (1964, F)
Fail-Safe (1964, F; 2000, TV)
JFK (1991, F)
Nixon (1995, F)
Path to War (2002, D)
Presidential Man (2002, TV)
Thirteen Days (2000, F)
Truman (1995, D)
The West Wing (1999–, TV)
Wilson (1944, F)

Bibliography

Beschloss, Michael. *Reaching for Glory: Lyndon Johnson's Secret White House Tapes, 1964–1965.* New York: Simon & Schuster, 2001.

Brinkley, Alan, and Davis Dyer, eds. *The Reader's Companion to the American Presidency.* Boston: Houghton Mifflin, 2000.

Cronin, Thomas E., and Michael A. Genovese. *The Paradoxes of the American Presidency.* New York: Oxford University Press, 1998.

Fisher, Louis. *Presidential War Power.* Lawrence: University Press of Kansas, 2000.

Hunter, Robert E. "Who's in Charge Here? Technology and the Presidency in *Fail-Safe* (1964) and *Colossus* (1970)." In Peter Rollins and John E. O'Connor, eds., *Hollywood's White House: The American Presidency as Film and History,* 200–234. Lexington: University Press of Kentucky, 2003.

Lehmann, Chris. "The Feel-Good Presidency: The Pseudo Politics of *The West Wing.*" In Peter Rollins and John E. O'Connor, eds., *Hollywood's White House: The American Presidency as Film and History,* 275–276. Lexington: University Press of Kentucky, 2003.

Levine, Myron. "The Transformed Presidency: The Real Presidency and Hollywood's Reel Presidency." In Peter Rollins and John E. O'Connor, eds., *Hollywood's White House: The American Presidency as Film and History,* 380–397. Lexington: University Press of Kentucky, 2003.

May, Ernest W. *The Kennedy Tapes: Inside the White House During the Cuban Missile Crisis.* Cambridge, MA: Harvard University Press, 1997.

——. "*Thirteen Days.*" *The American Prospect* 12.1 (January 2001): 5.

Morris, Dick. *Behind the Oval Office.* New York: Random House, 1997.

Rollins, Peter C., ed. *Hollywood as Historian: American Film in a Cultural Context.* 2d ed. Lexington: University Press of Kentucky, 1998.

Rollins, Peter, and John E. O'Connor. *The West Wing: The American Presidency as Television Drama.* Syracuse, NY: Syracuse University Press, 2003.

——, eds. *Hollywood's White House: The American Presidency as Film and History.* Lexington: University Press of Kentucky, 2003.

Schlesinger, Arthur M., Jr. *The Cycles of American History.* Boston: Houghton Mifflin, 1986.

——. *The Imperial Presidency.* New York: Columbia University Press, 1994.

Sorkin, Aaron. *The West Wing Script Book.* New York: Newmarket Press, 2002.

Tulis, Jeffrey K. *The Rhetorical Presidency.* Lawrence: University Press of Kansas, 1995.

[RON BRILEY]

Private Schools

Private or independent schools have played an important role in American education from colonial times into the twenty-first century. Promoting serious scholarship along with a commitment to service, independent schools such as Groton and Exeter have produced leaders in business, education, and public service, including presidents Franklin D. Roosevelt, John F. Kennedy, and George H. W. Bush. However, advocates of public education sometimes perceive private, or independent, schools as elitist institutions, perpetuating class divisions within an egalitarian society. A more balanced view is provided by Lawrence A. Cremin, who, in his multivolume history of American education, asserts that private nonsectarian schools in America cater to "particular kinds and classes of students with curricula featuring one or another emphasis not to be found, or at least perceived as not to be found, in the public schools—traditional academic emphases, progressive emphases, or artistic emphases."

Nevertheless, Cremin's definition provides for some ambiguity regarding private schools, an attitude that is well exemplified in popular film. Hollywood increasingly turned to the subject of education in the post–World War II period, reflecting the film industry's search for new markets and its recognition that the affluent society of the 1950s had produced teenagers with disposable income. Cinematic treatments of the public school, both positive and negative, have historically dominated the nation's theaters, while less numerous films depicting private education generally extol the virtues of heroic individuals, both students and teachers, who battle against the forces of conformity and prejudice. These films are usually set in a boarding-school environment or military school, ignoring the fact that the nonpublic school community in the United States is dominated by parochial and day schools.

Cinematic depiction of private education often focuses upon the British antecedents of the American boarding school. In *Goodbye, Mr. Chips* (1939), Robert Donat, in an Academy Award–winning performance, portrays a teacher in an English boys' school who devotes his life to his students following the death of his young wife. (The film was remade as a musical in 1969, with Peter O'Toole in the Donat role.) But such dedication may also lead to a dangerous overzealousness, as exemplified by the provocative *The Prime of Miss Jean Brodie* (1969). In other films dealing with the British school system, teachers such as Mr. Chips or Jean Brodie do not rise up to challenge the conventional wisdom. The rigidity, and even cruelty, of the system leads to revolution in director Lindsay Anderson's *If...* (1968), featuring Malcolm McDowell as a student who takes to the gun in order to challenge his school's and society's class system. *Another Country* (1984), directed by Julian Mitchell, explores the 1930s school friendship between Guy Burgess and Donald McLean, who in the 1950s spied for the Soviet Union while working for the British government. The central argument of the film is that Burgess's homosexuality made him just as much of an outsider as MacLean's marxism.

Indeed, the theme that private schools, especially same-sex boarding schools, encourage homosexuality and lesbianism is one found in several Hollywood films. In the 1936 film adaptation of Lillian Hellman's *These Three,* director William Wyler reduced the sexually provocative play, concerning student accusations of lesbianism leveled against the headmistresses of a girls' school, to a drama of unrequited love. However, in his 1962 remake, *The Children's Hour,* Wyler was able to tackle the sexual issues of the play more directly. Homosexuality and the boarding school is also addressed in *Tea and Sympathy* (1956), starring Deborah Kerr as a resident teacher's wife who provides a sensitive ear for a young student whose lack of "manly" qualities is criticized by his father and housemaster. The film implies that, through sympathy and understanding, homosexual tendencies may be reduced or cured. Although by today's standards the film's sexual politics are backward, the film deserves credit for considering a subject that was a virtual taboo during the 1950s.

Perhaps the most commercially successful film confronting private boarding schools, and the parents who send their children to such institutions, is *Dead Poets Society* (1989). In Peter Weir's film, Robin Williams portrays English teacher John Keating, who is determined to challenge the conformist traditions of the school and its curriculum. Attempting to foster intellectual curiosity among his students, Keating encourages them to rip pages from their textbooks and "seize the day." Tragedy arises when one of the students, inspired by Keating, decides to pursue his passion for acting. The boy's business-minded father confronts his son, who commits suicide. Keating is blamed for the boy's death and dismissed from his position, but his students assert their support and love by holding a demonstration, standing on their desks and calling Keating, "Captain, my Captain," after the famous Walt Whitman poem dedicated to Abraham Lincoln. The film was popular at the box office, but many critics were less enthusiastic. Jo Keroes argues that *Dead Poets Society* fails either to recognize the latent homosexuality in Keating's relationship with his boys or deal with whether Keating is instilling independent thinking or creating followers in the fashion of Jean Brodie. Instead of pursuing these more difficult questions, the film is satisfied with slamming the private-school environment for undermining individualism.

Prejudice and the private school is also the subject of *School Ties* (1992), in which Brendan Fraser portrays a talented quarterback who receives a football scholarship to the elite St. Matthew School. Like *Dead Poets Society,* Robert Mandel's film attempts to depict the 1950s as a conformist society. Fraser decides to conceal his background, but an athletic and romantic rival reveals the quarterback's Jewish identity. Following in the tradition of *Gentleman's Agreement* (1947), *School Ties* deserves credit for its condemnation of anti-Semitism, but a danger may be that with its 1950s setting, younger audiences will assume that anti-Semitism lacks relevance for contemporary America. Prep-school exploitation of athletes is also examined in the documentary *Hoop Dreams* (1994), which investigates the treatment of black athletes Arthur Agee and William Gates at St. Joseph, a predominantly white Catholic school.

Bias, along with violence, is also a theme in Hollywood's condemnation of private military schools in such films as *Taps* (1981), *Lords of Discipline* (1983), and *Toy Soldiers* (1991). Of these films, *Taps* is probably most notable for its production values and cast, including George C. Scott, Timothy Hutton, Sean Penn, and Tom Cruise. In Horace Becker's film, the conformity of military education and discipline leads to tragedy when a group of cadets takes up arms upon learning that their revered school and traditions will be razed to make way for a condominium development.

A more positive portrayal of the prep-school environment is provided in the 1972 film adaptation of the classic novel *A Separate Peace,* by John Knowles, a Phillips Exeter graduate. Set during the early years of World War II at the fictitious Devon School in New England, *A Separate Peace* examines the unlikely friendship between the athletic Finny and the introvert Gene, who must cope with his best friend's death in a tragic accident. The novel uses the private school setting to explore issues of youth and war in what many critics consider a coming-of-age masterpiece. Nevertheless, the glossy film production by director Larry Peerce, featuring Parker Stevenson and John Heyl, fails to capture some of the novel's introspective depth.

Scent of a Woman (1992) also provides what film critic Roger Ebert terms the classic prep-school hero; a misfit "who learns to stand up for what he believes." Charlie (Chris O'Donnell) is a scholarship student at an elite private school. His weekend job is to take care of cynical Colonel Slade (Al Pacino), who is blind but hardly helpless as he guides Charlie on a jaunt through New York City in which the young man gains new insights into life. Colonel Slade, who is really a romantic, then accompanies Charlie back to school, and, by exposing the hypocrisy of the school's administration, he prevents his young protégé from being expelled.

In 1998, Hollywood indicated that it was perhaps ready to move beyond the negative stereotypes of private schools with the release of *Rushmore.* In director Wes Anderson's film, Rushmore Academy student Max Fisher (Jason Schwartzman) rivals one of the school's parents and leading contributors, Herman Blume (played by comedian Bill Murray in a critically acclaimed performance), for the affections of teacher Miss Cross (Olivia Williams). This offbeat comedy depicts the adolescent behavior of both Fisher and Blume while presenting teachers, parents, and the private school world as tolerant of individual differences and quite compatible with the public school Fisher attends after being expelled from Rushmore.

Yet, less than positive images of private education continue to be a Hollywood mainstay. *Outside Providence* (1999) tells the story of Tim Dunphy (Shawn Hatosy), whose working-class father (Alec Baldwin) sends him to private school in the belief that his drug-happy son will straighten up there, away from the influence of his friends. However, Dunphy finds little to distinguish the behavior of prep-school students from those in the public sector—and certainly plenty of drugs. In *Finding Forrester* (2000), director Gus Van Sant has reclusive author William Forrester (Sean Connery) rescue his young protégé Jamal Wallace (Rob Brown) from the clutches of a frustrated prep-school English teacher (F. Murray Abraham).

The ambivalence exhibited by popular film toward independent education has tended to perpetuate negative stereotypes of private schools. The prep-school traditions of excellence and service are all too often missing from the cinema.

References

Filmography

Another Country (1984, F)
The Browning Version (1951, F)
The Children's Hour (1962, F)
Class (1983)
Dead Poets Society (1989, F)
Finding Forrester (2000, F)
Flirting (1989, F)
Goodbye, Mr. Chips (1939, 1969, F)
The Headmaster (1970–71, TV)
Hoop Dreams (1994, D)
If. . . (1968, F)
The Lawrenceville Stories (1987, TV)
Lords of Discipline (1983, F)
Outside Providence (1999, F)
The Prime of Miss Jean Brodie (1969, F)
Rushmore (1998, F)
A Separate Peace (1972, F)
Scent of a Woman (1992, F)

School Ties (1992, F)
Taps (1981, F)
Tea and Sympathy (1956, F)
These Three (1936, F)
Toy Soldiers (1991, F)

Bibliography

Considine, David M. *The Cinema of Adolescence.* Jefferson, NC: McFarland, 1985.

Cremin, Lawrence A. *American Education: The Metropolitan Experience, 1876–1980.* New York: Harper & Row, 1988.

Farber, Paul, Eugene F. Provenzo Jr., and Gunilla Holm, eds. *Schooling in the Light of Popular Culture.* Albany: State University of New York Press, 1994.

Groome, Thomas H. *Christian Religious Education: Sharing Our Story and Vision.* San Francisco: Jossey-Bass, 1980.

Kane, Pearl R. *Independent Schools, Independent Thinkers.* San Francisco: Jossey-Bass, 1992.

Keroes, Jo. *Tales out of School: Gender, Longing, and the Teacher in Fiction and Film.* Carbondale: Southern Illinois University Press, 1999.

McPhee, John. *The Headmaster: Frank L. Boyden of Deerfield.* New York: Farrar, Straus & Giroux, 1985.

Palladino, Grace. *Teenagers: An American History.* New York: Basic Books, 1996.

[RON BRILEY]

Public High Schools

Since the days when Horace Mann served as Massachusetts Commissioner of Education in the mid-nineteenth century, Americans have celebrated public schooling as the solution for democracy's discontents. Mann insisted that public investment in education would create wealth and foster democratic citizenship in the young republic. These principles resonated with champions of education throughout the nineteenth and twentieth centuries. In his multivolume history of American education, Lawrence A. Cremin argues that America has tried to define itself through the educational process. And, according to Cremin, the central purpose assigned to education has contributed to the political conflict over what should be taught. Educational reform thus may be viewed as the battle for America's soul.

This struggle intensified after World War II. According to historian Diane Ravitch, "the American crusade against ignorance required that the opportunity for education be made available to all young people, without regard to race, creed, national origin, sex, or family background." However, such high expectations often led to disillusionment by the century's end.

The crusade for equal opportunity in education encountered barricades in the inequitable funding for public schools, contributing to what Jonathan Kozol called "savage inequalities" in American schools. More conservative critics of American education, pointing to the 1983 Committee on Educational Excellence report entitled *A Nation at Risk,* assert that growing demands on the schools to serve a variety of social goals, such as sex education, have usurped functions once reserved for the family. The result of the schools' expanding mission has been a decline in basic skills and a lack of moral education, reflected in such violent encounters as the 1999 massacre of thirteen students and a teacher at Columbine High School in Littleton, Colorado. What is needed, these reformers assert, is a return to basics in education, exemplified by the standards movement and the debate over vouchers.

Accordingly, as the United States enters the twenty-first century there remains considerable conflict over how American education may claim the promise of American life. But both liberals and conservatives agree on the centrality of education to American citizenship and prosperity. This consensus is well represented in Hollywood's depiction of public education, and especially the American high school, which has been a staple of the film industry in the post–World War II period. Just as the nation has sought to define itself through education, the film industry has examined modern American through the lens of the public high school. Hollywood's high school includes nostalgia, sexuality, humor, escapism, music, learning, love, growth, and violence in an environment where courageous teachers often battle against indifferent school administrators and students struggle to maintain their individuality against the conformity often demanded by educational institutions.

In the early years of Hollywood, public education and high school were rarely the focus of filmmakers. School merely served as a backdrop to the Our Gang comedies and Andy Hardy series, featuring Mickey Rooney. Heroic teachers, who made a difference in the lives of their students, were usually depicted in a British setting, with films such as *Goodbye, Mr. Chips* (1939), *How Green Was My Valley* (1941), and *The Corn Is Green* (1945).

However, all of this changed in post–World War II America, where a growing affluence and middle class contributed to the rise of mass education through high school and the development of a teen culture and population with disposable income. Confronted with a challenge from television and other forms of leisure, Hollywood responded by exploiting the teen audience with topics and images which would appeal to youth, while simultaneously encoding more conservative messages for older viewers.

Perhaps the prototype high school film is director Richard Brooks's *The Blackboard Jungle* (1955). The film begins with the rock and roll anthem "Rock around the Clock," which, according to Grace Palladino in *Teenagers*, "marked the official inception of teenage rebel culture." The 1950s concern with juvenile delinquency is examined as teacher Rick Dadier (Glenn Ford) must deal with the ignorance of school bureaucracy, cynicism of fellow teachers, and hostility of angry students such as Miller (Sidney Poitier). With a sense of authority and compassion—what some psychologists might call tough love—Dadier is able to overcome physical threats and internal doubts, winning the respect of both students and colleagues. Emphasizing individual responsibility, *Blackboard Jungle* fails to examine the reason for teen dissatisfaction; however, one police detective blames World War II and mothers working outside the home. Similar themes of a rebellious image, coupled with a conservative message, are explored in *Rebel Without a Cause* (1955). James Stark (James Dean) is a disaffected youth seeking acceptance. Finding little solace in school or his dysfunctional family, Stark is reintegrated into society through the compassion and toughness of his probation officer.

In the 1960s, Hollywood returned to the theme of the courageous teacher battling against social indifference. *Up the Down Staircase* (1967), based upon the novel by Bel Kaufman, tells the story of first-year teacher Sylvia Barrett (Sandy Dennis), who battles bureaucratic and administrative barriers to reach the lower-class students of Calvin Coolidge High. Barrett compassionately resists the sexual advances of a student, who assumes that the teacher could care only for his body, and, in the film's conclusion, she refuses to accept a transfer to a more affluent school.

With *To Sir with Love* (1967), Sidney Poitier, the youthful foil of Rick Dadier in *Blackboard Jungle*, portrays teacher Mark Thackery. Accepting a teaching position in London's East End, Thackery gets the attention of his unruly students by demanding respect and instituting a practical curriculum to meet their needs. Along the way, he must gently thwart the advances of a white female student, although the social and racial implications of the relationship are only considered in an oblique fashion. But the image of the black teacher is a rare one for Hollywood. More typical is the white instructor confronting an African American student body. In *Conrack* (1974), based upon the memoir *The Water Is Wide* by Pat Conroy, Jon Voight plays a white teacher who wants to raise the intellectual and social horizons of his black pupils, living in isolation on a South Carolina island. While appreciated by his students, Conrack is loathed by his administrators and fired for taking his charges across the river to trick or treat in a white neighborhood. Films focusing upon school from an African American student perspective are rare, but director Michael A Schultz's *Cooley High* (1975) is a welcome exception. All too often, Hollywood has African Americans in the streets rather than in the schools.

In most 1970s films dealing with high school, blacks are absent, as is any type of caring adult

FIGURE 50. *Blackboard Jungle* (1955). After cynical teachers and incompetent public school administrators turn away from the juvenile-delinquency problem in urban public schools, Richard Dadier (Glenn Ford) refuses to be intimidated when student Artie West (Vic Morrow) brandishes a knife in his class. Courtesy Metro-Goldwyn-Mayer.

presence. George Lucas's *American Graffiti* (1973) provides an adolescent world in which the protagonist Curt (Richard Dreyfuss) must establish his individuality by leaving the conformist atmosphere of high school. While *Graffiti* champions escaping the adolescent concerns of automobiles and the elusive girl in the Thunderbird, the film version of the Broadway hit *Grease* (1978) places a nostalgic spin upon the juvenile delinquency and high school days of the 1950s, a nostalgia updated with the popular television series *Welcome Back, Kotter* (1975–79). The series featured a multiethnic cast, as did its near-contemporary *The White Shadow* (1978–81), suggesting that television was more open than film to the presence of minorities and caring teachers alike.

Less nostalgic and perhaps more reflective of the harassment and cruelty that often accompany the insecurities of adolescence is the film adaptation of Stephen King's *Carrie* (1976). In the title role, Sissy Spacek unleashes telekinetic powers against those peers who made her a subject of ridicule. But the ultimate adolescent fantasy may be the cult classic *Rock 'n' Roll High School* (1979). With the punk music of The Ramones blasting in the background, students respond to the insipid school administration by blowing up the high school. Some might deplore the film's violent conclusion, but it is a stretch to equate this film's adolescent tongue-in-cheek humor with the school violence of the 1990s. A much more pessimistic and sadistic film is *Class of 1984* (1982), in which a teacher seeks revenge against a psychopathic group of students who raped his wife in the halls of the high school.

Alongside these cruel images, Hollywood continued to offer the image of the heroic teacher battling against the apathy of students, bureaucrats, and society. In *Teachers* (1984), Nick Nolte portrays Alex Jarrell, whose idealism is rekindled when the school system is sued for awarding a diploma to an illiterate student. However, teachers were superfluous to most teen and high school films of the 1980s, where a traditional academic education was simply an obstacle placed in the path of adolescents seeking a good time or an understanding of the "real" world.

One of the best films of this genre is Amy Heckerling's *Fast Times at Ridgemont High* (1982), chronicling the exploits of Southern California teens reveling in sex, drugs, and rock' n' roll. In one memorable scene from the film, Jeff Spicoli (Sean Penn) dismays his history teacher, Mr. Hand (Ray Walston), by having a pizza delivered during class; in another, he gives a stoner reading of the founding of the American republic.

But the king of 1980s adolescent cinema has to be director John Hughes, whose films enjoyed considerable commercial success during the decade. In *The Breakfast Club* (1985), teens serving a Saturday school detention learn that they have common aspirations and problems, which their identities as rebel, nerd, brain, social queen, and jock tend to obscure. In *Ferris Bueller's Day Off* (1986), Matthew Broderick stars in the story of a popular teen who outwits school administrators, avoiding a meaningless history test on European socialism by skipping school for the day. Along the way, he helps his friend Cameron confront his materialistic parents. In the world of John Hughes, teenagers are spontaneous and fun loving, while the adult community of school is boring, irrelevant, and sometimes downright cruel. In the self-absorbed adolescents of Hughes, perhaps nowhere more insufferable than in his *Pretty in Pink* (1986), one may perceive parallels with Ronald Reagan's America of the 1980s and what liberal critics labeled as an era of greed and selfishness. The same critique of high schoolers as incipient Republicans plays through the frames of period movies such as *Three O'Clock High* (1987), *Hiding Out* (1987), and *Plain Clothes* (1988).

While the adolescents of Hughes's films seek to cope with high school through teenage angst or pranks, the high school students of the cult favorite *Heathers* (1988) adopt a more cynical approach to dealing with peer pressures. Taking revenge upon a clique of girls named Heather who dominate campus social life, Winona Ryder and Christian Slater portray disillusioned students who embark upon a series of revenge murders, which they try to disguise as suicides. The black humor of *Heathers* shows the dark side of school life, demonstrating how harassment and ridicule may lead to violent retaliation. It is the Hollywood film that may have the most light to shed on the real-life murders at Columbine.

Nevertheless, the heroic celluloid image of the teacher was able to withstand *Heathers* and John Hughes. In *Hoosiers* (1986), Gene Hackman portrays washed-up basketball coach Norman Dale, who finds redemption taking the small town of Hickory to the state championship in basketball-crazed Indiana. The film suggests that high school athletics may forge a sense of community, but the exploitative nature of prep sports is noted in such films as the documentary *Hoop Dreams* (1994), *All the Right Moves* (1983), and *Varsity Blues* (1998).

Two other high school films of the late 1980s offer positive portrayals of school life based upon real life figures and stories. In *Lean on Me* (1989), Morgan Freeman stars as controversial New Jersey teacher turned principal Joseph Clark, who turned around one of the state's toughest schools with a regime of high standards and strict discipline, including patrolling the halls with baseball bat in hand. Whereas *Lean on Me* offers an African American hero, *Stand and Deliver* (1988), originally produced for public television before its theatrical release, engages the Latino community, often neglected by Hollywood. *Stand and Deliver* tells the story of Jamie Escalante (Edward James Olmos) inspiring his students of an East Los Angeles barrio to take and pass the advanced placement test in calculus; indeed, the students retake the exam when the Educational Testing Bureau expresses reservations regarding the validity of test scores. While extolling the individual achievement of Escalante and his students, the film offers little in the way of systematic changes for the inequities in American education.

With *Dangerous Minds* (1995), Hollywood returned to the more typical story of a white teacher rescuing and providing guidance for minority students. But the twist in *Dangerous Minds,* based on the memoir *My Posse Don't Do Homework* by Louanne Johnson, is that the motivational white teacher is female, albeit a former marine and portrayed by Michelle Pfeiffer. While the film was commercially successful, a spin-off television series for ABC was short-lived.

While Pfeiffer's portrayal of Louanne Johnson continues the heroic tradition established by Rick Dadier in *Blackboard Jungle,* many teachers may better identify with Gene Holland (Richard Dreyfuss) in *Mr. Holland's Opus* (1996). Foregoing his ambitions as a composer, Holland takes what he assumes will be a temporary teaching position in a middle-class suburban school. After three decades, his compositions are not well known, but he has inspired a generation of students. The subplot of dealing with his deaf son may strike a note of familiarity with many teachers struggling to maintain a balance between family life and an all-consuming profession.

But anyone wishing to romanticize high school might do well to consult director Richard Linklater's *Dazed and Confused* (1993), which focuses upon the last day of high school for a group of students in Austin, Texas, in 1976. Scenes of sex, drinking, drugs, and cruelty abound as the teens appear to undertake a meaningless passage into the adult world, the emotional territory of Terry Zwigoff's fine film *Ghost World* (2001). Disaffected or marginalized teens may also find reason to identify with the protagonists of Sofia Coppola's *The Virgin Suicides* (1999) and the television series *Freaks and Geeks* (1999–2000), which ran for little more than a season but found an instant cult following. However, affluent, suburban students may better identify with the character of Cher (Alicia Silverstone) in Amy Heckerling's brilliant satire *Clueless* (1995), loosely based on Jane Austen's classic novel *Emma.* Although Cher and her wealthy friends are indeed clueless, they are not mean-spirited, and there is a desire to make a better world. Furthermore, all adults are not villains intent upon foiling the pleasures of young people. The film has considerably more "heart" than the Fox Television series *Beverly Hills 90210,* with which it is often compared. Another literary take on high school comes with *10 Things I Hate About You* (1999), a witty adaptation of William Shakespeare's *Taming of the Shrew.*

As we enter the twenty-first century, Hollywood continues to find high school a fertile ground to plow. In films such as *The Faculty* (1998), teachers (who turn out to be extraterrestrials) find violence as the only way to deal with their unruly charges. High school nostalgia remains rampant with the popular *Never Been Kissed* (1999), featuring Drew Barrymore as an undercover reporter who returns to high school, finding fun and love. While teachers are maligned in *Teaching Mrs. Tingle* (1999), the heroic nature of educators is celebrated in such films as *Music of the Heart* (1999), featuring Meryl Streep, and the Fox Television series *Boston Public* (2000–2002). The more sophisticated possibilities of the high school film genre are evident in Alexander Payne's *Election* (1999), depicting Matthew Broderick—who had portrayed Ferris Bueller thirteen years earlier—as a teacher attempting to sabotage the student-body presidential election of overachiever Tracy Flick (Reese Witherspoon).

With the common experience of high school shared by its potential audience, Hollywood will continue to tap this rich vein. In its treatment of the public school, the film industry perpetuates stereotypes of rebellious minority students and inspiring white teachers, nostalgic longing, insipid administrators and adults, and the all-knowing adolescent, while occasionally telling a true and moving story. In this wide-ranging tapestry, Hollywood does touch upon the diversity of the American experiment in public education championed in the educational reforms of Horace Mann and the promise of American life.

References

Filmography

All the Right Moves (1983, F)
American Graffiti (1973, F)
The Blackboard Jungle (1955, F)
Boston Public (2000–2002, TV)
The Breakfast Club (1985, F)
Carrie (1976, F)
Class of 1984 (1982, F)
Clueless (1995, F)
Conrack (1974, F)
Cooley High (1975, F)
Dangerous Minds (1995, F)
Dazed and Confused (1993, F)
Election (1999, F)
The Faculty (1998, F)
Fame (1980, F)
Fast Times at Ridgemont High (1982, F)
Ferris Bueller's Day Off (1986, F)
Freaks and Geeks (1999–2000, TV)

Ghost World (2001, F)
Grease (1978, F)
Head of the Class (1986–91, TV)
Heathers (1988, F)
Hiding Out (1987, F)
Hoop Dreams (1994, F)
Hoosiers (1986, F)
Lean on Me (1989, F)
Mr. Holland's Opus (1996, F)
Music of the Heart (1999, F)
My Bodyguard (1980, F)
Never Been Kissed (1999, F)
Peggy Sue Got Married (1986, F)
Plain Clothes (1988, F)
Pretty in Pink (1986, F)
Pump up the Volume (1990, F)
Rebel Without a Cause (1955, F)
Rock 'n' Roll High School (1979, F)
Room 222 (1969–74, TV)
Stand and Deliver (1988, F)
Teachers (1984, F)
Teaching Mrs. Tingle (1999, F)
10 Things I Hate About You (1999, F)
Three O'Clock High (1987, F)
To Sir with Love (1967, F)
Up the Down Staircase (1967, F)
Varsity Blues (1998, F)
The Virgin Suicides (1999, F)
Welcome Back, Kotter (1975–79, TV)
White Shadow (1978–81, TV)
Zebrahead (1992, F)

Bibliography

Considine, David M. *The Cinema of Adolescence.* Jefferson, NC: McFarland, 1985.

Cremin, Lawrence A. *American Education: The Colonial Experience, 1607–1783.* New York: Harper & Row, 1970.

——. *American Education: The Metropolitan Experience, 1876–1980.* New York: Harper & Row, 1988.

——. *American Education: The National Experience, 1783–1876.* New York: Harper & Row, 1980.

——. *Public Education.* New York: Basic Books, 1976.

Doherty, Thomas Patrick. *Teenagers and Teenpics: The Juvenilization of American Movies in the 1950s.* Boston: Unwin Hyman, 1988.

Farber, Paul, Eugene F. Provenzo Jr., and Gunilla Holm, eds. *Schooling in the Light of Popular Culture.* Albany: State University of New York Press, 1994.

Goldstein, Ruth M. *The Screen Image of Youth.* Metuchen, NJ: Scarecrow,1986.

Joseph, Pamela Bolotin, and Gail Burnaford, eds. *Images of Schoolteachers in Twentieth-Century America.* New York: St. Martin's, 1994.

Keroes, Jo. *Tales Out of School: Gender. Longing, and the Teacher in Fiction and Film.* Carbondale: Southern Illinois University Press, 1999.

Kozol, Jonathan. *Savage Inequalities: Children in American Schools.* New York: HarperCollins, 1992.

National Commission of Excellence in Education. *A Nation at Risk.* Washington, DC: U.S. Government Printing Office, 1983.

Palladino, Grace. *Teenagers: An American History.* New York: Basic Books, 1996.

Pettigrew, Terrence. *Raising Hell: The Rebel in the Movies.* New York: St. Martin's, 1986.

Ravitch, Diane. *The Troubled Crusade: American Education, 1945–1980.* New York: Basic Books, 1983.

Sizer, Theodore. *Horace's Compromise: The Dilemma of the American High School.* Boston: Houghton Mifflin, 1984.

VI. Places

★ ★ ★ ★ ★ ★ ★

[JOHN C. TIBBETTS]

The Midwest

On the night of December 5, 1854, ten idealistic young men camped out in a crude log cabin in central territorial Kansas. After noting "the beautiful conformation of the land," they drew up the Articles of Association for the town of Topeka. A few hours later, lightning struck the cabin and burned it to the ground. Like a slap on the backside of a newborn baby, lightning thus christened the birth of Kansas and the genesis of what came to be called the "Middle West." It is perhaps no less a quirk of circumstances that three decades later it was from this very same Topeka that real estate developer Harvey Henderson Wilcox journeyed to Southern California and bought up 120 acres of flatland that he christened "Hollywood." Thus, an unlikely but enduring alliance was established between the Middle West and Hollywood that has persisted to this day.

The midwestern character and the films that depict it have been midwifed by diverse circumstances of politics, geography, and weather. As Henry Nash Smith has pointed out, the Middle West lies between the dynamic regions of remote western frontier settlement and the eastern regions of cities and social stratification (143). Thus, it embodies the pastoral ideal, that middle region that lies suspended between untainted wilderness and urban-industrial evils. The immigrants and settlers—many of them extremists from conservative proslavery and liberal free-state factions—came from Yankee, Middle Atlantic, and Old South cultural traditions, as well as from regions as diverse as Germany, Scandinavia, Ireland, and Eastern Europe. The fertile land could reward their hard work, but the harsh environment and isolation threatened to destroy their will and determination. As the country expanded westward over two centuries, geographical referents such as "Middle" and "West" changed many times. Today's perception, as James R. Shortridge notes in his exhaustive study of the subject, is that the Middle West includes twelve states—North Dakota, South Dakota, Minnesota, Wisconsin, Michigan, Illinois, Indiana, Ohio, Nebraska, Iowa, Kansas, and Missouri. The inclusion of a thirteenth state, Oklahoma, is problematic. "Because of its location and early heritage," Shortridge writes, "Oklahoma has historically been called Southern or Southwestern, but Middle West affiliation exists in its wheat-growing north and west" (25, 118).

The Myth of the Garden

In the many films about nineteenth-century immigrants and homesteaders—a story genre that historian Wayne Franklin has dubbed the "settlement narrative"—filmmakers have tried to evoke the drama of transforming a wilderness into a garden, what Scott MacDonald describes as "the original settlers' wonder at where we are, something of the original explorers' excitement in transforming the possible into the actual, and something of the original settlers' understanding of the practical failures of their surroundings" (115–116). Pride of place among these pictures belongs to a duet of films by Swedish director Jan Troell, *The Emigrants* (1970) and *The New Land* (1971). They depict the travails of Swedish farmers Karl and Kristine Oscar during their hazardous sea voyage to America, trip inland by steamboat, and trek across the northern plains to the Minnesota Territory. The climactic image in the first film haunts the memory: after striding the raw grasslands searching for the best place to stake out his farm, Karl Oscar sinks a stick deep into the soft loam. Satisfied at last, he leans back against a tree, a slow smile spreading across his face. Paradoxically, implicit in this love of the earth is what the Kansas-born psychiatrist Karl Menninger claims is a deep-seated ambivalence: "What is really the nature of the soil? Is it the dirt? Is civilization largely built on overcoming it, or built up on the taboo of dirt, overcoming a natural affection for it?" (Hall, 37). There is no doubt of the convictions of at least one prominent midwesterner. Walt Disney, according to Richard Schickel, spent his career banishing the dirt and disorder that marked the hard days of his boyhood on a farm in Marceline, Missouri: he was "conditioned by the hatred of dirt and of the land that needs cleansing and taming and ordering and even paving over before it can be said to be in genuinely useful working order" (53). There never would be a speck of grime on Mickey Mouse's gloves, in Snow White's cottage, or in the theme parks.

Disney's chief rival in tidying up an unpleasant midwestern boyhood was Darryl F. Zanuck, who spent most of his years at Twentieth Century–Fox forging a cinematic antidote to the miserable childhood he had endured in his native Wahoo, Nebraska. Typical is *State Fair* (1945), adapted from a novel by Phil Stong, about the adventures of a rural Iowa family at the annual fair. The famed Broadway team of Rodgers and Hammerstein contributed six songs, including an opening number that is a virtual catalogue of midwestern farm stereotypes—each verse of the song, "Our State Fair," is passed from one member of the Frake family to another, including the family's prize pig Blue Boy. (*State Fair* had been filmed previously, with Will Rogers in 1933, and would be remade one more time in 1962, with Pat Boone and Alice Faye.)

The Serpent in the Garden

If Disney and Zanuck left the realities of rural, agrarian life far behind, other movies reflected a disenchantment with the agrarian ideal, reflecting the darker truths etched in Kansan E. W. Howe's novel *The Story of a Country Town* (1883)—a book that marked, in John William Ward's words, "The moment when the myth of the garden in America gave way to the wasteland of broken dreams" (Howe, 304). D. W. Griffith's *A Corner in Wheat* (1909) put his newly developed crosscutting editing strategies into the service of contrasting the squalid life of poor farmers with the opulent surroundings of the capitalists who were exploiting their labors.

One of the screen's most trenchant indictments of the failure of the land and the consequent defeat of those who try to homestead it appeared in Robert Benton's classic *Bad Company* (1972). A group of young men treks westward from Ohio in order to evade Civil War conscription. But instead of finding the anticipated freedom and opportunity of the West, they encounter only corruption and thievery. While riding through the Flint Hills of southeastern Kansas, they receive a warning from a passing farmer: "We tried farming the first year; the twisters wiped us out. Next year, it was the cattlemen. Then, just pure rotten soil. Ain't nobody got no money, 'ceptin' a few; and even if you do have, ain't a damn thing worth havin'. Rains so damned much it'll give you the chilblains. Dry spell come along and you near choke with the dust. That is, if a bushwhacker don't come along and take your last dollar. I mean it, boys—turn around and go on back." But, of course, the boys don't turn back. As they cross Kansas, they fall in with a gang of thieves—"rough types," as idealistic Drew Dixon (Barry Brown), notes wryly in his journal. With a life of crime as the only available option for survival, Drew's "high expectations" are blasted: "I have tried to look on the bright side of all this," he says with a perfect deadpan, "but I can't think what it would be."

Pare Lorentz's *The Plow That Broke the Plains* (1936) and *The River* (1937) investigated the uncoordinated industrial exploitation of the land that, with the Great Drought of the 1930s, had disrupted the Mississippi Valley's ecological system. Images of the worn faces of farm wives, blighted land, and blistered farmhouses, counterpointed by Missouri composer Virgil Thomson's folkish rendering of cowboy songs, church hymns, and pop tunes, created a sense of the Midwest that was general rather than specific. "Our heroine is the grass, the villain the sun and the wind, our players the actual farmers living in the Plains country," said Lorentz. "It is a melodrama of nature—the tragedy of turning grass into dust" (MacCann, 66). This was rather a departure from the Dust Bowl photographs of Walker Evans and Dorothea Lange, which tended to display a sharper focus and more dispassionate, apolitical objectivity. A clear political agenda lay behind it all. "Only by quality dramatization of the goals of the New Deal," said Lorentz, "could government films win the minds (and the votes) of the American people" (Rollins, 39). As historian Peter C. Rollins has noted, "We are assured that we can surrender our responsibility to government planners who will solve our economic and ecological problems for us" (47).

John Ford's *The Grapes of Wrath* (1940), adapted from John Steinbeck's novel, likewise smacks more of Roosevelt's New Deal liberalism than Steinbeck's Jeffersonian agrarianism. Representative of the "Okies," Dust Bowl migrants who left their dispossessed, blighted farms to seek their fortunes in California—modern archetypes, according to historian Russell Campbell, of the homeless and persecuted Israelites fleeing Egypt to Canaan (108)—the Joad family (Henry Fonda as Tom, Jane Darwell as Ma, and Charley Grapewin as Grampa) encounters in California the same opposing forces of banks and corporate landholders they had presumed to leave behind ("Them sons-a-bitches at their desks," says one character, "they jus' chopped folks in two for their margin o' profit"). Nunnally Johnson's script tempers Steinbeck's revolutionary socialism, omitting references to the takeover of California agriculture by large-scale industry and the revolutionary solidarity among the dispossessed roadside camp population. Rather, its primary foci are the tragedy of despoiled land, the family as the basic unit of community, and the durability of human dignity. Steinbeck's miserable ending, the shriveled remnants of a family struggling to escape a flood, is changed to an upbeat speech by Ma Joad (adapted by producer Darryl F. Zanuck from a speech two-thirds of the way through the book): "We'll go on forever, Pa; we're the people." The last scene of the film depicts the Joads' leaving a government camp and departing into the broad sunlight in search of work.

FIGURE 51. *Bad Company* (1972). Drew Dixon (Barry Brown, left) and one of his gang (John Savage, right) resort to robbing children to survive in Kansas. Going west to reap its supposed benefits and freedom, a disillusioned group of young men turns to crime. Courtesy Paramount Pictures and Jaffilms.

More recently, Richard Pearce's *Country* (1984) and Jocelyn Moorhouse's *A Thousand Acres* (1997), adapted from Jane Smiley's novel of the same name, reveal how public foreclosure and private greed threaten the midwest-

FIGURE 52. *The Grapes of Wrath* (1940). The Joad family packs its belongings to flee the Dust Bowl of their native Oklahoma for the presumed riches of California. Courtesy Twentieth Century-Fox.

ern farm idyll. In the latter film, not only does the acreage of the Cook family—which has been in the family for three generations—become the focal point of a contested legal battle, but poisonous water has seeped into the well and is killing the family. Finally, after squabbles have split the family apart, the land stands unoccupied and uncultivated. Images of glowing vistas of fertile fields and open skies are reduced to a tiny view visible through the window of the now-deserted farmhouse. The promise of three generations and a thousand acres have diminished to a single point of light.

City life in the Midwest has likewise been portrayed with ambivalence. Hoosier writer Booth Tarkington's idyllically picaresque "Penrod" stories, originally written for *Cosmopolitan* in 1914, were brought to the screen in the silent era by Marshall Neilan (*Penrod,* 1922) and William Beaudine (*Penrod and Sam,* 1923) and to the talkies in two Doris Day musicals, Roy del Ruth's *On Moonlight Bay* (1951) and David Butler's *By the Light of the Silvery Moon* (1953). This sort of musical Americana reached its peak in 1962 when Warner Bros. brought Meredith Willson's *The Music Man* to the screen. The schemes of con man Harold Hill (Robert Preston) in River City, Iowa, were accompanied by turn-of-the-century music from the Sousa and George M. Cohan era, replete with barbershop quartets and marching bands. "This vanished, almost mythical past is a fantasy burgeoning from the seeds of remembrance and counterpointing present reality," notes Joseph Andrew Casper (43).

In striking contrast is Orson Welles's *The Magnificent Ambersons* (1942), based on the Pulitzer Prize–winning novel by Hoosier writer Booth Tarkington. Industrialization overtakes the midwestern city of Midland—an encroachment embodied by the character of Eugene Morgan (Joseph Cotten), the progressive, maverick manager of an automobile factory. The arrogant, aristocratic George Amberson (Tim Holt), scion of a family of aristocrats, suffers his "comeuppance" and is reduced to the status of a common laborer. The opening scenes of the Amberson mansion ablaze with Christmas lights are replaced in the conclusion with tracking shots through a darkened house now ruined and empty. "The potential for a great civilization existed in the fertile land, and a vision of this greatness had been glimpsed by the first generation of settlers," notes James R. Shortridge, but "the second generation had lost sight of the dream. Corrupted by an obsession with the material side of success, they broke the pastoral tie" (45).

All four of William Inge's major plays, *Come Back, Little Sheba* (1950), *Picnic* (1953), *Bus Stop* (1955), and *Dark at the Top of the Stairs* (1957)—reflections of the playwright's own experiences growing up in the southeast Kansas town of Independence—came to the screen in the 1950s and early 1960s in versions by Daniel Mann, Josh Logan, and Delbert Mann. In addition, Elia Kazan directed Inge's Academy Award–winning screenplay of *Splendor in the Grass* in 1961. Beneath their deceptively monotonous, commonplace surfaces lay themes of loneliness, frustration, sexual inhibition, loss, despair, and, perhaps above all, the human need for love (Voss, 183). Their screen incarnations, like their theatrical originals, present graphic protraits of repressed characters living out isolated lives of moral confusion and tarnished ideals amidst the middlewestern spaces from which the young playwright had fled as a youth.

Most recently, Clint Eastwood's *The Bridges of Madison County* (1992) revisits these themes. Indeed, it may be regarded as a latter-day *Picnic*: The arrival in Iowa farm country of dashing Robert Kincaid (Clint Eastwood), an itinerant photographer on assignment, unleashes the passions of Francesca (Meryl Streep), a lonely farm wife. While their brief but intense affair—played out against the isolation of rural farm country—illuminates their desperate inner needs, it also throws into stark relief the emotional and physical obstacles blocking their chance for a more prolonged, fulfilling relationship. The enormous appeal of both the film and the book (which to date has sold more copies than the King James version of the Bible) attests to the enduring popularity of this sort of bittersweet rural idyll, to which Omaha-born director Alexander Payne added an ironic twist with his films *Citizen Ruth* (1996), *Election* (1999), and *About Schmidt* (2002).

Fanatics, Frauds, and Outlaws

Crisscrossing the midwestern landscape, sometimes under cover of darkness, sometimes amidst a hail of gunfire, and sometimes under the star-spangled glare of the revival tent marches a succession of opportunists, drifters, and self-righteous zealots. John Brown and William Clarke Quantrill sit astride the years of the Kansas-Missouri Border Wars (1856–1865), their faces lit from below as if by the flames of their conflicting free-state and proslavery ideologies. "The early settlers of Kansas were the extremists of the nation," writes David Hinshaw, "men from the North and East who flocked there to incorporate their conviction into law." (12) Raymond Massey brought a stern authority to his two screen portrayals of the fanatical Brown in Michael Curtiz's *Santa Fe Trail* (1941) and Charles Marquis Warren's *Seven Angry Men* (1955). Although the former was intended to be a vehicle for Errol Flynn as the swashbuckling Jeb Stuart, it was the saturnine Massey who stole the show ("I am a David armed with the power and the glory!"). However, Robert Buckner's script tap-danced around the slavery issue so carefully that it almost managed to avoid it altogether. This sample of the dialogue is typical:

> George Armstrong Custer [Ronald Reagan]: "There's a purpose behind [Brown's] madness."
> Jeb Stuart [Errol Flynn]: "It's not our job to say who's right or wrong."

On the other hand, the enigmatic Quantrill, on screen as in life, proved to be a more elusive character to pin down. In Raoul Walsh's *Dark Command* (1940), Quantrill is a schoolteacher named "Cantrell" (Walter Pidgeon) who is wholly apolitical—"You're not fighting for the North," he tells his guerilla band, "and you're not fighting for the South; you're fighting for what's coming for you!"—and whose attack on Lawrence, Kansas, is motivated primarily by the loss of his girlfriend to rival John Wayne. In Ray Enright's *Kansas Raiders* (1950), Quantrill (Brian Donlevy) is a proslavery martinet who dreams of bolstering Robert E. Lee's sagging fortunes by taking the Civil War into the regions west of Missouri. And in Edward Berndt's *Quantrill's Raiders* (1958), he is a vicious, womanizing thug (Leo Gordon) who is so inept as a soldier that he is unable to consummate the Lawrence raid. There are fragments of truth in all of these Hollywood reconstructions, but the politics behind the struggle over "Bleeding Kansas" have been largely ignored, with the notable exception of Taiwanese director Ang Lee's *Ride with the Devil* (1999).

A different breed of zealot swarmed across the Middle West after the turn of the century. Hard on the heels of a different kind of civil war, the conflict between evolutionary theorists and religious fundamentalists, tent-show preachers and revival shouters delivered a pentecostal message of deliverance to lower and middle-class citizens starved for practical answers to hard times. Religious fervor is part of the Plains States character, wrote William Inge, a consequence of the realization that in the face of earth and sky man is not all-powerful: "That may explain why people in the Plains States are (I believe) more solemnly religious than those in other parts of the nation" (Averill, ed., 157). Among the Bible-thumping brethren, however, were con artists all too willing to exploit their flocks for easy money. Frank Capra's *The Miracle Woman* (1931) stars Barbara Stanwyck as a disillusioned preacher's daughter who used sex and faked miracles to con the suckers. In Sinclair Lewis's *Elmer Gantry* (1927), adapted to the screen by Richard Brooks in 1960, the eponymous Elmer is a charismatic, fast-talking, thoroughly unscrupulous evangelist from Terwillinger College in Kansas. Although censorial pressures forced Brooks to temper the novel's anticlericalism and place the unordained Gantry outside the mainstream of pentecostal religion, the film cannily exploits Burt Lancaster's exuberant athleticism as Gantry in a way that recalls the antics of that real-life "calliope of Zion," ex-baseball player and native of Ames, Iowa, Billy Sunday. More recently, films such as *The Rainmaker* (1956), based on a play N. Richard Nash (and also starring Burt Lancaster), and *The Apostle* (1997), written and directed by Robert Duvall, have explored the uneasy relationships between miracle and illusion, faith and fraud.

Meanwhile, in the 1920s and 1930s, backcountry bandits such as Bonnie and Clyde were glorified and vilified, by turns, for largely the same reasons that Quantrill and the James Boys had been exploited as dime-novel protagonists, engaging in what Richard Slotkin describes as "an extreme but morally justifiable form of resistance to the invasion of their region first by Yankees and then by banks and railroads chartered by the Republican government of the state" (133). David Newman and Robert Benton's screenplay for *Bonnie and Clyde* (1967) dramatized the eponymous characters' two-year binge of robbery and murder on the back roads of Texas, Missouri, and Kansas. Its blend of reality and legend was served up with a soupçon of French New Wave sensibility. Director Arthur Penn saw affinities between the early 1930s and his own time, and he wanted to make "a modern film whose action takes place in the past" (Murray, 241). Moreover, Clyde's sexual ambiguity and the film's veering from seriocomic slapstick to graphically staged violence appealed to a divided American scene of urban riots, racial unrest, anti-Vietnam protests, and a dropout drug culture.

Among modern takes on real-life midwestern bandits and killers, Richard Brooks's *In Cold Blood* (1967) stands out. It is based on Truman Capote's book, a classic in what came to be called "the new journalism," blending factual reportage with novelistic techniques (Karl, 561–562). Capote's recounting of two ex-convicts' grisly shotgun murders in 1959 of a farming family in Holcomb, Kansas—a region of prairie lands and wheat fields seventy miles east of the Colorado border ("a lonesome area that other Kansans call 'out there,'" writes Capote)—was an eerie evocation of a place and a cast of characters that defied easy analysis. Both book and film employed that quintessential feature of the midwestern landscape, the vanishing point—the convergence of those archetypal elements of the prairie, the highway and the farmhouse—as a metaphor for the fatal intersection of the nomadic killers and the peacefully domestic Clutter family. The crosscutting between highway and farmhouse during the first third of the story predestines their ultimate collision. The subsequent violence, when it comes, is as sudden and inscrutable as a prairie lightning strike.

Miracles in the Wheat

Paradoxically, the flattest and most prosaic of midwestern landscapes may conceal unimaginable terrors and wonders. Swirling around the stoic, impassive form of that quintessential Kansan, Buster Keaton, were all manner of floods, cyclones and other disasters. "I used to daydream an awful lot in pictures," he said with typical understatement. "I could get carried away and visualize all the fairylands in the world."

Thus, as in Stephen King's *Children of the Corn* (1984), rows of tall corn conceal a mysterious, elemental "Corn God." In *Strategic Air Command* (1955), *Dr. Strangelove* (1964), and *Fail-Safe* (1964), fields of Nebraska wheat cover up underground silos filled with nuclear missiles—assuring that, in the event of nuclear confrontation, the Midwest would be a primary strike target, as dramatized in Nicholas Meyer's *The Day After* (1985). And in *Field of Dreams* (1989), an Iowa meadow spawns the ghosts of "Shoeless Joe" Jackson and the rest of the Chicago "Black Sox" baseball team.

It is weirdly appropriate that *Field of Dreams* closely resembles Steven Spielberg's *Close Encounters of the Third Kind* (1977). In both, two spiritually damaged fathers ("Ray" and "Roy," respectively) leave their families in the Midwest (Ray Neary in Muncie, Indiana, and Roy Kinsella in Dyersville, Iowa) to follow premonitions of a weird visitation (Neary's vision of a high tower; Kinsella's hearing of a mysterious voice intoning, "If you build it, he will come"). Each man finds his grail in the end (Ray follows an alien into a waiting spaceship; Roy plays a game of catch with the ghost of his father). The topography of both films are reverse images of each other: the landing site in *Close Encounters* resembles a ball diamond where the two "teams" of earthly scientists and extraterrestrial visitors engage in a kind of cosmic ball game; and the playing field in *Field of Dreams* functions as a "launching pad" for Roy's imagination. Each is a typically midwestern location, a secure, protected area bounded and measured. Each is safe. Each is home.

Disruption and separation have ended in discovery and reconciliation. This is the message embodied in that greatest of midwestern classics, *The Wizard of Oz* (1939), based on L. Frank Baum's novel. Readers of Baum's original story, published in 1900, will recall Dorothy's spirited defense of her home at the expense of the more glamorous Oz: "No matter how dreary and gray our homes are, we people of flesh and blood would rather live there than in any other country, be it ever so beautiful. There is no place like home" (Averill, ed., 2). And Disney's *Return to Oz* (1985)—not so much a remake of the MGM classic as an adaptation of Baum's later books, *The Land of Oz* and *Ozma of Oz*—prompted Billina, the talking chicken, to remark: "If this is Oz, I'll take my chances in Kansas!" But maybe it's not simply that Kansas is a place to escape from or to return to; rather, it's a place that one never leaves at all. Thus, the 1939 MGM film blurs the distinctions between Kansas and Oz by casting Ray Bolger, Jack Haley, Bert Lahr, and Margaret Hamilton in dual roles as the inhabitants of *both* regions, confirming a similarity that borders on identity. Small wonder that popular myth has begun to confuse the two and regard them both as interchangeable regions. At this writing, entrepreneurs are planning to locate a "Wizard of Oz" theme park in Johnson County, Kansas.

The dream of the Midwest is best expressed in the metaphor of the solitary soul standing midway between the broad sky and level earth, seeking that magical vanishing point where the individual and the community, the commonplace and the miraculous, freedom and responsibility, dream and reality, and yes—Hollywood and Kansas—meet—and merge.

References

Filmography

Abe Lincoln in Illinois (1938, F)
About Schmidt (2002, F)
The Apostle (1997, F)
Babbitt (1934, F)
Bad Company (1972, F)
Badlands (1973, F)
Bonnie and Clyde (1967, F)
The Bridges of Madison County (1992, F)
Bus Stop (1955, F)
By the Light of the Silvery Moon (1953, F)
Children of the Corn (1984, F)
Citizen Ruth (1996, F)
Close Encounters of the Third Kind (1977, F)
Come Back, Little Sheba (1952, F)
A Corner in Wheat (1909, F)
Country (1984, F)
Dark at the Top of the Stairs (1960, F)
Dark Command (1940, F)
The Day After (1985, F)
Days of Heaven (1978, F)
Dodsworth (1936, F)
Dr. Strangelove, or: How I Learned to Stop Worrying and Love the Bomb (1964, F)
Election (1999, F)
Elmer Gantry (1960, F)
The Emigrants (1970, F)
Fail-Safe (1964, F)
Field of Dreams (1989, F)
The Grapes of Wrath (1940, F)
In Cold Blood (1967, F)
Kansas City (1996, F)
Kansas Raiders (1950, F)
The Magnificent Ambersons (1942, F)
The Miracle Woman (1931, F)
Mr. and Mrs. Bridge (1993, F)
The Music Man (1962, F)
Native Sons (1940, F)
Natural Born Killers (1996, F)
Needful Things (1994, F)
The New Land (1971, F)
Penrod (1922, F)
Penrod and Sam (1923, F)
Picnic (1955, F)
Oklahoma! (1955, F)
One Week (1920, F)
On Moonlight Bay (1951, F)
O Pioneers! (1996, F)
Our Daily Bread (1932, F)
The Plow That Broke the Plains (1936, D)
Prime Cut (1972, F)
Quantrill's Raiders (1958, F)
The Rainmaker (1956, F)
Return to Oz (1985, F)
Ride with the Devil (1999, F)
The River (1937, D)
Santa Fe Trail (1941, F)
Sarah Plain and Tall (1997, F)
Seven Angry Men (1955, F)
Splendor in the Grass (1961, F)
State Fair (1933, F; 1945, F; 1962, F)
Steamboat Bill, Jr. (1928, F)
Strategic Air Command (1955, F)
They Live by Night (1947, F)
A Thousand Acres (1997, F)
True-Heart Susie (1919, F)
The Wizard of Oz (1939, F)
Young Mr. Lincoln (1939, F)
You Only Live Once (1937, F)

Bibliography

Averill, Thomas Fox. "Oz and Kansas Culture." *Kansas History* 12.1 (1989): 2–12.

——, ed. *What Kansas Means to Me.* Lawrence: University Press of Kansas, 1991.

Bell, Elizabeth, Lynda Haas, and Laura Sells, eds. *From Mouse to Mermaid: The Politics of Film, Gender, and Culture.* Bloomington: Indiana University Press, 1995.

Benton, Thomas Hart. *An Artist in America.* Columbia: University of Missouri Press, 1983.

Campbell, Russell. "Trampling Out the Vintage: Sour Grapes." In Gerald Peary and Roger Shatzkin, eds., *The Modern American Novel and the Movies,* 107–118. New York: Frederick Ungar, 1978.

Casper, Joseph Andrew. *Vincente Minnelli and the Film Musical.* New York: A. S. Barnes, 1977.

Farber, Manny. *Movies.* New York: Hillstone, 1971.

Fellman, Michael. *Inside War: The Guerilla Conflict in Missouri During the American Civil War.* New York: Oxford University Press, 1989.

Frazier, Ian. *Great Plains.* New York: Farrar, Straus & Giroux, 1989.

Hall, Bernard H., ed. *A Psychiatrist's World: The Selected Letters of Karl Menninger.* New York: Viking, 1949.

Hinshaw, David. *A Man from Kansas: The Story of William Allen White.* New York: Putnam's, 1945.

Howe, W. W. *The Story of a Country Town.* New York: Twayne, 1962.

Karl, Frederick R. *American Fictions: 1940–1980.* New York: Harper & Row, 1983.

Kerr, Walter, *The Silent Clowns.* New York: Knopf, 1975.

Leslie, Edward E. *The Devil Knows How to Ride: The True Story of William Clarke Quantrill and His Confederate Raiders.* New York: Random House, 1996.

MacCann, Richard Dyer. *The People's Films.* New York: Hastings House, 1973.

MacDonald, Scott. "Re-Envisioning the American West." *American Studies* 39.1 (1998): 115–146.

McLoughlin, William Gerald. *Billy Sunday Was His Real Name.* Chicago: University of Chicago Press, 1955.

Meyer, Nicholas. "*The Day After,* Bringing the Unwatchable to TV." *TV Guide,* 19–25 November 1983.

Mordden, Ethan. *Rodgers & Hammerstein.* New York: Abrams, 1992.

Murray, Lawrence L. "Hollywood, Nihilism, and the Youth Culture of the Sixties: *Bonnie and Clyde.*" In John E. O'Connor and Martin A. Jackson, eds., *American History/ American Film: Interpreting the Hollywood Image,* 237–256. New York: Frederick A. Ungar, 1979.

Quanatic, Diane Dufva. "The Unifying Thread: Connecting Place and Language in Great Plains Literature." *American Studies* 32.1 (1991): 67–83.

Rollins, Peter C. "New Deal Documentaries." In Peter C. Rollins, ed., *Hollywood as Historian: American Film in a Cultural Context,* 32–48. 2d ed. Lexington: University Press of Kentucky, 1998.

Sanford, Charles L. *The Quest for Paradise.* Urbana: University of Illinois Press, 1961.

Schickel, Richard. *The Disney Version.* New York: Simon & Schuster, 1968.

Shorer, Mark. *Sinclair Lewis: An American Life.* New York: McGraw-Hill, 1961.

Shortridge, James R. *The Middle West: Its Meaning in American Culture.* Lawrence: University Press of Kansas, 1989.

Slotkin, Richard. *Gunfighter Nation: The Myth of the Frontier in Twentieth-Century America.* New York: Atheneum, 1992.

Smiley, Jane. *A Thousand Acres.* New York: Ivy Books, 1996.

Smith, Henry Nash. *Virgin Land: The American West as Symbol and Myth.* New York: Knopf, 1950.

Sobchack, Vivian. "*The Grapes of Wrath* (1940): Thematic Emphasis Through Visual Style." In Peter C. Rollins, ed., *Hollywood as Historian: American Films in a Cultural Context,* 68–87. 2d ed. Lexington: University Press of Kentucky, 1998.

Thomson, Virgil. *Virgil Thomson.* New York: Da Capo, 1967.

Toplin, Robert Brent. *History by Hollywood: The Use and Abuse of the American Past.* Urbana: University of Illinois Press, 1996.

Voss, Ralph. *A Life of William Inge.* Lawrence: University of Kansas Press, 1989.

White, William Allen. *The Autobiography of William Allen White.* New York: Macmillan, 1946.

[JAMES HANLAN]

The "New" West and the New Western

Frederick Jackson Turner's 1893 essay "The Frontier in American History" shaped the view of generations of academicians, who expanded on and revised Turner's ideas about the nature of American exceptionalism. Turner saw many of the nation's best characteristics—such as democracy, individualism, and opportunity—as arising out of America's longstanding encounter with the frontier. In 1950 Henry Nash Smith's *Virgin Land* magnificently summarized and critiqued the impact of the West on the American imagination. In *Nature's Metropolis: Chicago and the Great West* (1991), William Cronon further revised historical views by demonstrating the inextricable ecological and economic links between urban and frontier communities. Western historical literature is vast and rich; it includes Robert Dykstra's work on cattle towns, Richard McGrath on frontier violence, and Robert Utley on Indians, among other contributions to a large body of scholarship. Michael Malone's *Historians and the American West* (1983) explores some of that vast literature. Likewise, Jane Tompkins's *West of Everything: The Inner Life of Westerns* (1992) treats the relationship between film and western life in a thematic fashion, analyzing the ways in which westerns have portrayed death, women, the use of landscape, and animals, and setting these themes amid complex historical factors.

In contrast to recent scholarly work, the Turnerian image of the West has had an enduring popularity and has influenced Hollywood's representations. Never far ahead of the popular, Theodore Roosevelt, in *The Winning of the West* (1907), reflected this perspective; his opinions influenced both government policy and popular culture. (Roosevelt advocated the view that "peace by the sword" in a war against "savages" was the most righteous expression of true manhood.)

The western film long stood as a unique genre for the American film industry. Westerns were typically set on the American frontier during the late nineteenth or early twentieth century (1865–1915) and followed formula themes: the conflict of good versus evil, villain versus hero, lawman versus outlaw, settlers versus Indians. The background was glorious and sweeping, nothing less than the panorama of the entire American West, where a well-endowed and generous nature awaited subordination and romance waited to bloom. The western hero was typically a lawman, a man of principle and integrity with a clear moral compass, a sense of rugged individualism, and a (reluctant) willingness to use violence to the extent needed to assure the triumph of good. The formula became well established and predictable in the hundreds of low-budget westerns made from the 1920s through the 1940s. The formula western reinforced established social values and mores and assured audiences that the forces of good and evil were easily distinguishable; most important, they promised that good would triumph despite the trials of adversity. Cowboy star Tom Mix appeared in more than three hundred films of this kind, while his contemporary William S. Hart made more than sixty-five films, ending in the late 1920s. For generations facing first the economic turmoil of the Great Depression and then the terrors of World War II, this formula offered solace.

During the 1950s, western films began to expand the themes with which they dealt in both variety and sensitivity. As early as 1943, William Wellman's *The Ox-Bow Incident,* based on the novel by Walter Van Tilburg Clark, called moral certainty into doubt. The stereotypical portrayal of the good lawman and the bad outlaw began to fade as the main characters in western films came to be seen as complex and fallible human beings whose moral and ethical ambiguities were worthy of exploration. The transformation and redefinition of the western film into a sophisticated and mature genre by revisionist filmmakers would enable it to counteract a decline in popularity in the late 1960s. In an era of space exploration, a different kind of frontier captured the imagination of a new generation of moviegoers, often using themes similar to those of the classic western but in a different setting, perhaps best exemplified by George Lucas's *Star Wars* series. The "New Western" genre that emerged in the 1970s continued the earlier revisionist trend and revived the popularity of the western as a vehicle for the exploration of contemporary social concerns. In the process, it called into question almost all of the formulas of the older western film.

The Evolving Portrayal of Native Americans

By the 1960s, American Indians, like other minority groups, had begun to reassert their rights and identity with vigor. Vine Deloria's *Custer Died for Your Sins* (1969) affirmed the strength and validity of Indian culture and called for an end to cultural oppression. In *Little Big Man* (1970), based on Thomas Berger's novel, director Arthur Penn presented an alternative form of captivity narrative. Taken captive and raised by Indians, Dustin Hoffman's character, Jack Crabb, referred to Indians as "human beings" and reflected that although there was an endless supply of white men, there was but "a limited supply of human beings." Penn's film presented white settlers as the real savages, randomly slaughtering Indian women and children. In addition, their leader, George Armstrong Custer, was portrayed as an impetuous madman in "a world without human beings [which] has no center to it." This countercultural critique of American society was reflected in the film's prediction that "human beings will soon walk a road that leads nowhere." *Little Big Man*'s portrait of Custer can usefully be contrasted with that presented in the PBS documentary *Last Stand at Little Big Horn* (1992), narrated by Pulitzer Prize–winning Native American writer N. Scott Momaday. Using journals, oral accounts, and ledger drawings as well as archival and feature film footage, the documentary contrasts white and Indian perspectives on "Manifest Destiny." The New Western, like earlier versions of the genre, reflected the social concerns of the era in which the films were produced. By the 1970s, Americans had come to question the wisdom of their own government and, following on the civil rights movement, were willing to reconsider the role accorded to minorities. Like John Ford's *Cheyenne Autumn* (1964), Penn's film exhibited sensitivity toward and admiration of the Native American.

Kevin Costner's *Dances with Wolves* (1990) further extended Hollywood's reinterpretation of the American Indian. Many Native Americans praised Costner's film for its portrayal of their peoples' everyday lives. Graham Greene, who portrayed Kicking Bird, was honored in 1997 with the National Aboriginal Achievement Award for his body of work. In its citation of Greene, the award praised his role as Kicking Bird for portraying all that was good in aboriginal life and experience; the citation also referred to the Costner film as one of the most important pieces of film in American Indian history. PBS contributed to the reinterpretation of Native American culture with *Geronimo and the Apache Resistance* (1988) and documented complex land swindles in *Indians, Outlaws and Angie Debo* (1988). Likewise, PBS's *In the White Man's Image* (1991) portrays as cultural genocide the efforts of the Carlisle School for Indians, where Indian children were housed for "white immersion" experiences to integrate them into the mainstream in the 1870s. The New Western thus both reflected an awareness of the worthiness of cultures once dismissed as primitive and the sensibilities of an America inured to excessive violence. As Peter C. Rollins and John E. O'Connor observe in *Hollywood's Indian* (1998), film long played a crucial part in shaping the popular image of the American Indian. Revisionist film continued the manipulation, but toward new ends.

Reflections of the 1960s

The films of Sam Peckinpah reflect a darker view of human nature adopted by a society exposed to televised reports from the Vietnam battlefields. Peckinpah's *The Wild Bunch* (1969) opened with a scene of children gleefully observing fire ants slaughtering a scorpion. This scene was followed by, and interspersed with, the confrontation of vigilantes with a gang of outlaws. In a typical Peckinpah reversal, familiar categories of good and evil were exchanged: it was the outlaws with whom the audience came to sympathize and the lawmen—depicted as agents of an exploitative railroad—who were of questionable moral authority. Peckinpah's outlaws were men seeking independence, identity, and reassurance of their manhood in a rapidly changing world where big business and big government threatened personal autonomy. The film was set on the Mexican border in 1913, shortly before "Black Jack" Pershing engaged in futile pursuit of the famous Mexican bandit Pancho Villa—a theme developed in greater depth by PBS's *The Hunt for Pancho Villa* (1993). Peckinpah saw General Pershing's payrolls as a suitable target for the outlaws—perhaps the last target they would have before modernity rendered "outlaws" obsolete. The Mexican rebel forces were viewed sympathetically as peasants striving for independence, while their government and the American army alike were simply on the wrong side of the moral equation. In the spirit of the 1960s, Peckinpah focused extensively, almost lovingly, on the violence of the confrontation. Forces that would have unquestionably represented good in the earlier western genre now were seen as conniving and evil. The "lawmen" were more than willing to shoot down innocent men, women, and children in order to kill the outlaws: any means to an end. The parallels with Lieutenant William Calley's "wasting" of a hamlet in Vietnam in 1968 and Peter Arnett's famous report of a military assertion that a hamlet sometimes had to be destroyed in order to be saved would be strong and inescapable. (While the film was playing in theaters, contemporary newspaper headlines revealed the horrors of the My Lai massacre.) In Peckinpah's world, the forces breaking the law used minimal violence, whereas the forces that represent the law used massive destructive force in defense of a dubious establishment selfishness. Symbols of a new technology of death emerged in the film with the use of the machine gun and a reference to flying machines used to kill. The closing scene of *The Wild Bunch* was marked by devastation and buzzards; a peasant society had been torn apart by war and violence. Furthermore, any remaining individualists or rebels had been "wasted."

When *The Wild Bunch* was released in 1969, critics hailed it as a milestone, some claiming it to be the most important American film since Orson Welles's *Citizen Kane* (1941). The balletic shootouts were both denounced and admired, with director Peckinpah being labeled the "Picasso of Violence." The scholarly analysis of violence on the frontier presented by Roger D. McGrath in *Gunfighters, Highwaymen, and Vigilantes* (1984) certainly reveals a less sensationalistic history of the use of force. Clearly, Peckinpah was addressing his own time: from the Watts riot of 1965 (which caused the deaths of thirty-four people) through the summer of 1968, American cities erupted in violence. For many Americans, the nonviolent approach of Martin Luther King Jr. seemed to have died with him in 1968, leaving Peckinpah's western film as a reflection of the times.

In sharp contrast with Peckinpah's obsession with bloodletting, George Roy Hill's *Butch Cassidy and the Sundance Kid* (1969) reveals that one of the main characters, Cassidy, never shot a man until a confrontation made violence mandatory. Paul Newman (as Butch) and Robert Redford (as Sundance), both Hollywood legends, present rustlers, bandits, and robbers in a thoroughly likeable—almost innocent—way. Director Hill assures his audience that "most of what follows is true" at the outset of the film, indicating that the film would play against existing western myths; indeed, the portrayal of Butch and Sundance is colored by the legend that emerged and grew in the almost seven decades following Butch and Sundance's adventures. Despite the directorial statement, the function of Hill's movie is to entertain in a tale of two likeable rogues characterized by charm, loyalty, and 1960s-style nonconformism as redeeming qualities. They represent the closing of the American West, and their flight to South America suggested that American modernity was driving out our last individualists. It is in only this interpretive framework that the film is "accurate," rather than in the sense of presenting any historical objectivity. The disillusionment with authority figures and distrust of big business setting in by the late 1960s may have been the most "accurately" presented interpretation conveyed by this film. The two engaging outlaws are incredulous when told that Mr. E. H. Harriman, legendary leader of the Union Pacific Railroad and father of diplomat W. Averill Harriman, a name recognizable by informed filmgoers, has tired of *their* picking on *him* and has determined to have them eliminated. A powerful establishment had to suppress the irrepressible individualists.

The 1970s and Beyond

Robert Altman's *McCabe & Mrs. Miller* (1971) picked up the theme of the individual victimized by business interests and turned most of the stereotypes of the western film upside down. Rather than being met with the wide vistas of the American West, a landscape full of beauty, Turnerian potential, and gifted by nature, the film opens at a dismal, isolated mining town with the ironic name of Presbyterian Church. More than the landscape is drab; the characters themselves are presented in anything but an heroic mode. McCabe (Warren Beatty), an inept and bungling would-be entrepreneur, is saved from the folly of his own incompetence by Mrs. Miller (Julie Christie), a shrewd madame with few illusions about life or romance. The usual romantic gender roles are reversed here: the man is love-struck, the woman cold and calculating. Although Constance Miller is capable and tough, neither the film nor the new western genre adequately readdresses the role of women in the West. The women in the film are prostitutes, their lives governed by commerce. Commerce eventually proves the undoing of McCabe when he foolishly refuses to sell out his "business interests" in the bordello. He naively relies on the promises of lawyer Samuels (modeled after Mark Twain) that the trusts will be brought under control and "won't be able to lift one little finger against you." Mrs. Miller recognizes the folly of this advice and urges McCabe to get out of town. When he refuses, Constance Miller wastes no time mourning her lost love and turns instead to her true love, an opium pipe. In the end Altman presents his audience with a nihilistic vision of society: men and women mistrust one another, nature has turned hostile to human values, a philistine world of business and commerce has triumphed, and drugs have created an escapist stupor for their victims. In the closing scenes of the film, McCabe is hunted down by gunslingers in a blizzard, while Mrs. Miller becomes lost in an opium cloud. Not even youth held redeeming potential; the one naive and likable character in the film, a young cowboy, is gunned down by a remorseless, would-be gunslinger who is with the bounty hunters pursuing McCabe for the mining company.

Altman's allegorical account of life in a mining town contrasts with a documentary view, *Out of the Depths—The Miner's Story* (1988), produced for PBS as part of Bill Moyers's *A Walk Through the Twentieth Century* series. Moyers worked with scholars at the University of Colorado to produce an oral history account of the life of mineworkers at the beginning of the twentieth century that includes accounts of the Ludlow massacre (1914) as well as personal reminiscences of everyday life. The PBS version more closely reflects the work of scholars such as Rodman W. Paul, whose considerably older *Mining Frontiers of the Far West, 1848–1880* (1963) presents a detailed, factual analysis of mining communities.

FIGURE 53. *McCabe & Mrs. Miller* (1971). John McCabe (Warren Beatty, right) ponders an offer by Sears (Michael Murphy, left), the owner of a mining company, to purchase his land and profitable bordello. Egotistical and ignorant of the economic changes and powerful entrepreneurs moving into the West, McCabe refuses to sell, leading to his death. Courtesy Warner Bros.

In *McCabe & Mrs. Miller*, the only black characters are a wagon driver and his wife. In most earlier western genre films blacks are almost invisible. John Ford's *Sergeant Rutledge* (1960), made toward the end of the fabled director's career, focuses on an African American trooper in the Ninth Cavalry wrongfully accused of rape and murder. Contemporary reviewers praised Woody Strode, who played Rutledge, but greeted Ford's film with mixed reactions. Black journalists sensed that the film was historically important both for the industry and for audiences, while white journalists were less enthusiastic, with one calling it an embarrassingly bad film. Years later the film was recognized as an important cinematic contribution to the understanding of race in the turbulent 1960s. In his revisionist film *Posse* (1993), African American director and star Mario Van Peebles continued in Ford's footsteps by putting his race at the very center of the American West. The film contrasts establishment with disestablishment by stressing both the number of African Americans who participated in western settlement and portraying black disenfranchisement and the terror of the Ku Klux Klan—all matters touched on as well in Mel Brooks's broad farce *Blazing Saddles* (1974), one of the few mainstream films of the time with an African American lead actor.

The Influence of Television

Although the attractiveness of the classic western theme declined for producers of feature films, television continued to grind out western stories. Unlike the genre of commercial television, though, the works of filmmaker Ken Burns and his associates for public television were carefully researched and presented the commentary of prominent scholars on the complex issues of western settlement, community life, environment and geography, racial and ethnic conflict, and economic development. In his two-hour series entitled *Lewis & Clark: The Journey of the Corps of Discovery* (1997), Burns presented a thoughtful interpretation of an epic expedition in which a broad spectrum of scholarly views were aired—especially those of Stephen Ambrose and John Allen. Burns's severest critics have pointed out that the flaws of his approach are the inherent failings of a melodramatic medium, while Robert B. Toplin has urged filmmakers to make the public aware that historical interpretation involves debate and the making of judgments about conflicting interpretations of the past. Leon Litwak and Daniel Walkowitz have suggested that Burns tends to take a vintage nineteenth-century approach, stressing visual beauty and military details while avoiding difficult and vexing political questions. In particular, Walkowitz sees a substantial divergence between the values of historians and underwriters such as the National Endowment for the Humanities and General Motors. As of 1996, the auto giant had provided ten years of support for Burns's work and agreed to provide corporate underwriting for all of Burns's films through the year 2000. Perhaps in response to this mainstream corporate support, Burns pointed to the limitations of scholars who speak to an increasingly smaller audience of academic specialists; in contrast, Burns stressed that his films are intended to engage and excite a large popular audience.

Burns acted as producer for a nine-part series, *The West* (1996), directed by Stephen Ives, an associate in Burns's New Hampshire center. Burns and Ives consciously downplay the culture of violence romanticized by gunslinger stories and films, stressing instead the process of settlement of a vast territory by a heterogeneous people. Although this approach much more closely parallels scholarly work on the West than do Hollywood films, ironically, in a 1996 interview about the series, Burns acknowledged that the single most influential filmmaker in shaping his own views was John Ford, whom Burns credited with both promoting the western myth and simultaneously going beyond it.

An Enduring Genre

Although the popularity of the western film has declined as the genre has grown more sophisticated, the western remains nonetheless an enduring theme in both American film and American literature. The resurgent appeal of the western genre on television has been demonstrated in the success of *Lonesome Dove* (1989), a miniseries based on Larry McMurtry's Pulitzer Prize–winning novel. The miniseries gave rise to sequels that proved popular for their rejuvenation of traditional western themes, perhaps reflecting a return to a Turnerian view in the age of Ronald Reagan, whose visage has been advocated as a suitable addition to the Mount Rushmore pantheon. While Reagan's popularity as president has outlived his reputation both as host of the television series *Death Valley Days* and as an actor in western films, the genre itself has proven remarkably adept in its ability to represent changing contemporary interpretations of our national life. Cast in celluloid and videotape rather than stone, the ever-evolving images of the western film continually present themselves anew to the consciousness of new generations of filmgoers.

References

Filmography

Blazing Saddles (1974, F)
Butch Cassidy and the Sundance Kid (1969, F)
Cheyenne Autumn (1964, F)
Dances with Wolves (1990, F)
Geronimo and the Apache Resistance (1988, D)
The Hunt for Pancho Villa (1993, D)
Indians, Outlaws and Angie Debo (1988, D)
In the White Man's Image (1991, D)
Last Stand at Little Big Horn (1992, D)
Lewis & Clark: The Journey of the Corps of Discovery (1997, D)
Little Big Man (1970, F)
Lonesome Dove (1989, TV)
The Man Who Shot Liberty Valance (1962, F)

McCabe & Mrs. Miller (1971, F)
The Outlaw Josey Wales (1976, F)
Out of the Depths—The Miners' Story (1988, D)
The Ox-Bow Incident (1943, F)
Posse (1993, F)
The Searchers (1956, F)
Sergeant Rutledge (1960, F)
Stagecoach (1939, F)
Tombstone (1993, F)
Unforgiven (1992, F)
The West (1996, D)
The Wild Bunch (1969, F)

Bibliography

Allen, John L. *Passage Through the Garden: Lewis and Clark and the Images of the American Northwest.* Urbana: University of Illinois Press, 1975.

Ambrose, Stephen E. *Undaunted Courage: Meriwether Lewis, Thomas Jefferson and the Opening of the American West.* New York: Simon & Schuster, 1996.

Calder, Jenni. *There Must Be a Lone Ranger: The American West in Film and in Reality.* New York: McGraw-Hill, 1977.

Cronon, William. *Nature's Metropolis: Chicago and the Great West.* New York: Norton, 1991.

Dykstra, Robert. *The Cattle Towns.* New York: Knopf, 1968.

Hitt, Jim. *The American West from Fiction (1823–1976) into Film (1909–1986).* Jefferson, NC: McFarland, 1990.

Malone, Michael, ed. *Historians and the American West.* Lincoln: University of Nebraska Press, 1983.

Manchel, Frank. "Losing and Finding John Ford's *Sergeant Rutledge* (1960)." *Historical Journal of Film, Radio, and Television* 17.2 (1997): 245–259.

Mitchell, Lee Clark. *Westerns: Making the Man in Fiction and Film.* Chicago: University of Chicago Press, 1996.

Paul, Rodman W. *Mining Frontiers of the Far West, 1848–1880.* New York: Holt, Rinehart and Winston, 1963.

Rollins, Peter C., and John E. O'Connor, eds. *Hollywood's Indian: The Portrayal of the Native American in Film.* Lexington: University Press of Kentucky, 1998.

Slotkin, Richard. *Gunfighter Nation: The Myth of the Frontier in Twentieth-Century America.* New York: Atheneum, 1992.

Smith, Henry Nash. *Virgin Land: The American West as Symbol and Myth.* New York: Knopf, 1950.

Tompkins, Jane P. *West of Everything: The Inner Life of Westerns.* New York: Oxford University Press, 1992.

Tuska, Jon. *The American West in Film: Critical Approaches to the Western.* Westport, CT: Greenwood, 1985.

Utley, Robert, and Wilcomb Washburn, eds. *American Heritage History of the Indian Wars.* New York: Bonanza Books, 1977.

[JOSEPH DORINSON AND GEORGE LANKEVICH]

New York City

New York is America's metropolis, a quintessential urban drama where the dreams, disappointments, and dangers of life are naked and intense. Its enduring power has made the city a favorite subject for both historians and filmmakers, and images from Gotham's history fill the minds of Americans. One of the oldest cities on the continent, Manhattan offers a panorama of themes ranging from wilderness post to revolutionary sparkplug, from vibrant seaport to immigrant ghetto, from capital of the United States to core of capitalist enterprise. As we enter the new millennium, New York's position as "capital of the world" is unquestioned, and the city revels in its fabled diversity. It is equally home to international bankers and street peddlers, diplomats and drug dealers, fashion models and displaced persons, the frightened newcomer and the establishment WASP.

Change is built into the very fabric of New York, a continuing process of "creative destruction." Manhattan is physically a continuous work-in-progress, a site for architectural innovation that contains more skyscrapers than any other world metropolis. Incessant change makes New York difficult to love, because it is constantly obliterating its own heritage. Beyond such construction is the constant flow of immigration that has characterized the city for over two centuries and made it a melting pot of peoples: Germans, Irish, Jews, Italians, and Slavs in the nineteenth century; Puerto Ricans, Vietnamese, Dominicans, Chinese, and Russians in contemporary times. A composite of so many forces, New York is unique, and the endless source of fascination for historians who research its past and artists who seek its hidden dramas.

The diversity of New York demands historical analysis. More than 1,100 volumes have attempted to illuminate facets of local history. Arguably, the most impressive of these studies arrived in 1995, when the *Encyclopedia of New York City* brought together 680 authors to write 4,300 articles about the national metropolis. If a single theme emerged from their efforts, it was that the infinitely complex "Big Apple" eluded comprehensive description, even in a tome of 1,320 pages. Edwin G. Burrows and Mike Wallace won a Pulitzer Prize in 1999 for *Gotham*, a text of 1,236 pages that relates New York's story only up to 1898. The authors conclude that their subject is best defined commercially: "Sharp practice and money making and real estate lie somewhere near the core of New York's genetic material" (xv). Despite vast erudition and enormous length, neither of these justly acclaimed volumes exhausted its subject. The collision of dreams and reality, shifting yet constant, will no doubt provide the substance of many more studies each year.

History's inability to capture the essence of New York has long furnished an opportunity for filmmakers, who probe the "naked city" through the individual stories of its people. Film, more than words, has the ability to convey the dynamic of a "city that never sleeps." It is fitting that the great metropolis has been a favorite setting for moviemakers, for the American film industry was born in New York.

On May 9, 1893, two years before the Lumière brothers thrilled Paris, Thomas Edison demonstrated his Kinetoscope process to a packed audience at the Brooklyn Institute of Arts and Sciences. The first film showed men hammering an anvil and then having a beer. Within a year, Charles Chinnock filmed a boxing match from a Brooklyn rooftop, and, as early as May 1895, eidoloscope shorts were being shown in Manhattan. Edison developed a portable camera so that crews could film everyday city wonders, from a bucolic Central Park to elevated trains to the joys of Coney Island; hundreds of popular nickelodeons were in business by 1910. For over a century, from flickering kinetoscopes such as *Around New York in 15 Minutes* (1905) to modern documentaries such as *The New Metropolis: A Century of Greater New York* (1998) and Ric Burns's magnificent twelve-hour paean *New York* (1999), the city has been a star of American movies.

Until 1920 New York was also the center of movie production. The first version of *Ben Hur* (1907) was shot in Brooklyn, and film's first *Romeo and Juliet* (1909) was filmed at Bethesda Fountain in Central Park. Companies such as Biograph, Vitagraph, Kalem, and Pathé were among the thirty in New York attempting to monopolize movie production in the early 1900s. The creation of Hollywood after 1910 ended that dream. Nevertheless, corporations such as Universal (1912) and Fox (1914) and moguls such as Samuel Goldfish (Goldwyn) began in New York before going west. Others remained, with William Randolph Hearst's Cosmopolitan Studio, Fox, and the Astoria Studio being the largest; Astoria alone made 110 silent films before 1927. It was in Manhattan that the Fox Corporation tested audio techniques and where *Movietone News* premiered in 1927. In the same year, *The Jazz Singer* (the first "talkie") traced the rise of a nice Jewish boy from the Lower East Side to stardom. Yet the move to California was inexorable, and by 1937 not a single feature film was made entirely in New York. Still, politically charged documentary films flourished, and classics such as *New York Hooverville* (1932), *The City* (1939) and *Native Land* (1941) were all produced in the city.

"The influence of New York on the cinema constitutes a unique cultural relationship," the writers of the WPA's *New York Panorama* (1938) correctly remark (284). In a real sense Americans have two hometowns, their own and New York City. Every citizen knows the harshness of immigrant life, the elitism of Park Avenue, the crassness of Madison Avenue, the rowdiness of the Bowery, and the glitter of Broadway, even if these New York locations were never experienced personally. The earliest American films had a New York edge, dealing openly with urban problems, assimilation, and social conflict. D. W. Griffith's *The Musketeers of Pig Alley* (1912) and *Intolerance* (1916) and offshoots of Fritz Lang's *Metropolis* (1926) certainly offered different views of the city, but all recognized its inherent dramatic possibilities. From glorious penthouse to squalid slum, New York provides directors with extremes of success and failure, altruism and social pathology, danger and romance. The city had everything for filmmakers, but it could also repel ordinary Americans. Movies warned them that New York was best experienced at a distance; it was Sodom on the Hudson, a city of ambition, vice, and cruelty, where virtue counted for little. Yet it was endlessly fascinating. It is not surprising that the American Film Institute's list of the one hundred best films includes twenty-three set in the city, from *Citizen Kane* (#1) to *Yankee Doodle Dandy* (#100).

New York taught America that "going to the movies" could be a special occasion. By the time of World War I, when personages such as Gloria Swanson, Marion Davies, Norma Talmadge, and Pearl White lived in Manhattan, it was essential that studios have theaters as spectacular as their stars. The first movie "palace" probably was Samuel "Roxy" Rothafel's 1,800-seat Regent Theater (1913) in Harlem; by 1927 he would open a "cathedral" to motion pictures on Broadway where six thousand patrons watched shows in refrigerated comfort. Every studio created its own version of filmgoer's heaven, and so the Strand (1914), the Rivoli (1917), the Capital (1919), and the Paramount (1926) were born. After 1920 the Loews Corporation built dozens of lavish theaters in every city borough to present the films of MGM. The culmination of all this effort came on December 27, 1932, when Radio City Music Hall opened, offering film and stage shows (Rockettes) that thrilled audiences for fifty years. Unlike most of the palaces, Radio City survives today, with its restored interior designated a New York landmark.

As Americans made moviegoing their greatest source of entertainment, what did they learn about New York? "All the nations under heaven," Frederick Binder and David M. Reimers observe, gravitate to New York City, drawn to Gotham in search of success, love, adventure, escape, or privacy. In the 1930s, as the Depression engulfed the nation, no other city offered the immigrants, the poor, the ambitious, and the already rich a greater sense of opportunity. It was the one place offering everyone a new deal. *King Kong* (1933) established a checkered pattern in black and white of innocence in conflict with corruption. Wrenched from his natural habitat, Kong retaliates against a cruel city but is brought down by technology and by unrequited love for beauty, as represented by Fay Wray. In the climactic scenes, the Empire State Building—completed only in 1931 and already symbolic of New York—is equally the star, and it easily survives Kong's assault. Busby Berkeley charted happier endings in his musicals, especially *42nd Street* (1933), where chorus girls start as understudies and come out as stars. The Empire City represents survival of the fittest, but the hard city would always reward talent. All around glittering Broadway were dark, horrific slums such as *Hester Street* (1975). Whether immigrant or native-born, troubled teenagers such as the Dead End Kids discovered that grinding poverty and a hostile environment could often lead to crime. Life in New York could alienate anyone: Babyface Martin (Humphrey Bogart) in *Dead End* (1937), Vito Corleone in *The Godfather* (1972), and Travis Bickle in *Taxi Driver* (1976). Hollywood did try to teach the kids that crime does not pay. In *Angels with Dirty Faces* (1938), two boys from the slums take different paths: Pat O'Brien becomes a priest and James Cagney a criminal. Because sociologists in the 1930s stressed the environment (nurture) over heredity (nature), Father Jerry Connelly converts the Dead End Kids through basketball but needs help from Cagney to die doing a "good deed." Abandoning his usual strut and swagger, Cagney complies. Feigning panic and fear, he goes to the electric chair as an object lesson.

The films of the 1930s began the long relationship of New York with the crime story, for in the metropolis, according to Daniel Bell, crime functions as "a queer ladder of success." Its pervasive presence reflects a distortion of American values (128). Robert Warshow describes the urban gangster as the contemporary "tragic hero" (86–88). The modern New York criminal comes in many versions: John Garfield preys on local fishermen in *Out of the Fog* (1941), Humphrey Bogart plays a psychopathic killer in *The Enforcer* (1951), Lee J. Cobb portrays a vicious labor racketeer in *On the Waterfront* (1954), Peter Falk embodies crazed killer Abe Reles, who jumps or is pushed to his death in *Murder Inc.* (1960). All, however, show the baleful effects of having to succeed by any means. More bureaucratized crime was presented by Marlon Brando, Al Pacino, and Robert De Niro, who put their stamp on Mafioso portraiture in *The Godfather* (1972) and *The Godfather, Part II* (1974). Harvey Keitel hooked up with De Niro as a petty crook to walk the *Mean Streets* (1973) of Greenwich Village, while Joe Pesci and Ray Liotta joined De Niro's criminal fraternity in *GoodFellas* (1990). In pursuit of international drug traffickers, Gene Hackman starred in the greatest car chase ever filmed in *The French Connection* (1971) under the McDonald Avenue El in Brooklyn. But Hackman's Popeye Doyle was a flawed cop, for the city seems to corrupt even its sworn defenders, as shown in *Detective Story* (1951), *Serpico* (1973), *Fort Apache, the Bronx* (1981), *A Bronx Tale* (1993), and *Cop Land* (1997), among many other films.

If life in Manhattan burned with intensity, the movies discovered that ordinary life could be found in the outer boroughs. Brooklyn became the perfect example of a city, nestled in New York, where release, recreation, and happiness beckoned. Betty Grable starred in *Coney Island* (1943), a film that captures the glory of America's first amusement area. Subsequently, Coney Island is featured such movies as *The Little Fugitive* (1953), about a Bensonhurst boy who runs away from home and school. Ten years later, Shirley Clarke's *Cool World* (1963) traces the odyssey of a black youngster who descends into a now seedy Coney Island in search of adventure. In the classic buddy movie *Butch Cassidy and the Sundance Kid* (1969), the protagonists party in Coney Island before departing for their crime spree in South America. From the streets of Brooklyn, recognizable film types emerged. Cops, cab drivers, sports fanatics, hustlers, and fools are personified by Jimmy Durante, Jack Carson, Frank Sinatra, Danny Kaye, Sam Levine, William Bendix, Richard Conte, Woody Allen, Phil Silvers, Mae West, Martha Raye, and Lana Turner. No World War II film was complete unless its "universal platoon" featured a resident of "the borough of churches." William Bendix became the quintessential Brooklyn soldier in *Wake Island* (1943) and *Guadalcanal Diary* (1943) (see "World War II: Feature Films"). His fatal trip in *Lifeboat* (1944) showed how a gritty Brooklynite stoically faces death.

New York films have always honored strong women. Alice White in *Show Girl* (1928), Alice Faye in *Girl from Brooklyn* (1938), Betty Grable in *Sweet Rosie O'Grady* (1943), and Rita Hayworth in *Cover Girl* (1944) showed how independent women could master both men and the metropolis. Joan Blondell in *A Tree Grows in Brooklyn* (1945) sensitized Americans to the triumphs and tribulations of ordinary women, while Rosalind Russell successfully addressed every problem of urban existence in *My Sister Eileen* (1942), *Auntie Mame* (1958), and *A Majority of One* (1962). The tradition of the smart, talented and complex New York woman is continued by Faye Dunaway in *Network* (1976), Jill Clayburgh in *An Unmarried Woman* (1978), Tracy Camilla Johns in *She's Gotta Have It* (1986), Cher in *Moonstruck* (1987), Melanie Griffith in *Working Girl* (1988), Renée Zellweger in *A Price above Rubies* (1998), Jennifer Lopez in *Maid in Manhattan* (2002)—and, of course, Dustin Hoffman in *Tootsie* (1982).

It is appropriate that the Statue of Liberty, symbolic of New York City, is a woman. This beacon of freedom, coupled with that magnificent skyline, makes you want to sing in harmony with a soundtrack emitting the unforgettable melodies of Irving Berlin, Cole Porter, George Gershwin, Jerome Kern, and Richard Rodgers. In the 1930s, Americans longed for fascinating rhythm and yearned for happy days. It was *Swing Time* (1936) that propelled Fred Astaire and Ginger Rogers into superstardom. The New York musical embraced many of the clichés issuing from the "American Dream"—including the challenges and the dangers of success. Witness *Tin Pan Alley* (1940), *Ziegfield Girl* (1941), *Babes on Broadway* (1941), *Yankee Doodle Dandy* (1942), *Cover Girl* (1944), *On the Town* (1949), *The Band Wagon, Kiss Me Kate* (both 1953), *Guys and Dolls* (1955), *The Joker Is Wild* (1957), *Bells Are Ringing* (1960), *West Side Story* (1961), *Funny Girl* (1968), *Sweet Charity* (1969), and *New York New York* (1977). These films trumpeted the inspiring American success story, which Frank Sinatra captured in the memorable lyric: "If you can make it here, you can make it anywhere."

In addition to its unique people, Brooklyn has a bridge that illuminates many films. Completed in 1883, the great bridge is both a conduit and metaphor, as American-studies scholars David McCulloch and Alan Trachtenberg have demonstrated. The Brooklyn Bridge made the consolidation of greater New York inevitable. "The City," however, is located on one end of its imposing span. Manhattan is the destination for New Yorkers on the make. Thus, John Travolta has to cross over the bridge after *Saturday Night Fever* (1977) possesses him. Johnny Weismuller, the "Ape Man," jumps from the bridge in *Tarzan's New York Adventure* (1942). Frank Sinatra is inspired to croon a love song in *It Happened in Brooklyn* (1947). Gene Kelly dances across it in *On the Town* (1949), doomed Meryl Streep drinks champagne on it in *Sophie's Choice* (1982), Kurt Russell performs various death-defying acrobatics on it in *Escape from New York* (1981), and the working-class Long Islanders of *The Brothers McMullen* (1995) regard it with awe. Other means of transport are available to ambitious New Yorkers. Melanie Griffith takes the Staten Island Ferry to Wall Street for fame, fortune, and Mr. Right in *Working Girl.* She has a Ford (Harrison) in her future. And the lonely, homely Bronx butcher of *Marty* (1955) takes the subway to find love in a Manhattan ballroom, while Paul Mazursky rides it to sever umbilical ties to a predatory mother in *Next Stop, Greenwich Village* (1976).

Directors love New York because its well-known locations immediately establish a sense of place, class, status, and ambience. It is a city of the "haves," "have-nots," and "wannabes." Their respective lifestyles elicit the style and substance of most film scripts. The intersection of high, low, and middle has always generated enormous profit for Hollywood. Starting in 1934, a series of six *Thin Man* films coupled William Powell and Myrna Loy as high-society detectives who glide through society exuding charm and wit while consuming copious amounts of alcohol. Vicariously, viewers enjoyed the end of spoiled rich girl Claudette Colbert's journey into the muscular, bare-chested embrace of Clark Gable in *It Happened One Night* (1934). Viewers also laughed at the role reversals in *My Man Godfrey* (1936) which featured William Powell as a rich man pretending to be poor—a rich man who devotes himself to helping his new friends from the "Hooverville" along the East River.

Obviously, New York, the microcosm of America, believes that rich is better. Morris Townsend (Montgomery Clift) makes money his goal in the futile pursuit of plain but wealthy Catherine Sloper (Olivia de Havilland) in *The Heiress* (1949); years later, the haunting Henry James saga reappeared with the more apt original title, *Washington Square* (1997). Truman Capote's Holly (Audrey Hepburn) does "it" lightly for money in *Breakfast at Tiffany's* (1961). For the love of money, Max Bialystock (Zero Mostel) sleeps with old ladies and cons them out of their savings in *The Producers* (1968). Gordon Gekko (Michael Douglas) almost convinces the audience and nearly seduces the idealistic Buddy Fox (Charlie Sheen) to believe that "greed is good" in *Wall Street* (1987). Money is power, and power in New York is always intimidating. *Citizen Kane* (1941), *Meet John Doe* (1941), *The Great Gatsby* (1949, 1974), *Executive Suite* (1954), *The Sweet Smell of Success* (1957), and *Network* (1976) all preach the gospel of success, and rarely does the "little man" strike back unless he is a prince among paupers like Howard (Woody Allen) in *The Front* (1976) or an irredeemable rebel like Murray Burns (Jason Robards Jr.) in *A Thousand Clowns* (1965).

Whether engaged in pride, prejudice, or patriotism, New York has always fought for the American way of life. Spying and subversion became a concern in the fight against fascism. *Confessions of a Nazi Spy* (1939), *All Through the Night* (1942), *Saboteur* (1942), and *The*

House on 92nd Street (1945)—the last a brilliant example of quasi-documentary filmmaking—established the genre. The films crafted during the Cold War, however, seemed devoid of such creative fire: sparked more by the "great fear" of communist infiltration than a love for artistic presentation. This foible also pertains to the allegedly subversive *A King in New York* (1957) by an aging Charlie Chaplin and *Daniel* (1983) based on a novelized account of Ethel and Julius Rosenberg. Beyond a stirring *On the Waterfront* (1954)—Elia Kazan's cinematic rationale (or rationalization) for informing—the rest of the anticommunist films, such as *I Was a Communist for the FBI* (1951), can be cast into a trash heap in New Jersey.

During these turbulent years, New Yorkers continued to cope with "lives of quiet desperation" as in *The Lost Weekend* (1945), *Marty* (1955), *12 Angry Men* (1957), *A View from the Bridge* (1962), *The Pawnbroker* (1965), *Dog Day Afternoon* (1975), and *Taxi Driver* and *Network* (both 1976) that sometimes erupt in rage ("I am mad as hell and won't take it anymore!") and violence. We learn from *Last Exit to Brooklyn* (1990) that for many, like Jean-Paul Sartre, there is no exit from hell. A creative and desperate soul could change genders, like Dustin Hoffman in *Tootsie.* A destructive and desperate soul man could start a riot on a steamy summer's day with Spike Lee in *Do the Right Thing* (1989)—or hide from the streets, as do the New Yorkers of Lee's *Summer of Sam* (1999).

Hollywood shunned the New York proletariat. For a glimpse into how the other half lived, viewers had to tune in to television. *The Goldbergs,* led by matriarch Molly; *The Honeymooners'* Ralph and Alice; and *All in the Family*'s Archie and Edith provided the only mass-mediated slice of working-class life in New York. Later police dramas like *NYPD Blue* sustained this tradition. Most viewers, however, were exposed to middle-class singles or upper-class professionals like *CPW, The Cosby Show, Spin City, Veronica's Closet,* and *Friends.* Perhaps the need for escape into fancy matched the concern for profit.

It was after World War II that America experienced social engineering with Hollywood in tow: charting the route out of the asphalt and into the trees. New York's planning czar, Robert Moses, paved the way with new roads. Thousands of urban residents followed the exodus into suburbia. There one found splendor in the crabgrass frontier where *Mr. Blandings Builds His Dream House* (1948). *The Man in the Grey Flannel Suit* (1954), however, soon discovered that he could not escape from trouble. *Goodbye Columbus* (1965) meant farewell to New York City and hello to Westchester and the pools haunted by *The Swimmer* (1968). Though Philip Roth's novel originally pitted Newark against Short Hills, New Jersey, Hollywood shifted locales because of New York's universality. White flight, urban blight, and territorial fights ensued. The tax base eroded. The city pitched toward bankruptcy in the early 1970s. No film has fully chronicled that story although the machinations of Al Pacino's *City Hall* (1996) seem to demonstrate that this, too, will come.

What saved the city? The clue to survival, embedded in history, can be found in the films that chronicle city life across the decades. More than any other city, New York has the power to laugh at itself. Staccato bursts of laughter issued primarily from the Marx Brothers in *A Night at the Opera* (1935). Fortified with S. J. Perelman scripts, Groucho—the "shnorrer" as explorer—and his brothers plunged into gleeful nihilism. "When I came to this country, I didn't have a nickel in my pocket. Now, I have a nickel in my pocket." To that pillar of piety and symbol of WASP stolidity, Margaret Dumont, in *A Day at the Races* (1935), he proposes: "Marry me, and I'll never look at another horse." In response to one of her inane comments, Groucho quips: "That remark covers a lot of territory. As a matter of fact, you cover a lot of territory. Is there any truth to the fact that they're going to tear you down and put up an office building?" No one—person or profession—remained safe from Marx's demolition derby.

The tradition of Jewish humor animates Neil Simon in *The Odd Couple* (1968), *Plaza Suite* (1971), *The Prisoner of Second Avenue* (1974), and *The Sunshine Boys* (1975), and Woody Allen in films such as *Manhattan* (1979), *Stardust Memories* (1980), *Broadway Danny Rose* (1984), *The Purple Rose of Cairo* (1985), *Hannah and Her Sisters* (1986), and *Radio Days* (1987). Arguably the best film of this brilliant—if neurotic—New Yorker is *Annie Hall* (1977), which paints a vivid contrast between Anglo-Saxon and New York urban-ethnic culture. Alvie Singer (Woody himself) refuses to move (unlike the Dodgers and the movies) to Los Angeles, where "the only cultural advantage is that you can make a right turn on a red light." He knows that the air is clear there only because "they take their garbage and make it into television shows."

Sports provide both social identity and personal escape. In the arenas, people of all classes, ethnicities and cultures gather. They speak a common language and build community. In addition, sports heroes serve as role models for youngsters. Gary Cooper gave a fine interpretation of Lou Gehrig in *The Pride of the Yankees* (1942), while Babe Ruth still waits for an actor equal to his gargantuan stature in baseball (see "Babe Ruth and Lou Gehrig"), for both William Bendix in *The Babe Ruth Story* (1948) and John Goodman in *The Babe* (1992) proved unequal to the task. Trailblazer Jackie Robinson played himself opposite Ruby Dee as his beloved wife, Rachel, in *The Jackie Robinson Story* (1950). Paul Newman put on a new face to play boxing champion Rocky Graziano in *Somebody Up There Likes Me* (1956). When three major New York sports teams crested in 1969–70—the Mets in baseball, the Jets in football, and the Knicks in basketball—they brought city residents together and no doubt contributed to Mayor John Lindsay's successful bid for reelection. Later, Ken Burns crafted a compelling documentary on baseball with New York City as a major focal point. The best of this genre, Martin Scorsese's *Raging Bull* (1980) provided a gritty look at the boxing game through the troubled life of Jake LaMotta.

Even today, New York remains the city of immigrants and their children. From early settlers seeking their fortune to the more recent Yuppies, Gotham continues to lure the "huddled masses" and the upwardly mobile classes. This trend is effectively, indeed comically, related in a film tradition that began with *The Immigrant* (1917). Modern variations on this theme resonate in *America, America* (1963), *Moscow on the Hudson* (1984), *Coming to America* (1988), *Green Card* (1990), *A Pyromaniac's Love Story* (1995), and the low-budget "sleeper" *The Brothers McMullen*, while *Hester Street* (1975) and *Little Odessa* (1994) transmit discordant notes in the movement toward Americanization.

Beyond money and power, New York also fulfills the romantic needs of "strangers in the night." Whether in the clutches of *The Seven Year Itch* (1955) or ensnared by *The Goodbye Girl* (1977); unable to blot out *An Affair to Remember* (1957) or erase *Stardust Memories*, Eros thrives in Gotham. If love seems better the second time around, casual sex can be prohibitively expensive in *All About Eve* (1950), *The Apartment* (1960), *Midnight Cowboy* (1969), and *Fatal Attraction* (1987). America's love/hate affair with city continues in cinematic makeovers. *The Out-of-Towners* (1970) projected a dangerous city tempered somewhat by Neil Simon's humor. A remake in 1999 starring Steve Martin and Goldie Hawn was less funny to be sure; but the new version etched a less acid, more positive portrait with a happy ending. Despite the obligatory mugging, Martin gets the job and Hawn the luxury apartment. In short, they take Manhattan. Love, tolerance, and tourism convey an upbeat message. New York can arouse the *Sleepless in*

Seattle (1993), can overcome fake orgasms in *When Harry Met Sally* (1989) and provide true orgasmic feasts in the world's best restaurants. Here in the global city, one finds an open-door policy toward single mothers, ailing children, gay men and women, creative eccentrics, and the process of metamorphosis through love experienced by Jack Nicholson and Helen Hunt in *As Good as It Gets* (1997), a James Brooks film that projects the miracle of resurrection. Like the proverbial phoenix emergent from the ashes, New York is back because of its gritty, resilient, immigrant "never-say-die" populace.

The Turning Point (1977) serves as metaphor for that pivotal decade, the 1970s. New York became the dominant subject for filmmakers. The Academy of Motion Pictures, Arts and Sciences awarded Oscars to *Midnight Cowboy* (1969), *The French Connection* (1971), *The Godfather* (1972), *The Godfather, Part II* (1974), *Annie Hall* (1977), and *Kramer vs. Kramer* (1979). In addition to inspiring the best American movies in the last decades of the twentieth century, Gotham recaptured its lost status as a producer of films as well as Hollywood's prime location. Astoria Studios reopened in 1975 and has produced such films as *Thieves* (1975), *Ransom* (1996), and *First Wives Club* (1996), as well as an abundance of TV shows. During the long tenure of Mayor Ed Koch (1978–90), the city joyfully welcomed film companies, and in the 1980s no less than sixty films were shot annually. Labor costs and recalcitrance caused a downturn early in the 1990s, but, as the century ended, New York was the locale for 213 features in 1997 and 221 in 1998. In the process, filmmaking enriched the city by $3 billion a year. By 2000 Queens alone had four studios. Chelsea Pier attracted filmmakers and a major sound stage development was planned for the government-divested Brooklyn Navy Yard. Fittingly, the Museum of the Moving Image (1988) chose to locate itself in New York, a city that has more film students than the rest of America. Like *auteurs* such as Woody Allen, Martin Scorsese, Sidney Lumet, and Spike Lee, these students will never have to leave New York to examine the great spectrum of human possibility. The city will remain vital to the history of film in America—and the essence of American identity.

References

Filmography

An Affair to Remember (1957, F)
All About Eve (1950, F)
All Through the Night (1942, F)
Angels with Dirty Faces (1938, F)
Annie Hall (1977, F)
The Apartment (1960, F)
Around New York in 15 Minutes (1905, D)
Arsenic and Old Lace (1944, F)
As Good as It Gets (1997, F)
Auntie Mame (1958, F)
Babes on Broadway (1941, F)
The Blackboard Jungle (1955, F)
Breakfast at Tiffany's (1961, F)
A Bronx Tale (1993, F)
The Brothers McMullen (1995, F)
Bye, Bye Braverman (1968, F)
Citizen Kane (1941, F)
The City (1939, F)
City Across the River (1949, F)
City Hall (1996, F)
Coney Island (1943, F)
Cool World (1963, F)
Cop Land (1997, F)
Cover Girl (1944, F)
Crossing Delancey (1986, F)
Dead End (1937, F)
Detective Story (1951, F)
Dog Day Afternoon (1975, F)
Do the Right Thing (1989, F)
Don Juan Quilligan (1945, F)
The Enforcer (1951, F)
Escape from New York (1981, F)
Executive Suite (1954, F)
Fatal Attraction (1987, F)
Fort Apache, The Bronx (1981, F)
42nd Street (1933, F)
The French Connection (1971, F)
Girl from Brooklyn (1938, F)
The Godfather (1972, F)
The Godfather, Part II (1974, F)

The Goodbye Girl (1977, F)
GoodFellas (1990, F)
Great Expectations (1998, F)
The Great Gatsby (1949, 1974, F)
Green Card (1990, F)
Guys and Dolls (1955, F)
Hannah and Her Sisters (1986, F)
The Heiress (1949, F)
Hester Street (1975, F)
The House on 92d Street (1945, F)
Intolerance (1916, F)
It Happened in Brooklyn (1947, F)
It Happened One Night (1934, F)
The Jazz Singer (1927, F)
The Joker Is Wild (1957, F)
A King in New York (1957, F)
King Kong (1933, F)
Last Exit to Brooklyn (1990, F)
The Little Fugitive (1953, F)
Little Odessa (1994, F)
Lost in Yonkers (1993, F)
The Lost Weekend (1945, F)
Love on the Run (1936, F)
Maid in Manhattan (2002, F)
A Majority of One (1962, F)
Manhattan (1979, F)
Marty (1955, F)
Mean Streets (1973, F)
Meet John Doe (1941, F)
Midnight Cowboy (1969, F)
Miracle on 34th Street (1947, F)
Moonstruck (1987, F)
Moscow on the Hudson (1984, F)
Mr. Deeds Goes to Town (1946, F)
Murder Inc. (1960, F)
The Musketeers of Pig Alley (1912, F)
My Man Godfrey (1936, F)
My Sister Eileen (1955, F)
Native Land (1941, D)
Network (1976, F)
The New Metropolis: A Century of Greater New York (1998, D)
New York (1999, D)
New York Hooverville (1932, D)
New York New York (1977, F)
New York Stories (1989, F)
New York Town (1941, F)
Next Stop, Greenwich Village (1976, F)
The Odd Couple (1968, F)
On the Town (1949, F)
On the Waterfront (1954, F)
Out of the Fog (1941, F)
The Out-of-Towners (1970, F; 1999, F)
The Pawnbroker (1965, F)
Plaza Suite (1971, F)
The Pride of the Yankees (1942, F)
The Prisoner of Second Avenue (1974, F)
Prizzi's Honor (1985, F)
The Producers (1968, F)
A Pyromaniac's Love Story (1995, F)
Queens Logic (1991, F)
Raging Bull (1980, F)
Saturday Night Fever (1977, F)
Scent of a Woman (1992, F)
Serpico (1973, F)
The Seven Year Itch (1955, F)
She's Gotta Have It (1986, F)
Show Girl (1928, F)
Silent Movie (1976, F)
Sleepless in Seattle (1993, F)
Stardust Memories (1980, F)
Summer of Sam (1999, F)
Sweet Rosie O'Grady (1943, F)
The Sweet Smell of Success (1957, F)
Swing Time (1936, F)
The Taking of Pelham One Two Three (1974, F)
Tales of Manhattan (1942, F)
Tarzan's New York Adventure (1942, F)
Taxi Driver (1976, F)
A Thousand Clowns (1965, F)
Tin Pan Alley (1940, F)
Tootsie (1982, F)
A Tree Grows in Brooklyn (1945, F)
An Unmarried Woman (1978, F)
A View from the Bridge (1962, F)
Wall Street (1987, F)
Washington Square (1997, F)
Weekend at the Waldorf (1945, F)
When Harry Met Sally (1989, F)
Wonder Man (1945, F)
Working Girl (1988, F)
Yankee Doodle Dandy (1942, F)
Ziegfield Girl (1941, F)

Bibliography

Basinger, Jeanine. *The World War II Combat Film: Anatomy of a Genre.* New York: Columbia University Press, 1986.

Bell, Daniel. *The End of Ideology.* New York: Free Press, 1964.

Belton, John. *American Cinema/American Culture.* New York: McGraw-Hill, 1994.

Bennett, Michael, et al. *Rediscovering New York.* Orlando, FL: Harcourt Brace, 1995.

Bergman, Andrew. *We're in the Money: Depression America and Its Films.* New York: New York University Press, 1971.

Berrol, Selma C. *The Empire City: New York and Its People.* New York: Praeger, 1995.

Binder, Frederick M., and David M. Reimers. *All the Nations Under Heaven: An Ethnic and Racial History of New York City.* New York: Columbia University Press, 1995.

Burns, Ric, and James Sanders. *New York: An Illustrated History.* New York: Knopf, 1999.

Burrows, Edwin G., and Mike Wallace. *Gotham: A*

History of New York City. New York: Oxford University Press, 1999.

Cowden, Gary, ed. *A Political Companion to American Film.* Chicago: Lakeview Press, 1994.

Desser, David, and Lester D. Friedman. *American-Jewish Filmmakers: Traditions and Trends.* Urbana: University of Illinois Press, 1993.

Dorinson, Joseph. "Brooklyn: The Elusive Image." *Journal of Long Island History* 1.2 (1989): 128–135.

Durgnat, Raymond. *The Crazy Mirror: Hollywood Comedy and the American Image.* London: Faber & Faber, 1969.

Fraser, George MacDonald. *The Hollywood History of the World.* New York: Fawcett Columbine, 1988.

Freeman, Joshua B. *Working Class New York: Life and Labor Since World War II.* New York: New Press, 2000.

Fyne, Robert. *The Hollywood Propaganda of World War II.* Metuchen, NJ: Scarecrow, 1994.

Gelmis, Joseph. "Brooklyn in the Movies." *Brooklyn Bridge* 4.8 (1999): 58–63.

Jackson, Kenneth T. *Crabgrass Frontier: The Suburbanization of the United States.* New York: Oxford University Press, 1985.

——, ed. *The Encyclopedia of New York City.* New Haven: Yale University Press, 1995.

Lankevich, George J. *American Metropolis: A History.* New York: New York University Press, 1998.

Manbeck, John, and Mike Olshan. "Brooklyn in the Movies." *New Brooklyn* 5.3 (1983): 58–62.

Mast, Gerald, and Bruce F. Kawin. *A Short History of the Movies.* 6th ed. Boston: Allyn & Bacon, 1996.

Rollins, Peter C., ed. *Hollywood as Historian: American Film in a Cultural Context.* Lexington: University of Kentucky Press, 1998.

Stern, Lee Edward. *The Movie Musical.* New York: Pyramid, 1974.

Warshow, Robert. *The Immediate Experience.* New York: Doubleday, 1962.

White, David Manning, and Richard Avedon. *The Celluloid Weapon: Social Comment in the American Film.* Boston: Beacon Press, 1972.

[MARY MALLOY]

The Sea

Perhaps uniquely among the historical subjects that appear in film, the interpretation of the maritime experience is often more influenced by a centuries-old literary tradition than it is by actual events that occurred at sea. Seafaring themes—such as the test against nature, the isolation of a community and the consequential requirement that members confront each other, the mysteries of the unexplored, and the encounter with the exotic—make for compelling drama. Into such a framework Homer laid the *Odyssey*, the Arabs set *Sinbad*, and Shakespeare put *The Tempest*. Each story had at its heart real navigational enterprises, but fact and legend became so intertwined in the telling as to become almost inseparable. Such a strong and persistent literary tradition has been extremely influential. Many writers have felt that relationships between human beings, and between human beings and the natural world, can be examined more intensively on the deck of a ship than on land, and filmmakers have followed them out to sea.

The sea can be thought of as both a romantic canvas and a real place to work: while the former is everywhere in film, the latter is practically invisible. Extraordinary maritime adventures are more easily accessible in American movies than ordinary day-to-day commerce, with the result being that the carrying of cargo—the backbone of the American maritime experience—is almost never illustrated, while sea-monster attacks and pirate escapades are commonplace. This creates something of a dilemma for the teacher who wants to use films to document the business of seafaring and its important role in American history, but it simultaneously allows for the exploration of broad cross-disciplinary themes.

Maritime History as American History

American history can be defined in maritime terms before 1850, when America turned its back on the sea and began to face "the West." Most Americans have ancestors who came here as shipboard immigrants and, with few exceptions, major U.S. cities are or were seaports. Until the transcontinental railroad was completed in 1869, it was still easier to travel from the East to the West Coast by sea, and the transportation of information, goods, and people was and is dependent on shipping to a far greater extent than is generally acknowledged.

The romantic sailors regularly depicted in literature and on film bear little resemblance to their working counterparts of the age of sail. The working sailors of the nineteenth century, for instance, were mostly poor. About 20 percent of the shipboard company was made up of African Americans, but an equal or greater percentage were immigrants who spoke languages other than English, and, when the ship docked, members of the crew went ashore to find themselves at the bottom of the societal hierarchy. The crew was also made up entirely of men, and the inability of the community, in its working environment, to generate a conventional love story for dramatic purposes has made it less than interesting for filmmakers and their audiences. Some writers, including

Herman Melville and Joseph Conrad, set works shipboard specifically because they wanted to deal with human issues other than romantic love. With the exception of movies about war on the sea, however, filmmakers have not generally followed their example, and even *Moby-Dick* was first filmed (in 1925 and again in 1930) with a love triangle at the center of the storyline.

What films can do that printed sources for maritime history cannot, however, is place us on the deck of a ship. Some films, such as Victor Fleming's *Captains Courageous* (1937), were made at a time when actual working vessels could be filmed in their ocean environment, and the black-and-white images of those schooners on the Grand Banks of Newfoundland add powerfully to our understanding of the lives of fishermen.

From the *Mayflower* to the War of 1812

The voyage of the *Mayflower,* carrying the citizens who would found the first successful British colony in America, is a logical place to begin an examination of the role of seafaring in American history. Two films have been made of the enterprise. Spencer Tracy plays the captain of the *Mayflower* in *Plymouth Adventure* (1952). A credible replica of the ship was made for this film by the Australian ship historian Alan Villiers. More than half of the movie takes place on shipboard, and a storm scene is quite convincing. But, as with many attempts to film events of maritime history, Hollywood could not resist a romantic subplot, and Spencer Tracy's failed attempt to seduce Gene Tierney (as the wife of Governor William Bradford) and her subsequent death by accident or suicide draw us away from the historical material. Romantic entanglements on shipboard also play a role in the 1979 movie *Mayflower: The Pilgrims' Adventure,* where Anthony Hopkins takes the helm as captain of the ship and Jenny Agutter provides a romantic foil.

The rapid growth of the New England colonies was built on a base of maritime commerce. Seasonal cycles of fishing, farming, and foresting, culminated in shipments of salt cod, agricultural products, and timber from the Atlantic seaboard to the West Indies and Europe. A complex commercial network was developed that also included slaves from Africa, sugar products from the Caribbean, and manufactured goods from England. British regulations and parliamentary support for the trade monopolies of the East India and South Seas Companies kept ships from the American colonies confined to the Atlantic ocean; a capable shipbuilding industry grew steadily throughout the colonial period, however, along with navigational knowledge and experience. When the independent United States emerged at the end of the Revolutionary War, American merchants were ready to launch into world trade. Voyages around the Cape of Good Hope to the Indian Ocean and Canton were followed quickly by the first ventures beyond Cape Horn to the Pacific. Unfortunately, none of the maritime commerce of the colonial period, or that of the Federalist traders who emerged after the Revolution, has yet been dramatized on film.

With the rise of independent trade came the need for a navy to protect it. Unlike their British counterparts, American moviemakers never found the development or history of the sailing navy a very compelling subject. *Old Ironsides,* a 1926 silent film about the USS *Constitution,* and the 1959 movie *John Paul Jones* are the only offerings, and neither has very good depictions of shipboard scenes.

The Age of Expansion

The rise of the United States merchant marine and the expansion of Americans into the Pacific were documented by Richard Henry Dana in *Two Years Before the Mast,* an autobiographical account of a voyage around Cape Horn from Boston to California, published in 1840. Dana, a Harvard student who worked his passage as a common seaman, introduced Americans to the culture of seafaring, the plight of sailors, and to the coast of California with its transient population of Americans, Hawaiians, Spaniards, Russians, and Native Americans. An extremely influential work, which inspired James Fenimore Cooper and Herman Melville to introduce a more realistic quality into their own descriptions of the shipboard world, Dana's book was also the principle account of California used by the thousands of men who traveled there in the Gold Rush.

A movie of *Two Years Before the Mast* was made in 1944 and released in 1946, but, except for the title, it bears little resemblance to Dana's book. As portrayed by Brian Donlevy, Dana is a middle-aged man on a mission to reveal the truth about the violent treatment of sailors; Alan Ladd is a spoiled young rich man who, despite the fact that his father owns the brig *Pilgrim,* is nonetheless shanghaied aboard and then abused by the captain. Filmed entirely on a Hollywood soundstage, the film captures none of the book's important sense of the community on shipboard or the coast of California.

Relationships between American sailors and the native people they encountered on a voyage were seldom realized with any full humanity in the films produced in the first decades of American movies. Three film versions of the story of the 1789 mutiny led by Fletcher Christian against Captain William Bligh of the *Bounty* (in 1935, 1962, and 1984) show the development of relationships between British sailors and Tahitian women, and the evolution of the depiction over the five decades is interesting. In *All the Brothers Were Valiant* (1953), Betta St. John plays the Gilbert Island wife of one of a pair of whaling brothers from New Bedford, Massachusetts, as an exotic, though expendable character. She dies conveniently at the hands of robbers in order to enable her husband (Stewart Granger) to vie with his brother (Robert Taylor) for the *real* love of his life, played by Ann Blyth. Though the movie also goes awry with an unnecessary subplot about stolen pearls, the whaling scenes in *All the Brothers Were Valiant* are solid in their technical details. Two earlier versions of the Ben Ames Williams novel were filmed in 1922 and 1928.

The movie that most effectively explores the complex relationship of transient shipboard outsiders to native Pacific Islanders is *Hawaii* (1966), based on James Michener's novel of the same name. The voyage of missionaries Julie Andrews and Max von Sydow to Polynesia from Boston was filmed aboard the brigantine *Romance,* a North Sea trader refit for the movie by Alan Villiers. The interaction of the New Englander missionaries with both Hawaiians and American sailors, who visited the islands by the thousands in the first half of the nineteenth century, is shown in lavish detail, with attention paid to the ethnographic treatment of Hawaiian traditional life.

The greatest number of American sailors came to Hawaii and other South Sea Islands aboard whaling ships, which identified almost every point of land within the vast reaches of the Pacific in their constant search for whales, wood, water, fresh provisions, and sexual partners. Herman Melville challenged his readers to name another industry that had worked such dramatic changes upon "the whole broad world . . . as the high and mighty business of whaling," by which he meant the rush to the Pacific of American whalemen in the first half of the nineteenth century, the consequent charting of that ocean, and the interaction of as many as twenty thousand men a year with Pacific Islanders on the decks of American ships.

The earliest films of whaling were made when the industry was still operational, though much in decline, off the coast of New England. The silent film *Down to the Sea in Ships* (1923), was able to bring cameras out onto actual whaling vessels during the course of filming and consequently is a valuable document of the industry. There is a silly subplot as Clara

Bow, making her film debut, disguises herself as a boy and signs on board the voyage. This dramatic device of the "woman in disguise" was popular in the plays of Shakespeare and continues to fascinate audiences of seafaring drama to this day, though attempts by historians to identify more than a handful of women who participated as crew aboard sailing vessels before the middle of the twentieth century have been unsuccessful.

Another film using the title *Down to the Sea in Ships,* but bearing no resemblance to the silent version, was made in 1949 and stars Lionel Barrymore as the crusty Captain Joy, who brings his grandson (Dean Stockwell) with him on his final voyage before retiring. A joyless Richard Widmark plays the first mate as a stoic New Englander. Twentieth Century–Fox built the *Pride of Bedford,* a full-sized replica of a whaling ship, in its studio, and had whale blubber shipped down from a whaling station on Vancouver Island to provide a realistic look to the scenes of processing the whale on deck; the early industrial technology demonstrated in the film is impressively accurate.

Herman Melville's great whaling novel *Moby-Dick* has been filmed four times. The intricate subtleties of the book, filled with parables and metaphorical allusions to race relations, the exploitation of nature and native peoples, and the expansionist tendencies then in the forefront of American politics, are, for the most part, lost in the movie versions. Screenwriters reduced the novel down to the bare bones of the plot and, in the earliest versions, did not even leave much of that.

John Barrymore played Ahab in two different filmed versions of *Moby-Dick,* a silent version entitled *The Sea Beast,* in 1925, and again as a talkie in 1930. In both movies, Barrymore's Ahab has a love interest, and in each the plot revolves around the contest between Ahab and his brother Derek for the love of the girl. (Dolores Costello played Esther in *The Sea Beast* and married Barrymore soon after the film was made; Joan Bennett played Faith in the subsequent version.) Though the opening line of *Moby-Dick* is arguably the most famous in all of American literature, there was no opportunity to use it in either film inasmuch as the character of Ishmael was cut as an unnecessary diversion from the basic love triangle.

When director John Huston took up *Moby-Dick* as a cinematic project in 1955, he was determined to capture the spirit of Melville's novel as well as the plot. Ray Bradbury wrote the screenplay, and the result is a brooding, philosophical Ahab, wonderfully played by Gregory Peck. The larger issues—those that cannot be easily captured in soliloquies—are, of necessity, abandoned in the movie. In a television version of *Moby-Dick* made for the USA cable network in 1997, Patrick Stewart, best known as the admirable captain of the starship *Enterprise* in *Star Trek: The Next Generation,* turns in a disappointing performance as Ahab; his terrible wig commands as much attention as Ahab's monomaniacal ranting. The filmmakers were not so careful with the whaling technology as in earlier versions, and the cliffs of southern Australia are a bothersome stand-in for the sandy beaches of Nantucket. (John Huston used an Irish coastal village to play the role of New Bedford with equally questionable—though more interesting—results.)

The story of three shipwrecked whalemen ashore in the Arctic, their dependence on the native residents for survival, and the resulting cultural confusion that unfolds tragically, is beautifully told in Philip Kaufman's *The White Dawn* (1974), based on the novel by James Houston. Starring Timothy Bottoms, Warren Oates, and Lou Gossett Jr., the film was made largely on location on Baffin Island with people from the local Inuit community of Iqaluit.

The Sea Wolf, Jack London's drama of the sealing trade is the most often filmed sea novel. Nine versions have been made, three of them in the silent era. The best known is the Michael Curtiz version of 1941, wherein the screenwriter, Robert Rossen, made an extraordinary decision in changing the character of the righteous and pious Maude Brewster into an ex-con (Ida Lupino) on the lam. The story was filmed again in 1994 for cable television by the Turner Network, and the character of poor Maude was modeled on Ida Lupino's film character rather than the character described by London. Though sealing is nominally the reason for the voyage, it served London primarily as a backdrop for exploring the philosophical questions about natural/scientific man vs. civilized/religious man. Simplified into a struggle between good and evil, the filmed versions do not attempt to dramatize the seal hunt, but they do give viewers a good sense of the confinement that a ship represents when hostile forces share the limited space with little hope for escape.

The seal hunt was again, nominally, the subject of *The World in His Arms* (1952). Gregory Peck plays "The Boston Man," who commands a sealing schooner making regular runs between San Francisco and the coast of Alaska. Ann Blyth has a ridiculous role as a Russian countess, and Anthony Quinn is almost as ridiculous as a Portuguese rival to Peck. The movie highlights San Francisco as the undisputed capitol of American maritime commerce on the West Coast, and it includes terrific footage of two schooners in a race for port.

Even as American interests expanded into the Pacific, the working trades that had fueled the Atlantic economy from the first ventures of Europeans into the waters of the New World continued in an unbroken tradition along the Atlantic seaboard and south to the Caribbean. Fishing is the oldest and most common ocean occupation, but it has limited dramatic potential. The best fishing movie is *Captains Courageous* (1937), which uses extensive footage shot aboard actual fishing schooners. The story is based on the Rudyard Kipling novel, and in alterations made by screenwriters Marc Connelly and Dale Van Every the central dramatic flaw of the book is resolved. The transformation of Harvey Cheyne from irritating brat to

FIGURE 54. *Moby Dick* (1956). Captain Ahab (Gregory Peck) commands his ship in search of the great white whale. John Huston's 1955 film attempted to capture both the environment of the novel and philosophical brooding of Ahab. Courtesy Moulin Productions.

dependable lad is more believable in the screen version, where a younger Harvey bonds with the fatherly Spencer Tracy as the Portuguese fisherman Manuel.

The slave trade, which was one corner of the "triangle trade" that also included New England fish and West Indian sugar products, continued well into the nineteenth century. Though dominated by British merchants, especially from the port of Liverpool, Americans participated in the slave trade from colonial times to the eve of the Civil War. Most American vessels involved in the slave trade were owned in states where the practice of slavery was abolished earliest. Ships from Rhode Island dominated the trade in the colonial period, but were surpassed by Massachusetts vessels after the Revolution. Many of the slaves carried as hostage cargo on these ships never came to the United States but were transported instead to the Caribbean or Brazil.

Until the middle of the nineteenth century, three times as many people had crossed the Atlantic Ocean as slaves from Africa as had crossed it as immigrants from Europe. More than 24,000 voyages were made in the slave trade, transporting more than ten million people in bondage to the Americas, some 600,000 of them into the plantations of the American

FIGURE 55. *Captains Courageous* (1937). Director Victor Fleming capitalized on the opportunity to film fishermen and their schooners around the Grand Banks of Newfoundland. These images provide a strong realistic element that blends into the staged scenes. Courtesy Metro-Goldwyn-Mayer.

South. This difficult subject has been mostly avoided by Hollywood. In 1937 two films appeared that had scenes aboard slave-trading vessels, but the scenes below decks were secondary to the romantic drama of the white protagonists in both *The Slave Ship* and *Souls at Sea.*

It was the 1977 television miniseries *Roots* that first brought the horrifying conditions of the slave ship to the screen. It took another twenty years before the subject was seriously tackled again, this time in Steven Spielberg's film *Amistad,* the historical details of which have been the subject of an interesting series of commentaries. *Amistad* tells the story of a slave revolt in 1839 aboard a Spanish-owned vessel on the coast of Cuba. Sailing east by day under the watchful eye of Cinqué, the leader of the revolt, and north by night when navigated by the captured Spanish crew, the *Amistad* ended up near Long Island, where it was seized by the U.S. Navy. The rebel slaves were imprisoned in Connecticut for eighteen months while a series of trials decided their fate. Spielberg's movie makes a powerful statement about the empowerment of the Africans in the judicial process and about the inspirational influence of Cinqué on John Quincy Adams, who argued the case before the United States Supreme Court.

Historians, beginning with Simon Schama in a January 1998 article in the *New Yorker,* described key aspects of the movie as "feel-good fantasy" and "fabulously fictitious." In a response to Schama in the *National Review* published the following month, Stanley Kauffmann said that the movie "may not be historically exact, but it is dramatically and thematically apt." That same month Gary Rosen went even further than Schama in an article in *Commentary* called "*Amistad* and the Abuse of History." According to Rosen, "The facts at issue in Spielberg's *Amistad* are not picayune details, quibbles over the compressing or simplifying of what is a very complex tale. Such things are to be expected in a dramatization. What Spielberg has done in relating this 'shared piece of American history' is more fundamental. He has misrepresented, in a way that can only be intentional, the racial relations that form the very heart of the events he depicts" (48). A firestorm of letters appeared in response, one written by two noted historians, Lesley Herrman and Steven Mintz, who supported the motives of the filmmaker and said that "despite some important distortions and omissions, *Amistad* does what films can do and history texts cannot: it brings the past to life." Rosen responded that "in this mendacious retelling, the *Amistad* affair becomes a tale of multicultural collaboration, and thus a predictable reflection of the present rather than a meaningful window on the past."

A key issue for discussion is whether a film that purports to tell a true story reflects more the time in which the story took place, or the time in which the story, through the film, is told. History serves a purpose in allowing us to deal with sensitive and controversial issues, like race relations, from a temporal distance. If the objective of the filmmaker is to introduce such difficult topics for debate, then the way in which known events of the past are manipulated for that purpose must be made clear.

Cecil B. De Mille's *Reap the Wild Wind* (1942) explores the world of marine salvage on the Carolina and Florida coasts with the coming of steamships after the middle of the nineteenth century. John Wayne stars as Captain Jack Stuart, a man who makes his living picking up the pieces after a shipwreck but longs to command the new steamer *Southern Cross.* Raymond Massey as his competition is not just a salvager but also a wrecker, who purposefully causes the destruction of ships by using false signal lights on shore. Paulette Goddard plays the love interest, a spunky young woman who actually ventures to sea in a hurricane to rescue the survivors a shipwreck. The exaggerated plot is replete with multiple shipwrecks, stowaways, women in disguise, gunfights, and even an attack by a giant squid. While it is not a great source of historical detail, De Mille paints an interesting picture of the society on shore that supported maritime endeavors, including a turn by Ray Milland as a lawyer representing the commercial interests of the ship owner. *Reap the Wild Wind* is also interesting for the underwater scenes filmed on a shipwreck set De Mille had built in the main tank of the Pacific Marine Museum in Santa Monica, some of the first extensive underwater footage to appear in a movie.

War on the Sea

Few films depict American naval action before World War I. The Civil War is dramatized in only one maritime film, *Ironclads: The Monitor and the Merrimac* (1988), though both the Union and Confederate navies made extensive use of ships for blockading ports and raiding the opposition's seagoing commerce. *Ironclads* is most notable for its attention to the rapidly advancing technology of some of the first steamships employed in sea battles. The Spanish-American War was set in motion by the sinking of the battleship *Maine* in Havana harbor in February 1898, but that incident has never made it into a movie except as a passing reference.

Navy sailors began to be of dramatic interest to the American public in the years following World War I, however, and a number of lighthearted Navy movies appeared between the wars and into the early years of World War II. A number of these films were musicals, including *Here Comes the Navy* (1934), with Jimmy Cagney, and *Follow the Fleet* (1936), with Fred Astaire and Ginger Rogers. Others in the genre were *Hit the Deck* (1930, 1955), *In the Navy* (1941), and *Navy Blues* (1941). As light romance, a navy story requires a good amount of time spent on shore, and all these movies bowed to that necessity. The ships in these films were generally populated by amusing swabbies who were actually just average American Joes doing their part in a crazy, mixed-up world. (The stereotypical mix included a scared young Iowa farm boy, a smart-alecky Brooklyn native of Italian or Jewish extraction, the Boston-born son of an immigrant Irish mother, and the wealthy scion of a *Mayflower* family; African Americans were occasionally included in minor roles.)

During and after World War II, more serious films about naval activities began to appear, focusing more on shipboard action. Three excellent documentaries, *The Battle of Midway* (1942), *Torpedo Squadron* (1943), and *We Sail at Midnight* (1943) were made by director John Ford, who served as a lieutenant commander in the U.S. Navy during the war and was promoted later to the position of two-star admiral in the naval reserves. Ford also made a dramatic film about PT boat crews, *They Were Expendable* (1945), which starred another U.S. Navy veteran, Robert Montgomery. The best dramatic movies of this period were made in England (where the national identity continued to be more closely tied to the maritime world), and include *In Which We Serve* (1942).

Merchant mariners, whose crucial role in wartime is often overlooked by historians, are well represented in *Action in the North Atlantic* (1943), which stars Humphrey Bogart as the captain of a freighter. Other noncombatants unexpectedly caught up in the war are the occupants of Alfred Hitchcock's *Lifeboat* (1944), the surviving passengers and crew from a liner hit by a torpedo fired by a German U-boat. Tallulah Bankhead stars as the haughty rich woman, while Walter Slezak plays the captain of the German submarine, which was also sunk in the encounter. Made entirely on a single wet set, *Lifeboat* explores the psychology of the occupants who have survived disaster only to find themselves still caught in a desperate and potentially hopeless situation.

It took a decade after the war was over for filmmakers to be able to approach it with a more historical eye, and again the British achieved excellence with *The Cruel Sea* (1952). When John Ford began the project of making *Mr. Roberts,* which appeared in 1955, he had the Navy's full cooperation, and scenes were shot in the Pacific on board the USS *Hewell.* Set in the late years of the war on a naval cargo vessel, *Mr. Roberts* stars Henry Fonda (who, like Ford, had served in the Navy, spending some two years in the South Pacific and rising to the rank of lieutenant). The film captures the routine and repetitive tasks that make up the sailor's day. Made around the same time, an excellent series of twenty-six half-hour television documentaries, *Victory at Sea,* is now available through PBS video outlets. Two American presidents can be found in films depicting World War II naval activities: Ronald Reagan stars in *Hellcats of the Navy* (1956), while John F. Kennedy is depicted (by Cliff Robertson) in *PT 109* (1963).

Korean War action is very well represented by *The Bridges at Toko-Ri* (1955), based on a novel by James Michener and starring William Holden as Harry Brubaker, a flier and World War II veteran who is angry to have been called back up from the reserves for service on an aircraft carrier off the coast of Asia. The shipboard scenes are convincing, and the subplots serve to enhance our understanding of Brubaker's relationships with his wife (Grace Kelly), his captain (Frederic March), and the pilot of a rescue helicopter (Mickey Rooney) who is asked to risk his life to save Brubaker's. There is also a nod to the complexity of cross-cultural relationships, as Mickey Rooney's character finds that his Japanese fiancée has abandoned him for another American sailor while he was at sea.

The dramatic potential of a ship, with its confined space, placement within an unsurvivable element, dependence on technology, and captive characters, is heightened when the vessel becomes a submarine, as the large number of submarine titles attest. Films exploring these themes include: *The Seas Beneath* (1931), *Hell Below* (1933), *Submarine Patrol* (1938), *Crash Dive* (1943), *Destination Tokyo* (1944), *Submarine Command* (1951), *The Enemy Below* (1957), *Torpedo Run* (1958), *Up Periscope* (1959), and *Grey Lady Down* (1978). Among the best of the submarine films is *Run Silent Run Deep* (1958), which was followed only a year later by the silly *Operation Petticoat* (1959), in which the inability of the submarine crew to deal with female nurses in their isolated world provides the comic structure.

Nuclear issues are powerfully dealt with in the submarine films *On the Beach* (1959), *Ice Station Zebra* (1968), and *Crimson Tide* (1995). The latter also wonderfully outlines the hierarchy of command and the pressures of decision making in the nuclear age. In *The Hunt for Red October* (1990), the captain of a Russian submarine (Sean Connery) defects with the most advanced nuclear submarine in the Soviet arsenal. The threat of nuclear power and Cold War politics is also the subject of *The Bedford Incident* (1965), directed by and staring Richard Widmark. The film explores what happens when a nuclear weapon is accidentally discharged, with the response being decided largely at the level of individual command rather than national policy. Herman Wouk's novel, *The Caine Mutiny,* which explores a fictional mutiny in the U.S. Navy during World War II, but from a Cold War perspective, was made into an effective movie in 1954, starring Humphrey Bogart as the paranoid Captain Queeg.

Technology on the High Seas

Except for naval movies, steamships are generally represented in film only if they sink. *Little Old New York* (1940) purports to be an account of Robert Fulton's development of the steamship, but liberal dramatic license makes it less than useful for historical purposes. Eugene O'Neill's four plays about men working on steam freighters were combined by screenwriter Dudley Nicols into *The Long Voyage Home* (1940), directed by John Ford. John Wayne is improbable as the Scandinavian sailor, Ole Olson, but the dim and grimy world of the tramp steamer is well represented. The best-known steamship, *Titanic,* wrecked in 1912, has inspired five major movies, the most recent of which (1997) became a media phenomenon. Appearing the same year as *Amistad,* James Cameron's film inspired a very different sort of debate among historians and movie critics. Florence King, writing in the *National Review* in January 1998, remarks that the release of *Titanic* ended the important, though often painful, discussion of *Amistad*: "America changed boats. *Amistad* was sunk, as it were, by *Titanic,* the whitest event in history."

Cameron's *Titanic* is breathtaking in its special effects. The ship is exactingly recreated, from the opulence of its first-class accommodations and public rooms right down to the boilers. The viewer gets a sense of being on the ship; the tremendous size of the *Titanic* and of the crowd on board is beautifully conveyed. The finding of the wreck and subsequent interest in salvaging material from it is also introduced, and the computer-generated model of how the ship wrecked and sank works very well in guiding the audience through subsequent events in the film.

The weakness of *Titanic* is in the characters and plotline that are laid over the historical material. The well-known first-class passengers, including Mr. and Mrs. John Jacob Astor, William Guggenheim, Mr. and Mrs. Isadore Strauss, and the ever-present Molly Brown, circulate in the background. Except for Molly, who rose up from the lower classes by marrying a tycoon, the social and financial elite are depicted here mostly as imbeciles.

The Sea in the New Millennium

The role that the sea once played so strongly in the imagination of writers and filmmakers has been, in the late twentieth century, largely replaced by outer space. The notion of a diverse crew confined in a capsule, placed in a dangerous environment, dependent on technology and each other, and then subjected to natural hardships and encounters with alien cultures is still compelling and popular, but the venue has changed. The sea is now depicted not so much as vast, dangerous, and mysterious, but as a fragile environment that needs to be protected. Human beings are now seen as a danger to the sea rather than the other way around.

For a time, in the 1970s, however, the sea fought back, as a series of monsters from the marine environment took revenge against arrogant or thoughtless humanity. *Jaws* (1975), the movie that propelled director Steven Spielberg to fame, was based on a novel by Peter Benchley and showed the horrific consequences of disregarding nature. The sequels were less effective as the shark's motives became anthropomorphized and a less believable, and consequently less scary, enemy on a rampage replaced the soulless killing machine. *Orca* (1977) and other less than effective efforts followed in the wake of *Jaws.*

The first nautical movie of the new millennium, *The Perfect Storm* (2000), based on the best-selling book by Sebastian Junger, synthesizes many of the stalwart salty themes with a good dose of environmental consciousness and a respect for nature. Overfishing and pollution have pushed the swordfish stocks—and their pursuers—further out to sea, where the environment is still beyond the control of humans, despite high-technology equipment, satellite forecasting, and years of experience. Men, and now women as well, face down the environment to the best of their ability but find themselves humbled by the power of nature.

The relentless surge of the sea is the continuous feature in all these films. Human activity changes, technology advances, social conditions evolve, public policy is directed or misdirected, power changes hands, the environment is degraded, but the relationship between the sea and the people who travel on it or into it remains fundamentally unchanged.

References

Filmography

Action in the North Atlantic (1943, F)
All the Brothers Were Valiant (1953, F)
Amistad (1997, F)
The Battle of Midway (1942, D)
The Bedford Incident (1965, F)
The Bounty (1984, F)
The Bridges at Toko-Ri (1955, F)
The Caine Mutiny (1954, F)
Captains Courageous (1937, F)
Crash Dive (1943, F)
Crimson Tide (1995, F)
The Cruel Sea (1952, F)
Destination Tokyo (1944, F)
Down to the Sea in Ships (1923, F; 1949, F)
The Enemy Below (1957, F)
Follow the Fleet (1936, F)
Grey Lady Down (1978, F)
Hawaii (1966, F)
Hell Below (1933, F)
Hellcats of the Navy (1956, F)
Here Comes the Navy (1934, F)
Hit the Deck (1930, F; 1955, F)
The Hunt for Red October (1990, F)
Ice Station Zebra (1968, F)
In the Navy (1941, F)
In Which We Serve (1942, F)
Ironclads: The Monitor and the Merrimac (1997, D)
Jaws (1975, F)
John Paul Jones (1959, F)
Lifeboat (1944, F)
Little Old New York (1940, F)
The Long Voyage Home (1940, F)
Mayflower: The Pilgrims' Adventure (1979, F)
Moby-Dick (1925, F; 1930, F; 1956, F; 1997, TV)
Mr. Roberts (1955, F)
Mutiny on the Bounty (1935, F; 1962, F)
Navy Blues (1941, F)
Old Ironsides (1926, F)
On the Beach (1959, F)
Operation Petticoat (1959, F)
Orca (1977, F)
The Perfect Storm (2000, F)
Plymouth Adventure (1952, F)
PT 109 (1963, F)
Reap the Wild Wind (1942, F)
Run Silent Run Deep (1958, F)
The Sea Beast (1925, F)
The Seas Beneath (1931, F)
The Sea Wolf (1941, F; 1994, TV)
The Slave Ship (1937, F)
Souls at Sea (1937, F)
Submarine Command (1951, F)
Submarine Patrol (1938, F)
They Were Expendable (1945, F)
Titanic (1997, F)
Torpedo Run (1958, F)
Torpedo Squadron (1943, D)
Two Years Before the Mast (1946, F)
Up Periscope (1959, F)
Victory at Sea (1955, TV)
We Sail at Midnight (1943, D)
The White Dawn (1974, F)
The World in His Arms (1952, F)

Bibliography

Kauffmann, Stanley. "Response to 'Clio at the Multiplex.'" *National Review,* 16 February 1998.
King, Florence. "Misanthrope's Corner." *National Review,* 26 January 1998.
Labaree, Benjamin W., et al., eds. *America and the Sea: A Maritime History.* Mystic, CT: Mystic Seaport Museum, 1998.
Mahan, Alfred T. *The Influence of Sea Power Upon History.* New York: Dover, 1987.
Rosen, Gary. "*Amistad* and the Abuse of History." *Commentary,* February 1998. (See also letters to the editor and Rosen's reply, June 1998.)
Schama, Simon. "Clio at the Multiplex: What Hollywood and Herodotus Have in Common." *New Yorker,* 19 January 1998.
Thomas, Tony. *The Cinema of the Sea: A Critical Survey and Filmography, 1925–1986.* Jefferson, NC: McFarland, 1988.

[JOHN C. TIBBETTS]

The Small Town

In William Wellman's *Magic Town* (1947), pollster Lawrence Smith (James Stewart) claims that a small town named Grandview embodies the statistical average of the nation. "Just like the country," he exclaims, "the same percentage of males, females, farmers, labor, Democrats, Republicans, everything!" But when the good citizens of this "America in a capsule" learn they have attracted nationwide attention, they begin to behave like caricatures in their own drama. "Okay, now," one citizen admonishes another, "you're the typical American. Act like it!" The town collapses under the burden of its self-consciousness.

FIGURE 56. *Magic Town* (1947). Pollster Lawrence Smith (James Stewart) plays basketball with the adolescents of "Grandview." Smith claims that the town demographically and ideologically is representative of the United States. This creates much publicity at the expense of "Grandview's" close-knit community. Courtesy RKO Radio Pictures and Robert Riskin Productions.

During the years spanning the Hollywood studio film (roughly the 1920s to the mid-1960s) and the postmodern era, filmmakers doggedly pursued the dream of a "magic town" that would embody the essence of the American experience. However, the resulting films have been more autobiographical and self-referential in nature than indicative of any reality studied by sociologists and historians—like, for example, the classic series of studies generated by Robert S. and Helen M. Lynd's *Middletown* researches, begun in 1929, which conducted a sociological study of Muncie, Indiana, a town "as representative as possible of contemporary American life" (7). In other words, Hollywood films about small towns have not typified America as much as they have mirrored that quintessential "magic town," Hollywood itself.

Throughout the studio era, Hollywood's pursuit of the small-town paradigm, a "representative anecdote" of the nation at large, was driven by the personal artistic agendas of a handful of influential filmmakers and targeted to an audience composed primarily of middle-class whites, especially "average citizen's wives," between the ages of fourteen and forty-five. These compounds of personal and corporate myths were tagged, labeled, and exhibited to a receptive public, even if their self-conscious artifice separated them from any reality outside the movie theaters.

From 1910 until 1940, filmmakers Walt Disney, Frank Capra, Darryl F. Zanuck, and Louis B. Mayer, as well as actors such as Mary Pickford and Will Rogers, envisioned cinematic small towns as simulacra of "home," of lost childhood experiences reconfigured into idealized locales. In her notable series of films for

Artcraft in 1917–18, particularly *Rebecca of Sunnybrook Farm* (1917), Pickford, who had been working since age five and had never known a "normal" childhood of her own, invested fictional sleepy towns like Riverboro, Maine, with the kind of sentiment and picaresque humor she drew from the popular adolescent fiction of contemporary writers like Kate Douglas Wiggin and Eleanor H. Porter.

Walt Disney transformed and idealized a miserable, abused childhood on a farm near Marceline, Missouri, into the scrubbed, buffed and polished experience of his theme parks. Significantly, Marceline's reconstituted "Main Street" is the only area in the parks through which every visitor must pass. Moreover, it reappears constantly in Disney's films, its barnyards serving as the backdrops for the antics of Mickey Mouse, its quaint front porches and gabled roofs as settings for Hayley Mills's *Pollyanna* (1960) and *Summer Magic* (1963). "All the harshness, inconsistencies, and filth of the original [Marceline] have been removed," notes commentator Scott MacDonald. "The recreated Main Street apparently represents the past that America wants to believe existed" (140–141).

Frank Capra celebrated in his movies the small-town life he had never known as an Italian immigrant come to America at age five. After years of hardships and rootless wanderings, he found a "home" at Columbia Pictures (a "small town," aptly enough, compared to the larger "communities" of major studios like MGM and Paramount). He gained enough artistic independence to remake his life into a series of Horatio Alger–like fables where small-town idealists like Longfellow Deeds (Gary Cooper) of Mandrake Falls, Jefferson Smith (James Stewart) of Willet Creek, and George Bailey (Stewart) of Bedford Falls overcome corrupt, big city corporate lawyers (*Mr. Deeds Goes to Town,* 1936); crooked politicians (*Mr. Smith Goes to Washington,* 1939); and greedy bankers (*It's a Wonderful Life,* 1946). Whether these pictures are true populist fables of pluralistic democracy has long been debated (see, e.g., Phelps; Richards); however, what is evident is that at the very least the films confirm the ideal of the "town meeting": Capra "seems to be saying that society and the individuals within it will be qualitatively better," writes Glenn Alan Phelps, "only when each individual is given a large degree of responsibility for his own actions *and* for the actions of his community" (390).

Likewise, another immigrant, MGM studio chief Louis B. Mayer, regained his lost childhood in the mythical setting of Carvel, Idaho, the location during the mid-1930s and early 1940s of the enormously popular "Andy Hardy" series starring Mickey Rooney and Lewis Stone. Here, Mayer could "set aside the difficulties of his youth," wrote critic Bosley Crowther, and extol his "elaborate affection for the family and . . . American home life" (237).

Similarly, the "Homeville" comedies of Will Rogers—*Dr. Bull* (1932), *Judge Priest* (1933), *David Harum* (1934), and *Steamboat 'Round the Bend* (1935)—may be regarded as idyllic transformations of the otherwise troubled scenes of Rogers's boyhood in Oolagah, Oklahoma Territory. As Peter C. Rollins notes, in these films "Uncle Will" could preside over preindustrial southern towns "purposefully insulated from contemporary strains and pressures" and from "the world of ethical confusion, depression, and impending war" (59). It is not coincidental, by the way, that some of these pictures were released by producer Darryl F. Zanuck of the newly formed Twentieth Century–Fox studio. Zanuck was busily making a career out of reconfiguring the miseries of his boyhood in Wahoo, Nebraska, into the idealized confections of small-town American life. He would perform the same function in crafting the background settings and cultural milieu for his other great star of the 1930s, Shirley Temple (*Captain January,* 1936; *Rebecca of Sunnybrook Farm,* 1937).

But, as Ima Honaker Herron has demonstrated in her enormously informative study

The Small Town in American Drama, this popular image of the American village as a "resort of peace" and "haven of democracy" had been under review—in drama and literature, at least—ever since E. W. Howe's novel *The Story of a Country Town* (1883) exposed the tiny fictional Kansas villages of Fairview and Twin Mounds as victims of their own isolation, blighted by intellectual stagnation and provincialism. Howe's novel, writes John William Ward, "is the earliest expression in our fiction of disenchantment with . . . the simplicities and virtues of rural life" (302). Additionally, as that citizen of the quintessential American small town, Emporia, Kansas, newspaper editor William Allen White pointed out in his *Autobiography* that the new century's increasingly urbanized collectivistic way of life was threatening the ideal of village democracy (626).

The small town that was Hollywood in those days—and it has been argued that studio-era Hollywood was indeed an insular, self-contained "community" composed of a "mature oligopoly" of vertically integrated studios (Schatz, 9–11)—was also reeling from internal and external shocks. Beginning in the 1920s, union organizers, government antitrust investigators, and state and industry censors were threatening to disrupt its balance of power. Moreover, the economic problems stemming from the Depression were plunging most of the major studios into bankruptcy and receivership, necessitating a takeover by New York banking interests. Small wonder that an embattled Hollywood could identify with the crises contemporaneously afflicting small-town life, subsequently locating many of its so-called problem films in villages and small communities. Thus, Sinclair Lewis's novel, *Main Street,* a sensational attack on the smug materialism of the American town (the fictional Gopher Prairie, Minnesota), attracted filmmakers as early as 1922 (it was remade in 1936 under another title, *I Married a Doctor*). Elsewhere on screen, small towns erupted in mob violence (Cecil B. De Mille's *This Day and Age,* 1933; Fritz Lang's *Fury,* 1935; Clarence Brown's *Intruder in the Dust,* 1949); racist bigotry (Archie Mayo's *Black Legion,* 1937; Gordon Parks's *The Learning Tree,* 1969); jingoistic patriotism (Preston Sturges's *Hail the Conquering Hero,* 1944); and social and political corruption (Robert Rossen's *All the King's Men,* 1949). The narrow confines of these communities—cultural, social, and racial—acted like pressure cookers that brought these problems to a boil.

Alfred Hitchcock's *Shadow of a Doubt* (1943) brought to wartime American audiences the disturbing news that there was a skeleton in the closet of small-town hearth and home. "Uncle Charlie" (Joseph Cotten), unbeknownst to his relatives, is a serial killer on the lam. Like a modern-day serpent in the garden of small town America, he informs his innocent niece, also named Charlie (Theresa Wright), that her "ordinary little town" of Santa Rosa, California, does not at all resemble her "peaceful, stupid dreams": "How do you know what the world is like? Do you know the world is a foul sty? Do you know if you ripped the fronts off houses you'd find swine? The world's a hell! What does it matter what happens in it?" Even though Uncle Charlie ultimately perishes under the wheels of a train, the ominous shadow of his presence seems to linger. The sun will never again shine quite so brightly on this community.

Many Cold War movies confirmed paranoid fears that communist insurgency would not only find its easiest target in the complacency of American small towns but was already suspected of operating unchecked in Hollywood itself. This warning appeared either in the guise of science fiction—as in *Invasion of the Body Snatchers* (1956), Don Siegel's adaptation of Jack Finney's classic novel about a race of soulless, extraterrestrial "pod people" who attempt to take over Santa Mira, California—or outright political propaganda, as in *Red Nightmare* (1962), an overwrought

FIGURE 57. *Shadow of a Doubt* (1943). Alfred Hitchcock uses a serial killer, "Uncle Charlie" (Joseph Cotten), to unsettle forever the peace and tranquility that is the privilege of small town America. Courtesy Skirball Productions and Universal Pictures.

parable of how vulnerable a quiet country village can be to imminent Communist takeover, a scenario revisited in John Milius's similarly overwrought *Red Dawn* (1984), set in small-town Colorado.

By the time postmodern horror film cycles appeared in the 1970s and 1980s, American urbanization had left many small towns mere backwater anomalies, useless, vestigial reminders of a nation haunted by its loss of individual opportunity and community identity. Similarly, Hollywood's studio system was itself in shambles, torn apart by, among other things, the government's antitrust actions that forced the studios to sell off their theater chains and by the competitive inroads of commercial television. Small wonder that serial killers now stalked the streets of Haddonfield, Illinois, in John Carpenter's *Halloween* (1978) and the unidentified town of Wes Craven's *Nightmare on Elm Street* series; that unemployed butchers in a tiny Texas town resorted to cannibalism in Tobe Hooper's *Texas Chainsaw Massacre* (1974); that vampires infested Stephen King's *Salem's Lot* (1979) and the small desert towns of Kathryn Bigelow's *Near Dark* (1987); and that the minions of Satan himself blew into Green Town, Illinois, in Ray Bradbury's *Something Wicked This Way Comes* (1983).

Today, as Hollywood increasingly grinds out product targeted directly to cable networks and commercial television, its image of a "magic town," appropriately enough, looks more and more like a television sitcom. The immaculately groomed, picture-perfect villages of Seahaven, in Peter Weir's *The Truman Show* (1998), and the black-and-white Pleasantville in Gary Ross's 1998 film of the same name, are imitations of the 1950s television communities of *Leave It to Beaver* and *The Adventures of Ozzie and Harriet.* Once Truman Burbank (Jim Carrey) and George Parker (William H. Macy) realize they have been unwitting participants in media-reconstructed, prefabricated realities, the conformist walls come tumbling down and chaos reigns. Only then, it is implied, can their lives *really* begin. Magic Town is only a myth on the way toward a larger reality. The mailing address that playwright Thornton Wilder provides for Grovers Corners, New Hampshire, in *Our Town* applies to Seahaven and Pleasantville: they are only dots lost in the vast inscrutability of a larger mystery.

References

Filmography

The Adventures of Ozzie and Harriet (1952–66, TV)
All the King's Men (1949, F)
The Andy Griffith Show (1960–68, TV)
Andy Hardy Comes Home (1958, F)
Black Legion (1937, F)
David Harum (1934, F)
Dr. Bull (1932, F)
Ethan Frome (1994, F)
A Family Affair (1937, F)
Fury (1935, F)
Hail the Conquering Hero (1944, F)
Halloween (1978, F)
High Noon (1951, F)
I Married a Doctor (1936, F)
Intruder in the Dust (1949, F)
Invasion of the Body Snatchers (1956, F; 1978, F)

It's a Wonderful Life (1946, F)
Judge Priest (1933, F)
The Learning Tree (1969, F)
Leave It to Beaver (1957–63, TV)
Magic Town (1947, F)
Main Street (1922, F)
Meet John Doe (1940, F)
Mr. Deeds Goes to Town (1936, F)
Mr. Smith Goes to Washington (1939, F)
Near Dark (1987, F)
Nightmare on Elm Street (1984, F)
Our Town (1940, F)
Pleasantville (1998, F)
Pollyanna (1960, F)
The Rainmaker (1956, F)
Rebecca of Sunnybrook Farm (1917, F; 1937, F)
Red Dawn (1984, F)
Salem's Lot (1979, F)
Shadow of a Doubt (1943, F)
Smalltown, U.S.A.: A Farewell Portrait (1964, D)
So Dear to My Heart (1945, F)
Something Wicked This Way Comes (1983, F)
Steamboat 'Round the Bend (1935, F)
Steamboat Willie (1928, F)
Summer Magic (1963, F)
The Texas Chainsaw Massacre (1974, F)
This Day and Age (1933, F)
The Truman Show (1998, F)

Bibliography

Crowther, Bosley. *Hollywood Rajah: The Life and Times of Louis B. Mayer.* New York: Holt, Rinehart & Winston, 1960.

Herron, Ima Honaker. *The Small Town in American Drama.* Dallas: Southern Methodist University Press, 1969.

Howe, E. W. *The Story of a Country Town.* 1883. New York: Twayne, 1962.

Lewis, R. W. B. *The American Adam: Innocence, Tragedy, and Tradition in the Nineteenth Century.* Chicago: University of Chicago Press, 1955.

Lynd, Robert S., and Helen M. Lynd. *Middletown: A Study in Modern American Culture.* New York: Harcourt, Brace & World, 1929.

MacDonald, Scott. "Reenvisioning the American West." *American Studies* 39.1 (1998): 115–146.

Phelps, Glenn Alan. "The 'Populist' Films of Frank Capra." *The Journal of American Studies* 13.3 (1979): 377–392.

Richards, Jeffrey. "Frank Capra and the Cinema of Populism." *Film Society Review* 7 (1972): 38–46, 61–72.

Rollins, Peter C. *Will Rogers: A Bio-Bibliography.* Westport, CT: Greenwood, 1984.

Schatz, Thomas. *The Genius of the System: Hollywood Filmmaking in the Studio Era.* New York: Pantheon, 1988.

Shortridge, James R. *The Middle West: Its Meaning in American Culture.* Lawrence: University Press of Kansas, 1989.

Wheeler, Thomas C., Ed. *A Vanishing America: The Life and Times of the Small Town.* New York: Holt, Rinehart & Winston, 1964.

White, William Allen. *The Autobiography of William Allen White.* New York: Macmillan, 1946.

[OWEN W. GILMAN JR.]

The South

From the early years of the American film industry to the present, the South has been an enduring subject of interest to both filmmakers and moviegoers. Practically everyone knows some segments of its story. The premiere of *Gone with the Wind* in 1939 was a carefully crafted extravaganza designed to catch the full attention of the nation. Subsequently, *Gone with the Wind* was reissued at intervals in a pattern set to ensure that the romance of Scarlett O'Hara and Rhett Butler—coupled to the mystique of Tara and Twelve Oaks—would be the most watched and most widely known Hollywood story for a half century. Well before the national hoopla surrounding *Gone with the Wind,* however, the South had been vigorously established as a powerful presence on the silver screen. From the beginnings of film, even as the actual region underwent significant cultural change, movies set in the South attracted audiences, and those audiences "learned" a lot of southern history in the process.

Southerners are people of memory and tradition, with the past always shadowing the present. Historians confronted this pattern formally in the years after World War II, and it is particularly well represented in C. Vann Woodward's famous 1960 essay collection *The Burden of Southern History.* The scholarly rigor of Woodward's work challenged many cherished nostrums of southern culture and social practice that had been a staple of films about the South throughout the first half of the twentieth century. Those films had constructed a popular view of the South's history, but by Woodward's death in the final month of the century, his revisionist work had been confirmed and extended by a host of junior colleagues such as Drew Gilpin Faust and Eugene Genovese. Furthermore, the substance of those revisions had also been reflected in films from the last half of the twentieth century.

In "The Historical Dimension" section of *The Burden of Southern History,* Woodward acknowledges the key role of southern writers from the 1920s onward as they looked deep into the past to discern truths of the present, noting that "they have not set up as defenders of a cause, either one lost or still sought" (38). Although the first film in this study of the South and history, *The Birth of a Nation,* proceeded from a novelist's vision that was darkly enraptured with a lost cause, quite a number of subsequent film treatments of the South fit rather more closely within Woodward's argument. Any approach to history and the South in film must attend to writers from the South and the literary works that attempt to distill the good from the bad, the real from the ideal, the permanent from the impermanent in their native region. Quite a few pieces of this rich and strong writing have proven to be readily adaptable to film presentation.

Writers know particulars, and the South's history has strong distinguishing features. Although the South actually subdivides into numerous smaller sections defined by particular features of natural environment, habit, custom, and even dialect—Savannah, the setting of *Midnight in the Garden of Good and Evil* (1998), would never be confused with the area around Grandfather Mountain in western North Carolina, the setting of *Songcatcher* (2001), or with east Texas, the setting of *Terms of Endearment* (1983)—the whole region nevertheless has a distinct quality of "place" about it. A sense of enduring history is more palpable here than elsewhere in America, as is the closeness of relationship between people and particular, distinct spots of land.

Americans are enthralled with newness and change. At an accelerating rate, the years of the twentieth century have introduced new notions that have displaced the old in America. Of all the geographical areas of the United States, the South best represents a pattern of resistance to change, an adherence to old customs and values (see Eugene Genovese's *The Southern Tradition*). The South's conservatism has been well documented in a wide range of political, social, and economic conditions, some deeply lamentable and some potentially salutary. As Americans struggled to process all the consequences of development, they simultaneously sought a means to review and recall matters lost in the passing of cultural time. Films about the South frequently address this issue and fill a lingering national need to pay homage to old ways of life.

America is a land of hard conflicts. The "more perfect union" goal of the preamble to the Constitution has presented tough challenges over time. The most obstinate challenge of all involves race relations. Even though all parts of the country have struggled to achieve racial harmony (on this point, John Egerton recalls in *Shades of Gray*, Malcolm X once observed that the South "is anywhere south of the Canadian border), the South's particularly infamous experience with race has made it a logical and enduring location for film consideration of this key national dilemma.

Even as portions of the real, modern South have become beacons for a future rich in the wonder of global communications—most prominently represented in Ted Turner's cable television news empire (ultimately blended into AOL Time Warner) and his huge collection of American movie classics—a long and storied past still shadows the threshold of a new millennium. At last, the South has achieved rich diversity, and yet, the South keeps the permanence of memory safe from deletion or erasure.

In light of this interest, however, southern history has been exceedingly malleable, a matter of steadily evolving perspective. At almost any time, from D. W. Griffith's legendary effort to make the South distinguished and justified in its racism and prejudice in *The Birth of a Nation* (1915) through to Clint Eastwood's film adaptation of *Midnight in the Garden of Good and Evil*, viewers of any film with a southern location should understand that the director's perspective and the cinematographer's lens are of as much historical interest as any point of cultural past framed in the narrative. This cautionary point is explored in fine detail by Jack Temple Kirby's *Media-Made Dixie* (1977), which demonstrates convincingly how much the South is a construct of popular culture, with film laying its foundation.

Films Make History

Any examination of the intersection of the South, film, and history must begin with *The Birth of a Nation*, for, as D. W. Griffith solidly established numerous key narrative film techniques—a matter of achievement warranting forty-fourth place on the 1998 American Film Institute (AFI) list of the top one hundred American movies—he simultaneously introduced a long-lasting impression of the South as it might be placed in history. Griffith's effort clearly bears the stamp of his time and personal background. As a consequence, *The Birth of a Nation* reveals the temper of the nation in 1915. Following the Civil War and a subsequent interlude of federally managed "Reconstruction," the white community reclaimed key forms of power late in the nineteenth century. C. Vann Woodward's *Strange Career of*

Jim Crow (1955) skillfully delineates the key steps in this pattern of cultural regression at the turn of the last century; more recently, Eric Foner notes in *The Story of American Freedom* (1998) that "boundaries of exclusion had long been intrinsic to the meaning of American freedom" (107). Looking backward from the vantage point of the early twentieth century, southern writers idealized the Old South, providing a nostalgic and mythic veneer to plantation life, a disposition which would survive for several generations in Hollywood following Griffith's vigorous and influential lead.

As the practice of segregation gained momentum in the early years of the twentieth century, most explicitly in the South but tacitly in the rest of the nation, the idea of white superiority once again was widespread, a viewpoint with long-lasting consequence. Griffith's film and its representation of the past materially contributed to the breadth and depth of this egregious social condition. The reach of the film was extraordinary, except for some areas where the recently created NAACP mounted protests and some few locales (Kansas, Chicago, Newark, Atlantic City, St. Louis) where the movie was banned for a time. The film was screened for President Woodrow Wilson in the White House, with Wilson reporting satisfaction. In the main, Americans felt comfortable with the Cameron family of the South as the Camerons tried to recover control over their region's destiny.

To see *The Birth of a Nation* is to fathom the deep gulf between white and black in American culture in the twentieth century—all foregrounded in the South and from a white point of view. Griffith was a Kentuckian. His father had been a colonel in the Confederate Army, and he enthralled his son with yarns of his past, which included slaveholding. Thus, when Griffith began making his most influential film, it was natural for him to draw upon the fiction of a North Carolinian, Thomas Dixon, most especially Dixon's novel (and subsequent stage drama) *The Clansman,* a bestseller in 1905. Dixon's racism is virulent and unabated. Griffith's film adaptation tempered the racism just enough to appeal to a much broader audience, but the bias against persons of color is devastating nevertheless, perhaps most provocatively in the famous suicidal leap from a cliff that Flora Cameron (Mae Marsh) takes to avoid the pursuit of a drunken, sex-crazed African American named Gus (Walter Long). This scene and others equally inflammatory were used to justify the creation of the Ku Klux Klan as a force to assert white dominance. Everett Carter treats the lamentable impact of Griffith's film with fine discernment, noting creation of the "Plantation Illusion": "a debasement of epic powers in which those powers pander to popular taste instead of attempting to reach a whole vision, sinewed with moral responsibility" (19).

An effective counterpoint to the mythos of white supremacy was a long time coming in films set in the South. Two books by Thomas Cripps, *Slow Fade to Black* and *Making Movies Black,* account in painstaking detail for the slowness of change in representing African Americans. Two movies from the 1970s, both developed for television broadcast, finally completed the shift.

First came *The Autobiography of Miss Jane Pittman* (1974), adapted by Tracy Keenan from a novel by Ernest Gaines, with Cicely Tyson in the lead role. This made-for-television production stands more than half a century on end, for finally the camera lens looks at America from the perspective of an African American. Jane Pittman's long life reaches from the plantation days before the Civil War all the way to the civil rights agitation of the late 1950s and early 1960s. Her history parallels the history of her region—mainly southern Louisiana. Viewers of this production see the impact of a century upon the central subject of the film, a black woman. As the movie follows Miss Jane to the end of her life, the legacy of D. W. Griffith in film treatment of the African American is at last displaced.

Just three years later, Alex Haley's family saga *Roots* was adapted for broadcast over several nights in January 1977. This production reached a huge audience, claiming about 85 percent of possible viewers, more people than had enjoyed *Gone with the Wind* in their living rooms when it finally reached television on two nights in early November 1976. Although historians have questioned the accuracy of some details in *Roots,* the narrative nevertheless does yeoman work as a powerful counterweight to the long-lasting white frame of reference in representing the South, and it set the stage for subsequent reinterpretations of southern history from an African American perspective.

Following *The Autobiography of Miss Jane Pittman* and *Roots,* it became possible for films to move with increasingly precise historical focus into smaller-scale examinations of race relations in the South. The treatments range from the recent consideration of segregation's darkest last days in *Ghosts of Mississippi* (1996), through scrutiny of the hierarchy of color in *Mississippi Masala* (1992), to meditations on friendship across racial lines in *Driving Miss Daisy* (winner of the Academy Award for best picture in 1989), *Forrest Gump* (best picture of 1994 and seventy-first on the AFI list), and *Cookie's Fortune* (1999)—these last films both being anticipated in part by the determined buddy bonding between the characters played by Sidney Poitier and Tony Curtis in *The Defiant Ones* (1958).

Sometimes, however, recent film treatment of the South's battle with racism still sets history askew, as happened in *Mississippi Burning* (1988). In Mark Carnes's useful and provocative *Past Imperfect* (1995), William H. Chafe's commentary on *Mississippi Burning* clearly shows how the film neglects the important contributions of many black activists in propelling change in Mississippi and spotlights instead the work of two white FBI men, played by Gene Hackman and Willem Dafoe. This production shows that it remains entirely possible for casting decisions and star appeal, key ingredients in the movie industry's calculus, to drive history into distortion. Robert Brent Toplin acknowledges the problem in shifting narrative focus to the FBI figures, but observes that the film nevertheless represents the "ugliness and viciousness of racial prejudice in the South about as well as any Hollywood film of the post–World War II period" (26).

The Old Plantation Place: A Long-Lasting Myth

Between *The Birth of a Nation* and *The Autobiography of Miss Jane Pittman* are a host of finely made films that reflect the intrigue that Hollywood producers and directors, in concert with film viewers nationwide, all found in the South as the twentieth century developed. On the surface of life in the South, where most of these films concentrate their efforts at verisimilitude in rendering the historical past, much is available to delight the eye. Quite a number of these films use the plantation myth as a key point of departure. Again and again, the structured social order and decorum of a departed world are evoked in scenes of plantation life, whether at "Portobello" in King Vidor's *So Red the Rose* (1935, based on Stark Young's 1934 successful novel) or out at "Halcyon" in William Wyler's *Jezebel* (1938), a countryside location presumed safe from the population density and human waste pollution that was thought to contribute to suffering in the city of New Orleans during an 1850s outbreak of yellow fever (familiarly known in the film as "Yellow Jack"). The plantation myth movies, of which *Gone with the Wind* (1939, fourth on the 1998 AFI list) is king and the recent *The Patriot* (2000) a strange reflex, present strong and appealing images of an agrarian world where landowners are mainly chivalrous and workers (slaves) mostly hibernate in a cocoon of cotton. Exceptions to this pattern are sometimes represented—as clear exceptions.

Hollywood in the 1930s had a boom period for projecting a positive, uplifting vision of antebellum plantation life. Mythic visions reigned. Closely detailed, thoroughly objective scholarship about the actual conditions of the slavery period in the South—and also about the South throughout the years following the Civil War—was still some decades in the future (including such works as Drew Gilpin Faust's *James Henry Hammond and the Old South,* C. Vann Woodward's *The Strange Career of Jim Crow,* Eugene D. Genovese's *Roll, Jordan, Roll,* and Eric Foner's *Reconstruction*). The kind of painstaking examination of the master/slave relationship that distinguishes Faust's study of J. H. Hammond's South Carolina plantation, Silver Bluff (on the Savannah River about 175 miles northwest of Savannah), is way beyond the sweeping broad strokes found in movie portraits of the southern plantation during the decade before World War II. Hammond fathered children by his female slaves, actions which, by Faust's account, involved more than "casual sex," extending to "strong, troubling, conflicting emotions about these women and their offspring" (87). William Faulkner struck close to the heart of this highly vexed matter with his most ambitious novel, *Absalom, Absalom!* (1936), but Faulkner, who had put in time as a Hollywood scriptwriter, knew Thomas Sutpen's story was not at all right for the movie business of his time, and not just because of restrictions against miscegenation in the Motion Picture Production Code. (See Robert Sklar's *Movie-Made America* for a useful commentary on this particular taboo.) During this period, when investments were made for historical accuracy, mostly the money went into columned facades, elaborate gowns, and sweeping circular staircases.

Occasionally, as in the case of *So Red the Rose,* where an elaborate, specially constructed mansion was carefully fitted out with period furniture, it was also possible to link the backgrounds of key production people with the South. King Vidor, the director, was from Texas; Robert Cummings, who played a Texan visiting "Portobello" in Mississippi in the film, claimed Texas for his personal background; both Randolph Scott, in a lead male role, and Margaret Sullavan, as Valette, were from families linked to Virginia. Anything that could contribute to the aura of southern gentility was especially valued. The mint julep was a frequent key prop, typically concocted by the main house servant and prized by all true southerners. Much ado is made of Cato's mastery of the mint julep formula in *Jezebel.* One of these fancy libations is generously—and surprisingly—handed back to Cato himself by Preston Dillard (a New Orleans banker played stiffly by Henry Fonda) when he arrives at Halcyon.

The fullest flowering of the South on film, with magnolias frequently in bloom, took place between 1929 and 1941, a time marking the appearance of roughly one quarter of all the films listed for serious consideration in Edward Campbell's *The Celluloid South* (1981). The reason for this profusion of movies with southern settings is fairly simple. As the national economy went far "south" following the stock market crash of 1929, the American movie audience was more than prepared to hanker after nostalgia about the Old South. (William E. Leuchtenburg provides excellent background for this situation in *The Perils of Prosperity, 1914–1932.*)

What reality had stolen from American life, films restored. Real farmers went through terrifying times. The whole nation lurched further and further away from a rural, agricultural center, part of a demographic shift ongoing throughout the twentieth century but impelled harshly by the hardships of farm life during the Great Depression. This moment generated grave anxiety regarding the consequences of this change. Thus, film viewers relished the relief of watching an ordered social and economic system totally rooted in the land and (apparently) self-sufficient. In *Jezebel,* Miss Julie (a scheming Jezebel in biblical terms, played by Bette Davis) tells Preston Dillard (Henry Fonda) that he could not be content in the North, that he is really part of the "country," the South—however quick and dangerous it might be. The whole mix is mighty romantic. This condition stands behind the widespread appeal of several Will Rogers films from the mid-1930s: *In Old Kentucky* (1935), *Judge Priest* (1934), and *Steamboat 'Round the Bend* (1935), all John Ford–directed films that transported viewers back to a harmonious past—but a past that never existed. When song and dance were added to this concoction, as in the Shirley Temple–Bill "Bojangles" Robinson numbers in *The Littlest Rebel* (1935) or in Bing Crosby's songs from *Mississippi* (1935), audiences were afforded a resonant antidote to the dissonant, strident realities of the 1930s.

In *I'll Take My Stand* (1930), frequently labeled "an agrarian manifesto," twelve southern writers, among them John Crowe Ransom and Allen Tate, constructed a vigorous case for privileging the farm over the factory, for trying to keep the South's economy and culture based both on values linked to agriculture and on the intimacy with nature. Despite the vehemence of this colorful collection of essays by diverse southern talents, there was no staying the progress of industrialization or even preventing growth of urbanization and suburbanization in the South. The fact that industrialization eventually swept through the South, along with exploitative labor practices, is demonstrated powerfully in Martin Ritt's *Norma Rae* (1979), for which Sally Field garnered an Academy Award for her portrayal of a woman trying to unionize workers and that, Robert Brent Toplin writes, drew useful attention to the union's dispute with the J. P. Stevens company. However, through the 1930s the whole nation indulged a fantasy of being close to the land through the plantation myth films.

Tara Forever: Land and Its Ownership

A land fixation is most dramatically represented in Scarlett O'Hara's love for Tara. As Eric Foner has shown in *The Story of American Freedom* (1998), the idea of freedom has changed substantially—from generation to generation—over the course of the American experience. One of the earliest foundations for the freedom concept in America was land ownership. This notion—the option for free people to own their own land—was broadly assumed in the various agitations leading up to the revolt of the English colonies late in the eighteenth century. An image of the yeoman farmer was central to Jeffersonian democracy, and it proved to have extraordinary staying power.

Possession of land is a key issue in Margaret Mitchell's Pulitzer Prize–winning and best-selling novel of 1936. The O'Hara family came to America from Ireland because Gerald O'Hara had killed a rent agent for an English landowner. In the old world of Europe, ordinary people could not own land. In contrast, in the new world, Gerald was able to become an important landowner. He also became a slaveholder, for the freedom to own property extended to chattel, a point of obvious tension and conflict as northern abolitionists scrutinized the conditions of slavery. In Eric Foner's view, the right of one person to claim to dominance over another has roots in the rise of freedom as a function of property possession. Although the Civil War ended chattel slavery, the centrality of property ownership stayed strong in the southern philosophy. The turbulence of the Great Depression threatened many people and their assumptions about freedom in owning land, however. On this issue of ownership, Margaret Mitchell's story, written over a ten-year period from 1926 to 1936, is completely a text of its time, and so is the movie that came of it.

Land ownership is made an explicit central concern in the film. Standing in the fields of Tara, early in the movie, Gerald O'Hara (Thomas Mitchell) lectures his daughter Scarlett (Vivien Leigh) on the value of land for the culture he cherishes: "Why, land is the only thing in the world worth working for, worth fighting for, worth dying for because it's the only thing that lasts." Such a declaration resounds with consequence for southerners of many generations. Against the backdrop of national economic stress in the 1930s, these words of a plantation owner would reach many sympathetic and understanding ears, as would remarkably similar words from Muley Graves in John Ford's 1940 film adaptation of John Steinbeck's *Grapes of Wrath.* The feisty Scarlett learns her lesson well and becomes determined, albeit with a habit of procrastination, to sustain her life through her link to the land.

The Civil War eventually comes to Tara, which is ransacked by northern troops during Sherman's march to the sea—on which, see Ross McElwee's delightful quasi-documentary *Sherman's March* (1986), itself a fine exploration of southernness. The first part of *Gone with the Wind* then closes with an extremely powerful scene in which Scarlett, facing the devastation of Tara, falls to her knees. The inability of a radish pulled from the earth to appease her hunger sets up one of the most impassioned and memorable oaths in American film history: "As God is my witness, they're not going to lick me. . . . I'm going to live through this and when it's over I'm never going to be hungry again. No, not any of my folks! If I have to lie, steal, cheat or kill, as God is my witness I'll never be hungry again." Tara—the land—is the place of sustenance, the place where the future will be made right. For that reason, at the end of the film, as Rhett departs, Scarlett has a steadfast response: "Tara . . . Home. I'll go home, and I'll think of some way to get him back. After all, tomorrow is another day." This land-rootedness is distinctively southern, but, at the close of one of America's most difficult decades and following a pattern wherein many Americans gave up their links to the land, Scarlett's need to return to Tara resonated with a mass audience.

Toward a Modern, Tawdry, Complex South

With the 1940s and World War II, films about the South underwent powerful change. Jean Renoir's superb effort in *The Southerner* (1945) signals part of the shift, for it foregrounds the life of the poor, not the landed gentry. Although James Agee found that Renoir's film romanticized poverty in a way that ran counter to his own and Walker Evans's efforts to understand the South in *Let Us Now Praise Famous Men* (1941), *The Southerner* nevertheless pointed the way to the future. There would still be a small place for a kind of sweetness and light in representation of the Old South, most pointedly sustained in Walt Disney's *Song of the South* (1946), based loosely on Joel Chandler Harris's Uncle Remus folk tales. However, the central vision of the South from the early 1940s onward would mirror national cultural trends toward a focus on systematic alienation and displacement. Increasingly in films about the South, the dark side of human affairs would predominate. In film, "noir" became normative. Whether proceeding from original film scripts or coming from film adaptations of published fiction, films centered on the South for the past fifty years have steadily pushed forward in three ways: considering how far and how hard people fall from grace, showing how violent will be the means to the fall, and discovering how close to showing explicit sex the film can go in the process. In the last half-century, as Hollywood went, so went films about the South, albeit with southern versions often carrying the "gothic" label.

The rough and tawdry underside of human life appeared with considerable force in John Ford's 1941 film adaptation of Erskine Caldwell's *Tobacco Road* (1932), which, along with *God's Little Acre* (1933, film 1958), became best-selling narratives of the southern white lower class—although still above the condition of the African American. Caldwell was a native Georgian, and the South he projected in his works—and that made it into film versions—was one defined by poverty, tenantry, hard times, and, increasingly, depravity.

The depravity theme worked its way into a host of films about the South. The film adaptation of Lillian Hellman's play *The Little Foxes*

(1941), centered on the aims and means of avaricious cruelty, led the way in deromanticizing southern life in the modern era. The 1949 film version of Robert Penn Warren's *All the King's Men* caught the irony of having even a leader elected to serve the people's interests become ensnared by dark impulses, most notably sexual ones. Willie Stark (played by Broderick Crawford in an Academy Award–winning performance), the quintessential populist, strays outside marriage for sex, as does Louisiana governor Earl Long (played by Paul Newman) in the 1989 film *Blaze.* For decades, in reel life as well in real life, the South would have a vanguard place in the story of men overwhelmed by prurient emotions. Television news shows from January 1998 to January 1999 in America were filled with lurid details of just such a story, trashing the man from Hope, Arkansas.

Sex and Violence, Southern Style

The cinematic lurch into sex as a feature of southern life was the product, in large part, of a singular playwright. Tennessee Williams was responsible for the material used in seven films from 1951 to 1962, almost always in the same pattern. This theme was explosively introduced in the first work, *A Streetcar Named Desire* (1951), with Vivien Leigh as the plummeting, sexually needy Blanche DuBois and Marlon Brando as the sexually supercharged, brutish Stanley Kowalski. The scene is New Orleans. New Orleans has all the charm of a cramped, congested, contagious city. It's the New Orleans of *Jezebel,* without the remedy of an escape to a plantation. Blanche has only a fading recollection of "Belle Reve," an illusion of gentility, the beautiful dream of a lost past where moonlight was kind to ladies and gentlemen alike. Although the film was subjected to last-minute Legion of Decency censorship, what survived the cut made the main point clear. In the city, Blanche is no match for Stanley. Brutal sexuality triumphs over beauty. As a result, the modern, industrialized South proves to be a hard and ugly place.

Arthur Penn's *The Chase* (1966), based on a Horton Foote novel with a screenplay by Lillian Hellman, extends the South's sexual morass from the city to a Texas small town and rural setting. Marlon Brando plays a decent but troubled local sheriff who tries to contain a crowd impelled by raging hormones and incessant adulterous impulses. White folks are the main culprits in the ensuing mayhem, but their moral deficiencies also put blacks at risk. A remark made by a black mother to her son at the beginning of the story as they observe an escaped white prison convict on the road, "Let white men take care of white men's problems," seems prudent—but also problematic, given the pervasive interconnection of races in the South. Penn's next film, *Bonnie and Clyde* (1967), covered some of the same geographic region but simplified matters by concentrating on white people's violence against other white people, with it all driven somehow by repressed sexual torment.

The brutal South is vividly represented in three works from the late 1960s and early 1970s: *Cool Hand Luke* (1967), *Easy Rider* (1969), and *Deliverance* (1972). The first blends more or less standard prison fare with 1960s antiestablishment sentiment and plenty of sexual longing, all tropes echoed in Joel and Ethan Coen's rollicking *O Brother, Where Art Thou?* (2000). *Easy Rider* features an explosive confrontation between the South's conservatism and the rebellions of youth during the 1960s. When long hair, drugs, and antiauthoritarianism took to the road on motorcycles in the Deep South, resolution was found in the blast of a shotgun at close range. As the characters played by Peter Fonda and Dennis Hopper discover, the country South stood fast—with guns at the ready—against the newfangled challenges of the counterculture.

Another kind of violent encounter appears in *Deliverance,* based on James Dickey's novel of the same name, when four suburbanites from Atlanta decide to have a whitewater canoeing experience before "progress" dams a river. Dickey's lifelong enthusiasm for things primal becomes more evident the deeper his protagonists venture into the wilderness. Human beasts inhabit those backwoods, and several kinds of violence, including sexual, become manifest before the story ends back in the protected suburbs of Atlanta.

To Kill a Mockingbird

Amid the clichéd films of the South from the 1950s to the 1990s, an occasional gem stands apart. Such is the case with a movie from the early 1960s, another successful adaptation of a southerner's novel. Besides *The Birth of a Nation* and *Gone with the Wind,* people mostly know the South in film from *To Kill a Mockingbird* (1963, thirty-fourth on the AFI list). Horton Foote developed a superb screenplay from Harper Lee's Pulitzer Prize–winning novel. Gregory Peck justly received an Academy Award for best actor for his masterful portrait of Atticus Finch, a lawyer with a sense of human duty that transcends the color line. For much of what Harper Lee did in her novel, William Faulkner's *Intruder in the Dust* (1948, film 1949) provided a model of sorts. In each case, a black man is falsely accused of a crime. In each case, young white children have a role in propelling justice. But there are strong changes, too. Faulkner's young Charles Mallison is split into the two Finch children, with Scout, the spunky girl, being a guaranteed audience pleaser whether in print or on screen in the person of Mary Badham; moreover, Faulkner's renaissance lawyer Gavin Stevens evolves into Atticus Finch in *To Kill a Mockingbird,* a loving and wise father, a courageous face-the-lynch-mob individualist, and a compassionate human being capable of rising above social prejudice when justice calls.

Martin Luther King Jr. delivered his famous "I Have a Dream" speech on the National Mall in Washington in 1963. As America inched slowly toward King's dream, *To Kill a Mockingbird* dovetailed with the mood of the nation. After Kim Stanley's voiceover introduction from a grown-up Scout, the film takes a long, deliberate look at a place in the past, the economically depressed world of the 1930s in Macon, Georgia. Not surprisingly, this look backward takes the form of a fond reminiscence, for such a viewpoint reflects a long-standing southern disposition to engage the past with empathy. The sense of place in *To Kill a Mockingbird* is palpable, tellingly realized in small details of food, family, community, and custom—all sensibly evocative of the South. The key conflict of the film centers on racial justice. While Atticus Finch does not succeed in saving his African American client from wrongful conviction or from death, the film nevertheless gave dignified voice and significant substance to the South's slow emergence from the grasp of bigotry and race conflict, which is the longest and deepest story to be told in the history of the South.

FIGURE 58. *To Kill a Mockingbird* (1963). The confrontation between the lawyer Atticus Finch (Gregory Peck) and a racist white, Bob Ewell (James Anderson), in front of an African American defendant's (Brock Peters) home, illuminates the differences between how whites and blacks lived in the South in the 1930s. Courtesy Universal International Pictures and Pakula-Mulligan Brentwood Productions.

The Diverse South

As the twentieth century closed, the South was many things. There was not only Robert Altman's postmodern *Nashville* (1975), a Moral Majority South run amok, but also the hardscrabble Appalachian South of *Coal Miner's*

Daughter (1980), *The River* (1984), and *Winter People* (1989); the Deep South of *Steel Magnolias* (1989), *The Big Easy* (1987), and *Grande Isle* (1992), Kelly McGillis's adaptation of Kate Chopin's *The Awakening*; the endlessly corrupt South of John Grisham's books-to-films canon and John Sayles's *Matewan* (1987) and *Sunshine State* (2002); the violent, racially charged South of Billy Bob Thornton's *Sling Blade* (1996), Carl Franklin's *One False Move* (1992), and Marc Forster's *Monster's Ball* (2001); and, finally, with echoes of all that has gone before but without a hint of nostalgia, the Jonathan Demme–Oprah Winfrey adaptation of Toni Morrison's *Beloved* (1998), which is the South deep in time. *Beloved* came to the screen through the commitment of one of America's most extraordinary media megastars, one fit to match up well with the likes of Ted Turner and his Atlanta-based empire, which was, until the moment it was sold to Time Warner, always looking forward, expanding into a larger and brighter future. Set off against that important powerful contemporary southern impulse, one determined to make the years to come better and bolder, the story of *Beloved* carries the heavy burden of history, constraints and all, which the South represents consistently and steadfastly to the American film industry.

The South's Claim on History

Given its unique investment in maintaining an enduring sense of history, the South will remain a place especially inviting to filmmakers who wish to explore the American historical record on a large screen. The linkage of place to history is so profound that it is difficult to render a film story in the South without invoking its past. Such historical references may be relatively subtle, as in the naming of Forrest Gump (played by Tom Hanks), which honors the memory of Nathan Bedford Forrest, a famous Confederate cavalry commander in the Civil War and founder of the Ku Klux Klan, but they nevertheless have consequence. In Gump's case, history haunts a person everywhere because it must be lived down. Forrest's eventual friendship with Bubba Blue, a black man from his Vietnam combat unit, thus corrects the errors of a past symbolized in his name. The Gump "Life is like a box of chocolates" phenomenon proved to be so strong and so appealing that it spawned a restaurant franchise based on the West Coast, Bubba Gump Shrimp Co.

More importantly, *Forrest Gump* (based on Winston Groom's 1986 novel) illustrates how completely the South and southern culture would stake out ownership of American history. Forrest Gump, a loveable innocent with a heart of gold, wanders in fine picaresque fashion through all the major historical moments of his generation: he is with Kennedy; he is with Johnson; he is with Nixon; he is with the peace protesters at the Washington Monument; he is with the Chinese as the Cold War ends. Forrest Gump, archetypal southerner, is ubiquitous in modern history. The South may have lost the Civil War, but as the twenty-first century opens, Americans who employ cinematic paradigms of the past to define their own identities must incorporate southern history in the process. As Forrest Gump goes, so goes the nation.

This pattern, with writers in the lead, pursuing history as if by deeply rooted instinct, is noted by Dewey Grantham in the conclusion of *The South in Modern America* as he appraises the future for the long-enduring and continuing pattern of distinctiveness in southern culture. The differences Grantham spotlights are attractive for film treatment, thus assuring that films will always be part of the South's history.

References

Filmography

All the King's Men (1949, F)

The Autobiography of Miss Jane Pittman (1974, TV)

Beloved (1998, F)
Blaze (1989, F)
The Big Easy (1987, F)
The Birth of a Nation (1915, F)
Bonnie and Clyde (1967, F)
The Chase (1966, F)
Coal Miner's Daughter (1980, F)
Cookie's Fortune (1999, F)
Cool Hand Luke (1967, F)
The Defiant Ones (1958, F)
Deliverance (1972, F)
Driving Miss Daisy (1989, F)
Easy Rider (1969, F)
Forrest Gump (1994, F)
Ghosts of Mississippi (1996, F)
God's Little Acre (1958, F)
Gone with the Wind (1939, F)
Grand Isle (1992, F)
In Old Kentucky (1935, F)
Intruder in the Dust (1949, F)
Jezebel (1938, F)
Judge Priest (1934, F)
The Little Foxes (1941, F)
The Littlest Rebel (1935, F)
Matewan (1987, F)
Midnight in the Garden of Good and Evil (1998, F)
Mississippi (1935, F)
Mississippi Burning (1988, F)
Mississippi Masala (1992, F)
Monster's Ball (2001, F)
Nashville (1975, F)
O Brother, Where Art Thou? (2000, F)
One False Move (1992, F)
The Patriot (2000, F)
Roots (1977, TV)
Sherman's March (1986, D)
Sling Blade (1996, F)
Songcatcher (2001, F)
Song of the South (1946, F)
So Red the Rose (1935, F)
The Southerner (1945, F)
Steamboat 'Round the Bend (1935, F)
Steel Magnolias (1989, F)
A Streetcar Named Desire (1951, F)
Sunshine State (2002, F)
Terms of Endearment (1983, F)
Tobacco Road (1941, F)
To Kill a Mockingbird (1963, F)
Winter People (1989, F)

Bibliography

Boles, John H. *The South Through Time: A History of an American Region.* Englewood Cliffs, NJ: Prentice-Hall, 1995.

Campbell, Edward D. C., Jr. *The Celluloid South: Hollywood and the Southern Myth.* Knoxville: University of Tennessee Press, 1981.

Carnes, Mark C., ed. *Past Imperfect: History According to the Movies.* New York: Henry Holt, 1995.

Carter, Everett. "Cultural History Written with Lightning: The Significance of *The Birth of a Nation.*" In Peter C. Rollins, ed., *Hollywood as Historian: American Film in a Cultural Context,* 9–19. 2d ed. Lexington: University Press of Kentucky, 1998.

Cripps, Thomas. *Making Movies Black: The Hollywood Message Movie from World War II to the Civil Rights Era.* New York: Oxford University Press, 1993.

——. *Slow Fade to Black: The Negro in American Film, 1900–1942.* New York: Oxford University Press, 1977.

Egerton, John. *Shades of Gray: Dispatches from the Modern South.* Baton Rouge: Louisiana State University Press, 1991.

Faust, Drew Gilpin. *James Henry Hammond and the Old South: A Design for Mastery.* Baton Rouge: Louisiana State University Press, 1982.

Foner, Eric. *Reconstruction: America's Unfinished Revolution, 1863–1877.* New York: Harper & Row, 1988.

——. *The Story of American Freedom.* New York: Norton, 1998.

French, Warren, ed. *The South and Film.* Jackson: University Press of Mississippi, 1981.

Genovese, Eugene D. *Roll, Jordan, Roll: The World the Slaves Made.* New York: Vintage, 1976.

——. *The Southern Tradition: The Achievement and Limitations of an American Conservatism.* Cambridge, MA: Harvard University Press, 1994.

Grantham, Dewey W. *The South in Modern America: A Region at Odds.* New York: HarperCollins, 1994.

Heider, Karl G., ed. *Images of the South: Constructing a Regional Culture on Film and Video.* Athens: University of Georgia Press, 1993.

Kirby, Jack Temple. *Media-Made Dixie: The South in the American Imagination.* Baton Rouge: Louisiana State University Press, 1978.

Leuchtenburg, William E. *The Perils of Prosperity, 1914–1932.* Rev. ed. Chicago: University of Chicago Press, 1993.

Sklar, Robert. *Movie-Made America: A Cultural History of American Movies.* Rev. ed. New York: Vintage, 1994.

Smith, Stephen A. *Myth, Media, and the Southern Mind.* Fayetteville: University of Arkansas Press, 1985.

Tindall, George. *The Emergence of the New South, 1913–1945.* Baton Rouge: Louisiana State University Press, 1967.

Toplin, Robert Brent. *History by Hollywood.* Urbana: University of Illinois Press, 1966.

Woodward, C. Vann. *The Burden of Southern History.* Baton Rouge: Louisiana State University Press, 1960.

——. *The Strange Career of Jim Crow.* 3d ed. New York: Oxford University Press, 1974.

[SUSAN OPT AND MICHAEL DENISON]

Space

The dream of space flight has been around as long as humankind has been telling stories. With the advent of film, the stories of exploring that frontier moved from printed page to the theater screen. Early cinematic audiences were delighted by Georges Méliès's 1902 film version of Jules Verne's *A Trip to the Moon,* clips of which would later be shown as human beings actually touched down on the moon in 1969. But the reality of space exploration, as manifest in the U.S. space program, has often varied from the dreams of the writers and filmmakers. Historian H. J. P. Arnold explains, "The latter, quite rightly, concentrate upon engineering, technological and scientific matters and ignore the vagaries of political considerations" (235). Cinematic portrayals of the U.S. space program—from the early days of rocket-shaped vehicles exploring outer space to the latter-day shuttle astronauts who save Earth from impending doom—have, to some extent, reflected the issues and emphases of the space program. Yet, although documentaries have kept audiences informed of the space program's technological progress, feature films have only rarely focused on the space program itself.

NASA: The History

Historians note that many factors, such as technology, society, and politics, have influenced the development of the U.S. space program. Two main questions have always dominated decisions about conquering the space frontier: Why do it? What is the best way to do it? As the program moved forward, answers have changed. Historians typically describe the U.S. space program as evolving in three stages—pre-Sputnik, post-Sputnik, and post-Apollo.

The early, pre-Sputnik days of space flight development were characterized by loners, amateurs, and rocket-society members who received little outside funding for their work yet designed and tested much of the technology that would be essential in upcoming decades. During World War II, the U.S. government became interested in military rocket applications, and in the 1950s it worked on developing reconnaissance satellites. As to the reason for space flight, historian Roger Launius notes, "Before the Sputnik crisis, space enthusiasts were motivated by an expansive view of human voyages of discovery, exploration and settlement of the moon and other planets of the solar system and eventual interstellar travel" (6). However, he adds that these objectives rarely motivated political leaders to invest heavily in space ventures.

Manned flight was envisioned as a possibility for space travel, but unmanned flight was an easier probability. These early decades of space flight attempts were riddled with failures—rockets often exploded on launch pads or veered off course. But, during this pre-Sputnik era, Americans became aware that reaching space was a possibility, and the agenda for the future U.S. space agency—the National Aeronautics and Space Administration (NASA)—began to take shape. In 1951, rocket scientist Wernher von Braun outlined a space program beginning with cargo rockets and space shuttles, then moving to large space stations, and finally advancing to manned moon and Mars landings (Heppenheimer, 89–90).

The scenario von Braun proposed for a rational, long-term development of a space program was shattered on October 4, 1957, when Americans learned of the Soviet satellite *Sputnik* circling overhead. Almost overnight, U.S. attitudes toward space flight shifted to concern that the Cold War enemy would come to dominate the heavens. Space flight capability symbolized technological progress and advancement. Furthermore, it was widely assumed that Third World nations would ally themselves with the more technologically advanced nation (Launius, 155). The Soviet Union would also launch the first spacecraft to fly by the moon, *Luna I,* in 1959, and put the first man in space in 1961—once again challenging American claims about the superiority of a free society.

In response to the perceived Soviet threat, NASA was created in 1958 to organize and oversee the U.S. space program, and President Kennedy, in 1961, set the goal of landing a man on the moon before the end of the decade. This mission stimulated what many describe as the most rapid advance in technology ever experienced in human history, culminating in the 1969 *Apollo 11* moon landing.

In the post-Sputnik days, the question of why do it was suddenly clear—national security and world leadership depended on it. Thus, NASA emerged out of America's need to demonstrate the viability of its culture and way of life as opposed to that of the Soviets. As to how to do it, manned flight seemed the only option. Americans in space would serve to signal the superiority of democracy over communism. Visionaries at the time predicted space stations, moon bases, and trips to Mars—space exploration was just beginning, and its possibilities were limitless. NASA "became the symbol for American technical, scientific, and operational superiority," write Wendy Alter and James Logan, two former NASA employees.

But as soon as it began, so did it seem to end. Historians view NASA as reaching its golden years during the 1960s. After the moon landing in July 1969, public attention to—and government funding for—further moon landings and space exploration began to wane. Historians attribute this decline in interest to a combination of the high costs of the Vietnam War, soaring budget deficits, and wrenching domestic strife. Although the harrowing flight of *Apollo 13* in April 1970 captured world interest briefly, after *Apollo 17* the remaining four moon missions were scrubbed.

In looking back, historians characterize the Apollo Project as an anomaly in the space program's development because it arose out of political pressures rather than from a carefully chartered technological path. Early expectations were that NASA would return to the original proposed course of developing a space station and eventually head out to Mars. But, again, because of political and social concerns, this return, too, was not to be. Three decades after humans beings walked on the moon, only parts for a space station were beginning to be ferried into orbit and travel to Mars was still limited to survey probes such as *Viking* and *Pathfinder.*

In 1972 NASA began work on a space shuttle, launched in 1981, that was designed as a cheap alternative to a space station. Unlike the earlier space missions, the shuttle has been viewed more as a workhorse than as a vehicle to explore the new frontier, so it has never achieved mythological status. Instead, the program has been plagued by cost overruns, unmet expectations, and tragedies such as the *Challenger* explosion in January 1986. NASA itself has undergone much criticism in recent years for its bureaucracy and turf struggles. The shuttle program received a brief moment of attention in 1998, when John Glenn, America's first man to orbit the earth in 1962 and now its oldest astronaut, rode aboard the shuttle *Discovery.*

With the race to the moon won and the Cold War largely a thing of the past, the answer to the question of "why do it" has become less clear in the post-Apollo days. Although proponents of the space program have pointed out the many benefits of space travel (such as the enhancement of communications, navigation, and weather-watch systems, among others), program costs dominated the talk of the 1990s. Although the ideal of exploring a new frontier still prompts discussion of space travel, it competes with demands that the United States rejuvenate its cities and farms. And, once again, the question of manned versus unmanned space flight is part of the public debate. In the twenty-first century, to travel beyond Earth's orbit, space enthusiasts must turn to the movies.

NASA: The Films

Where space and America converge in film, whether in futuristic dramas such as *Star Trek: The Motion Picture* (1979) or *Solaris* (1972, 2002), space-horror films such as *Event Horizon* (1997) or *Alien* (1979), or even airy comedies such as *Space Truckers* (1997) or *Airplane II* (1982), NASA or some thinly disguised version of it is almost certain to be involved somehow. No viewer today could avoid comparing and contrasting any space film with past, existing, or planned NASA program counterparts. Media coverage and NASA documentaries have trained the public to recognize the "right" way that spacesuits, shuttlecraft, lunar excursion modules, and zero-gravity movement should look. And filmmakers have had to respond in kind, creating more technically sophisticated movies to meet those demanding audience expectations.

This was not the case, however, in the pre-Sputnik years. Films before 1957 were not under such restrictions concerning verisimilitude. They featured storylines ranging from exploration to fighting off alien forces, low-budget special effects with impractical spacecraft, spacesuits that looked like trapeze costumes, and huge computers with hundreds of gaily flashing lights. The film serial *Flash Gordon* (1936) and television's *Captain Video* (1949) and *Buck Rogers* (1950) are examples from this era. Space flight was not portrayed as an organized government effort, but rather as an undertaking of military, commercial, or private groups. These films were referred to as "space operas," just as westerns were referred to as "horse operas." One exception was *Destination Moon* (1950), director George Pal's first genre film, about a trip to the moon. Besides being the first motion picture to use star technology and effects, it also quite accurately predicted the technological space race between the United States and the Soviet Union. Although, in general, the films before 1957 are scientifically laughable, they have a certain charm and emotional attraction. Americans look on space movies much as they look on westerns, as important and beloved parts of their cultural heritage. The advent of NASA, however, would transform the attitude toward space.

The post-Sputnik days were replete with documentaries educating the American public and promoting the U.S. space program. A steady stream flowed directly out of NASA—which had, after all, original footage. These ranged from dry explanations of scientific experiments and the latest equipment to films peddling jingoistic propaganda about the wonders of America's space program. Following World War II precedent, Walt Disney joined in supporting the government's efforts with the film *Man in Space* in 1959.

In the feature film arena, the comedy *The Reluctant Astronaut* (1967) parodied the U.S-Soviet space race. It was released just as the Gemini program was ending and Apollo beginning. The film featured scenes at the Houston Space Center, Mission Control, and Cape Kennedy. Up until this time in real life, NASA's only first was a fourteen-day space endurance record, set in 1965. But in the world of movies, the United States beat the Soviets at putting a bumbling janitor (Don Knotts) into space. Despite the comedic angle, the movie promoted the real-life NASA image of an astronaut as being a courageous hero—an image that supported the mythology developing about the space program and would be repeated in almost all NASA-related films to come.

A year later, just after the United States accomplished another first—orbiting men around the moon in Apollo 8—Stanley Kubrick's classic *2001: A Space Odyssey* (1968) debuted. Even now, more than three decades after its initial release, audiences are still awed by its challenging themes, scientific accuracy, and stunning cinematography. In 1998, the American Film Institute listed it as one of the one hundred best American films. While not about NASA directly, the movie reflects Wernher von Braun's vision for the U.S. space program set in 1951—traveling by shuttlecraft to space stations, from space stations to moon bases, and from moon bases to the outer frontiers of space. Among the scientific matters the film deals with accurately are artificially induced gravity, eating and voiding in the absence of gravity, hibernation, time delays in communication with Earth, explosive decompression, artificial-intelligence computers run amok, and the likelihood that our eventual encounter with an intelligence much greater than our own may be far beyond our immediate understanding. (The last point is echoed particularly well in 1997's *Contact,* starring Jodie Foster.) However, the "why" of space flight differs from the reality of the post-Sputnik era. In *2001,* the motivation was scientific exploration, not international competition. In 1968 as well, Robert Altman's *Countdown* was released. This underseen gem shows the lives of astronauts in much the same way that *The Right Stuff* would in later years, again reinforcing the cultural mythology developing around the U.S. space program.

One year after *2001* portrayed space flight as a routine operation of the future and man walked on the moon, the movie *Marooned* (1969), directed by John Sturges, reminded audiences of the riskiness of the venture. The film's focus on technical glitches and the uncertainty of the long-term effects of space flight on human beings highlights the dark potentiality of space travel, rarely mentioned in the glory days of NASA. The film, released right after the *Apollo 12* launch, almost foreshadows the real life crisis NASA would face with *Apollo 13* and the possibility of cooperation between the two space-race giants (a Soviet cosmonaut saves, at the last minute, an American astronaut). In fact, the 1994 documentary *Moonshot* suggests that *Marooned* helped set the stage for the eventual 1975 joint U.S.-Soviet *Apollo-Soyuz* flight. Despite the loss of one astronaut in *Marooned,* NASA is still portrayed as a heroic institution, ready to overcome any obstacle. In fact, NASA provided technical advisers during filming, and the movie won an Academy Award for special effects. However, it was not a box-office hit, which cinema critic John Brosnan blames on the real moon landing that took place the year of the film's release, "an event that tended to make the cinema's space age activity look rather out of date" (184).

It was almost a decade after the *Apollo 11* landing before NASA appeared on the feature screen again, this time as a villain in Peter Hyams's *Capricorn One* (1978). As NASA is preparing for the first manned Mars mission, it discovers a major technical flaw in the spacecraft that will result in disaster. Rather than scrub the flight and lose program funding, Dr. James Kelloway (Hal Holbrook) of NASA decides to fake the mission on a soundstage and then murder the astronauts. This film is one of the few that truly reflects the issues being raised in post-Apollo years about the "how" and "why" of space flight.

In 1983, the first feature film to recount actual NASA history was released—Philip Kaufman's *The Right Stuff,* based on Tom Wolfe's historical novel about the Mercury space program. The film deals not only with the history of the program but also with the politics of the space race, the personal lives of the astronauts

FIGURE 59. *Marooned* (1969). A mishap prevents the return of three astronauts to earth, raising questions about the reliability of technology and the logic behind and safety of manned space travel. The film's realism sent a disconcerting message to the nation upon its release after *Apollo 12* and before the crisis of *Apollo 13.* Courtesy Columbia Pictures.

and their families, and the mythic ethos surrounding some very brave test pilots. The film delineates how the real-life NASA created and exploited the heroic mythology of the astronauts. Ironically, at the same time, Kaufman reinforces the heroic myth. The film, which stars Sam Shepard, Scott Glenn, Ed Harris, Dennis Quaid, and Fred Ward, was a roaring success, and newspaper reviews of the time suggest that the film's release, just as John Glenn was running for U.S. Senate, may have contributed to his successful bid for office. The image from the film of the astronauts in their spacesuits walking abreast straight toward the camera has become a potent and widely imitated symbol of the space age. Later this scene would be reenacted as a cinematic allusion in *Armageddon* (1998), as the astronauts leave Earth to save humanity from certain destruction, and in *Space Cowboys* (2000), as the elderly test pilots set out to save humanity from a rogue satellite weapon.

The only other major feature film to deal specifically with NASA history appeared in 1995—director Ron Howard's *Apollo 13.* Based on astronaut Jim Lovell's book *Lost Moon,* the movie recounts the story of the 1970 *Apollo 13* flight, in which a scheduled moon-landing mission had to be aborted after an oxygen tank on the craft exploded. The film, released on the twenty-fifth anniversary of the flight, takes a NASA failure—a story NASA had avoided telling since 1970—and transforms it into a success of heroic proportions. NASA is portrayed in a man-against-failed-technology struggle, but with the involved human elements also carefully drawn and powerfully acted by Tom Hanks, Bill Paxton, Kevin Bacon, and Gary Sinise. Although the audience knows that all ended well, viewer interest and suspense are sustained by intercutting from technological challenges aloft to family anxieties on the ground. *Apollo 13* serves as a reminder of the golden years of NASA, when Yankee ingenuity ruled and Americans could overcome any challenge.

Two years later, *The Right Stuff* and *Apollo 13* would be parodied in Disney's *The Rocketman* (1997) in which a nerdy computer genius serves as a last-minute replacement on the first manned mission to Mars. This comic story is probably less a comment on NASA than on the rising social importance in America of the so-called nerds. With no national crisis motivating the space program, Disney could play with the topic. However, the film does reflect the more cosmopolitan atmosphere of the real-life NASA, with women and minorities featured as astronauts.

In the post-Apollo days, without a Soviet antagonist to prompt the U.S. space program, filmmakers have had to turn to outer world threats to find gripping conflict. In two blockbuster films of 1998, *Armageddon,* directed by Michael Bay, and *Deep Impact,* directed by Mimi Leder, amateurs and astronauts do more than save the free world as in the days of Apollo—they save the globe itself. In both productions, the heroes travel via NASA shuttles to incoming asteroids that threaten to destroy the earth. In *Armageddon,* however, NASA is portrayed as an inept bureaucracy that has to call for the assistance of a ragtag group of civilian deep-sea oil drillers to help save humankind, rough-hewn men of Earth, not unlike the test pilots who were called in to help during the Mercury program. In *Deep Impact,* NASA astronauts make the ultimate sacrifice to save the world—their lives. Both movies point to a possible reason for the real-life NASA to continue space exploration—one day the fate of the world may depend on space technology.

In recent years, NASA has also been featured in a few more films, such as Brian De Palma's *Mission to Mars,* Anthony Hoffman's *Red Planet,* and Clint Eastwood's *Space Cowboys* (all 2000). The first two films use NASA as little more than a nameplate on their respective space vehicles, although Eastwood's film does depict behind-the-scenes political maneuvering and offer musings on obsolescence. It also alludes to NASA's glory years and suggests, much like *Armageddon,* that today's NASA suffers from ineptitude.

Film and television documentaries in the post-Apollo years have ranged from continuing public education about current space technology to remembrances of the space program's golden era. Often these documentaries have been released to coincide with a twenty-fifth, thirtieth, or fortieth anniversary of a space-related achievement. For example, in 2002, Fox News Network aired *To the Moon and Beyond: Celebrating Apollo 17* to commemorate the thirtieth anniversary of the last moon mission. Among the best of these documentaries are *The Dream Is Alive* (1985), an IMAX film shot by the astronauts themselves aboard the space shuttles, which features glorious shots of the earth from space; *For All Mankind* (1989), a National Geographic film nominated for the Academy Award for best documentary; *Racing for the Moon* (1989), an ABC retrospective on the space race and the glory days; *Space Station* (2002), an IMAX film shot aboard the International Space Station; and *Moonshot* (1994), released on the twenty-fifth anniversary of the moon landing, which recounts Alan Shepard and Deke Slayton's memories of the space program. "Keeping the dream alive" is a direct quotation from Deke Slayton, and by intercutting between the glorious past and the seemingly pedestrian present, the film implies that the dream will die if the United States does not have the imagination and resources to rekindle the flame.

In April 1998, HBO premiered the twelve-hour docudrama *From the Earth to the Moon,* executive producer and host Tom Hanks's dream project—telling the stories of all twelve manned Apollo missions. The series—which recreated virtually every shot from the beginnings of the race to the moon in 1961 to the last Apollo landing in 1972 and, at $68 million, was the most expensive single original TV project in history—received seventeen Emmy nominations. President Bill Clinton, after previewing the miniseries, remarked that the growth of the space program reflected the growth of the United States since the 1960s. He added, "President Kennedy wanted us to become the world's leading space-faring nation, and we have. I want us to continue that distinction well into the twenty-first century. It is profoundly important to us" (383).

NASA's Right Stuff

In its history, NASA has fared well in motion pictures. Aside from *Capricorn One,* the movies and documentaries generally portray the space agency as one that can meet any challenge and continually create new American heroes. Even in *Capricorn One,* the villain is not really the space agency itself but a few misguided zealots willing to do anything to save the program—including deceiving the public. Although in the real world NASA has suffered budget cuts, technological disappointments, and social criticism, in the world of film the glory days continue, and the strong emotional resonance that has been built up between NASA and the entire genre of space movies continues. In an age of bureaucracy and corporate mergers, the frontier myth of Americans as practical, adaptable individualists and explorers retains its power. And NASA will go down in film history as having had "the right stuff."

References

Filmography

Airplane II (1982, F)
Alien (1979, F)
Apollo 13 (1995, F)
Armageddon (1998, F)
Capricorn One (1978, F)
Close Encounters of the Third Kind (1977, F)
Contact (1997, F)
Countdown (1968, F)
Dark Star (1974, F)
Deep Impact (1998, F)
Destination Moon (1950, F)
Destination Space (2000, D)
Diamonds Are Forever (1971, F)
The Dream Is Alive (1985, D)
Event Horizon (1997, F)
For All Mankind (1989, D)
From the Earth to the Moon (1998, D)
Man in Space (1959, F)
Marooned (1969, F)
Mission to Mars (2000, F)
Moonraker (1979, F)
Moonshot (1994, D)
Planet of the Apes (1968, F; 2001, F)
Project X (1987, F)
Racing for the Moon (1989, D)
Red Planet (2000, F)
The Reluctant Astronaut (1967, F)
The Right Stuff (1983, F)
Rocketman (1997, F)
Solaris (1972, F; 2002, F)
Space Cowboys (2000, F)
Space Station (2002, D)
Space Truckers (1997, F)
Stargate (1994, F)
Star Trek: The Motion Picture (1979, F)
To the Moon (1999, D)
To the Moon and Beyond: Celebrating Apollo 17 (2002, D)
A Trip to the Moon (1902, F)
2001: A Space Odyssey (1968, F)

Bibliography

Alter, Wendy, and James S. Logan. "NASA Goes to Ground." *Whole Earth Review,* May 1992.

Arnold, H. J. P., ed. *Man in Space: An Illustrated History of Spaceflight.* New York: Smithmark, 1993.

Bizony, Piers. "Politics of Apollo." *Omni,* July 1994.

Brosnan, John. *Future Tense: The Cinema of Science Fiction.* New York: St. Martin's, 1978.

Clinton, William J. "Remarks at the Screening of *Earth to the Moon.*" Weekly Compilations of Presidential Documents 383.2 (9 March 1998).

Dewaard, E. John, and Nancy Dewaard. *History of NASA: America's Voyage to the Stars.* New York: Exeter, 1984.

Heppenheimer, T. A. *Countdown: A History of Space Flight.* New York: Wiley, 1997.

Heppenheimer, T. A., and Frederic Smoler. "Lost in Space: What Went Wrong with NASA?" *American Heritage,* November 1992.

Launius, Roger D. *Frontiers of Space Exploration.* Westport, CT: Greenwood, 1998.

Menville, Douglas, and R. Reginald. *Things to Come: An Illustrated History of the Science Fiction Film.* New York: Times Books, 1977.

National Aeronautics and Space Administration. History of Space Exploration. Available online at: www.ksc.nasa.gov./history.

Opt, Susan K. "American Frontier Myth and the Flight of Apollo 13: From News Event to Feature Film." *Film & History* 26.1–4 (1996): 40–51.

Taylor, L. B. *For All Mankind: America's Space Program of the 1970s and Beyond.* New York: Dutton, 1974.

Warren, Bill. *Keep Watching the Skies! American Science Fiction Movies of the Fifties.* 2 vols. Jefferson, NC: McFarland, 1982–86.

Wright, Gene. *Science Fiction Image: The Illustrated Encyclopedia of Science Fiction in Film, Television, Radio and the Theater.* New York: Facts on File, 1983.

[DAVID E. WILT]

Suburbia

Suburbia is as much a state of mind as it is a particular geographic location. Popular culture—especially movies and television but also books, novels and stories, even advertising—has cemented the image of a suburban lifestyle in the public consciousness as the embodiment of the American dream. But is this dream actually a nightmare? Since the 1950s, films have frequently depicted suburbs as outwardly pleasant places to live but regimented and stultifying yet spiced with unsavory outbreaks of promiscuity, vice, and violence.

Historians and social scientists have long debated the significance of the American suburb. Kenneth T. Jackson writes that "suburbia symbolizes the fullest, most unadulterated embodiment of contemporary culture; it is a manifestation of such fundamental characteristics of American society as conspicuous consumption, a reliance upon the private automobile, upward mobility, the separation of the family into nuclear units, the widening division between work and leisure, and a tendency toward racial and economic exclusiveness" (4). But psychiatrist Bernard Gordon, in his study of Bergen County, New Jersey, sees another side of suburban living: "Why do we needle the typical American about his shiny mass-produced house and car, his manners and more? Possibly because he represents the great sad joke of our time. Having amassed a wealth that used to be the subject of fairy tales, he often finds that he isn't happy at all" (28). These two viewpoints—suburbia as the embodiment of American culture and suburbia as a breeding ground for malaise and discontent—have characterized the debate over suburbia in America since the early twentieth century.

For many, the word "suburbs" evokes the post–World War II American phenomenon that started with tract housing developments such as Levittown. But although suburbs have actually existed for centuries, it was not until the advent of public transportation systems in the nineteenth century that it was convenient for people to live a significant distance from the city center—where business, industry, and cultural activities were located—and yet travel there on a regular, daily basis. Railroads were followed by the horse-drawn streetcar, the cable car, and the electric streetcar or "trolley" as means of opening up the land surrounding cities for settlement by those who would travel to work in the city, "commuters." The private automobile, which became affordable with the introduction of the Ford Model T in 1908, contributed to the spread of suburban communities (and eventually, the decline of public transportation), although it would be several decades before the nation's road system caught up to the huge increase in car ownership.

The growth of American suburbs was not driven solely by advances in transportation. Just because people *could* live outside the city did not mean they would *want* to live there. The suburban experience in the United States was also a function of factors such as the abundance of relatively cheap land, high wages, advances in home building design (which reduced the cost of construction), and the desire to own a private, family home, which meant a detached house on a plot of land. Suburbs were perceived as clean, healthy, safe, and private, the opposite of overcrowded ghettos in the city.

The Depression and World War II temporarily slowed the construction of new homes and the production of private automobiles, but as soon as the war ended, the process of suburbanization resumed at an even greater rate. It was during this period that criticism of the suburbs began to be heard. Funds for public transportation were diverted to highways; the decline of America's city centers increased. Critics suggested that suburban living weakened the extended family by leaving housewives and children isolated during the day. Furthermore, the suburban lifestyle, though available to many more Americans than before, was still largely restricted to certain socioeconomic and racial segments of society.

Although suburbia is still the "quintessential physical achievement of the United States" (Jackson, 4), over the past several decades steps have been taken in an attempt to mitigate some of its problems. Intensive efforts have been made to revitalize some cities, and public transportation has regained some support for ecological and economic reasons. As the supply of cheap and available suburban land becomes exhausted, some predict a gradual return to city living for the middle class, as has occurred in Chicago, for example. However, although suburbs may change, they are unlikely to disappear.

Early Film Images of Suburbia

Films with recognizably "suburban" themes and settings date back to the first decade of the century, in comedy shorts such as *The Suburbanite* (1904) and *The Suburbanite's Ingenious Alarm* (1908). The mechanics of suburban living—and its companion, the commute to work—figure in the plot of *The Commuters* (1915), which concerns businessmen who use the excuse that they are working late to stay in the city and have a wild "boys' night out." Similarly, the depiction of "suburban sin"—so popular in novels and films of the 1950s and 1960s—may be found as early as *Let's Be Fashionable* (1920), which takes place in "the suburban community of Elmhurst, where it is considered fashionable for married couples to engage in harmless affairs" (American Film Institute, *F1*, 511).

The occasional use of suburbia as a setting or a plot device persisted into the 1930s, although few films seriously addressed the topic of suburbia and its impact on society. The plot of *The Night of June 13* (1932) involves a man whose wife committed suicide because she was jealous that he was riding to the commuter rail station with an attractive neighbor! In *Mama Runs Wild* (1938), a married couple moves to the "Paradise Park" development. The housewives try to shut down the local tavern, the men rebel, and eventually there is a *Lysistrata*-style war between the sexes. Although the protagonist of *Three Men on a Horse* (1936) lives in a "cookie-cutter sub-development" (American Film Institute, *F3*, 2199), his commute by bus does have one positive benefit: only on this daily trip to work can he unfailingly pick the winners of horse races.

Suburban life—despite its foibles—was by no means considered undesirable. Home ownership was still part of the American dream, although the Depression made buying a home of one's own more difficult to achieve. In 1939, the American Institute of Planners sponsored the production of a documentary film for the upcoming New York World's Fair. Documentary filmmaker Pare Lorentz wrote the script, based the ideas of urban planner and historian Lewis Mumford. The result was *The City* (1939), directed by Ralph Steiner and Willard Van Dyke. This film begins by lauding New England small towns: the sense of community, the convenience, the pleasant and healthy lifestyle. *The City* then illustrates the pitfalls of life in modern, overcrowded, dirty, and hectic industrialized cities. Acknowledging America's inability to return to the bucolic pleasures of small-town life, the final section of the picture suggests the development of "green communities," where the advantages of small towns could be combined with the new industrial economy. The film calls for the construction of planned communities, utilizing modern technology and mass transit, as an alternative to decaying cities. In 1964, Lewis Mumford supervised the production of six new short films—made under the auspices of the Canadian Film Board—further examining the relationships between the city and society.

Suburbs in 1940s Hollywood

Although, as Robert Fishman notes "the two great symbols of postwar Los Angeles—the tract of endlessly repeated suburban houses and the freeway—were developed in the 1930s" (172), suburbia as a nationwide phenomenon, with its own media identity, is rooted in the years after World War II. "The boys came marching home in 1945 and 1946, produced babies, and looked for homes to house their families. Instant suburbs, thrown up by developers, without professional planning or architectural assistance, supplied the homes and the GIs moved in" (Donaldson, 39). Levittown, a name synonymous with tract housing developments, consisted of seventeen thousand homes on Long Island. At first, films and other forms of popular culture portrayed suburbanization as a positive move toward fulfillment of the American dream—to own a "piece of land." *It's a Wonderful Life* (1946) illustrates this point: George Bailey's (James Stewart) goal as manager of a building and loan society is to help his fellow citizens buy homes in the "Bailey Park" subdivision. The happy homeowners can raise their children in clean, healthful surroundings, instead of renting sordid tenements from the sinister Mr. Potter (Lionel Barrymore).

Some films dealing with flight from the city to the suburbs eschew the stereotyped image of tract housing, choosing to depict their protagonists—usually for comic effect—trying to rehabilitate decrepit older homes. These films, even those set beyond the suburbs in truly rural areas, carry a double message. They reiterate the American desire for a private home outside the city; they also exaggerate some of the more mundane aspects of home ownership, such as repair and maintenance. As opposed to apartment dwellers whose maintenance needs are handled by various and sundry employees of the building's owner, suburban homeowners must emulate their pioneer ancestors and become members of the "do it yourself" fraternity, or rely on eccentric and unreliable outside contractors. An early example of this type of film is *George Washington Slept Here* (1942), in which Jack Benny and Ann Sheridan move from a New York City high-rise apartment to a rundown Pennsylvania farmhouse. *Mr. Blandings Builds His Dream House* (1948) has a similar premise, this time with Cary Grant and Myrna Loy as the urban refugees who move to the clean air of the suburbs, only to discover that their dream house is a wreck. As the influx of "home improvement" programs on television attest, the theme continues to be a topical one, and has served as the basis for such films as *The Money Pit* (1986) and *Life as a House* (2001).

The 1950s and 1960s: Suburbia for All

The names of housing developments, real and filmic, hint at the appeal of suburban living: Bailey Park, Paradise Park, Sunrise Hills, Elmhurst, Cuesta Verde. "The suburbanite tries to escape from the noisy dirty city to the lap of nature" (Donaldson, 55), or at least to some approximation of nature. The American belief in the nobility of the farmer had to be tempered with the realistic needs of everyday life, and, for most, the suburbs were a satisfactory compromise. Films critical of suburbia point out exactly how much "nature" most suburbanites encountered: in *Poltergeist* (1981), for example, the only tree visible in the entire development is a huge, gnarled, dead specimen (which eventually comes to life and tries to swallow the family's son). Both *Poltergeist* and the much earlier *No Down Payment* (1957) show that the "piece of land" homeowners purchased was often so narrow that the next house was literally an arm's length away.

And yet, by the 1950s, suburban living had become a middle-class ideal: between 1934 and 1954, the population of the suburbs grew by 75 percent, while the total population of the United States increased by just 25 percent. It should be noted that both in real life and in popular culture, "suburbia" had a dichotomous meaning. There were upper-middle-class suburbs (Connecticut was the archetype), where well-paid executives and other white-collar workers lived, commuting each day to the metropolis by train. On the other hand were the massive Levittown-like subdivisions, populated by young families of more modest means, whose breadwinner often commuted by car to his job. Befitting their economic and social differences, the lives and problems of the residents of these two types of suburbs were depicted as quite dissimilar. The protagonist (Gregory Peck) of *The Man in the Gray Flannel Suit* (1956), for example, is a war veteran living in a mortgaged home in Connecticut; however, his home and white-collar city job are distinctly superior to those of the veteran (Cameron Mitchell) living in tract housing in *No Down Payment* who manages a gas station and whose neighbors are salesmen, small businessmen, and the like.

Nonetheless, both types of suburbia were tarred with the same brush in popular culture, when the phenomenon was considered as the central theme of a novel or film. More often than not, suburban life was either ignored or used—generally without comment—as just one more setting in a film. Hollywood, particularly, found more excitement in exotic and urban locales than in the suburbs. In 1955, for example, at least 60 percent of Hollywood's

FIGURE 60. *No Down Payment* (1957). Glowing in the charms of suburban life in a new housing development in California, Jerry Flagg (Tony Randall, right) enjoys a drink with a neighbor as his wife (Sheree North) and the children play Monopoly. When the Flaggs face a monetary crisis that threatens their home, tragedy ripples throughout the community, taking the form of alcoholism, murder, and divorce. Courtesy Twentieth Century-Fox.

output absolutely excluded suburbia because most of the movies were period films (including westerns), took place in foreign locales, or were clearly restricted to specific urban or truly rural settings.

Television, on the other hand—and particularly the situation comedy—has long been a fertile source for images of suburbia. But it was not always so. The Kramdens and the Nortons in *The Honeymooners* lived in New York City apartments, as befitting the economic status of Ralph and Ed (bus driver and sewer worker, respectively). In *I Love Lucy,* Lucy and Ricky Ricardo also lived in a New York apartment, albeit a nicer one than the Kramdens'. However, in the last season of the series the Ricardos moved to the suburbs—not a Levittown tract house, of course, but an upscale Connecticut town. This new location provided new material for jokes, including gags about two quintessential suburban pastimes, lawn mowing and backyard barbecues.

The Dick Van Dyke Show featured an archetypal suburban situation: Rob Petrie lives in a detached house in New Rochelle, and commutes every day to his office in New York City.

Laura Petrie is a housewife and mother. Ironically, perhaps as part of an antisuburban backlash in popular culture, *That Girl*'s protagonist moves from New Rochelle to New York City as the series opens (in 1966). Although situation comedy will never desert the suburbs entirely (TV's *The Simpsons* is proof of this), many popular shows of the past several decades—particularly those that do not center on a nuclear family in its home—have returned to city locations, including such productions as *Seinfeld, Friends,* and *Frasier.*

Films, TV shows, and books of the late 1950s dealing with the suburban phenomenon were almost universally critical of the "multitude of uniform, unidentifiable houses, lined up inflexibly at uniform distances . . . inhabited by people of the same class, the same income, the same age group, witnessing the same television performances . . . conforming in every outward and inward respect to a common mold" (Mumford, 486). *No Down Payment* focuses on four couples in the Sunrise Hills housing development. During the course of the film, rape, murder, alcoholism, racism, and divorce are all highlighted. *Rebel Without a Cause* (1955) shows that young couples are not the only ones suffering from suburban angst: teenage children of the middle class, despite the nice homes they live in and the material goods bestowed upon them by their parents, are still rootless and prone to random acts of senseless violence and vandalism. Their parents discover that living in a detached house in a "nice neighborhood" is no substitute for the personal attention they are now too busy to give their children. James Dean became a symbol for a generation of Americans stifled by the materialism of this world.

The melodramatic, even lurid, topics of pictures like *No Down Payment* and *Rebel Without a Cause* are not that different from those portrayed in Hollywood's small towns (for example, *Peyton Place,* 1957). The setting makes the difference: implicit is the criticism that the suburban dream has a sinister lining. It is easy to suggest that, in order to make an interesting film, Hollywood would naturally choose to "accentuate the negative," but the negative image of suburbia was not just a creation of popular culture: *The Split-Level Trap,* a 1960 sociological study, begins almost like a Stephen King novel: "What has been happening to these people? What is so terribly wrong, in this pretty green community?" (Gordon, 19).

In 1960s and 1970s cinema, suburbia seemed a little less like hell, but there were still many critical and satirical images in films such as *Bachelor in Paradise* (1961), in which travel writer Bob Hope is assigned to live in and study a suburb, another "exotic" location. As the only bachelor in the development of Paradise Valley, Hope's character is home all day and surrounded by curious housewives, leading to the expected comic romantic entanglements. Suburbia as a setting for illicit sex, a subtext of Frank Perry's excellent film *The Swimmer* (1968), gave rise to exploitation films such as *Sin in the Suburbs* (1962), *Suburban Roulette* (1968), and *Suburban Girls Club* (1968). All three of these films feature organized "sex clubs" that attempt to spice up the lives of bored suburbanites, especially housewives—a phenomenon of the 1960s and 1970s subtly critiqued, with fine use of period detail, in Ang Lee's *The Ice Storm* (1997).

However, the suburban state of mind was by now so ingrained that many films were set in suburbia without comment. As with television, the norm was now a detached house in suburbia, often larger and somewhat more luxurious than those in which the audience lived, but certainly, as Leslie Felperin writes, "instantly recognisable, with well-manicured lawns stretching a few tens of feet in front of tract houses, white convenience stores and lurid malls . . . anonymous locations with little presence in the films themselves. . . . Suburbia, constantly on our screens, is seldom allowed to convey the character, specificity and local identity that cinema allows cities and countryside alike" (15).

The 1980s and 1990s: Suburban Hell

Criticism of the conformity of suburbia in the 1950s and 1960s did not come primarily from the counterculture of the day but rather from the intelligentsia. Starting in the late 1960s, the middle-class connotation of suburban living did draw the fire of rebellious youth, who (in theory, if not reality) rejected suburbia to live in rural communes and urban neighborhoods such as San Francisco's Haight-Ashbury and New York's Greenwich Village. As time went by, the pendulum swung back once more, and in the past several decades the liberal establishment—represented by Hollywood—has once again chosen suburbia as a target.

Poltergeist is one of the more barbed attacks, lightly camouflaged as a horror film. The California housing development of Cuesta Verde is depicted as a place where families can raise their children in nice homes (even though one prospective buyer complains "I can't tell one house from another"), but it is also sun-baked and mosquito-infested, and the homes are so close to one another that one man's TV remote control wreaks havoc on his neighbor's set. The real horror underlying Cuesta Verde is not revealed until the conclusion: the development was built over a cemetery, and the undead "residents" resent their new, living neighbors. Clearly, the film strives for a metaphor about the spiritual corruption underlying suburbia.

Neighbors (1981), based on a Thomas Berger novel, relates how the arrival of two unconventional neighbors disrupts the boring suburban life of Earl Keese (John Belushi). At film's end, Earl abandons his home and family—even setting his home on fire—and drives off to an undetermined destination with the bizarre Vic and Ramona (Dan Aykroyd and Cathy Moriarty), freed from the shackles of bourgeois conventionality.

Other idiosyncratic assaults on the suburban mythos include *Parents* (1989), which is set in the 1950s and opens with aerial shots of a housing development. The father in this film insists "We have to fit in" with the other residents, which basically means not revealing his cannibalistic tendencies! *The 'Burbs* (1989) commences with an extended zoom-in on the Universal Studios globe corporate logo, down to mid-America, then down to an aerial shot of a specific area, winding closer and closer until it singles out Mayfield Place, a suburban neighborhood (albeit not tract housing: these are rather large Victorians) which is replete with eccentric neighbors surrounding the home of Ray Peterson (Tom Hanks). *Meet the Applegates* (1990) relates the adventures of a group of giant, intelligent insects who assume human form and try to "fit in" as a typical, middle-class suburban family. In the TV spin-off *The Coneheads* (1993), the pinheaded alien visitors do not even try to camouflage themselves as they go through the stereotypical actions of suburbanites. These films mock the conventional image of suburbia, showing that even aliens, cannibals, and giant insects can be assimilated into a *Father Knows Best*–style society. *Next Friday* (2000) contains an interesting variation on the Hollywood image of suburbia: Watts resident Craig (Ice Cube) is sent to live in Rancho Cucamonga with his uncle and cousin in order to avoid a vengeance-seeking gangster. The lily-white suburbs have become integrated, as the residents include whites, African Americans, and Hispanics, a phenomenon the comedy *Blast from the Past* (1999) has fun with as well.

Pleasantville (1998) goes a step further: although the television-show "universe" to which the film's two protagonists are transported is "perfect," its drab sterility enforces conformity and represses emotion among its inhabitants. As the two interlopers begin to affect the stultified world, the film changes from black and white to color. In *American Beauty* (1999), the ideal suburban lifestyle is revealed to be an empty shell. Although the film dwells on the sexual aspects rather excessively (infidelity, voyeurism, exhibitionism, repressed and open homosexuality, and the sexual attraction between a middle-aged man—played by Kevin Spacey—and his teenage daughter's friend are just some of the plot devices), *American Beauty* is not merely an updated version of *Suburban Roulette,* but rather an examination of the empty lives led by some who outwardly seem to have obtained their piece of the "American dream."

Suburbia in the Magnifying Glass

In the words of Kenneth T. Jackson, "for those on the right, [suburbia] affirms that there is an 'American way of life' to which all citizens can aspire. To the left, the myth of suburbia has been a convenient way of attacking a wide variety of national problems, from excessive conformity to ecological destruction" (4). The image of suburbia in post–World War II popular films and television is just as contradictory. For five decades, Hollywood has been almost subliminally presenting the suburban lifestyle as the norm for middle-class America: the city is the domain of the rich, the poor, and young single professionals. Families live in detached houses in housing developments: children ride their bikes or skateboards, neighbors drop over for coffee and conversation, fathers leave for work every morning and do yard work and have cookouts on the weekend. For the most part, this is the good life to which ordinary Americans aspire.

But Hollywood periodically chooses to hold up a magnifying glass to suburban life: neighbors are at best wacky and eccentric, and at worst psychotic, violent, and vengeful; home ownership condemns one to lifelong indebtedness and is fraught with the need for constant, back-breaking maintenance and expensive repairs; bored suburban housewives turn to extramarital affairs, alcohol, drugs, and even devil worship to shatter the monotony of their days. Children run wild, "hang out," drink alcohol and take drugs, participate in mindless sex and violence. Or, at the opposite end of the spectrum, residents of suburbia are stereotyped, identical plastic robots, creatures of a consumer-oriented middle-class society, incapable of independent thought or creativity.

None of these images is, of course, completely accurate. However, such a widely divergent group of images suggests that the concept of suburbia is still capable of provoking controversy even after so many years.

References

Filmography

American Beauty (1999, F)
Bachelor in Paradise (1961, F)
Blast from the Past (1999, F)
Boys' Night Out (1962, F)
The 'Burbs (1989, F)
The City (1939, D)
The Commuters (1915, F)
The Coneheads (1993, TV)
Edward Scissorhands (1990, F)
George Washington Slept Here (1942, F)
Good Neighbor Sam (1964, F)
The Ice Storm (1997, F)
It's a Wonderful Life (1946, F)
Let's Be Fashionable (1920, F)
Life as a House (2001, F)
Mama Runs Wild (1938, F)
The Man in the Gray Flannel Suit (1956, F)
Meet the Applegates (1990, F)
The Money Pit (1986, F)
Mr. Blandings Builds His Dream House (1948, F)
Neighbors (1981, F)
Next Friday (2000, F)
The Night of June 13 (1932, F)
No Down Payment (1957, F)
Parents (1989, F)
Peyton Place (1957, F)
Pleasantville (1998, F)
Poltergeist (1981, F)
Rebel Without a Cause (1955, F)
Sin in the Suburbs (1962, F)
Suburban Girls Club (1968, F)
The Suburbanite (1904, F)
The Suburbanite's Ingenious Alarm (1908, F)
Suburban Pagans (1968, F)
Suburban Roulette (1968, F)
SubUrbia (1997, F)
Suburbia Confidential (1966, F)
The Swimmer (1968, F)
Three Men on a Horse (1936)
Welcome to the Dollhouse (1998, F)

Bibliography

American Film Institute. *The American Film Institute Catalog of Motion Pictures Produced in the United States: Film Beginnings, 1893–1910.* Lanham, MD: Scarecrow, 1998.

——. *The American Film Institute Catalog of Motion Pictures Produced in the United States: F1, Feature Films 1911–1920.* Berkeley: University of California Press, 1988.

——. *The American Film Institute Catalog of Motion Pictures Produced in the United States: F2, Feature Films 1921–1930.* Berkeley: University of California Press, 1997.

——. *The American Film Institute Catalog of Motion Pictures Produced in the United States: F3, Feature Films 1931–1940.* Berkeley: University of California Press, 1993.

——. *The American Film Institute Catalog of Motion Pictures Produced in the United States: F6, Feature Films 1961–1970.* Berkeley: University of California Press, 1997.

Donaldson, Scott. *The Suburban Myth.* New York: Columbia University Press, 1969.

Duany, Andres, Elizabeth Plater-Zyberk, and Jeff Speck. *Suburban Nation: The Rise of Sprawl and the Decline of the American Dream.* New York: Farrar, Straus & Giroux, 2000.

Felperin, Leslie. "Close to the Edge." *Sight & Sound* 7.10 (October 1997): 15–18.

Fishman, Robert. *Bourgeois Utopias: The Rise and Fall of Suburbia.* New York: Basic Books, 1987.

Gordon, Richard E., Katherine K. Gordon, and Max Gunther. *The Split-Level Trap.* New York: Bernard Geis Associates, 1961.

Jackson, Kenneth T. *Crabgrass Frontier: the Suburbanization of the United States.* New York: Oxford University Press, 1985.

Kay, Jane Holtz. *Asphalt Nation.* New York: Crown, 1997.

Mumford, Lewis. *The City in History.* New York: Harcourt, Brace & World, 1961.

Rothman, William. "Hollywood and the Rise of the Suburbs." *East-West Film Journal* 3.2 (1989): 96–105.

Silverstone, Roger, ed. *Visions of Suburbia.* London: Routledge, 1997.

[MARK BUSBY]

Texas and the Southwest

A lone rider appears silhouetted against the sky. A brilliant sun shines mercilessly on the solitary horseman riding across the screen amid a rocky, dusty landscape of buttes and mesas and the massive arms of the distinctive cactus of western film as it looms almost humanlike in the background. Yet this icon of the "western," the saguaro, is decidedly southwestern, growing only in the Sonoran Desert of southern Arizona and northern Mexico.

Although the Library of Congress includes hundreds of books on "western" film, almost nothing turns up on a genre called "southwestern." However, because older definitions of the "Greater Southwest" include Texas, New Mexico, and Arizona, plus parts of Oklahoma, Colorado, Utah, Nevada, and southern California, as well as northern Mexico, and almost every recognizable western trait is more truly southwestern, the label "southwestern" is a more accurately descriptive. Still, defining the Southwest is not a simple task. As the noted folklorist J. Frank Dobie concludes (partly out of exasperation) in *Guide to Life and Literature of the Southwest:* "The principal areas of the Southwest are . . . Arizona, New Mexico, most of Texas, some of Oklahoma, and anything else north, south, east, or west that anybody wants to bring in" (iv).

As well as covering a rather broad area, the region's prehistory and history reflect the lives and interaction of diverse peoples. Its compelling prehistory has often been subject of documentaries about native bands that populated the region. The Anasazi, builders of cave dwellings at Mesa Verde at the four corners of Colorado, New Mexico, Arizona, and Utah and at Chaco Canyon in New Mexico, have been evaluated effectively in *The Anasazi* (1985) and *The Anasazi and Chaco Canyon* (1994).

Alvar Nuñez Cabeza de Vaca was the first European to contact the many native peoples and to travel the Southwest after he shipwrecked and washed up near present-day Galveston, Texas, in 1528, wandering through Texas, New Mexico, and Mexico before returning to Spain in 1536. His stories of golden cities to the west led Coronado to search for the seven cities of gold in 1540. The explorer's story was dramatized in a feature film, *Cabeza de Vaca* (1991) by Spanish filmmaker Nicolás Echevarría. The film is unsatisfying, partly because the lush river scenes make Texas look like the Amazon valley and because the film transforms Cabeza de Vaca's *mala cosa,* an evil spirit, into a malicious dwarf.

When Juan Oñate settled New Mexico in 1598, he brought cattle and horses, animals that would eventually transform the natural environment through overgrazing and alter the human landscape when the Plains Indians—particularly the Comanches and Apaches—became lords of the plains on horseback. Filmmakers have found little in this period of interest, except for the often-told story of Zorro in colonial California, most recently in Martin Campbell's *The Mask of Zorro* (1998).

After Mexico won its independence from Spain in 1821, the Mexican government offered land grants in Texas to Anglo settlers such as Moses Austin and his son Stephen; the Anglo migration into the Southwest began and pointed to the major events to shape the region in the nineteenth century—Texas independence, the U.S. war with Mexico, the discovery of gold in California, the Civil War, Indian wars, and the growth of the cattle industry. One of the signal events, of course, was the massacre at the Alamo, dramatized notably in an early film, *Martyrs of the Alamo* (1915), directed by Christy Cabanne and featuring Douglas Fairbanks; and, most famously, in *The Alamo* (1960) directed by and starring John Wayne, in a long, talky epic.

The major American film genre, of course, is the western, recognized by being set in the nineteenth century, with cattle, cowboys, horses, Indians, and outlaws. And the cowboy is primarily a Texan and southwestern figure. After the Civil War, when Texas veterans discovered their homes and livelihood in disarray, with herds of wild cattle roaming the land, some enterprising veterans began to round up the cattle, which began the trail drives that are the heart of cowboy legend. That life lasted about twenty-five years, from 1870 to 1895, when barbed wire, the opening of train service, and economic downturns ended the golden days of trail driving. Still, the cowboy is internationally recognizable as an American icon—a symbol of frontier freedom and independence.

In the twentieth century, southwestern history reveals a schism between urban and rural life, particularly the transitions from ranch to farm to oil to computers to tourism, all within the context of the clash and cooperation of the region's diverse cultures: Indian, Spanish, Anglo, and African American.

The Classic Southwestern

Just as famed historian Frederick Jackson Turner proclaimed the closing of the western frontier in 1893, frontier life burst upon American popular culture. It came through Buffalo Bill's Wild West Show, through dime and half-dime novels, and through the first western film, Edwin S. Porter's *The Great Train Robbery* in 1903, a year after the first serious western novel, Owen Wister's *The Virginian.* In that year the first major trail-drive novel, Andy Adams's *The Log of a Cowboy,* was released.

Turner defined the frontier as the "meeting point between savagery and civilization." As commentators such as Will Wright have noted, the classic western and southwestern film focuses on oppositions about characters who are either inside or outside of society, good or bad, strong or weak, and, most importantly, enact a struggle between wilderness and civilization. The classic plot, as identified by Wright, involves actions in which the hero enters a social group to which he is unknown and reveals special abilities that place him in a distinct status. After villains threaten the society, the hero fights and defeats them, making the society safe so that it accepts the hero and gives him a unique status. Often, because he has been violent, he must leave the social group after defeating the villains. A variation on the classical plot involves the hero's relentless need for revenge for some past wrong.

The preeminent southwestern film classic is John Ford's *Stagecoach* (1939) in which Ford lifted John Wayne from B-western obscurity and set him on the path as America's favorite movie star. Wayne's initial appearance in the film takes place along the trail after the stagecoach leaves Tonto, Arizona, for Lordsburg, New Mexico. It suggests his mythic stature, as his image fills the screen when the camera tracks up to him standing with his rifle and saddle. Against the spectacular backdrop of Monument Valley, with a post–Civil War, nineteenth-century setting, Ford has the coach and its passengers journey into the wilderness where the confrontation with the forces of nature and savagery will bring out the best qualities in the microcosm of American society. *Stagecoach* clearly turns on the civilization/savagery dichotomy as the agents of savagery, both Geronimo (and his Apaches) and the murderous white men, the Plummers, are counterpointed by representatives of civilization. Between them as a mediating figure is the Ringo Kid (Wayne), who sits symbolically on the floor of the stagecoach and talks of borders.

Ringo's outlaw status and name suggest the most durable southwestern figure, Billy the Kid, who has been the subject of numerous films over the years, including Kurt Neumann's *The Kid from Texas* (1950) with Audie Murphy, Arthur Penn's *The Left Handed Gun* (1958) with Paul Newman, Sam Peckinpah's *Pat Garrett and Billy the Kid* (1973) with Kris Kristofferson, Christopher Cain's *Young Guns* (1988) and Geoff Murphy's *Young Guns II* (1990), both with Emilio Estevez, and many others.

Another recognizable southwestern subgenre, one that draws from the history of the cowboy, is the trail-drive film, with several versions of Emerson Hough's novel, *North of 36,* adapted for the silver screen, including an eponymous version released in 1924, a year after the novel was published. It was remade in 1931 as *The Conquering Horde* and again in 1938 as *The Texans* with Randolph Scott and Walter Brennan. The actual trail drive lends itself to narrative, inasmuch as it includes a journey with a clear beginning, middle, and end, punctuated by obstacles such as river crossings, thunderstorms, sandstorms, hailstorms, wind, lightning, stampedes, Indians, quicksand, drought, rustlers, and snakes. The ultimate trail-drive film, critic Don Graham argues, is Howard Hawks's *Red River* (1948), with its ambiguous melding of history, legend, and region. The title evokes the Biblical overtones of the Red (Sea) River, with an echo of epic activity and empire building, and recalls the drive's slogan, "Beef for hungry people." The made-for-television film *Lonesome Dove* (1989), starring Robert Duvall and Tommie Lee Jones and based on Larry McMurtry's 1984 novel of the same name, revisits *Red River* and the trail-drive period, and many historians have praised it for its overall faithfulness to historical fact.

Transitional Films

In the 1950s the classic southwestern moved beyond traditional plots and characters toward allegorical statements about contemporary concerns. A major transitional film is Fred Zinnemann's *High Noon* (1952), which has many of the traditional plot elements but reverses Wright's classic pattern: the hero begins inside society and ends outside of it. For a traditionalist like John Wayne, the changes were unacceptable. In a 1971 interview, Wayne described *High Noon* as "the most un-American thing I've ever seen in my whole life. The last thing in the picture is ole Coop putting the United States marshal's badge under his foot and stepping on it." Wayne recalled the final scene incorrectly, for Will Kane only drops his badge. Still, Gary Cooper's Kane displays traditional and nontraditional elements of the western hero in this transitional film. Like other heroes, he is resolute and determined, strong-willed and capable. He is a "man," in contrast to his youthful deputy, Harvey (Lloyd Bridges).

Screenwriter Carl Foreman, blacklisted as a result of the House Committee on Un-American Activities (HUAC), later explained that he had adapted the town of Hadleyville from Mark Twain's Hadleyburg to attack the cowardice of Hollywood. He also said that he had written the film as an explicit attack on the country's fear of Sen. Joseph McCarthy's anticommunist bullying. *High Noon* takes place in a southwestern landscape where "good" violence must confront "evil" violence to overcome chaos. As an anti-McCarthy allegory, the film condemns the complacency of the town with its sham democracy and craven boosterism, stated most fatuously by Thomas Mitchell as the mayor.

High Noon signaled that the southwestern film was changing, and other Texas and southwestern films of the 1950s pursued new directions. Delmer Davies's *Broken Arrow* (1950) featured Indians in a new and sympathetic light; it stressed that Native Americans had their own form of governance and were not simply representatives of savagery. John Ford's *The Searchers* (1956) presented a new variation on the vengeance hero, with John Wayne on a monomaniacal quest to find a niece captured by Comanches. His racism is so vicious that it saps his humanity and renders him as barbaric as the "savages" he set out to find. Ford uses a number of plot and visual devices to indicate how Wayne's Ethan Edwards mirrors the "savage" Comanche Chief Scar (Henry Brandon): Ethan shows his cruelty when he reproduces Comanche ceremonies by shooting the eyes out of an Indian corpse (so its spirit will wander); later, in the most brutal onscreen violence of the film, Ethan scalps Scar. As the Texan searchers ride across Monument Valley in the foreground with the Comanches riding parallel in the background, Ford establishes a visual image of the identification between savagery and civilization.

Another important film of the 1950s that concerns the sweep of Texas history is George Stevens's *Giant* (1956), an epic tale of the shift from a cattle to an oil economy. Bick Benedict (Rock Hudson) owns the sprawling Texas ranch, Riata (based on the King Ranch), and, after marrying a wealthy easterner (Elizabeth Taylor), he begins to establish a dynasty. Oil changes their lives, especially the life of Jett Rink (played by James Dean in his last movie and based on Texas wildcatter Glenn McCarthy). Dean's JR becomes fabulously wealthy when he hits oil on the small bit of Riata left to him when Bick's sister dies. The film examines attitudes toward gender and race from the 1920s to the 1950s, issues that would become even more prominent in the next decade.

Where *Giant* is the ultimate ranch film, other southwestern films examined farming in the Southwest. Famed French filmmaker Jean Renoir adapted George Sessions Perry's Pulitzer Prize–winning novel *Hold Autumn in Your Hand*, about a year in the life of a central Texas sharecropper, as *The Southerner* in 1940, exploring the demise of small family farms in the Southwest and documenting an era in American history when many people led rural lives in constant contact with—and at the mercy of—changing climates. A year later John Ford filmed *The Grapes of Wrath*, John Steinbeck's famous novel about uprooted Okies forced off their farms traveling Highway 66 west. Terrence Malick's *Days of Heaven* (1978) studies new immigrants and the American dream in the Texas panhandle in 1916, where the possibility of realizing the dream is palpable until the reality of violence and a plague of grasshoppers intrude. This film dramatizes a powerful sense of ambivalence toward the natural: both good and bad fortune are linked essentially with natural conditions and natural events, and the characters' fates are determined by the whims of nature rather than human action. Similarly, Robert Benton's *Places in the Heart* (1984) explores the vicissitudes of cotton farming in the 1930s near Waxahachie in north central Texas.

The 1960s

The 1960s ushered in a decade of "new westerns," with John Huston's *The Misfits* in 1961 and then three releases in 1962: David Miller's *Lonely Are the Brave*, John Ford's *The Man Who Shot Liberty Valence*, and Sam Peckinpah's *Ride the High Country*. These end-of-the-frontier narratives signaled a movement from the classic western's glorification of the hero to an interest in antiheroes and outsiders. For example, *Hud* (1963), based on Larry McMurtry's first novel, *Horseman, Pass By*, shifts from the book's focus on the initiation of its narrator Lonnie (Brandon DeWilde) to the amorality of Hud (Paul Newman) and examines how the frontier world represented by Homer Bannon (Melvyn Douglass) is being replaced in 1950s Texas. *The Misfits, Lonely Are the Brave*, and *Hud* point to a continuing trend in southwestern film, the anachronistic southwestern, where films with post-1940s settings look back to a frontier past. More recent films like Stephen Frears's *The Hi-Lo Country* (1999) and especially Billy Bob Thornton's *All the Pretty Horses* (2000) follow this trend. Thornton's film, based on Cormac McCarthy's highly celebrated novel, was long anticipated but disappointed many reviewers. Thornton's original four-hour film was cut by almost two hours and left out the depth of McCarthy's ambivalent look at the changing Southwest.

The 1960s saw other new types of southwestern films. Italian director Sergio Leone's "spaghetti" westerns with Clint Eastwood in *For a Few Dollars More* (1965), *The Good, the Bad, and the Ugly* (1966), and *A Fistful of Dollars* (1967) are set in some vague but iconic Southwest—usually hot, dry, and peopled with brown-skinned characters, with Eastwood wearing his trademark serape. The spaghetti westerns, inexpensive productions filmed in arid southern Spain, helped rejuvenate the southwestern genre in the 1960s; their emphasis on violence clearly reflects a major issue of the Vietnam era.

Arthur Penn's *Bonnie and Clyde* (1967) transformed the outlaw tale into the ultimate film for the 1960s counterculture, using historical Texas bank robbers Clyde Barrow (Warren Beatty) and Bonnie Parker (Faye Dunaway) as its antiheroes. The young outlaws are opposed by a stiff, moralistic older generation. Penn, drawing from the French New Wave films, notably Jean-Luc Godard's *Breathless,* includes psychosexual themes, mixes the comic and tragic, and brings film violence to a different level, especially in the concluding, graphic, slow-motion scene in which Texas Rangers riddle Bonnie and Clyde with hundreds of bullets.

Another change in the traditional western pattern that began to become popular at the end of the 1950s and continued into the 1960s was what Wright calls the "professional plot," seen in such films as Howard Hawks's *Rio Bravo* (1959) and Richard Brooks's *The Professionals* (1966). In this formula variant, the heroes are hired to protect a society incapable of defending itself. The heroes band together into a group with special abilities, affection, and loyalty. Ultimately they fight the villains and either settle down or die together.

The most significant southwestern film at the end of the 1960s was Sam Peckinpah's *The Wild Bunch,* which draws carefully from a specific historical era. Peckinpah worked with the western genre throughout his tempestuous career. *The Wild Bunch* foreshadows the novels of Cormac McCarthy by focusing on a specific historical moment along the border between Texas and Mexico. Set in 1913, the film suggests how the older world is about to be irrevocably changed against the backdrop of the Mexican Revolution, the legislated morality of Prohibition, the looming World War I conflict, the disappearance of the older world of horses and outlaws and concomitant imminent industrial transformation of the Southwest.

The Wild Bunch acknowledges that the basic appeal of the western has been its emphasis on violence and dramatizes explicitly, in repeated slow-motion scenes of gunfire and blood, the reality of that assumption. The plot is constructed so that the aging leader of the bunch, William Holden, plagued by the knowledge of his past mistakes and aware of the changing world in which he lives ("We've got to start thinkin' beyond our guns. Those days are closin' fast"), realizes that the only redemptive possibility in a world of violence is by the existential act of a dramatic exit in a final, flaming, brutal act based on the only principle that they have learned to live by—the band must act together. This furious scene, when the band fatalistically attacks General Mapache's troops, is in counterpoint to the film's famous opening sequence where the bunch rides into an ambush in San Rafael, Texas, but escapes as delighted children burn a mound of ants attacking a scorpion. (Much of Peckinpah's social vision in this landmark film is explored in Paul Seydor's 1996 documentary *The Making of "The Wild Bunch,"* with Ed Harris reading Peckinpah's comments about the film. Seydor interviews other principals, such as Edmond O'Brien and Peckinpah's daughter.)

The Wild Bunch emphasizes how the southwestern is a border film, a strong subgenre reflected in a number of other productions about the region: Orson Welles's *Touch of Evil* (1958); Jack Nicholson's *Goin' South* (1978); Australian director Fred Schepisi's *Barbarosa* (1982), from a script by the Texas-born William D. Wittliff; and John Sayles's *Lone Star* (1996).

FIGURE 61. *The Wild Bunch* (1969). A gang of outlaws—Pike Bishop (William Holden), Dutch Engstrom (Ernst Borgnine), Lyle Gorch (Warren Oates), Tector Gorch (Ben Johnson), and Angel (Jaime Sanchez)—transports guns and munitions to a Mexican revolutionary, oblivious to the impact of their actions to the politics and landscape of the Southwest. Courtesy Warner Brothers/Seven Arts.

The 1970s to the 1990s

In the 1970s and 1980s southwestern films set in the traditional nineteenth-century Southwest were in decline, partially because of the colossal failure of Michael Cimino's *Heaven's Gate* (1980), which investors, shying away from the genre, cited as a clear example of Hollywood excess. Earlier, Mel Brooks's *Blazing Saddles* (1974) sent up the traditional genre, but several southwestern films set in the twentieth century examined small-town southwestern life. Peter Bogdanovich's *The Last Picture Show* (1971) softened the harsh satire of Larry McMurtry's novel but still treated small-town life critically. Other small southwestern films of the period include Jack Hicks's *Raggedy Man* (1981); Robert Benton's *Tender Mercies* (1983), *Places in the Heart* (1984), and *Nadine* (1987), set in Austin in 1954, when it was a small town; and Kevin Reynolds's *Fandango* (1985), with a young Kevin Costner visiting Marfa, Texas, where *Giant* was filmed. An ironic film with a small-town Texas title is Wim Wenders's *Paris, Texas* (1984), with a screenplay by dramatist Sam Shepard. This film uses the arid, southwestern desert landscape around Terlingua as an ironic mirror of the bleak, urban sprawl of Houston.

In 1990 Peter Bogdanovich directed *Texasville,* the sequel to his earlier triumph, *The Last Picture Show.* Allison Anders's *Gas, Food, Lodging* (1992) concerns a truck-stop waitress and her two daughters, who live in a Laramie, New Mexico, trailer park, all echoing elements of Martin Scorsese's *Alice Doesn't Live Here Anymore* (1974), filmed in Tucson but set in Phoenix, Arizona. Clint Eastwood's *A Perfect World* (1993) starred Eastwood and Kevin Costner and uses murder, Texas Rangers, and car chases to explore the familiar issue of violence. Lesser-known independent films set in small towns were also produced in the 1990s, including Tim McCanlies's *Dancer, Texas Pop. 81* (1998) and Mark Illsley's *Happy, Texas* (1999). A locally popular documentary with a similar focus on the small town is *Hands on a Hard Body* (1998), which sympathetically captures the spirit of a contest in Longview, Texas, where the last person standing with his or her hand on a pickup truck wins the truck.

Southwestern City Films

Although small southwestern towns have gotten the most film treatment, some of the major cities have been important settings. James Brooks's *Terms of Endearment* (1983), based on another McMurtry novel, focuses on Houston and won five Academy Awards. A sequel, *The Evening Star* (1996), directed by Robert Harling, is also set in Houston and features the last performance by Ben Johnson. James Bridges's *Urban Cowboy* (1980) takes vestiges of the old world inside Houston honkytonks; John Travolta's performance created a neo-cowboy clothing craze and made riding mechanical bulls popular. No film has influenced the popular image of Dallas as much as the television series about oilman J. R. Ewing, but its setting for a number of films is important. The Dallas Cowboys' football team yielded Ted Kotcheff's *North Dallas Forty* (1979), an examination of the macho world of Texas football. Errol Morris's acclaimed documentary *The Thin Blue Line* (1988), examines the killing of a Dallas policeman in 1976. Likewise, the city of John Kennedy's assassination is important to Oliver Stone's *JFK* (1991) and Jonathan Kaplan's *Love Field* (1992). Austin's post-1960s dropout culture permeates Richard Linklater's *Slacker* (1991) and *Waking Life* (2001), while the multiculturalism of San Antonio is featured in Gregory Nava's *Selena* (1997). Another important southwestern city's history is explored in Barry Levinson's *Bugsy* (1991), with Warren Beatty dramatizing "Bugsy" Siegel's role in building Las Vegas.

North Dallas Forty points to another subgenre of Texas films, the football film, which includes Stan Dragoti's *Necessary Roughness* (1991), a humorous look at college football, and Brian Robbins's *Varsity Blues* (1999), an examination of the "win at any cost" mentality in a small Texas high school.

Diverse Southwesterns

In the late 1980s and 1990s, the western and southwestern film genre was adapted for Native American, feminist, African American, and Mexican American issues. One film, Louis Malle's *Alamo Bay* (1985), extends the concerns to the conflicts over shrimp harvests that occasionally led to violence between Texan and Vietnamese American fishermen along the Gulf Coast. Jonathan Wacks's *Powwow Highway* (1989) follows two contemporary Cheyenne men from Montana to New Mexico, merging the traditional road movie with a poignant quest for racial heritage. Similarly, Chris Eyre's *Smoke Signals* (1998) follows two Coeur d'Alene Indians as they travel from Idaho to Arizona to retrieve the remains of the father of one of them. Walter Hill's *Geronimo* (1993) takes a new look at the title figure. Ridley Scott's *Thelma and Louise* (1991) begins in Arkansas and then becomes a feminist, southwestern, buddy road film as Susan Sarandon and Geena Davis travel through Oklahoma, heading for Mexico. Maggie Greenwald's *The Ballad of Little Jo* (1993), Sam Raimi's *The Quick and the Dead* (1994), and Jonathan Kaplan's *Bad Girls* (1994) revise the western from a feminist perspective.

Mario Van Peebles's *Posse* (1993) adapts the western for African Americans. Earlier southwestern films that are concerned with African American characters and themes include John Ford's *Sergeant Rutledge* (1960) about a black soldier in the Southwest, and *Black Like Me* (1964), based on Texas writer John Howard Griffin's book about darkening his skin chemically and then traveling through the South and back to Texas. Other films trace the lives of important African American southwesterners: Gordon Parks's *Leadbelly* (1974) traces the life of the famous bluesman Huddie Ledbetter, who spent years in Texas and Louisiana prisons until he was discovered by Texas folklorist John Lomax. Similarly, Jeremy Kagan's *Scott Joplin* (1977) follows the life of ragtime's most famous practitioner, who was born in Texarkana.

Films that focus on Mexican American life include Robert Young's *The Ballad of Gregorio Cortez* (1982), based on a groundbreaking book by Chicano scholar Américo Paredes; Robert Redford's *The Milagro Beanfield War* (1989), which dramatizes the politics of water rights and the tensions between Anglo newcomers and Hispanic residents specifically in late-twentieth-century northern New Mexico, but—by implication—throughout the Southwest; Severo Perez's *And the Earth Did Not Devour Him* (1994), based upon Tomás Rivera's story of a young south Texas migrant worker and his family in the 1950s; and Gregory Nava's *Selena* (1997), based on the life and death of the enormously popular Tejana singer. Richard Rodriguez's $7,000 student project *El Mariachi* (1991) was remade with a large budget as *Desperado* (1995). Both border films focus on Hispanics, but they are violent action films rather than examinations of culture, their violence accelerated in Rodriguez's *From Dusk Until Dawn* (1996).

Probably the most significant southwestern film of the 1990s is John Sayles's *Lone Star* (1996). Like novelist Cormac McCarthy, Sayles uses the border between Texas and Mexico both as a physical setting and as a metaphor for the mestizo world that characterizes the Southwest, a mixture of cultures, histories, motives, hopes, and desires. The film crosses borders between Texas and Mexico, parent and child, past and present, African American and Indian, even sexual relations between brother and sister. True to its revisionist nature, the film ends not by remembering the Alamo, but with language that banishes the single symbol of cultural confrontation from collective memory.

It seems clear that the western film is often southwestern, harkening back to the cultural experiences of the region—Indian, Mexican, African American, and Anglo, particularly the cowboy tradition—adapting the recognizable elements for contemporary circumstances or examining a world where the older values have been altered or forgotten. Even if the actual region seems endangered by parking lots and megamalls, the Southwest of buttes, mesas, and saguaro cactus will live forever in the imagination.

References

Filmography

The Alamo (1960, F)
Alamo Bay (1985, F)
Alice Doesn't Live Here Anymore (1974, F)
All the Pretty Horses (2000)
The Anasazi (1985, D)
The Anasazi and Chaco Canyon (1994, D)
And the Earth Did Not Devour Him (1994, F)
Bad Girls (1994, F)
The Ballad of Gregorio Cortez (1982, F)
The Ballad of Little Jo (1993, F)
Barbarosa (1982, F)
Black Like Me (1964, F)
Blazing Saddles (1974, F)
Bonnie and Clyde (1967, F)
The Border (1982, F)
Broken Arrow (1950, F)
Bugsy (1991, F)
Cabeza de Vaca (1991, F)
The Conquering Horde (1931, F)
Dancer, Texas Pop. 81 (1998, F)
Days of Heaven (1978, F)
Desperado (1995, F)
El Mariachi (1991, F)
The Evening Star (1996, F)
Fandango (1985, F)
A Fistful of Dollars (1967, F)
For a Few Dollars More (1965, F)
From Dusk Until Dawn (1996, F)
Gas, Food, Lodging (1992, F)
Geronimo (1993, F)
Giant (1956, F)
Goin' South (1978, F)
The Good, the Bad, and the Ugly (1966, F)
The Grapes of Wrath (1941, F)
The Great Train Robbery (1903, F)
Hands on a Hard Body (1998, D)
Happy, Texas (1999, F)
Heaven's Gate (1980, F)
High Noon (1952, F)
The Hi-Lo Country (1998, F)
Hud (1963, F)
JFK (1991, F)
The Kid from Texas (1950, F)
The Last Picture Show (1971, F)
Leadbelly (1974, F)
The Left Handed Gun (1958, F)
Lonely Are the Brave (1962, F)
Lonesome Dove (1989, TV)
Lone Star (1996, F)
Love Field (1992, F)
The Making of "The Wild Bunch" (1996, D)
The Man Who Shot Liberty Valence (1962, F)
Martyrs of the Alamo (1915, F)

The Mask of Zorro (1998, F)
The Milagro Beanfield War (1989, F)
Nadine (1987, F)
Necessary Roughness (1991, F)
North Dallas Forty (1979, F)
North of 36 (1924, F)
Paris, Texas (1984, F)
Pat Garrett and Billy the Kid (1973, F)
Places in the Heart (1984, F)
Posse (1993, F)
Powwow Highway (1989, F)
The Quick and the Dead (1994, F)
Red River (1948, F)
Ride the High Country (1962, F)
Scott Joplin (1977, F)
The Searchers (1956, F)
Selena (1997, F)
Sergeant Rutledge (1960, F)
Slacker (1991, F)
Smoke Signals (1998, F)
The Southerner (1940, F)
Stagecoach (1939, F)
Tender Mercies (1983, F)
Terms of Endearment (1983, F)
The Texans (1938, F)
The Thin Blue Line (1988, D)
Touch of Evil (1958, F)
Urban Cowboy (1980, F)
Varsity Blues (1999, F)
Waking Life (2001, F)
The Wild Bunch (1969, F)
Young Guns (1988, F)
Young Guns II (1990, F)

Bibliography

Dobie, J. Frank. *Guide to Life and Literature of the Southwest.* Dallas: Southern Methodist University Press, 1952.

Graham, Don. *Cowboys and Cadillacs: How Hollywood Looks at Texas.* Austin: Texas Monthly Press, 1983.

John, Elizabeth A. H. *Storms Brewed in Other Men's Worlds: The Confrontation of Indians, Spanish, and French in the Southwest, 1540–1795.* Norman: University of Oklahoma Press, 1996.

Lavender, David. *The Southwest.* Albuquerque: University of New Mexico Press, 1984.

Mitchell, Lee Clark. *Westerns: Making the Man in Fiction and Film.* Chicago: University of Chicago Press, 1996.

Wright, Will. *Sixguns & Society: A Structural Study of the Western.* Berkeley: University of California Press, 1975.

[MICHAEL BIRDWELL]

The Trans-Appalachian West

After the French and Indian War, England's King George III issued a proclamation in 1763 forbidding settlement west of the Appalachian Mountains. Defying paper barriers, however, intrepid pioneers and land speculators pushed into the forbidden territory. The establishment of Watauga (in what is now eastern Tennessee) and Richard Henderson's Transylvania Company's illicit land trade increased tensions between colonists and the crown. After the American Revolution, the Continental Congress passed three land ordinances designating new territory for settlement across the Appalachians. The lands included the Southwest Territory, which comprised the present states of Kentucky and Tennessee, and the Northwest Territory, which encompassed the entire Ohio Valley (and future states of Ohio, Illinois, Indiana, Michigan, and Wisconsin). As Americans migrated west into the Ohio Valley, the trans-Appalachian frontier eventually included all territory between the Appalachian Mountains and the Mississippi River.

Frederick Jackson Turner articulated the frontier's importance to American history in his famous "frontier thesis" (1893). America's frontier experience, Turner argued, represented a unique event in world history, providing a crucible that forged a distinctive American character, while representing limitless possibility and optimism. Turner's thesis inspired a flurry of historical writing about frontier life and values that has continued into our own time.

Among Turner's disciples, Henry Nash Smith examined the impact of the frontier myth in his classic work, *Virgin Land* (1950). Smith argued that myth proved more potent than historical reality, inspiring Manifest Destiny and helping define America's self-image. Abundant free land fueled notions of democracy while buttressing a belief that Americans were a chosen people ready to inherit a new Promised Land. The new Canaan, however, allowed competing desires to grow up side by side: the desire to conquer and tame nature vied with the desire to return to nature, creating tension between agriculture and industry as true heirs to the frontier. "The frontier of agricultural settlement was universally recognized as the line separating civilization from savagery," and the frontiersmen represented the first cultural shock troops into the wilderness (215). Part of the frontier's allure was its very wildness. Pioneers believed that the land needed to be tamed; however, by doing so, they often destroyed what had attracted them in the first place—open spaces, bountiful land, social equality, and the lack of oppressive institutions. Nostalgia for land lost to industrial progress and the celebration of frontier heroes from Daniel Boone to Buffalo Bill kept the frontier myth alive.

Martin Ridge and Ray Allen Billington used Turner's thesis as the basis for their survey text *Westward Expansion: A History of the American Frontier* (1984), stressing the frontier experience as the central theme of U.S. history. The myth of the New World garden and Americans as the chosen people explained westward expansion and our national identity. John Winthrop claimed that his Puritans came to the

New World to "create a New Zion" and were responding to the command of God. Such pronouncements shaped a mindset inherent in American notions of the frontier and progress.

Some historians, such as Walter Prescott Webb, writing in the 1930s, argued that Turner's work was based on the "frontier" he found in his native Wisconsin and that Turner's ideas were parochial at best. By the Vietnam era many historians found Turner's thesis inadequate, overlooking the importance of minorities, non-Anglo Europeans, women, and the West's varied geography and topography. No one monolithic West existed in American history, they argue; rather, there were many Wests. Just as Native American tribes differ in myriad ways, so too did pioneers who flocked to the frontier. Many post-Vietnam scholars view the Turner thesis as facile, simplistic, and overly idealistic. Anti-Turnerians begged for a "new" western history, which struggled to find its footing at first but continues in the work of Donald Worster, Richard White, and Patricia Nelson Limerick, among other scholars. (For an examination of how the debate Turner sparked continues to blaze, see Gerald Nash's *Creating the West* and John Mack Faragher's afterword to *Rereading Frederick Jackson Turner.*)

As Malcolm Rohrbough notes, "Generally speaking, the frontier of the trans-Appalachian West from 1775 to 1850 was an experience of high expectations" for land ownership and the promise of a new beginning. Pioneers' high hopes "carried them through the hard struggle of the first few years, when the forest wilderness, the canebrakes, or the prairie land had to be subdued yard by yard." With them they carried the trappings of Western civilization, harboring a "sense that the structure of the New World was not in its final form and that something important might come out of it for them. As a more permanent world of institutions took shape around them, they came to realize that the New World was no longer new" (397). The trans-Appalachian West set the stage for the frontiers to follow, providing a pattern for westward settlement and its attendant problems, including race relations, slavery, industrialization, and the formation of various sociopolitical institutions.

The trans-Appalachian hero of print and screen owes his origin to the literary work of James Fenimore Cooper. Inspired by frontier legends of Daniel Boone made popular by John Filson's 1784 biography of the Kentucky patriarch, Cooper created a solitary, taciturn hero known by various names—Natty Bumppo, Deerslayer, Leatherstocking, and Hawkeye. Though Cooper wrote a number of novels about the frontiersman who knew the secret ways of Native Americans and could be a member of both white society and the expansive wilderness, *The Last of the Mohicans* (1826) proved to be the one most often filmed. Hawkeye represented the nexus between civilization and savagery, a man who fits comfortably in neither world. As such, the literary hero located himself on the frontier where the two value systems collided: Hawkeye emerged repeatedly onscreen, acting as a mirror to the times.

The Early Film Frontier

In its various incarnations *The Last of the Mohicans* often raised questions about the proper relationship between pioneers and Native Americans. D. W. Griffith told Hawkeye's story in *Leatherstocking* (1903), a film that demonized both Indians and the British in the wake of America's recent recognition as a world power. The "closing" of the frontier in 1889 was no distant memory for many filmgoers. The Spanish-American War (1898) and America's role in quelling the Boxer Rebellion in China (1900) rekindled American pride and desire for expansion beyond the continental United States. Griffith hailed from postbellum Kentucky, raised on stories of Daniel Boone and the Civil War. His version of *The Last of the Mohicans* reflected his romantic attitudes about American expansion and celebrated America's foray into empire.

Many silent films from 1903 to 1928 examined the trans-Appalachian West. Silent-era treatments of the transmontane West tended to demonize Native Americans and valorize expansion as a God-given birthright for Euro-Americans. Evocative of a confident young country embarking on world empire, silent films reflected America's new role as a world power.

During the 1930s, movie audiences looked to Hollywood for escape and potential solutions to economic and spiritual depressions plaguing the country. Many films reflected their anxiety as Americans looked for the possibility of a better life. The rediscovery of frontier heroes Daniel Boone and Davy Crockett (as well as Andrew Jackson and Abraham Lincoln) by academics and filmmakers during the Depression and World War II mirrored events and attitudes in American society (O'Connor, 99–100). The Depression caused national soul-searching as many people felt worthless, could find little satisfying work, and felt betrayed by the American Dream.

The administration of Franklin D. Roosevelt played an active role in restoring public faith in the country and federal government. The Works Progress Administration (WPA) employed hundreds of writers, artists, composers, and filmmakers to resuscitate faith in the dream. Many looked to the frontier for inspiration, and during the war years, its heroes—who often used violence to insure their futures—acted as fitting symbols for a country at war. Boone, Crockett, and Lincoln represented canny, self-reliant men who could rise to any occasion and defeat any enemy.

In 1932 and 1936 *Last of the Mohicans* emerged again, first as a serial and later as a feature film. The serials, a staple of the Depression era, made Hawkeye (Harry Carey Sr.) a favorite among young viewers, but it strayed significantly from Cooper's novel. Hawkeye acted more like a cowboy dressed in buckskin than a pioneer. The series, though entertaining, gave audiences little sense of the realities of the trans-Appalachian West. Western hero Randolph Scott played Hawkeye in the 1936 film, which presented the British in a favorable light, unlike the serial, which employed English characters for contempt or comic relief. In both, Native Americans were treated in keeping with the traditional cowboy film, representing a violent threat to frontier families. Both the serial and the feature film offered adventure and escapist fare while engendering a sense of pride in American expansion. Embodying the best characteristics of Americans—individualism, integrity, honesty, patriotism, democratic virtues, love of liberty, and generosity—they indicated that American history is a story of triumph over adversity. Just as the heroes of the trans-Appalachian frontier overcame tremendous obstacles to make the land their own and secure their destiny, 1930s-era Americans would weather the Depression and be stronger for it.

In the late 1930s and early 1940s, Harry Warner instituted a series of patriotic short subjects, the *Old Glory* series, to instruct and entertain American audiences about U.S. history. All received A-film budgets, and most were filmed in Technicolor. Of the fourteen installments released before December 1941, four related to the trans-Appalachian frontier: *The Man Without a Country* (1937), *The Romance of Louisiana* (1938), *The Monroe Doctrine* (1939), and *Old Hickory* (1939). Drawing on images of the frontier and its heroes, the films were thinly veiled calls to action. *The Man Without a Country* dramatized Edward Everett Hale's story about a fictional American implicated in the Burr Conspiracy (1806). After his arrest, Lieutenant Philip Nolan denounces the United States and is forever banished, forcing him to a lonely, guilt-ridden life with no place to call home. The American Legion praised the film for its frank discussion of the importance of patriotism in troubled times. Likewise, the *Monroe Doctrine* presented a clear message to the world to leave the United States and its sphere of influence alone—or else! Though the

Old Glory series lost money, Warner allowed schools, churches, and civic groups to screen episodes free of charge. The series earned Harry Warner and his studio a special Academy Award for public service, and the fourteen films are worthy of further attention by scholars.

Although Warner Bros. called for preparedness, most studios favored isolationism. Some used frontier films to make their point. *Allegheny Uprising* (1939), produced by RKO, depicts an Anglo-Indian alliance as the major impediment to westward expansion. Venal settlers engage in illegal commerce with Indians with the tacit approval of the British authorities. Their avarice threatens the lives of peaceful settlers on the frontier. Based on actual events that took place in western Pennsylvania in 1760, the film dramatizes a frontier revolt against British authority. The movie simplifies the conflict, acting primarily as a backdrop for a love story between Jim Smith (John Wayne) and Janie McDougall (Claire Trevor). Smith defies British authorities personified by the foppish Captain Swanson (George Sanders), who displays all "the intelligence of a badly inbred poodle" (Roberts and Olson, 173). Angered by British duplicity, Smith cobbles together a ragtag band of frontiersmen called the "Black Boys" (who often disguise themselves as Indians) against the corrupt and effete redcoats. At film's end, Smith vows to assert his personal independence and lead like-minded individuals farther west into the wilderness to escape English tyranny. The film has less to do with tribulations on the frontier than with world events in 1939. Stridently anti-British, *Allegheny Uprising* is a plea for American isolation.

Drums Along the Mohawk, produced by Darryl Zanuck at Twentieth Century-Fox, directed by John Ford, and starring Henry Fonda and Claudette Colbert, opened one week after *Allegheny Uprising* (November 10, 1939). It presents a more earnest depiction of life on the frontier. Set in New York's Mohawk Valley, it examines the lives of brave pioneers trying to carve out an existence in the wilderness on the eve of the American Revolution, a period during which some five thousand Mohawk Indians under war chief Joseph Brant allied with the British against Americans on the frontier. Paying careful attention to historic details, the filmmakers created an entire frontier community—not merely a lone hero. Colbert's character, a genteel upper-class woman, provides a dramatic contrast between gentrified life in the city and rigors of the frontier. Zanuck insisted that the pace of the film be slow to accentuate the privations pioneers endured. By contrast, quicker-paced battle scenes involve men and women fighting together to save their homes. Zanuck wanted the audience to identify with characters on a human level and drew conscious parallels to the suffering endured by Americans during the Great Depression. The film depicts the Battle of Oriskany (which occurred near present-day Utica in August 1777), conflating that battle with other frontier skirmishes of the Revolution in one of the film's most powerful sequences.

Set at a later time on the trans-Appalachian frontier, *Stand Up and Fight* (1939) examines the impact of a transportation revolution upon the region. An atypical trans-Appalachian western film, it placed emphasis upon the second generation of pioneers. Beginning at the Cumberland Gap in 1844, Robert Taylor played a Maryland entrepreneur and aristocrat determined to extend the Baltimore & Ohio Railroad across the mountains. Many frontier folk proved hostile to the iron horse, chief among them the head of a competing stagecoach line (Wallace Beery). The film pitted the two men in a struggle of technological progress versus the status quo while flirting with problems caused by slavery. (Beery's character, who stood in the way of progress, was engaged in illicit slave trading.) Though fiction, the movie pointed to real conflicts created by social class, industrialization, resistance to change, and slavery.

Northwest Passage (1940), set in 1759 during the French and Indian War, recounted the

FIGURE 62. *Allegheny Uprising* (1939). Jim Smith (John Wayne) lies wounded after a successful revolt against the British for selling guns to the Indians, jeopardizing the settlement of the Trans-Appalachian frontier. Courtesy RKO Radio Pictures.

story of ranger Major Robert Rogers (Spencer Tracy). Based on Kenneth Roberts's popular novel and directed by King Vidor, it is filled with inaccuracies but is also splendid viewing. Originally intended to be the first installment in a two-part epic, the second half was never filmed, nor was the promised passage ever seen. Rogers's Rangers set out to destroy the Abenaki Indians' stronghold at St. Francis, near the Canadian border, in hopes of ending the war. The action film makes excellent use of Technicolor and is buoyed along by Herbert Stothart's rousing score. In spite of the film's distorted historic details, it captures the spirit of frontier life and indirectly changed American attitudes toward intervention in the European struggle.

The Postwar Frontier and Cold War Themes

Surprisingly, no major studio produced films about the trans-Appalachian frontier once the United States declared war on December 8, 1941. War films tended to be about World War II, while views of the frontier were dominated by trans-Mississippi westerns. Once the war ended, however, filmmakers returned to the trans-Appalachian West.

Cecil B. De Mille's *Unconquered* (1947), starring Gary Cooper, marked a return to the prerevolutionary West. Much of the film centers on the buying and selling of an indentured servant (Paulette Goddard) and an opportunist (Howard Da Silva) who traffics willfully with the enemy. Though the film attempts to present the politics of the era, it degenerates into an unsatisfactory love story. *Unconquered* was filmed during a difficult time in Hollywood. The United States had emerged triumphant from World War II only to face a Cold War that was heating up on the home front. In 1947 the House Committee on Un-American Activities (HUAC) began holding hearings in Hollywood. During the 1930s, when capitalism seemed doomed, many people in Hollywood—including most of those called before HUAC—had toyed with communism. Their flirtation with this political ideology returned to haunt them during the Cold War. Moguls closed ranks, cooperating with the investigation. Director Cecil B. De Mille presented information to HUAC and California's own Communist Party watchdog, the Tenney Committee. Friendly witness Robert Taylor singled out Howard Da Silva, the opportunist who collaborated with the British in *The Unconquered.* Gary Cooper joined the conservative Motion Picture Alliance, denouncing Hollywood's fellow travelers before the committee. Thus, though *The Unconquered* did poorly at the box office, the film's story about enemies in one's midst reflected what was occurring in the movie colony.

FIGURE 63. *Unconquered* (1947). A Virginia militia captain (Gary Cooper, right) becomes embroiled in the "buying and selling of an indentured servant" as he struggles to prevent Seneca Indians from acquiring guns and threatening Fort Pitt. Courtesy Paramount Pictures.

John Wayne (who also produced the film) portrayed a coonskin-capped volunteer returning from the Battle of New Orleans (January 8, 1814) in *The Fighting Kentuckian* (1949). Stopping in Alabama on his way home, John Breen (Wayne) falls in love with a French general's daughter (Vera Ralston). Meanwhile, the community of Alabama pioneers falls prey to villainous land grabbers; in response, pioneers turn to the experienced fighter and war hero to save them. Though a standard action feature with a convoluted plot, *The Fighting Kentuckian* offered Wayne an opportunity to enhance his onscreen persona. Republic, a poverty-row studio with a reputation for cheapness and formula, fashioned a film with some inspired casting and credible actors. Among them is Oliver Hardy playing pioneer Willie Paine in a seriocomic performance without Stan Laurel. Though formulaic, the film presented Breen as a man struggling to decide where his allegiance lay, while depicting the tenuous nature of frontier life and the struggle to create a community in a hostile environment—very much a metaphor for the times.

Burt Lancaster produced, directed, and starred in *The Kentuckian* (1955), a story about a frontiersman and his son migrating to Texas in the 1830s. Filmed on location near Owensboro, Kentucky, it accurately depicts the land between the Appalachian Mountains and the Mississippi River. Based on Felix Holt's novel *The Gabriel Horn,* it was adapted by the novelist A. B. Guthrie Jr. The painter Thomas Hart Benton designed the film's poster, which depicts Lancaster as a pioneer—a larger-than-life figure in buckskin literally towering over the landscape with his son and dog by his side, a true mythic hero.

The film portrayed difficulties of traveling west in an era without adequate roads and bridges and where dangers were real. Lancaster's Big Eli Wakefield lives by his wits on his journey west. Indians provide no threat in this movie; instead, other Euro-Americans do. This trans-Appalachian frontier, populated with tough, unscrupulous men, challenges Big Eli's assumptions about himself and fellow man. As he and Little Eli travel, the son grows more knowledgeable and adaptable to the changing milieu. Walter Matthau, in his screen debut, depicted a sadistic saloonkeeper who publicly humiliates Big Eli, horsewhipping him in the street. (As long as Big Eli remained in the wilderness he knew what to do, but in towns he faltered.) By the film's end Little Eli becomes the savior of his father and heir to the dream of Texas and freedom. J. W. Williamson observes that *The Kentuckian* "is a pretty straightforward story about the loss of American virility due to an obsession with business and money and the spreading cancer of cities" (90).

From Camelot to Clinton

John Ford, George Marshall, and Henry Hathaway codirected a sprawling Cinerama epic of both the trans-Appalachian and trans-Mississippi West with the episodic film *How the West Was Won* (1963). Ostensibly a story of one family's journey across the American continent, the film presented a survey of frontier history from 1803 to 1890. Told in five segments, the narrative follows the fictional Prescott family through historic settings, beginning with the Erie Canal. Painted with a broad brush, the epic includes a series of historic figures and events. The Prescott family encounters river pirates, hazardous rapids, buffalo stampedes, Indian attacks, and other challenges. Though filled with an impressive cast (including James Stewart, Walter Brennan, Henry Fonda, Lee J. Cobb, John Wayne, and Gregory Peck) the film lacks a cohesive storyline and often bends history to fit its episodic structure. Some segments provide dramatic insight about the difficulty of life on the frontier, and the film vividly portrays those hardships. Unlike the Prescotts' breakneck adventures, life, for most pioneers, was typified by brief moments of intense action followed by mind-numbing boredom. The film captures the hope inherent in the frontier spirit that John F. Kennedy had rekindled. In his inaugural address of 1961, President Kennedy had promised a new frontier, and here was a movie reminding audiences how invigorating and expansive the original frontier had been. Unlike later, Vietnam-era productions, this film is a celebration of America as a sprawling, dangerous land filled with promise, where ordinary people can brush elbows with heroes and where the only limitations are the ones Americans make for themselves.

Max von Sydow and Liv Ullman starred in an earnest depiction of the lives of Swedish immigrants to Minnesota in the 1850s in Jan Troell's gritty film *The Emigrants* (1972). Told from the immigrants' point of view, it exposes not only the physical hardships of eking out a life on the frontier but also the cultural chauvinism encountered by non-English speakers. The film follows the arduous journey over sea and land from Sweden to the American interior. Excellent in its depictions of characters and period details, *The Emigrants* provides a believable glimpse of frontier life for average pioneers. A worthy sequel, *The New Land*, followed in 1973.

Charlton Heston and Brian Keith teamed up to tame the frontier in the buddy picture *The Mountain Men* (1980). The film stretches the boundaries of the trans-Appalachian West from the Ohio Valley to the Rockies. A story of two aging trappers in the last days of the fur trade, the film accurately depicts the annual rendezvous associated with the heyday of the trapping. Authentic costumes, inspired by Frederic Remington's nineteenth-century illustrations, enhance the film's visuals. Nostalgia for a simpler time, when people could rely on themselves rather than outside agencies, pervades the film. In an era of runaway inflation, gas lines, and residual effects of Vietnam and Watergate, *The Mountain Men* presented a bygone virile America. It mirrored the campaign rhetoric of Ronald Reagan in 1980, who tapped the mythology of the frontier, and renewed faith in the American Dream.

Hawkeye and Chingachgook fought the French and Indian war on television in 1985 in a serialized version of James Fenimore Cooper's *The Last of the Mohicans.* More faithful to the source material than previous versions, the TV show made good use of locations and credible costuming. Steve Forrest portrayed Hawkeye as an older, more introspective hero, a war-weary pioneer seeking peace and stability on a contested frontier. He acts as mediator between greedy settlers and Indians intent on retaining their homelands. The miniseries reflected the mood of a country in the pall of a "Vietnam syndrome" ten years after the fall of Saigon: the world was no longer black and white between heroic pioneers and their opponents; rather, it was complicated by competing goals, conflicting values, and racial misunderstanding.

In 1992 Michael Mann directed *Last of the Mohicans,* using Native Americans in roles formerly held by Caucasians. Casting Native American activist Russell Means as Hawkeye's mentor Chingachgook added gravity and importance to this beautifully photographed film. Wes Studi (Magua) delivered a powerful performance, and his vengeful actions propelled the story. Mann's version, however, leaves uninformed viewers with the impression that the 1757 massacre at Fort William Henry was the primary cause of the American Revolution. But, more graphically violent than preceding versions, Mann's battle scenes, often filmed in slow motion with a quasi-rock score, achieve a near balletic quality. Filmed in the Smoky Mountains near Asheville, North Carolina, the landscape is as much a character as the humans—as it was in Cooper's novels. Mann deviates from the novel, producing a visually stunning film with a high degree of historical detail—but not necessarily accuracy. His stylized shots, framing, and rapid cross-cutting, associated with his television series *Miami Vice,* creep into the film. This is especially evident in the painterly romantic sequences between Hawkeye (Daniel Day-Lewis) and Alice (Madeline Stowe) and the action sequences, often filmed in slow motion.

Into the Twenty-First Century

Though the trans-Appalachian West of feature films often had more in common with the cowboy film genre, it has proved an important subject for filmmakers. The West east of the Mississippi created some of the early republic's most familiar heroes, from Daniel Boone to Abraham Lincoln, both of whom embody American notions of optimism, self-reliance, and democratic spirit. The most enduring figure to incorporate different generations' attitudes continues to be James Fenimore Cooper's Hawkeye. As Frederick Jackson Turner pointed out, all attempts at writing history reflect problems of the present, and presentism has long been a part of American film. The earliest depictions of the trans-Appalachian region reflected ideals of Americans on the verge of the so-called American Century, demonizing Native Americans, non-Anglo Europeans, and women. Other films reflected American questions about World War II, the Cold War, Vietnam, and our changing role as a superpower. Later depictions, by contrast, examined ecological issues; they presented a more multicultural region, problems systemic in competing cultures vying for the same space, and the role of women as a "civilizing force." The trans-Appalachian West continues to be fertile ground for filmic investigations, including films such as *Hoosiers* or *Major League* (1989).

In *Hoosiers,* Dennis Hopper portrays a former high school basketball hero named "Shooter" who has lost his way in the post–World War II Midwest. He looks backward to the trans-Appalachian frontier for guidance, dressing in a blanket coat and worn-out top hat, and his diction reflects the speech of the early nineteenth century. He lives a quasi-frontier existence in a crude, decaying structure without electricity, warmed by a fire and lit with lanterns. Shooter, an anachronism in dress, speech, and behavior, rises to the occasion to help lead his son's basketball team to victory in the state championships.

Likewise, in *Major League,* a baseball parody centering on the Cleveland Indians, a band of athletic misfits put together by the team's unscrupulous owner, who hopes for a losing season so she can move the team. Charlie Sheen plays the out-of-control pitcher "Wild Thing," who embodies the ethos of the trans-Appalachian frontier. A loner who bristles against authority, Wild Thing brings a gritty excitement to the staid game of baseball, especially when the team begins a winning streak, insuring that the team will stay in Cleveland. The trans-Appalachian frontier, with its emphasis on individual ability, a sense of adventure, and Manifest Destiny, continues to infuse the plots and characters of modern movies.

References

Filmography

Allegheny Uprising (1939, F)
The Daniel Boone Show (1964–70, TV)
Davy Crockett, King of the Wild Frontier (1954–55, TV; 1955, F)
Drums Along the Mohawk (1939, F)
The Emigrants (1972, F)
The Fighting Kentuckian (1949, F)
How the West Was Won (1963, F)
The Kentuckian (1955, F)
Leatherstocking (1903, F)
The Last of the Mohicans (1932, F; 1936, F; 1992, F)
The Man Without a Country (1937, F; 1973, TV)
The Monroe Doctrine (1939, F)
Northwest Passage (1940, F)
Old Hickory (1939, F)
The Romance of Louisiana (1938, F)
Unconquered (1947, F)

Bibliography

Brownlow, Kevin. *The War, the West and the Wilderness.* New York: Knopf, 1984.
Cameron, Kenneth M. *America on Film: Hollywood and American History.* New York: Continuum, 1997.
Cronon, William, George Miles, and Jay Gitlin. *Under an Open Sky: Rethinking America's Western Past.* New York: Norton, 1992.
Faragher, John Mack, ed. *Rereading Frederick Jackson Turner: "The Significance of the Frontier" and Other Essays.* New Haven: Yale University Press, 1994.
Meyers, Jeffrey. *Gary Cooper: American Hero.* New York: Morrow, 1998.
Morgan, Ted. *A Shovel Full of Stars: The Making of the American West, 1800 to the Present.* New York: Simon & Schuster, 1995.
Nash, Gerald. *Creating the West: Historical Interpretations, 1890–1990.* Albuquerque: University of New Mexico Press, 1991.
Navasky, Victor. *Naming Names.* New York: Viking, 1980.
O'Connor, John E. "Drums Along the Mohawk." In John E. O'Connor and Martin A. Jackson, eds., *American History/American Film: Interpreting the Hollywood Image,* 99–102. New York: Frederick Ungar, 1979.
Pitts, Michael R., ed. *Hollywood and American History: A Filmography of Over 250 Motion Pictures Depicting U.S. History.* Jefferson, NC: McFarland, 1984.
Roberts, Randy, and James Olson. *John Wayne: American.* New York: Free Press, 1995.
Rohrbough, Malcolm. *The Trans-Appalachian Frontier: People, Societies, and Institutions, 1775–1850.* New York: Oxford University Press, 1978.
Slotkin, Richard. *Fatal Environment: The Myth of the Frontier in the Age of Industrialization, 1800–1890.* New York: Harper & Row, 1985.
——. *Gunfighter Nation: The Myth of the Frontier in Twentieth Century America.* New York: Atheneum, 1992.
——. *Regeneration Through Violence: The Mythology of the American Frontier, 1600–1860.* New York: Harper & Row, 1973.
Smith, Henry Nash. *Virgin Land: The American West as Symbol and Myth.* Cambridge, MA: Harvard University Press, 1950.
Williamson, J. W. *Hillbillyland: What the Movies Did to the Mountains and the Mountains Did to the Movies.* Chapel Hill: University of North Carolina Press, 1995.

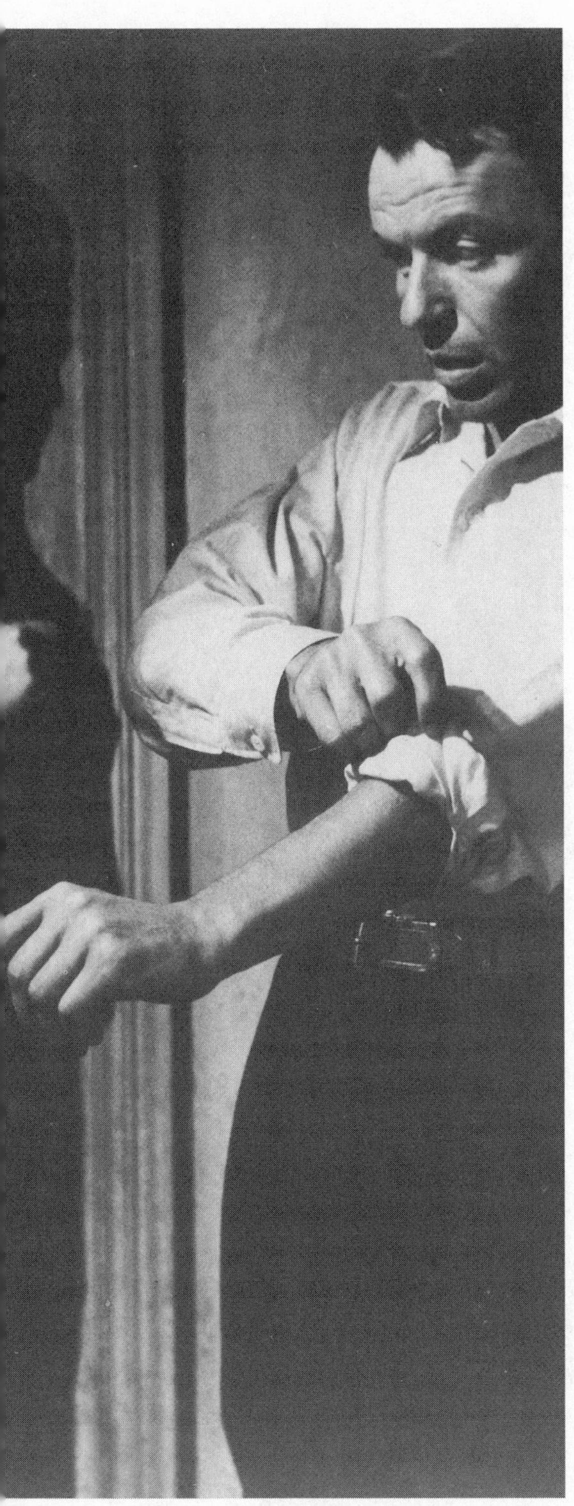

VII. Themes and Topics

★ ★ ★ ★ ★ ★ ★

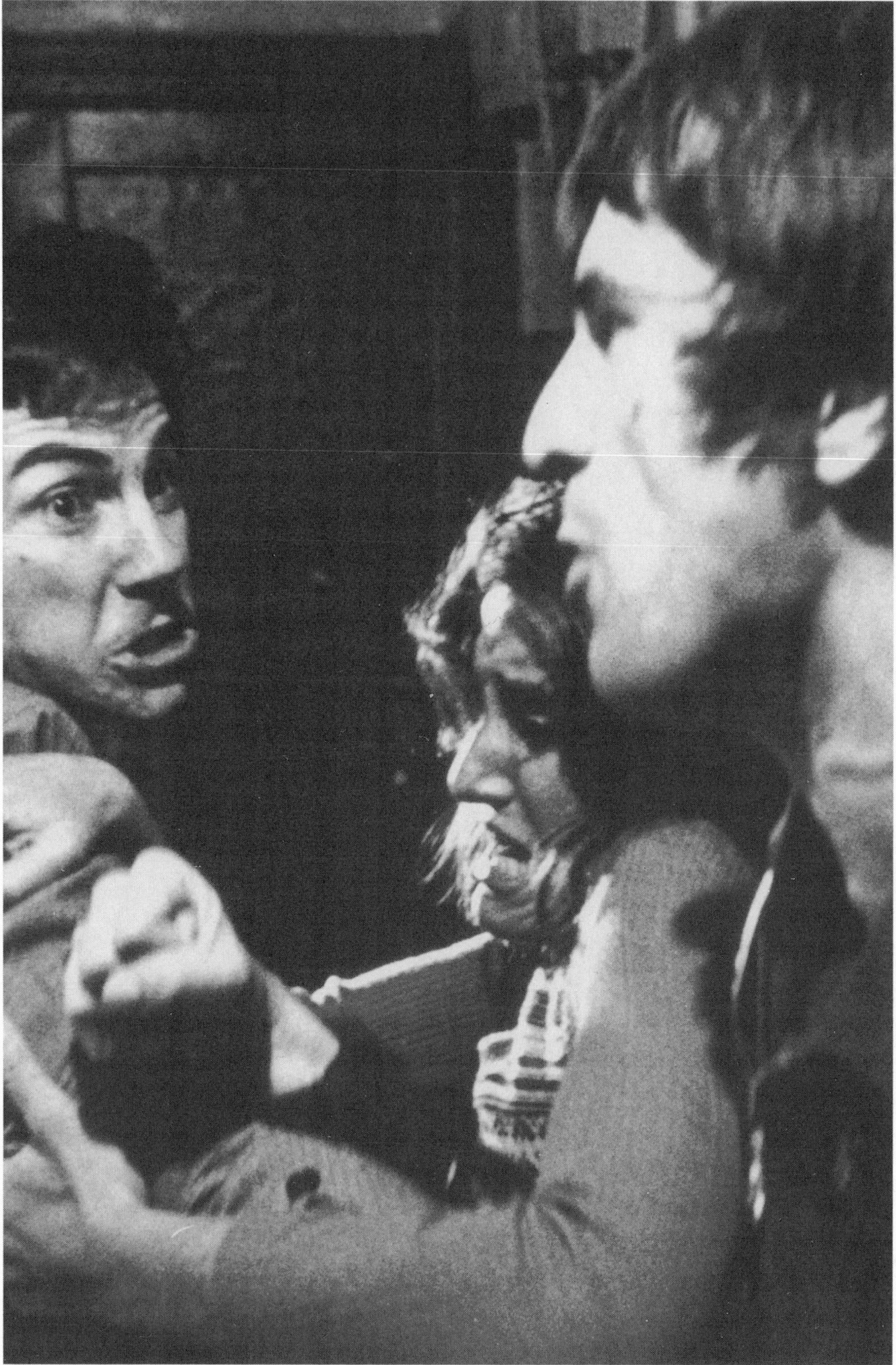

[RONALD W. WILSON]

Crime and the Mafia

In a classic article written in 1953, "Crime as an American Way of Life," sociologist Daniel Bell described crime as an alternative ladder of success. With other avenues of opportunity closed off by discrimination and a lack of education, organized crime provided a way to fulfill aspirations of entrepreneurship and social mobility. According to Bell, "Crime, in many ways, is a Coney Island mirror, caricaturing the morals and manners of society. The jungle quality of the American business community, particularly at the turn of the century, was reflected in the mode of 'business' practiced by the coarse gangster elements, most of them from new immigrant families, who were 'getting ahead,' just as Horatio Alger had urged" (128). As both society and business changed, Bell continued, so did the types and organization of crime; significantly, crime films reflect these same changes.

In the 1850s, ethnic gangs dominated the crime scene in large metropolitan areas; for example, in New York City, the Five Pointers, the Cherry Hill Gang, the Dead Rabbits, and the Hudson Dusters were but a few of the immigrant gangs that formed for mutual protection and profit. In 1891 New Orleans chief of police William Hennessey was assassinated by members of a secret society of Italian immigrants that was referred to as "the Mafia." In the early part of the twentieth century an extortion racket operated in New York; it was known by members of the Italian community as *la Mano Nera,* the Black Hand. In 1919 the Eighteenth Amendment to the Constitution went into effect, outlawing the manufacture, sale, distribution, and transportation of alcoholic beverages. This attempt to legislate morality provided a profitable opportunity for the many factions of immigrant gangsters to organize for illegal activities; once Prohibition was repealed in 1933, they turned to other options. The early 1940s "Murder, Inc." trials revealed a subsidiary arm of organized crime that was used primarily as an execution squad. In 1946 the Hobbs Act was passed, the first piece of legislation designed specifically to combat organized crime. Individual crime leaders such as Al Capone and Charles "Lucky" Luciano were removed from power by law enforcement rather than criminal means. In the 1950s and 1960s both the Kefauver Committee and the McClellan Committee investigated the extent of organized crime. The terms "Mafia" and "Cosa Nostra" were frequently used to describe an underworld network of organized criminal activity. In 1970, noting the growing influence of organized crime, President Nixon signed into law the Organized Crime Control Act. Title IX was the Racketeer Influence and Corrupt Organizations Act (RICO), which would become the most potent legislative weapon against organized crime. It listed twenty-four activities (such as bribery, extortion, and murder) associated with organized criminal activity, expanded the definition of conspiracy, and gave law enforcement the tool of "asset forfeiture"—the seizure of assets, proceeds, and instrumentalities of crime. The Witness Security and Protection Program was also a part of this legislation, as were fewer restrictions on the use of electronic surveillance (wiretapping and electronic bugs) by law enforcement personnel. RICO allowed a more effective attack on organized gambling, prostitution, narcotics trafficking, and loan-sharking because it criminalized the acquisition, maintenance, or control of a business funded through illegal activities.

Crime and violence became an important part of the American cultural mythos. Cultural icons such as Jesse James, Billy the Kid, and the Dalton Gang were representative of the outlawry that was a part of the literature and myths about the settling of the American West in the nineteenth century. With the coming of industrialization and urbanization in the twentieth century, a different cultural image was required. David E. Ruth has argued that the media gangster was a central cultural figure who helped Americans negotiate a bumpy transition into the changing social world of the twentieth century: "The gangster represented a reformulation of longstanding concerns for a new cultural context. As staged in the underworld, the city was a disorderly place of dangerous strangers, of rapacious capitalists, of unmanly men and unwomanly women, of seekers of pleasure and shirkers of responsibility" (8). Similarly, cultural historian Richard Slotkin views the gangster as an extension of the frontier myth, suggesting that just as violence was inexorably linked with the nation's expansion in the nineteenth century, so, too, was it a part of the urban "frontier" of the twentieth (260–265).

Even before the advent of motion pictures, crime was a regular feature of newspapers, dime novels, plays, novels, and songs. Many film and social historians have attempted to explain America's fascination of the genre. One of the earliest and most influential was by Robert Warshow, who asserted cryptically that the gangster represented the "no" to the great American "yes." (Warshow links the gangster's popularity to the American dream of success.) Genre critics Stanley J. Solomon and Stuart Kaminsky have emphasized the crime films specially constructed moral universe where the only value was getting ahead. Solomon and Kaminsky also have speculated on the attraction of the crime film, asserting that it provides a "vicarious experience of continual action, violence, social deviation, corruption, and a determined drive for power" (Solomon, 158). Solomon also claimed that the crime genre allowed prurient glimpses into otherwise avoided subcultures.

The Silent Era: From Gangs to Gangsters

The preoccupation of early crime films with urban crime parallels the social reform concerns of the Progressive era (1879–1920). Progressive reformers exposed the conditions of tenement districts of metropolitan areas, which they saw as breeding crime as a result of a corrupt social environment. Jacob Riis's famous book *How the Other Half Lives* (1890) recorded those egregious conditions with a still camera. That the center of the early film industry was the metropolitan New York area influenced the atmospherics of many early crime films. D. W. Griffith's *Musketeers of Pig Alley* (1912) is generally considered to be the first "gangster" film. In 1915 two feature films were released that further added to the growing genre, Raoul Walsh's *The Regeneration* and Maurice Tourneur's *Alias Jimmy Valentine. The Regeneration* is considered the oldest surviving feature-length gangster film. The subject of "white slavery," widely reported in the press, as well as the focus of a Rockefeller White Slavery Report (1912), provided fodder for two "exploitation" films: *Traffic in Souls* (1913), directed by George Loane Tucker, and *Inside the White Slave Traffic* (1913), directed by Frank Beal. Both films relied heavily on real-life incidents, as well as documentary footage, for an air of authenticity. The advent of Prohibition gave rise to the increase in both underworld activity and films about crime.

The crime film was seriously affected by two quite different events in the late 1920s: the coming of sound in 1927 and the St. Valentine's Day Massacre in 1929: sound was to add considerably to the action-oriented material of the crime genre, while the St. Valentine's Day Massacre in Chicago catapulted Al Capone and others into the headlines. According to Jonathan Munby, "Although a criminal and an ethnic to boot, Al Capone gained credibility as a new national hero in the context of Prohibition, a piece of legislation universally despised across class and ethnic lines. Capone bucked not only the entire system of nativist middle-class idealism rooted in commitment to the work ethic and the deferment of gratification. The gangster's popularity reached new heights in the aftermath of the Wall Street crash, an event that removed the economic platform on which Prohibition's credibility was rested" (37). Although it was a late silent film, Joseph von Sternberg's *Underworld* (1927), written by Chicago newspaperman-turned-playwright Ben Hecht, set the standard for the 1930s gangster genre. In 1929 the ambush of seven members of "Bugs" Moran's gang in Chicago provided an additional incentive for filmmakers to satisfy public curiosity. The addition of sound to the moving image allowed audiences to hear not only the famous gunplay, but also the colorful argot of America's urban underworld.

The Great Depression and the Production Code

The early 1930s witnessed a flourish of criminal activity from the establishment of organized crime to the exploits of numerous rural bandits throughout the Midwest. The gangland murders of Salvatore Maranzano and Giuseppe "Joe the Boss" Masseria in 1931 led to the formation of the "Commission," a board of directors that would oversee the Mafia. The old-style Italian Mafia was out, and the "syndicate" was in. In addition, during the early 1930s numerous hoodlums with colorful names were making headlines throughout the Midwest. Pretty Boy Floyd, Ma Barker, Bonnie Parker and Clyde Barrow, John Dillinger, and Machine Gun Kelly became household names, and newspapers across the nation closely followed their activities.

Mervyn LeRoy's *Little Caesar* (1930), based on a novel of the same name by W. R. Burnett and starring Edward G. Robinson, ushered in a cycle of brutal gangster antiheroes. William Wellman's *The Public Enemy* (1931) and Howard Hawks's *Scarface* (1932) embellished the film industry's depiction of crime. These films chronicled the rise and fall of their protagonists in a way that mirrored the American success story; indeed, many scholars have viewed this initial crime-film cycle as a parodic reflection of the American success myth. The drive to be a success in business is a basic theme running through American literature, especially at the turn of the century. Film historians have noted a parallel in the early 1930s gangster films. Andrew Bergman, for instance, compares the gangster film to both the Horatio Alger mythos of success ("from rags to riches") and Andrew Carnegie's success formula found in a famous speech entitled "The Road to Business Success." Carnegie's vision emphasized the individual accomplishment of success from at the bottom by being exceptional, breaking orders, and inventing new ones. Couched within a context of social Darwinism, this image was particularly applicable to the early gangster film, where the basic formula followed a rise-and-fall pattern of success and failure within a context demanding survival of the fittest.

Several factors led to the demise of the classic gangster cycle of the early 1930s: the implementation of the 1927 Production Code by the Hays Office, the repeal of the Eighteenth Amendment, and President Franklin D. Roosevelt's "war on crime." The repeal of prohibition in 1933 removed any need for rumrunners and racketeers, and the press turned to celebrating the exploits of rural and "folk" bandits such as Pretty Boy Floyd, Bonnie and Clyde, and John Dillinger. President Roosevelt's subsequent "war on crime" and the glo-

FIGURE 64. *Scarface* (1932). Tony Camonte (Paul Muni, center), once an unmannered hood, with his boss John Lovo (Osgood Perkins) and Lovo's girlfriend Poppy (Karen Morley), basking in the opulence provided by the fruits of the crime industry. Tony, also called Scarface, vies for the attention of Poppy and eventually her companionship as he plans to push out Lovo. A revisionist gangster film, *Scarface* is an early depiction of criminals who believe they have access to the myth of American success. Courtesy Caddo and United Artists.

rification of J. Edgar Hoover's "G-men" shifted the public fascination from lawbreakers to law enforcers. Also factoring into this cultural shift was the implementation of the Production Code in 1934. Threats of theater boycotts by such pressure groups as the Catholic Legion of Decency caused Hollywood to enforce its Production Code. One of the central concerns of Hollywood's critics was its glorification of criminal activity. The now-famous Payne Studies of 1933 had "proven" that America's youth was harmfully influenced by the content of gangster films. The Payne Studies, which were condensed into the popular volume *Our Movie Made Children* (1933), provided many examples of youth who robbed banks and stores claiming to have been inspired by what they had seen on screen. Movie content, as a result, became a popular topic for editorials and homilies. As a consequence of this backlash, the gangster hero was supplanted by federal agents. Warner Bros.' *"G" Man* (1935), starring James Cagney, and *Bullets or Ballots* (1936), with Edward G. Robinson, canonized a new law-and-order image for America, ironically with the very actors who had enjoyed such success as gangsters.

The 1940s and Postwar Developments

The gangster figure virtually disappeared from domestic films from 1941 to 1945; it was easy enough to simply replace gangsters with Nazi villains in such films as *All Through the Night* (1942) and *Casablanca* (1942). During the mid-1940s, films based on the hard-boiled fiction of Dashiell Hammett and James M. Cain saw a marked increase in production, particularly from Paramount Studios, whose releases included *This Gun for Hire* (1942), *The Glass Key* (1944), and *Double Indemnity* (1944). Film historian Carlos Clarens suggests that the film noir developed, at least partially, as a response to Joseph Breen's refusal to allow the production of gangster pictures during the war years. With the one exception of Max Nosseck's *Dillinger* (1945), no real-life criminals were portrayed on screen until Don Siegel's *Baby Face Nelson* (1957). The Breen Office supplemented a thirteenth section to the MPAA code while the Hollywood Ten were refusing to testify before the House Committee on Un-American Activities. The section read: "No picture shall be approved dealing with the life of a notorious criminal of current or recent times which uses the name, nickname or alias of such notorious criminal in the film, nor shall a picture be approved if based on the life of such notorious criminal unless the character shown in the film be punished for crimes shown in the film committed by him" (quoted in Clarens, 192). The fear that the exploits of real criminals, when portrayed on the screen, would influence audiences was a prominent concern of the public and the Hays Office. The dormancy of the gangster film allowed for other crime genres to develop: particularly, the police procedural, the caper film, and the syndicate film.

In January 1950 the Senate Special Committee to Investigate Crime in Interstate Commerce was formed. Headed by Senator Estes

Kefauver of Tennessee, the committee, due primarily to the broadcast of its hearings on television, became not only the most important probe of organized crime in America, but riveting TV drama as well. Rather than hold Senate hearings strictly in Washington, Kefauver opted to travel to key cities (fourteen in all) to show the ubiquity of organized criminal activity. Films following in the wake of the Kefauver hearings include *711 Ocean Drive* (1950) *The Enforcer* (1951), *The Racket* (1951), *Hoodlum Empire* (1952), *Captive City* (1952), *The Big Heat* (1953), *The Big Combo* (1955), and *New York Confidential* (1955). Jonathan Munby has suggested, "While some of these [films] use the syndicate milieu as an opportunity to valorize institutions such as the FBI and to demonize unions, most of them take as their central dramatic interest not so much the fight between 'good' and 'bad' institutions, but the fact that nothing (including the judicial system, politics, real estate, the union, and trade) is immune to graft and mob control" (133).

Another event, the so-called Apalachin Conference, contributed to yet another cycle of crime films. The New York State Police raided a meeting of mobsters in Apalachin, New York, on November 14, 1957. Before this incident, the FBI had always refused to admit the existence of a so-called Mafia, emphasizing that most organized crime was on the local, rather than national, level. The raid, along with the gangland murder of Albert Anastasia in 1957, spurred a "retro-gangster" cycle of films that scoured the underworld for pseudohistorical film biographies (with the relaxation of the censorship code, biographies were all right as long as the gangsters were dead). This cycle included *Machine Gun Kelly* (1958), *The Bonnie Parker Story* (1958), *Al Capone* (1959), *Pretty Boy Floyd* (1960), and *The Rise and Fall of Legs Diamond* (1960). The cycle ended in 1967 with Roger Corman's celluloid reenactment of The St. Valentine's Day Massacre, with Jason Robards Jr. as Al Capone. It should also be noted that the interest in retro-gangsterism extended to television during this period: the Quinn-Martin series *The Untouchables*, starring Robert Stack as Eliot Ness, premiered on ABC in 1959 and ran successfully for the next four years.

One legacy of the crime films of the 1950s was that the word "Mafia" became synonymous, in the public sphere, with any type of "organized" criminal activity. The 1960s provided an additional boost to filmic interest in the Mafia, with the testimony of Joseph Valachi before the McClellan Committee in 1963, as well as U.S. Attorney General Robert Kennedy's "war on crime." With the end of the Production Code and the establishment of a new film ratings system in 1968, the crime film—like all other film genres—entered a more graphic era, a liberation that paralleled the violent events and cultural upheavals of the 1960s.

Rural Gangsterism and Rogue Cops: The 1960s

The cataclysmic countercultural movement of the 1960s fueled a growing distrust of the establishment. The assassinations of President John F. Kennedy in 1963 and of Dr. Martin Luther King and Robert F. Kennedy in 1968, along with the violence engendered by the student protest movement, were also emblematic of the social upheaval and unrest of the time. This increasing violence was reflected in the films of the period, particularly of the last part of the decade.

The year 1967 was a watershed for the crime-film genre. Two films were significant because of recent sociocultural developments of the 1960s. Arthur Penn's *Bonnie and Clyde* and John Boorman's *Point Blank* represent, as John Cawelti observes, "a new set of generic constructs more directly related to the imaginative landscape of the second half of the twentieth century" (200). *Bonnie and Clyde*, based loosely on the story of Clyde Barrow and Bonnie Parker, venerated two youthful rural bandits as cult heroes. The advertising slogan for the film read, "They were young, they were in love, they killed people." This advertisement and the film itself targeted a youthful, rebellious audience whose angst and anger at the establishment were reflected in the exploits of the criminal couple. *Point Blank,* starring Lee Marvin as an individualistic antihero named simply Walker, not only initiated a rogue male series of films (particularly rogue cops in films such as *Madigan, Bullitt,* and *Coogan's Bluff*), but it also arguably began the neo-noir cycle that flourished in the 1970s with such films as *Chinatown, The Long Goodbye,* and *The Big Sleep.*

The Godfather and Family

Many of the crime films of the 1970s reflect a growing concern over the disintegration of both the family and society. The Watergate scandal and the Vietnam conflict contributed to this sense of despair. Concern over the rise in urban crime and the ineffectiveness of the police unleashed a number of vigilante films such as *Dirty Harry* (1971), *Walking Tall* (1973), and *Death Wish* (1974). "Neo-noir" became a critical term for a number of films that were a "contemporary rendering of the *noir* sensibility" (Erikson, 321). This "noir sensibility" and the accompanying paranoia and pessimistic view of a corrupt society fit in well with the tenor of the times. Notable among "neo-noirs" were Roman Polanski's *Chinatown* (1974), Arthur Penn's *Night Moves* (1975), and Martin Scorsese's *Taxi Driver* (1976). The legacy of Watergate can also be seen in a number of conspiracy films released during the 1970s, most notably *Executive Action* (1973), *The Conversation* (1974), *The Parallax View* (1974), *Three Days of the Condor* (1975), *The Domino Principle* (1976), and *All the President's Men* (1976).

Two of the most significant crime films of this decade reintroduced the gangster into American film. Francis Ford Coppola's *The Godfather* (1972) and Martin Scorsese's *Mean Streets* (1973) reflect the disintegration of traditional values in a changing society. Based on Mario Puzo's best-selling book, *The Godfather* is an epic gangster saga that traces the history of the Corleone family. Don Corleone (Marlon Brando) is the aging head of the family, and his son Michael (Al Pacino) inherits his mantle. As Carlos Clarens observes, "*The Godfather* is also about the transition from the archaic, relatively honor-bound order of Don Corleone to the more pragmatic and less scrupulous regime of his younger son, who would develop the family business into an impersonal corporation" (278). The film relates the story of the Corleone family and its struggles to stay intact as a criminal organization. Both *The Godfather* and its sequel/prequel, *The Godfather II* are constructed with an epic sweep that chronicles the violent history of a powerful and influential criminal family within a social history of immigration and social aspiration. Both films illustrate the transition from "traditional" culture and values to American culture.

Martin Scorsese's *Mean Streets,* and many of his subsequent crime films, detail the everyday life of the lower echelons of the criminal world. More gritty than Coppola's grandiosely romantic *Godfather* saga, Scorsese's film evokes the life and times of the petty street hoods in New York's Little Italy. In this world, as in the real world, violence erupts suddenly. Criminality in Scorsese's films is a result of the environment, the neighborhood. In *Mean Streets,* Charlie (Harvey Keitel) and his friends often go to see movies at the neighborhood theater, where Scorsese indulges in some reflexivity (and perhaps social commentary) by showing the audience brief clips from violent genres (a western, a horror film, and a gangster film). In many ways Scorsese demystifies the gangster film in such a way that it is a precursor to the contemporary crime film's genre bending and revisionism.

The Modern Crime Film

A major FBI crackdown on organized crime throughout the 1980s resulted in the impris-

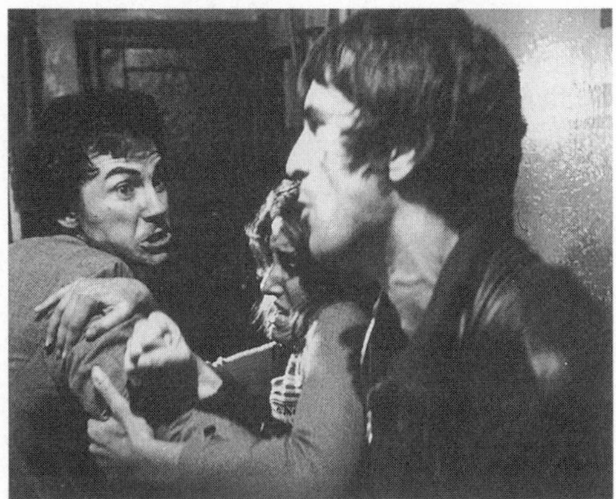

FIGURE 65. *Mean Streets* (1973). Charlie Cappa (Harvey Keitel), angered at Johnny Boy Civello's (Robert De Niro) attitude and inability to take an unpaid loan seriously, spontaneously breaks out into another fight in the hallway of a tenement building, with Cappa's girlfriend Teresa Ronchelli (Amy Robinson) caught in the middle. Martin Scorsese brought a raw and explosive cinematic style to gangsters and Italian family life before the genre took a different stylistic direction. Courtesy Taplin-Perry-Scorsese Productions.

onment of John Gotti on June 23, 1992. Gotti had inherited the mantle of leader of the Gambino mob following Carlo Gambino's death (from natural causes) in 1976. With Gotti and other major Mafia figures gone, a multiethnic succession of organized crime began to assert itself. Many ethnic groups began to forge a loose confederation of organized crime. These include the Dixie Mafia in the South, Latin American gangs in the Southwest, white ethnic groups across the nation, Asian groups in New York and San Francisco, and Italian and Cuban groups. New to this melting pot of organized criminal activity was the Russian Mafia, which was ousted from its native country after the fall of the Soviet Union. Black gangs became more prominent in the 1980s. This multiethnic grouping of organized crime began to surface in motion pictures during the late 1980s and 1990s.

The era saw the debut of several black filmmakers in the crime film genre. Influenced by current events, as well as the increasing popularity of "gangsta rap" music, three key films revitalized the gangster genre within a different sociocultural context: *New Jack City* (1991) directed by Mario Van Peebles; *Menace II Society* (1993), directed by Allen and Albert Hughes; and *Boyz N the Hood* (1991), directed by John Singleton. The streets of America's inner cities were the primary locales for these crime films and their many successors, such as Spike Lee's critically acclaimed *Clockers* (1995), whose roots lay in contemporary life and culture.

The multiculturalism of the crime film can also be seen in several other features during this period: Latino gangsters in *American Me* (1992), directed by Edward James Olmos, and *Mi Vida Loca* (My crazy life) (1994), directed by Allison Anders; the Asian American gangster in Michael Cimino's *Year of the Dragon* (1988); and the Russian Mafia in *Romeo Is Bleeding* (1993), directed by Peter Medak, and *Little Odessa* (1994), directed by James Grey.

The crime genre was also represented on the small screen in American homes during the 1980s and 1990s. Two nonfiction series debuted in 1988: *America's Most Wanted* (Fox) and *Unsolved Mysteries* (NBC). Both series dealt with real-life crimes and criminals and sought the support and advice of a captivated public in apprehending criminals and solving crimes. Likewise, a video-*verité* program entitled *Cops* (Fox), which debuted in 1989, followed police officers and detectives at work. The success of this low-budget series led to popular spin-offs along the same lines, among them *FBI: The Untold Stories* (ABC) and *True Detectives* (CBS). Another interesting and controversial series, which debuted on HBO in January 1999, was *The Sopranos*, a hybrid soap opera and crime drama that centered on a New Jersey Mafia family. The series literally put the mobster "on the couch," seeking psychotherapy for panic attacks, revealing traumatic memories of a father's violent death and family pressures brought on by a domineering mother and challenging adolescent children. The language used in the series mirrored the billingsgate of the early gangster films of the

1930s, providing the audience with a rich lexicon of mobster jargon. Not surprisingly, the series was not without its detractors; several Italian American groups protested (and filed lawsuits) over the ethnic stereotypes depicted in the series. It should be noted that this was also a criticism of the popular 1960s crime series *The Untouchables*—yet audiences were fascinated by the forbidden pleasures of both programs.

During the 1990s a further transformation in the contemporary crime film has made of it an alternative, ideological commentary on the times. Nicole Rafter has labeled this subgenre the "critical crime film," pointing to the absence of a traditional, admirable hero and its pervasive sense of hopelessness. Rafter notes, "Recently, a few innovative filmmakers have rebelled against crime films' tradition of safe critique and sanitized rebellion, developing a critical alternative of alienated, angry movies that subject viewers to harsh realities and refuse to flatter either their characters or their audiences" (11). This group of filmmakers and films include Joel and Ethan Coen's *Miller's Crossing* (1990) and *Fargo* (1996); David Lynch's *Blue Velvet* (1986) and *Lost Highway* (1997); Martin Scorsese's *GoodFellas* (1990) and *Casino* (1995); Quentin Tarantino's *Reservoir Dogs* (1992) and *Pulp Fiction* (1994); and Bryan Singer's *The Usual Suspects* (1995). More recently, Steven Soderberg's *The Limey* (2000), Christopher Nolan's *Memento* (2001), and Scorsese's *Gangs of New York* (2002) explored further permutations along these same lines. The crime film continues to express the dark side of the American dream, challenging filmmakers and audiences alike with stylistic innovations and hyperbolic narrative techniques in its combination of entertainment and sociocultural critique.

References

Filmography

Alias Jimmy Valentine (1915, F)
All Through the Night (1942, F)
American Me (1992, F)
Angels with Dirty Faces (1938, F)
Armored Car Robbery (1950, F)
Asphalt Jungle (1950, F)
Baby Face Nelson (1957, F)
The Big Combo (1955, F)
The Big Heat (1953, F)
Bonnie and Clyde (1967, F)
Boyz N the Hood (1991, F)
Bullets or Ballots (1936, F)
Captive City (1952, F)
Casablanca (1942, F)
Clockers (1995, F)
The Conversation (1974, F)
Dillinger (1945, F)
Donnie Brasco (1997, F)
Double Indemnity (1944, F)
The Enforcer (1951, F)
Gangs of New York (2002, F)
The Glass Key (1944, F)
"G" Man (1935, F)
The Godfather (1972, F)
The Godfather II (1974, F)
GoodFellas (1990, F)
Hoodlum Empire (1952, F)
Inside the White Slave Traffic (1913, F)
Little Caesar (1930, F)
Little Odessa (1994, F)
Mean Streets (1973, F)
Menace II Society (1993, F)
Mi Vida Loca (1994, F)
The Musketeers of Pig Alley (1912, F)
New Jack City (1991, F)
Point Blank (1967, F)
The Postman Always Rings Twice (1946, F)
Public Enemy (1931, F)
Pulp Fiction (1994, F)
The Racket (1951, F)
The Regeneration (1915, F)
Reservoir Dogs (1992, F)
Romeo Is Bleeding (1993, F)
Scarface (1932, F; 1983, F)
711 Ocean Drive (1950)
The St. Valentine's Day Massacre (1967, F)
This Gun for Hire (1942, F)
Underworld (1927, F)
Year of the Dragon (1988, F)

Bibliography

Altman, Rick. *Film/Genre.* London: British Film Institute, 1999.

Asbury, Herbert. *The Gangs of New York.* New York: Knopf, 1928.

Bell, Daniel. *The End of Ideology.* Cambridge, MA: Harvard University Press, 1988.

Bergman, Andrew. *We're in the Money: Depression America and Its Films.* New York: New York University Press, 1971.

Brownlow, Kevin. *Behind the Mask of Innocence: Sex, Violence, Prejudice, Crime Filmsof Social Conscience.* New York: Knopf, 1990.

Cawelti, John G. "*Chinatown* and Generic Transformation in Recent American Films." In Barry Keith Grant, ed., *Film Genre Reader,* 183–201. Austin: University of Texas Press, 1986.

Clarens, Carlos. *Crime Movies: An Illustrated History of the Gangster Genre from D. W. Griffith to Pulp Fiction.* New York: Da Capo, 1997.

Erikson, Tod. "Kill Me Again: Movement Becomes Genre." In Alain Silver and James Ursini, eds., *Film Noir Reader,* 319–323. New York: Limelight Editions, 1996.

Hardy, Phil, ed. *The Overlook Film Encyclopedia: The Gangster Film.* Woodstock, NY: Overlook Press, 1998.

Martin, Richard. *Mean Streets and Raging Bulls: The Legacy of Film Noir in Contemporary American Cinema.* Lanham, MD: Scarecrow, 1997.

McArthur, Colin. *Underworld USA.* London: Secker & Warburg, 1972.

Moore, William Howard. *The Kefauver Committee and the Politics of Crime, 1950–1952.* Columbia: University of Missouri Press, 1974.

Munby, Jonathan. *Public Enemies, Public Heroes: Screening the Gangster from* Little Caesar *to* Touch of Evil. Chicago: University of Chicago Press, 1999.

Neale, Steve. *Genre and Hollywood.* New York: Routledge, 2000.

Peterson, Virgil W. *The Mob: 200 Years of Organized Crime in New York.* Ottawa, IL: Green Hill, 1983.

Pitkin, Thomas Monroe, and Francesco Cordasco. *The Black Hand: A Chapter in Ethnic Crime.* New York: Littlefield, Adams, 1977.

Potter, Claire Bond. *War on Crime: Bandits, G-Men, and the Politics of Mass Culture.* New Brunswick, NJ: Rutgers University Press, 1998.

Powers, Richard Gid. *G-Men: Hoover's FBI in American Popular Culture.* Carbondale: Southern Illinois University Press, 1983.

Rafter, Nicole Hahn. *Shots in the Mirror: Crime Films and Society.* New York: Oxford University Press, 2000.

Ruth, David L. *Inventing the Public Enemy: The Gangster in American Culture, 1918–1934.* Chicago: University of Chicago Press, 1996.

Ryan, Patrick J. *Organized Crime: A Reference Handbook.* Santa Barbara, CA: ABC-CLIO, 1995.

Shadoian, Jack. *Dreams and Deadends: The American Gangster/Crime Film.* Cambridge, MA: MIT Press, 1977.

Sifakis, Carl. *The Encyclopedia of American Crime.* New York: Facts on File, 1982.

Slotkin, Richard. *Gunfighter Nation: The Myth of the Frontier in Twentieth-Century America.* New York: Atheneum, 1992.

Smith, Dwight C. *The Mafia Mystique.* New York: Basic Books, 1975.

Solomon, Stanley J. *Beyond Formula: American Film Genres.* New York: Harcourt, Brace, Jovanovich, 1976.

Warshow, Robert. *The Immediate Experience.* Garden City, NY: Doubleday, 1974.

Yaquinto, Marilyn. *Pump 'Em Full of Lead: A Look at Gangsters on Film.* New York: Twayne, 1998.

[JENNIFER TEBBE-GROSSMAN]

Drugs, Tobacco, and Alcohol

Drugs, tobacco, and alcohol are controversial subjects in American culture, and our records of their use are full of contradictions. Consumers of these products praise their therapeutic effectiveness or their indulgent, naughty, and exuberant qualities; however, the government has exercised increasingly stringent controls. As David Courtwright illustrates in his discerning study *Dark Paradise,* this process began through taxation in the mid-nineteenth century, and with the increased awareness of addiction by the health professions, it moved to regulation on the municipal and state level. In the twentieth century, the criminalization of drug taking developed, owing largely to how American society perceived changes in the populations that indulged in drugs and alcohol—from the respectable upper middle classes in the later nineteenth century to racial and immigrant groups and working-class urban white males who were blamed for addicting the emerging new middle classes engaged in professional careers. The era of narcotics control began with the movement toward such policies as the Harrison Narcotics Act in 1914 and Prohibition—passed in 1920 and then repealed under the Roosevelt administration in 1933. Since the 1960s, public health education, the rise of new therapies and treatment facilities, drug trafficking control, and severe criminal-justice sanctions have prevailed. The control of individual "bad habits" also extended to tobacco consumption. In 1998, a team of state attorneys general negotiated a settlement with the tobacco industry containing agreements on repaying and relieving states of medical costs for smoking-related illnesses, restraining advertising and marketing campaigns to prevent targeting of children and teens, and funding research programs and public-health-education antismoking campaigns. The settlement endorsed future legislative reforms in developing national standards on smoking in public places, substantial new FDA regulation, and comprehensive civil and criminal enforcement procedures.

Although science and medical research led the efforts to fight substance abuse in the late twentieth century, crusades articulating moral and religious values about health and fitness and such disease-related behaviors as drug use, drinking, and smoking are as alive and well at the beginning of the twenty-first century as they were in the temperance eras. In discussing alcohol, the medical sociologist Joseph Gusfield forcefully argues that since the 1980s, "public health attempted to bring alcohol use more fully into the medical frame. These efforts to 'sanitize,' secularize, and objectify the drinking event have had little impact. If the evangelical churches no longer own the public problem of drinking in the United States, the ghost of that ownership still retains its hold in the assumption that the moral life is also the healthy life; that sobriety is virtue and drinking is villainous; that illness is a sign of sin and health the reward of virtue" (223–224).

Historians of American film argue that motion pictures instruct as well as entertain. Film narratives and visual images influence Americans in their views about when consumption is socially acceptable and when it is addiction. Not surprisingly, Hollywood films portray our national ambivalence by providing audiences with conflicting messages about appropriate responses to the consumption of drugs, alcohol, and tobacco. These range from the nightmarish depiction of alcoholism with James Cagney in *Come Fill the Cup* (1951) and Susan Hayward in *I'll Cry Tomorrow* (1955) to the tacit approval of drug-taking behavior with emerging young stars of the 1980s in *Fast Times at Ridgemont High* (1982) and The *Breakfast Club* (1985).

Alcohol

In Hollywood's nickelodeon and silent films, filmmakers entertained with melodramatic stories often taken from sensationalist newspaper headlines, introducing subjects of medicine and public health to large popular audiences. Alcoholism, the saloon, and the dangers they presented to the American family were frequent subjects, allowing filmmakers to explore seamier human needs and desires, arouse audience emotions and yet still please temperance crusaders (and potential censors). Whether in such films as *The Drunkard's Fate* (1909), promoted by Selig Films as a temperance lesson, or *The Weaker Mind* (1913), which introduced hereditary factors in an era rife with racial theories, alcoholism was a popular subject for melodrama.

In the 1920s and early 1930s, despite the Motion Picture Producers and Distributors Association's (MPPDA) edicts on depicting drinking on the screen, many films portrayed alcohol consumption not as a questionable pastime, but as an intimate everyday activity for sophisticated Americans. Still, that liquor was harmful to family values was made clear in classic films such as Charlie Chaplin's *City Lights* (1931) and D. W. Griffith's *The Struggle* (1931).

In the 1930s, as Prohibition was repealed, Alcoholics Anonymous was formed, and many government councils were established to study the problems of alcoholism. Hollywood continued to present conflicting images of drink throughout the era of the Great Depression. There were popular wealthy sophisticates, personified by Nick and Nora Charles in *The Thin Man* (1934), who seemed to quaff champagne and cocktails morning to night, or the weakling alcoholic as seen in *A Star Is Born* (1937), which tells the story of a woman who struggles her way to the top of Hollywood stardom only to lose her former leading man to drink. *A Star Is Born* reflected growing concerns about the offscreen behavior of Hollywood denizens. Two years later, John Ford's western *Stagecoach* (1939) portrayed what was to become a stereotypical figure often played for "comic relief"—an alcoholic doctor who only sobers up to perform a lifesaving operation. *The Philadelphia Story* (1940) portrays wealthy socialites Tracy Lord (Katharine Hepburn) and C. K. Dexter Haven (Cary Grant) who break up because of Dexter's alcoholism and ironically reconcile when he forsakes alcohol just as the haughty Tracy discovers champagne's sparkle. The Arts & Entertainment Network documentary *Prohibition: 13 Years That Changed America* (1997) examines how Americans developed this love-hate relationship with alcohol, attributing the problem to religion, family values, corruption, racial prejudice and immigrant intolerance, and social and political reform efforts.

The classic "social problem" film *The Lost Weekend* (1945), directed by Billy Wilder, exhibits the distinction between using and abusing alcohol that developed in American society after the repeal of Prohibition. Ray Milland plays Don Birnam, a writer who succumbs to his self-destructive love of liquor as he pursues his lonesome quest for drink from one bleak bar and liquor store to the next. Milland's character Birnam is representative of a wave of post–World War II Hollywood films that focused on a middle-class character's struggle with drink. The film's denouement has Birnam grinding out a cigarette in his whiskey glass, symbolizing that he will recover by writing an autobiography of his addiction and reform. *The Lost Weekend* was the first of a series of films about alcoholics that earned Academy Awards for their male stars.

Films about alcohol in the second half of the twentieth century continued to give audiences the socially acceptable drunk who makes them laugh. Well received by critics, the wealthy misfit characters played by Jimmy Stewart in *Harvey* (1950) and Dudley Moore in *Arthur* (1981) connect their drinking to personal liberation and lovability, and they come to happy endings—which do not include such real-life consequences as liver failure, stroke, or fatal car accidents, nor do they require that Elwood P. Dowd or Arthur give up their bubbly.

The commercially and critically successful *Days of Wine and Roses* (1962) considered the impact of alcoholism on a middle-class family: a husband (Jack Lemmon) and wife (Lee Remick) who fall victim to "social drinking." Lemmon is saved when he joins Alcoholics Anonymous, while Remick, less lucky, finds refuge in a squalid hotel room on skid row. The film depicts a growing public awareness of successful recovery from alcohol addiction outside of the "self-control" paradigm in its focus on the AA program. Both Lemmon and Remick received Academy Award nominations, and Henry Mancini and Johnny Mercer won an Academy Award for best song with their haunting theme "Days of Wine and Roses."

Despite health policy shifts in the immediate post–World War II years, which identified alcoholism as a "medical condition" (and funded research and treatment programs), films about alcoholism in the 1970s and 1980s returned to a focus that emphasizes a moralism of self-control. In *The Verdict* (1982) Frank Galvin (Paul Newman) may be a drunk who has destroyed his family and career, but he regains much of his dignity by being a good lawyer for a working-class family. In *Tender Mercies* (1983), alcoholic songwriter Mac Sledge (Robert Duvall) appears to recover his talent, reject his past with an alcoholic country singer ex-wife, and find sobriety, redemption, and family values in the home of a Christian woman (Tess Harper). Both Newman and Duvall received Academy Award nominations for their performances. Few women were given alcoholic roles in this period, although Jane Fonda received critical acclaim in the thriller *The Morning After* (1987), in which she plays a failed alcoholic actress who lays claim to a better life free of alcohol with the help of a former cop (Jeff Bridges) who has also renounced his drinking past.

FIGURE 66. *The Lost Weekend* (1945). Don Birman (Ray Milland) defined for decades the image of the isolated, lonely alcoholic falling tragically from the middle class. Courtesy Paramount Pictures.

In the decade of the 1990s, with the increasing prominence of the health and fitness movement and the formation of such advocacy groups as Mothers Against Drunk Driving (MADD), alcohol regulation took on even greater moral resonance. The most critically acclaimed "alcoholic" film of this decade is *Leaving Las Vegas* (1995), based on John O'Brien's novel of the same name. The film follows Ben (Nicholas Cage), a screenwriter who loses his family and job in Los Angeles and departs for the palaces of consumption culture in Las Vegas, planning to drink and die. There are no upright loved ones who try to save him from his demons, only a prostitute,

Sera (Elizabeth Shue), who grants unconditional love and acquiesces in his request that "you can never, never ask me to stop drinking." Unlike earlier treatments, *Leaving Las Vegas* keeps the harsh realities of alcoholism in focus: the vomiting, seizures, rages, public scenes, and steady deterioration. The film identifies Ben and Sera as the ultimate social deviants—there are no appeals for self-control or medical treatment solutions. There is no *Lost Weekend*-style happy ending. Elizabeth Shue received a nomination and Nicholas Cage won an Academy Award for their performances. The popular actress Sandra Bullock received no such accolades for her work in the recovery tale *28 Days* (2000), which pictures alcoholism as an alternately madcap and depressive experience, and which audiences did not rush to see.

Drugs

Drug laws such as the Harrison Narcotics Act of 1914 were a social expression of not only the need for stronger government regulation of opiates, cocaine, and heroin, but also increased concern about "criminal" segments in our society. Americans blamed "foreigners"—the Chinese for opium, the Mexicans for marijuana, and American blacks for cocaine—when they began to criminalize drugs. They also constructed a new class of drug user, the "social deviant," a young, lower-class, urban male who mostly obtained the drugs from new immigrants or black Americans and used drugs "for kicks." This new group's drug use led to criminal activity. Eric Schaefer argues that "drug films" did not portray the plight of this underclass drug user. Rather, in such films as *The Drug Traffic* (1923) and *Human Wreckage* (1923) they consistently focused on the tragedies of younger middle-class Americans, particularly the new young overworked professionals—especially physicians or lawyers—who become addicted to and then socially marginalized in the world of "drug-pushers."

In *Modern Times* (1936), one of the few films with a major filmmaker and star to satirize drugs, Charlie Chaplin's Little Tramp mistakes cocaine for sugar and loads it onto his bowl of cereal. The scene is played for laughs: Charlie's humble character becomes a lion of courage and, under the influence of the "sweetener," saves prison officials from being taken hostage during an escape attempt. Nonetheless, as American films became more popular with middle-class audiences, major studios increasingly avoided drug themes—especially after drug-abuse scandals involving Hollywood stars in the 1920s.

"Exploitation" drug films on the other hand, played from the 1930s through the early 1950s, often as midnight features. *Reefer Madness* (1936, also known under the titles *Tell Your Children, The Burning Question, Doped Youth,* and *Love Madness*) promoted the moral dangers of marijuana to America's youth. Although it did not receive Motion Picture Code approval, like other exploitation films, it reflected the values of federal narcotics officials. It depicted ordinary high school students who, enticed to smoke marijuana, are forced down a path of prostitution, attempted rape, murder, incarceration, and suicide. Rediscovered in the early 1970s, it attained status as a drug film cult classic when it was redistributed as part of a fund raising effort for (the pro-marijuana) National Organization for the Reform of Marijuana Law (NORML). *Reefer Madness* played widely on college campuses and in commercial movie theaters—to the raucous laughter of college students who rejected its sermonic messages.

The Man with the Golden Arm (1955), a commercial success directed by Otto Preminger and featuring Frank Sinatra and Kim Novak, was released without a Production Code seal of approval. Adapted from Nelson Algren's novel, the film dealt openly with the "social problem" of heroin addiction. Franky Machine (Sinatra) is released from prison and a drug rehabilitation program. He returns to his old world of nightclubs and gambling and is portrayed sympathetically as a victim of environmental circumstances, a deranged wife, and dishonest friends. The supportive nightclub hostess Molly (Novak) stands by Franky during dramatic bouts of withdrawal, and in the end, Franky and Molly walk away together. The film affirms the new faith in professional rehabilitation, lifestyle change, and honest love. By the end of the 1950s, the Production Code allowed a broader treatment of drug behaviors and more major motion picture studio drug films followed.

In the 1960s, there was a significant increase in the use of marijuana, LSD, and heroin by inner-city minorities, returning Vietnam veterans, and—in large numbers—the white middle-class baby boomers in rebellion. A number of Hollywood low-budget films about drugs were produced by the middle of the decade, such as *The Trip* (1967) directed by Roger Corman, scripted by Jack Nicholson, and starring Peter Fonda as Paul, a TV-commercial producer undertaking a personal journey with the drug LSD. Seth Cagin and Philip Dray note the exploitative "cheesiness of the production," but also point out an important element related to a number of films of the time: *The Trip* "documents LSD as an agent of social change. Within the film, on an individual level, Paul undergoes a catharsis and learns how to love. Allegorically and socially, this matches the impact of acid on the generation of alienated rebels it transformed into hippies" (60–61).

Easy Rider (1969), made for just over $500,000, was written, acted, produced, and directed by Fonda and Dennis Hopper, who made back their production costs in the first few days of distribution. The film has since grossed over $60 million worldwide and, as Peter Biskind notes, is the first major motion picture of the 1960s that "defined a sensibility, opened Hollywood to the counterculture" (75). Drug use is central to the film, and some critics argue that audiences interpreted this use

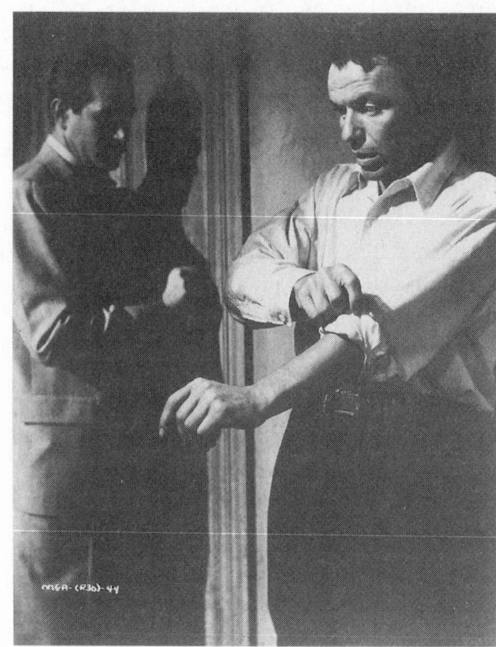

FIGURE 67. *The Man with the Golden Arm* (1955). Frankie Machine (Frank Sinatra) gave the heroin addict a starry eye and haunting look, winning him an Academy Award for best actor. Otto Preminger's film was released without scrutiny by the Hays Office and the Production Code approval seal. But by affirming the benefits of drug rehabilitation and showing faith in the perseverance of the human spirit, the film helped loosen Production Code restrictions. Courtesy Carlyle Productions.

and the heroes' quest as a political statement about freedom. Other critics have said that the film sent an ambivalent message, especially citing the soundtrack, which included rock and roll lyrics condemning "the pusher," and many sequences that questioned the entire "drug scene" and pointed to its casualties. Near the end of the film, Captain America (Fonda) concedes that "we blew it"—a statement some critics interpreted as a condemnation of the drug culture lifestyle, though others thought it referred to the main characters' attempts to make a profit from drugs rather than share them freely.

The 1970s and early 1980s maintained conflicting representations of drug use in films. *The French Connection* (1971), loosely adapted from a book by Robin Moore, was set in New York City and won several Academy Awards for depicting the largest police seizure of pure heroin from drug smugglers at the time. Gene Hackman's portrayal of a tough, brutal narcotics cop, "Popeye" Doyle, was a box-office success. *The French Connection* established a genre of films that attempted to dramatize the workings and effects of the drug trade, from stories about Columbia drug cartels to smaller examinations of the lives of drug dealers and drug takers in urban and suburban communities.

Cheech and Chong's *Up in Smoke,* a box-office windfall in 1978, was representative of films playing drug use and users for big laughs, as was that year's *Animal House,* which put in a good word for alcohol and tobacco as well. Other early 1980s films such as *The Big Chill* (1983) and *The Breakfast Club* (1985) led audiences to believe that smoking a little marijuana allowed middle-class Americans to open up their personal feelings to one another—without leading to addiction or more intense drug use. However, later films of the 1980s such as *Clean and Sober* (1988) and *Drugstore Cowboy* (1989) were produced during the era of the "Just Say No" and "War on Drugs" campaigns, and they returned to the themes of drug use as a threat to middle-class vitality and morality. The lead characters in these two films (Michael Keaton and Matt Dillon, respectively) successfully fight their addictions; their loved ones or accomplices in drug-taking behaviors do not. Rehabilitation programs and treatment facilities play an important role in recovery, presenting realistic images of the difficulties encountered on a long road to life without addiction.

In the 1990s, statistics from the Substance Abuse and Mental Health Services Administration showed that drug use was still a part of American culture. Marijuana use, while rising, was half of what it was in 1979. Cocaine use had leveled, but heroin use was on the rise with first-time users. Health scholars note more acceptance of drugs, especially among younger Americans. Government policy seems unclear: judges provide harsh sentences for possession of small amounts of marijuana; public-health funding is freely spent on television commercials and school programs aimed at preventing drug abuse and sending messages of health fitness; and yet, voters in some states approve marijuana use for what is labeled "medicinal purposes."

Hollywood has reflected these tensions in American society with a resurgence of films, including seemingly nostalgic homages to the 1970s or early 1980s: *Fear and Loathing in Las Vegas* (1998), *The Last Days of Disco* (1998), *Studio 54* (1998), and *Blow* (2001). Other films, such as *Prozac Nation* (2003), based on Elizabeth Wurzel's best-selling 1997 memoir, and Catherine Hardwicke's *Thirteen* (2003), immersed audiences in the darker world of drug addiction by showing the destructive effects of prescription- and illicit-drug use among adolescents and young adults. Some films revisited the theme of the talented artist on drugs: the writer in *Permanent Midnight* (1998), the photographer in *High Art* (1998), and the singer in *Why Do Fools Fall in Love?* (1998). Some, including *Illtown* (1997), *Another Day in Paradise* (1999), and *Narc* (2002), explore the violent nightmare of drug dealing. And some, such as *PCU* (1994) and *Half Baked* (1998), return to the Cheech and Chong sensibility, portraying drugs as good clean fun.

In the 1990s, significant documentary films addressed drugs in a historical context, including *Berkeley in the Sixties* (1990) and *Breaking Boundaries, Testing Limits* (1991). They focused on the decade of the 1960s, stressing that advocates of a "drug culture" should be seen in a separate context from political reform efforts whether from the right or left. Other documentaries, particularly *The Hemp Revolution* (1995), blamed Hollywood for demonizing marijuana—arguing that marijuana should be seen in the context of the role hemp has played in American history and environmental and health reform—George Washington and others grew it, for instance, as a product for medicinal use and a source of fuel, oil, food, and fiber. The broadest historical overview of illegal drugs, attempting a span from ancient times to the present, can be found in a four-part series produced by the History Channel, *Hooked: The History of Illegal Drugs* (2000). The series examines opiates, cocaine, amphetamines and barbiturates, marijuana, LSD, ecstasy, and so-called smart drugs. Bruce Sinofsky's documentary *Hollywood High* (2002), made for the American Movie Classics cable network, is particularly acute in its analysis of Hollywood "drug movies" from *Reefer Madness* (1936) to *Requiem for a Dream* (2000). It offers thoughtful commentary on themes from drug movies by many of those associated with their production—directors, actors, and screenwriters.

Tobacco

The 1998 tobacco settlement illustrated that the state has a responsibility for addressing the problems of tobacco addiction. At the same time, Allan Brandt, a medical historian, successfully argues that "the emphasis on personal responsibility for risk taking and disease has come at the very moment when cigarette smoking is increasingly stratified by education, social class, and race" (503). Both of these perspectives can be seen in recent motion pictures, and the debate can also be reflected in earlier twentieth-century films. Perhaps no other commodity has caused such an outcry as the prevalence of cigarettes and cigars in major motion pictures. Mass-market tobacco advertising in the early twentieth century featured celebrities promoting smoking as a democratic, indulgent, and pleasurable behavior that was easily accessible to all.

Innumerable films of the 1940s, but especially *Casablanca* (1942) and *Now, Voyager* (1942), provided indelible images of smoking. As Richard Klein emphasizes in *Cigarettes Are Sublime,* Rick, in *Casablanca,* establishes the archetypal heroic male lead: "The Humphrey Bogart cigarette, held between thumb and index, allows the tough guy to smoke and to show his knuckles." In nearly every World War II film, the cigarette is "the soldier's friend" (175–176), and women enjoy them too. In the Bette Davis "tear-jerker," *Now, Voyager,* for instance, a dowdy daughter rejects her strict upbringing and a mentally unstable diagnosis. Together with a new fashionable attire and drinking habit, smoking symbolizes the transformation Davis's character undergoes in rebelling against a domineering mother. In the closing scene, Davis and her newfound beloved seal their declaration of undying (and unrequited) love by sharing a cigarette.

By the 1970s, with the release of the Surgeon General's Report on the health risks of cigarette smoking in 1964 and the successes of the antismoking advocacy organizations in stigmatizing the cigarette smoker, smoking by lead characters in American films had significantly decreased. With Norman Lear directing, Dick Van Dyke and Bob Newhart were featured in the comedy *Cold Turkey* (1971), about an entire town trying to quit smoking as part of a contest with public-health-education messages. In the 1990s, despite publicly funded antismoking advertising campaigns primarily directed at teenagers, the cigarette as an icon returned, with a major character seen smoking in more that half of the movies released between 1990 and 1995. The updated, romantic, noirish murder mysteries *Dead Again* (1991) and *Basic Instinct* (1992) deliberately link cigarette smoking—especially efforts to quit by the major male protagonist—to plot themes connecting power and intimacy. Although few motion pictures of the 1990s have featured smoking as the subject of the film, *Smoke* (1995) and its sequel *Blue in the Face* (1995) made men with their tobacco, including the cigar, the center of attraction: Harvey Keitel and the male patrons of his smoke shop brood about the connection between smoking and the soul. The young, "hip" characters of *200*

Cigarettes (1999), including Ben Affleck and Christina Ricci, wander around the East Village in New York City on New Year's Eve, looking for love and sex, with cigarettes featured prominently as a connective plot device. And when someone like Julia Roberts (as a beguiling food critic in *My Best Friend's Wedding* [1997]), Will Smith and Jeff Goldblum (heroes who save earth from aliens in *Independence Day* [1996]), or Gene Hackman (the woebegone patriarch of *The Royal Tenenbaums* [2001]) lights up, advocacy groups and former first lady Hilary Clinton have been quick to protest the increasing "glamorization" of smoking in films and television. While stopping short of supporting censorship, they have urged legislators to caution filmmakers about "placing" tobacco products. Two contemporary documentaries address the issues of Hollywood celebrities and smoking: *Dying for a Smoke* (1994) features film stars as advocates who favor or oppose tobacco interests, while *Smoke That Cigarette* (1995) decries glamorizing smoking in movies and television.

Robert Zemeckis on Smoking, Drinking and Drugging in the 20th Century: In Pursuit of Happiness (1999) is part of a series featuring documentary film in which celebrated Hollywood directors were commissioned to look at issues around the millennium. Zemeckis's documentary uses rapid juxtaposition of commentary from experts (with specific contributions from historians) and clips from films—from the silent era to the present—as well as other mass-media documents. Zemeckis relies heavily on his own film to illustrate arguments about the addictive impulse, including *Romancing the Stone* (1984) and *Who Framed Roger Rabbit?* (1988). The film is especially good in portraying contrasting images of the glamorization of cigarettes and alcohol with images of the stigmatization and criminalization associated with cocaine, marijuana, and opiates. Zemeckis makes it clear that an awareness of social class, race, and ethnicity as complex factors must be addressed in any viewing of how Hollywood portrays addictive substances.

References

Filmography

Animal House (1978, F)
Another Day in Paradise (1999, F)
Armistead Maupin's "More Tales" (1998, TV)
Armistead Maupin's "Tales of the City" (1994, TV)
Arthur (1981, F)
Barbarians at the Gate (1993, TV)
Basic Instinct (1992, F)
Berkeley in the Sixties (1990, D)
The Big Chill (1983, F)
Blow (2001, F)
Blue in the Face (1995, F)
The Breakfast Club (1985, F)
Breaking Boundaries, Testing Limits (1991, D)
Bright Leaf (1950, F)
Bright Lights, Big City (1988, F)
Casablanca (1942, F)
City Lights (1931, F)
Clean and Sober (1988, F)
Cold Turkey (1971, F)
Come Fill the Cup (1951, F)
The Country Girl (1954, F)
Days of Wine and Roses (1962, F)
Dead Again (1991, F)
Drugstore Cowboy (1989, F)
The Drug Traffic (1923, F)
The Drunkard's Fate (1909, F)
Dying for a Smoke (1994, D)
Easy Money (1983, F)
Easy Rider (1969, F)
Fast Times at Ridgemont High (1982, F)
Fear and Loathing in Las Vegas (1998, F)
The French Connection (1971, F)
Half Baked (1998, F)
Harvey (1950, F)
A Hatful of Rain (1957, F)
The Hemp Revolution (1995, D)
High Art (1998, F)
Hollywood High (2002, TV)
Human Wreckage (1923, F)
I'll Cry Tomorrow (1955, F)
Illtown (1997, F)
I'm Dancing as Fast as I Can (1982, F)
The Insider (1999, F)
The Last Days of Disco (1998, F)

Leaving Las Vegas (1995, F)
Less Than Zero (1987, F)
The Lost Weekend (1945, F)
The Man with the Golden Arm (1955, F)
Midnight Express (1978, F)
Modern Times (1936, F)
The Morning After (1987, F)
My Best Friend's Wedding (1997, F)
My Name Is William W. (1989, TV)
Narc (2002, F)
Now, Voyager (1942, F)
Parrish (1961, F)
PCU (1994, F)
Permanent Midnight (1998, F)
The Philadelphia Story (1940, F)
Postcards from the Edge (1990, F)
Prohibition: 13 Years That Changed America (1997, D)
Prozac Nation (2003, F)
Reefer Madness (1936, F)
Requiem for a Dream (2000, F)
Robert Zemeckis on Smoking, Drinking and Drugging in the 20th Century: In Pursuit of Happiness (1999, D)
Romancing the Stone (1984, F)
The Rose (1979, F)
The Royal Tenenbaums (2001, F)
Rush (1991, F)
Sid and Nancy (1986, F)
Smoke (1995, F)
Smoke That Cigarette (1995, D)
Stagecoach (1939, F)
A Star Is Born (1937, F)
The Struggle (1931, F)
Studio 54 (1998, F)
Tender Mercies (1983, F)
The Thin Man (1934, F)
Thirteen (2003, F)
The Trip (1967, F)
28 Days (2000, F)
200 Cigarettes (1999,F)
Up in Smoke (1978, F)
The Verdict (1982, F)
The Weaker Mind (1913, F)
Where the Buffalo Roam (1980, F)
Who Framed Roger Rabbit? (1988, F)
Why Do Fools Fall in Love? (1998, F)
A Woman Under the Influence (1974, F)

Bibliography

Biskind, Peter. *Easy Riders, Raging Bulls: How the Sex-Drugs-and-Rock 'n' Roll Generation Saved Hollywood.* New York: Simon & Schuster, 1998.

Brandt, Allan M. "The Cigarette, Risk, and American Culture." In Judith Leavitt and Ronald Numbers, eds., *Sickness and Health in America: Readings in the History of Medicine and Public Health,* 494–505. Madison: University of Wisconsin Press, 1997.

Cagin, Seth, and Philip Dray. *Hollywood Films of the Seventies: Sex, Drugs, Rock 'n' Roll, and Politics.* New York: Harper & Row, 1984.

Courtwright, David T. *Dark Paradise: Opiate Addiction in America Before 1940.* Cambridge, MA: Harvard University Press, 1982.

Denzin, Norman K. *Hollywood Shot by Shot: Alcoholism in American Cinema.* New York: Aldine de Gruyter, 1991.

Gusfield, Joseph R. "Alcohol in America: The Entangled Frames of Health and Morality." In Allan M. Brandt and Paul Rozin, eds., *Morality and Health,* 220–229. New York: Routledge, 1997.

Klein, Richard. *Cigarettes Are Sublime.* Durham, NC: Duke University Press, 1993.

Kluger, Richard. *Ashes to Ashes: America's Hundred-Year Cigarette War, the Public Health, and the Unabashed Triumph of Philip Morris.* New York: Knopf, 1997.

Musto, David F., ed. *Drugs in America: A Documentary History.* New York: New York University Press, 2002.

Peiss, Kathy. *Cheap Amusements: Working Women and Leisure in Turn-of-the Century New York.* Philadelphia: Temple University Press, 1986.

Schaefer, Eric. *Bold! Daring! Shocking! True! A History of Exploitation Films, 1919–1959.* Durham, NC: Duke University Press, 1999.

Sloan, Kay. *The Loud Silents: Origins of the Social Problem Film.* Urbana: University of Illinois Press, 1988.

Starks, Michael. *Cocaine Fiends and Reefer Madness: An Illustrated History of Drugs in the Movies.* New York: Cornwall, 1982.

Stevens, Jay. *Storming Heaven: LSD and the American Dream.* New York: Harper & Row, 1987.

Sullum, Jacob. *For Your Own Good: The Anti-Smoking Crusade and the Tyranny of Public Health.* New York: Free Press, 1998.

[ANTHONY CHASE]

Elections and Party Politics

In one of the earliest motion pictures dealing with elections and the American political process, the silent film *Going to Congress* (1924), Will Rogers plays a naive backcountry politician who is given sound advice by a local cobbler: "If you see a man coming with a black bag, either shoot him or resign before he can get to you." Because the film was made just after the Teapot Dome scandal of 1923, newspaper reports of which made famous reference to "a little black bag," film audiences no doubt recognized the same reference from *Going to Congress.* "What is a government trust between friends," asked Will Rogers, according to biographer Donald Day, "especially if there is a little black bag with enough money in it?" (140).

From Harding and Teapot Dome to Nixon election-campaign scandals, during which self-designated "bag man" Anthony Ulasewicz testified to capers that Watergate historian Stanley Kutler suggests might have been scripted by Damon Runyon, corruption and chicanery have run like a red thread through both American political history and its reflection on the silver screen. In Tim Robbins's black comedy *Bob Roberts* (1992), an underground newspaper reporter, referring to Frank Capra's best-known political film, claims that "there are no Mr. Smiths in Washington. Mr. Smith has been bought. Just a bunch of deal makers."

But that is not all there is to either the history or the films. On the contrary, motion pictures have often provided a rather subtle and sophisticated reflection upon the contradictions of political aspiration in the United States. Themes as old as those explored by the master of Renaissance political philosophy, Niccolo Machiavelli—such as the relation between ends and means, virtue and power—have often helped shape a dramatic tension at the heart of films capable of both riveting contemporary audiences, as well as, in retrospect, telling us something important about the national experience. Lord Acton said it: power tends to corrupt and absolute power corrupts absolutely. But just how much in the real world can actually be accomplished by those who are outside the circle of power—or who simply stand aside?

Sympathy for the Devil

The Reader's Companion to American History (1991) logically surveys the development of American party politics chronologically, beginning with 1789, and provides a capsule summary of every presidential election since the Federalists and Republicans first squared off. Similarly, the opening credit sequence for Franklin Schaffner's film of Gore Vidal's *The Best Man* (1964) includes portraits or photographs, in proper historical sequence, of every American president from George Washington to Lyndon Johnson. That represents a tough way to survey movies about U.S. elections, however; motion-picture political history generally begins around the Civil War and takes place mostly after World War I.

Two books quite useful for thinking through political films, *Hollywood as Historian* (1998) and *Reel Politics* (1987), are organized around when the films chronicled were themselves made and how they reflect on their own time. But films specifically dealing with elections and party politics seem to reveal a consistent set of themes that cut across boundaries of time and place, current policy controversy or particular debating points. We may not remember much today about the crisis over Quemoy and Matsu, but film of the famous Nixon-Kennedy TV debates will be shown again every election season as long as television has a political impact. So the films reviewed here are categorized generically as classical Hollywood dramas, new realist cinema, and objective documentaries, with thematic structure given pride of place.

Another, perhaps more comfortable, name for "deal making" is "compromise." In an imperfect world, the party politician is confronted with the necessity of compromise, giving something up to get something in return. The difference between an astute political bargain and an illegal bribe can make all the difference in the world. How the deal is characterized and what it makes of those it touches is often the central issue in the classical Hollywood drama of party campaigns and popular elections.

There are those who play the game and those who refuse, those who are willing to risk compromise and those who are not. Broderick Crawford won an Academy Award for his performance as Willie Stark in Robert Rossen's *All the King's Men* (1949), based on the Robert Penn Warren novel about the thinly disguised Louisiana governor, Huey Long. Crawford's Stark is the premier example in film of a politician who makes a pact with the devil and, while rising to high office, eventually is destroyed. Having begun as a man of the people, power eventually becomes for Stark an end in itself, and his assassination seems fated. So does Richard Nixon's fall in a host of films, including *All the President's Men* (1976), *Secret Honor* (1984), and *Nixon* (1995). Different from both the populist Stark and the paranoid Nixon, progressive if "blandly selfish" young politico Joe Tynan (Alan Alda), in *The Seduction of Joe Tynan* (1979), is also taken in by the promise of power—and pays a heavy price in the loss of his family's love and trust.

Art of the Possible?

It is not the case, however, that resisting the temptation to wheel and deal represents a standard cinematic prescription for good (or effective) government. Early on, in the Darryl F. Zanuck–produced biopic *Wilson* (1944), Princeton University's president enters politics on a high note, refusing to bargain with an entrenched "New Jersey boss system." But high-minded principles are not enough, by themselves, to get the job done. By the end of the film, Wilson is forced to leave office without achieving his main reform, the League of Nations, owing to stiff opposition from a phalanx of jacks-in-office with more clout than all the New Jersey kingpins combined: the U.S. Congress.

In Frank Capra's *State of the Union* (1948), Grant Matthews (Spencer Tracy) is a successful American entrepreneur who has a brief fling with politics, mainly just to "show 'em how it's done." Like Warren Beatty in *Bulworth* (1998)—or Ross Perot in his quixotic third-party machinations—he shoots from the hip and tells it like it is, whether the voters like it or not. But Matthews's simple message starts to catch on, and he thus (inevitably) falls into the hands of spin doctors who start making him into a serious, and increasingly conventional, presidential candidate. In the nick of time, and with moral prodding from his idealistic wife, played by Katharine Hepburn, Matthews denounces politics as corrupt and corrupting and throws in the towel. Matthews's self-respect remains intact, but what about the country? With what sort of choice do the voters end up?

William Russell (Henry Fonda), in *The Best Man,* declines to use bogus evidence of homosexual conduct against a political opponent and thus preserves his personal integrity but, at the same time, ends his political career. Fonda is perfectly cast as the dryly circumspect

FIGURE 68. *State of the Union* (1948). Millionaire republican presidential candidate Grant Matthews (Spencer Tracy), separated from Mary Matthews, his wife (Katharine Hepburn) requests she return to his side to help his campaign image. She does and recognizes the abandonment of the values he stood for at the start of the campaign, convincing him to announce on a radio broadcast his withdrawal from the election. Courtesy Liberty Films.

intellectual who, in the end, does not have the stomach for old-fashioned political infighting. Like Grant Matthews in *State of the Union,* he, too, opts for a decent private life and walks away from politics. Another Tracy character, based upon Boston's infamous Mayor Curley in John Ford's *The Last Hurrah* (1958), has plenty of stomach for machine politics and ward heeling, but he is unwilling to compromise with either the Yankee aristocrats and bankers who really run the city or the slick Madison Avenue campaign style their candidate employs. Instead of throwing in the towel, this time Tracy, his honor the mayor, is thrown out of office.

The Last Hurrah's scenes of despondent campaign workers, cronies, and ward bosses staring defeat in the face are reminiscent of the newsroom calamity confronted by Charley Kane's outfit as the votes tally up in Orson Welles's legendary *Citizen Kane* (1941). The headline "Kane Elected" is replaced by one that reads "Fraud at Polls!" across page one of Kane-owned papers. Refusing to deal with Boss Jim Geddes, and ignoring pleas from his own wife, Kane must soon deal with his own private life's being exposed to public view. "Caught in love nest" with a "singer," the William Randolph Hearst–based character (played by Welles himself) is, overnight, like Tracy's Irish bellwether, out of politics. Even Kane's fate is not as grim as that of Gary Cooper's Long John Willoughby in Frank Capra's *Meet John Doe* (1941). Willoughby/John Doe is a well-intentioned hobo who gets sucked into a complex political conspiracy engineered by D. B. Norton, a protofascist businessman who uses Willoughby to front a deceptively attractive people's party then dispenses with the chump once Willoughby starts to figure things out. Except for the fact that "you just can't kill Gary Cooper," the movie's forlorn hero, rejected and himself disillusioned, probably would have committed suicide on Christmas Day by jumping off city hall. In end the, Capra opted for a more ambiguous finale to the picture.

Film critic Andrew Sarris, Capra biographer Joseph McBride, and political analyst Brian Neve all point to a similarity between some of the political values propagated by Capra's populist films and the very ideologies he seeks to target. "There seems to be no role," argues Neve, "for an authentic politics in [*Meet John Doe*], apart from the moralistic 'John Doe' clubs, which seem so dependent on their leader that they are hardly distinguishable from the threatening totalitarianism of the Norton junta" (50–51). Part of Neve's observation can be applied to nearly all of the films discussed here. Within the classical Hollywood drama of elections and parties, across the decades, whether protagonists are destroyed by deal making (or their inability to control its consequences) or are conversely rendered superfluous by a refusal to even be tainted by compromise, an authentic politics appears genuinely impossible, nothing more than pipedream. It is hard to avoid the conclusion that a deep suspicion of politics and politicians remains a profound sentiment reflected in American film and, perhaps inescapably, American political history as well.

Railsplitter Statesman

Now, there are exceptions—films which look at politics differently and thus structure their dilemmas at an angle to the dominant form. Gore Vidal wrote the screenplay for *The Best Man,* is cast as a liberal senator in *Bob Roberts,* and wrote an important novel about Abraham Lincoln, which provides the basis for Lamont Johnson's film *Lincoln* (1993). John Travolta's Governor Stanton, in Mike Nichols's *Primary Colors* (1998), cynically asks his aide, Henry, "Don't you think Abe Lincoln was a whore before he became President?" What is remarkable about *Lincoln* is that it neither portrays the railsplitter as a saint (see John Ford's wonderful *Young Mr. Lincoln*) nor debunks the Lincoln myth, but rather does what so few classical Hollywood dramas even seem able to imagine: It shows a real-world politician with a confident grasp of the relation between ends and means. Rejecting advice to "let the errant sisters go," Lincoln argues that a house divided against itself cannot stand and solemnly pledges to keep the Southern states in the Union. His refusal to compromise leads him not *out* of politics but *into* war, that is, politics by other means, in von Clausewitz's famous formulation. Resolving fierce conflicts between North and South, Republicans and Democrats, abolitionists and their opponents within his own party, indeed within his cabinet, instead of tearing Lincoln apart makes him a better, stronger leader.

"Gentlemen," says President Lincoln, addressing a group of party and congressional leaders early in the war on the subject of campaign promises, "you and I are politicians. We know that our principles are, on occasion, slightly modified, sometimes greatly modified, by what is practical and possible." Lincoln is explaining his personal commitment to abolishing slavery in the South when he feels the time is right and he has the legal authority to do so. Whether on abolition, the selection of generals to lead the northern army, or his own reelection, Lincoln is shown to be a shrewd politician, often hemmed in by events, but usually able to manipulate them to his advantage.

Although circumstances portrayed in the film involving Lincoln's handling of his wife's financial misconduct—and her alleged selling of an advance copy of one of his speeches to a big city newspaper—are at odds with those recounted in David H. Donald's masterful biography, the tone and flavor of Lincoln's handling of the office seem about right. Appalled by the mounting casualties the war entails on both sides, Lincoln still does not lose faith in his own ability to calibrate the relation between ends and means. It is just this capacity for political authenticity that is so rare in American film history. Unlike so many other silver-screen politicians, rather than remaining aloof, on the one hand, or selling out, on the other, Lincoln rises to the occasion.

Cinema/Truth

Beyond the classical Hollywood drama, the second main category of motion pictures in this field is that of new realist cinema. The genre may not be all that new—it really begins with *The Candidate* (1972)—and "realism" is not used here to signify a heightened degree of historical or political accuracy. The essence of this group of films is that they *look* real; they have a surface or stylistic verisimilitude that not only is foreign to classical Hollywood narrative cinema but that also tends to become the central focus of the films themselves: the medium is the message. What is their angle on history? According to this group of movies, the selling of the president—the utilization of sophisticated human and technological resources to win at all costs—has gradually displaced the original point of holding public office. Whether such a perspective represents cynicism, realism, or candor is perhaps a crucial question of contemporary American public life.

Michael Ritchie's *The Candidate* is a transitional film. Robert Redford's character, Bill

McKay, is glib but not jaded, skeptical but still willing to give the system a chance to work. The film glances back over its shoulder at the classical dramatic tradition in quite self-conscious ways: McKay's conservative political opponent stands before huge portrait posters a lot like those unfurled earlier by Charles Foster Kane; a voice blaring over the sound system at a political rally is none other than that of Broderick Crawford, who brought Willie Stark to life. But the handheld camera point of view, the "live at five" pacing of the film, and the feeling of really being inside a political campaign, warts and all, make *The Candidate* a model for subsequent developments within the genre. Amazingly, the conservative/liberal byplay between Redford and his opponent tracks almost word for word campaign debates between George Bush and Bill Clinton, in spite of the fact that *The Candidate*'s screenplay was written by Jeremy Larner, a Eugene McCarthy speechwriter, twenty years before the Bush-Clinton presidential campaign of 1992.

FIGURE 69. *The Candidate* (1972). Bill McKay (Robert Redford), a presidential candidate, campaigns close to the people. Using a narrative perspective from inside campaign headquarters and such cinematic techniques as handheld, point-of-view shots, *The Candidate* contributed to the narrative and stylistic approach of future campaign films. Courtesy Redford-Ritchie Productions and Warner Bros.

This cinema verité approach to the historical reconstruction of elections and party politics has been pursued in both nonfiction films—for example, *The War Room* (1993), dealing with Bill Clinton's first presidential campaign, and *A Perfect Candidate* (1996), following Oliver North's first senatorial campaign—and fiction films such as *Bob Roberts* and *Primary Colors. Wag the Dog* (1998) quickly achieved notoriety when President Clinton ordered antiterrorist bombing raids in the wake of mounting impeachment pressures. It suggests the ultimate lengths to which spin doctors and media consultants might go to "change the lead" on the evening news. While *Wag the Dog* explores, at one level, how con jobs actually work and, at a presumably more elevated level, the "relation between illusion and reality" (themes common to films scripted or directed by *Wag the Dog*'s screenwriter, David Mamet), the movie also provides a critique of how modern political campaigns are conducted. The harrowing escape of a refugee girl from a burning village in Albania, for example, turns out to have been manufactured in a California movie studio. Whatever one thinks of its political cynicism, this scene is fascinating at the level of pure visual artifice: a bag of Tostitos is placed in the desperate girl's arms for the time being, a frightened cat will be digitally substituted for the taco chips in postproduction.

To be sure, there are plenty of politicians on the take, as well as brutally amoral campaign strategists, in *The American President* (1995), *The Big Brass Ring* (1999), and *The Contender* (2000). But what is surprising is that at the center of all three films are political leaders with real courage and an abiding commitment to real values. Lobbyist Sydney Wade (Annette Bening) and President Andrew Shepherd (Michael Douglas) in *The American President,* Governor William Blake Pellarin (William Hurt) in *The Big Brass Ring,* and both Senator Laine Hanson (Joan Allen) and President Jack Evans (Jeff Bridges) in *The Contender* have been around the block and know perfectly well that politics can be a dirty game. But when the chips are down, they seem to discover new resources within themselves and take the high road, however much it represents a real stretch. These films reflect tawdry current events (sex scandals, impeachment, ineptly conducted elections) much less than they seem to anticipate the kind of national spirit that came to the fore in the United States after the terrorist attacks of September 2001 on the World Trade Center and Pentagon. It was not just Honest Abe who could rise to the occasion in a time of crisis or national peril.

Just the Facts

The final approach to making films of political history is objective documentary. *The War Room* is in fact a documentary but belongs primarily in the category of new realist cinema. Carefully tracking the day-to-day experiences and perspectives of Clinton campaign managers, James Carville and George Stephanopoulos, this film (by the noted documentarians D. A. Pennebaker and Chris Hegedus) captures perfectly the personalities of two contemporary spin doctors. But describing the traditional documentary film as "objective" does not mean that it is politically neutral; rather, what is most striking about this sort of filmmaking is that (unlike *The War Room,* a "hot" new realist film essay) documentary appears to stand back and view its subject matter at arm's length, with a cold eye, without "tilt"—merely documenting a political campaign or life, for the record.

A staple of school and public libraries, *Just Around the Corner* (1986), narrated by Alexander Scourby, does a first-rate job of introducing viewers to an often neglected subject: the impact of third-party candidates in U.S. political history. Watching and listening to the real Huey Pearce Long speak from the stump makes clear, in a way that *All the King's Men* does not, exactly why Long had such a devoted following.

The PBS *American Experience* documentaries provide state of the art coverage for presidents Kennedy, Johnson, and Nixon. *LBJ* (1991), narrated by David McCullough, includes an interview with presidential advisor Clark Clifford, who describes Johnson as "a great, hurtling locomotive running down the track," while the film cuts to an image of Johnson, Stetson on his head, arm stretched out, apparently directing the nation. Only those familiar with Richard Pipes's remarkable photograph "Campaign 1960," shown by the Museum of Modern Art as part of its "American Politicians" exhibition in 1994, will realize that, inexplicably, the makers of *LBJ* have chosen to simply crop a concerned and restraining John Fitzgerald Kennedy out of this picture. It is precisely the tension between Kennedy and Johnson in the photo that makes it one of the most startling and memorable pictures in the history of American photography. Kennedy ended up on *LBJ's* cutting room floor, a vivid reminder that just as elections involve choices among candidates, filmmaking necessarily requires choices among images.

References

Filmography

All the King's Men (1949, F)
All the President's Men (1976, F)
The American President (1995, F)
The Best Man (1964, F)
The Big Brass Ring (1999, F)
Bob Roberts (1992, F)
Bulworth (1998, F)
The Candidate (1972, F)
Citizen Kane (1941, F)
The Contender (2000, F)
Going to Congress (1924, F)
High Crimes and Misdemeanors (1990, D)
Just Around the Corner (1986, D)
The Last Hurrah (1958, F)
LBJ (1991, D)
Lincoln (1993, TV)
The Manchurian Candidate (1962, F)
Meet John Doe (1941, F)
Nixon (1995, F)
A Perfect Candidate (1996, D)
Primary Colors (1998, F)
Secret Honor (1984, F)

The Seduction of Joe Tynan (1979, F)
Seven Days in May (1964, F)
State of the Union (1948, F)
Wag the Dog (1998, F)
The War Room (1993, D)
What Happened to Bill Clinton? (1995, D)
Wilson (1944, F)
Young Mr. Lincoln (1939, F)

Bibliography

Burgoyne, Robert. *Film Nation: Hollywood Looks at U.S. History.* Minneapolis: University of Minnesota Press, 1997.

Chase, Anthony. *Movies on Trial: The Legal System on the Silver Screen.* New York: New Press, 2002.

Christensen, Terry. *Reel Politics.* New York: Basil Blackwell, 1987.

Day, Donald. *Will Rogers: A Biography.* New York: David McKay, 1962.

Ferro, Marc. *Cinema and History.* Detroit: Wayne State University Press, 1988.

Foner, Eric, and John A. Garraty, eds. *The Reader's Companion to American History.* Boston: Houghton Mifflin, 1991.

Donald, David H. *Lincoln.* New York: Simon & Schuster, 1995.

Kutler, Stanley I. *The Wars of Watergate.* New York: Knopf, 1990.

McBride, Joseph. *Frank Capra: The Catastrophe of Success.* New York: Simon & Schuster, 1992.

Museum of Modern Art. *American Politicians: Photographs from 1843 to 1995.* New York: Abrams, 1994.

Neve, Brian. *Film and Politics in America.* London: Routledge, 1992.

Quart, Leonard, and Albert Auster. *American Film and Society since 1945.* 2d ed. Westport, CT: Praeger, 1991.

Rollins, Peter C., ed. *Hollywood as Historian.* 2d ed. Lexington: University Press of Kentucky, 1998.

Rosenstone, Robert. *Visions of the Past: The Challenge of Film to Our Idea of History.* Cambridge, MA: Harvard University Press, 1995.

Toplin, Robert Brent. *History by Hollywood.* Urbana: University of Illinois Press, 1996.

Vidal, Gore. *The American Presidency.* Monroe, ME: Common Courage Press, 1998.

[JUNE SOCHEN]

Feminism and Feminist Films

Feminism is a twentieth-century ideology. The previous century had a woman's-rights movement in the United States that concentrated on gaining women the right to vote, to attend college, and to own property. The feminist movement, born in the 1910s, declared women to be equal with men in every significant way. Although feminists witnessed the passage of the Nineteenth Amendment in 1920, giving women the right to vote, they quickly concluded that suffrage alone would not guarantee women's equality. In 1923, they proposed an Equal Rights Amendment to eliminate all forms of discrimination. The bill languished in Congress for many years. Many women reformers, who did not define themselves as feminists, did not support the ERA and concentrated on helping working-class women improve their situation.

Women's lives changed dramatically after 1920 thanks to both material circumstances and the efforts of feminists and women reformers. The growth of the middle class, with more education and healthcare available for more women, enabled more American women than ever before to live longer, to have smaller families, and to be homemakers, volunteer community activists, and workers outside of the home. But these improvements were seriously interrupted by the Great Depression and World War II.

A second wave of feminism emerged in the late 1960s in an atmosphere of liberation to seek women's equality in all areas of life. The baby-boom generation, born during the optimistic post-1945 period, came of age in the late 1960s and provided feminism with a new generation of leaders and followers. The rhetoric became bolder and the subject matter more controversial, with television coverage, a large cohort of sympathetic listeners, and a more receptive government in place.

The Equal Rights Amendment passed Congress in 1972 (though it never was ratified by a sufficient number of states); the Supreme Court ruled in *Roe v. Wade* in 1973 that women had a legal right to abortion under certain conditions; and affirmative action programs gave women job opportunities they had never had before. Though the feminist revolution is by no means complete, young women coming of age today play basketball, attend college, marry, have a few children, and try to balance family and career.

Hollywood studios have dealt with feminism in fits and starts. Never comfortable with assertive women or movies that preach, filmmakers often approached the subject of the "new woman," as many feminists were called in the 1910s, with caution, if not censure. When they portrayed a woman as independent and competent, they were sure to emphasize her physical beauty more than her mental qualities. Ever mindful of the culture's deep-seated commitment to women as the second sex, screenwriters, directors, and producers camouflaged their feminists in traditional heroine garb. Occasionally, when the writer was a woman (such as Ruth Gordon), or the male director was especially sympathetic to strong women (George Cukor), a feminist portrayal was created. Screen writer Kate Corbally wrote the 1913 *What 80 Million Women Want,* a favorable portrait of women's suffrage. The year before, however, in the silent film *The Suffragette* (1912), women reformers seeking the vote were portrayed as overbearing and tough; as wives, they henpecked their husbands.

Filmmakers Lois Weber and Dorothy Arzner were among the small group of women working in Hollywood during the silent era. Weber directed, wrote, and produced more than four hundred features, primarily in the 1910s. In a few of them, she treated explosive social issues such as birth control, a favorite topic of the most advanced feminists. In *Where Are My Children?* (1916), Weber drew a sophisticated portrait of the subject; she contrasted the behavior of an idealistic doctor who dispensed birth control information to poor women (an illegal action that resulted in a jail term for him) to that of a rich doctor who performed abortions on rich women unwilling to spoil their figures during pregnancy. Censorship boards in various cities protested the showing of the movie.

In a 1927 interview, Weber said that "the schoolroom blackboard will one day be supplanted by the motion picture screen." However, her frustration with her critics' unwillingness to grant her artistic freedom, combined with studio reluctance to deal with controversial subjects, led to a decline in her moviemaking in the 1920s. Women directors remained a distinct minority as most studios hesitated to allow women to control a major film budget, to produce a movie on their own, or to direct features. (The situation obtains today.)

Dorothy Arzner stands out as another exceptional example of a working woman director in late silent and early sound movies. Although she made fewer movies than Weber, her film heroines were always spirited and outspoken. In *Our Dancing Daughters* (1928), Joan Crawford stars as a young flapper interested in good times. In one scene, she jumps onto a table during a party, raises her champagne glass and declares: "To Myself. I have to live with myself until I die, so I hope I like myself!"

Many screenwriters during the silent period were women; Frances Marion, Anita Loos, Salka Viertel, and Jeanie Macpherson were among the most prominent. Loos wrote many screen treatments as well as the screenplay for the very popular *The Women* (1939); Viertel wrote many Garbo movies; and Macpherson wrote the majority of director Cecil B. De Mille's scripts. Though all women screenwriters did not write feminist stories, when they had the opportunity to write a feature that starred a strong woman, they did so.

Salka Viertel's script for Garbo in *Queen Christina* (1933) is a good example. In it, Garbo portrayed the historical Queen of Sweden as an independent thinker and an antiwar monarch. Christina, according to Viertel via Garbo, read Molière and wished to pursue her own life while ruling the kingdom. Not only is a woman treated respectfully in this movie, but she is also a leader with her own ideas for her kingdom. But because this movie is a romance as well as a historical drama, love brings Christina down and forces her to abdicate her kingdom for the man she loves (a foreigner). Cultural values are thus upheld, though most of the movie treats audiences to a portrait of woman as both thinker and activist.

The Golden Years, 1933–1955

The feminist crusade for the Equal Rights movement continued during the Depression years but had no success. New Deal legislation, however, improved working conditions for women and men, thereby fulfilling some of the reformers' goals. But because the Depression and war years required strength from everyone, Hollywood made innumerable movies featuring strong women. Katharine Hepburn played the quintessential feminist in A *Bill of Divorcement* (1932), *Sylvia Scarlett* (1935), and *The Philadelphia Story* (1940). She was a career woman in *Christopher Strong* (1932), *A*

Woman Rebels (1936), and *Woman of the Year* (1942), an aristocrat in *Holiday* (1938), *The Philadelphia Story* (1940), and most of her other films. As an aristocrat, she had independent wealth and could pursue whatever wacky or sane plan she had (*Bringing Up Baby,* 1939).

Take-charge mothers such as Greer Garson in *Mrs. Miniver* (1942) shared with other strong women the feminist label. Though feminist film critic Molly Haskell finds shortcomings in many 1930s films, she agrees that they featured a variety of women coping with life's challenges, unlike more recent films where there have been fewer portrayals of women's lives. Movies during the golden era featured women as pilots, journalists, doctors, lawyers, and athletes. Besides Hepburn, Rosalind Russell often played the lead. In *His Girl Friday* (1940), she was a successful investigative reporter. Though romance remained a vital component in all of these independent-woman films, the star clearly had a distinct identity and mind of her own.

In *Woman of the Year* (1942), the first time Hepburn played opposite Spencer Tracy (in a screenplay written by Ruth Gordon and her husband Garson Kanin), Hepburn plays an internationally famous journalist (modeled after Dorothy Thompson and *New York Times* writer Anne O'Hare McCormick), while Tracy is the sportswriter on the same newspaper. The George Stevens film has both comic and melodramatic elements; in sharp contrast to most romances, the couple marries early in the movie, with career conflicts (mainly her very busy schedule) and the adoption of a child (which Hepburn does for public relations reasons) creating strife. One of the most famous scenes occurs after they separate and Hepburn tries to win him back by cooking breakfast. The scene is done silently and with comic effect, for the career woman does not know a waffle iron from a coffeepot. Consequently, she messes up everything she touches. The scene ends when her commotion wakes Tracy and he tells her that she can be both a wife and a writer. How the two demanding careers can be reconciled is not explained.

Bette Davis played a reporter in *Front Page Woman* (1935) as well as a "working girl" in *Marked Woman* (1937). Journalism was clearly one of the newest, most visible, and exciting professions for women, and Hollywood responded accordingly. But in all of the cinematic treatments of independent women, romance always trumps career, and the domestic scene is woman's ultimate venue. The unspoken assumption—that marriage takes precedence over a woman's profession—prevailed in "feminist" films, just as it did in all other films as well as in society. One of the most predictable and popular storylines was that of the too serious and too masculine professional woman who needed the love of a good man to humanize—or rather womanize—her.

Davis, one of the greatest actresses of the 1930s generation, could also play an aristocrat (*Jezebel,* 1938) or a career woman. Given her strong personality, she was usually a woman in charge. In *All About Eve* (1950), directed by Joseph L. Mankiewicz, she plays a mature theatrical actress with fewer and fewer roles available to her. Davis, who was in her forties at that point, demonstrated that older women could be sexy and glamorous. Anne Baxter plays the ingénue who tries to sabotage and replace her. Ultimately, Eve Harrington (Davis) comes to terms with her aging and wins the man she loves. (Davis won the Academy Award for her performance; the production received the award as best picture of 1950.)

Feminist Marriages

Arguably the best and most unusual example of a feminist marriage in 1930s movies was *The Thin Man* series. Beginning in 1934, Myrna Loy and William Powell starred as Nora and Nick Charles, an upper-class couple who find themselves solving mysteries in spite of their best intentions to avoid all trouble. In all six movies, which ranged from 1934 to 1947, they drink martinis, speak witty lines, and share

FIGURE 70. *Woman of the Year* (1942). Tess Harding (Katharine Hepburn, standing at center rear), an internationally recognized reporter dedicated only to the *New York Daily*, marries the paper's sportswriter, Sam Craig (Spencer Tracy). Harding, an outspoken feminist, also frequently speaks at affairs, giving her little time for marriage. Still, Harding tries to prove that she can be a helpmeet and journalist at the same time. Courtesy Metro-Goldwyn-Mayer.

each adventure as equals. The novelty of the characterization and plot engaged audiences, with the five sequels providing testimony to their enduring popularity.

Another "couple" who made many movies together, though not based on the same characters, were Katharine Hepburn and Spencer Tracy; beginning with *Woman of the Year* (1942) and continuing sporadically over the years until Stanley Kramer's *Guess Who's Coming to Dinner* (1967), they displayed the strengths and problems facing a strong-willed couple. In *Adam's Rib* (1949), directed by George Cukor, for example, both are lawyers who oppose each other in the courtroom in a case that deals with women's rights. It threatens to end their marriage, but love wins out. In *Pat and Mike* (1952), also directed by Cukor, she is a professional athlete, and he is her coach.

A New Era

Although the first generation of sound actresses easily played feminist types, Hollywood selected a very different second generation after 1945. Young actresses who could have picked up the mantle from the Hepburns and Davises were ignored in favor of the single-image glamour girl. Ava Gardner, Rita Hayworth, and Lana Turner enjoyed prominence, as did the two superstars of the 1950s, Elizabeth Taylor and Marilyn Monroe. None of these actresses portrayed career women or independent aristocratic types with clearly defined identities. Rather, they were usually shaped and determined by their great beauty. Romance was the genre in which they excelled, not independent-woman films, and the great beauty of Taylor and sensuality of Monroe decided their screen image.

In fact, Hollywood films since the 1940s have rarely focused upon feminist women, even within a comic or romantic plot line. The major exception to this trend was when women's liberation became a subject of public discussion in the 1970s. Movies such as *Network* (1976), *The Turning Point* (1977), *An Unmarried Woman* (1978), *The China Syndrome* (1979), and *Norma Rae* (1979) had career women, divorced women, working women, and frustrated wives as the central characters. But these movies remained exceptions rather than pioneers in a new genre with many followers.

Between 1970 and 1990, only four out of the twenty-one Academy Award–winning movies featured women. More often, Mafia bosses (the *Godfather* movies), soldiers (*Patton, The Deer Hunter,* and *Platoon*), and other assorted heroes such as Gandhi and Rocky dominated the movie screen. Not only were feminist romances absent from the screen, but roles for women in any genre became rarer and rarer. Hollywood relied on the tried-and-true formulas of thrillers and adventures, with women being incidental to the story. Television became the home for discussion of independent women in the 1970s, with Mary Tyler Moore, Carole Burnett, Valerie Harper, Bonnie Franklin, and other actresses dominating primetime.

The Turning Point (1977), directed by Herbert Ross, starred two mature actresses, Anne Bancroft, best known for her role as the seductress of young college graduate Benjamin Braddock in *The Graduate* (1967), and Shirley MacLaine, a film veteran. It offered a rare look at women who had made their choices and now, in middle age, had to evaluate the meaning and value of their decisions. Both women had been ballerinas, but MacLaine's character married and had a family, while Bancroft went on to become a world-famous ballerina and was now nearing the end of her career. Who had made the better choice? Had both? Neither? The movie offers no easy answers, but it explores the subject in a fresh way, something not often seen in a Hollywood movie. In the sense that the questions raised are feminist, the film qualifies as a thoughtful exploration of an important subject.

In the 1980s, Meryl Streep emerged as the most interesting actress capable of playing a wide variety of screen roles. She has been aptly dubbed a worthy successor to Hepburn and Davis. Her portrayal in *Sophie's Choice* (1982) of a Polish woman survivor of World War II was a sterling performance. Streep has not always or only played feminist roles, but her women are always strong and unusual. In *Silkwood* (1983), she plays an unwitting reformer, a working woman who discovers dangerous conditions for workers exposed to radiation. In possibly her greatest part, as writer Isak Dinesen in *Out of Africa* (1985), she runs a plantation in East Africa, starts writing, and has a love affair. This movie, presented in grand epic style, combined the best of the romantic genre with the independent-woman film.

While Streep was nominated eight times for the Academy Award from 1981 to 1995, she was joined by other strong actresses such as Jodie Foster, Susan Sarandon, Sally Field, and Jessica Lange. These women dominated the few juicy roles available for actresses during this period, though not all were necessarily feminist roles. Foster played a working-class woman raped in *The Accused* (1988) and a tough federal officer in the scary *Silence of the Lambs* (1991). Sarandon has been nominated five times for the Academy Award since 1981, with her most popular role being in *Thelma and Louise* (1991).

Feminist film critics have divided on whether this film, directed by Ridley Scott, was a positive statement for feminist ideas or not. In it, two working-class women leave their homes and their men for what is originally thought to be a brief vacation. It turns out to be their final journey, but, in the course of the adventure, they both learn a lot about themselves. Sarandon's performance in *Bull Durham* (1988) may offer a more interesting look at a sexually liberated woman who is crazy about baseball and chooses a new lover every season from the hometown semipro team. Her frequent commentaries on life, love, and freedom present viewers with a rare look at an audaciously independent woman.

With fewer movies starring women, let alone independent women, those that treat women respectfully and look at their dilemmas receive a lot of attention from feminist critics lamenting the long drought in women's films. *Working Girl* (1988) was an interesting example of a movie that touches many themes concerning women. It depicts a working-class woman (Melanie Griffith) who wants to be a player in the heady world of mergers and acquisitions while she works as secretary to a career-driven MBA type (Sigourney Weaver). The woman boss, of course, behaves like a competitive, dog-eat-dog man and steals an idea of Griffith's in order to advance her own career. Harrison Ford acts as the colleague and romantic interest. Directed by Mike Nichols, the movie offers a social satire of the career woman as man in disguise versus the sexy career-woman-wannabe who also wants romance. Griffith says, in her first meeting with Ford, that she has "a head for business and a bod for sex. Is that wrong?" Indeed, this movie might more accurately be labeled a postfeminist film in that it seeks to combine the traditional roles for women with the new ones. The challenge in film, and in life, is to find the proper combinations.

Two recent documentaries offer opposite views of feminism: *Gloria Steinem* (1994) is an interview with the founder of *Ms.* magazine and explores the origins of her feminist thinking. *Has Feminism Gone Too Far?* (1996) asks feminist writers Camille Paglia and Christina Sommers why they have developed doubts about the direction of contemporary feminism. Viewed together, they offer the audience lively and contrasting opinions on the state of feminism in the 1990s.

References

Filmography

The Accused (1988, F)
Adam's Rib (1949, F)
All About Eve (1950, F)
Bull Durham (1988, F)
A Century of Women (1994, D)
The China Syndrome (1979, F)
Gloria Steinem (1994, D)
Guess Who's Coming to Dinner (1967, F)
Has Feminism Gone Too Far? (1996, D)
His Girl Friday (1940, F)
Jezebel (1938, F)
Marked Woman (1937, F)
Network (1976, F)
Norma Rae (1979, F)
Out of Africa (1985, F)
Pat and Mike (1952, F)
The Philadelphia Story (1940, F)
Queen Christina (1933, F)
Silence of the Lambs (1991, F)
Silkwood (1983, F)
Sophie's Choice (1982, F)
The Suffragette (1912, F)
Thelma and Louise (1991, F)
The Thin Man (1934, F)
The Thrill of It All (1963, F)
The Turning Point (1977, F)
An Unmarried Woman (1978, F)
Where Are My Children? (1916, F)
Woman of the Year (1942, F)
Women Get the Vote (1962, D)
Working Girl (1988, F)

Bibliography

Cott, Nancy F. *The Grounding of American Feminism.* New Haven: Yale University Press, 1989.
Erens, Patricia, ed. *Issues in Feminist Film Criticism.* Bloomington: Indiana University Press, 1990.

Evans, Sara. *Born for Liberty: A History of Women in America.* New York: Free Press, 1989.

Riley, Glenda. *Inventing the American Woman: An Inclusive History.* Arlington Heights, IL: Harlan Davidson, 1995.

Sochen, June. *From Mae to Madonna: Women Entertainers in Twentieth-Century America.* Lexington: University Press of Kentucky, 1999.

Welsch, Janice R. *Film Archetypes: Sisters, Mistresses, Mothers and Daughters.* New York: Arno, 1978.

[JOSEPH MILLICHAP]

Railroads

Just as railroads permeate American geography and pervade American history, trains likewise prove ubiquitous in American film. Our movies thus complement the complicated, often ambiguous relations among nature, culture, and technology represented by the American railroad. Images of the train in American film rarely achieve artistic ambivalence, however. Unlike our literature or our graphic arts, American movies only occasionally freight their railroads with complex cultural messages or important symbolic meanings. Trains in American films function more often as devices to impart motion to their pictures or to move along their characters, plots, settings, and symbols. Therefore, an approach to screen railroads by way of film genre, rather than by historic era, better reveals the importance of trains as generic American cultural symbols.

In its most general definition, the railroad—the system of metal tracks over which locomotive engines draw trains of various vehicles on flanged wheels to transport people and cargo between terminals—is a technology for converting natural energy into cultural power. In other words, the technology of the railroad mediates between nature and culture. Technology is never neutral, though, for it confronts us with ambiguous messages. We rejoice in its energy and its ability to overcome the inertia of the material world, but we resist its power, its momentum to alter our relation to nature through the evolution of our culture.

Railroads transported American history from the agricultural innocence of the early nineteenth century to the postindustrial experience of the late twentieth century by shaping American geography into a spatial network of cities and towns located in zones of standardized time. Metal rails and steam engines seemed almost a natural pairing, one that allowed our young nation to expand where it would, not just along its natural or man-made waterways. "Railroad iron is the magician's rod," Emerson remarked in his essay "The Young American" (1844), "in its power to invoke the sleeping power of land and water." At the other end of the lines of track laid from the established coastal cities, new settlements in the Midwest burgeoned as thriving urban centers; Chicago was soon the fastest-growing city in the world after the railroads arrived not long before the Civil War.

A railroad map of the United States in 1861 illustrates why the South lost the Civil War: whereas the Northern states were stitched tightly together in a thick web of iron rails, the Southern states were rather loosely knitted. The South's indifference to technology not only contributed to its losing the Civil War, but it also cost it those transport, communication, and manufacturing capabilities that it had developed. Within a generation after the war, however, railroads not only reconstructed the South but also transformed the West from an open frontier to a prosperous and sophisticated American region, another piece in the puzzle of our national identity. Even as the western frontier closed along with the nineteenth century, the golden age of American trains ensued in the opening decades of the twentieth century. After World War II, our century saw a long decline of American railroading under the pressures of restrictive regulation and increased competition, though this declension was reversed in recent decades following government deregulation and rapid consolidation.

Among the technologies transforming America at the turn of the twentieth century were the pioneering efforts of Thomas A. Edison and others on the new frontier of film. For subject matter, Edison and his imitators turned their cameras on the everyday America that surrounded them, in particular anything in motion. Trains, moving at mile-a-minute speeds by then, became an important subject for the new medium. Early film titles include the *Empire State Express* (1896), a "kinematograph" of the era's fastest "flyer." Often, unsuspecting nickelodeon audiences panicked at the sight of a speeding express charging at them by way of the camera's magic. Appropriately enough, our first narrative feature film is generally considered Edison's *The Great Train Robbery* (1903).

Unfortunately, these early instances of railroad images became the patterns for American film. On the one hand, the movies were compelled to record the physical reality of American railroads, except for the occasional use of models in low-budget train wrecks, and even the documentation of railroads was soon surpassed by the even more exciting technologies of automobiles, airplanes, and spacecraft. On the other hand, trains were essentially an oversized prop in most narrative films. For example, *The Great Train Robbery* uses its turn-of-the-century locomotive and cars as devices of action and setting, though novels of the same era—such as Frank Norris's *The Octopus* (1899) and Theodore Dreiser's *Sister Carrie* (1900)—employ railroads as multifaceted cultural markers. Even the film adaptations of literary classics excised their railroad images, perhaps as much in terms of production cost as for any other reason.

Railroads in movies tend to be discovered in those film genres that could derive the greatest advantage from their inherent narrative and graphic qualities—in particular, their paradoxical movement and confinement. The western, the mystery/adventure, and the comedy/musical could make the most of these contrasts, as the screen presence of trains confirms. Yet these generic uses also reconstruct the history of American railroads from a pioneering period in the nineteenth century, to the new triumphs during and after the Civil War, to the golden age of named expresses and fast freights in the twentieth century, to the era of decline and regeneration in the second half of our century. Although the early development of railroads in the East and Midwest was mentioned incidentally in historical dramas and biographies, the movie images of the pioneering period derive from the construction of the great western rail lines.

The first transcontinental railroad became the stuff of epic westerns from John Ford's silent classic *The Iron Horse* (1924) to Cecil B. De Mille's studio sound saga *Union Pacific* (1939). These narratives focused on fictive conflicts rather than on historical facts; in the former, hero George O'Brien avenges his father's death even as he spans the Continental Divide with iron rails; in the latter, Joel McCrea survives a dramatic if unhistorical train wreck. Other examples from the golden age of westerns featured other construction projects: the historical Royal Gorge War in *Denver and Rio Grande* (1951), the best-known western line in *Santa Fe* (1951), and the Civil War era in *Kansas Pacific* (1953). Characterization becomes murkier in these post–World War II efforts, and the heroism of the entire enterprise is deconstructed in more recent and revisionist westerns. The classic of this later mode remains Sergio Leone's *Once Upon a Time in the West* (1969), which recycles not just plot and setting but even characterization when western icon Henry Fonda portrays the hired killer Frank, the agent of the venal railroad barons.

Westerns were concerned with more than railroad construction; destruction proved almost as important in exciting scenes of train wrecks and robberies. The "rails across the plains" epics mentioned earlier often presented spectacular derailments or wild Indian raids as temporary setbacks to be overcome before the completion of "the iron road." Again, *The Great Train Robbery* set a pattern that would extend throughout the century. Variations are found in both the silent and early sound eras, though not as many as might be anticipated—probably because of the low budgets assigned to matinee westerns. Features such as *The Great K&A Train Robbery* (1926), with Tom Mix and an uncredited John Wayne, or *Jesse James* (1939), with Tyrone Power and Henry Fonda as the train-robbing James brothers, were recast in postwar classics such as *Carson City* (1951), starring Randolph Scott and Raymond Massey, and reprised in revisionist fare like *Butch Cassidy and the Sundance Kid* (1969), with Paul Newman and Robert Redford. Interesting variations with outlaws trying to escape from aboard speeding trains include John Wayne's *The Train Robbers* (1973) and Charles Bronson's *Breakheart Pass* (1976). Again, the ultimate revisionism is found in the so-called spaghetti westerns, the domain of Sergio Leone and a few other directors, mostly Spanish and Italian.

Racing trains provided great action props in nonwestern settings as well. For example, the historical Andrews Raid during the Civil War was twice recaptured: first in Buster Keaton's silent classic *The General* (1927) and later in Disney's *The Great Locomotive Chase* (1956). The hobo's life while riding the rails supplied other adventure, especially during the 1930s, in movies as different as *Emperor of the North* (1973), directed by Robert Aldrich; *Bound for Glory* (1976), the story of Woody Guthrie; and *Boxcar Bertha* (1972), Martin Scorsese's first studio film as director. Modern outlaws also used trains for scams or escapes, as in the comedic *Silver Streak* (1976), with Gene Wilder and Richard Pryor, or the violent *Runaway Train* (1985), starring Jon Voight and Eric Roberts.

Trains have always provided effective settings for mysteries because of their confined spaces and inexorable movement toward their destinations. Many of the classic examples are set abroad even if made in the United States. Interesting American settings are found in two of Alfred Hitchcock's classics, *Strangers on a Train* (1951) and *North by Northwest* (1959). In both films, the train journeys seem to symbolize the inexorable fates of the doomed characters, while other forms of transport and movement are contrasted in symbolic terms—the destructive merry-go-round in the former and the threatening biplane in the latter.

Musicals and comedies have also made good use of the tight constrictions and rapid movements provided by trains. American railroads quickly became one of the major props of silent slapstick comedy, most notably in the works of Buster Keaton, that master of film and other technologies, but also in the shorts and features of Mack Sennett, Charlie Chaplin, and Harold Lloyd. The transfer of the stage musical and the sophisticated comedy to the silver screen in the early sound era coincided with the golden age of American rail travel on romantically named Pullman Limiteds. Soon enough, these famous names became the titles of 1930s features such as *Twentieth Century* (1934), an early effort of Howard Hawks featuring John Barrymore and Carole Lombard as a disaffected Broadway couple wooing once more on the New York Central flagship express to Chicago that provides the title. *Streamline Express* (1935), *Florida Special* (1936), and *Broadway Limited* (1941) soon followed, albeit with less famous passengers on board. More historic use of railroad settings included *The Harvey Girls* (1946), a musical extravaganza with Judy Garland, Cyd Charisse, and Angela Lansbury as three ingénues going west as singing waitresses in the Harvey House restaurants along the Santa Fe railway. Other aspects of show business involving railroads appeared in *Chattanooga Choo Choo* (1984), *The Greatest Show on Earth* (1952), and *Some Like It Hot* (1959).

Recent filmic treatments of railroads demonstrate a postmodern blurring of traditional genres, one that complements the ambiguous recent history of both industries. Examples include the science-fiction comedy *Back to the Future III* (1990), which employs a nineteenth-century steam locomotive as a time-travel device. The black comedies *Planes, Trains, and Automobiles* and *Throw Momma from the Train* (both 1987) featured trains; Steve Martin and John Candy became strange bedfellows in the former, while Danny DeVito and Billy Crystal spoofed Hitchcock's train movies in the latter. Even seriocomic features such as *Stand by Me* (1986) or *Fried Green Tomatoes* (1991) used fine ensemble casts to develop contradictory images of railroads, as did the superb *End of the Line* (1988), which pays homage to the dying short-haul railroad in the age of Reaganomics while offering scenes worthy of Frank Capra.

Even more than Hollywood's employment of trains within the traditional genres, these more recent efforts demonstrate that movie railroads are for the most part props intended to support entertainment values. Although the historical reality and artistic symbolism of American railroads are more often discovered in our literature or our graphic arts than in our movies, the sheer persistence of the train in American film complements its place as a significant artistic marker within our culture. In turn, all these re-created images of trains project the historical importance of railroads in America during an era when they are somewhat neglected, as well as their centrality to the American creative imagination still struggling to understand the development of our culture.

References

Filmography

Back to the Future III (1990, F)
Bound for Glory (1976, F)
Boxcar Bertha (1972, F)
Breakheart Pass (1976, F)
Broadway Limited, (1941, F)
Butch Cassidy and the Sundance Kid (1969, F)
Carson City (1951, F)
Chattanooga Choo Choo (1984, F)
Denver and Rio Grande (1951, F)
Emperor of the North (1973, F)
End of the Line (1988, F)
Florida Special (1936, F)
Fried Green Tomatoes (1991, F)
The General (1927, F)
The Greatest Show on Earth (1952, F)
The Great K&A Train Robbery (1926, F)
The Great Locomotive Chase (1956, F)
The Great Train Robbery (1903, F)
The Harvey Girls (1946, F)
The Iron Horse (1924, F)
Jesse James (1939, F)
Kansas Pacific (1953, F)
Keystone Cops (1985, D)
North by Northwest (1959, F)
Once Upon a Time in the West (1969, F)
Planes, Trains, and Automobiles (1987, F)
Runaway Train (1985, F)
Santa Fe (1951, F)
Silver Streak (1976, F)
Some Like It Hot (1959, F)
Stand by Me (1986, F)
Strangers on a Train (1951, F)
Streamline Express (1935, F)
Throw Momma from the Train (1987, F)
The Train Robbers (1973, F)
Twentieth Century (1934, F)
Union Pacific (1939, F)

Bibliography

Douglass, George H. *All Aboard: The Railroad in American Life.* New York: Marlowe, 1992.

Gordon, Sarah H. *Passage to Union: How the Railroads Transformed American Life, 1829–1929.* Chicago: Ivan Dee, 1996.

Jensen, Oliver. *The American Heritage History of Railroads in America.* New York: American Heritage, 1975.

Marx, Leo. *The Machine In the Garden: Technology and the Pastoral Ideal in America.* New York: Oxford University Press, 1964.

Schivelbusch, Wolfgang. *The Railway Journey: The Industrialization of Time and Space in the 19th Century.* New York: Urizen, 1979.

[**WILLIAM E. BRIGMAN**]

Sexuality

Movies emerged as a part of popular culture during the first of two major sexual revolutions of the twentieth century. By the turn of the century, industrialization and urbanization had already changed the sexual mores of the working class, and the mores of the middle class were on the edge of a transformation. The city moved courtship off the porch and into nightclubs, darkened movie theaters, and private spaces; in addition, the automobile provided both escape from parental oversight and semiseclusion. "By World War I," Sharon Ullman points out, "the Victorian assumptions about sexuality which dominated Progressive rhetoric were in tatters. Public imagery of women no longer conveyed purity and chastity" (42).

World War I accelerated the change in sexual attitudes. The soldiers who went abroad were exposed to European sexual attitudes and practices; concurrently, standards were modified at home. Sexual roles changed as women became more active outside the home. With fathers abroad and mothers at work, unchaperoned middle-class adolescents created a new sexual ethic. Subsequent studies by Alfred Kinsey found that around 1915 a major shift occurred in the erotic experiences of American women. Although traditional moralists tried to limit the effects of the changed social and sexual attitudes resulting from the war, they were only partially successful in combating what amounted to a revolution in morals. The youths of the 1920s embraced the Jazz Age: sex was the cornerstone of the new lifestyle. They carried hip flasks, drank in speakeasies, petted in parked cars, and justified their rebellion against the Puritan tradition with allusions to Sigmund Freud and Havelock Ellis. Sexuality appeared to dominate all of American culture in the late 1920s.

The Great Depression produced a noticeable shift in the sexual climate. There was a change of emphasis: the revolution was being consolidated rather than advanced. The prosperity of the 1920s encouraged experimentation; the scarcity of the Depression reinforced traditional values. At the same time, it made their implementation very problematic. Restricting sexuality to marriage was difficult, inasmuch as the marriage rate dropped by more than 20 percent. On the other hand, sexual activity did not halt: the sale of contraceptives skyrocketed, and a survey found that over 70 percent of males and females engaged in premarital sex.

World War II accelerated the move from traditional sexual mores: courtship, chastity, and marital fidelity were early casualties of the war. Courtships and marriages were accelerated to accommodate forty-eight-hour leaves or to create the illusion of stability for soldiers about to go abroad. And, once abroad, soldiers were sexually active. An Army survey in 1945 found that more than 80 percent of soldiers who had been away from home more than two years had regular sexual relations with the women where they were stationed; indeed, half of the married soldiers had extramarital relations. Many sweethearts and spouses back home also had active sex lives: 650,000 children were born out of wedlock during the war.

Moreover, the large-scale entry of women into the workplace changed perceptions of sexual roles.

After the war, there was a major attempt at retrenchment. During the 1950s, sexual-purity campaigns merged with Cold War fears: political nonconformists were denounced; homosexuals, who had expanded their subculture during World War II, were pushed back into the closet; comic books were investigated for their sexual and subversive content; and married couples in movies slept in separate beds. However, the strenuous campaign to reestablish traditional sexual values was undermined by both science and commercialism. Alfred Kinsey's two books on sexuality, published in 1948 and 1953, stimulated an examination of sexual habits and values. In December 1953, Hugh Hefner's *Playboy* began publishing glossy nude pictorials and celebrating a hedonistic sexual philosophy. By the end of the decade, it had more than a million readers, only about half of whom were single men.

By the 1960s, Americans lived in a society where sexual activity was accepted as an important source of personal happiness for both sexes. A major factor was the introduction of the birth control pill, which almost eliminated fear of pregnancy. However, the wars over sexuality had not ended. Although there was a large, vocal counterculture practicing and advocating a liberated sexuality, there was no national consensus on this volatile subject. Rather, the increase in sexuality, including premarital intercourse, was merely an acceleration of a trend that had been growing since the beginning of the century.

Homosexuality, which had been forced underground in the 1950s, spawned a nationwide gay rights movement after the Stonewall riot (June 1969) in New York City, which resulted from a police raid on a gay bar. Homosexuality also emerged from the movie closet with *The Boys in the Band* (1969) and *The Killing of Sister George* (1968). Today, more than half of the states have repealed antisodomy laws, and the Clinton White House featured an HIV liaison officer.

Although the blight of AIDS, which was widely publicized by the death of Rock Hudson in October 1985, cast a pall over the sexual revolution, it did not reverse it. Sex and sexual portrayal in the media—both straight and gay—are staples of American life.

Sex in the Movies

Moralists quickly perceived movies as a threat to traditional sexual mores and began an unending struggle to mold film content to fit their values. Although censorship was strongest from 1934 to 1968, movies have seldom been without some level of distortion caused by sexual censorship. As a result, movies are not as reliable a reflection of the sexual world as they may be of other areas.

Some of the early films reflected the dramatic changes in sexual attitudes caused by industrialization and urbanization. These early explorations offered "no single moral vision" but indicated that "sexuality remained an uncharted area open to exploration" (Ullman, 1). When sexuality came to mainstream film in *Traffic in Souls* (1913), it was supposedly based on New York vice investigations. The movie set the pattern for films that used social abuses, abortion, and women's rights as a pretext to introduce sexual themes. However, it was not until the first sex-film star, Theda Bara, appeared in *Cleopatra* (1917)—with her breasts cradled by two gold snakes—that sexuality was projected in such a way as to influence social fashions. That same year, another sex symbol, Clara Bow, dubbed the "It" girl, appeared nude in *Hula* (1917).

Films also reflected the changing attitudes toward sex, marriage, and divorce in the "flapper" and speakeasy era after World War I. Female stars such as Gloria Swanson, Clara Bow, Louise Brooks, and Greta Garbo conveyed an open, frank attitude toward sexuality that would have been unacceptable to the Victorians of the prewar era. Likewise, the new male sex symbol, Rudolph Valentino, generated female responses that destroyed the Victorian belief that women were uninterested in sex.

Director Cecil B. De Mille, who had highlighted bath scenes, bare breasts, and orgies in his early biblical epics, modified his approach to produce movies challenging the prevailing view of marriage as a nonsexual relationship. For example, in *Why Change Your Wife?* (1920), a nagging Gloria Swanson reclaims her husband from another woman by dressing sexily, a theme to reemerge three-quarters of a century later with Jamie Lee Curtis in *True Lies* (1994).

Ignoring the evidence, critics blamed the decline in theater attendance at the beginning of the Depression on "too much sex" in the movies. But Hollywood, on the brink of bankruptcy, saw things differently and turned to gold diggers, screwball comedies, and gangster films. Paralleling the difficulties of the economic world, sex in the movies lost its romantic quality and became a commodity. Marlene Dietrich, Joan Crawford, Jean Harlow, and Barbara Stanwyck portrayed gun molls, mistresses, B-girls, and two-timing prostitutes who used sex as a key to their hard-won success. The male star also changed: the Latin lovers and all-American boys of the 1920s were deemed inadequate. The new stars—Clark Gable, James Cagney, Gary Cooper, and Cary Grant—were both more rugged and more sophisticated.

Into this milieu sauntered Mae West, a forty-year-old veteran of vaudeville and Broadway—and more. Her caricature of amoral sexuality in *I'm No Angel* (1933) and *She Done Him Wrong (*1933) was a huge success and almost single-handedly saved the Paramount studio from bankruptcy, returning ten times the investment. However, her libidinous repartee made her a ripe target for censors. In 1934, the Catholic Church, highly offended by De Mille's *Sign of the Cross,* created the Legion of Decency to enforce a previously ineffectual Production Code (Walsh, 66–143). Because Catholics constituted one-third of the potential domestic audience, a negative evaluation by the legion could kill a movie. Not only was Mae West's career sharply curtailed, but for the next thirty years every element of film production was also closely scrutinized by the industry's own censor, the Hays Office, and the legion to protect traditional values (Leff and Simmons, 19–32).

While the censors were trying to clean up the movies, other media offered more sexual titillation. *Esquire* began publishing in late 1933. Other magazines featured provocative pictorials. Many mainstream comics featured buxom women, and a new form of eight-page hardcore comics was created. Meanwhile, traveling stag film exhibitions attracted many otherwise respectable males.

With a few notable exceptions, such as *The Miracle of Morgan's Creek* (1944), wartime movies did not reflect the new reality. In wartime films, women were loyal to their men in service; adultery was harshly punished; and soldiers did not curse. *Casablanca* (1942) offered romantic obsession, male camaraderie, and a patriotic ending. After all, as Rick Blaine (Humphrey Bogart) says, "the problems of three little people don't amount to a hill of beans."

However, at the end of the war, the disillusionment generated by the Depression, the stresses of war, and the fears and disappointment of difficult adjustments to peacetime resulted in what amounted to a backlash. A new genre, film noir, which first appeared in 1941 with John Huston's *The Maltese Falcon,* came of age in 1946–47. From the viewpoint of gender relations, film noir was grounded in the glorification of the pinup during the war, the changed expectations of both sexes, and the suspicions and paranoia of the war increased by "Dear John" letters. *The Blue Dahlia* (1946) encapsulated the immediate postwar experience: a soldier returns from the war to discover his world destroyed; his wife is unfaithful or dead; his business partner has cheated him; his

FIGURE 71. *The Sign of the Cross* (1932). Cecil B. De Mille's epic of debauchery and decadence in Rome included scenes of sex and sadism. The film's release resulted in the Catholic Church's establishing the Legion of Decency. Courtesy Paramount Pictures.

job is gone. In a more general sense, Hollywood used the works of Dashiell Hammett, James Cain, and Raymond Chandler, mystery writers whose femmes fatales used sex as a tool and took betrayal below what it had been in the gangster films of the 1920s. In film noirs such as *Gilda* (1946), *The Big Sleep* (1946), and *The Postman Always Rings Twice* (1946), wives were uncontrollable; husbands were cuckolds or worse. In short, the women of film noir were very attractive, very sexy, very aggressive, and very untrustworthy. The Production Code could outlaw bawdiness, but it could not outlaw the radiant sexuality of a Lauren Bacall or a Barbara Stanwyck.

Conformity seemed to prevail in both the society and the movies of the early 1950s, but the seeds of change were being sown as movie directors competed with television by including sexual tidbits in old film formulas and adapting novels and plays that dealt with adultery, sexual activity, fornication, or homosexuality. Tennessee Williams was a favorite source. His *Streetcar Named Desire* (1947, play; 1951, film) was one of Hollywood's first excursions into truly adult filmmaking. It starred a brutal and aggressive Marlon Brando, who was the prototypical male of the 1950s, and grossed over $4 million.

The first major skirmishes in the war against the Production Code occurred after Otto Preminger released *The Moon Is Blue* (1953) and *From Here to Eternity* (1953) without Code approval. The box-office success of the films foretold the Production Code's death. Equally important, the Supreme Court ruled in *Jacobellis v. Ohio* that *The Lovers* (1958), a softcore tale of a repressed wife seeking fulfillment through adultery, was not obscene. In a concurring opinion, Justice Potter Stewart made the oft-quoted remark that, although he could not define obscenity, "I know it when I see it."

Meanwhile, the development of the "nudie-cutie" in the exploitation genre paved the way for the return of nudity to mainstream films. *The Immoral Mr. Teas* (1959) blurred the boundary of acceptability by playing in theaters that had never screened erotic films. Facing the threat of nudie-cuties and—more important, of foreign art films—Warner Bros. included nude scenes in *Splendor in the Grass* (1961)—only to cut them before release.

Sex themes, however, were flourishing. *Anatomy of a Murder* (1959) dealt with rape and homicide and featured strong language. In *A Summer Place* (1959), Sandra Dee is required to have her virginity affirmed by a doctor after she spends a shipwrecked, unchaperoned evening with Troy Donahue. Films about love and prostitution, but without nudity, such as *Butterfield 8* (1960), *The World of Suzie Wong* (1960), *Breakfast at Tiffany's* (1961), *Never on Sunday* (1960), and *Irma la Douce* (1963), were artistic and commercial successes.

Another sign of the coming liberation of the movies was George Cukor's *The Chapman Report* (1962), a takeoff, nine years after its publication, of the first Kinsey studies on sexual behavior of women. Despite its perverse fixation on sexually frustrated and nymphomaniacal housewives, the film contained no nudity, but a decade later it was one of the early "daring" offerings by the new cable TV network, Home Box Office (HBO).

Whatever the explanation, the film industry was increasingly out of touch with changing sexual mores, and change was inevitable. The ban on nudity was broken with director Sidney Lumet's *The Pawnbroker* (1965), in which a nude scene, shot from the rear, was deemed essential to the plot and received Code approval. (John Ford's *In Harm's Way,* released the same year, featured a similar scene.) One year later, Michelangelo Antonioni's *Blowup* (1966), released without Code approval, was the first mainstream film to offer a glimpse of female genitalia.

Cold War fears combined with sex to produce the James Bond spy-film franchise of the 1960s and beyond. Featuring beautiful women, lots of sexual innuendo, and a lack of realism, the spy genre's audience appeal insulated it from the censors and provided release from the real fears of nuclear war. In contrast to the vicarious sex and violence of the spy genre, the late 1960s also saw the development of a new kind of hero who reflected changing gender views: the sensitive, insecure male struggling with his sexuality and relationships. The classic example was Dustin Hoffman in *The Graduate* (1967), who set the stage for future portrayals of males with humor, sensitivity, and character as an alternative to the handsome, roguish, and apparently emotionless male of the past.

In the short run, however, "adult" movies, which had been a separate industry since 1915, moved center stage when a softcore Swedish film, *I Am Curious (Yellow)* (1968) became popular. Subsequent "documentaries" about the end of film censorship in Denmark set the stage for *(Behind) The Green Door* (1972), one of the breakthrough American-made hardcore movies. The next year *Deep Throat* (1973) and *The Devil in Miss Jones* (1973) were among the top ten films in gross revenues. Surveying these novel developments, *The New York Times* coined the phrase "porno chic," wondering if a new genre was being created to address a changing lifestyle.

Overwhelmed by the sexual revolution and the threat of more explicit foreign films, the Production Code was replaced in 1968 by a new rating system. By 1970, it was almost impossible to find a non-Disney film without at least partial nudity, and many went further. *Beyond the Valley of the Dolls* (1970) featured a lesbian, a male prostitute, a female transvestite, and an eighteen-year-old virgin in the same bed; mainstream films such as Paul Mazursky's *Bob & Carol & Ted & Alice* (1969) and Mike Nichols's *Carnal Knowledge* (1971) were similarly daring. The capstone was *Last Tango in Paris* (1973), starring Marlon Brando and Maria Schneider. Although there are only about ten minutes of sexual activity—in which Brando keeps his pants on—the buttery image of anal intercourse was the talk of many suburban parties of the sort so brilliantly portrayed in Ang Lee's film *The Ice Storm* (1997). Clearly, at this point, the sexual barrier in mainstream cinema had fallen.

By the mid-1970s, sex had become an integral part of American cinema and, to a significant extent, reflected sexual concerns in the society, albeit through the lens of the box office. Homosexuality came out of the movie closet with *The Boys in the Band* (1969). Lesbianism became an acceptable screen topic after *The Killing of Sister George* (1968). *La Cage aux Folles* (1978)—as a show and as a film—was a major hit with both gay and straight audiences. Transvestites and transsexuals were central characters in *The Rocky Horror Picture Show* (1975) and *Victor/Victoria* (1982). Even incest received sensitive treatment in Louis Malle's *Murmur of the Heart* (1971) and played a pivotal role in *Chinatown* (1974), in which the femme fatale, Evelyn Cross Mulwray (Faye Dunaway) admits that she had borne a child by her father, Noah Cross (John Huston).

Greater openness led to more diversity and explicitness in film, but old themes still flourished. The prostitute who fascinated the 1960s became a more complex character thanks to Jane Fonda in *Klute* (1971); Jodie

Foster in *Taxi Driver* (1976); Brooke Shields in *Pretty Baby* (1978); Richard Gere in *American Gigolo* (1981); Rebecca De Mornay in *Risky Business* (1983); Jamie Lee Curtis in *Trading Places* (1983); and Julia Roberts in *Pretty Woman* (1990). Glenn Close updated Theda Bara's vamp in *Fatal Attraction* (1987), and Kathleen Turner reprised a 1940s theme in *Body Heat* (1981). These movies were precursors of a new genre—sexual thrillers—made possible by relaxed sexual standards that encouraged explicit portrayals of sexual activity. The classic is *Basic Instinct* (1992), which opens with a torrid intercourse scene with a murderous climax. Many feminists saw the whole genre as an attack on the women's movement. Whether the charge is valid or not, the motif of woman as evil and dangerous returned to the movies of the 1990s.

Three recent movies illustrate the freedom and constraints of contemporary filmmakers in dealing with sexual issues. *Primary Colors* (1998) was very loosely based on allegations of sexual misconduct by a president still in office. And, ironically, 1997 saw the reemergence of censorship with the remake of Vladimir Nabokov's *Lolita.* The previous version was directed by Stanley Kubrick in 1962; this time, Adrian Lyne's version was produced under the close supervision of an attorney to protect the producers from child pornography charges, criticism that also attended the 1999 release of Sam Mendes's *American Beauty.* Thus, as movies gain more freedom to deal with more graphic sexual material—and must do so if they are to compete with television fare such as *Sex in the City*—the struggle over film content continues.

References

Filmography

American Beauty (1999, F)
American Gigolo (1981, F)
Anatomy of a Murder (1959, F)
Basic Instinct (1992, F)
(Behind) The Green Door (1972, F)
Beyond the Valley of the Dolls (1970, F)
The Big Sleep (1946, F)
Blowup (1966, F)
The Blue Dahlia (1946, F)
Bob & Carol & Ted & Alice (1969, F)
Body Heat (1981, F)
The Boys in the Band (1969, F)
Breakfast at Tiffany's (1961, F)
Butterfield 8 (1960, F)
Carnal Knowledge (1971, F)
Casablanca (1942, F)
The Chapman Report (1962, F)
Chinatown (1974, F)
Cleopatra (1917, F)
Deep Throat (1973, F)
The Devil in Miss Jones (1973, F)
Fatal Attraction (1987, F)
From Here to Eternity (1953, F)
Gilda (1946, F)
The Graduate (1967, F)
I Am Curious (Yellow) (1968, F)
The Ice Storm (1997, F)
The Immoral Mr. Teas (1959, F)
Irma la Douce (1963, F)
The Killing of Sister George (1968, F)
Klute (1971, F)
La Cage aux Folles (1978, F)
Last Tango in Paris (1972, F)
Lolita (1962, F; 1997, F)
The Maltese Falcon (1941, F)
The Miracle of Morgan's Creek (1944, F)
The Moon Is Blue (1953, F)
Murmur of the Heart (1971, F)
Never on Sunday (1960, F)
The Pawnbroker (1965, F)
The Postman Always Rings Twice (1946, F; 1981, F)
Pretty Baby (1978, F)
Pretty Woman (1990, F)
Primary Colors (1998, F)
Risky Business (1983, F)
The Rocky Horror Picture Show (1975, F)
The Sheik (1921, F)
The Sign of the Cross (1934, F)
Splendor in the Grass (1961, F)
A Streetcar Named Desire (1951, F)
A Summer Place (1959, F)
Taxi Driver (1976, F)
Trading Places (1983, F)
Traffic in Souls (1913, F)
True Lies (1994, F)
Victor/Victoria (1982, F)
Why Change Your Wife? (1920, F)
The World of Suzie Wong (1960, F)

Bibliography

Black, Gregory D. *Hollywood Censored: Morality Codes, Catholics, and the Movies.* New York: Cambridge University Press, 1994.

D'Emilio, John, and Estelle B. Freedman. *Intimate Matters: A History of Sexuality in America.* New York: Harper & Row, 1988.

Jacobs, Lea. *The Wages of Sin: Censorship and the Fallen Woman Film, 1928–1942.* Berkeley: University of California Press, 1977.

Kinsey, Alfred C., Wardell Pomeroy, and Clyde E. Martin. *Sexual Behavior in the Human Male.* Philadelphia: W. B. Saunders, 1948.

Kinsey, Alfred C., Wardell Pomeroy, Clyde E. Martin, and Paul H. Gebhard. *Sexual Behavior in the Human Female.* Philadelphia: W. B. Saunders, 1953.

Knight, Arthur, and Hollis Alpert. "The History of Sex in Cinema." *Playboy,* November 1969.

——. "The History of Sex in Cinema, Part 1: The Original Sin." *Playboy,* April 1965.

——. "The History of Sex in Cinema, Part 2: Compounding the Sin." *Playboy,* May 1965.

——. "The History of Sex in Cinema, Part 3: Hollywood's Flaming Youth." *Playboy,* June 1965.

——. "The History of Sex in Cinema, Part 4: The Twenties." *Playboy,* August 1965.

——. "The History of Sex in Cinema, Part 5: Sex Stars of the Twenties." *Playboy,* September 1965.

——. "The History of Sex in Cinema, Part 6: The Thirties." *Playboy,* November 1965.

——. "The History of Sex in Cinema, Part 7: The Thirties." *Playboy,* February 1966.

——. "The History of Sex in Cinema, Part 8: Sex Stars of the Thirties." *Playboy,* April 1966.

——. "The History of Sex in Cinema, Part 9: The Forties." *Playboy,* August 1966.

——. "The History of Sex in Cinema, Part 10: The Forties." *Playboy,* September 1966.

——. "The History of Sex in Cinema, Part 11: Sex Stars of the Forties." *Playboy,* October 1966.

——. "The History of Sex in Cinema, Part 12: The Fifties." *Playboy,* November 1966.

——. "The History of Sex in Cinema, Part 14: Sex Stars of the Fifties." *Playboy,* January 1967.

——. "The History of Sex in Cinema, Part 15: Experimental Films." *Playboy,* April 1967.

——. "The History of Sex in Cinema, Part 16: The Nudies." *Playboy,* June 1967.

——. "The History of Sex in Cinema, Part 17: The Stag Film." *Playboy,* November 1967.

——. "The History of Sex in Cinema, Part 18: The Sixties." *Playboy,* April 1968.

——. "The History of Sex in Cinema, Part 19: The Sixties." *Playboy,* July 1968.

——. "The History of Sex in Cinema, Part 20: Sex Stars of the Sixties." *Playboy,* January 1969.

Leff, Leonard J., and Jerold L. Simmons. *The Dame in the Kimono: Hollywood, Censorship, and the Production Code from the 1920s to the 1960s.* New York: Grove Weidenfeld, 1990.

Pascall, Jeremy, and Clyde Jeavers. *A Pictorial History of Sex in the Movies.* London: Hamlyn, 1975.

Petersen, James R. *The Century of Sex: Playboy's History of the Sexual Revolution.* New York: Grove Press, 1999.

Quarles, Mike. *Down and Dirty: Hollywood's Exploitation Filmmakers and Their Movies.* Jefferson, NC: McFarland, 1993.

Ullman, Sharon R. *Sex Seen: The Emergence of Modern Sexuality in America.* Berkeley: University of California Press, 1997.

Walsh, Frank. *Sin and Censorship: The Catholic Church and the Motion Picture Industry.* New Haven: Yale University Press, 1996.

[**ROBERT B. TOPLIN**]

Slavery

Many scholars speak of American "exceptionalism," noting that the people of the United States enjoyed greater freedom, opportunity, and democracy over their history than other peoples of the world, including Europeans. The U.S. experience with slavery, however, contrasts sharply with this positive and optimistic interpretation. Americans were unable to find peaceful political solutions to the crisis of slavery. Nearly four million African Americans lived in bondage by the 1850s, and the struggle to win their freedom contributed significantly to the divisions that drew the country into four years of bloody civil war. In the nineteenth century, Americans disagreed vigorously as they interpreted the lessons of their country's painful experience with slavery, and they continued these debates into the twentieth century not only in writing but also, eventually, through their portrayals in motion pictures and television programs.

Interpretations of the past often reflect perspectives of the present. As new views about politics, society, and the law come into vogue, these considerations make an impact on views of the past. Changes in popular attitudes about slavery are especially noticeable around the time of World War II. Before the war, books and especially movies tended to tell the history of slavery from the perspective of southern whites. After the war, books, motion pictures, and television programs gave greater attention to the African American perspective.

The Historical Debate

Before the 1940s, many writers treated slavery in the United States as a rather benign institution. They drew attention to the paternalistic attitudes of masters, observing that whites often treated their black servants and agricultural workers like members of an extended family. Some of these writers also viewed slavery as a "school of civilization," arguing that the institution trained Africans for participation in American culture. One of the most influential of these historians was Ulrich Bonnell Phillips, whose books *American Negro Slavery* (1918) and *Life and Labor in the Old South* (1929) challenged the nineteenth-century abolitionists' claim that slavery was unusually harsh.

Interpretations of the African American experience in the antebellum South changed rather dramatically after World War II. Revulsion against Hitler's racism and the extermination of six million Jews in the Holocaust contributed to growing concern about the rights of minorities. In the postwar years, America's historical record of prejudice and oppression came under greater scrutiny and criticism. Kenneth M. Stampp's *The Peculiar Institution* (1956) attacked many of the conclusions found in Phillips's work. Stampp showed that African Americans suffered tremendously under slavery. He observed that slaves reacted in a variety of ways to their oppression. Some ran away, and a few rebelled. Most recognized that outright resistance was impossible because it could excite violent reactions from the whites. Stampp's broad message was clear: slaves were generally unhappy with their condition and eager for freedom.

A number of studies soon followed that demonstrated ways in which blacks coped with their difficult condition in slavery. In *Roll, Jordan, Roll* (1974), Eugene D. Genovese showed that slaves found a sense of personal dignity and salvation through religious practices, and John Blassingame revealed in *The Slave Community* (1972) that blacks often protected themselves on farms and plantations through a complex network of personal and familial relationships with their fellow slaves. Both of these studies argue that the enslaved were not simply victims of an oppressive system. African Americans devised effective ways to limit the master's power over their lives and to resist the pressures of an exploitative work regime.

American society's growing resistance to racism and broadening commitment to civil rights in the decades after World War II also brought heightened attention to the history of racial prejudice in the United States. Not surprisingly, historians reported that important sources of racial bigotry could be found in the country's experience with slavery. In *White Over Black* (1968), Winthrop Jordan reported that Englishmen exhibited racial fears even before they had become broadly involved with slavery in North America. The growth of slavery in British colonies of the Western Hemisphere tended to intensify these prejudiced attitudes. Carl N. Degler argues that the treatment of blacks in the American South was not worse than the treatment they received in Brazil (the second largest slave society in the Americas), but racial prejudice in the antebellum United States became much more severe than in Brazil's slave society because Americans usually viewed all people with some African ancestry as black. George M. Fredrickson contributed to the scholarship on prejudice by showing that the racism of many white southerners evolved. During the revolutionary period, a number of white southerners talked about emancipation, equality, and the rights of all men, notes Fredrickson in *The Black Image in the White Mind* (1971). Then, as the southern whites' dependence on cotton profits grew and they came under challenge from antislavery leaders, racial views hardened. White southerners increasingly treated their "peculiar institution" in an uncompromising way, and they argued that their supposedly "inferior" slaves were incapable of handling freedom.

The treatment of slavery in popular entertainment roughly paralleled these trends. Before World War II, interpretations in motion pictures often reflected elements of Phillips's views on slavery. After the war, movies (as well as films on television) often reflected the perspectives advanced by scholars such as Stampp, Genovese, and Fredrickson. The Hollywood and TV versions of history exaggerated these interpretations. They accentuated the messages with emotion-laden pictures and portrayals that hammered viewers with strong criticisms of slavery's role in antebellum southern life.

Filmic Views of Slavery before World War II

The Birth of a Nation presented the most influential early perspective on slavery from the motion picture business. Based on a book, *The Clansman,* by North Carolina writer Thomas Dixon, the 1915 movie gave audiences a highly biased view of slavery, the Civil War, and Reconstruction. Its brief segments dealing with slavery portrayed blacks as generally happy with their condition. Plantations appeared idyllic, and the movie suggested that whites demonstrated a paternalistic concern for their slaves' well-being. A caption in the film blamed slavery for the Civil War, saying, "The bringing of the African to America planted the first seeds of disunion."

Black leaders publicly criticized the racist nature of D. W. Griffith's influential movie. They particularly objected to the film's negative images of the blacks during Reconstruction. An editorial in the African American publication *The Crisis* called the movie "a sordid and lurid melodrama" that characterized the black man "either as an ignorant fool, a vicious rapist, a venal and unscrupulous politician, or a faithful but doddering idiot." The *New York Globe* suggested that the movie fomented "race antipathy that is the most sinister and dangerous feature of American life." *Birth of a Nation* nevertheless became an extraordinary box-office success. Within a year of its opening, an estimated three million viewers had seen the movie. Its popularity contributed to the revival of the Ku Klux Klan in the 1915–25 period.

Gone with the Wind (1939), another popular historical epic about the Civil War, also delivered memorable depictions of slavery in the antebellum South. Like Griffith's classic, *Gone with the Wind* displayed a paternalistic attitude on the part of the masters and painted an idyllic picture of life on the plantations. One of the movie's most negative characterizations of a black figure showed actress Butterfly McQueen disintegrating into a state of panic when she needed to assist in delivering a baby. Nevertheless, the movie's depictions were an improvement over the simplistic and critical portrayals of blacks in *The Birth of a Nation.* African Americans in *Gone with the Wind* were friendly individuals, not the dangerous aggressors seen in *Birth of a Nation. Gone with the Wind* also featured a strong black character: Hattie McDaniel, in a role that won her an Academy Award, played a loyal but tough servant who is not afraid to berate Scarlett O'Hara when her behavior threatens to demean the family's reputation.

Post–World War II Views of Slavery

Just as books about slavery published after World War II began to reflect a more critical approach to slavery, Hollywood, too, began to treat the institution more negatively in movies dealing with southern themes. One of the significant early signs of change appeared in *Band of Angels* (1957), in which Sidney Poitier plays a talented but unhappy slave under the control of his master, Hamish Bond (Clark Gable), a rakish former slave trader who feels remorse about his dishonorable profession. *Band of Angels* also cast Yvonne DeCarlo in the role of Amantha Starr, a tragic mulatto. DeCarlo plays a beautiful debutante from Kentucky who was sold to the slave markets of New Orleans with her father's estate. In dealing with these ugly elements of slavery, *Band of Angels* presented a picture of antebellum times that contrasted starkly with the "moonlight and magnolias" view evident in many of Hollywood's earlier productions.

Television also began to contribute to the revision of popular views on slavery. The most notable impact came from *Roots,* an immensely successful dramatic series that appeared on ABC in 1977. In a multiepisode format that looked like a prime-time soap opera, *Roots* stressed the horror of the black experience in slavery. It began with stories about the travails of a young African male who had been captured by white slave traders and forced to labor in Virginia. The drama then followed the lives of his descendants as they experienced whippings, sexual harassment, separation from their families, and other abuses. Based on a popular book by author Alex Haley, *Roots* pulled at the heartstrings of Americans of whatever ethnicity. It broke all audience records for a new television drama, and in the aftermath of its broadcast many schools and colleges scheduled classroom discussions about its treatment of history.

Some observers raised questions about *Roots'* presentation of history. Historian James Brewer Stewart complained that the drama did not show ambiguities and complexities in the master-slave relationship, and *Time*'s reviewer, Richard Schickel, claimed that the miniseries offered "almost no new insights, factual or emotional" about slavery. Schickel considered the TV movie "a handy compendium of stale melodramatic conventions." The chorus of positive responses, especially from ordinary viewers, drowned out these negative reactions.

Other made-for-television dramas attempted to cash in on the popularity of *Roots,* such as *Freedom Road* (1979) and *Beulah Land* (1980), but they presented whites and blacks in such one-dimensional, stereotypical characterizations that they tended to bore audiences. A more sophisticated treatment soon appeared in a PBS series called *A House Divided* (now marketed in video stores under the title *Half Slave/Half Free*). The programs of *A House Divided,* developed by historian Robert Brent Toplin, dramatized the lives of three real-life figures from the years of slavery and the Civil War: Denmark Vesey, Solomon Northup, and Charlotte Forten. These dramas conveyed the negative assessment of slavery evident in Kenneth M. Stampp's book, but they also communicated ideas from the newer research about the slaves' coping efforts seen in books by Eugene D. Genovese and John Blassingame, who showed that slaves found spiritual and communal strength in their practice of religion and in their ties to an extended family. The dramas corrected the tendency in *Roots* and its imitators to portray almost all slaveholders as insensitive exploiters. For example, one of the films, entitled *Solomon Northup's Odyssey,* showed an African American working under three different masters. One was a kindly individual whose good intentions were undermined by the slave system. A second master was a vicious, poorly educated individual who was jealous of Northup's intelligence and skills. The third respected Northup but drove him hard nevertheless in order to maximize profits on his plantation.

In the late 1960s and early 1970s Hollywood movies tended to go to extremes in countering the old images of slavery seen in movies such as *Birth of a Nation* and *Gone with the Wind.* A new genre appeared called "blaxploitation films" that stressed the brutal aspects of slavery, revealed the horrors associated with slave breeding, viewed slaves as seething rebels, and portrayed white masters and mistresses as hungry for sexual escapades with the African Americans on their plantations. These R- and X-rated films, such as *Slaves* (1969), *The Quadroon* (1971), *Mandingo* (1975), *Drum* (1976), and *Passion Plantation* (1978) contained lots of lust and violence. Characterizations were often stereotypical, featuring male slaves as Nat Turners and their white owners as deeply flawed individuals. Interestingly, no major motion picture of the period dramatized the story of Nat Turner, although some Hollywood producers talked about bringing William Styron's controversial novel *The Confessions of Nat Turner* (1967) to the screen.

Caleb Deschanel's 1988 film *Crusoe,* starring Aidan Quinn and Ade Sapara, brought a nuanced view of the slavery issue to its retelling of Daniel Defoe's famed novel, portraying the Robinson Crusoe character as a Virginia slave trader whose eyes are slowly opened to the evils of his work. A sophisticated treatment of slavery appeared on television in 1990 in the form of a documentary series. In *The Civil War,* filmmaker Ken Burns identified slavery as the principal cause of the great conflict. Burns's film showed a famous photograph of an African American with scars on his back from whippings and presented other disturbing pictures of life in bondage. Burns also provided a sympathetic treatment of the abolitionists who attacked slavery. *The Civil War* effectively communicated criticisms of slavery previously explored by historians such as Stampp, Genovese, and Blassingame. Some white southerners objected to the series, arguing that it presented a biased interpretation of sensitive issues (they claimed that Burns exhibited a pro-Yankee, pro-abolitionist perspective), but most journalists and historians gave the film high marks for its treatment of history.

In 1997 Steven Spielberg entered the cinematic debates about slavery with his big-screen production of *Amistad.* Based on a real historical event, *Amistad* portrays the mutiny of Africans on a Spanish slave ship. It follows the

Africans' experiences after Americans intercepted the ship off the coast of New England. The movie shows that the authorities placed the captives behind bars while abolitionists and slave interests fought over their fate. At the end of the film, the elderly ex-president of the United States, John Quincy Adams (Anthony Hopkins), successfully defends their freedom before the U.S. Supreme Court.

Spielberg received much praise for his powerful emotional statement about the horrors of the African slave trade. The opening scenes in the movie, depicting vicious treatment of blacks, including wholesale murder, presented especially frightening images. Some historians objected to the artistic liberties taken by the filmmaker, however. They noted, for example, that the dedicated abolitionist Lewis Tappan (who made tremendous personal commitments to free the blacks in the Amistad case) appeared in the movie as an opportunist who was willing to sacrifice the slaves' interests to serve his own purposes. Critics also pointed to a booklet Spielberg's movie company distributed to the nation's schools that encouraged classroom discussions about characters and incidents in the movie. Scholars observed, for instance, that the instructional materials recommended discussions about the movie character Theodore Joadson (Morgan Freeman), a black abolitionist. Joadson was not a real figure from history, noted the critics; he was an invention of the filmmakers.

Sensitive treatment of the African American experience in bondage continued in 1998 with the appearance of a four-part PBS documentary series, *Africans in America.* The film series traced the history of African Americans from the early colonial period through the Civil War. It gave most of its attention to the struggle of enslaved blacks to cope with and overcome slavery. The documentary described the horrors of life in bondage, giving attention to the slave trade, the breakup of families, and the influence of racism on both North and South. The film maintained that blacks were not passive victims of oppression. It focused on the work of black abolitionists as well as the efforts of blacks in slavery that attempted to escape or rebel against their condition. Despite these achievements, *Africans in America* presents little of the complex new understanding of history that scholars have been providing in recent decades, and it gives almost no hint that historians have disagreed considerably in interpreting the story of slavery in America.

References

Filmography

Africans in America (1998, D)
Amistad (1997, F)
The Birth of a Nation (1915, F)
The Civil War (1990, D)
Crusoe (1988, F)
Drum (1976, F)
Glory (1989, F)
Gone with the Wind (1939, F)
Half Slave/Half Free (1984, D)
Mandingo (1975, F)
Roots (1977, TV)

Bibliography

Berlin, Ira. *Many Thousand Gone.* Cambridge, MA: Belknap Press, 1998.

Blassingame, John. *The Slave Community: Plantation Life in the Antebellum South.* New York: Oxford University Press, 1972.

Campbell, Edward D. C., Jr. *The Celluloid South: Hollywood and the Southern Myth.* Knoxville: University of Tennessee Press, 1981.

Cripps, Thomas. *Making Movies Black: The Hollywood Message Movie from World War II to the Civil Rights Era.* New York: Oxford University Press, 1993.

——. *Slow Fade to Black: The Negro in American Film, 1900–1942.* New York: Oxford University Press, 1977.

Degler, Carl N. *Neither White nor Black: Slavery and Race Relations in Brazil and the United States.* New York: Macmillan, 1971.

Frederickson, George M. *The Black Image in the White Mind.* New York: Harper & Row, 1971.

Genovese, Eugene D. *Roll, Jordan, Roll: The World the Slaves Made.* New York: Pantheon, 1974.

Kirby, Jack Temple. *Media-Made Dixie: The South in the American Imagination.* Baton Rouge: Louisiana State University Press, 1978.

Leab, Daniel J. *From Sambo to Superspade: The Black Experience in Motion Pictures.* Boston: Houghton Mifflin, 1975.

Stampp, Kenneth M. *The Peculiar Institution.* New York: Knopf, 1956.

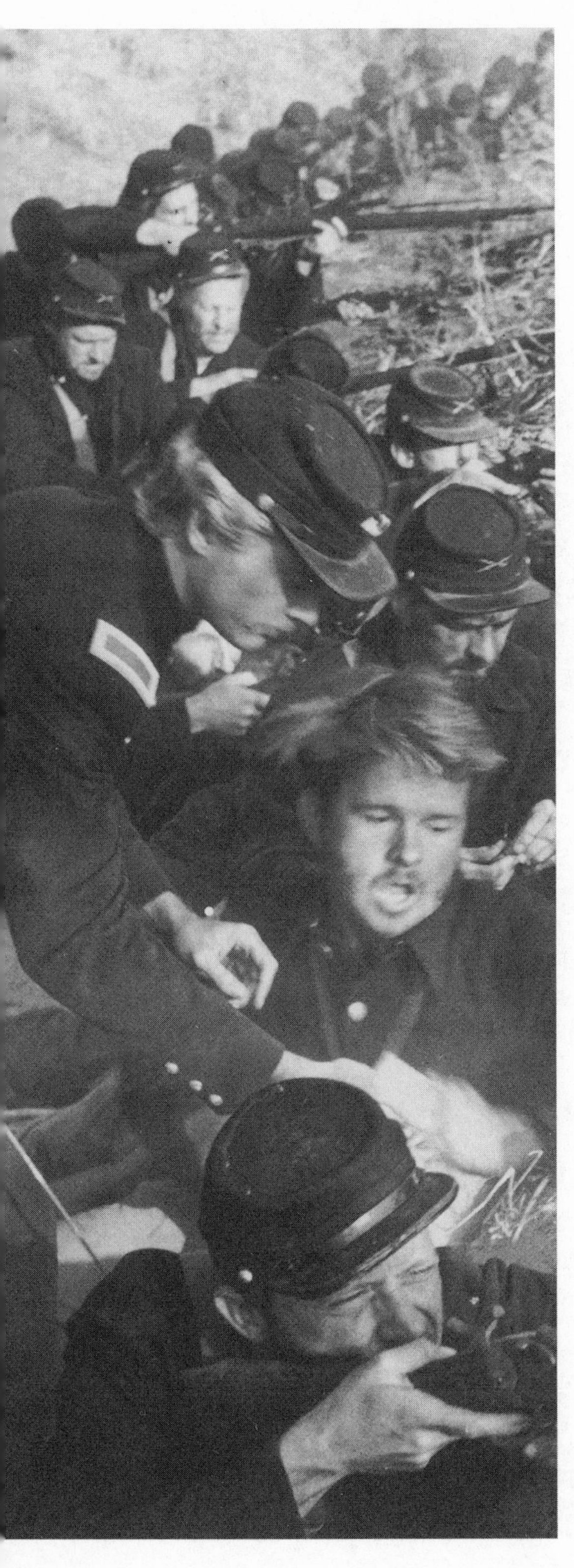

VIII.
Myths and Heroes

★ ★ ★ ★ ★ ★ ★

[CHARLES J. MALAND]

The American Adam

The American Adam has been an animating myth in American literature and culture since the early nineteenth century. Along with such myths as the success myth, the myth of virgin land, and the manifest destiny of Americans to populate and develop the continent, it has helped define key ingredients in the national self-image. Related in interesting ways to a number of these other cultural myths, the myth of the American Adam has also been evident in American films.

As related by such cultural historians as R. W. B. Lewis, David W. Noble, and Giles Gunn, the myth of the American Adam is rooted in the first half of the nineteenth century. Even before that time, many colonists believed that the settlers in the New World would construct a new harmonious society—a City on a Hill—exempt from the institutional limitations and corruptions of the Old World. During the early nineteenth century, the notion of American exceptionalism became even more widespread. Its advocates held that the United States, because of its democratic political institutions, its emergent individualism, and its vast western frontier, constituted a unique social and political experiment on the world stage. Emerging in this New World Garden would be a model democratic society, celebrating the common man and extending individual freedom far beyond anything imagined in Europe. Affected by this vision, the New England transcendentalists and their followers celebrated the self-reliant individualist in such works as Ralph Waldo Emerson's *Nature* and "The Divinity School Address"; Henry David Thoreau's *Walden*; and Walt Whitman's "Song of Myself." Combined with the perceived triumph of the common man in Andrew Jackson's election to the presidency in 1828, this optimistic vision spurred the dream that the United States had shed the burdens of the past and was creating a new, more perfect human society.

From these hopes about the rich possibilities of American life emerged the character of the American Adam. He was, in Whitman's words, "a single, separate self," often orphaned, estranged from parents, or with an uncertain, unknown past. Like the original Adam before the fall, he was an innocent—optimistic about the possibilities of man's place in nature, untested by experience, and often either unaware of or skeptical about the shaping and limiting constraints of human community. As defined in the literary and historical analyses of Lewis and Noble, the drama of this cultural myth emerged from the conflict between the American Adam and the social or natural forces that tested his optimism and innocence. Writers with a hopeful view of human nature created works that celebrated the ability of the self to transcend social limitations, evident, for example, in Thoreau's *Walden* and Whitman's *Leaves of Grass.* Others, such as Nathaniel Hawthorne in "My Kinsman, Major Molineaux" or Herman Melville in "Benito Cereno" and *Billy Budd,* cast a more complex and critical eye on the place of innocence in a fallen world. The core of the Adamic cultural myth emerged in the dialectic between these optimistic and pessimistic visions of human experience.

The myth of the American Adam is also related in important ways to the myth of the American frontier and the American success myth. James Fenimore Cooper's Natty Bumppo, for example, knows the frontier world and is most comfortable there, but at times he also acts to bring about the best forces of civilization, even if it may destroy his world. When Frederick Jackson Turner and later historians emphasized the centrality of the frontier in shaping the American character from the 1890s on, one version of the American Adam was transmuted into the solitary and often romantic cowboy hero. Similarly, as the United States became more urban and industrial in the later nineteenth century, the American Adam often transformed into a country or small-town innocent who went to the city and had his innocence tested there, thus linking the Adams to the American success myth, perhaps most memorably in F. Scott Fitzgerald's *The Great Gatsby*.

The American Adam in Film

As Robert Ray has convincingly argued, American film narratives since the establishment of the studio era have drawn on nineteenth-century American cultural myths and narrative conventions. This tendency has clearly been true of the myth of the American Adam, but with some changes from the mid-nineteenth-century literary tradition. Although the dream of the American Adam first established itself when the United States was primarily an agrarian society, American movies are a product of an urban industrial and postindustrial civilization that has played an increasingly large role on the world stage, and the forces confronting cinematic American Adams have evolved, particularly when the films have contemporary settings.

One early manifestation of the American Adam emerged in silent film comedy. Although one could discuss Harry Langdon's persona in such films as *The Strong Man* (1926), the dominant comic Adam was, of course, Charlie Chaplin's tramp. Chaplin solidified the tramp's persona at Essanay and Mutual between 1915 and 1917. In many of those films, and in most of the other comedies through *Modern Times* (1936), the tramp yearns for love and basic human needs like food and shelter, facing a world of antagonists physically stronger or financially more powerful than he is. Although his past is unknown, he faces the threats against him with physical agility, good humor, and resilience. Whether he ends the film with the girl (*The Gold Rush*, 1925), without her (*The Circus*, 1928), or in abeyance (*City Lights*, 1931), he manages to avoid being broken by the forces against him.

King Vidor's *The Crowd* (1928) offers a silent-era study of difficulties confronting the innocent hero in the city. Its hero, Johnny Sims (James Murray), is a key cinematic American Adam, born on July 4, 1900, in a paradigmatic small town. Johnny's father dreams he will become president, but he dies when Johnny is only twelve. Nevertheless, Johnny still dreams of succeeding when he goes to New York in the 1920s. Exhibiting some of the alienation of the 1920s Lost Generation, the film shows how Johnny struggles anonymously in the urban mass society. Unable to earn promotion above his tedious desk job at an insurance company, he also struggles in his marriage after his daughter is run over by a truck and killed. Instead of achieving a life of freedom, fulfillment, and acclaim, Johnny ends up just another struggling member of the crowd.

One of the most memorable American Adams created during the cultural nationalism of the late 1930s, Jefferson Smith (James Stewart) in Frank Capra's *Mr. Smith Goes to Washington* (1939) resembles Johnny Sims in that he has no father and leaves small-town life for the big city. Named a U.S. senator to fill out the term of one who dies in office, Smith, like some of his more optimistic nineteenth-century progenitors, is also closely associated with nature (he is the leader of a Boy Scouts–like group and sponsors a bill to establish a National Boy's Camp) and is connected to the political traditions of American liberty and individualism. Although his political idealism is tested and almost crushed by the power of Jim Taylor (Edward Arnold), a corrupt machine politician, Smith sticks to his principles and, against all odds, exposes the political machine while retaining his Adamic vision. Very much in the tradition of Emerson and Thoreau, Capra urges one to retain idealistic political principles when political compromise, represented in the film by Senator Paine (Claude Rains), seems both more tempting and lucrative. In doing so, Capra makes Jefferson Smith one of the most compellingly romantic American Adams of twentieth-century American film.

From early on in film history, the Western became a dominant film genre, and the cowboy hero has often functioned as a kind of American Adam. One, the Ringo Kid (John Wayne), in John Ford's *Stagecoach* (1939), appeared the same year as Jefferson Smith. Orphaned when the Plummer brothers kill his parents, Ringo has been imprisoned unjustly and has broken out of prison to avenge the murders. Depicted as an innocent and wronged common man, he is kind to the marginal members of the group traveling in a stagecoach across Indian country—especially the drunken Doc Boone (Thomas Mitchell) and the prostitute Dallas (Claire Trevor). As with many cowboy Adams, Ringo uses redemptive violence at the film's conclusion, killing all three of the Plummers, thus ridding society of evil and helping establish greater social harmony and stability. (The title character of *Shane* [1953], played by Alan Ladd, is a close Adamic relative of Ringo's.) Although Ringo is bathed in the optimistic glow of Popular Front politics, director Ford would later take a memorable and darker look at the individualist (yet less innocent) cowboy hero via Ethan Edwards (John Wayne) in *The Searchers* (1956). By 1970, following the turmoil of the 1960s, Dustin Hoffman, as the Indian scout Jack Crabb in *Little Big Man,* could play an American Adam who stands the social vision of the traditional Western on its head. Orphaned by a Pawnee raid as a child, Crabb is raised by the Cheyenne and observes both white and Native American cultures close range, concluding, in contrast to the conventional western, that white society is corrupt and that only among the Cheyenne, led by Old Lodge Skins (Chief Dan George), can he find a genuinely harmonious and humane society.

Other heroes in important American films of the 1940s and 1950s might be explored within the lens of the Adamic myth, including the title character of Orson Welles's *Citizen Kane* (1941). Although he has memories of a happy childhood and shows idealism and vitality in his young adulthood, Charles Foster Kane (Welles) ends up with a life of domination, acquisition, and loneliness, convinced he would have become a "really great man" except for the childhood trauma of parental separation and the burden of great wealth. *Casablanca*'s (1942) individualist hero with a mysterious past, Rick Blaine (Humphrey Bogart), is also an American Adam. In this case, however, the ethos of World War II requires that the isolated and isolationist Adam recognize the evil Nazi threat to the American garden and commit himself to fighting for the antifascist cause. More generally, the private detective movie heroes spawned by novelists like Raymond Chandler and Dashiell Hammett, although grizzled and cynically aware of urban corruption, are often related to the American Adam by the romantic individualism at the core of their character.

A memorable American Adam from the 1950s is Terry Malloy (Marlon Brando) in *On the Waterfront* (1954). Orphaned and raised by his brother Charley (Rod Steiger) and an evil surrogate father, Johnny Friendly (Lee J. Cobb), Terry yearns to shed the feeling that he is nothing but a bum, just as he dreams of finding love and integrity in a life that seems to be passing him by. Designed in part as a veiled, ambivalent defense of Kazan's own testimony before the House Committee on Un-American Activities in the McCarthy era, *On the Waterfront* depicts Terry, prodded by Edie (Eva Marie Saint), Father Barry (Karl Malden), and his own brother's death, achieving the integrity he yearns for by informing about Friendly's union corruption, fighting him, and destroying his power. Terry's character finds a descendant in the hero of the eponymous *Rocky* (1976), which features another parentless, failing, and innocent Adam, Rocky Balboa (Sylvester Stallone), who yearns for something better.

FIGURE 72. *On the Waterfront* (1954). Terry Malone (Marlon Brando) stands alone against the control of union corruption as his colleagues look on. Brando brought out the complex characteristics of the "American Adam." Courtesy Columbia Pictures and Horizon Pictures.

It is probably true that in nineteenth-century literature the American Adam appeared most often in what Nina Baym has aptly termed "melodramas of beset manhood." In a similar vein, American films since the early 1970s have presented him most memorably in such male action genres as gangster films, science fiction films, and war films.

Although *The Godfather* (1972) and *The Godfather II* (1974) are fundamentally a family gangster tragedy—an American House of Atreus—they are linked to the Adamic myth by Michael Corleone (Al Pacino). Although he has parents, the college graduate and war hero Michael is certainly played as an innocent early in the first film, insisting to his girlfriend Kay (Diane Keaton) that he is not a part of the family's violence and corruption. Separate from them and different, he shares his father Vito's (Marlon Brando) dream that he become a legitimate and respected member of the American society, a senator or a judge. But despite Vito's kind manners and celebration of Old World family loyalty, his power is based on violence, and Michael's murders of two rivals draw him into the maelstrom of the family business. His innocence corrupted, Michael becomes the new Godfather, overseeing the destruction of the family, becoming as isolated by the end of the second film as Charles Foster Kane was in his old age.

The Adamic myth is also central in *Star Wars* trilogy (*Star Wars,* 1977; *The Empire Strikes Back,* 1980; *Return of the Jedi,* 1983), where the youthful Luke Skywalker (Mark Hamill), parentless and raised by relatives, passionately yearns to grow up by fighting against the powerful forces of the Empire. Drawing on archetypal narrative patterns after discussions with Joseph Campbell, screenwriter/director George Lucas allows Luke to fight valiantly and successfully in the first film. By the third, however, his American Adam learns that the evil Darth Vader is his real father, and he is forced to confront the disturbing possibility—usually neglected in action films—that good and evil may be less a question of us versus them than of contending forces within oneself.

Oliver Stone's two Vietnam films both feature Adamic protagonists: Chris Taylor (Charlie Sheen) in *Platoon* (1986) and Ron Kovic (Tom Cruise) in *Born on the Fourth of July* (1989). Unlike the American Adam during World War II—who learns, like Rick Blaine, that the cause is worth fighting for—Stone's heroes come to see war and the American involvement much differently. (Given that the movies are a popular medium and that public support for World War II was much more pronounced than support for Vietnam, this should not be surprising.) *Platoon* opens when Chris, a "cherry" estranged from his parents (though not from his grandmother), arrives in Vietnam with other replacements, and it traces his growing experience and horror at the war, caught between the good Sergeant Elias (Willem Dafoe) and the evil Staff Sergeant Barnes (Tom Berenger), a brutal man who permits the massacre of Vietnamese civilians. A dark picture of American involvement in Vietnam emerges when Barnes, afraid of evidence Elias has against him, leaves him, wounded, to die in the midst of an attack, and later when Chris kills the wounded Barnes in retaliation. The film ends with Chris looking back after the war, observing that in retrospect the war seems actually to be within him and that memories of Elias and Barnes were still fighting for his soul.

FIGURE 73. *Born on the Fourth of July* (1989). The Vietnam War film resurrected and revised the "American Adam" in Ron Kovic (Tom Cruise). Kovic returns home a paraplegic and shuns the social system and the patriotism he once embraced. Here, in his wheelchair, he is caught in the mayhem of an antiwar rally. Courtesy Ixtlan Corporation.

Ron Kovic (Tom Cruise) in *Born on the Fourth of July* is an Adamic product of the patriotic American 1950s and 1960s. Growing up in a small community on Long Island, he attends annual Independence Day parades and plays war with his playmates, his imagination fueled by John Wayne war films played on television. Although he does not start out estranged from his parents, he is portrayed as an innocent, mouthing platitudes he has heard from his mother or from politicians on TV, and is surprised when his father (Raymond J. Barry), a World War II veteran, worries just before his induction about the wisdom of fighting a war thirteen thousand miles from home. The war turns out nearly to destroy him: his unit carelessly kills women and children, he kills a buddy whom he mistakes for an attacking enemy soldier, his superior officers cover up both incidents, and finally he is shot in a battle and paralyzed permanently from the waist down. He returns home, and the rest of the film traces his movement from patriotic supporter of the war, to anguished doubter about the wisdom of his sacrifice, and finally to active spokesman for the Vietnam Veterans Against the War. Here the American Adam loses his innocence, blames his milieu for instilling thoughtless patriotism within him, and rejects all he had believed in, finally committing himself to opposing the war that cost both his health and the lives of many of his buddies.

In both literature and film, the myth of the American Adam has focused primarily on male protagonists, although women, like Henry James's innocent Daisy Miller, do exist. Rooted in the belief of American exceptionalism, the hope that the United States can avoid the corruptions of the Old World and create a model society, the American Adam, innocent and often orphaned, serves as a metaphor for a national self-image of a model democratic society, freed from the burdens of the past to face the future with enthusiasm. Although some American Adams, like Jefferson Smith and the Ringo Kid, retain their idealistic vision and succeed, it may be more common, particularly for films with contemporary settings made during times of social critique or reform, for the Adamic hero to be disillusioned or even destroyed by his confrontation with the harsh realities of contemporary society. The title characters of *Forrest Gump* (Tom Hanks, 1994) and *The Truman Show* (Jim Carrey, 1998) show that cinematic American Adams still fascinated viewers in the media-dominated, postindustrial 1990s and beyond, although, as Daniel Bell has argued, the belief in American exceptionalism may be declining as our world shrinks and global markets expand. Only time will tell whether and how the myth will persist in the new century.

References

Filmography

Born on the Fourth of July (1989, F)
Casablanca (1942, F)
The Circus (1928, F)
Citizen Kane (1941, F)
City Lights (1931, F)
The Crowd (1928, F)
The Empire Strikes Back (1980, F)
Forrest Gump (1994, F)
The Godfather (1972, F)
The Godfather II (1974, F)
The Gold Rush (1925, F)
Little Big Man (1970, F)
Modern Times (1936, F)
Mr. Smith Goes to Washington (1939, F)
On the Waterfront (1954, F)
Platoon (1986, F)
Return of the Jedi (1983, F)
The Searchers (1956, F)
Shane (1953, F)
Stagecoach (1939, F)
Star Wars (1977, F)
The Strong Man (1926, F)
The Truman Show (1998, F)

Bibliography

Baym, Nina. "Melodramas of Beset Manhood." *American Quarterly* 33.2 (1981): 123–139.

Bell, Daniel. "The End of American Exceptionalism." *Public Interest* 41 (1975): 193–229.

Gunn, Giles. "The Myth of the American Adam." In Richard Dorson, ed., *Handbook of American Folklore,* 79–85. Bloomington: Indiana University Press, 1983.

Hartz, Louis. *The Liberal Tradition in America.* New York: Harcourt, 1955.

Lewis, R. W. B. *The American Adam: Innocence, Tragedy, and Tradition in the Nineteenth Century.* Chicago: University of Chicago Press, 1955.

Lipset, Seymour. *American Exceptionalism: A Double-Edged Sword.* New York: Norton, 1996.

Noble, David. *The Eternal Adam and the New World Garden: The Central Myth in the American Novel Since 1830.* New York: George Braziller, 1968.

Ray, Robert. *A Certain Tendency of the Hollywood Cinema, 1930–1980.* Princeton: Princeton University Press, 1985.

Slotkin, Richard. *Gunfighter Nation: The Myth of the Frontier in Twentieth-Century America.* New York: Atheneum, 1992.

[ROBERT C. DOYLE]

The American Fighting Man

America has witnessed a long series of wars on the silver screen. Unlike most written histories of human conflict, often impersonalized by statistics and arrows on maps, feature films thrive on the personal dimension of war. Especially for young male viewers, the combat film has enjoyed a special attraction: whether in times of struggle or after major conflicts, American war films have held up role models of bravery in the name of democratic principles. Furthermore, Hollywood has taken a leading role in propagandizing for our country during its struggles—at least until the Vietnam War, when Hollywood productions often took a decidedly antiwar stance.

Antecedents include memoirs and diaries, personal narratives, autobiographies, and fictional accounts of battles, many of which described the taming of the American wilderness. Soldiers such as Ethan Allen (*The Narrative of Colonel Ethan Allen,* 1807) and Joseph Plumb Martin (*A Narrative of a Revolutionary Soldier,* 1830) pictured themselves as human monuments. With a clear mission, they followed a classical Roman code that emphasized martial virtue, serious regard for discipline and authority, personal integrity, guided ambition, and duty (Cunliffe, 154–155). Not until the end of the Civil War in 1865 did the symbolic opposition of civilization and savagery subside. By the end of the nineteenth century, Americans began to worry more about populist threats to their democratic institutions and economic opportunities and less about the frontier (Höbling, 297–298). By the twentieth century, Americans saw themselves as noble and moral crusaders for liberal democratic traditions that included the rule of law, progress, freedom, and individual rights. In the early 1940s American soldiers fought World War II for both moral virtue and national defense, and from 1945 to 1991 they became reluctant but committed warriors in the various hot flashes of the Cold War.

In terms of combat and its aftermath, Hollywood films have succeeded in painting pictures of the American Fighting Man as a multidimensional cultural figure. Although they marked their subjects idiosyncratically, directors such as D. W. Griffith early in the century, John Ford, John Huston, William Wyler, and Frank Capra in midcentury, and Oliver Stone, John Frankenheimer, Edward Zwick, and Steven Spielberg at the end of the century continued to focus on the traditional themes within the context of the classical code. As directors, they brought audiences to the battlefield and showed the technical details of war to those unfamiliar with the front lines; reminded veterans of their reliance on the code's idealism and that their sacrifices were not made in vain; and showed that Americans were citizen soldiers rather than militarists, shaped by the culture's particular interpretation of a specific conflict at a given time.

The Civil War

One of the directors who first painted the American soldier using the classical code was D. W. Griffith in *The Birth of a Nation* (1915). Although he favored the postwar antireconstructionist and racist views of the Ku Klux

Klan, Griffith created lucid battle scenes showing Civil War combat in terms of bravery, sacrifice, discipline, authority, personal integrity, and duty under fire in an epic style that later films emulated. For example, Matthew Broderick's portrayal of Colonel Robert Gould Shaw in Edward Zwick's *Glory* (1989), the story of the 54th Massachusetts Volunteer Infantry, brought to life the actions, motivations, and conflicts of one of the most aggressive fighting units in the Union Army. Zwick showed the racial divide in nineteenth-century America and rightly credited the 175,000 African Americans who went into harm's way between 1862 and 1865 as United States Colored Troops (USCT). Zwick noted only briefly in an epilogue that the 54th was not completely destroyed in South Carolina; after the fight at Fort Wagner near Charleston on July 18, 1863, the regiment went on to fight more battles and finished the Civil War with a distinguished combat record (Cornish, 153–156).

Audie Murphy's convincing portrayal of Private Henry Fleming in John Huston's classic film version of Stephen Crane's novel *Red Badge of Courage* (1951), perhaps, surpasses all the other attempts before and after to show the inner struggles of the American Fighting Man. As a volunteer Union infantryman, Fleming (Audie Murphy) is so desperate about being caught between cowardice (crushed by the horrors of war) and bravery (performance in the face of fear and mortal danger) that he inflicts a minor wound on himself to mark his initiation to soldiering. After moving to the rear and temporary safety, he watches the stoic but tragic death of the Tall Soldier, which motivates his return to his unit and his determination to fight until the war is won.

That this Civil War film was made and released during the Korean War (1950–53) and that its star won the Medal of Honor during World War II made this visualization of the American Fighting Man especially significant. *The Red Badge of Courage* (1951), like many other war films, identifies what J. Glen Gray, a combat veteran of World War II, called the phenomenon of *Homo furens,* the "furious man," the warrior. Gray concludes that combat is fully capable of generating a transformation of the whole person when war represses civilian habits of the mind in order to focus on the situation at hand. This transformation makes soldiers, especially citizen soldiers, different kinds of creatures for life (27–28). Historian John Keegan also notes that soldiers are not like other men; the experience of war throws them into what Keegan calls "the spell of an entirely different world" (xvi). Such is the phenomenon, but it seldom happens in isolation; instead it takes place as a process in the company of others.

FIGURE 74. *The Red Badge of Courage* (1951). Director John Huston traces Henry Fleming's (Audie Murphy) fear of war, panic at the front lines, and flight from battle. Later Fleming comes to his senses and courageously returns to his company. Courtesy Metro-Goldwyn-Mayer.

The Primary Unit in Battle

John Huston recreates in *The Red Badge of Courage* what sociologists call the primary unit, a universal social group that shares several distinct qualities such as size, cohesion, homogeneity, mission, and pride. Characteristically, military primary units are small and distinct. They often carry numerical designations, but they also are identified by patches, songs, mascots, and nicknames that create group consciousness; hierarchies are apparent by rank and deference. Films such as Edward

Ludwig's *The Fighting Seabees* (1944), William Keighley's *The Fighting 69th* (1940), and Samuel Fuller's *The Big Red One* (1980) serve as eponymous examples. These groups achieve tight coherence despite vast differences in backgrounds and experiences. Likewise, a deep ethical consistency takes hold in whatever mission is assigned, and soldiers take a pride in a nearly total self-sufficiency.

These small ad hoc social units, called fire teams, platoons, companies, battalions, regiments, squadrons, or ships' crews, consist of geographically varied groups held together not only by rank structure but also by interdependence. Such was the case in Tay Garnett's *Bataan* (1943), which shows the primary unit in an idealized 1940s melting pot of European immigrants and African Americans, much as the television series *Combat!* would do in the 1960s. In *Platoon* (1986), Oliver Stone's fire teams consisted not so much of immigrants but black and white Americans from cities like Brooklyn and Memphis and country boys from the farms of Iowa, Georgia, Tennessee, or Kansas. Stone's narrator, an introspective, middle-class young man named Chris Taylor (Charlie Sheen), has gone to Vietnam willingly—"I volunteered. Can you believe that?"—and noted the crosscultural and sometimes bitterly divided social composition of his primary unit. It was clear in *Platoon* that Stone wanted to show these divisions, but like Steven Spielberg's *Saving Private Ryan* (1998), the film also shows an essential basic economy: everybody counts in battle. Individual members may function as a community divided against itself behind the lines, but they united during the adversity of battle.

Whether in terms of individuals or in primary units, films have also shown what Rupert Wilkinson called the plain-man hero: skilled soldiers take care of themselves and others in the primary unit. They are dynamic people who celebrate action, speed, and efficiency (Wilkinson, 5–7, 9); they are soldiers who can face adversity bravely and resolve to close with the enemy when necessary. Thus, the American soldier in film emerges as a complex of frontier myths and images formulated in part from an anticourtier Puritan tradition that thrives on severe tensions and human conflicts between self-sacrifice, righteous striving, and self-indulgence. Such was the case with Marine Sergeant Stryker (John Wayne) in Allan Dwan's *Sands of Iwo Jima (*1949), one of the most copied figures in film. John Wayne's two highly polemical films *The Alamo (*1960) and *The Green Berets* (1968) highlight the complex central characters similarly in this respect, as plain men justly brought to war by totalitarian adversaries.

Some plain-man characters were officers; others were sergeants, corporals, or privates. Some were good; others were evil. As Stone shows in *Platoon,* soldiers knew who these people were in their units; in reality, every unit has them. Stone's tough plain-man character Staff Sergeant Barnes (Tom Berenger) calls his rival, Sergeant Elias (Willem Dafoe) a "waterwalker," which means that Elias was not a plain man like him but a Christlike innocent who must be sacrificed for the survival of the platoon. In the end, Sergeant Barnes cannot survive the combat environment either, and Stone's use of the fratricide theme is dialectically very powerful: two heroes die to give birth to a third, a composite figure who can live in peace.

Propaganda

Propaganda in wartime is both necessary and desirable. Sam Adams is remembered neither as a soldier nor as a Boston brewer, but as the master propagandist of the American Revolution. Tom Paine was no less a personality in this respect. During the Civil War, newspaper editorialists fought their war in printed words; in modern times, it was Frank Capra. By the early 1940s, motion pictures had become a vitally important aspect of American culture, and Frank Capra was one of Hollywood's top directors (Masalowski, 68).

During World War II, more than ten million Americans were inducted into the armed services, and 2,670,000 actually trained for combat. At the request of General George C. Marshall and the Office of War Information (OWI), Frank Capra produced the *Why We Fight* series of propaganda films to orient and motivate soldiers for the shooting war. Combat is anything but glamorous, and Capra and his fellow artists offered an anxious America compelling reasons for their sacrifice. As master mythmakers before the war, they knew well that concepts concerning political, social, and economic freedom were powerful and seductive tools, especially to explain to their audiences what legalists call *jus ad bellum,* the reasons for going to war, in terms of justice, legality, and morality. Modern critics have often condemned these propaganda efforts as manipulative, but they worked despite the critics, because some wars have to be fought. Although Capra's films were popular with civilian audiences, John Ford's *Battle of Midway* (1942), William Wyler's *Memphis Belle* (1944), and John Huston's short documentary *Battle of San Pietro* (1944) really brought the war home to American civilians. In these examples and many more, Hollywood contributed mightily to the war effort from 1941 to 1945 and beyond by convincing audiences that America's soldiers personified democracy, freedom, and idealism.

Some ex-soldiers, such as Michael Lee Lanning in *Vietnam at the Movies* (1994), criticize Hollywood films for being unrealistic depictions of the fighting man's experiences (24). Others, such as the French novelist Pierre Boulle, argue that individual experiences can scarcely be set down as a continuous narrative that corresponds to the procession of each hour, because it would bore an audience as much as it did most soldiers (170). Mark Carnes writes in *Past Imperfect* (1995) that Hollywood history fills irritating gaps in the historical record and polishes dulling ambiguities and complexities. "The final product," wrote Carnes, "gleams, and it sears the imagination" (9). One can only conclude that the experience of war on film has charged the human imagination with a paradox: on one hand, films recreate the act of war with ever-increasing realism; one the other, they rely heavily on fictional substitutes for reality—created, retained, and refined through the prism of human memory, which often survive longer in the public mind than unfiltered, naked historical facts.

References

Filmography

The Alamo (1960, F)
Apocalypse Now (1979, F)
Back to Bataan (1945, F)
Bataan (1943, F)
Battle of Midway (1942, D)
Battle of San Pietro (1944, D)
The Big Red One (1980, F)
The Birth of a Nation (1915, F)
The Boys in Company C (1978, F)
The Bridge on the River Kwai (1957, F)
Combat! (1962–67, TV)
The Deer Hunter (1978, F)
The Fighting Seabees (1944, F)
The Fighting 69th (1940, F)
Full Metal Jacket (1987, F)
Glory (1989, F)
Go Tell the Spartans (1978, F)
The Great Escape (1963, F)
The Green Berets (1968, F)
Hamburger Hill (1987, F)
Hanoi Hilton (1987, F)
Hearts and Minds (1974, D)
Heroes (1977, F)
Hogan's Heroes (1965–71, TV)
The Iron Triangle (1989, F)
King Rat (1965, F)
The Manchurian Candidate (1962, F)
Memphis Belle (1944, D)
Platoon (1986, F)
The Purple Heart (1944, F)
The Rack (1956, F)
The Red Badge of Courage (1951, F; 1974, TV)
Sands of Iwo Jima (1949, F)
Saving Private Ryan (1998, F)
Slaughterhouse-Five (1972, F)
Son of the Morning Star (1991, TV)

Stalag 17 (1953, F)
Three Came Home (1950, F)
Uncommon Valor (1983, F)
Victory at Sea (1952–53, TV)
Von Ryan's Express (1965, F)
The War at Home (1978, D)
When Hell Was in Session (1976, TV)
Why We Fight (1943–45, D)

Bibliography

Auster, Albert, and Leonard Quart. *How the War Was Remembered: Hollywood and Vietnam.* New York: Praeger, 1988.

Boulle, Pierre. *My Own River Kwai.* Trans. Xan Fielding. New York: Vanguard, 1966.

Carnes, Mark, ed. *Past Imperfect: History According to the Movies.* New York: Henry Holt, 1995.

Cornish, Dudley Taylor. *The Sable Arm: Black Troops in the Union Army, 1861–1865.* Lawrence: University Press of Kansas, 1987.

Cunliffe, Marcus. *George Washington: Man and Monument.* New York: New American Library, 1982.

Garland, Brock. *War Movies.* New York: Facts on File, 1987.

Gray, J. Glen. *The Warriors: Reflections on Men in Battle.* New York: Harcourt Brace, 1959.

Höbling, Walter. "Discourse of War in U.S. Novels." In Groupe de Recherches en Etudes Anglophones de Mains, ed., *Guerre et littérature dans le monde anglophone,* 294–302. Le Mans: Université du Maine, 1988.

Karsten, Peter. *The Military in America: From the Colonial Era to the Present.* New York: Free Press, 1980.

Keegan, John. *A History of Warfare.* New York: Random House, 1993.

Lanning, Michael Lee. *Vietnam at the Movies.* New York: Fawcett, 1994.

MacDonald, J. Fred. *Television and the Red Menace: The Video Road to Vietnam.* New York: Praeger, 1985.

Masalowski, Peter. "Reel War vs. Real War." *MHQ: The Quarterly Journal of Military History* 10.4 (1998): 68–75.

Medved, Michael. *Hollywood vs. America.* New York: HarperCollins, 1992.

Rollins, Peter, and John E. O'Connor, eds. *Hollywood's World War I Motion Picture Images.* Bowling Green, OH: Bowling Green State University Popular Press, 1997.

Sklar, Robert. *Movie-Made America: A Cultural History of American Movies.* New York: Random House, 1975.

Slotkin, Richard. *Gunfighter Nation: The Myth of the Frontier in Twentieth-Century America.* New York: Atheneum, 1992.

Wilkinson, Rupert. *American Tough: The Tough-Guy Tradition and American Character.* New York: Harper & Row, 1986.

Wills, Garry. *John Wayne's America: The Politics of Celebrity.* New York: Simon & Schuster, 1997.

[THOMAS DOHERTY]

Democracy and Equality

"What then is the American, this new man?" asks Hector St. John de Crèvecouer in a primal passage from *Letters from an American Farmer* (1782), answering his own question with a melting-pot vision of democracy and equality. "He is an American, who, leaving behind him all his ancient prejudices and manners, receives new ones from the new mode of life he has embraced, the new government he obeys, and the new rank he holds. . . . Here individuals of all nations are melted into a new race of men, whose labors and posterity will one day cause great changes in the world." Like all vital traditions, America's myth of democracy and equality endures first because it has cultural resonance for a nation that has largely met Crèvecouer's expectations and second because it is carefully preserved and ritually performed. In the age of the moving image, the generous embrace of Hollywood cinema has expressed the best hopes of the American experiment in self-government and the dream—often deferred, never surrendered—of equality.

It is a matter of no little irony, not to say embarrassment, that the first great feature film in the American motion picture tradition was D. W. Griffith's *The Birth of a Nation* (1915), a fierce celebration of inequality. Enthusiastically blurbed by no less a film critic than President Woodrow Wilson, the "history written in lightning" told a sinister, revisionist version of the Civil War and Reconstruction, wherein a heroic Ku Klux Klan rode to the rescue of southern democracy and virginal womanhood alike. Griffith's Confederate hallucination ranks as but the most notorious rendering of a conventional attitude toward American race relations. In film, as in American life, African Americans were the conspicuous exception to the national ethos of fair dealing and open admission: demeaned, demonized, and erased from the American pageant. Just as Jim Crow segregated African Americans in the nation's theaters, Hollywood restricted 10 percent of the population into segregated screen space. Always, however, the main rule was not so much offensive stereotypes as pervasive invisibility. Whole genres and film cycles in the classical Hollywood canon may unspool without so much as a glimpse of a black face. Another touchstone depiction of the Civil War, *Gone with the Wind* (1939) is of a kind in its matter-of-fact subjugation of the servant class: neutered men and bovine woman, faithful retainers and squealing incompetents.

Other shades of Americans found the screen a more tolerant and open-minded medium. *The Jazz Singer* (1927), the epochal first sound film, was as much an assimilationist as a technological landmark. In America, a Jewish kid from the Lower East Side could transform himself from a *schlemiel* named Jacob Rabinowitz into a Broadway superstar named Jack Robin. Bantering with Yiddish vernacular in the intertitles, *The Jazz Singer* taught that ethnic immigrants could have it both ways—living the American dream while still getting to sing the Kol Nidre in synagogue. Toss off "the feudal and the old" and embrace the "democratic and modern," the poet Walt Whitman had demanded of his fellow artists a generation earlier in *Democratic Vistas* (1871).

The theatrical space of the motion picture venue itself, from peep show to nickelodeon to an evening's entertainment in an ornate motion picture palace, traces the upward mobility of the movies as an art form: from an urban, working-class vice indulged in by immigrants to a respectable, middle-class diversion. Spreading wide its social glue, Hollywood configured its ideal audience as a broad, undifferentiated Public, a family of man comprising all ages, classes, and ethnicities. At the same time, however, the star system held rigidly to an antidemocratic caste prejudice, a hierarchy of royalty in which some screen faces were to the medium born. The shimmering close-up is the best way to tell who is validated, and before the camera lens, all men, and especially women, are not created equal.

Mainly, though, both in front of and behind the screen, the Hollywood melting pot stirred up a creative mix of exotic ingredients: German directors, Swedish screen goddesses, Italian gangsters, brawling Irishmen, Jewish wisecrackers, Latin lovers, and sidekicks of Asian, African, and Native American lineage. After 1934, the rigorous enforcement of the Production Code leavened out the promiscuous interbreeding that invigorated the silent and early sound era: the Production Code's injunction for "respectful treatment" of "national feelings" often meant to ignore the swarthiest of hyphenated Americans. Still, if Anglo-American surnames and chiseled North European features got the best lines and most flattering close-ups, Hollywood made room for its own not so huddled masses: accented bit players, character actors, and against-the-grain stars, usually at Warner Bros., the gritty "working class studio" built on the backs of Edward G. Robinson, James Cagney, Paul Muni, and Bette Davis in films such as *Little Caesar* (1930), *The Public Enemy* (1931), *I Am a Fugitive from a Chain Gang* (1932), and *Dangerous* (1935), respectively.

Hollywood delivered its lessons in American civics most sternly in the "great man" biopics of the 1930s and 1940s, a genre of high seriousness and big budgets featuring an Olympian pantheon of Founding Fathers, military leaders, and great scientists. So glorious was the stature of certain Americans that their exemplary lives were uncontainable in a single feature film: *Young Mr. Lincoln* (1939) and *Abe Lincoln in Illinois* (1940), *Young Tom Edison* (1940) and *Edison the Man* (1940). Moreover, the biopic genre was supple enough to turn likely foreigners of sufficient independence of mind into honorary American character types in *The Story of Louis Pasteur* (1936), *The Life of Emile Zola* (1937), and *Dr. Ehrlich's Magic Bullet* (1940). Though constrained by both political expediency and the Production Code, a few didactic and ideologically charged films managed to admit that, the New Deal notwithstanding, discontent and injustice existed in Great Depression America. The compromised genre of Hollywood "social consciousness" in the 1930s included preachments against unfair labor conditions (*Black Fury,* 1935), lynching (*Fury,* 1936), and ethnic (though not racial) intolerance (*Black Legion,* 1936).

World War II changed everything. The egalitarian ethos and unifying requirements of wartime mobilization meant a marshalling of all Americans under the banner of "Americans All." The Warner Bros. platoon offers perhaps the most enduring tableaux of the American melting pot, a multicultural unit of average guys, from different regions, with different skills, working and fighting shoulder to shoulder against a pureblooded race of Aryans and Sons of Heaven. In *Bataan* (1943), *Air Force* (1943), *Guadalcanal Diary* (1943), and *The Purple Heart* (1944), the War Department seemed to issue American ethnicities with demographic precision, one type per platoon: Brooklyn Jews, Italian American Romeos, Iowa farm boys, Boston Irishmen, crusty old-timers nicknamed "Pops," and the lone wolf recalcitrant who by the end reel dies for his buddies and the Allied cause. Office of War Information and official military propaganda told the same story, most notably in Frank Capra's *Why We Fight* series (1942–45), a seven-part guidebook in American democracy and equality that opens and closes with the pealing of the Liberty Bell. Perhaps the biggest break with the black-and-white past on film was the Capra unit's *The Negro Soldier* (1944), a forthright avowal of racial equality given the stamp of government approval.

The promulgation of American values during wartime had a not totally unintended consequence. Lofty rhetoric beamed at the self-styled master races of Nazi Germany and imperial Japan boomeranged back to native shores, forcing a confrontation with the regional contradictions to an egalitarian ethos that looked so good on screen. First in the wartime film, where divisive antagonism was of necessity put on hold for the duration, and then in the postwar social problem film, where for the first time the exceptions to equality were addressed bluntly, if often tendentiously, on the American screen, Hollywood began practicing what it preached. In affirming a myth that was still not a reality, the postwar social problem film showcased the domestic aberrations and submitted the obvious solution. Of course, by the time Hollywood articulated the answer to the social problem, most Americans were primed to listen to the lessons in tolerance for the disabled (*The Best Years of Our Lives,* 1946; *The Men,* 1950), Jews (*Crossfire,* 1947; *Gentleman's Agreement,* 1947), and African Americans (*Pinky,* 1949; *Home of the Brave,* 1949; *No Way Out,* 1950). *Bright Victory* (1951) exemplifies several of the core elements and best impulses: a white southerner and a black southerner, each blinded in combat, become fast friends during convalescence, the blinded white man ultimately opening his eyes to the equality of the black man.

With the breakup of the Hollywood studio system in the 1950s, new space opened up for independent and hence independent-minded productions. Prodded by competition from television, challenged by Italian neorealism and the French New Wave, and abetted by the slackening of Production Code censorship, American cinema turned away from the myth of mere entertainment to engage subject matter that the first generation of studio moguls had studiously avoided: downbeat melodrama, political controversy, and noirish fatalism.

During the Cold War, American culture tended to define itself by its antagonist: to conjure the Soviet menace was to affirm its opposite. The terror of the antidemocratic alternative surfaced with hysterical force in the anticommunist cycle bracketed by *The Red Menace* (1949) and *Big Jim McLain* (1952), melodramas of subversion whose contempt for due process and constitutional niceties oozed from every frame. In the science fiction film, the same forebodings arose in a series of more compelling and longer-lived allegories of extraterrestrial invasion and attack. Acting out fantasies of national insecurity whose real meaning was transparent even at the time, alien death rays obliterated Washington, D.C., in *Earth vs. the Flying Saucers* (1956), and flying insects battled the U.S. Air Force in *The Deadly Mantis* (1957). Closer to home, the subversive suspicion that equality was conformity, freedom a chimera in a consumer society, was captured in the title of the most evocative political allegory of the Cold War, *Invasion of the Body Snatchers* (1956), where vegetable "pod people" take over the souls of the citizens of a small American community, although to all outward appearances the town remains the same. Yet some of the best evidence of a sustaining faith in America as the last, best hope of mankind came in the films that claimed to fear for its survival. *A Face in the Crowd* (1957), *The Manchurian Candidate* (1962), and *Seven Days in May* (1964) condemned homegrown demagogues and internal threats that, like Senator Joseph McCarthy himself, were exposed by television and defeated by good men doing the right thing. With suggestive timing, the connection was underscored in Emile de Antonio's landmark documentary *Point of Order!* (1963), a deft compilation of kinescope clips from the Army-McCarthy hearings of 1954.

The civil rights movement that galvanized America from the mid-1950s to the late 1960s arrived in Hollywood most notably in the gradual admission of African Americans into less separate and more equal screen space. The power to engender identification, to make one person the same size as another, and to frame the world from the perspective of an outcast character makes film an apt medium for color-coded lessons in equality. *The Defiant Ones* (1958) featured an exemplary cinematic epiphany: a girl being rescued by Sidney Poitier sees the black man looming over her, and the spectator adopts her racist vision, though his white partner and not he is the true threat. In fact, race was but one of many prejudices being cast off onscreen. *The Graduate* (1967) and *Funny Girl* (1968) showcased faces that in an earlier decade would have been relegated to sidekick status and rhinoplasty.

Ironically, as the Hollywood screen was becoming more tolerant, television was usurping its cultural centrality. One result was the fragmentation of the mass audience for motion pictures into segmented and specialized tastes—art house cinema, teenpics, blaxploitation, chick flicks, and so on. The noisiest and most numerous slice of the new motion picture demographic was the baby-boomer-bred counterculture of the 1960s, whose obvious landmark was *Easy Rider* (1969), a western on motorcycles that, for all its alleged radicalism, held firmly to the traditional verities: getting back to the land, lighting out for the territory, and pursuing happiness. "This used to be a helluva country," laments a patriotic dropout (played by Jack Nicholson) during a moment of clarity in the marijuana haze.

By the mid-1970s, in the wake of Vietnam and Watergate, overtly political filmmaking such as *The Parallax View* (1974) and *Three Days of the Condor* (1975) came to see American democracy as an underhanded conspiracy, a system run not by the sovereign will of the American people but by a secret cabal of sinister bureaucrats and uniformed martinets. Explicitly, Hollywood continues to be more likely to deny the promise of American life than to affirm it. The paranoid style of filmmaking is epitomized by Oliver Stone's *JFK* (1991) and *Nixon* (1995), where the names of presidents announce not great-man biopics but deranged psychodramas.

Against the dark vision of contemporary America as a betrayer of its own principles, the best proof of the endurance of the democratic, egalitarian ethos in motion picture art remains the character of the man (it almost always is a man) at the center of the typical Hollywood narrative. Whether superspy or private detective, agent of the state or his own agenda, he is a rugged individual who exudes a native disdain for authority and a ready kinship with the common folk. In the high testosterone action-adventure blockbusters issued in roman numerals—the *Rocky, Rambo,* and *Lethal Weapon* cycles—he also acts out an interracial bond of American brotherhood. Whatever his race and occupation, the virile adventurer who takes no guff from the rich and powerful remains the favorite hero that "the American, this new man" looks up to on screen: Clint Eastwood in the *Dirty Harry* series, Bruce Willis in the *Die Hard* series, Eddie Murphy in the *Beverly Hills Cop* series, and so on, ad infinitum.

At the approach of the new millennium, as if looking back over the first full century of the moving image to relive its most dramatic tour of duty, Hollywood returned to the event that, in retrospect, served as its single most vital fount of democratic myth-making. Beginning with Steven Spielberg's brilliant, moving *Saving Private Ryan* (1998) and cresting with Michael Bay's boneheaded, tedious *Pearl Harbor* (2001), an extraordinary explosion of World War II–minded narratives cut across the precincts of American popular culture. From the programming of the History Channel to the top slots on the best-seller lists, reverent paeans to what television anchorman and World War II chronicler Tom Brokaw dubbed "the greatest generation" proliferated, not least in the revival of the combat film genre. On a cultural level, the retrospective glance backward expressed the filial impulse of baby boomer sons to give one final salute to their World War II fathers fading away. On a technical level, the fin de siècle cycle of combat films was a tribute to the power of Computer Graphics Imaging to render the spectacle and carnage of the battlefield persuasively and cost effectively on the big screen. Yet whether set amid the beaches of Normandy (*Saving Private Ryan*), the jungles of a Pacific atoll (*The Thin Red Line*, 1998; *Windtalkers*, 2002), or for that matter the urban jungles of Somalia (*Black Hawk Down*, 2001) or the Central Highlands of Vietnam (*We Were Soldiers*, 2002), the new wave of combat films held true to the generic baseline of a multicultural brotherhood forged by conduct and courage, not color or class. In *We Were Soldiers*, the gruff but caring Colonel Harold Moore (Mel Gibson) affirms the democratic ethos to his assembled troops before mustering out for the crucible of combat in Vietnam. "We're not leaving home," he tells them. "We're going to what home was always supposed to be." In the aftermath of September 11, 2001, another date that will live in infamy, the wartime background assumed added resonance and immediate relevance: the shock of awakening to a fiery conflagration, the celebration of the heroism of men in uniform, and the reaffirmation of the common values held by all Americans.

Among a cascade of images and narratives that express the American myth of democracy and equality, one scene can serve as an archetypal representation: the breathless montage in Frank Capra's *Mr. Smith Goes to Washington* (1939). Mouth agape and teary-eyed, the young and idealistic Sen. Jefferson Smith (Jimmy Stewart) takes a tour of the Capitol. The secular shrines swirl around him, patriotic music trumpets on the soundtrack, and phrases on parchment flash across the screen as if written by the hand of God. Before the altar of democracy at the Lincoln Memorial, Smith shares a reverent moment with some fellow American acolytes: an dignified old black man come to pay homage to the Great Emancipator, and a Jewish refugee, smiling as his grandson reads the words emblazoned on the wall, dedicated—like so much of Hollywood cinema—to the proposition that all men are created equal.

References

Filmography

Abe Lincoln in Illinois (1940, F)
Air Force (1943, F)
Bataan (1943, F)
The Best Years of Our Lives (1946, F)
Big Jim McLain (1952, F)
The Birth of a Nation (1915, F)
Black Fury (1935, F)
Black Hawk Down (2001, F)
Black Legion (1936, F)
Bright Victory (1951, F)
Crossfire (1947, F)
Dangerous (1935, F)
The Deadly Mantis (1957, F)
The Defiant Ones (1958, F)
Dr. Ehrlich's Magic Bullet (1940, F)
Earth vs. the Flying Saucers (1956, F)
Easy Rider (1969, F)
Edison the Man (1940, F)
A Face in the Crowd (1957, F)
Funny Girl (1968, F)
Fury (1936, F)
Gentleman's Agreement (1947, F)
Gone with the Wind (1939, F)
The Graduate (1967, F)
Guadalcanal Diary (1943, F)
Home of the Brave (1949, F)
I Am a Fugitive from a Chain Gang (1932, F)
Invasion of the Body Snatchers (1956, F)
The Jazz Singer (1927, F)
JFK (1991, F)

The Life of Emile Zola (1937, F)
Little Caesar (1930, F)
The Manchurian Candidate (1962, F)
The Men (1950, F))
Mr. Smith Goes to Washington (1939, F)
The Negro Soldier (1944, D)
Nixon (1995, F)
No Way Out (1950, F)
The Parallax View (1974, F)
Pearl Harbor (2001, F)
Pinky (1949, F)
Point of Order! (1963, D)
The Public Enemy (1931, F)
The Purple Heart (1944, F)
The Red Menace (1949, F)
Saving Private Ryan (1998, F)
Seven Days in May (1964, F)
The Story of Louis Pasteur (1936, F)
The Thin Red Line (1998, F)
Three Days of the Condor (1975, F)
We Were Soldiers (2002, F)
Why We Fight (1942–45, D)
Windtalkers (2002, F)
Young Mr. Lincoln (1939, F)
Young Tom Edison (1940, F)

Bibliography

Belton, John. *America Cinema/American Culture.* New York: McGraw-Hill, 1994.
Boorstin, Daniel J. *The Americans: The Democratic Experience.* New York: Random House, 1973.
Fuchs, Lawrence. *The American Kaleidoscope: Race, Ethnicity, and the Civic Culture.* Middletown, CT: Wesleyan University Press, 1990.
Sklar, Robert. *Movie-Made America: A Cultural History of American Movies.* New York: Random House, 1975.

[R. PHILIP LOY]

The Frontier and the West

The migration west from the Atlantic Ocean to the Pacific Ocean and the ever-moving frontier it created have enthralled the American imagination and served as a source for distinctive American myths and legends. James Fenimore Cooper's *Leather-Stocking Tales* featured Natty Bumppo, America's first fictional westerner. The "West" in four of Cooper's tales was western New York, yet the heroic, self-reliant qualities Cooper assigned to Natty Bumppo forever shaped the popular image of the westerner. The real and fictional exploits of Daniel Boone and Davy Crockett captivated American imagination as settlers crossed the eastern mountain ranges into the old Northwest Territory, the present states of Kentucky and Tennessee, and on to the Mississippi River and the Great Plains. Nineteenth-century novels, dime novels, theater, and Wild West shows cultivated widespread fascination with the North American frontier, but filmed entertainment quickly became the primary genre through which western myths and legends were communicated.

Three frontier images dominated western films for the first sixty years of the century: the West as a place of individual redemption and regeneration as individuals undertook self-discovery and self-assertion; the West as empty space, a vast desert to be transformed by courageous persons into a productive garden; and the West as a place where savagery and lawlessness confronted civilization. Projected onto motion-picture screens, those images interacted with myths such as the hardy pioneer braving untold dangers to settle the West; the lonely, determined cowboy pushing great herds of Texas Longhorns to Kansas railheads; or the solitary peace officer doing battle with lawless elements. Events such as the Battle of the Little Bighorn, the gunfight at the O.K. Corral, and the James gang's raid on the bank in Northfield, Minnesota, and individuals such as Jesse James, Wyatt Earp, William Hickok, Cochise, Sitting Bull, Chief Joseph, Calamity Jane, and Annie Oakley became the material of America's legends.

Historians played an important role in the development of these legends as they articulated the centrality of the frontier in American history. In 1893 Frederick Jackson Turner read a paper, "The Significance of the Frontier in American History," at a meeting of the American Historical Association. Turner developed a "frontier hypothesis" in which he argued that the dominant element molding American character was the contraction of free land as the nation spread westward. Half a century later, Henry Nash Smith published *Virgin Land: The American West as Symbol and Myth.* In that monument of American-studies scholarship, Smith developed the binary concepts of savagery/civilization and garden/desert, which have shaped all subsequent writings on the West as myth.

However, from the silent screen to the early 1960s, Hollywood productions shaped popular perceptions of the American West far more than did historians. Richard Maltby concurs: "The formulation of the myth of the frontier preceded the events that would provide its content, and the ideological framework provided by the myth governed the choice of material for Western history. . . . The history exists because the legend exists" (39). And silent-era cinephile Kevin Brownlow observes, "So affectionate have we grown toward the Western that to suggest it reflects more wishful thinking than history seems blasphemous" (224).

The Silent Era

George M. Anderson's screen character, Bronco Billy, pioneered the film myth of the West as a place of personal redemption; however, it was William S. Hart's films, such as *Hell's Hinges* (1916), *The Return of Draw Egan* (1916), and *The Narrow Trail* (1917), that made the conversion of the bad man a central motif of western feature-length films, and Hart was also among the first to bring the Hickok legend to the screen when he starred in *Wild Bill Hickok* (1923). *The Virginian* (1914), with Dustin Farnum in the title role, was the first screen adaptation of Owen Wister's famous novel and highlighted the struggle to bring civilization to the lawless Wyoming frontier. Both *The Covered Wagon* (1923) and *The Iron Horse* (1924) portray the twin themes of overcoming the savagery and lawlessness of the frontier West so that it could become a civilized garden where farms and towns thrived. Overall, westerns of the silent era were positive expressions of nationalistic sentiments, celebrating the West as a place of personal regeneration, egalitarian democracy, and the superiority of Anglo-Saxon culture.

Westerns from 1930 to 1960

For the most part, western films continued to accept uncritically the images of the West cultivated during the silent era and to perpetuate the notion that western films were historically accurate. *The Big Trail* (1930), John Wayne's first starring role, and *Union Pacific* (1939) mirror the themes found in *The Covered Wagon* and *The Iron Horse.* Wayne portrays a wagon-train scout who constantly admonishes the prospective settlers not to be discouraged by either man-made or natural impediments during their migration to Washington Territory. *Cimarron* (1931), which won an Academy Award for best picture, celebrates the opening of the Cherokee Strip and Oklahoma's push for statehood (1889–1907). *The Virginian* (1929), with Gary Cooper in a role with which he would be identified for the rest of his life, stresses the heroic individual who places justice above friendship and hence brings order to a lawless frontier. The first two films in John Ford's 1940s cavalry trilogy, *Fort Apache* (1948) and *She Wore a Yellow Ribbon* (1949), celebrate the expansion of the white West at the expense of Native Americans who were forced onto reservations and the role the U.S. Army played in the "taming" of the West.

Western films of the era also featured prominent historical personalities. *Santa Fe Trail* (1940) is an interesting western in which the historical figures of Jeb Stuart (Errol Flynn) and George Custer (Ronald Reagan) are paired to frustrate John Brown's (Raymond Massey) attempts to manipulate unsuspecting runaway slaves for his own political purposes in pre–Civil War Kansas. In 1941, Errol Flynn assumed Reagan's role and portrayed George Custer in the well-received *They Died with Their Boots On* (1941). *The Plainsman* (1937) brings Wild Bill Hickok (Gary Cooper), Buffalo Bill (James Ellison), and Calamity Jane (Jean Arthur) together in a historically unrealistic but very entertaining film. Barbara Stanwyck starred in an equally fanciful portrayal of the famed sharpshooter in *Annie Oakley* (1935). *My Darling Clementine* (1946), John Ford's widely acclaimed tale, tells how Wyatt Earp and his brothers cleaned up Tombstone, Arizona. The historicity of each figure was shaped to fit popular perceptions, just as motion-picture portrayals of those individuals dominated public understanding.

In the 1930s and 1940s, badmen were glamorized in numerous westerns, including *Billy the Kid* (1930), *Jesse James* (1939), *The Return of Frank James* (1940), *When the Daltons Rode* (1940), *Belle Starr* (1941), *Bad Men of Missouri* (1941), and *The Outlaw* (1943). The famed Hispanic outlaw Joaquin Murrieta was recast in both *The Avenger* (1931) and *Robin Hood of El Dorado* (1936). In nearly every instance, the outlaw is depicted as someone who resists the evil influences of greedy industrialists or bankers and then seeks personal vindication for a life outside the law.

Nearly all of the westerns produced between 1930 and 1960 are set in the trans-Mississippi West; however, a few feature eastern locations. *Drums Along the Mohawk* (1939) stars Henry Fonda in a Revolutionary War drama set in the Mohawk Valley of New York. George Montgomery appeared in three 1950s colonial-type westerns. Two of them, *The Iroquois Trail* (1950) and *The Pathfinder* (1953), are based loosely on James Fenimore Cooper novels, and *Fort Ti* (1953) is set in the Revolutionary War. *Seminole* (1953) is the saga of U.S. Army efforts to subdue the Seminole Indians in Florida. *Davy Crockett, King of the Wild Frontier* (1955) was among the most popular films of the decade. This Disney production created a national craze, and for a while it seemed as if every child in America owned a coonskin cap.

Hollywood westerns of the 1930s and 1940s were positive expressions of the myths and legends derived from the frontier experience, and they were useful as the nation came to grips with the national challenges of the two decades. More than a few people were convinced that the Depression was the result of malfeasance by wealthy bankers and industrialists concerned only about profits, so it is not surprising that western outlaws were recast as victims of those same forces. To a country searching for vindication and meaning in the carnage of World War II, westerns reminded Americans that they were heirs to hardy pioneers and resolute frontier sheriffs. The answer to contemporary national problems of the 1930s and 1940s seemed to lie back in an imagined egalitarian rural past rather than in the realities and complexities of an urban industrial present.

In the twenty years following the end of World War II, westerns continued, for the most part, to portray positively the images, myths, and legends that had dominated the genre; however, increasingly it challenged them as well. *Broken Arrow* (1950) and *Hondo* (1953) portray Indians—Apaches in this instance—as family-oriented people open to reasoned argument and friendship with whites. *The Gunfighter* (1950) and *Shane* (1953) emphasize the lonely, alienated life of a gunfighter—not the heroic image that had characterized the genre in the previous decades. Even John Wayne, the quintessential exponent of traditional western myths and legends, changed characters. *The Searchers* (1956) depicts Wayne as an Indian-hating psychopath searching for a niece kidnapped by marauding Comanches; he intends to kill her because after living as an Indian she will longer be fit to rejoin white society. James Stewart in films such as *The Naked Spur* (1953), Randolph Scott in efforts such as *Ride Lonesome* (1959), and Joan Crawford in *Johnny Guitar* (1954) reshaped the hero and heroine into a lonely, revenge-obsessed individual, not the self-denying hero of traditional myths and legends. In *Lonely Are the Brave* (1962), clearly a revisionist western, Kirk Douglas portrays a cowboy who affirms the traditional images of the West; unfortunately, Douglas and his horse are killed by a truck on a modern highway while fleeing from a sheriff's posse—an ignominious demise for the hero.

Westerns Since 1960

Reflecting the renaissance of national pride during the Kennedy era, early-1960s westerns returned to the images, myths, and legends that had shaped the genre of an earlier era. *The Alamo* (1960), a massive undertaking by John Wayne, captures all of the legendary elements of that tragic event. *How the West Was Won*

(1962) is an epic expression of the trek west. *Ride the High Country* (1962) counterpoises new and old images of westerns, but in the end the old images triumph. To a nation buffeted by a rapidly changing social order and war in Vietnam, the values implicit in the images, myths, and legends of westerns seemed hopelessly dated by the middle of the decade. Westerns responded either by parodying the genre, as in *Cat Ballou* (1965) or *Little Big Man* (1970), or by associating the West with the excessive and often vivid violence of *The Wild Bunch* (1969).

As "New West" writers began to challenge traditional interpretations of American history and as the country reacted to numerous public scandals, westerns films nearly disappeared. However, the last fifteen years of the twentieth century saw a mild resurgence of the genre. Not surprisingly, the films reflected the changed realities and sensitivities of the country as well as the ideology of "New West" historians such as Gene M. Gressley, Patricia Nelson Limerick, and Gerald D. Nash as well as American-studies scholars such as Richard Slotkin and Jane Tompkins. In *Pale Rider* (1985), villains use hydraulic mining and ravage the landscape in their wanton search for gold. *Dances with Wolves* (1990) portrays white people as insensitive destructors of both Native American culture and the natural environment. Native Americans, according to this Kevin Costner film, lived in harmony with each other and their environment. *Tombstone* (1993) and *Wyatt Earp* (1994) provide more historically accurate accounts of both Wyatt Earp's life and the events surrounding the gunfight at the O.K. Corral. In Clint Eastwood's *Unforgiven* (1992), violence appears as a pointless waste of human life practiced by either cowards or men who could kill only when drunk.

By the end of the twentieth century, the images closely associated with westerns and the myths and legends derived from those images had been largely discarded by post–World War II generations. Younger generations, slightly amused by the genre, did not accept the images of the United States closely associated with westerns. New urban-based images, myths, and legends were being fashioned, ones not easily adapted to westerns; hence, the genre is having minimal impact on America's understanding of itself in the first years of the new millennium.

References

Filmography

The Alamo (1960, F)
Annie Oakley (1935, F)
The Avenger (1931, F)
Bad Men of Missouri (1941, F)
Belle Starr (1941, F)
The Big Trail (1930, F)
Billy The Kid (1930, F)
Broken Arrow (1950, F)
Cat Ballou (1965, F)
Cimarron (1931, F)
The Covered Wagon (1923, F)
Dances with Wolves (1990, F)
Davy Crockett, King of the Wild Frontier (1955, F)
Drums Along the Mohawk (1939, F)
Fort Apache (1948, F)
Fort Ti (1953, F)
The Gunfighter (1950, F)
Hell's Hinges (1916, F)
Hondo (1953, F)
How the West Was Won (1962, F)
The Iron Horse (1924, F)
The Iroquois Trail (1950, F)
Jesse James (1936, F)
Johnny Guitar (1954, F)
Little Big Man (1970, F)
Lonely Are the Brave (1962, F)
My Darling Clementine (1946, F)
The Naked Spur (1953, F)
The Narrow Trail (1917, F)
The Outlaw (1943, F)
Pale Rider (1985, F)
The Pathfinder (1953, F)
The Plainsman (1937, F)
The Return of Draw Egan (1916, F)
The Return of Frank James (1940, F)
Ride Lonesome (1959, F)
Ride the High Country (1962, F)
Robin Hood of El Dorado (1936, F)

Santa Fe Trail (1940, F)
The Searchers (1956, F)
Seminole (1953, F)
Shane (1953, F)
She Wore a Yellow Ribbon (1949, F)
They Died with Their Boots On (1941, F)
Tombstone (1993, F)
Unforgiven (1992, F)
Union Pacific (1939, F)
The Virginian (1914, F; 1929, F)
When the Daltons Rode (1940, F)
Wild Bill Hickok (1923, F)
The Wild Bunch (1969, F)
Wyatt Earp (1994, F)

Bibliography

Brownlow, Kevin. *The War, the West, and the Wilderness.* New York: Knopf, 1979.

Buscombe, Edward, ed. *The BFI Companion to the Western.* New York: Da Capo, 1988.

Cawelti, John G. *The Six-Gun Mystique.* 2d ed. Bowling Green, OH: Bowling Green State University Popular Press, 1984.

Gressley, Gene M., ed. *Old West/New West.* Norman: University of Oklahoma Press, 1994.

Lenihan, John H. *Showdown: Confronting Modern America in Western Film.* Urbana: University of Illinois Press, 1985.

Maltby, Richard. "A Better Sense of History: John Ford and the Indians." In Ian Cameron and Douglas Pye, eds., *The Book of Westerns,* 34–49. New York: Continuum, 1996.

Slotkin, Richard. *Gunfighter Nation: The Myth of the Frontier in Twentieth-Century America.* New York: Atheneum, 1992.

Smith, Henry Nash. *Virgin Land: The American West as Symbol and Myth.* New York: Random House, 1950.

Tompkins, Jane. *West of Everything: The Inner Life of Westerns.* New York: Oxford University Press, 1992.

[DAVID E. WILT]

Hollywood's Detective

One of the most enduring characters in American popular culture is the private detective. The concept of the private investigator dates back to the nineteenth century: Edgar Allan Poe's Auguste Dupin and Arthur Conan Doyle's Sherlock Holmes were fictional counterparts to the real-life Allan Pinkerton and Monsieur Lecoq. They were joined in the twentieth century by Philo Vance, Sam Spade, Philip Marlowe, Mike Hammer, Travis McGee, Fletch, and hundreds (perhaps thousands) of others in virtually every manifestation of popular culture, and the genre shows no signs of disappearing.

The private detective who appears in novels, television shows, and films bears little resemblance to his real-life model. The very idea of a *private* detective implies that justice (however it may be defined) can only be obtained by paying for it, while those without money are forced to rely upon an overburdened, tax-supported police and court system. In the late nineteenth and early twentieth centuries, private detective agencies such as the Pinkertons were notorious for their involvement in union-busting activities on the behalf of large corporations. In fiction, of course, the private detective—and others who assume this mantle, including "renegade" police detectives such as Dirty Harry Callahan, crusading reporters, Perry Mason–like lawyers, and so on—generally takes the side of the underdog against the more powerful, a reversal of the situation of the real-life private eye whose rates largely limit his clientele to the wealthy.

The strength of the detective film resides in the universality of its theme. The detective hero is involved in a quest for truth and justice, although the definition of these two concepts may vary from year to year and film to film. This quest may take place in a variety of time periods—past, present, and even future—and various geographical locations. A large part of the quest involves interviews—ranging from those with completely cooperative subjects to violent confrontations—as opposed to investigation of physical evidence. Thus, the detective-film plot is character-based and allows for the presentation of a wide spectrum of personalities, social classes, sexes, races, and religions—indeed, a panorama of American society.

However, the popularity of the detective hero may be rooted in something even more fundamental: the protagonist's role as audience surrogate. At best, the detective is a powerful, competent figure who is unswerving in his (or her) pursuit of the truth, and who makes sure justice is served; even at his worst, the detective is at least someone who makes the effort, who has defined values and a personal code of honor that places him at the service of the oppressed, even if a just outcome may be in conflict with his personal interest.

The Rise of the Private Eye: 1920–1941

The detective in fiction and film has taken many forms. One of these appears in what author Raymond Chandler called "the traditional or classic" detective story, epitomized by Sherlock Holmes, Hercule Poirot, and Philo Vance, which poses "problems in logic and deduction" (5–6). This type of detective has continued to thrive, as evidenced by the popularity of Ellery Queen, Agatha Christie's Miss Marple, and even television's Jessica Fletcher (*Murder, She Wrote*). However, the detective-hero who has achieved the most enduring success is the contemporary, urban private eye, whose roots stretch back to the early years of the century, but who really took form in the 1920s in a magazine entitled *Black Mask.*

In the words of John G. Cawelti, "the hard-boiled detective is a traditional man of virtue in an amoral and corrupt world" (152). The "hard-boiled" school of fiction emerged in the 1920s after the savagery of World War I had concluded. The decade was marked by lawless excess, the result of the great, failed experiment of Prohibition, an effort to legislate morality that backfired in spectacular fashion. Rather than a cool, intellectual detective solving the mystery of the murdered nobleman in his locked library, audiences were ready for a different kind of hero who would respond appropriately to gangsters, kidnapers, murderous anarchists, and other—real and imagined—modern menaces: "The hard-boiled detective metes out the just punishment that the law is too mechanical, unwieldy, or corrupt to achieve" (Cawelti, 143).

Two of the first proponents of hard-boiled fiction were Carroll John Daly and Dashiell Hammett. Daly never managed to break free of the lower levels of the popular fiction universe, but Hammett succeeded in reaching the best-seller stratum. Two of Hammett's characters achieved immortality via Hollywood: Sam Spade, hero of *The Maltese Falcon,* and Nick Charles, protagonist (with his wife Nora) of *The Thin Man* and its sequels. These characters represent the opposite ends of the detective spectrum: Spade is a professional private investigator who detects for a living, while the affluent Nick and Nora Charles solve crimes as a whimsical hobby.

Although it was not the first private eye film by any stretch of the imagination (it was not even the first adaptation of the book: Hammett's novel had been filmed twice before, in 1931 and 1936), John Huston's version of *The Maltese Falcon* (1941) remains for many the quintessential example of the genre, just as the world-weary, middle-aged Sam Spade (Humphrey Bogart) in his dark suit and fedora has become a cultural icon as the detective. The milieu is proto–film noir, a menacing urban landscape populated with sinister villains and their henchmen, femmes fatales, hostile and sometimes dumb cops, the slumming rich, and the working poor. *The Maltese Falcon* does not so much invent the conventions of the private eye genre as it assembles them into a cohesive form. The concept of the city as the center of sin and violence and the class and society aspects of the characters were clearly not original to *The Maltese Falcon,* and may be found in many other films, novels, and stories. And without being overtly political, the film still manages to reflect American feelings about the international situation: Spade, minding his own business, is reluctantly dragged into a dispute which does not really concern him. His loyalty (to his dead partner) and gallant nature (as a gentleman, he cannot refuse Brigid O'Shaughnessy's plea for help) force him to confront a gang of foreign enemies. Although Hammett's novel was written long before the outbreak of World War II, 1941 audiences could easily project their own attitudes onto the film version.

The *Thin Man* films, on the other hand, are glossy Hollywood representations of high society. These prewar film adaptations of Hammett's work (*The Thin Man* series consisted of six pictures, four of which were released before World War II) not only serve as good examples of the styles of their respective studios (Warner Bros. and MGM) but also represent the opposite poles of prewar film: hard-boiled realism on the one hand (although *The Maltese Falcon* is certainly not as "proletarian" as other Warner Bros. productions of the 1930s and early 1940s) and frothy escapism on the other

FIGURE 75. *The Maltese Falcon* (1941). Sam Spade (Humphrey Bogart, left) attentively absorbs the conversation of Joel Cairo (Peter Lorre, standing at center), Kasper Gutman (Sydney Greenstreet, seated), and Iva Archer (Gladys George). Spade maintains composure and a hard edge while unraveling the deceptions and confusion of international espionage. Courtesy First National Pictures and Warner Bros.

(*The Thin Man* films are as much screwball comedies as they are detective stories). There were numerous other films of the 1930s featuring detective heroes, but characters such as Charlie Chan, Bulldog Drummond, Mr. Moto, Mr. Wong, and Sherlock Holmes were—as exotic "foreigners"—closer to the traditional detective than the hard-boiled version.

Detectives During World War II

By the time World War II arrived, Dashiell Hammett's writing career had long since faded. Another *Black Mask* magazine alumnus, Raymond Chandler, was making his mark. Chandler's Philip Marlowe is one of the most famous detective characters in literature; however, although Marlowe appeared in four films in the 1940s, one in the 1960s, and three more versions in the 1970s, Humphrey Bogart's Sam Spade remains a more recognizable screen image than any of the seven movie Marlowes (Dick Powell, Bogart, George Montgomery, Robert Montgomery, James Garner, Elliott Gould, and—in two films—Robert Mitchum). Marlowe is the archetypical private detective as knight errant, hard-boiled and violent when necessary, but sensitive, well-read, and compassionate at times. Sam Spade tracks down the killer of his partner almost begrudgingly, prodded by a sense of duty; Marlowe, although he is also a detective for hire, acts out of a sense of what he believes is morally correct.

The private detective film flourished in the 1940s. In addition to the earliest Chandler adaptations—*The Falcon Takes Over* and *Time to Kill* (both 1942), in which "Philip Marlowe" was replaced by existing characters The Falcon (George Sanders) and Mike Shayne (Lloyd Nolan), and the first true Marlowe film, *Murder, My Sweet* (1944)—there were numerous B-movie series featuring Boston Blackie, the Lone Wolf, and Ellery Queen, as well as one-shot films with detective protagonists. The lawlessness and desperation of the Prohibition and Depression years were supplanted by the war: even in films not directly dealing with wartime issues, film historian Martin Rubin suggests that "the detective film can be seen as a response to the regimentation and deindividualized conflict of the war. . . . The detective is often a neutral who becomes personally committed in the course of the action, working out a private accommodation between self-reliance and social responsibility" (88). The ranks of the enemies of society were rife with war profiteers, traitors, and spies, in addition to more mundane criminals.

Postwar Detectives and Film Noir: 1946–1959

Chandler's quintessential private eye continued his noble quest in the postwar era in *The Big Sleep* (1946), *The Brasher Doubloon* (1947), and *Lady in the Lake* (1947). However, with the end of the great crusade against fascism came the turmoil of a confused peace. Major changes in society were both exciting and frightening. In this era, some movie detectives were being portrayed in a rather morally ambiguous light. The postwar film noir *Out of the Past* (1947) stars Robert Mitchum as a private eye who betrays his client's trust for the love of a woman (ultimately revealed to be duplicitous and unworthy of him) and in the end pays with his life. Noir protagonists were prone to such victimization, and the image of the detective as moral arbiter suffered as a result. One film that demonstrates not only how clearly the image of the hard-boiled detective had become a part of American popular culture, but also the way it melded with film noir is the parody *My Favorite Brunette* (1947), which begins with its detective-protagonist (Bob Hope) relating his story in flashback from his cell on death row.

Another postwar detective phenomenon was diametrically opposed to the noir detective as fall guy: Mickey Spillane's ultraviolent Mike Hammer, the central character in a string of best-selling novels beginning with 1947's *I, the Jury*. Historian Henry Bamford Parkes suggests that "the *ne plus ultra* (or so one hopes) of the American frontier myth of an isolated natural virtue at war with the corruption of society was reached . . . in the novels of Mickey Spillane. The Spillane hero . . . has an innate sense of justice which is not supported by the official representatives of law and order. . . . The popularity of Spillane's novels, like that of its political analogue, McCarthyism, is a most disturbing phenomenon" (293). The misogynistic, brutal, and anticommunist adventures of Hammer were brought to the screen in bowdlerized form several times during the 1950s and early 1960s; Robert Aldrich's *Kiss Me Deadly* (1955) was the best of the lot, although depicting Mike Hammer (Ralph Meeker) as a sleazy and unpleasant sort, far removed from the sardonic but trustworthy Sam Spade and Philip Marlowe. Screen versions of Spillane's detective in the 1980s and 1990s (including numerous TV movies) were more conventional genre efforts, although society had finally caught up with Spillane, and Hammer's propensity for shocking violence was now practically commonplace.

Through the 1960s, detective films generally eschewed overt political commentary, the occasional picture like *Big Jim McLain* (1952) to the contrary. This film stars John Wayne as a House Committee on Un-American Activities (HUAC) investigator tracking down communist spies in Hawaii. Instead, social and political changes were alluded to in more subtle ways, whether in film noir's air of postwar malaise or the McCarthy-like paranoia of Mike Hammer. Organized crime, once seen as a bit quaint, was elevated to the status of a vast conspiracy by the Kefauver hearings and the stern public warnings of J. Edgar Hoover's FBI. Plots that once centered on murders, blackmail, and unsavory family secrets now dealt with corruption on the municipal, state, and even national and international level. Detectives were not necessarily portrayed more realistically, but increasingly they were shown to be human, even flawed, rather than noble, and their victories were often Pyrrhic.

Private Eyes in the Vietnam Era and Beyond

The 1960s were not an especially good decade for film detectives—although the genre never completely disappeared and fictional investigators Lew Archer (renamed Harper for the 1966 film of that title, played by Paul Newman), Tony Rome (Frank Sinatra in *Tony Rome* [1967] and *Lady in Cement* [1968]), and Virgil Tibbs (Sidney Poitier in 1967's *In the Heat of the Night*) made the transition to the screen—but as the decade came to a close, and then in the post-Vietnam and post-Watergate 1970s, the genre underwent a significant resurgence with such countercultural films as *Klute* (1971) and *The Big Fix* (1978). Chandler's Philip Marlowe showed up in four features released between 1969 and 1978, three with contemporary settings that attempted to show how the hard-boiled detective would function in modern America.

Roman Polanski's *Chinatown* (1974), is a period film that presents a revisionist look at the "classic" private eye of the 1930s and 1940s. The genre's archetypal elements are present, but the tribulations of detective Jake Gittes (Jack Nicholson) are more closely linked to those of a film noir fall guy than to hard-boiled Sam Spade and Philip Marlowe: Gittes is tricked by a client, has his nostril slit for being "too nosy," and even though he "solves the case," the villains are not brought to justice or even foiled in their nefarious plan. *Chinatown* (and its 1990 sequel *The Two Jakes*) is just one example of a genre film that reflects a cynical attitude about traditional beliefs and values (numerous 1970s westerns also demonstrate this revisionist trend). A new wave of anti-establishment filmmakers such as Polanski and Robert Altman took advantage of the post-Vietnam disillusionment of some in the American film audience to challenge the fundamental underpinnings of societal beliefs. These films reflected just one trend in society—not the only one—but they are notable because they so clearly clash with familiar genre conventions.

A more assertive private eye appeared in *Shaft!* (1971) and its sequels, demonstrating that the genre could still be played straight and that audiences would still respond to a traditional detective film (albeit one with a contemporary level of sex and violence) in which the hero punishes the guilty and manages to walk away victorious. John Shaft (Richard Roundtree) is also just one of many private eyes of the late 1960s and 1970s who broke the white, middle-aged male stereotype: the theater and TV screens of the era were crowded with black detectives, female detectives, elderly detectives, disabled detectives, fat detectives, rich detectives, teenaged detectives, married detectives, and so on, ad infinitum. *Shaft!* is also illustrative of the "blaxploitation" films of the period: the civil rights movement not only affected society as a whole, but it also engendered an awareness of black pride and spawned numerous films that tried to cash in on this trend. While many blaxploitation films are familiar genre productions, a number include some political commentary in an attempt to be more relevant to their target audience.

Films, TV shows, and novels that center on the efforts of the police to solve crimes are known as "police procedurals;" the protagonists of these works—think Sgt. Joe Friday of *Dragnet*—are only peripherally related to detective heroes like Sam Spade. In the police procedural, teamwork is paramount; the de-

FIGURE 76. *Chinatown* (1974). Jake Gittes (Jack Nicholson) is beaten by thugs while investigating a case that constantly eludes him. In the revisionist *Chinatown* (1974), Gittes lacks style and control, unable to recognize he is being deceived and incapable of achieving any form of justice. Courtesy Paramount Pictures.

tective hero may have some help from friends and acquaintances, but he is essentially a loner, one man (or, more rarely, a woman) standing against the forces of evil. The series of films that began with *Dirty Harry* (1971) feature a police detective as their protagonist, but Harry Callahan (Clint Eastwood) is definitely not a team player; the second film in the series, *Magnum Force* (1973), makes this even clearer, for Callahan is pitted against a "death squad" of uniformed motorcycle cops instead of more traditional threats such as killers, bank robbers, and terrorists. At odds with his own superiors and the liberal (and therefore ineffectual) justice system, Callahan works alone and cuts through red tape with bullets from his .357 magnum. He is "the emblem of public rage directed against problems without solutions" (Ruehlmann, 12) and is not bound by the artificial rules of behavior that restrain other policemen. In essence, he has the best (and worst) of both worlds: an official imprimatur (although it can be withdrawn, subjecting him to censure and the loss of his livelihood) and the freedom to act as he sees fit. Films such as the *Dirty Harry* and *Death Wish* series (the second starring Charles Bronson as a vigilante whose enemies are police officials as much as criminals) illustrate the distrust of the "establishment" that appears in many motion pictures of the 1970s and beyond.

The detective hero seems to be infinitely adaptable and resilient, and so the character continues to appear in films and TV shows with surprising frequency. Parodies such as the popular *Ace Ventura, Pet Detective* (1994) and *Who Framed Roger Rabbit?* (1988) vie with more "serious" efforts such as *Kill Me Again* (1989), *Dead Again* (1991), and *Kiss the Girls* (1997). Detectives come in all sizes, sexes, and colors, and are situated in past (*Devil in a Blue Dress,* 1995), present (*V. I. Warshawski,* 1991), and future (*Blade Runner,* 1982) settings.

Civilization vs. Anarchy

It has been said that "the private eye novel was a Western that took place somewhere else" (Ruehlmann, 5). To a certain extent, this comparison also applies to films, although the similarity may chiefly be found in both genres' use of an independent, even isolated protagonist who fights on the side of civilization against the forces of anarchy. However, the theme and structure—and, of course, setting—of a western is fundamentally different than that of a detective film, where urban issues and challenges are paramount. Perhaps more significantly, detective films still flourish, whereas westerns are a virtually extinct form. Why is this so?

The hard-boiled detective emerged in the aftermath of World War I and was formed by the sensibilities of Prohibition-era America. In succeeding decades, the detective hero adapted to the society he encountered: the Depression, World War II, the McCarthy era, Vietnam, and beyond. Regardless of the specificities of his situation, the detective hero is a champion of morality confronted by immoral forces. As

John G. Cawelti writes, "Whether his vision of evil is political or metaphysical, the hard-boiled detective has rejected the ordinary social and ethical pieties and faces a world he has learned to understand as fundamentally corrupt, violent, and hostile" (150). The western hero vanished when the concept of the American frontier disappeared; but only in a perfect world, free of crime and corruption, would the detective hero become extinct.

References

Filmography

The Big Fix (1978, F)
Big Jim McLain (1952, F)
The Big Sleep (1946, F)
Blade Runner (1982, F)
The Brasher Doubloon (1947, F)
Chinatown (1974, F)
Death Wish (1974, F)
Devil in a Blue Dress (1995, F)
Dirty Harry (1971, F)
The Drowning Pool (1975, F)
The Falcon Takes Over (1942, F)
Farewell, My Lovely (1975, F)
The Girl Hunters (1962, F)
Harper (1966, F)
In the Heat of the Night (1967, F)
I, the Jury (1953, F; 1982, F)
Kill Me Again (1989, F)
Kiss Me Deadly (1955, F)
Klute (1971, F)
Lady in Cement (1968, F)
Lady in the Lake (1947, F)
The Long Goodbye (1973, F)
Magnum Force (1973, F)
The Maltese Falcon (1941, F)
Marlowe (1969, F)
Murder, My Sweet (1944, F)
My Favorite Brunette (1947, F)
My Gun Is Quick (1957, F)
Out of the Past (1947, F)
Shaft! (1971, F)
Shaft in Africa (1973, F)
Shaft's Big Score (1972, F)
Time to Kill (1942, F)
Tony Rome (1967, F)
The Two Jakes (1990, F)
V. I. Warshawski (1991, F)

Bibliography

Baker, Robert A., and Michael T. Nietzel. *Private Eyes: One Hundred and One Knights—A Survey of American Detective Fiction, 1922–1984.* Bowling Green, OH: Bowling Green State University Popular Press, 1985.

Cawelti, John G. *Adventure, Mystery, and Romance.* Chicago: University of Chicago Press, 1976.

Chandler, Raymond. *The Simple Art of Murder.* New York: Houghton Mifflin, 1950.

Cocchiarelli, Joseph J. *Screen Sleuths: A Filmography.* New York: Garland, 1992.

Collins, Max Alan, and James L. Traylor. *One Lonely Knight: Mickey Spillane's Mike Hammer.* Bowling Green, OH: Bowling Green State University Popular Press, 1984.

Geherin, David. *The American Private Eye: The Image in Fiction.* New York: Frederick Ungar, 1985.

Hunt, William R. *Front-Page Detective: William J. Burns and the Detective Profession, 1880–1930.* Bowling Green, OH: Bowling Green State University Popular Press, 1980.

Parkes, Henry Bamford. *The American Experience: An Interpretation of the History and Civilization of the American People.* New York: Random House, 1947.

Pitts, Michael R. *Famous Movie Detectives.* Metuchen, NJ: Scarecrow, 1979.

Rubin, Martin. *Thrillers.* New York: Cambridge University Press, 1999.

Ruehlmann, William. *Saint with a Gun: The Unlawful American Private Eye.* New York: New York University Press, 1974.

Slotkin, Richard. *Gunfighter Nation: The Myth of the Frontier in Twentieth-Century America.* New York: Atheneum, 1992.

Tuska, Jon. *The Detective in Hollywood.* Garden City, NY: Doubleday, 1978.

——. *In Manors and Alleys: A Casebook on the American Detective Film.* New York: Greenwood, 1988.

Wilt, David. *Hard Boiled in Hollywood.* Bowling Green, OH: Bowling Green State University Popular Press, 1991.

[JOHN C. TIBBETTS]

The Machine in the Garden

Many nineteenth-century American observers greeted what Ralph Waldo Emerson called "the whistle of the locomotive in the woods" with a mixture of awe and anxiety. When Nathaniel Hawthorne heard a train's "startling shriek" shatter the stillness of Concord Woods on the morning of July 27, 1844, he worried it would usher "the noisy world into the midst of our slumbrous peace." Painter George Catlin feared it would destroy "the grace and beauty of Nature"; and Thoreau regarded it as "a fate" that "never turns aside" (Nash, 13, 100).

Theirs was both a lament and a prophecy. The locomotive was just one of the new forces invading and despoiling the American Garden. For transplanted Europeans and hardy settlers, the New World had held out the hope of a New Eden, of fresh beginnings, of the promise of the regenerative power of bountiful, natural terrain. Here especially, between the raw wilderness of the remote western frontier and the industrialized cities of the eastern seaboard, was a "garden," a "great interior valley," as cultural historian Henry Nash Smith described it in his classic *Virgin Land* (123). Smith and other cultural commentators, including Roderick Nash, Leo Marx, and Charles L. Sanford, regard this middle region as "one of the dominant symbols of nineteenth century American Life," a significant metaphor of American cultural mythology—a delicately poised equilibrium between innocence and experience, chaos and order, hope and disillusionment (Smith, 123).

The "Machine in the Garden" myth defines an essentially American ambivalence toward the contradictory conditions of pastoral promise and material experience. The myth has become a pervasive theme in American film; moreover, the apparatus and effects of the film medium—in a larger sense, media technology in general—constitute a new Machine in the Garden of American art, society, and sensibility whose effects are still being gauged.

The Machine in the Garden in American Society and Literature

The locomotive that invaded Hawthorne's garden is a convenient index of the new "forces," as Henry Adams catalogued them from the vantage point of the early twentieth century in his *The Education of Henry Adams* (privately published in 1907)—forces that (in his view at least) threatened to dehumanize the New American. Within his lifetime, Adams saw an agricultural America become a predominantly urban industrial society. Steam power, electrical energy, radium, and photographic technologies were only a few technological spin-offs of scientific discovery. The rise of monopolies, mass communications, mechanical reproduction of art forms, as well as the proliferation of evolutionary theory, phenomenology, naturalism, and feminism were among their inevitable consequences. Man had "maundered among the magnets," wrote Adams wittily, and "had translated himself into a new universe which had no common scale of measurement with the old" (381).

Novelists in the late nineteenth century seized on the "Machine in the Garden" myth as a useful paradigm to understand contemporary anxieties and uncertainties. For example, Frank Norris's *The Octopus* (1899), probably influenced by the railroad-related imagery and themes of Zola's *La Bête Humaine*, written a decade earlier, portrayed the Pacific and Southwestern railway as a monopoly, an "octopus" that was dispossessing farmers of their lands in the San Joaquin Valley. Early in the story, the character of Presley, a poet, watches in horror as a locomotive—"filling the air with the reek of hot oil, vomiting smoke and sparks"—smashes through a herd of sheep grazing on the tracks: "It was a slaughter, a massacre of innocents. The iron monster had charged full into the midst, merciless, inexorable." Not only were bleeding, mutilated bodies left in its wake, but a sense of irrecoverable loss: "The sweetness was gone from the evening, the sense of peace, of security, and placid contentment was stricken from the landscape" (50).

The Motion Picture: A New Machine in the Garden?

In the mid-1890s, just as historian Frederick Jackson Turner was proclaiming the end of the frontier, another technology was disrupting the peace and harmony of the American Garden. Like the locomotive, it moved on gears and wheels and penetrated the darkness with its cyclopean eye. Audiences who had gathered in theaters in New York City and Boston in late December 1896 and early 1897 to witness Thomas Edison's "Vitascope" motion-picture projection device scattered in panic at the sight on the screen of a locomotive steaming down the track straight toward them. "It seemed as if the train were dashing down upon the audience," one observer reported, "the rushing of steam, the ringing of bells and the roar of the wheels making the scene a startlingly realistic one" (Musser, 178).

No sooner did viewers adjust to these crude black-and-white illusions flickering on the big screen, than their perceptual—read "pastoral"—complacency was disturbed again by a succession of new shocks and effects—"attractions," as historian Tom Gunning describes them. In the late 1920s, sudden, unnerving bleats and blaats of sound from the early talkies assailed the ears; in the early 1930s, Technicolor hues bloomed like hothouse flowers; in the early 1950s, 3-D and widescreen processes shattered the proscenium; and today's "virtual reality" and holographic projections surround and engulf the senses in a totality of synesthetic experience.

Each successive technological innovation has stripped away a protective veil of illusion. As long as a picture image's illusion was "partial," as Rudolph Arnheim has argued—that is, delimited by fixed boundaries and deprived of color, sound, and dimension—the viewer could exist in a happy state of complicity with the screen, suspended between belief and doubt, his imagination commingling with the illusion. He was, in effect, the shepherd happy in his Arcadia. But when filmmakers kept upping the ante with increasingly realistic effects, they upset that harmonious equipoise, subjecting the viewer to the insistent, multisensory proddings of those new mechanical gods of the screen, Showscan and IMAX. In sum, asserts Gunning, the film medium's unprecedented potential for *realism* has always been its primary power—"its ability to convince spectators that the moving image was, in fact, palpable and dangerous . . . swallowing, in its relentless force, any consideration of representation—the imaginary perceived as real" (819).

Meanwhile, as early as 1906, borne on the rails of the Southern Pacific Railroad, filmmakers were invading the Garden of the San Fernando Valley and the northwest sector of the city of Los Angeles. The sounds of their bulldozers, hammers, and clattering cameras shattered the bucolic stillness of the fig orchards and orange groves. They re-created the area in their own image. They invaded Hollywood Boulevard and brought in New York–style shops and delicatessens. They appropriated the once-quiet streets for staged car chases and train wrecks. They established their own cities (like Carl Laemmle's Universal City) and built their own railroad lines. And in the heart of Hollywood, on Wilton Place, they erected the area's first synagogue. The solid, conservative denizens of Los Angeles recoiled in shock. Their placid existence would never be the same again.

The Machine in the Garden in Hollywood Films

Hollywood films have represented the "Garden" in many ways, as a rural farm, a small town, an innocent childhood, a baseball game, the hopeful vision of a newly arrived immigrant—that is, any state of order and harmony that is disrupted or threatened in some way by the "Machine," which may be, by turns, a polluting factory, a "forbidden" science, warfare, an extraterrestrial space ship, or an atomic bomb.

To recount even a fair sampling of these titles from all the popular genres is quite beyond the scope of this essay. A few will have to suffice. Issues of ecology and land reclamation surface in John Ford's epic of the dust bowl migrations, *The Grapes of Wrath* (1940), and the cautionary tales of John Boorman's *The Emerald Forest* (1985), John McTiernan's *Medicine Man* (1992), and Robert Altman's *Short Cuts* (1993). In the Ford film, Caterpillar tractors come hard on the heels of dust storms and drought to uproot the "Okies" from their farms. "They come, they come and pushed me off," wails Muley (John Qualen) to his neighbor, Tom Joad (Henry Fonda), his voice counterpointing images of formations of tractors, their mechanical throats chuckling while their iron paws stamp and flatten his farm house; "they come with the 'cats, the caterpillar tractors. . . . And for every one of them there was ten-to-fifteen families throwed right of their homes . . . throwed right out into the road." In the Boorman and McTiernan films, bulldozers present a threat to the ecological balance of the Brazilian rainforests. Environmental pollution is the overriding theme of the Altman picture—the helicopters' spread of Malathion insecticide over Los Angeles creates a fogbank that poisons and corrupts everything and everybody in the multitiered story.

Many westerns, such as David Miller's *Lonely Are the Brave* (1962), Ford's *Cheyenne Autumn* (1964), and Kevin Costner's *Dances with Wolves* (1990), deal with the demise of those archetypal figures of western myth, the cowboy and the Indian (both shepherds of their own Arcadia, if you will). In the first, a ruggedly individualist cowboy (Kirk Douglas) flees on horseback from pursuing helicopters, jeeps, and diesel trucks. Crushed under the wheels of the truck, he lies dying while a moving epitaph—an elegy to the departed romance of the West—is spoken over his body. The latter two films indict the greed and corruption of "Manifest Destiny" that has appropriated and despoiled the Garden of the Native American, expelling its peoples from their lands.

On a lighter note, many musicals thrive on the spectacle of con men, rock stars, and devils invading the Gardens of old-fashioned Americana—Mr. Applegate (Ray Walston) wields his infernal powers to corrupt the institution of baseball in *Damn Yankees* (1958); rock 'n' roll idol Conrad Birdie (Jesse Pearson) introduces the teenagers of the sleepy town of Sweet Apple to sexually suggestive music in *Bye, Bye Birdie* (1963); Harold Hill (Robert Preston) hatches a plot to swindle the gullible yokels of River City, Iowa, in *The Music Man.*

In a spate of science fiction, fantasy, and horror films beginning in the Cold War era, many Machines of both earthly and extraterrestrial origin have invaded America's Garden of complacency and conformity. The atomic bomb is either an impending threat to planetary survival (Sidney Lumet's *Fail-Safe,* 1964) or a global destroyer (Stanley Kubrick's *Dr. Strangelove,* 1964). Weird extraterrestrials, armed with deadly weapons, threaten the planet in popular classics such as Robert Wise's *The Day the Earth Stood Still* (1951) and George Pal's *The War of the Worlds* (1953).

Literal replays of the Machine in the Garden metaphor include Jack Clayton's *Something Wicked This Way Comes* (1983), wherein an infernal locomotive brings death and damnation into the idyllic hamlet of Green Town, Illinois; and Douglas Trumbull's *Silent Running* (1972), which chronicles the threats to earth's last remaining garden, a dome floating in deep space and superintended by a latter-day version of Virgil's pastoral shepherd, Freeman Lowell (Bruce Dern). But perhaps no science fiction film better exemplifies the Machine in the Garden myth than Kubrick's *2001: A Space Odyssey* (1969). The black monolith that periodically appears and astonishes protohominid and astronaut alike is nothing less than a cosmic intruder into the Garden of Man, whose every appearance precipitates yet another stage in human evolution.

Last, among the many pertinent comedies is that nifty little cartoon by Chuck Jones called "Duck Amuck." For most of its length, Daffy Duck—a maniacal Virgilian shepherd if there ever were one—is persecuted by an unknown outside force that invades his space with a giant pencil and almost erases him out of existence. In this case, it turns out that the sadistic agency of his confusion is none other than that embodiment of the urban slickster and con man, Bugs Bunny! "Ain't I a stinker?" smiles the Wabbit.

Television and Video in the Garden

Many motion pictures have depicted proliferating media and communications technologies as latter-day Machines in the American Garden. This reflects, in the words of Jonathan Romney, "the mindset of a society still beginning to come to terms with the implications of media and political manipulation" (39).

The mere presence of a television set is enough to disrupt the family idyll in Barry Levinson's *Avalon* (1990) and Albert Brooks's *Reel Life* (1973). *Avalon* is an affecting elegy to the blasted hopes of an immigrant family come to America. The saga of the Krichinsky family (based on Levinson's mother's family) begins with the arrival of Sam Krichinsky (Armin Mueller-Stahl) in Baltimore in 1914 as he looks ahead to a new start in this Paradise he calls, appropriately, Avalon ("It was the most beautiful place you've ever seen in your life!"). By the story's end, however, America's urban push has despoiled the Krichinsky garden, and the family members have fled to the suburbs. "I keep getting farther and farther away from Avalon," Sam laments. The film concludes with a reprise of Sam's initial vision of Avalon, but now we know it to be no longer a shining hope but a failed dream.

More to the point of this discussion, *Avalon* is a critique of the invasion of the American Garden by that one-eyed monster—television. From the very moment a television set invades the Krichinsky home in the early 1950s, family relationships begin to deteriorate. It is amusing, at first, to see everybody grouped before the set, attracted to the sheer novelty of the test patterns. Later, however, they become so preoccupied with sitcoms, quiz shows, and movies that they spend more and more time watching, and they gradually cease talking to each other. Family gatherings begin to resemble wakes, whose participants sit, stunned, before the flickering set. The Thanksgiving dinner tradition, where hitherto people talked and laughed together around the big table, is replaced by a silent cluster of TV trays around the tube. Finally, old Sam Krichinsky sits alone in his room in the nursing home, the television set his only companion.

Reel Life is a satiric take on the 1972 PBS documentary series *An American Family*. The twelve-hour series documented a seven-month period in the life of the William C. Loud family of Santa Barbara, California. During that time, the family, generally regarded as a "candy box" ideal of the American home, underwent severe disruptions, resulting in revelations of, among other things, ongoing marital infidelity (the parents ultimately divorced) and the homosexuality of one of the family members. Brooks's *Reel Life* mercilessly indicts the cinema-verité filmmaking practices of *An American Family* as a calculating, meddlesome, and disruptive intrusion of privacy. Brooks portrays himself as the opportunistic director who not only has no compunction about invading the homes of his subjects, but who does not scruple to engage in a disastrous affair with one of the family members.

The New Technological Garden

Recent motion pictures reverse the Machine in the Garden paradigm. In Alex Proyas's *Dark City* (1998) and Peter Weir's *The Truman Show* (1998), the Machine now is the Garden, a new kind of media-driven pastoral space of technological perfection and urban anonymity. The peaceful tranquility of Hawthorne's Concord Woods has been replicated by the artificially controlled and/or computer-generated wraparound environments of television studios, malls, theme parks, and bubble-dome cities.

In these films the disruptive force that now invades the Garden and shatters its illusions is not the intrusive Machine, but, ironically, the *hand of man.* The protagonists of *Dark City* and *The Truman Show,* John Murdoch (Rufus Sewell) and Truman Burbank (Jim Carrey), respectively, beat their fists against the machine-tooled facades of their bubble cities and dream of a counter Arcadia, a tropical paradise—for Murdoch it is a place called "Shell Beach," and for Truman it is the Fiji Islands.

References

Filmography

An American Family (1972, D)
Angels with Dirty Faces (1938, F)
Avalon (1990, F)
Bad Company (1971, F)
Black Diamond Express (1896, SF)
Bye, Bye Birdie (1963, F)
Cheyenne Autumn (1964)
Close Encounters of the Third Kind (1977, F)
The Conversation (1974, F)
Crash (1997, F)
Damn Yankees (1958, F)
Dances with Wolves (1990, F)
Dark City (1998, F)
The Day the Earth Stood Still (1951, F)
Dead End (1936, F)
Demon Seed (1977, F)
Dr. Strangelove, or: How I Stopped Worrying and Learned to Love the Bomb (1964, F)
EdTV (1999, F)
The Emerald Forest (1985, F)
Enemy of the State (1998, F)
Fail-Safe (1964, F)
Full Metal Jacket (1987, F)
Gattaca (1997, F)
The General (1926, F)
The Grapes of Wrath (1940, F)
Lonely Are the Brave (1962, F)
The Magnificent Ambersons (1942, F)
Medicine Man (1992, F)
Millennium Man (1999, F)
The Music Man (1962, F)
1984 (1955, F; 1984, F)
Paths of Glory (1957, F)
The Red Badge of Courage (1951, F)
Reel Life (1973, F)
Robocop (1987, F)
Sex, Lies, and Videotape (1989, F)
Short Cuts (1993, F)
Silent Running (1972, F)
Something Wicked This Way Comes (1983, F)
Star Trek: First Contact (1996, F)
Terminator 2 (1991, F)
THX 1138 (1970, F)
To Kill a Mockingbird (1962, F)
The Truman Show (1998, F)
2001: A Space Odyssey (1969, F)
Videodrome (1982, F)
War of the Worlds (1953, F)

Bibliography

Adams, Henry. *The Education of Henry Adams.* 1907. Boston: Houghton Mifflin, 1974.
Arnheim, Rudolph. "The Two Authenticities of the Photographic Media." *Journal of Aesthetics and Art Criticism* 51.4 (1993): 537–540.
Brosnan, John. *Future Tense: The Cinema of Science Fiction.* New York: St. Martin's, 1978.
Davis, Keith F. *An American Century of Photography: From Dry-Plate to Digital.* New York: Abrams, 1990.
Fielding, Raymond. *A Technological History of Motion Pictures and Television.* Berkeley: University of California Press, 1983.

Gunning, Tom. "An Aesthetic of Astonishment: Early Film and the (In)credulous Spectator." In Leo Braudy and Marshall Cohen, eds., *Film Theory and Criticism*, 818–832. New York: Oxford University Press, 1999.

Marx, Leo. *The Machine in the Garden: Technology and the Pastoral Ideal.* New York: Oxford University Press, 1964.

Minnis, Stuart. "Digitalization and the Instrumentalist Approach to the Photographic Image." *Iris* 25 (1998): 1–11.

Mitchell, William. *The Reconfigured Eye: Visual Truth in the Post-Photographic Era.* Cambridge, MA: MIT Press, 1992.

Musser, Charles. *The Emergence of Cinema.* New York: Scribner's, 1993.

Nash, Roderick. *Wilderness and the American Mind.* New Haven: Yale University Press, 1982.

Romney, Jonathan. "The New Paranoia: Games Pixels Play." *Film Comment* 34.6 (1998): 39–43.

Sanford, Charles I. *The Quest for Paradise: Europe and the American Moral Imagination.* Urbana: University of Illinois Press, 1961.

Schivelbusch, Wolfgang. *The Railway Journey: The Industrialization of Time and Space in the 19th Century.* New York: Urizen, 1979.

Smith, Henry Nash. *Virgin Land: The American West as Symbol and Myth.* Cambridge, MA: Harvard University Press, 1950.

Susman, Warren I. *Culture as History: The Transformation of American Society in the Twentieth Century.* New York: Pantheon, 1984.

[HANNU SALMI]

Success and the Self-Made Man

The myth of personal success has been characteristic of American culture and society at least since the mid-nineteenth century. Its roots date back to the eighteenth-century individualism embedded in the culture of enlightenment and best exemplified by Benjamin Franklin's famous *Autobiography.* The underlying idea that a citizen himself can determine his own future and change his life for the better lies at the core of modern culture. In the eighteenth century, the ideal citizen was represented as a male figure, and the myth of success applied to males only.

The son of a Unitarian minister, Horatio Alger Jr. (1832–1899) has been identified as the quintessential spokesman for this myth. Although it cannot be said that he invented the idea, he certainly is the most famous mediator and interpreter of the Self-Made Man. Alger was initially a pastor, but after his first assignment he moved to New York City and started a career as a freelance writer. In most of his 135 books, Alger addressed a young male audience and described how a ragged street boy could attain a respected place in the community—that virtue and success were *not* incompatible.

Despite such alluring titles as *Fame and Fortune* and *Striving for Fortune,* Alger did not, as often has been stated, depict boys who alone and unaided rise to the top. Neither did he speak in an unqualified way for individualistic free enterprise. As John G. Cawelti has shown, a typical Alger hero "is established in a secure white-collar position, either as a clerk with the promise of a junior partnership or as a junior member of a successful mercantile establishment," (109) but none of them achieves immediate economic or political prominence.

Still, by the end of the nineteenth century, the expression "Horatio Alger story" was used to refer to a very successful career and even carried materialistic connotations. "Fame" and "fortune" became more important in the popular imagination than "modesty," "respect," and "hard work." The most idolized self-made men in American culture were either successful manufacturers or technological innovators, such as Andrew Carnegie and Thomas A. Edison. Carnegie, a success philosopher himself, argued, however, that success always requires character and, to acquire money, one must undergo a process of education and self-denial. If one loses modesty, wealth will soon vanish.

Self-making as a contradictory process, including both self-denial and money making, modesty and richness, has been a fruitful starting point for the film medium. Indeed, success has been one of the central themes in cinema right from the start. Despite the crucial role of "success," there still is no comprehensive study of its mythic treatment in cinema. One could, however, mention Bernard B. Scott's book *Hollywood Dreams and Biblical Stories* (1994), which includes a chapter on Horatio Alger's legacy in Hollywood cinema. Furthermore, there are excellent studies of the Self-Made Man in American culture as a whole. In addition to John G. Cawelti's *Apostles of the Self-Made Man* (1965), Irvin Wyllie's *The Self-Made Man in America* (1954), Richard Weiss's *The American Myth of Success from Horatio Al-*

ger to Norman Vincent Peale (1969), David Madden's *American Dreams, American Nightmares* (1970), and Richard Huber's *The American Idea of Success* (1971) are all noteworthy. Those who are interested in Horatio Alger's legacy might find Carol Nackenoff's *The Fictional Republic: Horatio Alger and American Political Discourse* (1994) worth consulting. A fascinating reexamination of the myth is Jeffrey Louis Decker's *Made in America: Self-Styled Success from Horatio Alger to Oprah Winfrey* (1997), analyzing the changing rhetoric of personal success. In the late twentieth century, the emphasis of this rhetoric has moved from religious "character" to psychological "personality" and celebrity "image."

Self-Making and Nation Building

During the nineteenth century, the image of the Self-Made Man was often connected to the genesis of the American nation. In the Old World, traditional society limited the possibilities of breaking the boundaries of social classes, but in the United States, the promise of upward mobility seemed to open infinite personal frontiers.

The myth of personal success was actually a much-needed instrument in a country that had to reassure newcomers about the possibilities of their future. It claimed that those who worked hard and were honest and punctual would inevitably find their place on the social ladder. The myth resonated with a quasi-religious message: for millions of European immigrants, America was a "promised land" with endless opportunities. At the turn of the century, from the 1870s to the 1920s, this myth had a crucial role in the process of assimilation of dozens of ethnic groups.

But the reality did not always meet these promises. Charles Chaplin's *The Immigrant* (1917) showed future-oriented newcomers whose optimism was hindered by the fact that the "promised land" did not actually welcome outsiders. In his spectacular vision of "the birth of a nation," *Heaven's Gate* (1980), Michael Cimino portrayed the difficulties of the settlers in the Wyoming of the 1890s. The immigrant settlers had to fight for their rights against cattle barons whose thirst for power and property not only made the fulfillment of the American Dream impossible but severely endangered the very lives of the lower classes.

In the process of nation building, the role of great men has also been stressed in the cinema. Innovators like Thomas A. Edison and Alexander Graham Bell have been presented in an adoring manner: they have been glorified both as successful self-made men and as crucial American characters whose contribution has had nationwide or even global influence. These kinds of filiopietistic biographies were especially popular from 1930 to 1960. In addition to such films as *The Story of Alexander Graham Bell* (1939), *Young Tom Edison* (1940), and *Edison the Man* (1940), great men of politics were also turned into role models. John Ford's classic *Young Mr. Lincoln* (1939) described the self-making of a future president and also emphasized the importance of "modesty," "respect," and "hard work"—in the sense of Horatio Alger.

All biographies of the classical Hollywood era tend to promote the idea of a self-made man. In a way, the basic notion that success is something inherent, something that does not come "from outside" but that is in a great man by birth, seems to be in contradiction with the democratic ideal that, in America, everybody makes his own future. However, often these films have elements of Horatio Alger's notion of self-education: to be a genius, natural talent is not enough. One has to cultivate one's own character, to be humble and hard-working. This idea becomes visible, for example, in Glenn Miller's struggle to find his personal style, his own sound, in Anthony Mann's *The Glenn Miller Story* (1954).

If there were a filmmaker inspired by Horatio Alger in Hollywood, the one who most obviously comes to mind is the Sicilian immigrant Frank Capra, the director of numerous populist comedies. He did not really tell stories about people who advance from rags to riches. Instead, he argues that the American Dream has been misunderstood and that the adoration of success had led to false passion for making money, to a domination of greed over more humane sentiments. In *Meet John Doe* (1941), a hobo (Gary Cooper) is made a celebrity by a newspaper reporter (Barbara Stanwyck) working in cooperation with scheming politicians. This success, created and exploited by media, is inauthentic itself, but, in Capra's vision, this exception does not mean that the myth of success is an illusion; it has only been used for selfish purposes by politicians who have forgotten their duties and by a media that has forgotten the responsibilities that go along with the freedom of speech. Many Capra films, like *Mr. Deeds Goes to Town* (1936) and *Mr. Smith Goes to Washington* (1939), clearly would like to reelevate and reappraise the role of a self-made man: the myth is revived by going back to its rural and sincere origins in America's small towns.

Ambiguity of Success

In literature and popular culture, the myth of success often is Janus-faced. It is eclipsed by a certain ambiguity because external signs and internal essence, richness and character always intertwine, and the American Dream is in danger of turning into a nightmare, becoming either an individual or a social horror. Despite the fundamental belief that all citizens are equal, implanted in a traditional Alger story, already during the 1910s, the descriptions of immigrant self-made men in literature and cinema tended to become critical.

In his novel *The Rise of David Levinsky* (1917), Abraham Cahan portrayed how an immigrant of Russian Jewish origin gained material success in his new home country but lost his cultural heritage. As John Higham notes in his introduction to Cahan's novel, "since he could not forget what he had betrayed, the path of commercial achievement ended in spiritual loss and emptiness" (vi–vii). At the end of the novel, Levinsky has everything—thousands of things that had been a forbidden fruit to him are at his command—but, still, "money is no measure of value." His past and his present "do not comfort well"; he never can get what he lost through his economic rise (524–525).

During the 1920s, the myth of the white, Anglo-Saxon, self-made man started to decline. As Jeffrey Louis Decker has pointed out, Scott F. Fitzgerald's novel *The Great Gatsby* (1925) is a critique of uplift stories. Gatsby has illicit business associations with immigrant gangsters—successful bootleggers—which are presented as necessary for advancement in the post–World War I era. On the other hand, there had been growing suspicion of immigrants during and after the war: in the late 1920s, xenophobic, anti-immigrant sentiments were fueled by premonitions of economic decline.

This atmosphere became visible on the screen in the early 1930s, when gangster movies gained popularity. The American melting pot was failing to assimilate immigrants, and the struggle for success found violent, illegal forms. Such films as *Little Caesar* (1930) and *The Public Enemy* (1931) explored inverted and distorted images of the American Dream, turned into a nightmare. "Despite all the gunplay, mayhem, and omnipresence of death, the gangster film of the early thirties served primarily as a success story," writes Andrew Bergman, adding, "That Americans were attracted to outlaws during the Depression's most wrenching years is an undeniable and useful fact, but the manner in which the outlaws operated only reinforced some of the country's most cherished myths about individual success" (6–7). Yet here is an interesting paradox: gangsterism and entrepreneurial corruption worked strongly against the traditional myth of personal success because they limited the possibilities of a citizen, but gangster *movies* focused on the individuals, not on organized crime as a social institution that was jeopardizing American individualism. Thus, the films became advocates of the success myth, irrespective of their violent and antisocial subject matter.

When the struggle for success replaces other values, illegal methods seem to be unavoidable. Francis Ford Coppola's *Godfather* saga (in three parts, made in 1972, 1974, and 1990) is an illuminating example, although one should keep in mind that, in later gangster movies, it is not only the matter of individual prosperity but the collective success of "the family" as well.

Yet the ambiguity of success had been explored by filmmakers before the peak of cinematic gangsterism. Erich von Stroheim's *Greed* (1925) traces an obsession for money and the destructive power of money lust. King Vidor's *The Crowd* (1928), on the other hand, shows a man who does not even have the opportunity to achieve success. The big city, according to Vidor, does not offer prospects for upward mobility; indeed, retrogression often seems more likely. When the daughter of the central character is suddenly killed, everything starts to move downwards: he loses his job and is about to commit suicide. At the last moment, he decides to start again, right from the bottom, and takes a job as a sandwich-board carrier.

Perhaps the most well-known of the success stories of Hollywood is *Citizen Kane,* directed by Orson Welles in 1941. Like Abraham Cahan's novel over two decades earlier, it succeeds in revealing the loneliness of success, how selfishness and greed, in the end, separate individuals from the community. Charles Foster Kane falls morally along his way to the top, just like the protagonist of *All the King's Men* (1949) and many other movies in the anti-success genre. In the end, he lives alone in his castle, Xanadu. His last word heard during the claustral preface of the film, does not refer to luxury but to something very personal, something he lost as a child and could never replace with material things.

Success in the Media World

Citizen Kane described the world of media that was to become the most common background for success stories in the 1950s. *Sweet Smell of Success* (1957), written by Clifford Odets together with Ernest Lehman and directed by Alexander Mackendrick, offered a sour study of journalism, set in New York City. In the year of its release, it was widely regarded as an attack on gossip columnist Walter Winchell. His cinematic sharp-edged alter ego, J. J. Hunsecker (Burt Lancaster), was a powerful, merciless journalist whose stories could either make or break a career. His right-hand man is a press agent, Sidney Falco (Tony Curtis), who supports himself hunting down items for Hunsecker's writings. *Sweet Smell of Success* was strongly influenced by its left-wing scriptwriter, Clifford Odets, whose sharp and scorching lines unmask the cynicism of the media world.

Many other films of the 1950s discuss the role of media in the formation of success: here fame and fortune can be acquired not only by hard and humble work, as Alger suggested, but through publicity—by becoming a popular singer or an actor. Hollywood itself had become a symbol of fame already during the 1920s and 1930s. William A. Wellman's *A Star Is Born* (1937) had captured well the hustle of the dream factory. This story of stardom was to inspire later filmmakers: it was remade in 1954 by George Cukor and in 1976 by Frank Pierson. During the 1950s, such films as *Sunset Boulevard* (1950) and *The Big Knife* (1955) continued to emphasize Hollywood mythology. Paradoxically, at the same time, film production was in crisis and a new medium, television, was transforming viewing habits and patronage.

Modern success can be born without any entrepreneurial activity, through the means of publicity, especially advertising. George Cukor's *It Should Happen to You* (1953) tells a story of Gladys Glover (Judy Holliday) who is haunted by her own ordinariness. She rents a

FIGURE 77. *Sweet Smell of Success* (1957). Sidney Falco (Tony Curtis), a publicity agent and toady of hateful newspaper columnist J. J. Hunsecker (Burt Lancaster), strides confidently down a New York street. Courtesy Hill-Hecht-Lancaster Productions.

huge billboard on Columbus Circle in New York City with her last savings. She even succeeds in getting six other billboards and, soon, her name is known everywhere in New York. She becomes a pure product of publicity. Finally, she realizes the absurd state of things and returns, happily, to anonymity. In this film, Cukor was making a comment on the huge changes in the media environment after World War II. Surely, the film industry was not nonpartisan in this cultural conflict: the spokesmen of the old media openly criticized new technologies such as television and, simultaneously, the modern lifestyle it extolled—a lifestyle supposedly filled with meretricious and conspicuous consumption.

Frank Tashlin directed a number of satires about television and advertising. *Will Success Spoil Rock Hunter?* (1957) tells a story of an advertising-jingle writer, Rock Hunter (Tony Randall), who is striving to advance his position at a company, although the president openly despises him. Hunter convinces a movie sex symbol (Jayne Mansfield) to endorse his ad campaign, and his career starts to skyrocket. The film laughs at the persistent ambition to advance up the corporate ladder by any means possible. Heaven's door itself seems to open for Rock Hunter when he gets his own key to the executive washroom. Although there is a certain critical point in this satire, there seems to be a traditional undertone within. Just as Gladys Glover finally perceives the senselessness of empty success and returns to ordinary life, Rock Hunter learns that the girl next door can offer much more genuine happiness than his career at the agency.

The Return of the Self-Made Man (and Woman)

Success defined as economic well-being can be found in a high percentage of American films; fantasies of money have long been an essential part of entertainment and still are. During the depression era, such daydreams were especially popular. In *Gold Diggers of 1933,* Ginger Rogers, supported by chorus girls holding giant coins, sang an ode for earthly well-being: "We're in the money. We've got a lot of what it takes to get along. We never see a headline about a breadline today." To see backstage musicals of the early 1930s only as escapist fantasies or as counterimages of the depression era is not enough; they served to revitalize the myth of success.

In Hollywood cinema, making money has been mainly a male privilege. There are, however, examples of self-made women, but they seem to be rare, at least as protagonists of the stories. Michael Curtiz's *Mildred Pierce* (1945) shows an ambitious mother (Joan Crawford) who works hard in order to give her daughter (Ann Blyth) a good education. Mildred achieves an enormous success and is ready to sacrifice everything for her daughter. Finally, money proves to be meaningless—and Mildred cannot buy a better life for herself or her spoiled offspring.

During recent decades, female protagonists have become much more common as successful characters. In Garry Marshall's *Pretty Woman* (1990), a ruthless businessman, Edward Lewis (Richard Gere), needs an escort and hires prostitute Vivian Ward (Julia Roberts) to be his companion at some social events. As Bernard B. Scott notices, Vivian is depicted as an Alger hero who, finally through marriage, rises from rags to riches. In the end, she "is not a fallen woman but a working woman" (134). The film does not actually stress the instrumentality of sex as a means to success, but, in many other Hollywood stories, sex and success seem to intertwine. In Barry Levinson's *Disclosure* (1994), this coupling is obvious. Tom Sanders (Michael Douglas) works in a computer company in Seattle. On her first day at DigiCom, Meredith Johnson (Demi Moore) tries to use her sexual appeal in order to influence Tom. Irritated by his refusal, Meredith tells their boss (Donald Sutherland) that Tom has sexually harassed her. *Disclosure* has a clearly male perspective when describing an unprincipled female trying to make a success in business world through every possible means.

In classical Hollywood cinema, African Americans and other ethnic minorities were on the margins: the Self-Made Man was predominantly a myth for white Anglo-Saxons. During the last decades, there have been, however, many success films with black protagonists. In his comedy *Coming to America* (1988), John Landis tells a story about a wealthy African prince (Eddie Murphy) who emigrates to the United States in search of love. A perhaps more interesting case is Walter Hill's *Brewster's Millions* (1985), in which a minor-league baseball player, Montgomery Brewster, has to spend $30 million in thirty days in order to inherit $300 million. This story, based on George Barr McCutcheon's novel (1902), had been filmed four times before. The leading role was performed by white actors Edward Abeles (1914), Fatty Arbuckle (1921), Jack Buchanan (1935), and Dennis O'Keefe (1945), but in the 1985 adaptation, Richard Pryor was given the opportunity to explore an African American version of success.

During the 1980s and 1990s, there was also a revival of the white Self-Made Man in Hollywood. Instead of emphasizing the qualities of Horatio Alger, many recent films, especially from the late 1970s onward, stressed the importance of physical strength through conditioning as a basis for personal success. Think of the lead characters of *Rocky* (1976), *Pumping Iron* (1977), and *First Blood* (1982): here self-education has taken the form of bodybuilding, and the role of a self-made man has been presented as crucial in defending American values. So often in the Sylvester Stallone films, personal success has again been identified with a renewal of a proud national identity.

There seems, however, to be a touch of Horatio Alger's spirit left in the American mainstream cinema, especially in its attempts to return to the age of innocence. *Forrest Gump* (1994), directed by Richard Zemeckis, follows the life of a humble person who, irrespective of his casual appearances in media, makes his own way—and succeeds. The film is certainly an ironical comment on recent American history, but it also suggests that there always is a place in American hearts for modest, hardworking, decent citizens.

References

Filmography

All the King's Men (1949, F)
The Big Knife (1955, F)
Brewster's Millions (1914, F; 1921, F; 1935, F; 1945, F; 1985, F)
Citizen Kane (1941, F)
Coming to America (1988, F)
The Crowd (1928, F)
Disclosure (1994, F)
Edison the Man (1940, F)
First Blood (1982, F)
Forrest Gump (1994, F)
The Glenn Miller Story (1954, F)
The Godfather (1972, F)
The Godfather, Part II (1974, F)

Gold Diggers of 1933 (1933, F)
Greed (1925, F)
Heaven's Gate (1980, F)
The Immigrant (1917, F)
It Should Happen to You (1953, F)
Little Caesar (1930, F)
Meet John Doe (1941, F)
Mildred Pierce (1945, F)
Mr. Deeds Goes to Town (1936, F)
Mr. Smith Goes to Washington (1939, F)
Pretty Woman (1990, F)
The Public Enemy (1931, F)
Rocky (1976, F)
A Star Is Born (1937, F; 1954, F; 1976, F)
The Story of Alexander Graham Bell (1939, F)
Sunset Boulevard (1950, F)
Sweet Smell of Success (1957, F)
Will Success Spoil Rock Hunter? (1957, F)
Young Mr. Lincoln (1939, F)
Young Tom Edison (1940, F)

Bibliography

Adams, James Truslow. *The Epic of America.* Boston: Little, Brown, 1931.

Bergman, Andrew. *We're in the Money: Depression America and Its Films.* New York: New York University Press, 1971.

Cahan, Abraham. *The Rise of David Levinsky.* 1917. New York: Harper & Row, 1960.

Cawelti, John G. *Apostles of the Self-Made Man.* Chicago: University of Chicago Press, 1965.

Decker, Jeffrey Louis. *Made in America: Self-Styled Success from Horatio Alger to Oprah Winfrey.* Minneapolis: University of Minnesota Press, 1997.

Durgnat, Raymond, and Scott Simmon. *King Vidor, American.* Berkeley, Los Angeles: University of California Press, 1988.

Huber, Richard. *The American Idea of Success.* New York: McGraw-Hill, 1971.

Madden, David, ed. *American Dreams, American Nightmares.* Carbondale: Southern Illinois University Press, 1970.

Nackenoff, Carol. *The Fictional Republic: Horatio Alger and American Political Discourse.* New York: Oxford University Press, 1994.

Naremore, James. *The Magic World of Orson Welles.* New York: Oxford University Press, 1978.

Scott, Bernard B. *Hollywood Dreams and Biblical Stories.* Minneapolis: Fortress Press, 1994.

Susman, Warren I. *Culture as History: The Transformation of American Society in the Twentieth Century.* New York: Pantheon, 1984.

Weiss, Richard. *The American Myth of Success from Horatio Alger to Norman Vincent Peale.* New York: Basic Books, 1969.

Wyllie, Irvin. *The Self-Made Man in America: the Myth of Rags to Riches.* New Brunswick, NJ: Rutgers University Press, 1954.

★ CONTRIBUTORS

Peter C. Rollins
General Editor
Film and History
www.filmandhistory.org

Ray Arsenault
Civil Rights
Department of History
University of South Florida

Robert Baird
Indian Leaders; Journalism and the Media
Department of English
University of Illinois at Urbana-Champaign

Scott Baugh
Mexican Americans
Department of English
Texas Tech University

Mike Birdwell
Antebellum Frontier Heroes; The Trans-Appalachian West to 1861
Department of History
Tennessee Tech University

Bill Brigman
Sexuality
Department of Social Sciences
University of Houston–Downtown

Ron Briley
Private Schools; Public High Schools
Sandia Preparatory School
Albuquerque, New Mexico

Alicia Browne
The Civil War and Reconstruction
Independent scholar
Tuscaloosa, Alabama

Mark Busby
Texas and the Southwest
Center for the Study of the Southwest
Southwest Texas State University

Anthony Chase
Christopher Columbus; Congress and the Senate; Elections and Party Politics
Shepard Broad Law Center
Nova Southeastern University

Solomon Davidoff
Jewish Americans
New England Institute of Art and Communications

Michael Denison
Space
Cottey College

Thomas Doherty
Democracy and Equality
American Studies and Film Studies
Brandeis University

Stacey Donahue
Italian Americans
Department of English
Central Oregon Community College

Joe Dorinson
New York City
Department of History
Long Island University–Brooklyn Campus

Robert Doyle
The American Fighting Man
Department of History
Franciscan University

Robert Fyne
World War II: Feature Films
Department of English
Kean University

Owen Gilman
The South
Department of English
St. Joseph's Jesuit University–Philadelphia

Ron Green
Children and Teenagers in the Twentieth Century
Casady School
Oklahoma City, Oklahoma

Thomas Halper
City and State Government
Department of Political Science
Baruch College, City University of New York

James Hanlan
The "New" West and the New Western; The Political Machine
Humanities Department
Worcester Polytechnic Institute

Zia Hasan
The 1970s
Vice President's Office
Claflin University

Dale Herbeck
Football
Department of Communications
Boston College

Peter Holloran
Catholic Americans; Irish Americans
Department of History
Worcester State College

Terry Hong
Asian Americans
Asian Pacific American Program
Smithsonian Institution

Edward Ingebretsen
The Puritan Era and the Puritan Mind
Department of English
Georgetown University

Carlton Jackson
The 1930s
Department of History
Western Kentucky University

Martin A. Jackson
Abraham Lincoln; Harry Truman
Independent scholar
New York City

Jacqueline Kilpatrick
Native Americans
Department of Humanities
California State University–Channel Islands

Lawence Kreiser
The Civil War and Reconstruction
Department of History
University of Alabama

Phil Landon
The Cold War; The Korean War
Department of English
University of Maryland–Baltimore County

George Lankevich
New York City
Professor Emeritus, Department of History
City University of New York

Chris Lovett
The 1960s
Department of History
Emporia State University

R. Philip Loy
The Frontier and the West
Department of Political Science
Taylor University

Charles Maland
The American Adam
Department of English
University of Tennessee

Mary Malloy
The Sea
Sea Education Association
Woods Hole, Massachusetts

Gregory McNamee
Baseball
Independent scholar
Tucson, Arizona

Joseph Millichap
The 1890s; Railroads
Department of English
Western Kentucky University

Steven Mintz
The Family
Department of History
University of Houston

Douglas Muzzio
City and State Government
School of Public Affairs
Baruch College, City University of New York

Jessica Muzzio
City and State Government
School of Law
Rutgers University

Douglas Noverr
Babe Ruth and Lou Gehrig
Department of American Thought and Language
Michigan State University

William J. Palmer
The 1980s
Department of English
Purdue University

Sarah Pearsall
Women from the Colonial Era to 1900
Department of Modern History
University of St. Andrews, Scotland

Susan Opt
Space
Communications Department
University of Houston–Victoria

Peter C. Rollins
The Presidency After World War II; The Vietnam War; World War I; World War II: Documentaries
Department of English
Oklahoma State University

Michael J. Riley
Militias and Extremist Political Movements
Roswell Museum
Roswell, New Mexico

Hannu Salmi
Success and the Self-Made Man
Department of History
University of Turku, Finland

James Sandos
Westward Expansion and the Indian Wars
Department of History
University of Redlands

Cotten Seiler
The American Revolution; The Founding Fathers
American Studies Department
Dickinson College

Jack G. Shaheen
Arab Americans
Independent scholar
Hilton Head, South Carolina

Michael Shull
African-Americans After World War II; Franklin and Eleanor Roosevelt; The Labor Movement and the Working Class; Radicals and Radicalism; Robber Barons, Media Moguls, and Wall Street Power Elites
Rhetoric and Communications Department
Mount St. Mary's College

June Sochen
Women in the Twentieth Century; Feminism and Feminist Films
Department of History
Northeastern Illinois University

Jennifer Tebbe-Grossman
Drugs, Tobacco, and Alcohol
Department of American Studies and Political Science
Massachusetts College of Pharmacy

John D. Thomas
George Washington
Independent scholar
Chicago, Illinois

John Tibbetts
The Machine in the Garden; The Midwest; The 1920s; The Small Town
Department of Radio, TV, and Film
University of Kansas

Robert B. Toplin
Slavery
Department of History
University of North Carolina–Wilmington

Don Whaley
Richard Nixon
Department of Political Science
Salisbury University

Ron Wilson
Crime and the Mafia
Department of Radio, TV, and Film
University of Kansas

Davd Wilt
Hollywood's Detective; The Labor Movement and the Working Class; Radicals and Radicalism; Robber Barons, Media Moguls, and Wall Street Power Elites; Suburbia
University Library
University of Maryland at College Park

James Yates
The Mexican-American War and the Spanish-American War
Department of English
Northwestern Oklahoma State University

★ Index

This index contains entries for historical eras, events, people, institutions and movements; cultural themes; film titles, actors, directors, and producers; book authors and titles; and film art techniques. The principal article focusing on each topic is identified with boldfaced locators: **326–329**.